MACROECONOMICS

MACROECONOMICS

Douglas McTaggart
Bond University
Christopher Findlay
University of Adelaide
Michael Parkin
University of Western Ontario

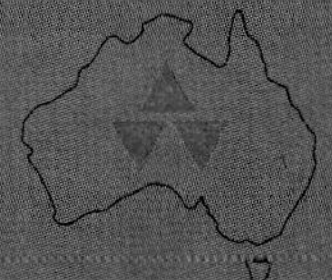

ADDISON-WESLEY PUBLISHING COMPANY

Sydney • Wokingham, England • Reading, Massachusetts
Menlo Park, California • New York • Don Mills, Ontario
Amsterdam • Bonn • Singapore • Tokyo • Madrid
San Juan • Milan • Paris • Mexico City • Seoul • Taipei

© 1992 Addison-Wesley Publishers Ltd.
© 1992 Addison-Wesley Publishing Company Inc.

All rights reserved. No part of this publication may be reproduced, stored in a retrieval system, or transmitted in any form or by any means, electronic, mechanical, photocopying, recording or otherwise, without the prior written permission of the publisher.

Many of the designations used by manufacturers and sellers to distinguish their products are claimed as trademarks. Addison-Wesley has made every attempt to supply trademark information about manufacturers and their products mentioned in this book.

ACQUISITIONS EDITOR: K. Andrew Semmens
PRODUCTION MANAGER: Stephen Bishop
PRODUCTION EDITOR: Susan Keany
PRODUCTION COORDINATOR: Susan Lewis
PRODUCTION CONTROLLER: Jim Allman
COPY-EDITORS: Lesley Dow, Andrew Kelly and Venetia Nelson
COVER DESIGN: John Windus, incorporating the painting *Forces at Play* by Denise Green, reproduced by permission of Denise Green and Delaney Galleries. © Denise Green. All rights reserved.
PHOTOGRAPHER FOR INTERVIEWS: Mishka Golski and Dona Haycraft
DESIGN: Pronk & Associates
Designers and Partners
TYPESETTER: Uniskill Ltd, Oxford
PRINTER: R.R. Donnelley & Sons

First printed 1992. Reprinted 1994

National Library of Australia Cataloguing-in-Publication Entry

McTaggart, Douglas, 1953-
Macroeconomics.

Australian ed.
Includes index.
ISBN 0 201 53936 7.

1. Macroeconomics. I. Findlay, Christopher. II. Parkin, Michael, 1939
-III. Title. (Series: Australian business studies series).

339

Text and photo credits appear on p. I-15 which constitutes a continuation of the copyright page.

DEDICATION

To
Pam, Andrew, Cameron and Lachlan
Tania, Marek and Kasia

ABOUT THE AUTHORS

DOUGLAS McTAGGART is an Associate Professor of Economics teaching in the School of Business at Bond University. He earned a degree in economics at the Australian National University before taking a PhD at the University of Chicago. His first academic appointment was at VPI in the United States, where he remained for several years, before returning to a visiting position at the University of Adelaide. From there he moved to Bond. His research interests lie mainly in the area of macroeconomics and monetary theory. Apart from these areas, he has also researched and published in the fields of game theory and applied microeconomics.

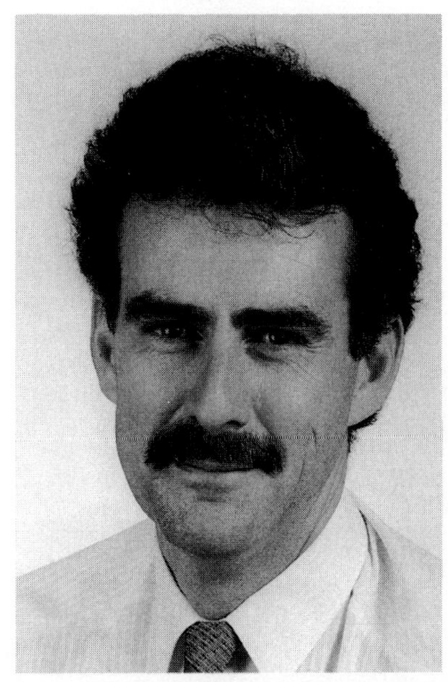

CHRISTOPHER FINDLAY was educated at the University of Adelaide and at the Australian National University (ANU). He was a Research Fellow in the Department of Economics in the Research School of Pacific Studies at the ANU before moving to Adelaide. He is now an Associate Professor in the Department of Economics at the University of Adelaide. He is also a Research Associate of the Australia–Japan Research Centre at the ANU. His chicf interest is Australia's international trade. He works on Australia's trade in services, especially air transport, on Australia's trade with Asia and on the minerals and energy sector in the Asia–Pacific region. He has written books and journal articles and contributed to edited volumes on these issues.

MICHAEL PARKIN was educated at the University of Leicester. Currently in the Department of Economics at the University of Western Ontario, Professor Parkin has held faculty appointments at the Universities of Sheffield, Leicester, Essex and Manchester and has lectured extensively throughout Canada, the United States, Europe, Australia and Japan. He has served as managing editor of the Canadian Journal of Economics and on the editorial boards of the American Economic Review and the Journal of Monetary Economics. Professor Parkin's research on macroeconomics, monetary economics and international economics has resulted in 160 publications in the American Economic Review, the Journal of Political Economy, the Review of Economic Studies, the Journal of Monetary Economics, the Journal of Money, Credit and Banking and dozens of other journals and edited volumes.

BRIEF CONTENTS

PART 1 **Introduction** 1

CHAPTER 1 What is Economics 3
CHAPTER 2 Making and Using Graphs 26
CHAPTER 3 Production, Specialization and Exchange 44
CHAPTER 4 Demand and Supply 64

PART 8 **Introduction to Macroeconomics** 89

CHAPTER 22 Inflation, Unemployment, Cycles and Deficits 92
CHAPTER 23 Measuring Output and the Price Level 112
CHAPTER 24 Aggregate Demand and Aggregate Supply 138

PART 9 **Aggregate Product Markets** 169

CHAPTER 25 Expenditure Decisions and GDP 172
CHAPTER 26 Expenditure and Income 208

PART 10 **Money, Interest, and the Dollar** 235

CHAPTER 27 Money, Banking and Prices 238
CHAPTER 28 The Reserve Bank of Australia, Money and Interest Rates 262
CHAPTER 29 Interest Rates and Exchange Rates 295

PART 11 **Macroeconomic Problems** 325

CHAPTER 30 Monetary and Fiscal Influences on Aggregate Demands 327
CHAPTER 31 Unemployment and Aggregate Supply 364
CHAPTER 32 Inflation 396
CHAPTER 33 Expansions and Contractions 423

PART 12 **Macroeconomic Policy** 447

CHAPTER 34 Stabilizing the Economy 450
CHAPTER 35 Federal Surpluses and Deficits 476

PART 13 **The World Economy** 499

CHAPTER 36 Trading with the World 501
CHAPTER 37 The Balance of Payments and the Dollar 529

PART 14 **Growth, Development and Comparative Systems** 553

CHAPTER 38 Growth and Development 556
CHAPTER 39 Comparing Economic Systems 575

TABLE OF CONTENTS

PART 1 INTRODUCTION

Talking with Heinz Arndt 1

CHAPTER 1 *What is Economics?* 3

Economic Questions in the World Today 5
- Production, Consumption and Technological Change 5
- Wages and Earnings 5
- Unemployment 5
- Inflation 6
- Government 6
- International Trade 6
- Wealth and Poverty 6

Scarcity 7
- Economic Activity 7
- Choice 8
- Competition and Cooperation 9

The Economy 12
- What is an Economy? 12
- The Economy's Working Parts 13
- Coordination Mechanisms 14
- Closed and Open Economies 16

Economic Science 17
- What Is and What Ought to Be 17
- Observation and Measurement 17
- Economic Theory 18
- Economic Models 18
- Microeconomic and Macroeconomic Models 22
- Model, Theory and Reality 22

Reading Between the Lines
Scarcity, Costs and Choice 10

Our Advancing Knowledge
Adam Smith and the Birth of Economic Science 20

Summary* 23

Key Terms* 24

Problems* 25

* Summary, Key Terms and Problems appear at the end of most chapters.

CHAPTER 2 *Making and Using Graphs* 26

Graphing Data 28
Graphing a Single Variable 28
Two-Variable Graphs 28
Time-Series Graphs 28
Scatter Diagrams 32

Graphs Used in Economic Models 35
Variables That Go Up and Down Together 35
Variables That Move in Opposite Directions 35
Relationships That Have a Maximum and a Minimum 35
Variables That Are Independent 37

The Slope of a Relationship 38
The Definition of Slope 38
Calculating Slope 38

Graphing Relationships Between More Than Two Variables 40
Other Things Being Equal 40

CHAPTER 3 *Production, Specialization and Exchange* 44

The Production Possibility Frontier 46
A Model Economy 46
On the Frontier Is Best 47

Opportunity Cost 48
The Best Alternative Forgone 48
Measuring Opportunity Cost 48
Increasing Opportunity Cost 49
The Shape of the Frontier 50
Everything Has an Increasing Opportunity Cost 50
Production Possibilities in the Real World 50

Changing Production Possibilities 51
The Cost of Shifting the Frontier 51
Capital Accumulation and Technological Change 51
Economic Growth in the Real World 52

Gains From Trade 54
Comparative Advantage: Kylie Meets Jason 54
Achieving the Gains from Trade 55
Productivity and Absolute Advantage 55

Exchange in the Real World 56
Property Rights 56
Money 57

Reading Between the Lines
Overcoming Obstacles to the Gains from Trade 58

CHAPTER 4 *Demand and Supply* 64

Demand 66
What Determines the Quantity Demanded? 66
The Law of Demand 66
Demand Schedule and Demand Curve 66
Willingness to Pay 67
A Change in Demand 67
Movement Along Versus a Shift in the Demand Curve 68

Supply 69
What Determines the Quantity Supplied? 71
The Law of Supply 71
The Supply Schedule and the Supply Curve 71
Minimum Supply Price 71
A Change in Supply 71
Movement Along Versus a Shift in the Supply Curve 72

Price Determination 74
Price as a Regulator 74
Equilibrium 75

Predicting Changes in Price and Quantity Traded 76
A Change in Demand 76
A Change in Supply 77
Changes in Both Supply and Demand 80
Walkmans, Houses and Coffee 84

Our Advancing Knowledge
Discovering the Laws of Demand and Supply 78

Reading Between the Lines
Supply and Demand in Action: Increasing Market Demand 82

PART 8 INTRODUCTION TO MACROECONOMICS

Talking with James Tobin 89

CHAPTER 22 *Inflation, Cycles, Unemployment, Deficits and Surpluses* 92

Inflation 94
Inflation Rate and the Price Level 95
The Recent Inflation Record 95
Inflation and the Value of Money 96
Is Inflation a Problem? 96
The Problem of Unanticipated Inflation 96
The Problem of Anticipated Inflation 97
Indexing 98

Gross Domestic Product 98
Nominal GDP and Real GDP 99
Real GDP — the Record 99
The Importance of Real GDP 100

The Business Cycle 101

Unemployment 102
What is Unemployment? 102
Measuring Unemployment 102
The Unemployment Record 103
Types of Unemployment 103
Full Employment 104
The Costs of Unemployment 105
Unemployment and the Business Cycle 106
The Stock Market and the Business Cycle 106
Inflation and the Business Cycle 107

The Government and International Accounts 108
The Government Accounts 108
The International Accounts 108

CHAPTER 23 *Measuring Output and the Price Level* 112
The Circular Flow of Expenditure and Income 114
Circular Flows in a Model Economy 114
Income and Expenditure Accounts 118

Australia's Income and Expenditure Accounts 120
The Expenditure Approach 120
The Income Approach 121
Factor Cost and Market Price 123
The Production Approach 123
Aggregate Expenditure, Production and Income 125

Price Level and Inflation 126
Consumer Price Index 126
GDP Deflator 127
Inflation and Relative Price Changes 128
The Consumer Price Index and the Cost of Living 130

Real GDP, Aggregate Economic Activity and Economic Welfare 131
Economic Welfare and Real GDP 134

Reading Between the Lines
The National Income Accounts 132

CHAPTER 24 *Aggregate Demand and Aggregate Supply* 138

Aggregate Demand 140
Why the Aggregate Demand Curve Slopes Downward 141
Changes in the Quantity of Real GDP Demanded 143
Changes in Aggregate Demand 144
Shifts in the Aggregate Demand Curve 146

Aggregate Supply 147
Two Macroeconomic Time Frames 147
Short-Run Aggregate Supply 147
Long-Run Aggregate Supply 151
Changes in Short-Run Aggregate Supply 152
Changes in Both Long-Run and Short-Run Aggregate Supply 153

Macroeconomic Equilibrium 154
Determination of Real GDP and the Price Level 154
Macroeconomic Equilibrium and Full Employment 155
Aggregate Fluctuations and Aggregate Demand Shocks 157
The Effects of a Change in Short-Run Aggregate Supply 160

Trends and Cycles in the Australian Economy 160
One View of the Economy in 1989/90 160
Growth, Inflation and Cycles 162
Microeconomic Reform and Macroeconomic Performance 163

Reading Between the Lines
Profit Expectations and Aggregate Demand 148

Our Advancing Knowledge
The Evolution of Modern Macroeconomics 158

PART 9 AGGREGATE PRODUCT MARKETS

Talking with Robert E. Lucas, Jr 169

CHAPTER 25 *Expenditure Decisions* 172

The Components of Aggregate Expenditure 174
Relative Importance of the Components of Aggregate Expenditure 174
Relative Volatility of the Components of Aggregate Expenditure 174

Consumption Expenditure and Saving 176
The Consumption Function and the Saving Function 177
The Average Propensities to Consume and to Save 178
The Marginal Propensities to Consume and to Save 179
The Australian Consumption Function 180
Shifts in the Consumption Function 181
The Aggregate Consumption Function 182

Investment 186
What Determines Investment? 186
Investment Demand 189
Investment Demand in Australia 191

Net Exports 192
Exports 192
Imports 193
Net Exports Function 193

Aggregate Expenditure and Real GDP 194
Aggregate Expenditure Schedule 195
Aggregate Expenditure Curve 195
Autonomous and Induced Expenditure 195
Slope of the Aggregate Expenditure Curve 197

Equilibrium Expenditure 198
When Expenditure Equals Real GDP 198
Convergence to Equilibrium 198

Appendix A: *Net Present Value and Investment* 204

Calculating Net Present Value 204
Expected Inflation and Real Interest Rate 205

Investment Demand 206

Appendix B: *The Simple Algebra of Income Determination* 207

Our Advancing Knowledge
Consumption and Saving 184

CHAPTER 26 *Expenditure and Income* 208

Autonomous Expenditure Multipliers 210
A Change in Autonomous Expenditure 210
The Paradox of Thrift 211
Calculating the Multiplier 212
The Multiplier and the Marginal Propensity to Spend 212
Why is the Multiplier Greater than 1? 214

Fiscal Policy Multipliers 216
Government Purchases Multiplier 216
Transfer Payments Multiplier 216
Tax Multiplier 217
Balanced Budget Multiplier 218
Automatic Stabilizers 218
Automatic Stabilizers and the Goverment Deficit 219
A Change in the Marginal Tax Rate 222

The Multiplier in Australia 224
The Australian Multiplier in 1990/91 224
The Multiplier in Recession and Recovery 225

Aggregate Expenditure and Aggregate Demand 226
Aggregate Expenditure and the Price Level 226

Real GDP, the Price Level and the Multipliers 227
Aggregate Demand Curve and Autonomous Expenditure 227
Equilibrium GDP and the Price Level 228

Reading Between the Lines
Net Exports and Aggregate Expenditure 220

PART 10 MONEY, INTEREST AND THE DOLLAR
Talking with Sir Leslie Melville 235

CHAPTER 27 *Money, Banking and Prices* 238

What is Money? 240
The Definition of Money 240
The Functions of Money 240
Different Forms of Money 242
Money in Australia Today 244

Financial Intermediaries 248
Banks 248
Other Financial Intermediaries 251
The Economic Functions of Financial Intermediaries 251
Financial Innovation 252
How Banks Create Money 253
Real World Money Multipliers 255
Bank Panic and Failure 255
Branch Banking Versus Unit Banking 255

Money and the Price Level 256
Money in the AD-AS Model 257
The Quantity Theory of Money 257
Historical Evidence on the Quantity Theory of Money 259
International Evidence on the Quantity Theory of Money 259

CHAPTER 28 *The Reserve Bank of Australia, Money and Interest Rates* 262

The Reserve Bank of Australia 264
- The Origins of the Reserve Bank 264
- The Structure of the Reserve Bank 265
- Constitutional Position of the Reserve Bank 266
- The Functions of the Reserve Bank 266
- Prudential Supervision 266
- Monetary Policy 267
- International Constraints on the Reserve Bank 267
- Monetary Policy Tools Prior to Deregulation 268
- Financial Market Deregulation 269
- Monetary Policy Tools Following Deregulation 270
- The Reserve Bank's Balance Sheet 271
- A Simple Model of Open Market Operations 273
- The Payments System 273
- Open Market Operations and the Money Market 274
- The Multiplier Effect of an Open Market Operation 275
- The Australian Money Multiplier 278

The Demand for Money 281
- The Motives for Money Holding 281
- The Influences on Money Holding 282
- The Demand for Real Money 284
- Shifts in the Demand Curve for Real Money 285
- The Demand for Money in Australia 286

Interest Rate Determination 286
- Interest Rates and Asset Prices 287
- Money Market Equilibrium 288
- Changing the Interest Rate 290
- The Reserve Bank in Action 291
- Profiting by Predicting the Reserve Bank's Actions 291

CHAPTER 29 *Interest Rates and the Exchange Rate* 295

Foreign Exchange 297
- Foreign Exchange Regimes 298
- Recent Exchange Rate History 298

Exchange Rate Determination 300
- The Exchange Rate and the Demand for Australian Dollar-Denominated Assets 302
- The Exchange Rate and the Supply of Australian Dollar-Denominated Assets 303
- Shifts in the Supply Curve of Dollar-Denominated Assets 304
- The Market for Australian Dollar-Denominated Assets 305
- The Exchange Rate Regime and Foreign Exchange Reserves 307
- Monetary Policy and the Exchange Rate 307
- Managing Exchange Rate Fluctuations 310
- Monetary Policy, Terms of Trade Variations and the Exchange Rate 311
- Government Surpluses and Deficits in the 1980s 313

Arbitrage, Prices and Interest Rates 314
- Arbitrage 314
- Purchasing Power Parity 315
- Interest Rate Parity 316
- A World Market 318

Monetary Independence 318
- Interdependence with a Fixed Exchange Rate 318
- Independence with a Flexible Exchange Rate 320
- A Paradox? 321

Reading Between the Lines
- *Managing the Exchange Rate* 308

PART 11 MACROECONOMIC PROBLEMS

Talking with Geoff Harcourt 325

CHAPTER 30 *Monetary and Fiscal Influences on Aggregate Demand* 327

Money, Interest and Aggregate Demand 329
Aggregate Demand and Aggregate Supply 329
Spending Decisions, Interest and Money 329
Equilibrium Expenditure and the Interest Rate 330

Monetary Policy and Aggregate Demand 332
The Initial Effect of a Change in the Money Supply 332
Adjustment Process 332
Other Transmission Channels 336

Fiscal Policy and Aggregate Demand 337
Initial Effect of Fiscal Policy Package 337
Adjustment Process 337
Crowding Out and Crowding In 340
The Exchange Rate and International Crowding Out 340

The Relative Effectiveness of Monetary and Fiscal Policy 341
The Effectiveness of Monetary Policy 341
The Effectiveness of Fiscal Policy 343
The Lags of Monetary and Fiscal Policy 345
The Keynesian–Monetarist Controversy 347
Influencing the Composition of Aggregate Demand 349
Assigning Monetary and Fiscal Policy Goals 349

Real GDP and the Price Level 350

The Short-Run Effects on Real GDP and the Price Level 350

The Long-Run Effects on Real GDP and the Price Level 351

Appendix: The *IS–LM* Model of Aggregate Demand 355
Equilibrium Expenditure and Real GDP 355
The *IS* Curve 357

Money Market Equilibrium 357
The *LM* Curve 358
The Equilibrium Interest Rate and Real GDP 359

The Aggregate Demand Curve 359
The Effects of a Change in Price Level on the *LM* Curve 360
The *LM* Curve Shift 360
The Aggregate Demand Curve Derived 360
Fiscal Policy and Aggregate Demand 360
Monetary Policy and Aggregate Demand 362

CHAPTER 31 *Unemployment and Aggregate Supply* 364

The Short-Run Aggregate Production Function 366
The Marginal Product of Labour 367
Economic Growth and Technological Change 367
Variable Growth Rates 368
The Australian Short-Run Aggregate Production Function 368

The Demand for Labour 369
Diminishing Marginal Product and the Demand for Labour 370
Shifts in the Demand for Labour Curve 371
The Australian Demand for Labour 371

The Supply of Labour 372
The Determination of Hours per Worker 373
The Participation Rate 374
Intertemporal Substitution 374

Wages and Employment 374
The Flexible Wage Theory 374
The Sticky Wage Theory 378

Unemployment 384
Indivisible Labour 384
Job Search and Unemployment 384
Unemployment with Flexible Wages 386
Unemployment with Sticky Wages 390

Reading Between the Lines
Achieving Wage Flexibility 382
Reading Between the Lines
Measuring Unemployment 392
Our Advancing Knowledge
Unemployment: Waste or 'Natural 388

CHAPTER 32 *Expectations and Inflation* 396

Inflation 398
Anticipated Inflation 398
Unanticipated Inflation 398

Demand Inflation 399
Sources of Increasing Aggregate Demand 399
Inflation Effect of an Increase in Aggregate Demand 399
Wage Response 399
A Price–Wage Inflation Spiral 400
Anticipating Increases in Aggregate Demand 401

Supply Inflation and Stagflation 401
Sources of Decreasing Aggregate Supply 401
Inflation Effect of a Decrease in Aggregate Supply 402
Aggregate Demand Response 402
A Cost–Price Inflation Spiral 402

Inflation Expectations 403
The Cost of Wrong Forecasts 404
Minimizing the Losses from Wrong Expectations 404
How People Form Expectations in the Real World 404
How Economists Predict People's Forecasts 405
The Rational Expectation of the Price Level 405
Rational Expectation with Sticky Money Wages 406
Rational Expectation with Flexible Wages 407
Theory and Reality 407

Rational Expectations Equilibrium 407
Sticky Versus Flexible Wages 408
Individuals in a Rational Expectations Equlibrium 409
Anticipated Inflation 409
Inflationary Expectations and Policy Credibility 412

Interest Rates and Inflation 413
Expectations of Inflation and Interest Rates 413
Inflation and Interest Rates in Australia 414
Money Supply and Interest Rates Again 415

Inflation over the Business Cycles: The Phillips Curve 416
The Phillips–Curve Approach 416
The Phillips Curve in the Short Run 416
The Phillips Curve in the Long Run 417
Variable Natural Rate of Unemployment 418
The Phillips Curve in Australia 418

Reading Between the Lines
Inflationary Expectations 410

CHAPTER 33 *Expansions and Contractions* 423

Australia's Economic Performance in the 1980s 425
The 1980–1983 Business Cycle 426
The 1983–1986 Business Cycle 428
The 1986–1990 Business Cycle 429

Money, Interest Rates and Expenditure over the Business Cycle 430
Changes in Expenditure 433

Business Cycles and the Australian Labour Market 433
The Expansion in 1981/82 433
The Contraction in 1982/83 434
The Wages Accord 436

Another Great Depression? 437
What the Great Depression Was Like 437
The Great Depression in the Rest of the World 439
Government Policy and the Depression in Australia 442
The Stock Market Crash 444
Can it Happen Again? 444

Reading Between the Lines
The Task of Managing Policy 410

PART 12 MACROECONOMIC POLICY

Talking with John Nevile 447

CHAPTER 34 *Stabilizing the Economy* 450

The Stabilization Problem 452
Macroeconomic Policy Targets 452
Macroeconomic Performance Indexes 452

The Key Players 455
The Government of Australia 455
The Reserve Bank of Australia 456
The Australian Council of Trade Unions 456
Employer Organizations 456

The Policy Instruments 456
Fiscal Policy 457
Monetary Policy 457
Wages and Incomes Policies 457
Trade and Industry Policy 458

Alternative Approaches to Stabilization Policy 460
Fixed Rules and Feedback Rules 460
The Two Rules in Action 460
Advantages of Feedback Rules 462
Implementing Feedback Rules — the Problems 462
Advantages of Fixed Rules 468

Stabilizing the Australian Economy 469
The Reserve Bank's Monetary Targeting 469
Using a Checklist 469
Destabilizing Monetary Policy, 1987/88 to 1990/91? 472
Wages Policy and the Accord 473

Reading Between the Lines
Guessing Future Policy Directions 464

Our Advancing Knowledge
The Quantity Theory and Monetarism 470

CHAPTER 35 *Federal Deficits and Surpluses* 476

The Sources of the Deficit or Surplus 478
The Federal Budget since 1953/54 478
Federal Government Revenue 480
Outlays 481
The Evolving Budget 482
The Budget and the Business Cycle 483
The Surplus in Expansion and Recession 484

The Real Deficit or Surplus 484
The Government's Real Deficit or Surplus 485
Real and Nominal Federal Deficits and Surpluses in Australia 487

Financing a Deficit 487
Debt Financing and Money Financing in Australia 488
Money Versus Debt Financing 489
Unpleasant Arithmetic 490

Arguments Against a Deficit 491
A Burden on Future Generations? 491

Our Advancing Knowledge
David Ricardo and the Deficit 494

PART 13 THE WORLD ECONOMY

Talking with Max Corden 499

CHAPTER 36 *Trading with the World* 501

Patterns and Trends in International Trade 503
Australia's International Trade 503
The Balance of Trade 508

Opportunity Cost and Comparative Advantage 508
Opportunity Cost in Pioneerland 508
Opportunity Cost in Magic Empire 509
Comparative Advantage 509

The Gains from Trade 509
Reaping the Gains from Trade 509
Balanced Trade 510
Changes in Production and Consumption 510
Calculating the Gains from Trade 512
Gains for All 512
Absolute Advantage 512
Gains from Trade in Reality 513
A Puzzle 513
Where Will the Jobs Come From? 515

Trade Restrictions 515
The History of Protection 515
How Tariffs Work 518
Non-tariff Barriers 520
How Quotas and VERs Work 520
Why Quotas and VERs Might Be Preferred to Tariffs 522
Dumping 522
Measurement of the Effects of Protection 523
Why is International Trade Restricted? 523
Compensating Losers 524
The Political Outcome 525
Industry Policy Debates in the 1990s 525
International Agreements 525

Reading Between the Lines
Sources of Comparative Advantage 516

CHAPTER 37 *The Balance of Payments and the Dollar* 529

Financing International Trade 531
Balance of Payments Accounts 531
Australia's Balance of Payments Accounts 533

International Borrowing and Lending 537
Borrowing to Consume or Invest 537
Australia's International Borrowing 538

Current Account Balance 539
Sector Balances 539
Bookkeeping and Behaviour 544
Government Sector Balance and Current Account 544
Effects of Government Sector Balance on Private Sector Balance 545
Effects of Government Sector Balance on Current Account Balance 545

Net Exports and the Dollar 546
Prices and the Exchange Rate 546
Money Prices in Two Countries 547
Prices of Exports and Imports 547
The Dollar and the Balance of Trade 547
Equilibrium Exchange Rate 548
The Private Sector Balance, Net Exports and the Exchange Rate 548
Stabilizing the Exchange Rate 550
The 'Real'/'Nominal' Distinction 550

Reading Between the Lines
The Issue of Foreign Debt 540

PART 14 GROWTH, DEVELOPMENT AND COMPARATIVE SYSTEMS

Talking with Helen Hughes 553

CHAPTER 38 *Growth and Development* 556

The International Distribution of Income 558
The World Lorenz Curve 559

Growth Rates and Income Levels 560

Inputs, Technological Progress and Economic Growth 560
Capital Accumulation 562
Technological Change 562

Contributors to Economic Growth 563
Capital Accumulation 564
High Saving Rate 564
International Debt 566
Foreign Aid 567
Population Growth 567
The Underdevelopment Trap 568
Population Control 568
Trade and Development 569
Foreign Investment 570
Structural Change 570
Aggregate Demand Stimulation and Growth 570
An East Asian Model 572

Settler Economies: Resources and Growth 572

CHAPTER 39 *Comparing Economic Systems* 575

The Fundamental Economic Problem 577
Scarcity 577
Getting on to the Production Possibility Frontier 577
Producing the Right Quantities of Goods and Services 577
The Distribution of Economic Well-Being 578

Alternative Economic Systems 578
Capitalism 579
Socialism 580
The Pros and Cons of Capitalism 580

Varieties of Capitalism 581
Japan 581
Welfare State Capitalism 583

The Former Soviet Union/New CIS 584
History 584
Planning and Command System 585
The Market Sector 588
Performance 588
The Reforms of 1987 and 1991 589
Problems in Soviet Reform 589
Options for Reform 590

China 591
The 1978 Reforms 592
Issues in the Chinese Reforms 594

Glossary G-1

Index I-1

PREFACE

To change the way students see the world: this is our aim in teaching economics and in writing this book.

Economics teaches students to use the economist's lens to view the world more clearly. At every point in the writing, development and production of this book, we have tried to put ourselves in the student's place. We have repeatedly recalled our own early struggles to master this discipline and drawn on the learning experiences of the several thousand students whom we have been privileged to teach.

Three assumptions (or are they facts?) about students have been our guiding principles in determining the content, organization, features and visual appearance of this book. First, students are eager to learn, but they are overwhelmed by the seemingly endless claims on their time, interests and energy. As a result, they want to be told — and in a convincing way — just *why* they are being asked to study a particular body of material. They want to be motivated by a demonstration of its relevance to their everyday experience. Second, once motivated, students want to be presented with a thoughtful, clear and logical explanation, so that they can understand and begin to apply what they have learned. They do not want to be handed loosely related facts and anecdotes. Third, students are more interested in the present and future than in the past. They want to learn the economics of the 1990s so that, as they enter the twenty-first century, they will be equipped with the most up-to-date tools available to guide them.

Content and Organization

This book seeks to be truly modern and accurate and, at the same time, to respect and reflect the heritage of timeless principles that have been distilled from the scholarship of economists over the past two centuries.

Many core economic principles have been around for more than one hundred years and other important elements, especially parts of the theory of the firm and Keynesian macroeconomics, have been with us for more than fifty years.

However, economics has also been developing and changing rapidly during the past few decades, and although all economics texts pay some attention to these more recent developments, they have not succeeded in integrating the new and the traditional. They have created a patchwork quilt rather than a seamless web. We have worked hard to avoid this patchwork approach and to present new ideas in a new way, incorporating them into the body of timeless principles in order to weave a coherent pattern.

Among the many recent developments that you will find in this book are rational expectations, efficient markets, game theory, public choice theory, aggregate demand and aggregate supply, and real business cycle theory. Yet the presence of modern topics does not translate into 'high level'. Nor does it translate into 'bias'. The presentation has been designed to make recent developments in economics thoroughly accessible to the beginning student. Furthermore, where these modern theories are controversial, the more traditional theories that they are seeking to replace are also presented and the two (or more) approaches are evaluated and compared. Thus, for example, in macroeconomics, all the alternative 'schools' — Keynesian, monetarist, rational expectations and real business cycle — are given an even-handed treatment.

But this book does have a point of view on one issue. It is that economics is a serious, lively and evolving science — a science that seeks to develop a body of theory powerful enough to explain the economic world around us and that pursues its tasks by building, testing and rejecting economic models. In some areas the science has succeeded in its tasks, but in others it has some way to go and controversy persists. Where matters are settled, we present what we know in the clearest possible light; where controversy persists, we present the alternative viewpoints.

The existence of controversy and disagreement has implications for the organization of an economics course. As a consequence, we have paid special attention to ensuring that this book can be used in a wide variety of ways.

Flexibility

There is legitimate disagreement about how best to teach the principles of economics. Most fundamentally, there is disagreement about the best order in which to present microeconomics and macroeconomics. We have chosen to do microeconomics first, but the book has been written to accommodate courses that put macroeconomics first. The microeconomics and macroeconomics chapters do not depend on each other; concepts and terms are defined and ideas are developed independently in each of the two halves.

Macroeconomics In recognition of the diversity in approaches to teaching macroeconomics — and believing strongly that diversity is appropriate in unsettled parts of the discipline — we have paid special attention to writing these chapters so that they can be used in a variety of ways. We think that the most natural way to teach macroeconomics is as it is presented here. But several other sequences also work well.

We have long been puzzled by the way economics texts present the aggregate demand and aggregate supply model. *Aggregate* demand and *aggregate* supply analysis is more difficult than demand and supply analysis. Yet most books devote a full and thoughtful chapter to the demand and supply model and then present the aggregate demand and aggregate supply model in just a few pages. We have recognized the inherently more difficult nature of the aggregate model and have tried to present an equally careful development of that model in Chapter 24, which parallels our development of the microeconomic demand and supply model in Chapter 4.

Chapter 24 on aggregate demand and aggregate supply serves as an overview of the rest of the macroeconomics material. Alternatively, it can be read as a synthesis of the individual components of aggregate demand and aggregate supply and can be studied after Chapter 31.

For those instructors who like to teach the *IS–LM* model, it is presented in an appendix, but one that is longer, more gentle and (we hope) more teachable than is commonly found.

Special Features

Artwork

One of the most important tools for economists is graphical analysis, yet students often find this method of analysis extremely challenging and even a stumbling block. Recognizing this fact and always keeping it in mind, we and the developmental and art editors at Addison-Wesley have taken extraordinary care in designing the artwork.

We began by observing a distinction between diagrams that represent models and those that display data. Model-based diagrams emphasize analysis and abstraction, whereas empirical graphs emphasize shapes, patterns and visual correlations. It makes good pedagogical sense to differentiate these two kinds of figures in order to help students work with them. As a signal to students, we set our model-based diagrams on a white background, and the empirical graphs on a manila background.

Our aim in the model-based art (see the sample figure below) is to show clearly 'where the economic action is'. To achieve this, we use a consistent format which includes:

* Highlighting shifted curves, points of equilibrium and the most important features in red.

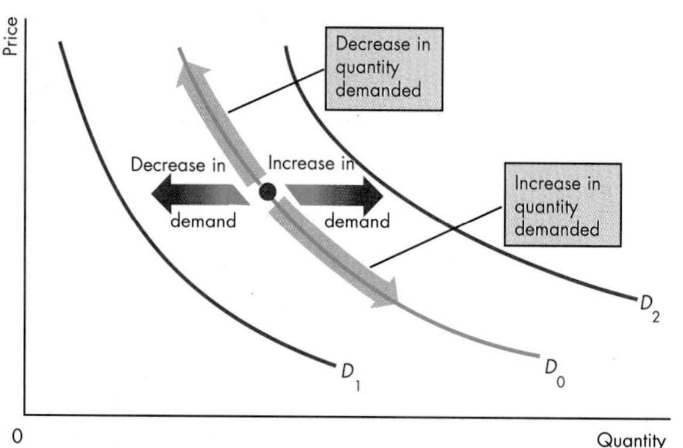

* Using arrows in conjunction with colour to lend directional movement to what are usually static presentations.
* Pairing graphs with data tables from which the curves have been plotted.
* Using colour consistently to emphasize the content, and referring to the colour in the text and captions.
* Labelling key pieces of information in graphs with boxed notes.
* Rendering each piece electronically, so that precision is achieved.

The design of the artwork has been developed with the study and review needs of the student in mind. We have included complete, informative captions that encapsulate the major points in the graph, so that students can preview or review the chapter by skimming through the art.

The Interviews

An important aim of an economics course is to develop, in students, the ability to reason like economists. To aid this process, this book enables students to eavesdrop on a series of conversations that we conducted with fourteen eminent people; these people have contributed either to economics as a discipline, or to the formation and execution of economic policy, or both. There is an interview at the beginning of each part of the book. It has been a great joy to learn from these creators or users of economics something about how they view their area of specialization, about their unique contributions to economics, and also about their general insights which are relevant to beginning students.

Each interview has been carefully edited to be self-contained and the necessary concepts and terms are defined informally within each one. Since each interview discusses topics that are introduced formally in the following group of chapters, students can use it as a preview to some of the issues they are about to encounter. A more careful reading afterwards will give students a fuller appreciation of the discussion. Finally, the whole series of interviews can be approached as an informal symposium on the subject matter of economics as it is practised today.

Reading Between the Lines

Another common aim of an economics course is to develop the student's ability to use economics to analyse current events reported in the media. Recognizing this need, we have developed a feature that may, we hope, be fruitful. Each 'Reading Between the Lines' feature contains three passes at a story. It begins with a facsimile of an actual (usually abbreviated) newspaper or magazine article. It then presents a digest of the article's essential points. Finally, it provides an economic analysis of the news story. We believe that students, using this feature, will learn how to do more than just notice the relevance of economics to modern life. We hope that they will also develop the ability to ask good questions, to evaluate the quality of information presented in the media, and to use economic models to deepen their understanding of the economic world around them.

Our Advancing Knowledge

Another group of special essays reveals the birth and development of economic ideas, not just as abstract models, but as intimately tied to the people and circumstances that formed them.

Learning Aids

We have developed a careful pedagogical plan to ensure that this book complements and reinforces formal teaching. Each chapter contains the following pedagogical elements:

* *Objectives.* A list of chapter objectives that enables students to set their goals before embarking on a chapter.

* *Chapter openers.* Economic vignettes, questions, puzzles or metaphors that motivate the analysis and that are resolved in the chapter.
* *Highlighted in-text reviews.* Succinct summaries at the end of many main sections.
* *Key terms.* Highlighted within the text, these concepts form the first part of a three-tiered review of economic vocabulary. These terms are repeated, with page references, at chapter ends and they are compiled in the end-of-book glossary.
* *End-of-chapter study material.* Summaries organized around major headings; lists of key terms with page references; and problems. We have worked hard to make the problems interesting, challenging and useful for students.

Design

The design has an important place in the overall pedagogical plan. Our aim with the design of special features was to evoke the colourful feeling of non-textbook print media, notably magazines and annual reports, thus reinforcing the connection of economics to the real world. In the text itself, we sought a scrupulously clear and honest look that would let the models being presented speak for themselves.

The Teaching and Learning Package

In conjunction with the authors of the supplements and Addison-Wesley we have put a tremendous amount of effort into ensuring that each component of the package will help students and instructors derive the maximum benefit from the textbook.

Study Guide Prepared by Teresita Bentick of the University of Adelaide, the *Study Guide* offers a wide range of challenging questions and has been carefully coordinated with the main textbook. Each chapter contains: Chapter in Perspective, Learning Objectives, Helpful Hints, Self-Test and Answers to Self-Test.

Computerized Test Bank Prepared by Terry Alchin of the University of Western Sydney, this package offers 3000 multiple-choice questions. Computerized Test Items Software for qualified adopters is available for IBM-PC compatible microcomputers and Macintosh computers. Hard copy is available on request from Addison-Wesley.

Instructor's Manual Prepared by Pasquale Sgro of Deakin University, the *Instructor's Manual* includes detailed chapter outlines and teaching suggestions, a list of relevant transparencies, answers to problems in the textbook and a flexibility guide prepared by Michael Parkin.

Acetates/Transparency Masters Reproductions of many of the key figures are available to qualified adopters of the textbook.

Student Graph Package Key graphs from the text are reproduced in a consumable format. This inexpensive supplement will allow the student to concentrate on the content of the lecture rather than redrawing the instructor's overhead material.

Reading Between the Lines Includes 85 news articles dealing with important economic principles, each followed by a series of analytical questions. An extension of the 'Reading Between the Lines' feature found in the text.

Economic Times An economic journal of the world events prepared by Michael Parkin. This supplement can be used with the textbook to review key concepts as they apply to current events and will be updated on a bi-annual basis.

Economics in Action This software has been prepared by Doug McTaggart, Michael Parkin, Christopher Findlay, Robin Bade and Paul Davis for both the IBM–PC (and compatibles) and the MAC platforms. It is an interactive tutorial and quizzing program, fully menu driven in a windowing environment. Not simply an electronic paging program, **IHTutor** establishes the state-of-the-art for interactive computer-based learning (CAL).

Student Edition Software Full-function versions of leading software adapted for student purchase only are available from Addison-Wesley, including Student Edition Software for Lotus™1-2-3™, MathCAD™, MINITAB™ and dBASE IV™.

Acknowledgements

One of the great pleasures of writing an introductory text is the opportunity it affords to learn from so many generous friends and colleagues. Although the extent of our debts cannot be fully acknowledged here, it is nevertheless a joy to record our gratitude to the many people who have helped, some without realizing just how helpful they were.

Michael Parkin, in the Preface to his original US edition of *Economics*, acknowledged the generous colleagues and friends from around the world whose advice and suggestions were invaluable. He paid particular tribute to Robin Bade who was almost a co-author of that edition and who became a co-author of the subsequent Canadian edition.

Doug McTaggart and Christopher Findlay acknowledge the comments and suggestions received from those listed in the Review Board. We have made every attempt to heed advice where given. We are particularly grateful to some individuals who spent more time that we could have reasonably expected and provided detailed comments on various drafts of the manuscript. We would be remiss if we did not single out for mention John Lodewijks and Geoffrey Kingston of the University of New South Wales, David Round of the University of Adelaide and Margaret Freebairn of the Swinburne Institute of Technology. Binh Tran-Nam, now at the University of New South Wales, also provided useful comments and corrected some errors that might otherwise have slipped through. Bruce Chapman from the ANU ably re-directed us on the chapters concerning labour markets. Alan Powell, Director of the Impact Project, generously provided us with data on supply and demand elasticities and Allan Potter, from Pacific Power, provided the data on the costs of producing electricity.

Christopher Findlay is also grateful to his colleagues at the University of Adelaide for discussing many points with him. Teresita Bentick, a partner in this venture, through her work on the *Study Guide*, was another important contributor of comments and ideas. Other Adelaide colleagues who spent time with the authors included Ian McLean, Kym Anderson and Cliff Walsh. Ray Lewis at Adelaide re-read and checked the manuscript for us, and Stephen Woodland provided expert assistance in gathering data and producing charts.

Finally, we are deeply grateful to the team at Addison-Wesley. Andrew Semmens opened the batting in the project with us. He was backed by Susan Lewis and Wendy Rapee. We are also grateful for the contribution of the editorial team of Andrew Kelly, Lesley Dow and Venetia Nelson.

The empirical test of this textbook's value will be made by its users. We would appreciate hearing from instructors and students about how we might improve the book in future editions.

Douglas McTaggart
School of Business
Bond University
Gold Coast
Queensland 4229
Australia

Christopher Findlay
Department of Economics
University of Adelaide
Box 498 GPO
Adelaide 5001
Australia

Michael Parkin
Department of Economics
University of Western Ontario
London, Ontario N6A 5C2

REVIEWERS

Terry Alchin	*University of Western Sydney*
Jonathan Baldry	*University of New England*
Jeff Carmichael	*Bond University*
Peter Drysdale	*Australian National University*
Cathy Fletcher	*Monash University*
Margaret Freebairn	*Swinburne Institute of Technology*
Dudley Jackson	*University of Wollongong*
Steven Kemp	*Curtin University of Technology*
John King	*La Trobe University*
Geoffrey Kingston	*University of New South Wales*
Don Lamberton	*Circit (Centre for International Research on Communication and Information Technology)*
John Lodewijks	*University of New South Wales*
Ian McDonald	*University of Melbourne*
Ian McLean	*University of Adelaide*
Ron McIver	*University of South Australia*
Judith Milne-Pott	*Royal Melbourne Institute of Technology*
Yew-Kwang Ng	*Monash University*
Keith Norris	*Murdoch University*
Graham Richards	*Monash University*
David Round	*University of Adelaide*
Pasquale Sgro	*Deakin University*
Yanis Varoufakis	*University of Sydney*
Don Wright	*University of Sydney*

Part 1

Introduction

Talking with Heinz Arndt

Professor Heinz Arndt was until his retirement Professor of Economics in the Research School of Pacific Studies at the Australian National University. He is still writing and doing research on issues in economic development and macroeconomics. Christopher Findlay spoke to him about the origins of his interest in economics and some current issues.

What attracted you originally to economics?

It seemed to me to be much more hard headed and rigorous than the other social sciences, something one could get one's teeth into. Economics has the most rigorous methodology, which involves putting forward hypotheses that can be tested with the econometric apparatus. This methodology distinguishes economics from other social sciences.

Does that make economics scientific?

The only way people knew how to make economics 'scientific' was to imitate the approach of the physical sciences. The trouble is that economics is a moral science where rigorous testing of positive hypotheses is only part of the story. At every point, in order to draw inferences about policy, you have to inject value judgements and that involves a very considerable capacity to judge, to combine inferences from facts with trade-offs between all sorts of objectives.

'economics is a moral science'

What do you think of the public's perception of economists?

Part of the public's perception is that economists disagree violently — you know the joke — if you put all the economists in the world end to end they would never reach a conclusion! On the other hand, despite these complaints, economists are held in great respect almost like religious prophets, because on economic policy issues the public prefers a judgement by an economist to one by a politician.

Can we date the emergence of an economics profession?

There were no professional economists, that is, people who regarded themselves as economists much more than 100 years ago. It was the Keynesian revolution in the 1930s that made the public think about economists as professionals. Keynesian prescriptions for dealing with depressions gave economists considerable status, and that has lasted through the post-war years.

Do you think that economists can adequately encapsulate the trade-offs we might want to make between growth and the environment? Some public comment suggests that we cannot do that.

That may be true. On the other hand I'm extremely sceptical about the religion of environmentalism and its emergence as a luxury consumption good of the middle class. The problem is to dissociate that sort of position from sensible discussion of the trade-offs between rising living standards and environmental protection. For two decades the trade-off was between growth and equity but environmentalism has slowly taken over. For relatively well-to-do members of our society it may be easy to disparage growth but for the whole society it may not be.

'the public's perception is that economists disagree violently'

Is it possible for economists to comment on these sorts of debates without injecting their personal values?

No it's not. I think that it is important to state your own value premises as best you can. It certainly helps to be aware of your prejudices and to try to warn your readers. In the light of their own value judgements economists should try to come to the best judgement they can. The advantage of economists is that they make trade-offs in the light of a better understanding of the operation of the economic system and a better knowledge of the facts.

What are your views of the importance or lack of importance of Australia's foreign debt?

I belong to the group that believes that it is bad for a country to run up an enormous foreign debt, borrowing year by year to finance a large current account deficit. It's a dubious proposition, as argued by some people, that the debt and the current account deficit don't matter. The notion that foreign debt is a bad thing so long as it's incurred by government borrowing but doesn't matter if it's incurred by private borrowing depends on a very extreme view of the rationality of profit maximizing business people.

'it is bad for a country to run up an enormous foreign debt'

Could it not be the case that the high capital inflow reflects the investment opportunities in Australia?

The crucial variable is our international competitiveness. I see the current account deficit as the result of declining international competitiveness. This deficit is financed by capital inflow, attracted by high interest rates. The other view is the one you mention, that the current account deficit reflects the capital inflow which is attracted to Australia by the investment opportunities. The current account deficit in this view is the consequence of the capital account surplus. This perspective is too complacent. There are many things we need to do to increase competitiveness and reduce the current account deficit.

'treat economics as a social science which is relevant to the real world'

What piece of advice would you give to persons first starting their study of economics?

Economics is an exciting and important subject. They should study it with as much history, politics and geography as possible, do the quantitative work in maths and stats they have to, but treat economics as a social science which is relevant to the real world and where ultimately they will have to make their own judgements.

If you would like to read more about Professor Arndt, and how he came to live and work in Australia, look in your library for his autobiography entitled *A Course Through Life: Memoirs of an Australian Economist*, published in 1985 by the National Centre for Development Studies at the Australian National University in Canberra.

Chapter 1

What is Economics?

After studying this chapter, you will be able to:

- State the kinds of questions that economics tries to answer.
- Explain why all economic questions and economic activity arise from scarcity.
- Explain why scarcity forces people to make choices.
- Define opportunity cost.
- Describe the function and the working parts of an economy.
- Distinguish between positive and normative statements.
- Explain what is meant by an economic theory and how economic theories are developed by building and testing economic models.
- Distinguish between positive and normative statements.

Seven Big Questions

Seven big questions give an overview of economics. They are: Q How do people choose what to consume and how to produce, and how are these choices affected by the discovery of new ways of doing things — new technologies? Q What determines people's incomes and why do some people receive much larger rewards than do others whose efforts appear to be similar? Q What are the causes of unemployment and why are some groups more severely affected by unemployment than others? Q Why do prices rise and why do some countries sometimes experience rapid price increases while others have stable prices? Q How does the scope of government influence economic life and what happens when the government has a budget deficit or surplus? Q What determines the pattern and volume of trade between nations and what are the effects of tariffs and quotas on international trade? Q What causes differences in wealth among nations, making the people in some countries rich and in others poor?

These seven questions that provide an overview of economics are big questions for two reasons. First, they affect the quality of human life with great intensity. Second, they are hard questions to answer. They generate passionate argument and debate, and just about everybody has an opinion about them. Self-appointed experts abound. One of the hardest things for students of economics, whether beginners or seasoned practitioners, is to stand clear of the passion and emotion, and to approach their work with the detachment, rigour and objectivity of a scientist.

In this chapter, we will explain how economists try to find answers to economic questions.

Economic Questions in the World Today

Just about every time you pick up a newspaper, open a magazine, or turn on your radio or television, you are bombarded with economic information and confronted with economic questions. Economics is already a major part of your life. Let's look at the economic reality that surrounds you with some examples that illustrate the seven big questions that economics tries to answer.

Production, Consumption and Technological Change

If you wanted to watch a movie in your home in 1975, you had to rent a movie projector and a screen — as well as the movie itself. The cost of such entertainment would have been as high as what a theatre would have paid to show the movie to several hundred people. Only the rich could afford to watch movies in the comfort of their own homes.

In 1978, the video cassette recorder (VCR) became available to Australian consumers. Its typical price tag was $1300 (which in today's dollars is nearly $3500). Since that time, the price of VCRs has steadily fallen so that today you can buy a reliable machine for $500. A video can be rented for a few dollars a day and can be bought for less than $20. In just a few years, watching a movie at home changed from a luxury available to the richest few to an event enjoyed by millions.

Advances in technology affect the way we *consume*. We now watch far more movies at home than we did a decade ago because new technologies have lowered the cost.

New technologies also affect the way we *produce* things. Johnny Wilder, Jr., was a successful popular musician in the 1970s with such hits as 'Boogie Nights' and 'Always and Forever'. A car accident in 1979 left Wilder paralysed from the neck down. Today, Wilder again produces music but of a new kind. The artist now works with a Macintosh computer and synthesizers controlled by his breath and by beams of light.

We hear a great deal these days about lasers. Their most dramatic use may be in the types of weapons systems that were used with great effect in the recent Gulf War. 'Smart bombs' and laser-guided defence systems have changed the way generals think about conducting war. But lasers have been having an impact on our daily routines for some time now. They scan prices at the supermarket checkout. They create holograms on credit cards, making them harder to forge. Neurosurgeons and eye surgeons use them in our hospitals.

New technologies affect the way that we produce goods and services and the examples that we have given illustrate the first big economic question:

How do people choose what to consume and how to produce, and how are these choices affected by the discovery of new ways of doing things — of new technologies?

Wages and Earnings

On a crisp, bright winter day on the ski slopes at Perisher, a 23-year-old instructs some beginning skiers in the snowplow turn. For this pleasant and uncomplicated work, the young woman, who quit school after year 11, is paid $50 for a one hour session, perhaps giving a couple of sessions a day.

In a lawyer's office in the centre of a busy city, a 23-year-old office manager handles a large volume of correspondence, filing, scheduling and meetings. He arrives home most evenings exhausted. He has a bachelor's degree in English and has taken night courses in computer science and word processing. He receives $8 an hour for his work.

In 1990, Australian golfer Greg Norman earned $1,165,477 in prize money playing golf on the United States PGA Tour. He played in 17 tournaments, winning two of them. Over the same year, another Australian golfer, Ian Baker-Finch, who went on to win the British Open in 1991, played seven more tournaments than Norman on the same tour, and only won $611,492. A similar phenomenon can be seen in the headquarters of large corporations. Chief executive officers who work no harder (and in some cases, even less hard) than the people immediately beneath them receive far higher salaries than their subordinates.

Situations like these raise the second big economic question:

What determines people's incomes and why do some people receive much larger rewards than others whose efforts appear to be similar?

Unemployment

During the Great Depression, the four years from 1929 to 1933, unemployment afflicted almost one fifth of the labour force in the industrial world. For months and in some cases years on end, many families had no income other than meagre payments from the government or from private charities. In the 1950s and 1960s, unemployment rates stayed below 5 per cent in most countries and in some — for example, Japan, Britain and Australia — below 2 per cent. During the 1970s and early 1980s, unemployment steadily increased so that by 1983 almost 10 per cent of the Australian labour force was looking for work. In 1989, the Australian unemployment rate had fallen to below 7 per cent. But by 1991, it had risen back up to 10 per cent.

Unemployment affects different groups unequally. When the average unemployment rate in Australia was 6.6 per cent — as it was in 1988/89 — the unemployment rate among young people 15 to 19 years old was 16.5 per cent. For young women aged 15 to 19 it was 18.5 per cent.

These facts raise the third big economic question:

What are the causes of unemployment and why are some groups more severely affected than others?

Inflation

Between August 1945 and July 1946, prices in Hungary rose by an average of 20,000 per cent per month. In the worst month, July 1946, they rose 419 quadrillion per cent (a quadrillion is the number 1 followed by 15 zeros).

In 1985, the cost of living in Bolivia rose by 11,750 per cent. This meant that in downtown La Paz a McDonald's hamburger that cost 20 bolivianos on January 1 cost 2370 bolivianos by the end of the year. That same year, prices were rising at a rate of 6.8 per cent per year in Australia but at only 3.2 per cent in the United States. But in the late 1970s, prices in Australia and the United States were rising at a rate in excess of 10 per cent a year.

These facts raise the fourth big economic question:

Why do prices rise and why do some countries sometimes experience rapid price increases while others have stable prices?

Government

The government touches many aspects of life. It maintains the army, air force and navy, for our national defence. It provides law enforcement, health care, social security and education.

The cost of government has increased dramatically over the years. In the early 1900s, the Federal government took in taxes and spent about 4 cents out of every dollar earned, and State and local governments took in and spent about 2 cents — for a total of about 6 cents for every dollar earned. Government budgets were balanced. In 1988/89 the Federal government collected 26 cents in taxes out of every dollar earned, and spent 24 cents, thereby generating a 2-cent surplus, or a 2-cent excess of taxation over spending for every dollar earned. The Federal government thus saved 2 cents in every dollar earned. If you add State and local government spending to that of the Federal government, savings fell to less than 1 cent in every dollar earned by Australians because State and local governments operated at a deficit. But by 1991/92 the Federal government was again spending more than it was collecting in taxes.

These facts about government raise the fifth big economic question:

How do government spending and taxes influence economic life and what happens when the government has a deficit or a surplus?

International Trade

In the 1960s, cars and trucks on Australian roads were mostly Holdens, Fords, Chryslers or British Leylands. By the late 1980s, Toyotas, Hondas, Nissans, Mitsubishis and Hyundais were a common sight on these same roads. By 1989 almost one-fifth of all new cars sold in Australia were imported. The proportion of imports was about the same as in the late 1950s but the big change has been in the increase in the market share of Japanese and Korean brands.

Cars are not exceptional. The same can be said of television sets, clothing and computers.

Governments regulate international trade in cars and in most other commodities. They impose taxes on imports, called tariffs, and also establish quotas, which restrict the quantities that may be imported.

These facts raise the sixth big economic question:

What determines the pattern and the volume of trade between nations and what are the effects of tariffs and quotas on international trade?

Wealth and Poverty

At the mouth of the Pearl River in south-east China is a small rocky peninsula and a group of islands with virtually no natural resources. But this bare land supports about 5.6 million people who, though not excessively rich, live in rapidly growing abundance. They produce much of the world's fashion goods and electronic components. They are the people of Hong Kong.

On the eastern edge of Africa bordering the Red Sea, a tract of land more than a thousand times larger supports a population of 45 million people — only eight times that of Hong Kong. The region suffers such abject poverty that in 1985 rock singers from Europe and North America organized one of the most spectacular world-wide fund-raising efforts ever seen — Live Aid — to help them. These are the desperate and dying people of Ethiopia.

Hong Kong and Ethiopia, two extremes in income and wealth, are not isolated examples. The poorest two-thirds of the world's population consumes about 15 per cent of all things produced. The richest 20 per cent of the world's population — living in rich countries such as the United States, Canada, Western Europe, Japan, Australia and New Zealand — consumes 70 per cent of the world's output.

These facts raise the seventh big economic question:

What causes differences in wealth among nations, making the people in some countries rich and in others poor?

Later in this chapter, we will explain how economists try to find answers to economic questions. But before doing that, let's go back to the seven big questions. What do these questions have in common? What distinguishes them from non-economic questions?

Scarcity

All economic questions arise from a single and inescapable fact: you can't always get what you want. We live in a world of scarcity. An economist defines **scarcity** to mean that wants always exceed the resources available to satisfy them. A child wants a 90-cent can of soft drink and a 50-cent pack of chewing gum but has only $1 in her pocket. She experiences scarcity. A student wants to go to a party on Saturday night but also wants to spend that same night catching up on late assignments. She also experiences scarcity. The rich and the poor alike face scarcity. The government of Australia with its enormous budget, around $100 billion in 1990/91, faces scarcity. It would like to be able to spend more on defence, health, education, welfare and other services than it currently is able to. Even parrots face scarcity — there just aren't enough crackers to go around.

'Not only do I want a cracker – we all want a cracker!'

Drawing by Modell; © 1985 The New Yorker Magazine, Inc.

Wants do not simply exceed resources; they are unlimited. In contrast, resources are limited, or finite. People want good health and a long life, material comfort, security, physical and mental recreation, opportunities for personal development and the preservation of many aspects of their natural environment.

None of these wants is satisfied for everyone; and everyone has some unsatisfied wants. While many Australians have all the material comfort they want, many do not. No one feels entirely satisfied with his or her state of health and length of life. No one feels entirely secure, and no one — not even the wealthiest person — has the time to enjoy all the travel, vacations and art that he or she would like. Not even the wisest and most knowledgeable philosopher or scientist knows as much as he or she would like to know.

We can imagine a world that satisfies people's wants for material comfort and, perhaps, even security. But we cannot imagine a world in which people live as long and in as good a state of health as they would like. Nor can we imagine people having all the time, energy and resources to enjoy all the sports, travel, vacations and art that they would like. Natural resources and human resources — in the form of time, muscle-power and brain-power — as well as all the dams, roads, buildings, machinery, tools and other equipment that have been built by past human efforts amount to an enormous heritage, but they are limited. Our unlimited wants will always outstrip the resources available to satisfy them.

Economic Activity

The confrontation of unlimited wants with limited resources results in economic activity. **Economic**

activity is what people do to cope with scarcity. **Economics**, then, is the study of how people use their limited resources to try to satisfy unlimited wants. Defined in this way, economic activity and economics deal with a wide range of issues and problems. The seven big questions posed earlier are examples of the more important problems economists study. Let's see how those questions could not arise if resources were infinitely abundant and scarcity did not exist.

With unlimited resources, there would be no need to devise better ways of producing more goods. Studying how we all spend our time and effort would not be interesting because we would simply do what we enjoyed without restriction. There would be no wages. We would do only the things that we enjoyed because there would be enough goods and services to satisfy everyone without effort. Unemployment would not be an issue because no one would work — except for people who wanted to work simply for the pleasure that it gave them. Inflation — rising prices — would not be a problem because everything would be free. Questions about government intervention in economic life would not arise because there would be no need for government-provided goods and no taxes. We would simply take whatever we wanted from the infinite resources available. There would be no international trade since, with complete abundance, it would be pointless to transport things from one place to another. Finally, differences in wealth among nations would not arise because we would all have as much as we wanted. There would be no such thing as rich and poor countries — all countries would be infinitely wealthy.

You can see that this science fiction world of complete abundance would have no economic questions. It is the universal fact of scarcity that produces economic questions.

Choice

Faced with scarcity, people must make *choices.* When we cannot have everything that we want, we have to choose among the available alternatives. Because scarcity forces us to choose, economics is sometimes called the science of choice — the science that explains the choices that people make and predicts how changes in circumstances affect their choices.

To make a choice, we balance the benefits of having one more of one thing against the costs of having less of something else. Balancing benefits against costs and doing the best within the limits of what is possible is called **optimizing.** There is another word that has a similar meaning — *economizing.* **Economizing** is making the best use of the resources available. Once people have made a choice and have optimized, they cannot have more of *everything.* To get more of one thing means having less of something else. Expressed in another way: in making choices, we face costs. Whatever we choose to do, we could always have chosen to do something else instead.

Opportunity Cost Economists use the term opportunity cost to emphasize that making choices in the face of scarcity implies a cost. The **opportunity cost** of any action is the best alternative forgone. If you cannot have everything that you want, then you have to choose among the alternatives. The best thing that you choose not to do — the best forgone alternative — is the cost of the thing that you choose to do.

Dollar Cost We often express opportunity cost in terms of dollars. But this is just a convenient unit of measurement. The dollars spent on a book are not available for spending on a compact disc (CD). The opportunity cost of the book is not the dollars spent on it but the CD forgone.

Time Cost The dollar cost of a good is only part of its opportunity cost. Another part is the time spent obtaining the good. If you take an hour off work to visit your dentist, the opportunity cost of that visit (expressed in units of dollars) is the amount that you paid to your dentist plus the wages that you lost by not being at work. Again, it's important to keep reminding yourself that the opportunity cost is not the dollars involved but the goods that you could have bought with those dollars.

External Cost Not all of the opportunity costs that you incur are the result of your own choices. Sometimes others make choices that impose opportunity costs on you. And your own choices can impose opportunity costs on others. For example, when you cannot get onto a bus at rush hour, you have to bear the cost of the choices made by all the other people who filled the bus. If you managed to get on the bus, you have imposed an opportunity cost on those left waiting in the line.

Marginal Cost A marginal cost is an extra cost resulting from changing the scale or type of activity undertaken. Opportunity cost is a marginal cost. For example, suppose your dentist's office is on the route that you always take from home to work. When you visit the dentist, you break your journey but don't change your route and it doesn't cost any more to get to work. And the amount you spent on the bus from home to the dentist's office is not part of the opportunity cost of your dental work. But now suppose your dentist moves. To get to her office, you have to make a detour from your normal journey to work. The cost of that detour is part of the opportunity cost of visiting the dentist.

Best Alternative Forgone It's important, in measuring opportunity cost, to value only the best alternative forgone. To make this clear, consider the following example. You are supposed to attend a lecture at 8.30 on a Monday morning. There are two alternatives to attending this lecture: stay in bed for an hour or go jogging for an hour. You cannot, of course, stay in bed and go jogging for that same hour. The opportunity cost of attending the lecture is not the cost of an hour in bed and the cost of jogging for an hour. If these are the only two alternatives that you would contemplate, then you have to decide which one you would do if you did not go to the lecture. The opportunity cost of attending a lecture for a jogger is an hour of exercise; the opportunity cost of attending a lecture for a late sleeper is an hour in bed.

Scarcity implies cost — opportunity cost. It also implies one other fundamental feature of human life — competition.

Competition and Cooperation

Competition If wants exceed resources, wants must compete against each other for what is available. **Competition** is a contest for command over scarce resources. In the case of the child with $1.00 in pocket money who wants a soft drink and chewing gum that add up to $1.40, the soft drink and gum compete for the $1.00 in her pocket. For the student who has allowed assignments to accumulate, the party and the assignments compete with each other for Saturday night. For the government, defence and social services compete with each other for limited tax dollars.

Scarcity also implies competition between people. If it is not possible to have everything that you want, then you must compete with others for what is available. In modern societies, competition has been organized within a framework of almost universally accepted rules that have evolved. This evolution of rules is itself a direct response to the problem of scarcity. Not all societies, even modern societies, employ identical rules to govern competition. For example, the way that economic life is organized in Australia differs greatly from that in China. In Chapter 39, we examine these differences and compare alternative economic systems. For now, we will restrict our attention to the rules that govern competition in Australia.

A key rule of competition is that people own what they have acquired through voluntary exchange. People can compete with each other by offering more favourable exchanges — for example, selling something for a lower price or buying something for a higher price. But they cannot compete with each other by simply taking something from someone else.

Cooperation Perhaps you are thinking that scarcity does not make competition inevitable and that cooperation would better solve economic problems. **Cooperation** means working with others to achieve a common end. If we cooperated instead of competing with each other, wouldn't that eliminate economic problems? This line of reasoning is appealing because it emphasizes the possibility that we might be able to solve our economic problems by using reason. Moreover, examples abound of cooperation as a solution to economic problems. We cooperate when we agree to rules of the game that limit competition to avoid violence. Marriage partners cooperate. Most forms of business also entail cooperation. Workers cooperate with each other on the production line; members of a management team cooperate with each other to design, produce and market their products; management and workers cooperate; business partners cooperate. Cooperation can even occur at the national economic policy level as, for example, when the government, unions and employers agreed upon the Accord process in 1983.

Common as it is, cooperative behaviour neither solves the economic problem nor eliminates competition. Almost all cooperative behaviour implies some prior competition to find the best individuals with whom to cooperate. Marriage provides a good example. Although marriage is a cooperative affair, unmarried people compete intensely to find a marriage partner. Similarly, although workers and management cooperate with each other, firms compete for the best workers and workers compete for the best employers. Professionals such as lawyers and doctors compete with each other for the best business partners.

Competition does not end when a partner has been found. Groups of people who cooperate compete with other groups. For example, although a group of lawyers may have formed a partnership and may work together, they will be in competition with other lawyers.

Scarcity, Costs and Choice

Hydro-scheme: Forests Lose but Ozone Wins

A 1988 plan for a hydro-electric power scheme in Queensland's far north has re-emerged with new vigour and a new edge to the old environmental debate which focused on damage to forests and loss of rare fauna.

For the first time in Australia, arguments over the projected boost to greenhouse gas emissions from a coal- or gas-fuelled alternative power scheme, are being used as a major counter-argument to the environmental negatives, including the loss of world heritage listed forests south of Ravenshoe.

The Premier, Mr Goss, pushed this argument yesterday as he fired up the national debate on the proposed Tully–Millstream hyro-electric project by revealing that he intended to talk directly to the Prime Minister, Mr Hawke, and push for a decision 'as soon as possible'.

The go-ahead for the scheme would ultimately depend on the Federal government's decision because of the legal and constitutional requirements applying to the project, which would claim 15 per cent of the 900,000 ha of world heritage forests in the far north.

Weighty task force studies, put before State Cabinet in Brisbane yesterday and later released publicly by Mr Goss, argue that the next best option to the Tully–Millstream hydro-electric scheme, a coal- or gas-fired project, would push an additional 48.6 million tonnes of carbon dioxide equivalent into the atmosphere.

This figure, calculated over an estimated 50-year life of the hydro-scheme was, according to the studies, equivalent to roughly 19 per cent of the present total annual carbon dioxide emissions from fossil fuels in Australia.

In pure financial terms, the hydro advantage is measured at $270 million, $30 million of which is proposed for compensation in terms of environmental research and replacement national parks.

Financial Review
Tuesday 9 April 1991
By Murray Massey

The Essence of the Story

- The Queensland Government is committed to increasing the supply of electricity in the state by building a new power plant. The alternatives are either a gas- or coal-fired power scheme or a hydro-scheme.

- The hydro-scheme would entail the use of land currently set aside as would heritage listed forest.

- The gas- or coal-fired scheme would release large quantities of carbon dioxide into the atmosphere.

- In weighing up the costs and benefits, the Queensland government has come down on the side of the hydro-scheme. But both options have been costed by the government and a final decision will be made following discussion of the reports outlining the benefits and costs of the different options.

Background and Analysis

- Both electric power and envirnomentally undisturbed forest areas are scarce goods. In this instance, provision of one means having less of the other.

- In terms of alternative land use, the opportunity cost of building a hydro-electric plant is the loss of protected forest area and the consequent damage to the fauna and flora.

- The opportunity cost of retaining the forest area undisturbed is the need to build an alternative gas- or coal-fired power plant.

- But this alternative to the hydro-scheme increases greenhouse gas emissions by 19 per cent and imposes considerable environmental costs itself.

- In addition, the gas or coal option costs an extra $270 million to build and run — that is, has a further opportunity cost in terms of foregone goods and services to the value of $270 million.

Conclusions

- Four scarce goods enter into consideration here: power, forests, air and other goods and services. Because they are all scarce, choices must be made which involve choosing more of some of these goods and less of others.

REVIEW

Economics is the study of the activities arising from scarcity. Scarcity forces people to make choices. Economists try to understand the choices that people make. To make choices, people optimize. To optimize, they evaluate the costs of alternative actions. We call these opportunity costs, to emphasize that doing one thing removes the opportunity to do something else. Scarcity also implies that people must compete with each other. ■

You now know the types of questions that economists try to answer and that all economic questions and economic activity arise from scarcity. In the following chapters, we are going to study economic activity and discover how a modern economy such as that of Australia works. But before we do that, we need to stand back and take an overview of our economy. What exactly do we mean by 'the economy'?

The Economy

What is an economy? How does an economy work? Rather than trying to answer these questions directly, let's begin by asking similar questions but on a more familiar subject. What is an aeroplane? How does an aeroplane work?

Without delving into the detail that would satisfy an aeronautical engineer, most of us could take a shot at answering these two questions. We would describe an aeroplane as a flying machine that transports people and cargo. To explain how an aeroplane works, we would describe its key components — fuselage (or body), wings and engines, and also perhaps its flaps, rudder, and control and navigation systems. We would also explain that as powerful engines move the machine forward, its wings create an imbalance in air pressure that lifts it into the air.

This example nicely illustrates four things. First, it is hard to explain what something is without saying what it does. To say that an aeroplane is a machine does not tell us much. We have to go beyond that and say what the machine is for, and how it works.

Second, it is hard to explain how something works without dividing it up into components. Once we have described something in terms of its components, we can explain how those components work and how they interact with each other.

Third, it is hard to explain how something works without leaving out some details. Notice that we did not describe an aeroplane in all its detail. Instead, we isolated the most important parts in order to explain how the whole works. We did not emphasize the inflight movie system, the seat belts or the colour of the paint on the wings. We supposed that these things were largely, or even totally, irrelevant to an explanation of how an aeroplane works.

Fourth and finally, there are different levels of understanding how something works. We gave a superficial account of how an aeroplane works. An aeronautical engineer would have given a deeper explanation and experts in the individual components — engines, navigation systems, control system and so on — would have given an even more detailed and precise explanation than a general engineer.

Now let's return to questions about the economy. What is an economy? How does it work?

What is an Economy?

An **economy** is a mechanism that allocates scarce resources among competing uses. This mechanism achieves three things:

- What
- How
- For whom

1 *What* goods and services will be produced and in *what* quantities? How many VCRs will be made and how many movie theatres will be built? How many restaurants will open up and how many grocery stores? How many high performance cars will be built, and how many trucks and station-wagons?

2 *How* will the various goods and services be produced? Will a supermarket operate with three checkout queues and operators using laser scanners or six checkout queues and operators keying in prices by hand? Will workers weld station-wagons by hand or will robots do the job? Will farmers keep track of their income, expenditure and stock numbers by using paper and pencil records or personal computers? Will credit card companies use computers to read charge slips in Sydney or ship paper records to cities in Asia for hand processing?

3 *For whom* will the various goods and services be produced? The distribution of economic benefits depends on the distribution of income and wealth.

Figure 1.1 A Picture of the Economy

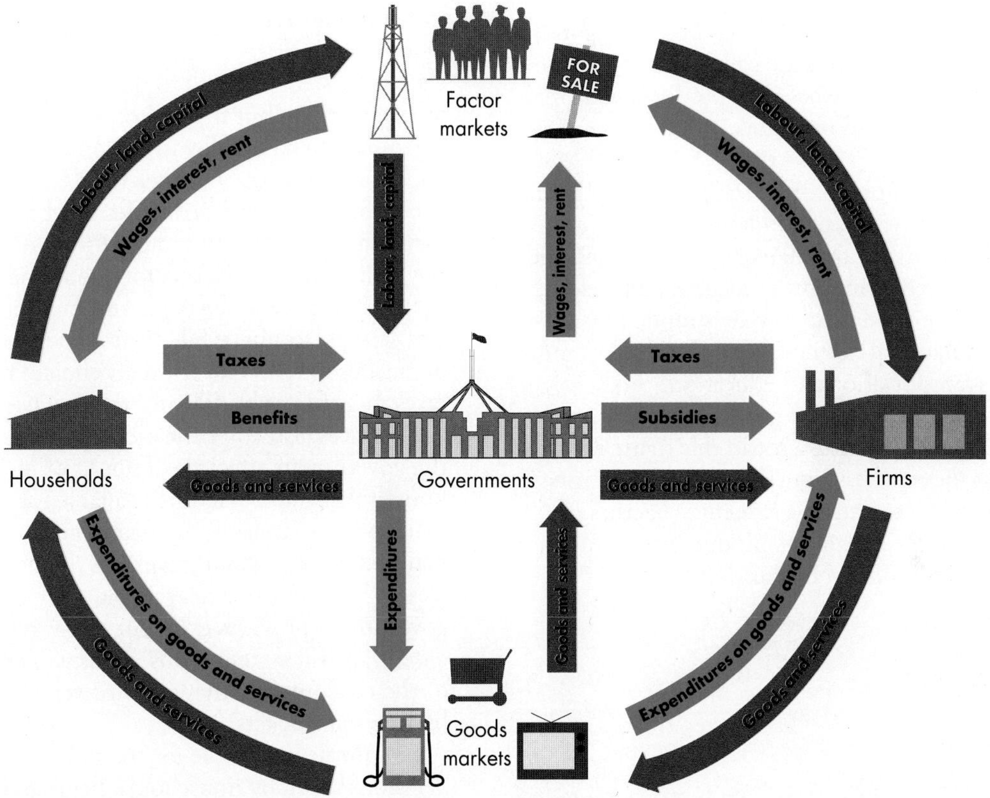

The economy has three groups of decisionmakers: households, firms and governments. It also has two groups of markets: factor markets and goods markets. Households provide factors of production to both firms and governments through factor markets. Firms and governments pay households wages, interest, rent and profits in exchange. Firms supply goods and services to households and to governments through goods markets. Households and governments pay firms for these goods and services. In addition, governments provide goods and services directly to households and firms. Households and firms pay taxes to government and governments make transfer payments — subsidies and benefits — to firms and households. In this figure, flows of goods, services, land, labour and capital are represented by the red arrows. Money and other expenditures are shown by the green arrows.

Those with a high income and great wealth consume more goods and services than those with low income and little wealth. Who gets to consume what thus depends on income. Will the ski instructor consume more than the lawyer's secretary? Will the people of Hong Kong get to consume more than the people of Ethiopia?

The Economy's Working Parts

To understand how an economy works, we must identify its major working parts and see how they interact with each other. The working parts of an economy and the interrelations between them are illustrated in Fig. 1.1. The working parts of the economy fall into two categories:

- **Decisionmakers** — any person or organized group of persons that make choices
- **Coordination mechanisms** — arrangements that make the choices of one person or group compatible with the choices of others

Decisionmakers Decisionmakers fall into three groups:

- Households
- Firms
- Governments

A **household** is any group of people living together as a decisionmaking unit. Every individual in the economy belongs to a household. Some households consist of a single person while others consist either of families or of groups of unrelated individuals, such as two or three students sharing an apartment.

A **firm** is an organization that produces goods and services. All producers are called firms, no matter how big they are or what they produce. Car makers, farmers, banks and insurance companies are all firms.

A **government** is an organization that has three functions: the provision of goods and services to households and firms, the management of economic policy and the redistribution of income and wealth. Examples of the goods and services supplied by government are national defence, law enforcement, public health, transportation and education.

You can see these three groups of decisionmakers in Fig. 1.1. You can also see in this figure the decisions that they make. Households supply factors of production to firms and governments. **Factors of production** are the economy's productive resources, usually classified under three headings:

- Labour
- Land
- Capital

Labour is the brain-power and muscle-power of human beings; **land** is natural resources of all kinds; **capital** is all the equipment, buildings, tools and other manufactured goods that can be used in production. Households sell or rent factors of production to firms and governments and receive an income in payment for their supply. Households also receive benefits from the government and pay taxes to the government. With what is left, households buy goods and services produced by firms.

Firms hire factors of production from households and choose how to use them to produce goods and services. They also decide what goods and services to produce and in what quantities. Expenditures by households and governments on goods and services are received by firms. Firms use these receipts to make payments to households for the factors of production supplied. Firms also receive subsidies from and pay taxes to governments.

Governments decide on the scale of purchases of factors of production from households and of goods and services from firms. They also decide on the scale of provision of goods and services to households and firms, as well as on the rates of benefits, subsidies and taxes.

Coordination Mechanisms

Perhaps the most striking thing about the choices made by households, firms and governments, as illustrated in Fig. 1.1, is that they surely must come into conflict with each other. For example, households choose how much work to do and what type of work to specialize in, but firms choose the type and quantity of labour to employ in the production of various goods and services. In other words, households choose the types and quantities of labour to sell and firms choose the types and quantities of labour to buy. Similarly, in markets for goods and services, households choose the types and quantities of goods and services to buy, while firms choose the types and quantities to sell. Government choices regarding taxes, benefits, subsidies and the provision of goods and services also enter the picture. Taxes taken by the government affect the amount of income that households and firms have available for spending and saving. Also, decisions by firms and households depend on the types and quantities of goods and services governments make available. For example, if the government provides excellent highways but a dilapidated railroad system, households will allocate more of their income to buying motor vehicles and less to buying train tickets.

How is it possible for the millions of individual decisions taken by households, firms and governments to be consistent with each other? What makes households want to sell the same types and quantities of labour that firms want to buy? What happens if the number of households wanting to work as economics lecturers exceeds the number that universities want to hire? How do firms know what to produce so that households will buy their output? What happens if firms want to sell more hamburgers than households want to buy?

There are two mechanisms that can achieve a coordination of individual economic choices:

- Command mechanism
- Market mechanism

A **command mechanism** is a method of determining *what, how* and *for whom* goods and services are produced, based on the authority of a ruler or ruling body — such as a king or a ruling political party. Although undergoing rapid change, examples of the use of command mechanisms in the modern world are in the former USSR, some other Eastern European countries, China, North Korea and Vietnam. In those economies, central planning bureaus, to varying degrees, make decisions about *what* will be produced, *how* it will be produced and *for whom* it will be produced. We will study command economies and compare them with other types of economies at the end of our study of economics, in Chapter 39.

A **market mechanism** is a method of determining *what, how* and *for whom* goods and services are produced, based on individual choices coordinated through markets. In ordinary speech, the word *market* means a place where people buy and sell goods such as fish, meat, fruits and vegetables. In economics, the word *market* has a more general meaning. A **market** is any arrangement that facilitates the voluntary buying and selling (trading) of a good, service or factor of production.

As an example of a market, consider that in which oil is bought and sold — the world oil market. The world oil market is not a place. It is all the many different institutions, buyers, sellers, brokers and so on who buy and sell oil. The market is a coordination mechanism because it pools together the separate plans of all the individual decisionmakers who try to buy and sell any particular good. Decisionmakers do not have to meet in a physical sense. In the modern world, telecommunications have replaced direct contact as the main link between buyers and sellers.

Markets are classified according to the types of things traded in them. Figure 1.1 shows the two types of market. The markets in which goods and services are traded are called **goods markets**. The markets in which factors of production are traded — markets for labour, land and capital — are called **factor markets**. These markets enable the plans of individual households and firms and the government to be coordinated and made consistent with each other.

The Australian economy relies extensively on the market as the mechanism for coordinating the plans of individual households and firms. There is, though, an element of command in the Australian economy. Markets do not operate in isolation of the legal framework established and enforced by the government sector of the economy. In recognition of the role played both by command and market coordination mechanisms, modern economies are referred to as mixed economies. A **mixed economy** is one that uses both market and command mechanisms to coordinate economic activity.

The US economy is also a mixed economy but one that relies more heavily on the market than does the Australian economy. In both countries, actions taken by the government sector modify the allocation of scarce resources, changing *what, how* and *for whom* the various goods and services are produced.

How Market Coordination Works The market coordinates individual decisions through price adjustments. To see how, think about the market for hamburgers in your local area. Suppose that the quantity of hamburgers being offered for sale is less than the quantity that people would like to buy. Some people who want to buy hamburgers will not be able to do so. To make the choices of buyers and sellers compatible, buyers will have to scale down their appetites and more hamburgers will have to be offered for sale. An increase in the price of hamburgers will produce this outcome. A higher price will encourage producers to offer more hamburgers for sale. It will also curb the appetite for hamburgers and change some lunch plans. Fewer people will buy hamburgers and more will buy meat pies (or some other alternative to hamburgers). More hamburgers (and more meat pies) will be offered for sale.

Now imagine the opposite situation. More hamburgers are available than people want to buy. In this case, the price is too high. A lower price will discourage the production and sale of hamburgers and encourage their purchase and consumption. Decisions to produce and sell and to buy and consume are continuously adjusted and kept in balance with each other by adjustments in prices.

In some cases, prices get stuck or fixed. When this happens, some other adjustment has to make the outcomes of choices by individuals consistent. Customers waiting in lines and stocks of inventories operate as a temporary safety valve when the market price is stuck. If people want to buy more than the quantity that firms have decided to sell, and if the price is temporarily fixed, then one of two things will have to happen. Firms wind up selling more than they would like and their inventories will shrink; or, lines of customers will develop and only those who get to the head of the line before the goods run out will be able to make a purchase. The longer the line or the bigger the decline in inventories, the more prices will have to adjust to keep buying and selling decisions in balance.

We have now seen how the market solves the question of *what* product and in *what* quantity to produce — how many hamburgers to make. The market also solves the question of *how* to produce in similar fashion. For example, hamburger producers

Figure 1.2 International Linkages

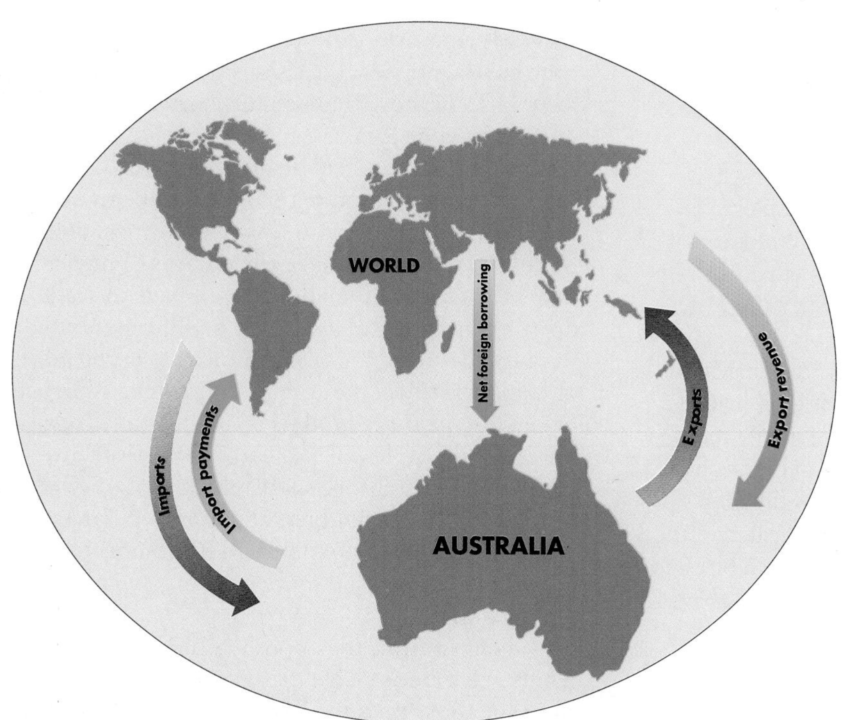

The Australian economy exports and imports goods and services. It receives a flow of revenue from its exports of goods and services and makes payments for imports. The difference between these two flows is the country's net foreign borrowing or lending. Australia has traditionally been a net borrower.

can use gas, electric power or charcoal to cook their hamburgers. Which fuel is used depends in part on the flavour that the producer wants to achieve and on the cost of the different fuels. If a fuel becomes very expensive, as did oil in the 1970s, less of it will be used and more of other fuels will be used in its place. By substituting one fuel for another as the costs of the different fuels change, the market solves the question of how to produce.

Finally, the market helps solve the question of *for whom* to produce. Skills, talents and resources that are in very short supply will command a higher price than those in greater abundance. The owners of rare resources and skills will obtain a larger share of the output of the economy than the owners of those resources in abundant supply.

Closed and Open Economies

The economy depicted in Fig. 1.1 is a closed one. A **closed economy** is one that has no links with any other economy. The only truly closed economy is that of the entire world. The Australian economy is an open economy. An **open economy** is one that has economic links with other economies. Firms in an open economy export some of their production to other countries, rather than selling only to households within their own country. Firms, households and governments in an open economy also buy some of the goods and services that they use from firms in other countries. These imports and exports of goods and services are illustrated in Fig. 1.2. The total values of exports and imports are not necessarily equal to each other. The difference between those two values is the net amount that a country lends to or borrows from the rest of the world.

In Australia, the payment for imports of goods and services has typically exceeded the receipts from exports of goods and services. The consequence of our importing more goods and services than we export is that Australia is a net borrower from the rest of the world. We will study the international linkages between the Australian economy and the rest of the world in Chapter 36.

R E V I E W

An economy is a mechanism that determines what is produced, how it is produced and for whom it is produced. In the Australian economy, these choices are made by households, firms and government, and they are coordinated through markets. Governments influence these choices by taxing, subsidizing, regulating and lawmaking. The Australian economy is an open economy, having extensive links with other economies. ■

We have now described an economy in about as much detail as we described an aeroplane. But we're about to become the economic equivalent of aeronautical engineers. We're going to build economies that fly! To do that, we have to understand the principles of economics as thoroughly as aeronautical engineers understand the principles of flight. To discover these principles, economists approach their work with the rigour and objectivity of natural scientists — they do economic science.

Economic Science

Economic science, like the natural sciences (such as physics and biology) and the other social sciences (such as political science, psychology and sociology), is an attempt to find a body of laws of nature. All sciences have two components:

- Careful and systematic observation and measurement
- Development of a body of theory to direct and interpret observations

All sciences are careful to distinguish between two types of statements:

- Statements about what *is*
- Statements about what *ought* to be

What is and What Ought to Be

Statements about what *is* are **positive statements.** Statements about what *ought* to be are **normative statements.** Let's illustrate the distinction between positive and normative statements with two examples.

First, consider the controversy over the hole in the ozone layer. The question 'Is it possible to design and make products which do not emit gases that reduce the ozone layer?' is positive. The question 'Ought we to try to reduce emissions of ozone-depleting gases?' is normative. Second, consider the economic controversy over tax reform. The question 'Will a switch in the tax base encourage saving and make people work harder?' is positive. The question '*Should* more reliance be placed on consumption rather than income taxes?' is normative. Science — whether natural, social or economic — tries to discover and catalogue positive statements that are consistent with what we observe in the world. Science is silent on normative questions. It is not that such questions are unimportant. On the contrary, they are often the most important questions of all. Nor is it that scientists as people do not have opinions on such questions. It is simply that the activity of doing science cannot settle a normative matter and the possession of scientific knowledge does not equip a person with superior moral precepts or norms. A difference of opinion on a positive matter can ultimately be settled by careful observation and measurement. A difference of opinion on a normative matter cannot be settled in that way. In fact, there are no well-defined rules for settling a normative dispute and sometimes reasonable people simply have to agree to disagree. When they cannot, political and judicial institutions intervene in order for decisions to be made. We settle normative disagreements in the political, not the scientific, arena. The scientific community can, and often does, contribute to the normative debates of political life. But science is a distinct activity. Even though scientists have opinions about what ought to be, those opinions have no part in science itself.

Now let's see how economists attempt to discover and catalogue positive statements that are consistent with their observations and that enable them to answer economic questions such as the seven big questions that we reviewed earlier.

Observation and Measurement

Economic phenomena can be observed and measured in great detail. For example, we can catalogue the amounts and locations of natural and human resources. We can describe who does what kind of work, for how many hours and how they are paid. We can catalogue the things that people produce, consume and store, and their prices. We can describe in detail who borrows and who lends and at what interest rates. We can also catalogue the things that government taxes and at what rates, the programmes it finances and at what cost.

Our list is not exhaustive. It gives a flavour, though, of the array of things that economists can describe through careful observation and measurement of economic activity.

In today's world, computers have given us access to an enormous volume of economic description. Government agencies around the world, national statistical bureaus, private economic consultants, banks, investment advisors and research economists working in universities generate an astonishing amount of information about economic behaviour.

But economists do more than observe and measure economic activity, crucial as doing that is. Describing something is not the same as understanding it. You can describe your digital watch in great detail, but that does not mean you can explain what makes it work. Understanding what makes things work requires the discovery of laws. That is the main task of economists — the discovery of laws governing economic behaviour. How do economists go about this task?

Economic Theory

We can describe in great detail the ups and downs, or cycles, in unemployment, but can we explain *why* unemployment fluctuates? We can describe the fall in the price of a VCR or a pocket calculator and the dramatic increase in its use, but can we explain the low price and popularity of such items? Did the fall in the price lead more people to use pocket calculators, or did their popularity lower the costs of production and make it possible to lower the price? Or did something else cause both the fall in the price and the increase in use?

Questions like these can be answered only by developing a body of economic theory. An **economic theory** is a reliable generalization that enables us to understand and predict the economic choices that people make. We develop economic theories by building and testing economic models. What is an economic model?

Economic Models

You have just seen an economic model. To answer the question 'What is an economy and how does it work?' we built a model of an economy. We did not describe in all its detail all the economic actions that take place in Australia. We concentrated our attention only on those features that seemed important for understanding economic choices, and ignored everything else. You will perhaps better appreciate what we mean by an economic model if you think about more familiar models.

We have all seen model trains, cars and aeroplanes. Although we do not usually call dolls and stuffed animals models, we can think of them in this way. Architects make models of buildings and biologists make models of DNA (the double helix carrier of the genetic code).

A model is usually smaller than the real thing that it represents. But models are not always smaller in scale (for example, the biologist's model of the components of cells) and, in any case, the scale of a model is not its most important feature. A model also shows less detail than its counterpart in reality. For example, all the models we have mentioned resemble the real thing in *appearance*, but they are not usually made of the same substance nor do they work like the real thing that they represent. The architect's model of a new high-rise shows us what the building will look like and how it will conform with the buildings around it — but it does not contain plumbing, telephone cables, lift shafts, air conditioning plants and other interior workings.

All the models that we have discussed (including those that are typically used as toys) represent something that is real, but they lack some key features. The model abstracts from the detail of the real thing. It includes only those features needed for the purpose at hand. It leaves out the inessential or unnecessary. What a model includes and what it leaves out is not arbitrary; it results from a conscious and careful decision.

The models that we have just considered are all 'physical' models. We can see the real thing and we can see the model. Indeed, the purpose of those models is to enable us to 'visualize' the real thing. Some models, including economic models, are not physical. We cannot look at the real thing and look at the model and simply decide whether the model is a good or bad representation of the real thing. But the idea of a model as an abstraction from reality still applies to an economic model.

An **economic model** is an artificial or imaginary economy, or part of an economy. It has two components:

- Assumptions
- Implications

Assumptions form the foundation on which a model is built. They are propositions about what is important and what can be ignored; about what can be treated as being constant and, therefore, reliably used to make predictions.

Implications are the outcome of a model. The link between a model's assumptions and its implications is a process of logical deduction.

Let's illustrate these components of a model by building a simple model of your daily journey to lectures. The model has three assumptions:

1 Lectures begin at 9.00 a.m.

2 The bus ride takes 30 minutes.

3 The walk from the bus to the lecture theatre takes five minutes.

The implication of this model is that to be in at the lecture on time, you have to be on the bus by 8.25 a.m.

The assumptions of a model depend on the model's purpose. The purpose of an economic model is to understand how people make choices in the face of scarcity. Thus in building an economic model, we abstract from the rich detail of human life and focus only on behaviour that is relevant for coping with scarcity. Everything else is ignored. Economists know that people fall in love and form deep friendships; that they experience great joy and security or great pain and anxiety. But economists assume that, in seeking to understand economic behavior, they may build models that ignore many aspects of life. They focus on one and only one feature of the world: people have wants that exceed their resources and so, by their choices, have to make the best of things.

Assumptions of an Economic Model Economic models are based on four key assumptions:

1 *People have preferences.* Economists use the term **preferences** to denote likes and dislikes and the intensity of those likes and dislikes. People can judge whether one situation is better, worse or just as good as another one. For example, you can judge whether for you, one loaf of bread and no cheese is better, worse or just as good as a half a loaf of bread and 100 grams of cheese.

2 *People are endowed with a fixed amount of resources and a technology that can transform those resources into goods and services.* Economists use the term **endowment** to refer to the resources that people have and the term **technology** to describe the methods of converting those endowments into goods and services.

3 *People economize.* They choose how to use their endowments and technologies in order to make themselves as well-off as possible. Such a choice is called a rational choice. A **rational choice** is the best possible course of action from the point of view of the person making the choice. Each choice, no matter what it is or how foolish it may seem to an observer, is interpreted, in an economic model, as a rational choice.

Choices are made on the basis of the information available. With hindsight, and with more information, people may well feel that some of their past choices were bad ones. This fact does not make such choices irrational. Again, a rational choice is the best possible course of action, from the point of view of the person making the choice, *given that person's preferences and given the information available when the choice is made.*

4 *People's choices are coordinated.* One person's choice to buy something must be matched by another person's choice to sell that same thing. One person's choice to work at a particular job must be matched by another person's choice to hire someone to do that job. The coordination of individual choices is made either by a market mechanism or a command mechanism.

Assuming that people's choices are somehow coordinated does not imply that the relevant coordination mechanism chosen is without flaws.

Implications of an Economic Model The implications of an economic model are the equilibrium values of various prices and quantities. An **equilibrium** is a situation in which everyone has economized — that is, all individuals have made the best possible choices in the light of their own preferences and given their endowments, technologies and information — and in which those choices have been coordinated and made compatible with the choices of everyone else. Equilibrium is the solution or outcome of an economic model.

The term equilibrium conjures up the picture of a balance of opposing forces. For example, a balance scale can be said to be in equilibrium if a kilogram of cheese is placed on one side of the balance and a one-kilogram weight is placed on the other side. The two weights exactly equal each other and so offset each other, leaving the balance arm horizontal. A soap bubble provides another excellent physical illustration of equilibrium. The delicate spherical film of soap is held in place by a balance of forces of the air inside the sphere and the air outside it.

This second physical analogy illustrates a further important feature of an equilibrium. An equilib-

Adam Smith and the Birth of Economic Science

Adam Smith

In the year that colonists in America revolted against Britain, a Scottish thinker touched off a different kind of revolution. For it was in 1776 that Adam Smith published *An Inquiry into the Nature and Causes of the Wealth of Nations*, the book that began economics as a science. Even today, more than two hundred years after its publication, the book is reprinted, reinterpreted and reread repeatedly.

Smith led a quiet, scholarly life. He was born in 1723 in Kirkaldy, Scotland, a small community near Edinburgh where he spent his first 14 years. At the remarkably early age of 14, he became a student at the University of Glasgow. He graduated at 17 and then went on to Oxford University where he spent the next six years. His first major academic appointment, at age 28, was as Professor of Logic, and subsequently as Professor of Logic and Moral Philosophy, at Glasgow. After 13 years at Glasgow, Smith became a tutor to a wealthy Scottish duke who lived in France. After Smith spent two years in that position, the duke gave him a pension — an income for the rest of his life — of £300 a year. (An income of this size would have bought a great deal in the eighteenth century, when the average wage was about £30 a year.)

With the financial security of a pension, Smith devoted the next ten years of his life — from 1766 to 1776 — to his great treatise. He was writing his *Wealth of Nations* at a time when the British economy was undergoing what came to be called the Industrial Revolution. New technologies were being invented and applied to the manufacture of cotton and wool products, iron, transportation and agriculture. The prevailing intellectual climate held that Britain needed to be protected from cheap foreign imports so that the nation could build up its stock of gold and finance its continuing process of industrialization.

Smith scoffed at this idea and developed a massive case against protection and in favour of 'free trade'. *The Wealth of Nations* argued that when each person makes the best economic choice possible, that choice leads, as if by 'an invisible hand', to the best economic outcome for society as a whole. This best possible social outcome arises not because people pay attention to the needs of others but from self-interest. Said Smith, 'It is not from the benevolence of the butcher, the brewer or the baker, that we can expect our dinner, but from their regard to their own interest'.[1]

The Wealth of Nations proposed that all economic behaviour can be understood as the rational pursuit of self-interest. The book begins much like the one that you are now studying, but much more profoundly, for Smith's was the first systematic treatment of these ideas. Smith explained how specialization, exchange and the development of money lead to massive increases in goods and services. He applied his basic theory to a sweep of human history, starting from the fall of the Roman Empire. He explained the rise and progress of towns and cities, how commerce between towns and farmlands benefits both, and why free international trade leads to improved living standards. He also applied the theory of rational self-interest to explain why the universities of the eighteenth century were organized not for the benefit of the students but, as he put it, 'for the ease of the professors'. He even used his theory to explain the proliferation of new religions.

Many thinkers had written earlier on economic questions, but Smith was the first to make a science of economics.

It was Smith who provided so broad and authoritative an account of the known economic doctrine that henceforth it was no longer permissible for any subsequent writer on economics to advance his own ideas while ignoring the state of general knowledge. A science consists of interacting practitioners, and henceforth no one could decently ignore Smith's own work and in due time the work of Malthus, Ricardo and the galaxy of economists who populated the first half of the nineteenth century.[2]

This first essay on our advancing knowledge in economic science has been devoted to Adam Smith, who stands alone as the founder of this discipline. Subsequent essays in this series will give you a taste of how various branches of the subject have advanced from this founding father through to the present. The goal is to enable you to see how the science of economics advances and perhaps even to inspire you to become one of that community of scholars seeking to deepen our understanding of economic phenomena.

---

1 Adam Smith, *An Inquiry into the Nature and Causes of the Wealth of Nations*, ed. Edwin Cannan, with a new preface by George J. Stigler (Chicago: University of Chicago Press, 1976), p. 18.

2 George J. Stigler, 'Nobel Lecture: The Process and Progress of Economics', *Journal of Political Economy* 91 (August 1983), pp. 529–45.

rium is not necessarily static but may be dynamic — constantly changing. By squeezing or stretching the bubble, you can change its shape, but its shape is always determined by the balance of the forces acting upon it (including the forces that you exert upon it).

An economic equilibrium has a great deal in common with that of the soap bubble. First, it is in a constant state of motion. At each point in time, each person makes the best possible choice, given the endowments and actions of others. But changing circumstances alter those choices. For example, on a busy day in Sydney, there are more cars looking for parking spaces than the number of spaces available. In this situation, the equilibrium number of free spaces is zero. But people do get to park. Individual cars are leaving and arriving at a steady pace. As soon as one car vacates a parking space, another instantly fills it. Being in equilibrium does not mean that everyone gets to park instantly. There is an equilibrium amount of time spent finding a vacant space. People hunting for a space are frustrated and experience rising blood pressure and increased anger. But there is still an equilibrium in the hunt for available parking spaces. Similarly, an economic equilibrium does not mean that everyone is experiencing economic prosperity. The constraints may be such that some people are very poor. Nevertheless, given their preferences, endowments, the available technologies and the actions of everyone else, each person has made the best possible choice and sees no advantage in modifying his or her current action.

Microeconomic and Macroeconomic Models

Economic models fall into two categories: microeconomic and macroeconomic. **Microeconomics** is the branch of economics that studies the decisions of individual households and firms. Microeconomics also studies the way that individual markets work and the detailed way that regulation and taxes affect the allocation of labour and of goods and services.

Macroeconomics is the branch of economics that studies the economy as a whole. It seeks to understand the big picture rather than the detailed individual choices. In particular, it studies the determination of the overall level of economic activity — of unemployment, aggregate income, average prices and inflation.

Of the seven big questions, those dealing with technological change, production and consumption, and wages and earnings are microeconomic. Those dealing with unemployment, inflation and differences in wealth among nations are macroeconomic.

Model, Theory and Reality

People who build models often get carried away and start talking as if their model *is* the real world — as if their model is reality. No matter how useful it is, there is no sense in which a model can be said to be reality.

A model is an abstract entity. It lists assumptions and their implications. When economists talk about people who have made themselves as well-off as possible, they are not talking about real people. They are talking about artificial people in an economic model. This is an important but easily misunderstood fact.

Economic theory bridges the gap between an economic model and the real world. Economic theory proposes that the economic behaviour of people in actual economies can be predicted by using models in which people who make rational choices interact with each other in an equilibrium. Economists develop models based on this idea to explain all aspects of economic behaviour. But economic models have to be tested.

To test an economic model, its implications are matched against actual events in the real world. That is, the model is used to make predictions about the real world. The model's predictions may correspond to or be in conflict with the facts. It is by comparing the model's predictions with the facts that we are able to test a model. The process of developing economic theories by using models is illustrated in Fig. 1.3. We begin by building a model. The model's implications are used to generate predictions about the world. These predictions and their test form the basis of a theory. When predictions are in conflict with the facts, either a theory is discarded in favour of a superior alternative or we return to the model building stage, modifying our assumptions and creating a new model. Economics itself provides guidance on how we might discover a better model. It prompts us to look for some aspect of preferences, endowments, technology or the coordination mechanism that has been overlooked.

Economics is a young science and a long way from having achieved its goal. Its birth can be dated fairly precisely in the eighteenth century with the publication of Adam Smith's *The Wealth of Nations* (see Our Advancing Knowledge, pp. 20–21). In the

Figure 1.3 How Theories are Developed

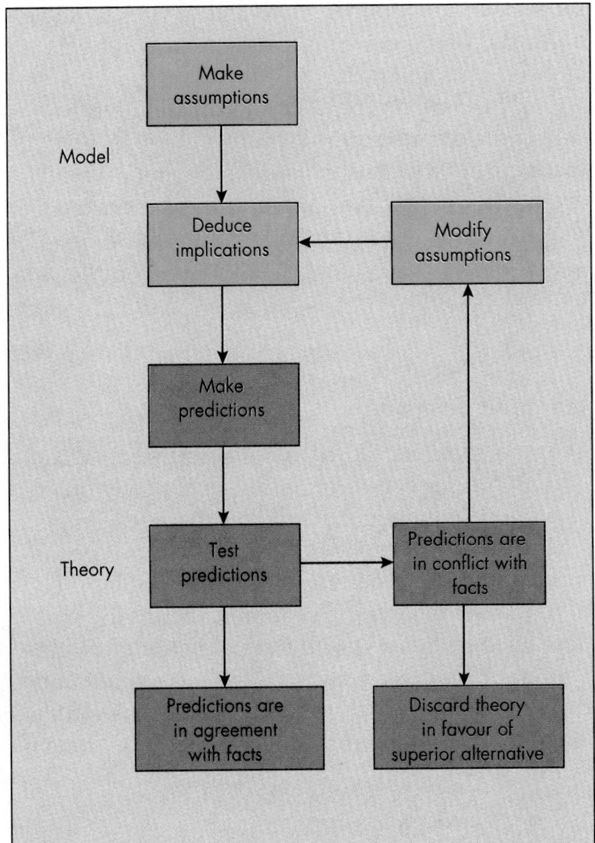

Economic theories are developed by building and testing economic models. An economic model is a set of *assumptions* about what is important and what can be ignored and the *implications* of those assumptions. The implications of a model form the basis of *predictions* about the world. These predictions are tested by being checked against the facts. If the predictions are in conflict with the facts, either the theory is discarded in favour of a superior alternative or the model-building process begins anew with modified assumptions. It is only when predictions are in agreement with the facts that a useful theory has been developed.

closing years of the twentieth century, economic science has managed to discover a sizeable number of useful generalizations, many of which we will reveal in this book. In many other areas, however, we are still going around the circle — changing assumptions, performing new logical deductions, generating new predictions and getting wrong answers yet again. The gradual accumulation of correct answers gives most practitioners some faith that their methods will, eventually, provide usable answers to the big economic questions.

As we make progress, though, more and more things become clearer and seem to fit together. Theoretical advances lead to deeper understanding. This feature of economics is shared with scientists in all fields. As Albert Einstein, the great physicist, said: 'Creating a new theory is not like destroying an old barn and erecting a skyscraper in its place. It is rather like climbing a mountain, gaining new and wider views, discovering new connections between our starting point and its rich environment. But the point from which we started still exists and can be seen, although it appears smaller and forms a tiny part of our broad view gained by the mastery of the obstacles on our adventurous way up'. [1]

■ In the next chapter, we will study some of the tools that economists use to build economic models. Then, in Chapter 3, we will build an economic model and use that model to understand the world around us and to start to answer some of the seven big economic questions.

SUMMARY

Seven Big Questions

Economics tries to answer difficult questions that affect our daily lives. These questions concern the production and consumption of goods and services; wages and earnings; unemployment; inflation; government spending, taxation and regulation; international trade; and the distribution of wealth and poverty in Australia and throughout the world. There are no

[1] These words are attributed to Einstein in a letter by Oliver Sacks to *The Listener*, 88, No. 2279 (30 November 1972), p. 756.

easy answers to the big economic questions, which must be approached in a scientific manner. (pp. 4–7)

Scarcity

All economic questions arise from the fundamental fact of scarcity. Scarcity means that wants exceed resources. Human wants are effectively unlimited but the resources available to satisfy them are finite.

Economic activity is what people do to cope with scarcity. Scarcity forces people to make choices. Making the best choice possible from what is available is called optimizing. In order to make the best possible choice, a person weighs the costs and benefits of the alternatives.

Opportunity cost is the cost of one choice in terms of the best forgone alternative. The opportunity cost of any action is the best alternative action that could have been undertaken in its place. Attending a lecture instead of staying in bed has an opportunity cost — the cost of one hour of rest.

Scarcity forces people to compete with each other for scarce resources. People may cooperate in certain areas, but all economic activity ultimately results in competition among individuals acting alone or in groups. (pp. 7–12)

The Economy

The economy is a mechanism that allocates scarce resources among competing uses, determining *what, how* and *for whom* the various goods and services will be produced.

The economy's working parts are divided into two categories: decisionmakers and coordination mechanisms. Economic decisionmakers are households, firms and governments. Households decide how much of their factors of production to sell to firms and government, and what goods and services to buy from firms. Firms decide what factors of production to hire and which goods and services to produce. Governments decide on the scale of purchases of factors of production from households and of goods and services from firms. They also decide on the scale of provision of goods and services to households and firms, as well as on the rates of benefits and subsidies and taxes.

There are two types of coordination mechanisms: the command mechanism and the market mechanism. The Australian economy relies mainly on the market mechanism, but the actions taken by the government sector do modify the allocation of scarce resources. The Australian economy is therefore a mixed economy. (pp. 12–17)

Economic Science

Economic science, like the natural sciences and the other social sciences, attempts to find a body of laws of nature. Economic science seeks to understand what *is* and is silent about what *ought* to be. Economists try to find economic laws by developing a body of economic theory, and economic theory, in turn, is developed by building and testing economic models. Economic models are abstract, logical constructions that contain two components: assumptions and implications. An economic model has four key assumptions:

1 People have preferences

2 People have a given endowment of resources and technology

3 People economize

4 People's choices are coordinated through market, or command mechanisms

The implications of an economic model are the equilibrium values of various prices and quantities that result from each individual doing the best that is possible, given the individual's preferences, endowments, information and technology, and given the coordination mechanism. (pp. 17–23)

KEY TERMS

Assumptions, p. 18
Capital, p. 14
Closed economy, p. 16
Command mechanism, p. 14
Competition, p. 9
Cooperation, p. 9
Coordination mechanisms, p. 13
Decisionmakers, p. 13

Economic activity, p. 7
Economic model, p. 18
Economic theory, p. 18
Economics, p. 8
Economizing, p. 8
Economy, p. 12
Endowment, p. 19
Equilibrium, p. 19
Factor markets, p. 15
Factors of production, p. 14
Firm, p. 14
Goods markets, p. 15
Government, p. 14
Household, p. 13
Implications, p. 19
Labour, p. 14
Land, p. 14
Macroeconomics, p. 22
Market, p. 15
Market mechanism, p. 15
Microeconomics, p. 22
Mixed economy, p. 15
Normative statements, p. 17
Open economy, p. 16
Opportunity cost, p. 8
Optimizing, p. 8
Positive statements, p. 17
Preferences, p. 19
Rational choice, p. 19
Scarcity, p. 7
Technology, p. 19

PROBLEMS

1 Illustrate each of the seven big questions with your own examples.

2 Which of the following are part of your opportunity cost of being a student? Explain why they are or are not.
   a) The money you spend on haircuts.
   b) The holidays you would have taken if you had been working rather than being a student.
   c) The tapes and CDs that you don't have because you've had to spend so much on economics textbooks.
   d) The amount you pay for your lunch in the cafeteria each week.
   e) The $20,000 annual salary you could have made in your uncle's supermarket.

3 List some examples of opportunity costs that you have incurred today.

4 Give some examples of opportunity costs you incurred that are the results of someone else's actions.

5 Give some examples of opportunity costs incurred by someone else that are the result of your actions.

6 Which of the following statements are positive and which are normative?
   a) Low rents will restrict the supply of housing.
   b) High interest rates lower the demand for mortgages and new homes.
   c) No family ought to pay more than one-quarter of its income to rent decent housing.
   d) Owners of flats ought to be free to charge whatever rent they like.
   e) The government ought to restrict the rents that landlords are allowed to charge.

7 You have been hired by a company that makes and markets tapes, records and CDs. Your employer is going to start selling these products in a new market that has a population of 100 million people. A survey has revealed that 40 per cent of this market buys only popular music and 5 per cent of it buys only classical music. No one buys both types of music. The average income of the pop music fan is $10,000 a year and that of the classical fan is $50,000 a year. It has also been discovered that people with low incomes spend one-quarter of 1 per cent of their income on tapes, records and CDs while those with high incomes spend 2 per cent of theirs. You have been asked to predict how much is likely to be spent in this market on pop music and classical music in one year. Build a model to answer this question. List your assumptions and work out their implications. Draw attention to the potential for unreliability in your answers. Why might your model give wrong answers?

Chapter 2

Making and Using Graphs

After studying this chapter, you will be able to:

- Make and interpret a time-series graph and a scatter diagram.
- Distinguish between linear and nonlinear relationships and relationships that have a maximum and a minimum.
- Define and calculate the slope of a line.
- Graph relationships among more than two variables.

Three Kinds of Lies

Benjamin Disraeli, British prime minister in the late nineteenth century, is reputed to have said that there are three kinds of lies: lies, damned lies and statistics. One of the most powerful ways of conveying statistical information is in the form of a picture — a graph. Thus graphs, too, like statistics, can tell lies. But a good graph does not lie. Indeed, it reveals data and helps its viewer to see and think about relationships that would otherwise be obscure. Graphs are a surprisingly modern invention. They first appeared in the late eighteenth century, long after the discovery of mathematically sophisticated ideas such as logarithms and calculus. But today, especially in the age of the personal computer and the video display, graphs have become almost more important than words. The ability to make and use graphs is as important as the ability to read and write. How do economists use graphs? What are the different types of graphs that economists use? What do economic graphs reveal and what can they hide? What are the main pitfalls that can result in a graph that lies? It will be clear to you from the seven big questions that you studied in Chapter 1 that the problems that economics seek to solve are difficult ones. You will also suspect, and rightly so, that hardly anything in economics has a single cause. Variations in the quantity of ice cream consumed are not caused merely by variations in the air temperature or in the price of cream but by at least these two factors and probably several others as well. How can we drawn graphs of relationships that involve several variables, all of which vary simultaneously? How can we interpret such relationships?

In this chapter, we are going to look at the different kinds of graphs that are used in economics. We are going to learn how to make them and read them. We are going to look at examples of useful graphs as well as misleading graphs. We are also going to study how we can calculate the strength of the effect of one variable on another.There are no graphs or techniques used in this book that are more complicated than those explained and described in this chapter. If you are already familiar with graphs, you may want to skip or at least only skim this chapter. Whether you study this chapter thoroughly or give it a quick pass, you should regard it as a handy reference chapter to which you can return if you need additional help in understanding the graphs that you encounter in your study of economics.

Graphing Data

Graphing a Single Variable

Graphs represent a quantity as a distance. Figure 2.1 gives two examples. Figure 2.1(a) shows temperature, measured in degrees Celsius, as the distance on a scale. Movements from left to right represent increases in temperature. Movements from right to left represent decreases in temperature. The point marked zero represents zero degrees Celsius. To the right of zero, the temperatures are positive. To the left of zero, the temperatures are negative (as indicated by the minus sign in front of the numbers).

Figure 2.1(b) provides another example. This time altitude, or height, is measured in thousands of metres above sea level. The point marked zero represents sea level. Points to the right of zero represent metres above sea level. Points to the left of zero (indicated by a minus sign) represent depths below sea level.

There are no rigid rules about the scale for a graph. The scale is determined by the range of the variable being graphed and the space available for the graph.

Each of the two graphs in Fig. 2.1 show just a single variable. Marking a point on either of the two scales indicates a particular temperature or a particular height. Thus the point marked *a* represents 100°C, the boiling point of water. The point marked *b* represents 10 metres below sea level, the height of Lake Eyre.

Graphing a single variable as we have done does not usually reveal much. Graphs become powerful when they show how two variables are related to each other.

Figure 2.1 Graphing a Single Variable

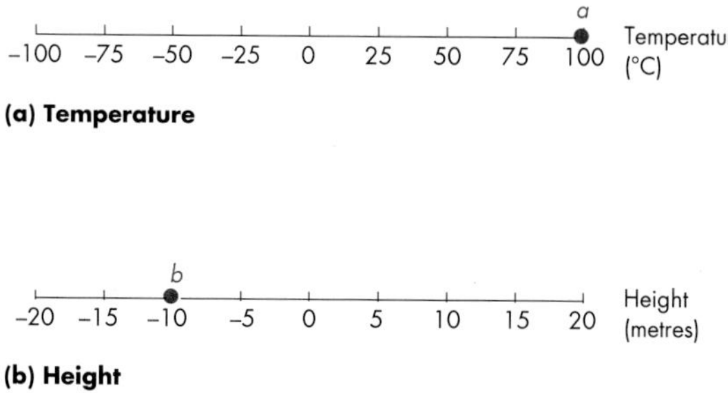

All graphs have a scale that measures a quantity as a distance. The two scales here measure temperature and height. Numbers to the right of zero are positive. Numbers to the left of zero are negative.

Two-Variable Graphs

To construct a two-variable graph, we set two scales perpendicular to each other. Let's continue to use the same two variables as those in Fig. 2.1. We will measure temperature in exactly the same way, but we will turn the height scale to a vertical position. Thus temperature is measured exactly as it was before but height is now represented by movements up and down a vertical scale.

The two scale lines in Fig. 2.2 are called **axes.** The vertical line is called the ***y*-axis** and the horizontal line is called the ***x*-axis.** The letters *x* and *y* appear on the axes of Fig. 2.2. Each axis has a zero point shared by the two axes. The zero point, common to both axes, is called the **origin**.

To represent something in a two-variable graph, we need two pieces of information. For example, Mount Kosciusko is 3456 metres high and, on a particular day, the temperature at its peak is −10°C. We can represent this information in Fig. 2.2 by marking the height of the mountain on the *y*-axis at 3456 metres and the temperature on the *x*-axis at −10°C. We can now identify the values of the two variables that appear on the axes by marking point *c*.

Two lines, called coordinates, can be drawn from point *c*. **Coordinates** are lines running from a point on a graph perpendicularly to its axes. The line running from *c* to the *x*-axis is the ***y*-coordinate**, because its length is the same as the value marked off on the *y*-axis. Similarly, the line running from *c* to the vertical axis is the ***x*-coordinate**, because its length is the same as the value marked off on the *x*-axis.

Now let's leave the top of Mount Kosciusko, at 3456 metres and −10°C, and take a trip in a 4WD vehicle. We are exploring Lake Eyre, 10 metres below sea level. Outside it is a sweltering 40°C. We are at the point marked *d* in Fig. 2.2. Our *y*-coordinate is −10 metres and our *x*-coordinate is 40°C.

Economists use graphs similar to this one in a variety of ways. Let's look at two examples.

Time-Series Graphs

One of the most common and powerful graphs used in economics is the time-series graph. A **time-series graph** measures time (for example, in years or months) on the *x*-axis and the variable or variables in which we are interested on the *y*-axis.

Figure 2.2 Graphing Two Variables

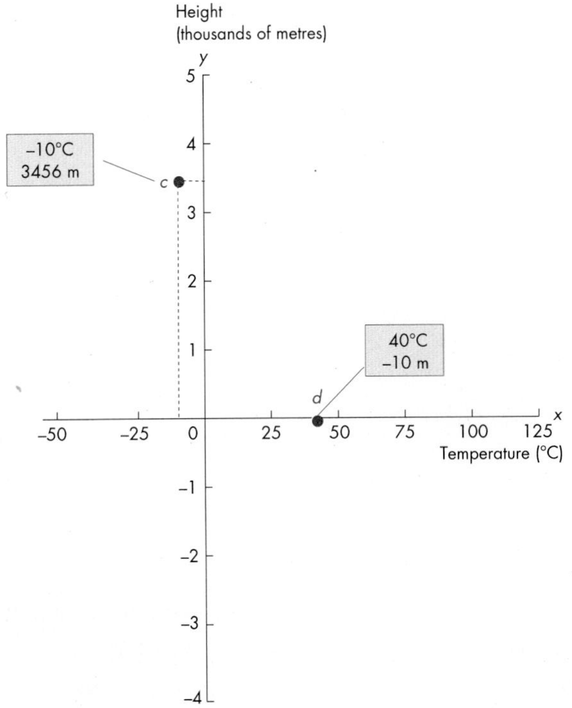

The relationship between two variables is graphed by forming two axes perpendicular to each other. Height is measured here on the *y*-axis and temperature on the *x*-axis. Point *c* represents the top of Mount Kosciusko, 3456 metres above sea level (measured on the *y*-axis), with a temperature of –10°C (measured on the *x*-axis). Point *d* represents –10 metres with a temperature of 40°C.

Figure 2.3 illustrates a time-series graph. Time is measured in years on the *x*-axis. The variable that we are interested in — the Australian unemployment rate (the percentage of the labour force unemployed) — is measured on the *y*-axis. The time-series graph conveys an enormous amount of information quickly and easily:

1 It tells us the *level* of the unemployment rate — when it is *high* and *low*. When the line is a long way from the *x*-axis, the unemployment rate is high. When the line is close to the *x*-axis, the unemployment rate is low.

2 It tells us *how* the unemployment rate *changes* — whether it *rises* or *falls*. When the line slopes upward, as in the early 1930s, the unemployment rate is rising. When the line slopes downward from left to right, as in the early 1940s, the unemployment rate is falling.

3 It tells us the *speed* with which the unemployment rate is *changing* — whether it is rising or falling *quickly* or *slowly*. If the line rises or falls very steeply, then unemployment is changing quickly, relative to past behaviour. If the line is not steep, unemployment is rising or falling slowly, relative to past behaviour. For example, unemployment rose sharply between 1930/31 and 1932/33. Unemployment also rose in 1965/66 and 1966/67 but more slowly. Similarly, when unemployment was falling in the early 1940s, it fell quickly between 1939/40 and 1941/42, but then it began to fall more slowly in 1942/43.

A time-series graph can also be used to depict a trend. A **trend** is a general tendency for a variable to rise or fall. You can see that unemployment had a general tendency to rise from the early 1970s to the early 1980s. That is, although there were ups and downs in the unemployment rate, there was overall an upward trend over that period.

Graphs also allow us to compare different periods quickly. It is apparent, for example, that the 1930s was different from any other period in the twentieth century because of exceptionally high unemployment. You can also see that unemployment fluctuated more wildly in the years before 1940/41 than it did in the years 1940/41 to 1970/71. The sawtooth pattern is more jagged in the period from 1900/01 to 1940/41 than it is in the period between 1940/41 and 1970/71.

We can thus see that not only does Fig. 2.3 convey a wealth of information, it does so in a much shorter space than we have used to describe only some of its features.

Misleading Time-Series Graphs Although time-series graphs are powerful devices for conveying a large amount of information, they can also be used to distort data and to create a misleading picture.

One common way of misleading is to place two graphs that have different scales, side by side. Figure 2.4 provides an illustration. This figure contains exactly the same information as Fig. 2.3, but the information is packaged in a different way. In Fig. 2.4(a), the scale on the y-axis has been compressed; in Fig. 2.4(b), it has been expanded. When we look at the two parts of this figure as a whole, they suggest that unemployment was pretty stable during the first half

Figure 2.3 A Time-Series Graph

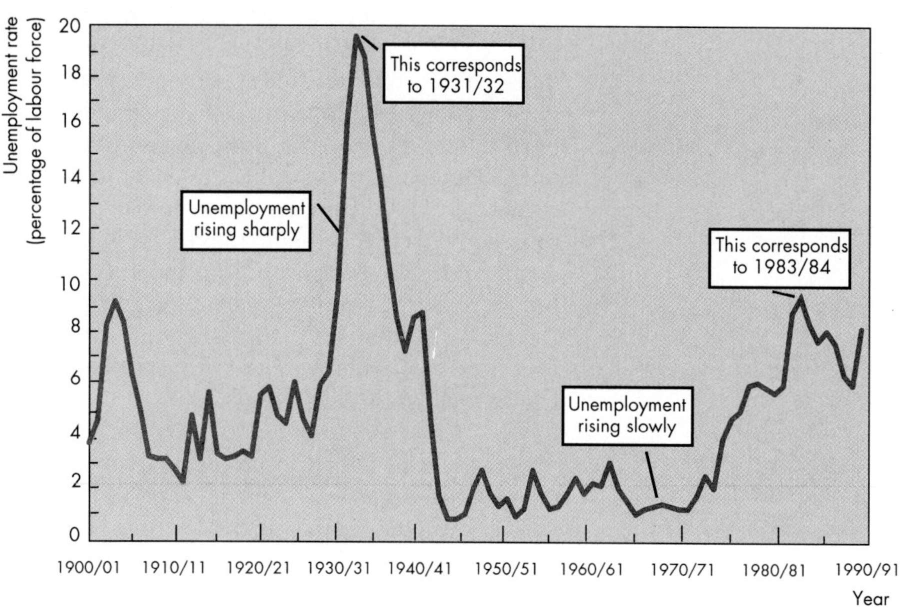

A time-series graph plots the level of a variable on the *y*-axis against time (days, weeks, months or years) on the *x*-axis. This graph shows the Australian unemployment rate each fiscal year from 1900/01 to 1990/91.

of this century but that it has trended upward dramatically in the last 40 years or so.

You may think that this graphical way of distorting data is so outrageous that no one would ever use it. If you scrutinize the graphs that you see in newspapers and magazines, you will be surprised how common this device is.

Omitting the Origin Sometimes a graph is drawn with the origin (0 on the vertical axis) omitted. Sometimes omitting the origin is precisely the correct thing to do, as it enables the graph to reveal its information. But there are also times when omitting the origin is misleading.

Figure 2.5 illustrates the effect of omitting the origin. In Fig. 2.5(a) and (b), you can see a graph of

Figure 2.4 Misleading Graphs: Squeezing and Stretching Scales

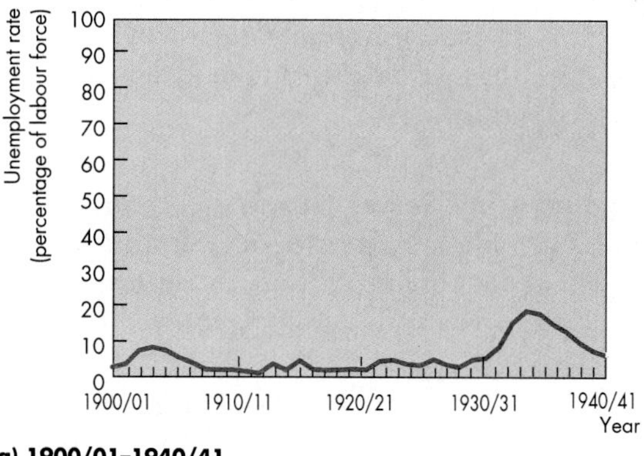

(a) 1900/01–1940/41

Unemployment rate
(percentage of labour force)
12
10
8
6
4
2
0
1940/41 1950/51 1960/61 1970/71 1980/81 1990/91
Year

(b) 1940/41–1990/91

Graphs can mislead by squeezing and stretching the scales. These two graphs show exactly the same thing as Fig. 2.3 — Australian unemployment from 1900/01 to 1990/91. Part (a) has squeezed the *y*-axis, while part (b) has stretched that axis. The result appears to be a low and stable unemployment rate before 1940/41 and a rising, highly volatile unemployment rate after that date. Contrast the lie of Fig. 2.4 with the truth of Fig. 2.3.

Figure 2.5 Omitting the Origin

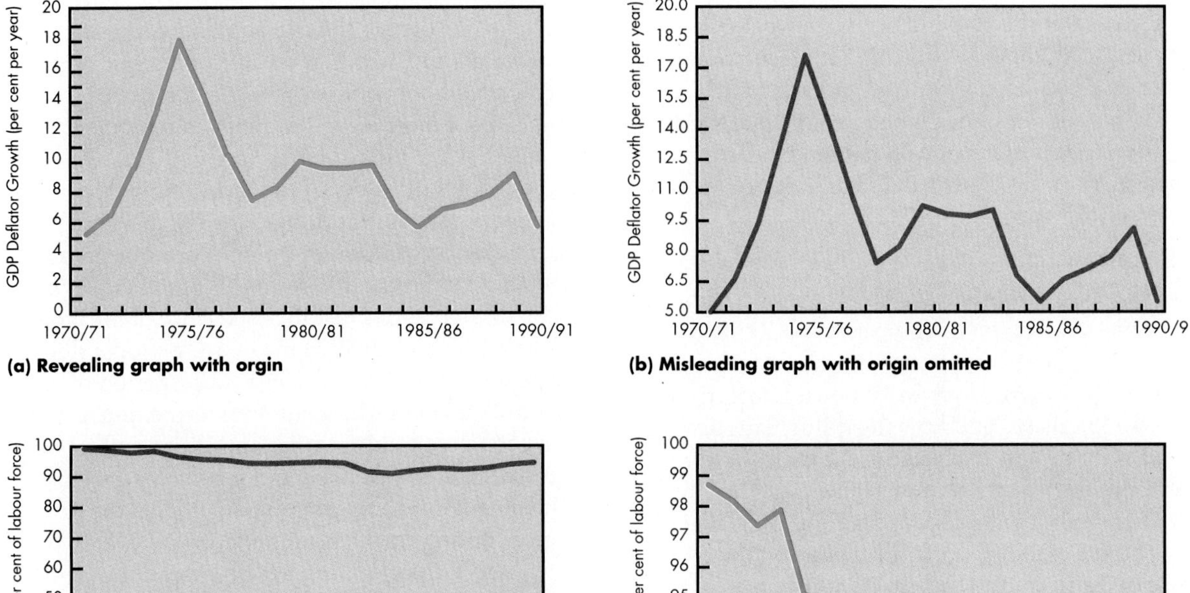

(a) Revealing graph with orgin

(b) Misleading graph with origin omitted

(c) Uninformative graph with origin

(d) Revealing graph with origin omitted

Sometimes the origin is omitted from a graph. This practice can be either revealing or misleading, depending on how it is used. Parts (a) and (b) graph the Australian inflation rate between 1970/71 and 1990/91. Part (a) is graphed with the origin and part (b) without it. Part (a) reveals a large amount of information about the level and changes in the inflation rate over this time period. Part (b) overdramatizes the rises and falls in inflation and gives no direct visual information about its level.

Parts (c) and (d) graph the employment rate. Part (c) contains an origin and part (d) does not. In this case, the graph with the origin is uninformative and shows virtually no variation in the employment rate. The graph in part (d) gives a clear picture of fluctuations in the employment rate and is more informative than part (c) about those fluctuations.

the inflation rate between 1970/71 and 1990/91. Fig. 2.5(a) includes the origin, and Fig. 2.5(b) does not. The graph in Fig. 2.5(a) provides a clear account of what happened to inflation over the time period in question. You can use that graph to describe all the features of inflation during that time period. But the graph in Fig. 2.5(b) is less revealing and distorts the picture. It fails to reveal the level of inflation. It focuses only on, and exaggerates the magnitude of, the increases and decreases in the rate of inflation. In particular, the increases in the inflation rate between 1970/71 and 1974/75 look enormous when compared with the increases that appear in Fig. 2.5(a). By omitting the origin, small percentage changes can be made to look very big.

Figure 2.5(c) and Fig. 2.5(d) graph the employment rate — the percentage of the labour force employed. Figure 2.5(c) includes the origin, and Fig. 2.5(d) omits it. As you can see, the graph in Fig. 2.5(c) reveals very little about movements in the employment rate. It seems to suggest that the employment rate was pretty constant and lying between 90 and 98 per cent. The main feature of Fig. 2.5(c) is an enormous amount of empty space and an inefficient use of the space available. Figure 2.5(d) shows the same information but with the origin omitted. The scale begins at 90 per cent. In this case, we can see very clearly the ups and downs in the employment rate. This graph does not provide a visual impression of the level of employment but it does provide a clear picture of variations in its rate.

The decision about whether to include or exclude the origin of the graph depends on what the graph is designed to reveal. To convey information about the levels of employment and inflation and variations in their rates, the graphs in Fig. 2.5(a) and Fig. 2.5(d) are almost equally revealing. By comparison, the graphs in Fig. 2.4(b) and Fig. 2.5(c) convey almost no information.

Comparing Two Time-Series Sometimes we want to use a time-series graph to compare two different variables. For example, suppose you wanted to know how the rate of growth of Gross National Expenditure (GNE) fluctuated and how those fluctuations compared with the rate of change in the trade surplus. You can examine two such series by drawing a graph of each of them in the manner shown in Fig. 2.6(a). The scale for the rate of growth in GNE appears on the right side of the figure and the scale for the percentage change in the trade surplus appears on the left. The blue line shows GNE growth and the red line shows the change in the trade surplus. You will probably agree that it is pretty hard work figuring out from Fig. 2.6(a) just what the relationship is between the rate of growth of GNE and the rate of change of the trade surplus. But it does look as if there is a tendency for the rate of change of the trade surplus to become smaller (red line goes downward) when the rate of growth of GNE increases (blue line goes upward). In other words, it seems as if these two variables have a tendency to move in opposite directions to each other.

In a situation such as this, it is often more revealing to flip the scale of one of the variables over, and graph it upside-down. Figure 2.6(b) does this. The rate of growth in GNE in Fig. 2.6(b) is graphed in exactly the same way as in Fig. 2.6(a). But the rate of change of the trade surplus has been flipped over. Now, instead of measuring the rate of increase in the surplus (a positive number) in the up direction and the rate of decrease in the surplus (a negative number) in the down direction, we measure the rate of increase in the deficit upward and the rate of decrease in the deficit downward. You can now see very clearly the relationship between these two variables. There is indeed a tendency for the rate of change in trade deficit to get bigger when the rate of growth of GNE gets higher. The relationship is very close but by no means exact.

Rates of Change Figure 2.7 illustrates another transformation that can help us interpret a time-series graph. Figure 2.7(a) shows the values of the GDP deflator for the period 1900/01 to 1990/91. The value of the index in 1984/85 is 100. A question often asked is whether the rate of inflation is rising or falling, or in other words, is the rate of increase of the general price level rising or falling? The rate of change of the price level is difficult to tell in terms of the values of the index plotted in Fig. 2.7(a). We need to work out values of the index as a proportion of the previous year. But that's exactly what a logarithmic transformation can do for us. The same graph with the *y*-axis rescaled in terms of logs is shown in Fig. 2.7(b). It suggests that the experience of inflation in Australia can be divided into three periods. The first period up to the mid-1940s was a period of generally low inflation, the second up to the mid-1970s was a period of moderate inflation, and since then we have experienced sustained and relatively rapid rates of inflation. Also the log scaling highlights the drop in prices during the Depression around 1930.

Time-series graphs, whether simple ones with a single variable or more complex ones such as those in Fig. 2.6 that show two variables, enable us to see how things change over time. But sometimes we are more interested in how variables relate to each other than in how they move over time. To study such relationships, we need to use a different but common kind of graph employed in economics — the scatter diagram.

Scatter Diagrams

A **scatter diagram** plots the value of one economic variable against the value of another. It measures one of the variables on the *x*-axis and the other variable on the *y*-axis.

Figure 2.8 illustrates three scatter diagrams. Figure 2.8(a) shows the relationship between total private consumption and national income. The *x*-axis measures national income and the *y*-axis measures total consumption. Each point represents total consumption and national income in Australia from 1970/71 to 1989/90. The years are identified by the two-digit numbers 'scattered' within the graph. For example, the point marked 85 tells us that in 1985/86 total consumption was $144 billion and national income was $240 billion. The pattern formed by the points in Fig. 2.8(a) tells us that when income rises, consumption also rises.

In Fig. 2.8(b), the *x*-axis shows the percentage of households owning a VCR and the vertical axis shows its average price. Each two-digit number represents a year. Thus the point marked 86 tells us that

Figure 2.6 Seeing Relationships in Time-Series Graphs

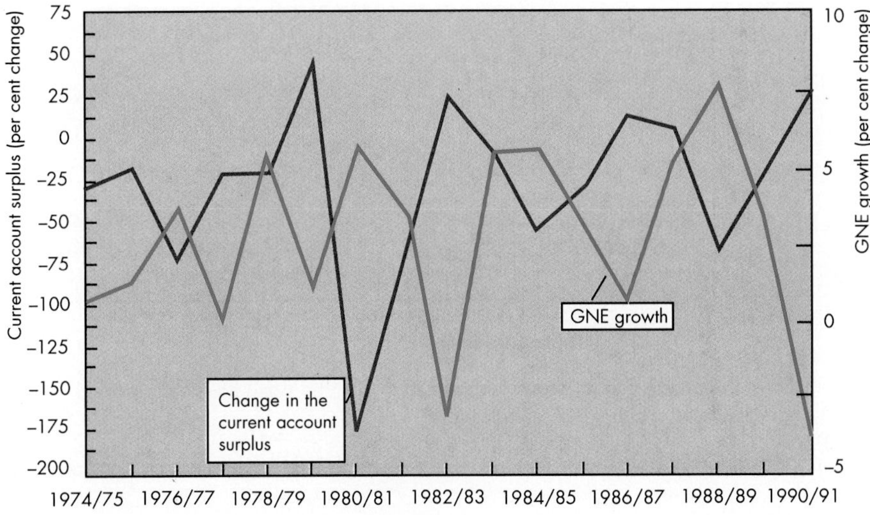

(a) GNE growth and current account surplus

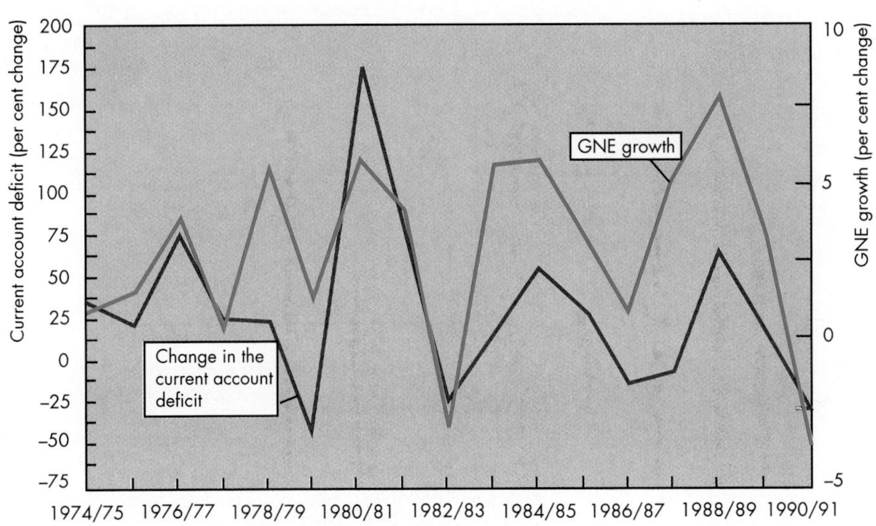

(b) GNE growth and current account deficit

A time-series graph can be used to reveal relationships between two variables. These two graphs show the rate of growth in GNE and the trade surplus between 1974/75 and 1990/91. The growth in GNE line is identical in the two parts. In part (a), percentage change in trade balance is shown measuring increases in surpluses upward and decreases downward (as negative numbers). It looks as if the percentage change in trade surplus gets bigger when the rate of growth of GNE slows, but not much else is shown by part (a). Part (b) inverts the scale on which rates of change in the trade balance are measured. Now a rate of increase in the trade deficit is measured in the up direction and a rate of decrease in the deficit in the down direction. The relationship between the rate of change in the trade deficit and the rate of growth of GNE is now clearer. There is a tendency for rates of changes in trade deficit and the rate of growth of GNE to move together.

the average price of a VCR in 1986 was $799 and that VCRs were owned by 51.7 per cent of all households. The pattern formed by the points in Fig. 2.8(b) tells us that as the price of a VCR falls, more people own one.

Figure 2.8(c) is another scatter diagram. Its *x*-axis measures the annual rate of growth of the M3 measure of the money supply in Australia and its *y*-axis measures the inflation rate. Again, each two-digit number represents a year. The point marked 85 tells us that in 1985/86 the increase in the money supply was 13 per cent and inflation was 8 per cent. The pattern formed by the points in Fig. 2.8(c) does not reveal a clear relationship — upward-sloping or downward-sloping — between the two variables. The graph thus informs us, by its lack of a distinct pattern, that there is no obvious relationship between these two variables.

Now that we have seen how we can use graphs in economics to represent economic data, let us exam-

Figure 2.7 Logarithmic Scaling

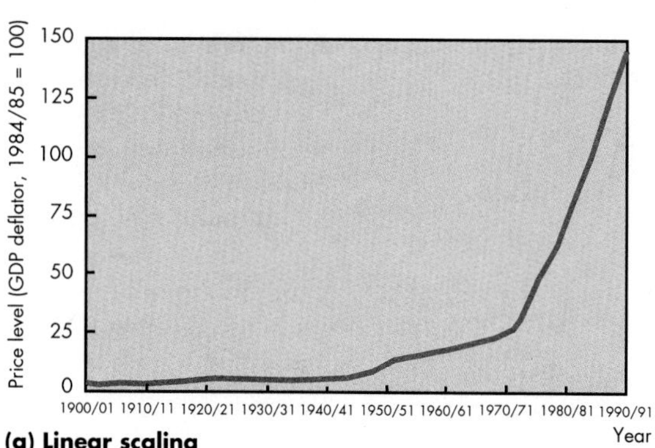

(a) Linear scaling

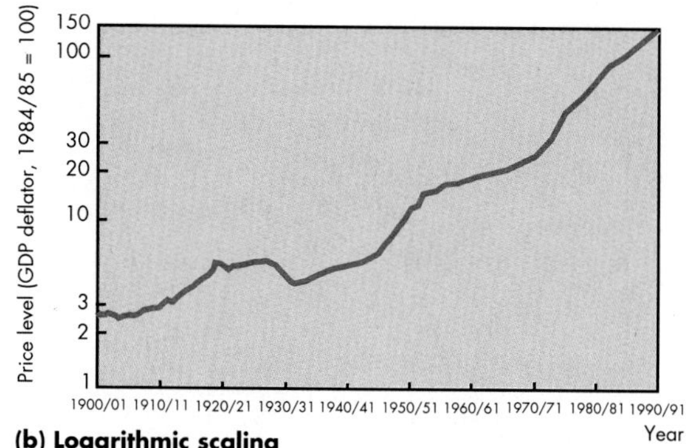

(b) Logarithmic scaling

The plot of the values of the GDP price deflator is shown in part (a). Part (b) shows the same data after the *y*-axis has been rescaled in terms of logarithmic values. Part (b) shows more clearly the rates of change of the price level.

Figure 2.8 Scatter Diagrams

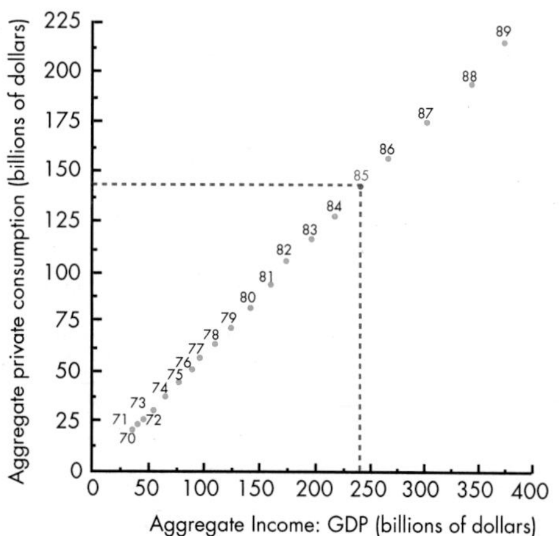

(a) Consumption and Income

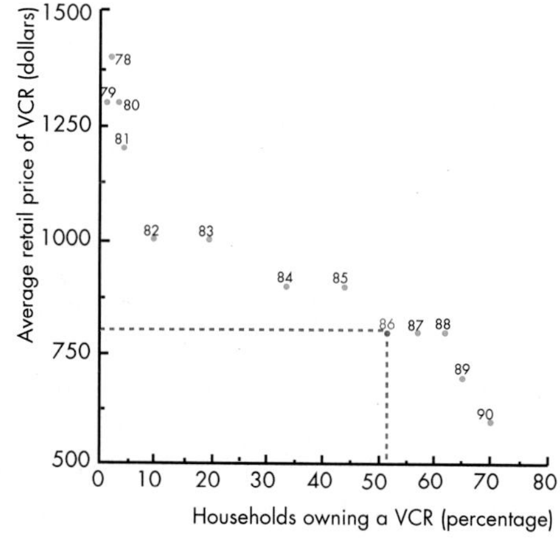

(b) VCR ownership and price

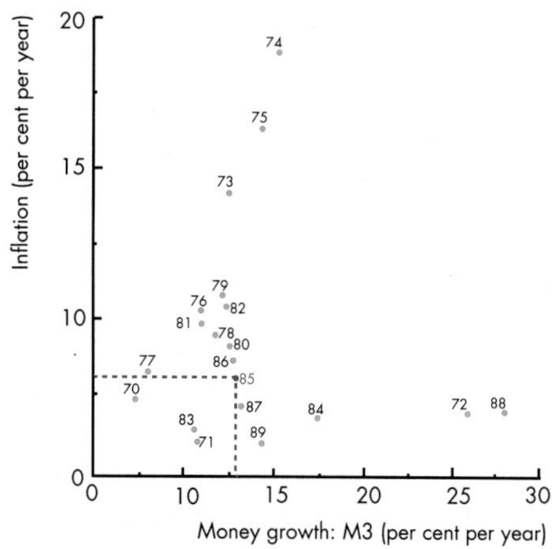

(c) Money and Inflation

A scatter diagram shows a relationship between two variables. Each point on these scatter diagrams represents an observation of two variables in a specific year. Part (a) shows that as income increases, so does consumption. Part (b) shows that as the price of a VCR falls, the share of households owning a VCR increases. Part (c) shows that there is no simple relationship between the inflation rate and increases in the money supply.

ine how economists use graphs in a more abstract way to construct and analyse economic models.

Graphs Used in Economic Models

Although you will encounter many different kinds of graphs in economics, there are some patterns which, once you have learned to recognize them, will instantly convey to you the meaning of a graph. There are graphs that show each of the following:

- Variables that go up and down together
- Variables that move in opposite directions
- Variables that are not related to each other at all
- Variables that have a maximum or a minimum

Let's look at these four cases.

Variables That Go Up and Down Together

Graphs that show the relationship between two variables that move up and down together are shown in Fig. 2.9. The relationship between two variables that move in the same direction is called a **positive relationship**. Such a relationship is shown by a line that slopes upward.

Figure 2.9(a) shows the relationship between the number of kilometres travelled in 5 hours and speed. For example, the point marked *a* tells us that we will travel 200 kilometres in 5 hours if our speed is 40 kilometres an hour. If we double our speed and travel at 80 kilometres an hour, we will cover a distance of 400 kilometres. The relationship between the number of kilometres travelled in 5 hours and speed is represented by an upward-sloping straight line. A relationship depicted by a straight line is called a **linear relationship**. A linear relationship is one that has a constant slope.

Figure 2.9(b) shows the relationship between distance sprinted and exhaustion (exhaustion being measured by the time it takes the heart rate to return to normal). This relationship is an upward-sloping one depicted by a curved line that starts out with a gentle slope but then becomes steeper.

Figure 2.9(c) shows the relationship between the number of problems worked by a student and the amount of study time. This relationship is illustrated by an upward-sloping curved line that starts out with a steep slope but then becomes more gentle.

There are three types of upward-sloping lines in the graphs in Fig. 2.9, one straight and two curved. But they are all called curves. Any line on a graph — no matter whether it is straight or curved — is called a **curve**.

Variables That Move in Opposite Directions

Figure 2.10 shows relationships between variables that move in opposite directions. A relationship between variables that move in opposite directions is called a **negative relationship**.

Figure 2.10(a) shows the relationship between the number of hours available for playing squash and the number of hours for playing tennis. One extra hour spent playing tennis means one hour less playing squash and vice versa. This relationship is negative and linear.

Figure 2.10(b) shows the relationship between the cost per kilometre travelled and the length of a journey. The longer the journey, the lower is the cost per kilometre. But as the journey length increases, the cost per kilometre decreases at a decreasing rate. This feature of the relationship is illustrated by the fact that the curve slopes downward starting out steep at a short journey length and then becoming flatter as the journey length increases.

Figure 2.10(c) shows the relationship between the amount of leisure time and the number of problems worked by a student. If the student takes no leisure, 25 problems can be worked. If the student takes 5 hours of leisure, only 20 problems can be worked (point *a*). Increasing leisure time beyond 5 hours produces a large reduction in the number of problems worked and, if the student takes 10 hours of leisure a day, no problems get worked. This relationship is a negative one that starts out with a gentle slope at a low number of leisure hours and becomes increasingly steep as leisure hours increase.

Relationships That Have a Maximum and a Minimum

Economics is about optimizing, or doing the best with limited resources. Making the highest possible profits or achieving the lowest possible costs of production are examples of optimizing. Economists make frequent use of graphs depicting relationships that have a maximum or a minimum. Figure 2.11 illustrates such relationships.

Figure 2.11(a) shows the relationship between rainfall and wheat yield. When there is no rainfall, wheat will not grow, so the yield is zero. As the rainfall increases up to 10 days a month, the wheat yield also increases. With 10 rainy days each month, the

Figure 2.9 Positive Relationships

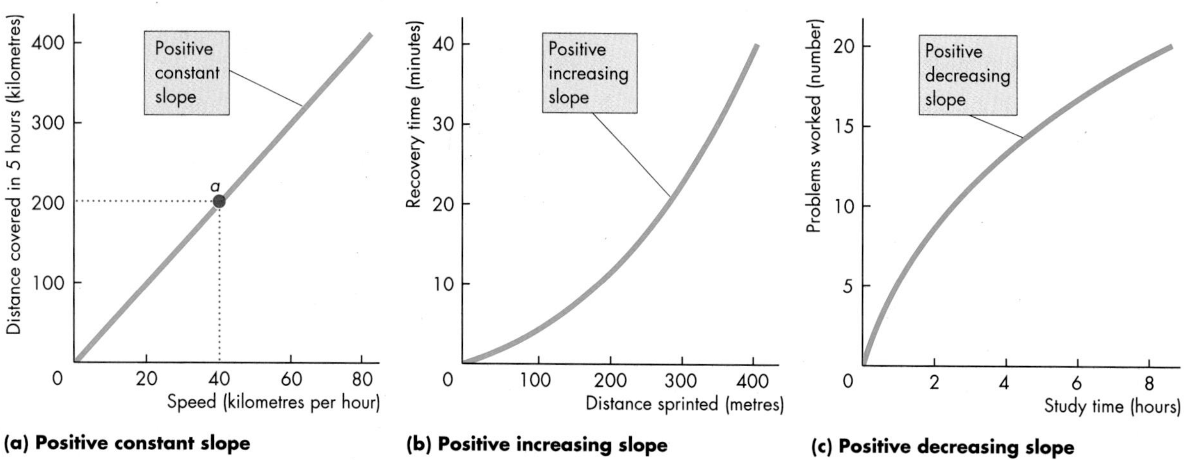

(a) Positive constant slope **(b) Positive increasing slope** **(c) Positive decreasing slope**

Each part of this figure shows a positive relationship between two variables. That is, as the value of the variable measured on the *x*-axis increases, so does the value of the variable measured on the *y*-axis. Part (a) illustrates a linear relationship — a relationship whose slope is constant as we move along the curve. Part (b) illustrates a positive relationship whose slope becomes steeper as we move along the curve away from the origin. It is a positive relationship with an increasing slope. Part (c) shows a positive relationship whose slope becomes flatter as we move away from the origin. It is a positive relationship with a decreasing slope.

wheat yield reaches its maximum at 20 bushels per hectare (point *a*). Rain in excess of 10 days per month starts to lower the yield of wheat. If every day is rainy, the wheat suffers from a lack of sunshine and the yield falls back almost to zero. This relationship is one that starts out positive, reaches a maximum, and then becomes negative.

Figure 2.11(b) shows the reverse case — a relationship that begins with a negative slope, falls to a minimum, and then becomes positive. An example

Figure 2.10 Negative Relationships

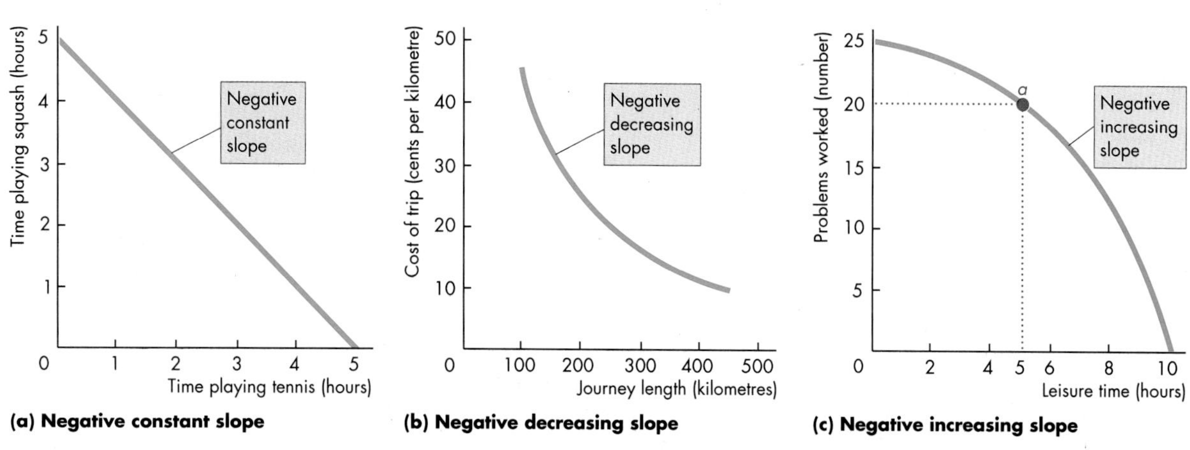

(a) Negative constant slope **(b) Negative decreasing slope** **(c) Negative increasing slope**

Each part of this figure shows a negative relationship between two variables. Part (a) shows a linear relationship — a relationship whose slope is constant as we travel along the curve. Part (b) shows a negative relationship of decreasing slope. That is, the slope of the relationship gets less steep as we travel along the curve from left to right. Part (c) shows a negative relationship of increasing slope. That is, the slope becomes steeper as we travel along the curve from left to right.

Figure 2.11 Maximum and Minimum Points

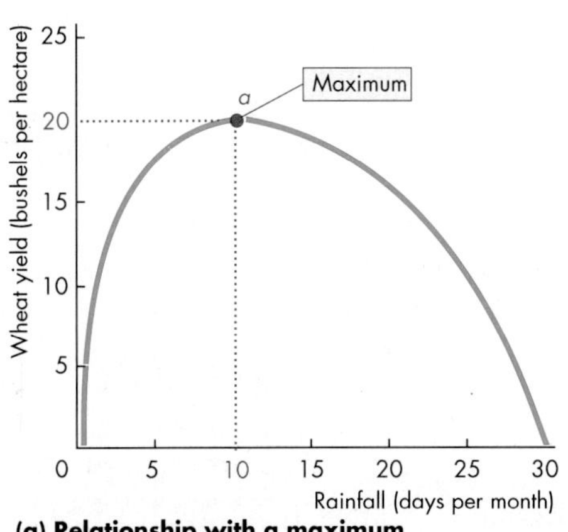

(a) Relationship with a maximum

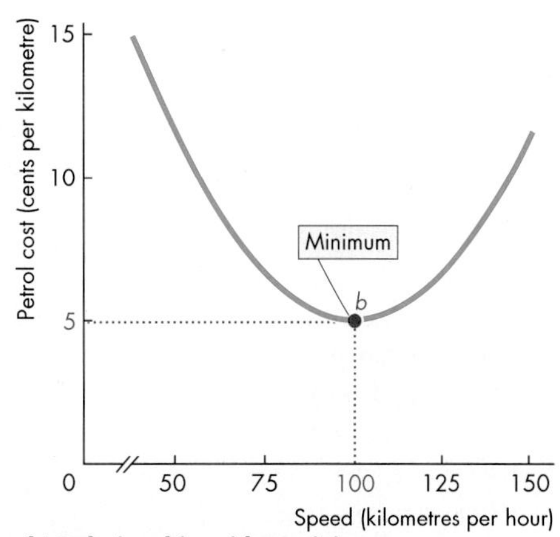

(b) Relationship with a minimum

Part (a) shows a relationship that has a maximum point, *a*. The curve rises at first, reaches its highest point, and then falls. Part (b) shows a relationship with a minimum point, *b*. The curve falls to its minimum and then rises.

of such a relationship is the petrol cost per kilometre as the speed of travel varies. At low speeds, the car is creeping along in a traffic snarl-up. The number of litres per kilometre is high so the petrol cost per kilometre is high. At very high speeds, the car is operated beyond its most efficient rate and, again, the number of litres per kilometre is high and the petrol cost per kilometre is high. At a speed of 100 kilometres an hour, the petrol cost per kilometre travelled is at its minimum (point *b*).

Variables That Are Independent

There are many situations in which one variable is independent of another. No matter what happens to the value of one variable, the other variable remains

Figure 2.12 Variables with No Relationship

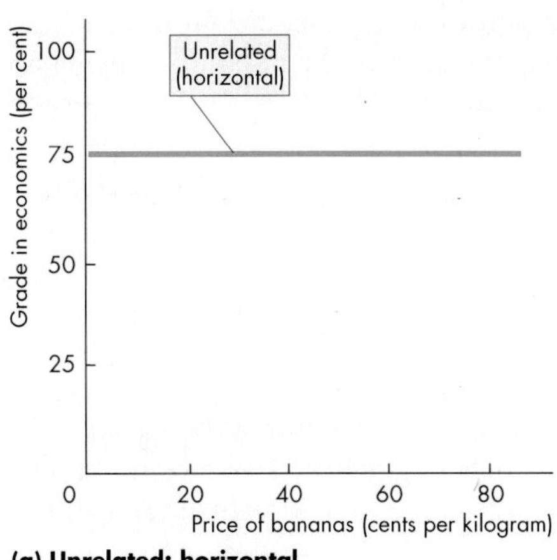

(a) Unrelated: horizontal

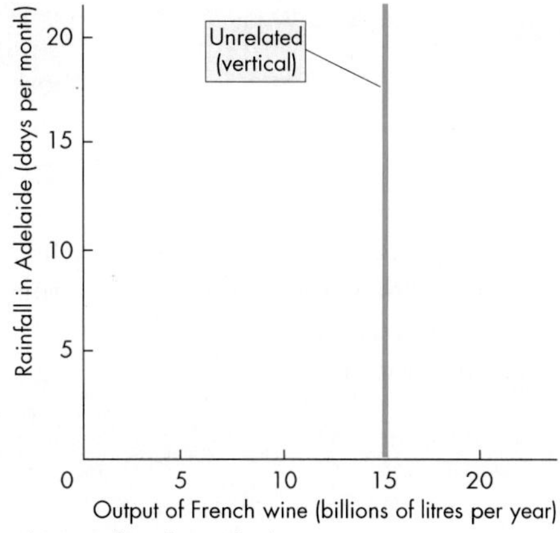

(b) Unrelated: vertical

This figure shows how we can graph two variables that are unrelated to each other. In part (a), a student's grade in economics is plotted at 75 per cent regardless of the price of bananas on the *x*-axis. In part (b), the output of the vineyards of France does not vary with the rainfall in Adelaide.

constant. Sometimes we want to show the independence between two variables in a graph. Figure 2.12 shows two ways of achieving this. In Fig. 2.12(a), your grade in economics is shown on the vertical axis against the price of bananas on the horizontal axis. Your grade (75 per cent in this example) does not depend on the price of bananas. The relationship between these two variables is shown by a horizontal straight line. In Fig. 2.12(b), the output of French wine is shown on the horizontal axis and the number of rainy days a month in Adelaide is shown on the vertical axis. Again, the output of French wine (15 billion litres a year in this example) does not change when the number of rainy days in Adelaide changes. The relationship between these two variables is shown by a vertical straight line.

Figures 2.9 through 2.12 illustrate ten different shapes of graphs that we will encounter in economic models. In describing these graphs, we have talked about curves that slope upward or slope downward and slopes that are steep or gentle. The concept of slope is an important one. Let's spend a little time discussing exactly what we mean by slope.

The Slope of a Relationship

The Definition of Slope

The **slope** of a relationship is the change in the value of the variable measured on the *y*-axis divided by the change in the value of the variable measured on the *x*-axis. We use the Greek letter Δ to represent 'change in'. Thus Δy means the change in the value of *y*, and Δx means the change in the value of *x*. The slope of the relationship between *x* and *y* is

$$\frac{\Delta y}{\Delta x}$$

If a large change in *y* is associated with a small change in *x*, the slope is large and the curve is steep. If a small change in *y* is associated with a large change in *x*, the slope is small and the curve is flat.

We can make the idea of slope sharper by doing some calculations.

Calculating Slope

A Straight Line The slope of a straight line is the same regardless of where on the line you calculate it. Thus the slope of a straight line is constant. Let's calculate the slopes of the lines in Fig. 2.13. In Fig. 2.13(a), when *x* increases from 2 to 6, *y* increases from 3 to 6. The change in *x* is +4 — that is, Δx is 4. The change in *y* is +3 — that is, Δy is 3. The slope of that line is

$$\Delta y/\Delta x = 3/4$$

In Fig. 2.13(b), when *x* increases from 2 to 6, *y* decreases from 6 to 3. The change in *y* is minus 3 — that is Δy is –3. The change in *x* is *plus* 4 — that is Δx is +4. The slope of the curve is

$$\Delta y/\Delta x = -3/4$$

Notice that the two slopes have the same magnitude (3/4), but the slope of the line in Fig. 2.13(a) is positive (+3/+4 = 3/4), while that in Fig. 2.13(b) is negative (–3/+4 = –3/4). The slope of a positive relationship is positive; the slope of a negative relationship is negative.

A Curved Line Calculating the slope of a curved line is more difficult. The slope of a curved line is not constant. Its slope depends on where on the line we calculate it. There are two ways to calculate the slope of a curved line: you can calculate the slope at a point on the line or you can calculate the slope across an arc of the line. Let's look at the two alternatives.

Slope at a Point To calculate the slope at a point on a curved line, you need to construct a straight line that has the same slope as the curve at the point in question. Figure 2.14 shows how such a calculation is made. Suppose you want to calculate the slope of the curve at the point marked *a*. Place a ruler on the graph so that it touches point *a* and no other point on the curve, then draw a straight line along the edge of the ruler. The straight red line in Fig. 2.14(a) is such a line. If the ruler touches the curve only at point *a*, then the slope of the curve at point *a* must be the same as the slope of the edge of the ruler. If the curve and the ruler do not have the same slope, the line along the edge of the ruler will cut the curve instead of just touching it.

Having now found a straight line with the same slope as the curve at point *a*, you can calculate the slope of the curve at point *a* by calculating the slope of the straight line. We already know how to calculate the slope of a straight line, so the task is straightforward. In this case, as *x* increases from 0 to 8 (Δx = 8), *y* decreases from 6 to 0 (Δy = –6). Therefore, the slope of the straight line is

$$\Delta y/\Delta x = -6/8 = -3/4$$

Thus the slope of the curve at point *a* is –3/4.

Figure 2.13 The Slope of a Straight Line

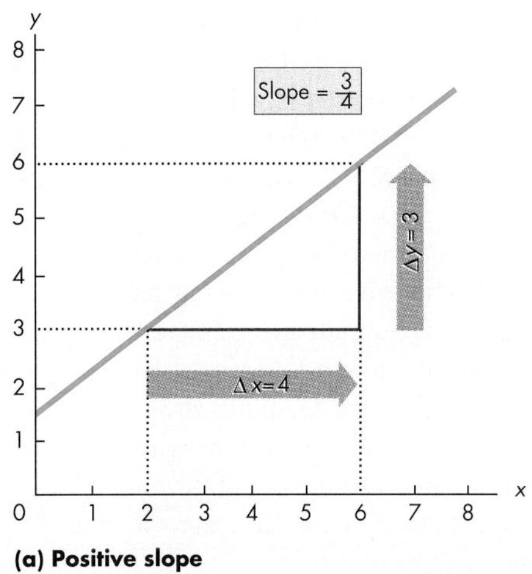

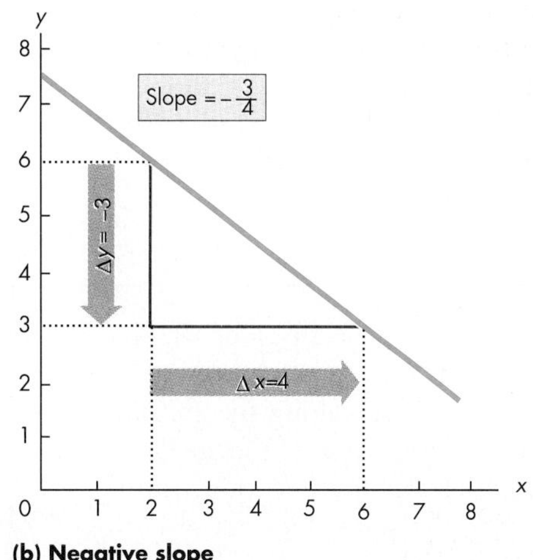

To calculate the slope of a straight line, we divide the change in the value of *y* by the change in the value of *x*. Part (a) shows the calculation of a positive slope — where both *x* and *y* go up together. When *x* goes up from 2 to 6, the change in *x* is 4 — that is, Δx equals 4. That change in *x* brings about an increase in *y* from 3 to 6, so that Δy equals 3. The slope ($\Delta y/\Delta x$) equals $\frac{3}{4}$. Part (b) shows a negative slope (when *x* goes up, *y* goes down). When *x* goes up from 2 to 6, Δx equals 4. That change in *x* brings about a decrease in *y* from 6 to 3, so that Δy equals –3. The slope ($\Delta y/\Delta x$) equals $-\frac{3}{4}$.

Figure 2.14 The Slope of a Curve

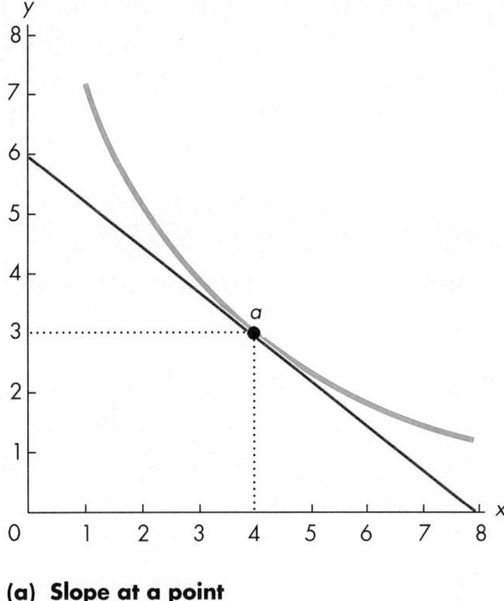

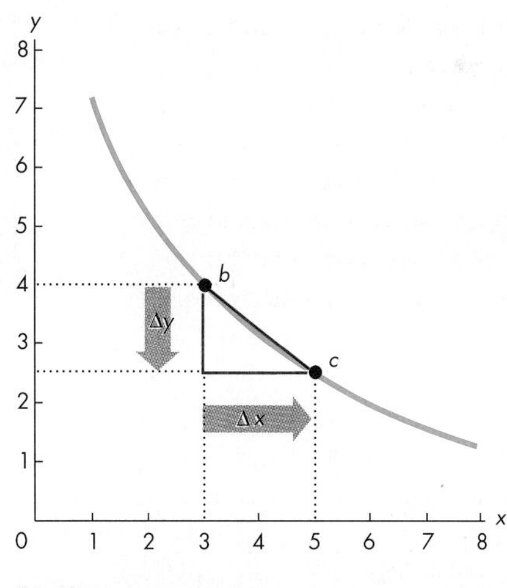

The slope of a curve can be calculated either at a point, as in part (a), or across an arc, as in part (b). The slope at a point is calculated by finding the slope of a straight line that touches the curve only at one point. One such straight line touches the curve at point *a*. The slope of that straight line is calculated by dividing the change in *y* by the change in *x*. When *x* increases from 0 to 8, Δx equals 8. That change in *x* is associated with a fall in *y* from 6 to 0, so Δy equals –6. The slope of the line is $-\frac{6}{8}$ or $-\frac{3}{4}$. To calculate the slope across an arc, we place a straight line across the curve from one point to another and then calculate the slope of that straight line. One such line is that from *b* to *c* in part (b). The slope of the straight line *bc* is calculated by dividing the change in *y* by the change in *x*. In moving from *b* to *c*, *x* goes up by 2, Δx equals 2, and *y* goes down by $1\frac{1}{2}$, Δy equals $-1\frac{1}{2}$. The slope of the line *bc is* $-1\frac{1}{2}$ divided by 2, or $-\frac{3}{4}$.

Slope Across an Arc Calculating a slope across an arc is similar to calculating an average slope. In Fig. 2.14(b), we are looking at the same curve as in Fig. 2.14(a) but instead of calculating the slope at point *a*, we calculate the slope for a change in x from 3 to 5. As x increases from 3 to 5, y decreases from 4 to $2\frac{1}{2}$. The change in y is $-1\frac{1}{2}$ ($\Delta y = -1\frac{1}{2}$). The change in x is +2 ($\Delta x = 2$). Therefore, the slope of the line is

$$\Delta y/\Delta x = (-1\tfrac{1}{2})/2 = -\tfrac{3}{4}$$

This calculation gives us the slope of the line between, points *b* and *c* and it represents a kind of average value of the slope along the arc *bc*. In this particular example, the slope of the arc *bc* is identical to the slope of the curve at point *a* in Fig. 2.14 (a). Calculating the slope does not always work out so neatly. You might have some fun constructing counter examples.

Graphing Relationships Between More Than Two Variables

We have seen that we can graph a single variable as a point on a straight line and we can graph the relationship between two variables as a point formed by the x and y coordinates in a two-dimensional graph. You may be suspecting that although a two-dimensional graph is informative, most of the things in which you are likely to be interested involve relationships among not just two variables but many. Examples of relationships among more than two variables abound. For example, consider the relationship between the price of ice cream, the air temperature and the amount of ice cream eaten. If ice cream is expensive and the temperature is low, people eat much less ice cream than when ice cream is inexpensive and the temperature is high. For any given price of ice cream, the quantity consumed varies with the temperature, and for any given temperature, the quantity of ice cream consumed varies with its price.

Other Things Being Equal

Figure 2.15 illustrates such a situation. The table shows the number of litres of ice cream that will be eaten each day at various temperatures and ice cream prices. How can we graph all these numbers? To graph a relationship that involves more than two variables, we consider what happens if all but two of the variables are held constant. This device is called *ceteris paribus*. ***Ceteris paribus*** is a Latin phrase that means 'other things being equal'. For example, in Fig. 2.15(a) you can see what happens to the quantity of ice cream consumed when the price of ice cream varies while the temperature is held constant. The line labelled 20°C shows the relationship between ice cream consumption and the price of ice cream when the temperature stays at 20°C. The numbers used to plot that line are those in the third column of the table in Fig. 2.15. The curve labelled 30°C shows the consumption of ice cream when the price varies and the temperature is 30°C.

Alternatively, we can show the relationship between ice cream consumption and temperature while holding the price of ice cream constant, as is shown in Fig. 2.15(b). The curve labelled 30 cents shows how the consumption of ice cream varies with the temperature when ice cream costs 30 cents, and a second curve shows the relationship when ice cream costs 15 cents. Fig. 2.15(c) shows the combinations of temperature and price that result in a constant consumption of ice cream. One curve shows the combination that results in 10 litres a day being consumed and the other shows the combination that results in 7 litres a day being consumed. A high price and a high temperature lead to the same consumption as a lower price and lower temperature. For example, 10 litres are consumed at 0°C and 30 cents per scoop and at 20°C and 60 cents per scoop.

■ With what you have now learned about graphs, you can move forward with your study of economics. There are no graphs in this book that are more complicated than those that have been explained here.

SUMMARY

Graphing Data

There are two main types of graphs used to represent economic data: time-series graphs and scatter diagrams. A time-series graph plots the value of one or more economic variables on the vertical axis (y-axis) and time on the horizontal axis (x-axis). A well-

Figure 2.15 Graphing a Relationship Among Three Variables

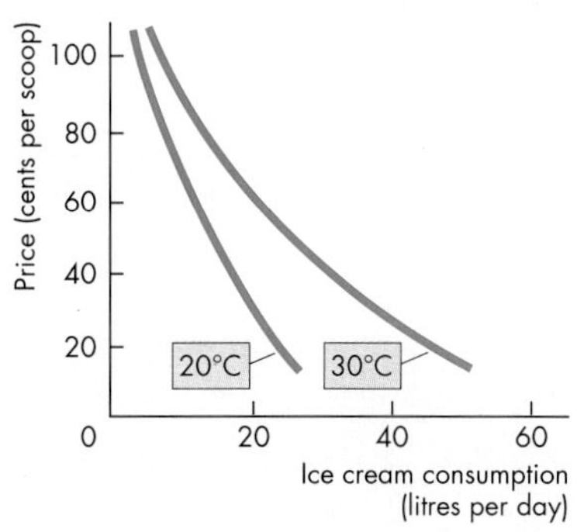

(a) Price and consumption at a given temperature

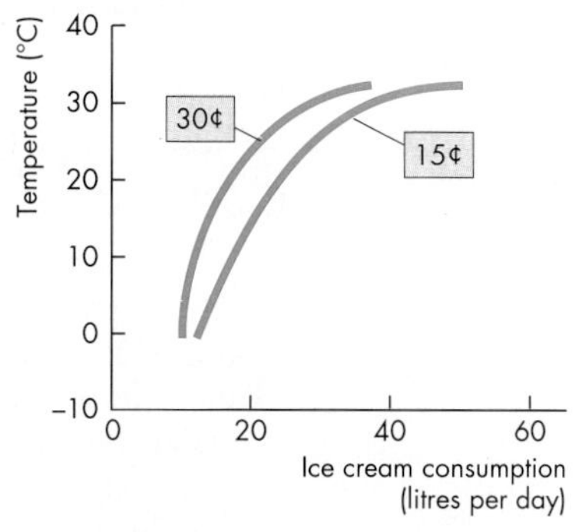

(b) Temperature and consumption at a given price

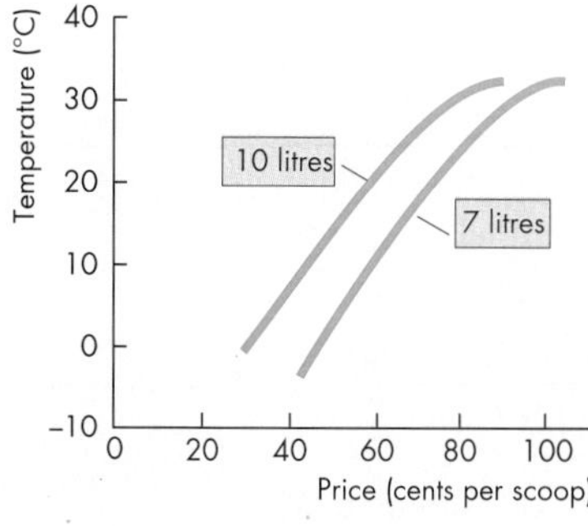

(c) Temperature and price at a given consumption

Price (cents per scoop)	**Ice cream consumption (litres per day)**			
	0°C	**10°C**	**20°C**	**30°C**
15	12	18	25	50
30	10	12	18	37
45	7	10	13	27
60	5	7	10	20
75	3	5	7	14
90	2	3	5	10
105	1	2	3	6

The quantity of ice cream consumed (one variable) depends on its price (a second variable) and the air temperature (a third variable). The table provides some hypothetical numbers that tell us how many litres of ice cream are consumed each day at different prices and different temperatures. For example, if the price is 45 cents per scoop and the temperature is 10°C, 10 litres of ice cream will be consumed. In order to graph a relationship between three variables, the value of one variable must be held constant. Part (a) shows the relationship between price and consumption, holding temperature constant. One curve holds temperature constant at 30°C and the other at 20°C. Part (b) shows the relationship between temperature and consumption, holding price constant. One curve holds the price at 30 cents and the other at 15 cents. Part (c) shows the relationship between temperature and price, holding consumption constant. One curve holds consumption constant at 10 litres and the other at 7 litres.

constructed time-series graph quickly reveals the level, direction of change and speed of change of a variable. It also reveals trends. Graphs sometimes mislead, especially when scales are stretched or squeezed to exaggerate or understate a variation.

Scatter diagrams plot the value of one economic variable associated with the value of another. These diagrams reveal whether or not there is a relationship between two variables and, if there is a relationship, its nature. (pp. 28–35)

Graphs Used in Economic Models

Graphs are used in economic models to illustrate relationships between variables. There are four cases: positive relationships, negative relationships, relationships that have a maximum or a minimum, and variables that are not related to each other. Examples of these different types of relationships are summarized in Fig. 2.9 through Fig. 2.12. (pp. 35–38)

The Slope of a Relationship

The slope of a relationship is calculated as the change in the value of y divided by the change in the value of x — $\Delta y/\Delta x$. A straight line has a constant slope, but a curved line has a varying slope. To calculate the slope of a curved line, we either calculate the slope at a point or across an arc. (pp. 38–40)

Graphing Relationships Between More Than Two Variables

To graph a relationship between more than two variables, we hold constant the values of all the variables except two. We then plot the value of one of the variables against the value of another. Holding constant all the variables but two is called the *ceteris paribus* assumption — other things being equal. (pp. 40–41)

KEY TERMS

Axes, p. 28
Ceteris paribus, p. 40
Coordinates, p. 28
Curve, p. 35
Linear relationship, p. 35
Negative relationship, p. 35
Origin, p. 28
Positive relationship, p. 35
Scatter diagram, p. 32
Slope, p. 38
Time-series graph, p. 28
Trend, p. 29
x-axis, p. 28
x-coordinate, p. 28
y-axis, p. 28
y-coordinate, p. 28

PROBLEMS

1 The inflation rate in Australia between 1970/71 and 1989/90 was as follows:

Year	Inflation Rate (% p.a.)
1970/71	4.8
1971/72	6.8
1972/73	6.0
1973/74	12.9
1974/75	16.7
1975/76	13.0
1976/77	13.8
1977/78	9.5
1978/79	8.2
1979/80	10.2
1980/81	9.4
1981/82	10.4
1982/83	11.5
1983/84	6.8
1984/85	4.3
1985/86	8.4
1986/87	9.3
1987/88	7.3
1988/89	7.3
1989/90	8.0
1990/91	5.3

Draw a time-series graph of these data, then use your graph to answer the following questions:

a) In which year was inflation highest?
b) In which year was inflation lowest?
c) In which years did inflation rise?
d) In which years did inflation fall?
e) In which year did inflation rise or fall the fastest?
f) In which year did inflation rise or fall the slowest?
g) What have been the main trends in inflation?

2 Interest rates on treasury notes in Australia between 1970 and 1990 were as follows:

Year	Interest Rate (% p.a.)
1970	5.5
1971	5.4
1970	5.5
1972	4.3
1973	5.9
1974	9.3
1975	7.5
1976	7.7
1977	8.5
1978	8.4
1979	8.9
1980	11.0
1981	13.2
1982	13.6
1983	11.0
1984	11.6
1985	16.0
1986	14.9
1987	12.2
1988	12.5
1989	16.8
1990	12.8

Use this data together with that in problem 1 to draw a scatter diagram showing the relationship between inflation and the interest rate. Use this diagram to determine whether there is a relationship between inflation and the interest rate and whether it is positive or negative.

3 Use the following information to draw a graph showing the relationship between x and y:

x	0	1	2	3	4	5	6	7	8
y	0	1	4	9	16	25	36	49	64

a) Is the relationship between x and y positive or negative?
b) Does the slope of the relationship rise or fall as the value of x rises?

4 Using the data in problem 3:
a) Calculate the slope of the relationship between x and y when x equals 4.
b) Calculate the slope of the arc when x rises from 3 to 4.
c) Calculate the slope of the arc when x rises from 4 to 5.
d) Calculate the slope of the arc when x rises from 3 to 5.
e) What do you notice that is interesting about your answers to (b), (c) and (d), compared with your answer to (a)?

5 Calculate the slopes of the following two relationships between x and y:

a)

x	0	2	4	6	8	10
y	20	16	12	8	4	0

b)

x	0	2	4	6	8	10
y	0	8	16	24	32	40

6 Draw a graph showing the following relationship between x and y:

x	0	1	2	3	4	5	6	7	8	9
y	0	2	4	6	8	10	8	6	4	2

a) Is the slope positive or negative when x is less than 5?
b) Is the slope positive or negative when x is greater than 5?
c) What is the slope of this relationship when x equals 5?
d) Is y at a maximum or at a minimum when x equals 5?

7 Draw a graph showing the following relationship between x and y:

x	0	1	2	3	4	5	6	7	8	9
y	10	8	6	4	2	0	2	4	6	8

a) Is the slope positive or negative when x is less than 5?
b) Is the slope positive or negative when x is greater than 5?
c) What is the slope of this relationship when x equals 5?
d) Is y at a maximum or at a minimum when x equals 5?

Chapter 3

Production, Specialization and Exchange

After studying this chapter, you will be able to:

- Define the production possibility frontier.
- Calculate opportunity cost.
- Explain why economic growth and technical change do not provide free gifts.
- Explain comparative advantage.
- Explain why people specialize and how they gain from trade.
- Explain why property rights and money have evolved.

Making the Most of it

We live in a style that most of our grandparents could not even have imagined. Medicine has cured diseases that terrified them. Most of us live in better and more spacious homes. We eat more, we grow taller, we are even born larger than they were. Our parents are amazed at the matter-of-fact way we handle computers. We casually use products — microwave ovens, graphite tennis rackets, digital watches — that didn't exist in their youth. Economic growth has made us richer than our parents and grandparents. But economic growth and technical change, and the wealth they bestow, have not liberated us from scarcity. Why not? Why, despite our immense wealth, do we still have to face costs? Why are there no 'free lunches'? We see an incredible amount of specialization and trading in the modern world. Each one of us specializes in a particular job — as lawyer, car maker, homemaker. We have become so specialized that only one in seventeen people in the workforce works in agriculture. Only one in six of us works in manufacturing. About two-thirds of all of us work in wholesale and retail trade, banking and finance, other services, and government. Why do we specialize? How do we benefit from specialization and exchange? How do money and the legal institution of private property extend our ability to specialize and increase production? These are the questions that we tackle in this chapter.

In this chapter we will begin by making the idea of scarcity more precise. Then we will go on to see how we can measure opportunity cost. We will also see how, when each individual tries to get the most out of scarce resources, specialization and exchange occur. That is, people specialize in doing what they do best and exchange their products with other specialists. We are also going to see why such social arrangements as private property and money exist and how they spring from people's attempts to make the most of their limited resources.

The Production Possibility Frontier

What do we mean by production? **Production** is the conversion of *land, labour and capital* into goods and services. We defined the factors of production in Chapter 1. Let's briefly recall what they are.

Land is all the gifts of nature. It includes the air, the water and the land surface, as well as the minerals that lie beneath the surface of the earth. Labour is all the muscle-power and brain-power of human beings. The voices and artistry of singers and actors, the strength and coordination of athletes, the daring of astronauts, the political skill of diplomats, as well as the physical and mental skills of the many millions of people who make cars and carpets, chewing-gum and glue, wallpaper and watering cans, are included in this category. Capital is all the goods that have been produced and can now be used in the production of other goods and services. Examples include the national highway system, the fine buildings of great cities, dams and power projects, airports and jumbo jets, car production lines, shirt factories and hot bread kitchens. A special kind of capital is called human capital. **Human capital** is the accumulated skill and knowledge of human beings, which arise from their training and education, building on their natural endowment of labour.

Goods and services are all the valuable things that people produce. Goods are storable and transferable. For example, you can stock up on bread, you can lend your car to someone else or you can collect spoons. But you can't stock up on a year's supply of haircuts. You can't have a haircut then transfer it to your friend. Things like haircuts are called services. They are not storable and once a service has been produced it can't be transferred to someone else. There are two types of goods: capital goods and consumption goods. We saw that **capital goods** are those that are used in the production of other goods or services. They can be used many times before they wear out. **Consumption goods** are those consumed and used up for their own enjoyment by households. Some consumption goods are also durable so they can be used many times before they wear out but many can also be used only once. Examples are toothpaste and apples. **Consumption** is the process of using up goods and services.

The amount that we can produce is limited by our resources and the technologies for transforming those resources into goods and services. That limit is described by the production possibility frontier. The **production possibility frontier** marks the boundary between production levels that can and cannot be attained. It is important to understand the production possibility frontier in the real world, but in order to achieve that goal more easily, we will first study an economy — a model economy — that is simpler than the one in which we live.

A Model Economy

Instead of looking at the real world economy with all its complexity and detail, we will build a model of an economy. The model will have features that are essential to understanding the real economy, but we will ignore most of reality's immense detail. Our model economy will be simpler in three important ways:

1 For the time being, we will suppose that everything that is produced is also consumed. This simplification means that, in our model, capital resources neither grow nor shrink. Later we will examine what happens if we consume less than we produce and add to capital resources.

2 In our model economy, there will be just two goods — even though in the real world we use our scarce resources to produce countless goods and services.

3 Although there are approximately five billion people living on this planet, our model economy initially has just one person, Kylie, who lives on a deserted island and has no dealings with other people.

Let's suppose that all the resources of Kylie's island economy can be used to produce two goods, grain and cloth. Suppose also that Kylie can work 10 hours each day. The amount of grain and cloth that Kylie can produce will depend on how many hours she devotes to producing them. Table 3.1 sets out Kylie's production possibilities for grain and cloth. If she does no work, she produces nothing. Two hours a day devoted to grain farming produces 6 kilograms of grain per month. Devoting more hours to grain increases the output of grain, but there is a decline in the extra amount of grain that comes from extra effort. The reason for this decline is that Kylie has to use increasingly unsuitable land for growing grain. At first, she plants grain on a lush, flat plain. Eventually, when she has used all the arable land, she has to start planting on the rocky hills and the edge of the beach. The numbers in the second column of the table show how the output of grain rises as hours devoted to cultivating it rise.

To produce cloth, Kylie gathers wool from the sheep that live on the island. The sheep are tame

Table 3.1 Kylie's Production Possibilities

Hours worked per day		Grain grown (kilograms per month)		Cloth produced (metres per month
0	either	0	or	0
2	either	6	or	1
4	either	11	or	2
6	either	15	or	3
8	either	18	or	4
10	either	20	or	5

If Kylie does no work, she produces no grain or cloth. If she works for 2 hours per day and spends the entire amount of time on grain production, she produces 6 kilograms of grain per month. If that same time is used for cloth production, 1 metre of cloth is produced but no grain. The last three rows of the table show the amounts of grain or cloth that can be produced per month as more hours are devoted to each activity.

and Kylie can catch and shear a constant number of sheep each hour. As she devotes more hours to collecting wool, and making cloth, her output rises at a constant rate.

If Kylie devotes all her time to growing grain, she can produce 20 kilograms of grain in a month. In that case, however, she cannot produce any cloth. Conversely, if she devotes all her time to making cloth, she can produce 5 metres a month but will have no time left for growing grain. Kylie can devote some of her time to grain and some to cloth but not more than 10 hours a day total. Thus she can spend 2 hours growing grain and 8 hours making cloth or 6 hours on one and 4 hours on the other (or any other combination of hours that add up to 10 hours).

We have defined the production possibility frontier as the boundary between what is attainable and what is unattainable. You can calculate Kylie's production possibility frontier by using the information in Table 3.1. These calculations are summarized in the table in Fig. 3.1 and graphed in that figure as Kylie's production possibility frontier. To see how we calculated that frontier, let's concentrate first on the table in Fig. 3.1.

Possibility *a* shows Kylie devoting no time to cloth and her entire 10-hour working day to grain. In this case, she can produce 20 kilograms of grain per month and no cloth. For possibility *b* she spends 2 hours a day making cloth and 8 hours growing grain, to produce a total of 18 kilograms of grain and 1 metre of cloth per month. The pattern continues on to possibility *f*, where she devotes 10 hours a day to cloth and no time to grain. These same numbers are plotted in the graph shown in Fig. 3.1. Metres of cloth are measured on the horizontal axis and kilograms of grain on the vertical axis. Points *a, b, c, d, e* and *f* represent the numbers in the corresponding row of the table.

Of course, Kylie does not have to work in blocks of 2 hours, as in our example. She can work 1 hour or 1 hour and 10 minutes growing grain and devote the rest of her time to making cloth. All other feasible allocations of Kylie's 10 hours will result in a series of production possibilities represented by the line that joins points *a, b, c, d, e* and *f*. This line shows Kylie's production possibility frontier. She can produce at any point on the frontier or inside it. These are attainable points. Points outside the frontier are unattainable. To produce at points beyond the frontier, Kylie needs more time than she has. By working 10 hours a day producing both grain and cloth, Kylie can choose any point she wishes on the frontier. By working less than 10 hours a day, she produces at a point inside the frontier.

On the Frontier Is Best

Kylie produces grain and cloth, not for the fun of it, but so that she can eat and keep warm. The larger the quantities of grain and cloth she produces, the more she can consume. Her wants for grain and cloth outstrip her production possibilities, and the best that she can do is to produce — and, therefore, consume — at a point *on* her production possibility frontier. To see why, consider a point such as *z* in the attainable region. At point *z*, Kylie can improve her situation by moving to a point such as *b* or *d* or to a point on the frontier between *b* and *d*, such as point *c*. Kylie can have more of everything on the frontier than at points inside it. At point *b*, she can consume more grain and no less cloth than at point *z*. At point *d*, she can consume more cloth and no less grain than at point *z*. At point *c* she can consume more grain and more cloth than at point *z*. Kylie will never choose points such as *z* because better choices, such as *c*, will always be available. That is, some point on the frontier is always better than a point inside the frontier.

We have just seen that Kylie wants to produce at some point on her production possibility frontier, but she is still faced with the problem of choosing the best point. In choosing between one point and another, Kylie is confronted with *opportunity costs*.

Figure 3.1 Kylie's Production Possibility Frontier

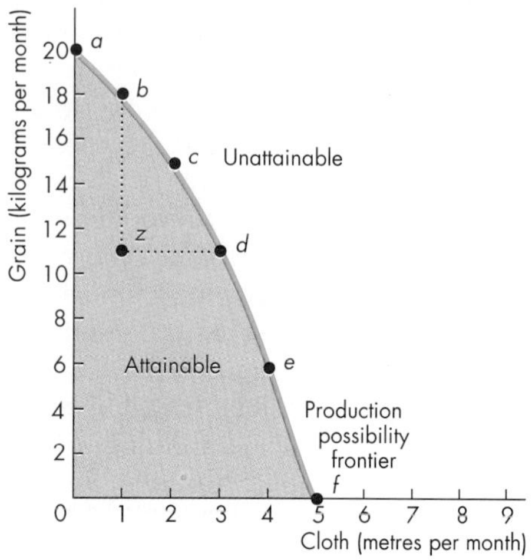

Possibility	Grain (kilograms per month)		Cloth (metres per month)
a	20	and	0
b	18	and	1
c	15	and	2
d	11	and	3
e	6	and	4
f	0	and	5

The table lists six points on Kylie's production possibility frontier. Row *e* tells us that if Kylie produces 6 kilograms of grain, the maximum cloth production that is possible is 4 metres. These same points are graphed as points *a, b, c, d, e* and *f* in the figure. The line passing through these points is Kylie's production possibility frontier, which separates the attainable from the unattainable. The attainable area contains all the possible production points. Kylie can produce anywhere inside this area or on the production possibility frontier. Points outside the frontier are unattainable. Kylie prefers points on the frontier to any point inside. Points between *b* and *d* on the frontier are better than point *z* inside the frontier because they give Kylie more of both goods.

At point *c*, for example, she has less cloth and more grain than at point *d*. If she chooses point *d*, she does so because she figures that the extra cloth is worth the grain forgone. Let's explore opportunity cost more closely and see how we can measure it.

Opportunity Cost

We've defined opportunity cost as the best alternative forgone: for a late sleeper, the opportunity cost of attending an early morning lecture may be an hour in bed; for a jogger, it may be an hour of exercise. The concept of opportunity cost can be made more precise by using a production possibility frontier such as the one shown in Fig. 3.1. Let's see what that curve tells us.

The Best Alternative Forgone

The production possibility frontier in Fig. 3.1 traces the boundary between attainable and unattainable combinations of grain and cloth. Since there are only two goods, there is no difficulty in working out what is the best alternative forgone. More grain can be grown only by paying the price of having less cloth, and more cloth can be made only by bearing the cost of having less grain. Thus the opportunity cost of producing an additional metre cloth is the grain forgone and the opportunity cost of producing an additional kilogram of grain is the cloth forgone. Let's put numerical values on the opportunity costs of grain and cloth.

Measuring Opportunity Cost

We are going to measure opportunity cost by using Kylie's production possibility frontier. We will calculate how much cloth she has to give up to get more grain and how much grain she has to give up to get more cloth.

If all Kylie's time is used to produce grain, she produces 20 kilograms of grain and no cloth. If she decides to produce 1 metre of cloth, how much grain does she have to give up? You can see the answer in Fig. 3.2. To produce 1 metre of cloth Kylie moves from *a* to *b* and gives up 2 kilograms of grain. Thus the opportunity cost of the first metre of cloth is 2 kilograms of grain. If she decides to produce an additional metre of cloth, how much grain does she give up? The answer can be seen in Fig. 3.2. This time, Kylie moves from *b* to *c* and gives up 3 kilograms of grain to produce the second metre of cloth.

Figure 3.2 Kylie's Opportunity Costs of Cloth

As Kylie increases her cloth production,
First 1 metre of cloth costs 2 kilograms of grain
Next 1 metre of cloth costs 3 kilograms of grain
Next 1 metre of cloth costs 4 kilograms of grain
Next 1 metre of cloth costs 5 kilograms of grain
Last 1 metre of cloth costs 6 kilograms of grain

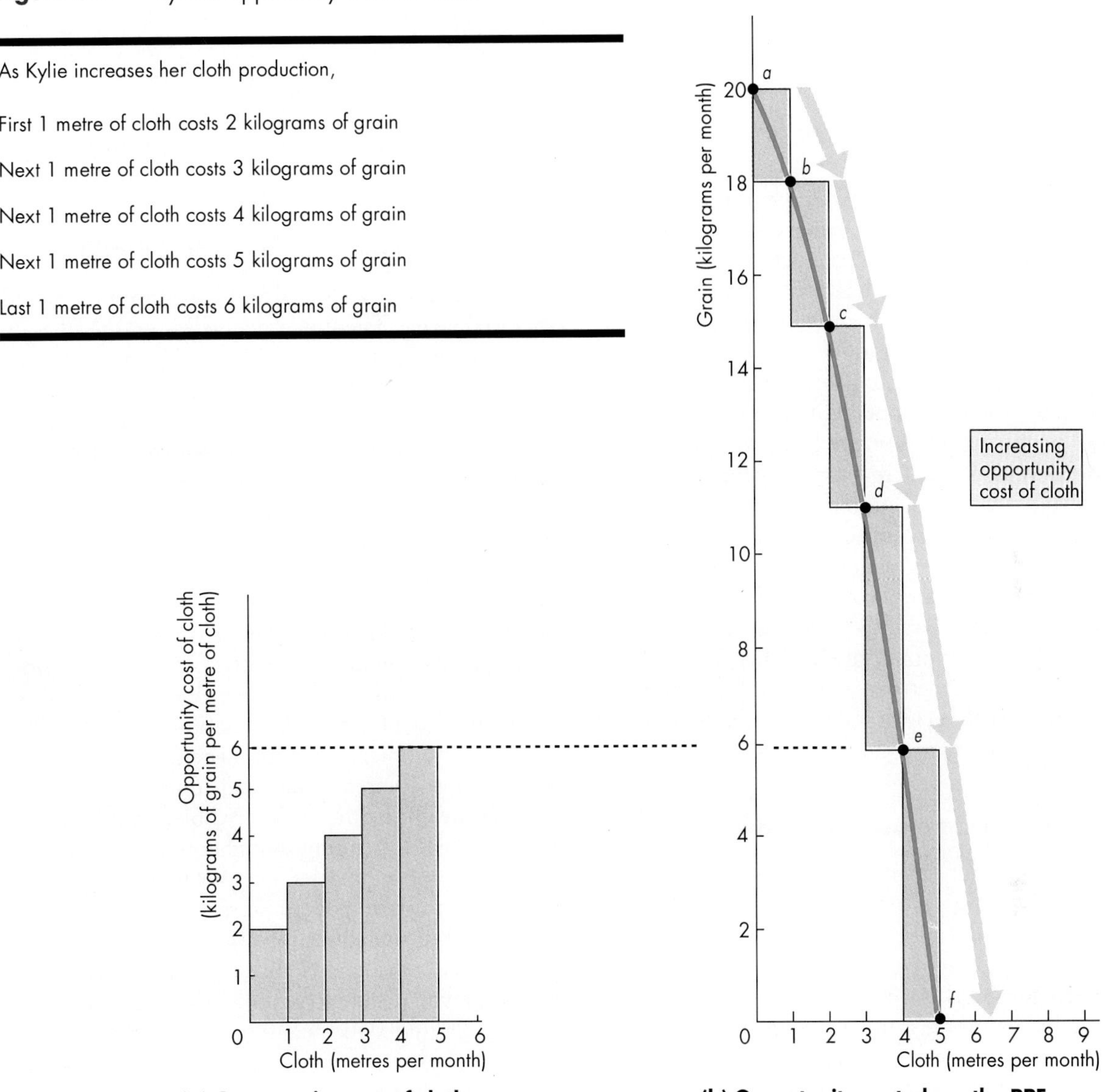

The table records Kylie's opportunity cost of cloth. The first metre of cloth costs 2 kilograms of grain. The next metre of cloth costs 3 kilograms of grain. The opportunity cost of cloth rises as Kylie produces more cloth, with the last metre of cloth costing 6 kilograms of grain. Part (a) of the figure shows the increasing opportunity cost of cloth, and part (b) shows increasing opportunity cost as Kylie moves along her outward-bowed production possibility frontier increasing her production of cloth and decreasing her production of grain.

These opportunity costs are set out in the table of Fig. 3.2. The first two rows set out the opportunity costs that we have just calculated. The table also lists the opportunity costs of moving between points *c, d, e* and *f* on Kylie's production possibility frontier of Fig. 3.1. You may want to work out another example on your own to be sure that you understand what is going on. Calculate Kylie's opportunity cost of moving from *e* to *f*.

Increasing Opportunity Cost

As you can see, opportunity cost varies with the quantity produced. The first metre of cloth costs 2 kilograms of grain. The next metre of cloth costs 3 kilograms of grain. The last metre of cloth costs 6 kilograms of grain. Thus the opportunity cost of cloth increases as Kylie produces more cloth. Figure 3.2(a) illustrates the increasing opportunity cost of cloth.

The Shape of the Frontier

Pay special attention to the shape of the production possibility frontier in Fig. 3.1. When a large amount of grain and not much cloth is produced — between points *a* and *b* — the frontier has a flatter slope. When a large amount of cloth and not much grain is produced — between points *e* and *f* — the frontier is steeper. The whole frontier bows outward. These features of the production possibility frontier are a reflection of increasing opportunity cost. You can see the connection between increasing opportunity cost and the shape of the production possibility frontier in Fig. 3.2(b). Between points *a* and *b,* 1 metre of cloth can be obtained by giving up a small amount of grain. Here the opportunity cost of cloth is low and the opportunity cost of grain is high. Between points *e* and *f,* a large amount of grain must be given up to produce 1 extra metre of cloth. In this region, the opportunity cost of cloth is high and the opportunity cost of grain is low.

Everything Has an Increasing Opportunity Cost

We've just worked out the opportunity cost of cloth. But what about the opportunity cost of grain? Does it also increase as more of it is produced? You can see the answer in Fig. 3.2. By giving up 1 metre of cloth to produce some grain, Kylie moves from *f* to *e* and produces 6 kilograms of grain. Thus the opportunity cost of the first 6 kilograms of grain is 1 metre of cloth. Moving from *e* to *d* you can see that the next 5 kilograms of grain cost 1 metre of cloth. Thus the opportunity cost of grain also increases as Kylie makes more grain.

Increasing opportunity cost and the outward bow of the production possibility frontier arise from the fact that scarce resources are not equally useful in all activities. For instance, some of the land on Kylie's island is extremely fertile and produces a high crop yield, while other land is rocky and barren.

Kylie uses the most fertile land for growing grain and gathers wool from the sheep which occupy the most barren areas. Only if she wants a larger amount of grain does she try to cultivate relatively barren areas, and only if she wants a larger amount of wool does she pursue less friendly sheep. If she uses all her time to grow grain, she has to use some very unsuitable, low-yielding land. Devoting some time to making cloth, and reducing the time spent growing grain by the same amount, produces a small drop in grain production but a large increase in the output of cloth. Conversely, if Kylie uses all her time to make cloth, a small reduction in wool-gathering yields a large increase of grain production.

Production Possibilities in the Real World

Kylie's island is dramatically different from the world that we live in. The fundamental lesson it teaches us, however, applies to the real world. The world has a fixed number of people endowed with a given amount of human capital and limited time. The world also has a fixed amount of land and capital equipment. These limited resources can be employed, using available but limited technology, to produce goods and services. Consequently, there is a limit to the goods and services that can be produced, a boundary between what is attainable and what is not attainable. That boundary is the real-world economy's production possibility frontier. On that frontier, producing more of any one good requires producing less of some other good or goods.

For example, a prime-ministerial candidate who promises better welfare and education services must at the same time, to be credible, promise either cuts in defence spending or higher taxes. Higher taxes mean less money left over for holidays and other consumption goods and services. The cost of better welfare and educational services is less of other goods. On a smaller scale but equally important, each time you decide to rent a video you decide not to use your limited income to buy some other good. The cost of one more video is one less of something else.

On Kylie's island, we saw that the opportunity cost of a good increased as the output of the good increased. Opportunity costs in the real world increase for the same reasons that Kylie's opportunity costs increase. Consider, for example, two goods vital to our well being — food and health care. In allocating our scarce resources, we use the most fertile land and the most skilful farmers to produce food. We use the best doctors and the least fertile land for health care. If we shift fertile land and tractors away from farming and ask farmers to do surgery, the production of food drops drastically and the increase in the production of health care services is small. The opportunity cost of health care services rises. Similarly, if we shift our resources away from health care toward farming, we have to use more doctors and nurses as farmers and more hospitals as hydroponic tomato factories. The drop in health care services is large, but the increase in food production small. The opportunity cost of producing more food rises.

This example is extreme and unlikely, but these same considerations apply to any pair of goods that you can imagine: guns and butter; housing for the poor and diamonds for the rich; wheelchairs and golf carts; television programmes and breakfast cereals. We cannot escape from scarcity and opportunity cost. More of one thing always means less of something else, and the more of anything that we have or do, the higher is its opportunity cost.

R E V I E W

The production possibility frontier is the boundary between the attainable and the unattainable. There is always a point on the frontier that is better than any point inside it. Moving from one point on the frontier to another means having less of one good to get more of another. The frontier is bowed outward or, equivalently, the opportunity cost of a good increases as more of it is produced. ■

Changing Production Possibilities

Although the production possibility frontier defines the boundary between what is attainable and what is unattainable, that boundary is not static. It is constantly changing. Sometimes the production possibility frontier shifts *inward*, reducing our production possibilities. For example, droughts or other extreme climatic conditions shift the frontier inward. Sometimes the frontier moves outward. For example, excellent growing and harvest conditions have this effect. Sometimes the frontier shifts outward because we get a new idea. It sometimes occurs to us that there is a better way of doing something that we never before imagined possible — we invent the wheel.

Over the years, our production possibilities have undergone enormous expansion. The persistent expansion of our production possibilities is called **economic growth**. As a consequence of economic growth, we can now produce much more than we could 100 years ago and quite a bit more than even 10 years ago. By the mid-1990s, if the same pace of growth continues, our production possibilities will be even greater. By pushing out the frontier, can we avoid the constraints imposed on us by our limited resources? That is, can we get our free lunch after all?

The Cost of Shifting the Frontier

We are going to discover that although we can and do shift the production possibility frontier outward over time, we cannot do so without incurring costs. The faster the pace of economic growth, the less we can consume at the present time. Let's investigate the costs of growth by examining why economies grow and prosper.

Two key activities generate economic growth: capital accumulation and technological progress. **Capital accumulation** is the growth of capital resources. **Technological progress** is the development of new and better ways of producing goods and services. As a consequence of capital accumulation and technological progress, we have an enormous quantity of cars and aeroplanes that enable us to produce more transportation than when we only had horses and carriages; and we have satellites that make transcontinental communications possible on a scale much larger than that produced by the earlier cable technology. But accumulating capital and developing new technology are costly. To see why, let's go back to Kylie's island economy.

Capital Accumulation and Technological Change

So far, we've assumed that Kylie's island economy can produce only two goods, grain and cloth. But let's now suppose that while pursuing some of the sheep, Kylie stumbled upon an outcrop of flintstone and a forest that she had not known about before. She realizes that she can now make some flintstone tools and start building fences around the grain and sheep, thereby increasing production of both of these goods. But to make tools and build fences, Kylie has to devote time to these activities. Let's continue to suppose that there are only 10 hours of working time available each day. Time spent making tools and building fences is time that could have been spent growing grain and making cloth. Thus to expand her future production, Kylie must produce less grain and cloth today so that some of her time can be devoted to making tools and building fences. The decrease in her output of grain and cloth today is the opportunity cost of expanding her production of these two goods in the future.

Figure 3.3 provides a concrete example. The table sets out Kylie's production possibilities for pro-

Figure 3.3 Economic Growth on Kylie's Island

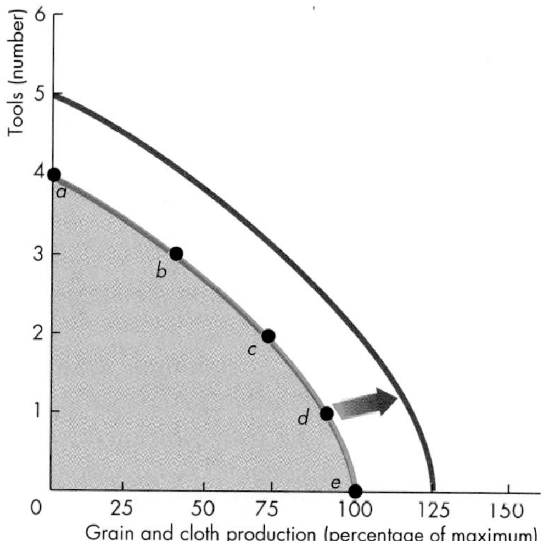

Possibility	Tools (number)	Corn and cloth production (per cent)
a	4	0
b	3	40
c	2	70
d	1	90
e	0	100

If Kylie devotes all her time to grain and cloth production, she produces no tools (row *e* of the table). As she devotes more time to tool production, she can produce successively smaller amounts of grain and cloth. If all her time is devoted to tool production (possibility *a*), no grain and cloth and four tools are produced. In the figure, the curve *abcde* is Kylie's production possibility frontier for tools and consumption goods (grain and cloth). If Kylie produces at point *e* (producing no tools), her production possibility frontier remains fixed at *abcde*. If she cuts her production of grain and cloth and makes one tool (producing at point *d*), her future production possibility frontier shifts outward as shown in the figure. The more tools and the less grain and cloth Kylie produces, the farther out the frontier shifts. The reduced output of grain and cloth is the opportunity cost of increasing future production possibilities.

ducing capital — tools and fences — as well as current consumption goods — grain and cloth. If she devotes all her working hours to grain and cloth production (row *e*), she produces no capital — no tools or fences. If she devotes enough time to producing one unit of capital a month (row *d*), her grain and cloth production is cut back to 90 per cent of its maximum possible level. She can devote still more time to capital accumulation and, as she does so, her grain and cloth production falls by successively larger amounts.

The numbers in the table are graphed in the figure. Each point, *a* through *e*, represents a row of the table. Notice the similarity between Figs. 3.3 and 3.1. Each shows a production possibility frontier. In the case of Fig. 3.3, the frontier is that between producing capital equipment — tools and fences — and producing current consumption goods — grain and cloth. If Kylie produces at point *e* in Fig. 3.3, she produces no capital and remains stuck on the production possibility frontier for grain and cloth shown in Fig. 3.1. But if she moves to point *d* in Fig. 3.3, she can produce one unit of capital each month. To do so, Kylie reduces her current production of grain and cloth to 90 per cent of what she can produce if all her time is devoted to those activities. In terms of Fig. 3.1, Kylie's current production possibility frontier for grain and cloth shifts to the left as less time is devoted to grain and cloth production and some of her time is devoted to producing capital goods.

By decreasing her production of grain and cloth and producing tools and building fences, Kylie is able to increase her production possibilities. An increasing stock of tools and fences make her more productive at growing grain and producing cloth. She can even use tools to make better tools. As a consequence, Kylie's production possibility frontier shifts outward as shown by the shift arrow. Kylie experiences economic growth.

But the amount by which Kylie's production possibility frontier shifts out depends on how much time she devotes to accumulating capital. If she devotes no time to this activity, the frontier remains at *abcde* — the original production possibility frontier. If she cuts back on current production of grain and cloth and produces one unit of capital each month (point *d*) her frontier moves out in the future to the position shown by the red curve in the figure. The less time she devotes to grain and cloth production and the more time to capital accumulation, the farther out the frontier shifts.

Economic growth is not a free gift for Kylie. To make it happen, she has to devote more time to producing tools and building fences and less to producing grain and cloth. Economic growth is no magic formula for abolishing scarcity.

Economic Growth in the Real World

The ideas that we have explored in the setting of Kylie's island apply with equal force to our real-world economy. If we devote all our resources to producing food, clothing, housing, vacations and the many other consumer goods that we enjoy, and none to research, development and accumulating capital, we will have no more capital and no better technologies in the future than we have at present. Our production possibilities in the future will be exactly the same as those today. If we are to expand our production possibilities in the future, we must produce fewer consumption goods today. The resources we free up today will enable us to accumulate capital and to develop better technologies for producing more consumption goods in the future than would otherwise have been possible. The cut in the output of consumption goods today is the opportunity cost of economic growth.

The recent experience of the world's biggest economies, the United States and Japan, provides a striking example of the effects of our choices on the rate of economic growth. In 1965, the production possibilities per capita in the United States were much larger than those in Japan (see Fig. 3.4). The United States devoted one-sixth of its resources to producing capital goods and the other five-sixths to producing consumption goods, as illustrated by point *a* in Fig. 3.4(a). But Japan devoted just under one-third of its resources to producing capital goods and only two-thirds to producing consumption goods, as illustrated by point *a* in Fig. 3.4(b). Both countries experienced economic growth, but the growth in Japan was much more rapid than the growth in the United States. Because Japan devoted a bigger fraction of its resources to producing capital goods, its stock of capital equipment grew more quickly than that of the United States and its production possibilities expanded more quickly. As a result, Japanese production possibilities per capita are now so close to those in the United States that it is hard to say which country has the larger per capita production possibilities. If Japan continues to devote a third of its resources to producing capital goods (at point *b* on its 1993 production possibility frontier), it will continue to grow much more rapidly than the United States and its frontier will move out beyond that of the United States. If Japan increases its production of consumption goods and reduces its production of capital goods (moving to point *c* on its 1993 production possibility frontier), then its rate of economic expansion will slow down to that of the United States. Australia, by comparison, devotes about one-quarter of its resources to producing capital goods — a higher share than that of the United States but not as high as Japan.

Figure 3.4 Economic Growth in the United States and Japan

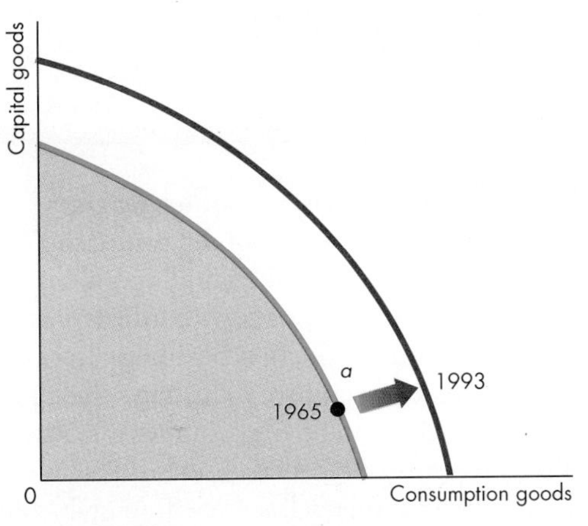

(a) United States

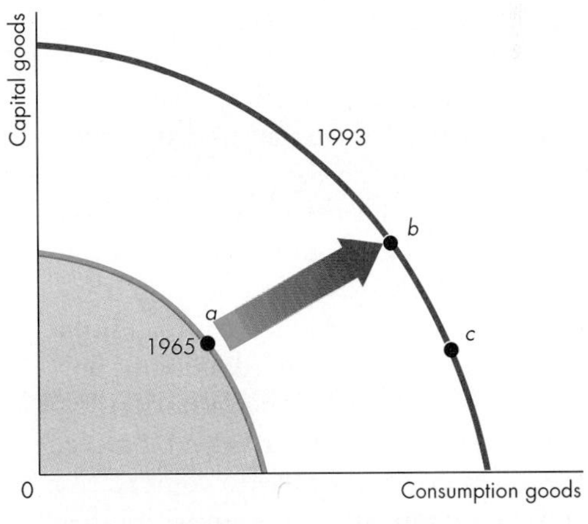

(b) Japan

In 1965, the production possibilities per capita in the United States, part (a), were much larger than those in Japan, part (b). But Japan devoted one-third of its resources to producing capital goods, while the United States devoted only one-sixth. Japan's more rapid increase in capital equipment resulted in its production possibility frontier shifting out more quickly than that in the United States. The two production possibilities per capita in 1993 are similar to each other. If Japan produces at point *b* on its 1993 frontier, it will continue to grow more quickly than the United States. If Japan increases consumption and produces at point *c* on its 1993 frontier, its growth rate will slow down to that of the United States.

R E V I E W

Economic growth results from the accumulation of capital and the development of better technologies. To reap the fruits of economic growth, we must incur the cost of fewer goods and services for current consumption. By cutting the current output of consumption goods, we can devote more resources to accumulating capital and to the research and development that lead to technological change — the engines of economic growth. Thus economic growth is not a free lunch. It has an opportunity cost — the fall in the current output of consumption goods. ■

Figure 3.5 The Gains from Specialization and Exchange

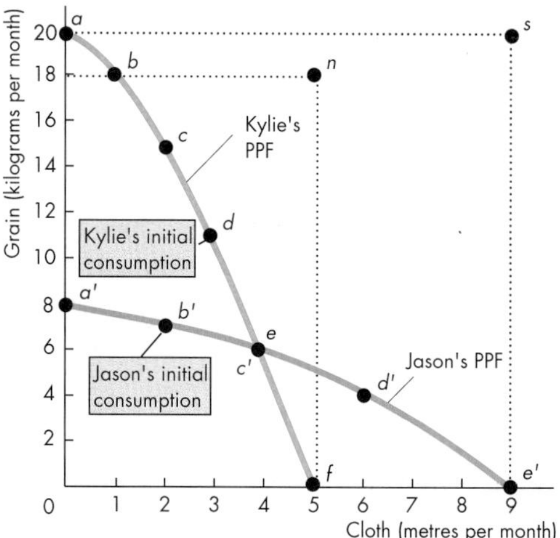

When Kylie and Jason are self-sufficient, Jason consumes 7 kilograms of grain and 2 metres of cloth (point *b′*) and Kylie consumes 11 kilograms of grain and 3 metres of cloth (point *d*). Their total production is 18 kilograms of grain and 5 metres of cloth (point *n*). Jason and Kylie can do better by specialization and exchange. Kylie, whose comparative advantage is in grain production, specializes in that activity, producing 20 kilograms a month (point *a*). Jason, whose comparative advantage is in cloth production, specializes in that activity, producing 9 metres of cloth a month (point *e′*). Total production is then 20 kilograms of grain and 9 metres of cloth (point *s*). If Kylie gives Jason 8 kilograms of grain in exchange for 5 metres of cloth, they each enjoy increased consumption of both grain and cloth. They each gain from specialization and exchange.

Gains From Trade

Can you think of someone who seems to excel at everything? Sometimes we think we know people like this! But generally when, for example, one person is more athletic than another, another may have a quicker mind or better memory. What one person does with ease, someone else finds difficult.

Comparative advantage: Kylie meets Jason

Differences in individual abilities mean that there are also differences in individual opportunity costs of producing various goods. Such differences give rise to comparative advantage — we say that a person has a **comparative advantage** in producing a particular good if that person can produce the good at a lower opportunity cost than anyone else.

People can produce for themselves all the goods that they consume or they can concentrate on producing one good (or perhaps a few goods) and then exchange some of their own products for the output of others. Concentrating on the production of only one good or a few goods is called **specialization.** We are going to discover how people can gain by specializing in that good at which they have a comparative advantage and then trading their output with others.

Let's return again to our island economy. Suppose that Kylie has discovered another island very close to her own and that, like her island, it has just one inhabitant — Jason. Kylie and Jason each have access to a simple boat that is adequate for transporting themselves and their goods between the two islands.

Jason's island, too, can produce only grain and cloth, but its terrain differs from that on Kylie's island. While Kylie's island has a lot of fertile grain-growing land and a small sheep population, Jason's island has little fertile grain-growing land and plenty of sheep. This important difference between the two islands means that Jason's production possibility frontier is different from Kylie's. Figure 3.5 illustrates these production possibility frontiers. Kylie's frontier is labelled 'Kylie's PPF' and Jason's is labelled 'Jason's PPF'.

Kylie and Jason can be self-sufficient in grain and cloth. **Self-sufficiency** is a situation in which people produce only enough for their own consumption. Suppose that Kylie and Jason are each self-sufficient. Kylie chooses to produce and consume 3 metres of cloth and 11 kilograms of grain a month, point *d.* Jason chooses to produce and consume 2 metres of cloth and 7 kilograms of grain a month, point *b′*. These choices are identified on their respective production possibility frontiers in Fig. 3.5. (Each could have chosen any other point on their own production possibility frontier.) Total production of grain and cloth is the sum of Kylie's and Jason's production: 18 kilograms of grain and 5 metres of cloth. Point *n* in the figure represents this total production.

Kylie's Comparative Advantage In which of the two goods does Kylie have a comparative advantage? We have defined comparative advantage as a situation in which one person's opportunity cost of producing a good is lower than another person's opportunity cost of producing that same good. Kylie, then, has a comparative advantage in producing whichever good she produces at a lower opportunity cost than Jason. What is that good?

You can answer the question by looking at the production possibility frontiers for Kylie and Jason in Fig. 3.5. At the points at which they are producing and consuming, Kylie's production possibility frontier is much steeper than Jason's. To produce more grain, Kylie gives up much less cloth than Jason. Hence Kylie's opportunity cost of a kilogram of grain is much lower than Jason's. This means that Kylie has a comparative advantage in producing grain.

Jason's Comparative Advantage Jason's comparative advantage is in producing cloth. His production possibility frontier at his production and consumption point is much flatter than Kylie's. This means that Jason has to give up much less grain to produce more cloth than Kylie does. Jason's opportunity cost of a metre of cloth is lower than Kylie's, so Jason has a comparative advantage in cloth production.

Achieving the Gains from Trade

Can Kylie and Jason do better than be self-sufficient? In particular, what would happen if each were to specialize in producing the good at which each has a comparative advantage and then trade with the other?

If Kylie, who has a comparative advantage in grain production, puts all her resources into growing grain, she can grow 20 kilograms (the amount labelled *a* on the vertical axis of Fig. 3.5). If Jason, who has a comparative advantage in cloth production, puts all his resources into making cloth, he can make 9 metres (the amount labelled *e′* on the horizontal axis). By specializing, Kylie and Jason together can produce 20 kilograms of grain and 9 metres of cloth (the amount labelled *s* in the figure). Point *s* shows the production of 20 kilograms of grain (all produced by Kylie) and 9 metres of cloth (all produced by Jason). Clearly, Kylie and Jason produce more cloth and grain at point *s* than they were producing at point *n*, when each took care only of his or her own requirements. Point *s* is a better point than *n* because, between them, Kylie and Jason have more of both grain and cloth than at point *n*.

To obtain the gains from trade, Kylie and Jason must do more than specialize in producing the good at which each has a comparative advantage. They must exchange the fruits of their specialized production. Suppose that Kylie and Jason agree to exchange 5 metres of cloth for 8 kilograms of grain. Kylie has 20 kilograms of grain and Jason has 9 metres of cloth before any exchange takes place. After the exchange takes place, Jason consumes 8 kilograms of grain and Kylie 12 kilograms of grain. Jason consumes 4 metres of cloth and Kylie 5 metres of cloth. Compared to the time when they were self-sufficient, Kylie now has 1 extra kilogram of grain and 2 extra metres of cloth, and Jason has 1 extra kilogram of grain and 2 extra metres of cloth. The gains from trade are represented by the increase in consumption of both goods that each obtains. They each consume at a point outside their own production possibility frontiers.

Productivity and Absolute Advantage

Productivity is defined as the amount of output produced per unit of inputs used to produce it. For example, Kylie's productivity in making cloth is measured as the amount of cloth she makes per hour of work. If one person has greater productivity than another in the production of all goods, that person is said to have an **absolute advantage**. In our example, neither Kylie nor Jason has an absolute advantage. Kylie is more productive than Jason in growing corn and Jason is more productive than Kylie in making cloth.

It is often suggested that people and countries that have an absolute advantage can outcompete others in the production of all goods. For example, it is often suggested that Australia cannot compete with Japan because the Japanese are more productive than we are. This conclusion is wrong, as you are just about to discover. To see why, let's look again at Kylie and Jason.

Suppose that a volcano engulfs Kylie's island, forcing her to search for a new one. And suppose further that disaster leads to fortune. Kylie stumbles on a new island that is much more productive than the original one, enabling her to produce twice as much of either corn or cloth with each hour of her labour. Kylie's new production possibilities appear in Table 3.2. Notice that she now has an absolute advantage.

We have already worked out that the gains from trade arise when each person specializes in producing that good with the lower opportunity cost. Jason's opportunity costs remain exactly the same as they were before. What has happened to Kylie's opportunity costs now that she has become twice as productive?

You can work out Kylie's opportunity costs by using exactly the same calculation that was used in the table of Fig. 3.2. Start by looking at Kylie's opportunity cost of grain. The first 12 kilograms of grain that Kylie grows cost her 2 metres of cloth. So the opportunity cost of 1 kilogram of grain is $^1/_6$ of a metre of cloth — the same as Kylie's original opportunity cost of grain. If you calculate the opportunity costs for Kylie's production possibilities *a* through *f*, you will discover that each of them has remained the same.

Since the opportunity cost of cloth is the inverse of the opportunity cost of grain, Kylie's opportunity costs of cloth also have remained unchanged. Let's work through one example. If Kylie moves from *a* to *b* to make 2 metres of cloth, she will have to reduce her grain production by 4 kilograms — from 40 to 36 kilograms. Thus the first 2 metres of cloth cost 4 kilograms of grain. The cost of 1 metre of cloth is, therefore, 2 kilograms of grain — again exactly the same as before.

When Kylie becomes twice as productive as before, each hour of her time produces more output, but her opportunity costs remain the same. One more unit of grain costs the same in terms of cloth forgone as it did previously. Since Kylie's opportunity costs have not changed and since Jason's have not changed, Jason continues to have a comparative advantage in producing cloth. Both Kylie and Jason can have more of both goods if Kylie specializes in grain production and Jason in cloth production.

The key point to recognize is that it is *not* possible for a person having an absolute advantage to have a comparative advantage in everything.

Table 3.2 New Production Possibilities

Possibility	Grain (kilograms per month)		Cloth (metres per month)
a	40	and	0
b	36	and	2
c	30	and	4
d	22	and	6
e	12	and	8
f	0	and	10

R E V I E W

Gains from trade come from comparative advantage. Unless two individuals have the same opportunity costs, each has a comparative advantage in some activity. Differences in opportunity costs provide the basis for comparative advantage and the gains from specialization and exchange. Even a person with an absolute advantage gains from specialization and exchange. ■

Exchange In The Real World

In the real world, where there are billions of people specializing in millions of different activities, gains from specialization and trade exist, but they are harder to exploit. Trade has to be organized. To organize trade, rules of conduct and mechanisms for enforcing those rules have evolved. One such mechanism is private property rights. Another is money. In the island economy of Kylie and Jason, direct exchange of one good with another is feasible. Direct exchange was observed in ancient societies, like that of the Aboriginal people, and in the arena of international trade it occasionally occurs today under the name of 'countertrade'. (See the Reading Between the Lines pp. 58–59). In most circumstances in the modern economy, however, direct exchange of one good for another is very cumbersome. To lubricate the wheels of exchange, societies have created money — a medium that enables indirect exchange of goods for money and money for goods. Let's examine these aspects of exchange arrangements in more detail.

Property Rights

Property rights are social arrangements that govern the ownership, use and disposal of property. **Property** is anything of value that is owned: it includes land and buildings — the things we call property in ordinary speech — and it also includes stocks and bonds, durable goods, plant and equipment. Finally, it includes **intellectual property** — the intangible product of creative effort. This type of property is protected by copyrights and patents on books, music, computer programs and inventions of all kinds.

What if property rights did not exist? What would such a world be like?

A World Without Property Rights Without property rights, people could take possession of whatever they had the strength to obtain for themselves. In such a world, people would have to devote a good deal of their time, energy and resources to protecting what they had produced or acquired.

In a world without property rights, it would be impossible to reap any gains from specialization and exchange. People would have no incentive to specialize in producing those goods at which they each had a comparative advantage. In fact, the more of a particular good someone produced, the bigger the chance that others would simply help themselves to it. Also, if a person could take the goods of others without giving up something in exchange, then there would be no point in specializing in producing something for exchange. In a world without property rights, no one would enjoy the gains from specialization and exchange, and everyone would specialize only in unproductive acts of piracy.

It is to overcome the problems that we have just described that property rights have evolved. Let's examine these property rights as they operate to govern economic life in Australia today.

Property Rights in Private Enterprise Capitalism
The Australian economy operates for the most part on the principles of private enterprise capitalism. **Private enterprise** is an economic system that permits individuals to decide on their own economic activities. **Capitalism** is an economic system that permits private individuals to own the capital resources used in production.

Under the property rights in such an economic system, individuals own what they have made, acquired in a voluntary exchange with others or been given. Any attempt to remove the property of someone against that person's will is considered theft, a crime punished by a sufficiently severe penalty to deter most people from becoming thieves.

It is easy to see that property rights based on these ideas can generate gainful trade: people can specialize in producing those goods that, for them, have the least opportunity cost. Some people will specialize in enforcing and maintaining property rights (for example, politicians, judges and police officers) and all individuals will have the incentive to trade with each other, offering the good in which they have a comparative advantage in exchange for the goods produced by others.

Although the Australian economic system is based on a system of private property with voluntary exchange, property rights even in this country have limits. Let's look at some of these.

Taxes Limit Private Property Rights The most important and pervasive limit on people's rights to private property comes from taxes. All of us have to pay taxes to Federal, State and local governments. Many people regard the taxes that they pay as a fair price for the services provided by government. Many others, however, regard the taxes that they pay as exorbitant. Taxing part of the property that people have created limits people's efforts to create more property and reduces their gain from specialized production.

Even though taxes constitute an intrusion into private property rights, the taxes themselves are not arbitrary. Everyone faces the same rules and can calculate the effects of their own actions on the taxes for which they will be liable.

Regulation Limits Private Property Rights
Other restrictions on private property rights prohibit certain kinds of voluntary exchange. For example, pharmaceutical manufacturers cannot place a product on the market without first obtaining approval from a government agency. The government controls or prohibits the sale of many types of drugs, and also restricts trading in human beings and their component parts — that is, it prohibits the selling of slaves, children and human organs.

These restrictions on the extent of private property and on the legitimacy of voluntary exchange, though important, do not, for the most part, seriously impede specialization and gainful trade. Most people take the view that the benefits of regulation — for example, prohibiting the sale of dangerous drugs — far outweigh the costs imposed on the sellers.

Let's now turn to the other social institution that permits specialization and exchange — the development of an efficient means of exchange.

Money

We have seen that well-defined property rights based on voluntary exchange allow individuals to specialize and exchange their output with each other. In our island economy, we studied only two people and two

Overcoming Obstacles to the Gains from Trade

Soviet Trading via Barter

Hugh Haslehurst-Smith of the giant Angliss food group wants to swap cans of Australian mutton for tins of salmon and crab.

Goodman Fielder Wattic hopes to sell Australian fats and oils but may have to take payment in the form of Siberian marble.

Such are the trials and tribulations of trying to do trade with the Soviet Union, especially at the time when hard-currency cash is scarce.

Direct barter trade, when no cash changes hands, already accounts for 5–10 per cent of Australia's $1 billion flow of exports to the USSR each year.

But an increasing amount of business between the two nations is now being channelled into so-called reciprocal deals — agreements which tie the Australian exporter to buying a set amount of Soviet goods.

Both Elders and Dalgety Farmers, which sell a large part of Australia's $767 million of wool exports to the Soviet Union, are old hands at reciprocal trading.

Ian McIvor, the general manager of Dalgety's international trading division, said in Vladivostok that increasing pressure was being exerted by Soviet authorities for reciprocal deals rather than cash wool sales.

Mr McIvor said Dalgety was now buying electrical motors from the USSR under such an arrangement.

The usual terms stipulate that Dalgety promises to buy motors to a certain value, in return for the Soviets purchasing five times that amount of wool.

Mr McIvor believes that more of Dalgety's trade with the USSR will be done this way this year.

'It is especially true of the Soviet Far East too, where cash is particularly short and where many organisations do not have the authority from Moscow to deal in hard cash', he said.

'But the difficulty is finding something that you know how to place in Australia and you've got to buy a hell of a lot of garden forks and cheap chairs to equate to a load of cattle or wool'.

In an effort to show Australian companies represented at the Vladivostok trade fair what products the USSR has to offer, a Soviet display has also been set up.

The potential exports range from computers and fur coats to marble, honey, china and dried deer penises.

Keen interest has already been shown by several Australian traders, including CRA, in the region's marble, which is considerably cheaper than comparable Italian exports.

Elders has already established that its main interest for reciprocal trade is in whitegoods, although some deals in scrap steel have also been negotiated.

For the Angliss group, trade with the USSR is less of a problem.

Mr Haslehurst-Smith is confident of being able to place almost any food commodity swapped for Australian meat products through its world-wide organisation.

Soon he hopes to sell $5–12 million of canned beef and mutton to the Soviet Far East region, products which have been specially formulated to suit Russian tastes.

In return, he is willing to accept canned salmon and crabmeat or frozen scallops.

'It is really important to make the effort in some form of two-way trade here', Mr Haslehurst-Smith said.

'It helps to cement the relationship. Otherwise, if it is just a one-way street all the time and your survival rate will be very short-term'.

Financial Review
Monday 9 July 1990
By Sue Neales in Vladivostok

The Essence of the Story

- Trade with the former Soviet Union, now the Commonwealth of Independent States (CIS) takes two forms:
    - Direct sales — Australian exports are sold to CIS traders in return for currency
    - Direct barter trade (sometimes called countertrade) — Australian exports are directly exchanged for CIS goods and no cash changes hands.
- In 1991 direct barter trade accounted for 5–10 per cent of the $1 billion flow of exports to the former Soviet Union. The amount of direct barter trade is expected to grow in the 1990s.
- Some companies have difficulty finding commodities they are willing to accept in return for exports to the CIS. Other companies with world-wide trading networks have fewer problems.

Background and Analysis

- The Commonwealth of Independent States is a centrally planned economy undergoing tremendous change.
- Most member countries of the CIS are currently working towards adopting a market based system.
- The predominant currency in the CIS, the rouble, is not convertible into other currencies and has little value on world markets, so cannot be used to buy imports.
- The country's foreign exchange resources are limited and central government approval is required for their use.
- The CIS, like other countries or unions, wants to specialize in the production of goods in which it has a comparative advantage. If trade were restricted to cash transactions, there would be few opportunities for the CIS, and its trading partners, to benefit from their comparative advantages and potential gains from trade would be lost.
- This difficulty is overcome by resorting to direct barter trade. But barter arises requires a 'double coincidence of wants'.
- To achieve this, the CIS authorities promote trade exhibits that advertise the range of products available.
- Companies with large trading networks are best placed to take advantage of direct barter in CIS products.

Conclusions

- When the potential gains from trade are lost because of the current institutional arrangements, new arrangements emerge to everyone's benefit.

goods. Exchange in such a situation was a simple matter. In the real world, however, how can billions of people exchange the millions of goods that are the fruits of their specialized labour?

Barter Goods can be simply exchanged for goods. This system is known as **barter.** However, exchanging goods only through the barter system severely limits the amount of trading that can take place. Imagine that you have chooks, but you want to get roses. First you must look for someone with roses who wants chooks. Economists call this **a double coincidence of wants** — when person A wants to sell exactly what person B wants to buy, and person B wants to sell exactly what person A wants to buy. As the term implies, such occurrences are coincidences and will not arise frequently. A second way of trading by barter is to undertake a sequence of exchanges. If you have oranges and you want apples, you may have to trade oranges for plums, plums for peaches, peaches for pineapples and then eventually pineapples for apples.

Trade in Aboriginal Australia was organized through the direct exchange of goods — barter. Aboriginal people bargained and haggled with each other over the value of the goods involved. The trading system was complex and the continent was crisscrossed by trade routes (see Fig. 3.6). Trade also occurred with the outside world.

Cumbersome though it is, quite a large amount of barter trade still takes place. For example, when British rock star Rod Stewart played in Budapest, Hungary, in August 1986, he received part of his compensation in Hungarian sound equipment, electrical cable and the use of a forklift truck. A significant part, up to 10 per cent, of Australia's exports to the Soviet Union are bartered for Soviet goods. For example, we receive electrical motors in return for raw wool, or tins of salmon in return for cans of mutton. This is called countertrade.

Although barter exchange does occur, it is an inefficient means of exchanging goods. Fortunately, a better alternative has been invented.

Figure 3.6 Aboriginal Trade Routes

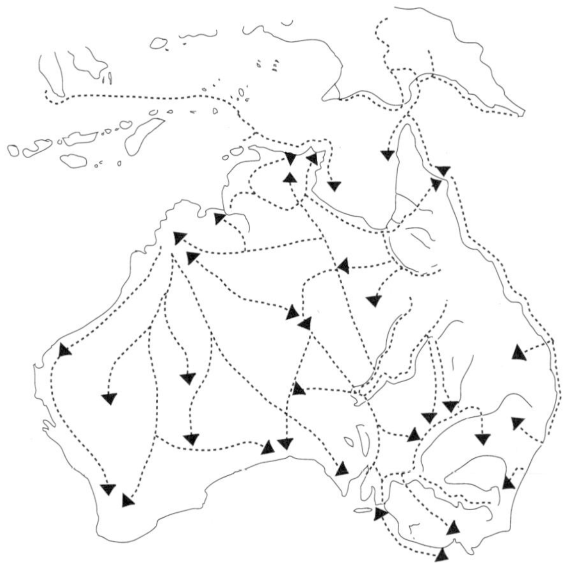

'From the Kimberey coast come pearlshells of various kinds, plain and incised, also bamboo necklaces, and certain types of boomerang. They are passed along, on one track, through the eastern Kimberleys: and back from the east come shovel-bladed spears with bamboo shafts, hooked spears, a variety of boomerang, wooden coolamon dishes, dilly bags and red ochre. The Lungga say they cannot make boomerangs properly: they prefer to import them from the east, west or south-west. The Walmadjeri trade their shields to the east, and Central Australian shields find they way into the Balgo camp near the head of the Canning Stock Route, just as do the typical Western Desert spearthrowers — into an area where the local throwers are quite differently designed. Kimberley pearlshells travelled right across Australia: one road down to Eyre's Peninsula in South Australia, through the Great Victoria Desert and Ooldea: another also to the Great Victoria Desert and Eucla, but via the Gascoyne and the Murchison'.[1]

Monetary exchange An alternative to barter is **monetary exchange** — a system in which some commodity or token serves as the **medium of exchange.** A medium of exchange is anything that is generally acceptable in exchange for goods and services. **Money** can also be defined as a medium of exchange — something that can be passed on to others in exchange for goods and services. In a monetary exchange system, people exchange money for goods and goods for money, but they do not directly exchange goods for goods.

Metals such as gold, silver and copper have long served as money. Most commonly, they serve as money by being stamped as coins. Primitive societies have traditionally used various commodities, such as sea shells, as money. During the US Civil War and for several years after, people used postage stamps as money. Prisoners of war in German camps in World War II used cigarettes as money. Even in the 1980s in Bucharest, the capital of Romania, people used ciga-

[1] R.M. and C.H. Berndt, *The World of the First Australians* (Sydney: Ure Smith, 1977).

rettes as money. Using cigarettes as a medium of exchange should not be confused with barter. Under the circumstances described, cigarettes play the role of money, and people buy and sell goods by using cigarettes as a medium of exchange.

In modern societies, governments provide paper money. The banking system also provides money in the form of cheque accounts. Cheque accounts can be used for settling debts simply by writing an instruction — writing a cheque — to the bank requesting that funds be transferred to another checking account. Electronic links between bank accounts, now becoming more widespread, enable direct transfers between different accounts without any cheques being written.

■ You have now begun to see how economists go about the job of trying to answer some important questions. The simple fact of scarcity and the associated concept of opportunity cost allow us to understand why people specialize, why they trade with each other, why they have social conventions that define and enforce private property rights, and why they use money. One simple idea — scarcity and its direct implication, opportunity cost — explains so much!

SUMMARY

The Production Possibility Frontier

The production possibility frontier is the boundary between what is attainable and what is not attainable. Production can take place at any point inside or on the production possibility frontier. But it is not possible to produce outside the frontier. There is always a point on the production possibility frontier that is better than a point inside it. (pp. 46–48)

Opportunity Cost

The opportunity cost of any action is the best alternative action forgone. The opportunity cost of acquiring one good is equivalent to the amount of another good that must be given up. The opportunity cost of a good increases as the quantity of it produced increases. (pp. 48–51)

Changing Production Possibilities

Although the production possibility frontier marks the boundary between the attainable and the unattainable, that boundary does not remain fixed. It changes, partly because of natural forces (changes in climate and the accumulation of ideas about better ways of producing) and partly by the choices that we make. If we use some of today's resources to produce capital goods and for research and development we will be able to produce more goods and services in the future. The economy will grow. But growth cannot take place without incurring costs. The opportunity cost of more goods and services in the future is consuming fewer goods and services today. (pp. 51–54)

Gains from Trade

A person has a comparative advantage in producing a good if that person can produce at a lower opportunity cost than anyone else. People can gain from trade if each specializes in the activity at which they have a comparative advantage. Each person produces the good for which their opportunity cost is lower than everyone else's. They then exchange part of their output with each other. By this activity, each person is able to consume at a point outside his or her individual production possibility frontier.

When a person is more productive than another person — he or she is able to produce more output from fewer inputs — that person has an absolute advantage. But having an absolute advantage does not mean there are no gains from trade. Even if someone is more productive than other people in all activities, so long as the other person has a lower opportunity cost of some good, then gains from specialization and exchange are available. (pp. 54–56)

Exchange in the Real World

Exchange in the real world involves the specialization of billions of people in millions of different activities. To make it worthwhile for each individual to specialize and to enable societies to reap the gains from trade, institutions and mechanism have evolved. The most important of these are private property rights, with a political and legal system to enforce them, and a system of monetary exchange. These institutions enable people to specialize, exchanging their labour for money and their money for goods, thereby reaping the gains from trade. (pp. 56–61)

KEY TERMS

Absolute advantage, p. 55
Barter, p. 60
Capital accumulation, p. 51
Capital goods, p. 46
Capitalism, p. 57
Comparative advantage, p. 54
Consumption, p. 46
Consumption goods, p. 46
Double coincidence of wants, p. 60
Economic growth, p. 51
Goods and services, p. 46
Human capital, p. 46
Intellectual property, p. 57
Medium of exchange, p. 60
Monetary exchange, p. 60
Money, p. 60
Private enterprise, p. 57
Production, p. 46
Production possibility frontier, p. 46
Productivity, p. 55
Property, p. 56
Property rights, p. 56
Self-sufficiency, p. 54
Specialization, p. 54
Technological progress, p. 51

PROBLEMS

1 Suppose that there is a change in the weather conditions on Kylie's island that makes the grain yields much higher. This enables Kylie to produce the following amounts of grain:

Hours worked per day	Grain (kilograms per month)
0	0
2	60
4	100
6	120
8	130
10	140

Her cloth production possibilities are the same as those that appeared in Table 3.1.

a) What are five points on Kylie's new production possibility frontier?
b) What are Kylie's opportunity costs of grain and cloth?
c) Comparing Kylie's opportunity cost of grain with that in the table in Fig. 3.2, has her opportunity cost of grain gone up, down or remained the same? Explain why.

2 Suppose that Jason has the following production possibilities:

Grain (kilograms per month)		Cloth (metres per month)
6	and	0.0
5	and	0.5
4	and	1.0
3	and	1.5
2	and	2.0
1	and	2.5
0	and	3.0

Kylie has the following production possibilities:

Grain (kilograms per month)		Cloth (metres per month)
3.0	and	0
2.5	and	1
2.0	and	2
1.5	and	3
1.0	and	4
0.5	and	5
0	and	6

Find the maximum quantity of grain and cloth that they can produce if each specializes in the activity at which he or she has the lower opportunity cost.

3 Suppose that Kylie has become twice as productive as in the previous problem and that she can now produce the following quantities:

Grain (kilograms per month)		Cloth (metres per month)
6	and	0
5	and	2
4	and	4
3	and	6
2	and	8
1	and	10
0	and	12

a) Show the effect of Kylie's increased productivity on her production possibility frontier.
b) Will it still pay Kylie to specialize and trade with Jason now that she is twice as productive?
c) Will it still pay Jason to trade with Kylie?

4 Consider a typically shaped production possibilities frontier — that is, it is downward sloping and bowed outwards, as in Fig. 3.1 — for an economy producing just two classes of goods — agricultural goods and manufactured goods. What are the effects on the frontier of the following changes:
   a) A prolonged drought
   b) A revolution in the science of robotics which makes all capital in manufacturing more productive
   c) Large scale immigration
   d) A war which leaves many people dead and much capital destroyed.

5 Society is often faced with the choice between 'guns' and 'butter'. That is, resources devoted to military uses are not equally useful for producing other goods.
   a) Depict this problem in a diagram.
   b) What is the opportunity cost for more weapons systems?

   Suppose that, through the political process, an allocation of resources between producing guns and butter has been arrived at. Suppose that the allocation of labour, capital and land is such that the choice leaves society on the production possibility frontier. Given its allocation, the military must decide how to allocate its fixed military budget between upgrading old weapons systems and developing new ones.
   c) Depict the choices facing military leaders.

   Now suppose that society decides to devote fewer resources to military uses, releasing those resources to produce more other goods — fewer guns, more butter.
   d) Show society's new choice in the diagram of part (a).
   e) What does this new allocation of resources mean for choices facing military leaders?

6 Economists often claim that 'There is no such thing as a free lunch'. What do they mean? Is it possible that, under some circumstances, there could be free lunches? Show diagrammatically.

Chapter 4

Demand and Supply

After studying this chapter, you will be able to:

- Explain how prices are determined.
- Explain why some prices rise, some fall and some fluctuate.
- Explain how quantities bought and sold are determined.
- Construct a demand schedule and a demand curve.
- Construct a supply schedule and a supply curve.
- Make predictions about price changes using the demand and supply model.

Slide, Rocket and Rollercoaster

Are these names of amusement park rides? No. They are commonly used descriptions of the behaviour of prices. There are lots of examples of price slides. One particular example is probably very familiar to you. In 1979, Sony began to market a pocket-sized cassette player that delivered its sound through tiny earphones. They named their new product the 'Walkman' and they gave it a price tag of around $300— more than $500 in today's money. Today Sony has been joined by many other producers of Walkman clones and you can buy a Walkman (or its equivalent), that's even better than the 1979 prototype, for less than one-tenth of the original price. During the time that the 'Walkman' has been with us, the quantity bought has increased steadily each year. Why has there been a long and steady slide in the price of the Walkman? Why hasn't the increase in the quantity bought kept its price high? Rocketing prices are also a familiar phenomenon. A well-publicized recent example is that of prices paid for houses in central locations in Sydney and other large cities. Huge increases in house prices have not deterred people from living in the centres of cities — on the contrary, their numbers have increased slightly in recent years. Why do people continue to seek housing in city centres when prices have rocketed so sharply? There are lots of price roller-coasters — cases in which prices rise and fall from season to season or year to year. Prices of coffee, strawberries and many other agricultural commodities fit this pattern. Why does the price of coffee rollercoaster even when people's taste for coffee hardly changes at all? Though amusement park rides provide a vivid description of the behaviour of prices, many of the things that we buy have remarkably steady prices. The audiocassette tapes that we play in a Walkman are an example. The price of a tape has barely changed over the past ten years. Nevertheless, the number of tapes bought has risen steadily year after year. Why do firms sell more and more tapes, even though they're not able to get higher prices for them and why do people willingly buy more tapes even though their price is no lower than it was a decade ago?

We will discover the answers to these and similar questions by studying demand and supply. We are first going to discover what determines the demand for different goods and the supply of them. Then we are going to discover how demand and supply together determine price. This powerful theory enables us to analyse many important economic events that affect our lives and even to make predictions about future prices.

Demand

The **quantity demanded** of a good or service is the amount that consumers plan to buy in a given period of time. Demands are different from wants. **Wants** are the unlimited desires or wishes that people have for goods and services. How many times have you thought that you would like something 'if only you could afford it' or 'if it weren't so expensive'? Scarcity guarantees that many — perhaps most — of our wants will never be satisfied. Demand reflects a decision about which wants to satisfy. If you demand something, then you've made a plan to buy it.

The quantity demanded is not necessarily the same amount as the quantity actually bought. The quantity that people actually buy and sell is called the **quantity traded**. Sometimes the quantity demanded is greater than the amount of goods available, so the quantity traded is less than the quantity demanded.

The quantity demanded is measured as an amount per unit of time. For example, suppose a person consumes one cup of coffee a day. The quantity of coffee demanded by that person can be expressed as one cup per day or seven cups per week or 365 cups per year. Without a time dimension, we cannot tell whether a particular quantity demanded is large or small.

What Determines the Quantity Demanded?

The amount that consumers plan to buy of any particular good or service depends on many factors. Among the more important ones are:

- The price of the good
- The prices of other goods
- Income
- Population
- Tastes

The theory of demand and supply makes predictions about the prices at which goods are traded and the quantities bought and sold. Our first focus, therefore, is on the relationship between the quantity demanded and the price of a good. To study this relationship, we hold constant all other influences on consumers' planned purchases. We can then ask: how does the quantity demanded of the good vary as its price varies?

The Law of Demand

The law of demand states:

Other things being equal, the higher the price of a good, the lower is the quantity demanded.

Why does a higher price reduce the quantity demanded? The answer is that each good, although unique, can usually be replaced by some other good. As the price of a good climbs higher, people buy less of that good and more of some substitute that serves almost as well.

Let's consider an example — blank audiocassette tapes, which we'll refer to as 'tapes'. Many different goods provide a similar service to a tape; for example, records, compact discs, prerecorded tapes, radio and television broadcasts, and live concerts. Tapes sell for about $3 each. If the price of a tape doubles to $6 while the prices of all the other goods remain constant, the quantity of tapes demanded will fall dramatically. People will buy more records and prerecorded tapes and fewer blank tapes. If the price of a tape falls to $1 while the prices of all the other goods stay constant, the quantity of tapes demanded will rise and the demand for records, albums and prerecorded tapes will fall dramatically.

Demand Schedule and Demand Curve

A **demand schedule** lists the quantities demanded at each different price, when all the other influences on consumers' planned purchases — such as the prices of other goods, income, population and tastes — are held constant.

The table in Fig. 4.1 sets out a demand schedule for tapes. For example, if the price of a tape is $1, the quantity demanded is 9 million tapes a week. If the price of a tape is $5, the quantity demanded is 2 million tapes a week. The other rows of the table show us the quantities demanded at prices between $2 and $4.

A demand schedule can be illustrated by drawing a demand curve. A **demand curve** graphs the relationship between the quantity demanded of a good and its price, holding constant all other influences on consumers' planned purchases. The graph in Fig. 4.1 illustrates the demand curve for tapes. By convention, the quantity demanded is always measured on the horizontal axis and the price is measured on the vertical axis. The points on the demand curve labelled *a* through *e* represent the rows of the demand schedule. For example, point *a* on the graph represents a quantity demanded of 9 million tapes a week at a price of $1 a tape.

The term **demand** refers to the entire relationship between the quantity demanded and the price of a good. The demand for tapes is described by both the demand schedule and the demand curve in Fig. 4.1.

Willingness to Pay

There is another way of looking at the demand curve: it shows the highest price that people are willing to pay for the last unit bought. If a large quantity is available, that price is low; but if only a small quantity is available, that price is high. For example, if 9 million tapes are available each week, the highest price that consumers are willing to pay for the 9 millionth tape is $1. But if only 2 million tapes are available each week, consumers are willing to pay $5 for the last tape available.

This view of the demand curve may become clearer if you think about your own demand for tapes. If you were given a list of possible prices of tapes, you could write down alongside each price your planned weekly purchase of tapes. On the other hand, if you were told that there is just one tape available each week, you could say how much you'd be willing to pay for it. If you were then told that there is one more tape available, you could say the maximum price that you will be willing to pay for that second tape. This process could continue, increasing the number of tapes by one, with you saying the maximum price that you're prepared to pay for each extra tape. The schedule of prices and quantities that you had arrived at would be your demand schedule.

Figure 4.1 The Demand Schedule and the Demand Curve

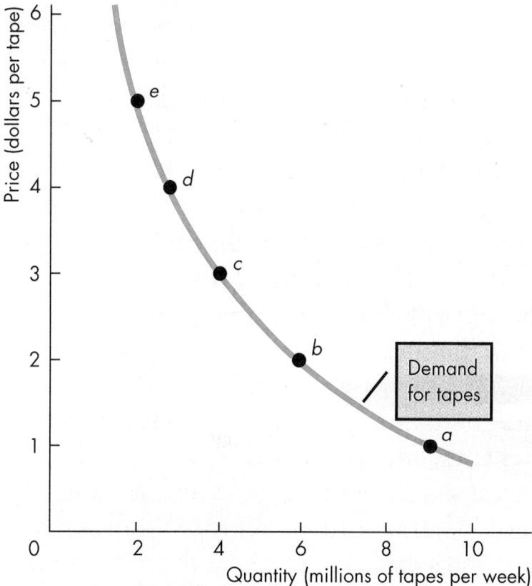

	Price (dollars per tape)	Quantity (millions of tapes per week)
a	1	9
b	2	6
c	3	4
d	4	3
e	5	2

The table shows a demand schedule listing the quantity of tapes demanded at each price if all other influences on buyers' plans are held constant. At a price of $1 a tape, 9 million tapes a week are demanded; at a price of $3 a tape, 4 million tapes a week are demanded. The demand curve shows the relationship between quantity demanded and price, holding everything else constant. The demand curve slopes downward: as price decreases, the quantity demanded increases. The demand curve can be read two ways. For a given price it tells us the quantity that people plan to buy. For example, at a price of $3 a tape, the quantity demanded is 4 million tapes a week. For a given quantity, the demand curve tells us the maximum price that consumers are willing to pay for the last tape bought. For example, the maximum price that consumers will pay for the 6 millionth tape is $2.

A Change in Demand

To construct a demand schedule and demand curve, we hold constant all the other influences on consumers' buying plans. But what are the effects of each of those other influences?

1. Prices of Other Goods. The quantity of tapes that consumers plan to buy does not depend only on the price of tapes. It also depends in part on the prices of other relevant goods. These other goods fall into two categories: substitutes and complements.

A **substitute** is a good that can be used in place of another good. For example, a bus ride substitutes for a train ride; a hamburger substitutes for a meat pie; a pear substitutes for an apple. As we have seen, tapes have many substitutes — records, prerecorded tapes, CDs, radio and television broadcasts, and live concerts. If the price of one of these substitutes increases, people economize on its use and buy more tapes. For example, if the price of records doubles, fewer records are bought and the demand for tapes increases — there is much more taping of other people's records. Conversely, if the price of one of these substitutes decreases, people use the now cheaper good in larger quantities, and they buy fewer tapes. For example, if the price of prerecorded tapes decreases, people play more of these tapes and make fewer of their own tapes — the demand for blank tapes falls.

The effects of a change in the price of a substitute occur no matter what the price of a tape. Whether tapes have a high or a low price, a change in the price of a substitute encourages people to make the substitutions that we've just reviewed. As a consequence, a change in the price of a substitute changes the entire demand schedule for tapes and shifts the demand curve.

A **complement** is a good used in conjunction with another good. Some examples of complements are meat pies and chips, party snacks and drinks, spaghetti and meat sauce, running shoes and jogging pants. Tapes also have their complements: Walkmans, tape recorders and stereo tape decks. If the price of one of these complements increases, people buy fewer tapes. For example, if the price of a Walkman doubles, fewer Walkmans are bought and, as a consequence, fewer people are interested in buying tapes — the demand for tapes decreases. Conversely, if the price of one of these complements decreases, people buy more tapes. For example, if the price of the Walkman halves, more Walkmans are bought and a larger number of people buy tapes — the demand for tapes increases.

2. Income. Another influence on demand is consumer income. When income increases, consumers demand more of most goods. When income decreases, consumers demand less of most goods. Higher average income means consumers demand more of most goods. Lower average income means consumers demand less of most goods.

Although an increase in income leads to an increase in the demand for most goods, it does not lead to an increase in the demand for all goods. Goods for which demand increases as income increases are called **normal goods**. Examples of normal goods are restaurant meals, clothing, art and entertainment. Goods that decrease in demand when income increases are called **inferior goods**. Examples of inferior goods are rice and potatoes. These two goods are a major part of the diet of people with very low incomes. As incomes increase, the demand for these goods declines as more expensive meat and dairy products are substituted for them.

3. Population. Demand also depends on the size of the population. The larger the population, the greater is the demand for all goods and services. The smaller the population, the less is the demand for all goods and services.

4. Tastes. Finally, demand depends on tastes. **Tastes** are an individual's attitudes or preferences toward goods and services. For example, a rock music fanatic has a much greater taste for tapes than does a tone-deaf workaholic. As a consequence, even if they have the same incomes, their demands for tapes will be very different. There is, however, a fundamental difference between tastes and all the other influences on demand. Tastes cannot be directly observed. We can observe the price of a good and of its substitutes and complements. We can observe income and population size. But we cannot observe people's tastes. Economists assume, as a first approximation, that tastes do not change or that they change only slowly, and that they are independent of all the other influences on demand. As we will see later, some firms use a lot of resources to advertise in an effort to shift people's tastes. Sometimes this is effective (see the Reading Between the Lines pp. 82–83), but for now we will assume that tastes do not change much.

A summary of influences on demand and the direction of those influences is presented in Table 4.1.

Movement Along Versus a Shift in the Demand Curve

Changes in the influences on buyers' plans cause either a movement along the demand curve or a shift in the curve. Let's discuss each case in turn.

Movement Along the Demand Curve If the price of a good changes but everything else remains the same, then we say that the quantity demanded of that good has changed. We illustrate the effect as a movement along the demand curve. For example, if the price of a tape changes from \$3 to \$5, the result is a movement along the demand curve, from point *c* to point *e* in Fig. 4.1.

A Shift in the Demand Curve If the price of a good remains constant but another influence on buyers' plans changes, we say that there is a change in demand for that good. We illustrate the change in demand as a shift in the demand curve. For example, a dramatic fall in the price of the Walkman — a complement of tapes — increases the demand for tapes. We illustrate this increase in demand for tapes with a new demand schedule and a new demand

Table 4.1 The Demand for Tapes

The law of demand	
The quantity of tapes demanded	
Falls if:	*Rises if:*
• The price of a tape rises	• The price of a tape falls
Changes in demand	
The demand for tapes	
Falls if:	*Rises if:*
• The price of a substitute falls	• The price of a substitute rises
• The price of a complement rises	• The price of a complement falls
• Income falls	• Income rises
• The population decreases	• The population increases

curve. Consumers demand a larger quantity of tapes at each and every price.

The table in Fig. 4.2 provides some hypothetical numbers that illustrate such a shift. The table sets out the original demand schedule and the new demand schedule resulting from a fall in the price of a Walkman. These numbers record the change in demand. The graph in Fig. 4.2 illustrates the corresponding shift in the demand curve. When the price of the Walkman falls, the demand curve for tapes shifts to the right.

A Change in Demand Versus a Change in Quantity Demanded The quantity demanded at a given price is shown by a point on a demand curve. The entire demand curve shows demand. It follows, then, that a **change in demand** is a shift in the entire demand curve. It also follows that a movement along a demand curve is a **change in the quantity demanded.** Figure 4.3 illustrates these distinctions. If the price of a good falls but nothing else changes, then there is an increase in the quantity demanded of that good (a movement down the demand curve D_0). If the price rises, but nothing else changes, then there is a decrease in the quantity demanded (a movement up the demand curve D_0). When any other influence on buyers' planned purchases changes, the demand curve shifts and there is a *change* (an increase or a decrease) *in demand.* A rise in income (for a normal good), in population or in the price of a substitute, or a fall in the price of a complement shifts the demand curve to the right (from D_0 to demand curve D_2). This represents an *increase in demand.* A fall in income (for a normal good), in population or in the price of a substitute, or a rise in the price of a complement shifts the demand curve to the left (from D_0 to demand curve D_1). This represents a *decrease in demand.*

R E V I E W

The quantity demanded is the amount of a good that consumers plan to buy in a given period of time at a particular price. Other things being equal, the quantity demanded of a good increases if its price falls. Demand can be represented by a schedule or curve that sets out the quantity demanded at each price. Demand describes the quantity that consumers plan to buy at each possible price, or the highest price that consumers are willing to pay for the last unit bought. Demand increases if the price of a substitute rises, if the price of a complement falls or if the population increases; demand decreases if the price of a substitute falls, if the price of a complement rises or if the population decreases.

The effect of a change in income depends on whether the good is normal or inferior. For a normal good, demand increases if income rises; and demand decreases if income falls. For an inferior good, demand decreases if income rises; and demand increases if income falls.

If the price of a good changes but all other influences on buyers' plans are held constant, there is a change in the quantity demanded and a movement along the demand curve. All other influences on consumers' planned purchases shift the demand curve. ■

Supply

The **quantity supplied** of a good is the amount that producers plan to sell in a given period of time at a particular price. The quantity supplied is not the amount firms would like to sell but the amount they definitely plan to sell. However, the quantity supplied is not necessarily the same amount as the quantity actually sold or traded. If consumers do not want to buy the quantity that firms plan to sell, then firms' sales plans will be frustrated. Like quantity demanded, the quantity supplied is expressed as an amount per unit of time.

Figure 4.2 A Change in the Demand Schedule and Shift in the Demand Curve

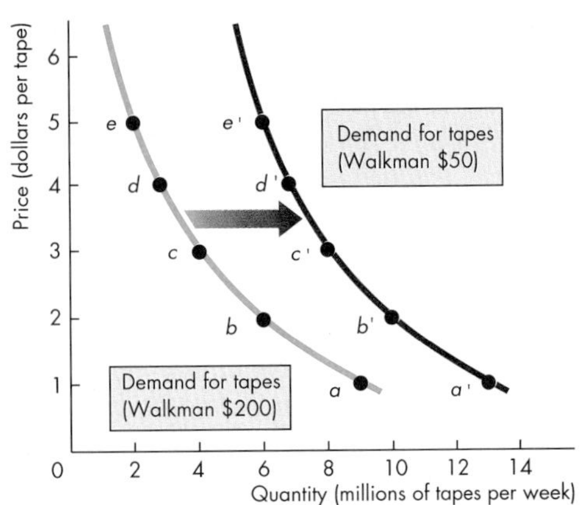

A change in any influence on buyers other than the price of the good itself results in a new demand schedule and a shift in the demand curve. Here a fall in the price of a Walkman — a complement of tapes — increases the demand for tapes. At a price of $3 a tape (row c of table), 4 million tapes a week are demanded when the Walkman costs $200 and 8 million tapes a week are demanded when the Walkman costs only $50. The demand curve shifts to the right, as shown by the shift arrow and the resulting red curve.

	Original demand schedule (price of Walkman $200)			**New demand schedule (price of Walkman $50)**	
	Price (dollars per tape)	**Quantity (millions of tapes per week)**		**Price (dollars per tape)**	**Quantity (millions of tapes per week)**
a	1	9	*a′*	1	13
b	2	6	*b′*	2	10
c	3	4	*c′*	3	8
d	4	3	*d′*	4	7
e	5	2	*e′*	5	6

Figure 4.3 A Change in Demand Versus a Change in the Quantity Demanded

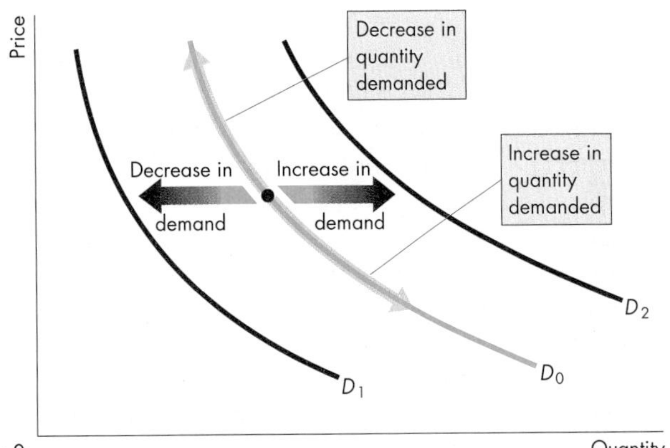

When the price of a good changes, there is a movement along the demand curve and a *change in the quantity of the good demanded.* For example, if the demand curve is D_0, a rise in the price of the good produces a decrease in the quantity demanded and a fall in the price of the good produces an increase in the quantity demanded. The arrows on demand curve D_0 represent these movements along the demand curve. If some other influence on demand changes, which increases the quantity that people plan to buy, there is a shift in the demand curve to the right (from D_0 to D_2) and an *increase in demand.* If some other influence on demand changes, which reduces the quantity people plan to buy, there is a shift in the demand curve to the left (from D_0 to D_1) and a *decrease in demand.*

What Determines the Quantity Supplied?

The quantity supplied depends on the number of firms supplying a good and the plans of each firm. The amount of any good that each firm plans to supply depends on many factors. Among the more important ones are:

- The price of the good
- The prices of other goods
- The prices of the factors of production used to produce the good
- The number of suppliers
- Technology

Since the theory of demand and supply makes predictions about prices and quantities traded, we focus first on the relationship between the price of a good and the quantity supplied. In order to study this relationship, we hold constant all the other influences on the quantity supplied. We ask: how does the quantity supplied of a good vary as its price varies?

The Law of Supply

The law of supply states:

Other things being equal, the higher the price of a good, the greater is the quantity supplied.

Why does a higher price lead to a greater quantity supplied of a good? The key to the answer is profitability. If the prices of the factors of production used to produce a good are held constant, a higher price for the good means a higher profit for the producer. Higher profits encourage existing producers to increase the quantity they supply. Higher profits also attract additional producers.

The Supply Schedule and the Supply Curve

A **supply schedule** lists the quantities supplied at each different price, when all other influences on the amount firms plan to sell are held constant. Let's construct a supply schedule. To do so, we examine how the quantity supplied of a good varies as its price varies, holding constant the prices of other goods, the prices of factors of production used to produce it and the state of technology.

The table in Fig. 4.4 sets out a supply schedule for tapes. It shows the quantity of tapes supplied at each possible price. For example, if the price of a tape is $1, no tapes are supplied. If the price of a tape is $4, 5 million tapes are supplied each week.

A supply schedule can be illustrated by drawing a **supply curve.** A supply curve graphs the relationship between the quantity supplied and the price of a good, holding everything else constant. Using the same numbers listed in the table, the graph in Fig. 4.4 illustrates the supply curve for tapes. For example, point *d* represents a quantity supplied of 5 million tapes a week at a price of $4 a tape.

The term **supply** refers to the entire relationship between the quantity supplied of the good and its price. The supply of tapes is described by both the supply schedule and the supply curve in Fig. 4.4.

Minimum Supply Price

Just as the demand curve has two interpretations, so too does the supply curve. So far we have thought about the supply curve and the supply schedule as showing the quantity that firms will supply at each possible price. But we can also think about the supply curve as showing the minimum price at which the last unit will be supplied. Looking at the supply schedule in this way, we ask what is the minimum price that brings forth a supply of a given quantity. For firms to supply the 3 millionth tape each week, the price has to be at least $2 a tape. For firms to supply the 5 millionth tape each week, they have to get at least $4 a tape.

A Change in Supply

To construct a supply schedule and supply curve, we hold constant all the other influences on suppliers' plans. Let's now consider these other influences.

1. Prices of Other Goods. The supply of a good can be influenced by the prices of other goods. For example, if an automobile assembly line can produce either sedans or stationwagons, the quantity of sedans produced will depend on the price of stationwagons and the quantity of stationwagons produced will depend on the price of sedans. These two goods are substitutes in production. An increase in the price of a substitute in production lowers the supply of the good. Goods can also be complements in production. Complements in production arise when two things are, of necessity, produced together. For example, extracting chemicals from coal produces coke, coal tar and nylon. An increase in the price of any one of these by-products of coal increases the supply of the other by-product.

Tapes have no obvious complements in production, but they do have substitutes: prerecorded tapes.

Figure 4.4 The Supply Schedule and the Supply Curve

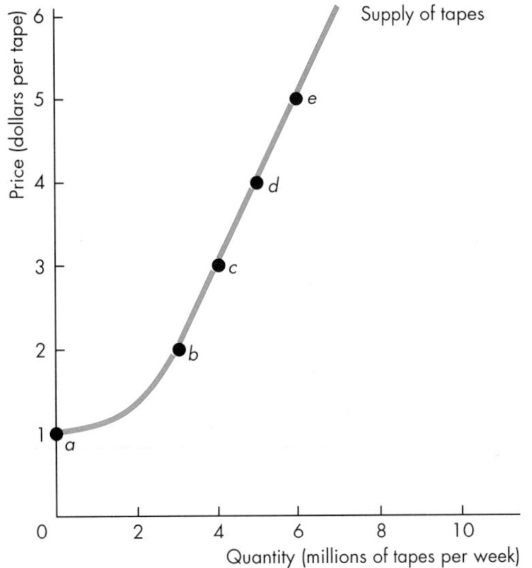

	Price of a tape (dollars)	Quantity of tapes supplied (millions per week)
a	1	0
b	2	3
c	3	4
d	4	5
e	5	6

The table shows the supply schedule of tapes. For example, at $2 a tape, 3 million tapes a week are supplied; at $5 a tape, 6 million tapes a week are supplied. The supply curve shows the relationship between the quantity supplied and price, holding everything else constant. The supply curve usually slopes upward: as the price of a good increases, so does the quantity supplied. A supply curve can be read in two ways. For a given price, it tells us the quantity that producers plan to sell. For example, at a price of $3 a tape, producers plan to sell 4 million tapes a week. The supply curve also tells us the minimum acceptable price at which a given quantity will be offered for sale. For example, the minimum acceptable price that will bring forth a supply of 4 million tapes a week is $3 a tape.

An increase in the price of prerecorded tapes will decrease the supply of blank tapes.

2. Prices of Factors of Production. The prices of the factors of production used to produce a good will exert an important influence on its supply. For example, an increase in the prices of the labour and the capital equipment used to produce tapes decreases the supply of tapes.

3. The Number of Suppliers. Other things being equal, the larger the number of firms supplying a good, the larger is the supply of the good.

4. Technology. New technologies that enable producers to use fewer factors of production will lower the cost of production and increase supply. For example, the development of a new technology for tape production by companies such as Sony and Minnesota Mining and Manufacturing (3M) has lowered the cost of producing tapes and increased their supply.

A summary of influences on supply and the directions of those influences is presented in Table 4.2.

Movement Along Versus a Shift in the Supply Curve

Changes in the influences on producers cause either a movement along the supply curve or a shift in it.

Table 4.2 The Supply of Tapes

The law of supply

The quantity of tapes supplied

Falls if:	*Rises if:*
• The price of a tape falls	• The price of a tape rises

Changes in supply

The supply of tapes

Falls if:	*Rises if:*
• The price of a substitute in production rises	• The price of a substitute in production falls
• The price of a complement in production falls	• The price of a complement in production rises
• The price of a factor of production used to produce tapes increases	• The price of a factor of production used to produce tapes falls
• The number of firms supplying tapes decreases	• The number of firms supplying tapes rises
	• More efficient technologies for producing tapes are discovered

Movement Along the Supply Curve If the price of a good changes but everything else influencing suppliers' planned sales remains constant, there is a movement along the supply curve. For example, if the price of tapes increases from $3 to $5 a tape, there is a movement along the supply curve from point *c* (4 million tapes a week) to point *e* (6 million tapes a week) in Fig. 4.4.

A Shift in the Supply Curve If the price of a good remains constant but another influence on suppliers' planned sales changes, then there is a change in supply and a shift in the supply curve. For example, as we have already noted, technological advances lower the cost of producing tapes and increase their supply. As a result, the supply schedule changes. The table in Fig. 4.5 provides some hypothetical numbers that illustrate such a change. The table contains two supply schedules: the original, based on 'old' technology, and another based on 'new' technology. With the new technology, more tapes are supplied at each price. The graph in Fig. 4.5 illustrates the resulting shift in the supply curve. When tape-producing technology improves, the supply curve of tapes shifts to the right, as shown by the shift arrow and the red curve.

A Change in Supply Versus a Change in Quantity Supplied The quantity supplied at a given price is shown by a point on a supply curve. The entire supply curve shows supply. **A change in supply** occurs whenever there is a shift in the supply curve. **A change in the quantity supplied** occurs when there is a movement along the supply curve.

Figure 4.6 illustrates and summarizes these distinctions. If the price of a good falls but nothing else changes, then there is a decrease in the quantity supplied of that good (a movement down the supply curve S_0). If the price of a good rises but nothing else changes, there is an increase in the quantity supplied (a movement up the supply curve S_0). When any other influence on sellers changes, the supply curve shifts and there is a *change in supply*. If the supply curve is S_0 and there is, say, a technological change that reduces the amounts of the factors of production needed to produce the good, then supply increases and the supply curve shifts to the red supply curve S_2. If production costs rise, supply decreases and the supply curve shifts to the red supply curve S_1.

REVIEW

The quantity supplied is the amount of a good that producers plan to sell in a given period of time at a particular time. Other things being equal, the quantity supplied of a good increases if its price rises. Sup-

Figure 4.5 A Change in the Supply Schedule and Shift in the Supply Curve

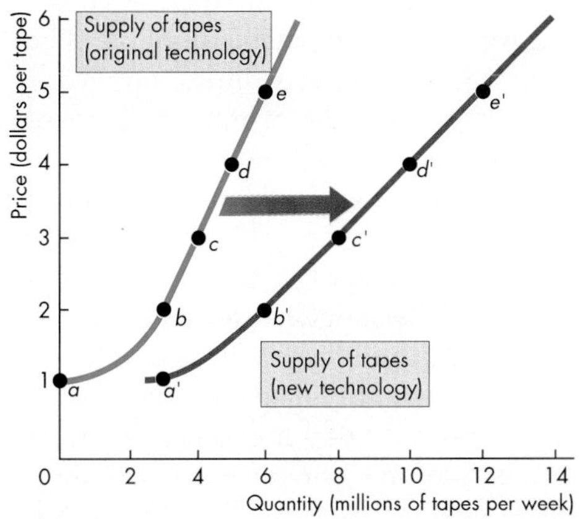

	Original Technology			New Technology	
	Price (dollars)	**Quantity (millions of tapes per week)**		**Price (dollars)**	**Quantity (million of tapes per week)**
a	1	0	*a′*	1	3
b	2	3	*b′*	2	6
c	3	4	*c′*	3	8
d	4	5	*d′*	4	10
e	5	6	*e′*	5	12

If the price of a good remains constant but another influence on its supply changes, there will be a new supply schedule and the supply curve will shift. For example, if Sony and 3M invent a new, cost-saving technology for producing tapes, the supply schedule changes, as shown in the table. At $3 a tape, producers sell 4 million tapes a week with the old technology and 8 million tapes a week with the new technology. Improved technology increases the supply of tapes and shifts the supply curve of tapes to the right.

Figure 4.6 A Change in Supply Versus a Change in the Quantity Supplied

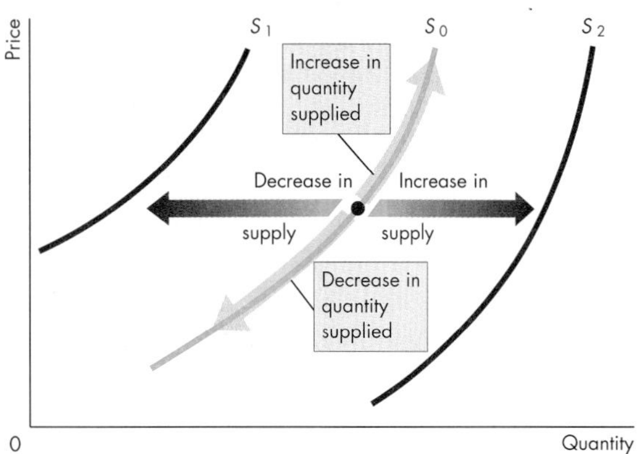

When the price of a good changes, there is a movement along the supply curve and a *change in the quantity of the good supplied.* For example, if the supply curve is S_0, a rise in the price of the good produces an increase in the quantity supplied, and a fall in the price produces a decrease in the quantity supplied. The arrows on curve S_0 represent these movements along the supply curve. If some other influence on supply changes, which increases the quantity that producers plan to sell, there is a shift in the supply curve to the right (from S_0 to S_2) and an *increase in supply.* If some other influence on supply changes, which reduces the quantity the producers plan to sell, there is a shift to the left in the supply curve (from S_0 to S_1) and a *decrease in supply.*

ply can be represented by a schedule or a curve that shows the relationship between the quantity supplied of a good and its price. Supply describes the quantity that will be supplied at each possible price or the lowest price at which producers will supply the last unit. Supply increases if the price of a substitute in production falls, if the price of a complement in production rises, if the prices of the factors of production used to produce the good fall or when technological advances lower the cost of production. If the price of a good changes but all other influences on producers' plans are held constant, there is a change in the quantity supplied and a movement along the supply curve. A change in any other influence on producers' plans shifts the supply curve. Changes in the prices of substitutes and complements in production, changes in the prices of factors of production or improvements in technology shift the supply curve and are said to change supply. ■

Now that we have studied demand and supply, let's bring these two concepts together and see how prices are determined.

Price Determination

We have seen that when the price of a good rises, the quantity demanded decreases and the quantity supplied increases. We are now going to see how adjustments in price achieve an equality between the quantities demanded and supplied.

Price as a Regulator

The price of a good regulates the quantities demanded and supplied. If the price is too high, the quantity supplied exceeds the quantity demanded. If the price is too low, the quantity demanded exceeds the quantity supplied. There is one price, and only one price, at which the quantity demanded equals the quantity supplied. We are going to work out what that price is. We are also going to discover that natural forces operating in a market move the price toward the level that makes the quantity demanded equal the quantity supplied.

The demand schedule shown in the table in Fig. 4.1 and the supply schedule shown in the table in Fig. 4.4 appear together in the table in Fig. 4.7. If the price of a tape is $1, the quantity demanded is 9 million tapes a week but no tapes are supplied. The quantity demanded exceeds the quantity supplied by 9 million tapes a week. In other words, at a price of $1 a tape, there is a shortage of 9 million tapes a week. This shortage is shown in the final column of the table. At a price of $2 a tape, there is still a shortage but only of 3 million tapes a week. If the price of a tape is $5, the quantity supplied exceeds the quantity demanded. The quantity supplied is 6 million tapes a week, but the quantity demanded is only 2 million. There is a surplus of 4 million tapes a week. There is one price and only one price at which there is neither a shortage nor a surplus. That price is $3 a tape. At that price the quantity demanded is equal to the quantity supplied — 4 million tapes a week. That quantity is also the quantity traded.

The market for tapes is illustrated in the graph in Fig. 4.7. The graph shows both the demand curve of Fig. 4.1 and the supply curve of Fig. 4.4. The de-

Figure 4.7 Equilibrium

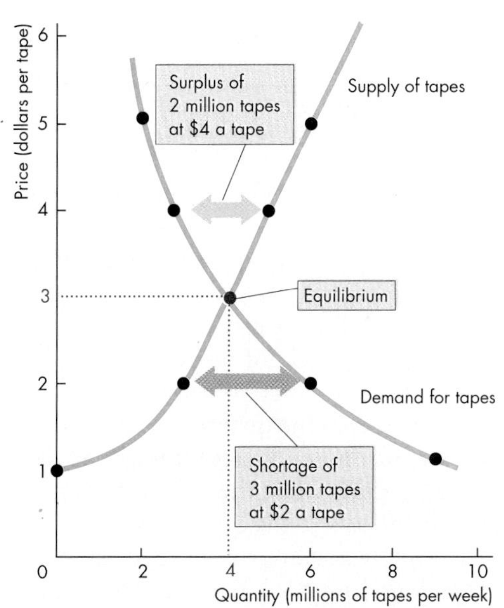

The table lists the quantities demanded and quantities supplied as well as the shortage or surplus of tapes at each price. (Note that the numbers in the final column of the table represent the shortages as negative numbers and the surpluses as positive numbers.) If the price of a tape is $2, 6 million tapes a week are demanded and 3 million are supplied. There is a shortage of 3 million tapes a week and the price rises. If the price of a tape is $4, 3 million tapes a week are demanded but 5 million are supplied. There is a surplus of 2 million tapes a week and the price falls. If the price of a tape is $3, 4 million tapes a week are demanded and 4 million are supplied. There is neither a shortage nor a surplus. Neither buyers nor sellers have any incentive to change the price. The price at which the quantity demanded equals the quantity supplied is the equilibrium price.

Price (dollars per tape)	Quantity demanded (millions of tapes per week)	Quantity supplied (millions of tapes per week)	Shortage (–) or surplus (+) (millions of tapes per week)
1	9	0	–9
2	6	3	–3
3	4	4	0
4	3	5	+2
5	2	6	+4

mand curve and the supply curve intersect when the price is $3 a tape, and the quantity traded is 4 million tapes a week. At prices above $3 a tape, the quantity supplied exceeds the quantity demanded. That is, there is a surplus of tapes. At $4 a tape the surplus is 2 million tapes a week, as shown by the arrow labelled 'Surplus' in the figure. At prices below $3 a tape, the quantity demanded exceeds the quantity supplied and there is a shortage of tapes, as shown by the arrow labelled 'Shortage'.

Equilibrium

We defined *equilibrium* in Chapter 1 as a situation in which opposing forces exactly balance each other and in which no one is able to make a better choice given the available factors of production and actions of others. So, in an equilibrium the price is such that opposing forces exactly balance each other. The **equilibrium price** is the price at which the quantity demanded equals the quantity supplied. To see why this situation is an equilibrium, we need to examine the behaviour of buyers and sellers a bit more closely. First, let's look at the behaviour of buyers.

The Demand Curve and the Willingness to Pay

Suppose the price of a tape is $2. In such a situation, producers plan to sell 3 million tapes a week. Consumers cannot force producers to sell more than they want to sell, so the quantity sold is also 3 million tapes a week. What is the highest price that buyers are willing to pay for the 3 millionth tape each week? The answer can be found on the demand curve in Fig. 4.7 — it is $4 a tape.

If the price remains at $2 a tape, the quantity of tapes demanded is 6 million tapes a week — 3 million tapes more than are available. In such a situation, the price of a tape does not remain at $2. Because people want more tapes than are available at that price and because they are willing to pay up to $4 a tape, the price rises. If the quantity supplied stays at 3 million tapes a week, the price rises all the way to $4 a tape.

In fact, the price doesn't have to rise by such a large amount because at higher prices the quantity supplied increases. The price will rise from $2 a tape to $3 a tape. At that price, the quantity supplied is 4 million tapes a week, and $3 a tape is the highest price that consumers are willing to pay. At $3 a tape, buyers are able to make their planned purchases and producers are able to make their planned sales. Therefore no one has an incentive to bid the price higher.

The Supply Curve and the Minimum Supply Price Suppose that the price of a tape is $4. In such a situation, the quantity demanded is 3 million tapes a week. Producers cannot force consumers to buy more than they want, so the quantity bought is 3 million tapes a week. Producers are willing to sell 3 million tapes a week for a price lower than $4 a tape. In fact, you can see on the supply curve in Fig. 4.7 that suppliers are willing to sell the 3 millionth tape each week at a price of $2. At $4 a tape, they would like to sell 5 million tapes each week. Because they want to sell more than 3 million tapes a week at $4 a tape, and because they would be willing to sell the 3 millionth tape for as little as $2, they will continuously undercut each other in order to get a bigger share of the market. They will cut their price all the way to $2 a tape if only 3 million tapes a week can be sold.

In fact, producers don't have to cut their price to $2 a tape because the lower price brings forth an increase in the quantity demanded. When the price falls to $3, the quantity demanded is 4 million tapes a week, which is exactly the quantity that producers want to sell at that price. So, when the price reaches $3 a tape, producers have no incentive to cut the price any further.

The Best Deal Available for Buyers and Sellers Both situations we have just examined result in price changes. In the first case, the price starts out at $2 and is bid upward. In the second case, the price starts out at $4 and producers undercut each other. In both cases, prices change until they hit the price of $3 a tape. At that price, the quantity demanded and the quantity supplied are equal and no one has any incentive to do business at a different price. Consumers are paying the highest acceptable price and producers are selling at the lowest acceptable price.

When people can freely make bids and offers and when they seek to buy at the lowest price and sell at the highest price, the price at which they trade is the equilibrium price — the quantity demanded equals the quantity supplied.

R E V I E W

The equilibrium price is the price at which the plans of buyers and sellers match each other — the price at which the quantity demanded equals the quantity supplied. If the price is below equilibrium, the quantity demanded exceeds the quantity supplied, buyers offer higher prices, sellers ask for higher prices and the price rises. If the price is above equilibrium, the quantity supplied exceeds the quantity demanded, buyers offer lower prices, sellers ask for lower prices and the price falls. Only when the price is such that the quantity demanded and the quantity supplied are equal are there no forces acting on the price to make it change. Therefore that price is the equilibrium price. At that price, the quantity traded is also equal to the quantity demanded and the quantity supplied. ■

The theory of demand and supply that you have just studied, is now a central part of economics. But that was not always so. Only 100 years ago, the best economists of the day were quite confused about these matters, which today even students in introductory courses find relatively easy to get right (Our Advancing Knowledge on pp. 78–79).

You'll discover in the rest of this chapter that the theory of demand and supply enables us to understand and make predictions about changes in prices — including the price slides, rockets and rollercoasters described in the chapter opener.

Predicting Changes in Price and Quantity Traded

The theory we have just studied provides us with a powerful way of analysing influences on prices and quantities traded. According to the theory, a change in price stems from either a change in demand or a change in supply. Let's look first at the effects of a change in demand.

A Change in Demand

What happens to the price of tapes and the quantity traded if demand for tapes increases? We can answer this question with a specific example. If the price of a Walkman falls from \$200 to \$50, the demand for tapes will increase as is shown in the table in Fig. 4.8. The original demand schedule and the new one are set out in the first three columns of the table. The table also shows the supply schedule.

The original equilibrium price was \$3 a tape. At that price, 4 million tapes a week were demanded and supplied. When demand increases, the price that makes the quantity demanded equal the quantity supplied is \$5 a tape. At this price 6 million tapes are traded each week. When demand increases, the price rises and the quantity traded increases.

We can illustrate these changes in the graph in Fig. 4.8. The graph shows the original demand for and supply of tapes. The original equilibrium price is \$3 a tape and the quantity traded is 4 million tapes a week. When demand increases, the demand curve shifts to the right. The equilibrium price rises to \$5 a tape and the quantity traded increases to 6 million tapes a week, as is highlighted in the figure.

The exercise that we've just conducted can easily be reversed. If we start at a price of \$5 a tape, trading 6 million tapes a week, we can then work out what happens if demand falls back to its original level. You will see that a fall in demand lowers price and decreases the quantity traded.

We can now make our first two predictions:

- When demand increases, the price rises and the quantity traded increases.
- When demand decreases, the price falls and the quantity traded decreases.

A Change in Supply

Let's ask what happens if supply changes. Again, we'll start out with a price of \$3 a tape and 4 million tapes a week being traded. Suppose that Sony and 3M have just introduced a new cost-saving technology for producing tapes. The new technology shifts

Figure 4.8 The Effect of a Change in Demand

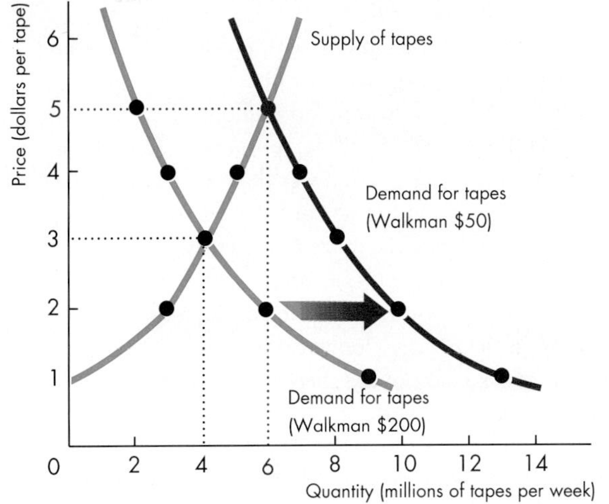

If the price of a Walkman is \$200, the quantity of tapes demanded and the quantity traded is 4 million tapes a week at a price of \$3 a tape. If the price of a Walkman falls from \$200 to \$50, the quantity of tapes demanded at a price of \$3 is 8 million tapes a week. If the price stays at \$3, there is a shortage of 4 million tapes a week. The quantities of tapes demanded and supplied are equal when the price is \$5 a tape and the quantity traded is 6 million tapes a week. The increase in demand raises the equilibrium price by \$2 and raises the equilibrium quantity traded by 2 million tapes a week.

Price (dollars per tape)	Quantity demanded (millions of tapes per week)		Quantity supplied (millions of tapes per week)
	Walkman \$200	Walkman \$50	
1	9	13	0
2	6	10	3
3	4	8	4
4	3	7	5
5	2	6	6

Discovering the Laws of Demand and Supply

Antoine-Augustin Cournot

How are the prices of goods and services determined? Why are some vital-to-life factors of production, such as the air that we breathe and the water that we drink, virtually free while luxurious but inessential commodities such as diamonds are so expensive? For centuries, people have puzzled over these and similar questions. The questions were finally answered when the theories of demand, supply and equilibrium price, that you have been studying in this chapter, were discovered and refined. But this discovery was not completed until the 1890s.

Let's transport ourselves back in time to the early part of the nineteenth century. We are planning to make a sizeable investment in railways and we are using the prevailing theory of prices to guide our decision. Economists believe that prices are determined by costs of production. So we predict that the price of railway transportation will stay in line with production costs and that a reasonable rate of return will be made on our investment. As a result, we (and millions of others) invest heavily in this new mode of transportation. Rates of return turn out to be much lower than we predicted. Why? What went wrong? Ignorant of the laws of demand and supply, we failed to realize that a massive increase in the supply of railway transportation services would drive their prices down and therefore lower the return on investing in them. Let's look at the main milestones on the road of discovery of the theory of demand and supply.

The road begins with the work of Antoine-Augustin Cournot. Cournot (1801–1877) was born near Dijon, France. In 1834, he became professor of mathematics at the University of Lyon. Four years later he published a book entitled *Recherches sur les principes mathématiques de la théorie des richesses (The Mathematical Principles of the Theory of Wealth).* In that book, Cournot wrote down the law of demand. But he wrote it in abstract mathematical language. Cournot's book was a work of amazing clarity, but because it used a mathematical language unfamiliar at that time to most students of economics, and because the book was in French, it did not have much influence until many years later. The first person to draw a demand curve was Arsène-Jules-Émile Juvenal Dupuit (1804–1866). Like Cournot, Dupuit was a Frenchman. He made profound contributions both as an engineer and an economic theorist. Dupuit's demand curve, which he called 'the curve of consumption' (*courbe de consommation*), appeared in 1844.

The law of demand was independently discovered a few years later and given its first practical application by Dionysius Lardner (1793–1859), an Irishman who was Professor of Philosophy at the University of London. In his book *Railway Economy*, published in 1850, Lardner drew and used a demand curve for transportation services.

The first person to draw a demand and supply curve together and to use demand and supply theory to determine price was Fleeming Jenkin (1833–1885), an Englishman who was also a Professor of Philosophy at the University of London. Jenkin's demand and supply curves appeared in a paper entitled 'The Graphic Representation of the Laws of Supply and Demand', published in 1870. Jenkin also was the first to use the theories of demand and supply to make predictions about the effects of taxes, in a paper entitled 'On the Principles Which Regulate the Incidence of Taxes', published in 1872.

Many others had a hand in the refinement of the theory of demand and supply, but the first thorough and complete statement of the theory, in terms sufficiently modern for it to be recognized as the same theory that you have studied in this chapter, was provided by Alfred Marshall (1842–1924). Marshall was a Professor of Political Economy at the University of Cambridge, and in 1890, he published a monumental treatise — *Principles of Economics.* Marshall's *Principles* was *the* textbook on this subject for almost half a century. In the preface to Principles, Marshall acknowledged his own debt to Cournot. He also expressed his view that the theory of demand and supply provides a unifying analysis applicable to all aspects of economics.

Although Marshall was an outstanding mathematician, he kept mathematics and even diagrams in the background. His own supply and demand diagram and discussion of how the equilibrium price arises appears only in a footnote. It is reproduced here. Although Marshall's diagram is far less striking than those you have been studying, note the strong similarities it has with Fig. 4.7.

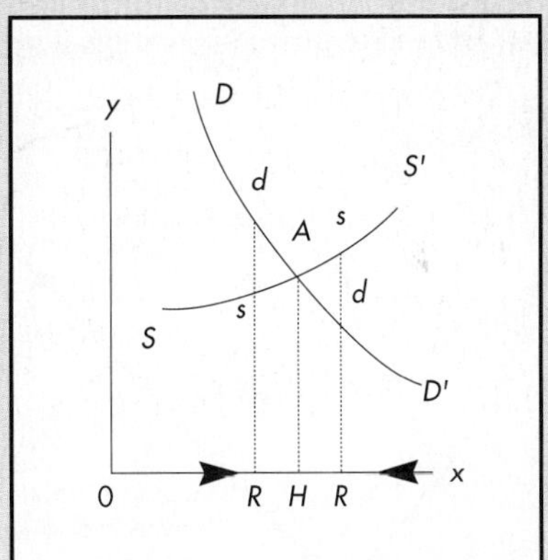

the supply schedule and the supply curve. The new supply schedule (the same one that was shown in Fig. 4.5) is presented in the table in Fig. 4.9. What is the new equilibrium price and quantity traded? The answer is highlighted in the table: the price falls to $2 a tape and the number of tapes traded rises to 6 million a week. You can see why by looking at the quantities demanded and supplied at the old price of $3 a tape. The quantity supplied at that price is 8 million tapes a week and there is a surplus of tapes. The price falls. Only when the price is $2 a tape is the quantity supplied equal to the quantity demanded.

The graph in Fig. 4.9 illustrates the effect of an increase in supply. The graph shows the demand curve for tapes and the original and new supply curves. The initial equilibrium price is $3 a tape and the original quantity traded is 4 million tapes a week. When the supply increases, the supply curve shifts to the right. The new equilibrium price is $2 a tape and the quantity traded is 6 million tapes a week, highlighted in the figure.

The exercise that we've just conducted can easily be reversed. If we start out at a price of $2 a tape with 6 million tapes a week being traded, we can work out what happens if the supply curve shifts back to its original position. You can see that the fall in supply increases the equilibrium price to $3 a tape and decreases the quantity traded to 4 million tapes a week. Such a fall in supply could arise from an increase in the cost of labour and raw materials.

We can now make two more predictions:

- When supply increases, the quantity traded increases and the price falls.
- When supply decreases, the quantity traded decreases and the price rises.

Changes in Both Supply and Demand

In the above exercises, we changed either demand or supply but only one at a time. If we change just one of these, we can predict the direction of change of the price and the quantity traded. If we change both demand and supply, we cannot always say what will happen to both the price and the quantity traded. For example, if both demand and supply increase, we know that the quantity traded increases but we cannot predict whether the price rises or falls. To make such a prediction, we need to know the relative importance of the increase in demand and supply. If de-

Figure 4.9 The Effect of a Change in Supply

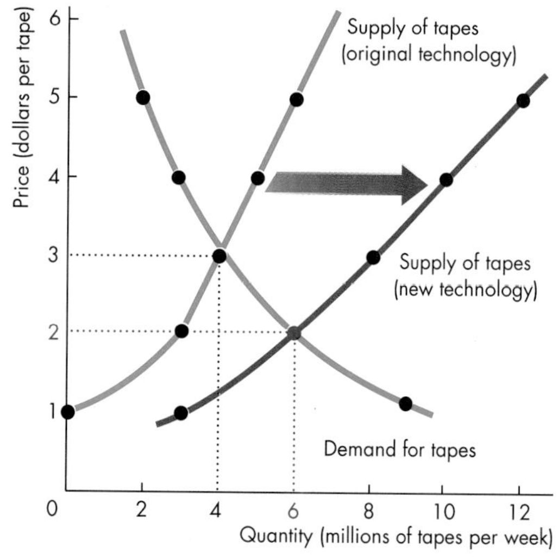

Price (dollars per tape)	Quantity demanded (millions of tapes per week)	Quantity supplied (millions of tapes per week)	
		Original technology	New technology
1	9	0	3
2	6	3	6
3	4	4	8
4	3	5	10

When the supply schedule changes as a result of introducing a new technology, the quantity of tapes supplied at $3 a tape exceeds the quantity demanded at that price. The quantity supplied is 8 million tapes at a price of $3. The table shows that the quantity demanded equals the quantity supplied when the price of tapes falls to $2. At this price, 6 million tapes are demanded and supplied each week. The new technology results in a shift in the supply curve to the right. The original technology supply curve intersects the demand curve at a price of $3 and at a quantity traded of 4 million tapes a week. The new technology supply curve intersects the demand curve at a price of $2 and a quantity traded of 6 million tapes a week. The increase in supply lowers the price of tapes by $1 and increases the quantity traded by 2 million tapes a week.

mand increases and supply decreases, we know that the price rises but we cannot predict whether the quantity traded increases or decreases. Again, to be able to make a prediction about the quantity traded, we need to know the relative magnitudes of the changes in demand and supply.

As an example of a change in both supply and demand, let's take one final look at the market for tapes. We've seen how demand and supply determine the price and quantity of tapes traded; how an increase in demand resulting from a fall in the price of a Walkman both raises the price of tapes and increases the quantity traded; how an increase in the supply of tapes resulting from an improved technology lowers the price of tapes and increases the quantity traded. Let's now examine what happens when both of these changes — a fall in the price of a Walkman (which increases the demand for tapes) and an improved production technology (which increases the supply of tapes) occur together.

The table in Fig. 4.10 brings together the numbers that describe the original quantities demanded and supplied and the new quantities demanded and supplied after the fall in the price of the Walkman and the improved tape production technology. These same numbers are illustrated in the graph. The original demand and supply curves intersect at a price of $3 a tape and a quantity traded of 4 million tapes a week. The new supply and demand curves also intersect at a price of $3 a tape but at a quantity traded of 8 million tapes a week. The rise in price brought about by an increase in demand is offset by the fall in price brought about by an increase in supply. So the price does not change. An increase in either demand or supply increases the quantity traded. Therefore when both demand and supply in-

Figure 4.10 The Effect of a Change in Both Demand and Supply

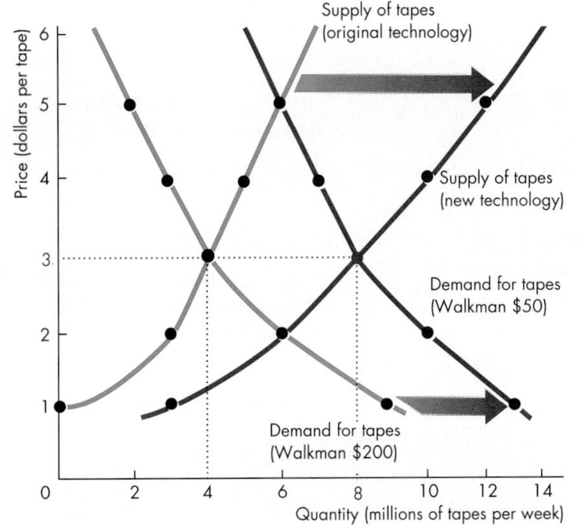

When a Walkman costs $200, the price of a tape is $3 and the quantity traded is 4 million tapes a week. A fall in the price of a Walkman increases the demand for tapes and improved technology increases the supply of tapes. The new technology supply curve intersects the higher demand curve at $3, the same price as before, but at a higher quantity traded of 8 million tapes a week. The simultaneous increase in both demand and supply increases the quantity traded but leaves the price unchanged.

Price (dollars per tape)	Original quantities (millions of tapes per week)		New quantities (millions of tapes per week)	
	Quantity demanded (Walkman $200)	Quantity supplied (Original technology)	Quantity demanded (Walkman $50)	Quantity supplied (New technology)
1	9	0	13	3
2	6	3	10	6
3	4	4	8	8
4	3	5	7	10
5	2	6	6	12

Supply and Demand in Action: Increasing Market Demand

Breakfast Cereal Producers Cash in on Health Concerns

The new generation of health-conscious consumers has meant more sales and higher prices for breakfast cereal producers.

In a recently released study of breakfast cereals, the industry research group Mintel said the cereal industry had been able to capitalise on the health craze to give new life to the breakfast cereal market.

By focusing on benefits such as the low sugar and salt content of their products, companies had increased the value of retail sales of breakfast cereals by 19.5 per cent in the 12 months to June 1990.

Consumption of breakfast cereals was reaching 10 kilograms per person a year, the report said.

In their pitch to sell more cereals, companies were targeting a consumer group Mintel has labelled 'health moderates'. These were consumers who were informed and environmentally aware, and who 'stood ready to embrace any product modification which recognised their demand for additive-free, organically grown or culprit-free food options'.

Mintel said 'health moderates' spent more than $1,732 per head on health products each year.

These health-conscious consumers were willing to pay 34 per cent more for a product which made health claims, although the product might be only slightly different from the standard product.

Such price tolerance had allowed the cereal industry and retailers to increase cereal prices by 13 per cent a year over the last five years, the report said.

Companies had expanded the cereal market through new products, and through making health claims on the cereal pack.

In the past, breakfast cereal marketing had concentrated on children, but the present focus on health, with companies trying to endow their products with a healthy image, had given an adult slant to cereal marketing.

Mintel noted that most cereal packets now made statements about the healthiness of the product to attract buyers, in preference to marketing ploys such as 'new size' or 'product of Australia'.

The most common health claims were those referring to what was not in the cereal, such as no salt, less sugar or less fat. The next most common claim was a reference to the fibre content of the cereal.

Financial Review
Tuesday, 22 January 1991
By Sam Hudson

The Essence of the Story

- Demand for breakfast cereals is rising.
- In 1989/90, prices of breakfast cereals rose by 13 per cent, the quantity sold rose by 6.5 per cent so that total sales rose by 19.5 per cent.
- Increased sales are attributed to an increase in demand for health products. Manufacturers are targeting this feature in advertising campaigns.
- Research has identified consumers, 'health moderates', who are prepared to pay 34 per cent more for a product which makes health claims.

Background and Analysis

- The consumption of breakfast cereal grew at a modest 1.5 per cent average annual rate between 1938/39 and 1978/79. Over the ensuing 10 years, the rate of growth in consumption doubled to over 3 per cent a year.

Year	Per capita consumption kg per year
1938/39	4.8
1948/49	6.1
1958/59	6.2
1968/69	6.8
1978/79	7.8
1987/88	10.2

- There are two types of consumer for breakfast cereals 'Norm' who place no value on the advertised health benefits of cereals; and 'Health Mods' who do.
- The demand for cereals by Health Mods is higher than the demand by Norms. At any given price, Health Mods buy more cereals than Norms. Equivalently, Health Mods are prepared to pay more for any given quantity of cereals.
- According to market research studies, Health Mods are prepared to pay 34 per cent more for cereals which might be only slightly different from the standard product.
- The demand curves for Norms and Health Mods are illustrated in part (a) of the figure. D_N is the demand curve for Norms; D_{HM} is the demand curve for Health Mods. For any quantity demanded, Health Mods are prepared to pay 34 per cent extra.
- The market demand for cereals is an average of the demand curve for Norms and the demand curve for Health Mods. The more Health Mods there are the closer is the market demand curve to D_{HM}.
- By introducing new products and making health claims on existing products, more consumers become Health Mods. Thus the market demand curve shifts to the right as demand becomes more heavily weighted in favour of Health Mods.
- The market supply curve is *S*. As market demand increases, both price and quantity traded increase and total sales increase. But the increase in price is less than 34 per cent for two reasons:
  - not all consumers become Health Mods.
  - the quantity supplied increases, so more cereals become available, limiting the price rise.

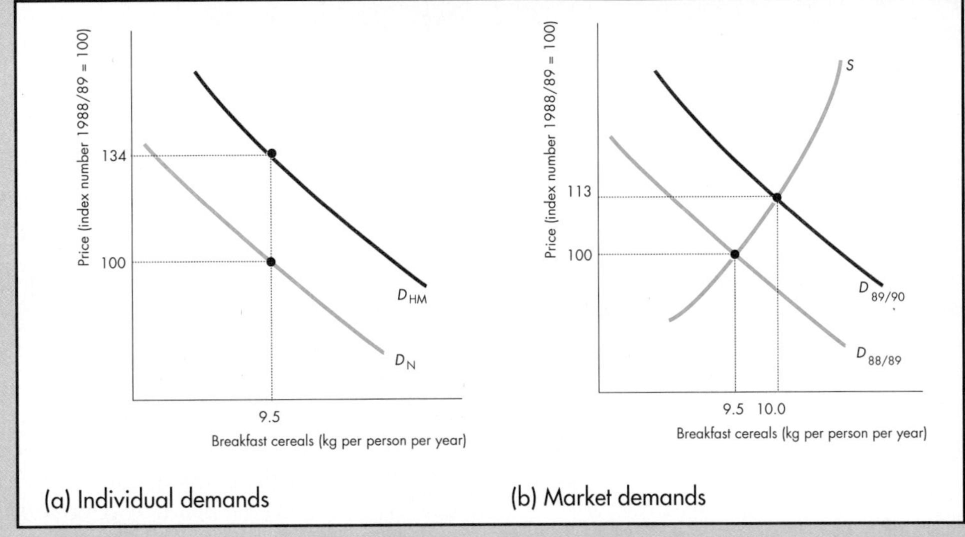

(a) Individual demands

(b) Market demands

crease, so does the quantity traded. Note that if demand had increased slightly more than shown in the figure, the price would have risen. If supply had increased by slightly more than shown in the figure, the price would have fallen. But in both cases the quantity traded would have increased.

Walkmans, Houses and Coffee

At the beginning of this chapter, we looked at some facts about prices and quantities traded of Walkmans, houses and coffee. Let's use the theory of demand and supply that we have just studied to explain the movements in the prices and the quantities traded of those goods. Figure 4.11 illustrates the analysis.

First, let's consider the Walkman, shown in Fig. 4.11(a). In 1980, using the original technology, the supply of Walkmans is described by the supply curve S_0. The 1980 demand curve is D_0. The quantities supplied and demanded in 1980 are equal at Q_0 and the price is P_0. Advances in technology and the building of additional production plants increase supply and shift the supply curve from S_0 to S_1. At the same time, increasing incomes increase the demand for Walkmans but not by nearly as much as the increase in supply. The demand curve shifts from D_0 to D_1. With the new demand curve D_1 and supply curve S_1, the equilibrium price is P_1 and the quantity traded is Q_1. The large increase in supply combined with a smaller increase in demand results in an increase in the quantity of Walkmans traded and a dramatic fall in their price.

Next, let's consider houses in the centre of the city, as in Fig. 4.11(b). The supply of houses is described by supply curve *S*. The supply curve is steep, reflecting the fact that there is a fixed amount of urban land and a fixed number of houses. As the number of young professionals increases and the number of two-income families increases, the demand for urban housing increases sharply. The demand curve shifts from D_0 to D_1. As a result, the price increases from P_0 to P_1 and the quantity traded also increases but not as dramatically as price.

Finally, let's consider the market for coffee, shown in Fig. 4.11(c). The demand for coffee is described by curve *D*. The supply of coffee fluctuates between S_0 and S_1. When growing conditions are good, the supply curve is S_1. When there are adverse growing conditions such as frost, the supply decreases and the supply curve is S_0. As a consequence of fluctuations in supply, the price of coffee fluctuates between P_0 (the maximum price) and P_1 (the minimum price). The quantity traded fluctuates between Q_0 and Q_1.

■ By using the theory of demand and supply, you will be able to explain past fluctuations in prices and quantities traded and also make predictions about future fluctuations. But you will want to do more than predict whether prices are going to rise or fall. You will want to predict by *how much* they will change when there is a change in demand or supply. To make such predictions, we need a quantitative measure of the relationship between the quantities demanded and supplied and price. In the next chapter, we study such a measure.

SUMMARY

Demand

The quantity demanded of a good or service is the amount that consumers plan to buy in a given period of time at a particular price. Demands are different from wants. Wants are unlimited, whereas demands reflect decisions to satisfy specific wants. The quantity that consumers plan to buy of any good depends on:

- The price of the good
- The prices of other goods — substitutes and complements
- Income
- Population
- Tastes

The demand schedule lists the quantities that will be demanded at each price, holding constant all other influences on consumers' planned purchases.

A demand curve graphs the quantity demanded at each price, holding everything else constant. A change in the price of a good produces a movement along the demand curve for that good. Such a movement is called a change in the quantity demanded. Changes in things other than the price of a good shift the demand curve. Such changes are said to change demand. (pp. 66–69.)

Figure 4.11 More Changes in Supply and Demand

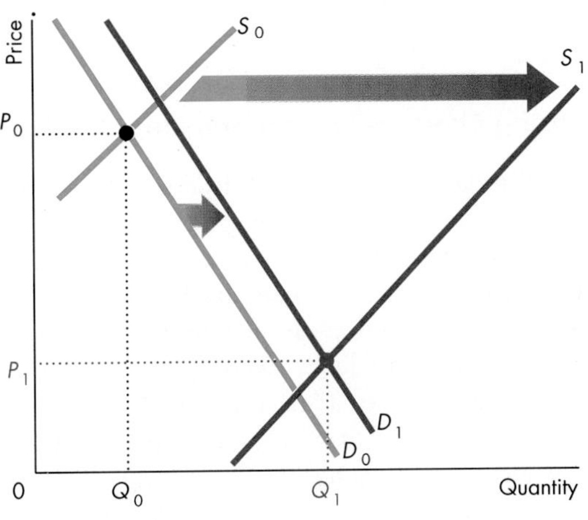

(a) Walkmans

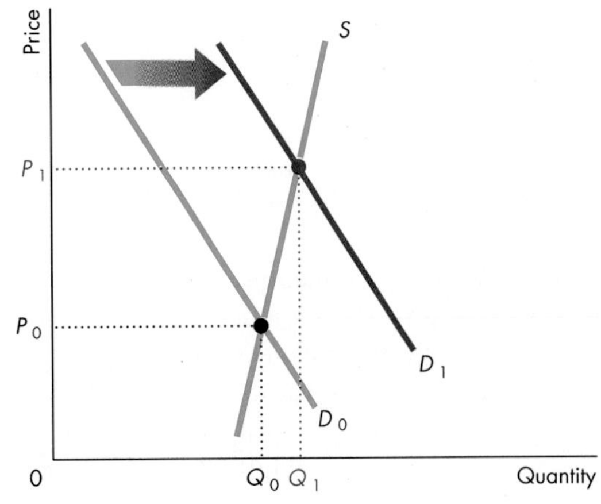

(b) Houses

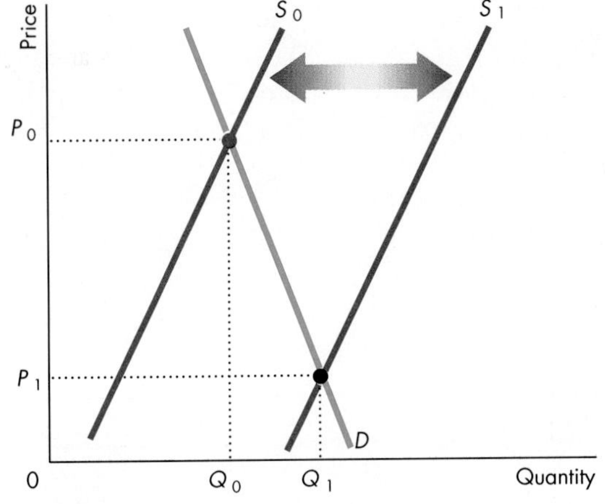

(c) Coffee

A large increase in the supply of Walkmans, from S_0 to S_1, combined with a small increase in demand, from D_0 to D_1, results in a fall in the price of Walkmans, from P_0 to P_1, and an increase in the quantity traded, from Q_0 to Q_1 (part a). An increase in the demand for houses produces a large increase in the price, from P_0 to P_1, but only a small increase in the quantity traded, from Q_0 to Q_1 (part b). Variations in the weather and in growing conditions lead to fluctuations in the supply of coffee, between S_0 and S_1, which produce fluctuations in the price of coffee, between P_0 and P_1, and in the quantity of coffee traded, between Q_0 and Q_1 (part c)

Supply

The quantity supplied of a good or service is the amount that producers plan to sell in a given period of time at a particular price. The quantity that producers plan to sell of any good or service depends on:

- The price of the good
- The prices of other goods
- The prices of the factors of production used to produce the good
- The number of suppliers
- Technology

The supply schedule lists the quantities that will be supplied at each price, holding constant all other influences on producers' planned sales. The supply curve graphs that relationship. Changes in the price of the good produce movements along the supply curve of that good. Such movements are called changes in the quantity supplied.

Changes in variables other than the price shift the supply curve. Such shifts are called changes in supply. (pp. 69–74)

Price Determination

Price regulates the quantities supplied and demanded. The higher the price, the greater is the quantity supplied and the smaller is the quantity demanded. At high prices, there is a surplus — an excess of the quantity supplied over the quantity demanded. At low prices, there is a shortage — an excess of the quantity demanded over the quantity supplied. There is one price and only one price at which the quantity demanded equals the quantity supplied. That price is the equilibrium price. At that price, buyers have no incentive to offer a higher price and suppliers have no incentive to sell at a lower price. (pp. 74–76)

Predicting Changes in Price and Quantity Traded

Changes in demand and supply lead to changes in price and in the quantity traded. An increase in demand leads to a rise in the price and to an increase in the quantity traded. A decrease in demand leads to a fall in price and to a decrease in the quantity traded. An increase in supply leads to an increase in the quantity traded and to a fall in price. A decrease in supply leads to a decrease in the quantity traded and a rise in price. (pp. 76–84)

KEY TERMS

Change in demand, p. 69
Change in the quantity demanded, p. 69
Change in the quantity supplied, p. 73
Change in supply, p. 73
Complement, p. 68
Demand, p. 67
Demand curve, p. 66
Demand schedule, p. 66
Equilibrium price, p. 75
Inferior goods, p. 68
Normal goods, p. 68
Quantity demanded, p. 66
Quantity supplied, p. 69
Quantity traded, p. 66
Substitute, p. 67
Supply, p. 71
Supply curve, p. 71
Supply schedule, p. 71
Tastes, p. 68
Wants, p. 66

PROBLEMS

1 Suppose that one of the following events occurs:

a) The price of petrol rises.
b) The price of petrol falls.
c) All speed limits on highways are abolished.
d) A new fuel-effective engine that runs on cheap alcohol is invented.
e) The population doubles.
f) Robotic production plants lower the cost of producing cars.
g) A law banning car imports from Japan is passed.
h) The rates for car insurance double.
i) The highway system is greatly improved.
j) The minimum age for drivers is increased to 19 years.
k) A massive and high-grade oil supply is discovered in Malaysia.
l) The environmental lobby succeeds in closing down all power stations which burn low quality coal.
m) The price of cars rises.
n) The price of cars falls.
o) The summer temperature averages 5° higher than normal and the winter temperature averages 5° lower than normal.
p) GMH stops making cars.

State which of the above events will:

1 Increase the quantity of petrol demanded.
2 Decrease the quantity of petrol demanded.
3 Increase the quantity of cars demanded.
4 Decrease the quantity of cars demanded.
5 Increase the quantity of petrol supplied.
6 Decrease the quantity of petrol supplied.
7 Increase the quantity of cars supplied.
8 Decrease the quantity of cars supplied.

9 Increase the demand for petrol.
10 Decrease the demand for petrol.
11 Increase the demand for cars.
12 Decrease the demand for cars.
13 Increase the supply of petrol.
14 Decrease the supply of petrol.
15 Increase the supply of cars.
16 Decrease the supply of cars.
17 Increase the price of petrol.
18 Decrease the price of petrol.
19 Increase the price of cars.
20 Decrease the price of cars.
21 Increase the quantity of petrol purchased.
22 Decrease the quantity of petrol purchased.
23 Increase the quantity of cars purchased.
24 Decrease the quantity of cars purchased.

2 The demand and supply schedules for chewing gum are as follows:

Price (cents per week)	Quantity demanded (millions of packs per week)	Quantity supplied (millions of packs per week)
10	200	0
20	180	30
30	160	60
40	140	90
50	120	120
60	100	140
70	80	160
80	60	170
90	40	180

a) What is the equilibrium price of chewing gum?
b) How much gum is bought and sold each week?

Suppose that a huge fire destroys one-half of the gum-producing factories? Supply decreases to one-half the supply shown in the above supply schedule.

c) What is the new equilibrium price of chewing gum?
d) How much gum is now bought and sold?
e) Has there been a shift in or a movement along the supply curve of chewing gum?
f) Has there been a shift in or a movement along the demand curve for chewing gum?
g) As the destroyed factories are gradually rebuilt, what will happen to:
(i) the price of chewing gum?
(ii) the quantity of gum traded?
(iii) the demand curve for chewing gum?
(iv) the supply curve of gum?

3 The demand for small and large cars depends on, amongst other things, the price of petrol. The demand schedules for both small and large cars, for low and high petrol prices, are as follows:

Petrol $0.70 per litre

Small cars Price ($'000)	Small cars Quantity demanded ('000 per year)	Large cars Price ($'000)	Large cars Quantity demanded ('000 per year)
10	28	28	20
12	26	30	18
14	24	32	16
16	22	34	14
18	20	36	12

Petrol $1.00 per litre

Small cars Price ($'000)	Small cars Quantity demanded ('000 per year)	Large cars Price ($'000)	Large cars Quantity demanded ('000 per year)
10	32	28	16
12	30	30	14
14	28	32	12
16	26	34	10
18	24	36	8

The supply schedules for small and large cars are as follows:

Small cars Price ($'000)	Small cars Quantity demanded ('000 per year)	Large cars Price ($'000)	Large cars Quantity demanded ('000 per year)
10	20	28	12
12	22	30	14
14	24	32	16
16	26	34	18
18	28	36	20

a) If petrol prices are low, what are the equilibrium prices of small cars and large cars?
b) If petrol prices are low, what are the numbers of small and large cars traded?

Suppose petrol prices now rise to $1.00 per litre.

c) What are the new prices and quantites of small and large cars traded?
d) Supposing that petrol and both small and large cars are complements in consumption, how can we explain the way the demand curves have shifted following the rise in petrol prices?

Part 8

Introduction to Macroeconomics

Talking with James Tobin

James Tobin has had a long and distinguished career in macroeconomics, extending the model suggested by Keynes, paying special attention to the demand for money, consumption and saving, fiscal and monetary policy, and economic growth. For most of his career, he has been at Yale University. He was a member of President John F. Kennedy's Council of Economic Advisers. For his many contributions, James Tobin received the Nobel Prize in economic science in 1981. Michael Parkin spoke with Professor Tobin about the challenges that face the economy.

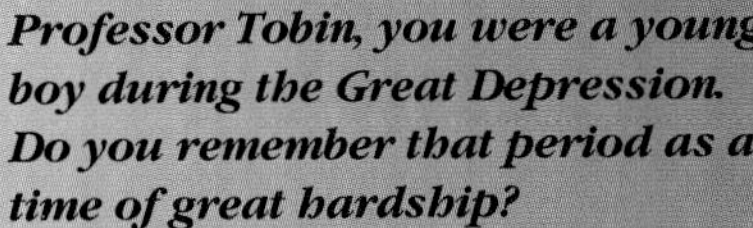

Professor Tobin, you were a young boy during the Great Depression. Do you remember that period as a time of great hardship?

Not of personal hardship, although my grandfather lost his job and his entire fortune when the bank of which he was president went under, and my father suffered serious losses when creditors took over the office building he had constructed in 1929. My father was a journalist at the University of Illinois. In 1932, my mother became the head of the local Family Service agency. Her job kept us aware of the ravages of the Depression. Our hometown, Champaign, Illinois was on the main rail line. Many poor people from the South, hoping for jobs and better lives in the North, got off the train in Champaign.

When did you first study economics?

As a Harvard sophomore in 1936. We met weekly with a tutor and discussed what we were reading or writing. My tutor was also my introductory economics teacher. He had just come back from a year in England, where he had heard a lot about a new book by John Maynard Keynes. He suggested that we read it. I was too green to understand that it was absurd for a sophomore to tackle *The General Theory of Employment, Interest, and Money.* So I plunged into it and got very excited about the book and about economics.

People usually refer to you as a Keynesian macroeconomist. Do you agree with that term?

I don't like labelling. I tried to contribute to economics, especially to macroeconomics. I tried to strengthen what we now call the microfoundations of macroeconomics. In the 1950s and 1960s we hoped that the Keynesian–Neoclassical controversy would soon be behind us, superseded by a synthesis of the two strands. Beginning with my first published article in 1940, which disagreed with Keynes about the relation between wages and employment, I wrote many pieces critical of *The General Theory*. Unfortunately, the old debates have been revived and magnified over the past two decades and we are far from a new synthesis. Today, if I have to be labelled — and considering the alternatives — I'm proud to be a Keynesian.

How would you characterize the controversy in macroeconomics? Has it stayed the same over the years, or is it different today?

The original controversy in the 1930s and 1940s was whether a capitalist market economy possesses reliable automatic mechanisms of adjustment, which would restore equilibrium between jobs and workers and between output and capacity whenever some shock to demand pushes the economy from full employment. Orthodox economists — Keynes called them Classical — said yes. Keynes said no. Today's New Classical macroeconomists are more extreme than their old Classical predecessors. They assert that the economy is *always* in full employment equilibrium. That the economy as a whole operates like a rational maximizing individual. Keynesians believe the economy can fall out of equilibrium and that government interventions can speed up recoveries.

'Today, if I have to be labelled — and considering the alternatives — I'm proud to be a Keynesian'

Given that macroeconomists still have important disagreements, can they use any of the same approaches? Might a Keynesian, for instance, use the idea of rational expectations, which is identified with the New Classical school?

Thoughtful economists of all sorts have long incorporated rational expectations in their models, to a limited degree. They would not postulate a stable, repetitive equilibrium that depended on expectations at odds with the actual values of variables. For example, if the interest rate is 2 per cent year after year, people would surely learn not to act on the expectation that it will become 4 per cent. But I think it stretches credibility to assume that ordinary business people and consumers can learn to form rational expectations in volatile economic environments whose structures even econometricians cannot discern.

I think rational expectations of

quantities like output and employment could have a place in Keynesian models. Those are important variables once the New Classical assumption that markets are always clearing is abandoned.

Many economists regard the macroeconomic performance of the early 1960s as a very successful period of moderate inflation, low unemployment and strong growth in real output. Was that the high point of macroeconomic management from which we've been sliding ever since?

Yes. I suppose I have a vested interest in believing that to be true — I helped to inaugurate the policy in 1961. And it was a pleasant period, when economists and policymakers were not as divided and combative as they are now. At the beginning of the Kennedy adminstration, unemployment was 7 per cent, considered unacceptably high in those days. Inflation was only 1 or 2 per cent, thanks in good part to the two recent Eisenhower recessions. We economists pushed for stimulative fiscal policy. We got some, but it took some time to bring President Kennedy and Congress to accept a major initiative. We were lucky when what looked like a hesitation in the recovery before our policies were firmly in place turned out to be temporary. The administration pursued a wage–price guidepost policy, seeking to get management and labour to agree to non-inflationary wage settlements and price decisions. By 1966 unemployment was down to 4 per cent and inflation was still around 2 per cent.

Were all the breaks good ones? Was there any bad luck?

The bad luck was the Vietnam War. Despite the advice of his Keynesian economists, President Johnson would not ask for a tax increase to finance his escalation of the war in 1966. His budget overheated the economy in the late 1960s. Unemployment fell to 3 per cent and inflation rose to 4 or 5 per cent. At the time, 5 per cent inflation was considered very serious, bad enough to induce President Nixon to introduce price controls. Today 5 per cent is accepted as 'zero' inflation, a reminder that attitudes are relative.

'It was a pleasant period, when economists and policymakers were not as divided as they are now'

What have we learned from the events of the 1970s?

Maybe what we should have learned is that those events were exceptional. There were two enormous shocks in oil and energy prices. A major increase in an important price raises the price index, but OPEC price shocks don't happen every year and shouldn't be incorporated into projections of overall inflation. What it was proper to worry about was the inflation potential of wage increases seeking to catch up with the increases in energy prices. The 1980s indicate that under normal circumstances, we experience less severe inflation.

We've just experienced seven years of economic recovery. How did economic policy contribute?

I give the Federal Reserve high marks for monetary policy since 1982. From October 1979 until 1982, the Fed was very monetarist. The overriding priority was to rid the economy of the temporary double-digit inflation that accompanied the second oil shock. Restrictive monetary policy and recession did bring it down to about 5 per cent. The strategy worked faster than I had expected — though not so fast as the optimists were suggesting. By 1982, unemployment reached its highest level since the Depression.

In 1982, Paul Volcker, the chairman of the Fed, turned both his policy and the economy around. Monetarism was displaced by concern for macroeconomic performance. The Fed fine-tuned the recovery, reducing unemployment as long as no new inflation threatened. By 1989 unemployment was down to 5 per cent, lower than the Fed and most economists thought 'inflation-safe' 10 years earlier.

Fiscal policy in the 1980s has been a radical departure from any previous federal administration in peacetime.

The tremendous reduction in taxes in 1981 along with the expansion of defence spending generated a series of deficits that raised federal public debt from 25 to 43 per cent of GNP over the eight years of the Reagan presidency.

Reagan's fiscal policy was a massive demand stimulus. The Fed had to worry about whether it would overheat the economy. It was like having two drivers in the same car. The fiscal driver had a heavy foot on the gas pedal. The monetary driver had to keep a foot on the brake. As I said, the Fed fine-tuned the brake quite well. But the by-products of this bizarre combination of policies have been disastrous — high interest rates, low capital investment, enormous trade deficits, threatening the living standards of future Americans.

'Students who understand the macro identities know more than most politicians and journalists'

What economic principles would you share with students?

First, opportunity cost — a simple, fruitful concept. Students can learn it; most people innocent of economics don't understand it. Second, fungibility — 'money mingles', a friend of mine liked to say. You can give people money, ostensibly for your own purpose, but the recipients will generally find a way to accommodate their own priorities. Third, economics students who understand the macro identities — for example, $Y = C + I + G + NX$ — know more than most politicians and journalists.

Chapter 22

Inflation, Cycles, Unemployment, Deficits and Surpluses

After studying this chapter, you will be able to:

- Define inflation and explain its effects.
- Define gross domestic product (GDP).
- Distinguish between nominal GDP and real GDP.
- Explain the importance of growth and fluctuations in real GDP.
- Define the business cycle.
- Define unemployment and explain its benefits and costs.
- Describe how unemployment, share prices and inflation fluctuate over the business cycle.
- Describe the balances on the government and international accounts.

Soon We Will All Be Millionaires

A litre of milk that cost 15 cents in 1955 now costs around $1. A loaf of bread costing 11 cents in 1955 now costs $1.25. The price of a modest car in 1955 was $2100; a similarly modest car today costs $15,000. Prices for most items have risen inexorably since the 1930s, the last time that prices actually fell. The same is true of wages. Average weekly earnings for male employees have risen from $31 in 1954 to $580 in 1991. If prices and wages continue to rise at the same rate over the next 35 years as they have done over the last 35 years the litre of milk will cost $5.77, the loaf of bread $14.20 and the modest car $107,142. The average weekly wage will be $10,271.60! We will all be millionaires, but will we be better off? What are the effects of persistently rising prices and wages? In 1991, for every nine people with jobs, one other person was unemployed, that is, looking for work but not finding it. Another unknown number of people had become discouraged about their chances of finding jobs and had stopped looking. Although unemployment has been unusually high through most of the 1980s, its level was modest compared with the 1930s — the years of the Great Depression. In the Depression's worst period, June 1931 to June 1932, nearly one-fifth of the labour force was unemployed. Unemployment fluctuates but it never disappears. At its lowest levels, in World War II, unemployment fell to just 1 per cent of the labour force. For most of the 1950s and 1960s, unemployment was under 2 per cent. And yet we do talk about 'full employment'. How can there be 'full employment' when there are people looking for work? Why is there always some unemployment? What are the costs of unemployment? At the depths of the Great Depression, in 1931/32, the value of all the goods and services produced in Australia was $1.2 billion. By 1990/91, 59 years later, the value of Australian output was $380 billion (more than 300 times its 1931/32 level). Between 1960/61 and 1990/91, the nation's output increased twenty-five-fold in value. How much of the growth in the value of our output is real and how much of it is an illusion created by inflation? Our economy does not follow a smooth and predictable course. From 1983 to 1987, the economy was on a course of sustained expansion: production grew, unemployment fell in all but one year, share prices rose and inflation was constant. Then, in October, 1987, the stock market crashed. Overnight, thousands of people found themselves poorer by millions of dollars. But the economy continued to expand until 1990. Production continued to grow and unemployment continued to fall. Expansions as strong and prolonged as that of the 1980s are unusual. Periods of expansion are usually punctuated by periods of contraction, which are sometimes severe ones. For example, 1982/83 and 1990/91 were such periods. In those years, production declined and unemployment rose rapidly. We call these waves of expansion and contraction business cycles. Which features of business cycles are similar from one cycle to another and which are different? Does the economy normally keep booming when the stock market crashes, as it did in 1987? Or do stock market crashes sometimes signal an upcoming contraction? We hear a lot these days about surpluses and deficits, particularly the government's surplus or deficit. Every year from 1970/71 to 1986/87, the Commonwealth government spent more than it raised in taxes — it ran a deficit. To cover the deficit, the government borrowed. Some of that borrowing was domestic and some was international. From 1987/88 to 1990/91 the government had a surplus. It used the surplus to retire past debt. But the recession of 1990/91 has led to a decline in the size of the surplus, and in 1991/92 a deficit re-emerged. How unusual is it for the government to have a surplus? Why does the size of the deficit or surplus vary with booms and recessions? Another deficit we hear a lot about is our international deficit — the value of the goods and services we buy from the rest of the world plus transfers (interest payments on foreign investment and foreign aid) we make less the goods and services we sell to the rest of the world. Every year since 1984/85 that deficit has exceeded $10 billion dollars a year. In 1989/90 it reached $22 billion (6 per cent of total output) but in 1990/91 it fell to $15 billion (4 per cent of total output). What happens when we spend more in the rest of the world than we earn? How do we make up the difference? And what are the consequences? The questions that we have just posed are the subject matter of macroeconomics — that branch of economics that seeks to understand the problems of rising prices, unemployment, fluctuating output, and government and international surpluses and deficits. It also studies the government's attempts to cope with these problems. The macroeconomic events through which we are now living are as exciting and tumultuous as any in history. Governments in Australia and around the world face a daily challenge to find policies that will give all of us a smoother macroeconomic ride.

With what you learn in these chapters, you will be better able to understand these macroeconomic policy challenges and the political debate that surrounds them. We begin our study of macroeconomics by looking at inflation.

Inflation

Inflation is an upward movement in the average level of prices. Its opposite is **deflation**, a downward movement in the average level of prices. Between inflation and deflation is price stability. **Price stability** occurs when the average level of prices is moving neither up nor down. The average level of prices is called the **price level** and is measured by a price index. A **price index** measures the average level of prices in one period as a percentage of their average level in an earlier period called the **base period.**

Price indexes in Australia go all the way back to Federation, and the story they tell is shown in Fig. 22.1. Over the 90-year period shown in that figure, prices have risen fifty-fold — an average annual rate of increase of 4.5 per cent. But prices have not moved upward at a constant and steady pace. In some periods, such as World War I, the Korean War and the years between 1973 and 1978, the increase was sharp and pronounced, exceeding 10 per cent a year in all of those years. At the opposite extreme are years in which prices have fallen. The last occasion on which this occurred in a sustained way was during the Great Depression of the 1930s, when prices fell steadily for a five-year period. Prices also fell in the early 1920s.

Perhaps the most striking fact revealed by Fig. 22.1 is the recent experience of high and *persistent* inflation. It took nearly forty years from 1900/01 for the price level to double. Because of the effects of

Figure 22.1 The Price Level, 1900/01–1990/91

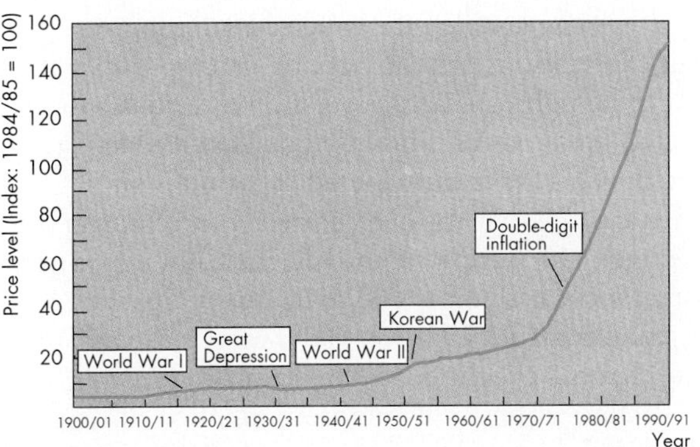

On average, prices have increased fifty-fold between 1900/01 and 1990/91. In some periods, such as World War I, the Korean War and the 1970s, price increases were rapid. In other periods, such as the 1950s and 1960s, increases were more moderate. At yet other times prices fell, such as in the early 1920s and the Great Depression years of the 1930s.

Sources: GDP deflator 1900/01 to 1947/48: M.W. Butlin, *A Preliminary Annual Data Base 1900/01 to 1973/74*, Reserve Bank of Australia, Research Discussion Paper 7701, May 1977; 1948/49 to 1991: Series NOQA.UD85_GDP, ABS Time Series Service, supplied by EconData's dX Data Service.

World War II, it took just twelve years to double again. But then the rate of inflation slowed and it took twenty years, over the 1950s and 1960s, for the price level to double again. Over the 1970s, however, the price level nearly trebled and over the 1980s it doubled again. The average annual rate of increase in prices over the last twenty years has been nearly 10 per cent (which means that the price level doubles every seven years).

Inflation Rate and the Price Level

The **inflation rate** is the percentage change in the price level. The formula for the annual inflation rate is

$$\text{Inflation rate} = \frac{\text{Current year's price level} - \text{Last year's price level}}{\text{Last year's price level}} \times 100$$

A common price index (one we'll learn more about in Chapter 23) is called the Consumer Price Index or simply the CPI. We can illustrate the calculation of the annual inflation rate by using this index. In June 1990, the CPI was 207.4 and in June 1991, it was 214.4. The inflation rate for 1990/91 is calculated using the above formula:

$$\text{Inflation rate} = \frac{214.4 - 207.4}{207.4} \times 100$$

$$= 3.4 \text{ per cent}$$

The Recent Inflation Record

Recent Australian economic history has seen some dramatic changes in the rate of inflation. The inflation rate between 1950/51 and 1990/91, as measured by the CPI, is shown in Fig. 22.2.

As you can see, the inflation rate was very high during the Korean War in the early 1950s. It settled down at a low and relatively constant rate for the second half of the 1950s and throughout the 1960s. In the early 1970s the inflation rate edged up, getting a major boost in 1973 from the first OPEC oil price

Figure 22.2 Inflation, 1950/51–1990/91

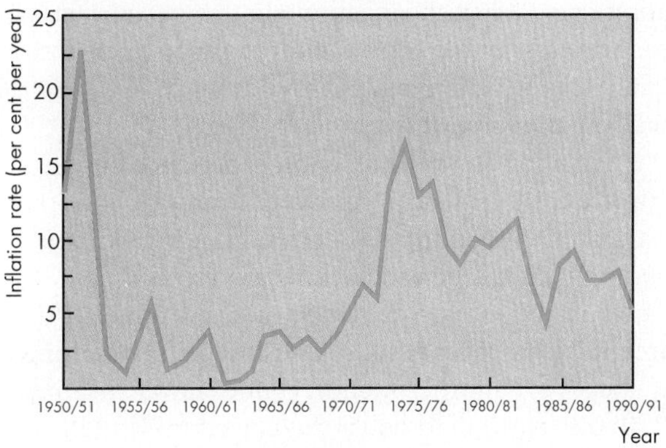

Inflation is a persistent feature of modern economic life in Australia. The inflation rate was very high during the Korean war. Inflation was low over the second half of the 1950s and throughout the 1960s. It began to edge up in the early 1970s, increasing rapidly following the first OPEC oil price shock in 1973. Inflation peaked at nearly 17 per cent in the year 1974/75, falling thereafter. It remained at a stubbornly persistent 7–8 per cent a year during the 1980s, but fell under the impact of the 1990/91 recession.

Sources: Consumer Price Index, 1950/51 to 1980/81: W.E. Norton and C.P. Aylmer, *Australian Economic Statistics*, Occasional Paper No. 8A, Reserve Bank of Australia; 1980/81 to 1990/91: Series RJDQ.V181 SM01 000A, ABS Time Series Service, supplied by EconData's dX Data Service.

shock. Although the inflation rate fell rapidly in the mid-1970s it stubbornly remained at the relatively high rate of 7–8 per cent over the 1980s. Under the impact of the recession, the rate of inflation did fall in 1990/91, just as it did in 1984/85.

Although the inflation rate has gone up and down over the years, since 1945 the price level has never fallen. The inflation rate has fallen from time to time, but the price level (see Fig. 22.1) has increased relentlessly, year after year. The price level falls only when the inflation rate is negative or less than zero. There has not been such a year in the period since 1945. Thus even in the year 1962/63, when the inflation rate was low (only 0.2 per cent), the price level was rising.

Inflation and the Value of Money

When inflation is present, money is losing value. The **value of money** is the amount of goods and services that can be bought with a given amount of money. When an economy experiences inflation, the value of money falls. In other words, you cannot buy as many groceries with $50 this year as you could last year. The rate at which the value of money falls is equal to the inflation rate. When the inflation rate is high, as it has been throughout the 1980s, money loses its value at a rapid pace. When inflation is low, as it was in 1962/63, the value of money falls slowly.

Inflation is a phenomenon experienced in all countries. But inflation *rates* vary from one country to another. When inflation rates differ by a lot and over a prolonged period of time, the result is a change in the foreign exchange value of money. A **foreign exchange rate** is the rate at which one money exchanges for another money. For example, in mid-1990, one Australian dollar exchanged for 75 US cents (US$0.75). Sixteen years earlier, in mid-1974, one Australian dollar exchanged for nearly 150 US cents (US$1.4875). Thus, since 1974, the value of the Australian dollar has halved in terms of the US dollar. This performance reflects the fact that the value of money in Australia has been falling more quickly than the value of money in the United States. We'll learn more about exchange rates and how they are influenced by inflation in Chapter 36.

Is Inflation a Problem?

Is it a problem if money loses its value and at a rate that varies from one year to another? It is, indeed, a problem, but to understand why, we need to distinguish between anticipated and unanticipated inflation. When prices are moving upward, most people are aware of that fact. They also have some notion about the rate at which they are rising. The rate at which people (on the average) believe that the price level will rise is called the **expected inflation rate**. But expectations may be right or wrong. If they turn out to be right, the actual inflation rate equals the expected inflation rate and inflation is said to be anticipated. That is, an **anticipated inflation** is an inflation rate that has been correctly forecast (on the average). To the extent that the inflation rate is not forecast correctly, it is said to be unanticipated. That is, **unanticipated inflation** is the part of the inflation rate that has caught people by surprise.

The problems arising from inflation differ depending on whether its rate is anticipated or unanticipated. Let's begin by looking at the problems arising from unanticipated inflation.

The Problem of Unanticipated Inflation

Unanticipated inflation is a problem because it produces unanticipated changes in the value of money. Money is used as the measuring rod of value in transactions that we undertake. Borrowers and lenders and workers and their employers all make contracts in terms of money. If the value of money varies, then the amounts *really* paid and received differ from those that people intended to pay and receive when they signed the contract. Measuring value with a measuring rod whose units vary is rather like trying to measure a piece of cloth with an elastic ruler. The size of the cloth depends on how tightly the ruler is stretched.

Let's take a look at the effects of unanticipated inflation by looking at what happens to agreements between borrowers and lenders and between workers and employers.

Borrowers and Lenders People often say that inflation is good for borrowers and bad for lenders. To see how that conclusion is reached — and also to see why it's not always correct — consider the following situation.

Sue borrows $5000 from the bank to buy a car and agrees to repay the loan with interest one year later. The agreed interest rate is 10 per cent a year. Sue repays the bank $5500 after one year.

Suppose that there is no inflation. The goods and services that can be bought with $5000 are the same after one year as they are when Sue borrows the money. In this situation, to pay the bank $500 in interest, Sue has to forgo the consumption of $500 worth of goods and services.

Now, in contrast, suppose that the economy is experiencing inflation at a rate of 10 per cent a year. In this case, when the loan is repaid with interest, although the bank receives $5500, the quantity of goods and services that it can buy with that money is exactly what it could have bought with $5000 a year earlier. (With a 10 per cent inflation rate, the price of a car, for example, will have risen from $5000 to $5500.) As far as Sue is concerned, although she pays the bank $500 in interest, that payment does not impose an opportunity cost on her. Over the year, the value of money has fallen. The $5000 that she borrowed is now worth only $4500 in terms of goods and services. This fall in the value of money cancels out the interest payment and leaves her having *really* paid no interest at all. Sue, the borrower, gains at the expense of the bank, the lender.

But the borrower does not always necessarily gain and the lender lose when there is inflation. Suppose that both Sue and the bank anticipate a 10 per cent inflation rate. They can act to offset the decreasing value of money by adjusting the interest rate that they agree upon. In this particular case, if they agree that 10 per cent is the appropriate interest rate with no inflation, they will agree to a 20 per cent interest rate when they expect a 10 per cent inflation rate. Let's see what happens in this case.

Sue repays the bank $6000 at the end of the year. Of this, $5000 is the repayment of the amount borrowed and $1000 (20 per cent of $5000) is the interest payment. Of the additional $1000 that Sue repays the bank, $500 is interest and the other $500 is compensation for the loss in the value of money. Sue *really* pays a 10 per cent interest rate and that's what the bank *really* receives.

If borrowers and lenders correctly anticipate the inflation rate, interest rates will be adjusted to cancel out inflation's effect on the interest *really* paid and *really* received. It is only when borrowers and lenders make errors in forecasting the future inflation rate that one of them gains and the other loses. But those gains and losses can go either way. If the inflation rate turns out to be higher than is generally expected, then the borrower gains and the lender loses. Conversely, if the inflation rate turns out to be lower than is generally expected, then the borrower loses and the lender gains.

Thus it is not inflation itself that produces gains and losses for borrowers and lenders. It is an *unanticipated increase* in the *inflation rate* that *benefits borrowers* and hurts lenders and an *unanticipated decrease* in the *inflation rate* that *benefits lenders* and hurts borrowers.

In Australia in the late 1960s and throughout the 1970s, the inflation rate kept rising and to some degree the rise was unanticipated, so borrowers tended to gain. In the 1980s, the inflation rate has been relatively constant and, therefore, anticipated. Neither lenders nor borrowers gain. On the international scene, many developing countries, such as Mexico and Brazil, borrowed large amounts of money in the late 1970s and early 1980s at high interest rates, in anticipation that an inflation rate of over 10 per cent a year would persist. These countries are now stuck with paying the interest on these loans without the extra revenue that they expected to receive from the higher prices for their exports.

Workers and Employers Another common belief is that inflation redistributes income between workers and their employers. Some people believe that workers gain at the expense of employers and others believe the contrary.

The previous discussion concerning borrowers and lenders applies to workers and their employers as well. If inflation increases unexpectedly, then wages will not have been set high enough. Profits are higher than expected and wages buy fewer goods than expected. Employers gain at the expense of workers. Conversely, if the anticipated inflation rate is higher than the actual inflation rate, wages will have been set too high and profits are squeezed. Workers are able to buy more with their income than was originally anticipated. In this case workers gain at the expense of employers.

During the 1960s and most of the 1970s, wages tended to grow faster than prices in Australia. In 1974/75, a year with extreme wage and price changes, wages grew by more than 25 per cent, while the CPI rose by less than 17 per cent. The buying power of earnings increased significantly as wages grew faster than anticipated changes in the inflation rate. However, with the advent of the Wages Accord, the rate of inflation has tended to exceed the amount expected and the buying power of earnings has actually declined over the last six years.

We've now seen the problems that unanticipated inflation can bring. Let's now turn to anticipated inflation.

The Problem of Anticipated Inflation

At low inflation rates, anticipated inflation is not considered by many economists to be much of a problem. But it becomes a serious problem when the anticipated inflation rate is extremely high.

At very high inflation rates, people know that money is losing value quickly. The rate at which money is losing value is part of the *opportunity cost* of holding on to money. The higher that opportunity cost, the smaller the amount of money people will want to hold. Instead of having a wallet full of banknotes and a large cheque account balance, people go shopping. They spend their incomes as soon as they are received and before they can lose value. The same is true for firms. Instead of hanging on to money they receive from the sale of their goods and services, they pay it out in wages as quickly as possible. High inflation rates thus induce people to increase the volume and frequency of their transactions. Transacting more often is less convenient and more costly than transacting less often.

In Germany, Poland, Austria and Hungary, in the 1920s, inflation rates reached extraordinary heights — often in excess of 50 per cent a month. In one extreme example, between the months of September and October 1921, wholesale prices in Germany rose by over 2400 per cent. Such high inflation rates are called **hyperinflations**. At the height of these hyperinflations, firms paid out wages twice a day and, as soon as they had been paid, workers rushed off to spend their wages before they lost too much value. To buy a handful of groceries, they needed a shopping trolley of bank notes. People who lingered too long in the coffee shop found that the price of their cup of coffee had increased between the time they placed their order and the time the bill was presented. With prices rising so rapidly, considerable quantities of resources were expended by sellers of goods and services just in changing prices of marked items and in maintaining up-to-date advertising. These costs are known today as 'menu costs'.

Such anticipated inflations brought economic chaos and disruption. Australia has never experienced inflations of that order. However, there is considerable disagreement today over just how much cost is associated with even the moderate levels of inflation experienced in Australia over the 1980s.

Indexing

It is sometimes suggested that the costs of inflation can be avoided by indexing. **Indexing** is a technique that links payments made under a contract to the price level. With indexing, Sue in our example above would not agree to pay back the car loan in terms of a set number of dollars; instead, she would agree to an indexing formula for calculating the number of dollars to pay. Similarly, with indexed wages a wage contract does not specify the number of dollars that will be paid to workers; instead, it specifies an indexing formula for calculating the number of dollars. These formulas take into account the inflation rate.

The amount of interest to be paid on bank deposits can also be linked to the inflation rate in order to avoid the opportunity cost of holding such deposits. Indexing is thought likely to be most important in preserving the buying power of pensions or other fixed incomes. Indexing is also used to limit the effects of inflation on long-term loans that people take to buy homes.

Adopting indexing to cope with changes in the value of money is not a simple matter for, as we will see in Chapter 23, there isn't a unique measure of the price level and, therefore, of the inflation rate. If borrowers and lenders and workers and employers are to index their contracts, they have to agree on the price index to be used to measure the inflation rate. Such agreements are hard to reach and increase the cost of engaging in transactions. Consequently, we see very few examples of indexation in our daily transactions.

R E V I E W

Inflation is an upward movement in the average level of prices and is measured as the percentage change in a price index. The inflation rate has risen and fallen since the 1930s, but the *price level* has only moved upward. The effects of inflation depend on whether it is unanticipated or anticipated. An unanticipated increase in the inflation rate benefits borrowers and hurts lenders, and an unanticipated decrease in the inflation rate benefits lenders and hurts borrowers. Anticipated inflation only becomes a serious problem when the inflation rate is extremely high. At such times, people spend money as soon as they receive it and there is a severe disruption of economic life. Indexing may reduce the costs of inflation but is costly to implement. ■

Gross Domestic Product

The value of all the final goods and services produced in the economy in a year is called **gross domestic product** or GDP. **Final goods and services** are goods and services that are not used as inputs in the production of other goods and services, but are bought by their final user. Such goods include consumption goods and services, and also new durable goods. Examples of final goods are cans of soft drink and cars. Examples of final services are motor vehicle insurance and haircuts.

Not all goods and services are 'final'. Some are called intermediate goods and services. **Intermediate goods and services** are those used as inputs into the production process of another good or service. Examples of intermediate goods are the windscreens, batteries and gearboxes used by car producers, and the paper and ink used by newspaper manufacturers. Examples of intermediate services are the banking and insurance services bought by car producers and news printers. Whether a good or service is intermediate or final depends on who buys it and for what purpose. For example, electric power purchased by a car producer or a printer is an intermediate good. Electric power bought by you is a final good.

When we measure gross domestic product, we do not include the value of intermediate goods and services produced. If we did, we would be counting the same thing more than once. When someone buys a new car from the local Ford dealer, that is a final transaction and the value of the car is counted as part of GDP. But we must not also count as part of GDP the amount paid by the dealer to Ford for the car or the amount paid by Ford to all its suppliers for the car's various parts.

If we want to measure GDP, we somehow have to add together all the final goods and services produced. Obviously, we can't achieve a useful measure by simply adding together the number of cars, newspapers, kilowatts of electric power, haircuts and motor vehicle insurance policies. To determine GDP, we first calculate the dollar *value* of the output of each final good or service. This calculation simply involves multiplying the quantity produced of each final good or service by its price. That is, we measure the output of each good and service in the common unit of dollars. We then add up the dollar values of the outputs of the different goods to arrive at their total value, which is GDP.

We measure GDP in dollars, but it is a mixture of real quantities — the numbers of final goods and services produced — and dollar quantities — the prices of the goods and services. A change in GDP, therefore, contains a mixture of the effects of changes in prices and changes in the quantities of final goods and services. For many purposes, it is important to distinguish price changes from quantity changes. To do so, we use the concepts of nominal GDP and real GDP. Let's examine these concepts.

Nominal GDP and Real GDP

Nominal GDP measures the value of the output of final goods and services using *current* prices. It is sometimes called *current dollar GDP*. **Real GDP** measures the value of the output of final goods and services using the prices that prevailed in some base period. An alternative name for real GDP is *constant dollar GDP*. Each measure refers to a specific time period, often a year, but sometimes a quarter (three months).

Comparing real GDP from one year to another enables us to say whether the economy has produced more or fewer goods and services. Comparing nominal GDP from one year to another does not permit us to compare the quantities of goods and services produced in those two years. Nominal GDP may be higher in 1990 than 1989, but that might reflect only higher prices, not more production.

The importance of the distinction between real GDP and nominal GDP is illustrated in Fig. 22.3. Real GDP is shown by the red area and nominal GDP is shown by the sum of the red and the green areas. The green area shows the inflation component of nominal GDP. In 1970/71, nominal GDP was $35 billion. By 1990/91, it had grown to $380 billion. But only part of that increase represents an increase in goods and services available — an increase in real GDP. Nominal GDP increased every year, but on two occasions — in 1982/83 and again in 1990/91 — the real component of GDP declined.

Real GDP — the Record

Estimates of real GDP in Australia go back to the 1860s. Figure 22.4 illustrates the record of real GDP since Federation. Two facts stand out. First, there is a general tendency for real GDP to increase. Second, the rate of upward movement is not uniform and sometimes real GDP actually declines. Precipitous declines have occurred in the early and later stages of World War I, the late 1920s, the early 1930s during the Great Depression and during and after World War II. More recently a decline occurred during the worldwide recession of the early 1980s. There were also periods in which real GDP grew extremely quickly — for example, the years before World Wars I and II.

In order to obtain a clearer picture of the changes in real GDP we'll consider separately the two general tendencies just identified:

- Trend real GDP
- Growth rate in real GDP

Figure 22.3 Gross Domestic Product, 1970/71–1990/91

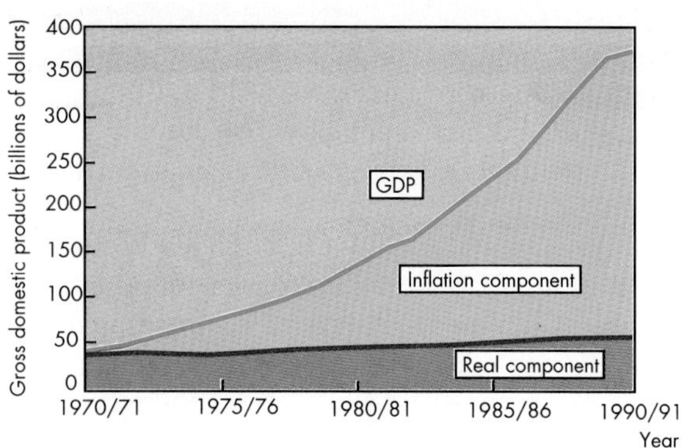

Gross domestic product increased more than ten-fold between 1970/71 and 1990/91. But much of that increase was the result of inflation. Real GDP, the increase in nominal GDP attributable to the increase in the volume of goods and services produced, has also increased but at a more modest pace. The figure shows how real GDP and the inflation components of nominal GDP have evolved. Nominal GDP has increased in every year, but real GDP fell in 1982/83 and in 1990/91.

Source: Gross Domestic Product: Series NODQ.UC_GDP, ABS Time Series Service, supplied by EconData's dX Data Service.

Trend real GDP is a measure of the general upward tendency or drift of real GDP that ignores its fluctuations. Trend real GDP rises for four reasons:

- Growing population
- Growing stock of capital equipment
- Growing stock of human capital
- Advancing technology

These forces have produced the general upward tendency that you can see in Fig. 22.4. Trend GDP is illustrated in Fig. 22.4 as a thin black line passing through the middle of the path actually followed by real GDP in its meanderings above trend (blue areas) and below trend (red areas).

The departures of real GDP from its trend are a measure of economic fluctuations. Another, more common, measure of economic fluctuations is the rate of growth of real GDP (annual percentage change). These growth rates appear in Fig. 22.5. As you can see, real GDP growth shows distinct cycles in economic activity that correspond to recession and depression events, and wartimes. Prior to both World War I and World War II real GDP grew very strongly. In the latter stages of and immediately after both wars, real GDP fell. Other major recessionary events are clearly identifiable in Fig. 22.5: the Great Depression, the post-Korean War recession and, more recently, the recessions of 1982/83 and 1990/91. A significant slow-down in the growth rate is evident following the oil price rises of the 1970s.

An interesting characteristic portrayed in Fig. 22.5 is the reduction in the magnitude of fluctuations in the entire period following World War II. Whether or not this change in the behaviour of real GDP was determined by the world economic environment or was the result of conscious policy choices by the Australian government is a matter of current debate.

The Importance of Real GDP

The upward trend in real GDP is the major source of improvements in living standards. The pace of this upward movement has a powerful effect on the stand-

Figure 22.4 Real GDP, 1900/01–1990/91

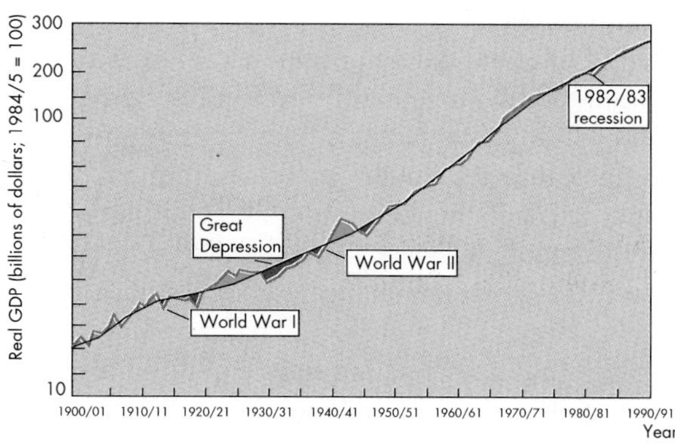

Real GDP has grown at an average rate of 3.3 per cent per year between 1900/01 and 1990/91. But the growth rate has not been the same in each year. In some periods, such as the years before World War I and World War II, real GDP expanded rapidly. In other periods, such as the Great Depression and, more recently, the recession of the early 1980s, real GDP declined. The general tendency of real GDP to increase is illustrated by trend real GDP.

Source: See Fig. 22.1.

Figure 22.5 Real GDP — Annual Growth Rate, 1900/01–1990/91

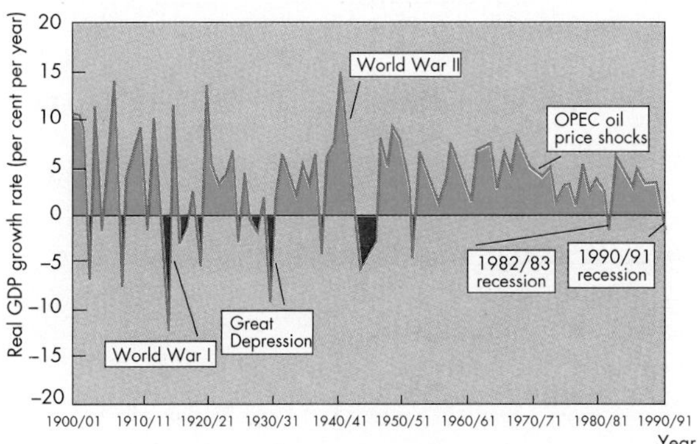

The uneven pace of increase of real GDP is illustrated by tracking the growth rate of real GDP. Rapid expansion of GDP occurred prior to World Wars I and II and during the late 1960s. Rapid contractions occurred following both Wars, during the Great Depression, in 1982/83 and in 1990/91. A significant slowdown in average growth rates occurred following the OPEC oil price shocks in the 1970s.

Source: See Fig. 22.1.

ard of living of one generation compared with its predecessor. For example, if real GDP trends upward at 1 per cent a year, it takes 70 years for real GDP to double. But with a trend of 10 per cent a year, real GDP doubles in just seven years. The Chinese and Korean economies were growing at that rate over the 1980s. Thailand and Singapore also grew at that rate in the late 1980s. With an average trend of 3.3 per cent a year, which Australia has achieved over the 90-year period shown in Fig. 22.5, real GDP doubles approximately every 22 years.

But an upward trend in real GDP has its costs. The more quickly we increase real GDP, the faster we deplete exhaustible resources such as oil and natural gas, and the more severe our environmental and atmospheric pollution problems become. Furthermore, the more quickly real GDP increases, the more we have to accept change, both in what we consume and in the jobs that we do. But increases in real GDP also bring benefits in the form of a greater volume and variety of consumption goods. These benefits have to be balanced against the costs. The choices that people make to balance these benefits and costs, acting individually and through government institutions, determine the actual pace at which real GDP increases.

As we have seen, real GDP does not increase at an even pace. In some years the economy booms and in other years it busts. Are the fluctuations in real GDP important? This question is a hard one to answer and one on which economists disagree. Some economists believe that fluctuations are costly and that when real GDP is below trend GDP, output is lost, and when real GDP is above trend GDP, bottlenecks and shortages arise. With output below trend, unemployment is high and the economy's stock of capital equipment is underused. If a downturn in real GDP can be avoided, average income and consumption levels can be increased. If large fluctuations above trend GDP can be controlled, shortages and bottlenecks can be avoided and inflation better kept in check.

An alternative view is that most of the fluctuations in real GDP represent the best possible response to the uneven pace of technological change. At times when technological progress is rapid, capital accumulation is also rapid, so total production increases as more new-technology capital is produced. Once a boom, which is driven by the exploitation of new technologies, has run its course, the economy temporarily drops into low gear, ready to accelerate with the next burst of technological progress and innovation. Since we are not able to order the pace of new technology to be smooth, we are only able to smooth the pace of economic growth by delaying the implementation of new technologies. Such delays would result in never-to-be-recovered waste.

Regardless of which position economists take, they all agree that depressions as deep and long as that which occurred in the early 1930s result in extraordinary waste and human suffering. The disagreements concern the more common and gentler ebbs and flows of economic activity that have occurred in the years since World War II, as we saw in Fig. 22.5.

Let's now take a more systematic look at the ebbs and flows of economic activity.

The Business Cycle

The **business cycle** is the periodic but irregular up and down movement in economic activity measured by fluctuations in real GDP and other macroeconomic variables. To identify the business cycle we focus our attention on the growth rate of real GDP since this variable gives a direct measure of the uneven pace of economic activity. A business cycle is not a regular, predictable or repeating phenomenon like the swings of the pendulum of a clock. Its timing is random and, to a large degree, unpredictable.

A business cycle is identified as a sequence of four phases:

- Contraction
- Trough
- Expansion
- Peak

These four phases are shown for three complete cycles in Fig. 22.6. This figure shows the growth rate of real GDP during the 1980s. Notice the four phases of the cycle. A **contraction** is a slow-down in the pace of economic activity, such as occurred between 1980/81 and 1982/83 or between 1987/88 and 1990/91. An **expansion** is a speed-up in the pace of economic activity, such as occurred between 1982/83 and 1983/84. A **trough** is the lower turning point of a business cycle, where a contraction turns into an expansion. Troughs occurred in 1982/83, 1986/87 and 1990/91. A **peak** is the upper turning point of a business cycle, where an expansion turns into a contraction. Peaks occurred in 1980/81, 1983/84 and 1987/88.

A recession occurs if a contraction is severe enough. A **recession** is a downturn in the level of economic activity, in which real GDP declines in *two successive quarters*. A deep trough is called a slump or a **depression.**

A characteristic of recessions and depressions is rising unemployment. Let's now look at the meaning of unemployment.

Figure 22.6 The Business Cycle

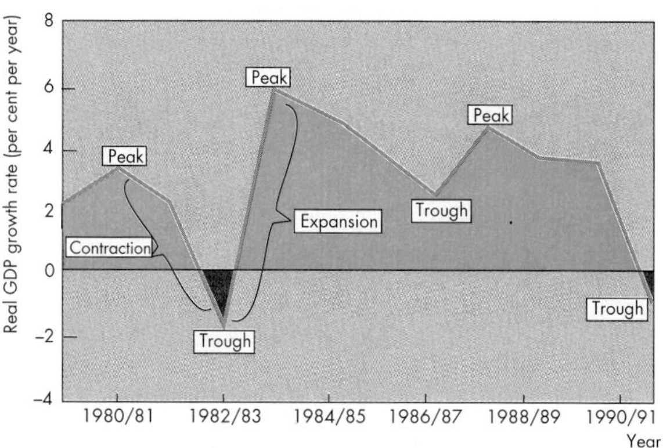

The business cycle has four phases: contraction, trough, expansion and peak. The experiences of the 1980s illustrate these phases.

Source: See Fig. 22.1.

Unemployment

At many times in Australia's history, unemployment has been a severe problem. For example, in February 1983, more than 750,000 people were seeking jobs. By November 1989, the number unemployed had fallen to fewer than 450,000. But by mid-1991 it had risen again to 850,000. What exactly is unemployment? How is it measured? How has its rate fluctuated? Are there different types of unemployment? What are the costs of unemployment?

What is Unemployment?

Each person over the age of 15 falls into one of three categories:

- Employed
- Unemployed
- Not in the labour force

Employment is measured as the number of adult workers (aged 15 and over) who have jobs. That is, the number of persons (15 and over) who worked for one hour or more, in the previous reference period; for pay, profit or commission; for themselves or somebody else. **Unemployment** is measured as the number of adult workers who are not employed and who are seeking jobs. To be classified as unemployed, a person must be able and willing to work, be actively seeking work and be without a job. Everyone who fits this description is unemployed. The **labour force** is the total number of employed and unemployed workers. The **unemployment rate** is unemployment expressed as a percentage of the labour force.

Measuring Unemployment

Unemployment is measured in Australia every month from the labour force survey section of the monthly population survey. The results of the survey appear in a publication of the Australian Bureau of Statistics called *The Labour Force.* This survey is used as the basis for the unemployment figures reported monthly in the news media.

To be counted as unemployed by the labour force survey, a person must be available for work and be in one of the following three categories:

1 Without work, but have made specific efforts to find a job within the previous 4 weeks
2 Waiting to be called back to a job from which he or she has been laid off for less than 4 weeks
3 Waiting to start a new job within the next 4 weeks and would have started in the reference period if the job had been available

Anyone surveyed who satisfies one of these three criteria is counted as unemployed. Part-time workers are counted as employed.

There are three reasons why the unemployment level as measured by the labour force survey may be misleading. Let's examine these.

Unrealistic Wage Expectations If someone is willing to work but only for a much higher wage than what is available, it does not make sense to count that person as unemployed. That is, if someone says that he or she is willing to work at McDonald's, but only for $30 an hour, then that person is not really available for work. From the way the statistics are collected, however, that person would be counted as unemployed.

Correcting the unemployment data to take account of wage and job expectations would result in a lower measured unemployment rate. But how much lower we do not know. A second factor works in the opposite direction.

Discouraged Workers Many people who fail to find a suitable job after prolonged and extensive search effort come to believe that there is no work available for them. They become discouraged and stop looking for work. Such people are called discouraged workers or the hidden unemployed. **Discouraged workers** are people who do not have jobs and would like work, but have stopped seeking work. Discouraged workers are not counted as unemployed by the labour force survey because they have not actively sought work within the previous 4 weeks. If discouraged workers were added to the unemployment count, the unemployment rate would be higher than the one currently measured. For example, recent estimates by Bruce Chapman, a labour economist at the Australian National University, suggest that including discouraged workers might increase measured unemployment rates by as much as 50 per cent in some years.[1]

Part-Time Workers As we have noted, part-time workers are counted as employed. But many part-time workers are available for and seek full-time work. The measured unemployment rate does not capture this element of part-time unemployment. This source of unemployment is a potentially important one.

The Unemployment Record

The Australian unemployment record since 1900/01 is set out in Fig. 22.7. The dominant feature of that record is the Great Depression in the early 1930s. During that episode of our history, almost 20 per cent of the labour force was unemployed. In recent years we have not experienced anything as devastating as the Great Depression although we have experienced periods of high unemployment rates. Two such periods are the early 1990s, when there was a sharp rise in unemployment, and the late 1970s and early 1980s, when there was a steady, persistent rise in unemployment. There have also been periods of low unemployment. The most extreme such period was from the early 1940s to the early 1970s when unemployment often fell to just 1 per cent of the workforce. The average unemployment rate over the 90-year period from 1900/01 to 1990/91 has been 5.1 per cent.

Unemployment is a highly charged topic. We chart the course of the unemployment rate as a measure of Australia's economic health with the intensity that a physician keeps track of a patient's temperature. What does the unemployment rate tell us about the economic health of the nation? Is a high unemployment rate a sign of economic ill-health? Let's address these questions by looking at the reasons why we experience unemployment.

Types of Unemployment

There are three types of unemployment:

- Frictional
- Structural
- Cyclical

Frictional Unemployment People are constantly changing their economic activities. Young people leave school and join the labour force. Old people leave the labour force and retire. People sometimes

[1] See Bruce Chapman, 'The Labour Market' in Stephen Grenville (ed.), *The Australian Macro-economy in the 1980s*. Reserve Bank of Australia, Sydney, 1990.

Figure 22.7 Unemployment, 1900/01–1990/91

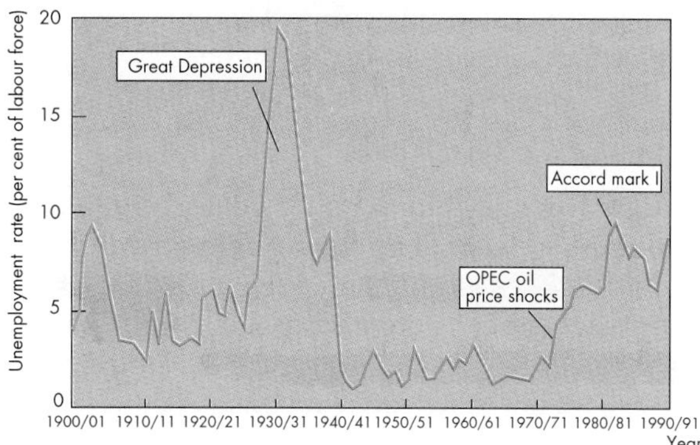

Unemployment is a persistent feature of economic life, but its rate varies considerably. At its worst — during the Great Depression — close to 20 per cent of the labour force was unemployed. Even in the most recent recessions, the unemployment rate climbed to over 10 per cent. From the early 1970s through to the early 1980s there was a general tendency for the unemployment rate to increase. From 1982/83 to 1989/90 the unemployment rate gradually decreased.

Sources: Unemployment rate: 1900/01 to 1958/59: M.W. Butlin, *A Preliminary Annual Data Base 1900/01 to 1973/74*, Reserve Bank Discussion Paper 7701, May 1977; 1959/60 to 1990/91: Series VNEQ.AN_RNV, NIF-10S Model Data, supplied by EconData's dX Data Service.

leave the labour force temporarily, perhaps to raise children or for some other reason, and then rejoin it. The fortunes of businesses are also constantly changing. Some are closing down and laying off their workers. At the same time, new firms are starting up and hiring workers.

This constant change results in unemployment. People don't usually take the first job that comes their way. Instead, they spend time searching out what they believe will be the best job available to them. By doing so, they can match their own skills and interests with the available jobs and find a satisfying job and income. Unemployment arising from this source is called frictional. That is, **frictional unemployment** is the unemployment arising from normal labour market turnover.

It is unlikely that frictional unemployment will ever disappear. The amount of frictional unemployment depends on the rate at which people enter and leave the labour force and on the rate at which jobs are created and destroyed. These factors in turn depend on the age, sex and occupational composition of the labour force and on the rate of technological change. The amount of time that people take to find a job is influenced by unemployment compensation. The more generous the rate of unemployment benefit, the longer the average time taken in job search and the higher is the rate of frictional unemployment.

Structural Unemployment Our economy is dynamic and ever-changing. Production and consumption change as new technologies are developed and exploited. Often such technological advance creates jobs in some industries and regions, and destroys jobs in others. The rapid expansion of jobs in the high-tech, computer-oriented sectors and the loss of jobs in traditional sectors such as cars and steel are important recent examples of this effect of technological change. Industries are sometimes concentrated in particular regions. Thus the decline of an industry can mean the decline of a region. **Structural unemployment** is the unemployment that results when industry concentrated in a particular region declines. The amount of structural unemployment varies and depends on the precise nature and regional concentration of technological change.

Cyclical Unemployment Our economy fluctuates, expanding quickly at some times and more slowly at others. It even shrinks on occasion. **Cyclical unemployment** is unemployment arising from a slow-down in the pace of economic expansion.

Measuring frictional, structural and cyclical unemployment and distinguishing one type of unemployment from another is controversial. It is not possible to provide a quantitative breakdown of the three types of unemployment.

Full Employment

At any given time, there are people looking for work and firms looking for people to employ — there are unemployed people and job vacancies. **Full employment** is a state in which the quantity of labour demanded equals the quantity of labour supplied. The unemployment rate at full employment is called the **natural rate of unemployment.** The natural rate of unemployment fluctuates because of fluctuations in frictional and structural unemployment.

There is controversy about the magnitude of the natural unemployment rate. Some economists believe that the natural rate of unemployment in Australia is between 5 and 6 per cent of the labour force.

Other economists believe that not only does the natural rate of unemployment vary but that it can be quite high, especially at times when demographic and technological factors point to a high frictional and structural unemployment rate.

The magnitude of the natural unemployment rate is a controversial and sometimes emotional issue because it is generally accepted that unemployment can be very costly. But what are the costs of unemployment?

The Costs of Unemployment

There are four main costs of unemployment. They are:

- Loss of output and income
- Loss of human capital
- Increase in crime
- Loss of human dignity

Let's examine each of these in turn.

Loss of Output and Income The most obvious cost of unemployment is the lost output and income that the unemployed would have produced if they had had jobs. How big this cost is depends on the natural rate of unemployment. If the natural rate really is between 5 and 6 per cent, the lost output from unemployment is enormous.

Arthur Okun, a US economist, studied the relationship between unemployment and aggregate output and formulated what came to be known as *Okun's Law* (see Our Advancing Knowledge, Chapter 31). Okun's Law, applied to Australian data, may be stated as follows:[2]

> Other things being equal, for every 1 percentage point increase in the unemployment rate, the nation's output of goods and services falls by 2.75 percentage points.

In 1990/91, 1 per cent of aggregate output in Australia was $3.8 billion. Thus a fall in the unemployment rate from 10 per cent to 7 per cent — a decrease in the unemployment rate of 3 percentage points — would increase the value of Australian output by 8.25 per cent, or over $31 billion. With an increase in output of this magnitude, every Australian could buy, on the average, close to an extra $1750 worth of goods and services each year. You can now see why those economists who believe that the natural rate of unemployment is constant also believe that the value of output lost in periods of high unemployment is very large.

Those economists who believe that the natural rate of unemployment itself varies think that the lost output cost of unemployment is small. If the unemployment rate is temporarily high because a lot of technical changes or changing patterns of demand, call for a higher than normal amount of labour turnover, then lowering the unemployment rate will prevent the necessary re-allocation of labour. To reap the full advantage of the new technologies or demand patterns, people need to change jobs. If they do not, both output and income will be lower than the new technologies could otherwise have achieved.

Loss of Human Capital A second, and important, cost of unemployment is the permanent damage that can be done to an unemployed worker by hindering his or her career development and acquisition of human capital. **Human capital** is the value of a person's education and acquired skills. It is measured as the amount of money that, invested at the average interest rate, would yield the same increment to income as that produced by the person's acquired skills. These skills include the mechanical and mental skills that we acquire in school as well as those that we develop on the job to complement our basic physical capacity. They also include our work habits and our ability to concentrate. Prolonged unemployment seriously lowers the value of a person's human capital. When unemployment is prolonged, human capital depreciates or deteriorates — skills are lost.

Increase in Crime A rise in the unemployment rate usually causes an increase in the amount of crime. When people cannot earn an income from legitimate work, they sometimes turn to crime. A high crime rate is also one of the costs of high unemployment.

Loss of Human Dignity A final cost that is difficult to quantify is the loss of self-esteem that afflicts many who suffer prolonged periods of unemployment. It is probably this aspect of unemployment that makes it so highly charged with political and social significance.

---

[2] See D.T. Nguyen and A.M. Siriwardana, 'The Relationship between Output Growth and Unemployment: A Re-examination of Okun's Law in Australia', *Australian Economic Review*, 81(1), 16–27, 1988.

R E V I E W

There have been enormous fluctuations in the unemployment rate in Australia but no matter how low its rate, unemployment never disappears. Some unemployment is frictional, arising from labour market turnover. Some is structural, arising from the decline in certain industries and regions. And some is cyclical, associated with the fluctuating pace of economic expansion. The natural rate of unemployment is that unemployment rate at which there is a balance between the quantity of labour demanded and the quantity supplied. This rate fluctuates with changes in the frictional and structural unemployment rate. The costs of unemployment include lost output and income, loss of human capital, an increase in crime and a loss of human dignity. ■

Unemployment and the Business Cycle

We have previously noted that real GDP is not the only variable that fluctuates over the course of the business cycle. Its fluctuations are matched by related fluctuations in a wide range of other economic variables. One of the most important of these is unemployment. In the contraction phase of a business cycle, the unemployment rate rises, and sometimes continues to rise into the expansion phase of a business cycle. As the economy continues in an expansion phase, the unemployment rate falls. This relationship between the unemployment rate and the phases of the business cycle is illustrated in Fig. 22.8. The GDP growth rate is calculated as the average of two years' real growth. Note that in the figure, the scale for the unemployment rate is reversed.

It is interesting to note that unemployment rose to very high levels during the Great Depression in the 1930s. However, during two contractions of similar magnitude but shorter duration, following both World Wars, the unemployment rate did not change much.

Figure 22.8 Unemployment and the Business Cycle

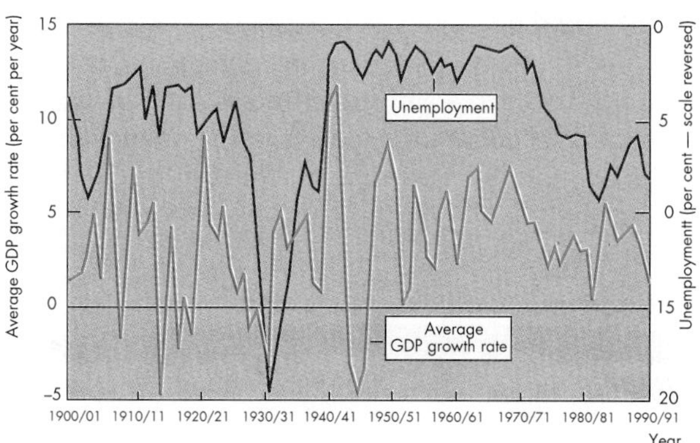

The figure shows the relationship between unemployment and the business cycle. The variations in average real GDP growth rate tell us when the economy is at a peak or trough or in a contraction or expansion phase of the business cycle. The unemployment rate is plotted in the same figure. The cycles in output are matched by the cycles in the unemployment rate.
Source: See Figs 22.1 and 22.7.

The Stock Market and the Business Cycle

Another indicator of the state of the economy, and perhaps the most visible of all such indicators, is provided by the stock market. Every weekday, news reports tell us of the day's events in the Sydney, Melbourne, New York and Tokyo stock exchanges. Movements in share prices attract attention partly for their own sake and also partly for what they might foretell about our *future* economic fortunes.

Do share prices fluctuate in sympathy with fluctuations in real GDP and unemployment? Is a stock market downturn a predictor of economic contraction? Is a stock market boom a predictor of economic expansion? To answer these questions, let's take a look at the behaviour of share prices and see how they relate to the expansions and contractions of economic activity.

Figure 22.9 tracks the course of inflation-adjusted share prices since March 1960. Actual share prices have increased much more than is indicated here because of inflation, but those purely inflationary price increases have been removed so that we can see what has 'really' happened to share prices — what the path of real share prices has been. The most striking feature of share prices is their extreme volatility and lack of any obvious cyclical pattern. One stock market crash, in October 1987, is indicated in the figure. There have also been periods of steadily falling prices over longer time horizons — throughout 1970 and 1973, for example. At other times there have been rapid increases in share prices, the most dramatic being that which preceded the 1987 crash. There were also strong increases in share prices in the late 1960s and 1972.

How do fluctuations in share prices correspond with the business cycle? While there are periods when the stock market provides information about

Figure 22.9 Real Share Prices, 1960–1990

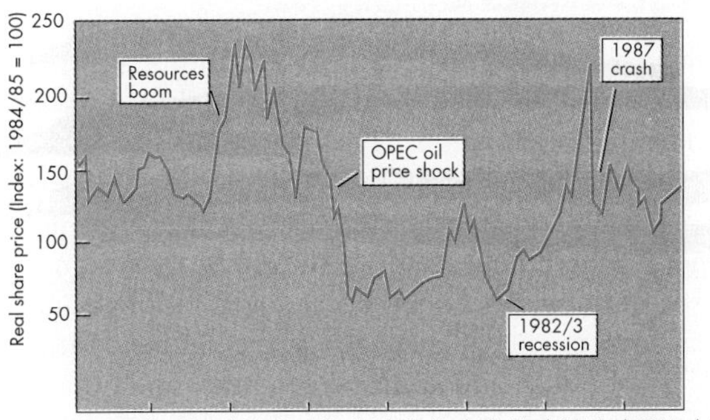

Share prices are among the most volatile elements of our economy. Real share prices (share prices measured to take out the effects of changes in the value of money) climbed strongly in the late 1960s. Then, throughout 1970 and 1971, share prices fell. After a short period of recovery, share prices again fell throughout 1973 and 1974. Share prices rose rapidly prior to the 1987 crash.

Source: All Ordinaries Share Price Index: Series FS MAS X SPAO, RBA Bulletin Database, supplied by EconData's dX Data Service, divided by GDP deflator.

where the economy is heading, the relationship between share prices and real output can best be described as loose. Generally speaking, the turning points in the stock market do not reliably predict the turning points in the economy. While there are some periods when the stock market and real GDP move together, there are more periods when their movements oppose each other. For example, the crash of 1987 occurred at a time when the economy, both in Australia and in the rest of the world, was expanding strongly.

When share prices collapsed in October 1987, many people drew parallels between that episode and the 1929 stock market crash. In 1930, the economy collapsed. In 1988, the economy continued to grow. Why were the two episodes so different? The key answer, and the key reason for the lack of a strong connection between share price fluctuations and the business cycle, is our inability to forecast the business cycle. Share prices are determined by people's expectations about future profitability of firms. Future profitability, in turn, depends on the state of the economy. Hence, share prices are determined by expectations about the future state of the economy. But those expectations turn out to be wrong about as often as they turn out to be right. Thus the movement in share prices is not an entirely reliable predictor of the state of the economy.

Inflation and the Business Cycle

We've looked at fluctuations in real variables: real GDP, the unemployment rate and real share prices. We've seen that there is a systematic relationship between fluctuations in real GDP and in the unemployment rate. We've also seen that there is little in the way of a systematic relationship between real share prices and the business cycle. How does inflation behave over the business cycle? Are fluctuations in its rate closely connected with the business cycle or does the inflation rate vary independently of the business cycle?

To answer these questions, let's look at the period since the 1950s. In Fig. 22.10 the rate of inflation is plotted along with the real GDP growth rate but inflation is plotted to lag two years behind real GDP. For example, the inflation rate plotted against 1981/82 is the rate of inflation occurring in 1983/84. As you can see, there was a general tendency for inflation to rise two years after real GDP rose. Similarly, inflation tended to fall two years after the rate of growth in real GDP fell. But the relationship was not always tight. It certainly broke down in the early 1970s when inflation rose rapidly after the growth rate of real GDP fell. This phenomenon of rising inflation and falling output growth rates is known as **stagflation**.

Following the rapid rise in the rate of inflation in the 1970s, the relationship between inflation and the business cycle was loosely re-established, although it will be increasingly strained as the Australian economy undergoes some of the reforms currently proposed. There is an important difference between the period of the 1950s and 1960s and the period of the 1970s and 1980s, however, which appears unrelated to the business cycle. That is, the average rate of inflation in the earlier period is much lower than in the later period.

The features of the relationship between inflation and real GDP fluctuations visible in Fig. 22.10 raise two questions. First, why is there a general tendency for inflation to move in sympathy with the business cycle? Second, why is that relationship such an imprecise one — that is, why are there large variations in the inflation rate that are independent of the business cycle phase through which the economy is passing? We'll begin to answer these questions in

Figure 22.10 Inflation and the Business Cycle, 1950/51–1990/91

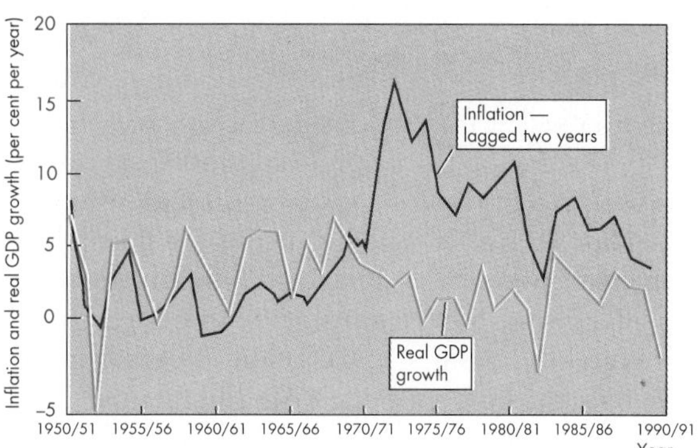

The figure shows the rate of inflation, lagged two years, along with the rate of growth of real GDP. Lagging inflation by two years means that the rate of inflation plotted against any one year is the rate that actually occurred two years later. For example, plotted against 1981/82 is the rate of inflation ocurring in 1983/84. This indicates that GDP growth (or decline) does not have an impact on the price level until up to two years later.

Until 1970/71, there was a close relationship between real GDP growth and lagged inflation. Whenever GDP growth increased, inflation rose two years later. And vice versa. The relationship broke down in the early 1970s, when GDP growth fell but inflation continued to rise. This was a period of stagflation.

The relationship was loosely re-established from the mid-1970s onwards, but at a higher average rate of inflation than prevailed during the 1950s and 1960s.

Source: See Figs 22.2 and 22.5.

Chapter 24 and get deeper and more thorough answers in Chapters 27 and 32.

We've now examined inflation, unemployment, real GDP fluctuations and business cycles. Let's turn now to our final topic, deficits and surpluses.

The Government and International Accounts

If you spend more than you earn, you have a deficit. To cover your deficit, you have to borrow or sell off some of the things that you own. If you spend less than you earn, you have a surplus that can be saved or used to pay off past borrowings. Just as individuals can have deficits or surpluses, so can governments and so can entire nations. These deficits and surpluses have attracted a lot of attention recently.

The Government Accounts

The balance on the government's accounts is the total revenue of the government sector less the total expenditure of that sector. The balance is a **surplus** if total revenues exceed total expenditures. It is a **deficit** if total expenditures exceed total revenues. The general government sector of the economy is composed of the Federal government, and the State and local governments. These governments spend on a variety of public and social programmes and obtain their revenue from taxes. Until recently, the government sector was usually in deficit. That deficit expanded rapidly from less than one billion dollars in 1973/74 (2 per cent of total output) to over eight billion dollars in 1983/84 (over 4 per cent of total output). Then the deficit of the general government sector fell rapidly, mainly because the Commonwealth government reduced its deficit to almost zero in 1987/88 and actually produced a surplus of nearly three billions dollars in 1989/90. However, the general government sector fell back into deficit in 1990/91 as a result of the recession in that year.

As recent experience confirms, the balance of the government budget is related to the business cycle. When the economy is expanding rapidly (in the expansion phase of the business cycle), tax receipts rise quickly and the government's spending on unemployment benefits decreases. Through this phase of the business cycle, the government's deficit decreases or its surplus increases. When the economy is in a contraction phase, tax receipts decline and unemployment benefits increase. In this phase, the government budget deficit gets bigger or its surplus smaller.

We'll study the government deficit more closely and at greater length in Chapter 35. In that chapter, we'll discuss the sources and consequences of deficits and surpluses.

The International Accounts

The difference between the value of all the goods and services that we sell to other countries (exports) and the value of all the goods and services that we buy from foreigners (imports), plus net income paid abroad and other transfers, is called the **current account balance**. If we sell more to the rest of the world than we buy from it, Australia has a current account surplus. If we buy more from the rest of the world than we sell to it, Australia has a current account deficit. Most of the time since 1950 Australia has had a current account deficit. In recent years, an already large current account deficit has increased substantially.

Borrowing from the rest of the world permits a country to pay for the goods and services that it is buying in excess of the value of those that it is selling. Persistently operating with a current account deficit means that a country is persistently borrowing from or selling equity to the rest of the world. Over time the total borrowings, called the external debt, increase, sometime to levels that cause concern. Mirroring one country's current account deficit and borrowing from the rest of the world is a current account surplus and lending to the rest of the world in some other countries. The most notable country on the opposite side of Australia's balance sheet is Japan, which has had a current account surplus and, in recent years, an increasing surplus.

The causes of these international surpluses and deficits and their consequences will be discussed at greater length in Chapter 36.

■ In our study of macroeconomics, we're going to find out what we currently know about the causes of inflation and of variations in its rate; we're also going to discover what we know about the causes of unemployment and the business cycle. We're going to discover why there are certain times when the stock market is a good predictor of the state of the economy and others when it is not. We're also going to discover why sometimes inflation and the business cycle move in sympathy with each other and why there are times when these variables follow separate courses. Finally, we're going to learn more about deficits and surpluses — on the government's accounts and the international account — their causes, their importance and their consequences.

The next step in our study of macroeconomics is to learn more about macroeconomic measurement — about how we measure gross domestic product, the price level and inflation.

SUMMARY

Inflation

Inflation is an upward movement in the average level of prices. To measure the average level of prices, we calculate a price index. The inflation rate is the percentage change in the price index over a given period.

Inflation is a persistent feature of Australian economic life, but the rate of inflation fluctuates. In the early 1960s, inflation was sometimes less than 1 per cent a year. Inflation increased through the 1960s and 1970s, hitting a peak of 17 per cent in 1974/75, and has remained high and relatively constant throughout the 1980s.

Inflation is a problem because it brings a fall in the value of money at an unpredictable rate. The more unpredictable the inflation rate, the less useful is money as a measuring rod for conducting transactions. Inflation makes money especially unsuitable for transactions that are spread out over time, such as borrowing and lending or working for an agreed wage rate. The inflation rate is the opportunity cost of holding money. (pp. 94–98)

Gross Domestic Product

Australia's total output is measured by its gross domestic product. Gross domestic product is the dollar value of all final goods and services produced in Australia in a given time period. Changes in gross domestic product reflect both changes in prices and changes in the quantity of goods and services available. To separate the effects of prices from real quantities, we distinguish between nominal GDP and real GDP. Nominal GDP is measured using current prices. Real GDP is measured using prices for some base year.

Real GDP grows, on average, every year, and this general upward tendency is called trend real GDP. But real GDP does not increase at a constant rate. Its rate of expansion fluctuates so that real GDP fluctuates around trend real GDP value. If the annual growth rate in real GDP is higher than the annual growth rate of the population, living standards rise but not without costs. The main costs of fast economic growth are resource depletion, environmental pollution and the need to face rapid and often costly changes in job type and location. The benefits of higher consumption levels have to be balanced against such costs. (pp. 98–101)

The Business Cycle

The business cycle is the periodic but irregular up and down movement in economic activity. The cycle has four phases: contraction, trough, expansion and peak. Deep troughs are called slumps or depressions. Deviations from trend in real GDP, or real GDP growth rates, measure the ebbs and flows in economic activity — the business cycle.

Unemployment fluctuates with fluctuations in real GDP. When real GDP is above trend GDP, unemployment is low; when real GDP is below trend GDP, unemployment is high. Real share prices often fluctuate in sympathy with the business cycle and sometimes a stock market crash precedes a recession, but it does not always do so.

There is no simple relationship between the inflation rate and the business cycle. Sometimes the inflation rate is high when there is a large positive fluctuation in real GDP and low when there is a large negative movement in real GDP. But there are other times when the inflation rate moves independently of the business cycle. Thus there are two types of forces at work generating inflation — those that are related to the business cycle and those that are not. (pp. 101–102)

Unemployment

Measured unemployment is the number of adult workers (aged 15 and over) who are not employed and who are actively seeking jobs. Measured employment is the number of adult workers holding jobs. The labour force is the sum of those unemployed and those employed. The unemployment rate is the percentage of the labour force unemployed. Unemployment is measured each month by a survey of households.

Unemployment was a major problem in Australia during the Great Depression years of the 1930s and became an important problem again in the 1970s and 1980s. Over the past 90 years the average unemployment rate has been 5.1 per cent.

Unemployment has some benefits. It provides people with the time and opportunity to search out the job that best matches their own skills and temperament. It also helps the economy respond to changing technologies and innovations.

The major costs of unemployment are the lost output and earnings that could have been generated if the unemployed had been working. Other major costs are a slow-down in the accumulation of human capital, or a rise in its depreciation rate, and, when unemployment is prolonged, crime and severe social and psychological problems for unemployed workers and their families. (pp. 102–108)

The Government and International Accounts

The government balance is the total revenue of the government sector less the total expenditure of that sector. To some degree the government surplus or deficit fluctuates over the course of the business cycle. In the past the government sector has persistently operated with a deficit, but recently it has created a surplus. That surplus or deficit varies with the business cycle.

A country's current account balance is the difference between the value of the goods and services that it sells to other countries and the value of the goods and services that it buys from the rest of the world. Australia has normally had a current account deficit and, in recent years, this deficit has grown in magnitude. Mirroring Australia's current account deficit is a current account surplus in some other countries. Japan is one of the countries that in recent years has had a large surplus. (pp. 108–109)

KEY TERMS

Anticipated inflation, p. 96
Base period, p. 94
Business cycle, p. 101
Contraction, p. 102
Current account balance, p. 108
Cyclical unemployment, p. 104
Deficit, p. 108
Deflation, p. 94
Depression, p. 102
Discouraged workers, p. 103
Employment, p. 102
Expansion, p. 102
Expected inflation rate, p. 96
Final goods and services, p. 98
Foreign exchange rate, p. 96
Frictional unemployment, p. 104
Full employment, p. 104
Gross domestic product, p. 98
Human capital, p. 105
Hyperinflation, p. 98
Indexing, p. 98
Inflation, p. 94
Inflation rate, p. 95
Intermediate goods and services, p. 99

Labour force, p. 102
Natural rate of unemployment, p. 104
Nominal GDP, p. 99
Peak, p. 102
Price index, p. 94
Price level, p. 94
Price stability, p. 94
Real GDP, p. 99
Recession, p. 102
Stagflation, p. 107
Structural unemployment, p. 104
Surplus, p. 108
Trend real GDP, p. 100
Trough, p. 102
Unanticipated inflation, p. 96
Unemployment, p. 102
Unemployment rate, p. 102
Value of money, p. 96

PROBLEMS

1 At the end of 1987 the price index was 172. At the end of 1988 the price index was 186. Calculate the inflation rate in 1988.

2 In a non-inflationary world, Joe and Mary are willing to borrow and lend at 2 per cent a year. Joe expects that inflation next year will be 4 per cent and Mary expects that it will be 8 per cent. Would Joe and Mary be willing to sign a contract in which one of them borrows from the other? Explain why or why not?

3 Will the Cone-Heads Ice Cream Parlour be able to agree with its employees on a wage rate for next summer if the employer expects that inflation next year will be 4 per cent while the employees' expectation of inflation is lower at 2 per cent? Explain your answer.

4 Obtain data on unemployment in your State. If the library that you use has the Australian Bureau of Statistics publication *The Labour Force*, you can get the data from there. Compare the behaviour of unemployment in your State with that in Australia as a whole. Why do you think your State might have higher or lower unemployment than the Australian average?

5 Obtain data on inflation in Australia, the United States, Japan and Germany since 1980. You will find this data in *International Financial Statistics* in the library. Draw a graph of the data and answer the following questions:

(a) Which country had the highest inflation rate?
(b) Which country had the lowest inflation rate?
(c) Which country had the fastest rising inflation rate?
(d) Which country had the fastest falling inflation rate?

6 On the basis of your discoveries in answering problem 5, what do you expect happened to the foreign exchange rates between the Australian dollar and the Japanese yen, the US dollar and the German mark? Check your expectation by finding these exchange rates in the *International Financial Statistics*.

Chapter 23

Measuring Output and the Price Level

After studying this chapter, you will be able to:

- Describe the circular flow of expenditure and income.
- Explain why aggregate expenditure, income and product are equal to each other.
- Explain the three ways in which gross domestic product (GDP) is measured — the expenditure approach, the income approach and the output approach.
- Explain how real GDP is measured.
- Explain how the cost of living is measured by the Consumer Price Index (CPI).
- Distinguish between two measures of the price level — the CPI and the GDP deflator.
- Distinguish between inflation and changes in relative prices.
- Distinguish between real GDP, aggregate economic activity and economic welfare.

Reading the Tea Leaves

Every three months, the Australian Bureau of Statistics (ABS) publishes the latest quarterly estimates of the gross domestic product or GDP — a barometer of our nation's economy. As soon as it is published, analysts pore over the data, trying, like tea readers, to understand the past and divine the future. But how do government accountants add up all the diverse, decentralized economic activity of the country to arrive at the number called GDP? And what exactly is GDP? We saw in the last chapter that the pace of expansion of GDP fluctuates and is occasionally interrupted by a period of contraction. We described these ebbs and flows of economic activity as the business cycle. But to reveal the business cycle, we have to measure the extent to which GDP has expanded because production has increased and the extent to which it has expanded because prices have risen. In other words, we have to distinguish between real GDP and nominal GDP. How do we go about measuring the real component of GDP and separating out the inflation component? From economists to homemakers, inflation watchers of all types pay close attention to the monthly publication of the Consumer Price Index or CPI. The government publishes new figures each month, and analysts in newspapers and on TV quickly leap to conclusions. How does the government determine the CPI? How well does it measure the consumer's living costs? If oranges go up in price by 40 per cent, and haircuts go up by only 4 per cent, are rising orange prices causing inflation? Most economic activity results in transactions taking place in markets for goods and services and factors of production. But not all economic activity results in such transactions. Some people make a living from crime. Others, although undertaking work that is legal, try to hide that fact and also try to hide the payment they receive in order to evade taxes or other regulations. And, finally, some people undertake economic activity that does not take place in the marketplace at all. Cooking meals, laundering shirts, mowing the lawn and washing the car are all examples of production activities that take place within the household. Are these activities taken into account when we measure GDP? If they are not taken into account, how important are they? And does it matter if they don't show up in GDP?

In this chapter, we're going to learn more about the macroeconomic concepts of GDP and the price level. We'll see how GDP is measured. We'll also see how the real and inflationary components of GDP are separately measured and identified. We'll learn how to calculate and interpret the CPI. Finally, we'll ask what GDP means: what does it tell us about our standard of living and economic welfare? We're going to begin by describing the circular flow of expenditure and income.

The Circular Flow of Expenditure and Income

The circular flow of expenditure and income provides the conceptual basis for measuring national expenditure, national income and national product. The theory and measurement of these variables has benefited greatly from contributions by Australian economists. A pioneer in the field was Colin Clark, an English born economist who spent many years in Australia, based mainly at the University of Queensland.

We'll see some of the key ideas and relationships more clearly if we begin with a model economy that is simpler than the one in which we live. In particular, we will suppose that our economy has no government sector and that it is closed off from the rest of the world. We'll then add some features to make our model economy correspond more closely with that of the real economy.

Circular Flows in a Model Economy

Our simplified model economy has just two kinds of economic institutions: households and firms.

Households:

- Receive incomes in exchange for the supply of factors of production to firms.
- Make expenditures on consumption goods and services bought from firms.
- Save some of their incomes.

Firms:

- Pay incomes to households for the factors of production hired (these payments include wages paid for labour, interest paid for capital, rent paid for land and profits).
- Receive revenue from the sale of consumption goods and services to households.
- Receive revenue from the sale of capital goods to other firms.
- Borrow to finance purchases of capital goods from other firms.

The economy has three types of markets:

- Goods (and services) markets
- Factor markets
- Financial markets

Two kinds of flows occur between households and firms. First, real objects are supplied by households to firms and by firms to households. Second, money passes between households and firms in exchange for these real objects.

The real flows from households to firms are the services of factors of production. That is, households supply factors of production — labour, capital and land — to firms. The real flows from firms to households are consumption goods and services. That is, firms produce popcorn and soft drinks, films and chocolate bars, microwave ovens and dry cleaning services and sell them to households. The total expenditure by households on consumption goods and services is called **consumption expenditure.**

Moving in the opposite direction to the real flows are money flows. These money flows represent the payments made in exchange for the real flows that have just been described. There is the flow of factor income payments made by firms to households. They include wages paid to households for their labour services, interest for the use of their capital, rents for the use of their land and profits to the owners of firms. The payments that firms make to households in exchange for factor services are the households' income. **Income** is the amount received by households in payment for the services of factors of production.

Firms do not sell all their output to households. First, some output may be added to inventory or stock. For example, if General Motors Holden produces 1000 cars and sells 950 of them to households, 50 cars will still remain unsold and GMH's stock of cars will increase by 50. Second, some output is new capital equipment that is sold to other firms. For example, IBM sells a mainframe computer to GMH. To pay for new capital equipment and additional stock, firms borrow from households in the financial markets. The purchase of new plant, equipment and building, and additions to inventories or stocks are called **investment.**

The money flows that we have just described are illustrated in Fig. 23.1. To help you keep track of the different types of flows, they have been colour-coded. The blue flow represents aggregate income — that is, total income received by all households in exchange for the services of factors of production. We denote aggregate income by Y.

The red flows represent expenditures on goods and services. The flow of consumption expenditure from households to firms is denoted by C. Investment — additions to inventory and purchases of new

Figure 23.1 The Circular Flow of Expenditure and Income Between Households and Firms

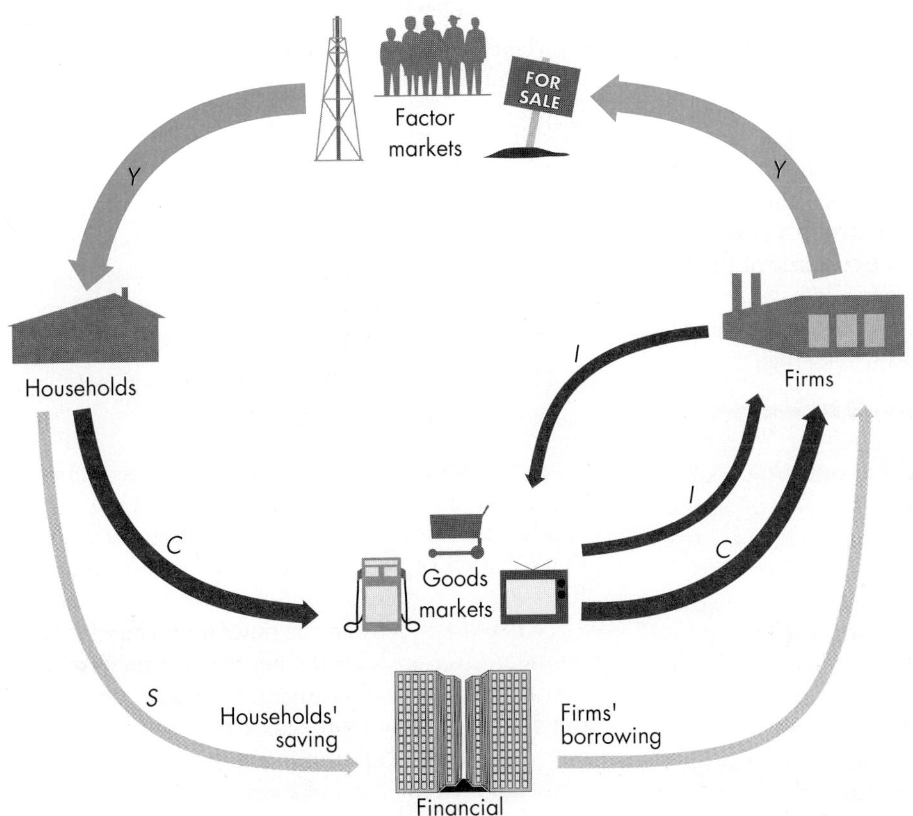

Three types of money flows are illustrated: payments for factors of production (blue), payments for final goods and services (red) and borrowing and lending (green). Households receive factor incomes from firms in exchange for the factor services supplied. Households purchase consumer goods and services from firms and firms purchase capital goods from other firms (and inventories from themselves). Households save part of their income and firms borrow to finance their purchases of capital goods and inventory holdings. Firms' receipts from the sale of goods and services are paid out to households as wages, interest, rent or profit. Aggregate expenditure (consumption expenditure plus investment) equals aggregate income. The value of output is also equal to aggregate income and aggregate expenditure.

capital goods — is denoted by *I*. Notice that investment expenditure is illustrated in the figure as a flow from firms through the goods markets and back to firms. It is illustrated in this way because some firms produce capital goods and other firms buy them. When a firm adds unsold output to inventory, we can think of the firm as buying goods from itself.

There are two additional flows in the figure shown in green. These flows do not represent payments made in exchange for the services of factors of production or for the purchases of goods and services. They are payments made in exchange for future commitments — they are loans. Households do not spend all their income — they save some of it. In this model economy, saving is the difference between household income and consumption expenditure. Saving (*S*) gets channelled through financial markets. Firms borrow the funds required to finance their purchases of new capital, equipment and inventory holdings in financial markets.

The flows illustrated in Fig. 23.1 give a complete description of all the money flows that occur in the model economy that we're studying. For present purposes, however, the most important of these flows are the payments for the services of factors of production (the blue flow) and the payments made in exchange for goods and services (the red flows). We're going to discover that the blue flow and the two red flows in aggregate are equal — that is, aggregate income and aggregate expenditure are equal. Let's see why.

Equality of Income and Expenditure To see the equality of aggregate income and aggregate expenditure, let's focus on firms. Notice first that there are two red arrows indicating flows of revenue to firms. They are consumption expenditure (C) and investment (I). The sum of these two flows is aggregate expenditure on final goods and services (more briefly, aggregate expenditure). Everything that a firm receives from the sale of its output it also pays out for the services of the factors of production that it hires. To see why, recall that payments for factors of production include not only wages, interest and rent paid for the services of labour, capital and land, but also profits. Any difference between the amount received by a firm for the sale of its output and the amount paid to its suppliers of labour, capital and land is a profit (or loss) for the owner of the firm. The owner of the firm is a household and the owner receives the firm's profit (or makes good the firm's loss). Thus the total income each firm pays out to households equals its revenue from the sale of final goods and services.

Since the above reasoning applies to each and every firm, for the economy as a whole, then

Aggregate income = Aggregate expenditure

Equality of Expenditure, Income and Value of Output The value of output is the value of all the goods and services produced by firms. There are two ways in which we can value the goods and services produced by firms. One is to value them on the basis of the cost of the factors of production used to produce them. The other is to value them on the basis of what the buyers have paid for them. But we've just discovered that aggregate expenditure equals aggregate income. That is, the total amount spent on the goods and services produced equals the total amount paid for the factors of production used to produce them. Thus the value of output equals aggregate income, which in turn equals aggregate expenditure. That is

Aggregate income = Aggregate expenditure = Value of output (GDP)

Government and Foreign Sectors In the model economy that we've just examined, we focused exclusively on the behaviour of households and firms. In real world economies, there are two other important institutions that add additional flows to the circular flow of expenditure and income: the government and the rest of the world. These institutions do not change the fundamental results that we've just obtained. Aggregate income is equal to aggregate expenditure and to the value of output, no matter how many sectors we consider and how complicated a range of flows we consider between them. Nevertheless, it is important to add the government and the rest of the world to our model so that we can see the additional expenditure and income flows that they generate. Let's now add these two sectors to our model economy.

The government:

- Receives tax revenue from, and pays benefits and subsidies to, households and firms.
- Makes expenditures on goods and services bought from firms.
- Borrows to finance the difference between its revenue and spending .

The rest of the world:

- Makes expenditures on goods and services bought from domestic firms and receives revenue from the sale of goods and services to domestic firms.
- Lends to (or borrows from) households and firms in the domestic economy.

The additional flows arising from the transactions between the government, the rest of the world, and households and firms, along with the original flows that we've already considered, are illustrated in Fig. 23.2.

Let's first focus on the flows involving the government. Net taxes are the net flows of money from households to the government.[1] These net flows are the difference between the taxes paid and benefits received. The flows of money from the government to households in the form of social benefits are called **transfer payments**. It is important not to confuse government transfer payments with government purchases of goods and services. The term 'transfer payments' is designed to remind us that these items are simply transfers of money and, as such, are a bit like taxes except that they flow in the opposite direction — they flow from government to households. Net taxes are illustrated in the figure as a green flow to remind you that this flow does not represent a payment in exchange for goods and services or a factor income. It is simply a transfer of financial resources from households to the government.

Government purchases of goods and services from firms are shown as the flow *G*. This flow is shown in red to indicate that it represents a money flow in exchange for goods and services. It is expenditure by government and revenue for firms. Al-

[1]The diagram does not show firms paying any taxes. You can think of taxes paid by firms as being paid on behalf of the households that own the firms. For example, a tax on a firm's profit means that the households owning the firm receive less income. It is as if the households receive all the profit and then pay tax on the profit. This way of looking at taxes simplifies Fig. 23.2, but does not change any conclusions.

Figure 23.2 The Circular Flow Including Government and the Rest of the World

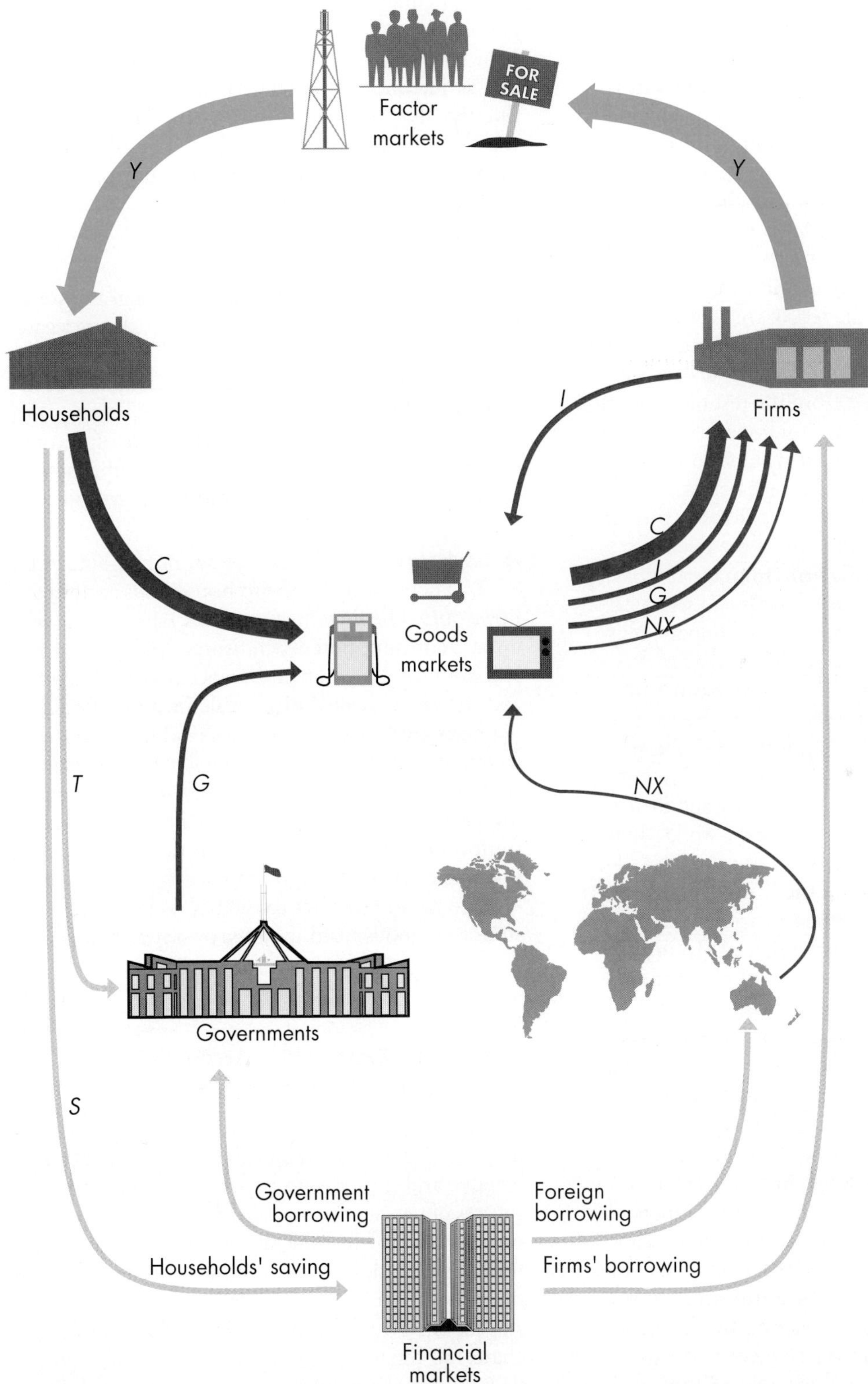

Three types of money flows between firms, households, government and the rest of the world are illustrated: payments for factors of production (blue), expenditures on final goods and services (red) and borrowing, lending and taxes (green). Firms hire factors of production and make income payments to households in exchange (*Y*). Households make consumption expenditures (*C*), firms undertake investment — purchase new capital goods from other firms and accumulate inventories — (*I*), government purchases goods and services from firms (*G*), and purchases of goods and services by the rest of the world minus the sum of purchases of goods and services from the rest of the world plus other transfers out result in net exports (*NX*) . The sum of consumption expenditure, investment, government purchases of goods and services, and net exports is equal to aggregate expenditure, which also equals aggregate income. The green flows illustrate household saving and tax payments, government borrowing, and borrowing by firms and the rest of the world.

though not indicated in the figure, some of these purchases are returned to households and firms in the form of government services.

The difference between the net taxes received by government and government expenditure on goods and services is the government's budget balance. If that balance is negative, the government is operating at a deficit, which it covers by borrowing in financial markets. Such borrowing is illustrated by the green flow in the figure.

Next, look at transactions with the rest of the world. The red flow labelled *NX* is net exports. **Net exports** are the difference between exports of goods and services to the rest of the world and imports of goods and services from the rest of the world. Other net transfers to the rest of the world, for example, foreign aid, are included in imports. This flow represents the money that flows from the rest of the world to domestic firms in exchange for goods and services produced by domestic firms. It is a net flow in the sense that it represents the difference between the value of the goods sold by domestic firms to the rest of the world (exports) and the sum of the value of goods purchased by domestic firms from the rest of the world (imports) and the value of goods and ser-vices given away (transfers). If exports exceed imports plus transfers, net exports are positive. There is a net flow into the domestic economy. To finance that net inflow, the rest of the world has to borrow from the domestic economy. This flow is illustrated by the green flow labelled foreign borrowing. (If imports plus transfers exceed exports, net exports are negative and there is a flow from domestic firms to the rest of the world. In this case, the domestic economy borrows from the rest of the world. That is, the rest of the world lends to the domestic economy through the financial markets. This case is not illustrated in the figure. To illustrate it, we simply reverse the directions of the flows of net exports and foreign borrowing.)

Now that we have introduced more elements of the real world into our model economy, let's check that aggregate expenditure still equals aggregate income.

Expenditure Equals Income Again Aggregate expenditure equals aggregate income in this more complicated economy just as it does in the economy that has only households and firms. To see this equality, focus on the expenditures on goods and services (the red flows) received by firms and on firms' payments for factor services (the blue flow). We now have four flows representing firms' revenues from the sale of goods and services — consumption expenditure (C), investment (I), government purchases of goods and services (G), and net exports (NX). The sum of these four flows is equal to aggregate expenditure on final goods and services. As before, everything that a firm receives from the sale of its output is paid out as income to the owners of the factors of production that it employs and to the households that have a claim on its profits. The blue factor income flow, therefore, equals the sum of the red expenditure flows. That is

$$Y = C + I + G + NX$$

Thus as we discovered in the case of the simpler model economy, aggregate income equals aggregate expenditure.

The value of output (GDP) also equals aggregate expenditure or aggregate income. This equality occurs because we can measure the value of output either as the sum of the incomes paid to the factors of production or as the expenditure on that output.

Households Let's next look at households in Fig. 23.2. There is one flow into households and three flows out. The flow in is income (Y). The flows out are consumption expenditure (C), saving (S) and net taxes (T). The difference between income and net taxes is called **disposable income.** Recall that net taxes are equal to total taxes paid minus transfer payments received. Thus disposable income is income plus transfer payments from the government minus taxes. **Saving** is disposable income minus consumption expenditure. With this definition of saving, it is clear that everything received by households — income and transfer payments — is spent on consumption goods, paid in taxes, or saved. That is

$$Y = C + S + T$$

Income and Expenditure Accounts

We can record the transactions shown in the circular flow diagram in a set of accounts, one for firms and one for households. Table 23.1(a) shows the firm's revenue and expenditure account. The first two sources of revenue are the sale of goods and services to households (C) and the sale of capital goods to other firms (I). In addition, firms now receive revenue from the sale of goods and services to the government (G) and for their sale of goods and services (net of purchases) to the rest of the world (NX). The sum of all their sources of revenue ($C + I + G + NX$) equals the payments made to the owners of factors of production (Y).

The households' income and expenditure account is shown in Table 23.1(b). Households receive income (Y) in payment for the factors of production supplied and spend that income on consumption goods (C), pay net taxes (T) and the balancing item, as before, is household saving (S).

Injections and Leakages The flow of income from firms to households and of consumption expenditure from households to firms is the circular flow of income and expenditure. Investment, government purchases of goods and services, and exports are called **injections** into the circular flow of expenditure and income. Net taxes, saving and imports are called **leakages** from the circular flow of expenditure and income. Let's take a closer look at these leakages and injections.

We have seen from the firms' accounts that

$$Y = C + I + G + NX$$

Let's break net exports into two components, exports of goods and services (EX) and imports of goods and services (IM). We will include net transfers to the rest of the world in imports. Thus

$$NX = EX - IM$$

Combining this equation with the previous one, you can see that

$$Y = C + I + G + EX - IM$$

We have also seen from the households' accounts that

$$Y = C + S + T$$

Since the left side of these two equations is the same, it follows that

$$I + G + EX - IM = S + T$$

If we add IM to both sides of this equation, we get

$$I + G + EX = S + T + IM$$

The left side of the equation shows the injections into the circular flow of expenditure and income and the right side the leakages from the circular flow. *The injections into the circular flow equal the leakages from the circular flow.*

Table 23.1 Firms' and Households' Accounts

(a) Firms

Revenue		Expenditure	
Sale of consumption goods and services	C	Payments to factors of production	Y
Sale of capital goods	I		
Sale of goods and services to government	G		
Sale of goods and services to rest of world *less* purchases of goods and services from rest of world	NX		
Total	Y		Y

(b) Households

Income		Expenditure	
Payments for supplies of factors of production	Y	Purchases of consumption goods and services	C
		Taxes paid *less* transfers received	T
		Saving	S
Total	Y		Y

Firms, shown in part (a), receive an income from the sale of consumption goods and services to households (C), capital goods to other firms (I), goods and services to government (G) and net exports (NX) or the difference between the value of their sales to the rest of the world and their purchases of goods from the rest of the world. Firms make payments for the services of factors of production (Y). The total income that firms pay equals their total revenue: $Y = C + I + G + NX$. Households, shown in part (b), receive an income for the supply of factors of production (Y). They buy consumer goods and services from firms (C) and pay net taxes (taxes minus transfers payments) to the government (T). The part of household income that is not spent on consumption goods or paid in net taxes is saved (S). Consumption expenditure plus taxes plus saving is equal to income: $Y = C + T + S$.

R E V I E W

Aggregate expenditure is the sum of consumer expenditure (C), investment (I), government purchases of goods and services (G) and exports of goods and services (EX) minus imports of goods and services

(IM). Aggregate expenditure equals the value of the final goods and services produced. It also equals the aggregate income (Y) of the factors of production used to produce these goods and services, that is:

$$Y = C + I + G + EX - IM$$

Households allocate aggregate income to three activities: consumption expenditure (C), taxes (net of transfer payments) (T) and saving (S), that is:

$$Y = C + S + T$$

Investment, government purchases and exports are *injections* into the circular flow of expenditure and income. Saving, taxes (net of transfers) and imports are *leakages* from the circular flow. Injections equal leakages, that is:

$$I + G + EX = S + T + IM$$ ■

The circular flow of income and expenditure, and the income and expenditure accounts of firms and households, are our tools for measuring GDP. Let's now see how the Australian Bureau of Statistics use these concepts to measure Australia's GDP.

Australia's Income and Expenditure Accounts

The Australian Bureau of Statistics uses three methods to measure GDP:

- Expenditure approach
- Income approach
- Production approach

Let's look at what is involved in using these three alternative ways of measuring GDP.

The Expenditure Approach

The **expenditure approach** measures GDP by adding together all final expenditures: private final consumption expenditure (C), private gross fixed capital expenditure plus the increase in stocks, or investment (I), government final consumption expenditure plus public gross fixed capital expenditure (G) and exports of goods and services less imports of goods and services, or net exports (NX). This approach is illustrated in Table 23.2. The figures provided refer to 1990/91 and are in billions of dollars. There is also a statistical discrepancy that we'll explain later. The table also includes the appropriate Australian National Accounts (ANA) terminology.

Consumption enters the national accounts as private final consumption expenditure. It is the aggregate expenditure on goods and services produced by firms and sold to households. It includes goods such as soft drinks, records, books and magazines as well as services such as insurance, banking and legal advice. It does not include the purchase of new houses, which is counted as part of investment.

Investment is the sum of private gross fixed capital expenditure and the increase in stocks. It includes expenditure on capital equipment by firms and expenditure on new houses by households. It also includes the change in firms' inventories. **Inventories** are the stocks of raw materials, semifinished products and unsold final products held by firms. Inventories are an essential input into the production process. If a firm does not hold inventories of raw materials, its production process can operate only as quickly as the rate at which new raw materials can be delivered. Similarly, if a firm does not have inventories of semifinished goods, processes at later stages of production may become disrupted as a result of breakdowns or accidents at earlier stages. Finally, by holding inventories of finished goods, firms can respond to fluctuations in sales, standing ready to meet an exceptional surge in demand. The stock of plant, equipment and buildings (including housing) is called the **capital stock**. Additions to the capital stock are investment.

Government expenditure is the sum of government final consumption expenditure and government gross fixed capital expenditure. It includes expenditure on goods, services and investment by all levels of government from Canberra to the local council. This item of expenditure includes the cost of providing national defence, law and order, street lighting and garbage collection. It does not include *transfer payments*. As we have seen, such payments do not represent a purchase of goods and services but rather a transfer of money from government to households.

Net exports are the difference between the value of exports and imports. When BHP sells steel to Hyundai, the Korean car producer, the value of that steel is part of Australia's exports. When you buy a new Hyundai, your expenditure is part of Australia's imports. The difference between what the country earns by selling goods and services to the rest of the world and what it pays for goods and services bought from the rest of the world is the value of net exports.

Table 23.2 GDP: The Expenditure Approach

Item	ANA terminology	Symbol	Amount (billions of dollars)	1990/91 percentage of GDP
Consumption	Private final consumption expenditure	*C*	229.7	60.5
Investment	Private gross fixed capital expenditure *plus* increase in stocks	*I*	58.8	15.5
Government expenditure	Government final consumption expenditure *plus* public gross fixed capital expenditure	*G*	90.1	23.7
Net exports	Exports of goods and services *less* imports of goods and services	*NX*	–0.9	–0.2
Statistical discrepancy		*SD*	1.8	0.5
Gross domestic product		*Y*	379.6	100

The expenditure approach measures GDP by adding together consumption expenditure, investment, government purchases of goods and services, and net exports. A statistical discrepancy is included. In 1990/91, GDP measured by the expenditure approach was $379.6 billion. The largest component of aggregate expenditure is expenditure on consumption goods and services — 60.5 per cent of GDP.

Source: Australian Bureau of Statistics, *Australian National Accounts: National Income and Expenditure,* ABS No. 5206.0, June 1991.

Table 23.2 shows the relative importance of the four items of aggregate expenditure. As you can see, consumption expenditure is by far the largest component of the expenditures that add up to GDP.

The statistical discrepancy is the difference between GDP as measured by the expenditure approach and GDP as measured by the income approach. Because they use data from different sources, these two approaches do not usually give the same numerical estimate of GDP, and a discrepancy arises. The discrepancy is included on the expenditure side simply because of convention and does not necessarily imply that the income approach is more accurate than the expenditure approach. The discrepancy is usually small relative to the aggregates being measured. In 1989/90 it was $7.5 billion, or 2 per cent of GDP but it fell to less than one-half of one per cent in 1990/91.

The Income Approach

The **income approach** measures GDP by adding together the incomes paid by firms to factors of production and two other items — depreciation and net indirect taxes — explained later in this chapter. All these income items, taken together represent the cost of producing GDP.

Incomes paid to factors of production fall into two categories:

- Wages, salaries and supplements
- Net operating surplus.

Wages, salaries and supplements are payments by firms to employees. They include net wages and salaries (take-home pay), taxes withheld from earnings, fringe benefits such as income paid in kind (for example, board), contributions to pension or superannuation schemes and workers' compensation for injuries.

Net operating surplus is the operating surplus of firms after allowing for the use of capital in the production process. Net operating surplus is calculated for different types of firms. They are:

- Private trading enterprises
- Public trading enterprises
- General government
- Financial enterprises

Private trading enterprises include corporate trading enterprises, that is, businesses that are assessable for income tax as companies; unincorporated trading enterprises, which include sole proprietorships, partnerships and trusts; and households that own their own house. Owner-occupied houses are treated as businesses wherein the owner of the house pays a market rent to him or herself. The Australian Bureau of Statistics estimates or imputes the amount of that rent, which would otherwise have been paid in the market for housing.

Public trading enterprises are government-owned enterprises and public enterprises that aim to cover their operating expenses by selling their output. Telecom, Qantas and State government electricity authorities are examples. All other government departments, offices and organizations, at all levels, are included in *general government.* This group also includes, as a matter of convention, all non-profit organizations.

Financial enterprises include banks and all other types of financial intermediary, such as building societies, insurance offices and superannuation funds. In order to cover costs, financial enterprises generate income by establishing a margin between interest received (for example, from mortgages and loans) and interest paid (for example, on deposits). In the national accounts, the interest received by financial intermediaries is divided into a pure interest component and a service charge for organizing the funds. That part of the service charge relating to consumer loans is treated as being paid by the customer and is included in private final consumption expenditure. The remaining service charge is classified as the 'imputed bank service charge' paid for by industry and is subtracted from the operating surplus of financial trading enterprises as it represents a transfer between industries. Thus the operating surplus of financial trading enterprises is often reported as negative.

Net operating surpluses are disposed of in a variety of ways. They can be distributed as dividend payments to the owners of the firms, interest payments made by firms or rents paid to some factors of production. Net operating surpluses can also be saved by firms as retained earnings.

Domestic factor incomes are the sum of wages, salaries and supplements, and the net operating surplus of private trading enterprises, public trading enterprises, general government and financial enterprises. Domestic factor incomes are that part of GDP accruing as income to the suppliers of the factors of production (land, labour, capital and enterprise).

Gross domestic product at factor cost is the sum of wages, salaries and supplements, and gross operating surplus. Gross operating surplus is the operating surplus of firms before allowing for the consumption of capital in the production process. The difference between gross domestic product at factor cost and domestic factor incomes (and between net and gross operating surplus) is accounted for by the depreciation of capital. **Depreciation**, also known as the 'consumption of fixed capital', is the reduction in the value of the capital stock that results from wear and tear and the passage of time. We've seen that investment is the purchase of new capital equipment and inventories. Depreciation is the opposite — the wearing out or destruction of capital equipment. Part of investment represents the purchase of capital equipment to replace equipment that has worn out. This investment does not add to the stock of capital; it simply maintains the capital stock. The other part of investment represents additions to the capital stock — the purchase of new additional plant, equipment and inventories.

We need to distinguish between gross and net investment. **Gross investment** is the amount spent on replacing depreciated capital and on net additions to the capital stock. The difference between gross investment and depreciation is called net investment. **Net investment** is the net addition to the capital stock. Let's illustrate these ideas with an example.

On 1 January 1990, Jumbuck Pty Ltd had a capital stock consisting of three knitting machines that had a market value of $7500. In 1990, Jumbuck bought a new machine for $3000. But during the year the machines owned by Jumbuck depreciated by $1000. By 31 December 1990, Jumbuck's stock of knitting machines was worth $9500. Jumbuck's purchase of a new machine for $3000 is the firm's gross investment. The firm's net investment — the difference between gross investment ($3000) and depreciation ($1000) — is $2000. These transactions and the relationship between gross investment, net investment and depreciation are summarized in Table 23.3.

If we add indirect taxes less subsidies to domestic factor incomes we get **net domestic product.** Net domestic product (NDP) is also gross domestic product less depreciation. NDP is a measure of the total flow of goods and services available after allowing for replacement of the stock of capital worn out in the production process.

Table 23.3 Capital Stock, Investment and Depreciation for Jumbuck Pty Ltd, 1990

Capital stock on 1 January 1990 (value of knitting machines owned at beginning of year)		$7500
Gross investment (value of new knitting machine bought in 1990)	$3000	
less Depreciation (fall in value of knitting machines during year 1990)	–$1000	
equals Net investment in 1990		$2000
Capital stock on 31 December 1990 (value of knitting machines owned at end of year)		$9500

Jumbuck's capital stock at the end of 1990 equals its capital stock at the beginning of the year plus net investment. Net investment is equal to gross investment less depreciation. Gross investment is the value of new machines bought during the year and depreciation is the fall in the value of Jumbuck's knitting machines over the year.

Factor Cost and Market Price

When we calculate GDP using the expenditure approach, we add together expenditures on *final goods and services.* These expenditures are valued at the prices people pay for the various goods and services. The price that people pay for a good or service is called the **market price**. There is another way of valuing a good — factor cost. **Factor cost** is the value of a good measured by adding together the costs of all the factors of production used to produce it. In the terminology introduced in Chapter 6, GDP at market prices (or simply GDP) is GDP calculated at *consumer prices.* GDP at factor cost is GDP calculated at *producer prices.* If the only economic transactions that take place are between households and firms — if there is no government — the market price and factor cost methods of measuring value are identical. But transactions involving the government can drive a wedge between these two methods of valuation. The source of that wedge is indirect taxes and subsidies.

An **indirect tax** is a tax assessed on producers when they produce or sell goods and services. Examples of indirect taxes are the sales taxes and excises on alcohol, petrol and tobacco products. Indirect taxes result in the consumer paying more than the producer receives for a good. For example, suppose that you pay a sales tax of 10 per cent. If you buy a chocolate bar that costs $1 to produce, you pay $1.10. The market price of the chocolate bar is $1.10. The total cost, including profit, of all the inputs used to produce the chocolate bar, is $1. The factor cost of the chocolate bar is $1.

A **subsidy** is a payment made by the government to producers. The payment may be to ensure a guaranteed price or to enable the maintenance of the price of the good or service below the cost of production. A subsidy also drives a wedge between the market price value and the factor cost value, but in the opposite direction to an indirect tax. A subsidy lowers the market price below the factor cost — consumers pay less for the good than it costs the producer to make the good.

To use the factor incomes approach to measure gross domestic product, we need to add indirect taxes to total GDP at factor cost and subtract subsidies. Table 23.4 summarizes these calculations and shows how the factor incomes approach leads to the same estimate of GDP as the expenditure approach. The figures are for 1990/91 and are in billions of dollars. The table also shows the relative importance of the various factor incomes. As you can see, wages, salaries and supplements (compensation of employees) is by far the most important factor income.

The Production Approach

The **production approach** measures GDP by summing the value added of each firm in the economy. **Value added** is the market value of a firm's output minus the value of inputs bought from other firms. Let's illustrate value added by looking at the production of a chocolate bar.

Table 23.5 takes you through the brief but sweet life of a chocolate bar. It starts with the producers of the raw materials that go into the chocolate bar. Milk, sugar, cocoa beans and electric power are produced by farmers and an electricity authority. Let's suppose (just for the purpose of this story) that these producers buy no inputs other than factor ser-vices — labour, capital and land. When the chocolate producer buys milk, sugar, cocoa beans and electric power, it pays for the value added by firms in those other sectors of the economy. The chocolate producer combines the milk, sugar and cocoa by using equipment driven by the electric power it purchases and operated by labour that it hires to make the chocolate bars. The payment made by the chocolate producer to the labour that it hires is part of the value added in the chocolate sector of the economy.

When the chocolate producer sells the chocolate bar to a wholesaler there is some more value added in the chocolate sector — the profit of the chocolate producer. That profit is obviously not the entire 72 cents received from the wholesaler for the chocolate bar. It is the difference between the 72 cents and all the previous expenditures. If you add up those expenditures, you will see that they total 60 cents, which means that the chocolate producer's profit is 12 cents. The value added in the chocolate sector is 40 cents — the wages of the workers (28 cents) and the profit of the producer (12 cents). When the wholesaler sells the chocolate bar to the retailer, there is some more value added. That value added is 8 cents and represents the profit of the wholesaler and the payments made by the wholesaler for labour and other factors of production hired. Finally, when the retailer sells the chocolate bar to you, there is yet further value added — 20 cents — which represents the retailer's profit and factor costs.

If we add up all the value added in the dairy, sugar, cocoa, electricity, chocolate, wholesale and retail sectors we see that they come to $1, the price paid by you for the chocolate bar. If we add up all the amounts received and paid, they total $3.12. That total has no economic meaning — it is a mixture of expenditure on intermediate goods and services and expenditure on the final good.

The story of the life of a chocolate bar illustrates an important distinction between expenditure on final goods and expenditure on intermediate goods.

Table 23.4 GDP: The Factor Incomes Approach

Item	Amount in 1990/91 (billions of dollars)	Percentage of GDP
Wages, salaries and supplements	193.9	51.1
Gross operating surplus		
Private trading enterprises:		
Corporate	56.1	14.8
Unincorporated	40.0	10.5
Dwellings owned by households	31.1	8.2
Public trading enterprises	15.2	4.0
General government	7.0	1.8
Financial enterprises	-9.0	-2.4
GDP at factor cost	334.5	
Indirect taxes less subsidies	45.1	11.9
Gross domestic product	379.6	100

The sum of all factor incomes equals GDP at factor cost. GDP equals GDP at factor cost plus indirect taxes minus subsidies. In 1990/91, GDP measured by the income approach was $379.6 billion. The compensation of employees — labour income — was by far the largest part of total factor incomes.

Source: See Table 23.2.

Final Goods and Intermediate Goods In valuing output, we count only expenditure on *final goods*. The only thing that's been produced and consumed in the example is a $1 chocolate bar. All the other transactions involve the purchase and sale of *intermediate goods*. To count the expenditure on intermediate goods and services as well as the expenditure on the final good involves counting the same thing twice, or more than twice when there are several intermediate stages, as there are in this example. Counting both expenditure on final goods and intermediate goods is known as **double counting**.

Milk, sugar, cocoa and electric power are all intermediate goods in the production of a chocolate bar — the final good. But the milk, sugar, cocoa and electric power that you consume directly yourself are final goods. Thus whether a good is intermediate or final depends not on what it is but on what it is used for.

Table 23.6 sets out the production approach to measuring GDP in Australia using data for 1989/90. At the time this book went to press, the 1990/91 production approach estimates were not available. The sum of the value added in all industries gives us the gross domestic product at factor cost. GDP is then

Table 23.5 Value Added in the Life of a Chocolate Bar

Transaction	Total amount paid/received (dollars)	Value added (dollars)	Industry in which value is added
Chocolate producer buys milk	0.04	0.04	Dairy
Chocolate producer buys sugar	0.08	0.08	Sugar
Chocolate producer buys cocoa beans	0.08	0.08	Cocoa
Chocolate producer buys electric power	0.12	0.12	Electricity
Chocolate producer pays labour	0.28	0.28	Chocolate
Chocolate producer sells to wholesaler	0.72	0.12	Chocolate
Wholesaler sells to retailer	0.80	0.08	Wholesale
Retailer sells to you	1.00	0.20	Retail
Total	$3.12	$1.00	

To produce a $1 chocolate bar, a chocolate producer buys milk, sugar, cocoa beans and electric power from other producers. The value of these inputs into the chocolate bar are part of the product — value added — of the dairy, sugar, cocoa and electricity sectors of the economy. The chocolate producer buys labour services and sells the chocolate bar to the wholesaler at a profit. Its labour cost and profit are part of the value added in the chocolate sector. The wholesaler sells to the retailer, providing a service and adding further value to the chocolate bar. Finally, the retailer sells to you, the customer, adding further value in the form of retail services. The sum of all the amounts paid and received — $3.12 — is a mixture of expenditure on intermediate goods and services and expenditure on the final good; it has no economic meaning. The sum of the value added in each sector equals final expenditure on the chocolate bar.

calculated by adding indirect taxes less subsidies to gross domestic product at factor cost.

Aggregate Expenditure, Production and Income

We've now studied the *concepts* of aggregate expenditure, aggregate production and aggregate income as well as the *measurement* of these concepts by the Australian Bureau of Statistics. The relationship between the three concepts and the relative importance of the components of each are illustrated in Fig. 23.3. This figure provides a snapshot summary of the entire preceding description of the national accounting concepts that you've studied in this chapter.

R E V I E W

GDP can be measured by three methods — the *expenditure approach* (the sum of consumption expenditure, investment, government purchases of goods and services, and exports minus imports), the *income approach* (the sum of wages, interest, rent and profit) and the *production approach* (the sum of the value added in each industry or sector of the economy). ■

So far, in our study of GDP and its measurement, we've been concerned with the dollar value of GDP and its components. But GDP can change either because prices change or because there is a change in the volume of goods and services produced — a change in *real* GDP. As we saw

Figure 23.3 Aggregate Expenditure, Production and Income

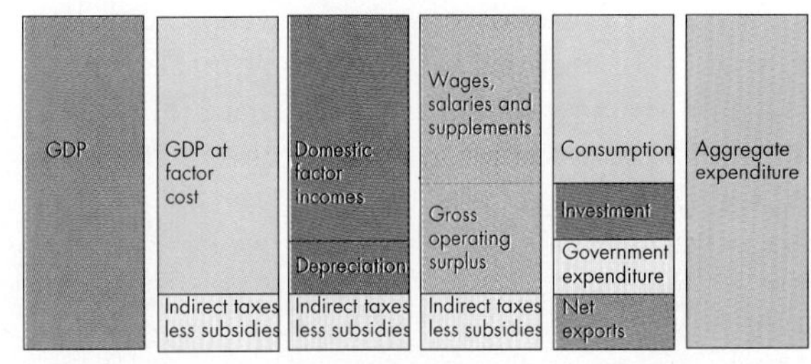

This figure emphasizes the equality between aggregate expenditure, the value of production (GDP) and aggregate income, and illustrates the relative magnitudes of the main components of each of these aggregate concepts.

Table 23.6 GDP: The Production Approach, 1989/90*

Industry	Value added in 1989/90 (billions of dollars)
Agriculture, forestry, fishing and hunting	15
Mining	17
Manufacturing	59
Electricity, gas and water	11
Construction	28
Wholesale and retail trade	68
Transport, storage and communications	28
Finance, property and business services	46
Public administration and defence	13
Community services	42
Recreation, personal and other services	16
Ownership of dwellings	34
Less Imputed bank service charge	–9
Gross domestic product at factor cost	328
Indirect taxes less subsidies	44
Gross domestic product at market prices	372

*1990/91 figures not available at time book went to press.

The production approach adds together the value added in each industry, which is gross domestic product at factor cost. To measure GDP, indirect taxes less subsidies are added to gross domestic product at factor cost. In 1989/90, GDP measured by the production approach was $372 billion.

Source: Australian Bureau of Statistics, *National Income and Expenditure Accounts*, ABS No. 5204.0, 1989/90.

in Chapter 22, the divergence between the dollar value of GDP and real GDP can be quite large. Let's now see how we measure the price level and distinguish between price changes and changes in real GDP.

Price Level and Inflation

Prices are constantly changing, some rising quickly, some slowly and some even falling. Because the prices of goods and services rise and fall at different rates, we use a price index to measure the average price level. First, we take a basket of goods and services and calculate its value. Then we express the value of the basket as a percentage of its value in some *base period.* Such a percentage is called a *price index.*

Table 23.7 shows you how to calculate a price index for the basket of goods that Tom buys. His basket is a very simple one. It contains 4 videos and 2 six-packs of soft drink. The value of Tom's basket in 1990 was $30. The same basket in 1991 cost $35.40. Tom's price index is $35.40 expressed as a percentage of $30. That is,

$$\frac{\$35.40}{\$30.00} \times 100 = 118$$

Notice that if the current period and the base period were one and the same, the price index would be 100.

There are two main price indexes used to measure the price level in Australia today: the Consumer Price Index and the GDP deflator. The **Consumer Price Index** (CPI) measures the average level of prices of the goods and services typically consumed by a metropolitan Australian household. The **GDP deflator** measures the average level of prices of all the goods and services that are included in GDP. We are now going to study the method used for determining these price indexes. In calculating the actual indexes, the Australian Bureau of Statistics processes millions of pieces of information. But we can learn the principles involved in those calculations by working through some simple examples.

Consumer Price Index

The *Consumer Price Index* measures the quarterly changes in the price of a basket of goods and services that account for a high proportion of expenditure by metropolitan wage and salary earning households.

To construct this price index, the Australian Bureau of Statistics first selects a base period. Currently the base period is 1980/81. It then selects a basket of goods — the quantities of 107 different goods and services that were typically consumed by urban households in the base period.

In the first two months of each quarter a team of observers descends on major urban centres across Australia to record the prices for these 107 items. When all the data is collected, the CPI is calculated by valuing the base period basket of goods at the current month's prices. That value is expressed as a percentage of the value of the same basket in the base period.

To see more precisely how the CPI is calculated, let's work through an example. Table 23.8 summarizes our calculations.

Table 23.7 Calculating a Price Index

Good	Quantity bought	1990 (base period) Price	1990 (base period) Expenditure	1991 (current period) Price	1991 (current period) Expenditure
Videos	4	$6.00	$24.00	$6.75	$27.00
Six-packs of soft drink	2	$3.00	$6.00	$4.20	$8.40
			$30.00		$35.40

Price Index for 1991 $= \frac{\$35.40}{\$30.00} \times 100 = 118$

A price index for 1991 is calculated in two steps. The first step is to value the goods bought in 1990, the base period, at the prices prevailing in both 1990 and 1991. The second step is to divide the value of those goods in 1991 by their value in the base period 1990, and multiply the result by 100.

Let's suppose that there are only three goods in the typical consumer's basket: oranges, haircuts and bus rides. The quantities bought and the prices prevailing in the base period are shown in the table. Total expenditure in the base period is also shown: the typical consumer buys 200 bus rides at 70¢ each and so spends $140 on bus rides. Expenditure on oranges and haircuts is worked out in the same way. Total expenditure is the sum of expenditure on the three goods, which is $210.

To calculate the price index for the current period, we need to discover the prices of the goods in the current period. We do not need to know the quantities bought in the current period. Let's suppose that the prices are those set out in the table under 'current period'. We can now calculate the current period's value of the basket of goods by using the current period's prices. For example, the current price of oranges is $1.20 a bag, so the current period's value of the base period quantity (5 bags) is 5 multiplied by $1.20, which is $6. The base period quantities of haircuts and bus rides are valued at this period's prices in a similar way. The total value in the current period of the base period basket is $231.

We can now calculate the CPI — the ratio of this period's value of the goods to the base period's value, multiplied by 100. In this example, the CPI for the current period is 110. The CPI for the base period is by definition 100, so that the overall increase in the price level for the period is 10 per cent.

GDP Deflator

The *GDP deflator* measures the average level of the prices of all the goods and services that make up GDP. It is calculated by dividing nominal GDP by real GDP and multiplying the result by 100. We use the term 'nominal GDP', because it measures the money value of output. Real GDP is a measure of the physical volume of output arrived at by valuing the current period output at prices that prevailed in a base period. Currently, the base period for calculating real GDP is 1984/85. We refer to the units in which real GDP is measured as '1984/85 dollars'.

Table 23.9 shows the values of nominal GDP, real GDP and the GDP deflator for selected years since 1974/75. As you can see, nominal GDP has increased much faster than real GDP. In fact, nominal GDP in 1990/91 is almost six times what it was in 1974/75, while real GDP is less than twice its 1974/75 value. The GDP deflator is 3.7 times higher in 1990/91 than it was in 1974/75.

We are going to learn how to calculate the GDP deflator by studying an imaginary economy. We will calculate nominal GDP and real GDP as well as the GDP deflator. To make our calculations simple, let's imagine an economy that has just three final goods: the consumption good is oranges; the capital good is computers; and the government good is pens. (Net exports are zero in this example.) Table 23.10 summarizes the calculations of nominal GDP, real GDP and the GDP deflator in this economy.

Let's focus first on calculating nominal GDP. We'll use the expenditure approach. The table shows the quantities of the final goods and their prices. To calculate nominal GDP, let's work out the expenditure on each good and then add the three expenditures. Consumption expenditure (oranges) is $4452,

Table 23.8 The Consumer Price Index (A Simplified Calculation)

Items in the basket	Base period Quantity	Price	Expenditure	Current period Price	Expenditure on base period quantities
Oranges	5 bags	$ 0.80 bag	$4.00	$1.20 per bag	$6.00
Haircuts	6	$11.00 each	$66.00	$12.50 each	$75.00
Bus rides	200	$ 0.70 each	$140.00	$0.75 each	$150.00
Total expenditure			$210.00		$231.00
	CPI = $\frac{\$210.00}{\$210.00} \times 100 = 100$			$\frac{\$231.00}{\$210.00} \times 100 = 110$	

A fixed basket of goods — 5 bags of oranges, 6 haircuts and 200 bus rides — is valued in the base period at $210. Prices change and that same basket is valued at $231 in the current period. The CPI is equal to the current period value of the basket divided by the base period value of the basket, multiplied by 100. In the base period the CPI is 100 and in the current period it is 110.

investment (computers) is $10,500, government purchases (pens) are $1060, so nominal GDP is $16,012.

Next, let's calculate real GDP. This is calculated by valuing the current period quantities at the base period prices. The table shows the prices for the base period. Real expenditure on oranges for the current period is 4240 bags of oranges valued at $1 per bag, which is $4240. If we perform the same types of calculations for computers and pens and add up the real expenditures, we arrive at a real GDP of $15,300.

To calculate the GDP deflator for the current period, we divide nominal GDP ($16,012) by real GDP ($15,300) and multiply the result by 100. The GDP deflator that we obtain is 104.7. If the current period is also the base period, nominal GDP equals real GDP and the GDP deflator is 100. Thus the GDP deflator in the base period is 100, just as it is for the CPI.

Inflation and Relative Price Changes

The inflation rate is calculated as the percentage increase in the price index. For example, in the case that we studied in Table 23.8, the CPI rose by 10 per cent from the base period to the current period. Underlying that change in the price index are the individual changes in the prices of oranges, haircuts and bus rides. No individual price rose by 10 per cent. The price of oranges rose by 50 per cent, the price of haircuts by 13.6 per cent and the price of bus rides

Table 23.9 Nominal GDP, Real GDP and the GDP Deflator

Year	Nominal GDP (billions of dollars)	Real GDP (billions of 1984/85 dollars)	GDP deflator (1984/85 = 100)
1974/75	65	163	39.9
1979/80	123	187	65.8
1984/85	216	216	100.0
1990/91	380	257	147.6

Nominal GDP measures the *money* value of output. Real GDP measures the *physical volume* of output. Nominal GDP values output in the prices that prevailed in the period in question. Real GDP values output in the prices of the base period. In the table, goods and services produced between 1974/75 and 1990/91 are valued in the prices that prevailed in 1984/85. The GDP deflator is equal to nominal GDP divided by real GDP, multiplied by 100. In 1984/85 the *base period*, the GDP deflator is 100. Nominal GDP in 1990/91 is six times what it was in 1974/75, real GDP is less than twice as high, and the GDP deflator is 3.7 times as high.

Source: Australian Bureau of Statistics, *Australian National Accounts: National Income and Expenditure Accounts*, ABS No. 5206.0, June 1991.

Table 23.10 Nominal GDP, Real GDP and the GDP Deflator: Simplified Calculations

Item	Current period Quantity	Price	Expenditure	Base period Price	Expenditure
Oranges	4240 bags	$1.05/bag	$4,452	$1/bag	$4,240
Computers	5	$2100 each	$10,500	$2000 each	$10,000
Pens	1060	$1 each	1,060	$1	$1,060
		Nominal GDP	$16,012	Real GDP	$15,300

GDP deflator = $\frac{\$16,012}{\$15,300} \times 100 = 104.7$

An imaginary economy produces only oranges, computers and pens. In the current period, nominal GDP is $16,012. If the current period quantities are valued at base period prices, we obtain a measure of real GDP, which is $15,300. The GDP deflator in the current period — which is calculated by dividing nominal GDP by real GDP in that period and multiplying the result by 100 — is 104.7.

by 7.1 per cent. This example captures a common feature of the world in which we live: it is rarely the case that all prices change by the same percentage amount. When the prices of goods rise by different percentages, there is a change in relative prices. The **relative price** is the ratio of the price of one good to the price of another good. For example, if the price of a bag of oranges is $0.80 and the price of a haircut is $11, the relative price of a haircut is 13 ¾ bags of oranges. It costs 13 ¾ bags of oranges to buy one haircut.

Prices and inflation, of course, mean a great deal to people. However, many people are confused by the difference between the inflation rate and relative price changes. Inflation and relative price changes are completely separate and independent phenomena. To see why this is true, we'll work through an example showing that, for the same relative price changes, we can have two entirely different inflation rates.

We will first learn how to calculate a change in relative prices. We can calculate the percentage change in a relative price as the difference between the percentage change in the price minus the inflation rate. Let's use again the calculations that we worked through in Table 23.8, now presented in Table 23.11(a). For example, the price of a bag of oranges rises from $0.80 to $1.20, or by 50 per cent. We have already calculated that prices on the average rose by 10 per cent. To calculate the percentage change in the relative price of a good, subtract the inflation rate from the percentage change in its price. The price of oranges increased relative to the average price of all goods by 50 per cent minus 10 per cent, which is 40 per cent. Bus rides fell in price relative to goods on the average by 2.9 per cent. The change in relative prices on the average is zero by definition. For every good whose relative price increases by *x* per cent there must be other goods whose relative prices fall by an average of *x* per cent.

In Table 23.11(b), we see that relative prices can change without inflation. In fact, part (b) illustrates the same changes in relative prices that occurred in part (a) but with no inflation. In this case, the price of oranges increases by 40 per cent to $1.12 a bag, the price of haircuts increases by 3.6 per cent to $11.40 a haircut and the price of bus rides falls by 2.9 per cent to $0.68 a ride. If you calculate the current and base period values of the basket in part (b), you will find that consumers spend exactly the same at the new prices as they do at the base period prices. There is no inflation, even though relative prices have changed.

We've now looked at two cases in which the relative price of oranges increases by 40 per cent. In one, inflation is 10 per cent; in the other, there is no inflation. Clearly, inflation has not been *caused* by the change in the price of oranges. In the first case, the price of each good increases by 10 per cent more than it does in the second case. Singling out the good whose relative price has increased most does not help us explain why all prices are rising by 10 per cent more in the first case than in the second case.

Any inflation rate can occur with any behaviour of relative prices. Relative prices are determined by supply and demand in the markets for the individual

Table 23.11 Relative Price Changes With or Without Inflation

(a) 10 per cent inflation

Item	Base period price	New price	Percentage change in price	Percentage change in relative price
Oranges	$ 0.80	$ 1.20	+ 50.0	+40.0
Haircuts	$11.00	$12.50	+ 13.6	+ 3.6
Bus rides	$ 0.70	$ 0.75	+ 7.1	− 2.9

(b) No inflation

Item	Base period price	New price	Percentage change in price	Percentage change in relative price
Oranges	$ 0.80	$ 1.12	+ 40.0	+40.0
Haircuts	$11.00	$11.40	+ 3.6	+ 3.6
Bus rides	$ 0.70	$ 0.68	− 2.9	− 2.9

A relative price is the price of one good divided by the price of another good. Relative prices change whenever the price of one good changes by a different percentage from the price of some other good. Relative price changes do not cause inflation. They can occur with or without inflation. In part (a), the price index rises by 10 per cent. In part (b), the price index remains constant. In both parts, the relative price of oranges increases by 40 per cent and that of haircuts by 3.6 per cent, and the relative price of bus rides falls by 2.9 per cent. The rise in the price of oranges cannot be regarded as the cause of the rise in the price index in part (a) because that same rise in the price of oranges occurs with no change in the price index in part (b).

goods and services. The price level and the inflation rate are determined independently of *relative* prices. To explain an increase (or decrease) in the inflation rate, we have to explain why all prices are increasing at a different rate and not why some prices are increasing faster than others. Not everyone understands this distinction.

The Consumer Price Index and the Cost of Living

Does the Consumer Price Index measure the cost of living? Does a 5 per cent increase in the CPI mean that the cost of living has increased by 5 per cent? It does not for three reasons:

- Substitution effects
- Arrival of new goods and disappearance of old ones
- Quality improvements

Substitution Effects A change in the CPI measures the percentage change in the price of a *fixed* basket of goods and services. The actual basket of goods and services bought depends on relative prices and on consumers' tastes. Changes in relative prices will lead consumers to economize on goods that have become relatively expensive and to buy more of those goods whose relative prices have fallen. If chicken doubles in price but the price of beef increases by only 5 per cent, people will substitute the now relatively less expensive beef for the relatively more expensive chicken. Because consumers make such substitutions, a price index based on a fixed basket will overstate the effects of a given increase in the general level of prices on the consumer's cost of living.

Arrival and Disappearance of Goods Discrepancies between the CPI and the cost of living also arise from the disappearance of some commodities and the emergence of new ones. For example, suppose that you want to compare the cost of living in 1990 with that in 1890. Using a price index that has horse feed in it will not work. Though that price featured in people's transportation costs in 1890, it plays no role today. Similarly, a price index with petrol in it will be of little use since petrol, while relevant today, did not feature in people's spending in 1890. Even comparisons between 1990 and 1980 suffer from this same problem. Compact discs and microwave popcorn that feature in our budgets in 1990 were not available in 1980.

Quality Improvements The consumer price index can overstate a true rise in prices by ignoring quality improvements. Most goods undergo constant quality improvement. For example, cars, computers and CD players get better year after year. Part of the increase in price of these items reflects the improvement in the quality of the product. Yet the CPI will regard such a price change as inflation. Attempts have been made to correct for this factor, which might contribute as much as 2 per cent a year on the average to the measured inflation rate.

Substitution effects, the arrival of new goods, the departure of old ones and quality improvements make the connection between the CPI and the cost of living imprecise. To reduce the problems that arise from this source, the Australian Bureau of Statistics updates the weights used for calculating the CPI from time to time. Even so, the CPI is of limited value for making comparisons of the cost of living over long periods of time. But for the purpose for which it was devised — calculating month-to-month and year-to-year rates of inflation — the CPI does a good job.

R E V I E W

The GDP deflator is a price index that converts nominal GDP to real GDP. It is calculated as the ratio of nominal GDP to real GDP (multiplied by 100). Real GDP values the current period's output at base period prices. The Consumer Price Index is a price index based on the consumption expenditures of a typical metropolitan family. It is calculated as the ratio of the value of a base period basket in the current period to its value in the base period (multiplied by 100).

A relative price is the price of one good relative to prices on the average. Relative prices are constantly changing but are independent of the inflation rate. Any pattern of relative price changes can take place at any inflation rate.

The CPI has limitations as a means of comparing the cost of living over long periods but does a good job of measuring year-to-year changes in the inflation rate. ■

Now that we've studied the measurement of GDP and the price level and know how *real* GDP is measured, let's take a look at what real GDP tells us about the aggregate value of economic activity, the standard of living and economic welfare.

Real GDP, Aggregate Economic Activity and Economic Welfare

What does real GDP really measure? How good a measure is it? What does it tell us about aggregate economic activity? And what does it tell us about the standard of living and economic welfare?

Economic welfare is a comprehensive measure of the general state of well-being and standard of living. Economic welfare depends on the following factors:

- The quantity and quality of goods and services available
- The amount of leisure time available
- The degree of ecomonic equality among individuals

Real GDP does not accurately measure the quantity or quality of all the goods and services that we produce and it provides no information on the amount of leisure time or the degree of economic equality. Its mismeasurement of production has errors in both directions. There are five limitations of real GDP as a measure of economic welfare:

- Underground real GDP
- Household production
- Environmental damage
- Economic equality
- Leisure time

Underground Real GDP The **underground economy** comprises all economic activity that is legal but unreported. Underground economic activity is unreported because participants in the underground economy withhold information to evade taxes or regulations. For example, avoiding safety regulations, minimum wage laws, social security payments or other fringe benefits are motives for operating in the underground economy. Attempts have been made to estimate the scale of the underground economy and

The National Income Accounts

National Accounting for Sustainable GDP

Poor Nauru. The 7500 inhabitants of the tiny island could once boast the highest per capita income in the world, thanks to the reported $100 million a year proceeds from bird dung exports. Nauru was the OPEC of the Pacific.

But after 80 years of extraction, the phosphate deposits are close to exhaustion, leaving the 22 square kilometre island looking like a lunar landscape. According to newspaper reports, there is little topsoil left, the locals have forgotten how to fish, a diet of junk food has produced widespread diabetes and the island is heavily in debt to foreigners.

Nauru provides the extreme case of where the traditional measures of economic well-being — Gross Domestic Product — can be highly misleading by confusing the depletion of valuable assets with the generation of income.

It prompts some economists to call for 'natural resource and environmental accounting' to gauge whether economic development is 'sustainable' or whether current rates of income and consumption are eating into the economy's stock of natural resources.

The national accounts measure of GDP is largely a cash-flow concept designed more for short-term macroeconomic stabilisation purposes than for measures of 'sustainable' income over the long run.

As the World Resources Institute has noted, the classical economists of the 18th and 19th centuries such as David Ricardo and Karl Marx regarded income as the return on three kinds of inputs or assets: natural resources (such as land), human resources (labour) and invested human-made capital.

But the neo-classical economists of the 19th century largely ignored the productive role and scarcity value of natural resources and instead concentrated on labour and capital.

This has meant that today's national accounts regard natural resources as a 'gift of nature' that were either in infinite supply or capable of regeneration. They do not deduct from 'income' any depletion of natural resource stocks.

This, of course, is contrary to business accounting, where depreciation of buildings and machinery and capital losses are routinely deducted from income. Otherwise, a company's measured 'income' would partly represent a reduction in its net worth.

Measures of Gross Domestic Product do not deduct depreciation of the economy's human-made capital stock. But this is because the rate of depreciation is (probably) fairly constant over time — so that net domestic product (or NDP) tends to run parallel with GDP. This is a more heroic assumption for depreciation of natural capital.

As well, environmental economists have criticized the national accounting treatment of so-called defensive or 'regrettable' spending on the environment. Spending on pollution abatement, soil conservation, air and water quality monitoring, water and sewerage treatment, waste disposal and cleaning up pollutants such as oil spills are basically a cost of economic activity. But, in national accounting, such expenditures are often treated as an increase in national income or output (as is increased spending on national defence).

OK, so what ought to be done? One approach would be to adjust directly traditional measures of GDP for resource depletion. By subtracting environmental protection expenditures from the GDP estimates contained in the traditional national accounts, a set of proposed satellite accounts would provide an estimate of 'environmentally adjusted GDP'.

And environmentally adjusted GDP minus environmental costs from the depletion or degradation of natural resources would give sustainable gross domestic product, or SGDP.

Australian Financial Review
1 June, 1990
Economics Extra By Michael Stutchbury

The Essence of the Story

- Nauru's national income accounts do not properly measure Nauru's income.
- Nauru's per capita GDP was high while its phosphate exports were high.
- Reliance on the phosphate exports allowed traditional skills to be ignored, and ultimately lost.
- Mining also degraded the environment to such an extent that other activities are now no longer viable.
- When Nauru's phosphate deposits are depleted, per capita GDP will be low.

Background and Analysis

- Modern national accounting practices measure product and income flows arising from current market transactions. These might not be a good indicator of current and future welfare.
- Welfare is better measured by wealth, which is the present discounted value of all current and future income flows.
- Current and future income flows depend on the availability of current and future labour and capital inputs. Thus if we want the national income accounts to provide an indicator of national welfare, they must be expanded to include some measure of the appreciation or depreciation of all forms of capital — physical, human and natural.
- Currently, only additions to the physical stock of capital are included in the national income accounts.
- The accounts ignore the following:
    - the rate of accumulation, net of depreciation, of human capital. (In Nauru's case, the loss of traditional fishing skills meant the inability to generate income when the phosphate deposits were depleted.)
    - the rate of accumulation of natural or environmental capital. (In Nauru's case, the mining of phosphate so degraded the land, eliminating the topsoil, that the land was unsuitable for other activity.)
- In addition, the national income accounts do not distinguish between those activities that create new goods and services and those that are directed at restoring physical, human and environmental capital that was consumed in the production processes of the economy. Thus 'defensive spending', such as pollution abatement, soil conservation and water quality monitoring, are really forms of replacement investment to be subtracted from GDP to give a measure of net domestic product.
- While difficult to construct, the Australian Bureau of Statistics has begun work on an environmentally adjusted set of national income accounts.

Conclusion

- Nauru's preoccupation with current levels of GDP, while they were high, may ultimately have led to an overall decline in welfare for Nauru's inhabitants. Ignoring the impacts of mining on Nauru's stock of human and natural capital has depleted them to the extent that GDP will fall as Nauru's phosphate deposits run down.

guesses range from 5 per cent to 15 per cent of GDP ($19–$56 billion).

Although not usually regarded as part of the underground economy, a great deal of other unreported activity takes place — economic activity that is illegal. In today's economy, various forms of illegal gambling, prostitution and drug trading are important omitted components of economic activity. It is impossible to measure the scale of illegal activities but guesses range from 1 to 2 per cent of GDP ($3–$6 billion).

Household Production An enormous amount of economic activity that no one is obliged to report takes place every day in our own homes. Changing a light bulb, cutting the grass, washing the car, washing a shirt, painting a door, and teaching a child to catch a ball are all examples of productive activities that do not involve market transactions and that are not counted as part of GDP.

Household production has become much more capital intensive over the years. As a result, less labour is now used in household production. For example, a microwave meal that takes just a few minutes to prepare uses a great deal of capital and almost no labour. Because we use less labour and more capital in household production, it is not easy to work out whether this type of production has increased or decreased over time. It is likely, however, that it has decreased as more and more people have joined the labour force.

Household production is almost certainly cyclical. When the economy is in recession, household production increases. Households whose members are unemployed buy fewer goods in the marketplace and provide more services for themselves. When the economy is booming, there is an increase in employment outside the home and household production decreases.

Environmental Damage The environment is directly affected by economic activity. The burning of hydrocarbon fuels is the most visible activity that damages our environment. But it is not the only example. The depletion of exhaustible resources, the mass clearing of forests and the pollution of lakes and rivers are other important environmental consequences of industrial production.

Resources used to protect the environment are valued as part of GDP. For example, the value of catalytic converters that help to protect the atmosphere from automobile emissions are part of GDP. But if we did not use such pieces of equipment and polluted the atmosphere instead, we would not count the deteriorating air that we were breathing as a negative in the GDP.

It is obvious that an industrial society produces more atmospheric pollution than a primitive or agricultural society. But such pollution does not necessarily increase as industrial societies become wealthier. One of the things that wealthy people value is a clean environment and they devote resources to protecting it. Compare the level of pollution in East Germany in the late 1980s with the level of pollution in Australia. East Germany, a relatively poor country, polluted its rivers, lakes and atmosphere in a way that is unthinkable in Australia.

Economic Equality A country might have a very large real GDP per person but also have a high degree of inequality. A few people might be extremely wealthy while the vast majority live in abject poverty. Such an economy would generally be regarded as having less economic welfare than one in which the same amount of real GDP was more equally shared. For example, average GDP per person in the oil-rich countries of the Middle East is similar to that of several countries in Western Europe, but much less equally distributed. Economic welfare is higher in those Western European countries.

Leisure Time Leisure time is obviously an economic good that adds to our economic welfare. Other things being equal, the more leisure we have, the better off we are. Our working time is valued as part of GDP but our leisure time is not. Yet from the point of view of economic welfare, that leisure time must be at least as valuable to us as the hourly wage that we earn. If it was not, we would work instead of taking the leisure.

Economic Welfare and Real GDP

Figure 23.4 provides a summary of the above discussion about real GDP and economic welfare. It also shows why the factors left out of real GDP could paint a misleading picture. If real GDP increases at the expense of other factors that affect economic welfare (see the arrows encroaching on leisure time and underground production), there will be no change in economic welfare. But if real GDP increases with no reduction (or even an increase) in the other factors, then welfare will increase (see the arrows expanding economic welfare).

Whether we get the wrong indications about economic welfare from changes (or differences) in real GDP depends on whether we are asking questions about the business cycle and economic welfare or whether we are comparing standards of living and economic welfare at different points in time or in different countries.

Figure 23.4 Real GDP and Economic Welfare

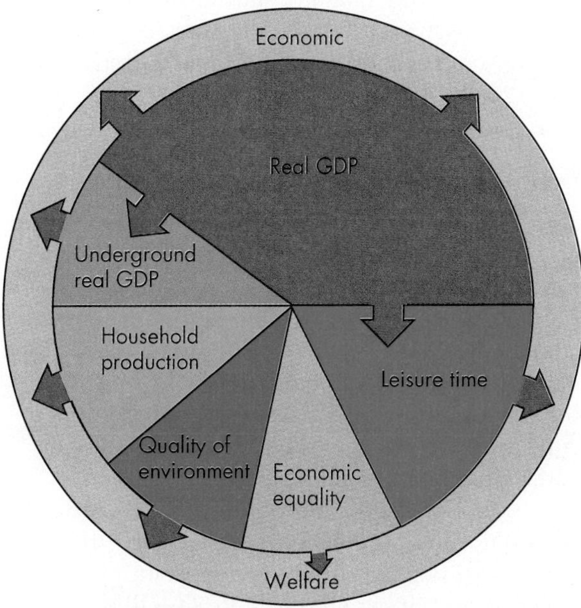

Real GDP is just one of the contributors to economic welfare. The others are production in the underground economy, household production, the quality of the environment, leisure time and economic equality. An increase in real GDP does not necessarily increase economic welfare and more information is needed to make welfare judgements and comparisons.

The Business Cycle and Economic Welfare The fluctuations in economic activity measured by real GDP probably overstate the fluctuations in total production and economic welfare. But the directions of change of the two are likely to be the same. Real GDP fluctuations probably overstate the fluctuations in economic welfare because when there is an economic downturn, household production increases and so does leisure time. When real GDP is growing quickly, leisure time and household production probably decline.

Standard of Living and Economic Welfare Comparisons For standard of living comparisons, the factors omitted from real GDP are probably very important. For example, in developing countries, the underground economy and the amount of household production are a much higher proportion of economic activity than in developed countries. This fact makes comparisons of GDP between countries such as Australia and Nigeria, for example, unreliable measures of comparative living standards unless the GDP data is supplemented with other information.

Using GDP data to gauge changes in living standards over time is also unreliable. Living standards depend only partly on the value of output. They also depend on the composition of that output. For example, a country may have the same GDP in two different years but in one of these years may produce more weapons and in the other more music. Consumers will not be indifferent as to which of these two products are produced.

Other factors affecting living standards include the amount of leisure time available, the quality of the environment, the security of jobs and homes, the safety of city streets and so on. It is possible to construct broader measures that combine the many factors that contribute to human happiness. Real GDP will be one element in that measure, but it will be by no means the whole of it.

■ In Chapter 22, we examined Australia's macroeconomic performance in recent years and over a longer sweep of history. In this chapter, we studied the methods used for measuring the macroeconomy and, in particular, the average level of prices and the overall level of real economic activity. In the following chapters, we're going to study some macroeconomic models — models designed to explain and predict the behaviour of real GDP, the price level, employment and unemployment, the stock market and other related phenomena. We start this process in the next chapter by examining a macroeconomic model of demand and supply — a model of *aggregate* demand and *aggregate* supply.

S U M M A R Y

The Circular Flow of Expenditure and Income

All economic agents — households, firms, government and the rest of the world — interact in the circular flow of income and expenditure. Households sell factors of production to firms and buy consumption goods and services from firms. Firms hire factors of production from households and pay incomes to households in exchange for factor services. Firms sell consumption goods and services to households and capital goods to other firms. Government collects taxes from households and firms, pays benefits under various social programmes to households and buys goods and services from firms. Foreigners buy goods from domestic firms and sell goods to them.

The flow of expenditure on final goods and services winds up as somebody's income. Therefore

$$\text{Aggregate income} = \text{Aggregate expenditure}$$

Furthermore, expenditure on final goods and services is a method of valuing the output of the economy. Therefore

$$\begin{matrix}\text{Aggregate} \\ \text{income}\end{matrix} = \begin{matrix}\text{Aggregate} \\ \text{expenditure}\end{matrix} = \begin{matrix}\text{Value of} \\ \text{output (GDP)}\end{matrix}$$

From the firm's accounts we know that

$$Y = C + I + G + EX - IM$$

and from the household's accounts we know that

$$Y = C + S + T$$

Combining these two equations we obtain

$$I + G + EX = S + T + IM$$

This equation tells us that injections into the circular flow (left-hand side) equal the leakages from the circular flow (right-hand side). (pp. 114–120)

Australia's Income and Expenditure Accounts

Because aggregate expenditure, aggregate income and the value of production are equal, national income accountants can measure GDP using one of three approaches: expenditure, income and production.

The expenditure approach adds together consumption expenditure, investment, government purchases of goods and services, and net exports to arrive at an estimate of GDP.

The income approach adds together the incomes paid to the various factors of production plus profit paid to the owners of firms. To use the income approach, it is necessary to make an adjustment from the factor cost value of GDP to the market price value by adding indirect taxes and subtracting subsidies. It is also necessary to add capital consumption (depreciation) in order to arrive at GDP.

The production approach sums the value added by each firm in the economy. In using the production approach, it is necessary to be careful to avoid double counting and only measure value added rather than total sales in each sector of the economy.

Actual GDP does not measure all the economic activity in the nation. It excludes crime, the underground economy and non-market activities. (pp. 120–126)

Price Level and Inflation

There are two major price indexes that measure the price level and inflation: the Consumer Price Index and the GDP deflator.

The CPI measures the average level of prices of goods and services typically consumed by a metropolitan family in Australia. The CPI is the ratio of the value of a base period basket of commodities at current period prices to the same basket valued at base period prices, multiplied by 100.

The GDP deflator is nominal GDP divided by real GDP, multiplied by 100. Nominal GDP is calculated by valuing the current period quantities produced at current period prices. Real GDP is calculated by valuing the current period quantities produced at base period prices.

In interpreting changes in prices, we need to distinguish between inflation and relative price changes. A relative price is the ratio of the price of one good to the price of another good. Relative prices are constantly changing. We cannot tell anything about the sources of inflation by studying which relative prices have changed most. Any relative price changes can occur with any inflation rate.

Because relative prices are constantly changing and causing consumers to substitute less expensive items for more expensive items, because of the disappearance of some goods and the arrival of new goods and because of improvements in the quality of goods, the CPI is an imperfect measure of the cost of living, especially when comparisons are made across a long time span. (pp. 126–131)

Real GDP, Aggregate Economic Activity and Economic Welfare

Real GDP is not a good measure of aggregate economic activity and economic welfare. It excludes production in the underground economy, household production, environmental damage and the contribution to economic welfare of equality and leisure. (pp. 131–135)

KEY TERMS

Capital stock, p. 120
Consumer Price Index, p. 126
Consumption expenditure, p. 114
Depreciation, p. 122
Disposable income, p. 118
Domestic factor incomes, p. 122
Double counting, p. 124
Economic welfare, p. 131
Expenditure approach, p. 120
Factor cost, p. 123
GDP deflator, p. 126
Gross domestic product at factor cost, p. 122
Gross investment, p. 122
Income, p. 114
Income approach, p. 121
Indirect tax, p. 123
Injections, p. 119
Investment, p. 114
Inventories, p. 120
Leakages, p. 119
Market price, p. 123
Net domestic product, p. 123
Net exports, p. 118
Net investment, p. 122
Production approach, p. 123
Relative price, p. 129
Saving, p. 118
Subsidy, p. 123
Transfer payments, p. 116
Underground economy, p. 131
Value added, p. 123

PROBLEMS

1 The following flows of money took place in an imaginary economy last year:

Item	Millions of dollars
Wages paid to labou	800,000
Consumption expenditure	650,000
Taxes paid on wages	200,000
Government payments to support the unemployed, sick, and aged	50,000
Firms' profits	200,000
Investment	250,000
Taxes paid on profits	50,000
Government expenditure on goods and services	200,000
Export earnings	250,000
Saving	200,000
Import payments	300,000

a) Calculate the GDP for this economy.
b) Did you use the expenditure approach, income approach or production approach to make this calculation?
c) Does your answer to 1(a) value production in terms of market prices or factor cost? Why?
d) Calculate the value added last year.
e) What extra information do you need in order to calculate net national product?

2 A typical family in an island economy consumes only apples, bananas and cloth. The base period is year 1. Prices in the base period are $2 for a bag for apples, $3 a kilogram for bananas and $5 a metre for cloth. The typical family spends $40 on apples, $45 on bananas, and $25 on cloth. In year 2, apples cost $3 a bag, bananas cost $3 a kilogram and cloth cost $8 a metre. Calculate the economy's Consumer Price Index for year 2 and the inflation rate between year 1 and year 2.

3 A newspaper in the economy in problem 2, commenting on the inflation figures that you have just calculated, runs the headline 'Steeply Rising Clothing Prices Cause Inflation'. Write a letter to the editor pointing out the weakness in the economic reasoning of the paper's business reporter.

4 An economy has the following real GDP and nominal GDP in 1989 and 1990:

Year	Real GDP	Nominal GDP
1990	$1000 billion	$1200 billion
1991	$1050 billion	$1386 billion
1992	$1200 billion	$1500 billion

a) What is the GDP deflator for 1991?
b) What is the GDP deflator for 1992?
c) What is the inflation rate as measured by the GDP deflator between 1991 and 1992?
d) What is the percentage increase in the price level between 1991 and 1992 as measured by the GDP deflator?

Chapter 24

Aggregate Demand and Aggregate Supply

After studying this chapter, you will be able to:

- Define aggregate demand and explain what determines it.
- Explain the sources of growth and fluctuations in aggregate demand.
- Define aggregate supply and explain what determines it.
- Explain the sources of growth and fluctuations in aggregate supply.
- Define macroeconomic equilibrium.
- Predict the effect of changes in aggregate demand and aggregate supply.
- Explain why real GDP grows.
- Explain inflation and why its rate varies, sometimes exploding as it did in the 1970s.
- Explain the world-wide recession of 1981/82 and its effects on Australia.
- Explain the effects of monetary policy during the 1980s.
- Explain the effects of microeconomic reform on macroeconomic performance.

What Makes Our Garden Grow

In the twenty years from 1970/71 to 1990/91, Australian real GDP almost doubled. In fact, a near doubling of Australia's real GDP every twenty years has been routine. What forces drive our economy's growth? At the same time as real GDP has been growing, our dollar has been falling in value — we've experienced persistent inflation. In 1990/91, you needed $200 to buy what $100 would have bought in 1980/81. The fall in the value of the dollar that occurred in the 1980s was steady and continuous. What causes inflation? Why does it persist over many decades? Why did it explode in the 1970s and persist in the 1980s and into the 1990s? The Australian economy doesn't grow in a smooth, even expansion. Instead, it ebbs and flows over the business cycle. What makes real GDP grow unevenly, sometimes speeding up and sometimes slowing down or even shrinking? Recent years have shown great turbulence in the economy. In 1983/84, the unemployment rate shot up to its highest level since the Great Depression. Between 1983/84 and 1989/90 it fell. In 1990/91 it rose rapidly. Over the same period, real GDP has gone from shrinking in 1982/83 to rapid growth in 1983/84 and then to more moderate but sustained growth in the subsequent six years. In 1990/91 it again fell. Can we make sense of such rapid economic change? Sometimes our economy is hit with a big disturbance — for example, the financial deregulation throughout the 1980s, including floating the exchange rate in 1983; the collapse in the prices exporters received in 1985/86; and the tight monetary policy in 1989/90. How do developments such as these affect prices and production?

To answer questions like these, we need a model — a macroeconomic model. Our first task in this chapter is to build such a model. The particular macroeconomic model that we'll study contains three concepts: aggregate demand, aggregate supply and macroeconomic equilibrium. It is known as the aggregate demand — aggregate supply model. The aggregate demand–aggregate supply model is a big picture overview model that plays a role in macroeconomics similar to the demand and supply model in microeconomics. Just as the demand and supply model enables us to explain and predict fluctuations in prices and quantities of individual goods and services, so the aggregate demand and supply model enables us to explain and predict fluctuations in the price level and real GDP. Our second task in this chapter is to use the aggregate demand and supply model to answer questions such as those that we've just posed. You'll discover that this powerful theory of aggregate demand and aggregate supply enables us to analyse and predict many important economic events that have a major impact on our lives.

Aggregate Demand

The aggregate quantity of goods and services produced (real output) is measured as real GDP — GDP valued in constant dollars. The average price of all these goods and services is measured by the GDP deflator. We are going to build a model that determines the values of real GDP and the GDP deflator. The model that we will build is based on the same concepts of demand, supply and equilibrium that we met in Chapter 4. But here the good is not tapes, the market we considered in Chapter 4 — it is real GDP — and the price is not the price of tapes — it is the GDP deflator.

The **aggregate quantity of goods and services demanded** is the sum of the quantities of consumption goods and services demanded by households, of investment goods demanded by firms, of goods and services demanded by governments and of net exports demanded by foreigners. Thus the aggregate quantity of goods and services demanded depends on decisions made by households, firms, governments and foreigners. When we studied the demand for tapes, in Chapter 4, we summarized the buying plans of households in a demand schedule and a demand curve. Similarly, when we study the forces influencing aggregate buying plans, we summarize the decisions of households, firms, governments and foreigners by using an aggregate demand schedule and an aggregate demand curve.

An **aggregate demand schedule** lists the quantity of real output (GDP) demanded at each price level, holding constant all other influences on buying plans. The **aggregate demand curve** plots the quantity of real GDP demanded against the price level. **Aggregate demand** refers to the relationship between the quantity of real GDP demanded and the price level.

Figure 24.1 shows an aggregate demand schedule and aggregate demand curve. Each row of the table corresponds to a point in the figure. For example, row c of the aggregate demand schedule tells us that if the GDP deflator is 130, the level of real GDP demanded is 240 billion in 1984/85 dollars. This row is plotted as point *c* on the aggregate demand curve.

Figure 24.1 The Aggregate Demand Schedule and Aggregate Demand Curve

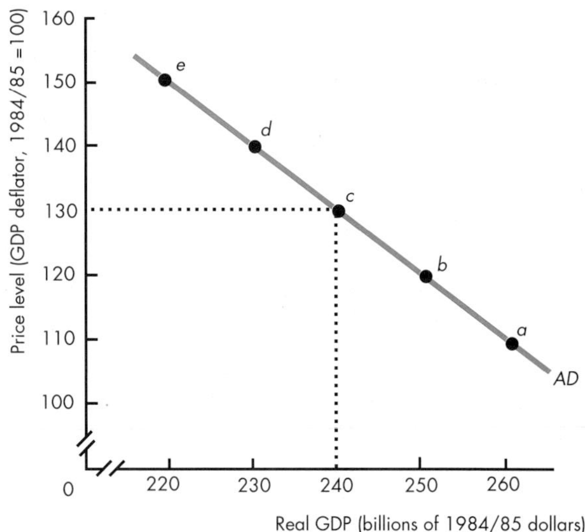

	Price level (GDP deflator)	Real GDP (billions of 1984/85 dollars)
a	110	260
b	120	250
c	130	240
d	140	230
e	150	220

The aggregate demand curve (*AD*) traces the quantity of real GDP demanded as the price level varies, holding everything else constant. The aggregate demand curve is derived from the schedule in the table. Each point from *a* through to *e* on the curve corresponds to the row in the table identified by the same letter. Thus when the price level is 130, the quantity of real GDP demanded is 240 billion in 1984/85 dollars, illustrated by point *c* in the figure.

In constructing the aggregate demand schedule and aggregate demand curve, we hold constant all the influences on the quantity of real GDP demanded other than the price level. The effect of a change in the price level is shown as a movement along the aggregate demand curve. A change in any of the other influences on the quantity of real GDP demanded results in a new aggregate demand schedule and a shift in the aggregate demand curve. First, let's concentrate on the effects of a change in the price level on the quantity of real GDP demanded.

You can see from the downward slope of the aggregate demand curve, and from the numbers that describe the aggregate demand schedule, that the higher the price level, the smaller is the quantity of real GDP demanded. Why does the aggregate demand curve slope downward?

Why the Aggregate Demand Curve Slopes Downward

It's easy to understand why the demand curve for a single good slopes downward. If the price of Coca-Cola rises, the quantity of Coca-Cola demanded falls because people switch to drinking Pepsi-Cola and other substitutes. It's also easy to understand why the demand curve for a whole class of goods and services slopes downward. If the prices of Coca-Cola, Pepsi-Cola and all other soft drinks rise, the quantity of soft drink demanded falls because people switch from drinking soft drink to other substitute drinks and other goods. But it's less easy to see why the demand curve for *all* goods and services slopes downward. If the price of all goods increases and people demand a smaller quantity of *all* goods, what do they demand a larger quantity of? What do they substitute for goods and services?

There are three types of substitutes for the goods and services that make up real GDP. They are:

- Money and financial assets
- Goods and services in the future
- Goods and services produced in other countries

People may plan to buy a smaller quantity of the goods and services that make up real GDP and hold a larger quantity of money or other financial assets. They may plan to buy a smaller quantity of goods and services today but a larger quantity at some future time. Also, people may decide to buy a smaller quantity of the goods and services made in Australia and buy a larger quantity of goods and services made in other countries. These decisions are influenced by the price level and those influences result in the aggregate demand curve sloping downward.

Corresponding to these three decisions, we can identify three separate effects of the price level on the quantity of real GDP demanded. In the jargon of economists, they are:

- Real money balances effect
- Intertemporal substitution effect
- International substitution effect

Real Money Balances Effect The **real money balances effect** is the influence of a change in the quantity of real money on the quantity of real GDP demanded. The **quantity of money** is the quantity of currency, bank deposits and deposits at other types of financial institutions (such as building societies) held by households and firms. **Real money** is a measure of money based on the quantity of goods that it will buy. Real money is measured as dollars divided by the price level. For example, suppose that you have $500 in the bank. The quantity of money that you are holding is $500. Suppose that you continue to hold $500 and that the price level increases by 25 per cent. Then your real money holdings decrease by 25 per cent. That is, the $500 of money that you are holding will now buy what $400 would before the price level increase.

The real money balances effect is the influence of the quantity of real money on the quantity of goods and services bought. *Other things being equal, the larger the quantity of real money that households and firms are holding, the larger is the quantity of goods and services bought.* To understand the real money balances effect, let's think about how the Sony Corporation's spending plans are influenced by its real money holdings.

Suppose that Sony has $20 million in the bank. Suppose, furthermore, that Sony has decided that it doesn't want to change the way it's holding its assets. It doesn't want to have less money and more capital equipment in its production and distribution plants. And it doesn't want to sell off some of its productive assets in order to hold more money.

Now suppose that the prices of most goods and services, and the average price level, fall. Suppose that among the prices that fall are those of office buildings, computers, movie studios and all the other things that Sony owns and operates. The money that Sony is now holding buys more goods than it would before. Sony's got *more* real money. But its other assets are now worth less than before. This fall in the price level has increased Sony's holdings of real money and decreased the value of its holdings of capital equipment. Sony will now take advantage of the fact that it's holding a larger amount of real money to buy some additional capital equipment. But new buildings, plant and machinery are some of the goods that make up real GDP. Thus Sony's decision to use some of its extra real money to buy more plant and equipment results in an increase in the quantity of goods and services demanded — an increase in real GDP demanded.

Although Sony is a multinational giant, if only Sony behaves in this way, real GDP demanded will not increase much. The real money balances effect will be tiny. But if everyone behaves like Sony, the aggregate quantity of goods and services demanded will be larger than before. This increase in the quantity of goods and services demanded results from a fall in the price level.

Intertemporal Substitution Effect The substitution of goods now for goods later or of goods later for goods now is called **intertemporal substitution**. An example of intertemporal substitution is your decision to buy a new Walkman today instead of waiting until the end of the month. Another example is IBM's decision to speed up its installation of a new computer production plant. Yet another example is your decision to postpone that longed-for vacation.

There are two influences on intertemporal substitution:

- Current prices compared with expected future prices
- Interest rates

Current Prices Low current prices relative to expected future prices encourage people to change the timing of their purchases of capital goods — plant and equipment, houses and consumer durable goods — shifting some of that spending from the future to the present. High current prices relative to expected future prices discourage people from buying capital goods now and encourage them to shift some of that spending from the present to the future.

For example, suppose you are planning to buy a new car. You have made your decision on the basis of current car prices and your expectation of the price level one year from now. All things considered, you've decided that next year is the best time for you to make a purchase. Then you discover that for the next two weeks only, car makers are offering once-in-a-lifetime special discounts. Should you bring forward your purchase to take advantage of the current low prices? For a big enough discount, you will. That is, for a low enough current price, relative to your expectation of the future price, you will buy now rather than later.

Similarly, a firm might shelve a decision to install some new machines on learning that their prices have just increased as a result of a temporary shortage. In this case the current price has increased relative to the expected future price, and the purchase is postponed.

Your impulsive purchase of a car when car prices fall or a single firm's postponement of the purchase of some new machines when their prices rise would not change *aggregate* demand — at least, not by much. But recall that the 'price' we are considering is the price level, an index of all prices. If the price level rises or falls, all other things — including future prices — held constant, everyone and every firm contemplating *when* to make a purchase will be affected. Thus many decisions will be brought forward to the present when current prices fall, increasing aggregate demand. Similarly, many decisions to buy will be deferred to the future when current prices rise and the aggregate quantity of real GDP demanded will fall.

Interest Rates Low interest rates encourage people to borrow and thus encourage them to change the timing of their spending on capital goods, shifting some of that spending from the future to the present. High interest rates discourage people from borrowing and thus encourage them to change the timing of their spending on goods, shifting some of that spending from the present to the future.

Interest rates, in turn, are influenced by the quantity of real money. We have just seen that the quantity of real money increases if the price level falls. We've also seen that the more real money people have, the larger is the quantity of goods and services they demand. But people do not necessarily have to use all their additional real money to buy other goods. They may lend some of it to others or use some of it to decrease their own borrowing. Borrowers who have experienced an increase in their real money holdings now need to borrow less and so decrease their demand for loans. Lenders whose real money holdings have increased are now willing to lend even more and so they increase their supply of loans. A decrease in the demand for loans and an increase in their supply results in a fall in interest rates. And lower interest rates lead to an intertemporal substitution effect — shifting spending plans from the future to the present and increasing the quantity of goods and services demanded.

An increase in the price level decreases the quantity of real money and has the opposite effect on spending plans. With a decrease in the quantity of real money people, to some degree, decrease their spending plans (real money balances effect) and, to some degree, decrease their supply of loans or increase their demand for loans. As a consequence, interest rates increase and spending is shifted from the present to the future (intertemporal substitution effect).

The intertemporal substitution effect is the second reason why the aggregate demand curve slopes downward. A lower price level:

- Lowers current prices relative to expected future prices.
- Increases the quantity of real money.
- Increases the supply of loans.
- Decreases the demand for loans.

- Lowers interest rates.
- Shifts spending from the future to the present and increases the quantity of goods and services demanded.

Let's now look at the third reason why the aggregate demand curve slopes downward.

International Substitution Effect The substitution of domestic goods and services for foreign goods and services, or of foreign goods and services for domestic goods and services, is **international substitution**. An example of international substitution is your decision to buy a Holden car made in Adelaide instead of a Hyundai made in Korea. Another example of international substitution is the decision by the British government to equip its armed forces with US-produced weapons rather than weapons made in Great Britain. Yet another example is your decision to take a skiing holiday in Queenstown, New Zealand instead of Thredbo, New South Wales.

If the Australian price level falls, holding everything else constant, Australian-made goods become relatively cheaper and, therefore, more attractive relative to goods made in other countries. Australians will plan to buy more domestically produced goods and fewer imports; foreigners will plan to buy more Australian-made goods and fewer of their own domestically produced goods. Thus at a lower Australian price level, people and firms will demand a larger quantity of Australian-produced goods and services. International substitution gives us the third reason for the downward slope of the aggregate demand curve.

Changes in the Quantity of Real GDP Demanded

When the price level changes, other things remaining constant, there is a change in the quantity of real GDP demanded. Such a change is illustrated as a movement along the aggregate demand curve. Figure 24.2 illustrates changes in the quantity of real GDP demanded. It also summarizes the three reasons why the aggregate demand curve slopes downward.

Figure 24.2 Changes in the Quantity of Real GDP Demanded

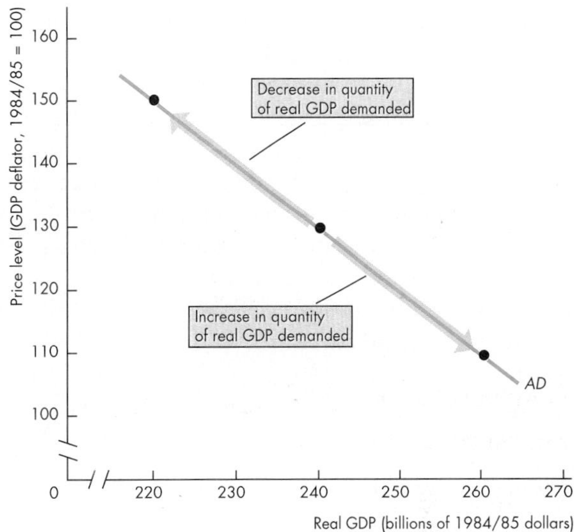

The quantity of real GDP demanded

Decreases if the price level increases	*Increases* if the price level decreases

because of:

Real money balances effect

An increase in the price level decreases the real money supply	A decrease in the price level increases the real money supply

Intertemporal substitution effect

An increase in the price level increases prices today relative to the future and increases interest rates	A decrease in the price level decreases prices today relative to the future and decreases interest rates

International substitution effect

An increase in the price level increases the cost of domestic goods and services relative to those from the rest of the world	A decrease in the price level decreases the cost of domestic goods and services relative to those from the rest of the world

R E V I E W

The aggregate demand curve traces the effects of a change in the price level — GDP deflator — on the aggregate quantity of goods and services demanded — real GDP demanded. The effect of a change in the price level is shown as a movement along the aggregate demand curve. Other things being equal, the higher the price level, the smaller is the quantity of real GDP demanded — the aggregate demand curve slopes downward.

The aggregate demand curve slopes downward for three reasons: money and goods are substitutes (real money balances effect); goods today and goods in the future are substitutes (intertemporal substitution effect); domestic goods and foreign goods are substitutes (international substitution effect). ■

Changes in Aggregate Demand

We've just seen that real GDP demanded varies when the price level varies. The effects of a change in the price level on real GDP demanded are shown as a movement along an aggregate demand curve. But the aggregate demand schedule and aggregate demand curve describe aggregate demand at a point in time, and aggregate demand does not remain constant. It is constantly changing. As a consequence, the aggregate demand curve is constantly shifting. The main influences on aggregate demand that shift the aggregate demand curve are:

- Government policy
- Interest rates
- Money and wealth
- International factors
- Expectations

Government Policy The government's decisions about its own purchases of goods and services and the taxes it collects and the transfer payments it makes have important influences on aggregate demand.

The scale of government purchases of goods and services has a direct effect on aggregate demand. If taxes are held constant, the more weapons, highways, schools and universities the government demands, the higher are government purchases of goods and services and so the higher is aggregate demand. Important changes in government purchases of goods and services that influence aggregate demand arise from the state of international tension and conflict. In times of war, government purchases increase dramatically.

A decrease in taxes increases aggregate demand. An increase in transfer payments — unemployment benefits, social security benefits and other welfare payments — also increases aggregate demand. Both of these influences operate by increasing households' *disposable* income — the income available for spending. The higher the level of disposable income, the greater is the demand for goods and services. Since lower taxes and higher transfer payments increase disposable income, they also increase aggregate demand.

This source of changes in aggregate demand has been an important one in recent years. In the mid-1970s, and again in early to mid-1980s, transfer payments under various social programmes increased considerably. More recently, tax cuts have increased household disposable income.

Interest Rates If, at a given price level, interest rates increase, aggregate demand decreases. Faced with higher interest rates, firms and households cut back on spending, especially investment, to avoid higher interest costs or to take advantage of higher returns on loans. This shifts the aggregate demand curve to the left.

We've just seen that interest rates change when the price level changes and that such changes lead to a movement along the aggregate demand curve. You may be wondering how it can be that interest changes play a part in explaining why the aggregate demand curve slopes downward and also why it shifts. It is because interest rates change for many reasons and, whatever the reason for a change in interest rates, their level influences aggregate demand. When interest rates change because the price level has changed, there is a movement along the aggregate demand curve. But when interest rates change for some reason other than changes in the price level, the aggregate demand curve shifts.

Recent changes in interest rates with very large impacts resulted from the tight monetary policies of the Reserve Bank of Australia during 1988 and 1989. Beginning in the second half of 1988, the Reserve Bank of Australia began to tighten monetary policy, pushing up interest rates in an attempt to quell the rising level of aggregate demand (just how the Reserve Bank achieves this is discussed in Chapter 28). Although it appeared to take some time for the policy to work, by mid-1990 all components of aggregate demand were rapidly falling. By the end of 1990 it was apparent that the high interest rate policy had dampened demand too much, leading to a recession.

Money and Wealth The greater the quantity of nominal money and the higher the level of aggregate wealth, the greater is the level of aggregate demand.

An easy way to illustrate how the quantity of nominal money affects aggregate demand is to imagine what would happen if the government loaded all the army's helicopters with millions of dollars worth of new $10 bills and sprinkled them like confetti across the nation. We would all stop whatever we were doing and rush out to pick up our share of the newly available money. We wouldn't, though, just put the money we picked up in the bank. We would spend some of it, so our demand for goods and services would increase. Though this story is pretty extreme, it does illustrate that a rise in the quantity of money increases aggregate demand.

In practice, the quantity of money is determined by the Reserve Bank of Australia and the banks (in a process described in Chapters 27 and 28). Also, in practice, changes in the quantity of money change interest rates and so have an additional influence on aggregate demand by affecting investment and the demand for consumer durables. When the Reserve Bank speeds up the rate at which new money is being injected into the economy, there's a tendency for interest rates to fall. When the Reserve Bank slows down the pace at which it is creating money, there's a tendency for interest rates to rise. Thus a change in the quantity of money has a second effect on aggregate demand, operating through its effects on interest rates.

As recent experience confirms, fluctuations in the quantity of money and in interest rates induced by those fluctuations have been among the most important sources of changes in aggregate demand.

The level of aggregate wealth also affects the level of aggregate demand. Wealthy people consume larger quantities of goods and services than do poor people. If everyone's wealth increases, aggregate wealth also increases and so does aggregate demand. This source of changes in aggregate demand exerts a steady upward influence as people become gradually more wealthy.

For example, a rising stock market increases the wealth of people holding a portfolio of shares. To the extent that the increase in the value of an individual's portfolio is perceived to be permanent, then that individual's wealth has increased and we would expect to see an increases in his or her demand. The same holds true for all portfolio holders. So a booming stock market, which is seen to be adding to permanent wealth, will increase aggregate demand.

International Factors There are three main international factors that influence aggregate demand:

- The foreign exchange rate
- Foreign prices
- Foreign income

We've seen that a change in the Australian price level, other things being equal, leads to a change in the prices of Australian-produced goods and services relative to the prices of goods and services produced in other countries. Another important influence on the price of Australian-produced goods and services relative to those produced abroad is the *foreign exchange rate.* The foreign exchange rate affects aggregate demand because it affects the prices that foreigners have to pay for Australian-produced goods and services, and the prices that we have to pay for foreign-produced goods and services.

Suppose that one Australian dollar is worth 70 US cents. A Chinese importer can buy one tonne of Australian wheat for $A265 or US$185. The same importer can buy a tonne of US winter wheat for US$190. In this case the Chinese importer will purchase Australian wheat. But will the same quantity of Australian wheat be sold if the Australian dollar rises to 75 US cents and everything else remains the same? At 75 US cents per Australian dollar, the Chinese importer pays US$199 to buy the same tonne of Australian wheat. Compared to US wheat, Australian wheat is now more expensive. The Chinese importer will purchase US wheat instead of Australian wheat. The demand for Australian wheat falls as the Australian dollar rises. So as the foreign exchange value of the dollar rises, everything else held constant, aggregate demand decreases.

There were huge swings in the foreign exchange value of the dollar during the 1980s, leading to large swings in aggregate demand.

Foreign prices also influence aggregate demand. The opportunity cost of Australian wheat in terms of US wheat might change, not only because Australian prices change (a movement along the demand curve) or because the exchange rate changes, but because the price of US wheat falls.

Suppose, for example, that US farmers have a bumper crop with a large surplus or perhaps the US government increases its subsidies to US wheat farmers. In either case, the price of US wheat might fall from US$190 a tonne to US$180 a tonne. US wheat is now cheaper than Australian wheat, which costs $A265 a tonne, that is, US$185 at an exchange rate of 70 US cents. The Chinese importer in our example will again purchase US wheat instead of Australian wheat. As the foreign prices of foreign goods fall, aggregate demand decreases due to the decline in exports.

The ratio of the Australian price of Australian goods exported to the Australian price of foreign goods imported is called the **terms of trade**. There were huge swings in the terms of trade over the 1980s, which also contributed to large swings in aggregate demand.

The third international factor influencing aggregate demand is foreign income. The income of foreigners affects the aggregate demand for domestically produced goods and services. For example, an increase in income in Japan and the United States increases the demand by Japanese and US consumers and producers for fuel, raw materials, agricultural and other products produced in Australia. These sources of change in aggregate demand have been important ones since World War II and have contributed significantly to changes in the terms of trade.

Expectations Expectations about all aspects of future economic conditions play a crucial role in determining current decisions. But two expectations are especially important: expectations about future inflation and expectations about future profit.

An increase in the expected inflation rate, other things being equal, leads to an increase in aggregate demand. The higher the expected inflation rate, the higher is the expected price of goods and services in the future and the lower is the expected real value of money and other assets in the future. As a consequence, when people expect a higher inflation rate, they plan to buy more goods and services in the present and hold smaller quantities of money and other financial assets.

A change in expected future profit changes firms' demands for new capital equipment. For example, suppose that there has been a recent wave of technological change that has increased productivity. Firms will expect that by installing new equipment that uses the latest technology, their future profit will rise. This expectation leads to an increase in demand for new plant and equipment and so to an increase in aggregate demand.

Profit expectations were pessimistic in 1981/82, after a very optimistic period, and led to a decrease in aggregate demand. Expectations were very optimistic during 1987/88, leading to an investment boom and a sustained increase in aggregate demand.

Time Lags The effects of all the influences on aggregate demand that we have just considered do not occur in an instant or in a predictable manner. A change in any of the influences on aggregate demand affects aggregate demand for many months following the initial change. For example, if the Reserve Bank increases the money supply, there might at first be no effect on aggregate demand at all. A little later, as people re-allocate their wealth, there is an increase in the supply of loans and a tendency for interest rates to fall. Later yet, some households and firms, confronted with lower interest rates, change their buying plans for consumer durables and capital goods. As more time passes, more households and firms change their plans and aggregate demand gradually increases. The total effect of the initial change in the quantity of money is spread out over many months. The next time the Reserve Bank takes exactly the same action, there is no guarantee that its effects will take place with exactly the same timing as before. The lags in the effects of influences on aggregate demand are spread out and variable. They are also, to a degree, unpredictable.

Now that we've reviewed the factors that influence aggregate demand, let's summarize their effects on the aggregate demand curve.

Shifts in the Aggregate Demand Curve

We illustrate a change in aggregate demand as a shift in the aggregate demand curve. Figure 24.3 illustrates two changes in aggregate demand. Aggregate demand is initially AD_0 (the same as in Fig. 24.1); AD_1 shows an increase in aggregate demand and AD_2 a decrease in aggregate demand.

The aggregate demand curve shifts to the right, from AD_0 to AD_1 when government purchases of goods and services increase, taxes are cut, transfer payments increase, interest rates fall, the money supply or wealth increase, the foreign exchange rate falls, prices or incomes in the rest of the world increase, expected future profits increase or the expected inflation rate increases.

The aggregate demand curve shifts to the left, from AD_0 to AD_2 when government purchases of goods and services decreases, taxes are increased, transfer payments decrease, interest rates rise, the money supply or wealth decrease, the foreign exchange rate rises, prices or incomes in the rest of the world decrease, expected future profits decrease or the expected inflation rate decreases.

R E V I E W

A change in the price level leads to a change in the aggregate quantity of goods and services demanded. That change is shown as a movement along the aggregate demand curve. A change in any other influence on aggregate demand shifts the aggregate demand curve. These other influences include:

Figure 24.3 Changes in Aggregate Demand

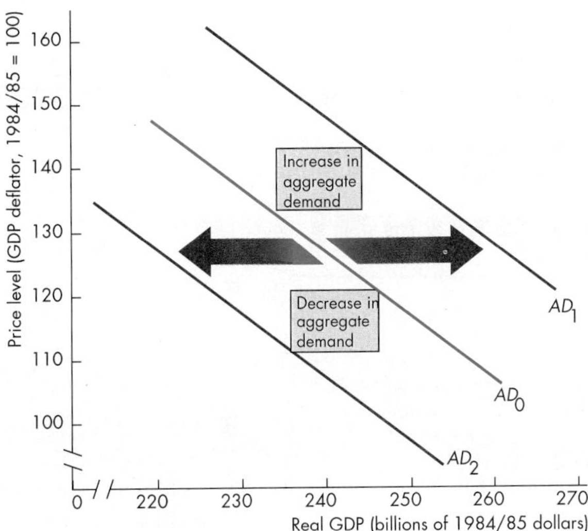

Aggregate demand

Decreases if	*Increases if*
• Government decreases spending or increases taxes	• Government increases spending or decreases taxes
• Interest rates rise	• Interest rates fall
• Money supply or wealth decreases	• Money supply or wealth increases
• Exchange rate increases or foreign prices decrease or foreign income decreases	• Exchange rate decreases or foreign prices increase or foreign income increases
• Expected inflation or expected profits decrease	• Expected inflation or expected profits increase

- Government policy
- Interest rates
- Money and wealth
- International factors
- Expectations ■

Aggregate Supply

The **aggregate quantity of goods and services supplied** is the sum of the quantities of all final goods and services produced by all firms in the economy. It is measured as real gross domestic product (GDP). In studying aggregate supply, we distinguish between two macroeconomic time frames: the short run and the long run.

Two Macroeconomic Time Frames

The **macroeconomic short run** is a period over which the prices of goods and services change in response to changes in demand and supply but wages, and possibly other input prices, do not change. The short run is identified as an important time frame because of the common observation that the prices of the goods and services we buy change frequently while wages change at less frequent intervals, often only once a year when new contracts are negotiated.

The **macroeconomic long run** is a period sufficiently long for all prices and wage rates to have adjusted to any disturbance so that the quantities demanded and supplied are equal in all markets (goods and services markets and labour markets). Thus in the macroeconomic long run, with wage rates having adjusted to bring equality between the quantities of labour demanded and supplied, there is full employment. In other words, unemployment is at its *natural rate.*

Short-Run Aggregate Supply

Short-run aggregate supply is the relationship between the aggregate quantity of final goods and services (real GDP) supplied and the price level (the GDP deflator), holding everything else constant.

We can represent short-run aggregate supply either as a short-run aggregate supply schedule or as a short-run aggregate supply curve. The **short-run aggregate supply schedule** lists quantities of real GDP supplied at each price level, holding everything else constant. The **short-run aggregate supply curve** plots the relationship between the quantity of real GDP supplied and the price level, holding everything else constant.

Figure 24.4 shows a short-run aggregate supply schedule and the corresponding short-run aggregate supply curve (labelled *SAS*). The figure gives two views of the short-run aggregate supply curve. Figure 24.4(a) shows the entire curve, and Fig. 24.4(b) zooms in on the intermediate range of the curve where the economy normally operates. Each row of the aggregate supply schedule corresponds to a point in the figure. For example, row *a′* of the short-run aggregate supply schedule and point *a′* on the curve

Profit Expectations and Aggregate Demand

Deepening Business Gloom Casts doubt on '91 Revival

Australian manufacturing is deeply recessed, with profits, output and new orders drying up in the final months of the year.

With business increasingly gloomy about its own prospects – scaling back expansion plans, shedding labour and battening down the hatches – Paul Keating's precariously balanced strategy for economic revival in 1991 is in jeopardy.

The CAI-Westpac survey of industrial trends, released yesterday, points to a sharp deterioration in business confidence in the manufacturing sector – with no improvement in sight – and signs that companies are fearing the current downturn will be just as bad as 1982–83.

New figures from the Bureau of Statistics, also issued yesterday, show that pre-tax corporate sector profits are being tightly squeezed – with manufacturing and retail earnings posting the most dramatic falls in the September quarter – and have been falling for the last five quarters.

The early signs are that the current downturn will be a lot longer and more painful than policymakers expected when deliberately engineering the current recession.

The battle going on within the Government's official family of economic advisers over further interest rate cuts is largely over the spurt to activity that rate cuts are likely to provide perhaps six months down the track.

Paul Keating conceded this week that the downturn would be more pronounced than anticipated, with unemployment rising further.

The housing sector remains weak, although falling mortgage interest rates are enticing first home buyers into the market.

A worrying sign for the Government is the often self-fulfilling pessimism of business during a recession.

According to the CAI-Westpac manufacturing survey, firms in all sectors of the industry reported sharp falls in employment, output, profitability, investment and new orders (the lifeblood of secondary industry) in the December quarter.

Two-thirds of firms reported a fall in new orders, while 11 per cent reported a rise. This 'net balance' of –55 per cent is the lowest result since March 1983.

As well, more than two-thirds of surveyed firms expect the general business situation to deteriorate even further in the next six months, while only 2 per cent predict an improvement.

This pessimism is coming, no doubt, from the state of company balance sheets.

In the three months to September companies employing more than 30 workers reported a 4 per cent seasonally adjusted decline in pre-tax profits.

Falling corporate earnings in a troubled economy is translating into business scaling back its investment plans.

Anecdotal and survey evidence suggests that despite the five percentage point fall in official interest rates this year, spending growth in new plant and equipment may reach 1982–83 rates.

The Treasurer told economists this week that the economic recovery would start in the middle of 1991, rather than at the beginning (as forecast in the August Budget). Mr Keating's optimism is based on a rebound in the housing industry, population growth, the January 1 tax cuts and the working of the stock cycle.

Economists generally agree that the tax cuts will boost consumption spending in the new year and that the housing sector (the first into the down-turn) will lead the economy out, with the Housing Industry Association expecting a near-capacity 139,000 housing starts in 1991.

Australian Financial Review
7 December 1990
By Tom Dusevic

The Essence of the Story

- By the end of 1990, the Australian economy was in recession.
- In the manufacturing sector, employment, output, profits and investment were falling.
- New orders for output also continued to fall, contributing to declines in business confidence.
- As expected future profits fell, firms scaled back future investment plans. This contributed to further declines in aggregate demand, which further undermined business confidence.
- Official interest rates had been reduced by 5 percentage points during 1990.
- There was disagreement within the government about the future direction of macroeconomic policy.
- Policymakers were unsure about whether the reductions in interest rates to date were sufficient to boost demand, or whether further reductions were necessary.

Background and Analysis

- The level of real GDP over the year to June 1990 was \$259 billion in 1984/85 dollars. We will suppose that this is the full employment level of real GDP.
- By March 1991, the level of real GDP had fallen to \$258 billion. The unemployment rate had risen from 6.7 per cent to 9.2 per cent of the labour force.
- Figure (a) illustrates the situation. LAS_{90}, is the long-run aggregate supply curve in June 1990, at the full-employment level of output. Equilibrium occurs where the short-run aggregate supply curve, SAS_{90}, intersects the aggregate demand curve, AD_{90}, at point *a*. The price level is at 145.2.
- The high interest rate policies of 1989 were intended to stop aggregate demand from moving too far to the right, into a state of overfull employment. They began to have an observable effect during 1990 and the aggregate demand curve shifted back to the left. By March 1991 the aggregate demand curve had shifted back to AD_{91}.
- Wages continued to rise over the period June 1990 to March 1991, even though unemployment was rising. Average weekly earnings rose from \$465 per week to \$497 per week. The rise in wages shifted the short-run aggregate supply curve to the left to SAS_{91}.
- Consequently, the March 1991 equilibrium was at point *b* with level of real GDP \$258 and the price level at 147.6.
- Beginning from point *b* in March 1991, the government is unsure of where the economy is going. Two possible outcomes are shown in Fig (b).
- In the first case, declining profit expectations — a result of the initial decline in demand — are causing firms to cut back investment plans. This translates into a further shift to the left of the aggregate demand curve. As aggregate demand falls again, profits expectations worsen and so a downward spiral begins. This outcome results in the expected aggregate demand for 1992 being $EAD_{0,92}$. Equilibrium occurs at point *c*. GDP falls further and unemployment continues to rise.
- In the second case, the lowering of interest rates throughout 1990, the tax cuts effective from 1 January 1991, and continued population growth are all expected to increase demand. The effects might be large enough to offset falling profit expectations and the aggregate demand curve could shift to the right, possibly to $EAD_{1,92}$. In this case, the economy has rebounded back to full employment at point *d*.
- The government is faced with a dilemma. Should it act to stimulate demand further by cutting interest rates again?
- If $EAD_{0,92}$ is the anticipated outcome, then perhaps it should. But if interest rates are lowered and $EAD_{1,92}$ is the actual outcome, then the economy will grow too strongly and overfull employment will result. This puts the government back in the position it started from in 1989, and interest rates would have to be raised. So the cycle would be perpetuated.

(a) The situation in March 1991

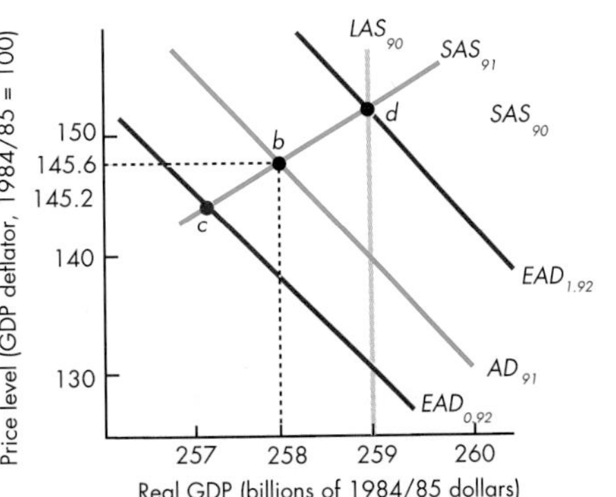

(b) What will the situation be in early 1992?

Conclusion

- Managing the economy is an especially difficult task for the government, complicated tremendously by the often self-fulfilling expectations of consumers and business people.

Figure 24.4 The Aggregate Supply Schedule and Aggregate Supply Curves

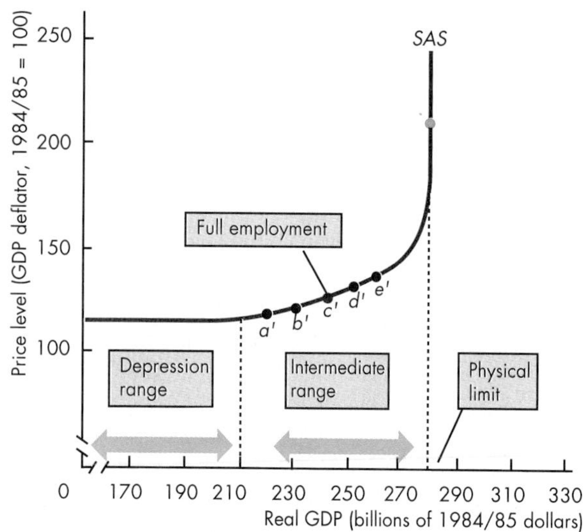

(a) The short-run aggregate supply curve

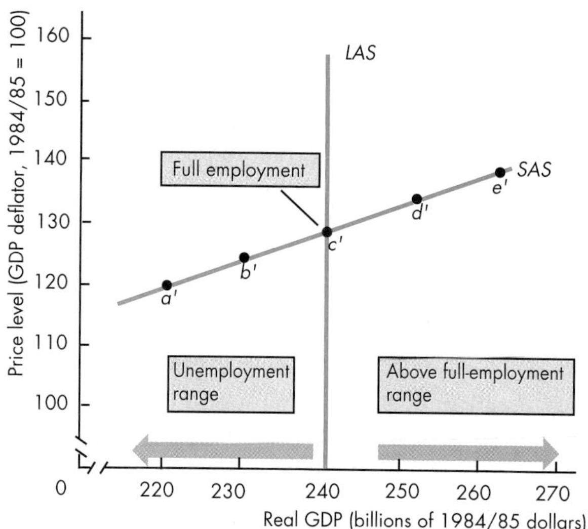

(b) The short-run and long-run aggregate supply curves

	Price level (GDP deflator)	Real GDP (billions of 1984/85 dollars)
Depression range	115	0 to 210
a′	120	220
b′	125	230
c′	130	240
d′	135	250
e′	140	260
Physical limit	Above 200	280

The short-run aggregate supply curve (*SAS*) traces the quantity of real GDP supplied as the price level varies, holding everything else constant. The short-run aggregate supply curves shown in this figure are derived from the schedule in the table. Part (a) shows the *SAS* curve over its entire range and part (b) zooms in on the intermediate range. In a depression, firms are willing to increase the quantity sold with no increase in price and the *SAS* curve is horizontal. At its physical limit, the economy can squeeze out no more production and the *SAS* curve becomes vertical. Normally the economy operates in the upward-sloping intermediate range. In that range, full employment occurs at *c′* where real GDP is $240 billion.

The long-run aggregate supply curve (*LAS*) in part (b) shows the relationship between full employment, real GDP and the price level. This level of real GDP is independent of the price level so the *LAS* curve is vertical as shown in part (b). At levels of real GDP below long-run level, unemployment is above the natural rate and at levels of real GDP above the long-run level, unemployment is below the natural rate, that is, above full employment.

tell us that if the price level is 120 (the GDP deflator is 120), the quantity of real GDP supplied is $220 billion in 1984/85 dollars.

Focus first on the entire short-run aggregate supply curve in Fig. 24.4(a). This curve has three ranges. It is horizontal over the depression range, upward sloping over the intermediate range and vertical at the physical limit of the economy's ability to produce goods and services. Why is the short-run aggregate curve horizontal in the depression range? Why does it slope upward over the intermediate range? And why does it eventually become vertical?

Depression Range When the economy is severely depressed, firms have lots of excess capacity and are anxious to sell whatever they can at the going price. They would be glad to sell more and willing to offer it for sale without the inducement of a higher price. Each firm has a horizontal supply curve, making the aggregate supply curve horizontal as well. The last time the economy was on the depression range of its *SAS* curve was in the 1930s.

The Intermediate Range Normally, the economy operates in the upward-sloping intermediate range of its *SAS* curve. That's why we've zoomed in on this range in Fig. 24.4(b), and it is this part of the *SAS* curve that we'll use in the rest of the book.

Over this upward-sloping portion of the short-run supply curve, an increase in prices induces firms to increase output and offer more goods to the market for sale. Suppose, for example, that car prices increase and car workers' wage rates remain constant. In this situation, General Motors Holden will increase its output and offer more cars for sale. It also hires more workers and increases the work hours of its existing workforce. Conversely, if car prices fall while car workers' wage rates remain constant, General Motors Holden decreases its output and offers fewer cars for sale. It lays off workers. All firms will respond in the same manner and the total quantity of output supplied will vary with the price level.

Thus changes in the price level, with wage rates held constant, lead to a change in the aggregate quantity of goods and services supplied and to changes in the level of employment and unemployment. The higher the price level, the higher is the aggregate quantity of goods and services supplied, the higher is the level of employment and the lower is the level of unemployment.

The Physical Limit to Real GDP At some level of real GDP, the short-run aggregate supply becomes vertical because there is a physical limit to the output the economy can produce. If prices increase while wages remain constant, each firm increases its output. It does so by working its labour overtime, hiring more labour and working its plant and equipment for longer hours. But there is a limit to the extent to which workers will accept overtime and there is a lower limit beyond which the unemployment rate cannot be pushed. There is also a limit beyond which firms will not want to operate their plant and equipment because of costly wear and tear and breakdowns. Once these limits have been reached, no more output can be produced no matter how high prices become, relative to wages. At that point, the short-run aggregate supply curve becomes vertical. In the example in Fig. 24.4, when the economy is operating at its physical limit, real GDP is $280 billion.

Long-Run Aggregate Supply

Long-run aggregate supply is the relationship between the aggregate quantity of final goods and services (real GDP) supplied and the price level (GDP deflator) when all prices, including wages, are flexible, so that there is full employment.

The Long-Run Aggregate Supply Curve Long-run aggregate supply is represented by the long-run aggregate supply curve. The long-run aggregate supply curve plots the relationship between the quantity of real GDP supplied and the price level when wage rates change along with the price level to achieve full employment. The long-run aggregate supply curve is vertical and is illustrated in Fig. 24.4(b) as the curve labelled *LAS*. In this example, full employment occurs when real GDP is $240 billion. If real GDP is less than this amount, a smaller quantity of labour is required and unemployment rises above its natural rate. The economy operates in the unemployment range shown in Fig. 24.4(b). If real GDP is greater than $240 billion, a larger quantity of labour is required and unemployment falls below its natural rate. The economy operates in the above full-employment range shown in Fig. 24.4(b).

Pay particular attention to the *position* of the *LAS* curve. It is a vertical line that intersects the short-run aggregate supply curve at point *c′* on its upward-sloping intermediate range. It does not coincide with the vertical part of the *SAS* curve where the economy is operating at its physical production limit.

Why is the long-run aggregate supply curve vertical? And why is long-run aggregate supply less than the physical limits to production?

Why the Long-Run Aggregate Supply Curve is Vertical The long-run aggregate supply curve is vertical because the level of real GDP at full employment does not depend on the price level. Full employment can occur at any price level. The key thing to remember about the long-run aggregate supply curve is that *two* things vary as we move along it: the price level and the wage rate. But the *real wage rate* — the wage rate relative to the price level — does not vary. With a given real wage rate, there is a unique level of employment and a unique level of real GDP. As the price level and the wage rate vary in step with each other, this level of real GDP does not change.

The Physical Limit to Production In the short-run, production (real GDP) can be increased above its long-run level by driving unemployment below its natural rate. When this occurs, there are more unfilled job vacancies than there are people looking for work. But such a situation cannot last forever. As firms compete with each other for the scarce labour resources, wages will rise faster than prices and output will gradually fall to its long-run level.

R E V I E W

The short-run aggregate supply curve shows the relationship between real GDP supplied and the price level, holding everything else constant. With no change in wage rates, an increase in the price level results in an increase in real GDP supplied. The short-run aggregate supply curve is upward sloping. But, in a severe depression, the short-run aggregate supply curve is horizontal. When the economy can produce no more output, the curve becomes vertical.

The long-run aggregate supply curve shows the relationship between real GDP supplied and the price level when wage rates change along with changes in the price level to maintain full employment. This level of real GDP is independent of the price level. The long-run aggregate supply curve is vertical. Its position tells us the level of real GDP at which the economy reaches full employment. This is a lower level of real GDP than the physical limit to production. ■

A change in the price level, with everything else held constant, results in a movement along the short-run aggregate supply curve. A change in the price level, with an accompanying change in wage rates that keeps unemployment at its natural rate, results in a movement along the long-run aggregate supply curve. But there are many other influences on real GDP supplied. These influences result in a change in aggregate supply and shifts in the aggregate supply curves.

Some factors change both short-run aggregate supply and long-run aggregate supply; others affect short-run aggregate supply but leave long-run aggregate supply unchanged. Let's examine these influences on aggregate supply starting with those that affect only short-run aggregate supply.

Changes in Short-Run Aggregate Supply

Wage Rates A very important influence on short-run aggregate supply that does not change long-run aggregate supply is the wage rate. Wage rates affect short-run aggregate supply through their influence on firms' costs. The higher the level of wage rates, the higher are firms' costs and the lower the quantity of output firms want to supply at each price level. Thus an increase in wage rates decreases short-run aggregate supply.

Why do wage rates affect short-run aggregate supply but not long-run aggregate supply? The answer lies in the definition of long-run aggregate supply. Recall that long-run aggregate supply refers to the quantity of real GDP supplied when wages have adjusted to achieve full employment. When the economy is producing its long-run aggregate supply, any change in wage rates is matched by an equivalent change in the price level. Real wages remain constant and so does output.

Interest Rates Interest rates, like wage rates, have an effect on the short-run costs of firms, and therefore on the short-run aggregate supply. This arises because the production process, itself, takes time. To bridge the time gap, many firms carry inventories. That is, output is produced and held in inventory. The firm's customers are then supplied directly out of inventory holdings. This eliminates the problem of customers having to place special orders with firms and then waiting for their particular production run. To finance their inventory holdings, firms need to acquire short-run operating funds or *operating capital.* The larger the output of the firm, the larger are inventory holdings and the larger is the operating capital requirement of the firm.

Operating capital can be met either from retained earnings or by direct borrowing. Either way, costs are incurred. If operating capital is supplied from retained earnings and used for current production, the firm forgoes the interest income it would have earned if the money had been left in the bank. Similarly, if operating capital is acquired by borrowing, interest must be paid. In both cases, when interest rates rise, the cost of operating short-run funds rises and firms' short-run costs rise. At a given price, the firm will be willing to supply less output to the market.

But changing interest rates do not affect long-run supply for the same reasons that changing wage rates do not.

Shift in the Short-Run Aggregate Supply Curve

A change in either wage rates or interest rates changes short-run aggregate supply and shifts the short-run aggregate supply curve. Figure 24.5 shows such a shift caused by a wage rate increase.

Long-run aggregate supply (*LAS*) intersects the original short-run aggregate supply curve (SAS_0) at the price level 130. Now suppose that wage rates increase from $13 an hour to $14 an hour. At the original level of wage rates, firms are willing to supply, in total, $240 billion worth of output at a price level of 130. They will supply that same level of output at the higher wage rate only if prices increase in the same proportion as wages have increased. With wages up from $13 an hour to $14 an hour, the price level that will keep the quantity supplied constant is 140. Thus the short-run aggregate supply curve shifts to SAS_1. There is a *decrease* in short-run aggregate supply.

A rise in interest rates would similarly shift the short-run aggregate supply curve to the left.

Changes in Both Long-Run and Short-Run Aggregate Supply

Five main factors influence both long-run and short-run aggregate supply. They are:

- The labour force
- The capital stock
- The availability of raw materials
- Technology
- Incentives

Figure 24.5 Changes in Short-Run Aggregate Supply

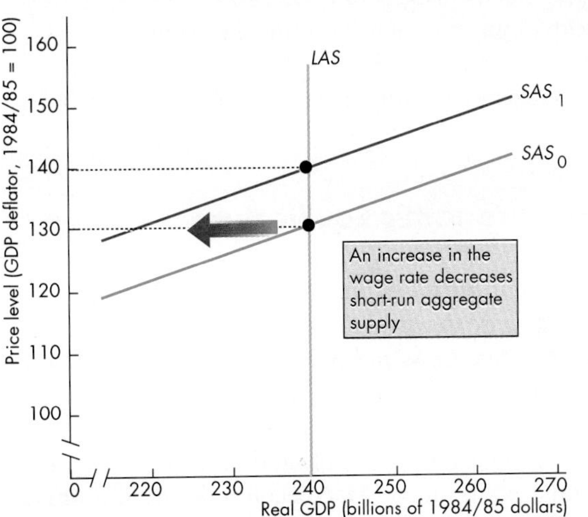

An increase in wage rates decreases short-run aggregate supply but does not change long-run aggregate supply. It shifts the short-run aggregate supply curve to the left and leaves the long-run aggregate supply curve unaffected. Such a change is shown here. The original short-run aggregate supply curve is SAS_0 and after the increase in the wage rate, the new short-run aggregate supply curve is SAS_1.

The Labour Force The larger the labour force, the larger is the quantity of goods and services produced.

The Capital Stock The larger the stock of plant and equipment, the more productive is the labour force and the greater is the output that it can produce. Also, the larger the stock of *human capital*— the skills that people have acquired through education and on-the-job training — the greater is the level of output.

The Availability of Raw Materials The availability of raw materials has an important effect on output. The discovery of new and easily accessed raw materials lowers their real cost and increases output. The depletion of materials has the reverse effect, lowering output.

Technology Technology influences aggregate supply in two distinct ways: one positive and permanent, the other negative but temporary.

Inventing new and better ways of doing things enables firms to produce more from any given amount of inputs. So, even with a constant population and constant capital stock, improvements in technology increase production and increase aggregate supply. This effect is positive and permanent.

Technological change creates new jobs and destroys old ones. It is rare that technological change affects all sectors of the economy and regions in the same way. Some sectors and all regions expand rapidly and others decline. An example is the explosive growth in the banking and financial services sector and the relative decline in the manufacturing sector during the 1980s. Other things being equal, the more rapid the rate of job creation and destruction, the larger is the rate of turnover of the labour force and the higher is the natural rate of unemployment. This effect is negative but temporary.

Incentives Aggregate supply is influenced by the incentives that people are offered. Two examples are unemployment benefits and investment tax credits. In Great Britain, unemployment benefits are much more generous, relative to wages, than in the United States. There is a greater incentive to find a job in

Figure 24.6 Changes in Aggregate Supply

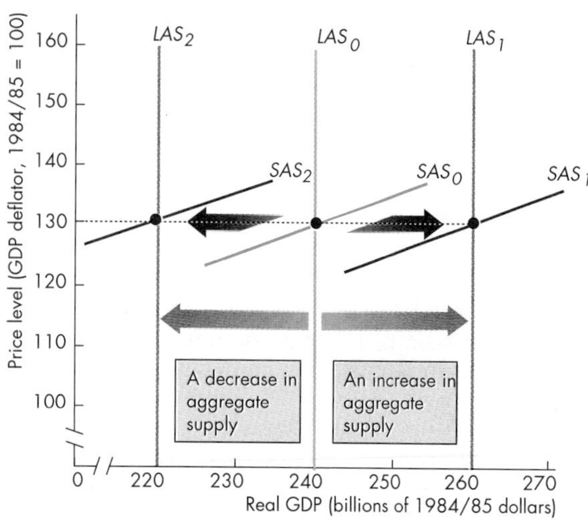

Aggregate supply

Decreases and both curves shift to the left if

- The labour force decreases
- The capital stock decreases
- Raw materials become less available or more costly
- Technological change increases the rate of job creation and destruction
- Incentives to work and invest in new plant and equipment are strengthened

Increases and both curves shift to the right if

- The labour force increases
- The capital stock increases
- Raw materials become more available or less costly
- Technological change increases the productivity of labour and capital
- Incentives to work and invest in new plant and equipment are strengthened

the United States than there is in Britain. As a result, Britain's natural unemployment rate is higher and long-run aggregate supply lower than would be the case if Britain had US unemployment compensation arrangements. Investment tax credits are credits that cut business taxes in proportion to the scale of a firm's investment in new plant and equipment. Such credits provide an incentive to greater capital accumulation and, other things being equal, increase aggregate supply.

Shifts in the Long-run and Short-Run Aggregate Supply Curves If any of the events that change long-run aggregate supply occur, the long-run aggregate supply curve *and the short-run aggregate supply curve* shift. Both curves shift in the same direction. Figure 24.6 illustrates an increase in long-run aggregate supply, with both curves shifting to the right, and also a decrease in long-run aggregate supply, with both curves shifting to the left. Initially, the long-run aggregate supply curve (LAS_0) and the short-run aggregate supply curve (SAS_0) intersect at a price level of 130 where real GDP is 240 billion 1984/85 dollars. An increase in the productive capacity of the economy that increases full-employment real GDP to 260 billion 1984/85 dollars shifts the long-run aggregate supply curve to LAS_1, and the short-run aggregate supply curve to SAS_1. A decrease in aggregate supply shifts the long-run aggregate supply curve to LAS_2 and the short-run aggregate supply curve to SAS_2. Long-run aggregate supply is now 220 billion 1984/85 dollars.

REVIEW

A change in wage rates changes short-run aggregate supply but leaves long-run aggregate supply unchanged. It shifts the short-run aggregate supply curve but does not shift the long-run aggregate supply curve.

Changes in the size of the labour force, the amount of capital stock, the availability of raw materials, the state of technology or the incentives people are offered change both short-run and long-run aggregate supply. Such changes shift short-run and long-run aggregate supply curves in the same direction. ■

Next, we'll study macroeconomic equilibrium.

Macroeconomic Equilibrium

Our purpose in building a model of aggregate demand and aggregate supply is to determine and predict changes in real GDP and the price level. To make predictions about real GDP and the price level, we need to combine aggregate demand and aggregate supply and determine macroeconomic equilibrium. **Macroeconomic equilibrium** occurs when the quantity of real GDP demanded equals the quantity of real GDP supplied. Let's see how macroeconomic equilibrium is determined.

Determination of Real GDP and the Price Level

We have seen that the aggregate demand curve tells us the quantity of real GDP demanded at each price level, and the short-run aggregate supply curve tells

Figure 24.7 Macroeconomic Equilibrium

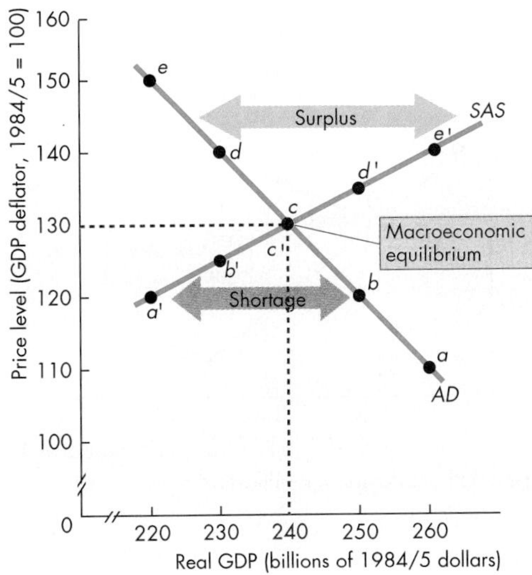

Macroeconomic equilibrium occurs when real GDP demanded equals real GDP supplied. Such an equilibrium is at the intersection of the aggregate demand curve (*AD*) and the short-run aggregate supply curve (*SAS*) — points *c* and *c′*. At price levels above 130 (for example, 140) there is an excess of the quantity of goods and services supplied over the quantity demanded — a surplus — and prices fall. At price levels below 130 (for example 120) there is an excess of the quantity of goods and services demanded over the quantity supplied — a shortage — and prices rise. Only when the price level is 130 is the quantity of goods and services demanded equal to the quantity supplied. This is the equilibrium price level. The quantity of goods and services traded at this price level is the equilibrium level of real GDP — 240 billion 1984/85 dollars.

us the quantity of real GDP supplied at each price level. There is one and only one price level at which the quantity demanded equals the quantity supplied. Macroeconomic equilibrium occurs at that price level. Figure 24.7 illustrates such an equilibrium at a price level of 130 and real GDP of 240 billion 1984/85 dollars (points *c* and *c′*).

To see why this position is an equilibrium, let's work out what happens if the price level is something other than 130. Suppose, for example, that the price level is 140. In that case, the quantity of real GDP demanded is $230 billion (point *d*) but the quantity of real GDP supplied is $260 billion (point *e′*). There is an excess of the quantity supplied over the quantity demanded, or a surplus of goods and services. Unable to sell all their output, firms willingly accept lower prices. Prices will be cut until the surplus is eliminated — at a price level of 130.

Next consider what happens if the price level is 120. In this case, the quantity of real GDP that firms supply is $220 billion worth of goods and services (point *a′*) and the quantity of real GDP demanded is $250 billion worth of goods (point *b*). The quantity demanded exceeds the quantity supplied. Aware of shortages, firms push their prices upward and continue to do so until the quantities demanded and supplied are in balance — again at a price level of 130.

Macroeconomic Equilibrium and Full Employment

Macroeconomic equilibrium does not necessarily occur at full employment. At full employment the economy is on its long-run aggregate supply curve. Macroeconomic equilibrium occurs at the intersection of the short-run aggregate supply curve and the aggregate demand curve — at the price level where the aggregate quantity of goods and services demanded equals the aggregate quantity of goods and services supplied. Macroeconomic equilibrium can occur at, below or above full employment. We can see this fact most clearly by considering the three cases shown in Fig. 24.8(b), (c) and (d).

In Fig. 24.8(a) the fluctuations of real GDP are shown for an imaginary economy over a five year period. In year 2, real GDP falls below its long-run level and there is a recessionary gap. A **recessionary gap** is the difference between long-run real GDP and actual GDP when actual is below its long-run level. In year 4, real GDP rises above its long-run level and there is an inflationary gap. An **inflationary gap** is the difference between long-run real GDP and actual real GDP when actual is above its long-run level. In year 3, actual real GDP and long-run real GDP are equal and the economy is at full employment.

These situations are illustrated in Fig. 24.8(b), (c) and (d) as the three types of macroeconomic equilibrium. In Fig 24.8(b) there is a below full-employment equilibrium. A **below full-employment equilibrium,** also called an unemployment equilibrium, is a situation in which macroeconomic equilibrium occurs at a level of real GDP below long-run GDP and there is a recessionary gap. The unemployment equilibrium illustrated in Fig. 24.8(b) occurs where aggregate demand curve AD_0 intersects short-run aggregate supply curve SAS_0 at a real GDP of 220 billion 1984/85 dollars and a price level of 130. There is a recessionary gap of 20 billion 1984/85

Figure 24.8 Three Types of Macroeconomic Equilibrium

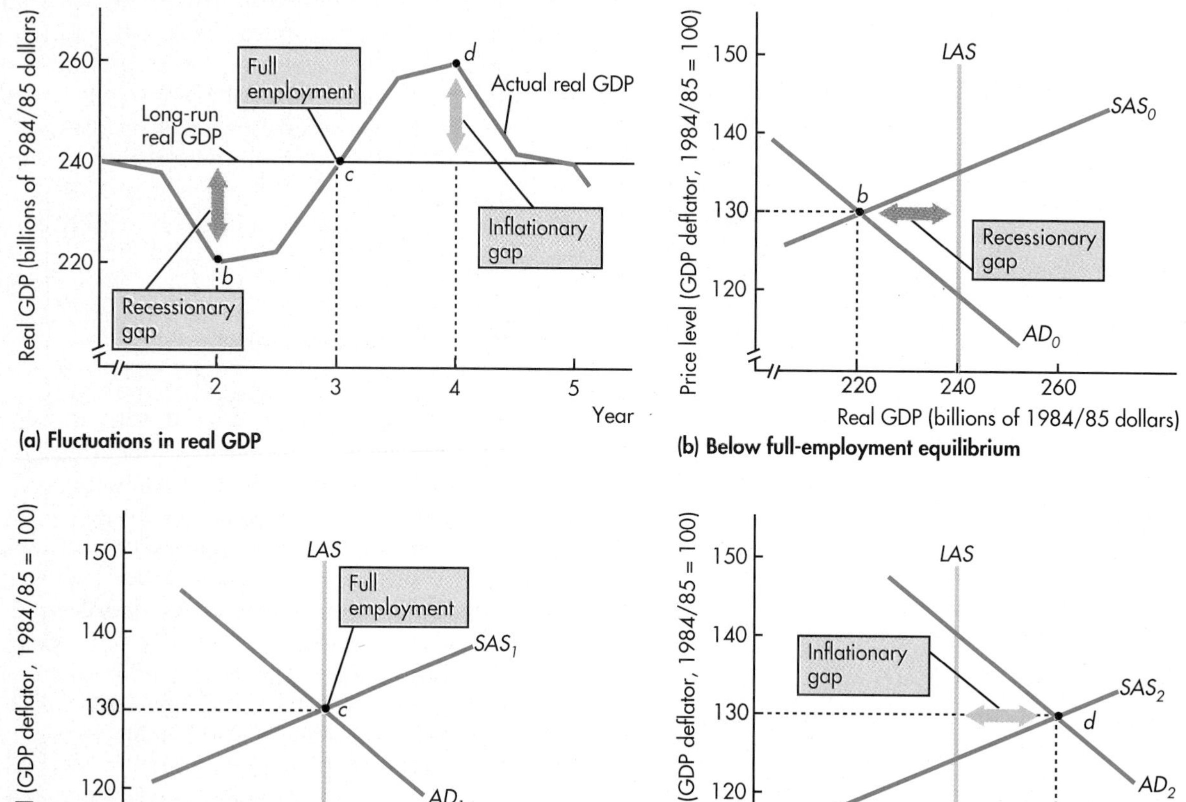

In part (a) real GDP in an imaginary economy fluctuates around its long-run level. When actual real GDP is below long-run real GDP, there is a recessionary gap (as in year 2). When actual real GDP is above long-run real GDP, there is an inflationary gap (as in year 4). When actual real GDP is equal to long-run real GDP, there is full employment (as in year 3).

The situation in year 2 is illustrated in part (b) where the aggregate demand curve (AD_0) intersects the short-run aggregate supply curve (SAS_0). The gap between that point of intersection and the long-run aggregate supply curve (*LAS*) is the recessionary gap. The situation in year 3 is illustrated in part (c) where the aggregate demand curve (AD_1) intersects the short-run aggregate supply curve (SAS_1) on the long-run aggregate supply curve (*LAS*). The situation in year 4 is illustrated in part (d) where the aggregate demand curve (AD_2) intersects the short-run aggregate supply curve (SAS_2). The gap between that intersection point and the long-run aggregate supply curve (*LAS*) is the inflationary gap.

dollars. The Australian economy was in a situation similar to that shown in Fig. 24.8(b) in 1990/91. In those years, unemployment was high and real GDP was substantially below trend.

Figure 24.8(c) is an example of full-employment equilibrium. **Full-employment equilibrium** is a macroeconomic equilibrium in which actual real GDP equals long-run real GDP. In this example, the equilibrium occurs where the aggregate demand curve AD_1 intersects the short-run aggregate supply curve SAS_1 at an actual and long-run real GDP of 240 billion 1984/85 dollars. The Australian economy was in a situation such as that shown in Fig. 24.8(c) in 1989/90.

Finally, Fig. 24.8(d) illustrates an above full-employment equilibrium. **Above full-employment equilibrium** is a situation in which macroeconomic equilibrium occurs at a level of real GDP above long-run real GDP and there is an inflationary gap. The above full-employment equilibrium illustrated in Fig. 24.8(d) occurs where the aggregate demand curve AD_2 intersects the short-run aggregate supply curve SAS_2 at a real GDP of 260 billion 1984/85 dollars and a price level of 130. There is an inflationary gap of 20 billion 1984/85 dollars. It was widely believed that, if the government had not changed policy in 1988/89, the Australian economy would have encountered a situation similar to that depicted in Fig. 24.8(d) in 1990/91.

The economy moves between the three types of equilibrium shown in Fig. 24.8 as a result of fluctuations in aggregate demand and in short-run aggregate supply. These fluctuations produce fluctuations in real GDP and in the price level.

You have now completed your first look at the aggregate demand–aggregate supply model. The story of its evolution is told in Our Advancing Knowledge in this chapter (pp. 158–159).

Next, we're going to put the model to work generating macroeconomic fluctuations. First we'll look at the effects of imaginary changes in aggregate demand and aggregate supply. Second we'll use the theory of aggregate demand and aggregate supply to interpret some recent events in the Australian economy.

Aggregate Fluctuations and Aggregate Demand Shocks

We're going to work out what happens to real GDP and the price level following a change in aggregate demand. Let's suppose that the economy starts out at full employment and, as illustrated in Fig. 24.9, is producing \$240 billion worth of goods and services at a price level of 130. The economy is on the aggregate demand curve AD_0, the short-run aggregate supply curve SAS_0 and on its long-run aggregate supply curve *LAS*.

Now suppose that the Reserve Bank of Australia takes steps to increase the quantity of money. With more money in the economy, people increase their demand for goods and services — the aggregate demand curve shifts to the right. Suppose that the aggregate demand curve shifts from AD_0 to AD_1 in Fig. 24.9. A new equilibrium occurs, where the aggregate demand curve AD_1 intersects the short-run aggregate supply curve SAS_0. Output rises to \$250 billion 1984/85 dollars and the price level rises to 135. The economy is now at an above full-employment equilibrium. Real GDP is above its long-run level and there is an inflationary gap.

The increase in aggregate demand has increased the prices of all goods and services. Faced with higher prices, firms have increased their output rates. At this stage, prices of goods and services have increased but factor prices, such as wage rates, have not changed. (Recall that as we move along a short-run aggregate supply curve, wage rates are constant.)

The economy cannot stay above its long-run aggregate supply and full-employment levels forever. Why not? What are the forces at work bringing real GDP back to its long-run level and restoring full employment?

If the price level has increased but wages have remained constant, workers have experienced a fall in the purchasing power of their wages. Furthermore, firms have experienced a fall in the real cost of la-

Figure 24.9 The Effect of a Change in Aggregate Demand

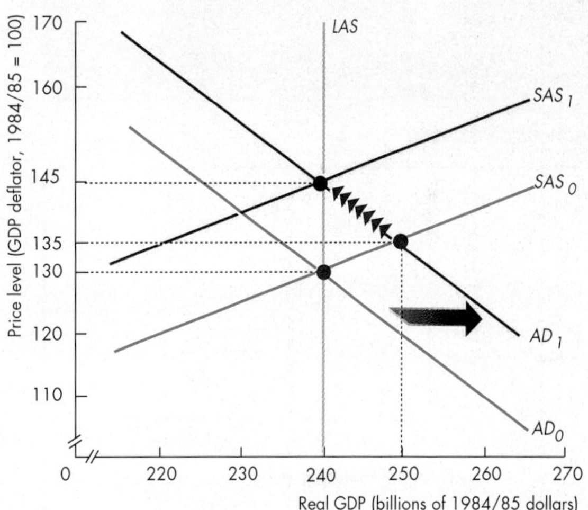

An increase in aggregate demand shifts the aggregate demand curve from AD_0 to AD_1. Real GDP increases from 240 billion to 250 billion 1984/85 dollars and the price level increases from 130 to 135. A higher price level induces higher wages and other factor prices, which in turn cause the short-run aggregate supply curve to move upward. As the *SAS* curve moves upward from SAS_0 to SAS_1, it intersects the aggregate demand curve AD_1 at higher price levels and lower real GDP levels. Eventually, the price level increases to 145 and real GDP falls back to 240 billion 1984/85 dollars — its full-employment level.

OUR ADVANCING KNOWLEDGE

The Evolution of Modern Macroeconomics

Jean-Baptiste Say

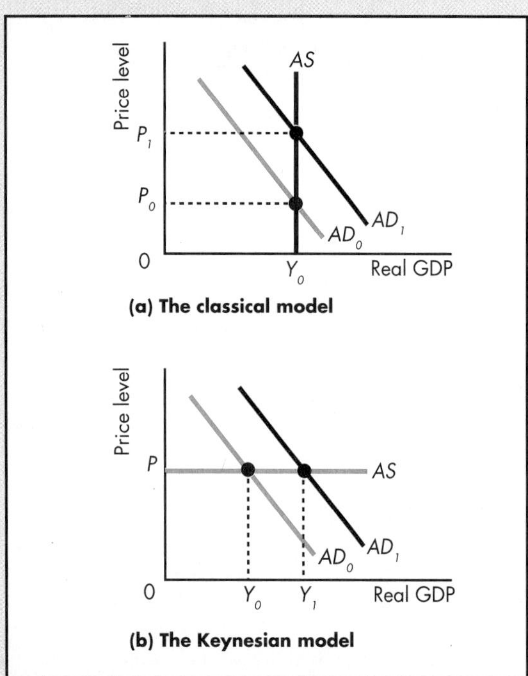

(a) The classical model

(b) The Keynesian model

Macroeconomics has been around for more than 200 years and one of the earliest macroeconomists was Jean-Baptiste Say. Born in Lyon, France, in 1767, Say worked as a journalist, a businessman manufacturing cotton and a professor of economics in Paris. His major book, *Traité d'économie politique (A Treatise on Political Economy)*, published in 1803, was a brilliant, more systematic and yet more compact presentation of Adam Smith's economics than Smith himself was able to write. By the early nineteenth century, Say was one of the most famous economists in both Europe and America and his *Traité* was used as a university textbook on both sides of the Atlantic.[1]

Say's most lasting contribution to macroeconomics was what came to be called Say's Law. Say's Law is the proposition that supply creates its own demand.

In the years following the Industrial Revolution in England and on the European continent, there was controversy as to whether the economy could continue expanding indefinitely or whether it would reach a limit beyond which there would not be sufficient demand to buy the goods and services that could be produced.

Say explained that the production of goods and services creates an income that is sufficient to purchase those goods and services — supply creates its own demand. Say's Law became the cornerpiece of what came to be called classical macroeconomics.

Classical Macroeconomics

Classical macroeconomics, building on the work of Adam Smith and Jean-Baptiste Say, gradually evolved until it was replaced by Keynesian macroeconomics in the 1930s. The classical system has five key elements. They are:

- The demand for labour and the supply of labour interact to determine the level of wages and employment.
- Given the level of employment and the economy's capital resources and technology, there is a unique aggregate quantity of real GDP supplied.
- The demand for and supply of loans determines

---

[1] Thomas Sowell, entry on Say in *The New Palgrave, A Dictionary of Economics*, edited by John Eatwell, Murray Milgate and Peter Newman (Stockton Press: New York, 1987), vol.4, p.249.

interest rates and the levels of consumption, saving and investment.

- The aggregate quantity of goods and services supplied creates a large enough income to enable those goods and services to be bought and adjustments in interest rates ensure that total spending equals total income.
- Aggregate demand determines only the price level. It has no effect on real GDP

The classical macroeconomic system can be summarized in an aggregate demand–aggregate supply diagram with a vertical aggregate supply curve (see Fig. (a)). The aggregate supply curve, *AS*, is vertical and its position is determined by the economy's resources and technology. The aggregate demand curve slopes downward and its position is determined by the quantity of money. If the aggregate demand curve is AD_0, the price level is P_0. If aggregate demand increases so that the aggregate demand curve shifts to AD_1, the price level increases to P_1, but real GDP remains constant at Y_0. In 1936, classical macroeconomics was delivered a serious blow, the onset of the Keynesian revolution.

Keynesian Macroeconomics

Keynesian macroeconomics was founded by John Maynard Keynes (see Our Advancing Knowledge, pp. 184–185). The centrepiece of Keynes' macroeconomic system is the **principle of effective demand** — the opposite of Say's Law and the proposition that the level of real GDP is determined by aggregate demand. Keynes argued that Say's Law was wrong and that there were impediments to the self-regulation of the economy that did not guarantee that supply would create its own demand. Instead, the quantity of goods and services supplied is determined by the demand for goods, not the supply. Keynes developed an economic model in which:

- Wages do not adjust to determine employment. The dollar value of wages is rigid and a large and persistent gap can emerge between the quantity of labour demanded and the quantity supplied.
- Interest rates do not adjust to ensure equality between saving and investment. If saving exceeds investment, spending falls short of income and income declines.

The Keynesian system can be described by an aggregate demand–aggregate supply model in which the aggregate supply curve is horizontal, such as that shown in Fig. (b). Here, because wages do not adjust to keep the quantities of labour demanded and supplied equal, the quantity of goods produced is free to vary and is not determined by labour market conditions and technology. Any quantity of goods and services (up to some maximum) can be produced. Thus the aggregate supply curve is horizontal over this range. In this situation, if aggregate demand increases from AD_0 to AD_1, there is an increase in real GDP from Y_0 to Y_1 and no change in the price level.

Neo-Classical Synthesis and Modern Macroeconomics

Modern macroeconomics can be seen as a mixture of classical and Keynesian macroeconomics and has been called the **neo-classical synthesis**. In the neo-classical synthesis, classical macroeconomics describes the long-run situation — the situation that prevails after a sufficient time lag for all factor prices to have adjusted in step with the prices of final goods and services. Keynesian macroeconomics is seen as being relevant for short-run adjustments over a time interval during which factor prices remain constant. In this case, however, the aggregate supply curve is not horizontal as in the extreme Keynesian model shown in Fig. (b), but is upward-sloping as shown in Fig. 24.4 in this chapter.

Modern macroeconomics pays careful attention to the distinction between aggregate demand and aggregate supply as schedules and the quantities of real GDP demanded and supplied as points on schedules. It also pays careful attention to the factors that make the short-run and long-run aggregate supply curves and aggregate demand curve shift and to the processes of adjustment of wages, prices and output.

The macroeconomics that you will study in the following chapters spells out these developments.

bour. In these circumstances, workers demand higher wages, and firms, anxious to maintain their employment and output levels, meet those demands. If firms do not raise wages, they either lose workers or have to hire less productive ones.

As wage rates rise, the short-run aggregate supply curve begins to shift. It moves upward from SAS_0 towards SAS_1. The rise in wage rates and the shift in the *SAS* curve produce a sequence of new equilibrium positions. At each point on the adjustment path, output falls and the price level rises. Eventually, wage rates will have risen by so much that the *SAS* curve is SAS_1, by which time the aggregate demand curve AD_1 intersects SAS_1 at a full-employment equilibrium. The price level has risen to 145, and output is back where it started, at its full-employment level. Real GDP is again back at its long-run level.

Throughout the adjustment process, higher wage rates raise firms' costs and, with rising costs, firms offer a smaller quantity of goods and services for sale at any given price level. By the time the adjustment is over, firms are producing exactly the same amount as initially produced, but at higher prices and higher costs. The level of costs relative to prices will be the same as it was initially.

We've just worked out the effects of an increase in aggregate demand. A decrease in aggregate demand has similar but opposite effects to those that we've just studied. That is, when aggregate demand falls, real GDP falls below its long-run level and unemployment rises above its natural rate. The lower price level increases the purchasing power of wages, and firm's output prices fall relative to their costs. Eventually, as the slack economy leads to falling wages, the short-run aggregate supply curve shifts downward and, gradually, full employment is restored.

The Effects of a Change in Aggregate Supply

Let's now work out the effects of a change in aggregate supply on real GDP and the price level. Figure 24.10 illustrates the analysis. Suppose that, as shown in Fig. 24.10(a), the economy is initially at full-employment equilibrium. The aggregate demand curve is AD_0 and the short-run aggregate supply curve is SAS_0. The long-run aggregate supply curve is LAS_0. Output is 240 billion 1984/85 dollars and the price level is 130.

Now suppose that the price of oil increases sharply, as it did when OPEC organized a worldwide embargo in 1973. As a result of the oil price rise, aggregate supply decreases and the long-run and short-run aggregate supply curves shift to the left, to LAS_1 and SAS_1. As a result of this change in aggregate supply the economy moves to a new equilibrium where the new short-run aggregate supply curve SAS_1 intersects the aggregate demand curve AD_0. The price level rises to 133 and real GDP falls to 235 billion 1984/85 dollars. Real GDP has fallen so the economy has experienced recession. But long-run real GDP has fallen by more than actual real GDP. So actual real GDP is *above* its long-run level. There is an inflationary gap. And there is worse to come!

Prices have increased, but wage rates have not. So real wages have fallen. In such a situation, firms try to hire more labour and workers try to get higher wages. Upward pressure on wages increases costs and the short-run aggregate supply starts to shift further to the left. As it does so, the price level rises even higher and real GDP falls even lower. The process comes to an end at a new long-run equilibrium, shown in Fig. 24.10(b), when the price level is 140 and real GDP is 230 billion 1984/1985 dollars.

We've now seen how changes in aggregate demand and aggregate supply influence real GDP and the price level. Let's now put our new knowledge to work and see how it helps us to understand Australia's macroeconomic performance.

Trends and Cycles in the Australian Economy

We're now going to use our new tools of aggregate demand and aggregate supply to interpret some recent trends and cycles in the Australian economy. We'll begin by looking at the state of the Australian economy in 1989/90.

One View of the Economy in 1989/90

Real GDP in 1989/90 was $259 billion (measured in 1984/85 dollars). The price level was 143. That is, the price level, measured by the GDP deflator, was 43 per cent higher in 1989/90 than in 1984/85. We can illustrate this state of the Australian economy by using the aggregate demand and aggregate supply model. Figure 24.11 shows the state of the economy in 1989/90. The aggregate demand curve (AD_{89}) cuts the short-run aggregate supply curve (SAS_{89}), at a price level of 143 and at a real GDP of $259 billion.

We do not know, with certainty, where the long-run aggregate supply curve was in 1989/90, as there is no single method for determining long-run aggregate supply. In Fig. 24.11 the long-run aggregate

Figure 24.10 The Effects of a Change in Aggregate Supply

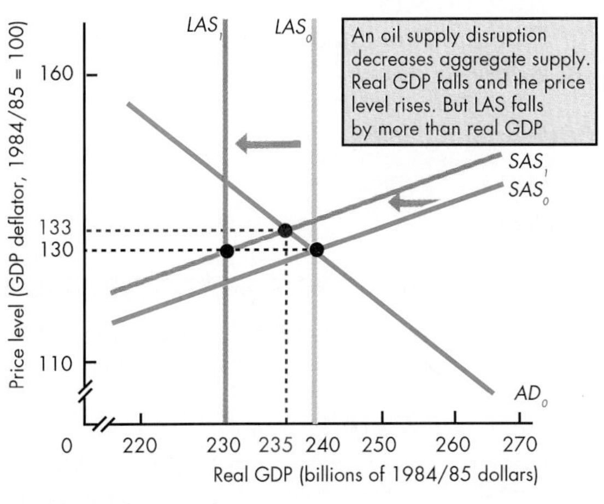

(a) Initial effect

(b) Long-run adjustment

An increase in the price of oil decreases aggregate supply and shifts the aggregate supply curves to the left, from LAS_0 to LAS_1 and from SAS_0 to SAS_1 in part (a). Real GDP falls from 240 billion to 235 billion 1984/85 dollars and the price level increases from 130 to 133. The higher oil price and higher prices in general start wages rising and the short-run aggregate supply curve starts to move further to the left in part (b). As it does so, real GDP falls further and the price level rises further. Eventually, real GDP falls to 230 billion 1984/85 dollars and the price level rises to 140.

supply curve (LAS_{89}) is based on the *assumption* that long-run aggregate supply in 1989/90 was also $259 billion in 1984/85 dollars. Thus actual real GDP was at the level of long-run aggregate supply and unemployment was at its natural rate. But by late 1990 the economy was in recession. What happened to change matters?

The years 1987/88 and 1988/89 were a time of strong growth in Australia. But with aggregate demand growing faster than real output, there was, during 1989, a widely held expectation that the economy was heading towards overfull employment. Fears of inflation and of a burgeoning trade deficit were widespread.

You can see why fears of inflation existed by comparing Fig. 24.11 with Fig. 24.9. In Fig. 24.9 we analysed what happens when aggregate demand increases to put real GDP above its long-run level. In such a situation there is pressure for wages to increase and, as they do so, for the short-run aggregate supply curve to shift upward.

The expectation held by many policymakers was that if aggregate demand continued to grow at its fast pace throughout 1990/91, then, because the economy was already at full-employment equilibrium, the aggregate demand curve would shift further to the right to EAD_{90} (expected aggregate demand in 1990/91). Prices would rise, eventually causing wages to rise, generating a shift upward of the short-run aggregate supply curve.

An added problem facing policymakers in Australia stemmed from the existence of the Wages Accord. The centralized mechanism for setting national wages appeared to work reasonably well in containing wages, when the rate of inflation was moderate and anticipated. But a burst of inflation that had not been accounted for in pre-arranged wage rises might have put pressure on unions to seek further wage rises outside the Accord system. This, of course, would have shifted the *SAS* curve upward again, possibly triggering a wage–inflation spiral.

With what appeared to be a consensus of opinion regarding the future expectation of increased inflation, the government began implementing a tight monetary policy as early as mid-1988. Attempting to use high interest rates to reduce aggregate demand,

Figure 24.11 The Australian Economy in 1989/90

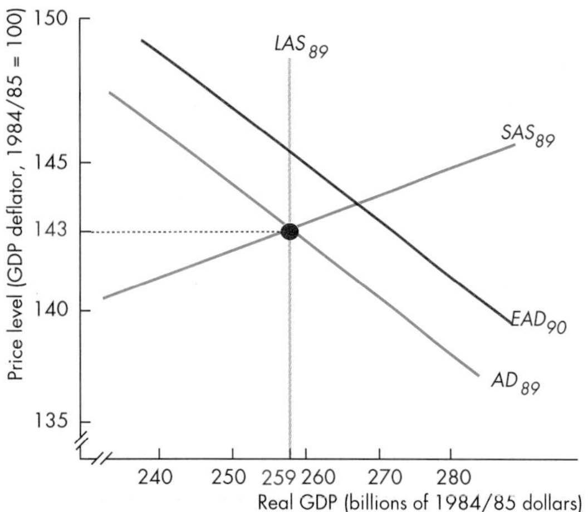

In 1989/90, the Australian economy was on the aggregate demand curve AD_{89} and the aggregate supply curve SAS_{89}. The price level was 143 and real GDP was 259 billion 1984/85 dollars. The long-run aggregate supply curve (LAS_{89}) and full-employment real GDP were at 259 billion in 1984/85 dollars, so that unemployment was at its natural rate. Policymakers believed that continued growth in aggregate demand would shift the aggregate demand curve to EAD_{90}. To forestall the possibility of inflation arising from overfull employment, aggregate demand was reduced by high interest rate policies. Unfortunately, the aggregate demand was reduced too much and a recession ensued.

so that the aggregate demand curve in 1990/91 continued to intersect long-run aggregate supply at full employment, it happened that the brakes were applied too hard and the actual aggregate demand curve shifted too far to the left and output fell as unemployment rose.

Growth, Inflation and Cycles

The economy is continually changing. If you imagine the economy as a video, then Fig. 24.11 is a freeze-frame. We're going to run the video again — an instant replay — but keep our finger on the freeze-frame button, looking at some important parts of the previous action. Let's run the video from 1960/61.

Figure 24.12 shows the state of the economy in 1960/61 at the point of intersection of its aggregate demand curve AD_{60} and short-run aggregate supply curve SAS_{60}. Real GDP was \$83.1 billion and the GDP deflator was 18.3.

By 1990/91, the economy had reached the point marked by the intersection of aggregate demand curve AD_{90} and short-run aggregate supply curve SAS_{90}. Real GDP was \$257 billion and the GDP deflator was 147.

There are three important features of the path followed by the economy traced by the dots. They are:

- Expansion
- Inflation
- Cycles

Figure 24.12 Aggregate Demand and Aggregate Supply, 1960/61 to 1990/91

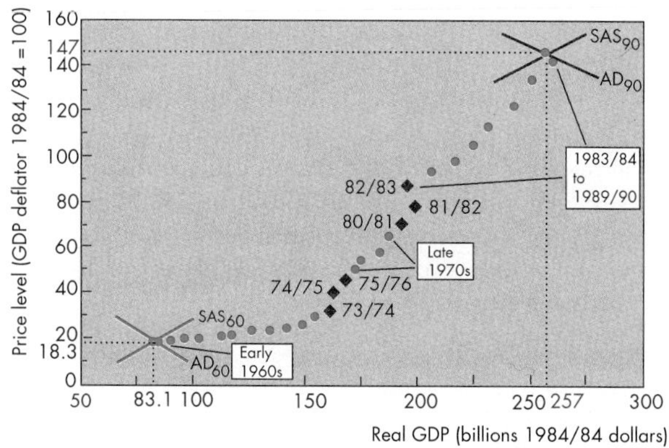

Each dot indicates the value of the GDP deflator and real GDP in a given year. In 1960/61, these variables were determined at the intersection of the aggregate demand curve AD_{60} and the short-run aggregate supply curve SAS_{60}. Each dot is generated by the gradual shift of the *AD* and *SAS* curves. By 1990/91, the curves were AD_{90} and SAS_{90}. Real GDP has grown and the price level has increased. But growth and inflation did not proceed smoothly. Real GDP grew quickly and inflation was moderate in the 1960s; real GDP growth sagged in 1973/74–1975/76 and again, more strongly, in the early 1980s. In 1982/83 real GDP actually contracted. The slow-down in the 1970s was caused by an unusually sharp increase in input prices (oil prices). The 1982/83 recession was caused by a slow-down in the growth of aggregate demand, which resulted from a slow-down in income growth in the rest of the world, and a speed-up in the rate of domestic wage increases. The period from 1983/84 to 1988/89 was one of strong, persistent recovery. But output fell again in 1990/91. Inflation was rapid during the 1970s, but moderated in the 1980s, although it was still high by world standards.

Source: See Fig 22.1.

Expansion Over the years, real GDP expands. The main force generating this expansion is an increase in long-run aggregate supply. Long-run aggregate supply increases because of population growth, the accumulation of capital — both physical plant and equipment and human capital — the discovery of new resources and the advance of technology.

Inflation The steady and persistent increase in prices results from a persistent increase in aggregate demand. Of all the factors that can shift the aggregate demand curve, one — the quantity of money — is the single most important factor leading to persistent and sustained increases in aggregate demand and the price level.

Cycles The pace of economic growth and inflation is uneven. The unevenness arises because both the expansion of short-run aggregate supply and the growth of aggregate demand do not proceed at a fixed, steady pace.

Let's examine the expansion, inflation and cycles in the period since 1960/61 by considering four time periods in Fig. 24.12.

First, you can see that, in the early 1960s, there was a strong increase in real GDP with only small increases in prices. This was a period of steady increases in long-run aggregate supply and of moderate increases in aggregate demand.

Second, look at the period from 1973/74 to 1975/76. In 1973 and 1974, a series of massive oil price increases put the Australian — and world — economy into a slow-down. Real GDP continued to increase but its growth rate was sharply reduced (especially in 1974/75) and the inflation rate increased to more than 10 per cent. The growth slow-down and increased inflation occurred because the increase in oil prices and wages shifted the short-run aggregate supply curve upward at a faster pace than the increase in aggregate demand. The result was a contraction with rising prices. Real GDP fell below its long-run aggregate supply level.

Third, look at the period from 1976/77 to 1982/83. The period begins with a renewed strength in real GDP growth but with continued high inflation. Inflation remains high and real GDP growth slows, eventually becoming negative in 1982/83. This period of continued inflation and slowing real GDP growth was partly the result of a battle between OPEC and the monetary authorities in other developed countries. OPEC increased the price of oil again in 1978. An inflationary recession ensued in the rest of the world. The Reserve Bank and other monetary authorities gave way and increased their money supplies, attempting to bring the Australian and other economies back to full employment. But as inflation became a problem in other countries, Australia's major trading partners, particularly the United States, restricted monetary growth in their countries in 1980/81 and 1981/82. With deteriorating conditions in Australia as a result of the world slow-down, demand for Australian exports declined. However, as inflation was still high, the Reserve Bank felt it had no option but to restrict the rate of growth of money in Australia in 1982/83. Interest rates rose to very high levels and aggregate demand fell.

You can see the effects of these influences in the figure. Aggregate demand increased but not at a fast enough pace to keep up with the upward movement of the short-run aggregate supply curve, resulting from wage and other factor price increases. As a consequence, by 1982/83, the upward movement of the short-run aggregate supply curve was so strong relative to the growth of aggregate demand that the economy went into a further deep recession and GDP fell.

Finally, look at the years 1983/84 to 1989/90. In this period, moderate wage growth as a result of the Wages Accord slowed the pace of the upward movement in the short-run aggregate supply curve. Sustained but steady growth in aggregate demand and in long-run aggregate supply kept the economy expanding. The economy moved from a recession with output well below its long-run aggregate supply level to full employment and perhaps beyond full employment.

With a renewed threat of inflation resulting from the buoyant conditions prevailing in 1987/88 and 1988/89, the government again moved to tighten monetary policy in 1988/89 and 1989/90. The policy was apparently slow to take effect but, by the second half of 1990, the economy was slowing down very rapidly. By late 1990, the economy had entered a recession with output falling and unemployment rising rapidly. As you can see, in 1990/91, output fell for only the second time since 1960/61.

The up-and-down swings in the Australian economy, Australia's relative lack of success in keeping inflation down and the progressively deteriorating net exports balance prompted many people to discuss ways to permanently improve Australia's long-run aggregate supply.

Microeconomic Reform and Macroeconomic Performance

Economists and politicians see reform as vital if Australia is to regain its place in the world economic league. Prominent among their proposals for reform is microeconomic reform. What is microeconomic reform? What are its macroeconomic effects?

Microeconomic reform is the attempt to increase output from *given* inputs of labour, capital and materials by making markets work more efficiently. Examples of microeconomic reform include removing barriers to international trade (for example, by reducing tariffs); removing barriers to competition in domestic markets (such as deregulating banking and finance markets); reforming the transport and communications systems (waterfront, coastal shipping and railways reform, privatizing some government owned and run monopolies, such as Telecom); removing barriers to competition in the labour market. What are the effects of these policies on real GDP and the price level?

The main effect of microeconomic reform (if it is successful) is to shift the long-run aggregate supply curve to the right. This is shown in Fig. 24.13. LAS_0 is the original long-run aggregate supply curve. After microeconomic reforms have been adopted, more real goods and services can be produced with the same amount of labour, capital and material inputs. The aggregate supply curve moves to the right, to LAS_1. Equilibrium real GDP increases and the price level falls. If, in addition, the reforms increase the marginal product of existing capital, firms might be induced to increase their level of investment and install new capacity. In this instance, the aggregate demand curve will shift to the right, from AD_0 to AD_1. With both curves shifting, the new equilibrium to emerge is at the point where real GDP has increased to $250 billion and the price level has dropped to 90.

By getting more output from given inputs, microeconomic reform brings about a one-time fall in the price level, and hence inflation, other things being constant. But if it also brings about permanently faster growth, because the level of investment and employment rise, then microeconomic reform might bring about a permanently lower inflation.

Public awareness of the need for microeconomic reform strengthened in the 1980s. But progress has been slow. Important reforms initiated by the government, so far, include deregulating financial markets; some personal income tax reforms (for example, cutting the top marginal rate from 60 per cent to 49 per cent); deregulating the production and sale of crude oil; share-dividend imputation; and elimination of the two airlines policy. Important gains have also been made in reducing industry protection.

Figure 24.13 Microeconomic Reform and Real Output and Prices

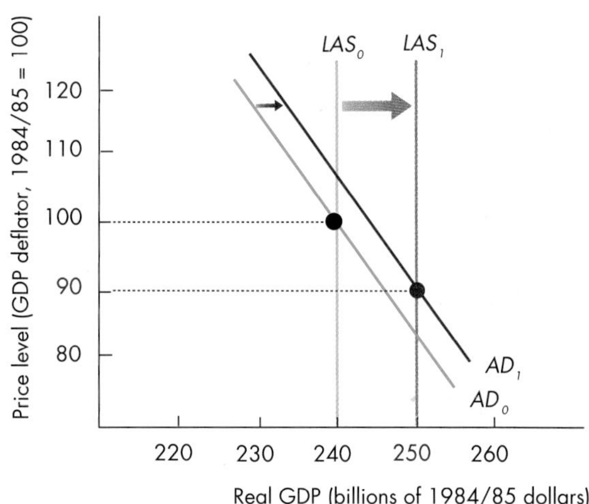

Initial aggregate supply is given by LAS_0 and aggregate demand by AD_0. In equilibrium, real GDP is $240 billion 1984/85 dollars and the price level is 100. After microeconomic reforms are adopted, the economy can get a larger quantity of output from the same inputs. The long-run aggregate supply curve moves to LAS_1. If the reforms also increase the marginal product of capital, firms will increase their investment in new machines, adding to aggregate demand. The aggregate demand curve shifts to the right to AD_1. The net effect is an increase in real GDP, to $250 billion, and a reduction in the price level, to 90.

The Industry Commission recently assessed the benefits from further microeconomic reform. By overhauling the coastal shipping services; improving rail systems and grain handling and storing services; improving pricing of road services; and improving postal, telecommunications and electricity services the Industry Commission estimated that the economy stood to benefit by $17.7 billion, or $1000 for every man, woman and child in Australia. Further, the CPI would fall by over 7 per cent and employment would rise by 0.6 per cent. The gains are obviously quite considerable.

The difficulty faced by governments is that the existing impediments to efficiency always benefit someone. So there is always strong opposition to reform from those groups who will suffer. And we are not always sure of the short-run effects of some reforms. Sometimes the desired outcome does not emerge. For example, there are claims that reforms directed at increasing competition among banks actually resulted in less competition and a higher (four-firm) concentration ratio. So governments are well aware of the benefits of microeconomic reform but traditionally have moved slowly in that direction.

This chapter has provided a model of real GDP and the GDP deflator that can be used to understand the growth, inflation and cycles that our economy follows. The model is a useful one because it enables us to keep our eye on the big picture — on the broad trends and cycles in inflation and output. But the model lacks detail. It does not tell us as much as we need to know about the components of aggregate demand — consumption, investment, government purchases of goods and services, and exports and imports. It doesn't tell us what determines interest rates or wages or even, directly, what determines employment and unemployment. In the following chapters, we're going to start to fill in that detail.

In some ways, the study of macroeconomics is like doing a large jigsaw puzzle. The aggregate demand and aggregate supply model provides the entire edge of the jigsaw. We know its general shape and size but we haven't filled in the middle. One block of the jigsaw contains the story of aggregate demand. Another, the story of aggregate supply. And when we place the two together, we place them in the frame of the model developed in this chapter, and the picture is complete.

SUMMARY

Aggregate Demand

Aggregate demand is the relationship between the aggregate quantity of goods and services demanded — real GDP demanded — and the price level — the GDP deflator. The aggregate demand curve slopes downward. A rise in the price level produces a movement along the aggregate demand curve, reducing the quantity of real GDP demanded. Factors that change aggregate demand shift the aggregate demand curve. (pp. 140–147)

Aggregate Supply

Aggregate supply is studied in two time frames: the long-run and the short-run. The macroeconomic short-run is a period in which the price of goods and services adjust but wages do not. The macroeconomic long-run is a period in which all prices and wage rates adjust to achieve full employment.

Short-run aggregate supply is the relationship between the aggregate quantity of final goods and services (real GDP) supplied and the price level (the GDP deflator) when money wages are held constant. The short-run aggregate supply curve slopes upward. With wage rates and all other influences on supply held constant, the higher the price level, the more output firms plan to sell.

Long-run aggregate supply is the relationship between the aggregate quantity of final goods and services (real GDP) supplied and the price level (GDP deflator) when prices and wage rates adjust to maintain full employment. The long-run aggregate supply curve is vertical — long-run aggregate supply is independent of the price level.

The factors that change short-run aggregate supply shift the short-run aggregate supply curve. Factors that change long-run aggregate supply also change short-run aggregate supply. Thus anything that shifts the long-run aggregate supply curve also shifts the short-run aggregate supply curve in the same direction. The most important of these factors are the size of the labour force, the capital stock, the availability of raw materials, the state of technology and incentives. (pp. 147–154)

Macroeconomic Equilibrium

Macroeconomic equilibrium occurs when the quantity of real GDP demanded equals the quantity of real GDP supplied. Macroeconomic equilibrium occurs at the intersection of the aggregate demand curve and the short-run aggregate supply curve. The price level that achieves this equality is the equilibrium price level, and the output level is equilibrium real GDP.

Macroeconomic equilibrium does not always occur at full employment, that is, at a point on the long-run aggregate supply curve. Unemployment equilibrium occurs when equilibrium real GDP is less than its long-run aggregate supply level. There is a recessionary gap and the unemployment level exceeds its natural rate. When equilibrium real GDP is above its long-run level, there is an inflationary gap and the unemployment level is below its natural rate.

An increase in aggregate demand shifts the aggregate demand curve to the right and increases both real GDP and the price level. If real GDP increases above its long-run level, input prices begin to increase and, as they do so, the short-run aggregate supply curve shifts to the left. The shift of the short-run aggregate supply curve to the left results in an even higher price level and lower real GDP. Eventually, real GDP returns to its long-run level.

A decrease in aggregate supply shifts the long-run and short-run supply curves to the left, lowering real GDP and increasing the price level. The initial decrease in real GDP and increase in the price level are intensified as wages respond to the supply shock and rising wages shift the short-run aggregate supply curve still further to the left. (pp. 154–160)

Trends and Cycles in the Australian Economy

Long-term growth in the Australian economy results from population growth, capital accumulation and technological change. Inflation persists in Australia because of steady increases in aggregate demand, in part, brought about by increases in the quantity of money. The Australian economy experiences cycles because the short-run aggregate supply and aggregate demand curves shift at an uneven pace.

A large increase in the price of oil in 1973 resulted in an inflationary slow-down in the mid-1970s. A replay in 1978 intensified the inflationary situation. World-wide restraint in aggregate demand growth in 1980/81 and 1981/82 resulted in a severe recession in Australia in 1982/83. This recession resulted in lower output. Even though factor price rises have been moderate, inflation has remained relatively high. The subsequent recovery in the second half of the 1980s appeared to some to be getting out of hand. Tight monetary policies were again implemented in 1988/89 and 1989/90 to moderate the rate of growth of aggregate demand, with the consequence that the economy entered a recession with falling output and rising unemployment.

Microeconomic reform is expected to have a direct effect on real GDP and the price level through its effect on long-run aggregate supply. The long-run effects on aggregate demand are likely to be negligible but the long-run aggregate supply curve will shift to the right as more output is generated by the same quantity of inputs. The price level will fall, inflation will temporarily slow and employment will increase. (pp. 160–165)

K E Y T E R M S

Above full-employment equilibrium, p. 157
Aggregate demand, p. 140
Aggregate demand curve, p. 140
Aggregate demand schedule, p. 140
Aggregate quantity of goods and services demanded, p. 140
Aggregate quantity of goods and services supplied, p. 147
Below full-employment equilibrium, p. 155
Full-employment equilibrium, p. 156
Inflationary gap, p. 155
International substitution, p. 143
Intertemporal substitution, p. 142
Long-run aggregate supply, p. 151
Long-run aggregate supply curve, p. 151
Macroeconomic equilibrium, p. 154
Macroeconomic long-run, p. 147
Macroeconomic short-run, p. 147
Microeconomic reform, p. 164
Quantity of money, p. 141
Real money, p. 141
Real money balances effect, p. 141
Recessionary gap, p. 155
Short-run aggregate supply, p. 147
Short-run aggregate supply curve, p. 147
Short-run aggregate supply schedule, p. 147
Terms of trade, p. 145

P R O B L E M S

1 Which of the following do not affect aggregate demand:
   a) Quantity of money?
   b) Interest rates?
   c) Technological change?
   d) Human capital?

2 Consider the following events:
   a) The labour force increases.
   b) Technology improves.
   c) The money wage rate increases.
   d) The quantity of money increases.

e) Foreign incomes increase.
f) The foreign exchange value of the dollar increases.

Sort these events into the following four categories:

Category A: Those that affect the long-run aggregate supply curve but not the short-run aggregate supply curve.

Category B: Those that affect the short-run aggregate supply curve but not the long-run aggregate supply curve.

Category C: Those that affect both the short-run aggregate supply curve and the long-run aggregate supply curve.

Category D: Those that have no effect on the short-run aggregate supply curve or on the long-run aggregate supply curve.

3 You are the prime minister's economic adviser and you are trying to figure out where the Australian economy is headed next year. You have the following forecasts for the *AD*, *SAS* and *LAS* curves:

Price level	Real GDP demanded	Real GDP supplied (billions of dollars)	
		short-run	long-run
140	550	350	460
150	500	400	460
160	450	450	460
170	400	500	460

This year, real GDP is $460 billion and the price level is 150.

The prime minister wants answers to the following questions:

a) What is your forecast of next year's real GDP?
b) What is your forecast of next year's price level?
c) What is your forecast of the inflation rate?
d) Will unemployment be above or below its natural rate?
e) Will real GDP be above or below trend? By how much?

4 Draw some figures similar to those in this chapter and use the information in problem 3 to explain:

a) What has to be done to aggregate demand to achieve full employment?
b) What is the inflation rate if aggregate demand is manipulated to achieve full employment?

5 The economy begins with the following *SAS*, *LAS* and *AD* curves

Price level	Real GDP demanded	Real GDP supplied (billions of 1984/85 dollars)	
		short-run	long-run
140	550	350	450
150	500	400	450
160	450	450	450
170	400	500	450

a) What is the equilibrium level of real GDP and the price level?

Successful implementation of reforms in the labour and financial markets increases *LAS* to 500 billion 1984/85 dollars.

b) What is the new level of real GDP and the price level?
c) What happened to inflation?

Because of the reforms, firms increase their rate of investment and real GDP demanded increases by $50 billion at every price level (that is, the *AD* curve shifts to the right by 50 billion 1984/85 dollars).

d) How are real GDP, the price level and the rate of inflation affected?

Part 9

Aggregate Product Markets

Talking with Robert E. Lucas, Jr

Robert E. Lucas, Jr is closely associated with the development of rational expectations macroeconomics. A professor of economics at the University of Chicago, Lucas first applied his ideas about rational expectations to the Phillips curve. Michael Parkin spoke with Professor Lucas about rational expectations macroeconomics, his views on other approaches to economics, and his views of economic policy.

You applied the idea of rational expectations to macroeconomics and to expectations about inflation. How has that hypothesis changed the way we think about things?

It ties down a loose end that shouldn't have been there. Any important economic decision depends upon what you think about the future. Rational expectations is just a way of dealing with that.

What do you see as the chief criticisms of the rational expectations hypothesis?

Here's the genuine difficulty people have with the idea. You would never discover the idea of rational expectations by introspection. Rational expectations describes something that has to be true of the outcome of a much more complicated underlying process. But it doesn't describe the actual thought process people use in trying to figure out the future. Our behaviour is adaptive. We try some mode of behaviour. If it's successful, we do it again. If not, we try something else. Rational expectations describes the situation when you've got it right.

Can you give an example?

In economics we're mostly concerned about repetitive events and decisions of some consequence. Our capitalist economy has been operating under pretty much the same laws for 200 years now. People aren't reacting to every monetary contraction as if it's the first time it ever happened. It's just inconceivable. I think people have developed certain ways of living with regular events as best they can.

What do you now think of the first rational expectations model that you proposed?

Rational expectations can be used in combination with a wealth of other assumptions to produce all kinds of different models. The particular models of business cycles that Tom Sargent and I, among others, advanced in the 1970s have run into hard times. In my case, I put a lot of emphasis on people having inadequate information about the quantity of money, and I think a lot of economists now feel that that's just too thin a reed to hang a theory of business cycles on. That it's just not that hard to get accurate information on the quantity of money, which, in the United States, is published every Friday. That's a criticism of a very specific model.

One of the most significant contributions of the 1980s has been real business cycle theory. How do you evaluate this approach?

Real business cycle theory asks what the time path of the economy's GNP or employment would be under the best possible macroeconomic policy. The early authors of this approach asked themselves what fraction of actual variation in GNP you could account for if you restrict yourself to the fluctuations in the rate of technological change. Their answer was, all of it. There's nothing left over for traditional macroeconomic theory to account for. I don't think that can be right.

'People aren't reacting to every monetary contraction as if it's the first time'

Why can't that be right?

Because you can't account for something like the events of 1929 to 1933 when real output fell by a quarter in four years, as if it resulted from the changes in the rate at which technology was decaying. The Depression didn't occur because production techniques got worse. Real business cycle theory suggests that real forces are much more important than we had thought and that the questions addressed by traditional macroeconomics are not as important as we once thought. That's the message.

How can we introduce monetary forces into a macroeconomic model that at the same time pays serious attention to real forces, one that shows fluctuations in price as well as in output?

I think that's a central unsolved problem that my 1972 paper on rational expectations, which we discussed earlier, addressed, only there I used deficiencies in people's information. There's also the approach that looks at fixed wage contracts, work done by John Taylor or Stanley Fischer. I'm much more sympathetic to that line of thought than I was 10 years ago. Why is it that people commit themselves to agreements to buy and sell at fixed nominal prices in a world where the value of a dollar is fluctuating all the time? Why would you tie your future decisions to some unit when you have no way of knowing what that unit is going to mean later on? That's a great question. No one yet knows the answer to it.

Some economists suggest that even at the level of pricing goods, not just labour and contracts, we should think of a rigidity that arises from 'menu costs'. The idea that you've got to publish your prices, to label the shelves, jars and bottles. And this is costly, so you won't change the price every minute. What do you think of this approach?

I think there's some truth to it. But it's criticized; it seems like a slim reed. People ask, do you mean to tell me that the Great Depression occurred because it was too much of a bother for supermarket clerks to put new price tags on the goods on their shelves? There's no question that there's something to this approach, but there's a question of how important it is. I think the details of individual price setting are very poorly understood. So when people adopt an assumption like rigid prices, I don't think we can afford to look down our noses at them.

'We can't afford to look down our noses at people who assume rigid prices'

You were a student of Milton Friedman, the architect of the movement called monetarism. How do you distinguish this approach from the kind of macroeconomics that you are responsible for creating?

I'm not that big on the distinction. I'm a monetarist. But the term does refer to several things. One aspect of what people call monetarism is just emphasis on the quantity of some monetary aggregate as a determinant of prices and of economic activity. In some ways, I think that the revolution has been so successful that it doesn't seem like a revolution any more. In this day and age, no one talks about the price level, exchange rates, or interest rates without talking about the quantity of money. In that sense, we're all monetarists. The second aspect of monetarism is a hostility toward government's continual management of the economy. The role of government, in a monetarist perspective, is to make its own behaviour on fiscal or monetary policy simple and predictable and then just to let the system operate without fine-tuning. That view, I think, is absolutely right.

'We don't want to manage the US economy. And we don't think anybody else should take the job either'

In recent years, we've experienced the biggest peacetime government budget deficit ever. How have you viewed the deficit over the years?

That's an embarrassing question for me because the deficit is not having the immediate unpleasant consequences I had predicted. My handle on the deficit is this. If you think of an economy in some kind of smooth, steady state, running a deficit year in and year out, what has to make up that deficit are changes in the monetary base. So I see large deficits that occur regularly as equivalent to a large rate of growth in the monetary base, which means inflation. I don't like deficits because they signal inflation. There's not a tight year to year connection, because you can issue bonds to cover the deficit, which are a promise either to raise taxes later or to print money later. But sooner or later it's the monetary base that fills the gap between government spending and tax revenues.

At the start of the Reagan administration, Tom Sargent and I wrote newpaper articles saying that the deficit would be inflationary. Well, that just hasn't happened. I'm in the process of rethinking about deficits. I'm sympathetic to people like Larry Kotlikoff, who suspects that the deficit might be an illusion as a result of inadequate accounting. That it just doesn't measure anything since things like future social security liabilities are arbitrarily excluded or included.

What is the context of your well-known debate with James Tobin?

Tobin views the role of macroeconomics to be to provide principles for guiding monetary and fiscal policy in order to keep the economy near what he thinks of as full employment. And he thinks if this isn't done, we'll have the Depression again. People like Sargent or Friedman or myself basically come and poke holes, saying 'Look, these principles you have for managing the economy are useless'. Our opponents in this debate tried to discredit us as economic managers, asking, 'Would you trust the management of the US economy to Lucas?'. We're not asking them to. We don't want the job, and we don't think anybody else should take it either.

Chapter 25

Expenditure Decisions

After studying this chapter, you will be able to:

- Describe the importance and degree of fluctuation in the components of aggregate expenditure.
- Explain how people make their consumption and saving decisions.
- Define and calculate the average and marginal propensities to consume and save.
- Explain how firms make their investment decisions and why there are large fluctuations in investment.
- Explain how export and import decisions are made and how net exports are determined.
- Derive the aggregate expenditure schedule and aggregate expenditure curve.
- Distinguish between autonomous expenditure and induced expenditure.
- Explain how the level of aggregate expenditure is determined

Fear and Trembling in the Shopping Aisles

'Consumer confidence falls to new low'. This headline, in The *Age*, of 20 June 1990, indicated the depth of pessimism pervading the Australian economy as it slid into a monetary-policy-induced recession in mid-1990. Even though interest rates were coming down, more people believed, according to a survey, that June 1990 was a bad time, rather than a good time, to buy household items. Why all the fear and trembling over what happens in the shopping aisles? Besides a few manufacturers and stores, who really cares whether people buy a lot of gifts for the holidays, or whether they continue to buy cars and VCRs after a stock market crash? How does this affect the rest of us? What makes people decide to spend less and save more? It's not only consumer spending that stirs up hope and fear in the economy. 'Investment pushes back recession fears', trumpeted the *Australian Financial Review*, on 28 November 1990. The story went on to say that the unexpected rise in investment in the September quarter reduced the chances of a recession and probably signalled the end of monetary policy easing in 1990. It was wrong on both counts. Another *Australian Financial Review* headline, a week later on 5 December 1990, said 'Rate cut despite rise in imports'. That is, even though import levels were still apparently high, monetary policy would continue to be eased in the face of an oncoming recession. It is clear that business investment, imports and exports all generate a lot of interest, uncertainty and emotion when it comes to the economy. How do these components of GDP affect us? How much of the country's spending do they make up, compared with consumer spending? Are fluctuations in these components of aggregate expenditure sources of fluctuations in our job prospects and living standards? What about the government's spending on goods and services? Is the government a source of instability in the economy or is the government's spending a stabilizing influence on aggregate expenditure?

In this chapter we're going to take a close look at consumption expenditure, investment, government purchases of goods and services, and net exports. First, we'll learn about their relative magnitudes and volatility. Second, we'll explain how consumption expenditure, investment and net exports are determined. Third, we'll see how these private components of aggregate spending, along with government purchases, interact to determine equilibrium aggregate expenditure and GDP.

Let's begin by looking at the components of aggregate expenditure.

The Components of Aggregate Expenditure

The components of aggregate expenditure are:

- Consumption expenditure
- Planned investment
- Government purchases of goods and services
- Net exports (exports minus imports)

Relative Importance of the Components of Aggregate Expenditure

What are the relative magnitudes of the components of aggregate expenditure? Which is the largest component? Figure 25.1 answers these questions for the years since 1960/61. By far the biggest portion of aggregate expenditure is consumption expenditure, which ranges between 58 and 62 per cent of GDP, averaging 59 per cent. The smallest portion is net exports, whose average value is –1.7 per cent, which reflects the fact that Australia is traditionally a net importer of goods and services. Investment ranges between 14 and 22 per cent of GDP and averages 18 per cent. Government purchases of goods and services are larger than investment, ranging between 23 and 26 per cent of GDP, and averaging 25 per cent. Currently, government purchases of goods and services account for nearly 24 per cent of GDP.

Relative Volatility of the Components of Aggregate Expenditure

Which of the components of aggregate expenditure are the most volatile — which fluctuate the most? Figure 25.2 answers this question. And that answer is investment and net exports. Consumption expenditure and government purchases of goods and services fluctuate much less than these two items.

In studying this figure, note that the vertical axis measures the extent to which the four compo-

Figure 25.1 The Components of Aggregate Expenditure, 1960/61–1990/91

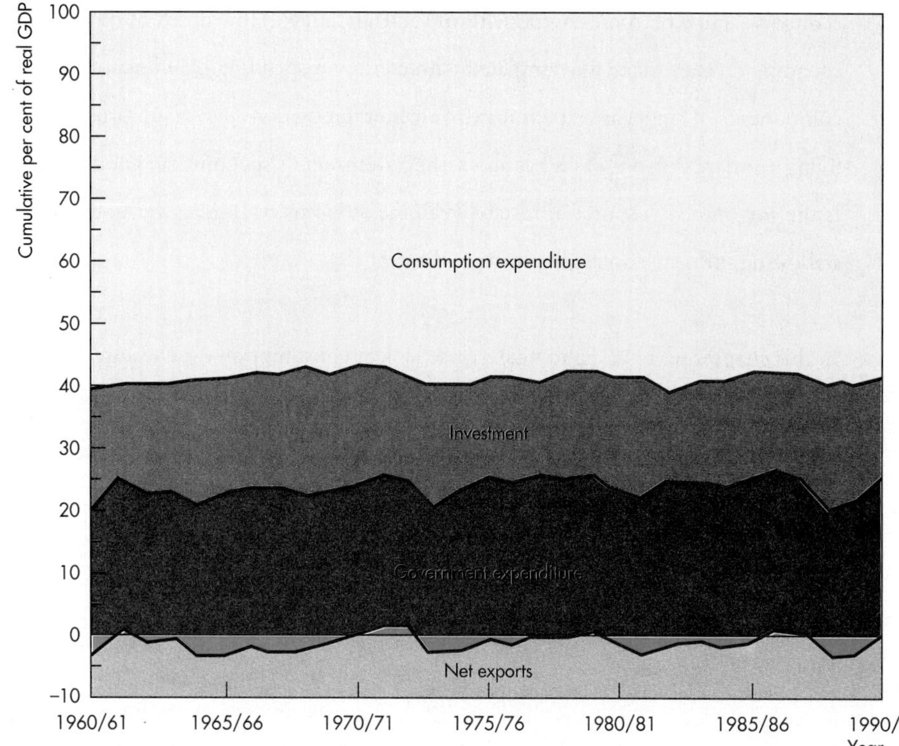

The biggest component of aggregate expenditure is consumption expenditure. It ranges between 58 and 62 per cent of GDP and averages 59 per cent. Investment averages 18 per cent of GDP, fluctuating between 14 and 22 per cent. Government expenditure on goods and services ranges between 23 and 26 per cent of GDP, averages 25 per cent of GDP and is currently 24 per cent. Net exports is the smallest item and averages approximately –1.7 per cent.

Source: ABS Time Series Service, supplied by EconData's dX Data Service.

Figure 25.2 Fluctuations in the Components of Aggregate Expenditure, 1960/61–1990/91

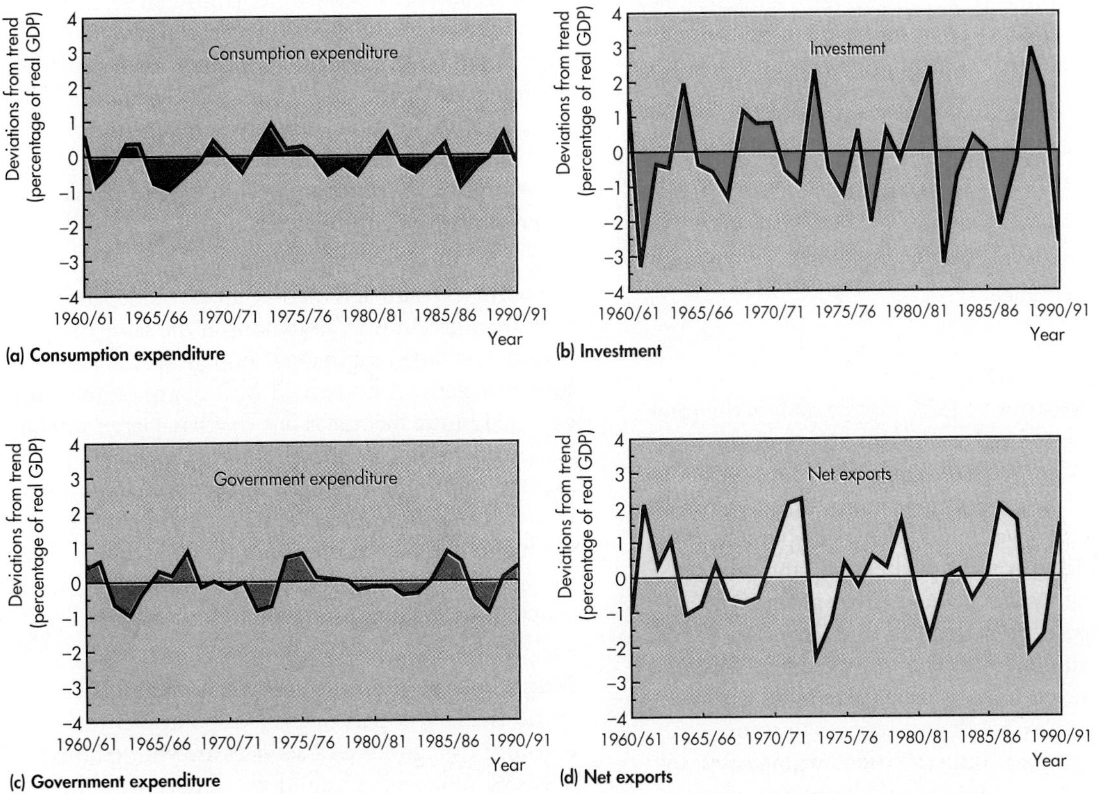

Fluctuations in the components of aggregate expenditure are shown as deviations from their own trends, expressed as percentages of GDP. Although consumption is the biggest component of aggregate expenditure, it is the one that fluctuates least, in percentage terms. Investment and net exports fluctuate most.

Source: See Fig. 25.1.

nents of aggregate expenditure deviate from their own trend values (as percentages of GDP). The scales on which each of the four variables are measured are identical, so the up and down movements in the lines give a precise indication of the relative volatility of the four components. Note that, although the fluctuations in consumption expenditure have a much smaller range than those in investment, the ups and downs of the two series move in sympathy with each other. Note also that the biggest decline in investment — in 1982/83 — occurred at precisely the time that the economy was at the trough of one of its most severe post-war recessions (a recession that we discussed in Chapters 22 and 24). Net exports are especially volatile and, to a large degree, represent a mirror image of fluctuations in consumption and investment. As both consumption and investment rise, the level of net exports declines.

Consumption expenditure, investment and net exports are the private components of aggregate expenditure. Government purchases of goods and services are determined by decisions made by governments in their interactions with voters. This is the *public* component of aggregate expenditure. In the material that follows, we're going to study the choices that determine the private components of aggregate expenditure. As we do so, we will hold prices constant and focus on other variables that affect the private components of aggregate expenditure. We will relax this assumption in later chapters. Let's now begin with the largest component — consumption expenditure.

Consumption Expenditure and Saving

Consumption expenditure is the value of the consumption goods and services bought by households. There are six main factors that influence a household's consumption expenditure:

- Disposable income
- Expected future income
- Wealth
- Stage in life
- Degree of patience
- Interest rates

Disposable Income *Disposable income* is the total income that households receive in exchange for supplying the services of factors of production, plus transfers from the government minus taxes. A household can do only two things with its disposable income: spend it on consumption goods and services or save it. Savings can be held either as financial assets (for example, bank deposits and shares) or as real assets (for example, housing and paintings). Disposable income saved today is usually set aside with consumption of future goods and services in mind.

As a household's disposable income increases, so does its expenditure on food and beverages, clothing, housing, transportation, medical care, and on most other goods and services. That is, a household's consumption expenditure increases as its income increases.

Expected Future Income Other things being equal, the higher a household's expected future income, the greater is its current consumption expenditure. That is, if there are two households that have the same disposable income in the current year, the household with the larger expected future income will spend a larger portion of current disposable income on consumption goods and services. Consider, for example, two households whose principal income earner is a senior executive in a large corporation. One executive has just been told of an important promotion that will increase the household's income by 50 per cent in the following years. The other has just been told that the firm has been taken over and that there will be no further employment beyond the end of the year. The first household buys a new car and takes an expensive foreign holiday, thereby increasing its current consumption expenditure. The second household sells the family's second car and cancels its holiday plans, thereby cutting back on its current consumption expenditure.

An important influence on expected future income is the state of consumer confidence. If people are uncertain about the future state of the economy they might be less certain about their own future employment prospects and, consequently, about their expected future income. Thus, when consumer confidence falls, expected future income falls and consumption expenditure declines. And conversely, when consumer confidence is high.

Wealth Wealth and income are not independent; they are different ways of looking at the same thing. Wealth has two components: human wealth and non-human wealth. A household with a large current and expected future income is one that has a large amount of human wealth. A household with large holdings of assets — non-human wealth — receives a large interest income from those assets. Other things being equal, the higher the two components of a household's wealth, the greater is its consumption expenditure (see Our Advancing Knowledge, pp. 184–185).

Stage in Life On the average, households that spend the largest part of their disposable income on consumption goods and services are young households with dependent children. Those who spend the smallest part of their disposable income on consumption goods and services are the middle-aged.

Degree of Patience The degree of patience varies from one person to another and from one household to another. Some, impatient to consume, do not worry if they run into debt. Others prefer to defer consumption and save instead. These personal characteristics influence the level of a household's consumption expenditure. The more impatient the household, the larger is its consumption expenditure, other things being equal.

Interest Rates The higher the interest rate, the lower is the level of consumption expenditure. High interest rates discourage consumption by making consumer loans more expensive or by making it more attractive for a household to save and lend part of its income to others.

Of the five influences on consumption expenditure, the most important one is the level of disposable income. Let's look at the relationship between consumption expenditure and disposable income more closely.

The Consumption Function and the Saving Function

The relationship between consumption expenditure and disposable income is called the **consumption function.** The relationship between saving and disposable income is called the **saving function.** We'll first examine the consumption function and saving function for an imaginary household. Then we'll study the consumption function in the Australian economy.

A household's consumption function and saving function are a statement about the household's consumption expenditure and saving plan at each possible level of disposable income. Figure 25.3 sets out the consumption function and saving function for the Hunter household. There are two important things to note about the Hunter household's consumption and saving functions. First, even if the Hunter household has no disposable income, it still consumes. It does so by having a negative level of saving. Negative saving is called **dissaving.** Households that consume more than their disposable income do so either by living off assets or by borrowing, a situation that cannot, of course, last forever.

Figure 25.3 The Hunter Household's Consumption Function and Saving Function

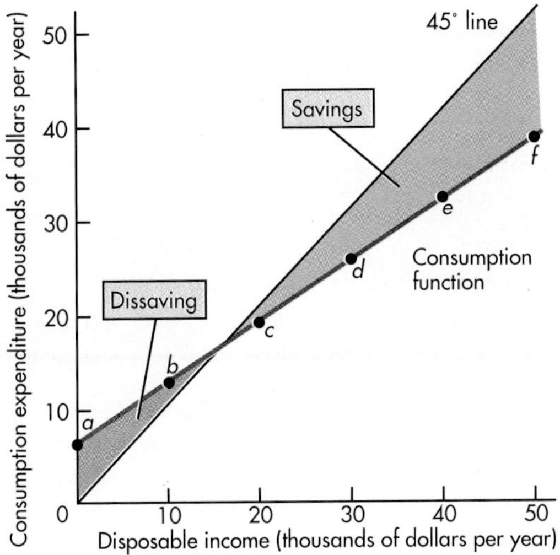

(a) Consumption function

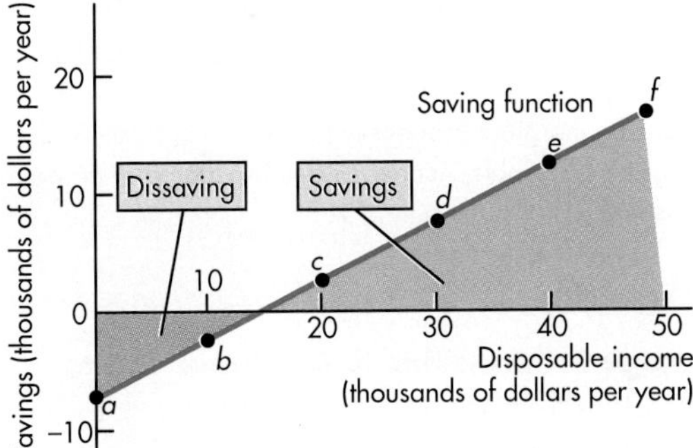

(b) Saving function

	Disposable income	Consumption expenditure	Saving
	(thousands of dollars per year)		
a	0	6	–6
b	10	12	–2
c	20	18	2
d	30	24	6
e	40	30	10
f	50	36	14

The table sets out the consumption and saving plan of the Hunter household at various levels of disposable income. Part (a) of the figure shows the relationship between consumption expenditure and disposable income (the consumption function). Part (b) shows the relationship between saving and disposable income (the saving function). Points *a* to *f* on the consumption and saving functions correspond to the rows in the table.

The 45° line in part (a) is the line of equality between consumption expenditure and disposable income. The Hunter household's consumption expenditure plus saving equals its disposable income. When the consumption function in part (a) is above the 45° line, saving is negative (dissaving occurs) and the saving function in part (b) is below the horizontal axis. When the consumption function is below the 45° line, saving is positive and the saving function is above the horizontal axis. At the point where the consumption function intersects the 45° line, all disposable income is consumed, saving is zero and the saving function intersects the horizontal axis.

Second, as the Hunter household's disposable income increases, so does the amount that it plans to spend on consumption and the amount that it plans to save. Since a household can only consume or save its disposable income, these two items always add up to disposable income. That is, consumption and saving plans are consistent with disposable income.

The Consumption Function The Hunter household's consumption function is plotted in Fig. 25.3(a). The horizontal axis measures disposable income and the vertical axis measures consumption expenditure (both in thousands of dollars). The points labelled *a* to *f* in the figure correspond with the rows having the same letters in the table. For example, point *c* indicates a disposable income of $20,000 and consumption of $18,000.

The 45° Line Figure 25.3(a) also contains a line labelled '45° line'. This line connects the points at which consumption, measured on the vertical axis, equals disposable income, measured on the horizontal axis. When the consumption function is above the 45° line, consumption exceeds disposable income; when the consumption function is below the 45° line, consumption is less than disposable income; and at the point where the consumption function intersects the 45° line, consumption and disposable income are equal.

The Saving Function The saving function is graphed in Fig. 25.3(b). The horizontal axis is exactly the same as that in Fig. 25.3(a). The vertical axis measures saving. Again, the points marked *a* to *f* correspond to the rows of the table.

There is a relationship between the consumption function and the saving function. We can see this relationship by looking at the two parts of the figure. When the saving function is below the horizontal axis, saving is negative (dissaving) and the consumption function is above the 45° line. When the saving function is above the horizontal axis, saving is positive and the consumption function is below the 45° line. When saving is zero, the saving function cuts the horizontal axis and when consumption equals disposable income, the consumption function cuts the 45° line. The level of disposable income at which the saving function cuts the horizontal axis is the same as that at which the consumption function cuts the 45° line — in this case, $15,000.

Table 25.1 Average and Marginal Propensities to Consume and to Save

(a) Calculating average propensities to consume and save

Disposable income (YD)	Consumption expenditure (C)	Saving (S)	APC (C/YD)	APS (S/YD)
(dollars per year)				
0	6,000	–6,000	—	—
10,000	12,000	–2,000	1.20	–0.20
20,000	18,000	2,000	0.90	0.10
30,000	24,000	6,000	0.80	0.20
40,000	30,000	10,000	0.75	0.25
50,000	36,000	14,000	0.72	0.28

(b) Calculating marginal propensities to consume and to save

Change in disposable income:	$\Delta YD = 10{,}000$
Change in consumption	$\Delta C = 6000$
Change in saving	$\Delta S = 4000$
Marginal propensity to consume	$MPC = \Delta C/\Delta YD = 0.6$
Marginal propensity to save	$MPS = \Delta S/\Delta YD = 0.4$

Consumption and saving depend on disposable income. At zero disposable income, some consumption is undertaken and saving is negative (dissaving occurs). As disposable income increases, so do both consumption and saving. The average propensities to consume and to save are calculated in part (a). The average propensity to consume — the ratio of consumption to disposable income — declines as disposable income increases; the average propensity to save — the ratio of saving to disposable income — increases as disposable income increases. These two average propensities sum to 1. Each additional — or *marginal* — dollar of disposable income is either consumed or saved.

Part (b) calculates the marginal propensities to consume and to save. The marginal propensity to consume is the fraction of the last dollar of disposable income spent on consumption goods and services. The marginal propensity to save is the fraction of the last dollar of disposable income saved. The marginal propensities to consume and to save sum to 1.

The Average Propensities to Consume and to Save

The **average propensity to consume** (APC) is consumption expenditure divided by disposable income. Table 25.1(a) shows you how to calculate the average propensity to consume. Let's do a sample calculation. At a disposable income of $20,000, the Hunter household consumes $18,000. Its average propensity to consume is $18,000 divided by $20,000, which equals 0.9.

As you can see from the numbers in the table, the average propensity to consume declines as disposable income rises. At a disposable income of $10,000, the household consumes more than its income, so its average propensity to consume is greater than 1. But at a disposable income of $50,000 the household consumes only $36,000, so its average propensity to consume is $36,000 divided by $50,000, which equals 0.72.

The **average propensity to save** (APS) is saving divided by disposable income. It too is calculated in Table 25.1(a). For example, when disposable income is $20,000 the Hunter household saves $2000, so that the average propensity to save is $2000 divided by $20,000, which equals 0.1. When saving is negative, the average propensity to save is negative. As disposable income increases, the average propensity to save increases.

As disposable income increases, the average propensity to consume falls and the average propensity to save rises. Equivalently, as disposable income increases, the fraction of income saved increases and the fraction of income consumed decreases. These patterns in the average propensities to consume and save reflect the fact that people with very low disposable incomes are so poor that their income is not even sufficient to meet their consumption expenditure. Consumption expenditure exceeds disposable income. As people become richer, with higher incomes, they are able to meet their consumption requirements with a lower and lower fraction of their disposable income.

The sum of the average propensity to consume and the average propensity to save is equal to one. These two average propensities add up to one because consumption and saving exhaust disposable income. Each dollar of disposable income is either consumed or saved.

You can see that the two average propensities add up to 1 by using the following equation:

$$C + S = YD$$

Divide both sides of the equation by disposable income to obtain:

$$C/YD + S/YD = 1$$

C/YD is the *average propensity to consume* and S/YD is the *average propensity to save.* Thus:

$$\text{APC} + \text{APS} = 1$$

The Marginal Propensities to Consume and to Save

The last dollar of disposable income received is called the marginal dollar. Part of that marginal dollar is consumed and part of it is saved. The division of the marginal dollar between consumption expenditure and saving is determined by the marginal propensities to consume and to save.

The **marginal propensity to consume** (MPC) is the fraction of the last dollar of disposable income that is spent on consumption goods and services. It is calculated as the change in consumption expenditure divided by the change in disposable income. The **marginal propensity to save** (MPS) is the fraction of the last dollar of disposable income saved. The marginal propensity to save is calculated as the change in saving divided by the change in disposable income.

Table 25.1 calculates the Hunter household's marginal propensities to consume and to save. Looking back at part (a) of the table, you can see that disposable income increases by $10,000 as we move from one row to the next — $10,000 is the change in disposable income. You can also see from part (a) that when disposable income increases by $10,000, consumption increases by $6000. The marginal propensity to consume — the change in consumption divided by the change in disposable income — is therefore $6000 divided by $10,000, which equals 0.6. The Hunter household's marginal propensity to consume is constant. It is the same at each level of disposable income. Out of a marginal dollar of disposable income, 60 cents is spent on consumption goods and services.

Table 25.1 also calculates the marginal propensity to save. You can see from part (a) of the table that when disposable income increases by $10,000, saving increases by $4000. The marginal propensity to save — the change in saving divided by the change in disposable income — is therefore $4000 divided by $10,000, which equals 0.4. The Hunter household's marginal propensity to save is constant. It is the same at each level of disposable income. Out of the last dollar of disposable income, 40 cents is saved.

The marginal propensity to consume plus the marginal propensity to save equals one. Each additional dollar must either be consumed or saved. In this example, when disposable income increases by $1, 60 cents more is spent and 40 cents more is saved. That is

$$\text{MPC} + \text{MPS} = 1$$

Marginal–Average Relations In the calculations we have just done, the marginal propensity to consume is less than the average propensity to consume, and as disposable income increases, the average propensity to consume falls.

This relationship between the marginal propensity to consume and the average propensity to consume is a feature of all marginal and average relations. You may appreciate the relationship more clearly if you think of a cricket batting average. Suppose that Allan Border comes in to bat with average runs per innings at 50. All his previous innings contributed to this average. His current innings is going to produce his marginal score. If he gets a century, his marginal score is better than his average and his average rises. If he makes a duck, his marginal score is worse than his average and his average falls.

You can see that this marginal–average relationship also holds in the case of saving. The marginal propensity to save is higher than the average propensity to save. As a consequence, as disposable income increases, so does the average propensity to save.

Saving is like a batsman making a century: the marginal propensity to save exceeds the average propensity to save, so the average propensity increases as disposable income increases — the score from the marginal innings exceeds the average, so the average increases as the number of innings increases. Consuming is like making a duck. The marginal propensity to consume is below the average propensity and the average propensity to consume decreases as disposable income increases — the marginal score is below the average score, so the average declines as the number of innings increases.

Marginal Propensities and Slopes The marginal propensity to consume is equal to the slope of the consumption function. You can see this equality by looking back at Fig. 25.3. In that figure, the consumption function has a constant slope that can be measured as the change in consumption divided by the change in income. For example, when income increases from $20,000 to $30,000 — an increase of $10,000 — consumption increases from $18,000 to $24,000 — an increase of $6,000. The slope of the consumption function is $6000 divided by $10,000, which equals 0.6 — the same value as the marginal propensity to consume that we've calculated in Table 25.1.

The marginal propensity to save is equal to the slope of the saving function. You can see this equality by again looking back at Fig. 25.3. In this case, when income increases by $10,000, saving increases by $4000. The slope of the saving function is $4000 divided by $10,000, which equals 0.4 — the same value as the marginal propensity to save that we calculated in Table 25.1.

We've studied the consumption and saving choices of a representative household. Let's now look at the consumption expenditure of actual households in Australia and see how that expenditure varies as disposable income varies.

R E V I E W

Consumption expenditure is influenced by six main factors: disposable income, expected future income, wealth, stage in life, degree of patience and interest rates. Households allocate their disposable income to either consumption expenditure or saving. The relationship between consumption expenditure and disposable income is the *consumption function* and the relationship between saving and disposable income is the *saving function.* The change in consumption expenditure divided by the change in disposable income is the *marginal propensity to consume* (MPC) and the change in saving divided by the change in disposable income is the *marginal propensity to save* (MPS). Because consumption expenditure plus saving equals disposable income, MPC + MPS = 1. ■

The Australian Consumption Function

Data for the Australian consumption function in 1988 is shown in Table 25.2. Each row represents disposable income and consumption expenditure averaged over a group of households. There are ten such rows, each showing the average disposable income and average consumption expenditure of households comprising 10 per cent of the population. The rows are arranged from the lowest to the highest income.

Consumption expenditure in Australia increases as disposable income increases. We can calculate the average and marginal propensities to consume using this data. First, let's calculate the average propensity to consume — consumption expenditure divided by disposable income. As you can see, the bottom 50 per cent of all households (rows *a–e*) consumed significantly more than their disposable income in 1988 — their average propensity to consume was greater than one. The average propensity to consume declines as income increases and the

Table 25.2 Disposable Income and Consumption Expenditure in Australia, 1988

Income group		Disposable income (dollars per week)	Consumption expenditure (dollars per week)	Average propensity to consume	Marginal propensity to consume
a	lowest 10 per cent	102	215	2.11	
					0.47
b	second 10 per cent	188	255	1.36	
					0.85
c	third 10 per cent	250	308	1.23	
					1.13
d	fourth 10 per cent	321	388	1.21	
					0.91
e	fifth 10 per cent	397	457	1.15	
					0.48
f	sixth 10 per cent	484	499	1.03	
					0.98
g	seventh 10 per cent	586	599	1.02	
					0.71
h	eighth 10 per cent	688	671	0.98	
					0.81
i	ninth 10 per cent	821	779	0.95	
					0.43
j	top 10 per cent	1258	967	0.77	

The rows record average disposable income and average consumption expenditure for Australian income groups ranging from the lowest to the highest. This data is used to calculate the average and marginal propensities to consume. The average propensity to consume — consumption expenditure divided by disposable income — declines as income increases. The marginal propensity to consume — the change in consumption divided by the change in disposable income — initially rises as income increases and then shows a tendency to decline. The marginal propensity to consume is less than the average propensity to consume.

Source: Australian Bureau of Statistics, *Household Expenditure Survey, 1988*, ABS Catalogue No. 6528.

group of households with the highest income has an average propensity to consume of 0.77.

Next, we'll calculate the marginal propensity to consume — the change in consumption expenditure divided by the change in disposable income. The marginal propensity to consume as disposable income increases between the lowest and second lowest income group is 0.47. As income increases through to the higher income groups, the marginal propensity to consume increases and then declines to only 0.43 for the highest income group. Middle-income Australians spend (row *e*) 90 cents of each additional dollar of disposable income received, while high-income Australians spend less than 45 cents of each additional dollar's worth of disposable income.

We saw in the case of the Hunter household, and in the case of the cricket batting scores, that when the marginal exceeds the average, the average increases; when the marginal is below the average, the average decreases. You can see the same relationship between the marginal and average propensities here. The marginal propensity to consume is below the average propensity to consume, and as disposable income increases the average propensity to consume declines.

Figure 25.4 plots the data in Table 25.2. Each point (from *a* to *j*) represents a row in the table. The line passing through these points is the Australian consumption function that describes the average relationship between consumption expenditure and disposable income across these income groups. Notice the similarity between the Australian consumption function in Fig. 25.4 and the Hunter household's consumption function in Fig. 25.3(a).

Shifts in the Consumption Function

We have noted that there are six main factors that influence a household's consumption expenditure, only one of which is disposable income. Those other factors — expected future income, wealth, stage in life,

Figure 25.4 The Australian Consumption Function in 1988

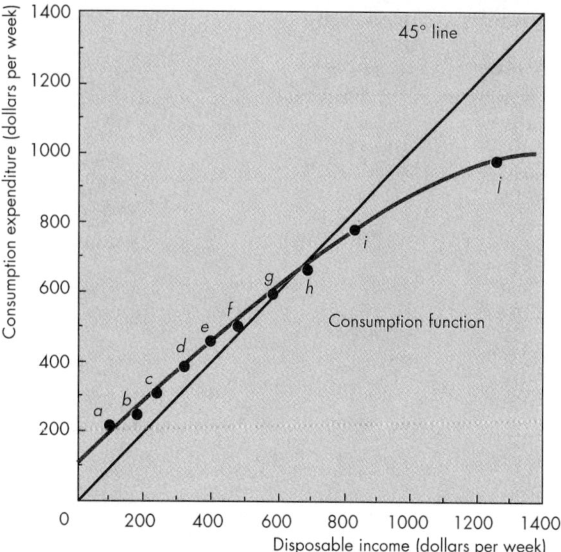

The Australian consumption function plots weekly household consumption expenditure on the vertical axis against weekly household disposable income on the horizontal axis. The consumption function shown here is based on disposable income and consumption expenditure data for ten income groups in 1988, as shown in Table 25.2. Points *a* to *j* on the consumption function correspond to the rows in the table. For example, the highest income households had an average weekly disposable income of $1258 in 1988 and a weekly consumption expenditure of $967. This consumption and disposable income is shown as point *j* on the consumption function. The consumption function is plotted as the line that most closely passes through points *a* to *j*.

degree of patience and interest rates — influence consumption expenditure and are represented by shifts in the consumption function. For example, an increase in expected future income shifts the consumption function upward; a decrease in expected future income shifts it downward. The consumption function shifts upward as a result of a decrease in interest rates. As a family progresses through its life cycle, its consumption function shifts upward as the number of children in the household increases and as the children get older. The consumption function then shifts downward when the children leave home and as the adults in the family approach retirement age.

You may have noticed from Table 25.2 that, in 1988, 70 per cent of all Australian households were consuming more than their income. That year was one with relatively low interest rates and an investment boom. Unemployment was falling and the majority of households expected a sustained period of prosperity with rising incomes. The influence of both these factors was sufficient to shift the consumption function upward so that the majority of households were either running down past savings or accumulating debt to finance their high levels of consumption.

The Aggregate Consumption Function

Our purpose in developing a theory of the consumption function is to explain the determination of aggregate expenditure and real GDP. So far, we have studied the relationship between consumption expenditure and disposable income for a typical household, and have described the average consumption function across households in Australia. We're now going to direct our attention away from the consumption function of an individual household and of households at different income levels and examine the aggregate consumption function.

The **aggregate consumption function** is the relationship between real consumption expenditure and real GDP. To obtain the aggregate consumption function, we first calculate the relationship between real consumption expenditure and real disposable income. This relationship is shown in Fig. 25.5(a). The vertical axis measures real consumption expenditure (in 1984/85 dollars) and the horizontal axis measures real disposable income (also in 1984/85 dollars). Each point identified by a dot represents real consumption expenditure and real disposable income for a particular year from 1960/61 to 1990/91. The line passing through these points is the time-series consumption function. The **time-series consumption function** is the relationship between real consumption expenditure and real disposable income over time. The slope of this consumption function, and hence the marginal propensity to consume, is 0.90.

It is important to understand why this time-series consumption function looks different from the consumption function for individual households that we examined in Fig. 25.4. The individual household consumption function tells us how consumption expenditure varies with disposable income across households in a given year. The time-series consumption function tells us how aggregate consumption expenditure varies with aggregate disposable income from one year to another. Equivalently, it tells us about the relationship between average consumption expenditure and average disposable income over time. Averaging over families with low incomes and high incomes, consumption expenditure represents 90

Figure 25.5 The Aggregate Consumption Function

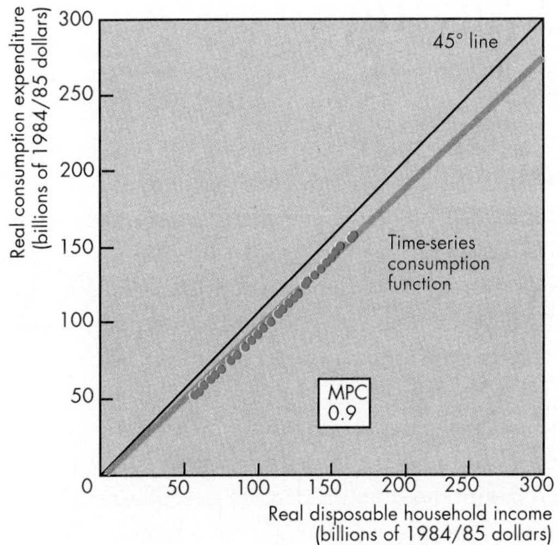

(a) Consumption as a function of disposable income

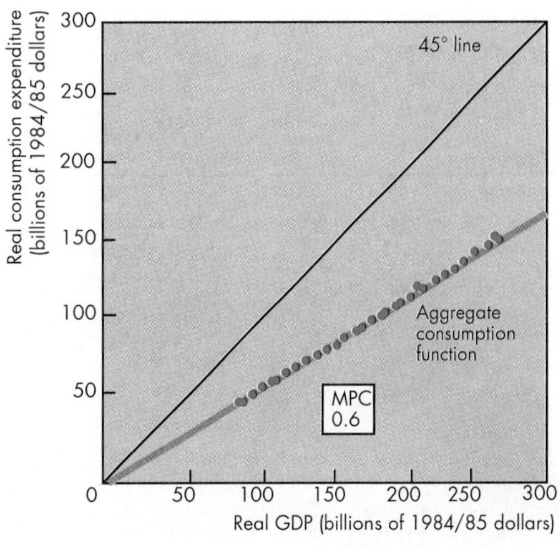

(b) Consumption as a function of real GDP

Real GDP (*Y*)	Disposable income (*YD* = 0.67*Y*)	Consumption expenditure (*C* = 0.90*YD* = 0.60*Y*)
	(billions of 1984/85 dollars)	
50	33.3	30
100	66.7	60
150	100.0	90
200	133.3	120
250	166.7	150
300	200.0	180

Source: Real Consumption Expenditure: Series NCQQ.UK85#; Real Disposable Income: Series NODQ.UC_HDI#; Real GDP: Series NOQA.UK85_GDP; ABS Time Series Service, supplied by EconData's dX Data Service.

Part (a) shows the Australian time-series consumption function — the relationship between real consumption expenditure and real disposable income — for each year between 1960/61 and 1990/91. Each point in the figure represents real consumption expenditure and real disposable income for a particular year. The marginal propensity to consume out of disposable income is approximately 0.90.

Part (b) shows the Australian aggregate consumption function — the relationship between real consumption expenditure and real GDP. This consumption function takes into account the fact that as real GDP increases, so too do net taxes. The marginal propensity to consume out of real GDP is approximately 0.6. The connection between the time-series consumption function and the aggregate consumption function is shown in the table. The tax rate is 33.33 per cent, so that disposable income is 0.67 times real GDP. The marginal propensity to consume out of disposable income is 0.9. Combining a tax rate of 33.33 per cent with a marginal propensity to consume out of disposable income of 0.9 gives a marginal propensity to consume out of real GDP of 0.6 (0.9 x 0.67 = 0.6).

cents in every dollar of disposable income. But there is a large amount of variation around this average and that variation is illustrated in the consumption function for individual households.

Figure 25.5(b) shows the aggregate consumption function — real consumption expenditure plotted against real GDP. To express consumption expenditure as a function of GDP, we need to establish the link between disposable income and GDP. That link is implicit in the definition of disposable income. Recall that we have defined disposable income as the difference between aggregate income and net taxes (net taxes are taxes minus transfer payments). Aggregate income is GDP. To work out the relationship between consumption and GDP, we need to know what happens to net taxes as GDP changes.

Net taxes increase as GDP increases. Almost all the taxes that we pay — personal taxes, corporate taxes and social security taxes — increase as our incomes increase. Transfer payments, such as social security and welfare benefits, decrease as our incomes

Consumption and Saving

Irving Fisher

By 1930, a consensus had emerged among economists concerning the determination of consumption and saving. That consensus was crystallized by Irving Fisher of Yale University in his classic work, *The Theory of Interest*, published in 1930.[1] The accepted view was that consumption and saving depend primarily on the real interest rate. A high real interest rate causes a decrease in consumption and an increase in saving. Fisher assumed that people have to be induced to decrease their spending with the reward of a high rate of return. The higher the reward, the greater is the tendency to put off consumption and to save.

This consensus received a revolutionary challenge from John Maynard Keynes of Cambridge, England, in his book, *The General Theory of Employment, Interest, and Money*, published in 1936. Keynes's idea was that consumption and saving do not depend on the interest rate but on the level of disposable income:

'The propensity to consume is a fairly stable function so that, as a rule, the amount of aggregate consumption mainly depends on the amount of aggregate income, . . . changes in the propensity itself being . . . a secondary influence. . . . The fundamental psychological law, upon which we are entitled to depend with confidence both a priori from our knowledge of human nature and from the detailed facts of experience, is that men are disposed, as a rule and on the average, to increase their consumption as their income increases, but not by as much as the increase in their income. That is to say, if ΔC is the amount of consumption and ΔY is income, C has the same sign as Y but is smaller in amount, i.e. $\Delta C / \Delta Y$ is positive and less than unity'.[2]

A little earlier than the time that Keynes was writing, Colin Clark, working in England, and Simon Kuznets, working at the University of Chicago, were beginning to compile national income data. This data fitted Keynes's theory remarkably closely.

During the 1940s and 1950s, a large amount of additional data was being collected — but this time by government bureaus. Official national income accounts were providing additional observations of consumption and income each year and, after 1947, each quarter-year. Cross-section data — that is, data on the consumption and income of individual groups of people classified by age, race and location — were also being collected. This new data revealed shortcomings in Keynes's theory. Even as early as the late 1940s, the Keynesian theory of the consumption function began to make important forecasting errors. Also, the cross-section data showed that the fraction of income consumed varied systematically, depending on whether people were young or old, black or white, or from urban or rural areas.

The anomalies and puzzles in the data brought forth two related new theories and advances in our understanding. The first of these was the *life-cycle hypothesis*

---

[1] Irving Fisher, *The Theory of Interest* (New York: the Macmillan Company. 1930).

[2] John Maynard Keynes, *The General Theory of Employment, Interest, and Money* (London: Macmillan, 1936), 96.

proposed by Franco Modigliani of the Massachusetts Institute of Technology (MIT); the second was the *permanent income hypothesis* proposed by Milton Friedman, then at the University of Chicago. Modigliani's work, done jointly with a young English economist, Richard Brumberg, was published in 1954.[3] Friedman's work was published three years later, in 1957, in a book entitled *A Theory of the Consumption Function.*[4]

Each of these scholars suggested that consumption is determined not by income but by wealth. Other things being equal, the wealthier an individual, the more that individual will consume. Income and wealth are related to each other, but not directly on a year-by-year basis. A wealthy person might have a low income in a particular year. A poor person might have a big income (a windfall) in a particular year. Random fluctuations in income not associated with fluctuations in wealth will produce small or even no fluctuations in consumption.

Modigliani's main contribution was to emphasize the relationship between an individual's stage of life and income and wealth. Young people with secure jobs may have a small income but be wealthy in the sense that their future incomes will grow. Such people therefore tend to consume a large fraction of their current income. People in mid-life have an income that is high relative to their wealth. They consume a small fraction of their income.

Friedman's main contribution was to emphasize the distinction between permanent and transitory changes in income. Permanent changes in income have a large effect on consumption while transitory changes have a small effect. The ideas of Modigliani and Friedman resolved most of the paradoxes of both the cross-section and time-series data. Both scholars received a Nobel Prize in economics, partly for their contributions in this area.

Another revolution in economics — the rational expectations revolution — began in the 1960s and gathered momentum in the 1970s. This revolution forced economists to change their views about Modigliani's and Friedman's theories of the consumption function. An important contribution to this reformulation is one made by Robert Hall of Stanford University in 1978.[5]

The rational expectations theory of the consumption function as proposed by Hall starts from the same point as Modigliani and Friedman: consumption depends on wealth. Wealth can be thought of as depending on all future income. The more income a person is going to earn in the future, whether in wages or interest, the wealthier that person is. People do not know how much they are going to earn in the future but, to make consumption decisions today, they have to form an expectation of what that future income will be. In forming their expectations, people will use all the information that is available. Having made a best estimate of their wealth, people will make consumption plans that achieve the best (in their assessment) allocation of consumption over time.

Expectations will change only as a result of 'news' — of new information not previously known. News arrives at random. As a consequence, people's estimates of how wealthy they are also change in a random fashion. Since consumption plans depend on wealth, these plans will also vary in a random fashion.

Changes in consumption from one period to another will reflect both the working out of a consumption plan, as Modigliani and Friedman sketched, and changes in plans due to new information. As a result, changes in consumption from one year to another will be random. The average value will reflect average long-run consumption plans but their changes from year to year will reflect changes in information and expectations about future wealth. No variable, other than current consumption, should be of any value for predicting future consumption.

Robert Hall's contribution is, for the time being, the most recent milestone in the path of our evolving understanding of consumption and saving. It is by no means the last word, though. Every month new contributions on this topic, some of which will turn out to be milestones when viewed in a longer perspective, are being published in the economics journals.

---

3 Franco Modigliani and Richard Brumberg, 'Utility Analysis of the Consumption Function: An Interpretation of Cross-Section Data', in *Post-Keynesian Economics,* ed. K.Kurihara (New Brunswick: Rutgers University Press, 1954).

4 Milton Friedman, *A Theory of the Consumption Function* (Princeton: Princeton University Press, 1957).

5 Robert E. Hall, 'Stochastic Implications of the Life-Cycle permanent Income Hypothesis: Theory and Evidence', *Journal of Political Economy* 86 (December 1978): 971–88

increase. (Social security benefits due to retirement do not vary with income but aggregate transfer payments do vary with income.) Since taxes increase and transfers decrease, net taxes clearly increase as incomes increase. There is, in fact, a tendency for net taxes to be a fairly stable percentage of GDP — about 33.33 per cent. If 33.33 per cent of GDP is paid in taxes net of transfers, 66.67 per cent of GDP is available as disposable income.

The table in Fig. 25.5 sets out the relationship between real GDP, disposable income and consumption expenditure. It incorporates the 66.67 per cent relationship between GDP and disposable income. For example, if real GDP is $300 billion, net taxes are $100 billion and, therefore, disposable income is $200 billion. The table also tells us what consumption expenditure is. We have seen that the marginal propensity to consume out of disposable income is 0.9. That is, out of each additional dollar of disposable income, 90 cents are consumed and 10 cents are saved. Thus if disposable income is $200 billion, consumption expenditure is 90 per cent of that amount, which is $180 billion.

Consumption as a function of real GDP — the aggregate consumption function — is shown in Fig. 25.5(b) as the straight line passing through the dots representing actual real consumption expenditure and real GDP for the years 1960/61 to 1990/91.

The change in consumption expenditure divided by the change in real GDP is the **marginal propensity to consume out of real GDP**. It is measured by the slope of the aggregate consumption function and depends on both the marginal propensity to consume and the relationship between disposable income and real GDP. Since 90 per cent (0.9) of disposable income is consumed and since 66.67 per cent (0.67) of GDP is available as disposable income, the fraction of GDP consumed is 0.6 ($0.9 \times 0.67 = 0.6$).

The story of the development of the theory of consumption and saving is told in Our Advancing Knowledge (pp. 184–185).

R E V I E W

Of all the influences on consumption expenditure, disposable income is the most important. Real consumption expenditure in Australia is a stable function of real disposable income. Real disposable income is, in turn, a stable function of real GDP. Therefore real consumption expenditure is a stable function of real GDP. In Australia today, each additional dollar of real GDP generates, on the average, an additional 60 cents of real consumption expenditure. ■

Let's now turn to the other main private component of aggregate expenditure — investment.

Investment

Gross investment is the purchase of new buildings, equipment and plant, or gross fixed capital expenditure, together with additions to inventories or increases in stock. It has two components: net investment and replacement investment. **Net investment** is the purchase of additions to existing capital. **Replacement investment** is the purchase of replacements for worn out or depreciated capital. Purchases of buildings, equipment and plant are usually the result of carefully laid plans. Some additions to inventories are similarly planned. However, some additions to inventories are the result of unanticipated falls in sales and are unplanned. Some reductions in inventories are the result of unanticipated increases in sales. Thus, while most investment is planned, some, resulting from unanticipated changes in inventories, is unplanned. We will focus on planned investment for now.

As we saw in Fig. 25.2, gross investment is a volatile component of aggregate expenditure. What determines the level of planned investment and why does it fluctuate so much? The answer lies in the investment decisions of firms. How does BHP decide how much to spend on a new steel mill? What determines IBM's outlays on new computer designs? How does Telecom choose what it will spend on fibre optic communications systems? And why are there times when firms invest at a high rate and other times at a low rate?

What Determines Investment?

The main influences on firms' investment decisions are:

- Interest rates
- Expected inflation
- Expected profit
- Existing capital

Interest Rates The lower the level of interest rates, the greater is the amount of investment. Firms sometimes pay for capital goods with money that they have borrowed, and sometimes they use their own funds — called retained earnings. Regardless of the method of financing an investment project, the interest rate is part of its *opportunity cost.* The interest paid on borrowing is a direct cost. But retained earnings could be lent to another firm at the going interest rate and the interest forgone is the opportunity cost of using retained earnings to finance an investment project. The lower the interest rate, the lower is the opportunity cost of any given investment project. Some projects that would not be profitable at a high interest rate become profitable at a low interest rate. The lower the interest rate, the larger is the number of investment projects that become profitable and, therefore, the greater is the level of investment.

For example, suppose that General Motors Holden (GMH) is contemplating building a new car assembly line in Elizabeth, South Australia, at a cost of $100 million. The assembly line is expected to produce cars for three years; then it will be scrapped completely and replaced with a new line that produces an entirely new range of models. The expected net revenue in each of the three years is the amount shown in Table 25.3.

Net revenue is the difference between the total revenue from car sales and the costs of producing those cars. In calculating net revenue, we do not take into account the initial cost of the assembly line or the interest that has to be paid on it. We take separate account of these costs. To build the assembly line, GMH plans to borrow the initial $100 million, paying the interest on the amount outstanding at the end of each year, and using its expected net revenue to pay off as much of the loan as it can each year. Does it pay GMH to invest $100 million in this car assembly line? The answer depends on the interest rate.

Case 1 shows what happens if the interest rate is 20 per cent a year. GMH borrows $100 million and at the end of the first year has to pay $20 million in interest. It has a net revenue of $20 million and so its total loan outstanding is unchanged after the first year — its total repayment just equalled its annual interest repayment. At the end of the second year, it again uses its total revenue of $20 million to pay the $20 million interest bill (20 per cent of the $100 million loan outstanding). At the end of the third year, GMH still owes $100 million. It can repay the loan with its total revenue for the year of $100 million but is left with the interest repayment of $20 million. So GMH makes a loss of $20 million on this project. That is, by the end of the third year, GMH has to find an extra $20 million, compared with what would have been the case if the project had not been undertaken.

Case 2 shows what happens if the interest rate is 10 per cent a year. In this case, GMH pays only $10 million interest at the end of the first year and so can reduce its outstanding borrowing to $90 million. In the second year, the interest payment on the loan is $9 million. In this year, the loan outstanding is reduced by a further $11 million ($20 million total revenue less $9 million interest repayment) to $79 million. In the third and final year of the project, the outstanding loan plus the interest on it amounts to $86.9 million ($79 million in outstanding loan plus $7.9 million interest repayment). But GMH earns $100 million in total revenue, which after paying off the loan plus interest, leaves $13.1 million profit.

You can see that, at an interest rate of 20 per cent a year, it does not pay GMH to invest in this car assembly plant. At a 10 per cent interest rate, it does pay. The lower the interest rate, the larger the number of projects, such as the one considered here, that yield a positive net profit. Thus the lower the interest rate, the larger is the scale of investment.

Expected Inflation The higher the expected inflation rate, the greater is the amount of investment. Higher expected inflation brings higher expected future net revenue. And the larger the expected future net revenue relative to the initial cost of an investment project, the larger is the return on the project.

In the GMH example above, the new car assembly plant costs $100 million to build in the current year, regardless of the inflation rate. But the higher the inflation rate, the faster car prices are rising. Wages and other production costs also rise faster as well. The gap between car prices and wages and other production costs also rises at the same rate as the inflation rate. Thus higher inflation leads to higher net revenue and, at a given level of interest rates, results in more investment projects being profitable.

The effect of expected inflation on investment is opposite to that of the interest rate. There is an important consequence of these opposing effects on a firm's investment decision. It is that investment depends on the real interest rate. The **real interest rate** is very closely approximated by the nominal interest rate minus the expected inflation rate. That is, the real interest rate is the actual interest rate paid adjusted

Table 25.3 Investment in Car Assembly Line

Cost of Assembly Line		**$100,000,000**
Expected Net Revenue:	**year 1**	**20,000,000**
	year 2	**20,000,000**
	year 3	**100,000,000**

Case 1: Interest rate is 20 per cent per year

	Interest payment	Net revenue	Reduction of principal	Loan outstanding
Initially	—	—	—	$100,000,000
End of year 1	$20,000,000	$20,000,000	—	100,000,000
End of year 2	20,000,000	20,000,000	—	100,000,000
End of year 3	20,000,000	100,000,000	$80,000,000	20,000,000

Loss: $20,000,000

Case 2: Interest rate is 10 per cent per year

	Interest payment	Net revenue	Reduction of principal	Loan outstanding
Initially	—	—	—	$100,000,000
End of year 1	$10,000,000	$20,000,000	$10,000,000	90,000,000
End of year 2	9,000,000	20,000,000	11,000,000	79,000,000
End of year 3	7,900,000	100,000,000	92,100,000	–13,100,000

Profit: $13,100,000

A new car assembly line costs $100 million to build and is expected to generate revenues of $20 million in the first year, $20 million in the second year and $100 million in the third year. The line will then be scrapped and replaced by a new one. In Case 1, the interest rate is 20 per cent a year. The revenue stream is too low to cover the total expense and the project is not worth undertaking. In Case 2, the interest rate is 10 per cent a year. The revenue stream is sufficient to repay the initial amount borrowed, pay all the interest and still leave a small profit. In this case, the project is worthwhile and is undertaken. The lower the interest rate, the larger is the number of projects that are profitable.

for the percentage change in the value of money arising from the expected inflation. You can see why it is the real interest rate that influences investment by considering again GMH's decision on whether to build a $100 million car assembly line.

We saw that with a 20 per cent interest rate, it does not pay to build the assembly line; with a 10 per cent interest rate, it does. Suppose that the interest rate is 20 per cent (as in Case 1 of Table 25.3). But also suppose that prices are expected to rise by 10 per cent a year. With rising prices, expected net revenue will also rise by 10 per cent a year. With expected net revenue rising by 10 per cent a year, the extra revenue enables more of the loan to be repaid each year and cuts the interest payments on the outstanding loan. The combined effect of a 20 per cent interest rate and a 10 per cent expected inflation rate is almost the same as the combined effect of a 10 per cent interest rate and no expected inflation. That is, the profit after three years when the interest rate is 20 per cent and the expected inflation rate is 10 per cent is approximately the same as the case in which the interest rate is 10 per cent and the expected inflation rate is zero.[1]

Thus, although investment is affected positively by lower interest rates and by higher expected inflation, we can combine these two influences into a single determinant of investment — the real interest rate. The lower the real interest rate, the higher is the level of investment.

Expected Profit The higher the expected profitability of new capital equipment, the greater is the amount of investment. To see why this proposition is correct, consider GMH's assembly line yet again. To decide whether or not to build the assembly line, GMH has to work out its net revenue. To perform that calculation, it has to work out the total revenue from car sales that, in turn, are affected by its expectations of car prices and the share of the market that it can attain. GMH also has to figure out its operating costs, which include the wages of its assembly workers and the costs of the products that it buys from other producers. The larger the net revenue that it anticipates, the more profitable is the investment project that generates those net revenues, and the more likely is it that the project will be undertaken.

Existing Capital A firm's existing capital influences its investment decisions in two ways. First, the larger the stock of capital, other things being equal, the greater is the amount of depreciation and the larger is the amount of replacement investment. Depreciation is not, however, a source of volatility in investment. It is a source of steady investment growth. Second, the higher the degree of utilization of existing capital, the larger is the amount of investment. When capital is underutilized, as in a recession, investment falls off. But when capacity is overutilized, as in a boom, investment increases.

Investment Demand

Investment demand is the relationship between the level of planned investment and the real interest rate, holding all other influences on the level of investment constant. The **investment demand schedule** is a list of the quantities of planned investment at each real interest rate, holding all other influences on investment constant. The **investment demand curve** graphs the relationship between the real interest rate and the level of planned investment, holding everything else constant. Some examples of investment demand schedules and investment demand curves appear in Fig. 25.6. The investment demand schedule and the position of the investment demand curve depend on the other influences on investment — expected profit and existing capital.

To calculate its expected profit on an investment, a firm has to do its best to foresee future events. The firm has to forecast the scale of demand for its output so that it can make a forecast of its revenue from sales. It has to forecast future technological developments and future prices of its inputs so that it can forecast its costs. Sometimes the firm will be pessimistic about the future. At other times it will be optimistic. Pessimistic expectations arise when a firm anticipates general business conditions to be poor or when it expects rapid technological change that makes current technology obsolete. Expectations are optimistic when the firm anticipates booming business conditions or when a new technology has become available that is not expected to be surpassed for a reasonable period of time. At yet other times, firms will be neither optimistic nor pessimistic. In such periods, profit expectations are average.

Fluctuations in firms' profit expectations are the main source of fluctuations in investment demand. The three investment demand schedules in the table in Fig. 25.6 give examples of investment demand under the three types of expectations. One example is with average profit expectations. In this case, if the real interest rate is 4 per cent a year, investment is \$100 billion. If the real interest rate decreases to 2 per cent a year, investment increases to \$120 billion. If the real interest rate increases to 6 per cent a year, investment decreases to \$80 billion. The second example is with optimistic profit expectations. In this case, investment is higher at each interest rate than it is when expectations are average. The third case is with pessimistic profit expectations. In this case, investment is lower at each interest rate than with average expectations.

The investment demand curve is shown in the figure. In Fig. 25.6(a), the investment demand curve (*ID*) is that for average expected profit. Each point (*a*, *b* and *c*) corresponds to a row in the table. A change in the real interest rate causes a movement along the investment demand curve. Thus if the real interest rate is 4 per cent a year, planned investment is \$100 billion. If the interest rate rises to 6 per cent a year, there is a movement up the investment demand curve (see blue arrow) and investment decreases to \$80 billion. If the interest rate falls to 2

[1]The proposition is demonstrated in Appendix A to this chapter (pp. 204–206).

Figure 25.6 The Investment Demand Schedule and Investment Demand Curve

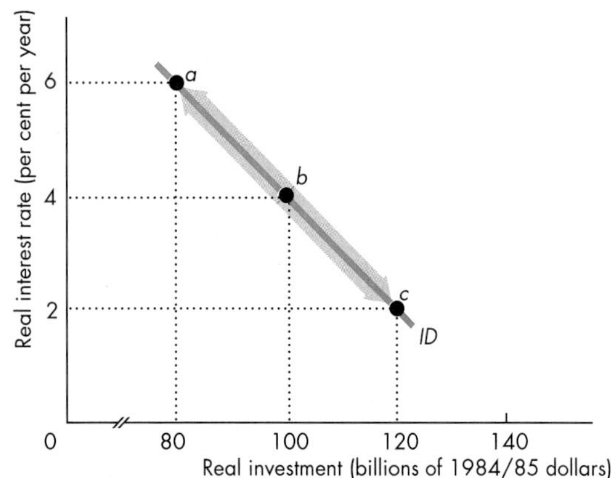

(a) The effect of a change in real interest rate

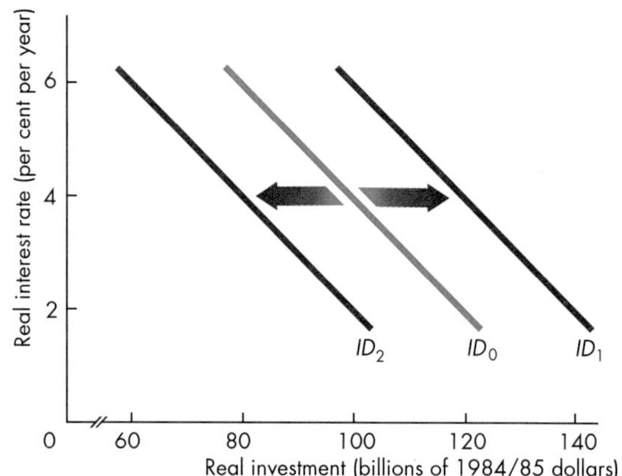

(b) The effect of a change in profit expectations

	Real interest rate (per cent per year)	Real investment (billions of 1984/85 dollars) Pessimistic	Average	Optimistic
a	6	60	80	100
b	4	80	100	120
c	2	100	120	140

The investment demand schedule lists the quantities of aggregate planned investment at each real interest rate. The table shows three investment demand schedules. As the real interest rate decreases from 6 per cent a year to 2 per cent a year, planned investment increases from $80 billion to $120 billion. The investment demand curve graphs the investment demand schedule in part (a). As the real interest rate rises from 2 per cent to 6 per cent, there is a movement along the investment demand curve from *c* to *a*. Investment plans are affected by the state of expectations of future profit. When profit expectations are average the investment demand curve is ID_0. Swings in expectations about future profit lead to shifts in the investment demand curve. If there is optimism about future profit, planned investment increases at each real interest rate and the investment demand curve shifts to the right to ID_1. If there is pessimism about future profit, planned investment decreases at each real interest rate and the investment demand curve shifts to the left to ID_2.

per cent a year, there is a movement down the investment demand curve (see blue arrow), and investment increases to $120 billion.

The effects of profit expectations are shown in Fig. 25.6(b). A change in profit expectations shifts the investment demand curve. The demand curve ID_0 represents average expected profit. When profit expectations become optimistic, the investment demand curve shifts to the right, from ID_0 to ID_1. When profit expectations become pessimistic, the investment demand curve shifts to the left, from ID_0 to ID_2.

The investment demand curve also shifts when there is a change in the amount of investment to replace depreciated capital. This influence leads to a steady rightward shift in the *ID* curve.

R E V I E W

Investment depends on the real interest rate, profit expectations and the scale of replacement of depreciated capital. Other things held constant, the lower the real interest rate, the higher is the level of investment. With optimistic profit expectations, the investment demand curve shifts to the right; with pessimistic profit expectations, it shifts to the left. Profit expectations are influenced by the business cycle. When the economy is expanding quickly, profit expectations are optimistic and investment demand is high. When the economy is expanding slowly (or contracting), profit expectations are pessimistic and investment demand is low. Investment to replace depreciated capital grows steadily over time. ■

We've just studied the theory of investment demand. Let's now see how that theory helps us to understand the fluctuations in investment that occur in the Australian economy.

Investment Demand in Australia

As we saw in Fig. 25.2, investment is one of the most volatile components of aggregate expenditure. In some years, investment is as much as 22 per cent of GDP and in others as little as 14 per cent of GDP. Let's see how we can interpret these fluctuations in investment with the theory of investment demand that we have just been studying.

We'll begin by looking at Fig. 25.7. It shows investment (in billions of 1984/85 dollars) between 1960/61 and 1990/91. It also shows the way in which gross investment is broken down between net investment and the replacement of depreciated capital — depreciation. As you can see, both depreciation and gross investment increase steadily over time. Depreciation follows a very smooth path. It reflects the fact that the capital stock grows steadily and smoothly. Net investment is the component of investment that fluctuates. You can see that fluctuation as the blue area between gross investment and depreciation.

Observe that in 1982/83, a year of recession, gross investment was not sufficient to cover the amount the capital stock depreciated. In that year, net investment was negative, that is, firms allowed their capital to deteriorate and the capital stock contracted.

The theory that we have just studied predicts that fluctuations in investment result from fluctuations in the real interest rate and in expectations of future profit. What is the relative importance of these two factors? Figure 25.8 answers this question. Each point in the figure represents a value of the real interest rate and net investment (as a share of GDP) for a given year. Real interest rate–investment combinations for the 1970s are represented by a diamond

Figure 25.7 Gross and Net Investment in Australia

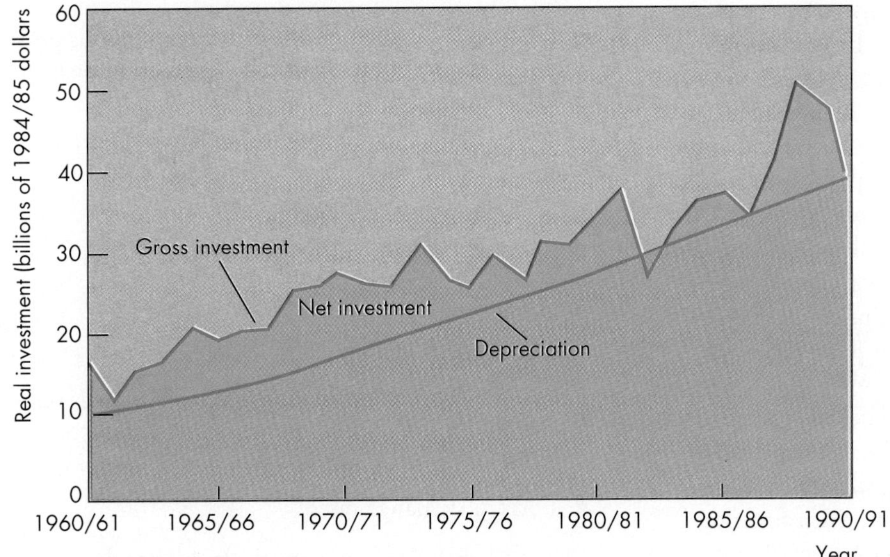

Gross investment is separated into two parts — the replacement of depreciated capital, which grows steadily, and net investment, which fluctuates.

Source: Gross Fixed Capital Expenditure: Series NODQ.UC_CAP#; Depreciation: NLDQ.UC_DEP_ENT#; ABS, Time Series Service supplied by EconData's dX Data Service.

Figure 25.8 Australian Investment Demand Curve

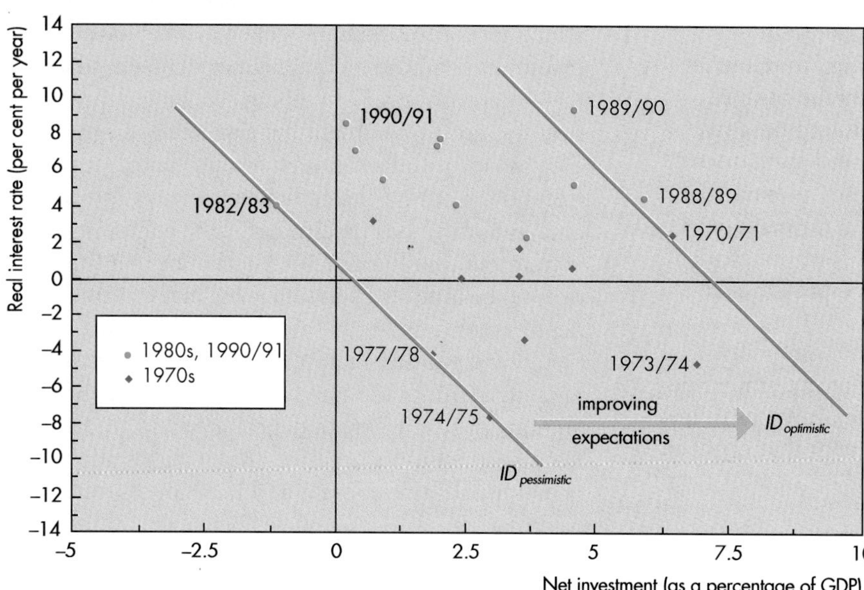

Each point in the figure represents the level of net investment, as a share of GDP, and the real interest rate in a given year. With pessimistic profit expectations, such as in 1974/75, 1977/78 and 1982/83, the Australian investment demand curve lies to the left. With optimistic profit expectations, such as in 1988/89 and 1989/90, the Australian investment demand curve shifts to the right. Swings in profit expectations are more important than real interest rates in creating fluctuations in net investment.

Source: See Fig. 25.7.

and those for the 1980s and for 1990/91 are shown by a circle. The figure also shows two investment demand curves. The curves are drawn for different expectations of future profit. As profit expectations fall the investment demand curve shifts to the left towards $ID_{pessimistic}$. As profit expectations improve the investment demand curve shifts to the right towards $ID_{optimistic}$.

Investment is high, on average, when real interest rates are low. The investment demand curve slopes downward. But there are large fluctuations in investment that occur independently of changes in the real interest rate. The investment demand curve shifts. It lies to the left in years of pessimism and recession, such as 1974/75, 1977/78 and 1982/83. It shifts to the right in years of optimism about future profits, such as 1970/71, 1988/89 and 1989/90. Fluctuations in investment resulting from changes in profit expectations are larger than those resulting from changes in interest rates.

Regardless of whether the fluctuations in investment are generated by shifts in the investment demand curve or movements along it, they have important effects on the economy. We'll find out what some of those effects are in Chapter 26.

Now we'll look at another private component of aggregate expenditure — net exports.

Net Exports

Net exports are the expenditure by foreigners on Australian-produced goods and services minus the expenditure by Australian residents on foreign-produced goods and services. That is, net exports are the value of Australian exports minus the value of imports. *Exports* are the sale of goods and services produced in Australia to the rest of the world. *Imports* are the purchase of goods produced in the rest of the world by firms and households in Australia.

Exports

Exports are determined by decisions made in the rest of the world and are influenced by four main factors:

- Real GDP in the rest of the world
- Degree of international specialization
- Prices of Australian-made goods and services relative to the prices of similar goods and services made in other countries
- Foreign exchange rates

Other things being equal, the higher the level of real GDP in the rest of the world, the greater is the demand by foreigners for Australian-made goods and services. For example, an economic boom in Japan increases that country's demand for Australian coal and iron ore, alumina, wool, wheat and tourism, and increases Australia's exports. A recession in Japan cuts its demand for those goods and decreases Australia's exports.

Also, the greater the degree of specialization in the world economy, the larger is the volume of exports, other things being equal. Over time, international specialization has been increasing. For example, the world aircraft industry is now heavily concentrated in the United States. While a small number of transcontinental airliners are built in Germany, France, Great Britain and the Soviet Union, most the world's major airlines buy their aircraft from the US companies Boeing or McDonnell-Douglas. Australia is a dominant exporter of coal, iron ore, bauxite, wool, wheat and other resource products. The distribution of specialized production world-wide is constantly changing. Many goods and services, notably in the consumer electronics industry, that were once made in North America in large quantities are now made almost exclusively in Japan, Hong Kong and other countries on the Asian rim of the Pacific Ocean.

Next, other things being equal, the lower the price of Australian-made goods and services relative to the prices of similar goods and services made in other countries, the greater is the quantity of Australian exports.

Finally, and again other things being equal, the lower the value of the Australian dollar, the larger is the quantity of Australian exports. For example, as the Australian dollar fell in value against most other currencies in 1985/86, the demand for Australian-made goods by those countries increased sharply.

Imports

Imports are determined by four main factors:

- Australia's real GDP
- Degree of international specialization
- Prices of foreign goods and services relative to the prices of similar goods and services made in Australia
- Foreign exchange rates

Other things being equal, the higher the level of Australia's real GDP, the larger is the quantity of Australian imports. For example, the period of rapid income growth in Australia between 1987 and 1989 brought a huge increase in Australian imports.

Also, the higher the degree of international specialization, the larger is the volume of Australian imports, other things being equal. For example, there is a high degree of international specialization in the production of VCRs. As a consequence, all the VCRs sold in Australia are now produced in other countries — mainly Japan and Korea.

Finally, and again other things being equal, the higher the prices of Australian-made goods and services relative to the prices of similar foreign-made goods and services, and the higher the value of the Australian dollar, the larger is the quantity of Australian imports.

It is often difficult to distinguish between the influence on Australian imports of high real GDP growth and the influence of a high value of the Australian dollar because the two are often moving in the same direction. When GDP growth is strong, income is high and so is demand for imports. But the dollar is also higher than average, reducing the relative price of imports and inducing people to substitute imported goods for domestic goods.

Net Exports Function

The **net exports function** is the relationship between net exports and real GDP, holding constant real GDP in the rest of the world, prices and the exchange rate. The net exports function can also be described by a net exports schedule, which lists the level of net exports at each level of real GDP, with everything else held constant. The table in Fig. 25.9 gives an example of a net export schedule.

In the table, real exports are a constant $45 billion — they are assumed to be independent of the level of real GDP in Australia. Imports increase by $0.15 billion for each $1 billion increase in real GDP. Real net exports, the difference between exports and imports, is shown in the final column of the table. When real GDP is $100 billion, net exports are $17.5 billion. Net exports decline as real GDP rises. At a real GDP of $217 billion, net exports are zero, and at real GDP levels higher than that, net exports become increasingly negative (imports exceed exports).

Exports and imports are graphed in Fig. 25.9(a) and the net exports function is graphed in Fig. 25.9(b). By comparing Fig. 25.9(a) and Fig 25.9(b) you can see that when exports exceed imports, net exports are above zero (there is a surplus) and when imports exceed exports, net exports are below zero (there is a

Figure 25.9 Net Exports Schedule and Net Exports Function

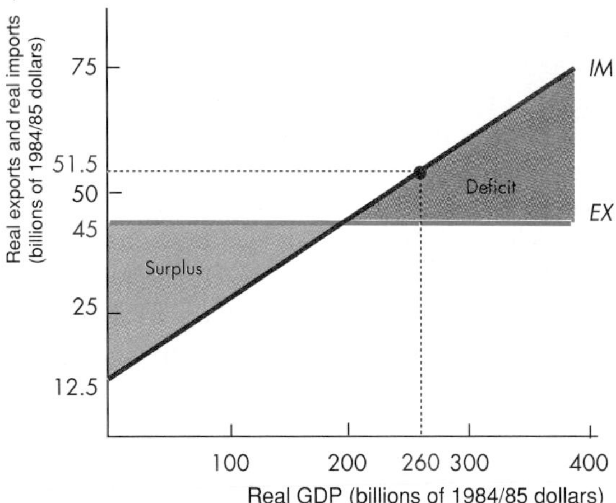

(a) Real exports and real imports

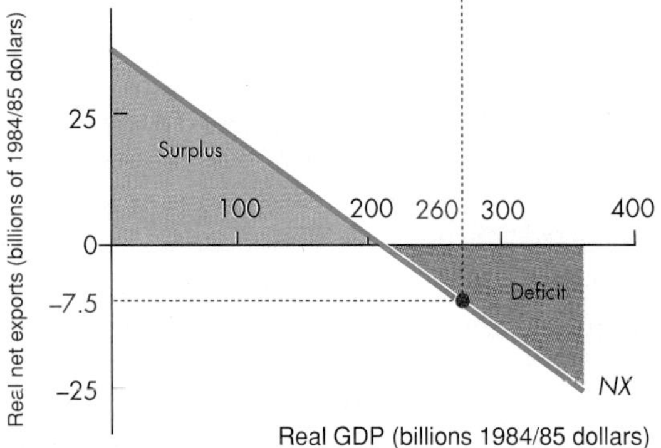

(b) Real net exports

Real GDP (Y)	Real exports (EX)	Real imports (IM)	Real net exports (EX – IM)
	(billions of 1984/85 dollars)		
0	45	12.5	30.0
50	45	20.0	25.0
100	45	27.5	19.5
150	45	35.0	10.0
200	45	42.5	2.5
250	45	50.0	–5.0
300	45	57.5	–12.5

The net exports schedule in the table shows the relationship between real net exports and real GDP. Real net exports are equal to real exports (*EX*) minus real imports (*IM*). Exports are assumed to be independent of real GDP but imports rise as real GDP rises. In the table, imports are 21 per cent of real GDP. Net exports fall as GDP rises.

Part (a) graphs the export and import schedules. Since exports are independent of real GDP, they are graphed as a horizontal line. Since imports rise as real GDP rises, they appear as an upward-sloping line. The distance between the export curve and the import curve represents net exports. Net exports are graphed in part (b) of the figure. The net exports function is downward sloping because the import curve is upward sloping. The real GDP level at which the net exports function intersects the horizontal axis in part (b) is the same as that at which the imports curve intersects the exports curve in part (a). That level of real GDP is $215 billion. Below that level of real GDP there is a surplus and above it there is a deficit. For example, if real GDP is $260 billion, imports exceed exports and net exports are –$7.5 billion.

deficit). When real GDP is $217 billion, there is a balance between exports and imports.

When real GDP is above $217 billion, exports exceed imports. For example, when real GDP is $260 billion, net exports are –$7.5 billion. These figures compare to those for Australia in 1989/90. In that year, real GDP was $259 billion, exports were $46 billion, imports were $55 billion and net exports were –$9 billion.

The position of the net exports function depends on real GDP in the rest of the world, on the degree of international specialization and on prices in Australia compared with those in the rest of the world. If real GDP in the rest of the world increases, the net exports function shifts upward. If Australian goods become cheap relative to goods in the rest of the world, the net exports function also shifts upward. A change in the degree of international specialization has an ambiguous effect on the position of the net exports function. If Australia becomes more specialized in goods for which there is an increase in world demand, the net exports function shifts upward. If Australian demand increases for goods in which the rest of the world specializes, the net exports function shifts downward.

Aggregate Expenditure and Real GDP

very important relationship is that between aggregate real expenditure and real GDP. **Aggregate expenditure** is the expenditure

that economic agents (households, firms, governments and foreigners) undertake in given circumstances. The relationship between aggregate real expenditure and real GDP may be described by either an aggregate expenditure schedule or an aggregate expenditure curve. The **aggregate expenditure schedule** lists the level of aggregate expenditure at each level of real GDP. The **aggregate expenditure curve** is a graph of the aggregate expenditure schedule.

Aggregate Expenditure Schedule

An aggregate expenditure schedule is set out in the table of Fig. 25.10. The data in this table is an example only and does not refer to the real world. However, it is of the same order of magnitude as the figures for the Australian economy in the late 1980s. The table shows not only aggregate expenditure but also its components. To work out the level of aggregate expenditure, we add the various components together.

The first column of the table shows real GDP and the second column shows consumption expenditure at each level of real GDP. For example, when real GDP is $100 billion, consumption expenditure is $77.5 billion. A $50 billion increase in real GDP generates a $32.5 billion increase in consumption expenditure. That is, the marginal propensity to consume is 0.65.

The next two columns show planned investment and government expenditure on goods and services. Recall that planned investment (total investment less unplanned changes in inventories) depends on the real interest rate and the state of profit expectations. Suppose that those factors are constant and, at a given point in time, generate a level of investment of $50 billion. Suppose also that this investment level is independent of the level of real GDP and is influenced solely by the real interest rate and expectations of profit that we are holding constant.

Government expenditure on goods and services is determined by decisions made by the Commonwealth, State and local governments. These purchases vary from year to year but, at any given point in time, their level has been determined by past decisions. Thus we'll suppose that this item is also fixed. Its value is $60 billion. That is, like investment, government purchases of goods and services are fixed at any given point in time and do not vary as real GDP varies.

The next three columns show exports, imports and net exports. Exports are influenced by events in the rest of the world and by our prices compared with prices in other countries, as well as the foreign exchange value of the Australian dollar. They are not directly affected by the level of real GDP. In the table, exports appear as a constant $40 billion. But imports do increase as real GDP increases. A $50 billion increase in real GDP results in $7.5 billion increase in imports. That is, the marginal propensity to import is 0.15. Thus net exports — the difference between exports and imports — also varies as real GDP varies. It decreases by $7.5 billion for each $50 billion increase in real GDP.

The final column of the table shows aggregate expenditure. This amount is the sum of consumption expenditure, planned investment, government expenditure on goods and services, and net exports.

Aggregate Expenditure Curve

The aggregate expenditure curve appears in the diagram in Fig. 25.10. Real GDP is shown on the horizontal axis and aggregate expenditure on the vertical axis. The aggregate expenditure curve is the red line labelled *AE*. Points *a* to *g* on that curve correspond to the rows in the table in Fig. 25.10. The *AE* curve is a graph of the last column, 'Aggregate expenditure', plotted against real GDP.

The figure also shows the components of aggregate expenditure. The constant components — planned investment, government expenditure on goods and services, and exports — are indicated by the horizontal lines in the figure. Consumption is the vertical distance between the line labelled $I + G + EX + C$ and that labelled $I + G + EX$.

To calculate the *AE* curve, we subtract imports from the $I + G + EX + C$ line. Imports are subtracted because they are not expenditure on *domestic* output. The purchase of a new car is part of consumption expenditure but if that car is a BMW, made in Germany, expenditure on it has to be subtracted from consumption expenditure to find out how much is spent on goods produced in Australia — on Australian GDP. Money paid to BMW for car imports from Germany does not add to aggregate expenditure in Australia.

Autonomous and Induced Expenditure

The components of aggregate expenditure that we've just considered can be divided into two broad groups:

- Autonomous expenditure
- Induced expenditure

Figure 25.10 Aggregate Expenditure Schedule and Aggregate Expenditure Curve

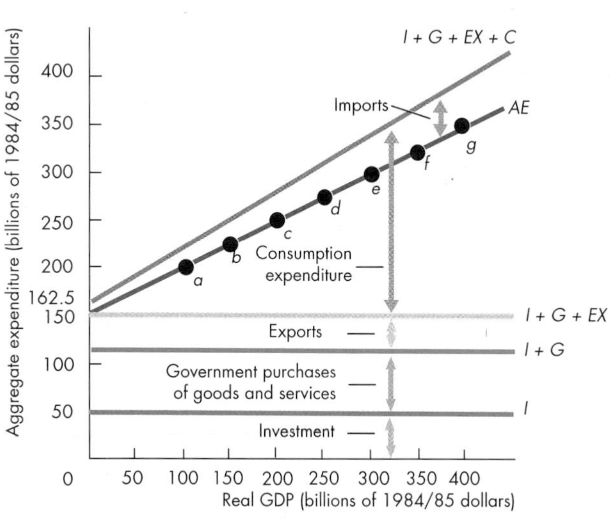

The aggregate expenditure function shows how aggregate expenditure varies as real GDP varies. The aggregate expenditure function may be described by an aggregate expenditure schedule (as shown in the table) or by an aggregate expenditure curve (as shown in the diagram). Aggregate expenditure is calculated as the sum of consumption expenditure, planned investment, government expenditure on goods and services, and net exports. For example, in row *a* of the table, if real GDP is $100 billion, aggregate consumption is $77.5 billion, investment is $50 billion, government expenditure on goods and services is $60 billion and net exports are $12.5 billion. Thus when real GDP is $100 billion, aggregate expenditure is $200 billion ($77.5 + $50 + $60 + $12.5 = $200). The expenditure plans are graphed as the aggregate expenditure curve *AE* in the figure, the line *ag*.

	Real GDP *(Y)*	**Consumption expenditure *(C)***	**Planned investment *(I)***	**Government purchases *(G)***	**Exports *(EX)***	**Imports *(IM)***	**Net exports *(NX)***	**Aggregate expenditure *(AE=C+I+G+NX)***
				(billions of 1984/85 dollars)				
a	100	77.5	50	60	40	27.5	12.5	200
b	150	110.0	50	60	40	35.0	5.0	225
c	200	142.5	50	60	40	42.5	–2.5	250
d	250	175.0	50	60	40	50.0	–10.0	275
e	300	207.5	50	60	40	57.5	–17.5	300
f	350	240.0	50	60	40	65.0	–25.0	325
g	400	272.5	50	60	40	72.5	–32.5	350

Autonomous expenditure is the sum of those components of aggregate expenditure that are not influenced by real GDP. These autonomous components of aggregate expenditure are planned investment, government expenditure on goods and services, exports and that part of expenditure on consumption and imports that does not vary with real GDP. In the example in Fig. 25.10, we have assumed that there is $12.5 billion of consumption expenditure and $12.5 billion in imports even if real GDP is zero. These components of expenditure are also part of autonomous expenditure.

Induced expenditure is the sum of those components of aggregate expenditure that do vary as real GDP varies. The induced components of aggregate expenditure are that part of consumption expenditure that varies with real GDP as well as imports. In the example in Fig. 25.10, each $50 billion increase in real GDP induces an additional $32.5 billion of consumption expenditure. This is the induced part of consumption expenditure. Imports are also part of induced expenditure since they increase as real GDP increases. But imports have to be *subtracted* from total spending to arrive at aggregate expenditure on real GDP.

Figure 25.11 Autonomous and Induced Expenditure

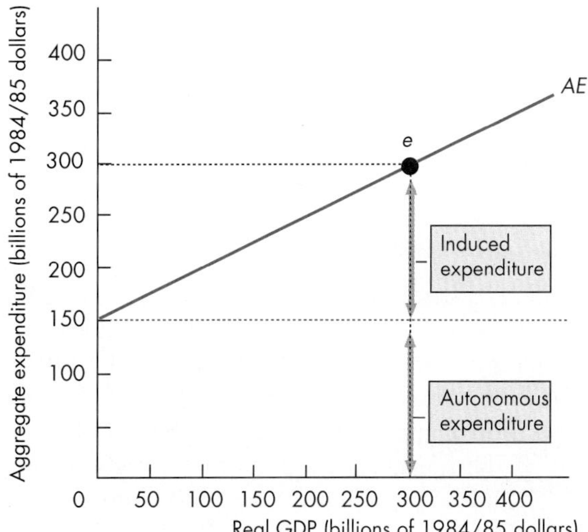

Autonomous expenditure, shown at the bottom of the figure, consists of planned investment, government expenditure on goods and services, exports, plus the autonomous component of consumption expenditure, less the autonomous component of imports. Induced expenditure consists of the remainder of consumption expenditure minus the remainder of imports. The sum of autonomous and induced expenditure is aggregate expenditure. For example, at point *e*, aggregate expenditure is $300 billion — $150 billion of autonomous expenditure and $150 billion of induced expenditure.

Autonomous expenditure and induced expenditure are shown in Fig. 25.11. Autonomous expenditure is made up of investment ($50 billion), government expenditure on goods and services ($60 billion), exports ($40 billion), plus the autonomous component of consumption expenditure ($12.5 billion), less the autonomous component of imports (–$12.5 billion). The sum of these items is $150 billion.

Induced expenditure increases by 50 cents for each $1 increase in real GDP. This increase is made up of 65 cents of consumption expenditure *minus* 15 cents of imports. For example, when real GDP is $300 billion, aggregate expenditure is also $300 billion (point *e* on the *AE* curve), which is made up of $150 billion of autonomous expenditure and $150 billion of induced expenditure. Autonomous expenditure remains at $150 billion regardless of the level of real GDP, but the induced component of aggregate expenditure rises from zero when real GDP is zero to $200 billion when real GDP is $400 billion.

Slope of the Aggregate Expenditure Curve

What determines the slope of the aggregate expenditure curve? The answer is the extent to which aggregate expenditure is induced by an increase in real GDP. As we've just seen, an increase in real GDP of $1 increases consumption by 65 cents and increases imports by 15 cents. The difference between these two, 50 cents, is the increase in induced expenditure.

Recall that the fraction of the last dollar of real GDP consumed is called the *marginal propensity to consume.* In Fig. 25.10, the marginal propensity to consume is 0.65. The fraction of the last dollar of real GDP spent on imports is called the **marginal propensity to import**. In this case, the marginal propensity to import is 0.15. The difference between these two marginal propensities is the marginal propensity to spend on domestic goods and services.

The **marginal propensity to spend (on domestic goods and services)** is the fraction of the last dollar of real GDP spent on domestic goods and services. In Fig. 25.11, a $1 increase in real GDP induces an increase in aggregate expenditure of 50 cents, so the marginal propensity to spend is 0.5.

Notice the distinction between the marginal propensity to consume and the marginal propensity to spend. The marginal propensity to consume is the fraction of the last dollar of income spent on all goods and services regardless of where in the world they are made. The marginal propensity to spend is the fraction of the last dollar of income spent on *domestically* produced goods and services. It equals the marginal propensity to consume minus the marginal propensity to import.

The marginal propensity to spend equals the slope of the aggregate expenditure curve. You can see this relationship by looking again at Fig. 25.11. If real GDP increases from $150 billion to $200 billion, an increase of $50 billion, aggregate expenditure increases from $225 billion to $250 billion, an increase of $25 billion. The slope of the aggregate expenditure curve equals the increase in aggregate expenditure divided by the increase in real GDP — ($25 billion ÷ $50 billion) = 0.5.

R E V I E W

Aggregate expenditure is the sum of consumption expenditure, planned investment, government expenditure on goods and services, and net exports. Aggregate expenditure is classified into two components: autonomous expenditure and induced expenditure. Planned investment, government expenditure on goods and services, exports and part of consumption and imports are autonomous. The other part of consumption expenditure minus imports is induced expenditure. Autonomous expenditure is independent of real GDP; induced expenditure varies as real GDP varies. The higher the level of autonomous expenditure, the greater is the level of aggregate expenditure. The fraction of the last dollar of income spent on domestic goods and services is called the marginal propensity to spend. The marginal propensity to spend equals the marginal propensity to consume minus the marginal propensity to import. The larger the marginal propensity to spend, the steeper is the slope of the aggregate expenditure curve. ■

We've now seen how to calculate the aggregate expenditure schedule and aggregate expenditure curve. We've seen that aggregate expenditure increases as real GDP increases. But what determines the point on the aggregate expenditure curve at which the economy operates?

Equilibrium Expenditure

Equilibrium expenditure occurs when aggregate expenditure equals aggregate output, or real GDP. If aggregate expenditure is different from real GDP then inventories or stocks are changing. If aggregate expenditure exceeds real GDP then stocks are falling as firms satisfy the surplus demand from previously accumulated output. If real GDP exceeds aggregate expenditure then stocks are rising as firms accumulate an unintended stock of unsold goods. These are added to the firms' inventories. Thus equilibrium occurs when unintended changes in inventory changes cease. Or when actual investment equals planned investment.

When Expenditure Equals Real GDP

The table in Fig. 25.12 shows different levels of real GDP in our model economy. Against each level of real GDP, the second column shows aggregate expenditure. Only when real GDP equals $300 billion is aggregate expenditure equal to real GDP. This level of expenditure is the equilibrium expenditure.

The equilibrium is illustrated in Fig. 25.12(a). The aggregate expenditure curve is *AE*. Since aggregate expenditure on the vertical axis and real GDP on the horizontal axis are measured in the same units and on the same scale, a 45° line drawn in Fig. 25.12(a) shows all the points at which aggregate expenditure equals real GDP. Such a line appears in the figure and is labelled '45° line'. Where the aggregate expenditure curve intersects the 45° line, at point *e*, equilibrium expenditure is determined.

Convergence to Equilibrium

You will get a better idea of why point *e* is the equilibrium if you consider what is happening when the economy is not at point *e*. Suppose that real GDP is $200 billion. You can see from Fig. 25.12(a) that in this situation aggregate expenditure is $250 billion (point *c*). Thus aggregate expenditure is higher than real GDP. How can real GDP be $200 billion if people spend $250 billion? If real GDP is $200 billion, the value of production is also $200 billion. The only way that people can buy goods and services worth $250 billion, when the value of production is only $200 billion, is if firms' inventories fall by $50 billion (point *c* in Fig. 25.12b). Since changes in inventories are part of investment, actual investment is lower than planned investment.

But this is not the end of the story. Firms have target levels for inventories and when inventories fall below those targets, production output is increased to restore inventories to their target levels. To restore their inventories, firms hire additional labour and increase output. Suppose that they increase output in the next period by enough to replenish their inventories. Aggregate output rises by $50 billion to $250 billion. But again, aggregate expenditure exceeds real GDP. When real GDP is $250 billion, aggregate expenditure is $275 billion (point *d* in Fig. 25.12a). Again, inventories fall but this time by less than before. With an output of $250 billion and expenditure of $275 billion, inventories fall by only $25 billion (point *d* in Fig. 25.12b). Again, firms hire additional labour, increase output, and real GDP increases still further.

The process that we have just described of expenditure exceeding income, inventories falling and output rising to restore the unplanned inventory reduction ends when real GDP has reached $300 billion. At this level of real GDP, there is an equilibrium. There are no unplanned inventory changes and firms do not change their output.

Next, let's perform a similar experiment to that above but in reverse, starting with a level of real GDP above the equilibrium. Suppose that real GDP is $400 billion. At this income level aggregate expendi-

Figure 25.12 Equilibrium Expenditure and Real GDP

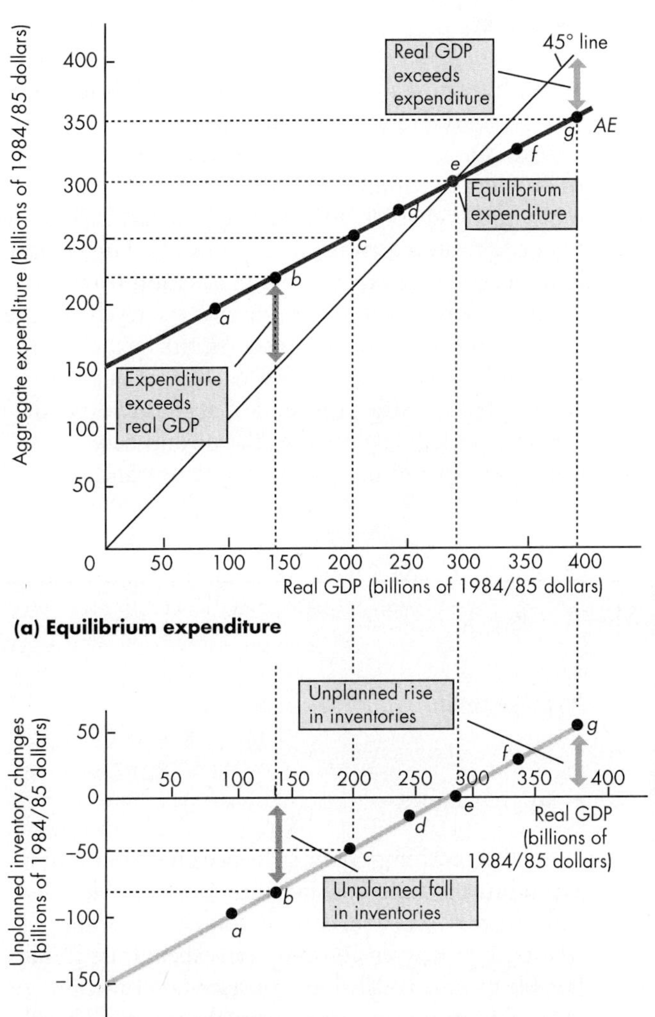

	Real GDP (*Y*)	Aggregate expenditure (*AE*)	Unplanned inventory changes (*Y* – *AE*)
	(billions of 1984/85 dollars)		
a	100	200	–100
b	150	225	–75
c	200	250	–50
d	250	275	–25
e	300	300	0
f	350	325	25
g	400	350	50

The table shows the aggregate expenditure schedule. When real GDP is $300 billion, aggregate expenditure equals real GDP. At GDP levels below $300 billion, aggregate expenditure exceeds GDP. At real GDP levels above $300 billion, aggregate expenditure is less than real GDP. The diagram illustrates equilibrium expenditure. The 45° line shows those points at which aggregate expenditure equals GDP. The aggregate expenditure curve is *AE* and actual aggregate expenditure equals real GDP. Equilibrium expenditure and real GDP are $300 billion. That GDP level generates expenditure that equals real GDP — $300 billion. At real GDP levels below $300 billion, aggregate expenditure exceeds real GDP and inventories fall — for example, point *b* in both parts of the figure. In such cases, firms increase output to restore their inventories and real GDP rises. At real GDP levels higher than $300 billion, aggregate expenditure is less than real GDP and inventories rise — for example, point *g* in both parts of the figure. In such a situation, firms decrease output to work off excess inventories and real GDP falls. Only where the aggregate expenditure curve cuts the 45° line is expenditure equal to real GDP. This position is equilibrium expenditure. There are no unplanned inventory changes and output remains constant.

ture is $350 billion (point *g* in Fig. 25.12a), $50 billion less than real GDP. With aggregate expenditure less than real GDP, inventories rise by $50 billion (point *g* in Fig. 25.12b) — there is an unplanned inventory build-up. With unsold inventories on their hands, firms cut back on production. They lay off workers, reduce the amount that they pay out in wages, and real GDP falls. If they cut back production by the amount of the unplanned increase in inventories, real GDP falls by $50 billion to $350 billion. At that level of real GDP, aggregate expenditure is $325 billion (point *f* in Fig. 25.12a). Again, there is an unplanned increase in inventories, but only of half the previous increase (point *f* in Fig. 25.12b). Again, firms will cut back production and lay off still more workers, reducing real GDP still further. Real GDP continues to fall whenever unplanned inventories increase. As before, real GDP keeps on changing until it reaches its equilibrium level of $300 billion.

Thus, if real GDP is below aggregate expenditure, inventories fall, firms increase output to restore their inventories and real GDP rises. If real GDP is above aggregate expenditure, unsold inventories prompt firms to cut back on production and real GDP falls. Only if real GDP equals aggregate expenditure are there no unplanned inventory changes and no changes in firms' output plans. In this situation, actual investment equals planned investment and real GDP remains constant.

R E V I E W

Equilibrium expenditure occurs when aggregate expenditure equals real GDP. If aggregate expenditure exceeds real GDP, inventories fall and firms increase output to replenish inventory levels. Real GDP increases and so does expenditure. If aggregate expenditure is below real GDP, inventories accumulate and firms cut output to lower inventory levels. Real GDP and aggregate expenditure decline. Only when aggregate expenditure equals real GDP are there no unplanned changes in inventories and no changes in output. Real GDP remains constant. ■

■ We have now discovered how the equilibrium levels of real GDP and aggregate expenditure are determined. Our next task is to study the sources of *changes* in the equilibrium.

In this chapter, we've studied the factors that influence private expenditure decisions, looking at each item of aggregate expenditure in isolation from the others. We have also looked at how the level of aggregate expenditure is determined. In the next chapter, we'll look more closely at how changes in autonomous spending affect the level of aggregate expenditure and we will explore the relationship between aggregate expenditure and aggregate demand.

S U M M A R Y

The Components of Aggregate Expenditure

The components of aggregate expenditure are:

- Consumption expenditure
- Planned investment
- Government purchases of goods and services
- Net exports

The largest component of aggregate expenditure is consumption expenditure. On average, 59 per cent of total expenditure comes from consumption. Investment accounts for 18 per cent and government purchases of goods and services for 25 per cent of the total, on average. Net exports, on average, are −1.7 per cent of GDP.

The components of aggregate expenditure that fluctuate most are investment and net exports. (pp. 174–176)

Consumption Expenditure and Saving

Consumption expenditure is influenced by six factors:

- Disposable income
- Expected future income
- Wealth
- Stage in life
- Degree of patience
- Interest rates

The most important influence on consumption expenditure is disposable income. As disposable income increases, so does consumption expenditure. The relationship between consumption expenditure and disposable income is called the consumption function. As disposable income increases, so too does saving. The relationship between saving and disposable income is called the saving function. At low levels of disposable income, consumption expenditure exceeds disposable income, which means that saving is negative (dissaving occurs). As disposable income increases, consumption increases but by less than the increase in disposable income. The fraction of each additional dollar of disposable income consumed is called the marginal propensity to consume. The fraction of each additional dollar of disposable income saved is called the marginal propensity to save. All the influences on consumption and saving, other than disposable income, shift the consumption and saving functions.

If we look at variations in disposable income and consumption expenditure across families, we see that for low income families, around 50 cents in each additional dollar of disposable income are spent on consumption goods and services. As incomes increase, the marginal propensity to consume increases and then, for higher income families, decreases. For the highest income families slightly less than 50 cents of each additional dollar of disposable income are consumed, on the average.

The relationship between aggregate consumption expenditure and aggregate disposable income over time is called the time-series consumption function. The time-series consumption function shows how aggregate consumption varies as disposable income varies from one year to the next. The average and marginal propensity to consume out of disposable income, on average, is 0.90. But there is a large variation around that average across individual families.

The relationship between real consumption expenditure and real GDP is called the aggregate consumption function. To calculate the aggregate consumption function, we take into account the difference between real disposable income and real GDP. Disposable income equals GDP plus transfer payments minus taxes. Transfer payments minus taxes are a fairly stable percentage of GDP. As a result, since consumption is a fairly stable percentage of disposable income, it is also a fairly stable percentage of GDP. Taxes net of transfers are approximately 33.3 per cent of GDP. Equivalently, disposable income is approximately 66.7 per cent, or two-thirds of GDP. Since consumption is 90 per cent of disposable income, and since disposable income is 66.7 per cent of GDP, consumption is 60 per cent of GDP, on average. (pp. 176–186)

Investment

The level of planned investment depends on

- Interest rates
- Expected inflation
- Expected profit
- Existing capital

The lower the interest rate, the higher is the level of investment; the higher the expected inflation rate, the greater is the level of investment. The higher the expected profit, the greater is the volume of investment. Interest rates and expected inflation have equal and opposite effects on investment. As a consequence, the two effects can be combined into a real interest rate effect. The higher the real interest rate, the lower is the volume of investment.

The main influence on investment demand is fluctuations in profit expectations. Sometimes expectations are optimistic and at other times pessimistic. Swings in the degree of optimism and pessimism lead to shifts in the investment demand curve. Swings in profit expectations are closely associated with business cycle fluctuations. When the economy is in an expansion phase, profit expectations are optimistic and investment is high. When the economy is in a contraction phase, profit expectations are pessimistic and investment is low.

Investment is also influenced by the existing stock of capital and its degree of utilization. The larger the stock of capital, the greater is the amount of depreciation and, other things being equal, the larger the amount of replacement investment. When capital is underutilized, as in a recession, investment falls off and when it is overutilized, as in a boom, investment increases. (pp. 186–192)

Net Exports

Net exports are the difference between exports and imports. Exports are determined by decisions made in the rest of the world and are influenced by GDP in the rest of the world, the degree of international specialization, Australian prices relative to prices of similar goods made in other countries and the foreign exchange rate. Imports are determined by Australian real GDP, the degree of international specialization, Australian prices relative to prices of similar goods made in other countries and the foreign exchange rate.

The net export function shows the relationship between net exports and Australian real GDP, holding constant all the other influences on exports and imports. (pp. 192–194)

Aggregate Expenditure and Real GDP

Aggregate expenditure is the sum of consumption expenditure, planned investment, government expenditure on goods and services, and new exports. Aggregate expenditure is either autonomous expenditure — expenditure independent of real GDP — or induced expenditure — expenditure which varies as real GDP varies. The fraction of the last dollar of income spent on domestic goods and services is called the marginal propensity to spend. The marginal propensity to spend equals the marginal propensity to consume less the marginal propensity to import. (pp. 194–198)

Equilibrium Expenditure

Equilibrium expenditure occurs when aggregate expenditure equals real GDP. If real GDP is above aggregate expenditure, real GDP falls. If real GDP is below aggregate expenditure, real GDP rises. Only when real GDP equals aggregate expenditure is real GDP constant and in equilibrium. The main influence bringing real GDP and aggregate expenditure into equality is the behaviour of inventories. When aggregate expenditure exceeds real GDP, inventories fall. To restore their inventories, firms increase output and this action increases real GDP. When aggregate expenditure is less than real GDP, inventories accumulate and firms cut back their output. This action lowers the level of real GDP. Only when there are no unplanned inventory changes do firms keep output constant and real GDP remains constant. (pp. 198–200)

KEY TERMS

Aggregate consumption function, p. 182
Aggregate expenditure, p. 194
Aggregate expenditure curve, p. 195
Aggregate expenditure schedule, p. 195
Autonomous expenditure, p. 196
Average propensity to consume, p. 178
Average propensity to save, p. 179
Consumption function, p. 177
Dissaving, p. 177
Equilibrium expenditure, p. 198
Gross investment, p. 186
Induced expenditure, p. 196
Investment demand, p. 189
Investment demand curve, p. 189
Investment demand schedule, p. 189
Marginal propensity to consume, p. 179
Marginal propensity to consume out of real GDP, p. 186
Marginal propensity to import, p. 197
Marginal propensity to save, p. 179
Marginal propensity to spend (on domestic goods and services), p. 197
Net exports function, p. 193
Net investment, p. 186
Real interest rate, p. 187
Replacement investment, p. 186
Saving function, p. 177
Time-series consumption function, p. 182

PROBLEMS

1 You are given the following information about the Batman family (Batman and Robin):

Disposable income (dollars per year)	**Consumption expenditure (dollars per year)**
0	10,000
10,000	15,000
20,000	20,000
30,000	25,000
40,000	30,000

a) Calculate Batman and Robin's marginal propensity to consume.
b) Calculate the average propensity to consume at each level of disposable income.
c) Calculate how much the Batman family save at each level of disposable income.
d) Calculate their marginal propensity to save.
e) Calculate their average propensity to save at each level of disposable income.

2 A car assembly plant can be built for $10 million and it will have a life of five years. At the end of five years, the plant will have a scrap value of $1 million. The firm will have to hire labour at a cost of $1 million a year and will have to buy parts and fuel costing another $1 million. If the firm builds the plant, it will be able to produce cars that will sell for $5 million each year. Will it pay the firm to invest in this new production line at the following interest rates:
a) 2 per cent a year?
b) 5 per cent a year?
c) 10 per cent a year?

3 You are given the following information about a hypothetical economy. The marginal propensity to consume out of disposable income is 0.8, and taxes net of transfer payments are one-quarter of national income. What is the marginal propensity to consume out of GDP in this economy?

4 You are given the following information about a model economy. The autonomous part of consumption is $80

billion. The marginal propensity to consume is 0.75. Planned investment is $400 billion; government purchases of goods and services are $600 billion; taxes are a constant $500 billion and do not vary as income varies. At equilibrium expenditure, what are the values of the following:

a) Real GDP?
b) Consumption?
c) Saving?
d) The average and marginal propensities to consume?
e) The average and marginal propensities to save?
f) Autonomous expenditure?
g) Induced expenditure?

Appendix A to Chapter 25

Net Present Value and Investment

To decide whether or not to undertake an investment project, we must calculate the project's net present value.

Calculating Net Present Value

Net present value is the sum of the present value of the stream of payments and receipts generated by an investment project. The *present value* of a future sum of money is the sum which, if invested in the present, accumulates to the future sum if it earns compound interest at a given rate. If the net present value of an investment project is positive, it pays to undertake the investment. If the net present value is negative, it does not pay to undertake the investment. Let's calculate a net present value.

An investment of $2775 is expected to yield the future stream of earnings of $1000 a year for three years. Thus an initial payment of $2775 results in a future receipt of $1000 in each of three years. Obviously, more comes back than is paid out. But the returns come later. To decide whether enough flows in later, we calculate the project's net present value. To calculate the net present value of a project, we use the formula

$$NPV = \frac{\$1000}{(1+i)} + \frac{\$1000}{(1+i)^2} + \frac{\$1000}{(1+i)^3} - \$2775$$

where i is the interest rate.

The higher the interest rate, the lower is the net present value. Table A25.1 sets out some calculations for three different interest rates. In part (a), an interest rate of 4 per cent a year is used. In this case, the net present value is zero. Let's see how that present value is calculated by using the above formula. The initial cost of the project ($2775) is paid out today, so its present value is exactly the same as the amount spent. The first $1000 of revenue from the project is received one year in the future. Its present value is $961. That is, if $961 is invested today at an interest rate of 4 per cent a year, it will accumulate to $1000 one year from today. The next $1000 is received two years hence. Its present value is $925. That is, if $925 is invested today for a two-year period at an interest rate of 4 per cent a year, it will accumulate to $1000 by the end of that period. Finally, the last $1000 is received three years hence and has a present value of $889. If $889 is invested today at an interest rate of 4 per cent a year, it will accumulate to $1000 after three years. Adding these present values together, and subtracting the present value of the initial cost of the project, gives the overall net present value for the project which, at an interest rate of 4 per cent a year, is zero.

Part (b) calculates the net present value at a lower interest rate — 2 per cent a year. In this case, the net present value of the project is positive at $108. Part (c) calculates the net present value at an interest rate of 6 per cent a year. This net present value is –$102.

At any interest rate lower than 4 per cent a year, it pays to undertake this investment project. But at an interest rate higher than 4 per cent a year, it does not pay to invest in the project.

Investment projects differ in their initial capital cost and in the receipts or revenue stream that they generate. To

Table A25.1 Net Present Value of an Investment Project

	Dollars paid	Dollars received	Present value (dollars)
(a) Interest rate: 4 per cent per year			
Initial cost of project	2775		–2775
Receipts after 1 year		1000	961
Receipts after 2 years		1000	925
Receipts after 3 years		1000	889
Net present value:			0
(b) Interest rate: 2 per cent per year			
Initial cost of project	2775		–2775
Receipts after 1 year		1000	980
Receipts after 2 years		1000	961
Receipts after 3 years		1000	942
Net present value:			108
(c) Interest rate: 6 per cent per year			
Initial cost of project	2775		–2775
Receipts after 1 year		1000	943
Receipts after 2 years		1000	890
Receipts after 3 years		1000	840
Net present value:			–102

decide which projects to undertake, a firm calculates the net present value of each project using the current interest rate at which it can borrow. All those projects that have a positive net present value are undertaken and all those that have a negative net present value are rejected. The lower the interest rate at which the firm can borrow, the larger is the number of projects that have a positive net present value and so the larger is the number of projects undertaken and the larger is the firm's investment.

Expected Inflation and Real Interest Rate

The real interest rate is the interest rate that people expect to earn after taking into account changes in the value of money. If you lend a dollar at an annual interest rate of i you will have $1 + i$ dollars at the end of the year. If prices are rising at an annual rate of π, you will need $1 + \pi$ dollars at the end of the year to buy what one dollar buys today. Your $1 + i$ dollars will only really be worth $(1 + i)/(1 + \pi)$ dollars. The interest that you have really earned is the amount that your money is really worth — $(1 + i)/(1 + \pi)$ — minus the dollar that you lent. That is:

$$\text{Real interest rate} = \frac{(1+i)}{(1+\pi)} - 1$$

In this formula, i is the interest rate (sometimes called the nominal interest rate) and π is the inflation rate. You can interpret this formula most easily by considering the case where the interest rate and the inflation rate are the same. Suppose that the interest rate and the inflation rate are each 6 per cent a year. Then the formula tells us that

$$\text{Real interest rate} = \frac{1.06}{1.06} - 1 = 0$$

That is, the interest that is paid when the interest rate is 6 per cent a year is enough to compensate for only the fall in the value of money, which means that no 'real' interest has been paid.

When neither inflation nor nominal interest rates are too high, an acceptable approximation to the real interest rate is:

$$\text{Real interest rate} = i - \pi$$

This is the formula we used earlier in this chapter.

Let's do one more calculation. If the interest rate is 6 per cent a year and the inflation rate is 1.92 per cent a year, the real interest rate is 4 per cent a year. To see this, put the numbers for interest rate and the inflation rate in the formula. We obtain:

$$\text{Real interest rate} = \frac{1.06}{1.0192} - 1$$

$$= 0.04 \text{ (4 per cent)}$$

Let's work out the net present value when the interest rate is 6 per cent a year and the expected inflation rate is 1.92 per cent a year, so that the real interest rate is 4 per cent a year. The calculations are summarized in Table A25.2. As before, the project costs \$2775. The receipts at the end of the first year are now higher because of inflation. With inflation expected to be running at 1.92 per cent a year, receipts will be expected to be \$1019. The present value of \$1019 at a 6 per cent interest rate is \$961. That is, if \$961 is invested today at an interest rate of 6 per cent a year, it accumulates to \$1019 after one year. At the end of the second year, the firm expects to receive \$1039. That is, over a two-year period, prices are expected to increase by 3.9 per cent. The present value of \$1039 two years hence is \$925. That is, if \$925 is invested today at an interest rate of 6 per cent a year, it accumulates to \$1039 after two years. With inflation expected to continue into the third year at the same rate, receipts are expected to increase to \$1059. The present value of \$1059 received three years in the future at an interest rate of 6 per cent is \$889. That is, if \$889 is invested today at an interest rate of 6 per cent a year, it accumulates to \$1059 three years in the future.

Adding the present value of the income stream and subtracting the present value of the cost of the project gives the net present value of the project. That net present value is zero.

Notice that when the interest rate is 6 per cent a year and expected inflation is 1.92 per cent a year, we obtain exactly the same net present value as we did in Table A25.1 with

Table A25.2 Present Value, Inflation and the Real Interest Rate

Interest rate: 6 per cent per year
Expected inflation rate: 1.92 per cent per year
Real interest rate: 4 per cent per year

	Current dollars	Real dollars	Present value (dollars)
Initial cost of project	–2775	–2775	–2775
Expected receipts after 1 year	1019	1000	961
Expected receipts after 2 years	1039	1000	925
Expected receipts after 3 years	1059	1000	889
Net present value:			0

no inflation and an interest rate of 4 per cent a year. But notice also that the real interest rate in Table A25.2 is 4 per cent a year. Comparing the numbers in Tables A25.1 and A25.2, you can see that the net present value of an investment project depends on the real interest rate. That is, the project that we are considering here has a net present value of zero when the real interest rate is 4 per cent a year. It makes no difference whether that real interest rate arises from an actual interest rate of 4 per cent a year and no inflation or an actual interest rate of 6 per cent a year and 1.92 per cent inflation. Either way, the net present value of the project is zero. The lower the real interest rate, the larger is the number of projects that have a positive net present value and that are undertaken.

Investment Demand

The investment demand schedule of the firm is obtained by calculating the total cost of all the projects that have a positive net present value at each interest rate. As the interest rate falls, the number of projects that are undertaken increases and the total amount of investment undertaken increases. Thus the firm's investment demand schedule shows an increase in the amount of planned investment as the real interest rate falls. Adding up all the planned investment projects of all the firms in the economy produces the aggregate investment demand schedule.

The net present value calculation of an investment project depends on the firm's best forecast of the future stream of revenue or receipts generated by the project. If firms have optimistic expectations, a larger number of projects will have positive net present values at each interest rate. If firms have pessimistic expectations about future revenue, a smaller number of projects will have positive net present values. Thus the number of projects that are undertaken at each interest rate depends on the degree of optimism or pessimism embodied in firms' forecasts of future revenue streams. Changes in the degree of optimism and pessimism lead to shifts in investment demand schedules.

Appendix B to Chapter 25

The Simple Algebra of Income Determination

In this Appendix we demonstrate that the results presented in tables and graphs can just as easily be derived using simple algebra. Let's look at how the value of real GDP can be calculated algebraically from aggregate expenditure.

First we need to calculate aggregate expenditure. As we discussed earlier in this chapter, aggregate expenditure is the sum of consumption expenditure, planned investment, government expenditure and net exports. That is:

$$AE = C + I + G + NX$$

Since net exports are given by exports minus imports:

$$AE = C + I + G + EX - IM$$

The consumption figures in Table 25.10 were based on the following consumption function:

$$C = 12.5 + 0.65Y$$

where the level of autonomous consumption is \$12.5 billion Y is real GDP in billions of 1984/85 dollars. The marginal propensity to consume is 0.65.

The import figures were based on the following import function:

$$IM = 12.5 + 0.15Y$$

The level of autonomous imports is 12.5 billion dollars. From Table 25.10 we see that:

$$I = 50$$

$$G = 60$$

$$EX = 40$$

where all variables are expressed in billions of 1984/85 dollars. Substituting all this information into the aggregate expenditure function we obtain:

$$\begin{aligned} AE &= C + I + G + EX - IM \\ &= (12.5 + 0.65Y) + 50 + 60 + 40 - (12.5 + 0.15Y) \\ &= 150 + (0.65 - 0.15)Y \\ &= 150 + 0.50Y \end{aligned}$$

Note that as real GDP rises by \$1, aggregate expenditure rises by 50 cents. The marginal propensity to spend is 0.65 minus 0.15 which equals 0.50.

Equilibrium occurs when aggregate expenditure equals the level of real GDP. That is, when

$$Y = AE$$

From above, this means that

$$Y = 150 + 0.5Y$$

or

$$\begin{aligned} Y - 0.5Y &= 150 \\ 0.5Y &= 150 \\ Y = 150/0.5 &= 300 \end{aligned}$$

This is the equilibrium value of real GDP identified in Figure 25.12.

Chapter 26

Expenditure and Income

After studying this chapter, you will be able to:

- Define and calculate the multiplier.
- Explain why changes in investment and exports produce changes in consumption expenditure and have multiplier effects on aggregate expenditure.
- Explain why changes in government expenditure have multiplier effects on aggregate expenditure.
- Explain why changes in taxes and transfer payments have multiplier effects on aggregate expenditure.
- Explain how the government can use fiscal policy in an attempt to stabilize aggregated expenditure.
- Explain the relationship between the aggregate expenditure and the aggregate demand.

Economic Amplifier or Shock Absorber

Jimmy Barnes breathes into a microphone at a barely audible whisper. The electronic signal picked up by the sensitive instrument travels along wires to a huge bank of amplifiers and then through high-fidelity speakers to the ears of the fans at his concert at the Sydney Entertainment Centre. Moving to a louder passage, Jimmy Barnes increases the volume of his voice and now, through the magic of electronic amplification, booms across the stadium drowning out every other sound. Wayne Goss, the Premier of Queensland, is being driven to a business meeting along one of Queensland's outback roads. (There are some pretty rough roads off the main routes.) He is dictating notes to a secretary who is taking down the words in impeccable shorthand. The car's wheels are bouncing and vibrating over some rough patches, but its passengers are largely undisturbed, and the shorthand notes are written without a ripple, thanks to the car's efficient shock absorbers. Investment and exports fluctuate like the volume of Jimmy's voice and the uneven surface of an outback road. How does the economy react to those fluctuations? Does it react like Wayne Goss's limousine, absorbing the shocks and providing a smooth ride for the economy's passengers? Or, does it behave like Jimmy Barnes' amplifier, blowing up the fluctuations and spreading them out to affect the many millions of participants in an economic rock concert? And is the economic machine built to a design that we simply have to live with, or can we modify it, changing its amplification and shock-absorbing powers? Finally, can the government operate the economic machine in a way that gives us all a smoother ride?

In Chapter 25, we discovered that consumption expenditure is a remarkably stable proportion of GDP and that the most volatile components of aggregate expenditure are investment and net exports. One goal of this chapter is to work out how fluctuations in planned investment and exports influence aggregate expenditure. Another goal is to discover the influence of taxes and government purchases of goods and services, and how fiscal policy may be used to stabilize aggregate expenditure. A third goal is to work out the relationship between equilibrium expenditure and aggregate demand. And the final goal of the chapter is to see how fluctuations in investment and exports as well as fiscal policy actions influence real GDP and the price level.

We are going to discover that the economy contains an important amplification unit that tends to magnify the effects of fluctuations in investment and exports resulting in a larger change in aggregate expenditure than the change in investment or exports that initiated it. But we are also going to discover that taxes and transfer payments act as a kind of shock absorber. They don't provide the smooth ride of a Ford LTD but they do a better job than the springs of a horse cart. Further, we're going to discover that the government can, to some degree, smooth out fluctuations in aggregate expenditure by varying taxes and its purchases of goods and services. Finally, we're going to discover that fluctuations in investment and exports and changes in fiscal policy affect both real GDP and the price level, and that those effects depend not only on equilibrium expenditure but also on aggregate supply.

Autonomous Expenditure Multipliers

We discovered in Chapter 25 how equilibrium expenditure is determined at the point of intersection of the aggregate expenditure curve and the 45° line. We're now going to discover how this equilibrium *changes* when there is a change in autonomous expenditure. Recall that autonomous expenditure consists of planned investment, exports and government purchases of goods and services. So that you can see the mechanisms at work as clearly as possible, we're going to begin by finding out what happens to aggregate expenditure and real GDP when the price level is constant.

Recall that the *aggregate expenditure curve* shows how aggregate expenditure varies as the level of real GDP varies, *other things remaining constant.* One of the things held constant along the aggregate expenditure curve is the price level. Thus when we study the forces that change equilibrium expenditure, we are working out what happens at a given price level. We discovered in Chapter 24 that the price level and real GDP are determined by aggregate demand and aggregate supply. Later in the chapter, we'll learn about the relationship between equilibrium expenditure and the aggregate demand–aggregate supply model and see how the ultimate effects of changes in autonomous expenditure also depend on aggregate supply.

A Change in Autonomous Expenditure

There are many possible sources of a change in autonomous expenditure. A fall in the real interest rate might induce firms to increase their planned investment. Booming business conditions may increase firms' optimism about future profits, adding yet more to their planned investment, as happened in Australia in 1988. Stiff competition in the car industry from Japanese and European imports might force GMH and Ford to increase their investment in robotic assembly lines. An economic boom in the United States and Japan might lead to a large increase in expenditure in those countries on Australian-produced goods (Australian exports). An increase in the number of working mothers might lead the Australian government to increase its expenditure on day-care facilities — an increase in government purchases of goods and services. These are all examples of increases in autonomous expenditure. What are the effects of such increases on aggregate expenditure? And do changes in autonomous expenditure affect consumers? Will they change their consumption expenditure?

Aggregate expenditure is set out in the table and illustrated in the diagram in Fig. 26.1. Autonomous expenditure initially is $150 billion. For each $50 billion increase in real GDP, induced expenditure increases by $25 billion. Thus the marginal propensity to spend out of real GDP is 0.5. Adding induced expenditure and autonomous expenditure together gives aggregate expenditure. Initially, equilibrium occurs when real GDP is $300 billion. This equilibrium can be seen in row *e* of the table, and in the figure where the aggregate expenditure AE_0 cuts the 45° line at the point marked *e*.

Now suppose that planned investment, government purchases and exports increase by an aggregate amount of $25 billion, so that autonomous expenditure becomes $175 billion. What is the new equilibrium? The answer is worked out in the final two columns of the table and illustrated in the diagram. When the new level of autonomous expenditure is added to induced expenditure, aggregate expenditure increases by $25 billion at each level of real GDP. The aggregate expenditure curve shifts upward to AE_1 — a parallel shift. That is, the vertical distance between AE_1 and AE_0 is $25 billion at all levels of real GDP. The new equilibrium, highlighted in the table (row f'), occurs where AE_1 intersects the 45° line and is at $350 billion (point f'). At this income level, aggregate expenditure equals real GDP. Autonomous expenditure is $175 billion and induced expenditure is also $175 billion.

Figure 26.1 An Increase in Autonomous Expenditure

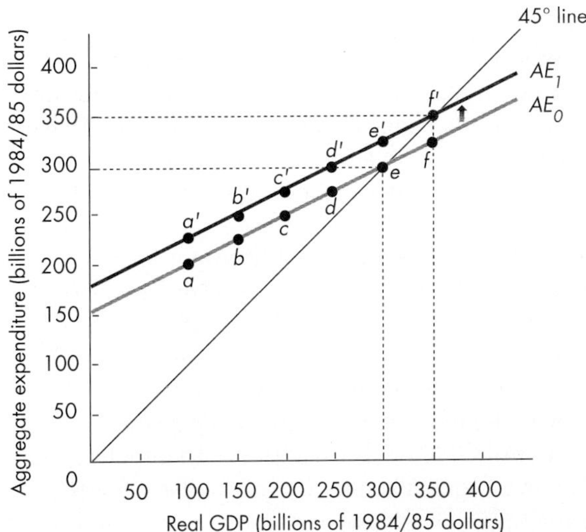

If autonomous expenditure increases from $150 billion to $175 billion, aggregate expenditure at each level of real GDP also increases by $25 billion. As shown in the table, the initial equilibrium expenditure of $300 billion is no longer the equilibrium. At that level of real GDP, aggregate expenditure is now $325 billion. The new expenditure equilibrium is $350 billion, where aggregate expenditure equals real GDP. The increase in real GDP is larger than the increase in autonomous expenditure. The figure illustrates the effect of the increase in autonomous expenditure. At each level of real GDP, aggregate expenditure is $25 billion higher than before. The aggregate expenditure curve shifts upward from AE_0 to AE_1 — a parallel shift. The new *AE* curve intersects the 45° line at *f*′ where real GDP is $350 billion — the new equilibrium point.

			Original			New	
Real GDP (*Y*)	**Induced expenditure (*N*)**		**Autonomous expenditure (A_0)**	**Aggregate expenditure (AE_0)**		**Autonomous expenditure (A_1)**	**Aggregate expenditure (AE_1)**
			(billions 1984/85 dollars)				
100	50	*a*	150	200	*a*′	175	225
150	75	*b*	150	225	*b*′	175	250
200	100	*c*	150	250	*c*′	175	275
250	125	*d*	150	275	*d*′	175	300
300	150	*e*	150	300	*e*′	175	325
350	175	*f*	150	325	*f*′	175	350
400	200	*g*	150	350	*g*′	175	375

Notice that equilibrium expenditure has increased by more than the increase in autonomous expenditure. Increased autonomous expenditure increases real GDP and the increase in real GDP produces an increase in induced expenditure. Aggregate expenditure increases by the sum of the initial increase on autonomous expenditure and the increase in induced expenditure.

Although we have just analysed the effects of an increase in autonomous expenditure, the same analysis applies to a decrease in autonomous expenditure. If autonomous expenditure is initially $175 billion, the initial equilibrium real GDP is $350 billion. If, in that situation, there is a cut in government purchases, exports or investment of $25 billion, then the aggregate expenditure curve shifts downward to AE_0. Equilibrium real GDP falls from $350 billion to $300 billion. The fall in real GDP is larger than the fall in autonomous expenditure. In both cases, the change in autonomous expenditure was amplified into a larger change for real GDP.

The Paradox of Thrift

Thrift is another word for saving. The thriftier a household, the more it saves. Also, the thriftier a household, the wealthier it becomes. By consuming less than its income, a household increases its income. It lends what it saves and earns interest on it.

What happens if we all become thriftier? Does aggregate income increase? We can work out one answer to this question by using the analysis that we've just performed.

Suppose that, initially, the aggregate expenditure curve is AE_1 in Fig. 26.1. Real GDP is $350 billion. Now suppose that there is an increase in thriftiness. As a result, autonomous expenditure decreases by $25 billion and, consequently, the aggregate expenditure curve shifts downward from AE_1 to AE_0. Equilibrium GDP and expenditure fall to $300 billion.

An increase in thriftiness has reduced real GDP. The fall in real GDP caused by an increase in saving is called the **paradox of thrift**. It is a paradox because an increase in thriftiness, which for an individual leads to an increase in income, leads, for the economy as a whole, to a decrease in income.

The paradox arises in this model because an increase in saving is *not* associated with an increase in investment. Although people save more, and there are more funds around, which could be loaned out, no one is undertaking additional borrowing and no one buys additional capital goods.

If at the same time that saving increases there was also an increase in investment, there would be no fall in income. An increase in saving shifts the *AE* curve downward but an increase in investment shifts it upward. If saving and investment each change by the same amount the *AE* curve does not shift. The result is no change in real GDP. But this is a short-run outcome.

There are further and much more important effects of saving and investment. They result in the accumulation of capital that enables incomes, both of individuals and the economy as a whole, to grow over time. Thus the paradox of thrift is not paradoxical after all. It is a consequence for current income only of increased saving with unchanged investment. In the long run, increased saving results in more capital and a higher level of real GDP.

We have now discovered that changes in autonomous expenditure shift the aggregate expenditure curve and change equilibrium real GDP. But how big are the changes? What determines the magnitude of the change in equilibrium real GDP brought about by a change in autonomous expenditure?

Calculating the Multiplier

Suppose that the economy appears to be heading for a recession. Profit prospects look bleak and firms are cutting investment. The world economy is heading toward recession and exports are falling. The question on everyone's lips is: How bad will the recession be? This is a hard question to answer but an important ingredient in the answer is working out the connection between a change in autonomous expenditure and the change in equilibrium aggregate expenditure. We've already seen that when autonomous expenditure changes, equilibrium expenditure and real GDP change by a larger amount. But what is the quantitative relationship between the change in autonomous expenditure and the change in equilibrium real GDP?

The **autonomous expenditure multiplier** (often abbreviated to simply the **multiplier**) is the amount by which a change in autonomous expenditure is multiplied to calculate the change in equilibrium aggregate expenditure and real GDP. To calculate the multiplier, we divide the change in equilibrium real GDP by the change in autonomous expenditure that brought about that change. Let's calculate the multiplier for the example in Fig. 26.1. Autonomous expenditure increases from $150 to $175 billion and equilibrium real GDP increases from $300 billion to $350 billion, an increase of $50 billion. That is

- Autonomous expenditure increases by $25 billion
- Real GDP increases by $50 billion

So, the multiplier is calculated as follows:

$$\text{Multiplier} = \frac{\text{Change in equilibrium real GDP}}{\text{Change in autonomous expenditure}}$$

$$= \frac{\$50 \text{ billion}}{\$25 \text{ billion}}$$

Thus a change in autonomous expenditure of $25 billion produces a change in equilibrium real GDP of $50 billion, a change that is twice as big as the initial change in autonomous expenditure. That is, the change in autonomous expenditure leads, like Jimmy Barnes' music-making equipment, to an amplified change in aggregate expenditure and real GDP.

The size of the multiplier depends on the marginal propensity to spend. Let's see how.

The Multiplier and the Marginal Propensity to Spend

Table 26.1 shows how to calculate the value of the multiplier. Part 1 introduces some definitions. It starts with the change in real GDP, ΔY. Our objective is to calculate the size of this change when there is a given change in autonomous expenditure, ΔA. Let's assume the change in autonomous expenditure is $50 billion. We're going to discover that the change in real GDP depends on the marginal propensity to spend, ε, which, in this example, we'll assume is equal to $\frac{2}{3}$. (Recall that the marginal propensity to spend is equal to the marginal propensity to consume out of real GDP minus the marginal propensity to import). The change in induced expenditure, ΔN, is equal to the change in real GDP (that we're working out) multiplied by the marginal propensity to spend. And the change in aggregate expenditure, ΔAE is the sum of the change in autonomous expenditure, ΔA, and the change in induced expenditure, ΔN. Finally, the multiplier k is defined as

$$k = \frac{\Delta Y}{\Delta A}$$

Part 2 of Table 26.1 sets out the calculations of the change in real GDP and the multiplier. The change in aggregate planned expenditure, ΔAE, is equal to the sum of the change in autonomous expenditure, ΔA, and the change in induced expenditure,

Table 26.1 Calculating the Multiplier

	Symbols and Formulas		Numbers
1. Definitions			
Change in real GDP	ΔY		
Change in autonomous expenditure	ΔA		50
Marginal propensity to spend	ε		$\frac{2}{3}$
Change in induced expenditure	$\Delta N = \varepsilon \Delta Y$		$\Delta N = (\frac{2}{3})\Delta Y$
Change in aggregate planned expenditure	$\Delta AE = \Delta A + \Delta N$		
The multiplier (autonomous expenditure multiplier)	$k = \Delta Y / \Delta A$		
The multiplier effect	$\Delta Y = k\Delta A$		
2. Calculations			
Aggregate expenditure	$AE = A + \varepsilon Y$		
Change in AE	$\Delta AE = \Delta A + \varepsilon \Delta Y$		$\Delta AE = 50 + \frac{2}{3}\Delta Y$
Change in equilibrium expenditure	$\Delta AE = \Delta Y$		
Replacing ΔAE with ΔY	$\Delta Y = \Delta A + \varepsilon \Delta Y$		$\Delta Y = 50 + \frac{2}{3}\Delta Y$
Subtracting $\varepsilon \Delta Y$ or $\frac{2}{3}\Delta Y$ from both sides	$\Delta Y - \varepsilon \Delta Y = \Delta A$		$\Delta Y - \frac{2}{3}\Delta Y = 50$
Factoring ΔY	$\Delta Y(1 - \varepsilon) = \Delta A$		$\Delta Y(1 - \frac{2}{3}) = 50$
Dividing both sides by $(1 - \varepsilon)$ or $(1 - \frac{2}{3})$	$\Delta Y = \frac{1}{(1 - \varepsilon)}\Delta A$		$\Delta Y = \frac{1}{1 - \frac{2}{3}} 50$
		or	$\Delta Y = \frac{1}{\frac{1}{3}} 50$
		or	$\Delta Y = 150$
Dividing both sides by ΔA or 50 gives multiplier	$\frac{\Delta Y}{\Delta A} = \frac{1}{(1 - \varepsilon)}$		$\frac{\Delta Y}{\Delta A} = \frac{150}{50} = 3$

The autonomous expenditure multiplier, or multiplier, is the ratio of the change in real GDP to a change in real autonomous expenditure. The multiplier effect is the change in real GDP brought about by a given change in autonomous expenditure — the change in autonomous expenditure multiplied by k. The table shows how to calculate the multiplier. The multiplier formula that results is $\Delta Y/\Delta A = 1/(1 - \varepsilon)$.

$\varepsilon\Delta Y$. In the numerical example it is equal to \$50 billion plus $\frac{2}{3}$ of the change in real GDP. Since, in equilibrium, the change in aggregate planned expenditure is equal to the change in real GDP, the change in real GDP is:

$$\Delta Y = \Delta A + \varepsilon \Delta Y$$

Using our numbers:

$$\Delta Y = 50 + \tfrac{2}{3}\Delta Y$$

This equation has just one unknown, ΔY, and we can find its value as shown in the next two rows of the table. Finally, dividing ΔY by ΔA gives the value of the multiplier which is:

$$k = \frac{1}{(1 - \varepsilon)}$$

Because the marginal propensity to spend is less than one, the multiplier, $\frac{1}{(1-\varepsilon)}$, is greater than 1. In the example, since ε is $\frac{2}{3}$, the multiplier is 3.

The larger the marginal propensity to spend, the larger is the multiplier. To see why, let's look at some further examples. If the marginal propensity to spend is 0 (if ε equals 0), an increase in real GDP would not lead to an increase in induced expenditure and the multiplier is 1. It is easy to see why. A \$1 change in autonomous expenditure changes real GDP by \$1 and, with no induced expenditure changes, that is the end of the matter.

If the marginal propensity to spend (ε) is $\frac{1}{2}$, \$1 of additional income induces 50 cents of additional expenditure. The multiplier is 2. This case is illustrated in Fig. 26.2(a). A \$25 billion increase in autonomous expenditure shifts the *AE* curve upward from AE_0 to AE_1 and increases equilibrium real GDP from \$300 billion to \$350 billion. An autonomous expenditure increase of \$25 billion increases equilibrium real GDP by \$50 billion, so the multiplier is 2.

If the marginal propensity to spend (ε) is $\frac{2}{3}$, the multiplier is 3. Figure 26.2 (b) illustrates this case. Here a \$25 billion increase in autonomous expenditure shifts the *AE* curve upward from AE_0 to AE_1 and increases equilibrium real GDP from \$300 billion to \$375 billion.

Why is the Multiplier Greater than 1?

The multiplier is greater than 1 because of induced expenditure — an increase in autonomous expendi-

Figure 26.2 The Multiplier and the Marginal Propensity to Spend

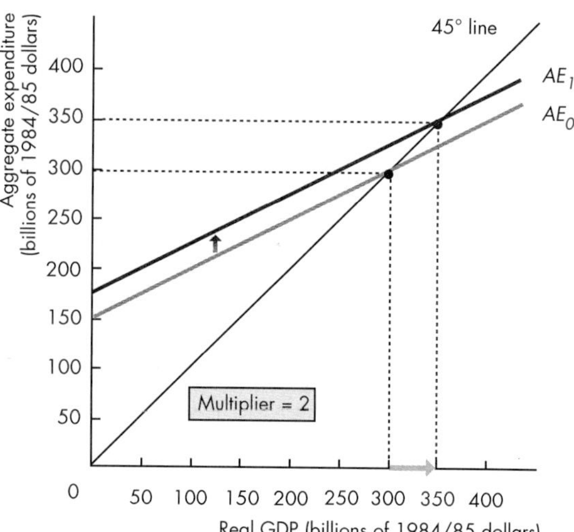

(a) Multiplier is 2

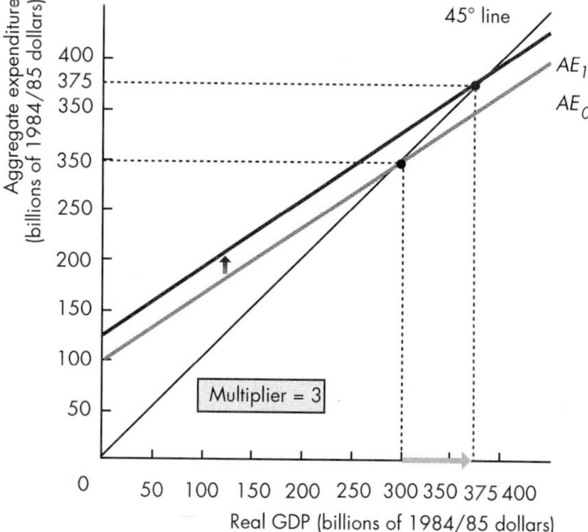

(b) Multiplier is 3

The size of the multiplier depends on the marginal propensity to spend. The multiplier formula, $k = 1/(1 - \varepsilon)$, tells us the relationship. If the marginal propensity to spend (ε) is $\frac{1}{2}$, the multiplier is 2. In this case, an increase of autonomous expenditure of \$25 billion shifts the *AE* curve upward from AE_0 to AE_1 in part (a). Real GDP increases from \$300 billion to \$350 billion. If e equals $\frac{2}{3}$, the multiplier is 3. In this case, a \$25 billion increase in autonomous expenditure shifts the aggregate expenditure curve upward from AE_0 to AE_1 in part (b). Real GDP increases from \$300 billion to \$375 billion, three times the size of the increase in autonomous expenditure.

ture induces an increase in consumption expenditure. If GMH spends $10 million on a new car assembly line, aggregate expenditure and real GDP immediately increase by $10 million. But that is not the end of the story. Engineers and construction workers now have more income and they spend part of the extra income on cars, microwaves, holidays and a host of other goods and services. Real GDP now rises by the initial $10 million plus the extra consumption expenditure induced by the $10 million increased income. The suppliers of cars, microwaves, holidays and other goods now have increased incomes and they, in turn, also spend part of their increase in income on consumption goods and services. Additional income induces additional expenditure, which creates additional income.

This multiplier process is illustrated in Fig. 26.3. In this example, the marginal propensity to spend, ε, is ⅔ as in Fig. 26.2(b). In round 1, there is an increase in autonomous expenditure of $25 billion. At that stage, there is no change in induced expenditure, so total expenditure increases by $25 billion. In round 2, the higher income induces higher consumption expenditure. Since the marginal propensity to spend, ε, is ⅔, an increase in income of $25 billion induces a further increase in expenditure of $16.67 billion.

This change in induced expenditure, when added to the initial change in autonomous expenditure, results in an increase in total expenditure of $41.67 billion. The round 2 increase in income induces a round 3 increase in expenditure. The process repeats through successive rounds as recorded in the table in Fig. 26.3. Each increase in income is two-thirds the size of the previous increase. The cumulative increase in income gradually approaches $75 billion. Even after only 10 rounds it has almost reached that level.

As the multiplier process depicted in Fig. 26.3 is working itself out, inventories and output are being adjusted in the manner described in Fig. 25.10. But you should not think of each expenditure round depicted in Fig. 26.3 as taking place in a fixed

Figure 26.3 The Multiplier Process

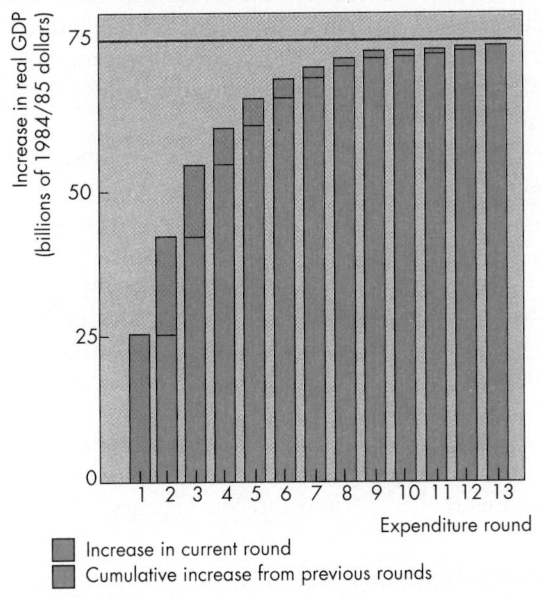

Expenditure round	Increase in expenditure	Cumulative increase in real GDP
	(billions of dollars)	
1	25	25
2	16.67	41.67
3	11.11	52.78
4	7.41	60.19
5	4.94	65.13
6	3.29	68.42
7	2.19	70.61
8	1.46	72.07
9	0.97	73.04
10	0.65	73.69
.	.	.
.	.	.
All others	1.31	75

Autonomous expenditure increases in round 1 by $25 billion. Real GDP also increases by the same amount. In round 2, the round 1 increase in real GDP induces an increase in expenditure of $16.67 billion. At the end of round 2, real GDP has increased by $41.67 billion. The extra $16.67 billion of real GDP in round 2 induces a further increase in expenditure of $11.11 billion in round 3. Total real GDP has increased by $52.78 billlion. This process continues until real GDP has eventually increased by $75 billion. The table stops counting after round 10 since the extra amounts become smaller and smaller. (Perhaps you would like to run the process further on your calculator. As a matter of interest, after 19 rounds you will be within $1 billion of the $75 billion total, and after 30 rounds within 1 cent of that total). The diagram shows you how quickly the multiplier effect builds up. The multiplier in this case is 3 because the marginal propensity to spend is ⅔ (see Table 26.1). The larger the marginal propensity to spend, the larger is the multiplier.

amount of calendar time. This multiplier process can take place in a single day or even a single instant. The amount of time that it takes is important.

It appears, then, that the economy does not operate like the shock absorbers on Wayne Goss's car. The economy's potholes and bumps are changes in autonomous expenditure — mainly brought about by changes in investment and exports. These economic potholes and bumps are not smoothed out but instead are amplified.

R E V I E W

Changes in autonomous expenditure change equilibrium expenditure and real GDP. The magnitude of the effect of a change in autonomous expenditure on equilibrium expenditure is determined by the multiplier. The multiplier, in turn, is determined by the value of the marginal propensity to spend. The higher the marginal propensity to spend, the larger is the multiplier. The multiplier acts like an amplifier. Fluctuations in autonomous expenditure — such as fluctuations in planned investment, government purchases of goods and services, or exports — change real GDP, introducing a change in consumption expenditure and having amplified effects on aggregate expenditure. ■

But the economic amplifier not only amplifies fluctuations in investment and exports. It also amplifies fluctuations in government expenditure on goods and services. Because of this fact, the government can take advantage of the multiplier in order to attempt to smooth out fluctuations in aggregate expenditure. Let's see how.

Fiscal Policy Multipliers

Fiscal policy is the attempt by government to smooth the fluctuations in aggregate expenditure by varying its purchases of goods and services, transfer payments and taxes. If the government expects a decline in investment or exports, it may attempt to offset the effects of the decline by increasing its own purchases of goods and services, increasing transfer payments or cutting taxes. But the government must figure out the size of the increase in purchases or transfers, or the size of the tax cut needed to achieve its goal. To make this calculation, the government needs to know the multiplier effects of its own actions. Let's study the multiplier effects of changes in government purchases, transfer payments and taxes.

Government Purchases Multiplier

The **government purchases multiplier** is the amount by which a change in government purchases of goods and services is multiplied to determine the change in equilibrium expenditure that it generates. Government purchases of goods and services are one of the components of autonomous expenditure. A change in government purchases has the same effect on aggregate expenditure as a change in any of the other components of autonomous expenditure. It sets up a multiplier effect exactly like the multiplier effect of investment or exports. That is

$$\text{Government purchases multiplier} = \frac{1}{(1-\varepsilon)}$$

By varying government purchases to offset changes in exports or investment, the government can attempt to keep total autonomous expenditure constant (or growing at a steady rate). Because the government purchases multiplier is the same size as the investment and exports multipliers, stabilization of autonomous expenditure would be achieved by increasing government purchases by $1 for each $1 decrease in those other items of autonomous expenditure.

In practice, using variations in government purchases to stabilize aggregate expenditure is not easy because the political decision process that produces changes in government purchases of goods and services operates with a long time lag. As a consequence, it is not possible to forecast the changes in private expenditure as far ahead as would be required to make this an effective instrument of macroeconomic stabilization policy.

A second way in which the government may seek to stabilize aggregate expenditure is by varying transfer payments. Let's see how this type of policy works.

Transfer Payments Multiplier

The **transfer payments multiplier** is the amount by which a change in transfer payments is multiplied to determine the change in equilibrium expenditure that it generates. A change in transfer payments influences aggregate expenditure by changing disposable income, which leads to a change in consumption expenditure. This change in consumption expenditure is a change in autonomous expenditure and it has a multiplier effect exactly like that of any other change in autonomous expenditure. But how large is the initial change in consumption expenditure? It is equal to the change in transfer payments multiplied by the marginal propensity to consume. If the marginal propensity to consume is c, a \$1 increase in transfer payments initially increases consumption expenditure by \$$c$. For example, if the marginal propensity to consume is 0.9, a \$1 increase in transfer payments initially increases consumption expenditure by 90¢. Therefore, the transfer payments multiplier is equal to c times the autonomous expenditure multiplier. That is

$$\text{Transfer payments multiplier} = \frac{c}{(1-\varepsilon)}$$

With a marginal propensity to consume of 0.9, and with a marginal propensity to spend, ε, of 0.5, the transfer payments multiplier is 1.8 (that is 0.9/0.5). Because the marginal propensity to consume is less than one, the transfer payments multiplier is smaller than the government purchases multiplier. As a consequence, to achieve a particular change in aggregate expenditure, a larger change in transfer payments is required than in government purchases of goods and services.

The use of variations in transfer payments to stabilize the economy has the same problems as the use of variations in government purchases of goods and services. The political process does not operate on the time scale required for timely changes in transfer payments to offset fluctuations in other components of autonomous expenditure.

Tax Multiplier

A third type of fiscal stabilization policy is to vary taxes. The effects of a change in taxes depend on whether the taxes are autonomous or induced. **Autonomous taxes** are taxes that do not vary directly with real GDP. Examples of such taxes are State and local government taxes such as those levied on the value of land (for example, water and sewerage rates). **Induced taxes** are taxes that vary directly with real GDP. Examples of induced taxes are personal income tax and sales taxes. Note that it is not the tax rate that varies with real GDP but, rather, it is the total amount of taxes collected. We'll study the effects of induced taxes later in the chapter. For now let's concentrate on changes in autonomous taxes and the autonomous tax multiplier.

The Autonomous Tax Multiplier The **autonomous tax multiplier** is the amount by which a change in autonomous taxes is multiplied to determine the change in equilibrium expenditure that it generates. An *increase* in taxes leads to a *decrease* in disposable income and a *decrease* in consumption expenditure. The amount by which consumption expenditure decreases, initially, is determined by the marginal propensity to consume. This initial response of consumption expenditure to a tax increase is exactly the same as its response to a decrease in transfer payments. Thus tax changes work like changes in transfer payments but in the opposite direction, and the autonomous tax multiplier equals the negative of the transfer payments multiplier. Because a tax *increase* leads to a *decrease* in expenditure, the tax multiplier is *negative.* It is:

$$\text{Autonomous tax multiplier} = -\frac{c}{(1-\varepsilon)}$$

With a marginal propensity to consume, c, of 0.9 and a marginal propensity to spend, ε, of 0.5, the autonomous tax multiplier is −1.8.

The autonomous tax multiplier effect is illustrated in Fig. 26.4. Initially, the aggregate expenditure curve is AE_0, and equilibrium expenditure is

Figure 26.4 Autonomous Tax Multiplier

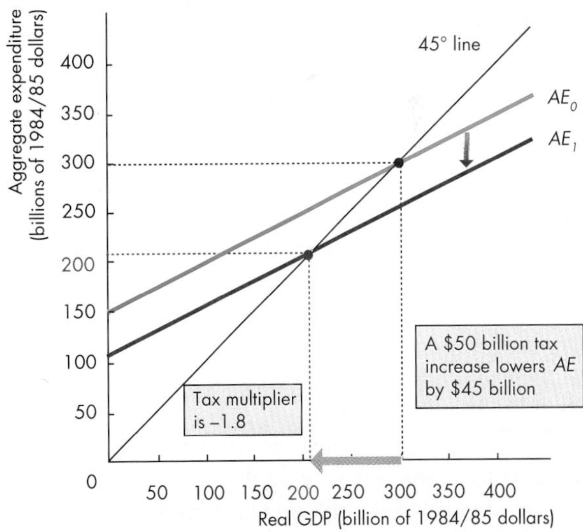

A \$50 billion increase in taxes reduces disposable income by \$50 billion dollars. Because the marginal propensity to consume out of disposable income is 0.9, consumption expenditure falls by only \$45 billion. The original aggregate expenditure curve, AE_0, shifts downward to AE_1. Equilibrium expenditure and real GDP fall by \$90 to \$210 billion. The tax multiplier is −1.8.

$300 billion. The slope of this curve is equal to the marginal propensity to spend, which in this example is 0.5. Taxes are increased by $50 billion and disposable income falls by that amount. With a marginal propensity to consume of 0.9, consumption expenditure decreases, initially, by $45 billion and the aggregate expenditure curve shifts downward by that amount to AE_1. Equilibrium expenditure and real GDP fall by $90 billion to $210 billion. The autonomous tax multiplier is –1.8.

Balanced Budget Multipliers

The **balanced budget multiplier** is the amount by which a change in government purchases of goods and services and in taxes of equal amounts is multiplied to determine the change in equilibrium expenditure that they generate. What is the multiplier effect of this fiscal policy action?

To answer we must combine the two multipliers that we have just worked out. We've seen that those two separate multipliers are:

$$\text{Government purchases multiplier} = \frac{1}{(1-\varepsilon)}$$

$$\text{Autonomous tax multiplier} = -\frac{c}{(1-\varepsilon)}$$

Adding these two multipliers together gives the balanced budget multiplier which is:

$$\text{Balanced budget multiplier} = \frac{(1-c)}{(1-\varepsilon)}$$

Because the marginal propensity to consume, c, is bigger than the marginal propensity to spend on domestic goods and services, ε, the balanced budget multiplier is less than one. For example, if the marginal propensity to consume is 0.9, and the marginal propensity to spend on domestic goods and services is 0.5, the balanced budget multiplier is 0.2 (that is, 0.1/0.5).

The balanced budget multiplier is illustrated in Fig. 26.5. Initially, the aggregate expenditure curve is AE_0. A $50 billion tax increase lowers aggregate planned expenditure by $45 billion and shifts the aggregate expenditure curve downward to AE_1. A $50 billion increase in government purchases increases aggregate planned expenditure by the entire $50 billion and shifts the aggregate expenditure curve upward to AE_2. The net shift in the aggregate curve is upward by $5 billion. Real GDP increases by that amount times the autonomous multiplier. Thus the balanced budget multiplier is positive but small. In this example, it is 0.2.

Figure 26.5 Balanced Budget Multiplier

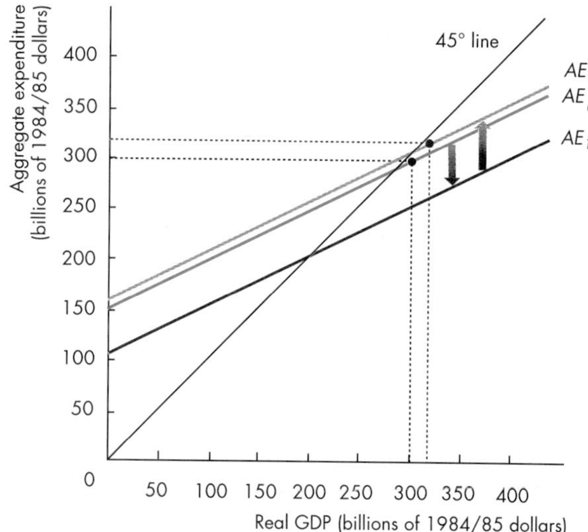

The initial aggregate expenditure curve is AE_0. A $50 billion dollar tax increase lowers aggregate expenditure by $45 billion. The aggregate expenditure curve shifts downward to AE_1. A $50 billion increase in government expenditure shifts the aggregate expenditure curve up by that amount, to AE_2. Equilibrium expenditure and real GDP rise by $5 billion overall. The balanced budget multiplier is 0.2.

This balanced budget multiplier result is an important one because it means that the government does not have to unbalance its budget and run a deficit in order to stimulate aggregate demand. But because the balanced budget multiplier is smaller than the multipliers for government purchases and taxes, the magnitude of the balanced budget changes would have to be larger to achieve a given effect on total spending.

A common drawback to all the fiscal policy actions that we have considered is that they take a long time in the legislative process to enact and, as a consequence, they are of limited value for stabilizing the economy. There is one feature of the tax and transfer payments system, however, that does help stabilize the economy and acts as an automatic stabilizer.

Automatic Stabilizers

Taxes and transfer payments act as automatic stabilizers. An automatic stabilizer is a mechanism that decreases the fluctuations in *aggregate* expenditure resulting from fluctuations in some *component* of aggregate expenditure. The automatic stabilizing effects of taxes and transfer payments means that they act like an economic shock absorber, making the aggregate effects of fluctuations in investment and exports smaller than they otherwise would be.

To see how taxes and transfer payments act as an economic shock absorber, let's see how a change in planned investment or exports affects equilibrium expenditure in two economies: in the first there are no induced taxes and transfer payments; in the second there are induced taxes and transfer payments similar to those in Australia today.

An Economy with No Induced Taxes and Transfer Payments In an economy with no induced taxes and transfer payments, the gap between GDP and disposable income is constant — it does not depend on the level of GDP. If the marginal propensity to consume is 0.9, the marginal propensity to consume out of GDP is also 0.9. That is, each extra dollar of GDP is an extra dollar of disposable income and induces an extra 90 cents of consumption expenditure. Suppose that there are no imports so that not only is the marginal propensity to consume 0.9, but so is the marginal propensity to spend.

What is the size of the multiplier if the marginal propensity to spend is 0.9? You can answer this question by using the formula

$$k = \frac{1}{(1 - \varepsilon)}$$

Substituting 0.9 for ε, the value of the multiplier is 10. In this economy, a $1 billion change in autonomous expenditure produces a $10 billion change in equilibrium expenditure. This economy has a very strong amplifier.

An Economy with Induced Taxes and Transfer Payments Contrast the economy that we have just described with one that has induced taxes and transfer payments.

The scale of induced taxes net of transfer payments is determined by the marginal tax rate. The **marginal tax rate** is the fraction of the last dollar of income that is paid to the government in net taxes (taxes minus transfer payments).

Let's assume that the marginal tax rate is 0.3. That is, each additional dollar of real GDP generates a tax for the government of 30 cents and a disposable income of 70 cents. If the marginal propensity to consume is 0.9 (the same as in the previous example), a $1 increase in real GDP increases disposable income by 70 cents and increases consumption expenditure by 63 cents (0.9 of 0.7 equals 0.63). In this economy, the marginal propensity to spend is 0.63. Substituting 0.63 for ε in the multiplier formula, the value of the multiplier is 2.7. The economy still amplifies shocks from changes in exports and investment but on a much smaller scale than the economy with no induced taxes and transfer payments. Thus, to some degree, induced taxes and transfer payments absorb the shocks of fluctuating autonomous expenditure. The higher the marginal tax rate, the greater the extent to which autonomous expenditure shocks are absorbed.

The existence of taxes and transfer payments that vary with real GDP help the shock-absorbing capacities of the economy. They don't produce the economic equivalent of the suspension of a Ford LTD but they do produce the economic equivalent of something better than the springs of a horse cart. As the economy fluctuates, the government's budget fluctuates absorbing some of the shocks, changing taxes and transfer payments, and smoothing the fluctuations in disposable income and expenditure.

Let's look at the effects of automatic stabilizers on the government's budget and its deficit.

Automatic Stabilizers and the Government Deficit

Because taxes and transfer payments fluctuate with real GDP, so does the government's deficit. Figure 26.6 shows how. Government purchases are part of autonomous expenditure and are independent of the level of real GDP. Recall, from the previous chapter, that we assumed the level of government purchases to be $60 billion. But taxes, net of transfer payments, increase as real GDP increases. There is a particular level of real GDP at which the government's budget is balanced — the deficit is zero. In Fig. 26.6, that level of real GDP is $270 billion. When real GDP is below that level there is a deficit, and when it is above that level there is a surplus.

As autonomous expenditure — investment and exports — fluctuate, bringing fluctuations in real GDP, taxes and the deficit also fluctuate. For example, a large increase in planned investment increases real GDP, increases taxes and lowers the deficit. The higher taxes act as an automatic stabilizer lowering disposable income and, to some degree, dampening the effects of the investment increase and moderating the rise in aggregate expenditure and real GDP. At the same time, they

Net Exports and Aggregate Expenditure

Export Sector Economy's Prop

Export industries, such as mining and agriculture, and the financial services sector were the props which held up the Australian economy in 1989–90 as industries dependent on domestic demand buckled under the weight of high interest rates.

Figures issued yesterday by the Australian Bureau of Statistics show that an 18.8 per cent increase in the real level of mining output, a 6.9 per cent growth in agricultural production and a 5.5 per cent increase in financial and business services were the underpinnings of the 1.2 per cent growth in overall national output over the year to June.

In contrast, manufacturing, construction, wholesale and retail trade, and the transport sector all fell sharply over the year, confirming the view that the economy has divided into two tiers of activity as domestic demand has collapsed and shifted the engine of growth to net exports.

The figures also show that agriculture joined the second tier of sagging sectors in the June quarter, falling 2.2 per cent after adjustment for seasonal factors and leaving an increase of 3.1 per cent in mining industry output to carry private sector growth.

Financial services were flat, while the recreation and personal services sector, which grew by a bare 0.3 per cent, and the largely public sector industries such as communications and community services were the only other industries to record positive growth in the June quarter.

The shift meant that overall output in the economy contracted by 1.4 per cent in industry revalued terms.

The shift to net exports and away from domestic demand as the wellspring of economic growth underpins the Budget strategy.

However, with demand for the rural commodity exports such as wool, wheat and sugar at low levels and world demand for mineral exports, apart from oil and gold, threatened by the effects on economic growth of the Gulf crisis, the risk is that these leading sectors will also weaken, pushing the overall economy into sharp contraction.

Australian Financial Review
26 September 1990
By Steve Burrell

Table 1

		June 1990	March 1991	Per cent change	Percentage contribution to growth in *AE*
		(billions of 1984/85			
Consumption	(C)	151	152	0.6	0.4
Investment	(I)	48	41	14.6	2.7
Government spending	(G)	64	65	1.6	0.4
Exports	(EX)	46	50	8.9	1.5
Imports	(IM)	55	53	3.6	0.8
Statistical discrepancy	(SD)	5	3	40.0	0.8
Aggregate expenditure	(AE)	259	258	0.4	0.4

Table 2

	Exchange rate US Dollar	Domestic CPI	OECD CPI
		Percentage change	
June 1990	77.8	7.7	5.8
March 1991	77.2	3.2	6.3

The Essence of the Story

- GDP grew 1.2 per cent in the year to 1989/90.
- However, the components of GDP grew at varying rates:
  - Output in the manufacturing, construction, wholesale and retail trade, and transport industries all fell sharply.
  - Mining output (18.8 per cent increase) and agricultural output (6.9 per cent increase) both grew strongly.
  - Both these industries are export oriented.
  - Output of financial services also grew (5.5 per cent increase).
- Real GDP growth is positive only because export growth is strong.
- Growth in the financial services sector appears to have ended.
- Since the export sector is the only component of aggregate expenditure contributing to positive growth, if world demand for Australian output falls, and exports decline, there will be a sharp contraction in domestic real GDP.

Background and Analysis

- Over the year to June 1990, economic growth was weak, and was positive only because of the contribution from net exports. This situation continued through the remainder of 1990 and into 1991. So as to maintain comparability with Reading Between the Lines in Chapter 24 (p. 148), where we analysed aggregate demand and supply in the period June 1990 to March 1991, Table 1 contains information on the components of aggregate demand over the same period.
- The table shows the levels of the components of aggregate expenditure in June 1990 and March 1991, the percentage change over the period, and also the contribution of each component to the growth in equilibrium aggregate expenditure.
- This last column is calculated by multiplying the growth in a component by its share in aggregate expenditure. For example, consumption expenditure grew by 0.6 per cent over the period. But it constitutes only 60 per cent of aggregate expenditure. Thus, its contribution to growth in aggregate expenditure is approximately 0.4 per cent (0.6 x 0.6).
- Between June 1990 and March 1991, equilibrium aggregate expenditure fell by 0.4 of 1 per cent.
- However, if we add up the contributions from domestic consumption, investment, government spending, and the statistical discrepancy, we see that their contribution to growth in equilibrium aggregate expenditure was –2.7 per cent.
- Offsetting this significant weakening of domestic spending was the contribution of net exports. Over the period exports grew by almost 9 per cent, contributing 1.5 percentage points to growth in equilibrium expenditure.
- Imports fell by 3.6 per cent, contributing a further 0.8 per cent to growth in equilibrium expenditure.
- On balance, net exports contributed 2.3 per cent to growth in equilibrium aggregate expenditure, almost enough to completely offset the decline in domestic spending.
- However, if the growth in net exports declined, and growth in domestic spending did not pick up to replace this shortfall, then equilibrium aggregate expenditure and real GDP would fall further.
- Why has net export growth remained strong as other components of aggregate expenditure have weakened? Certainly, growth in world output over the period June 1990 to March 1991 has not been strong. The United States, for example, entered into a recession at about the same time as Australia.
- One explanation might be found in the change in the relative price of Australian goods in terms of foreign goods. Table 2 provides some evidence relating to the changes in prices.
- Three things are apparent:
  - The exchange rate (see Chapter 29) weakened slightly. This, by itself, makes Australian-produced goods less expensive in foreign markets and makes foreign goods more expensive in Australian markets.
  - The rate of growth of domestic prices fell, while the rate of growth of foreign prices rose. These changes both reduce the relative price of Australian-produced goods in terms of foreign-produced goods.

Conclusion

If Australia can maintain lower prices than the rest of the world and if foreign income does not fall precipitously, it will be possible for the foreign sector to sustain aggregate expenditure while the domestic sector recovers from the effects of the high interest rate policies of 1988 and 1989.

Figure 26.6 The Government Deficit

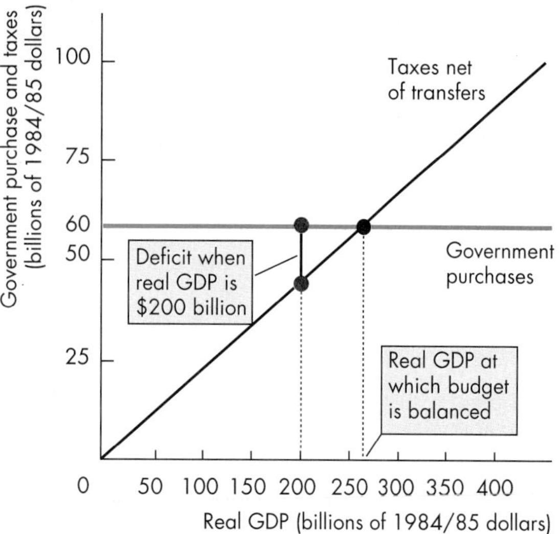

The figure shows how the government's deficit or surplus varies with real GDP. The level of government spending on goods and services is assumed to be part of autonomous expenditure and does not vary with real GDP. From the previous chapter, the level of government expenditure is $60 billion. Government revenue — taxes net of transfers — does vary with real GDP. As real GDP rises, revenue rises. When real GDP is $200 billion, taxes net of transfers are less than government spending so the government operates at a deficit.

bring a decrease in the government deficit (or an increase in the surplus).

Conversely, when a large decrease in planned investment is pushing the economy into recession, taxes fall and the deficit increases. The lower taxes act as an automatic stabilizer limiting the fall in disposable income and moderating the extent of the decline in aggregate expenditure and real GDP. But at the same time they increase the government deficit.

We've now seen how induced taxes and transfer payments influence the multiplier and how they bring fluctuations in the government budget as the total amount of tax collected varies with real GDP. But what happens to aggregate expenditure and real GDP if the government changes the marginal tax rate? Let's now answer this question.

A Change in the Marginal Tax Rate

Let's work out the effects of a change in the marginal tax rate on equilibrium expenditure and real GDP. Suppose that marginal tax rates have been cut, as they were in 1989 and then again in 1990. What are the effects of such a change in taxes on equilibrium expenditure and real GDP?

The immediate effect of a cut in the marginal tax rate is an increase in the marginal propensity to consume out of real GDP. For example, suppose that the marginal propensity to consume is 0.9 and that initially the marginal tax rate is 40 per cent. In this case, disposable income is 60 per cent of real GDP and the marginal propensity to consume out of real GDP is 0.54 (that is 0.9 times 0.6). If the marginal tax rate is cut to 30 per cent the marginal propensity to consume out of real GDP increases to 0.63 (that is 0.9 times 0.7).

Because a cut in the marginal tax rate increases the marginal propensity to consume out of real GDP, it also increases the marginal propensity to spend. Recall that the marginal propensity to spend measures the slope of the aggregate expenditure curve. Thus when taxes are cut the aggregate expenditure curve shifts upward and becomes steeper.

Figure 26.7 illustrates this effect when a cut in tax rates increases the marginal propensity to spend from 0.5 to 0.57. The table in the figure lists the effects that this change in the marginal propensity to spend has on induced expenditure and on aggregate planned expenditure, at each level of real GDP holding autonomous expenditure constant. Recall that induced expenditure equals real GDP multiplied by the marginal propensity to spend. The new induced expenditure, N_1, equals 0.57 times real GDP, whereas the original induced expenditure, N_0, equals 0.5 times real GDP. Aggregate planned expenditure equals induced expenditure plus the $150 billion of autonomous expenditure.

The aggregate expenditure curve associated with the larger marginal propensity to spend is shown as AE_1 in the diagram in Fig. 26.7. Since autonomous expenditure has not changed, the aggregate expenditure curve intersects the vertical axis at the same point as the original curve, AE_0. The AE_0 curve rotates upward. It does not shift in a parallel fashion; it becomes steeper.

The original equilibrium real GDP is $300 billion and the new equilibrium is $350 billion. Starting out at $300 billion, the higher marginal propensity to spend increases aggregate expenditure to $321 billion (see row *e'* of the table). But now aggregate expenditure exceeds real GDP, so real GDP increases (by the process described in Chapter 25, Fig. 25.12). Real GDP continues to increase until a

Figure 26.7 An Increase in the Marginal Propensity to Spend

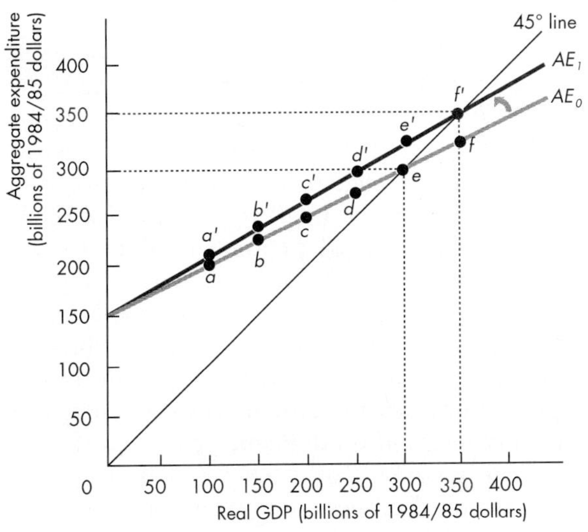

A tax cut increases the marginal propensity to spend from 0.5 to 0.57. Autonomous expenditure remains constant at $150 billion but induced expenditure increases. For example, when real GDP is $200 billion (row *c* of table), induced expenditure increases from $100 billion to $114 billion. In the figure, the aggregate expenditure curve shifts from AE_0 to AE_1. The aggregate expenditure curve becomes steeper because the marginal propensity to spend has increased. The new equilibrium occurs where aggregate planned expenditure equals real GDP — row *f'* in the table. In the diagram, the intersection of AE_1 and the 45° line determines equilibrium expenditure — $350 billion (point *f'*).

			Original			New	
Real GDP (Y)	**Autonomous expenditure (A)**		**Induced expenditure (N_0)**	**Aggregate expenditure (AE_0)**		**Induced expenditure (N_1)**	**Aggregate expenditure (AE_1)**
				(billions 1984/85 dollars)			
100	150	*a*	50	200	*a'*	57	207
150	150	*b*	75	225	*b'*	86	236
200	150	*c*	100	250	*c'*	114	264
250	150	*d*	125	275	*d'*	143	293
300	150	*e*	150	300	*e'*	171	321
350	150	*f*	175	325	*f'*	200	350
400	150	*g*	200	350	*g'*	229	379

new equilibrium is established. In the process, induced expenditure increases further. Only when real GDP is $350 billion has aggregate planned expenditure adjusted to the level required to attain a new expenditure equilibrium. You can verify this fact by noticing that at this level of real GDP, aggregate planned expenditure also equals $350 billion. That is, induced expenditure is $200 billion (real GDP of $350 billion multiplied by 0.57) and when this amount is added to autonomous expenditure of $150 billion, aggregate planned expenditure equals real GDP at $350 billion.

R E V I E W

The government purchases multiplier is equal to the autonomous expenditure multiplier. By varying its purchases of goods and services, the government can try to offset fluctuations in investment and exports. In practice, such actions are difficult to arrange because of time lags in the legislative process.

The transfer payments multiplier is equal to the marginal propensity to consume multiplied by the government purchases multiplier. A change in transfer payments works through a change in disposable income. Part of the change in disposable income is spent and part is saved. Only the part that is spent, that is determined by the marginal propensity to consume, has a multiplier effect.

The autonomous tax multiplier is negative — a tax increase leads to a decrease in equilibrium expenditure — but has the same magnitude as the transfer payments multiplier.

An equal change in both purchases of goods and services and taxes has a balanced budget multiplier effect on real GDP. The balanced budget multiplier is small, but positive.

Taxes and transfers that vary directly with GDP lower the value of the multiplier and act as an automatic stabilizer.

Changes in the marginal tax rate also have a multiplier effect. A cut in the marginal tax rate increases the marginal propensity to spend and increases real GDP. ■

We've now seen what determines the value of the autonomous expenditure multiplier, how the multiplier can be used by the government to influence aggregate expenditure by changing government purchases, transfer payments or taxes, and how, by its choice of the marginal rate of taxes (and transfer payments), the government can influence the magnitude of the autonomous expenditure multiplier. But so far we have studied model economies with hypothetical numbers. Let's now turn to the real world. What is the size of the marginal propensity to spend in Australia? How big is the multiplier in the Australian economy?

The Multiplier in Australia

The model economy that we studied earlier in this chapter has a marginal propensity to spend of 0.5 — each additional dollar of income induces 50 cents of expenditure. The multiplier is 2.

The marginal propensity to spend in Australia, and the resulting multiplier, are smaller than those in the model economy but the precise values are not known: there are a range of estimates.

The Australian Multiplier in 1990/91

In 1990/91, the marginal propensity to consume out of disposable income in Australia was 0.89, and disposable income was approximately 67 per cent (0.67) of GDP. Putting these two facts together, we can calculate that the marginal propensity to consume out of GDP was 0.6 ($0.67 \times 0.89 = 0.6$). Imports were 21 per cent of GDP. Using this percentage as an estimate of the marginal propensity to import gives a value of 0.21 (each dollar of income induces 21 cents of imports). Subtracting the marginal propensity to import from the marginal propensity to consume gives the marginal propensity to spend on domestic goods and services, which is 0.39 (that is 0.6 minus 0.21). With a marginal propensity to spend of 0.39, the multiplier is 1.64.[1] That is

$$k = \frac{1}{(1 - 0.39)} = \frac{1}{0.61} = 1.64$$

Thus in 1990/91, the multiplier in Australia was around 1.6.

Figure 26.8 The Multiplier in Australia

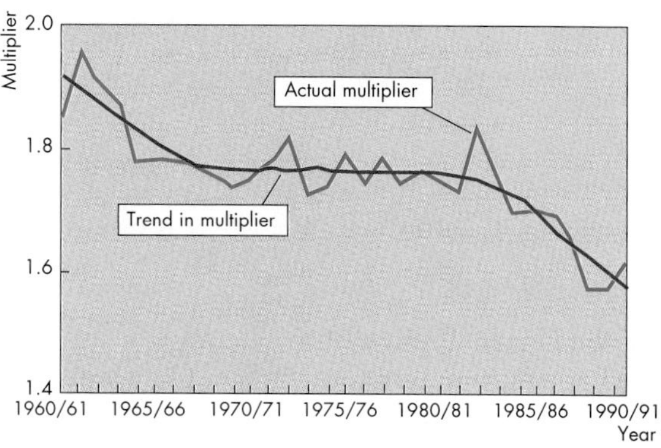

The decline in disposable income as a share of real GDP and the rise in the marginal propensity to import have both led to a trend decline in the multiplier, from almost 2.0 in the early 1960s to 1.6 in the late 1980s and early 1990s..

Source: From authors' calculations based on real disposable income, consumption, imports and GDP data from the ABS Time Series Service, supplied through EconData's Data Service.

[1] The numbers provide only a rough approximation to the true multipliers because we are using *average* values to estimate what is essentially a *marginal* concept. But as long as either (a) the autonomous components of consumption and imports are small relative to real GDP, or (b) the autonomous components of consumption and imports are roughly equal, then the average multiplier is close to the true multiplier.

The marginal propensity to spend has been falling over time in Australia. The marginal propensity to consume out of disposable income has risen slightly but disposable income has fallen as a share of GDP. And the marginal propensity to import has increased gradually over the years. In the 1970s, the marginal propensity to import was about 0.15. Today it is 0.21. If the marginal propensity to consume is 0.9, the share of disposable income out of GDP is 0.7 and the marginal propensity to import is 0.15, the marginal propensity to spend is 0.48. Thus, the multiplier is 1.9. That is

$$k = \frac{1}{(1 - 0.48)} = \frac{1}{0.52} = 1.92$$

This figure is a closer approximation to the multiplier as it applied in the 1960s and early 1970s. Figure 26.8 shows the multiplier, calculated as above, for the years 1960/61 to 1990/91. The decline of the multiplier in the 1960s and 1980s is clear. Notice also that the multiplier fluctuates around the trend. We discuss this aspect next.

Figure 26.9 Real GDP and the Multiplier

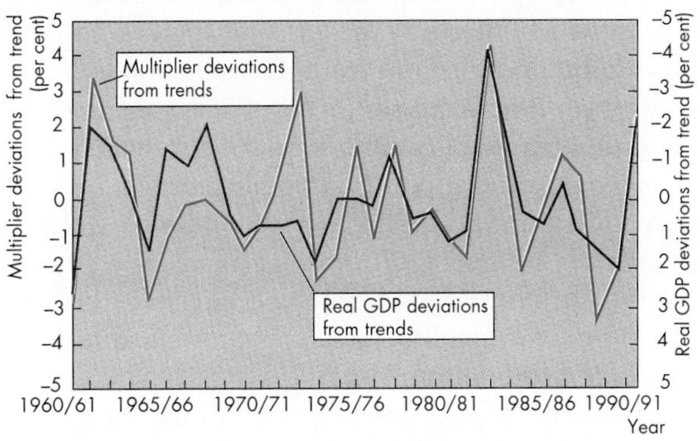

The deviations from trend in real GDP and the multiplier are shown. The scale for deviations from trend in real GDP is reversed. As income falls, consumption falls by less, the marginal propensity to consume rises and so the multiplier rises. This occurred in 1961/62, 1977/78, 1982/83 and 1990/91. As income rises, consumption rises by less, the MPC falls and so the multiplier falls. This levelling out response of consumption is called consumption smoothing and causes the multiplier to be countercyclical.

Source: See Fig. 26.8.

The Multiplier in Recession and Recovery

We've seen that the average value of the multiplier in the Australian economy in 1990/91 was 1.6 and that there has been a decline in the multiplier since the 1960s. Further, the fluctuations around trend are apparent. Are these fluctuations systematic? Does the multiplier take on the same value when the economy is going into a recession as when it is coming out and recovering? Or does its value vary and in some other systematic way? Answers to questions such as these are important for the design of policies to keep aggregate expenditure steady. How big an increase in government spending or cut in taxes is needed to avoid a recession? How big a cut in government spending or tax increase is needed to prevent the economy from overheating?

You can see the answers to these questions in Fig. 26.9. The figure shows the fluctuations in the multiplier and real GDP from their own trends. Note that the deviations of GDP from its trend are graphed with the scale reversed.

As you can see from the figure, there is a close negative relationship between deviations in the multiplier from its trend and deviations in real GDP from its trend. That is, when real GDP falls below trend, the multiplier rises above trend. A variable which exhibits this negative correlation with GDP is said to be **countercyclical**.

Why does the multiplier rise during a downturn or recession and fall during a recovery or boom? The answer to this question is that there are cycles in the marginal propensity to consume. When the economy goes into recession and income falls, households regard that income loss as temporary — the downturn is expected to be temporary and recovery will eventually come. Therefore they do not cut their consumption level by as much as the fall in income. Hence the marginal propensity to consume rises. During a boom period, when income is high, households expect that the good times cannot last and so consumption does not rise by as much as income. The marginal propensity to consume falls. As the marginal propensity to consume falls and rises, the multiplier falls and rises. So, in 1961/62, 1977/78, 1982/83 and 1990/91, when income was below trend, the multiplier was high. In 1980/81, when income was high, the multiplier was low. These expectational effects on consumption were discussed in Our Advancing Knowledge in the previous chapter.

One exception occurred in 1972/73, when the multiplier rose significantly while income was above trend. In this instance, household expectations must have been such that the increase in real GDP was expected to lead to further permanent increases in real GDP. Thus consumption rose by more than income.

Because consumption does not usually decline as much as income and does not rise as much as income over the business cycle, it acts, to some degree, like a shock absorber. This levelling out response by consumption is called **consumption smoothing.** ■

We have now explored the connection between changes in components of aggregate expenditure and changes in real GDP. But we have maintained the assumption that the price level is constant. In order to relax this assumption and to ascertain how changes in expenditure affect both the price level and the level of real output, we need to examine the relationship between aggregate expenditure and aggregate demand. This is our next task.

Aggregate Expenditure and Aggregate Demand

The aggregate demand curve is the relationship between the aggregate quantity of goods and services demanded and the price level. That is, the aggregate demand curve shows the quantity of real GDP demanded at each different price level. The aggregate expenditure curve tells us how aggregate expenditure varies as real GDP varies. The quantity of goods and services demanded is related to aggregate expenditure. Also, there is a connection between equilibrium expenditure and the aggregate demand curve. Let's explore the links between these concepts.

Aggregate Expenditure and the Price Level

In studying aggregate expenditure, we have distinguished between autonomous expenditure and induced expenditure. Induced expenditure varies with real GDP. Autonomous expenditure does not vary with real GDP. But autonomous expenditure is not constant. In fact, we have analysed the effects of changes in autonomous expenditure earlier in this chapter. Also, autonomous expenditure is not independent of other economic magnitudes. For example, a change in interest rates leads to a change in investment; a change in the foreign exchange rate leads to a change in exports. Autonomous expenditure is also influenced by the price level.

At a given price level, there is a given level of autonomous expenditure and a given level of aggregate expenditure. But if the price level changes, so does autonomous expenditure. Why? There are three main reasons, already explained fully in Chapter 24:

- Real balance effect
- Intertemporal substitution effect
- International substitution effect

A rise in the price level, other things held constant, decreases the real value of the money supply. The lower real money supply decreases aggregate planned expenditure — the *real balance effect.* The lower real money supply also brings higher interest rates and raises prices today relative to prices tomorrow. Both these changes lead to a decrease in consumption and investment — the *intertemporal substitution effect.* The higher price level, other things remaining the same, makes Australian-produced goods less competitive, increasing imports and decreasing exports — the *international substitution effect.*

All of these effects of a higher price level lower the level of aggregate expenditure at each level of real GDP. That is, they decrease autonomous expenditure and shift the aggregate expenditure curve downward. A decrease in the price level has the opposite effects to those described and shifts the aggregate expenditure curve upward.

Figure 26.10(a) illustrates these effects. When the price level is 100, the aggregate expenditure curve is AE_0, which intersects the 45° line at point *b.* Equilibrium expenditure and real GDP are $300 billion. If the price level increases to 125, the aggregate expenditure curve shifts downward to AE_1, which intersects the 45° line at point *a.* Equilibrium expenditure and real GDP are $200 billion. If the price level decreases to 75, the aggregate expenditure curve shifts upward to AE_2, which intersects the 45° line at point *c.* Equilibrium expenditure and real GDP are $400 billion.

When the price level changes, other things held constant, two things happen: there is a shift in the aggregate expenditure curve (that we've just examined) and a movement along the aggregate demand curve. Figure 26.10(b) illustrates these movements along the aggregate demand curve. At a price level of 100, the aggregate quantity of goods and services demanded is $300 billion — point *b* on the aggregate demand curve *AD.* If the price level increases to 125, the aggregate quantity of goods and services demanded falls to $200 billion. There is a movement along the aggregate demand curve to point *a.* If the price level decreases to 75, the aggregate quantity of goods and services demanded rises to $400 billion.

Figure 26.10 Aggregate Expenditure and Aggregate Demand

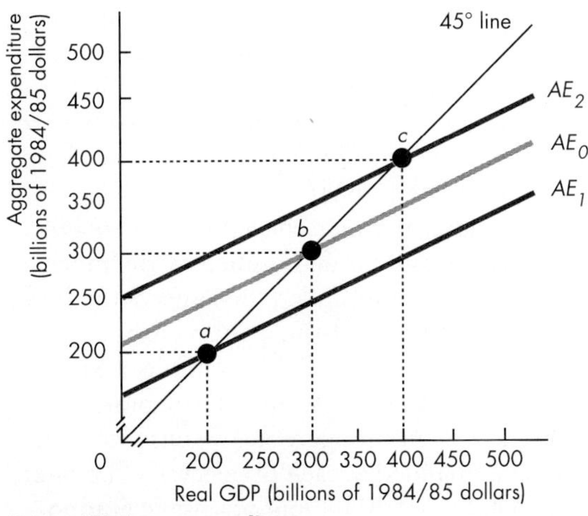

(a) Equilibrium expenditure

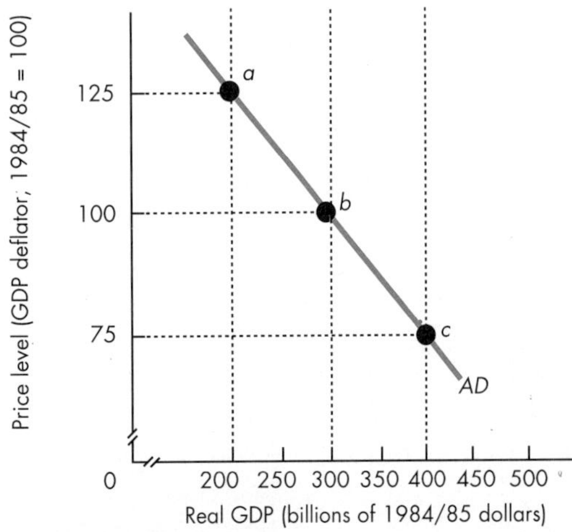

(b) Aggregate demand

The position of the aggregate expenditure curve depends on the price level. Suppose that when the price level is 100, the aggregate expenditure curve is AE_0, as shown in part (a). Equilibrium occurs where AE_0 intersects the 45° line at point *b*. The level of real GDP demanded is \$300 billion. In part (b) point *b* is a point on the aggregate demand curve (*AD*). At a price level of 100, the aggregate quantity of goods and services demanded is \$300 billion. Suppose that when the price level increases to 125, the aggregate expenditure curve shifts downward to AE_1. Equilibrium occurs at point *a* in part (a), where the aggregate quantity of goods and services demanded is \$200 billion. Thus, at a price level of 125 and an aggregate quantity of goods and services demanded of \$200 billion, point *a* is a point on the aggregate demand curve in part (b). If the price level falls to 75 and the *AE* curve shifts upward to AE_2, the equilibrium quantity of goods and services demanded occurs at point *c* where AE_2 intersects the 45° line. Point *c* in part (b) is another point on the aggregate demand curve. A change in the price level leads to a *shift* in the aggregate expenditure curve and to a movement *along* the aggregate demand curve.

There is a movement along the aggregate demand curve to point *c*.

At a given price level, equilibrium expenditure equals aggregate expenditure, which also equals the quantity of real GDP demanded. But the quantity of real GDP demanded at a given price level is a point on the aggregate demand curve. Thus for the expenditure equilibrium at each price level, there is a corresponding point on the aggregate demand curve. Changes in the price level *shift* the aggregate expenditure curve, changing the equilibrium level of aggregate expenditure and real GDP and produce movements *along* the aggregate demand curve.

Real GDP, the Price Level and the Multipliers

Now that we've seen the relationship between the aggregate demand curve and the equilibrium level of aggregate expenditure, let's work out what happens to aggregate demand, the price level and real GDP when there are changes in autonomous expenditure and fiscal policy. We'll start by looking at the effects on aggregate demand.

Aggregate Demand Curve and Autonomous Expenditure

We've just seen that the aggregate expenditure curve shifts when the price level changes. But it also shifts for a thousand other reasons. We studied some of these other sources of shifts in the aggregate expenditure curve earlier in this chapter — for example, a change in profit expectations that shifts the investment demand curve or a change in real GDP in Japan that increases that country's demand for Australian exports. Any factor other than the price level that shifts the aggregate expenditure curve also shifts the aggregate demand curve. Figure 26.11 illustrates these shifts.

Initially the aggregate expenditure curve is AE_0 in Fig. 26.11(a) and the aggregate demand curve is AD_0 in Fig. 26.11(b). The price level is 100. Now

Figure 26.11 Changes in Autonomous Expenditure and Aggregate Demand

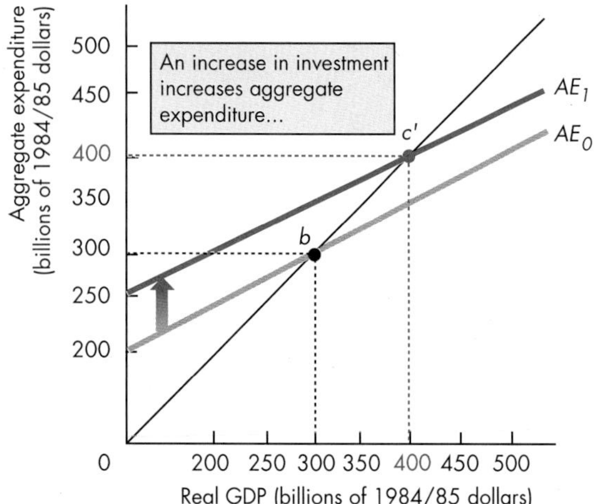

(a) Equilibrium expenditure

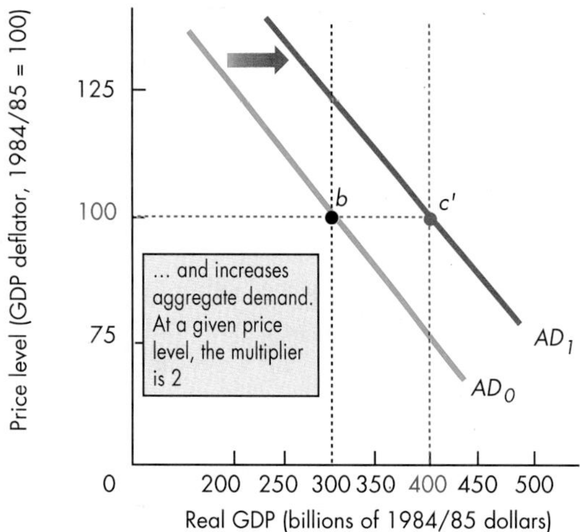

(b) Aggregate demand

The price level is 100. When the aggregate expenditure curve is AE_0 in part (a), the aggregate demand curve is AD_0 in part (b). An increase in autonomous expenditure shifts the aggregate expenditure upward to AE_1. The new equilibrium occurs where AE_1 intersects the 45° line at real GDP of $400 billion. The aggregate demand curve shifts to the right to AD_1. The magnitude of the shift to the right of the aggregate demand curve is determined by the change in autonomous expenditure and the size of the multiplier.

suppose that an increase in profit expectations leads to a rise in investment. Autonomous expenditure increases by $50 billion. If the price level remains at 100 the aggregate expenditure curve shifts upward to AE_1. This new, higher *AE* curve intersects the 45° line at an equilibrium expenditure of $400 billion. This amount is the aggregate quantity of goods and services demanded at a price level of 100, as shown by point *c′* in Fig. 26.11(b). Point *c′* lies on a new aggregate demand curve. The aggregate demand curve has shifted to the right to AD_1.

The distance by which the aggregate demand curve shifts to the right is determined by the multiplier. The larger the multiplier, the larger is the shift in the *AD* curve resulting from a given change in autonomous expenditure. In this example, a $1 billion increase in autonomous expenditure produces a $2 billion increase in the aggregate quantity of goods and services demanded at each price level. The multiplier is 2. That is, a $50 billion increase in autonomous expenditure shifts the aggregate demand curve to the right by $100 billion.

A decrease in autonomous expenditure shifts the *AE* curve downward and shifts the aggregate demand curve to the left. You can see this effect by supposing that the economy initially is on aggregate expenditure curve AE_1 and aggregate demand curve AD_1. There is then a decrease in autonomous expenditure and the aggregate expenditure curve falls to AE_0. The aggregate quantity of goods and services demanded falls to $300 billion and the aggregate demand curve shifts to the left to AD_0.

We can summarize what we have just discovered in the following way: an increase in autonomous expenditure arising from some source other than a change in the price level shifts the *AE* curve upward and shifts the *AD* curve to the right. The size of the shift of the *AD* curve is determined by the change in autonomous expenditure and the size of the multiplier.

Equilibrium GDP and the Price Level

In Chapter 24, we learned how to determine the equilibrium levels of real GDP and the price level as the intersection point of the aggregate demand curve and the short-run aggregate supply curve. We've now put aggregate demand under a more powerful microscope and discovered that changes in autonomous expenditure and fiscal policy shift the aggregate demand curve and that the magnitude of the shift depends on the size of the multiplier. But whether a change in autonomous expenditure results ultimately in a change in real GDP or a change in the price level or some combination of the two depends on aggregate supply.

Figure 26.12 Fiscal Policy with Unemployment

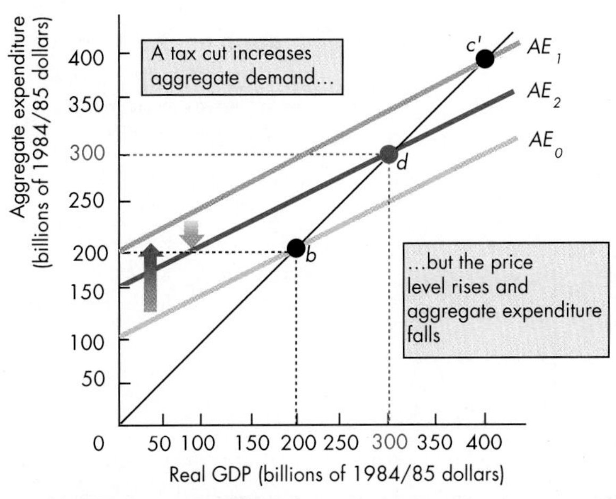

(a) Equilibrium expenditure

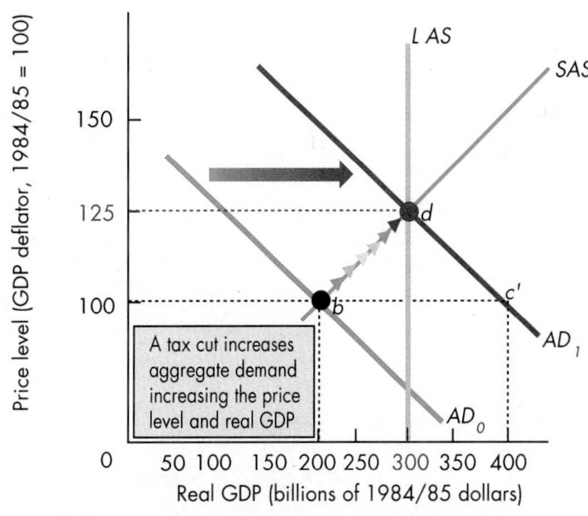

(b) Aggregate demand and aggregate supply

In part (a), the economy is initially in equilibrium with aggregate expenditure curve AE_0 intersecting the 45° line at point *b* where equilibrium expenditure and real GDP are both \$200 billion. In part (b) the aggregate demand curve is AD_0, the short-run aggregate supply curve is *SAS* and the equilibrium price level is 100. The economy is in an unemployment equilibrium.

A tax cut increases autonomous expenditure by \$100 billion. At the initial price level, the aggregate expenditure curve shifts upwards to AE_1 and equilibrium expenditure and real GDP increase to \$400 billion. With the higher level of autonomous expenditure, the aggregate demand curve shifts to the right to AD_1.

With the new aggregate demand curve, the price level rises to 125. At the higher price level, the aggregate expenditure curve shifts downward to AE_2. The new level of aggregate expenditure and real GDP is \$300 billion, the full-employment level. Fiscal policy has returned the economy to full employment.

We'll look at two cases. First we'll see what happens in the short run when the economy starts out in unemployment equilibrium. Then we'll look at a long-run full-employment situation.

An Increase in Aggregate Demand with Unemployment The economy is described in Fig. 26.12. In Fig. 26.12(a), the aggregate expenditure curve is AE_0, and equilibrium expenditure and real GDP are \$200 billion — point *b* on the 45° line. In Fig. 26.12(b), aggregate demand is AD_0, and the short-run aggregate supply curve is *SAS*. (Check back to Chapter 24 if you need to refresh your understanding of this curve.) Equilibrium is at point *b*, where the aggregate demand and short-run aggregate supply curves intersect. The price level is 100. The long-run aggregate supply curve is *LAS*. Since real GDP is \$200 billion, \$100 billion less than the full-employment level of real GDP, the economy is at an unemployment equilibrium.

Now suppose there is a tax cut that increases autonomous expenditure by \$100 billion. With the price level held constant at 100, the aggregate expenditure curve shifts upward to AE_1. Equilibrium expenditure and real GDP increase to \$400 billion — point *c′* on the 45° line. At constant prices and with a marginal propensity to spend of 0.5, the multiplier is 2 and the increase in aggregate expenditure is \$200 billion. In Fig. 26.12(b), the aggregate demand curve shifts to the right by \$200 billion — from AD_0 to AD_1. But with this new aggregate demand curve, the price level does not remain constant. It increases to 125, determined by the point of intersection, *d*, of the short-run aggregate supply curve (*SAS*) and the new aggregate demand curve (AD_1). And real GDP does not increase to \$400 billion, but to \$300 billion — the full-employment level.

At a price level of 125, the aggregate expenditure curve does not remain at AE_1. It shifts downward to AE_2, which intersects the 45° line at a level of aggregate expenditure and real GDP of \$300 billion.

As long as wages do not rise in response to the price increase, the short-run aggregate supply

Figure 26.13 An Increase in Aggregate Demand at Full-Employment

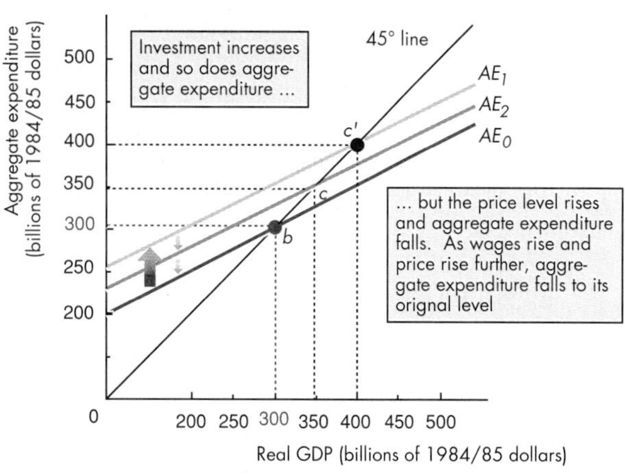

(a) Equilibrium expenditure

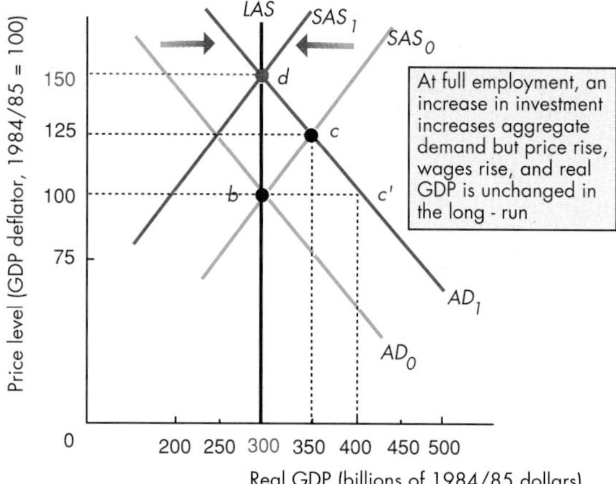

(b) Aggregate demand and aggregate supply

The economy begins at a full-employment equilibrium. In part (a), the aggregate expenditure curve is AE_0, with equilibrium expenditure and real GDP of $300 billion. In part (b), the aggregate demand curve is AD_0, short-run aggregate supply is SAS_0 and the price level is 100.

Suppose planned investment and exports increase by $50 billion. In part (a), the aggregate expenditure curve shifts upward to AE_1 and, in part (b), the aggregate demand curve shifts to the right to AD_1. At constant prices, equilibrium expenditure and real GDP increase to $400 billion. But, with wages constant, the price level rises to 125 and the aggregate expenditure curve shifts down to AE_2.

Since the economy is now at overfull employment, wages rise and the short-run aggregate supply curve shifts upward to SAS_1. Prices rise further. As prices continue to rise, the aggregate expenditure curve shifts back to its original position at AE_0. The final equilibrium occurs at the original level of equilibrium expenditure, but with a higher price level of 150.

curve will not shift upwards and the new equilibrium will remain at the full-employment level. In this instance, the tax cut has enabled the economy to expand and fully utilize unemployed labour.

Taking price level effects into account, the tax cut still has a multiplier effect on real GDP but the effect is smaller than it would be if the price level remained constant. In our example, the 'final' multiplier is 1. The steeper the slope of the short-run aggregate supply curve, the smaller is the multiplier effect on real GDP and the larger is the effect on the price level.

An Increase in Aggregate Demand at Full Employment Let's now see what happens when there is an increase in aggregate demand at full-employment. The economy is described in Fig. 26.13. In Fig. 26.13(a), the aggregate expenditure curve is AE_0, and equilibrium expenditure and real GDP are $300 billion — at point *b* on the 45° line. In Fig. 26.13(b), aggregate demand is AD_0, short-run aggregate supply is SAS_0 and the long-run aggregate supply curve is *LAS*.

Given the position of the long-run aggregate supply curve, $300 billion is the economy's full-employment level of real GDP. Now suppose that planned investment and exports increase, increasing autonomous expenditure by $50 billion. In Fig. 26.13(a), the aggregate expenditure curve shifts upward to AE_1 and in Fig 26.13(b), the aggregate demand curve shifts to the right to AD_1. At constant prices, aggregate expenditure and real GDP would have increased to $400 billion. But, as prices rise, the aggregate expenditure curve shifts down to AE_2. In the short-run, a new equilibrium will be achieved with real GDP at $350 billion. But this is at an over-full employment level of real GDP. The price level has risen from 100 to 125, and there is likely to be considerable pressure for wages to rise. At over-full employment, firms are scrambling to get enough workers to fulfil their production plans. As wages rise, the short-run aggregate supply curve shifts upward, to SAS_1. The price level rises further to 150 and real GDP falls back to the full-employment level.

The higher price level now lowers aggregate planned expenditure, and shifts the aggregate expenditure curve back to AE_0. The initial change in autonomous expenditure has been offset by a change in the opposite direction that is induced by the higher price level. With no change in autonomous expenditure, there is no shift of the aggregate expenditure curve and no change in the equilibrium quantity of goods and services demanded. The aggregate demand curve has shifted but there has also been a movement along the new aggregate demand curve, the combined effect of which is a higher price level and no change in real GDP. This result is not surprising if you think about the meaning of full-employment. If the economy is producing at its full-employment level when an increase in demand occurs, there is no capacity to increase real GDP, except in the short run. The long-run effect is a rise in prices with no change in real GDP. Only if the economy starts out with some slack can an increase in demand bring higher real GDP.

The two cases just examined indicate how a given increase in aggregate expenditure is allocated between increasing real GDP and increasing prices. When there are unemployed resources in the economy, beginning from an unemployment equilibrium, the increase in aggregate expenditure will induce an increase in real GDP, absorbing the unemployed workers, and the rise in prices will be mitigated. But when the economy begins with no unemployed resources, from a full-employment equilibrium, any gains in real GDP are temporary and prices must rise by enough to shift the aggregate expenditure curve back to its original position.

■ We have now studied the forces that influence the components of aggregate expenditure and have analysed the way the components interact with each other to determine aggregate expenditure and the position of the aggregate demand curve. Fluctuations in the aggregate expenditure curve and in the aggregate demand curve are caused by fluctuations in autonomous expenditure. An important element of autonomous expenditure is planned investment which, in turn, is determined by, among other things, the level of interest rates. But how are interest rates determined? That is the question to which we turn in the next chapter.

SUMMARY

Autonomous Expenditure Multipliers

An increase in autonomous expenditure increases aggregate expenditure and shifts the aggregate expenditure curve upward. Equilibrium expenditure and real GDP increase by more than the increase in autonomous expenditure. They do so because the increased autonomous expenditure induces an increase in consumption expenditure, and aggregate expenditure increases by the sum of the initial increase in autonomous expenditure and the increase in induced expenditure.

An increase in saving shifts the aggregate expenditure curve downward and decreases real GDP — the paradox of thrift. The paradox arises because the increase in saving does not automatically bring about an increase in investment. If investment and saving increased together, the aggregate expenditure curve would not shift and income would not fall. In the long run, additional saving enables more capital to be accumulated and makes incomes grow more quickly.

The autonomous expenditure multiplier (or simply multiplier) is the change in equilibrium real GDP divided by the change in autonomous expenditure that brought it about. The size of the multiplier, k, depends on the marginal propensity to spend, ε, and its value is given by the formula

$$k = \frac{1}{(1 - \varepsilon)}$$

Because the marginal propensity to spend is a number between 0 and 1, the multiplier, $1/(1 - \varepsilon)$, is greater than 1. The larger the marginal propensity to spend, the larger is the multiplier. The multiplier is greater than 1 because of induced expenditure — because an increase in autonomous expenditure induces an increase in consumption expenditure. (pp. 210–216)

Fiscal Policy Multipliers

There are three main fiscal policy multipliers:

- Government purchases multiplier
- Transfer payments multiplier
- Autonomous tax multiplier

The government purchases multiplier is the amount by which a change in government purchases of goods and services is multiplied to determine the change in equilibrium expenditure that it generates. Because government purchases of goods and services are one of the components of autonomous expenditure, this multiplier is equal to the autonomous expenditure multiplier. That is

$$\text{Government purchases multiplier} = \frac{1}{(1-\varepsilon)}$$

The transfer payments multiplier is the amount by which a change in transfer payments is multiplied to determine the change in equilibrium expenditure that it generates. Because a change in transfer payments influences aggregate expenditure by changing disposable income, this multiplier is equal to the marginal propensity to consume, c, times the autonomous expenditure multiplier. That is

$$\text{Transfer payments multiplier} = \frac{c}{(1-\varepsilon)}$$

The autonomous tax multiplier is the amount by which a change in autonomous taxes is multiplied to determine the change in equilibrium expenditure that it generates. A tax increase brings a decrease in equilibrium expenditure. The initial response of consumption expenditure to a tax increase is exactly the same as its response to a transfer payment decrease. Thus a tax change works like a change in transfer payments but its multiplier is negative. That is

$$\text{Autonomous tax multiplier} = -\frac{c}{(1-\varepsilon)}$$

If both government purchases of goods and services and taxes are changed together, and by the same amount, there is a balanced budget multiplier that combines the two separate multipliers. That is

$$\text{Balanced budget multiplier} = \frac{(1-c)}{(1-\varepsilon)}$$

Because the marginal propensity to consume, c, is bigger than the marginal propensity to spend, ε, the balanced budget multiplier is less than one.

The tax and transfer payments system acts as an automatic stabilizer — a mechanism that decreases the fluctuations in aggregate expenditure. In an economy with no induced taxes and transfer payments (and ignoring imports), the marginal propensity to spend is equal to the marginal propensity to consume, c, and the multiplier is:

$$k = \frac{1}{(1-c)}$$

This multiplier is much larger than the multiplier for an economy with taxes and transfer payments that vary with real GDP. In the latter case, the multiplier formula looks like the one above but c (the marginal propensity to consume) replaces ε (the marginal propensity to spend).

A change in the marginal tax rate changes equilibrium expenditure and real GDP. It does so by changing the marginal propensity to consume out of real GDP and changing the marginal propensity to spend. (pp. 216–224)

The Multiplier in Australia

The multiplier in the Australia is close to 1.6. But it fluctuates over the business cycle, rising in a recovery and falling in a recession. Some of the fluctuations in the multiplier are the result of consumption smoothing. The value of the multiplier has fallen, over time, because the marginal propensity to import has increased. (pp. 224–226)

Aggregate Expenditure and Aggregate Demand

The aggregate demand curve is the relationship between the aggregate quantity of goods and services demanded and the price level, other things held constant. A change in the price level brings a movement along the aggregate demand curve. The aggregate expenditure curve is the relationship between aggregate expenditure and real GDP, other things held constant. At a given price level and given level of real GDP, there is a given aggregate expenditure. A change in real GDP, at a given price level, changes aggregate expenditure and brings a movement along the aggregate expenditure curve. A change in the price level changes autonomous expenditure and shifts the aggregate expenditure curve. Thus a movement along the aggregate demand curve is associated with a shift in the aggregate expenditure curve. (pp. 226–227)

Real GDP, the Price Level and the Multipliers

A change in autonomous expenditure not caused by a change in the price level shifts the aggregate expenditure curve and also shifts the aggregate demand curve. The magnitude of the shift in the aggregate demand curve depends on the size of the multiplier and on the change in autonomous expenditure.

Real GDP and the price level are determined by both aggregate demand and aggregate supply. If an increase in aggregate demand occurs at an unemployment equilibrium, where the short-run aggregate supply curve is upward sloping, there is an increase in both the price level and real GDP. But the increase in real GDP is smaller than the increase in aggregate demand. The steeper the short-run aggregate supply curve, the larger is the change in the price level and the smaller is the change in real GDP.

If an increase in aggregate demand occurs at full employment, its long-run effect is entirely on the price level. Real GDP is unaffected. (pp. 227–231)

KEY TERMS

Automatic stabilizer, p. 218
Autonomous expenditure multiplier (or multiplier), p. 212
Autonomous tax multiplier, p. 217
Autonomous taxes, p. 217
Balanced budget multiplier, p. 218
Consumption smoothing, p. 226
Countercyclical, p. 225
Fiscal policy, p. 216
Government purchases multiplier, p. 216
Induced taxes, p. 217
Marginal tax rate, p. 219
Paradox of thrift, p. 212
Transfer payments multiplier, p. 216

PROBLEMS

1 You are given the following information about a hypothetical economy. The autonomous part of consumption is $100 million. The marginal propensity to consume out of disposable income is 0.8. Investment is $460 million; government expenditure on goods and services is $400 million; taxes are a constant $400 million and do not vary as income varies.
   a) Calculate the equilibrium levels of GDP and consumption.
   b) If government expenditure is cut to $300 million, what is the change in GDP and the change in consumption?
   c) What is the size of the multiplier?

2 Suppose that the tax laws are changed and instead of taxes being a constant $400 million they become one-eighth of GDP. Nothing else in problem 1 is changed.
   a) Calculate the equilibrium levels of GDP and consumption.
   b) If government expenditure is cut to $300 million, what is the change in GDP and the change in consumption?
   c) What is the size of the multiplier?

3 Suppose that the economy described in problem 1 has an absolute limit to its output of $3200 million. At that output level its aggregate supply curve is vertical.
   a) If the government increases its purchases of goods and services, what happens to the economy's aggregate demand curve and aggregate expenditure curve?
   b) What happens to the price level?

4 You are given the following information about the multiplier in an economy. Its average value is 2; in year A it is $\frac{1}{2}$ and in year B it is $3\frac{1}{2}$.
   a) Make an educated guess about the state of this economy in year A and year B.
   b) Was year A a recovery year or a recession year? Why?
   c) Was year B a recovery year or a recession year? Why?

Part 10

Money, Interest and the Dollar

Talking with Sir Leslie Melville

Sir Leslie Melville is one of the founders of economics as a profession in Australia. In 1929, he was appointed the first Professor of Economics at the University of Adelaide and since then has held a series of senior appointments in Australia. Christopher Findlay talked to Sir Leslie about his career.

What was it like being appointed to a foundation chair of economics at the time of the Great Depression?

It was an extremely busy time. There were very few economists in Australia. I was the only one working in South Australia. So I was involved in many meetings and conferences with other Australian economists like Copland and Giblin to discuss the policy options.

How did you become interested in economics?

I was studying science at Sydney University when I was persuaded that my career prospects would be brighter as an actuary. I switched courses and rather than finish my science degree, I took some economics subjects. Then I got a job as the Public Actuary of South Australia, and worked as well as an economics adviser to the State government.

Were there many debates among Australian economists about remedies for the Depression?

At this time there was little difference among economists in Australia. Copland and Giblin were willing to take more chances with public works expenditure than Shann or I were. But they did not feel very strongly about it. Later, during the 1930s, as young Keynesians began coming back from England the public works debate became stronger.

'public works had to be financed by the bank'

Why weren't you so keen on public works spending being used to give a stimulus to economy activity?

Wouldn't this have helped cut unemployment?

It might have, but only for a while. The main job, really, was to balance the budget and the overseas balance of payments. In those days, any increase in public works had to be financed by the banks and by an increase in the money supply. The United Kingdom was our only source of overseas funds; the United Kingdom wouldn't lend us a penny. We could have tried to increase spending but that would have meant increased pressure on our balance of payments and an unacceptable risk of defaulting on our loans. I thought the consequences of a default would create hysteria and be very bad for our long-run borrowing power.

Could the authorities have done better at managing the policy response to the Depression?

Yes, I think they could have. In 1932, it was recommended that the UK pound should be further devalued. Nominal wages could not be reduced but we thought a devaluation might reduce the spending power of wages and fixed incomes. If the devaluation succeeded in strengthening the balance of payments we would have recommended some increase in expenditure on public works. Without the depreciation, we thought an increase in public works expenditure financed in the only way possible at the time — by increasing the quantity of money — was too hazardous. We had, a short time earlier, stopped a flight of capital by drastic economies and we did not want a recurrence of that, with the potential for default on overseas loans.

Ironically, Keynes, when consulted, opposed our recommendation to devalue and suggested instead an increase in public works expenditure. This influenced the government to reject our recommendation of devaluation. But there was no possibility that the central bank would agree to use central bank credit to finance public works. So we fell between two stools.

'Ironically, Keynes, when consulted, opposed our recommendation to devalue'

In 1931, you started work at the Commonwealth Bank. What was that like?

At that time, the Commonwealth Bank was both a trading bank as well as playing the role of a central bank.

For example, it controlled the issue of notes in Australia. It had other powers as well. Later on, the other trading banks complained that it was not appropriate for the regulator of the banking system to be a trader as well. So in 1959, the Reserve Bank was created. This pleased the Commonwealth Bank people because then they could trade much more vigorously. Previously, they had been restrained to avoid criticism that they might be abusing their position as regulator.

You continued to be involved with the Reserve Bank, later as a Board member, but you also worked with the International Monetary Fund in Washington in the early 1950s. What was the big issue then?

The big issue was tariffs and non-tariff restraints to trade. Commonwealth countries had created the 'sterling area', that is, a system of higher restrictions on imports from countries outside the area. This led to a big argument between the United States and the United Kingdom. Indeed, I earned some bad marks by writing a paper arguing against the sterling area.

Your interest in a liberal trade policy continued into the 1960s when, after a term as Vice Chancellor of the Australian National University, you served as Chairman of the Tariff Board.

Yes, I did, but not for long. I resigned after two years. The Minister then was McEwen. He tried to bully the Board into higher protection. His position was that anybody who needed higher protection should get it. I didn't agree with that and so I resigned. I hope my resignation prompted greater academic interest in protection, like that shown by Max Corden.

'everyone should be able to pay the same taxes and get the same quality of service'

Another important official position you held, at the end of the 1960s, was Chairman of the Grants Commission.

The problem there was the payment of special grants to the smaller States. They lacked taxing power and their size raised the cost of providing services. The objective of the Grants Commission was that everyone should be able to pay the same taxes and get the same quality of service, wherever they were in Australia, as they would under a single government. That meant our job was to work out a formula for making transfers to the smaller States. And that still happens.

'the market is a poor judge of the correct rate of exchange'

Some economists argue that the determination of exchange rates should be left to the market. What do you think?

I disagree. Our experience of floating exchange rates suggests to me that the market is a poor judge of the correct rate of exchange. The correct rate depends on fundamental characteristics of the economy. It does not vary greatly from day to day, even year to year. But the market rates have been extra-ordinarily volatile. That volatility makes trade very difficult. It inhibits trade.

What's the solution?

Well, I would like to see a return to a Bretton Woods type of agreement, where countries agree to a stable set of exchange rates. You might argue

that the original Bretton Woods system collapsed by the end of the 1970s, but that was because the major industrial countries failed to complement the agreement on exchange rates with another to adopt fiscal and monetary policies compatible with those exchange rates. I was at the Bretton Woods meeting in 1944. The need for compatible macroeconomic policies was implicit in the agreement but we should have spelt it out explicitly.

The world economy may not now be able to return to such a tight system as the original Bretton Woods agreement. But at least we should decide on the desirability of some degree of exchange rate stability and ask the large industrial countries to undertake a greater degree of coordination of macroeconomic policy to achieve it.

You've held an extraordinary range of important jobs in your career.

Yes, and I think I was very fortunate. Economics as a profession in Australia really only dates from the 1930s. When I started work, as I said, I was the only economist in South Australia and I doubt there were any economists working in the Commonwealth Treasury at that time. So I had a lot of opportunities. But I did try to keep up a specialization in issues to do with money and banking.

Chapter 27

Money, Banking and Prices

After studying this chapter, you will be able to:

- Define money and describe its different forms.
- Describe the balance sheets of the main financial intermediaries.
- Explain the economic functions of banks and other financial intermediaries.
- Explain how banks create money.
- Explain why the quantity of money is an important economic magnitude.
- Explain the quantity theory of money.
- Describe the historical and international evidence on the relationship between the quantity of money and the price level.

Money Makes the World Go Around

Money, like fire and the wheel, has been around for a very long time. No one knows for sure how long or what its origins are. An incredible array of items has served as money — wampum (beads made from shells) were used by North American Indians; muskrat pelts were used in Upper Canada in the eighteenth and early nineteenth centuries; cowries (brightly coloured shells) were used extensively in India, China, Thailand, and parts of Africa; whales' teeth were used in Fiji; tobacco was used by early American colonists; large stone disks were used in the Pacific island of Yap; rum was a part, and sometimes all, of the wages paid to a sizeable section of the population in early colonial Australia; cigarettes and liquor have been used in more modern times; and even cakes of salt have served as money in Ethiopia, Africa, and Tibet. The Roman army was paid in salt — an allowance called 'salarium' (which is the origin of the word 'salary'). What exactly is money? Why has this rich variety of commodities served as money? Today, when we want to buy something, we can use coins or notes, or we can write a cheque or present a credit card. Are all these things money? When we deposit some coloured paper into a bank or building society, is that still money? And what happens when the bank or the building society lends the money in our deposit account to someone else? How can we get our money back if it's been lent out? Does lending by banks and building societies create money — out of thin air? The 1980s have seen dramatic changes in the types of accounts that banks and other financial institutions have been offering us, and also in the number and type of financial institutions. In the 1970s, we either had a savings account or a demand deposit (cheque account). The savings account earned interest and the cheque account didn't. Today, there are a wide variety of new types of accounts that provide us with the convenience of a cheque account and the income of a savings account. Why have these new kinds of bank accounts been developed? In the early 1980s, all financial institutions were domestically owned. By the end of the 1980s a number of foreign banks operated in Australia. What was the impact of this development? The biggest transaction that most people ever undertake is the purchase of a house. Few of us are wealthy enough to buy a house with our own funds. Instead, we have to borrow. The main source of funds to buy a house is the financial intermediary industry. Financial intermediaries obtain their funds from thousands of depositors, many of whom can withdraw their deposit at a moment's notice. But these institutions lend money on a very long-term basis — sometimes for as long as 30 years. When a financial intermediary is committed to long-term loans at a low interest rate and interest rates on deposits increase, these institutions get into trouble. Such was the situation in Australia in 1990 when some building societies found themselves in a desperate situation. In one instance, the Victorian government felt compelled to bail out the depositors of a faltering building society. Before the bail out, many feared that these institutions as a group were unsound. If building societies or banks collapse, does that mean that their depositors' money disappears with them? Q At certain times in our history, the quantity of money in existence has increased quickly. In other countries — such as China in the late 1940s, Israel in the early 1980s and some Latin American countries today — the quantity of money increased at an extremely rapid pace. Does the rate of increase in the quantity of money matter? What are the effects of an increasing quantity of money on our economy?

In this chapter, we'll study that useful invention, money. We'll look at the functions of money, the different forms that money takes, and the way money is defined and measured in Australia today. We'll also study banks and other financial institutions and learn how banks create money. Finally, we'll discover an important connection between the growth rate of the amount of money in the economy and the pace at which prices rise — the inflation rate. Whether we look at our own historical experience or at the contemporary experience of the major countries of the world, we see a clear and strong connection between the growth rate of the quantity of money and the inflation rate.

What is Money?

Let's begin by defining money.

The Definition of Money

Money is a medium of exchange. A **medium of exchange** is anything that is generally acceptable in exchange for goods and services. Without a medium of exchange, it would be necessary to exchange goods directly for other goods — an exchange known as barter. **Barter** is the direct exchange of goods for goods. For example, if you wanted to buy a hamburger, you could offer the used paperback novel that you've just finished reading or half an hour of your labour in the kitchen, in exchange for it. But barter can take place only when there is a double coincidence of wants. A **double coincidence of wants** is a situation that occurs when person A wants to buy what person B is selling, and person B wants to buy what person A is selling. That is, to get your hamburger, you'd have to find someone who's selling hamburgers and who wants a paperback novel or your work in the kitchen. The occurrence of a double coincidence of wants is sufficiently rare that barter exchange would leave most potential gains from specialization and exchange unrealized. The evolution of monetary exchange is a consequence of our economizing activity — of getting the most possible out of limited resources. We're going to study the institutions of monetary exchange that have evolved in the Australian economy. But first, we'll look at the functions of money.

The Functions of Money

Money has four functions. It serves as a

- Medium of exchange
- Unit of account
- Standard of deferred payment
- Store of value

Medium of Exchange Any commodity or asset that serves as a generally acceptable medium of exchange is money. Money guarantees that there will always be a double coincidence of wants. People with something to sell will always accept money in exchange for it, and people who want to buy will always offer money in exchange. Money acts as a lubricant that smooths the mechanism of exchange.

Unit of Account The **unit of account** is an agreed measure for stating the prices of goods and services. To get the most out of your budget you have to figure out, among other things, whether seeing one more film is worth the price you have to pay, not in dollars and cents, but in terms of the number of ice creams, sandwiches and coffees that you have to give up. It's not hard to do such calculations when all these goods have prices in terms of dollars and cents (see Table 27.1). If a film costs $6 and a sandwich costs $3, you know right away that seeing one more film costs you 2 sandwiches. If jelly beans are 50 cents a pack, one more film costs 12 packs of jelly beans. You need only one calculation to figure out the opportunity cost of any pair of goods and services.

But imagine how troublesome it would be if your local cinema posted its price as 2 sandwiches; and if the store posted the price of a sandwich as 2 ice-cream cones; and if the ice-cream shop posted the price of a cone as 3 packs of jelly beans; and if the lolly shop priced jelly beans as 2 cups of coffee! Now how much running around and calculating do you have to do to figure out how much a film is going to cost you in terms of the sandwich, ice cream, jelly beans or coffee that you must give up to see it? You get the answer for sandwiches right away from the sign posted on the cinema, but for all the other goods you're going to have to visit many different stores to establish the price of each commodity in terms of another and calculate prices in units that are relevant for your own decision. Cover up the column labelled 'Prices in money units' in Table 27.1 and see how hard it is to figure out the number of local phone calls it costs to see one film. It's enough to make a person give up films! How much simpler it is for everyone to express their prices in terms of dollars and cents.

Table 27.1 The Unit of Account Function of Money Simplifies Price Comparisons

Good	Price in money units	Price in units of another good
Film	$6.00 each	2 sandwiches
Sandwiches	$3.00 each	2 ice-cream cones
Ice cream	$1.50 per cone	3 packs of jelly beans
Jelly beans	$0.50 per pack	2 cups of coffee
Coffee	$0.25 a cup	1 local phone call

Money as a unit of account

One film costs $6 and coffee costs 25 cents, so one film costs 24 cups of coffee ($6.00/$0.25 = 24).

No unit of account

You go to a cinema and learn that the price of a film is 2 sandwiches. You go to a lolly shop and learn that a pack of jelly beans costs 2 cups of coffee. But how many cups of coffee does seeing a film cost you? To answer that question, you go to the convenience store and find that a sandwich costs 2 ice-cream cones. Now you head for the ice-cream store where an ice cream costs 3 packs of jelly beans. Now you get out your pocket calculator: 1 film costs 2 sandwiches or 4 ice-cream cones or 12 packs of jelly beans or 24 cups of coffee!

Standard of Deferred Payment A **standard of deferred payment** is an agreed measure that enables contracts to be written for future receipts and payments. If you borrow money to buy a house or if you save money to provide for retirement, your future commitment or future receipt will be agreed to in dollars and cents. Money is used as the standard for a deferred payment. Imagine the complexity of a world in which we did not use money as a standard of deferred payment. Instead of guaranteeing to repay your home loan in money, you and the lender must agree on a standard. You might agree to repay your loan in an agreed quantity of grade A beef. Both you and the lender will now bear a risk arising from uncertainty about the future price of beef. If beef rises in price relative to other goods, you will have struck a bad deal and the lender will have gained. If the price of beef falls relative to other goods, you will have gained and the lender will have lost. Since the prices of individual commodities fluctuate a great deal and cannot be predicted accurately, at least not a long way ahead, both borrowers and lenders would face much more risk than if money was used as the standard of deferred payment.

Using money as a standard of deferred payment is not entirely without risk for, as we saw in Chapter 22, inflation leads to unpredictable changes in the value of money. But, to the extent that borrowers and lenders anticipate inflation, its rate is reflected in the interest rates paid and received. Lenders, in effect, protect themselves by charging a higher interest rate and borrowers, anticipating inflation, willingly pay the higher rate.

Store of Value A **store of value** is any commodity that can be held and exchanged later for some other commodity or service. Most physical objects are stores of value. All financial assets, paper securities such as treasury bonds, and bank accounts are also stores of value. Services are not stores of value. Once a service has been performed, that is the end of the matter.

There are no stores of value that are completely safe and predictable. The value of a physical object, such as a house, a car or a work of art, as well as the value of a paper security and even of money itself, fluctuates over time. The more stable and the more predictable the value of a commodity, the better it can act as a store of value. Thus the higher and the more unpredictable the rate of inflation, the less useful is money as a store of value. It is essential that money be a store of value. Otherwise, it would not be acceptable as a medium of exchange.

Assets other than money provide some of the functions just discussed. For example, money is not the only store of value. But what makes money unique is that it is the only asset that provides all four functions — in particular, the medium of exchange function.

Different Forms of Money

Money can take four different forms:

- Commodity money
- Convertible paper money
- Fiat money
- Private debt money

Commodity Money **Commodity money** is a physical commodity that is valued in its own right and also used as a medium of exchange. An amazing array of items has served as commodity money at different times and places, several of which were described in the chapter opener. But the most common commodity monies have been coins made from metals such as gold, silver and copper. The first known coins were made in Lydia, a Greek city–state, at the beginning of the seventh century BC. These coins were made of electrum, a natural mixture of gold and silver.

Commodity money, mainly in the form of coin, sometimes in the form of rum, wheat or other produce, was the earliest money used in colonial Australia. Silver Spanish dollars, or 'pieces of eight' worth 5 shillings were used when available. Because there was a constant shortage of coin, in 1813, Governor Macquarie decided that a small hole should be cut in the centre of each Spanish dollar. The outer ring was still valued at 5 shillings. and the centre, or 'dump', valued of 1 shilling and 3 pennies. This improvisation had two effects. First, the quantity of money in circulation increased. Second, because the holey dollar, as the outer ring became known, was overvalued (it still exchanged for 5 shillings although it contained less silver), the tendency for it to be hoarded or exported was eliminated. Holey dollars were officially withdrawn from circulation in 1829.

Commodity money has considerable advantages but some drawbacks. Let's look at these.

Advantages of Commodity Money The main advantage of commodity money is that the commodity is valued for its own sake and can be used in ways other than as a medium of exchange. This fact provides a guarantee of the value of the money. For example, gold may be used to fill teeth and make rings; silver may be used to make tableware; cigarettes may be smoked; beads may be worn. The commodities that are most advantageous as money are the semi-precious metals such as gold and silver. Historically, these commodities were ideal because they were in constant demand by those wealthy enough to use them for ornaments and jewellery. Their quality was easily verified and they were easily divisible into units small enough to facilitate exchange.

Disadvantages of Commodity Money Commodity money has two main disadvantages. First, there is a constant temptation to cheat on the value of the money. Two methods of cheating have been commonly used — clipping and debasement. *Clipping* is reducing the size of coins, usually by an imperceptible amount, thereby lowering their metallic content. Governor Macquarie clipped, by a percepitble amount, the Spanish dollar. *Debasement* is creating a coin with a lower silver or gold content (the balance being made up of some cheaper metal).

This temptation to lower the value of money led to a phenomenon known as Gresham's Law, after the sixteenth-century English financial expert Sir Thomas Gresham. **Gresham's Law** is the tendency for bad money to drive out good money. Bad money is debased money; good money is money that has not been debased. It's easy to see why Gresham's Law works. Suppose that a person is paid with two coins, one debased and the other not. Each coin has the same value if used as money in exchange for goods. But one of the coins — the one that's not debased — is more valuable as a commodity than it is as a coin. It will not, therefore, be used as money. Only the debased coin will be used as money. It is in this way that bad money drives good money out of circulation.

A second major disadvantage of commodity money is that the commodity, valued for its own sake, could be used in ways other than as a medium of exchange if it was not being used as money — the commodity used has an opportunity cost. This cost creates incentives to find alternatives to the commodity itself for use in the exchange process. One such alternative is a paper claim to commodity money.

Convertible Paper Money Convertible paper money is a paper claim to a commodity that circulates as a medium of exchange. The first known example of paper money occurred in China during the Ming dynasty (AD 1368–1399). This form of money was also used extensively throughout Europe in the Middle Ages.

It was the inventiveness of goldsmiths and their clients that led to the increase and widespread use of convertible paper money. Because gold was valuable, goldsmiths had well guarded safes in which to keep their own gold. They also rented space to artisans and others who wanted to put their gold in safekeeping. The goldsmiths issued a receipt entitling the owner of the gold to reclaim their 'deposit' on demand. These receipts were much like the baggage check that you get when you travel by air.

Suppose that Isabella has a gold receipt indicating that she has 100 ounces of gold deposited with Samuel Goldsmith. She is going to buy a piece of land valued at 100 ounces of gold from Henry. There are two ways that Isabella might undertake the transaction. The first way is to go to Samuel, hand over her receipt and collect her gold, transport the gold to Henry and take title to the land. Henry now goes back to Samuel with the gold and deposits it there for safekeeping, leaving with his own receipt. The second way of doing this transaction is for Isabella simply to hand over her gold receipt to Henry, completing the transaction by using the gold receipt as money. Obviously, it is much more convenient to complete the transaction in the second way, provided Henry can trust Samuel. The gold receipt circulating as a medium of exchange is money. The paper money is *backed* by the gold held by Goldsmith. Also the paper money is *convertible* into commodity money.

Fractional Backing Once the convertible paper money system is operating and people are using their gold receipts rather than gold itself as the medium of exchange, goldsmiths notice that their vaults are storing a large amount of gold that is never withdrawn. This gives them a brilliant idea. Why not lend people gold receipts? The goldsmith can charge interest on the loan and the loan is created just by writing on a piece of paper. As long as the number of such receipts created is not too large in relation to the stock of gold in the goldsmith's safe, the goldsmith is in no danger of not being able to honour his promise to convert receipts into gold on demand. By this device, *fractionally-backed* convertible paper money was invented.

Fractional Backing in Australia There are important examples of fractionally backed convertible paper money in Australia's early colonial history.[1] The shortage of coin stimulated the creation of other forms of money and, by 1810, private promissory notes were circulating widely. These notes were convertible into 'sterling', which meant any form of money roughly equal in value and acceptability to bills drawn on the British Treasury. Sometimes they were convertible into 'currency', which meant forms of money with purely local acceptability, normally trading at a substantial discount in terms of sterling. At first these notes were issued by private citizens in the course of normal trade: usually an IOU in payment for goods received. Because they were so widely accepted, storekeepers began to make banking a part of their business by issuing notes that were not for specific payments. Governor Macquarie dubbed this practice 'petty banking' and noted that it created many opportunities for fraud. Various legal restrictions were imposed, from 1810 to 1817, in a largely unsuccessful attempt to curtail the practice of petty banking. Finally, in 1817 and with dubious legality, Macquarie chartered the first Australian bank, the Bank of New South Wales, in the hope that it would bring order to the monetary system.

The potential for the issuance of fractionally-backed notes was established with the Bank of New South Wales. It began by slowly issuing its own notes in denominations of 2s 6d, 5s, 10s, £1 and £5 (in pre-decimal currency) At first, note issue was slow because of competition from promissory notes in circulation. When a run on the Bank began, in 1820, there was only £5902 in outstanding notes backed by £6531 in coin, £16,111 in bills on the British Treasury and £11,369 in Commissariat Store receipts. By 1826 this position had changed and the Bank was in a precarious position because of competition from newly established banks issuing their own notes.

Until the establishment of the Commercial Banking Company of Sydney, in 1848, every colonial bank was, in law, a partnership, so that the share-

[1]For a lengthy but entertaining history of the early Australian monetary system, see S.J. Butlin, *Foundations of the Australian Monetary System*, Sydney University Press, 1953.

holders were subject to unlimited liability. (Royal charters granted by the British crown were valuable because they limited liability.) Because of the risks, all the banks held large reserves of cash. At this time, the proper ratio was generally agreed to be one-third cash to the sum of notes on issue plus deposits, high by today's standards.

In 1840, the British Treasury attempted to regulate the colonial banks by issuing the Colonial Banks Regulations. These regulations permitted note issue only up to the amount of paid-up capital in each bank. Effectively, this law eliminated fractional backing in Australia. Gradually, the restrictions were eased and, by 1856, banks could issue their own notes in an amount up to three times its specie (coin) and bullion (gold and silver) holdings.

The regulations remained unchanged until 1910. This period, from the mid-1800s to the early 1900s, was known as an era of 'free banking'.

Fiat Money **Fiat money** is an intrinsically worthless (or almost worthless) commodity that serves the functions of money. The term 'fiat' means by government order. Some of the earliest fiat monies were the continental currency issued during the American Revolution and the 'greenbacks' issued during the American Civil War. Greenbacks circulated until the restoration of the gold standard in 1879. Another early issue of fiat money was that of the so-called 'assignats' issued during the French Revolution. These early experiments with fiat money ended in rapid inflation because the amount of fiat money created was allowed to increase at a rapid pace, causing the money to lose value.

However, provided the quantity of fiat money is not allowed to grow too rapidly, it has a reasonably steady value in terms of the goods and services that it will buy. People are willing to accept fiat money in exchange for the goods and services they sell only because they know it will be honoured when they go to buy goods and services.

Fiat Money in Australia The bills and coins that we use in Australia today — collectively known as **currency** — are examples of fiat money. Because of the creation of fiat money, people are willing to accept a piece of paper with a special watermark, printed in coloured ink, and worth not more than a few cents as a commodity, in exchange for $100 worth of goods and services. The small metal alloy disk that we call a 50 cent piece is worth almost nothing as a piece of metal, but it pays for a local phone call and many other small commodities. The replacement of commodity money by fiat money enables the commodities themselves to be used productively while the tokens that we use as fiat money do not have a significant opportunity cost.

Fiat money in Australia had its origins in the *Australian Notes Act 1910*. Up to that time, all private banks issued their own notes. Effectively, the Note Act imposed a prohibitive tax on private note issue and Australian note issue became a function of the Australian Treasury. The first Australian notes were introduced in 1911.

In 1912, the Commonwealth Bank was established, mainly to create a national savings banking system that would compete with the private sector. It did take on some of the roles of a central bank — acting as banker to the government, for example. In 1920, responsibility for note issue was transferred to the Notes Board, whose chairman was also the Governor of the Commonwealth Bank. Then, in 1924, amendments to the Act establishing the Commonwealth Bank transferred to it full central banking power, along with responsibility for note issue. These notes were backed by nothing other than government debts held by the Commonwealth Bank, together with its holdings of gold and foreign exchange.

Private Debt Money In the modern world, there is a fourth important type of money — private debt money. **Private debt money** is a loan that the borrower promises to repay in currency on demand. By transferring the entitlement to be repaid from one person to another, such a loan can be used as money. For example, you give me an IOU for $10; I give the IOU to a bookseller to buy a biography of Adam Smith; you pay the holder of the IOU $10 — only now it's the bookseller holding the IOU.

The most important example of private debt money is the cheque account at a bank or other financial institution. A **cheque account** is a loan by a depositor to a bank, the ownership of which can be transferred from one person to another by writing an instruction to the bank — a cheque — asking the bank to alter its records. We'll have more to say about this type of money shortly. Before doing so, let's look at the different forms of money and their relative importance in Australia today.

Money in Australia Today

There are a number of measures of money in official use: **M0** (base money), **M1**, **M3** and **broad money**, which are defined in Table 27.2. Additionally, broad credit aggregates — lending by banks and credit by all financial institutions — are monitored. The most widely reported monetary aggregates are now M3 and broad money. Table 27.2 defines the aggregates, and some of the terms used to describe the components of the measures of money are set out in the compact glossary in Table 27.3.

Are All the Measures of Money Really Money?
We have defined money as a medium of exchange. Items that traditionally made up M1 — currency and current deposits (which used to refer to non-interest bearing cheque accounts held in trading banks) — fit that definition fairly closely. However, with the deregulation of the financial system in the 1980s, including the removal of the distinction between trading and savings banks, some types of deposits included in M1 are not obviously money. For example, the current accounts held in savings banks — passbook savings accounts or other interest-bearing current deposits — typically do not have associated cheque facilities, but these are part of M1. On the other hand, many types of deposits excluded from M1 are money. In fact, some types of deposit not even included in M3, but included in broad money, qualify as money. For example, you might have an account at a building society on which you can draw a payment order. To you, the payment order is effectively a cheque drawn on the building society. In practice, the building society normally would have an account at a bank, and the cheque you draw on your account draws directly on the building society's account held at the bank. Nonetheless, your cheque is still accepted as a ready means of payment or medium of exchange and yet your account held in the building society is not included in M1 or M3. It is counted in broad money.

Table 27.2 Official Measures of Money

M0 (base money)

- Holdings of notes and coin by the private sector
- Deposits of banks with the Reserve Bank
- Reserve Bank liabilities to the private non-bank sector

M1

- Notes and coin held by the private non-bank sector
- Current deposits with banks

M3

- M1
- All other bank deposits of the private non-bank sector

Broad money

- M3
- Borrowings from private sector non-bank financial institutions (NBFIs) less the latter's holdings of currency and bank deposits

Credit

- Bank bills outstanding
- Loans and other advances by financial intermediaries whose liabilities are included in broad money

The distinguishing characteristic of one asset from another, in terms of its 'moneyness', is the degree of liquidity associated with the asset. **Liquidity** is the degree to which an asset is instantly convertible into a medium of exchange at a known price. Assets vary in their degree of liquidity. Cash and cheque accounts are perfectly liquid because they are usable as a medium of exchange at all times and in all usual locations. Passbook and other savings accounts where the deposit is at call, that is can be withdrawn on demand, are also very liquid because, with minimal effort (perhaps a trip to the bank), they can also be converted into a medium of exchange. The liquidity of these accounts has been enhanced by the ability of account holders to undertake electronic funds transfer at point of sale (EFTPOS) transactions, that is, to purchase items at a shop and pay for them with an electronic transfer, usually by a debit card, directly out of their account into the shop's account. Various types of current account, held in both trading and savings banks, allow for transfers of funds by standing orders. You might, for example, automatically pay your rent or mortgage by an electronic transfer at a preset time every month.

Banks vary the degree of liquidity attached to other types of at call deposits by different means. Some investment savings accounts require minimum balances, and transactions must occur in fixed multiples of a given amount, usually $1000. Some savings accounts require the money to be deposited for at least seven days before it can be withdrawn. These restrictions reduce liquidity.

Less liquid than current deposits are fixed term deposits, which require money to be held in an account for a given length of time. While banks will

Table 27.3 Compact Glossary of the Components of Money

Currency	Private non-bank sector's holdings of notes and coin
Current deposits	Deposits in banks that are at call, that is, can be withdrawn on demand, sometimes called demand deposits
Interest-bearing current deposits	Current deposits that pay interest that were formerly mainly deposits in savings banks
Non-interest-bearing deposits	Current deposits that do not pay interest; were formerly mainly cheque current accounts at trading banks
Cheque accounts	A current deposit that may be withdrawn by writing a cheque
Debit card account	An account that may be drawn upon by a debit card, for example, Keycard and Handicard accounts. Transactions are possible from automatic tellers and via electronic funds transfer at point of sale (EFTPOS)
Passbook account	An account into which deposits are made or from which withdrawals are made via a passbook presented at the bank
Investment savings account	A form of passbook account
Statement savings account	An account that does not use a passbook. A debit card account is an example
Certificates of deposit	IOUs issued by banks for cash. Negotiable certificates of deposit are traded in the secondary market
Bank bills of exchange	Bank bills are negotiable securities issued by private agents. They are either accepted (unconditionally guaranteed) by a bank — 'bank accepted bills' — and sold in the bill market; or accepted by another company but backed by a bank — 'bank endorsed bills'. (Commonly called commercial paper outside Australia.)

usually allow individuals to withdraw their funds before the fixed term has expired, an interest rate penalty is applied. Some investment accounts require prior notice before the funds can be withdrawn. Some certificates of deposit, a form of fixed-term account, are readily marketable before the account matures, but at a price, which is unknown at the time of purchase. Thus considerable uncertainty is attached to early withdrawal.

At one time, the transition from M0 to M1 to M2 (now redundant) through to M3 and beyond was readily identifiable with a decreasing degree of liquidity as additional liabilities of the banking system were included. But the evolution of the financial system, both before and after the deregulation of the 1980s, has blurred the distinction between these definitions. Now the Reserve Bank and other observers often cite the usefulness of any given monetary aggregate as being directly related to the strength of the relationship between that aggregate and economic activity. Unfortunately, even these relationships may have changed as the financial system has evolved.

Figure 27.1 shows relative size of various monetary aggregates. As you can see, currency comprises only a small part of the overall money supply. Currency constitutes only 31 per cent of M1, its share falling as the definition of the money supply is broadened. Cheque accounts, mainly non-interest-bearing current accounts, have fallen in importance over the last two decades. Where they once comprised more than 70 per cent of trading banks' deposits, they now are less than 10 per cent of current deposit in banks.

In defining the money supply, we have included, along with currency, cheque accounts at banks and other financial institutions. We have not included the cheques that people actually write as part of the money supply.

It is important to understand why it is deposits that are money and not the cheques that people write when they make a payment.

Cheque Accounts are Money but Cheques are Not The best way to see why cheque accounts are money but cheques are not is to consider what happens when someone pays for goods by writing a

Figure 27.1 Relative Sizes of Different Measures of Money (billions of dollars)

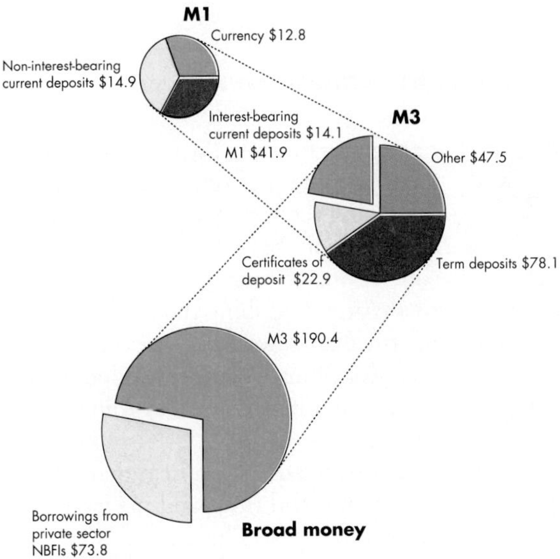

M1 (totalling $41.9 billion in June 1990) consists of currency and current deposits. It is roughly evenly split between currency, non-interest-bearing current deposits and interest-bearing current deposits. M3 (totalling $190.4 billion in June 1990) includes other bank deposits. M1 is just 22 per cent of M3. Broad money ($264.2 billion in June 1990) includes other liabilities of non-bank financial intermediaries (NBFIs). M3 constitutes nearly three-quarters of broad money.

Source: Reserve Bank Bulletin.

cheque. Let's suppose that Julie buys a bike for $200 from Tom's BMX Bikes. When Julie goes to Tom's bike shop she has $500 in her demand deposit account at the Hanging Rock Bank. Tom has $1000 in his demand deposit — at the same bank, as it happens. The total demand deposits of these two people is $1500. On 11 June, Julie writes a cheque for $200. Tom takes the cheque to Hanging Rock Bank right away and deposits it. Tom's bank balance rises from $1000 to $1200. But the bank not only credits Tom's account with $200, it also debits Julie's account $200, so that her balance falls from $500 to $300. The total demand deposits of Julie and Tom are still the same as before, $1500. Tom now has $200 more and Julie $200 less than before. These transactions are summarized in Table 27.4.

This transaction has not changed the quantity of money in existence. It has simply transferred money from one person to another. The cheque itself was never money. That is, there wasn't an extra $200 worth of money while the cheque was in circulation. The cheque simply served as a written instruction to the bank to transfer the money from Julie to Tom.

In our example, Julie and Tom use the same bank. Essentially the same story, though with additional steps, describes what happens if Julie and Tom use different banks. Tom's bank will credit the cheque to Tom's account and then take the cheque to a clearing house. Julie's bank will pay Tom's bank $200 and then debit Julie's account $200. This process can take a few days but the principles are the same as when two people use the same bank.

So, cheques are not money. But what about credit cards? Isn't having a credit card in your wal-

Table 27.4 Paying by Cheque

Date	Item	Debit	Credit	Balance
Julie's demand deposits account				
June 1	Opening balance			$500.00(CR)
June 11	Tom's BMX Bikes	$200.00		$300.00(CR)
Date	**Item**	**Debit**	**Credit**	**Balance**
Tom's BMX Bikes demand deposit account				
June 1	Opening balance			$1000.00(CR)
June 11	Julie buys bike		$200.00	$1200.00(CR)

*CR means 'credit': the bank owes the depositor

let and presenting the card to pay for a bike the same thing as using money? Why aren't credit cards somehow valued and counted as part of the quantity of money? We noted above that debit cards attached to bank accounts make those accounts more liquid. Why are credit and debit card accounts treated differently?

Credit Cards are Not Money When you pay by cheque you are frequently asked to prove your identity, often by showing your driver's licence. It would never occur to you to think of your driver's licence as money. Your driver's licence is just a means of identification — an ID.

A credit card is also an ID card, but one that enables you to borrow money at the instant a purchase is made on the promise of repaying later. When you make a purchase, you sign a credit card sales slip that creates a debt in your name. You are saying: 'I agree to pay for these goods when the credit card company bills me'. That is, you have created a non-negotiable security. Once you get your statement from the credit card company, you have to make the minimum payment due. To make that payment you need money — you need to have funds in your cheque account so that you can write a cheque to pay the credit card company.

Debit cards differ from credit cards in that debit cards do not allow you to write IOUs. They only allow you to draw upon existing deposits. Debit cards accounts are simply electronic cheque accounts and so are included in measures of money.

R E V I E W

Money has four functions: medium of exchange, unit of account, standard of deferred payment and store of value. Any durable commodity can serve as money, but modern societies use fiat money and private debt money rather than commodity money. An important component of money in Australia today is cheque accounts at banks and other financial institutions. Neither cheques nor credit cards are money. A cheque, or an EFTPOS transaction with a debit card, is an instruction to a bank to transfer money from one account to another. Money is the balance in the account itself. A credit card is an ID card that enables a person to borrow at the instant a purchase is made on the promise of repaying later. When repayment is made, money (currency or a cheque account) is used for the payment. ■

We've seen that the most important component of money in Australia is deposits at banks and other financial institutions. Let's take a look at the banking and financial system a bit more closely.

Financial Intermediaries

We are going to study the banking and financial system of Australia by first describing the variety of financial intermediaries that operate in Australia today. Then we'll examine the operations of banks and of other financial institutions. After describing the main features of financial intermediaries, we'll examine their economic functions, describing what they produce and how they make a profit. Finally, we'll explain how money gets created.

A **financial intermediary** is a firm that takes deposits from households and firms and makes loans to other households and firms. There are nine types of financial intermediaries whose deposits are components of the nation's money:

- Banks
- Money market corporations
- Finance companies
- Permanent building societies
- General financiers
- Credit cooperatives
- Cash management trusts
- Authorized money market dealers
- Pastoral finance companies

A compact glossary on these financial intermediaries and an indication of their relative importance is given in Table 27.5.

Let's begin by examining banks.

Banks

A **bank** is a firm, regulated under the *Banking Act 1959* to receive deposits and make loans. In 1990, there were 29 Australian-owned banks and 18 foreign-owned banks. All but three of the foreign-owned banks commenced operation in 1985/86. The scale and scope of the operations of banks can be seen by examining the balance sheet of all the banks added together.

A **balance sheet** is a statement that lists a firm's assets and liabilities. **Assets** are the things of value

Table 27.5 A Compact Glossary of Financial Intermediaries

Financial intermediary (approximate number, Sept. 1990)	Total assets (billions of dollars, Aug. 1990)	Main functions
Banks (47)	334	Companies regulated by the Reserve Bank and the Treasurer under the Banking Act 1959; funds are raised through deposits and distributed through loans
Money-market corporations (215)	54	Often called merchant banks, these are financial corporations which specialize in providing financial services, rather than lending their own funds, and raise funds by short-term borrowing from companies to finance business and investment
Finance companies (146)	41	Financial corporations that provide various types of loans including personal loans, finance for housing, instalment credit for retail sales and so on; they raise funds by borrowing from the public, mainly through debenture sales
Permanent building societies (50)	22	Cooperatives involved primarily in providing mortgage finance for owner-occupied housing, with funds collected from households
General financiers (140)	12	Similar to finance companies, but they do not borrow extensively from the public; rather they raise funds from small groups of investors, often related companies
Credit cooperatives (280)	8	Credit unions, which are non-profit institutions providing avenues for investment and borrowing by members; provide loans mainly for consumer durables
Cash management trusts	5	A sub-species of the general category of unit trusts, these are companies that allow small lenders to enter the wholesale sector of the financial system by aggregating small lots of funds provided by lenders into big enough parcels for the purchase of Treasury notes, bank bills and so on
Authorized money market dealers (9)	5	A select group of companies, with contractual relationships with the Reserve Bank, they undertake to foster the marketing of Commonwealth government securities and to provide facilities for the investment of overnight and short-term funds based on Commonwealth government securities
Pastoral finance companies (17)	2	Companies providing a range of services to rural businesses

that a firm owns. **Liabilities** are the things that a firm owes to households and other firms. Such a balance sheet — for all banks in June 1990 — is set out in Table 27.6. The left side — the assets — lists the items *owned* by the banks. The right side — the liabilities — lists the items that the banks *owe* to others.

The first thing to notice about the bank's balance sheet is that it includes both Australian dollar denominated and foreign currency denominated assets and liabilities. This reflects the removal of foreign exchange controls when the Australian dollar was floated in December 1983. As you can see from Table 27.6, only a small fraction of total assets and liabilities are in units of foreign currency. Foreign currency assets are loans or securities denominated in such currencies. Foreign currency liabilities are deposits made and repayable in the foreign currency.

Important though their foreign currency business is, it is business conducted in Australian dollars that constitutes the bulk of the business of the banks. Let's look at this more important aspect of their balance sheet, starting on the liability side.

Total Australian dollar liabilities of the banks in June 1990 were $297.2 billion. By far the most important component of these liabilities is the deposits. Your deposit at a bank is an asset to you but a liability to your bank. The bank has to repay you your deposit (and sometimes interest on it too) whenever you decide to take your money out of the bank. In effect, you have loaned your money to the bank.

We have discussed the various types of banks' deposit liabilities before in our discussion of the various definitions of money. The banks' liabilities are the **current deposits** (interest-bearing and non-interest-bearing), fixed deposits, certificates of deposit, investment savings accounts, statement savings accounts, passbook savings accounts and some others.

Why does a bank obligate itself to pay you your money back with interest? Because it wants to use your deposit to make a profit for itself. The bank borrows from you and uses the money to generate income. The assets side of the balance sheet tells us what the banks did with their $325.8 billion worth of borrowed resources in June 1990.

Table 27.6 The Balance Sheet of All Banks, June 1990

Assets (billions of dollars)		**Liabilities (billions of dollars)**		
Australian dollar assets		***Australian dollar liabilities***		
Coin, notes and cash balances with the Reserve Bank	2.1	Shareholders' funds		29.7
Non-callable deposits with the Reserve Bank	2.7	Deposits		
		current		
		interest bearing	15.6	
Public sector securities	22.1	non-interest-bearing	15.2	
			30.8	
Loans, advances and bills held	201.5			
		fixed	80.0	
		certificates of deposit	25.0	
Bills receivable	54.3	investment savings accounts	23.2	
		statement savings accounts	8.2	
Other Australian dollar assets	23.5	passbook accounts	9.1	
		other deposits	7.1	
		Total deposits		183.4
		Other borrowings		17.6
		Bill acceptance liabilities		56.2
		Other Australian dollar liabilities		10.3
Total Australian dollar assets	306.2	Total Australian dollar liabilities		297.2
Foreign currency assets	19.6	***Foreign currency liabilities***		**28.6**
Total assets	**325.8**	**Total liabilities**		**325.8**

First, the banks kept some of their assets in the form of deposits at the Reserve Bank of Australia and as cash in their vaults. (We'll study the Reserve Bank of Australia in Chapter 28.) The cash in a bank's vault plus its deposits at the Reserve Bank are called its **reserves**. You can think of a bank's deposit at the Reserve Bank as being similar to your deposit at your own bank. Banks use these deposits in the same way that you use your bank account. A bank deposits cash into or draws cash out of its account at the Reserve Bank and writes cheques on that account to settle debts with other banks.

If the banks kept all their assets in the form of deposits at the Reserve Bank and cash in their vaults, they wouldn't make any profit. But if they didn't keep *some* of their assets as cash in their vaults and as deposits at the Reserve Bank, they wouldn't be able to meet the demands for cash that their customers place on them. Nor would they be able to keep that automatic teller replenished every time you, your friends and all their other customers have raided it for cash for a midnight pizza.

The bulk of a bank's borrowed resources are put to work by making loans. Some of these loans are instantly convertible into cash and have virtually no risk. These very liquid assets are called **prime assets**, and are those assets that are instantly convertible into a medium of exchange with virtually no uncertainty about the price at which they can be converted. Prime assets include notes and coin, cash balances with the Reserve Bank, treasury notes and other Commonwealth government securities, and loans to authorized money market dealers secured against Commonwealth government securities. Banks are required to observe a **prime assets ratio (PAR)**, under which they must maintain prime assets equivalent to a fixed percentage of their assets. The PAR is currently set at 6 per cent.

Most of the banks' assets are the loans that they have made. A **loan** is a commitment of a fixed amount of money for an agreed period of time. Most of the loans made by banks are used by households for the purchase of owner-occupied housing and by corporations to finance capital equipment and inventories. But banks also make direct loans to households — personal loans. Such loans are used to buy consumer durable goods such as cars or boats. The outstanding balances on credit card accounts are also bank loans.

Banks make a profit by earning interest on loans, investment securities and liquid assets in excess of the interest paid on deposits and other liabilities. Also, banks receive revenue by charging fees for managing accounts.

Money is made up of the various liabilities of the banks. Personal savings deposits and other current deposits are the most important component of the M1 measure of money. And bank deposits are an important component of M3. But the deposit liabilities of banks are not the only components of the nation's money supply. Other financial institutions also take deposits that form part — and an increasing part — of the nation's money. Let's now examine these financial institutions.

Other Financial Intermediaries

There has always been a legal distinction in Australia between banks and other deposit-taking financial institutions. But the economic functions of other financial intermediaries have grown increasingly similar to that of banks and, today, their liabilities that serve as money constitute a growing fraction of the money supply. For example, the broad money definition of the money supply includes the deposit liabilities of other financial intermediaries such as credit unions, building societies, money market corporations, finance companies, cash management trusts and mortgage loan companies. These deposits accounted for 28 per cent of broad money in 1990. Let's consider the economic functions of financial intermediaries.

The Economic Functions of Financial Intermediaries

All financial intermediaries make a profit from a spread between the interest rate they pay on deposits and the interest rate at which they lend. Why can financial intermediaries borrow at a low interest rate and lend at a higher one? What services do they perform that makes their depositors willing to put up with a low interest rate and their borrowers willing to pay a higher one?

Financial intermediaries provide four main services:

- Minimizing the cost of obtaining funds
- Minimizing the cost of monitoring borrowers
- Pooling risk
- Creating liquidity

Minimizing the Cost of Obtaining Funds Finding someone from whom to borrow can be a costly business. Imagine how troublesome it would be if there were no financial intermediaries. A firm that was looking for $1 million to buy a new production plant would probably have to hunt around for several dozen people from whom to borrow in order to acquire enough funds for its capital project. Financial intermediaries lower those costs. The firm needing $1 million can go to a single financial institution to obtain those funds. The financial institution has to borrow from a large number of people, but it's not doing that just for this one firm and the million dollars it wants to borrow. The financial institution can establish an organization that spreads the cost of raising money from a large number of depositors.

Minimizing the Cost of Monitoring Borrowers
Lending money is a risky business. There's always a danger that the borrower may not repay. Most of the money which is lent is used by firms to invest in projects that they hope will return a profit. But sometimes those hopes are not fulfilled. Checking up on the activities of a borrower and ensuring that the best possible decisions are being made for making a profit and avoiding a loss is a costly and specialized activity. Imagine how costly it would be if each and every household that lent money to a firm had to incur the costs of monitoring that firm directly. By depositing funds with a financial intermediary, households avoid those costs. The financial intermediary performs the monitoring activity by using specialized resources that have a much lower cost than households would incur if they had to undertake the activity individually.

Pooling Risk As we noted above, lending money is risky. There is always a chance of not being repaid — of default. The risk of default can be reduced by lending to a large number of different individuals. In such a situation, if one person defaults on a loan, it is a nuisance but not a disaster. In contrast, if only one person borrows and that person defaults on the loan, the entire loan is a write-off. Financial intermediaries enable people to pool risk in an efficient way. Thousands of people lend money to any one financial intermediary and, in turn, the financial institution re-lends the money to hundreds, and perhaps thousands, of individual firms. If any one firm defaults on its loan, that default is spread across all the depositors with the intermediary and no individual depositor is left exposed to a high degree of risk.

Creating Liquidity Financial intermediaries create liquidity. We defined liquidity earlier as the ease and certainty with which an asset can be converted into a medium of exchange. The liabilities of some financial intermediaries are themselves a medium of exchange. Others are easily convertible into a medium of exchange and so are highly liquid.

Financial intermediaries create liquidity by borrowing short and lending long. Borrowing short means taking deposits but standing ready to repay them on short notice (and on even no notice in the case of demand deposits). Lending long means making loan commitments for a pre-arranged, and often quite long, period of time. For example, when a person makes a deposit with a building society, that deposit can be withdrawn on demand. The building society, however, makes a lending commitment for perhaps 20 years to someone buying a new house.

Financial Innovation

In their pursuit of a profit, financial intermediaries are constantly seeking better ways of delivering their product — of lowering the cost of obtaining funds and monitoring borrowers, pooling risk and creating liquidity. They are also inventive in seeking ways of avoiding the costs imposed on them by financial regulation. The development of new financial products and methods of borrowing and lending is called **financial innovation.**

The pace of financial innovation in Australia quickened in the 1970s and, following the release, in 1981, of the report of the Commission of Inquiry into the Australian Financial System (Campbell Committee), accelerated in the 1980s. The main impetus for financial innovation was the interaction between the high and rising inflation of the 1970s and the heavily regulated nature of banking. Rising inflation caused households to become more aware of interest rates, and they sought out deposits yielding the highest real rate of return. However, the banking sector was so regulated that it could not offer depositors the choices they were looking for. Thus the 1960s and 1970s saw the rapid growth of building societies, finance companies and credit unions offering financial services unavailable at banks. New financial institutions came on to the scene. The first cash management trust in Australia was created in 1980.

With the growth in non-bank financial intermediaries, the competitive position of traditional banks declined, leading to diminishing control by the Reserve Bank over both monetary policy and the prudential supervision of financial intermediation (see Chapter 28).

The Campbell Committee recommended reforms that increased the flexibility and efficiency of Australian financial markets by removing most of the inhibiting regulations. This provided a stimulus to the deregulatory trend first observed in the 1970s. Throughout the 1980s, new assets and new types of financial intermediaries emerged.

Other financial innovations resulted from technological change, most notably that associated with the increased use of computers and the decreased cost of long-distance communication. The spread in the use of credit cards and the development of international financial markets are consequences of technological changes.

R E V I E W

Most of the nation's money is made up of deposits in financial intermediaries. Of those financial intermediaries, banks are the most important. In the 1970s and 1980s, the deposit liabilities of financial institutions other than the banks became increasingly important as a result of financial innovation.

The main economic functions of financial intermediaries are minimizing the cost of obtaining funds, minimizing the cost of monitoring borrowers, pooling risk and creating liquidity. Financial intermediaries are constantly seeking new ways of making a profit and of avoiding the adverse effects of regulations on their activities. ■

Because banks and financial intermediaries are able to create liquidity and to create assets that are a medium of exchange — money — they occupy a unique place in our economy and exert an important influence on the quantity of money in existence. Let's see how money gets created.

How Banks Create Money

Money is created by the activities of banks and other financial institutions whose deposits circulate as a medium of exchange. In this section, we'll use the term 'banks' to refer to all these depository institutions.

As we saw in Table 27.6, banks don't have $100 in currency for every $100 that people have deposited with them. In fact, a typical bank today has about $2.60 in currency or on deposit at the Reserve Bank for every $100 deposited in it. No need for panic. Banks have learned, from experience, that these reserve levels are adequate for ordinary business needs. The fraction of a bank's total deposits that is held in reserves is called the **reserve ratio.** The value of the reserve ratio is influenced by the actions of a bank's depositors. If a depositor withdraws currency from a bank, the reserve ratio falls. If a depositor puts currency into a bank, the reserve ratio increases.

All banks have a desired reserve ratio. The **desired reserve ratio** is the ratio of reserves to deposits that banks regard as necessary in order to be able to conduct their business. The desired reserve ratio is determined partly by regulation (discussed in Chapter 28) and partly by what the banks regard as the minimum safety level for their reserve holdings. The difference between actual reserves and desired reserves are **excess reserves.**

Whenever banks have excess reserves, they are able to create money. When we say that banks create money, we don't mean that they have smoke-filled back rooms in which counterfeiters are busily working. Remember, most money is deposits, not currency. What they create is deposits and they do so by making loans. To see how banks create money we are going to look at a simple model of the banking system.

Let's suppose that the banks have a desired reserve ratio of 25 per cent. That is, for each dollar deposited, they want to keep 25 cents in the form of reserves. Alan, a customer of the Dundee Bank, decides to reduce his holdings of currency and put $100 in his deposit account at the bank. Suddenly, the Dundee Bank has $100 of new deposits and $100 of additional reserves. But with $100 of new deposits the Dundee Bank doesn't want to hold on to $100 of additional reserves. It has excess reserves. Its desired reserve ratio is 25 per cent so it plans to lend $75 of the additional $100 to another customer. Amy, a customer at the same bank, borrows $75. At this point, the Dundee Bank has new deposits of $100, new loans of $75 and new reserves of $25. As far as Dundee is concerned, that is the end of the matter. No money has been created. Alan has reduced his holdings of currency by $100 and increased his bank deposit by $100, but the total amount of money has remained constant. Although that's the end of the story for the Dundee Bank, it is not the end of the story for the entire banking system. What happens next?

Amy uses the $75 loan to buy a jacket from Julie. To undertake this transaction, she writes a cheque on her account with the Dundee and Julie deposits the cheque in the Hanging Rock Bank. The Hanging Rock Bank now has new deposits of $75

Table 27.7 Creating Money by Making Loans: Many Banks

Bank	Depositor	Borrower	New deposits	New loans	New reserves (dollars)	Increase in money	Cumulative increase in money
Dundee	Alan	Amy	100.00	75.00	25.00	0	
Hanging Rock	Julie	Bob	75.00	56.25	18.75	75.00	75.00
Morant	Andrew	Con	56.25	42.19	14.06	56.25	131.25
Sundowner	Geoff	Dale	42.19	31.64	10.55	42.19	173.44
Paris	David	Jenny	31.64	23.73	7.91	31.64	205.08
Malcolm	Sue	Ray	23.73	17.80	5.93	23.73	228.81
Green Card	John	Gail	17.80	13.35	4.45	17.80	246.61
Last Wave	Holly	Tony	13.35	10.01	3.34	13.35	259.96
Thunderdome	Jim	Jan	10.01	7.51	2.50	10.01	269.97
Gallipoli	Kym	Ken	7.51	5.63	1.88	7.51	277.48
Madmax	Lee	Diane	5.63	4.22	1.41	5.63	283.11
			.	.	.	.	.
			.	.	.	.	.
			.	.	.	.	.
All others			16.89	12.67	4.22	16.89	.
Total banking system			$400.00	$300.00	$100.00	$300.00	$300.00

and an additional $75 of reserves. The total amount of money supply is now $75 higher than before.

The Hanging Rock Bank doesn't need to hold on to the entire $75 that it has just received in reserves: it needs only a quarter of that amount — $18.75. The Hanging Rock Bank lends the additional amount, $56.25, to Bob who buys some used stereo equipment from Andrew. Bob writes a cheque on his account at the Hanging Rock Bank, which Andrew deposits in his account at the Morant Bank. The Morant Bank now has new deposits of $56.25, so the amount of money has increased by a total of $131.25 (the $75 lent to Amy and paid to Julie plus the $56.25 lent to Bob and paid to Andrew).

The transactions that we've just described are summarized in Table 27.7. But the story is still incomplete. The process that we're describing continues through the remaining banks and their depositors and borrowers, all the way down the list in that table. By the time we get down to the Madmax Bank, Ken has paid Lee $5.63 for a box of computer discs and so the Madmax Bank has new deposits of $5.63 and additional reserves of that same amount. Since it needs only $1.41 of additional reserves, it makes a loan of $4.22 to Diane, who in turn spends the money. By this time, the total amount of money has increased by $283.11, from the new deposits at each stage of the process listed in the first column of numbers in the table.

This process continues but with amounts that are now getting so tiny that we will not bother to keep track of them. All the remaining stages in the process taken together add up to the numbers in the second to last row of the table. The final tallies appear as the totals row at the bottom of the table. Deposits have increased by $400, loans by $300 and reserves by $100. The banks have created money by making loans. The quantity of money created is $300 — the same amount as the additional loans made. It's true that deposits have increased by $400, but $100 of that increase is Alan's original deposit. That increase in deposits does not increase the quantity of money. The currency that Alan deposited was already money. It is only the new deposits created by the lending activity of the banks that has increased the quantity of money in existence.

The ability of banks to create money does not mean that they can create an indefinite amount of money. The amount that they can create depends on the size of their reserves and on the desired reserve ratio. In this example, where the desired reserve ratio is 25 per cent, bank deposits have increased by four times the level of reserves. There's an important relationship between the change in reserves and the change in deposits.

The Simple Money Multiplier The **simple money multiplier** is the amount by which an increase in bank reserves is multiplied to calculate the effect of the increase in reserves on total bank deposits. The simple money multiplier is given by

$$\text{Simple money multiplier} = \frac{\text{Change in deposits}}{\text{Change in reserves}}$$

In the example that we've just worked through, the simple money multiplier is 4 — a $100 increase in reserves created the $400 increase in deposits.

The simple money multiplier is related to the desired reserve ratio. In our example, that ratio is 25 per cent (or $\frac{1}{4}$). That is,

$$\text{Desired reserves} = (\tfrac{1}{4}) \text{ Deposits}$$

Whenever desired reserves exceed actual reserves (a situation of negative excess reserves), the banks decrease their loans. When desired reserves are below actual reserves (a situation of positive excess reserves), the banks make additional loans. By adjusting their loans, the banks bring their actual reserves into line with their desired reserves, eliminating excess reserves. Thus when banks have changed their loans and reserves to make actual reserves equal desired reserves:

$$\text{Actual reserves} = (\tfrac{1}{4}) \text{ Deposits}$$

If we divide both sides of this equation by $\frac{1}{4}$ we obtain:

$$\text{Deposits} = [1/(\tfrac{1}{4})] \text{ Actual reserves}$$

If there is a change in reserves when desired reserves and actual reserves are equal, bank deposits change in order to satisfy the above equation. That is

$$\text{Change in deposits} = [1/(\tfrac{1}{4})] \text{ Change in reserves}$$

But $1/(\frac{1}{4})$ is the simple money multiplier. It is the amount by which the change in reserves is multiplied to calculate the change in deposits. In our example, this multiplier equals 4. The relationship between the simple money multiplier and the desired reserve ratio is

$$\text{Simple money multiplier} = \frac{1}{\text{Desired reserve ratio}}$$

Real World Money Multipliers

The money multiplier in the real world differs from the simple money multiplier that we have just calculated for two reasons. First, the desired reserve ratio of real world banks is much smaller than the 25 per cent that we have used here. Second, in the real world, not all the loans made by banks return to the banks in the form of reserves. Some of them remain outside the banks in the form of currency in circulation. This tendency for some of the loans to leave the banking system is called the **currency drain.** These two differences between the real world money multiplier and the simple money multiplier, which we have just calculated, work in opposing directions to each other. The smaller desired reserve ratio of real world banks makes the real world multiplier larger than the above numerical example. The cash drain makes the real world multiplier smaller. We study the actual values of real world money multipliers in the next chapter.

Bank Panic and Failure

Because banks lend most of their customers' deposits they could not pay out all their depositors on demand if they were required to do so. If one bank finds itself short of reserves, it can easily remedy the situation by borrowing from another bank. But suppose that the whole banking system is short of reserves. In such a situation, the banks are not able to pay their depositors' demands. Depositors, in turn, will become nervous about the security of their bank deposits and so will try to get even more of their money out of the bank. When the amount of currency the depositors are trying to withdraw from banks exceeds the amount that the banks have, there is a banking panic and banks fail.

The last time widespread bank panic and failure occurred in Australia was during the depression of the early 1890s. Failures occurred on a large scale in the United States during the Great Depression in the 1930s. Bank failures still occur in that country on a cyclical basis. In contrast, bank failure in Australia is extremely rare. Why have US banks failed more frequently than Australian banks?

Branch Banking Versus Unit Banking

The Australian banking system differs from that in the United States in many ways, but one is particularly important for its effects on bank solvency. Banking regulations in the United States prevent the emergence of large banks with many branches spanning the entire nation. In contrast, Australian law permits banks to have a large number of branches and to operate in all parts of the country.

Figure 27.2 Aggregate Demand, Aggregate Supply and the Quantity of Money

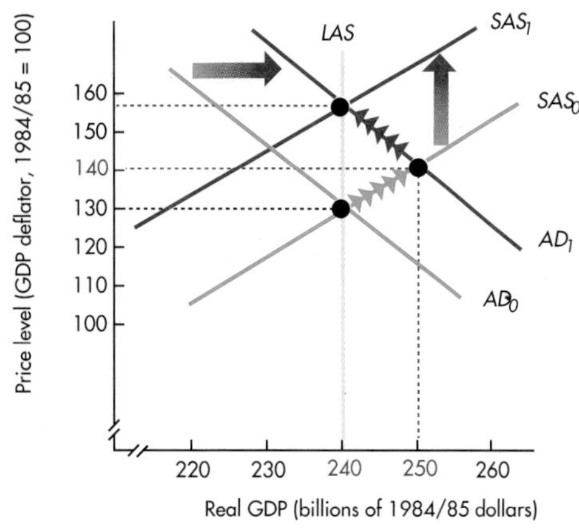

(a) From full employment

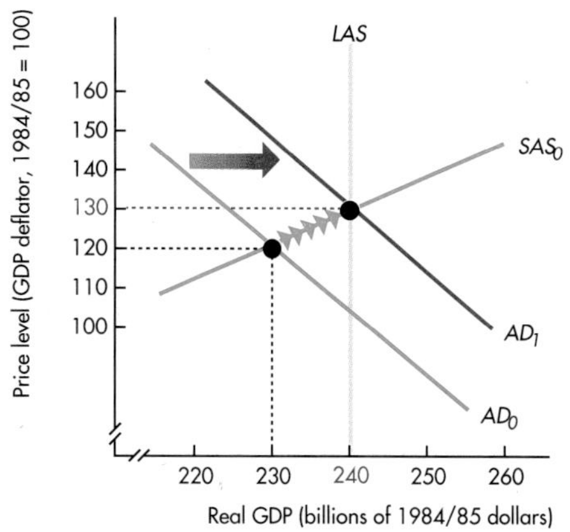

(b) From unemployment equilibrium

Part (a) shows the economy initially in full-employment equilibrium on its long-run aggregate supply curve, *LAS*. Initially, its short-run aggregate supply curve is SAS_0, and its aggregate demand curve is AD_0. The price level is 130 and real GDP is $240 billion. An increase in the quantity of money shifts the aggregate demand curve to AD_1. The price level increases to 140 and real GDP increases to $250 billion. The economy is at an above full-employment equilibrium. Wages and other input prices begin to rise and the short-run aggregate supply curve shifts upward to SAS_1. As it does so, real GDP falls back to its initial level and the price level increases to 156.

Part (b) shows the economy beginning from an unemployment equilibrium. Initially the aggregate demand curve is AD_0, the price level is 120 and equilibrium real GDP is $230 billion. An increase in the money supply shifts the aggregate demand curve to AD_1. Both the price level and real GDP increase. The price level rises to 130 and the full-employment level of real GDP is restored.

Four big banks — Westpac, Commonwealth, National Australia and ANZ — dominate the Australian banking system. These banks controlled over 65 per cent of the total assets of all banks in 1990. The growth and stability of these banks is assured by their extensive nation-wide branch network — 88 per cent of the banking industry's 5269 domestic branch offices were owned by these four banks. The existence of such a diverse network of branches has a major advantage in allowing the banks to diversify their risks much more effectively than US banks can. With a network of branch offices, losses on investments in one part of the country can be offset against profits in another part; unusually heavy drains of cash in one region can be offset by a deposit influx in another region. This was important in the recession of 1990/91 when the impact of the downturn varied between States (Victoria experiencing the sharpest downturn).

But the most important source of stability and security for our financial system arises from the existence of the Reserve Bank, an institution that monitors and regulates the banking and financial industry and seeks to maintain relatively stable and predictable conditions in markets for money and financial assets. We study this aspect of the financial system in Chapter 28.

Our next task in this chapter is to examine the effects of money on the economy and, in particular, the relationship between the quantity of money and the price level.

Money and the Price Level

We now know what money *is*. We also know that in a modern economy such as that of Australia today, most of the money is made up of deposits at banks and other financial institutions. We've seen that these institutions can actually create money — by making loans. Does the quantity of money created by the banking and financial system matter? What effects does it have? Does it matter whether the quantity increases quickly or slowly?

We're going to answer these questions first by refreshing our understanding of the aggregate demand–aggregate supply model and recalling the role played by money in influencing real GDP and the price level. Then we're going to consider a special theory of money and prices — the quantity theory of money. Finally, we'll look at some historical and international evidence on the relationship between money and prices.

Money in the AD–AS Model

In Chapter 24, we developed a model of aggregate demand and aggregate supply in which money plays an important role in influencing the aggregate demand curve. Figure 27.2 illustrates the model. The long-run aggregate supply curve is *LAS*. Figure 27.2(a) shows the economy initially in a full-employment equilibrium. The aggregate demand curve is AD_0 and the short-run aggregate supply curve is SAS_0. Equilibrium occurs where the aggregate demand curve AD_0 intersects the short-run aggregate supply curve SAS_0. The price level is 130 and real GDP is $240 billion.

Now suppose that there is an increase in the quantity of money. For the reasons discussed in Chapter 24 (see pp. 138–167), this increase in the quantity of money results in an increase in aggregate demand. The aggregate demand curve shifts to the right to become AD_1. The new equilibrium is at the intersection point of AD_1 and SAS_0. The price level rises to 140 and real GDP increases to $250 billion. But this is the short-run effect of an increase in the quantity of money. Over time, because the economy is at overfull employment, the prices of factors of production increase and, as they do so, the short-run aggregate supply curve shifts upward. The upward movement of the short-run aggregate supply curve leads to an even-higher price level and lower real GDP. If the long-run aggregate supply curve is unchanged, the long-run effect of an increase in the quantity of money occurs when the short-run aggregate supply curve has shifted upward to SAS_1, which intersects the aggregate demand curve AD_1, on the long-run aggregate supply curve, *LAS*. This equilibrium is at a price level of 156 with real GDP back at its original level of $240 billion.

The results are different if the economy starts from an unemployment equilibrium, as shown in Fig. 27.2(b). Initially, the aggregate demand curve is AD_0. Equilibrium occurs where the aggregate demand curve intersects the short-run aggregate supply curve, SAS_0. The price level is 120 and real GDP is $230 billion. Following the increase in the money supply, the aggregate demand curve shifts to the right (AD_1). It now intersects the short-run aggregate supply curve on the long-run aggregate supply curve, *LAS*. However, the increase in real GDP has absorbed previously unemployed factors and there is no additional pressure on wages, or other factor costs. The short-run aggregate supply curve does not change and the new equilibrium remains at the full-employment level of $240 billion. In this case the increase in the money supply has induced a permanent increase in output. By correctly choosing the increase in the quantity of money, it may even be possible to restore the full-employment level of output.

Beginning from full employment, the effects of the increase in the quantity of money are, first, to increase both real GDP and the price level and, second, to increase the price level yet further, while returning real GDP to its original full-employment level. That is, the short-run effect of an increase in the quantity of money is to increase both real GDP and the price level but the long-run effect of an increase in the quantity of money is to increase the price level only, leaving real GDP at its original level.

Beginning from an unemployment equilibrium, the effects of the increase in the quantity of money are to increase output, perhaps restoring the full-employment level of real GDP, and to increase prices. However, the increase in prices, when beginning from an unemployment equilibrium, is smaller than the increase in prices that ensues from an increase in the quantity of money at full employment.

Over long periods of time, economies tend to be near or at full employment much of the time. This close long-run relationship between the money supply and the price level is known as the quantity theory of money.

The Quantity Theory of Money

The **quantity theory of money** is the proposition that an increase in the quantity of money leads to an equal percentage increase in the price level. The original basis of the quantity theory of money is not the aggregate demand and aggregate supply model but the equation of exchange. The **equation of exchange** states the following:

$$\text{Quantity of money} \times \text{Velocity of circulation} = \text{Price level} \times \text{Real GDP.}$$

To understand the equation of exchange, let's start on the right-hand side — with the price level multiplied by real GDP. You will recognize this value as nominal GDP. That is, it is simply the total amount of expenditure on final goods and services valued in current dollars. The left-hand side of the equation of exchange can be thought of as defining the velocity of circulation. The **velocity of circulation** is the average

Figure 27.3 Money Growth and Inflation in Australia

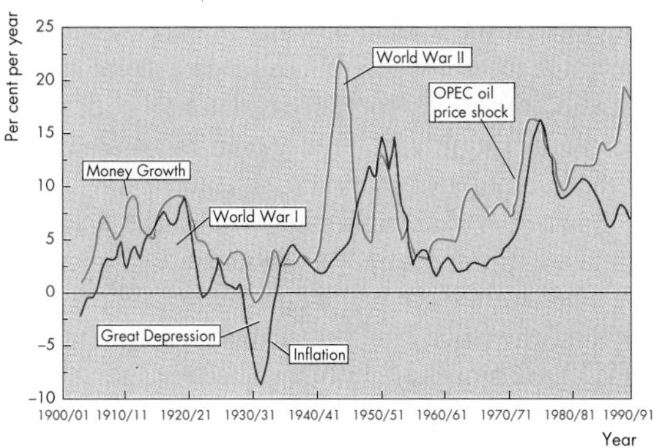

Four-year averages of money growth and inflation between 1900/01 and 1990/91 show that broad movements in the inflation rate are closely associated with changes in the money growth rate. But there are many independent changes in the inflation rate, indicating that money growth is not the only cause of inflation.

Sources: 1900/01 to 1959/60: Butlin; 1960/61 to 1990/91:RBA Bulletin Database, supplied through EconData's dX Data Service.

Figure 27.4 Money Growth and Inflation in the World Economy

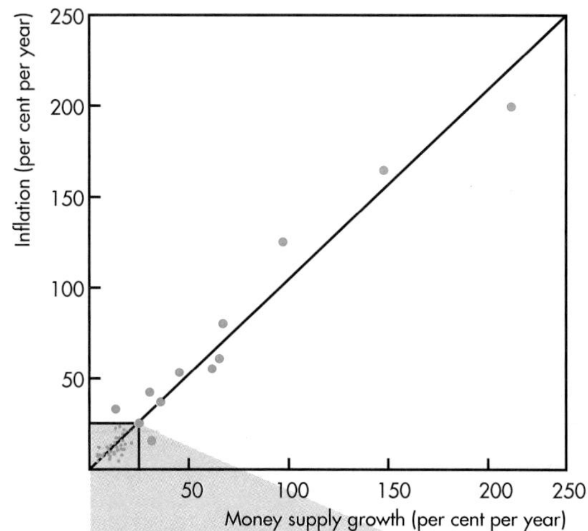

(a) All countries

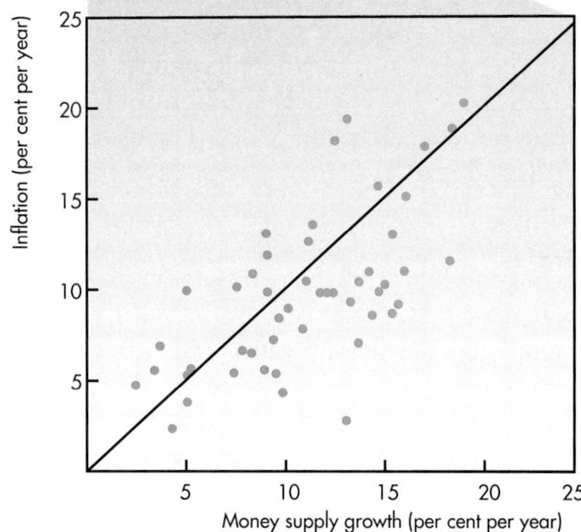

(b) Low-inflation countries

Inflation and money growth in 60 countries: low inflation countries in part (a) and high inflation countries in part (b) show that money growth is an important influence, though not the only influence, on inflation.

Source: Federal Reserve Bank of St. Louis, *Review*, May/June, 1988, 15.

number of times a dollar is used annually to buy the goods and services that make up GDP.

The equation of exchange is true by definition. It is fundamentally an accounting identity, so that there is no independent way of going out and measuring the velocity of circulation to check whether the equation is true. Rather, the velocity of circulation is whatever number it has to be to make the equation true.

The equation of exchange becomes the quantity theory of money by making two propositions:

- The velocity of circulation is a constant.
- Real GDP is not influenced by the quantity of money.

We can interpret the quantity theory of money in terms of our aggregate demand–aggregate supply model. The first proposition — that the velocity of circulation is a constant — implies that a change in the quantity of money shifts the aggregate demand curve by a very precisely stated amount. When the quantity of money increases, the aggregate demand curve shifts and its shift can be measured vertically by the percentage change in the quantity of money.

For example, in Fig. 27.2(a), the aggregate demand curve shifts from AD_0 to AD_1. That shift, measured by the vertical distance between the two demand curves, is 20 per cent. According to the quantity theory of money, a 20 per cent increase in the quantity of money shifts the aggregate demand curve upward by 20 per cent. The second proposition of the quantity theory of money — that real GDP is not affected by the money supply — can be interpreted as a statement about full-employment equilibrium. As you can see in Fig. 27.2, if a 20 per cent increase in the quantity of money increases aggregate demand from AD_0 to AD_1, in *full-employment equilibrium* the price level also increases by 20 per cent — an increase from 130 to 156 being a 20 per cent increase.

There are important factors influencing the velocity of circulation that result in its not being a constant. We discuss these factors in the next chapter. Also, because changes in the money supply have a short-run effect that is different from the long-run effect, the relationship between the quantity of money and the price level is not as precise as that predicted by the quantity theory of money. Finally, the economy is not always at full employment and a given increase in the quantity of money will produce different price level effects depending on how far from full employment it begins. With these qualifications in mind, it is interesting to ask to what extent the quantity theory of money correctly predicts the relationship between the quantity of money and the price level. Let's look at the relationship, both historically and internationally.

Historical Evidence on the Quantity Theory of Money

The quantity theory of money can be tested on the historical data of Australia by looking at the relationship between the growth rate of the quantity of money and the inflation rate. But, in looking at the historical evidence, we have to remember that the quantity theory of money is a proposition about long-run effects. We don't see long-run effects in the data. We see a sequence of short-run effects. But we can sharpen our focus on long-run effects and reduce the importance of short-run effects if we consider averages over periods longer than a year.

Figure 27.3 shows the historical relationship between the growth rate of the quantity of money (measured as M3) and the inflation rate in Australia for the 90 years between 1900/01 and 1989/90. The graph is constructed by plotting, for each year, the average money growth rate and inflation rate during that year and the previous three years — in what is called a four-year moving average. Thus the points plotted for 1988/89, for example, represent the average growth rate of the quantity of money for the years 1985/86 to 1988/89 and the inflation rate is the average inflation rate for that same four-year period.

Two things stand out in the figure. First, there is an unquestionable broad tendency for variations in the growth rate of the quantity of money to be associated with variations in the inflation rate. The build-up of inflation in the 1920s was accompanied by increases in the growth rate of the quantity of money. The falling prices of the Great Depression were associated with a decrease in the quantity of money. Increasing money supply growth during World War II brought increased inflation in the immediate postwar years, and steadily increasing money supply growth through the 1960s and 1970s brought steadily rising inflation through those decades. The second striking feature of this figure is the lack of precision in the relationship between these two variables. That is, there are many sub-periods in which there are obviously influences at work on the price level other than variations in the quantity of money.

What does the international evidence tell us?

International Evidence on the Quantity Theory of Money

The international evidence on the quantity theory of money is summarized in Fig. 27.4, which shows the inflation rate and the money growth rate for 60 countries. There is an unmistakable tendency for high money growth to be associated with high inflation.

But, like the historical evidence in Australia, this international data also tells us that money supply growth is not the only cause of inflation. Some countries have an inflation rate that exceeds the money supply growth rate, while others have an inflation rate that falls short of the money supply growth rate.

R E V I E W

The quantity of money exerts an important influence on the price level. An increase in the quantity of money increases aggregate demand. In the short run, that increase in aggregate demand increases both the price level and real GDP. In the long run, real GDP moves towards its original level and the price level continues to increase. The quantity theory of money predicts that an increase in the quantity of money produces an equivalent percentage increase in the price level. The historical and international evidence on the relationship between the quantity of money and the price level provides broad support for the quantity theory of money but also reveals important changes in the price level that occur independently of changes in the quantity of money. ■

■ In this chapter, we have studied the institutions that make up our banking and financial system. We've seen how the deposit liabilities of banks and other financial institutions comprise our medium of exchange — our money. Banks and other financial institutions create money by making loans. The quantity of money in existence has important effects on the economy and, in particular, on the price level.

In the next chapter, we're going to see how the quantity of money is regulated and influenced by the actions of the Reserve Bank. We're also going to discover how, by its influence on the money supply, the Reserve Bank is able to influence interest rates, thereby affecting the level of aggregate demand. It is through its effects on the money supply and interest rates and their wider ramifications that the Reserve Bank is able to help steer the course of the economy.

SUMMARY

What is Money?

Money has four functions: it is a medium of exchange, a unit of account, a standard of deferred payment and a store of value. The earliest forms of money were commodities. In the modern world, we use a fiat money system. The biggest component of money is private debt.

Official measures of money in use in Australia today are M0, M1, M3 and broad money. M1 and M3 include currency and deposits at banks. Broad money includes deposits at other financial institutions such as credit unions, building societies, cash management trusts and money market corporations. Various measures of lending and credit are also monitored. None of the official definitions of money corresponds exactly to the assets that function as money in Australia today. Money, the medium of exchange and means of payment, consists of currency and current deposits at banks (official M1) plus cheque accounts at non-bank financial institutions. The deposits that are included in M3 are highly liquid but must be converted into currency or current accounts to be directly used as a medium of exchange and the means of payment. Demand deposits are money but cheques and credit cards are not. (pp. 240–248)

Financial Intermediaries

The main financial intermediaries whose liabilities serve as money are banks, money market corporations, finance companies, building societies, general financiers, credit cooperatives, cash management trusts, authorized money market dealers and pastoral finance companies. All of these institutions take in deposits, hold cash reserves to ensure that they can meet their depositors' demands for currency, hold securities and make loans. Financial intermediaries make a profit by borrowing at a lower interest rate than that at which they lend. All financial intermediaries provide four main economic services: they minimize the cost of obtaining funds, minimize the cost of monitoring borrowers, pool risks and create liquidity. The continual search for profitable financial opportunities leads to financial innovation — to the creation of new financial products such as new types of deposits and loans.

Banks and other financial institutions create money by making loans. When a loan is made to one person and the amount lent is spent, much of it ends up as someone else's deposit. The total quantity of deposits that can be supported by a given amount of reserves (the simple money multiplier) is equal to 1 divided by the desired reserve ratio. (pp. 248–256)

Money and the Price Level

The quantity of money affects aggregate demand. An increase in the quantity of money increases aggregate demand. In the short run, this increase in aggregate demand increases the price level and real GDP. In the long run, if the economy begins from full employment, the price level continues to increase but real GDP returns to its original level. If the economy begins with some unemployment, the level of real GDP might increase sufficiently to eliminate the unemployment.

Since economies tend to be at or near full employment much of the time, the quantity theory of money states that there is a close relationship between increases in the money supply and increases in the price level. Both historical and international evidence suggest that the quantity theory of money is only correct in a broad average sense. The quantity of money does exert an important influence on the price level, but there are other important influences too. Nevertheless, other things being equal, the higher the growth rate of the quantity of money, the higher is the inflation rate. (pp. 256–259)

KEY TERMS

Assets, p. 248
Balance sheet, p. 248
Bank, p. 248
Barter, p. 240
Broad money, p. 244
Cheque account, p. 244
Commodity money, p. 242
Convertible paper money, p. 243
Currency, p. 244
Currency drain, p. 255
Current deposits, p. 250
Desired reserve ratio, p. 253
Double coincidence of wants, p. 240
Equation of exchange, p. 257
Excess reserves, p. 253
Fiat money, p. 244
Financial innovation, p. 252
Financial intermediary, p. 248
Gresham's Law, p. 242
Liability, p. 249
Liquidity, p. 245
Loan, p. 251
M0, p. 244
M1, p. 244
M3, p. 244
Medium of exchange, p. 240
Money, p. 240
Prime assets, p. 251
Prime assets ratio (PAR), p. 251
Private debt money, p. 244
Quantity theory of money, p. 257
Reserve ratio, p. 253
Reserves, p. 251
Simple money multiplier, p. 255
Standard of deferred payment, p. 241
Store of value, p. 241
Unit of account, p. 240
Velocity of circulation, p. 257

PROBLEMS

1 You are given the following information about a hypothetical economy: The banks have deposit liabilities of $300 billion. Their reserves are $15 billion.
   a) Using Table 27.6 as a guide, set out the balance sheet of the banks. Supply any missing numbers using your knowledge of the fact that total assets equal total liabilities.
   b) How much money is there in this economy if households and firms hold 10 times as much in their deposits as they do in cash?
   c) What is the simple money multiplier for this economy?

2 A new immigrant arrives in New Transylvania with $1000. The $1000 is put into a bank deposit. All the banks in New Transylvania have a desired reserve ratio of 10 per cent.
   a) What is the initial increase in the quantity of money of New Transylvania?
   b) What is the initial increase in the quantity of bank deposits when the immigrant arrives?
   c) How much does the immigrant's bank lend out?
   d) Using a format similar to that in Table 27.7, calculate the amount lent and the amount of deposits created at each 'round', assuming that all the funds lent are returned to the banking system in the form of deposits.
   e) By how much has the quantity of money increased after 20 rounds of lending?
   f) What is the ultimate increase in the quantity of money, in bank loans and in bank deposits?

3 An economy has a quantity of money of $1000 and GDP is $4000. What is the velocity of circulation in this economy?

Chapter 28

The Reserve Bank of Australia, Money and Interest Rates

After studying this chapter, you will be able to:

- Describe the role of the Reserve Bank of Australia.
- Describe the tools used by the Reserve Bank to influence the money supply and interest rates.
- Explain what an open market operation is.
- Explain how an open market operation works.
- Explain how an open market operation changes the money supply.
- Distinguish between the nominal money supply and the real money supply.
- Explain what determines the demand for money.
- Explain the effects of financial innovations on the demand for money in the 1980s.
- Explain how interest rates are determined.
- Explain how the Reserves Bank influences interest rates.

Fiddling with the Knobs

A young couple, planning to buy a first home, has found the perfect place. They're in luck — it is September 1966 and mortgages are plentiful at interest rates just over 6 per cent a year. Twenty years later, that same couple's daughter is looking for her first home. She too finds the perfect place, but mortgage rates have now reached 15.5 per cent a year. With much gnashing of teeth, she puts off her purchase until interest rates decline, making a mortgage affordable. However, by September 1989 mortgage rates are still higher at 17 per cent per year. Why do interest rates rise and fall? What determines interest rates? Are they determined by forces of nature? Or is somebody fiddling with the knobs somewhere? Q You suspect that someone is indeed fiddling with the knobs. For you've just read in your newspaper: 'The Reserve Bank is prepared to continue nudging interest rates higher in order to head off the threat of inflation'. And a few months earlier, you read: 'The Reserve Bank doesn't plan to push interest rates lower unless it sees further weakness in the economy'. What is 'the Reserve Bank'? Why would the Reserve Bank want to change interest rates? And how can the Reserve Bank influence interest rates? Q There is enough currency — coins and notes — circulating in Australia for every single individual to have a wallet stuffed with $750. There are enough cheque accounts in banks and other financial institutions for everyone to have $1700 in these accounts. There are enough other bank deposits for everyone to have a further $9000. Of course, not many people hold as much currency, cheque accounts and savings deposits as these averages. But these *are* the averages. Therefore, if most people don't hold this much, some people must be holding a great deal more. What determines the quantity of money that people hold? And what determines the form in which they hold it? Q The 1980s have seen a revolution in our banking and financial sector. At the beginning of that decade, most banks and other financial institutions offered just two kinds of deposit arrangements: a cheque account or a savings deposit. Cheques could be written on current or demand deposits but those deposits earned no interest; savings deposits earned interest but cheques couldn't be written on those accounts. Today, we are confronted with a rich variety of deposit arrangements: cheque accounts earn interest, at a rate which depends on such things as average daily balances. How has the developement of these new kinds of deposits influenced the amount of money that we hold? Q Credit cards have been around for a long time (Diners Club introduced the first card just after World War II). But there has been a virtual explosion in their use during the 1980s. Many people never use cash to buy petrol or a restaurant meal and many other commonly purchased items. But you can't buy everything with a credit card. For example, you feel like a midnight snack but your favourite spot doesn't accept credit cards and you're out of cash. No problem! You head straight for the automatic teller machine and withdraw what you need tonight and for the next few days as well. While walking out, you wonder to yourself: How much cash would I need to hold if I didn't have quick access to an automatic teller machine? How did people get cash for a midnight pizza before such machines existed? How have credit cards and computers affected the amount of money that we hold?

In the last chapter, we discovered that money is the currency (notes and coins) in circulation plus deposits at banks and other financial institutions. We also discovered that banks and financial intermediaries create money by making loans. Finally, we discovered that the quantity of money has an important effect on the price level. Increases in the quantity of money bring increasing prices. But we also saw that there is no precise relationship between the quantity of money and the price level — only a general tendency for the two to be correlated.

An important reason why the quantity of money and the price level do not have a precise relationship with each other is that the *velocity of circulation* of money fluctuates. In this chapter, we are going to discover what determines the velocity of circulation. We are going to discover that the velocity of circulation is determined by the demand for money. We are also going to discover that interest rates are determined in the market for money by the interaction of the demand for money and the supply of money.

But first we are going to study the Reserve Bank of Australia and learn how the Reserve Bank influences the quantity of money in its attempts to influence interest rates and, more generally, the overall level of aggregate demand and inflation. At the end of the chapter, we will return to the Reserve Bank and see how its operations in the 1980s generated huge swings in interest rates.

The Reserve Bank of Australia

The **Reserve Bank of Australia** is Australia's central bank. A **central bank** is a public authority charged with regulating and controlling a country's monetary and financial institutions and markets. The Reserve Bank is also responsible for the nation's monetary policy. **Monetary policy** is the attempt to control inflation, the foreign exchange value of our currency, and to moderate the business cycle by changing the quantity of money in circulation and adjusting interest rates. We are going to study the tools available to the Reserve Bank in its conduct of financial market supervision and monetary policy. We will also work out the effects of the bank's actions on interest rates. First, we will examine the origins and structure of the Reserve Bank.

The Origins of the Reserve Bank[1]

The Reserve Bank began operating as Australia's central bank on 14 January 1960, under the *Reserve Bank Act 1959*. Its duties and functions were further defined in the *Banking Act 1959* and the *Financial Corporations Act 1974*. Ministerial responsibility in terms of those acts is exercised by the Treasurer. Prior to 1959, Australia's central banking functions had been fulfilled by the Commonwealth Bank of Australia, which was established under the *Commonwealth Bank Act 1911*.

The Commonwealth Bank was originally established to carry on the general business of banking and the business of a savings bank. Its chief goals were to provide competition for the commercial banking sector and to establish a nation-wide savings system. However, the initial impetus for growth of the Commonwealth Bank was its role as banker to

[1] Material in this section draws heavily on a number of Reserve Bank publications, especially various issues of the Reserve Bank *Bulletin*. Particularly useful is the free publication *Reserve Bank in the Market Place*, Reserve Bank of Australia, April 1990.

the government. Gradually it assumed more of the functions of a central bank, including responsibility for note issue in 1924.

Prior to the outbreak of World War II, the Commonwealth Bank was given broad control over foreign exchange, bank liquidity, interest rates and the establishment of new banks under the *National Security (Banking) Regulations 1939–41.* These powers were formalized in the *Commonwealth Bank Act 1945* and the *Banking Act 1945.* It was at this stage the Commonwealth Bank was recognized as a central bank. Because the supervisory and prudential roles of a central bank clashed with the commercial trading and savings bank functions of the Commonwealth Bank, the central bank functions were removed from the Commonwealth Bank and placed with the newly created Reserve Bank under the 1959 legislation.

The Reserve Bank Act requires the Bank to

> 'contribute to the stability of the currency of Australia; the maintenance of full employment in Australia; and the economic prosperity and welfare of the people of Australia.'

In practice, the Reserve Bank has taken the view that the welfare of the people of Australia is best served by pursuing the first two goals: a stable currency and full employment. In this chapter we will learn about the tools the Reserve Bank employs to achieve these goals.

By the time that the Reserve Bank was created, most other countries already had a central bank. The first central banks had been established in Sweden and England as long ago as the seventeenth century. These earliest central banks were similar to the Reserve Bank in that they were set up as private banks to provide financial services to monarchs, who were the governments of their day. These banks gradually evolved into modern central banks, eventually becoming publicly owned corporations. Some central banks had quite different origins. The central bank in the United States, the Federal Reserve System, was established as a modern central bank in 1913. Similarly, the Bank of Canada was established as a central bank in 1935.

The Structure of the Reserve Bank

There are three key structural components in the Reserve Bank. They are:

- The Reserve Bank Board
- The Governor and Deputy Governor
- The senior staff.

The Reserve Bank Board The policy of the Reserve Bank is determined by the Board. It consists of, at most, ten members. Three members are the Governor, the Deputy Governor and the Secretary to the Treasury. The remaining seven are appointed by the government. It is a requirement that at least five of the seven appointed members are not associated with either the Commonwealth public service or the Reserve Bank. Over recent years, members have been drawn from the rural sector, manufacturing, mining, retailing, the trade union movement and the universities. The Board usually meets once a month, most often in Sydney.

The Governor and Deputy Governor The Governor and Deputy Governor are both appointed by the government for terms of up to seven years, with possible re-appointment. The Governor is responsible for the management of the Reserve Bank, subject to the policy of the Board. In the absence of the Governor, the Deputy Governor performs these duties.

There have been nine Governors prior to the present Governor of the Reserve Bank, Mr B.W. Fraser. Mr Fraser was appointed in September 1989 to hold office until September 1996. Previously, Mr Fraser was Secretary to the Treasury.

Senior Staff The senior staff of the Reserve Bank are housed in the head office in Sydney. Other offices are located in the capital city of each state, in New York and in London. A recent re-organization of the structure of the bank created four positions of Assistant Governor, each responsible for one of the major functional areas of the Reserve Bank's operations:

- Financial institutions
- Financial markets
- Economic policy/research
- Administrative

The senior staff in each of these areas formulate Bank policy and administer its functions. They are economists and central bankers with considerable national and international experience in monetary and financial affairs.

The staff in the *Financial Institutions* division have responsibility for the day-to-day supervision of banks and other financial intermediaries. They are responsible for the stability of the financial system as a whole. The staff in the *Financial Markets* division are responsible for the Bank's operation in domestic financial markets and foreign exchange markets. The *Economic Policy/Research* divison monitors and analyses macroeconomic developments in Australia and the rest of the world. They also provide medium-term research into various aspects of the Australian economy. The *Administrative* division manages the internal affairs of the bank.

Constitutional Position of the Reserve Bank

There are two different models for the relationship between a country's central bank and its central government:

- Independence
- Subservience

Independent Central Bank An independent central bank is one that has complete autonomy to determine the nation's monetary policy. Government public servants and elected officials may comment on monetary policy but the governor of the bank is under no obligation to take into account the views of anyone other than his own staff and board of directors.

The argument for an independent central bank is that it enables monetary policy to be formulated with a long-term view of maintaining stable prices and prevents monetary policy from being used for short-term political advantage. Countries that have independent central banks today are West Germany, the United States and Switzerland.

Subservient Central Bank Most central banks are subservient to their governments. In the event of a difference of opinion between the central bank and government, it is the government that carries the day and, if necessary, the central bank governor must resign if he or she is unwilling to implement the policies dictated by the government. The Reserve Bank has been in such a position since its creation. The Board of the Bank is obliged to report to the government from time to time. In the event of a disagreement over policy, the Reserve Bank Act lays down procedures for resolution of the differences. If a resolution cannot be achieved, the government can simply inform the Board of its policy and the Board is obliged to implement it. The government takes responsibility for the effects of its policy and must inform the Board that this is the case.

Those advocating subservience of the central bank take the view that monetary policy is essentially political in its effects and therefore must, like fiscal policy and indeed all other government policies, be subject to democratic control.

Although, ultimately, the Treasurer is responsible for Australia's monetary policy, this fact does not, by any means, reduce the Governor of the Reserve Bank to a position of impotence. Because of his expertise and authority in the field and because of the quality of the advice that he receives from the Bank's staff of senior economists and advisors, the Governor of the Bank has considerable power in both private and public discussions of monetary policy. Opinions would have to be sharply divided and on a range of crucial matters before a government would be willing to run the risk of seeing the Governor resign on a dispute over policy. Also, there are times when a government wants to pursue unpopular monetary policies and, at such times, it is very convenient for democratically elected officials to hide behind the authority of a relatively independent monetary agency such as the Reserve Bank.

The Functions of the Reserve Bank

The Reserve Bank has a number of important functions. It is the banker to the government; it is responsible for the issue of notes and coin; it supervises the financial system (prudential supervision); and it conducts monetary policy. We will now look at how the Reserve Bank handles the last two of these functions — prudential supervision and monetary policy.

Prudential Supervision

Prudential supervision consists of controls and requirements placed on banks by the Reserve Bank so as to protect investors and depositors, ensuring the stability of the financial system. It is not a guarantee against deposits, nor does it protect the shareholders of banks. The Reserve Bank only exercises prudential supervision over banks subject to the Banking Act. This excludes state banks, although they voluntarily adhere to the controls placed on other banks. It also excludes all other non-bank financial institutions, discussed in Chapter 27, some of which remain the responsibility of the various State governments.

The prudential system has, along with most aspects of the financial system, undergone changes in recent years. Up until the early 1980s there were no formal prudential liquidity requirements, although all banks voluntarily adhered to the LGS convention.

The **LGS convention** was a system under which each bank held a certain ratio of *L*iquid assets and *G*overnment *S*ecurities to their deposits. For trading banks this ratio was set at 18 per cent, while for savings banks the ratio was 7.5 per cent.

Since 1985, a more formal framework for supervising banks has been established. This framework is based upon three planks: capital adequacy, liquidity and concentration of risks.

Capital Adequacy Since 1988, banks have been required to have adequate capital. Capital, in this context, means the funds of the owners of the bank that are at risk in the business and available to meet losses. It is primarily shareholder funds and reserves. The current system is a risk-weighted system, where the assets of the bank are adjusted for a risk factor and then added up. Cash and short-term Commonwealth government securities carry no risk weighting; housing loans a 50 per cent weighting; and up to 100 per cent weighting on other private sector claims. Currently banks must maintain a minimum ratio of capital to risk weighted assets of 8 per cent.

Liquidity Banks require a minimum level of liquidity to ensure public confidence in the banking system. If you know that your bank has sufficient funds on hand to meet your withdrawals, whenever you want to make a withdrawal, then you are less likely to be concerned about the state of the bank and more likely to leave your money in the bank when you are not using it. This logic applies to all depositors. But by keeping large reserves of liquid assets on hand to meet possible withdrawals, no matter how unlikely they might be, banks forgo the income they could otherwise be earning by lending your deposit, and other deposits, out. So there are competing forces on banks: the desire to keep more reserves on hand to maintain public confidence in the bank, opposed by the desire to keep fewer reserves so that they can acquire more interest-earning assets.

Recognizing that banks have an incentive to lower their reserves of liquid assets motivated the LGS convention. This has now been replaced by the **prime assets ratio (PAR)**, established in 1985. The PAR requires banks to keep, at all times, a minimum ratio of 'high quality liquefiable assets' or prime assets. Initially this ratio was set at 12 per cent. In May 1990 it was lowered to 6 per cent. PAR applies to all banks now that the distinction between savings and trading banks has been removed.

Concentration of Risks The Reserve Bank also monitors the balance sheets of banks, consolidated over each banking group, to ensure that any one bank, or group of banks, is not accumulating too much of any one type of asset. Concentration of assets — putting too many eggs in one basket — increases the overall riskiness of the bank. Banks must regularly report to the Reserve Bank and, if concentration rises, the bank's amount of capital must also rise.

Monetary Policy

Most people associate the Reserve Bank with the conduct of monetary policy in Australia. In general terms, this means influencing the pace of economic activity and the rate of inflation. How the Reserve Bank conducts monetary policy has changed considerably over the past ten years as financial markets have been deregulated. We will consider monetary policy as it was conducted pre-deregulation and how it is conducted now. But first we must consider the world environment in which Australian financial markets are placed and how this affects the conduct of monetary policy by the Reserve Bank.

International Constraints on the Reserve Bank

The Australian economy in general, and its monetary and financial system in particular, are closely integrated with the rest of the world. Economic integration has been a fact of Australian life since long before Federation. The sheer size and importance of the world money and financial markets make it essential that Australian financial institutions seek profitable business, that is, borrow and lend, not only in Australia but beyond its borders.

These facts of financial life in Australia place some restrictions on the range of actions that the Reserve Bank might take. It cannot, for example, ignore interest rate pressures that stem from world markets. Furthermore, the Bank must adopt some attitude toward the value of the Australian dollar. That value is determined in a market — a world-wide market — for foreign exchange. There is one fundamental choice that the Commonwealth government and the Reserve Bank must make that has far-reaching implications for the monetary policy that Australia can pursue: this choice is which of three possible foreign exchange regimes to adopt. The three possible choices are:

- A fixed exchange rate

- A flexible exchange rate
- A managed exchange rate

A **fixed exchange rate** is pegged by the country's central bank. For example, the Reserve Bank could adopt a fixed exchange rate defining the Australian dollar as being worth, say, one US dollar (or some other value). To make this exchange rate possible, the Reserve Bank would have to stand ready to buy US dollars or sell Australian dollars at this pre-determined, fixed exchange rate, and would have to hold sufficiently large reserves of US dollars to enable it to do so.

A **flexible exchange rate** is determined by market forces in the absence of any central bank intervention. A flexible exchange rate is often called a 'clean float'.

A **managed exchange rate** is influenced by central bank intervention in the foreign exchange market. Under a managed exchange rate regime, the central bank's intervention does not seek to keep the exchange rate fixed at a pre-announced level but does seek to smooth out wild fluctuations in the exchange rate.

A managed exchanged rate is sometimes called a 'dirty float', to distinguish it from a cleanly floated flexible exchange rate.

Before December 1983, Australia had a fixed exchange rate. However, the operation of the fixed exchange rate system varied. Until 1976, the exchange rate was fixed against the US dollar for lengthy periods at an official announced rate. Between 1976 and 1983 the system operated as a 'crawling peg', where the level was not announced but the Reserve Bank intervened very often making small adjustments to the actual rate. These fixed exchange rate regimes were coupled with extensive controls on international capital flows. On 9 December 1983, the Australian government floated the Australian dollar and abolished most of the exchange controls.

When a country fixes its exchange rate, its central bank has virtually no freedom of manoeuvre for determining an independent, national monetary policy. To make a fixed exchange rate work, the central bank must be willing to supply as much, or as little, national currency as people want to hold. The Reserve Bank cannot control the nation's money supply in such a situation. It is in the same type of situation as a monopolist selling fresh mountain spring water. The monopolist can determine a price at which to sell the water, leaving the market to decide how much to buy at that price, or can decide on a production rate, leaving the market to determine the price at which that quantity will be sold. The monopolist cannot choose both the price at which it will sell its output and the quantity that people will buy.

The Reserve Bank is a monopolist in the supply of Australian dollars. It can choose the quantity to supply but not the price at which it exchanges for other currencies (or for goods and services). Alternatively, the Reserve Bank can fix the price at which the Australian dollar exchanges for some other currency (for example, the US dollar) but in so doing, relinquishes control over the quantity of Australian dollars outstanding.

By choosing to permit the foreign currency value of the Australian dollar to fluctuate, the Reserve Bank retains control over Australian monetary policy, that is, over the Australian money supply and interest rates. How the Bank exercises that control is the subject matter of the rest of this chapter. How the foreign exchange markets work to determine the value of the Australian dollar and how the Bank's interest rate policies influence the dollar are the subject of Chapter 29.

Our next task in studying the Reserve Bank's monetary policy is to examine the policy tools that the Bank has at its disposal.

Monetary Policy Tools Prior to Deregulation

From its creation in 1959 until 1980, the Reserve Bank conducted monetary policy by directly regulating the activity of banks — rationing lending and imposing credit controls. The means of regulation used by the Reserve Bank were:

- Quantitative limits on bank lending
- Interest rate controls
- Minimum liquid assets ratios
- Limited entry into other markets
- Foreign exchange controls

Let's look at these controls in greater detail.

Quantitative Limits on Bank Lending Quantitative lending restrictions were guidelines, issued by the Reserve Bank to banks, which put limits on how much lending the banks could undertake. In some instances, the guidelines also specified, in general terms, who the banks should lend to. By directly restricting bank lending, the Reserve Bank put an immediate stop to the cycle of banks creating new money by making loans that create new deposits.

Interest Rate Controls The Reserve Bank controlled the interest rates banks could pay on deposits and charge on loans. These restrictions limited the banks' ability to attract new customers and expand the deposit base. If there was an increase in the demand for loans, for example, as a result of an economic boom, banks could not raise interest rates to attract new deposits. Instead they rationed available funds. This system worked in favour of existing borrowers, who had already established a good credit rating, and against new borrowers who had not yet had the opportunity to establish a good credit record.

Minimum Liquid Assets Ratios These were a combination of the LGS convention and statutory reserve requirements. **Statutory reserve requirements (SRDs)** were a specified fraction of deposits that banks were required to hold as cash reserves at the Reserve Bank. As we saw earlier, LGS assets, including cash reserves, were informal requirements that the banks hold a given fraction of total assets in the form of cash and government securities. By increasing the required cash reserve ratio (SRD) or the amount of LGS assets that banks had to hold, the Reserve Bank could effectively slow the pace at which banks lent to the private sector.

Limited Entry into Other Markets Banks were excluded from entry into other markets where they would have been able to raise funds and so increase their lending. In particular, banks were excluded from the short-term money market — the market where financial enterprises and other corporations borrow from and lend to each other for short periods of time.

Foreign Exchange Controls Foreign exchange controls restricted banks, and other enterprises, from borrowing in foreign capital markets. All funds available to banks for domestic lending had to be raised in the domestic market.

The controls that we have just reviewed restricted the balance sheets of banks and limited their ability to raise funds. Exclusion from the domestic short-term money market and foreign capital markets meant that banks were limited to raising funds through increasing the deposit base. But the controls on interest rates limited the banks' abilities to compete for deposits. Ultimately, the banks passively accepted deposits as they came and had little ability to manage their own liabilities.

On the other side of the balance sheet, the LGS and SRD ratios and the lending guidelines restricted the banks' abilities to dispose of whatever deposits they had. It placed limits on how much lending banks could undertake, and sometimes to whom. It meant that banks were largely unable to manage their assets.

For a period these controls appeared to be very effective. The Reserve Bank could quickly and effectively control the availability of funds which, as we saw in Chapter 24, directly affected aggregate demand through the real balance effect, and indirectly affected demand through interest rates. The Reserve Bank's access to its regulatory powers of control, not available to other private monopolists, meant that, for a time, it could control both the price and the quantity of money. But with the onset of high and rising inflation in the 1960s and 1970s the above policy instruments began to lose their effectiveness.

The first problem was that these controls applied only to banks and not to other financial intermediaries. As non-bank interest rates rose with inflation, depositors withdrew their money from banks and placed it with other non-bank financial intermediaries — building societies, credit unions, life insurnace offices and so on. New intermediaries were created such as cash management trusts, the first of which, started by merchant bank Hill Samuel (now Macquarie Bank), began operations in December 1980. In the 1950s, banks accounted for about 65 per cent of financial intermediation. By the early 1980s their share had fallen to less than 40 per cent.

The second problem was that, with quantity rationing, the banks had to decide *who* would get the limited funds. While some favoured customers could borrow at low interest rates, many other would-be borrowers could not. A major concern was that the system discriminated against low income earners.

The third problem arose when, world financial markets rapidly integrated in the early 1970s with the breakdown of the Bretton-Woods system of fixed exchange rates (see Chapter 29). The closer international financial linkages meant that the Reserve Bank could not both set the exchange rate and control the domestic money supply.

In short, the Reserve Bank was exercising less control over a diminishing part of financial intermediation. In response to the loss in effectiveness of monetary policy the authorities could only choose from two options: either they could extend the coverage of the regulatory net to all financial intermediaries, or they could remove the regulations applying to banks, that is, deregulate. The government chose the latter — it decided to deregulate.

Table 28.1 Major Financial Deregulations

December 1980	Interest rate ceilings on all trading and savings bank deposits removed
August 1981	Minimum term on certificates of deposit reduced to 30 days
March 1982	Minimum terms on many other fixed deposits removed. The requirement of one month's notice of withdrawal from savings bank investment accounts removed
December 1983	Australian dollar floated and most foreign exchange controls removed
August 1984	All remaining controls on bank deposits removed including minimum and maximum terms on bank deposits and restrictions on size of deposits; savings banks permitted to offer cheque facilities
February 1985	Foreign banks invited to take up banking licences
April 1985	Remaining ceilings on bank interest rates removed, except for some housing loans
May 1985	Prime assets ratio (PAR) replaces LGS convention
April 1986	Interest rate ceilings on new housing loans removed
August 1988	Capital adequacy guidelines issued
September 1988	The SRD ratio abolished and replaced by non-callable deposits
December 1989	Distinctions between savings and trading banks removed by changes to the Banking Act

Source: Reserve Bank, *Bulletin*, March 1990, pp. 40–41.

Financial Market Deregulation

Today's financial markets are almost completely free of direct regulation. This was achieved over the decade of the 1980s in several stages. Table 28.1 lists some of the more important deregulatory moves. These include the removal of almost all restrictions on bank interest rates and lending, the entry of new banks and other financial intermediaries, and the floating of the exchange rate and removal of foreign exchange controls.

Since the various deregulations removed the Reserve Bank's ability to directly control the quantity of financial intermediation, a new approach to monetary policy was required. The only possibility was for the Reserve Bank to follow the practices of other central banks world-wide, focusing on reserve requirements and open market operations. Rather than directly controlling financial intermediation, these policies rely more on market processes and on interest rates determined in those markets.

Monetary Policy Tools Following Deregulation

With the removal of all direct controls. the Reserve Bank has two main policy tools to achieve its objectives:

- Reserve requirements
- Open market operations

Reserve Requirements All banks in Australia are required to hold reserves, specified as a minimum percentage of deposits of various classes. From 1960 until 1988 required reserves were specified by the Statutory Reserve Deposit (SRD) ratio. Between 1981 and 1988 the level of SRDs was set at 7 per cent of deposits for trading banks. Since the rate of interest paid on SRDs was below market rates, this acted as a penalty on trading banks. Competition between banks, induced by the removal of some interest rate controls in the early 1980s, caused them to look closely at the costs of funding new lending. In order to avoid the SRD 'penalty', banks sought new funds outside their traditional deposit base. These new sources of funds were in the bank bill market and through offshore borrowing. These activities did not attract SRD penalties, and some were not even included on the balance sheets of banks. The growth in 'off-balance-sheet' banking further eroded the Reserve Bank's ability to conduct monetary policy.

As a result of the growth in off-balance-sheet banking, the SRD requirement was removed in September 1988 and replaced with non-callable deposits. **Non-callable deposits** are 1 per cent of total deposits of banks, which must be held on deposit at the Reserve Bank. Non-callable deposits are held separately from assets held under PAR. In order to minimize the penalty attached to this new form of required reserve, the Reserve Bank pays interest, which is set monthly at 5 per cent below the rate offered on some government securities. This means that the interest rate differential, a measure of the cost of holding reserves, does not increase when interest rates rise.

Now that SRDs have been abolished and replaced with non-callable deposits, the Reserve Bank has indicated that it does not intend to use variations in required reserves as a tool of monetary policy. This leaves open market operations as the only tool of monetary policy in a deregulated environment.

Open Market Operations **Open market operations** are the purchase or sale of Commonwealth government securities — Treasury bills and bonds — by the Reserve Bank in order to influence the money supply. When the Reserve Bank sells government securities, they are ultimately paid for with bank deposits. Thus reserves go down, and tighter monetary and credit conditions are created. With lower reserves, banks cut their lending and interest rates rise. Conversely, when the Reserve Bank buys government securities, its payment for them ultimately puts additional reserves in the hands of the banks and loosens credit conditions. With extra reserves, the banks increase their lending, and interest rates fall.

In order to understand the Reserve Bank's open market operations and their effects on banks' reserves, we first need to examine the structure of the Reserve Bank's balance sheet. We will then examine open market operations in a simplfied framework. The system as it operates in Australia is a little more complex and dealt with later.

The Reserve Bank's Balance Sheet

The balance sheet of the Reserve Bank for June 1990 is set out in Table 28.2. The assets on the left-hand side are what the Reserve Bank owns and the liabilities, on the right-hand side, are what it owes. Most of the Reserve Bank's assets are gold and foreign exchange. The most important aspect of the Reserve Bank's balance sheet is on the liabilities side.

The largest liability of the Reserve Bank is Reserve Bank notes on issue, or notes in circulation. These are the banknotes that we use in our daily transactions. Some of these banknotes are in circulation with the public and others are in the tills and vaults of banks and other financial institutions.

You may be wondering why Reserve Bank notes are considered a liability of the Bank. Banknotes are considered a liability of the bank that issues them because, when notes were invented, they gave their owner a claim on the gold reserves of the issuing bank. Such notes were *convertible paper money.* The holder of such a note could convert the note on demand into gold (or some other commodity such as silver) at a guaranteed price. Thus when a bank is-

Table 28.2 The Balance Sheet for the Reserve Bank, June 1990

Assets (millions of dollars)		**Liabilities (millions of dollars)**	
Commonwealth government securities		Capital and reserve funds	4,043
Treasury bills	—	Notes on issue	12,981
Treasury notes	378	Deposits of Australian banks	3,535
Other	1,609	Deposits of government	1,269
Gold and foreign exchange	21,461	Other liabilities	3,066
Loans, advances and bills held	115		
Other assets	1,331		
Total	24,894	Total	24,894

Source: Reserve Bank, *Annual Report*, 1990.

sued a note, it was holding itself liable to convert that note into a commodity. Modern banknotes are non-convertible. A **non-convertible note** is a banknote that is not convertible into any commodity and that obtains its value by government fiat or decree — hence the term fiat money. Such banknotes are considered the legal liability of the bank that issues them, but they are backed not by commodity reserves but by holdings of securities and loans. Reserve Bank notes are backed by the Reserve Bank's holdings of Commonwealth government securities.

Another important liability of the Reserve Bank is the deposits held there by banks. We saw these deposits as an asset in the balance sheets of the banks. The remaining liabilities of the Reserve Bank consists of items such as Federal and State government deposits in government bank accounts at the Reserve Bank, and accounts held by foreign central banks (such as the Bank of England and the Reserve Bank in the United States).

The two largest items on the liability side of the Reserve Bank's balance sheet make up most of the monetary base. The **monetary base** (often called M0) is the sum of Reserve Bank notes and coin held by the private sector, deposits of banks with the Reserve Bank and Reserve Bank liabilities to the private non-bank sector. Coins are produced by the Royal Australian Mint and are sold at face value to, and sub-

Table 28.3 An Open Market Operation: Reserve Bank buys CGS

(a) Banks sell securities

Effects on the balance sheet of the Reserve Bank

Change in assets (millions of dollars)		Change in liabilities (millions of dollars)	
Commonwealth government securities	+100	Banks' deposits (reserves)	+100

Effects on the balance sheet of the banks

Change in assets (millions of dollars)		Change in liabilities (millions of dollars)	
Banks' deposits (reserves)	+100		
Commonwealth government securities	−100		

(b) Public sells securities

Effects on the balance sheet of the Reserve Bank

Change in assets (millions of dollars)		Change in liabilities (millions of dollars)	
Commonwealth government securities	+100	Banks' deposits (reserves)	+100

Effects on the balance sheet of the banks

Change in assets (millions of dollars)		Change in liabilities (millions of dollars)	
Banks' deposits (reserves)	+100	Deposits	+100

Effects on the balance sheet of the public

Change in assets (millions of dollars)		Change in liabilities (millions of dollars)	
Deposits	+100		
Commonwealth government securities	− 100		

sequently issued by, the Reserve Bank. They do not appear, therefore, as a liability of the Reserve Bank.

By buying or selling government securities, the Reserve Bank can directly determine the scale of its own liabilities and exert a considerable influence upon the monetary base. Such purchases and sales of government securities are the Reserve Bank's *open market operations*. Let's see how open market operations work in a simplified framework.

A Simple Model of Open Market Operations

When the Reserve Bank conducts an open market operation in which it buys Commonwealth government securities, it increases the reserves of the banking system. When it conducts an open market operation in which it sells Commonwealth government securities, it decreases the reserves of the banking system. Let's study the effects of an open market operation by working out what happens when the Reserve Bank buys $100 million of Commonwealth government securities.

Open market operations affect the balance sheets of the Reserve Bank, the banks and the rest of the economy. Table 28.3 keeps track of the changes in these balance sheets. In the simple textbook model, the Reserve Bank buys Commonwealth government securities from banks or directly from the public. Table 28.3(a) works out what happens when banks sell the securities that the Reserve Bank buys.

If the Reserve Bank bought securities from the banks, the Reserve Bank pays for them by crediting the banks' deposit accounts at the Reserve Bank. The changes in the Reserve Bank's balance sheet are that its assets increase by $100 million (the additional Commonwealth government securities bought) and its liabilities also increase by $100 million (the additional bank deposits). The banks' balance sheet also changes but their total assets remain constant. Their deposits at the Reserve Bank increase by $100 million and their securities decrease by $100 million.

Table 28.3(b) deals with the case in which the Reserve Bank buys securities from the public. The Reserve Bank's holdings of Commonwealth government securities increase by $100 million and other agents' holdings of Commonwealth government securities go down by $100 million. The Reserve Bank pays for the securities by giving cheques drawn on itself to the sellers. The sellers take the cheques to the banks and deposit them. Bank deposits increase by $100 million. The banks in turn present the cheques to the Reserve Bank, which credits the banks' accounts with the value of the cheques. Banks' deposits with the Reserve Bank — their reserves — increase by $100 million.

Regardless of which of the two cases takes place, by conducting an open market purchase of securities, the Reserve Bank increases the banks' deposits with itself, that is, it increases the banks' reserves.

If the Reserve Bank conducts an open market *sale* of securities, the events that we have just traced occur in reverse. The Reserve Bank's assets and liabilities will decrease in value and so will the reserves of the banks.

The simple case of open market operations conducted through banks, and sometimes directly with the public, does occur in some countries. But in most countries, central banks deal with an exclusive group of dealers. This is the case in Australia. While the system in Australia works in exactly the same way as described above, and the effects of open market operations on the various balance sheets are ultimately the same, the details of operation are somewhat different.

Furthermore, the Reserve Bank's role in the payments system, and its role as banker to the government, require it to make open market operations decisions daily. This practice differs from that in many other countries. In the United States, for example, open market decisions are made once a month by the Federal Open Market Committee but are implemented daily. We will now look at the operation of the payments system in Australia and closely examine the role of authorized money market dealers.

The Payments System

Every day millions of transactions are undertaken in the normal course of business. Many of these transactions involve cheques, or other means of payment, drawn on one bank and deposited in another. How do the banks settle all these transactions among themselves? The process by which these settlements occur is called the **payments system**. The settlements occur through accounts each bank holds at the Reserve Bank, called **exchange settlement accounts**. The balances in exchange settlement accounts are known as **cash**. The calculations required to make settlement, that is, working out the net position of each bank at the end of the day, is done in a **Clearing House** in each State. At the close of the day's business, each clearing house adds up the transactions for each bank and informs the Reserve Bank. The next morning the Reserve Bank passes the balances into each bank's exchange settlement account. It credits those banks which, on the previous day, had an increase in total deposits and debits those banks which, on the previous day, had a decrease in total deposits. This process, known as interbank settlement, means that each bank must be ready to settle the morning after the transactions have cleared.

Banks are not allowed to overdraw their exchange settlement accounts. But since the Reserve Bank does not pay interest on those accounts, banks like to keep the balance near zero. So, if a bank is debited the morning after a day with heavy withdrawals, it must be able to acquire funds, or cash, quickly to restore the exchange settlement account to credit. Or if a bank is credited in the morning, it wants to quickly move the money into short-term money securities, so it begins to earn interest income. Intermediating in this very short-term interbank money market, or cash market, are the authorized money market dealers.

Authorized Money Market Dealers The **authorized money market dealers** are a select group of nine dealers with a special relationship with the Reserve Bank. The authorized dealers fulfil three roles. First, they are required to 'make the market' in Commonwealth government securities, that is, they must stand ready to quote to clients the prices at which they are prepared to buy or sell Commonwealth government securities. Second, because the authorized dealers make that market, the Reserve Bank, which deals mainly in short-term government securities, transacts almost exclusively with them. The authorized dealers are the conduit through which open market operations occur. Third, they provide the means by which banks and others can invest funds overnight. In return for fulfilling these roles, the Reserve Bank provides the authorized dealers with banking facilities and a steady business.

The authorized dealers take overnight loans from other financial intermediaries, not just banks. These non-bank intermediaries do not have exchange settlement accounts with the Reserve Bank. Instead they have accounts with banks. Transactions between these financial institutions and the authorized dealers are made using bank cheques, which are then processed through the clearing system. Thus the authorized dealers deal in two types of funds: exchange settlement funds, or cash, and bank cheque funds. Exchange settlement funds constitute the **official money market**; bank cheque funds constitute the **unofficial money market**. The authorized dealers thus provide a very important link between the official and the unofficial money markets. The interest rate determined in the official money market is called the **official cash rate**. It is often seen as the key indicator of the current stance of monetary policy.

Open Market Operations and the Money Market

If only banks and other intermediaries were involved in the payments system then the total quantity of funds would be unaffected by any day's transactions, as one bank's withdrawal is another bank's deposit. But when an institution with an account at the Reserve Bank writes cheques on its account, there is a net addition to the funds available to other banks. This is because funds deposited in the Reserve Bank are not loaned out in the multiplier process described in the previous chapter, and represent a drain of money out of the system. Writing a cheque on that account is therefore an injection of money.

Of course, the government is a very important institution with an account at the Reserve Bank. Government transactions affect the amount of money clearing and can add to or subtract from the total quantity of funds in the system. If the government pays out pension cheques, for example, these cheques are drawn against the government account in the Reserve Bank and deposited in other banks. Total funds in the system rise. On the other hand, when the government collects taxes and deposits them in its account, funds are withdrawn from the banking system.

When total funds in the system rise, it is said to be 'in surplus'. That is, the banks start the day with a credit to their exchange settlement accounts, possibly because of large government payments the previous day. The surplus funds are lent by the banks to the authorized dealers in the official money market. The dealers then lend this money to their other clients, banks and other financial intermediaries in the unofficial money market. This increases their reserves in the same way as we described in Table 28.3 If the days starts with the system 'in deficit', funds in the system have fallen and the banks start with a debit to their exchange settlement accounts, possibly because of large tax payments the day before. This shortfall is met by banks calling funds from the authorized dealers, simply by withdrawing deposits held with them, or by selling Commonwealth government securities, which the dealers must quote on. The dealers then sell the securities on the unofficial market. This reduces the reserves of banks and other financial intermediaries in the same way as described in Table 28.3.

Whether the system is in surplus, in deficit or balanced is known early in the morning, after the Domestic Markets Department at the Reserve Bank calculates the exchange settlements for that day using the information provided by the Clearing Houses. At 9.30 a.m. the Reserve Bank announces the position of the market: in surplus, deficit or balanced. At the same time it announces its dealing intentions for the day. This sets the scene for a monetary policy action, if the Reserve Bank so chooses.

To maintain a *steady* monetary policy the Bank would buy securities in just sufficient quantities as to offset any deficiency of funds in the system; or it would sell just enough securities to mop up any surplus. To *tighten* monetary policy the Bank would not buy sufficient securities to offset a deficit in the official money market; or would sell more securities than required to offset a surplus. To *ease* monetary policy the Bank would buy more securities than required to offset a deficit; or would leave the system in surplus by not selling as many securities are required to offset a given surplus in the official money market.

Since the Reserve Bank is involved in the market on a day-to-day basis, because it acts as a banker to both the banks and the government, it has the opportunity to undertake open market operations daily, either through explicit sales and purchases of Commonwealth government securities, or simply by inaction when the payments system finds itself in either deficit or surplus. But the major difference between the Australian system and the more classical textbook case, such as depicted in Table 28.3, is that the Reserve Bank does not use open market operations to affect directly the level of bank reserves, which are included as a component of the money base. Rather, the Bank deals only with the authorized dealers and it is the banks' loans held with the authorized dealers that are ultimately affected by open market operations. These are not a component of the money base.

However achieved, the effects of an open market operation on the balance sheets of the Reserve Bank and the banks that we've traced in Table 28.3 are not the end of the story — they are just the beginning. With an increase in their reserves, the banks are now able to make more loans — as the banks did in Chapter 27 (pp. 238–261) when Alan increased his deposit at the Dundee Bank. That has a big effect on the quantity of money for, again, as we saw in Chapter 27, by making loans banks themselves create money. Let's see how this multiple expansion of money comes about.

The Multiplier Effect of an Open Market Operation

The **money multiplier** is the amount by which a change in the monetary base is multiplied to determine the resulting change in the quantity of money.[2] We'll work out the multiplier effect of an open market operation for the case where the Reserve Bank wants to expand the money supply. The Bank could achieve this by buying securities from the authorized dealers. The authorized dealers are obliged to sell securities to the Reserve Bank if it asks to buy. Having sold securities to the Reserve Bank, the open market operations have increased the cash reserves of the dealers. There are two uses to which the dealers can put the extra funds: they can repay loans they had previously taken with banks and other non-bank clients; or they can buy securities from others in the market. In either case, the reserves of both banks and non-bank financial institutions increase. Even at this stage the money supply has not risen. The banks and the other financial intermediaries are simply holding additional, or excess, reserves and fewer Commonwealth government securities. But because the financial system as a whole has increased reserves, the sequence of events shown in Fig. 28.1 takes place. These events are:

- Banks and non-banks lend excess reserves.
- New loans are used to make payments.
- Households and firms receive payments from new loans.
- Some of the receipts are held as currency — a *currency drain.*
- Some of the receipts are deposited in banks and other intermediaries.
- Reserves increase (by the same amount as the increase in deposits).
- Desired reserves increase (by a fraction — the desired reserve ratio — of the increase in deposits).
- Excess reserves decrease, but remain positive.
- The money supply increases by the amount of the currency drain and the increase in bank deposits.

[2] In Chapter 27 we worked with the *simple* money multiplier, defined as the amount by which a change in bank reserves is multiplied to determine the resulting change in deposits. The *money multiplier* and the *simple money multiplier* are related but different concepts and must not be confused.

Figure 28.1 A Round in the Multiplier Process Following an Open Market Operation

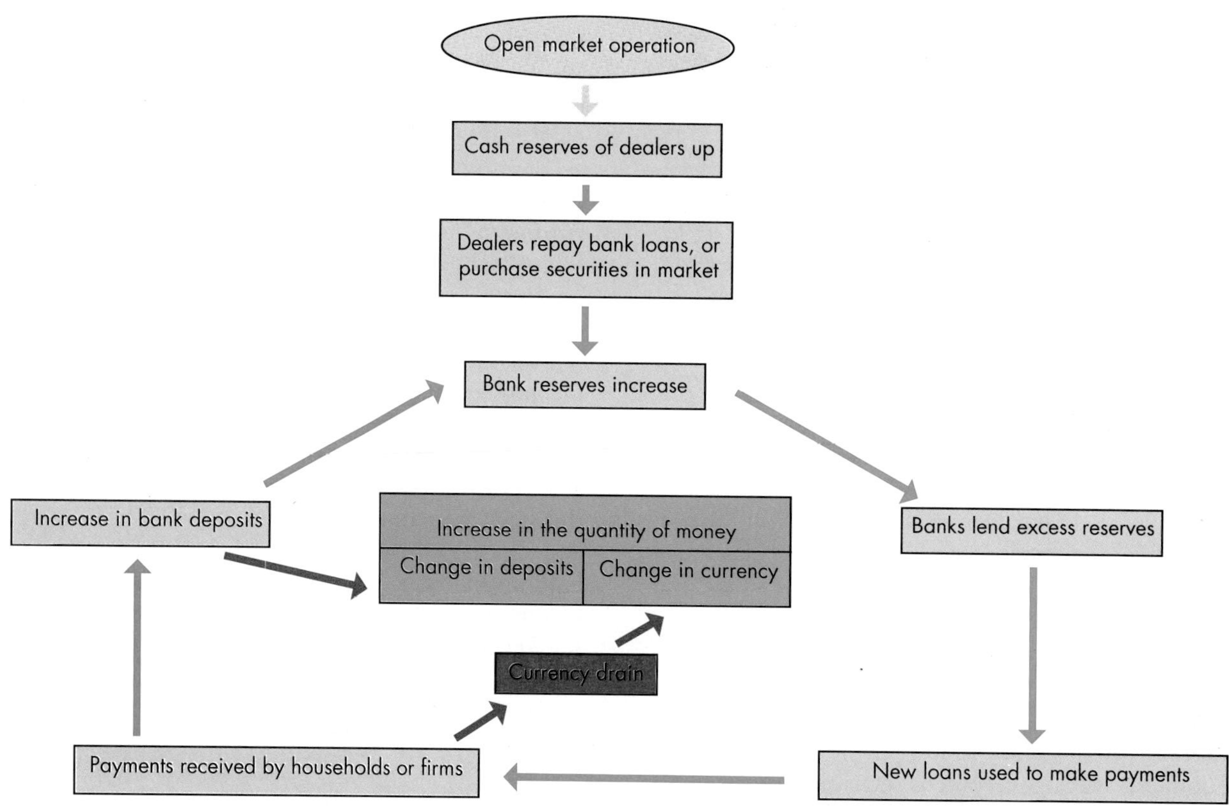

An open market purchase of Commonwealth government securities increases cash reserves of authorized dealers. They repay bank loans or loans to non-bank clients, or buy securities in the market. These actions increase the reserves of financial intermediaries, both bank and non-bank, and creates excess reserves. The excess is lent out and new loans are used to make payments. Households and firms receiving payments keep some of the receipts in the form of currency — a currency drain — and place the rest on deposit in financial intermediaries. The increase in deposits increases reserves, but also increases desired reserves. Desired reserves increase by less than actual reserves, so the financial intermediaries still have some excess reserves, though less than before. The process repeats until excess reserves have been eliminated. There are two components to the increase in the quantity of money: the currency drain and the increase in deposits.

The sequence just described is similar to that which we studied in Chapter 27 except that there we ignored the currency drain. The sequence repeats in a series of 'rounds', but each round begins with a smaller quantity of excess reserves than did the previous one. The process continues until excess reserves have finally been eliminated.

Table 28.4 keeps track of the magnitudes of new loans, the currency drain, the increase in deposits and reserves, the increase in desired reserves and the change in excess reserves at each round of the multiplier process. The initial open market operation has increased the reserves in the financial system but, since deposits have not changed, there is no change in desired reserves. Excess reserves are $100 million. These reserves are loaned out. When the money borrowed from the financial intermediaries is spent, some of it returns in the form of additional deposits and some of it leaks out of the banking system in the form of a currency drain. In the table, we're assuming that two-thirds of what is lent comes back in the form of deposits and one-third drains off and is held by households and firms in the form of currency. Thus when the initial $100 million of excess reserves is loaned out, $66.67 million comes back to them in the form of deposits and $33.33 million

Table 28.4 The Multiplier Effect of an Open Market Operation

Round	Excess reserves at start of round	New loans	Change in deposits	Currency drain	Change in reserves	Change in desired reserves	Excess reserves at end of round	Change in quantity of money
			(millions of dollars)					
1	100.00	100.00	66.67	33.33	66.67	2.00	64.67	100.00
2	64.67	64.67	43.11	21.56	43.11	1.29	41.82	64.67
3	41.82	41.82	27.88	13.94	27.88	0.84	27.04	41.82
4	27.04	27.04	18.03	9.01	18.03	0.54	17.49	27.04
5	17.49	17.49	11.66	5.83	11.66	0.35	11.31	17.49
6	11.31	11.31	7.54	3.77	7.54	0.23	7.31	11.31
7	7.31	7.31	4.88	2.44	4.88	0.15	4.73	7.31
8	4.73	4.73	3.15	1.58	3.15	0.09	3.06	4.73
9	3.06	3.06	2.04	1.02	2.04	0.06	1.98	3.06
10	1.98	1.98	1.32	0.66	1.32	0.04	1.28	1.98
	.	.	.	.	.	.	.	.
	.	.	.	.	.	.	.	.
All others		3.62	2.41	1.21		0.07		3.62
Total		283.02	188.68	94.34		5.66		283.02

drains off and is held outside the system as currency. The quantity of money has now increased by $100 million — the increase in deposits plus the increase in currency holdings.

The increased deposits now produce an increase in the desired reserves of the financial intermediaries. Assume that the desired reserve ratio is 3 per cent. This means that an increase in deposits of $66.7 million generates an increase in desired reserves of $2 million. But actual reserves have increased by the same amount as the increase in deposits — $66.7 million. Therefore, excess reserves are now $64.67 million. At this stage we have completed round 1. We have been around the circle shown in Fig. 28.1. The system still has excess reserves but the level has fallen from $100 million at the beginning of the round to $64.67 million at the end of the round. Round 2 now begins.

When the excess reserves of $64.67 are lent, and the loans spent, two-thirds — $43.11 million — come back in the form of deposits and one-third — $21.56 million — drains off as currency. The quantity of money has now increased by a further $64.67 million for a total increase of $164.67 million.

The process that we've just described keeps on repeating. Table 28.4 shows the first ten rounds in this process and collapses all the remaining ones into the next-to-last row of the table. At the end of the process, the quantity of money has increased by slightly more than $283 million.

The accumulated increase in deposits, currency and the quantity of money is illustrated in Fig. 28.2. As you can see, when the open market operation takes place (labelled OMO in the figure), there is no initial change in either the quantity of money or its components. Even after the authorized dealers have transacted with their clients, both bank and non-bank, there is no change in the money supply. Then, after the first round of lending, the quantity of money increases by $100 million — the size of the open market operation. In successive rounds, the quantity of money and its components continue to increase but by successively smaller amounts until, after 10 rounds, currency, deposits and the quantity of money have almost reached the value to which they are ultimately heading.

Because we have been considering the reserves and lending policy of *all* financial intermediaries, the definition of money we are concerned with here is broad money. If we had restricted our attention to the behaviour of banks only, not all financial intermediaries, then we would have been looking at the narrower definition of money, M3. For the same open market operation considered above, M3 would rise by less than broad money because some of the additional reserves and deposits are held in non-banks, and thus represent a drain out of M3.

Figure 28.2 The Multiplier Effect of an Open Market Operation

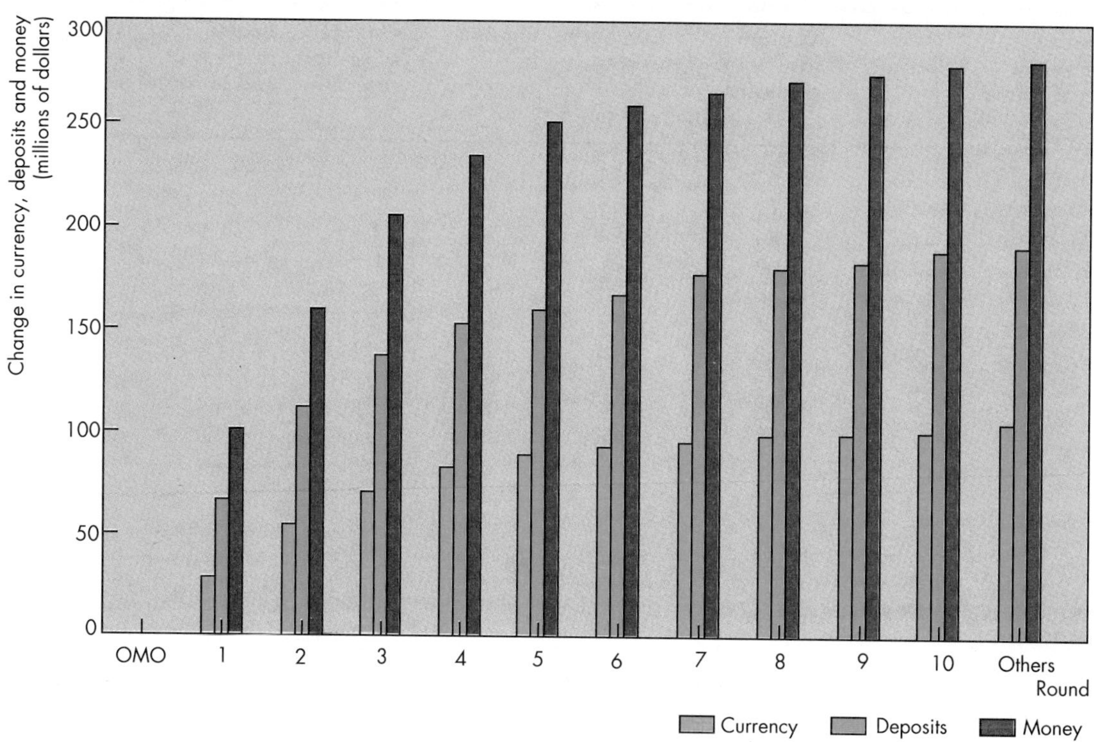

An open market operation (OMO) in which Commonwealth government securities are bought from the authorized dealers has no immediate effect on the money supply but, as the dealers repay past loans or purchase securities in the market, excess reserves are created in the banking system. When loans are made with these reserves and the loans are used to buy goods and services, deposits and currency holdings increase. Each time new loans are spent, part of the loan returns to the financial system in the form of additional deposits and additional reserves. Intermediaries continue to increase their lending until excess reserves have been eliminated. The magnitude of the resulting increase in the money supply is determined by the money multiplier.

What determines the size of the money multiplier and how big is the money multiplier in Australia?

The Australian Money Multiplier

The money multiplier is calculated as the ratio of the quantity of money to the monetary base. That is

$$\text{Money multiplier} = \frac{\text{Quantity of money}}{\text{Monetary base}}$$

The size of the money multiplier depends on which definition of money we're considering. The values of the M1 and M3 multipliers in Australia between 1970 and 1990 are set out in Fig. 28.3. As you can see, the M1 multiplier ranges between 1.5 and 2.5, and the M3 multiplier ranges between 5.3 and 10.3. There are a number of observations that can be drawn from the diagram. First, both multipliers were quite variable prior to 1981. This is the result of disintermediation. **Disintermediation** is the process whereby people withdraw their deposits from banks and deposit them in non-bank financial intermediaries. With disintermediation, the deposit base of the banks is reduced, and narrow measures of the money supply fall. This occurred in Australia because interest rates on bank deposits were controlled by the Reserve Bank and could not rise as interest rates on deposits in non-bank financial intermediaries did. For example, when interest rates available outside banks rose, as they did in the period 1972 to 1974, deposits were withdrawn from trading and savings banks and deposited in other fi-

Figure 28.3 The Money Multipliers

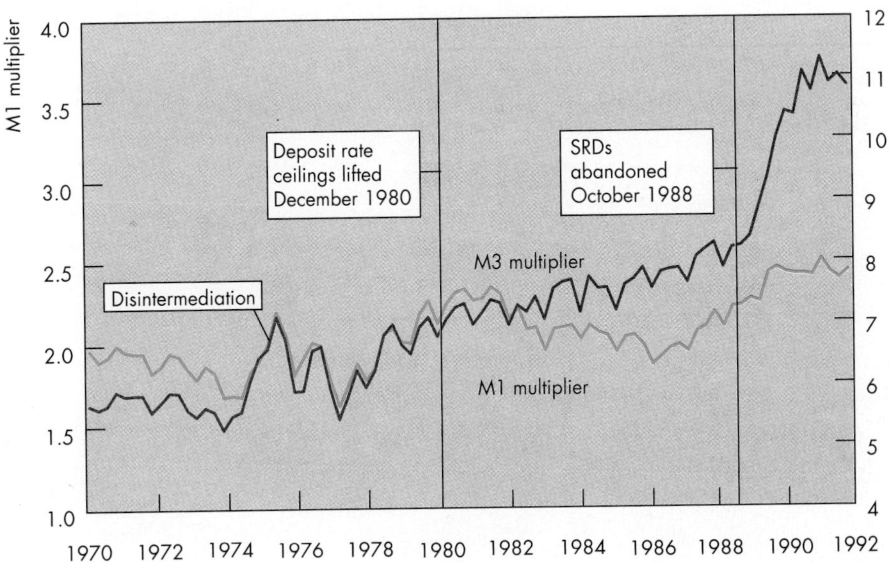

The money multipliers for both M1 and M3 exhibit a great deal of variability prior to 1981 because of disintermediation. When deposit rate ceilings were lifted in 1981, there was less shifting of deposits in and out of M1 and M3 accounts, and the multipliers settled down. In October 1988 SRDs were abolished and the M3 multiplier rose as banks borrowed less in the bank bill market and more actively sought deposit sources of funds instead.

Source: M1: Series VNEQ.AC_$LM1; M3: Series VNEQ.AC_$LM3 from the NIF-10S Model Data; and Monetary Base: Series DMAMB, RBA *Bulletin* Database, all supplied by EconData's dX Data Service.

nancial intermediaries, such as building societies. The money supply, measured as M1 or M3, fell and the multipliers fell. But as interest rates fell from 1975 to 1976, deposits were placed back in banks and the multipliers rose. There is a clear break in the behaviour of the multipliers from 1981 onwards as a result of the removal of interest rate ceilings on trading and savings bank deposits.

Between 1981 and 1988, the money multipliers exhibited considerably more stability, although there were still substantial variations in them as the financial system continued to be deregulated. As other deposits in banks began to compete with current deposits in trading banks, funds moved out of current deposits into fixed deposits. The M1 multiplier fell, while the M3 multiplier rose. The most dramatic change occurred in the M3 multiplier in 1989 when, in the space of one year, it rose from 8.5 to 10.5. This was the effect of the abolition of SRDs. Banks brought more of their business 'back on balance sheet', transacting much less business in the bank bill market. In other words, banks pursued fewer funds in the bank bill market and more funds from traditional deposit sources, and this is reflected in a larger measured M3.

The monetary base is like the base of an inverted pyramid of money. The monetary base itself is divided into currency and reserves. Each dollar of currency creates a dollar of money. Each dollar of reserves supports a multiple of itself as money and the larger the multiple, the broader the definition of money. By changing the monetary base indirectly through its transactions with authorized money market dealers, the Reserve Bank changes reserves. The change in reserves has a multiplier or magnification effect on the quantity of money outstanding.

It is expected that as the financial system finishes adjusting to the past decade of deregulation, the money multipliers will exhibit a stable relationship because their values depend on two ratios that, under normal circumstances, do not vary much. These ratios are:

- Currency holdings of households and firms as a fraction of total deposits
- Reserve holdings of banks as a fraction of total deposits

Table 28.5 shows how the money multiplier depends on these two ratios. It also provides numbers that illustrate the M1 money multiplier. Currency

Table 28.5 Calculating the Money Multiplier

	In general	Numbers for MI
1. The variables		
Currency	C	
Reserves	R	
Monetary base	MB	
Deposits	D	
Money supply	M	
Money multiplier	mm	
2. Definitions		
The monetary base is the sum of currency and reserves	$MB = C + R$	
The money supply is the sum of deposits and currency	$M = D + C$	
The money multiplier is the ratio of the money supply to the monetary base	$mm = M/MB$	
3. Ratios		
Currency to deposits	C/D	0.45
Reserves to deposits	R/D	0.15
4. Calculations		
Begin with the definition	$mm = M/MB$	
Use the definitions of M and MB to give	$mm = \frac{D+C}{C+R}$	
Divide top and bottom by D to give	$mm = \frac{1 + C/D}{C/D + R/D}$	$= \frac{1 + 0.45}{0.45 + 0.15}$
		$= 2.4$

holdings of households and firms are approximately 0.45 times the chequable deposits that make up M1. Equivalently, currency makes up 31 per cent of M1 and deposits 69 per cent. Reserve holdings, non-callable deposits at the Reserve Bank and other reserves are approximately 15 per cent (0.15) of the deposits in M1. We used this value for the desired reserve ratio in the above calculation. Combining these ratios in the formula derived in the table shows that the M1 money multiplier is 2.4.

R E V I E W

The Reserve Bank is the nation's central bank. The Reserve Bank influences the quantity of money in circulation by changing the excess reserves of the banking system. Potentially, it has two instruments at its disposal: reserve requirements and open market operations. The Bank has stated that it will not use reserve requirements as a tool of monetary policy. This leaves only open market operations. Open market operations are conducted with the authorized money market dealers whose clients are the banks and other non-bank financial intermediaries. Open market operations not only change the excess reserves of the financial system but also set up a multiplier effect. When excess reserves are lent, some of the loans 'drain' out of the financial system, but others come back in the form of new deposits. The intermediaries continue to lend until the currency drain and the increase in their desired reserves have eliminated excess reserves. The multiplier effect of an open market operation depends on the scale of the currency drain and the size of the banks' desired reserve ratio. ■

The Reserve Bank's objectives in conducting open market operations, or taking other actions that influence the quantity of money in circulation, are not simply to affect the money supply for its own sake. Its objective is to influence the course of the economy — especially the level of output, employment and prices. But these effects are indirect. The Reserve Bank's immediate objective is to move interest rates up or down. To work out the effects of the Reserve Bank's actions on interest rates, we need to work out how and why interest rates change when the quantity of money changes. We'll discover the answer to these questions by studying the demand for money.

The Demand for Money

The amount of money we *receive* each week in payment for our labour is income — a flow. The amount of money that we hold in our wallet or in a deposit account at the bank is a stock. There is no limit to how much income — or flow — we would like to receive each week. But there is a limit to how big a stock of money each of us would like to hold, on the average.

The Motives for Money Holding

Why do people hold a stock of money? Why do you carry coins and bills in your wallet, and why do you keep money in a deposit account at your neighbourhood bank?

There are three main motives for holding money:

- Transactions motive
- Precautionary motive
- Speculative motive

Transactions Motive The main motive for holding money is to be able to undertake transactions and to minimize the cost of transactions. By carrying a stock of currency, you are able to undertake small transactions such as buying your lunch at the canteen. If you didn't carry a stock of currency, you'd have to go to the bank every lunchtime in order to withdraw enough cash. The opportunity cost of these transactions, in terms of your own lost study or leisure time, would be considerable. You avoid those transactions costs by keeping a stock of currency large enough to make your normal purchases over a period of perhaps a week in length.

You also keep a stock of money in the form of deposits at the bank to make your transactions such as paying the rent on your flat or paying your bookshop bill. Instead of having a stock of bank deposits for these purposes, you might put all your assets into the stock or bond market — buying BHP shares or Commonwealth government securities. But if you did that, you would have to call your broker and sell some shares and bonds each time you needed to pay the rent or the bookshop. Again, you'd have to pay the opportunity cost of such transactions. Instead, by holding larger stocks of bank deposits, those costs can be avoided.

Individual holdings of money for transactions purposes fluctuate during any week or month. But aggregate money balances held for transactions purposes do not fluctuate much because, what one person is spending, someone else is receiving.

Firms' money holdings are at their peak just before the moment at which they pay their employees' wages. Households' money holdings are at a peak just after wages have been paid. As households spend their incomes, their money holdings decline and firms' holdings of money increase. Firms' holdings of money are actually quite large and it is this fact that makes average money holdings appear to be so large. Average money holdings of households are much lower than the economy-wide averages presented in the chapter opener.

Precautionary Motive Money is held as a precaution against unforeseen events that require unplanned purchases to be made. For example, on an out-of-town trip you carry some extra money in case your car breaks down and has to be fixed. Or, if you are shopping at the January sales you take with you more money than you are planning on spending in case you come across a real bargain that you just can't pass up.

Speculative Motive The final motive for holding money is to avoid losses from holding shares or bonds that are expected to fall in value. For example, suppose that, a week before the stock market crash of October 1987, you had predicted the crash. On the Friday afternoon before the markets closed, you would have sold all your shares and put the proceeds into your bank deposit account for the weekend. This temporary holding of money would persist until share prices had fallen to their lowest predicted level. Only then would you reduce your bank deposit and buy shares again.

The Influences on Money Holding

What determines the quantity of money that households and firms choose to hold? There are three important influences on this quantity:

- Prices
- Real expenditure
- The opportunity cost of holding money

The higher the level of prices, other things being equal, the larger is the quantity of money that people will want to hold. The higher the level of real expenditure, other things being equal, the larger the quantity of money that people plan to hold. The higher the opportunity cost of holding money, the smaller is the quantity of money that people plan to hold.

These influences on individual decisions about money holding translate into three macroeconomic variables that influence the aggregate quantity of money demanded:

- The price level
- Real GDP
- The interest rate

Price Level and the Quantity of Money Demanded The quantity of money measured in current dollars is called the **nominal quantity of money**. The nominal quantity of money demanded is proportional to the price level. That is, other things being equal, if the price level (GDP deflator) increases by 10 per cent, people will want to hold 10 per cent more nominal money than before. What matters to people is not the number of dollars that they hold but the buying power of those dollars. Suppose, for example, that to undertake your weekly expenditure on movies and soft-drink you carry an average of $20 in your wallet. If your income and the prices of movies and soft-drink increased by 10 per cent you would increase your average cash holding by 10 per cent to $22.

The quantity of money measured in constant dollars (for example, in 1984/85 dollars) is called *real money*. Real money is equal to nominal money divided by the price level. The quantity of real money demanded is independent of the price level. If the price level as measured by the GDP deflator is 200, people will want to hold, on the average, the same quantity of real money as they would if the GDP deflator was 100. Doubling the price level doubles the quantity of nominal money demanded but leaves the quantity of real money demanded unchanged.

Real GDP and the Quantity of Real Money Demanded An important determinant of the quantity of real money demanded is the level of real income — for the aggregate economy, real GDP. As you know, real GDP and real aggregate expenditure are two sides of the same transaction. The amount of money that households and firms demand depends on the amount of spending that they want to do. The higher the expenditure — the higher the income — the larger is the quantity of money demanded. Again, suppose that you hold an average of $20 to finance your weekly purchases of movies and soft-drink. Now imagine that the prices of these goods and of all other goods remain constant but that your income increases. As a consequence you now spend more and you also keep a larger amount of money on hand to finance your higher volume of expenditure.

The Interest Rate and the Quantity of Money Demanded The higher the level of interest rates, other things being equal, the lower is the quantity of real money demanded. Equivalently, the higher the level of interest rates, the higher is the velocity of circulation of money. The velocity of circulation is the ratio of real GDP to the quantity of real money demanded.[3] It measures how much work a given amount of money does. A high velocity of circulation means that money is circulating quickly so that each dollar coin and each dollar of chequable deposits is doing a lot of work. A low velocity of circulation means that currency and chequable deposits are circulating slowly.

---

[3] In Chapter 27 we defined the velocity of circulation using the equation of exchange:

$$MV = PY$$

where M is the quantity of nominal money, V is the velocity of

Continued

Though there are physical limits to how quickly money can circulate, the velocity of circulation can vary greatly. For example, suppose that four people have just a single one-dollar coin between them. At 9 a.m., Ann is holding the dollar coin and the other three people have no money at all. Ann uses the dollar coin at 9 a.m. to buy two cups of coffee from Bob. Bob uses the same dollar coin at lunchtime to buy a sandwich from Rick. Rick uses the dollar coin in the afternoon to buy an ice-cream cone from Debbie, who in turn uses it in the evening to rent a video from Ann. Ann holds the dollar coin overnight and the same sequence of transactions repeats itself the next day.

In this example, a single one-dollar coin has produced \$4 worth of transactions in a single day — involving coffee, a sandwich, ice cream and a video. The dollar coin has circulated quickly. A small amount of money has produced many transactions with a high velocity of circulation.

These same transactions could have occurred with a low velocity of circulation and a larger quantity of money. For example, the four people could have started and ended the day with a dollar, buying and selling the same goods as before. In the first example, the velocity of circulation is 4 — \$4 worth of expenditure is financed with a one dollar coin. In the second example, the velocity of circulation is 1 — \$4 worth of transactions are financed with \$4 worth of money.

Does the velocity of circulation matter? It does. Do people care how quickly they turn their money over? They do. There are both costs and benefits in having a high velocity of circulation.

The Costs of a High Velocity of Circulation The main cost of a high velocity of circulation is that people have to transact frequently. They also may have to transact at inconvenient times. For example, in the above story when there is only one dollar, only one person holds the dollar coin at any one time, so none of the others can make a purchase until they have made their sale. Debbie couldn't rent her video until she had sold the ice cream. Rick couldn't buy his ice cream until he had sold a sandwich, and so on. But if each person in the story starts and ends the day holding one dollar, any of the transactions could be undertaken at any time during the day. For example, it might be much more convenient for Debbie to rent the video on her way to work, before Ann has bought her breakfast, rather than having to run around to Ann's video rental shop in the late afternoon. It might be even more convenient to rent three videos at a time and hang on to them for three days, thereby visiting the video store just twice a week rather than every day. However, to do so, Debbie would need at least as much money as the price of three videos. Economizing on transactions — transacting less frequently — always requires a larger quantity of money than transacting frequently. These are the main costs of a high velocity of circulation — the increased costs of doing business.

The Benefits of a High Velocity of Circulation

What are the benefits of a high velocity of circulation of money? A high velocity of circulation means that a small quantity of money is being held relative to the amount of expenditure being undertaken. The lower the quantity of money held, the greater is the quantity of other assets that can be held. Cash in your pocket doesn't earn interest. Some bank deposits do earn interest, but at lower rates than other assets such as bonds and stocks. By holding less money and holding more assets that earn a higher interest rate than do bank deposits, people can increase their incomes. This the main benefit of a high velocity of circulation — a large interest income.

Interest Rate and Opportunity Cost You already know the fundamental principle that as the opportunity cost of something rises, people try to find substitutes for it. Money is no exception to this principle. The opportunity cost of holding money is the interest that could be earned on other assets. The higher the interest rate, the higher is the opportunity cost of holding money and the more people will try to find substitutes for money and economize on their holdings of money. The main substitute for holding money is more frequent transactions. By transacting more frequently and in smaller amounts, people can undertake a given amount of economic activity with a smaller amount of real money. The higher the opportunity cost of holding money, the lower is the quantity of money demanded and the higher is the

---

circulation, P is the price level and Y is real GDP. Dividing this equation by P gives:

$$(M/P)V = Y$$

and then dividing by the real quantity of money (M/P) gives:

$$V = Y/(M/P)$$

This shows that the velocity of circulation is equal to the ratio of real GDP to the real money supply.

frequency of transactions. Or in other words, the higher the interest rate, the higher is the velocity of circulation.

REVIEW

The quantity of money demanded depends on the price level, real GDP and the interest rate. The quantity of nominal money demanded is proportional to the price level. Real money is the nominal quantity of money divided by the price level. The quantity of real money demanded increases as real GDP increases. The opportunity cost of holding money is the interest rate. The benefit from holding money is the avoidance of frequent transactions. The higher the opportunity cost of holding money (the higher the interest rate), the smaller is the quantity of real money demanded and the higher is the velocity of circulation. ■

The Demand for Real Money

The **demand for real money** is the relationship between the quantity of real money demanded and the interest rate, holding constant all other influences on the amount of money that people wish to hold. To make the demand for real money more concrete, let's consider an example. A person's demand for real money can be represented as a demand schedule for real money. Such a schedule sets out the quantity of real money that a person wants to hold at a given level of real income for different levels of the interest rate.

Figure 28.4 sets out some numbers for the Hunter household. The household's real income is $20,000 a year. The price level is 1 or the GDP deflator is equal to 100, so the quantity of money is the same whether we measure it in nominal terms or real terms. The table tells us how the quantity of real money demanded by the Hunter household changes as the interest rate changes. For example, in row *a*, when the interest rate is 7 per cent a year, the Hunter household holds $2400 of money, on the average. When the interest rate is 5 per cent a year, real money holdings increase to $3000, and when the interest rate falls to 3 per cent a year, real money holdings increase to $4000. The figure also graphs the Hunter household's demand curve for real money (*MD*).

The demand curve for real money slopes downward. The reason for this relationship between the amount of real money held and the interest rate is that the opportunity cost of holding money falls as the rate of interest falls. At an interest rate of 3 per cent, the opportunity cost of holding money is small and the Hunter household holds a large average level of real money balances. But at an interest rate of 7 per cent, the opportunity cost of holding money is high, so the Hunter household holds a smaller average level of real money.

Figure 28.4 The Hunter Household's Demand for Real Money

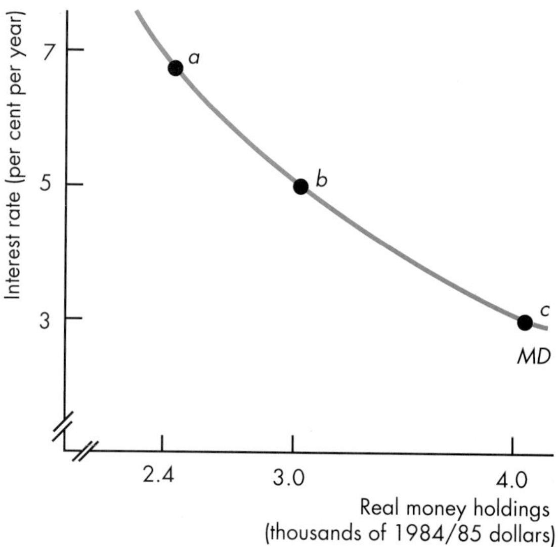

Hunter household's real income is $20,000; price level is 1

	Nominal interest rate (per cent per year)	Real money holdings (thousands of 1984/85 dollars)
a	7	2.4
b	5	3.0
c	3	4.0

The table shows the Hunter household's demand schedule for real money. The lower the interest rate, the larger is the quantity of real money that the household plans to hold. The graph shows the household's demand curve for real money (*MD*). Points *a*, *b* and *c* on the curve correspond to the rows in the table. A change in the interest rate leads to a movement along the demand curve. The demand curve for real money slopes downward because the interest rate is the opportunity cost of holding money. The higher the interest rate, the larger is the interest forgone on holding another asset.

Shifts in the Demand Curve for Real Money

The demand curve for real money shifts when

- Real income changes
- Financial innovation occurs

Changes in Real Income An increase in real income shifts the demand curve for real money to the right and a decrease shifts it to the left. The effect of real income on the demand curve for real money is shown in Fig. 28.5. The table shows the effects of a change in real income on the quantity of real money demanded when the interest rate is constant at 5 per cent. Look first at row *b* of the table. It tells us that when the interest rate is 5 per cent and real income is $20,000, the quantity of real money demanded by the Hunter household is $3000. This row corresponds to point *b* on the demand curve for real money MD_0. Continuing to hold the interest rate constant, if real income falls to $12,000, the quantity of real money held falls to $2400. Thus the demand curve for real money shifts from MD_0 to MD_1 in Fig. 28.5. If the Hunter household's real income increases to $28,000, the quantity of real money held by the household increases to $3600. In this case, the demand curve shifts to the right from MD_0 to MD_2.

Financial Innovation Financial innovation also results in a change in the demand for real money and a shift in the demand curve for real money. The most important such innovation in recent years has been the development of highly liquid deposits with banks and other financial institutions that make it possible for people to convert such deposits quickly and easily into a medium of exchange — to money. These innovations have been brought about partly as a result of deregulation of the financial sector and partly by the availability of low-cost computing power.

Computers are an important part of the story of financial innovation because they have dramatically lowered the cost of keeping records and making calculations. Interest-bearing cheque accounts, for example, have to have balances and interest payments calculated on a daily basis. Doing such calculations manually, although technologically feasible, would be very costly.

Now that banks have access to a vast amount of extremely low-cost computing power, they can offer a wide variety of deposit arrangements that make it convenient to convert non-medium of exchange assets into medium of exchange assets at extremely low cost. The development of these arrangements has led to a decrease in the demand for money.

The availability of low-cost computing power in the financial sector is also responsible, in large degree, for the widespread use of credit cards. Again, keeping the records and calculating the interest and outstanding debt required to operate a credit card system is feasible manually but too costly to undertake.

Figure 28.5 Changes in the Hunter Household's Demand for Real Money

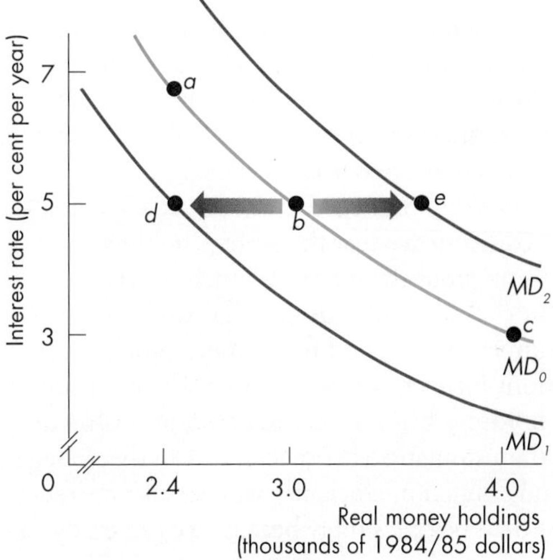

Interest rate is 5 per cent; price level is 1

	Real income (thousands of 1984/85 dollars)	Real money holdings (thousands of 1984/85 dollars)
d	12	2.4
b	20	3.0
e	28	3.6

A change in real income leads to a change in the demand for real money. The table shows the quantity of real money held by the Hunter household at three different levels of real income when the interest rate is constant at 5 per cent. The graph shows the effects of a change in real income on the demand curve for real money. When real income is $20,000 and the interest rate is 5 per cent, the household is at point *b* on the demand curve for real money MD_0. When real income falls to $12,000, the demand curve is MD_1 and, at a 5 per cent interest rate, the household is at point *d*. When real income rises to $28,000, the demand curve shifts to MD_2. With an interest rate of 5 per cent, the household is at point *e*.

No one would find it worthwhile to use plastic cards, shuffle sales slips and keep records if all the calculations had to be done manually (or even using pre-electronic mechanical calculating machines). This innovation — low-cost computing power — has also lowered the demand for money. By using a credit card to make purchases, it is possible to operate with a much lower stock of money. Instead of holding money for transactions purposes through the month, it is possible to charge purchases to a credit card, paying the credit card bill on, or a day or two after, payday, with the consequence that the average holding of money throughout the month is much lower.

The financial innovations that we have just considered affect the demand for money. Some financial innovations have changed the composition of our money holdings but not its total amount. One of these is the automatic teller machine. On the average, we can now function efficiently with smaller currency holdings than before, simply because we can easily obtain currency at almost any time or place. Although this innovation has decreased the demand for currency and increased the demand for deposits, it has probably not affected the overall demand for real money.

R E V I E W

We can represent the demand for money by a demand curve for real money. That demand curve for real money shows how the quantity of real money demanded varies as the interest rate varies. When the interest rate changes, there is a movement along the demand curve for real money. Equivalently, there is a change in the velocity of circulation of money. Other influences on the quantity of real money demanded shift the demand curve for real money. An increase in real income shifts the demand curve to the right; financial innovations that develop convenient near-money deposits shift the demand curve to the left. ■

Now that we have studied the theory of the demand for real money, let's look at the facts about money holdings in Australia and see how they relate to real income and the interest rate.

The Demand for Money in Australia

We've just seen that the demand curve for real money, which shows how the quantity of real money demanded varies as the interest rate varies, shifts whenever there is a change in real GDP or when there is a financial innovation influencing money holding. Because these factors that shift the demand curve for real money are changing all the time in the real world, it is not easy to 'see' the demand curve for real money for a real world economy.

The reason we are interested in examining the demand curve for real money is so that we can discover how that demand curve shifts as a result of changes in income and in the other factors that influence it. A good way of approaching this task is to study the demand for money measured not in dollars but as a percentage of GDP. We know that the demand for money changes when GDP changes. By measuring the amount of money held as a percentage of GDP, we are able to isolate the effects of interest rates, financial innovation and other factors, on the demand for money. Also, the amount of money held expressed as a percentage of GDP is related to the velocity of circulation of money. We've just discovered that changes in the velocity of circulation are equivalent to movements along the demand curve for real money. When the velocity of circulation is high, the amount of money held as a percentage of GDP is low. One is the inverse of the other.

Figure 28.6 shows the relationship between the interest rate and the velocity of circulation of M1 and M3; Fig. 28.6(a) deals with M1 and Fig. 28.6(b) with M3. As you can see from the figures, there was, prior to 1981, a distinct positive relationship between interest rates and velocity (the inverse of the demand for real money). Since 1981, that is, post-deregulation, that relationship has become less obvious — more so for M3 than M1.

We've now studied the factors that determine the demand for real money and have discovered that, other things held constant, the quantity of real money demanded decreases when the interest rate increases. We have also studied the way in which the Reserve Bank can influence the quantity of money supplied. We are now going to combine our models of the demand side and supply side of the money market and discover how the average level of interest rates is determined.

Interest Rate Determination

An interest rate is the percentage yield on a financial security such as a bond or a share. There is an important relationship between the interest rate and the price of a financial asset.

Figure 28.6 The Velocity of Circulation of M1 and M3

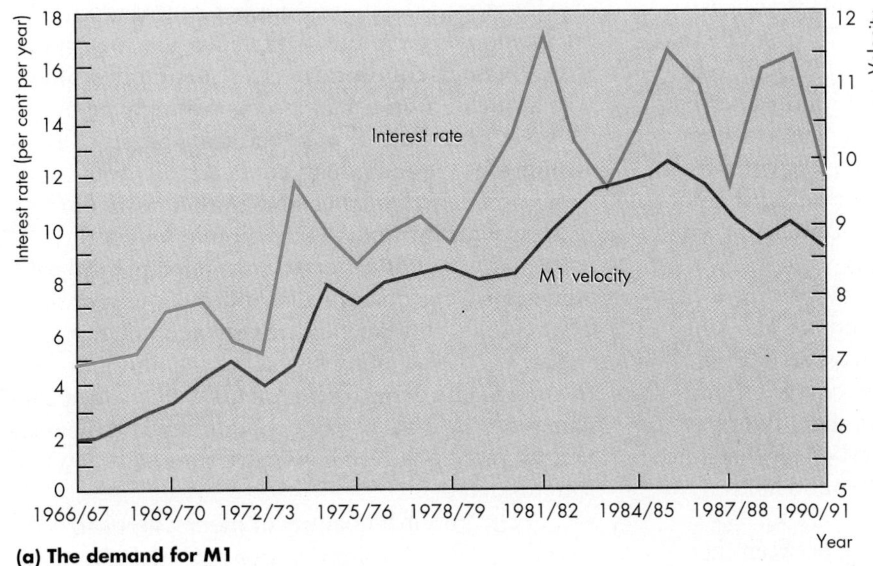

(a) The demand for M1

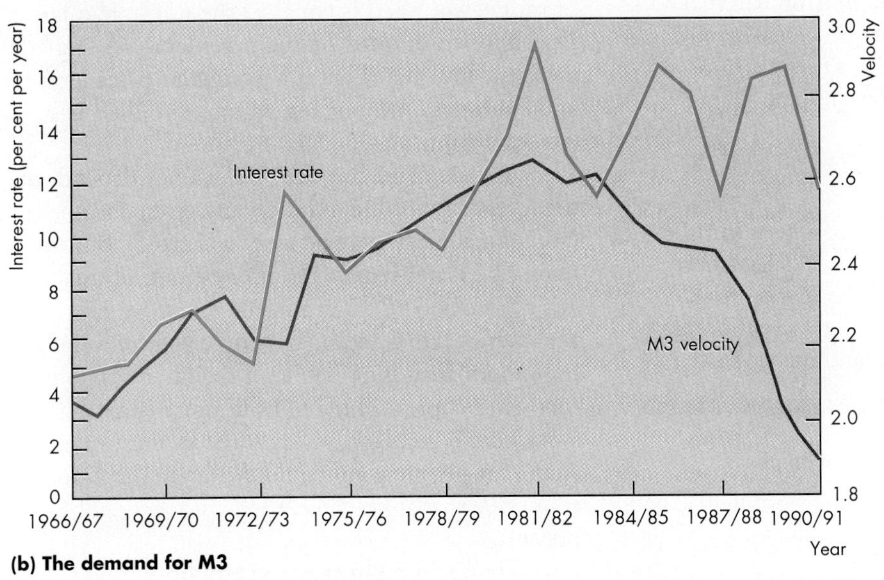

(b) The demand for M3

In part (a), the velocity of circulation — GDP per unit of M1 — is graphed against the interest rate (the commercial bill rate). Up to the early 1980s, there is a clear positive relationship between these two variables. As the interest rate rose, so did the velocity. Equivalently, demand for M1 declined as the opportunity cost of holding cash rose.

Part (b) shows the velocity of circulation of M3. Again, the relationship is quite strong up until the early 1980s. Since then it appears to have broken down, indicating a shift in the demand for M3.

Source: Commercial Bill Rate: Series VNEQ.UN_RCB, from NIF-10S Model Data; M1 and M3: see Fig. 28.3.

Let's spend a moment studying that relationship before analysing the forces that determine interest rates.

Interest Rates and Asset Prices

A bond is a promise to make a sequence of future payments. There are many different possible sequences but the most simple one, for our purposes, is the case of a bond called a perpetuity. A **perpetuity** is a bond that promises to pay a certain fixed amount of money each year forever. The issuer of such a bond will never buy the bond back (redeem it); the bond will remain outstanding forever, and will earn a fixed dollar payment each year. The fixed dollar payment is called the *coupon.* Since the coupon is a fixed dollar amount, the interest rate on the bond varies as the price of the bond varies. Table 28.6 illustrates this fact.

First, the table shows the formula for calculating the interest rate on a bond. The interest rate (r) is the coupon (c) divided by the price of the bond (p) all multiplied by 100 to convert it into a percentage. The table goes on to show some numerical examples for a bond whose coupon is $10 a year. If the bond costs $100 (row *b* of Table 28.6), the interest rate is 10 per cent a year. That is, the holder of $100 worth of bonds receives $10 a year.

Rows *a* and *c* of Table 28.6 show two other cases. In row *a*, the price of the bond is $50. With the coupon at $10, this price produces an interest rate of 20 per cent — $10 returned on a $50 bond holding is an interest rate of 20 per cent. In row *c* the bond costs $200 and the interest rate is therefore 5 per cent — $10 return on a $200 bond holding is an interest rate of 5 per cent.

There is an inverse relationship between the price of a bond and the interest rate earned on the bond. As a bond price rises, the bond's interest rate declines. Understanding this relationship will make it easier for you to understand the process whereby the interest rate is determined. Let's now turn to studying how interest rates are determined.

Money Market Equilibrium

The interest rate is determined at each point in time by equilibrium in the markets for financial assets. We can study that equilibrium in the market for money. We've already studied the determination of the supply of money and the demand for money.

Table 28.6 Interest Rate and Price of Bond

Formula for interest rate

r = interest rate, c = coupon, p = price of bond

$$r = (c/p)100$$

Examples

	Price of bond (dollars)	Coupon (dollars)	Interest rate (per cent per year)
a	50	10	20
b	100	10	10
c	200	10	5

We've seen that money is a stock. When the stock of money supplied equals the stock of money demanded, the money market is in equilibrium. *Stock equilibrium* in the money market contrasts with *flow equilibrium* in the markets for goods and services. A **stock equilibrium** is a situation in which the available stock of an asset is willingly held. That is, regardless of what the available stock is, conditions are such that people actually want to hold precisely that stock and neither more nor less. A **flow equilibrium** is a situation in which the quantity of goods or services supplied per unit of time equals the quantity demanded per unit of time. The equilibrium expenditure that we studied in Chapter 26 is an example of a flow equilibrium. So is the equality of aggregate real GDP demanded and supplied. Let's study stock equilibrium and the market for money and see how it determines the level of interest rates.

The nominal quantity of money supplied is determined by the policy decisions of the Reserve Bank and by the lending actions of banks and other financial intermediaries. The real quantity of money supplied is equal to the nominal quantity supplied divided by the price level. At a given moment in time, there is a particular price level and so the quantity of real money supplied is a fixed amount.

The demand curve for real money depends on the level of real GDP. And on any given day, the level of real GDP may be treated as fixed. But the interest rate is not fixed. The interest rate adjusts to achieve stock equilibrium in the money market. If the interest rate is too high, people will try to hold less money than is available. If the interest rate is too low, people will try to hold more than the stock that is available. When the interest rate is such that people want to hold exactly the amount of money that is available, then a stock equilibrium prevails.

Figure 28.7 illustrates an equilibrium in the money market. The quantity of real money supplied is $3 billion. The table sets out the quantity of real money demanded at three different interest rates when real GDP is constant at $300 billion and the price level is constant at 1 (the price index equals 100).

At a 5 per cent interest rate, the quantity of real money demanded is $3 billion, which equals the quantity of real money supplied. The equilibrium interest rate is 5 per cent. If the interest rate is above 5 per cent, people will want to hold less money than is available. At an interest rate below 5 per cent, people

Figure 28.7 Money Market Equilibrium

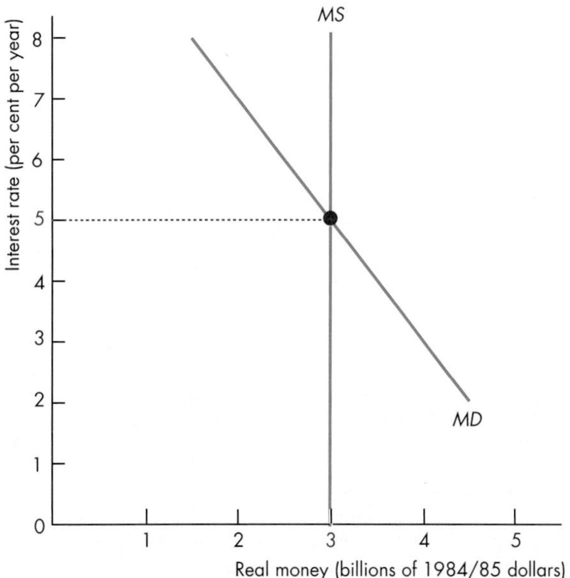

Real GDP is $300 billion; price level is 1

Interest rate (per cent per year)	Quantity of real money demanded (billions of 1984/85 dollars)	Quantity of real money supplied (billions of 1984/85 dollars)
7	2	3
5	3	3
3	4	3

Adjustments in the interest rate achieve money market equilibrium. If real GDP is $300 billion dollars, the demand for real money is given by curve *MD*. If the supply of real money is $3 billion (curve *MS* in the figure), the equilibrium interest rate is 5 per cent. At interest rates above 5 per cent, the quantity of real money demanded is less than the quantity supplied, so interest rates will fall. At interest rates below 5 per cent, the quantity of real money demanded exceeds the quantity supplied, so interest rates will rise. Only at 5 per cent is the quantity of real money in existence willingly held.

5 per cent interest rate, the amount of money available is willingly held.

How does money market equilibrium come about? To answer this question let's perform a thought experiment. First, imagine that the interest rate is temporarily at 7 per cent. In this situation, people will want to hold only $2 billion in real money even though $3 billion exist. But since $3 billion exist, people must be holding them. That is, people are holding more money than they want to. In such a situation, they will try to get rid of some of their money. Each individual will try to re-organize his or her affairs in order to lower the amount of money held and take advantage of the 7 per cent interest rate by buying more financial assets. But everybody will be trying to buy financial assets, and nobody will be trying to sell them at a 7 per cent interest rate. There is an excess demand for financial assets such as bonds. When there is an excess demand for anything, its price rises. So with an excess demand for financial assets, the prices of financial assets will rise. We saw earlier that there is an inverse relationship between the price of a financial asset and its interest rate. As the price of a financial asset rises, its interest rate falls.

As long as anyone is holding money in excess of the quantity demanded, that person will try to lower his or her money holdings by buying additional financial assets. Financial asset prices will continue to rise and interest rates will continue to fall. Only when the interest rate has moved down to 5 per cent will the amount of money in existence be held willingly. That is, people's attempts to get rid of unwanted excess money do not result in reducing the amount of money held in aggregate. Instead, those efforts result in a change in the interest rate that makes the amount of money available willingly held.

The thought experiment that we have just conducted can be performed in reverse by supposing that the interest rate is 3 per cent. In this situation, people want to hold $4 billion even though only $3 billion are available. To acquire more money, people will sell financial assets. There will be an excess supply of financial assets, so their prices will fall. As the prices of financial assets fall, the yield on them — the interest rate — rises. People will continue to sell financial assets and try to acquire money until the interest rate has risen to 5 per cent, where the amount of money available is the amount that they want to hold.

The determination of the equilibrium interest rate is illustrated in the diagram in Fig. 28.7. The real money supply is the vertical curve *MS* at $3 billion. The demand curve for real money *MD* cuts the supply curve at an interest rate of 5 per cent. At interest rates above 5 per cent, there is an excess of the quantity of real money supplied over the quantity of real money demanded. At interest rates below 5 per cent, there is an excess of the quantity of real money demanded over the quan-

quantity of real money demanded over the quantity of real money supplied. The only interest rate that makes the quantity of real money available willingly held is 5 per cent.

Changing the Interest Rate

Imagine that the economy is sagging and the Reserve Bank wants to encourage additional aggregate demand and spending. To do so, it wants to lower interest rates and encourage more borrowing and more investment. What does the Reserve Bank do? How does it fiddle with the knobs to achieve lower interest rates?

The Reserve Bank undertakes an open market operation, buying government securities from authorized dealers. The dealers then have too much cash. They repay loans to banks and other financial intermediaries. They also buy government securities in the market. As a consequence, the reserves of banks and other financial intermediaries increase, the monetary base increases and banks start making additional loans. The money supply increases.

Suppose that the Reserve Bank undertakes open market operations on a scale sufficiently large to increase the money supply from $3 billion to $4 billion. As a consequence the supply curve of real money shifts to the right, as shown in Fig. 28.8(a), from MS_0 to MS_1, and the thought experiment that we conducted earlier now becomes a real world event. The interest rate falls as individuals attempt to reduce their money holdings and buy additional financial assets. When the interest rate has fallen to 3 per cent, people are willingly holding the higher ($4 billion) stock of real money that the Reserve Bank and the banking system have now created.

Conversely, suppose that the economy is overheating (demand for real output is growing faster than supply) and the Reserve Bank fears inflation. The Reserve Bank decides to take action to slow down spending and cuts the money supply. In this case, the Bank undertakes an open market sale of securities. As it does so, it mops up reserves and induces the financial intermediaries to cut down the scale of their lending. They make a smaller quantity of new loans each day, retiring other loans, until the stock of loans outstanding has fallen to a level consistent with the new lower level of reserves. (Before deregulation, the Reserve Bank could simply have directed the banks to cut lending in order to try and achieve the same ends.) Suppose that the Reserve Bank undertakes an open market sale of securities on a scale big enough to cut

Figure 28.8 The Reserve Bank Changes the Interest Rate

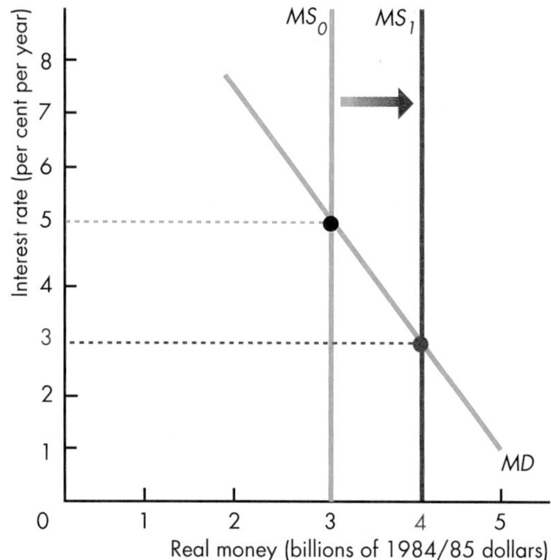

(a) An increase in the money supply

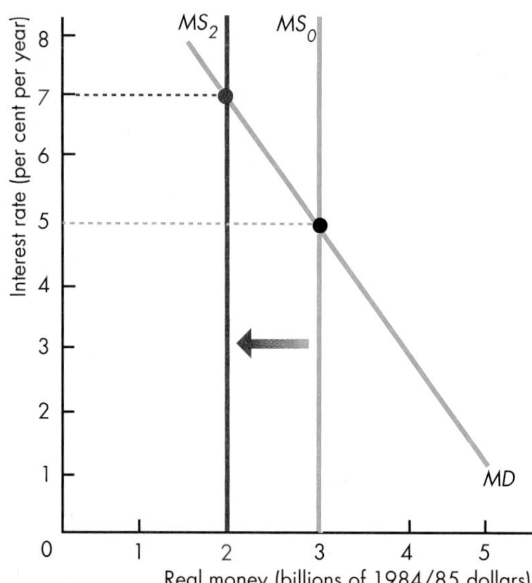

(b) A decrease in the money supply

In part (a), the Reserve Bank conducts an open market purchase of securities, increasing the money supply to $4 billion. The real money supply shifts to the right. The new equilibrium interest rate is 3 per cent. In part (b), the Reserve Bank conducts an open market sale of securities, decreasing the real money supply to $2 billion. The money supply curve shifts to the left, and the interest rate rises to 7 per cent. By changing the money supply, at a given real GDP and price level, the Reserve Bank can adjust short-term interest rates daily or weekly.

the real money supply to \$2 billion. Now the supply of real money curve shifts to the left, as shown in Fig. 28.8(b), from MS_0 to MS_2. With less money available, people attempt to acquire additional money by selling interest-earning assets. As they do so, financial asset prices fall and interest rates rise. Equilibrium occurs when the interest rate has risen to 7 per cent, at which point the new lower real money stock of \$2 billion is willingly held.

The Reserve Bank in Action

All this sounds nice in theory, but does it really happen? Indeed, it does, and sometimes with dramatic effect, because the Reserve Bank cannot always achieve its goals with the precision it would like. This propensity for making errors is sometimes very costly. Let's look at a recent episode in the life of the Reserve Bank, that started in 1987 and lasted until 1990.

Easing Monetary Policy At the beginning of 1987, the Australian economy was still emerging from the 1985/86 slow-down caused by a collapse in the terms of trade. To stimulate faster growth, the Reserve Bank eased monetary conditions by buying Commonwealth government securities and increasing the rate of growth of the money base, injecting cash into the system. This in turn reduced the official cash rate and increased the rate of growth of broader money aggregates such as M3. The stock market crash in October 1987 prompted fears of a recession so money growth rates were increased further. The effects of these policy decisions can be seen in Fig. 28.9. In Fig. 28.9(a) the rate of growth of the money base is graphed against the official cash rate — the interest rate determined in the official cash or money market. The impact of the money base on M3 can be seen in Fig. 28.9(b).

As monetary policy was eased and the rate of growth of the money base increased during 1987 the official cash rate fell. Between January 1987 and April 1988 the cash rate fell from more than 16 per cent to 10 per cent. Over that period, the relationship between the money base and M3 (and other broad aggregates) was reasonably stable with the M3 growth rate increasing with that of the money base.

Policy Tightening (1988/89) The declining interest rates, induced by the monetary easing, stimulated growth. However, unknown to policymakers at the time was the very strong rebound in the terms of trade, which was further stimulating growth — perhaps too much when coupled with the rapidly growing money supply. By mid-1988 the economy was growing very rapidly and signs of excess demand were emerging causing fears of renewed inflation. Of particular concern was the decline in net exports.

In reactions to these concerns, the Reserve Bank stopped easing monetary policy in early 1988 and began tightening policy in mid-1988 by slowing the rate of growth of the money base. That is, the Reserve Bank reduced the rate at which it was buying Commonwealth government securities and injecting cash into the system. Consequently, the official cash rate began to increase, which in turn increased all interest rates. The tightening of monetary policy is evident in Fig. 28.9(a).

However, as part of the general move towards deregulation, SRDs were abolished in October 1988. As discussed in the previous chapter, this led to an expansion of 'on-balance-sheet' banking throughout 1989 and M3 grew very rapidly, even as the money base growth rate was declining. The result of this policy change was that the contractionary effects of the monetary tightening were not felt for some time and the economy continued to grow, even though interest rates were rising. In September 1989, the growth rate of M3 peaked at over 30 per cent a year.

Policy Easing Again (1990/91) Throughout the latter third of 1989 and into 1990, the growth rate of M3 collapsed. By early 1990, the Reserve Bank was concerned that the belatedly felt effects of the previous tightening might be worse than anticipated and it eased monetary policy in January, February, April and further on into 1990. Monetary policy continued to be eased into 1991. The subsequent increase in the rate of growth of the money base is apparent in Fig. 28.9(a).

During the period 1987–1990, the Australian economy experienced some very high rates of growth and then some very low rates of growth. It would appear that attempts to fine-tune monetary policy at the same time as deregulatory changes are being felt and the terms of trade are experiencing wild swings have not always been successful.

Profiting by Predicting the Reserve Bank's Actions

Day by day, even minute by minute, the Reserve Bank can influence interest rates and the money supply by its open market operations. By increasing the supply of money, the Reserve Bank can lower short-term interest rates; by lowering the supply of money,

Figure 28.9 Recent Monetary Policy

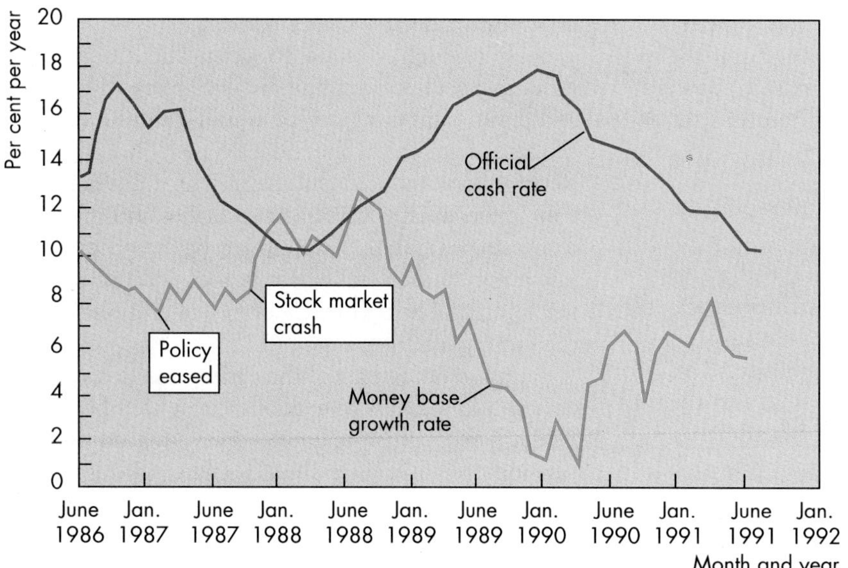

(a) Open market operations and the cash rate

(b) The effects of abolishing SRDs

Part (a) shows the relationship between the rate of growth of the money base and the official cash rate. When the money base growth rate is increasing the official cash rate is falling, as occurred in 1987 and 1990. When the rate of growth of the money base is decreasing the official cash rate is increasing, as occurred in 1988.

Part (b) shows the relationship between the money base growth rate and the rate of increase of M3. This relationship is apparently stable up until October 1988 when SRDs were abolished, freeing up bank reserves.

Source: See Figs. 28.3 and 28.6.

the Reserve Bank can increase interest rates. Holders of financial assets know about the powers of the Reserve Bank. They also know about another relationship that we have worked out: the higher the interest rate, the lower is the price of a bond, and the lower the interest rate, the higher is the price of a bond. They can also put these two things together and know that, if they can predict changes in monetary policy, then they can predict future interest rates and future bond prices. Predicting future bond prices is a potentially profitable activity. Predicting that interest rates are going to fall is the same as predicting that bond prices are going to rise — a good time to buy bonds. Predicting that interest rates are going to rise is the same as predicting that bond prices are going to fall — a good time to sell bonds.

Because predicting the Reserve Bank's actions is profitable, a good deal of effort goes into that activity. This is why financial markets and the financial press appear to drool over any statement, no matter how insignificant, uttered by the Prime Minister, Treasurer or Governor of the Reserve Bank. The eager journalists and financial market participants hope that these statements will provide a clue as to future monetary policy. Similarly, any new economic statistics, which might bear upon the direction of future policy, are eagerly anticipated.

But *if* people do anticipate the Reserve Bank's monetary policy changes, then bond prices and interest rates will change as soon as the Reserve Bank's actions are foreseen. By the time the Reserve Bank actually takes its actions, those actions will have no effect. The effect will have occurred *in anticipation* of the Reserve Bank's actions. Only changes in the money supply that were not foreseen will change the interest rate at the time that those changes actually occur.

R E V I E W

At any given moment, the interest rate is determined by the demand for and the supply of money. The interest rate makes the quantity of money demanded equal to the quantity of money supplied. Changes in the interest rate occur as a result of changes in the money supply. When the money supply change is not predicted, interest rates will change at the same time as the change in the money supply. If a change in the money supply is foreseen, interest rates will start to change ahead of the change in the money supply. ■

■ In this chapter we've studied the determination of interest rates and discovered how the Reserve Bank can 'fiddle with the knobs' to influence interest rate levels as well as influence the quantity of money and the volume of bank lending. In the next chapter, we're going to look at the effects of the Bank's actions on that other, crucial barometer of the nation's financial health — the foreign exchange value of our dollar.

S U M M A R Y

The Reserve Bank of Australia

The Reserve Bank of Australia is the central bank of Australia. It is headed by a Governor, aided by a Deputy Governor and a staff of senior economists and other advisors, and directed by a Board of Directors representing a variety of regional and other interests. The Bank's main instrument for influencing the economy is its open market operations. By buying government securities in the market (an open market purchase), the Reserve Bank is able to increase the monetary base and the reserves available to banks. As a result, there is an expansion of bank lending and a fall in interest rates. By selling government securities, the Reserve Bank is able to decrease the monetary base and the reserves of banks and other financial institutions, thereby curtailing loans and putting upward pressure on interest rates. The overall effect of a change in the monetary base on the money supply is determined by the money multiplier, which in turn depends on the ratio of currency to deposits held by households and firms, and the ratio of reserves to deposits held by banks and other financial institutions. (pp. 264–281)

The Demand for Money

The quantity of money demanded is the amount of currency, demand deposits and other cheque accounts that people hold on the average. The quantity of money demanded is proportional to the price level, and the quantity of real money demanded depends on the interest rate and real GDP. A higher level of real GDP induces a larger quantity of real money demanded. A higher interest rate induces a smaller quantity of real money demanded. Fluctuations in the ratio of real GDP to real money (the velocity of circulation) are correlated with fluctuations in the interest rate. Technological change in the financial sector has also reduced the demand for money over the years. (pp. 281–286)

Interest Rate Determination

Changes in interest rates achieve stock equilibrium in the markets for money and financial assets. There is an inverse relationship between the interest rate and the price of a financial asset. The higher the interest rate, the lower is the price of a financial asset. Money market equilibrium achieves an interest rate and asset price that makes the quantity of real money available willingly held. If the quantity of real money is increased by the actions of the Reserve Bank, the interest rate falls and the prices of financial assets rise.

People attempt to profit by predicting the actions of the Reserve Bank. To the extent that they can predict the Reserve Bank, interest rates and the price of financial assets move in anticipation of the Reserve Bank's actions rather than in response to them. As a consequence, interest rates change when the Reserve Bank changes the money supply only if the Reserve Bank catches people by surprise. Anticipated changes in the money supply produce interest rate changes by themselves. (pp. 286–293)

KEY TERMS

Authorized money market dealers, p. 274
Central bank, p. 264
Clearing House, p. 273
Demand for real money, p. 284
Disintermediation, p. 278
Exchange settlement accounts, p. 273
Fixed exchange rate, p. 268
Flexible exchange rate, p. 268
Flow equilibrium, p. 288
LGS convention, p. 267
Managed exchange rate, p. 268
Monetary base, p. 272
Monetary policy, p. 264
Money multiplier, p. 275
Nominal quantity of money, p. 282
Non-callable deposits, p. 271
Non-convertible note, p. 272
Official cash rate, p. 274
Official money market, p. 274
Open market operations, p. 271
Payments system, p. 273
Perpetuity, p. 287
Prime assets ratio (PAR), p. 267
Reserve Bank of Australia, p. 264
Statutory reserve requirements (SRDs), p. 269
Stock equilibrium, p. 288
Unofficial money market, p. 274

PROBLEMS

1 You are given the following information about a hypothetical economy. The banks have deposits of $300 million. Their reserves are $15 million, two-thirds of which is in deposits with the central bank. The monetary base is $40 million. There are no coins in this economy.
   a) Set out the balance sheet of the banks. Supply any missing numbers using your knowledge of the fact that total assets equal total liabilities.
   b) What is the amount of currency in circulation?
   c) What is the money supply?
   d) What is the money multiplier?

2 Suppose that the central bank in the economy of problem 1 undertakes an open market purchase of securities of $1 million. What happens to the money supply? Explain why the money supply changes by more than the change in the monetary base?

3 You are given the following information about another imaginary economy. For each $1 increase in real GDP, the demand for real money increases by one third of a dollar, other things being equal. Also, if the interest rate increases by 1 percentage point (for example, from 4 per cent to 5 per cent), the quantity of real money demanded falls by $40. If the price level is 1, real GDP is $1000 and the real money supply is $133, what is the interest rate?

4 Suppose that the central bank in the economy of problem 3 wants to change the interest rate to 4 per cent. By how much would it have to change the real money supply to achieve that objective?

Chapter 29

Interest Rates and the Exchange Rate

After studying this chapter, you will be able to:

- Explain how the foreign exchange value of the dollar is determined.
- Explain why the foreign exchange value of the dollar fluctuated in the 1980s.
- Explain the effects of changes in the exchange rate.
- Explain what determines interest rates and why they vary so much from one country to another.
- Explain how international arbitrage links together prices in different countries.
- Explain why a fixed exchange rate ties interest rates and inflation rates together.
- Explain why a flexible exchange rate brings monetary independence.

Australia's Financial Insulator

'When America sneezes, the rest of the world catches cold'. This observation, made during the Great Depression years of the early 1930s, is regarded, by many, as an unavoidable fact of life. And in today's world, something similar might also be said of Australia's relationships with West Germany and Japan. It is certainly the case that when the world's largest economies experience booming conditions, some of the associated prosperity spills over into enhanced export sales by almost every other country. And when any of the big three economies go into recession, as the US economy did in 1981, the rest of the world, to some degree, goes into recession with it. But is there nothing that a country such as Australia can do to insulate itself from the world economic see-saw? In particular, how does the nation's financial and monetary policy, and its international monetary policy, act to moderate the influence of the rest of world on Australia? One potential cushion that we can place between ourselves and the rest of the world is the value of our dollar. How do fluctuations in the value of the Australian dollar affect the economic lives of Australians, and do they protect Australians from economic fluctuations originating in other countries? Our dollar does indeed fluctuate considerably in value. In 1973, one Australian dollar exchanged for almost US$1.50. (The symbol US$ stands for the US dollar and A$ stands for the Australian dollar.) At its lowest point, in 1986, it took just US$0.57 to buy A$1. Our exchange rate has returned from that low point and, at the end of 1991, A$1 could be bought for approximately US$0.77. Our dollar has fluctuated not only against the US dollar but against all the other major currencies of the world. Against many currencies, for example, the Japanese yen, it has persistently declined in value. In August 1970, A$1 would buy 450 Japanese yen. By mid-1990, our dollar was worth only 120 yen. What does the value of the dollar have to do with the prices of the things that we buy — the price of an English tweed coat, a Korean VCR, a Japanese car or a foreign holiday? Do Speedo swimsuits sold in Australia cost the same as the same swimsuits sold in the United States? What makes our dollar fluctuate in value against other currencies? Have the fluctuations been particularly extreme in recent years? Is there anything we can do to stabilize the value of the dollar? The world is becoming ever more integrated. In October 1987, when Wall Street crashed, so too did the stock markets of Japan, Western Europe and Australia. But, despite the fact that the world is getting smaller, there are enormous differences in the interest rates at which people borrow and lend around the world. For example, in October 1990, the Australian government was paying 12 per cent a year on its long-term borrowing. At the same time, governments in Sweden and Spain were paying more than 13 per cent. But in the United States the government was paying only 8.5 per cent, in West Germany only 9 per cent and in Japan and Switzerland barely more than 7 per cent. How can interest rates around the world diverge so widely? Why don't loans dry up in low interest rate countries with all the money flooding to countries where interest rates are high? Why aren't interest rates made the same everywhere by the force of such movements? Q At most times in our recent history, we have maintained a fixed value for the Australian dollar against other currencies. Only since 9 December 1983 have we allowed the Australian dollar to find its own value in the world market for foreign exchange. Does it matter whether the Australian dollar exchange rate is fixed or flexible? Is the exchange rate regime something that only affects specialists who deal in foreign exchange or does it affect more broadly the economic lives of all Australians?

During the 1980s, the issues of international economics have become important matters for all Australians. We're going to study these issues in this chapter. We're going to discover why the Australian dollar fluctuates so much against the values of other currencies; and why interest rates in Australia are so high compared with those in the United States, Japan, Germany and Switzerland but still relatively low compared with those in many other countries. We're going to study the market forces that link countries together and that determine the values of their currencies, as well as the international transmission of interest rates and price changes.

Foreign Exchange

Because the medium of exchange in any country is usually its own currency, when we buy foreign goods or invest in another country, we have to obtain some of that country's currency to make the transaction. When foreigners buy Australian-produced goods or invest in Australia, they have to obtain some Australian dollars. The Australian dollar is not accepted as a medium of exchange in other countries; foreign currencies are not accepted as a medium of exchange in Australia. We buy foreign currency and foreigners buy Australian dollars in the foreign exchange market.

The **foreign exchange market** is the market in which the currency of one country is exchanged for the currency of another. The foreign exchange market is not in one physical location like a downtown flea market or produce market. The market is made up of thousands of people — importers and exporters, banks, and specialists in the buying and selling of foreign exchange called foreign exchange brokers. The foreign exchange markets open on Monday morning in Auckland, Sydney and Melbourne, then in Tokyo, while it is still Sunday evening in New York. As the day advances, markets open in Zurich, London, Montreal, New York, and finally, Vancouver, Los Angeles and San Francisco. Around the time the West Coast markets in the United States are closing, Sydney is opening again for the next day of business. The sun virtually never sets on the foreign exchange market. Dealers around the world are continually in contact using computers linked by telephone. On any given day, billions of dollars change hands.

The price at which one currency exchanges for another is called a **foreign exchange rate**. For example, in September 1990 one Australian dollar bought 114 Japanese yen. The exchange rate between the Australian dollar and the Japanese yen was 114 yen per dollar. Exchange rates can be expressed either way. We've just expressed the exchange rate between the yen and the dollar as a number of yen per dollar. Equivalently, we could express the exchange rate in terms of dollars per yen. That exchange rate, in September 1990, was $0.008772 per yen. (In other words, a yen was worth slightly less than one cent.) In foreign exchange market terminology, an exchange rate quoted in terms of the local currency — for example, one yen trades for A$0.00872 — is called a *direct quote.* If the exchange rate is quoted in terms of the foreign currency — A$1 equals 114 yen — it is called an *indirect quote.* The Australian dollar is usually quoted indirectly.

The actions of the foreign exchange dealers make the foreign exchange market highly efficient. Exchange rates are almost identical no matter where in the world the transaction is taking place. If Australian dollars were cheap in London and expensive in Tokyo, within a flash, someone would have placed a buy order in London and a sell order in Tokyo, thereby increasing demand in one place and increasing supply in another, moving the prices to equality.

Foreign Exchange Regimes

Foreign exchange rates are of critical importance to millions of people. They affect the costs of our foreign holidays and our imported cars. They affect the number of dollars that we end up getting for the coal and wheat that we sell to Japan. Because of its importance, governments pay a great deal of attention to what is happening in foreign exchange markets and, more than that, often take actions designed to achieve what they regard as desirable movements in exchange rates. As we noted in Chapter 28, there are three ways in which the government and the Reserve Bank of Australia can operate in the foreign exchange market — three foreign exchange market regimes. They are:

- Fixed exchange rate
- Flexible exchange rate
- Managed exchange rate

A *fixed exchange rate* regime is one in which the value of the dollar is pegged by the Reserve Bank, usually at an announced rate. A *flexible exchange rate* regime is one in which the value of the dollar is determined by market forces with no intervention by the Reserve Bank. A *managed exchange rate* regime is one in which the Reserve Bank intervenes in the foreign exchange market to smooth out fluctuations in the value of the dollar, but does not seek to maintain the dollar at an absolutely constant value for a long period of time. Also, under a managed exchange rate regime, the Reserve Bank does not announce the value of the dollar that it wishes to achieve.

Recent Exchange Rate History

Towards the end of World War II, the major countries of the world set up the International Monetary Fund (IMF). The **International Monetary Fund** is an international organization that monitors balance of payments and exchange rate activities. The IMF, located in Washington, DC, came into being during World War II. In July 1944, at Bretton Woods, in the United States, 44 countries signed the Articles of Agreement of the IMF. The centrepiece of those agreements was the establishment of a world-wide system of fixed exchange rates between currencies. The anchor for this fixed exchange rate system was gold. One ounce of gold was defined to be worth US$35. Other currencies were pegged to either the US dollar or the UK pound sterling at a fixed exchange rate. For example, the Japanese yen was set at 360 yen per US dollar; the UK pound was set at US$2.80. The Australian pound was fixed against sterling at an equivalent Australian dollar rate of A$2.5050 per UK pound.

The fixed exchange rate regime under which most countries operated, the Bretton Woods system as it became known, served the world well during the 1950s and early 1960s. However, it came under increasing strain in the late 1960s and early 1970s. By 1971 the system had almost collapsed. In that year a new world-wide agreement on fixed exchange rates was reached — the Smithsonian Agreement — under which Australia fixed its exchange rate against the US dollar, at the rate of A$1 to US$1.2160. The Australian dollar went through a period where its value was at first increasing against the US dollar, until mid-1974, and then decreasing, with the government constantly adjusting the announced rate at which it was fixing the dollar. On 9 December 1983, the Australian government finally floated the Australian dollar. The value of the Australian dollar continued to vary throughout the 1980s, under what is best described as a managed float. During this time it has steadily lost value against most other currencies.

Figure 29.1(a) shows what has happened to the exchange rate of Australian dollars in terms of the US dollar since 1970. As you can see, the value of our dollar rose until mid-1974 and has fallen ever since. That is the Australian dollar first appreciated then depreciated. The increase in the value of one currency in terms of another currency is called **currency appreciation.** On the other hand, currency depreciation is the fall in the value of one currency in terms of another currency.

Just as the Australian dollar has fallen in value in terms of the yen and US dollar, so the yen and US dollar have risen in value in terms of the Australian dollar. You can see the depreciation of the Australian dollar and the appreciation of the US dollar as the mirror image of each other in Fig. 29.1(a) and (b).

There are as many exchange rates for the Australian dollar as there are currencies for which it can be exchanged. The Australian dollar falls in value against some currencies (as we've just seen in the case of the US dollar and the Japanese yen) and increases

Figure 29.1 Exchange Rates, 1970–1991

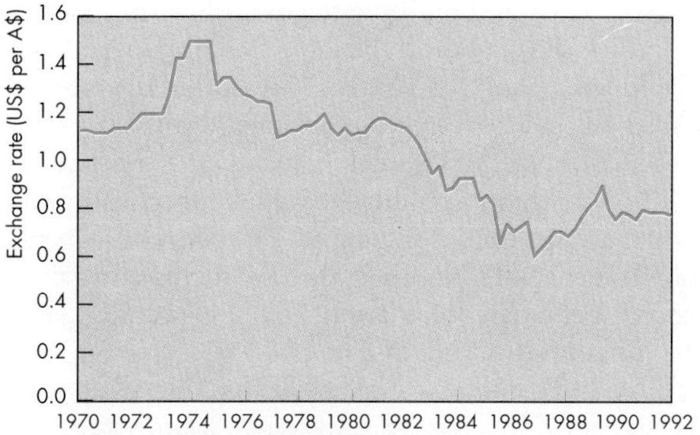

(a) US dollar–Australian dollar exchange rate

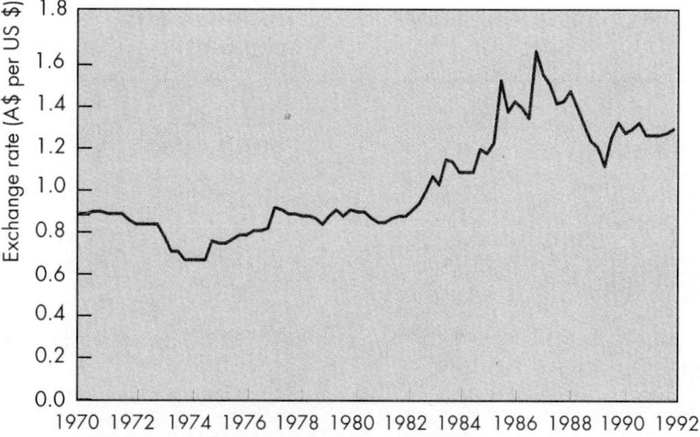

(b) Australian dollar–US dollar exchange rate

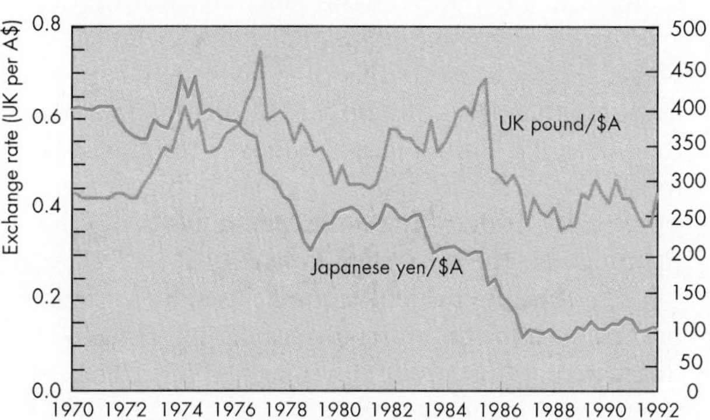

(c) UK pound and Japanese yen–Australian dollar exchange rate

The exchange rate is the price at which two currencies can be traded. Part (a) shows the US$–A$ exchange rate expressed in US dollars per Australian dollar. The Australian dollar has fallen in value — depreciated — against the US dollar since mid-1974. Part (b) shows the A$–US$ exchange rate in Australian dollars per US dollar. The price of US dollars in terms of Australian dollars has increased since mid-1974 — the US dollar has appreciated against the Australian dollar. The UK pound and Japanese yen–Australian dollar exchange rates are shown in part (c). The Australian dollar has steadily depreciated against the yen, but remained roughly constant against the pound.

Source: US$ exchange rate: Series FXRUSD; UK£ exchange rate: Series FXRUKPS; JP¥ exchange rate: Series FXRJY, RBA *Bulletin* Database, supplied by EconData's dX Data Service.

against others. To measure the average movement in the value of the Australian dollar, the Reserve Bank calculates the trade-weighted index for the Australian dollar. The **trade-weighted index** is an index that measures the value of the Australian dollar in terms of its ability to buy a basket of currencies of a group of countries, where the weight placed on each currency is related to its importance in Australia's international trade. The relative weights are adjusted as Australia's trade mix with other countries varies. Table 29.1 shows the weights as they were at 1 October 1990.

An example of the calculation of the trade-weighted index is set out in Table 29.2. Here we suppose that Australia trades with only three countries: the United States, Japan and the United Kingdom. Fifty per cent of the trade is with the United States, 30 per cent with Japan and 20 per cent with the United Kingdom. In year 1, the Australian dollar is worth 0.75 US dollars, or 100 Japanese yen, or 0.5 UK pounds.

Imagine putting these three foreign currencies into a 'basket' worth 100 Australian dollars, where 50 per cent of the value of the basket is in US dollars, 30 per cent in Japanese yen and 20 per cent in UK pounds. The table lists the contents of the basket. There are US$37.50, ¥3000 and £10. Converting these amounts of the three foreign currencies to Australian dollars at the exchange rates prevailing results in a basket worth A$100. Fifty dollars worth of the basket is in US dollars, $30 worth in Japanese yen and $20 worth in UK pounds. In year 1, the index number for the basket is 100 by definition.

Suppose that, in year 2, the exchange rates change in the way shown in the table. The US dollar stays constant, the Japanese yen goes up in value so that only 90 Japanese yen can be bought for one Australian dollar and the UK pound goes down in value

Table 29.1 Trade-Weighted Index

Country	Currency	Trade-weight (per cent)
Japan	yen	25.0862
United States	dollar	19.5653
United Kingdom	pound	5.6845
New Zealand	dollar	5.2665
West Germany	mark	5.1467
South Korea	won	4.3560
Taiwan	new dollar	4.1689
Singapore	dollar	3.5019
Italy	lira	2.9538
China	renminbi	2.6821
Hong Kong	dollar	2.4146
France	franc	2.2533
Canada	dollar	2.1590
Malaysia	ringgit	1.7617
Netherlands	guilder	1.7457
Indonesia	rupiah	1.6702
Switzerland	franc	1.4472
Papua New Guinea	kina	1.1883
Thailand	baht	1.1559
Sweden	krona	1.1435
Saudi Arabia	riyal	1.0582
Belgium	franc	1.0294
India	rupee	0.9594
United Arab Emirates	dirham	0.8167
USSR	rouble	0.7850

Source: Reserve Bank *Bulletin*, October 1990.

so that one Australian dollar buys 0.55 UK pounds. What is the change in the value of the basket?

The change is calculated in the final column of the table. Because the US dollar exchange rate is unchanged, the Australian dollar value of the US dollars in the basket remains constant at A$50. Because the Japanese yen has appreciated in value, more Australian dollars are now required to buy ¥3000. Thus the Australian dollar value of the Japanese yen in the basket is increased to A$33.33. Because the UK pound has decreased in value, fewer Australian dollars are required to buy the £10 in the basket. Thus the £10 are now worth A$18.18. The total number of Australian dollars required to buy the basket that was worth A$100 initially is now A$101.51.

Because more Australian dollars are now required to buy the basket of currency, the Australian dollar has decreased in value. To calculate the index number for the Australian dollar, we take the value of the basket in the first year — A$100 — divide it by the value of the basket in the second year — A$101.51 — and multiply the result by 100. This calculation is set out in the table and, as you can see, the index in year 2 is 98.51. That is, the Australian dollar has fallen in value, on average, against the other currencies in the basket, by about 1.5 per cent.

Note that the fall in the value of the Australian dollar against the Japanese yen is 10 per cent — a fall of ¥10 on ¥100. Note also that the increase in value of the Australian dollar against the UK pound is also 10 per cent — an increase of UK 5 pence on an initial value UK 50 pence. Why, if the Australian dollar has fallen in value by 10 per cent against the Japanese yen, and increased in value by 10 per cent against the UK pound, has it fallen in value on the average? The answer is that the Japanese yen has a bigger weight in the basket than does the UK pound, because Japan has a larger share of Australian trade than does the United Kingdom. As a result, the fall in value against the Japanese yen gets a bigger weight in the calculation of the index, the result being that the index for the Australian dollar falls.

In the above calculations we used hypothetical numbers. How the Australian dollar has actually fluctuated against other currencies on the average in recent years is shown in Fig. 29.2. As you can see, it fluctuated around a constant level until 1976 and then depreciated until 1987. It has remained steady against other currencies since 1987.

Exchange Rate Determination

What determines the foreign currency value of the dollar? Why has the dollar depreciated against the yen since 1970? Why was that depreciation particularly spectacular after 1985? Why did the dollar temporarily appreciate against the yen in 1982? These are difficult questions to answer but they are of vital importance to many people. We will answer them within a general framework based on the demand and supply analysis we have consistently applied throughout this book.

The foreign exchange value of the dollar is a price and, like any other price, is determined by demand and supply. But what exactly do we mean by the demand for and supply of dollars? There are, in fact, three different senses in which we can speak of the supply of and demand for dollars and all three

Table 29.2 Trade-Weighted Index Calculation

Currency	Exchange rates (units of foreign currency per Australian dollar)		Value of trade weights	Contents of basket	Value of basket (Australian dollars)	
	Year 1	**Year 2**			**Year 1**	**Year 2**
US dollar	0.75	0.75	0.50	US$37.50	50.00	50.00
Japanese yen	100.00	90.00	0.30	¥3000	30.00	33.33
UK pound	0.50	0.55	0.20	£10	20.00	18.18
Total			1.00		100.00	101.51

Trade-weighted index:

Year 1: 100.00

Year 2: $(100 \div 101.51) \times 100 = 98.51$

have featured, at various times, in the theories of the determination of the foreign exchange rate:

- Flow theory
- Monetary theory
- Portfolio balance theory

Let's consider each of these in turn.

Flow Theory The **flow theory of the exchange rate** is the proposition that the exchange rate adjusts to make the flow supply of dollars equal to the flow demand for dollars, where these flows are largely the result of international flows of goods and services. The flow supply of dollars in any given period thus depends on the value of Australian imports. Australian residents supply dollars in exchange for foreign currency in order to be able to buy foreign imports. The flow demand for dollars in any given period depends on the value of Australian goods (exports) that foreigners plan to buy during that period of time. Foreigners must buy Australian dollars before they are in a position to buy Australian goods and services. According to the flow theory of the exchange rate, the value of the exchange rate adjusts to keep the flow demand for a currency equals to its flow supply.

In addition to the flow demand and supply resulting from imports and exports, however, there is also a net flow demand or supply resulting from international borrowing and lending. Because the flow theory of the exchange rate does not explain how these net flows are determined, it has a serious shortcoming.

What does determine the flows of international borrowing and lending? They result from people's decisions about which assets to hold. People have to choose whether to hold domestic or foreign assets, and they also have to choose the currency in which their assets will be denominated. But these choices

Figure 29.2 Trade-Weighted Index

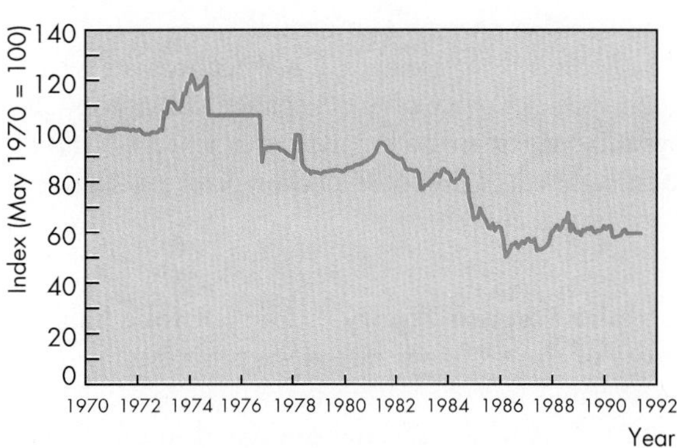

The trade-weighted index measures the value of the Australian dollar against the group of currencies of Australia's major trading partners. From 1970 to 1976 the value of the Australian dollar was roughly constant. From 1976 to 1987 the Australian dollar weakened against the basket of currencies in the index. Since then it has remained steady.

Source: TWI: Series FXRTWI, RBA *Bulletin* Database, supplied by EconData's dX Data Service.

are choices about stocks, not flows. The decision to *change* the stocks of assets held results in *flows,* but those *flows are the consequence of decisions about stocks.* Thus, in considering the determination of the exchange rate, even if we approach the matter from the point of view of the flow supply and demand for a currency, we cannot avoid considering the demand for a currency as a stock to hold rather than as a flow. The emphasis on the demand for a stock of currency gives rise to the other two theories of the exchange rate. Let's now turn to them.

Monetary Theory The **monetary theory of the exchange rate** is the proposition that the exchange rate adjusts to make the stock of a currency demanded equal to the stock supplied. The stock of a currency is identical to the *quantity of money.* In Chapter 28, we saw how the quantity of money in Australia — the quantity of Australian-dollar money — is determined by the behaviour of the banking system and the actions of the Reserve Bank. The quantity of money in Japan — the quantity of yen money — is determined by similar actions of the Bank of Japan; the quantity of US dollars is determined by similar actions of the Federal Reserve Board in the United States; and so on. According to the monetary theory, the exchange rate adjusts to ensure that the quantity of money in each currency supplied equals the quantity demanded. For example, if the demands for all currencies are unchanged and the supply of any one currency increases relative to others, then its price in terms of other currencies must fall.

Most international financial economists regard the monetary theory of the exchange rate as too narrow and suggest that a broader asset aggregate should be considered. This consideration gives rise to the portfolio balance theory.

Portfolio Balance Theory The **portfolio balance theory of the exchange rate** is the proposition that the exchange rate of any currency adjusts to make the stock of financial assets denominated in units of that currency demanded equal to the stock supplied. The total quantity of Australian dollar-denominated assets includes Australian dollar securities issued by the government and by firms. It also includes the Australian dollar liabilities of the Reserve Bank and the Australian dollar deposit liabilities of banks — the Australian money supply. But the money supply is just one part of the total quantity of Australian dollar-denominated assets. The exchange rate adjusts to make the total quantity of Australian dollar-denominated assets demanded equal to the quantity supplied.

In studying the forces that determine the exchange rate, we'll work with this third and broadest theory — the portfolio balance theory. We will examine the forces that influence the quantity of dollar-denominated assets demanded and supplied.

The Exchange Rate and the Demand for Australian Dollar-Denominated Assets

The law of demand applies to dollar-denominated assets just as it does to anything else that people value. The quantity of dollar-denominated assets demanded increases when the price of dollars in terms of foreign currency falls (the dollar depreciates) and decreases when the price of dollars in terms of foreign currency rises (the dollar appreciates). There are two separate reasons why the law of demand applies to dollars. First, there is a transactions demand. The lower the value of the dollar, the larger is the demand for Australian exports and the lower is our demand for imports. Hence the larger is the amount of trade financed by dollars. Foreigners demand more dollars to buy Australian exports and we demand fewer units of foreign currency and more dollars as we switch from importing to buying Australian-produced goods.

Second, there is a speculative demand arising from expected capital gains. Other things being equal, the lower the value of the dollar today, the higher is its expected rate of appreciation (or the lower is its expected rate of depreciation) in the future. Hence the higher is the expected gain from holding dollar-denominated assets relative to the expected gain from holding foreign currency assets. Suppose that you expect the dollar to be worth 110 Japanese yen at the end of one year. If today the dollar is worth 120 yen, you're expecting the dollar to depreciate by 10 yen. Other things being equal, you will not plan to hold dollar-denominated assets in this situation. Instead, you will plan to hold yen assets. But, if today's value of the dollar is 100 yen, then you're expecting the dollar to appreciate by 10 yen. In this situation, you will plan to hold dollar-denominated assets and take advantage of the expected rise in their value. Holding assets in a particular currency in anticipation of a gain in their value arising from a change in the exchange rate is one of the most important influences on the quantity demanded of dollar-denominated assets and of foreign currency assets. The more a currency is expected to appreciate, the greater is the quantity of assets in that currency that people want to hold.

Figure 29.3 shows the relationship between the foreign currency price of the Australian dollar and the quantity of dollar-denominated assets demanded — the demand curve for dollar-denominated assets. When the foreign exchange rate changes, other things being equal, there is a movement along the demand curve.

Any other influence on the quantity of dollar-denominated assets that people want to hold results in a *shift* in the demand curve. Demand either increases or decreases. These other influences are

- The Australian price level
- The price levels in other countries
- The interest rates on dollar-denominated assets
- The interest rates on foreign currency assets
- The expected future value of the dollar

Table 29.3 summarizes the above discussion of the influences on the quantity of dollar-denominated assets that people demand.

Figure 29.3 The Demand for Dollar-Denominated Assets

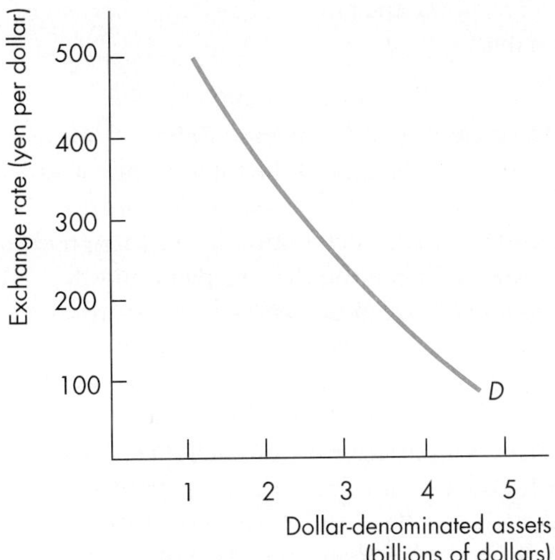

The quantity of dollar-denominated assets that people demand, other things held constant, depends on the foreign exchange rate. The lower the foreign exchange rate (the smaller the number of yen per dollar), the larger is the quantity of dollar-denominated assets demanded. The increased quantity demanded arises from an increase in the volume of dollar trade (the Japanese buy more Australian goods and Australians buy fewer Japanese goods) and an increase in the expected appreciation (or decrease in the expected depreciation) of dollar-denominated assets.

The Exchange Rate and the Supply of Australian Dollar-Denominated Assets

The supply of dollar-denominated assets includes domestic currency and all Australian dollar-denominated financial assets — bonds, debentures, shares and so on — and so is determined by the actions of many different groups of people in the economy. As we have already seen, the Reserve Bank of Australia is a very important supplier of dollar-denominated assets because it controls the money base — the quantity of Australian dollars in circulation. But the government, banks and firms also supply various types of Australian dollar-denominated assets. Whenever the government or a firm borrows, it sells a bond or a share and the supply of Australian dollar-denominated assets rises. Whenever a bank makes a loan, which is then deposited back in a bank, the supply of dollar-denominated assets rises.

However, of all the suppliers of dollar-denominated assets, only the Reserve Bank changes its behaviour in response to changes in the exchange rate. And the extent to which it does so depends on the exchange rate regime adopted. Figure 29.4 shows the supply curve of Australian dollar-denominated assets under the three possible exchange rate regimes.

Under a *fixed exchange rate regime,* the Reserve Bank stands ready to supply dollar-denominated assets, by buying or selling Australian dollars in exchange for foreign currency, at the chosen exchange rate. In effect, the Reserve Bank places a price ceiling and a price floor on the Australian dollar. Thus the supply curve of dollar-denominated assets is horizontal at the chosen exchange rate.

Under a *managed exchange rate regime* the Reserve Bank smooths fluctuations in the exchange rate, so that the supply curve of dollar-denominated assets is upward sloping. The higher the foreign exchange rate, the larger is the quantity of dollar-denominated assets supplied.

Under a *flexible exchange rate regime,* the Reserve Bank does not intervene in the foreign exchange market, so a fixed quantity of dollar-denominated assets is supplied, regardless of their price in terms of other currencies. That is, the supply of dollar-denominated assets from the Reserve Bank is independent of the exchange rate. As a consequence, under a flexible exchange rate regime, the supply curve of dollar-denominated assets is vertical.

Table 29.3 The Demand for Dollar-Denominated Assets

The law of demand	
The quantity of dollar-denominated assets demanded	
Increases if	*Decreases if*
• The foreign currency value of the dollar falls	• The foreign currency value of the dollar rises
Changes in demand	
The demand for dollar-denominated assets	
Increases if	*Decreases if*
• The price level falls	• The price level rises
• The price levels in other countries rise	• The price levels in other countries fall
• Interest rates on dollar-denominated assets rise	• Interest rates on dollar-denominated assets fall
• Interest rates on foreign currency assets fall	• Interest rates on foreign currency assets rise
• The dollar is expected to appreciate	• The dollar is expected to depreciate

Shifts in the Supply Curve of Dollar-Denominated Assets

The supply of Australian dollar-denominated assets changes over time as a result of any increase in the supply of dollar-denominated assets which is *not* the direct result of a change in the exchange rate: Important changes that shift the supply curve are:

- Changes in domestic monetary policy
- Changes in the government's budget
- Changes in the level of planned investment

Let's examine the effects of a change in each of these variables.

Figure 29.4 The Supply of Dollar-Denominated Assets

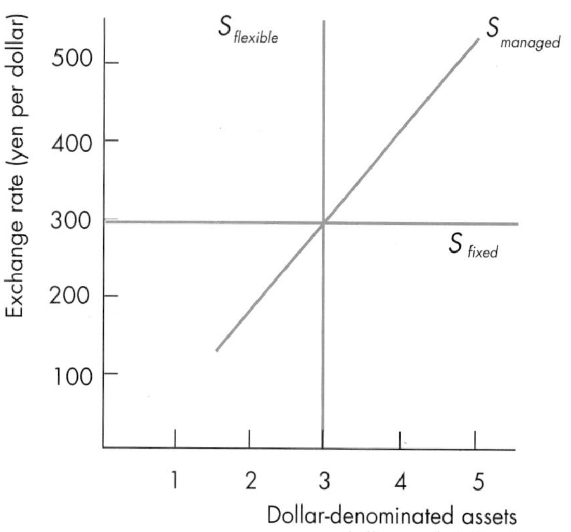

The slope of the supply curve of dollar-denominated assets depends on the exchange rate regime adopted by the Reserve Bank. Under a fixed exchange rate regime, the supply curve is horizontal at the chosen exchange rate. Under a flexible exchange rate regime, the supply curve is vertical. Under a managed exchange rate regime it is upward sloping.

Changes in Domestic Monetary Policy We have just discussed the changes in the total supply of Australian dollar-denominated assets that result from the Reserve Bank's direct intervention in the foreign exchange market. When the Reserve Bank buys foreign currency or foreign-currency-denominated assets, in an attempt to fix or manage the price of the Australian dollar, it increases the Australian money supply, and injects Australian dollars into the system, so that there is an increase in the total quantity of Australian dollar-denominated assets supplied. When the Reserve Bank sells foreign securities or foreign currency, it takes in existing Australian dollar bank deposits or notes, and the Australian money supply as well as the total supply of Australian dollar-denominated securities decrease. Such transactions are undertaken to achieve a particular exchange rate policy — an *external* goal.

Domestic monetary policy, on the other hand, is directed at *internal* goals, for example, achieving a particular interest rate, and is undertaken by the use of open market operations. As we saw in the previous chapter, open market operations are also transactions in dollar-denominated assets. A tightening of monetary policy — an open market sale of Commonwealth government securities — is an exchange of dollar-denominated securities for Australian dollars. Because the Reserve Bank exchanges one dollar-denominated asset for another, the total supply of dollar-denominated assets is unchanged. Similarly, an easing of monetary policy would leave the total supply unchanged. Thus the supply curve of dollar-denominated assets is unchanged immediately after an open market operation.

However, as we also saw in Chapter 28, there are consequences for the money supply which flow on from an open market operation. Directly, as a result of an open market purchase of government securities, there is an increase in bank reserves. With increased reserves, banks increase their level of lending. As money is lent out then redeposited in the banking system the money supply rises. That is, the total stock of dollar-denominated assets rises as a result of the multiplier effect on the changed money base — a consequence of the actions of banks but not directly because of the open market transaction itself.

Changes in the Government's Budget If the government has a budget deficit, the supply of Australian dollar-denominated assets increases. If the government has a budget surplus, the supply of dollar-denominated assets decreases. It is important to notice that the supply of Australian dollar-denominated assets increases when the government has a budget deficit, regardless of how the government finances that deficit. One way of financing the deficit is to sell bonds directly to the Reserve Bank. This method of financing a deficit results in an immediate increase in the money supply. In such a situation, the supply of Australian dollar-denominated assets increases. But, even if the government finances its deficit by selling bonds to households, firms or foreigners, so long as those bonds are denominated in Australian dollars, the total supply of Australian dollar-denominated assets increases.

It is possible for the Federal government or any of the State governments to finance a deficit by issuing bonds denominated in currencies other than the Australian dollar. For example, the Federal government has issued bonds denominated in US dollars. When the government finances its deficit by selling bonds denominated in units of the currency of some other country, then the supply of Australian dollar-denominated assets does not increase.

Changes in the Level of Planned Investment
Whenever firms increase planned investment and finance the new ventures by borrowing, or selling shares and equity, the supply of dollar-denominated assets rises. There will be no effect on the supply of dollar-denominated assets only if the firms borrow in foreign financial markets by selling foreign-currency-denominated bonds.

The effects of a change in domestic monetary policy, a change in the government's budget deficit or a change in the level of planned investment financed by borrowing all act to *shift* the supply curve of dollar-denominated assets. An expansionary monetary policy, an increase in the government's budget deficit or an increase in the level of planned investment shift the supply curve to the right. A decrease in any of them shifts the supply curve to the left.

This discussion of the influences that change the supply of dollar-denominated assets is summarized in Table 29.4.

The Market for Australian Dollar-Denominated Assets

Let's now bring the demand and supply sides of the market for Australian dollar-denominated assets together and determine the exchange rate. Figure 29.5 illustrates the analysis.

Table 29.4 Changes in the Supply of Dollar-Denominated Assets

The supply of dollar-denominated assets

Increases if	*Decreases if*
• The Reserve Bank undertakes an open market purchase of dollar-denominated securities	• The Reserve Bank undertakes an open market sale of dollar-denominated securities
• The government of Australia has a deficit	• The government of Australia has a surplus
• The level of planned investment rises	• The level of planned investment falls

Figure 29.5 Three Exchange Rate Regimes

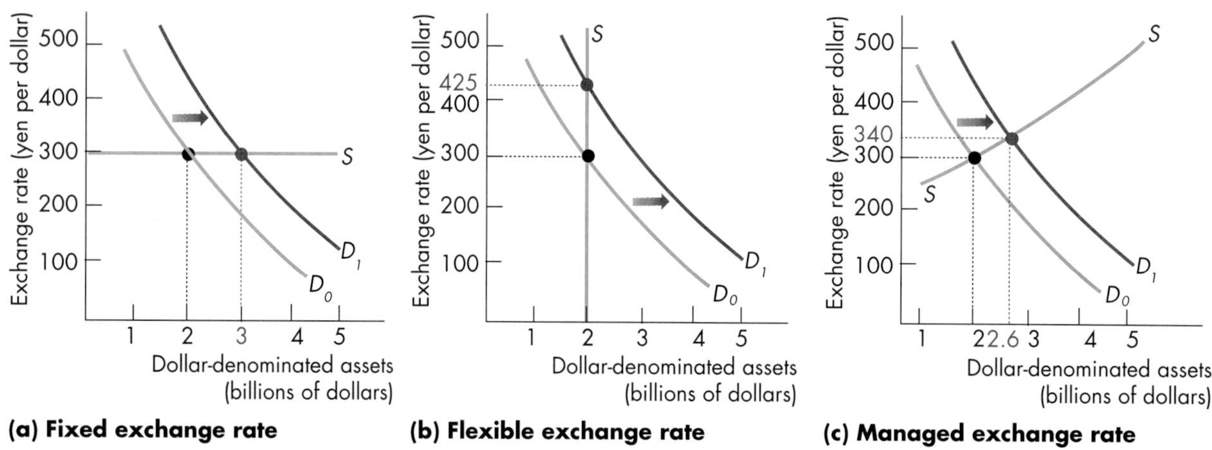

Under a fixed exchange rate regime — part (a) — the Reserve Bank stands ready to supply dollar-denominated assets or to take dollar-denominated assets off the market (supplying foreign currency in exchange) at a fixed exchange rate. The supply curve for dollar-denominated assets is horizontal. Fluctuations in demand lead to fluctuations in the quantity of dollar-denominated assets outstanding and to fluctuations in the nation's official holdings of foreign exchange. If demand increases from D_0 to D_1, the traded quantity of dollar-denominated assets increases from \$2 billion to \$3 billion.

Under a flexible exchange rate regime — part (b) — the Reserve Bank does not change the supply of dollar-denominated assets in response to changes in the exchange rate so that the supply curve is vertical. An increase in the demand for dollar-denominated assets from D_0 to D_1 results only in an increase in the value of the dollar — the exchange rate rises from 300 to 425 yen per dollar. The traded quantity of dollar-denominated assets remains constant at \$2 billion.

Under a managed exchange rate regime — part (c) — the supply curve of dollar-denominated assets is upward sloping, so that if demand increases from D_0 to D_1, the dollar appreciates but the quantity of dollar-denominated assets supplied also increases — from \$2 billion to \$2.6 billion. The Reserve Bank moderates the rise in the value of the dollar by increasing the quantity of dollar-denominated assets supplied but it does not completely prevent the exchange rate rise as it does in the case of fixed exchange rates.

Fixed Exchange Rate First, consider a fixed exchange rate regime, such as prevailed in Australia from 1945 to 1983. This case is illustrated in Fig. 29.5(a). The supply curve of dollars assets is horizontal at the fixed exchange rate of 300 yen per dollar. If the demand curve is D_0, 2 billion dollars worth of dollar-denominated assets is traded. An increase in demand to D_1 results in an increase in the traded quantity of dollar-denominated assets from \$2 billion to \$3 billion but no change in the yen price of dollars. To hold the price at 300 yen, the Reserve Bank must supply dollar-denominated assets, that is, sell Australian dollars in exchange for foreign currency. Its holdings of foreign exchange rise.

Flexible Exchange Rate Next look at Fig. 29.5(b), which shows what happens under a flexible exchange rate regime. In this case, the Reserve Bank does not change the supply of dollar-denominated assets in response to changes in the exchange rate and the supply curve of dollar-denominated assets is vertical at a traded quantity of \$2 billion. If the demand curve for dollars is D_0, the exchange rate is 300 yen per dollar. If the demand for dollars increases from D_0 to D_1, the exchange rate increases to 425 yen per dollar.

Managed Exchange Rate Finally, consider a managed exchange rate regime, which appears in Fig. 29.5(c). Here, the supply curve is upward sloping. When the demand curve is D_0, the exchange rate is 300 yen per dollar. If demand increases to D_1, the yen value of the dollar rises but only to 340 yen per dollar. Compared with the flexible exchange rate case, the same increase in demand results in a smaller increase in the exchange rate when it is managed. The reason for this is that the Reserve Bank increases the quantity supplied in the managed exchange rate case so as to moderate the increase in the exchange rate.

The Exchange Rate Regime and Foreign Exchange Reserves

There is an important connection between the foreign exchange rate regime and the country's foreign exchange reserves — the country's official holdings, by the Reserve Bank, of foreign currency. Under fixed exchange rates (as shown in Fig. 29.5a), every time there is a change in the demand for dollar-denominated assets the Reserve Bank must change the quantity of dollar-denominated assets supplied to match it. When the Reserve Bank has to increase the quantity of dollar-denominated assets supplied, it does so by offering dollar-denominated assets (bank deposits) in exchange for foreign currency (foreign bank deposits). In this case, the official holdings of foreign exchange increase. If the demand for dollar-denominated assets decreases, the Reserve Bank has to decrease the quantity of dollar-denominated assets supplied. The Reserve Bank does so by buying dollars back and using its foreign exchange holdings to do so. In this case, official holdings of foreign exchange decrease. Thus, with a fixed exchange rate, fluctuations in the demand for dollar-denominated assets result in fluctuations in official holdings of foreign exchange.

Under a flexible exchange rate regime, there is no Reserve Bank intervention in the foreign exchange market. Regardless of what happens to the demand for dollar-denominated assets, no action is taken to change the quantity of dollar-denominated assets supplied. Therefore there are no changes in the country's official holdings of foreign exchange.

With a managed exchange rate, official holdings of foreign exchange have to be adjusted to meet fluctuations in the demand for dollar-denominated assets, but in a less extreme manner than under fixed exchange rates. As a consequence, fluctuations in the official settlements balance are smaller under a managed exchange rate regime than under a fixed exchange rate regime.

Monetary Policy and the Exchange Rate

We have already discussed the effects on the supply curve of dollar-denominated assets of an open market operation intended to change the domestic money supply. In addition to the change in supply, there is a demand effect that we must consider. It arises because of the effects of a change in monetary policy on the domestic interest rate. As we saw in the previous chapter, the interest rate on dollar-denominated assets is changed following an open market operation, and this will change the demand for dollar-denominated assets. For example, the interest rate falls following an open market purchase of securities and this will reduce the demand for dollar-denominated assets. Thus a change in domestic monetary policy will affect both the supply curve and the demand curve for dollar-denominated assets.

Figure 29.6 considers the effects of an expansionary monetary policy — an open market purchase of Commonwealth government securities. The initial supply curve of dollar-denominated assets is S_0. The initial demand curve for dollar-denominated assets is D_0. The initial exchange rate is 300 yen per dollar. Directly following an open market purchase of Commonwealth government securities nothing happens, except that the banks now have more re-

Figure 29.6 Expansionary Monetary Policy and the Exchange Rate

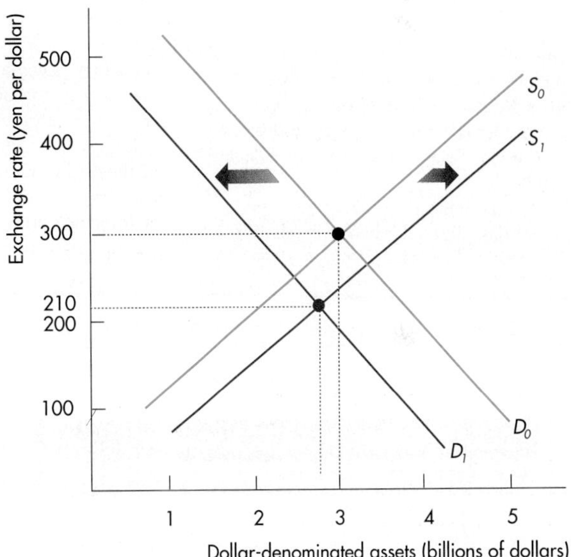

An open market purchase of domestic securities, intended to increase the domestic money supply, occurs when the Reserve Bank exchanges dollars for dollar-denominated assets. The total stock of dollar-denominated assets is unchanged. But as banks lend out their newly increased reserves, some of which are deposited back in banks, the money supply rises and the stock of dollar-denominated assets rises. The original supply curve, S_0, shifts to the right to S_1.

The increase in the money supply reduces the interest rate on dollar-denominated assets. Demand for them falls and the demand curve shifts from D_0 to the left, to D_1. The new equilibrium, with increased supply of and reduced demand for dollar-denominated assets, is achieved after the domestic currency depreciates.

Managing the Exchange Rate

Dollar Bounces Back After Reserve Sales

The Reserve Bank yesterday set off one of the most erratic days of trading in the dollar this year on local and international markets in a bid to stop its relentless advance.

The dollar traded within a US1c range as strong buying counteracted Reserve Bank selling.

The currency closed in local trading at US79.38c, compared with US79.51c locally on Thursday, and as it drifted slowly towards US79.40c in New York the United States Federal Reserve thumped it with a sell-off.

The currency plummeted to US78.56c after that move, which dealers said involved sales by the Reserve Bank through the US central bank.

'But it wasn't very effective and the dollar came right back again', one dealer said.

By the time local trade opened yesterday, the dollar had revived and moved to US79.04c.

Dealers said the Reserve Bank was flush with success after its bout of 'smoothing and testing' in New York on Thursday night.

'They hit the currency again late in the morning', one dealer said.

The central bank reportedly sold the dollar off through brokers and engaged in some direct trade on the market.

After the second bout of intervention the dollar lost only about 10 basis points and after the hiccup resumed its upward climb.

The chief economist at Macquarie Bank, Mr Bill Shields, said the Reserve Bank had acted in a 'predictable but not particularly successful' manner.

'The Reserve smooths and tests the market in an effort to affect its psychology or expectations… but in this case they have not been particularly successful', he said.

Mr Shields said the currency was well supported by exporters and foreign investors needing the funds to buy bonds.

Dealers said overseas buyers were busy picking up the parcels offered by the Reserve Bank for sale.

'The Japanese got some cheap Australian dollars to spend on bonds, that's for sure', another dealer said.

Other dealers said the currency would consolidate overnight before pushing back towards US80c.

The US dollar rose on the local market yesterday and finished at 1.6885 German marks from Dm1.6865 in New York, which matched Thursday's close.

The local dollar lost some ground against the trade-weighted index to end at 60.4 points from 60.5 points on Thursday.

It finished easier against the yen and closed at Y105.88 from Y105.91, and 45.83 pence from 46.03p.

But it rose against the New Zealand dollar to finish at $NZ1.3957 from $NZ1.3834 previously.

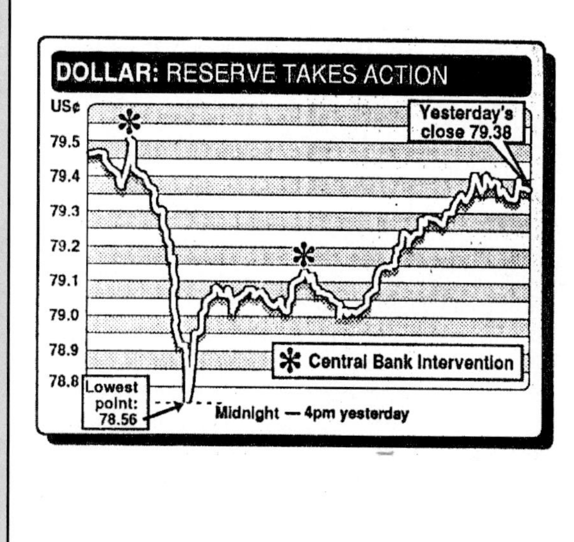

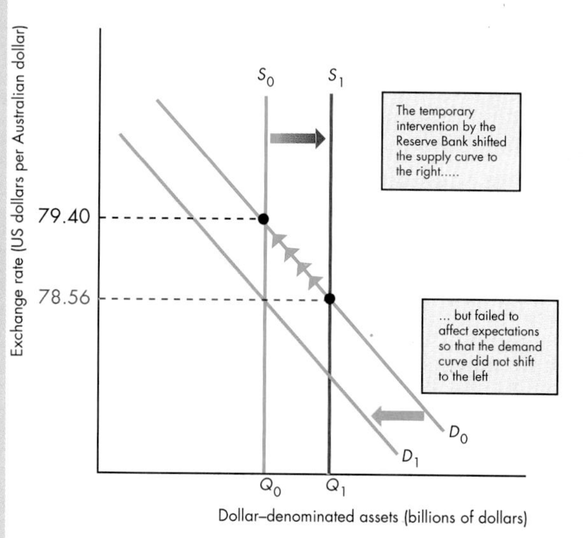

***The Weekend Australian*, 28–29 September 1991**
By Sally Fisher

The Essence of the Story

- Currencies are traded 24 hours a day, in markets around the world.
- On the evening of Thursday, 26 September 1991, the Australian dollar closed on the local market at US79.51 cents.
- It drifted to around US79.40 cents on the New York market, which opens after the local markets have closed.
- While it was night-time in Australia, the Reserve Bank sold off the Australian dollar on the New York market, using the United States central bank as its agent.
- The intervention drove the dollar down to US78.56 cents, roughly a one cent depreciation.
- But demand for the Australian dollar remained strong and it recovered to open at US79.04 cents on the local markets on the morning of Friday, 27 September 1991.
- Expecting to be able to hold the dollar down the Reserve bank 'hit' the currency again late on Friday morning. This time it sold the Australian dollar locally through brokers and also directly on the market.
- However continued 'support' for the currency carried it back to US79.40 cents by close of local business on Friday, back where it started the previous day.

Background and Analysis

- The value of the Australian dollar is determined mainly by market forces in a flexible foreign exchange market. But the Reserve Bank of Australia often tries to influence its value by buying or selling the currency in large quantities.
- Because foreign exchange markets are very large, in the absence of the types of controls on capital flows that existed prior to December 1983, it is very difficult for the Reserve Bank to control the value of the dollar directly.
- Rather, it attempts to affect the expectations of the market in order to get traders to act in a way that the Bank would like. Such was the case on Thursday, 26 September and Friday, 27 September 1991. The figure describes what happened.
- The market equilibrium at the close of business on the local market and the opening business in New York is given by the demand curve D_0 and supply curve S_0. The equilibrium value of the Australian dollar is US79.40 cents.
- The Reserve Bank wanted the currency lower. It temporarily increased the supply of Australian dollars to S_1 by selling off dollars in New York and again on local markets. The value of the dollar fell to US78.56 cents.
- The Reserve Bank was unable (or unwilling) to continue to sell Australian dollars to keep the exchange rate down. The supply curve moved back to S_0. The Bank had hoped to change market expectations and shift the demand curve to D_1, which would have reduced the equilibrium value of the local currency.
- But, demand from exporters converting their foreign currency gained from sales of Australian-produced goods to foreigners, and from foreigners wanting to buy Australian bonds (thus requiring domestic currency to do so) kept the demand curve at D_1.
- Thus the temporary intervention by the Reserve Bank was unsuccessful. The Australian dollar regained its lost value and returned to its initial equilibrium position.
- Those traders who bought the Australian dollar at US78.56 cents gained from the almost immediate appreciation. The annualized rate of return to those successful traders was of the order of 400 per cent. Evidently there are large gains to be had from being able to successfully predict the Reserve Bank's actions.

serves. The money supply, and the stock of dollar-denominated assets, rise only as the banks lend out some of their increased reserves. The supply curve shifts to the right, to S_1, as the money supply increases. In the domestic money market, the increase in the supply of money reduces interest rates on dollar-denominated securities. Demand for them falls and the demand curves shifts to the left to D_1. The ultimate effect of the expansionary *domestic* monetary policy in the foreign exchange market is that the exchange rate depreciates, in this example, to 210 yen per dollar.

But note that the Reserve Bank could have achieved a depreciation directly, had it so desired, by selling Australian dollar-denominated assets and buying foreign-currency-denominated assets in the foreign exchange market. This example highlights a very important connection between domestic monetary policy and exchange rate policy: that is, with respect to their effects on the exchange rate, open market operations are a very close substitute for foreign exchange market operations.

The other side of the coin is that operations in the foreign exchange market, designed to have a specific effect on the exchange rate, have important implications for the domestic money supply and, therefore, for domestic prices. For example, if the Reserve Bank intervenes in the foreign exchange market to hold down the value of the dollar, it sells Australian dollars and buys foreign currency. The supply of dollar-denominated assets rises and the price of them falls — the exchange rate depreciates. This means that the quantity of money has risen. If the Reserve Bank wants to insulate the domestic economy from the effects of the increased money supply it must somehow remove the new money from circulation. But the only tool at the Reserve Bank's disposal is an open market operation. It must sell Commonwealth government securities to mop up the increase in the money supply. The practice of undertaking an open market operation to offset the effects of a foreign exchange market intervention is known as **sterilization.** In Australia, the Reserve Bank routinely sterilizes open market operations two days after the foreign exchange market intervention itself.

Managing Exchange Rate Fluctuations

We've seen times when the Australian dollar–US dollar exchange rate has moved dramatically. These episodes have occurred even when the exchange rate was fixed by the Reserve Bank. On some of these occasions, for example in 1974/75 and 1985/86, the Australian dollar depreciated spectacularly. But on other occasions, for example in 1972/73 and 1987/88, it appreciated strongly. These large movements in the exchange rate are often interpreted as excessive volatility, and a case is made for the Reserve Bank to manage the exchange rate more closely, dampening down such large fluctuations. Let's consider the major influences on the exchange rate and assess whether or not the Reserve Bank can actually smooth out exchange rate fluctuations.

In Australia, one of the main reasons why the exchange rate has fluctuated so remarkably has been the large fluctuations in the terms of trade. Let's use our demand and supply framework to analyse the effects of a change in the terms of trade.

Changes in the Terms of Trade The terms of trade were defined in Chapter 24 as the ratio of export prices to import prices. The terms of trade rise

Figure 29.7 The Terms of Trade and the Exchange Rate Regime

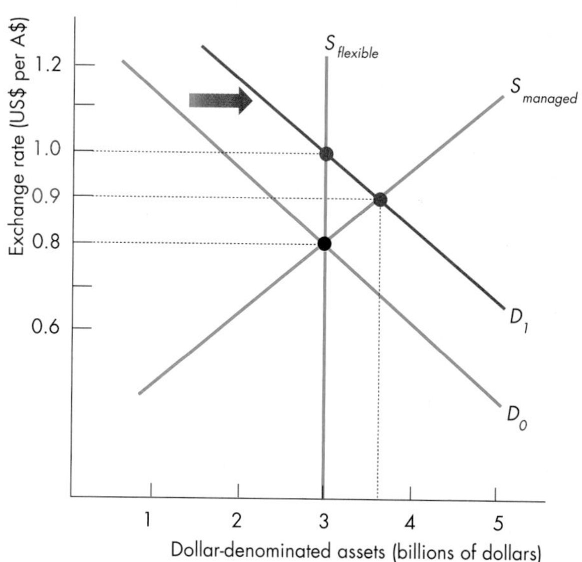

The figure shows the effects on the exchange rate of an improvement in the terms of trade resulting from an increase in prices received for exports. An improvement in the terms of trade shifts the demand for dollar-denominated assets out from D_0 to D_1. The exchange rate appreciates. The exchange rate appreciates from US$0.80 to US$1 per A$1 if the exchange rate is freely floating. But if the Reserve Bank is managing the exchange rate, it only appreciates to US$0.90.

(improve) if export prices rise or import prices fall. And the terms of trade fall (worsen) if export prices fall or import prices rise.

Figure 29.7 shows the effects of an increase in commodity export prices, which improves the terms of trade. Export prices rise, as world demand for Australian exports, principally mineral and agricultural products, is also rising. The transactions demand for dollar-denominated assets increases as the volume of trade increases, shifting the demand curve to the right, from D_0 to D_1. The dollar appreciates. If export prices fall, and the terms of trade fall, the demand for Australian exports falls and the demand for dollar-denominated assets falls, so that the demand curve shifts back to the left.

The size of the exchange rate appreciation (or depreciation) following a change in the terms of trade depends on the exchange rate regime adopted by the Reserve Bank. The change in the exchange rate is larger if the exchange rate is freely floating than if it is managed. In Fig. 29.7, following an improvement (increase) in the terms of trade, the exchange rate rises from US$0.80 to US$1 under a floating exchange rate regime. If the Reserve Bank manages the exchange rate, supplying more Australian dollar-denominated assets following the increase in the terms of trade, the rise in the exchange rate is only to US$0.90.

Figure 29.8 Recent Terms of Trade and Exchange Rate Variations

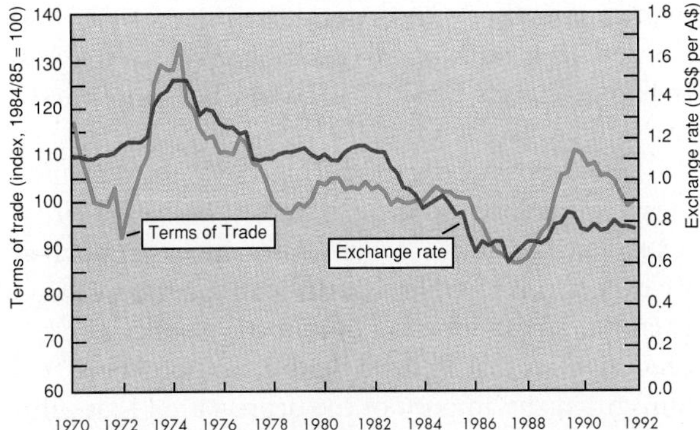

The terms of trade varied substantially from 1970 to 1990. There was a large rise in 1973/74 as commodity prices increased world-wide as a result of the oil price rises. Throughout 1975/76, the terms of trade fell. In 1985/86, the terms of trade fell again as export prices fell, but subsequently recovered in 1987/88. There is a close positive relationship between the exchange rate and the terms of trade over the entire period.

Source: Terms of trade: Series NPQQ.AD85TTR_INDEX, ABS Time Series Service; US$ exchange rate, Fig. 29.1, all supplied by EconData's dX Data Service.

Recent Terms of Trade Fluctuations Australia is in a unique position among developed countries because it imports a diverse collection of manufactured consumption and investment goods while it exports a relatively narrow set of primary commodities — minerals and agricultural raw materials. The prices of Australia's imports vary with world prices generally and do not exhibit an above average amount of variation compared to world prices generally. Australia's export prices, on the other hand, are determined in volatile commodity markets and do vary substantially over short periods of time. So the terms of trade that confront Australia vary greatly because of the variation in export prices. Figure 29.8 shows the terms of trade from 1970 to 1990 and the influence these variations have had on the US dollar exchange rate.

The large rise in the terms of trade in 1973/74 was the result of world-wide commodity price increases caused by the large increases in oil prices. Demand for energy spilled over into coal and other minerals, greatly benefiting Australian mining. As export prices fell in 1975/76, the terms of trade fell. Then in 1985/86, under the impetus of falling oil prices, export prices fell dramatically, causing the terms of trade to fall. The strong recovery in export prices in 1987/88 led to a sustained rise in the terms of trade.

On some occasions, the effects of changes in the terms of trade on the exchange rate have been dampened by offsetting domestic monetary policy. Let's see how the effects of terms of trade changes and changing monetary policies have caused variations in the exchange rate over two different episodes.

Monetary Policy, Terms of Trade Variations and the Exchange Rate

There have been two recent episodes during which the terms of trade changed dramatically. First, in 1985/86, the terms of trade fell substantially. Then in 1987/88 the terms of trade rose by much more than they had fallen two years earlier. In the same periods monetary policy was actively used. What were the effects of these disturbances on the exchange rate?

1985 to 1986 Between March 1985 and December 1986, the terms of trade declined by nearly 15

per cent as world prices for Australian exports fell. In the same period, the Australian dollar depreciated by 12 per cent. Figure 29.9(a) explains why this happened. At the beginning of 1985, the supply and demand curves for dollar-denominated assets were those labelled D_{85} and S_{85}. The exchange value of the Australian dollar was US$0.75 — where the supply and demand curves intersected.

As export prices fell during 1985, the demand curve shifted back to the left and the exchange rate depreciated. Did the dollar depreciate by as much as we expected it to? This is a difficult question to answer, but an examination of monetary policy at the time suggests that Reserve Bank action probably minimized the amount of the depreciation that actually occurred. In the Reserve Bank *Bulletin*, September 1986, the Bank reported that in response to the deteriorating balance of payments (see Chapter 37) a further tightening of monetary policy was necessary, 'continuing the trend which began in early 1985'. But the effects of the tight monetary policy were to reduce the money supply and increase interest rates. The reduction in the money supply shifted the supply curve back to the left. The increase in interest rates on dollar-denominated assets increased the demand for them, and the demand curve shifted to the right. At the same time, the Reserve Bank was selling foreign currency and buying Australian dollar-denominated assets as it attempted to prop up the Australian dollar.

So the sequence of events is as follows. The demand curve shifted back to the left following the fall in the terms of trade, to D_{86} in Fig. 29.9(a). The simultaneous tightening of monetary policy shifted the supply curve back to the left, to S^m_{86}, and shifted the demand curve back to the right to D^m_{86}. The sale of foreign currency by the Reserve Bank, which reduced the available dollar-denominated assets, was a direct intervention in the foreign exchange market and is shown by the positive slope of the supply curve — indicating that there is a managed exchange rate system. If the exchange rate regime had been perfectly flexible — a 'clean float' — the supply of dollar-denominated assets would have been fixed (that is, in perfectly inelastic supply) and the exchange rate would have fallen further. The tightening of domestic monetary policy is shown by the shift to the left of the supply curve and the shift to the right of the demand curve. Thus the actions of the Reserve Bank dampened the extent of the devaluation, which might have been expected from such a large fall in the terms of trade.

Figure 29.9 Terms of Trade Variations and Domestic Monetary Policy

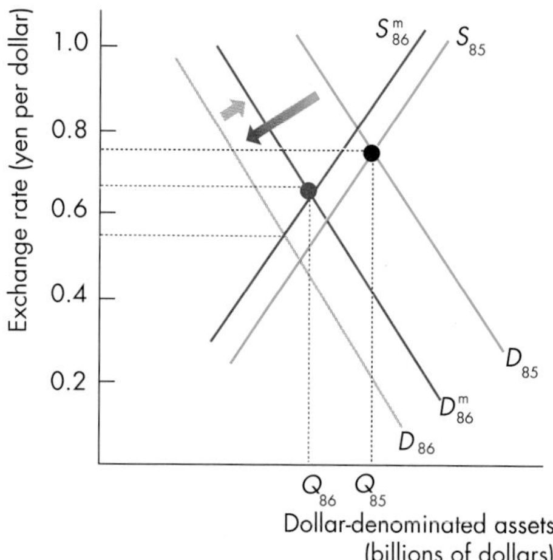

(a) 1985 to 1986

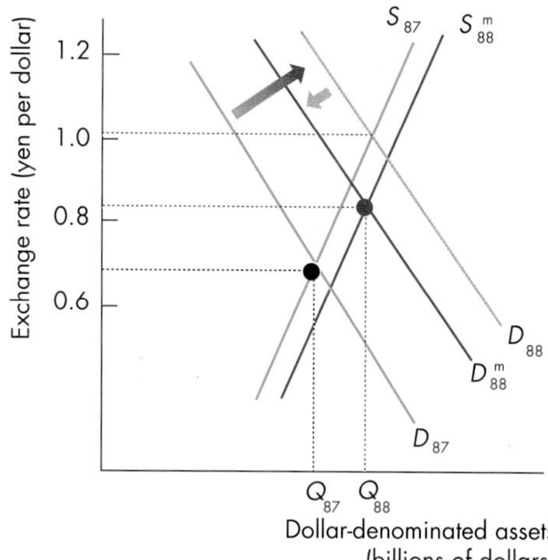

(b) 1987 to 1988

The period from March 1985 to December 1986 is shown in part (a). In 1985 the terms of trade collapsed, shifting the demand curve back to D_{86}. But the Reserve Bank tightened monetary policy at the same time, shifting the supply curve to the left to S^m_{86}. Interest rates rose, shifting the demand curve to the right, to S^m_{86}. The net effect is a smaller depreciation than would otherwise have occurred.

Part (b) shows the next two years, March 1987 to December 1988. In 1987 the terms of trade rose strongly. The demand for dollar-denominated assets increased strongly, shifting the demand curve to the right to D_{88}. The simultaneous loosening of monetary policy shifted the supply curve to the right, to S^m_{88}, and the lowered interest rates reduced the demand for dollar-denominated assets. The demand curve shifted back to S^m_{88}, reducing the net rise in the exchange rate.

1987 to 1988 Between March 1987 and December 1988 the terms of trade improved, strengthening by nearly 23 per cent. The US dollar–Australian dollar exchange rate appreciated by nearly 25 per cent. The strengthening terms of trade, and increased demand for Australian exports, increased the demand for Australian dollar-denominated assets. For a variety of reasons (some of which were discussed in the previous chapter) the Reserve Bank loosened monetary policy in 1987, causing interest rates to fall, leading to a shift to the right in the supply curve of dollar-denominated assets and a shift to the left in the demand curve for dollar-denominated assets. At the same time it was attempting to ease the effects of the exchange rate appreciation induced by the strong terms of trade by buying foreign currency denominated assets and selling dollar-denominated assets, leading to a movement along the supply curve in a managed exchange rate regime.

In Fig. 29.9(b) the situation at the beginning of 1987 is shown by the demand and supply curves D_{87} and S_{87}. The exchange rate was US$0.70. The rise in the terms of trade during 1987 and 1988 shifted the demand curve to D_{88}. However, the easing of monetary policy shifted the supply curve to the right to S^m_{88}, and the subsequent reduction in interest rates shifted the demand curve back to the left to D^m_{88}. Once again, the Reserve Bank's direct interventions in the foreign exchange market are indicated by the positive slope of the supply curve, while the effects of the change in domestic monetary policy is indicated by shifts in the curves.

In both the 1985/86 and 1987/88 episodes, large movements in the terms of trade induced large adjustments in the exchange rate. The changes were considerably dampened, however, by offsetting monetary policies adopted by the Reserve Bank and its direct management of the exchange rate. Therefore it would seem that, even though we have witnessed large variations in the exchange rate, those movements would have been even larger had the Reserve Bank not intervened.

Government Surpluses and Deficits in the 1980s

Fiscal policy in Australia has also seen some dramatic changes over the decade of the 1980s. These large variations would certainly have had long-term impacts on the exchange rate. As we have already seen, when the government runs a deficit, the supply of dollar-denominated assets increases, irrespective of how the deficit is financed. This causes the exchange rate to depreciate. When the government runs a budget surplus, the supply of dollar-denominated assets decreases and the exchange rate appreciates.

Up until the late 1980s it was usual for the Federal government, as it was for most Western governments, to operate at a deficit. In some countries these deficits were financed directly by creating money — selling government bonds directly to the central bank. Until the early 1980s, this was also partly true in Australia. For example, between 1975/76 and 1979/80 roughly 17 per cent of the government's total financing requirement was met by selling bonds (Treasury bills) directly to the Reserve Bank. This system changed with the introduction of tendering for government bonds in 1979 and 1982. (See Chapter 35 for a more complete discussion.) In the early 1980s, the government deficit increased rapidly, reaching a peak in 1983/84. In that year alone, the government sold almost $8 billion worth of debt. The effect of these bond sales is to shift the supply curve of dollar-denominated assets to the right and the exchange rate depreciates.

In 1985/86, the government changed its budgetary policy and began to work towards achieving a surplus. The first surplus was achieved in 1987/88. By 1989/90, the surplus amounted to nearly $8 billion dollars, or 2 per cent of GDP. Following our analysis, the effects of this policy reversal have been to cause the Australian dollar to strengthen or appreciate.

These swings in Federal government budget policy have occurred slowly relative to the changes in the terms of trade and monetary policy observed over the same periods. Thus, although we would expect longer run pressures on the exchange rate from changing fiscal policy, it has probably not added to the day-to-day, or even month-to-month, variability observed in the exchange rate.

R E V I E W

There are three possible foreign exchange rate regimes: fixed, flexible and managed. Under a fixed exchange rate regime, the Reserve Bank pegs the exchange rate but the foreign exchange reserves have to carry the burden of holding the exchange rate constant. A decrease in the demand for Australian dollar-denominated assets and an increase in the demand for foreign currency assets have to be met by lowering Australia's official holdings of foreign currency. Under a flexible exchange rate regime the Reserve Bank does not intervene in the foreign exchange markets. Australia's official holdings of foreign currency remain constant. Under a managed exchange rate regime the Reserve Bank smooths exchange rate fluctuations to a degree, but less strongly than under fixed exchange rates. Thus official holdings of foreign currency fluctuate less than under a fixed exchange rate regime. Under a flexible or a managed exchange rate regime, the exchange rate is determined by the demand for and supply of dollar-denominated assets.

Changes in the government's budget policy, planned investment from firms or domestic monetary policy all shift the supply curve of dollar-denominated assets. Domestic monetary policy, conducted by open market operations, is a close substitute for foreign exchange market interventions. Sterilization occurs when open market operations are undertaken to offset the effects on the domestic money supply of foreign exchange market interventions.

Variations in the prices received for Australia's exports, and the consequent variations in the terms of trade, cause large movements in the exchange rate. The recent actions of the Reserve Bank, through changing monetary policy, have dampened the fluctuations in the exchange rate caused by terms of trade fluctuations. ■

Arbitrage, Prices and Interest Rates

A**rbitrage** is the simultaneous act of buying low and selling high in order to make a profit on the margin between the two prices. Because both the low price and the high price are known when the transactions are made, arbitrage generates a riskless profit. Arbitrage has important effects on exchange rates, prices and interest rates. An increase in the quantity of purchases forces the buying price up. A decrease in the quantity of sales forces the selling price down. The prices move until they are equal and there is no arbitrage profit available. An implication of arbitrage is the law of one price. The **law of one price** states that any given commodity will be available at a single price.

The law of one price has no respect for national borders or currencies. If the same commodity is being bought and sold on either side of the Pacific Ocean, it doesn't matter that one of these transactions is being undertaken in Australia and the other in the United States or that one is using Australian dollars and the other US dollars. The forces of arbitrage bring about one price. Let's see how.

Arbitrage

Consider the price of a floppy disk that can be bought in either the United States or Australia. We will ignore taxes, tariffs and transport costs in order to keep the calculations simple, for these factors do not affect the fundamental issue.

Suppose that you can buy floppy disks in the United States for US$10 a box. Suppose that this same box of disks is available in Australia for A$15 a box. Where would it pay to buy disks — in Australia or in the United States? The answer depends on the relative costs of Australian and US money. If a US dollar costs A$1.50, then it is clear that the price of the disks is the same in both countries. Americans can buy a box of disks in the United States for US$10 or they can use US$10 to buy A$15 and then buy the disks in Australia. The cost will be the same either way. The same is true for Australians. Australians can use A$15 to buy a box of disks in Australia or could use A$15 to buy US$10 and then buy the disks in the United States. Again, there is no difference in the price of the disks.

Suppose, however, that a US dollar is less valuable than in the above example. In particular, suppose that a US dollar costs A$1.40. In this case, it will pay to buy the disks in the United States. Australians can buy US$10 for A$14 and therefore can buy the disks in the United States for A$14 a box compared with A$15 in Australia. The same comparison holds for Americans. Americans can use US$10 to buy A$14, but that would not be enough to buy the disks in Australia since the disks cost A$15 there. It therefore pays Americans also to buy the disks in the United States.

If the situation described above did prevail, there would be an advantage in switching the purchases of disks from Australia to the United States. Australians would mail-order direct to the distributors of disks in the United States and keep on doing so until the Australian price had fallen to A$14. Once that had happened, Australians would be indifferent as to whether they buy their disks in Australia or in the United States. Arbitrage would have eliminated the difference in prices between the two countries.

Perhaps you are thinking that this is a silly example since we don't rush out and order direct from the United States every time we want to buy a box of floppy disks. But the fact that there is a profit to be made means that it would pay someone to organize the importing of disks into Australia from the United States, thereby increasing the number of disks available here and lowering their price. The incentive to undertake such a move would be present as long as disks were selling for a higher price in Australia than in the United States.

Purchasing Power Parity

Purchasing power parity occurs when money has equal value across countries. (The word 'parity' simply means equality. The phrase 'purchasing power' refers to the 'value of money'. Thus 'purchasing power parity' translates directly to 'equal value of money'.) Purchasing power parity is an implication of arbitrage and of the law of one price. In the floppy disk example, when US$1 is worth A$1.40, US$10 will buy the same box of floppy disks that A$14 will buy. The value of money, when converted to common prices, is the same in both countries. Purchasing power parity thus prevails in this situation.

Purchasing power parity theory predicts that purchasing power parity applies to all goods and to price indexes, not just to a single good such as the floppy disk that we considered above. That is, if any goods or transportable services are cheaper in one country than in another, it will pay to convert money into the currency of that country, buy the goods in that country and sell them in another. By such an arbitrage process, all prices are brought to equality.

One test of the purchasing power parity theory that has been proposed is to calculate what is called the real exchange rate between two countries. The **real exchange rate** is the ratio of the price index in one country to the price index in another. The prices in the second country are converted to prices in the first, using the exchange rate between the two currencies. For example, the real exchange rate between the Australian dollar and the Japanese yen, expressed in units of Japanese goods per unit of Australian goods, is calculated by using the following formula:

$$\begin{array}{l}\text{Real exchange}\\ \text{rate between}\\ \text{Australian dollar}\\ \text{and Japanese yen}\end{array} = \frac{\begin{array}{l}\text{GDP deflator}\\ \text{in Australia}\end{array}}{\begin{array}{l}\text{GDP deflator}\\ \text{in Japan}\end{array}} \times \begin{array}{l}\text{yen per}\\ \text{dollar}\end{array}$$

To measure the real exchange rate between the Australian dollar and all other currencies, we calculate an index which is a weighted average of the real exchange rates between the Australian dollar and every other currency, where the weights reflect the importance of each other currency in Australian international trade. This calculation is similar to that of the trade-weighted index (of the nominal exchange rate) illustrated in Table 29.1.

There are large movements in the real exchange rate, and these movements lead some economists to conclude that the purchasing power parity theory is wrong. They argue that, if the purchasing power parity theory is correct, the real exchange rate index will remain close to 100. Any increase in the GDP deflator in Australia not matched by an equal percentage increase in the GDP deflator in Japan will be accompanied by a depreciation of the Australian dollar against the Japanese yen. The result would be an equal percentage change in Australian prices, when valued in Japanese yen, and in Japanese prices. Thus the real exchange rate index would remain at 100.

There is an important problem with this view of the implications of purchasing power parity for the real exchange rate. It arises from the fact that many goods and most services are not easily traded internationally. For example, it's lunch time in Adelaide, you are hungry and doughnuts are your thing. You don't have much choice but to buy your doughnut right there. You can't take advantage of the fact that doughnuts are cheaper in Hobart and begin an arbitrage operation. Doughnuts are examples of non-traded goods. A **non-traded good** is one that cannot be traded over long distances. Sometimes it is technically possible to undertake such a trade but prohibitively costly. In other cases, it is simply not possible to undertake the trade.

There are many examples of non-traded goods. Almost all the public services provided by the government are non-traded. You can't buy cheap street-sweeping services in Vietnam and sell them at a profit in Sydney. Many location-specific services, such as fast food, are also in this category. When goods cannot be traded over long distances, the goods are, strictly speaking, different goods. A fresh doughnut in Adelaide is as different from a fresh doughnut in Hobart as it is from a pancake across the street.

Arbitrage operates to bring about equality in prices of *identical* goods, not different goods. It does not operate to bring about equality between prices of similar-looking goods in widely differing locations. For this reason, tests of the purchasing power parity theory based on real exchange rates are faulty. In fact, for real exchange rates to stay constant every time the exchange rate changes, the prices of all goods will also have to change — the dollar will have to fall against all currencies and the doughnut!

An additional factor that influences the real exchange rate is the existence of tariffs, taxes and other restrictions on international trade. Such restrictions weaken the forces of arbitrage and prevent the same price from arising for the same commodity in different countries.

Arbitrage does not occur only in markets for goods and services. It also occurs in markets for assets. As a result, it tends to bring about another important equality or parity — interest rate parity.

Interest Rate Parity

Interest rate parity occurs when interest rates are equal across countries once the differences in risk are taken into account. Interest rate parity is a condition brought about by arbitrage in the markets for assets — markets in which borrowers and lenders operate.

At the beginning of this chapter, we noted some facts about interest rates in different countries. Those facts seem to suggest that interest rates are *not* equal in different countries. To make things concrete, let's look at a specific example. On 12 December 1990, it was possible to borrow money from a bank in New York at an interest rate of 7.73 per cent a year. On that same day, banks in Sydney were charging an interest rate of 12.88 per cent a year for a similar loan. Aren't these unequal interest rates? Isn't it possible for someone to borrow, say, a million dollars in New York at an interest rate of 7.73 per cent and lend that money in Sydney at 12.88 per cent a year, profiting from the 5.15 percentage point difference between the two interest rates? Such a transaction, done for a year, would produce a profit of $51,500, not bad for a few minutes' work! Also, apparently, an outcome that violates interest rate parity!

In fact, as you're about to discover, interest rates in Australia and the United States are almost equal — at least close enough to equality that you could not profit from the transactions just described.

The key to understanding why the interest rates are equal is to realize that when you borrow in New York you are borrowing *US dollars.* When the loan is due, you are committing yourself to repaying a certain number of *US dollars.* When you lend money in Australia — for example, by placing it on deposit in a bank — you are lending *Australian dollars* and the bank is obliged to repay *Australian dollars.* It's a bit like borrowing apples and lending oranges. But if you're borrowing apples and lending oranges, you've got to convert the apples to oranges. When the loans become due, you've got to convert oranges back into apples. The prices at which you do these transactions affect the interest rates that you pay and receive.

Let's look a bit more closely at the $1 million borrowing and lending operation that you might have done on 12 December 1990, and see how much you would have made (or lost) on the deal. Table 29.5 summarizes the events. Table 29.5(a) lists some data from 12 December 1990. It shows that commercial banks in New York were lending for three months at an interest rate of 7.73 per cent on that day. Banks in Sydney were offering the same three-month loans at an interest rate of 12.88 per cent. (These are annual interest rates.) We are supposing that you could charge the same interest rates as a bank could when you lend the money in Sydney. On that day, you can sell US dollars on the foreign exchange market at one US dollar for 1.3046 Australian dollars. That's the price at which you can convert the US dollars that you borrowed into the Australian dollars that you are going to lend. (Like the price at which you can sell oranges for apples.)

At the end of three months, you are going to have to convert Australian dollars back into US dollars to repay your New York bank loan and the interest on it. There are two ways in which you can do that transaction. You can wait until 12 March 1991, and take your chances on the exchange rate between the US dollar and the Australian dollar that prevails on that day. If you choose to do that, you will certainly be taking some risks. If the Australian dollar appreciates in that three-month period, you will stand to gain. If the Australian dollar depreciates, you will stand to lose.

But there is another way in which you can get the US dollars that you need to repay your bank loan on 12 March. You can enter into a contract on 12 December 1990, at a price agreed on that day, to buy a certain number of US dollars to be delivered on 12 March 1991. Such a contract is called a forward contract. A **forward contract** is a contract entered into at an agreed price to buy or sell a certain quantity of any commodity (including currency) at a specified future date. Forward contracts are traded on markets, and their prices are determined by supply and demand, in the same manner that any physical commodity is traded. There are forward markets in most agricultural products and in raw materials, as well as in currencies and stocks and bonds. The exchange rate in a forward contract is called a **forward exchange rate**. On 12 December 1990, the foreign exchange rate at which US dollars could be bought in the forward market for delivery three months in the future (on 12 March 1991) was A$1.3184 per US dollar. This means that the Australian dollar was expected to depreciate between 12 December and 12 March.

Table 29.5(b) sets out the transactions that you could have undertaken on 12 December 1990. You borrow US$1 million in New York and sell those US dollars at A$1.3046 per US dollar in exchange for A$1.3046 million. You loan that A$1.3046 million in Sydney on a three-month term. That's the end of your cash transactions on that day. At the same time, you enter into a forward contract, promising to buy enough US dollars for delivery on 12 March 1991 to convert your repaid loan and the interest on it. At an interest rate of 12.88 per cent per year, you will earn A$42,008 interest on your loan ($1,304,600 times 0.1288 divided by 4). Your total proceeds from the Sydney loan will be A$1,346,608 (A$1,304,600 + A$42,008) so you will need US$1,021,396. (Divide the 1,346,608 Australian dollars that you get back by 1.3184 Australian dollars per US dollar, the price that you agree to in the forward market, and you'll see that the answer is US$1,021,396.). You enter into a contract now to buy those 1.0214 million US dollars later in March at an agreed price of A$1.3184 per US dollar.

Table 29.5(c) tells us what happens on 12 March 1991. You receive your A$1,346,608 from your loan — principal of $1,304,600 plus a quarter of a year's interest (A$42,008). The total amount of Australian dollars you have is A$1.3466 million. You pay for your forward US dollar contract, which costs you A$1,346,608 million, and receive US$1,021,396. Last, you will repay the loan taken out with the New York bank that delivered the one million US dollars to lend in Sydney. At 7.73 per cent a year, you owe the bank US$1,019,325. (US$1,000,000 plus one quarter of one year's interest, $77,300 divided by 4.) In the end you have actually made some profit — US$2,071, or about 0.2 per cent. But this amount probably would not cover the brokers' and bank fees that must be paid. You would probably have made a loss when these transactions costs were included.

Suppose that the interest rates in Sydney and New York, the exchange rate and the forward exchange rate had been slightly different. Suppose that, instead of making a loss after transaction costs had been included, this set of transactions had returned a profit. How long would the profit opportunity exist? You and millions of people like you would be borrowing from banks in New York, converting US dollars into Australian dollars, lending them in Sydney, possibly by depositing them in an Australian bank, and taking out forward contracts to get the US dollars back to repay your US dollar loan at the end of the transaction period. Even if you could make only a few thousand dollars clear profit on a US$1 million contract, there would be nothing to stop

Table 29.5 International Borrowing and Lending

(a) Data on 12 December 1990

Bank lending rate in New York	7.73	per cent per year
Bank lending rate in Sydney	12.88	per cent per year
Price at which US dollars can be sold	1.3046	A$ per US$
Price at which US dollars can be bought for delivery in three months	1.3184	A$ per US$

(b) Transactions on 12 December 1990

Borrow	US$1 million in New York
Sell	US$1 million in exchange for A$1.3046 million
Lend	A$1.3046 million for three months in Sydney
Contract to buy US$	US$1.0214 million for delivery in three months at A$1.3184 per US$1

(c) Transactions on 12 March 1991

Receive	US$1.0214 million from loan repayment — deposit plus interest — converted into US dollars as forward contract fulfilled
Pay	US$1.0193 million to discharge debt with New York bank
Profit	US$0.0021 million

you from entering into a US$10 million or a US$100 million contract, which means that you could make a large income in the process. Or could you?

Think about what is going to happen to interest rates and exchange rates as you and everyone else attempt to profit. With an increased demand for loans from banks in New York, the interest rate there is going to increase. With an increased supply of loans and deposits to the banks in Sydney, the interest rate there will decrease. As more people offer US dollars in exchange for Australian dollars, the exchange rate will increase — more US dollars will have to be offered for an Australian dollar. And as more people try to buy US dollars in the forward market, the number of Australian dollars per US dollar in that market will increase. Every one of these changes reduces the possibility of making a profit by borrowing in New York and lending in Sydney, and these forces would operate until that profit opportunity had been wiped out. They will not operate to reverse the profit — that is, to make it profitable to borrow in Sydney and lend in New York. In such a situation, the reverse forces would be at work, again removing profit from international borrowing and lending actions.

In the situation that we've just described, interest rate parity prevails. The interest rate in New York — when the expected change in the price of the US dollar between December and March is taken into account — is almost identical to that in Sydney. It costs 7.73 per cent a year to borrow US dollars in New York but it costs nearly 13 per cent a year to borrow US dollars, convert them into Australian dollars and then convert them back into US dollars at a later date. It is in this sense that interest rates are equal. The Australian dollar interest rate in Sydney is the same as the Australian dollar interest rate in New York. The yen interest rate in New York is the same as the yen interest rate in Tokyo.

A World Market

Arbitrage in asset markets operates on a world-wide scale and keeps the world capital markets linked in a single global market. This market is an enormous one. It involves borrowing and lending through banks, in bond markets and in stock markets. The scale of this international business was estimated by Salomon Brothers, a merchant bank in the United States, at more than one thousand billion US dollars in 1986. It is because of international arbitrage in asset markets that the fortunes of the stock markets around the world are so closely linked. A stock market crash in New York makes its new low-priced stocks look attractive compared with high-priced stocks in Sydney, Toronto, Tokyo, Hong Kong, Zurich, Frankfurt and London. As a consequence, investors make plans to sell high in these other markets and buy low in New York. But before many such transactions can be put through, the prices in the other markets fall to match the fall in New York. Conversely, if the Tokyo market experiences rapid price increases and markets in the rest of the world stay constant, investors seek to sell high in Tokyo and buy low in the rest of the world. Again, these trading plans will induce movements in the prices in the other markets to bring them into line with the Tokyo market. The action of selling high in Tokyo will lower the prices there and the action of buying low in Frankfurt, London and New York will raise the prices there.

Monetary Independence

With what you have just learned about arbitrage and its effects on prices and interest rates, you can see why fixed exchange rates make one economy completely interdependent with another and why flexible exchange rates bring monetary and financial independence. Let's explore these issues.

Interdependence with a Fixed Exchange Rate

Suppose that Australia fixes its exchange rate against the US dollar and that through Reserve Bank actions in the foreign exchange market, it manages to hold the Australian dollar absolutely steady against the US dollar. Also, suppose that the Reserve Bank has large enough reserves of US dollars to be able to withstand any pressures that might make the exchange rate move.

The forces of arbitrage bring the prices of traded goods into line with each other on both sides of the Pacific Ocean. Where there are no tariffs or other trade restrictions, the prices are exactly the same regardless of whether a good is paid for in Australian dollars or US dollars — as in the example of disks that we reviewed earlier in this chapter. If there is an increase in prices in the United States, there is an increase of the same percentage in Australia, other things being equal. But other things are not necessarily constant and there may be a difference between the inflation rates in the United States and Australia. Nevertheless, a *change* in the inflation rate in the United States brings about a *change* in the inflation rate in Australia of an equal percentage magnitude. That is

$$\text{Inflation rate in Australia} = \text{Inflation rate in the United States} + \text{Other influences}$$

We saw how this process would work in our discussion of purchasing power parity.

Similarly, arbitrage in asset markets brings interest rates into equality in the two countries for assets having identical risks and other characteristics. For assets of differing risk, interest rates will differ both within Australia and between Australia and the United States. For example, when a bank makes a loan to BHP, that loan is less risky than one made to a small firm taking a highly speculative position in the market for some new computer software. The small software company pays a higher interest rate than BHP regardless of whether it borrows in US dollars or Australian dollars. Also, the software company pays the same interest rate regardless of whether it borrows in Melbourne or New York.

Because the average riskiness of loans in Australia might differ from that in the United States there may be a difference between the average interest rate here and in the United States. That difference reflects the difference in the average amount of risk in the two countries. Thus

$$\text{Interest rate in Australia} = \text{Interest rate in the United States} + \text{Risk differential}$$

Let's now work out what happens in Australia if the Federal Reserve System, the monetary authority in the United States, expands the rate at which money is created there. Suppose that the Federal Reserve System undertakes policies that speed up the growth of the money supply from 5 per cent a year to 10 per cent a year. This action eventually brings an increase in inflation in the United States of 5 per cent a year. The higher inflation rate increases interest rates in the United States by 5 percentage points. With higher inflation and higher interest rates in the United States, the forces of international commodity price arbitrage and interest rate arbitrage that we have just considered bring higher inflation and higher interest rates to Australia. But other factors may change. Abstracting from those other possible forces, the increased money supply growth in the United States has brought an increase in Australia's interest rates and Australia's inflation rates by amounts equal to the increases in those same variables in the United States.

Fixed Exchange Rates in Action How do fixed exchange rates work in practice? They work exactly like the theoretical description that you have just reviewed. During the 1960s, when the Australian dollar was fixed in value against the UK pound sterling, and when the pound sterling and most other currencies were fixed in value against the US dollar, inflation rates were remarkably similar around the world. So too were interest rates. As countries moved to flexible exchange rates, during the 1970s, inflation rates and interest rates diverged. In recent times, the major countries of Western Europe (including now the United Kingdom) have joined what is known as the European Monetary System (EMS). The **European Monetary System** is a fixed exchange rate system involving all the members of the European Community — the most important of which are West Germany, France and Italy. Since these countries have locked the values of their currencies together, their inflation and interest rates have come into closer alignment.

You can think of interest rates and inflation rates within a country as being a special case of fixed exchange rates. The Victorian dollar and the Queensland dollar are the same as the New South Wales dollar. The exchange rate between these dollars is fixed at one. Anything that changes the inflation rate in Victoria also, other things being equal, changes the inflation rate in Queensland and in New South Wales. Interest rates, similarly, are linked through the forces of arbitrage that we have described across Australia.

We've seen how fixed exchange rates bring financial interdependence between countries. Let's now see how flexible exchange rates break that interdependence and enable a country to insulate itself from financial shocks stemming from the rest of the world.

During the 1970s Australia still pursued a fixed exchange rate, by that time fixed directly to the US dollar. In 1973 and 1974, then again in 1978, the Western world was hit by the oil price shocks. At this time, Australia was self-sufficient in oil and so was not directly affected by the rise in oil prices — except for the increase in the terms of trade, which they induced. But most other Western countries, being oil and energy importers, tried to inflate their way out of the OPEC-induced recessions. With fixed exchange rates, these rapid rises in world inflation were quickly incorporated into the Australian inflation rate. For this reason, the Australian government decided to float the dollar at the end of 1983.

Independence with a Flexible Exchange Rate

The existence of a flexible exchange rate does not render international arbitrage forces ineffective. Instead, by making it possible for the value of one money to change in terms of another, it enables dollar prices (and interest rates) to change in one country while not changing in another and while respecting the laws and forces of arbitrage. To see how, first let's consider how flexible exchange rates insulate a country from inflation in another country.

We know that the basic forces of arbitrage ensure that

$$\text{Price in A\$} = \text{Price in US\$} \times \text{Exchange rate (A\$ per US\$)}$$

Consider again the case of disks. If disks cost $10 a box in the United States and if the exchange rate between the Australian and US dollars is A$1.25 per US$1, then the price of that same box of disks in Australian dollars is $12.50. Now suppose that prices of all goods increase in the United States by 10 per cent. The price of a box of disks increases to $11. Suppose at the same time, for reasons that we'll examine in a moment, that the Australian dollar appreciates against the US dollar by 10 per cent. The exchange rate changes to approximately A$1.14 per US$1. At this new exchange rate and new US dollar price, what is the Australian dollar price brought about by the forces of arbitrage? The answer is $12.50, the same as before.

But there are factors other than US prices and the exchange rate that can bring about price changes in Australia. Changes in tariffs, taxes or other non-monetary factors can influence the prices of goods in Australia relative to prices in the United States. Nevertheless, other things being equal, a change in the inflation rate in the United States does not translate into a change in the inflation rate in Australia unless the Australian dollar also stays constant against the US dollar. In general, since the exchange rate changes when the US inflation rate changes, there is some insulation of the Australian inflation rate from the US inflation rate. Inflation in the two countries is linked by the equation:

$$\text{Inflation rate in Australia} = \text{Inflation rate in the United States} - \text{Percentage appreciation of Australian dollars} + \text{Other influences}$$

If the US inflation rate increases and if the Reserve Bank wants to insulate Australians from that US inflation, it must take steps to ensure that the Australian dollar appreciates in value to offset the increase in US inflation.

Next, consider asset markets and the determination of interest rates. As we saw earlier, when one currency is expected to change in value against another currency, there is a difference between the levels of interest rates in the two countries. That difference equals the expected rate of change in the value of the currency. If the Australian dollar is expected to depreciate against the US dollar by 1 per cent a year, Australian interest rates are higher than US interest rates by that same 1 per cent a year. They may be higher still because of risk differentials. That is,

$$\text{Interest rate in Australia} = \text{Interest rate in the United States} - \text{Expected rate of appreciation of Australian dollar} + \text{Risk differential}$$

If interest rates rise in the United States and if the Reserve Bank wants to protect Australians from higher interest rates, it must take steps that produce an expected appreciation of the Australian dollar.

How does the Reserve Bank achieve financial insulation with a flexible exchange rate? It does so by ensuring that Australian monetary policy is geared toward Australian objectives and does not respond to changes in US monetary policy. Suppose, for example, that the same events occur that we analysed earlier in the case of fixed exchange rates. The Federal Reserve System increases the growth rate of the money supply in the United States by 5 percentage points (for example, from 3 per cent a year to 8 per cent a year). Inflation increases by 5 percentage points a year in the United States and US interest rates also increase by 5 percentage points. At the same time, the Reserve Bank makes no changes in its monetary policy. The money supply growth rate in Australia is held steady at its previous level. With no increase in the growth rate of the Australian money supply, there can be no increase in the Australian inflation rate. Prices in Australia continue to inflate at the same pace as before and interest rates remain at the same level as before. But, with higher inflation in the United States than in Australia, the Australian dollar appreciates. It appreciates by the difference between the two inflation rates. Also, with an inflation rate differential that is plain for everyone to see, people expect the appreciation of the Australian dollar to continue. As a consequence, the gap between interest rates in the

United States and in Australia equals the expected rate of appreciation of the Australian dollar.

Flexible Exchange Rates in Practice There is an enormous amount of evidence from the operation of flexible exchange rates that they do indeed provide financial independence. Countries such as Japan, West Germany and Switzerland have persistently, year-in and year-out, achieved lower inflation rates and lower interest rates than any other countries. They have done so by keeping the growth rate of the money supply in their own economies close to the growth rate of real GDP. As a consequence, they have achieved low inflation. Their currencies have appreciated against other currencies, and the expectation of continuing appreciation has kept their interest rates below those in other countries. By contrast, there are countries that have, over long periods, created money at a rapid pace — at an annual rate far in excess of the growth rate of real GDP. Examples are Australia, the United Kingdom, the Netherlands and Italy. In these countries, a rapid rate of money supply growth brings a higher-than-average inflation rate and currency depreciation. The expectation of continuing depreciation results in interest rates being higher than those in other countries.

In Australia, the Reserve Bank and the government have often directed monetary policy at issues relating to Australia's dealings with the rest of the world. On some occasions monetary policy has been directed at the balance of payments. At other times, monetary policy appears to have been directed at the exchange rate. Whenever monetary policy is used to target variables such as these, the Reserve Bank loses the independence of monetary policy achieved with freely flexible exchange rates.

A Paradox?

Many people complain that the Reserve Bank, from time to time, pursues too tight a monetary policy, thereby forcing Australian interest rates too high. These critics of the Bank say that, if the Bank permitted the money supply to grow at a faster pace, this could bring interest rates down. You have now learned that this advice and this conclusion are incorrect. If the Reserve Bank increased the Australian money supply, it could indeed bring a temporary decrease in interest rates. But if the Reserve Bank persistently increased the Australian money supply at a more rapid pace, once this monetary policy became correctly anticipated, interest rates in Australia would rise and the foreign exchange value of the Australian dollar would fall. In the longer run, loose monetary policy would have brought higher interest rates, not lower interest rates. To achieve low interest rates, the Reserve Bank would have to slow down the growth rate of the Australian money supply and maintain a lower average growth rate over several years. The consequence of this action would be lower inflation in Australia, an appreciating Australian dollar and lower interest rates in Australia than those in other countries.

Is this a paradox? Not really. A once-and-for-all (and unexpected) increase in the money supply brings a temporary decrease in interest rates. An ongoing and anticipated increase in the money supply brings higher interest rates, higher inflation and a depreciating currency.

■ You've now discovered what determines the foreign exchange value of a country's currency. That value is determined by the demand for and supply of assets denominated in that currency and is strongly influenced by monetary policy actions. A rapid increase in the supply of assets denominated in that currency will result in a decline in its value relative to other currencies.

You've also learned how international arbitrage links prices and interest rates together in different countries. International arbitrage does not occur in markets for non-traded goods, so there are variations in real exchange rates. But arbitrage operates in markets for traded goods and is especially powerful in markets for assets. Arbitrage in asset markets keeps interest rates equal around the world. Differences in national interest rates reflect the expectations of changes in exchange rates. Once these differences in exchange rates are taken into account, interest rates are equal across countries.

You've also discovered how fixed exchange rates lock inflation and interest rates across countries in step with each other and how flexible exchange rates bring the possibility of an independent monetary policy and insulation from monetary shocks stemming from the rest of the world.

In the following chapters, we're going to look at some broader macroeconomic issues. In particular, we're going to see how monetary and fiscal policy actions lead to fluctuations in aggregate demand and how these fluctuations, in turn, lead to changes in inflation and unemployment, and create booms and recessions.

SUMMARY

Foreign Exchange

Foreign currency is obtained in exchange for domestic currency in the foreign exchange market. The foreign exchange market operates 24 hours a day around the world. Central banks often intervene in foreign exchange markets. There are three types of foreign exchange rate regimes: fixed, flexible and managed. When the exchange rate is fixed, the government declares a value for the currency in terms of some other currency and the Reserve Bank takes actions to ensure that value of the exchange rate is maintained. To fix the value of the exchange rate, the Reserve Bank has to stand ready to supply dollar-denominated assets and take in foreign currency assets or to remove dollar assets from circulation in exchange for foreign currency assets. The country's foreign currency reserves fluctuate to maintain the fixed exchange rate.

A flexible exchange rate is one in which the central bank takes no action to influence the value of its currency in the foreign exchange market. The country's foreign reserves remain constant, and fluctuations in demand and supply of assets denominated in domestic currency lead to fluctuations in the exchange rate.

A managed exchange rate is one in which the central bank takes actions to smooth fluctuations that would otherwise arise but does so less strongly than under a fixed exchange rate regime. (pp. 297–300)

Exchange Rate Determination

In a flexible or managed exchange rate regime, the exchange rate is determined by the demand for and supply of dollar-denominated assets. The demand for dollar-denominated assets depends on the volume of dollar trade financed, the price level in Australia and in other countries, the interest rates on dollar-denominated assets, the interest rates on foreign currency assets and expected changes in the foreign exchange value of the dollar.

The supply of dollar-denominated assets depends on the exchange rate regime. Under fixed exchange rates, the supply curve is horizontal; under flexible exchange rates, the supply curve is vertical; under managed exchange rates, the supply curve is upward sloping. The position of the supply curve depends on the government's budget and the Reserve Bank's domestic monetary policy. The larger the budget deficit or the more rapidly the Reserve Bank permits the money supply to grow, the further to the right is the supply curve. Fluctuations in the exchange rate occur because of fluctuations in demand and supply of dollar-denominated assets and sometimes these fluctuations are large. Large fluctuations arise from changes in demand and supply that are interdependent. A shift in the supply curve often produces an induced change in the demand curve that reinforces the effect on the exchange rate. (pp. 300–314)

Arbitrage, Prices and Interest Rates

Arbitrage — buying low and selling high — keeps the prices of goods and services that are traded internationally close to equality across all countries. Arbitrage also keeps interest rates in line with each other.

Some goods are not traded internationally — they are non-traded goods. International arbitrage does not bring the prices of such goods into equality. For this reason, there are fluctuations in a country's real exchange rate — the purchasing power of the dollar at home compared with its purchasing power abroad.

Interest rates around the world look unequal, but the appearance arises from the fact that loans are contracted in different currencies in different countries. To compare interest rates across countries, we have to take into account changes in the values of currencies. Countries whose currencies are appreciating have low interest rates; countries whose currencies are depreciating have high interest rates. If the rate of currency depreciation is taken into account, interest rates are equal. (pp. 314–318)

Monetary Independence

With a fixed exchange rate, a country is unable to use monetary policy to control its inflation rate and interest rates. A change in inflation in the rest of the world, other things being equal, changes inflation in the domestic economy. It also changes interest rates.

With a flexible exchange rate, a country can insulate itself from inflation and interest rate shocks coming from the rest of the world. If, in the face of a higher inflation rate in the rest of the world, domestic monetary policy is held steady, the domestic inflation rate stays constant. The currency appreciates and interest rates in the domestic economy stay below those in the rest of the world.

To achieve lower inflation and lower interest rates than other countries, it is necessary for the Reserve Bank to maintain a lower average growth rate of the Australian money supply than the money supply growth rates that prevail in other countries. (pp. 318–321)

KEY TERMS

Arbitrage, p. 314
Currency appreciation, p. 298
Currency depreciation, p. 298
European Monetary System, p. 319
Flow theory of the exchange rate, p. 301
Foreign exchange market, p. 297
Foreign exchange rate, p. 297
Forward contract, p. 316
Forward exchange rate, p. 316
Interest rate parity, p. 316
International Monetary Fund, p. 298
Law of one price, p. 314
Monetary theory of the exchange rate, p. 302
Non-traded goods, p. 315
Portfolio balance theory of the exchange rate, p. 302
Purchasing power parity, p. 315
Real exchange rate, p. 315
Sterilization, p. 310
Trade-weighted index, p. 299

PROBLEMS

1. Suppose the interest rate on bank loans in Australia is 11 per cent a year. The interest rate on bonds in Japan is 4 per cent a year. In the foreign exchange market, dollars can be bought for yen at a rate of 80 yen per dollar. In the forward market, dollars can be bought for delivery in one year at a rate of 90 yen per dollar.
   a) How much would you gain or lose if you borrowed 1 million yen and invested the proceeds of the loan in Australian bonds, covering your transaction in the forward market?
   b) In which direction will the yen–dollar exchange rate and the interest rates in Australia and Japan be moving?
2. All the goods and services that are bought and sold in Australia are also bought and sold in Japan and there are no non-traded goods. Also, there are no tariffs or other impediments to trade between the two economies. Prices are rising in Australia at 7 per cent a year. Given the information presented in problem 1 about interest rates and foreign exchange rates, what is the inflation rate in Japan?
3. Do Japan and Australia have a fixed exchange rate or a flexible exchange rate?
4. Suppose the exchange rate between the dollar and the yen is fixed and that Japan does not change its monetary policy but Australia does. What happens to the inflation rate and to interest rates in the two economies?

Part 11

Macroeconomic Problems

Talking with Geoff Harcourt

Geoff Harcourt is Reader in the History of Economic Theory, and Fellow and President of Jesus College at Cambridge University in the United Kingdom. Before he moved to Cambridge in the early 1980s, he was Professor of Economics at the University of Adelaide where he was made Professor Emeritus in 1988. Recently, he has been working on the intellectual history of the circle of people who were either taught by or worked with Keynes and who tried to carry on the tradition associated with Keynes and the so-called Cambridge School. Christopher Findlay talked to Professor Harcourt about his view of economics and its importance.

Geoff, do you think of yourself as a member of this circle of intellectuals that you've been writing about?

Yes, I'm a member of the post-Keynesian circle. I've asked the question, 'Is there a coherent systematic scheme of thought called post-Keynesianism?' My answer is, 'No there isn't, and nor should there be'. Historically, a number of strands of theory, which come under the umbrella of post-Keynesian theory, have developed. They can be differentiated by the length of the time horizon to which they apply, for example, an interest in very short-run crises that can occur in the economy compared with an interest in the economy's long-run performance. While each strand may be internally coherent, the idea of a grand synthesis is really not on.

When we talk about Keynesianism in public debates, it's usually in the context of macroeconomic performance and, therefore, the application of the theory to short-run problems.

That's true, the Keynesians are interventionists; they're trying to tackle the level of aggregate demand and the idea they have at the back of their mind is that there is no automatic tendency, even in the long run let alone the short run, for effective demand to be at the full-employment level.

Is that how you see the major controversy in macroeconomics?

Yes, and that's what Keynes said. He said there were two sorts of people, those who think that, with much cranking and groaning, there is a tendency for the economy to operate correctly at full employment and with markets clearing, and those who think that there is no such tendency and that therefore you need to step in to create a different environment, help out, guide, direct and tame the forces of uncertainty as much as you can.

Is Keynesianism just about demand management?

Not at all. Keynesians recognize the importance of the aggregate supply function. Keynes said aggregate supply was just as important as aggregate demand, but he thought it was familiar. He used to say, 'It's our old friend the short-run supply curve writ large for the economy as a whole'. He thought we all knew about a short-run supply curve so why should he teach his grandparents to suck eggs? What was novel was his theory of aggregate demand. That was a tactical mistake by Keynes. If you knew that the aggregate supply curve was just as important as aggregate demand then when you got an oil price shock or an imported cost inflation, for example, you would know immediately that either shock would tend to raise the price level, reduce the level of activity and perhaps start an inflationary process. If the textbooks had been full of aggregate demand and aggregate supply, instead of IS–LM, which is purely demand, then Keynesianism might not have been thought to be vanquished the way it was.

How do you see the connections between these macro debates and micro policy discussions?

There is an absolutely false dichotomy between micro and macro, that is, you can't talk about micro without asking yourself what the macro background is, and you can't talk about macro without asking what your micro-economic foundations are. That's why I end up using a version of the solution to the Keynesian problems that feeds in micro foundations based on the world as we see it, such as mark-up pricing in the manufacturing and industrial sectors, and perhaps something more like competitive markets in the raw materials producing sector, though even that is now not a good stylized fact. In the Keynesian tradition, you've got swashbuckling, ruthless entrepreneurs driving the economy along, you've got class war and now you've got an organized and articulate working class fighting back against the capitalists.

These features of the world may be critical but it is extraordinarily difficult to incorporate all of them into a theoretical structure, at the same time.

That's one of the things that's happened in recent years. Modern theorists have now given up grand questions and grand overall designs and they tackle small definable problems in a manageable way. But I'm still a 'horses for courses' person; you make the model for the question you're asking.

Is modern neoclassical economics good at doing that?

Well, I think the point about neoclassical economics is that the basic

concepts are painfully simple but the detailed applications of them are intellectually very challenging. Parts of economics have to be very precisely and concisely defined. But I don't believe that truth only comes in the guise of a mathematical model. Keynes had very acute views on methods and his method was this — that in the social sciences there is a whole continuum of languages running all the way from intuition and poetry to formal logic and maths, and in any economic problem all of those languages may have a part to play for some aspects or some dimensions of the problem. If you feel that you are only theorizing when you're right down the precise end of the spectrum, then you may sever the link between the real world and the system of logic. You cut the umbilical cord between the two and can't get back to it, you've reduced the analysis to mere 'dry bones', so you never get back to illuminate the real world.

Do you think these differences in our vision of how the world works will ever be resolved?

Some people say we're all economists now, we all do it the same way, but that's just not true. There will always be schools of thought, contending ways of looking at things and, while I would call for open minds and the possibility that you might be wrong and the other fellow's right, it's ridiculous to say there's just one way of doing economics and we're all economists now. There are many sorts of economists. I've never understood why we can't be a broad church, learning from one another and showing tolerance towards one another while engaging in vigorous criticism as well.

How did you get interested in economics in the first place?

Well, that's funny, I was going to be a vet. I did economics as an extra subject when I was at secondary school in Victoria. After that I decided I'd be a school teacher and teach economics. I went to university and started doing economics. I was so excited by it. Subjects that I did in the first year of university showed me that the world wasn't like Glen Iris, heart of Barry Humphries land, where I lived. I was repelled by the injustices of various economic systems, what they did to those least able to defend themselves, and I thought there were more rational ways of organizing the world.

For the student who is doing a very first course in economics, what advice would you offer?

I would tell them to read Heilbroner's *The Wordly Philosophers*[1] for a start and get a sense of excitement, of wonderful people — because the best economists I've known have been wonderful human beings — and to get a sense of people going into a discipline because they don't like injustice and inequity, they want to know why it arises, and what can be done about it. If you look at economics like that and ask yourself how does the world work and what's the best way we find this out, and then what we can do about it, then you'll find economics a fabulous discipline, always a challenge, always something to do and always really interesting people, issues, and situations to learn about. But if you think it's just a dry-as-dust thing that you pull out of the sky, ready made, then you'll be bored out of your wits.

---

[1] Robert Heilbroner, *The Wordly Philosophers* (New York, Simon and Schuster).

Chapter 30

Monetary and Fiscal Influences on Aggregate Demand

After studying this chapter, you will be able to:

- Explain how monetary policy — a change in the money supply — influences interest rates and aggregate demand.
- Explain how fiscal policy — a change in government purchases or taxes — influences interest rates and aggregate demand.
- Explain what determines the relative effectiveness of monetary and fiscal policy on aggregate demand.
- Describe the Keynesian–monetarist controversy about the influence of monetary and fiscal policy on aggregate demand and explain how the controversy was settled.
- Explain how the mix of monetary and fiscal policy influences the composition of aggregate expenditure.
- Explain how monetary and fiscal policy influence real GDP and the price level in both the short run and the long run.

Pulling the Levers and Adjusting the Dials

Each year the Commonwealth and State governments approve budgets that determine the level of government expenditure on goods and services. By 1989/90, that total exceeded $60 billion — about one-sixth of GDP. These same governments also determine the scale of social programmes and the transfer payments associated with them, as well as the rules governing the taxes that we all have to pay. In 1989/90, transfer payments were a further $41 billion and taxes in excess of $114 billion, nearly one-third of GDP. Government expenditure, taxes and transfer payments are the levers of fiscal policy. How do these levers of fiscal policy influence the economy? In particular, how do they affect aggregate demand? How do they affect other variables that influence aggregate demand, such as interest rates and the exchange rate? Martin Place, Sydney, is the home of the Reserve Bank of Australia. Here the Bank pulls the nation's monetary policy levers. At some times, such as in 1982/83 and 1989/90, the Bank has used those levers to slow down the economy — increasing interest rates, slowing money growth and slowing the growth of aggregate demand. At other times, such as in 1987/88 and 1990/91, the Bank has used its monetary policy levers to speed up the economy — lowering interest rates, speeding up money growth and increasing aggregate demand. We've seen how the Reserve Bank's policy levers influence interest rates and the exchange rate. But how do the effects of the Bank's actions ripple through from interest rates and the exchange rate to the rest of the economy? How do they affect aggregate demand? Standing between Parliament and the Reserve Bank is the Department of Treasury headed by the Treasurer. Under our system of government, the Cabinet is ultimately responsible for all fiscal and monetary policy decisions and the Treasurer is a key player in the cabinet's deliberations on these policies. Between 1986/87 and 1990/91 the Federal government operated at a surplus — its expenditures were less than its receipts. This outcome was the result of a determined and conscious effort by the government to increase its level of saving. With fiscal policy firmly locked into place by the desire to generate surpluses, monetary policy became the 'swing instrument' of government policy. It was used to manage aggregate demand in the second half of the 1980s. Since both the fiscal actions of the government and the monetary actions of the Reserve Bank can increase or decrease aggregate demand, are these two methods of changing aggregate demand equivalent to each other? Does it matter whether a recession is avoided by having the Bank loosen up its monetary policy or by getting Cabinet to implement a tax cut? Do changes in taxes and government expenditure and changes in the money supply have to reinforce each other or can they offset each other? For example, when the Reserve Bank slowed down money growth and increased interest rates in 1988/89 and 1989/90 to reduce aggregate demand, could the government have reinforced the Bank's actions by taking actions of its own — increasing taxes or further decreasing government expenditure? Did the government's tax cuts in 1990 and 1991 act to offset the effects of the Reserve Bank's tighter monetary policy? Or, alternatively, if the government cuts government expenditure, creating fears of recession, could the Bank increase the money supply and keep GDP up, thereby avoiding recession?

We are going to answer these important questions in this chapter. You already know that the effects of monetary and fiscal policy are determined by the interaction of aggregate demand and aggregate supply. And you already know quite a lot about these two concepts. But this chapter gives you an even deeper understanding of aggregate demand and the way it is affected by the monetary policy actions of the Reserve Bank and the fiscal policy actions of the Federal government.

Although this chapter is about policy issues, it is not about the *conduct* of policy. It is a chapter about the *theory* of policy. It's important to get the theoretical foundations straight so that when we do come to study the conduct of policy, in Chapters 34 and 35, we will have a firm foundation on which to build.[1]

[1] It is possible to study stabilization policy in Chapters 34 and 35 without having previously studied the present chapter. But if you take the time and effort to study this chapter, you will find that you have an even deeper understanding of the discussion of policy issues in those later chapters.

Money, Interest and Aggregate Demand

Our ultimate goal is to understand how monetary and fiscal policy influence real GDP and the price level — and unemployment and inflation. But here we look only at their influences on aggregate demand. Before embarking on this study, let's see how it fits into the bigger picture.

Aggregate Demand and Aggregate Supply

Real GDP and the price level are determined by the interaction of *aggregate demand* and *aggregate supply* described in Chapter 24. In studying how monetary and fiscal policy influence *aggregate demand* we look at their effects on the position of the aggregate demand curve. In effect, we freeze the price level and ask questions about the directions and magnitudes of the shifts of the aggregate demand curve at a given price level. But the price level is not actually fixed. It is determined in the way described in Chapter 24.

Spending Decisions, Interest and Money

In working out the effects of monetary and fiscal policy on aggregate demand we'll use the aggregate expenditure model of Chapters 25 and 26. We can use this model because the aggregate expenditure curve tells us the level of aggregate planned expenditure at a given price level and equilibrium aggregate expenditure corresponds to a point on the aggregate demand curve (see Figure 26.10). Thus when equilibrium expenditure changes, the aggregate demand curve shifts.

We discovered in Chapter 25 that equilibrium expenditure depends on the level of autonomous expenditure. We also discovered that one of the components of autonomous expenditure — investment — varies with the interest rate. The higher the interest rate, other things held constant, the lower is investment, and hence the lower is autonomous expenditure and equilibrium expenditure. Therefore equilibrium expenditure and real GDP depend on the interest rate.

In Chapter 28 we saw how the interest rate is determined by equilibrium in the money market. We also saw that the demand for money depends on both real GDP and the interest rate. The higher the level of real GDP, other things held constant, the greater is the demand for money and the higher is the interest rate. Therefore the interest rate depends on real GDP.

We're now going to see how both real GDP and the interest rate are determined simultaneously. We'll then go on to see how the Reserve Bank's monetary policy and the government's fiscal policy affect both real GDP and the interest rate (at a given price level).

Equilibrium Expenditure and the Interest Rate

Let's see how we can link together the money market, where the interest rate is determined, and the market for goods and services, where equilibrium expenditure is determined. Figure 30.1 illustrates the linkages. The figure has three parts: Fig. 30.1(a) illustrates the money market; Fig. 30.1(b) shows investment demand; and Fig 30.1(c) shows aggregate planned expenditure and the determination of equilibrium expenditure. Let's begin with Fig. 30.1(a).

The Money Market The curve labelled *MD* is the demand for real money. The position of that demand curve depends on the level of real GDP. For a given level of real GDP, there is a given demand curve for real money. Suppose that the demand curve shown in the figure is the one that describes the demand for real money when real GDP is $300 billion. If real GDP is higher than $300 billion, the demand curve for real money is to the right of the one shown; if real GDP is below $300 billion, the demand curve for real money is to the left of the one shown.

The curve labelled *MS* is the supply curve of real money. Its position is determined by the monetary policy actions of the Reserve Bank, the behaviour of the banking system and the price level. At a given point in time, all these influences determine a quantity of money supplied that is independent of

Figure 30.1 Equilibrium Interest Rate and Real GDP

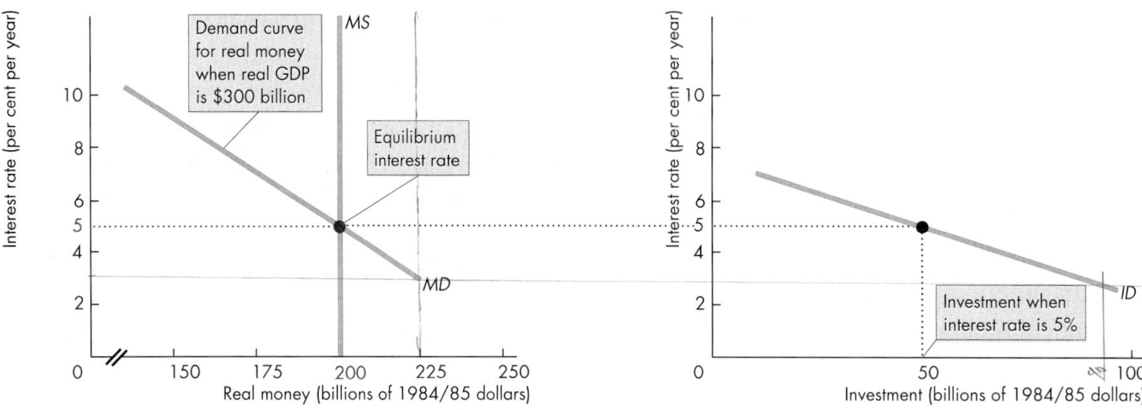

(a) Money and interest rate

(b) Investment and interest rate

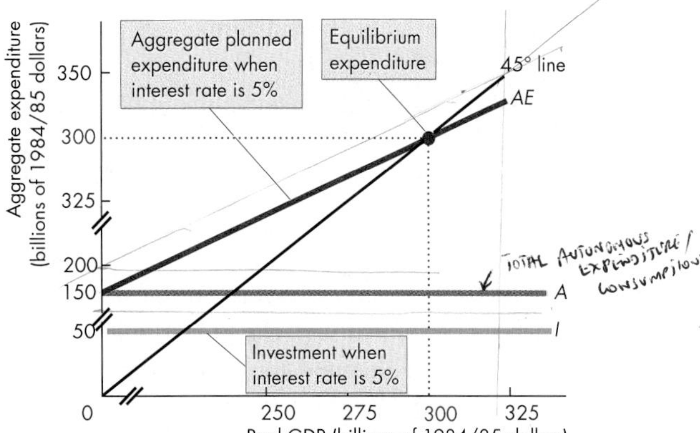

(c) Expenditure and real GDP

Equilibrium in the money market — part (a) — determines the interest rate. The money supply curve is *MS*. The demand curve for real money is *MD*. The position of the demand curve for real money is determined by real GDP. The demand curve for real money is *MD* when real GDP is $300 billion. The investment demand curve, *ID* in part (b), determines investment at the equilibrium interest rate determined in the money market. Investment is part of autonomous expenditure and its level determines the position of the aggregate expenditure curve (*AE*) shown in part (c). Where the aggregate expenditure curve intersects the 45° line, equilibrium expenditure and real GDP are determined. An equilibrium occurs when real GDP and the interest rate are such that the quantity of real money demanded equals the quantity of real money supplied, and aggregate planned expenditure equals real GDP.

the interest rate. Hence the supply curve for real money is vertical.

The equilibrium interest rate is determined at the point of intersection of the demand and supply curves for real money. In the economy illustrated in Fig. 30.1, that interest rate is 5 per cent.

Investment and the Interest Rate Next, let's look at Fig. 30.1(b) where investment is determined. The investment demand curve is *ID.* The position of the investment demand curve is determined by profit expectations and, as those expectations change, the investment demand curve shifts accordingly. For given expectations, there is a given investment demand curve. This curve tells us the level of planned investment at each level of the interest rate. But we already know the interest rate from equilibrium in the money market. When the investment demand curve is *ID* and the interest rate is 5 per cent, the level of planned investment is $50 billion.

Expenditure Equilibrium Figure 30.1(c) shows the determination of equilibrium expenditure. This diagram is similar to Fig. 26.4. The aggregate expenditure curve (*AE*) tells us aggregate expenditure at each level of real GDP. Aggregate expenditure is made up of autonomous expenditure and induced expenditure. Planned investment is part of autonomous expenditure. In this example, total autonomous expenditure is $150 billion. That is, investment is $50 billion and the other components of autonomous expenditure are $100 billion ($60 billion in government expenditure and $40 billion in exports). These amounts of investment and autonomous expenditure are shown by the horizontal lines in Fig. 30.1(c). Investment is *I* and total autonomous expenditure is *A.* Induced expenditure in this example (the induced part of consumption expenditure minus imports) equals 0.5 multiplied by real GDP. In other words, the marginal propensity to spend on real GDP is 0.5. (Recall from Chapter 26 that the marginal propensity to spend was 0.65 and the marginal propensity to import was 0.15).

Equilibrium expenditure is determined at the point of intersection of the *AE* curve and the 45° line. Equilibrium occurs when aggregate expenditure and real GDP are each $300 billion. That is, the level of aggregate demand is $300 billion.

The Money Market Again Recall that the demand curve, MD in Fig. 30.1(a), is the demand curve for real money when real GDP is $300 billion. We've just determined in Fig. 30.1(c) that, at the expenditure equilibrium, real GDP is also $300 billion. What happens if the level of real GDP that we discover in Fig. 30.1(c) is different from the value that we assumed when drawing the demand curve for real money in Fig. 30.1(a)? Let's perform a thought experiment to answer this question.

Suppose, when drawing the demand curve for real money, that we assume that real GDP is $275 billion. In this case, because there are fewer transactions at the lower level of GDP, less money is demanded and the demand curve for real money is to the left of the *MD* curve in Fig. 30.1(a). The interest rate will be lower than 5 per cent. With an interest rate below 5 per cent, investment is not $50 billion as determined in Fig. 30.1(b), but a higher amount. If investment is higher than $50 billion, autonomous expenditure will be higher and the *AE* curve is higher than the one shown in Fig. 30.1(c). If the aggregate expenditure curve is higher than *AE,* equilibrium expenditure and real GDP are larger than $300 billion. Thus, if we start with the demand curve for real money for a level of real GDP below $300 billion, expenditure equilibrium occurs at a level of real GDP above $300 billion. There is an inconsistency. The real GDP assumed in drawing the demand curve for real money is too low.

Next, let's reverse the experiment. Assume a level of real GDP of $325 billion. In this case, there are more GDP transactions, more money is demanded and the demand curve for real money will be to the right of the *MD* curve in Fig. 30.1(a). The interest rate will be higher than 5 per cent. With an interest rate higher than 5 per cent, investment is below $50 billion and the *AE* curve is lower than the one shown in Fig 30.1(c). In this case, expenditure equilibrium occurs at a level of real GDP that is below $300 billion. Again, there is an inconsistency. If we assume a level of real GDP of more than $300 billion to determine the position of the demand curve for real money, expenditure equilibrium occurs at a level of real GDP that is less than $300 billion.

Only if we use real GDP of $300 billion to determine the position of the demand curve for real money do we get a consistent story in the three parts of this figure. If the demand curve for real money is based on real GDP of $300 billion, the interest rate determined (5 per cent) delivers planned investment of $50 billion that, in turn, generates an expenditure equilibrium at the same level of real GDP that determines the position of the demand curve for real money. Thus equilibrium in the money market and expenditure equilibrium together determine real GDP and the interest rate, at a given level of prices.

Monetary Policy and Aggregate Demand

Suppose that the Reserve Bank is concerned that the economy is overheating and that inflation is about to accelerate. To slow down the economy, the Reserve Bank decides to reduce aggregate demand by decreasing the money supply. Let's work out the effects of the Bank's action on the interest rate and equilibrium expenditure.

The Initial Effect of a Change in the Money Supply

Suppose that the economy is in the situation illustrated in Fig. 30.1. The interest rate is 5 per cent, investment is $50 billion and real GDP is $300 billion. The Reserve Bank now cuts the real money supply by $25 billion, from $200 billion to $175 billion. In Fig. 30.2(a), the real money supply curve shifts to the left from MS_0 to MS_1. The immediate effect of this action, in the money market, is an increase in the interest rate from 5 per cent to 7 per cent. The higher interest rate leads to a fall in planned investment from $50 billion to $25 billion, as shown in Fig. 30.2(b).

The fall in planned investment lowers autonomous expenditure and so lowers aggregate expenditure. The fall in aggregate expenditure lowers the expenditure equilibrium and lowers real GDP, and the fall in real GDP decreases the demand for real money. The decrease in the demand for real money, in turn, has further effects on the interest rate. Let's look at the adjustment process.

Adjustment Process

To keep track of all these simultaneously occurring events, we're going to break the process up and study it in three parts:

- Equilibrium expenditure with a constant interest rate
- Induced changes in real GDP
- Induced changes in the interest rate

Equilibrium Expenditure with a Constant Interest Rate The real money supply decreased from

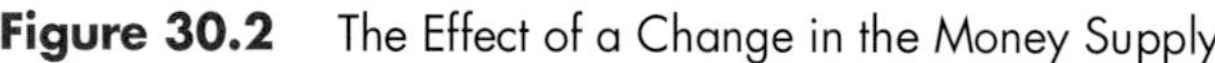

Figure 30.2 The Effect of a Change in the Money Supply

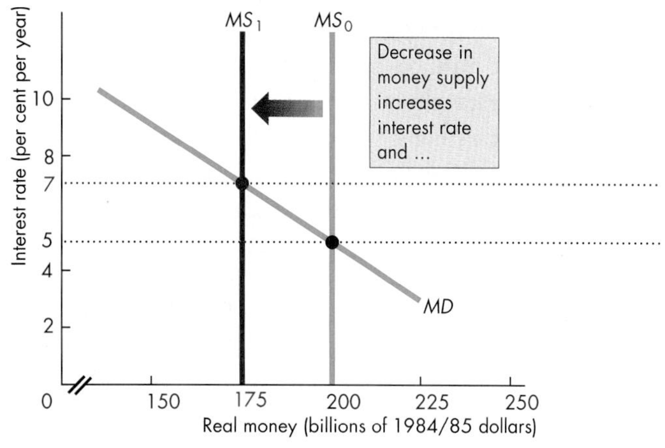

(a) Change in money supply

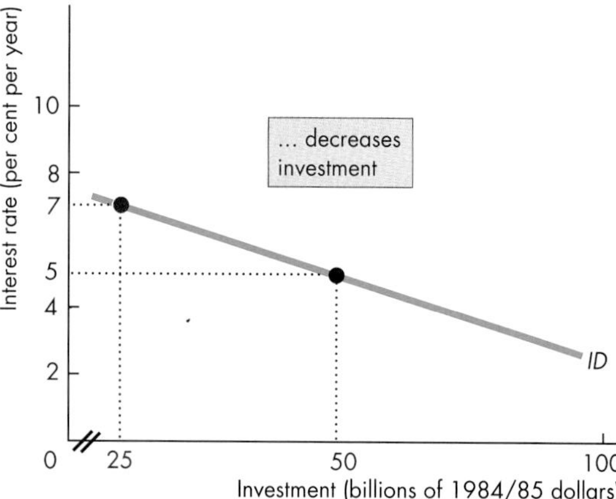

(b) Change in investment

A decrease in the money supply shifts the supply curve of real money from MS_0 to MS_1 in part (a). Equilibrium in the money market is achieved by an increase in the interest rate from 5 per cent to 7 per cent. At the higher interest rate, planned investment decreases, as shown in part (b).

$200 billion to $175 billion, and the real money supply curve shifted to the left from MS_0 to MS_1 in Fig. 30.2(a). The interest rate increased to 7 per cent. The higher interest rate lowered planned investment from $50 billion to $25 billion, as shown in Fig. 30.2(b). Let's work out what happens to equilibrium expenditure and real GDP if the interest rate remains at its new higher level of 7 per cent. With the interest rate at 7 per cent, investment falls to $25 billion, autonomous expenditure falls by the same amount as the fall in investment and the aggregate planned expenditure curve shifts downward from AE_0 to AE_1 in Fig. 30.3. That is, the *AE* curve shifts downward by $25 billion, the amount of the decrease in investment. When the aggregate expenditure curve is AE_1 equilibrium expenditure and real GDP are $250 billion.

The economy does not immediately jump from an equilibrium real GDP of $300 billion to one of $250 billion. *Equilibrium* real GDP has changed from $300 billion to $250 billion and actual GDP begins to move in the direction of the new equilibrium. But that process takes time, and during the adjustment process other changes take place that affect equilibrium real GDP so that the economy never actually gets to the point shown in Fig. 30.3. Let's now look at those other forces and see what course the economy actually takes.

Figure 30.3 The Effect of a Change in the Money Supply on Equilibrium Real GDP

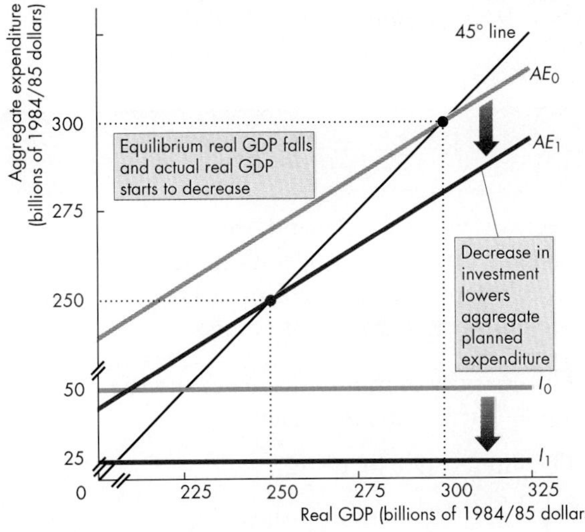

A decrease in the money supply increases the interest rate, lowers planned investment and results in a fall in aggregate expenditure. The *AE* curve shifts downward from AE_0 to AE_1. Equilibrium real GDP falls from $300 billion to $250 billion. Actual real GDP starts to decrease.

Induced Changes in Real GDP When planned investment decreases, the resulting decrease in aggregate expenditure sets up a multiplier process that gradually lowers the level of real GDP. We described this process in Chapter 25.

When aggregate expenditure decreases, it falls below real GDP. The gap between expenditure and real GDP is filled by an increase in inventories. This unexpected increase in inventories is part of *unplanned* investment. Thus, although planned investment decreases, as shown in Fig. 30.2(b), actual investment does not initially decrease by as much because of the unplanned increase in inventories.

With an unplanned increase in inventories, firms are anxious to restore inventories to their desired levels. To achieve this objective, firms cut back their production. As they do so, real GDP begins to fall.

So far, we've worked out two effects of a monetary policy action that increases interest rates. The first of these effects is a decrease in *equilibrium* expenditure and real GDP. We illustrated this effect in Fig. 30.3. The second effect, which we have just described, is an unplanned increase in inventories that initiates a process of falling *actual* aggregate expenditure and real GDP.

To keep track of what happens next, it is important to be clear about the distinction between actual real GDP and equilibrium real GDP. Actual real GDP is determined by actual expenditure — the sum of planned and unplanned expenditure. Equilibrium real GDP is determined by planned expenditure alone — by the *AE* curve. (Equilibrium real GDP is $250 billion at an interest rate of 7 per cent.) As the economy continues to adjust to a decrease in the money supply, *actual* real GDP continues to fall but *equilibrium* real GDP increases. (We will explain why in a moment.) The falling actual real GDP and rising equilibrium real GDP converge at a new equilibrium that we're now about to discover.

The fall in actual real GDP decreases the demand for real money. As a consequence, the demand curve for real money shifts to the left and the interest rate falls. A lower interest rate increases planned investment, from its new *lower* level, and makes the

AE curve start to shift upward. As the *AE* curve shifts upward, equilibrium expenditure and equilibrium real GDP increase. Let's see how the interest rate changes induced by falling real GDP bring about the new equilibrium.

Induced Changes in the Interest Rate The Reserve Bank has decreased the money supply. The interest rates is 7 per cent and planned investment has fallen but unplanned inventories are accumulating. Equilibrium real GDP has fallen to $250 billion and actual real GDP, which started out at $300 billion, is falling. With falling real GDP, the demand for money is decreasing and the demand curve for money is shifting to the left. The interest rate begins to fall and planned investment begins to increase.

Convergence to a New Equilibrium Figure 30.4 illustrates where this process ends up. Let's begin by looking at Fig. 30.4(a), which shows money market equilibrium. Actual real GDP begins to fall. Falling real GDP shifts the demand curve for real money to the left of MD_0. Suppose that the demand curve for real money, when real GDP is $275 billion, is MD_1. With this demand curve and the supply curve at MS_1, the equilibrium interest rate is 6 per cent.

When the interest rate is 6 per cent, investment is $37.5 billion, as shown in Fig. 30.4(b). Thus the fall in the interest rate from 7 per cent to 6 per cent increases planned investment from $25 billion to $37.5 billion.

The increase in planned investment from $25 billion to $37.5 billion shifts the *AE* curve upward from AE_1 to AE_2 in Fig. 30.4(c). When the aggregate expenditure curve is AE_2, equilibrium expenditure and equilibrium real GDP are $275 billion. But this level of real GDP is precisely the level that makes the demand curve for real money MD_1. When actual real GDP has fallen to $275 billion, the demand curve for real money has shifted to MD_1 and the interest rate has fallen to 6 per cent. Investment has increased to $37.5 billion ($I_2$) and aggregate planned expenditure has increased, so that equilibrium expenditure and equilibrium real GDP are also $275 billion. In this situation, aggregate expenditure equals real GDP and the quantity of money demanded equals the quantity supplied.

To check that the economy really does converge to a new equilibrium as shown in Fig. 30.4, let's rerun the economic video and hit the freeze-frame button before the equilibrium is reached.

Starting from the initial decrease in the money supply, let's freeze the picture when real GDP has fallen by only $12.5 billion and is at $287.5 billion. The demand curve for real money has not shifted as far to the left as MD_1 and the interest rate has not yet fallen to 6 per cent. It lies somewhere between 6 and 7 per cent. Planned investment is increasing but has not yet increased to $37.5 billion. It lies somewhere between $25 billion and $37.5 billion. The aggregate expenditure curve is shifting upward but is below AE_2, lying somewhere between AE_1 and AE_2. Aggregate expenditure is below real GDP, so actual real GDP is falling.

With actual real GDP falling, the demand curve for real money is shifting to the left; the interest rate is falling; planned investment is increasing; and the *AE* curve is shifting upward. Equilibrium real GDP is increasing. Inventories are accumulating and actual real GDP is decreasing. Eventually, actual real GDP and equilibrium real GDP become equal. When this occurs, their values are $275 billion as shown in Fig. 30.4(c).

The Aggregate Demand Curve Shifts Since equilibrium expenditure has fallen, given the price level, the aggregate demand curve (AD_0) has shifted to the left (to AD_1), as shown in Fig. 30.4(d).

R E V I E W

To decrease aggregate demand, the Reserve Bank undertakes an open market operation. It sells Commonwealth government securities. This action sets up the following sequence of events:

- The quantity of money decreases and the money supply curve shifts to the left.
- The interest rate increases.
- Planned investment decreases.
- Aggregate expenditure decreases.
- Equilibrium expenditure and equilibrium real GDP decrease.
- Unplanned inventories accumulate.
- Actual real GDP begins to fall.

Figure 30.4 The Convergence to a New Expenditure Equilibrium

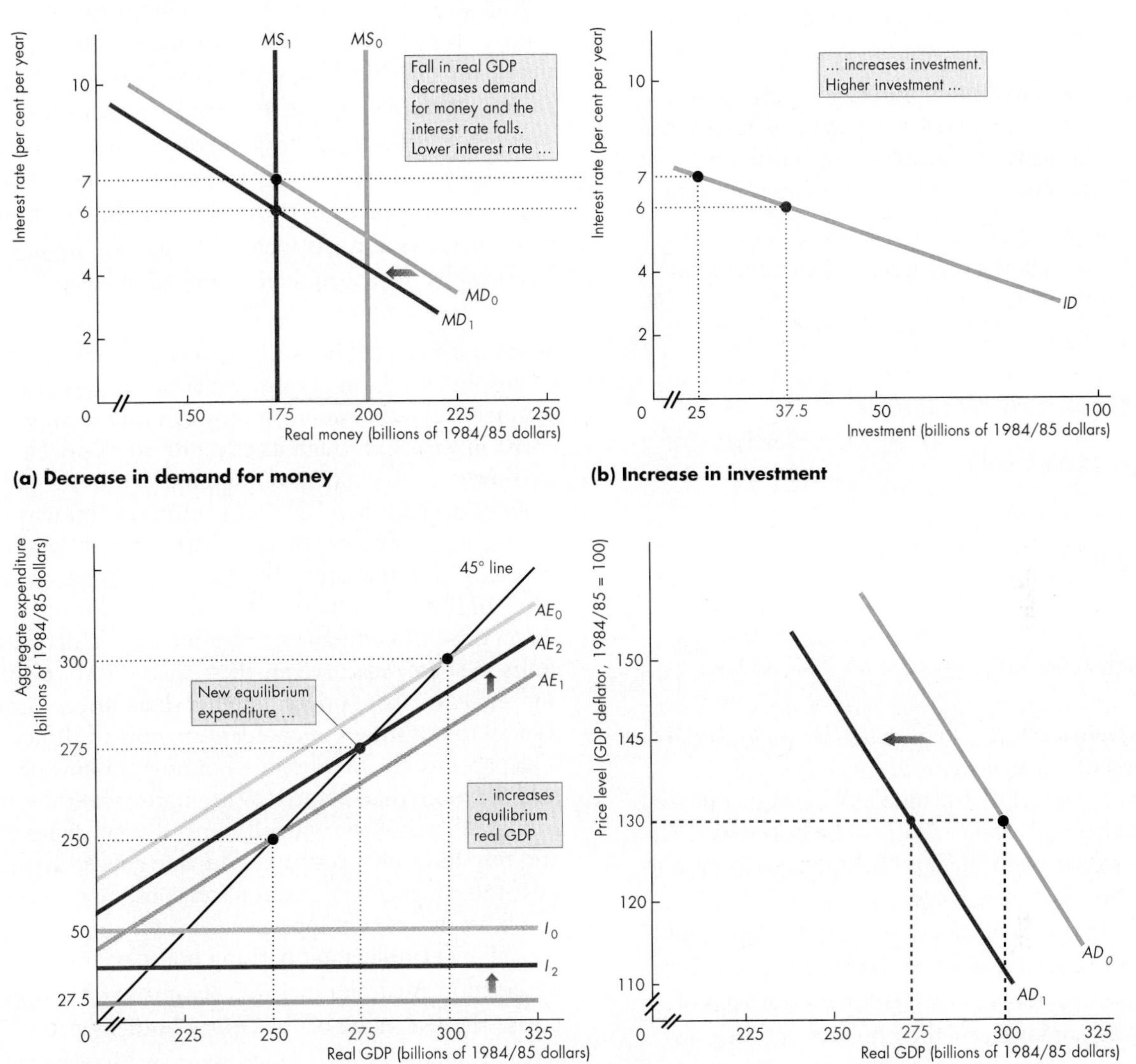

As real GDP falls, the demand curve for real money shifts to the left, from MD_0 to MD_1 as shown in part (a). The decrease in the demand for real money lowers the interest rate. As the interest rate falls, planned investment increases as in part (b). The increase in planned investment shifts the AE_1 curve upward to AE_2, as in part (c). During the process of adjustment, actual real GDP falls and aggregate expenditure increases. A new expenditure equilibrium occurs when real GDP and aggregate expenditure have converged to the same value. In the figure, the new expenditure equilibrium occurs at real GDP of $275 billion; see part (c). That level of real GDP makes the demand curve for real money MD_1, in part (a), which generates an interest rate of 6 per cent. At that interest rate, investment is $37.5 billion, in part (b), which in turn makes the aggregate expenditure curve AE_2, in part (c). At given prices, equilibrium expenditure has fallen and the aggregate demand curve shifts to the left from AD_0 to AD_1, as shown in part (d).

- Falling actual real GDP decreases the demand for money and shifts the demand curve for real money to the left.
- The shifting demand curve for real money decreases the interest rate.
- The falling interest rate increases planned investment.

- Increasing planned investment increases equilibrium expenditure and equilibrium real GDP.
- Falling actual real GDP and rising equilibrium real GDP converge.
- In the new equilibrium, the values of real GDP and the interest rate that make the quantity of real money demanded equal the quantity supplied also make aggregate planned expenditure equal to real GDP.
- With lower equilibrium expenditure at the original price level, the aggregate demand curve has shifted to the left. ■

Other Transmission Channels

There are three other important transmission channels of monetary policy:

- Real balance effect
- Wealth effect
- Exchange rate effect

Let's look at each of these in turn.

Real Balance Effect The *real balance effect* is the direct effect of a change in the real money supply on the quantity of real GDP demanded. We first met the real balance effect in Chapter 24. Let's see how it works.

An increase in the nominal money supply at a given price level increases the real money supply. With additional holdings of real money, households and firms plan to re-allocate their holdings of assets of all types. They want to lower their holdings of real money and increase their holdings of other assets. Some of these other assets are real assets — capital goods. To the extent that households convert their additional real money holdings into real assets, there is an increase in planned investment. This increase in investment is separate from the increase resulting from a lower interest rate. Even if the interest rate does not change, a larger holding of real money balances will, in general, trigger an asset re-allocation involving some additional spending on capital goods.

For example, the Reserve Bank might buy $100 million worth of government bonds from BHP. This open market operation increases the monetary base and increases BHP's real money holdings. To keep things simple, let's suppose that no change in the interest rate has occurred at this point in time. BHP is not going to sit on this extra $100 million of money for very long. It's going to put these financial resources to work acquiring profitable assets. Some of the money may be used to take over other firms and some of it may be used to buy new steel plants. To the extent that BHP buys new capital goods, there is an immediate increase in investment. If they take over other firms, the previous owners of these other firms have more real money and are able to undertake new investment of their own. Gradually, investment increases as firms spend the extra real money balances that the open market operation created.

Wealth Effect The **wealth effect** is the effect of a change in wealth on aggregate planned expenditure. An increase in the money supply can lead to an increase in wealth through its effect on stock prices. To see how this effect operates, suppose that in the previous example, when BHP sells some government securities to the Reserve Bank, it uses the $100 million proceeds from the sale to buy stock in other companies. BHP's action increases the demand for the shares of some companies. That increase in demand shifts the demand curve for these shares to the right and increases share prices. Higher share prices mean that all the existing shareholders are now wealthier. The paper assets that they are holding can now be sold for more than before. With higher wealth, some of these shareholders will sell some of their shares and buy additional consumer durable goods. To the extent that higher wealth stimulates consumption expenditure, it increases aggregate demand.

For example, rapidly rising house prices, as we observed in Australia in 1987/88 and 1988/89, increase the real value of the equity homeowners have in their asset. This increase in real wealth enables homeowners to increase all forms of consumption. Home equity loans are one way banks facilitate this. Thus the asset price inflation of the late 1980s may go a long way to explaining the very strong growth in the demand for goods and services in the same period.

Exchange Rate Effect An increase in the money supply can lead to a fall in the value of the dollar against other currencies — a depreciation — and to an increase in net exports. Since net exports are part of aggregate expenditure, this exchange rate effect is a further channel whereby monetary policy can influence aggregate demand. This channel of monetary policy is especially important in an economy that has a relatively large foreign trade sector as does Australia. It works in the following way.

An increase in the money supply lowers interest rates. If interest rates fall in Australia but do not fall in Japan and the United States, international investors will sell the now lower yielding Australian assets and buy the relatively higher yielding foreign assets. As they undertake these transactions, they sell Australian dollars and buy foreign currency. These actions decrease the demand for Australian dollars and increase the demand for foreign currencies. The result is a lower value of the Australian dollar against other currencies. (This mechanism is discussed in greater detail in Chapter 37.)

With the Australian dollar worth less, foreigners can now buy Australian-made goods at a lower price and Australians have to pay a higher price for the foreign goods that they buy. The result is a net increase in the demand for Australian-made goods, as Australians switch from buying expensive imports to cheaper, domestically produced goods and foreigners switch from buying their expensive, home-produced goods to cheaper imports from Australia.

This process also operates in the opposite direction, if the Reserve Bank undertakes a monetary policy action that lowers the money supply.

R E V I E W

A change in the money supply affects aggregate expenditure and real GDP through four channels: interest rates, real money balances, wealth and the foreign exchange rate. An increase in the money supply lowers interest rates, increases real money balances, increases wealth and lowers the value of the dollar against other currencies. As a consequence, aggregate expenditure and real GDP increase. Thus, at every price level, aggregate demand is higher and the aggregate demand curve shifts to the right. ■

Let's now turn to an examination of the effects of fiscal policy on aggregate demand.

Fiscal Policy and Aggregate Demand

Suppose the government is concerned that the economy is slowing down and that a recession looks likely. To head off the recession, the government decides to stimulate aggregate demand by using fiscal policy. It puts together a package of tax cuts and increases in its own purchases of goods and services that increase autonomous expenditure by $25 billion. Let's work out the effects of the government's action on the interest rate and on equilibrium expenditure and real GDP.

Initial Effect of Fiscal Policy Package

Suppose that the economy is in the situation illustrated in Fig. 30.1. This situation is shown again in Fig. 30.5. In Fig. 30.5(a) the aggregate expenditure curve is AE_0, autonomous expenditure is A_0, and equilibrium expenditure and real GDP are $300 billion. In Fig. 30.5(b) the demand for money is MD_0, the money supply is *MS* and the interest rate is 5 per cent. In Fig. 30.5(c), with an interest rate of 5 per cent, planned investment is $50 billion.

The government now introduces its fiscal policy package, cutting taxes and increasing its purchases of goods and services. Autonomous expenditure increases by $25 billion. The immediate effect of this increase is shown in Fig. 30.5(a). The autonomous expenditure line shifts upward by $25 billion to A_1 and the aggregate expenditure curve also shifts upward by $25 billion to AE_1.

The rise in autonomous expenditure and the consequent rise in aggregate expenditure increase equilibrium expenditure and real GDP. But the rise in real GDP increases the demand for real money. The increase in the demand for real money affects the interest rate, which in turn affects investment and equilibrium real GDP. Let's look at this adjustment process.

Adjustment Process

To keep track of all the simultaneously occurring events, we'll break up the adjustment process (as we did earlier in this chapter for monetary policy) and study it in three parts:

- Equilibrium expenditure with a constant interest rate
- Induced changes in real GDP
- Induced changes in the interest rate and investment

Equilibrium Expenditure with a Constant Interest Rate In Fig. 30.5(a), with aggregate planned expenditure at AE_1, equilibrium expenditure and real GDP is $350 billion, where the aggregate expenditure curve intersects the 45° line. The increase in

Figure 30.5 Fiscal Policy: Convergence to New Equilibrium

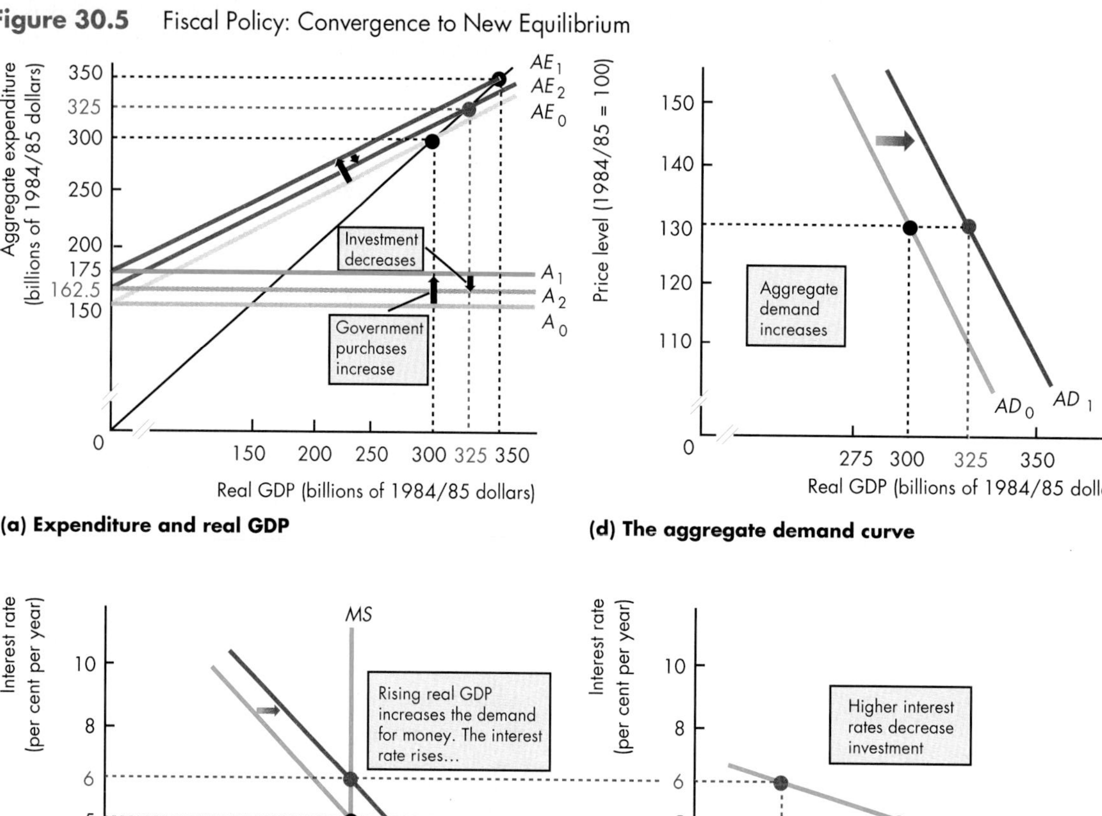

In part (a) the aggregate expenditure curve is AE_0, autonomous expenditure is A_0, and equilibrium expenditure and real GDP are $300 billion. In part (b) the demand curve for real money is MD_0, the real money supply is *MS*, and the interest rate is 5 per cent. In part (c), with an interest rate of 5 per cent, investment is $50 billion.

A $25 billion increase in government purchases of goods and services shift the autonomous expenditure line upward from A_0 to A_1 and the aggregate expenditure curve upward from AE_0 to AE_1.

Equilibrium expenditure and real GDP increase to $350 billion, in part (a). Actual real GDP begins to increase toward the new equilibrium. But rising real GDP increases the demand for money and the demand curve for real money shifts to the right raising the interest rate, as shown in part (b). The higher interest rate decreases investment, in part (c). Falling investment leads to falling aggregate planned expenditure and the aggregate expenditure curve shifts downward, lowering equilibrium real GDP. The new equilibrium occurs at $325 billion where the rising actual real GDP equals the falling equilibrium real GDP — part (a). The interest rate rises to 6 per cent — part (b) — and investment falls to $37.5 billion — part (c). Since equilibrium expenditure has risen, given the price level, the aggregate demand curve shifts as shown in part (d).

equilibrium real GDP is $50 billion, twice the $25 billion fiscal policy package. The multiplier is 2 because the marginal propensity to spend is 0.5 (that is, $1/(1 - 0.5) = 2$). This is the result that we discovered in Chapter 26 where we studied fiscal policy multipliers.

Induced Changes in Real GDP When autonomous expenditure increases, the resulting increase in aggregate expenditure sets up a multiplier process that gradually raises the level of real GDP. We described this process in Chapter 25 and used it to study monetary policy earlier in this chapter.

When aggregate expenditure increases, it rises above real GDP. The difference is met by a decrease in inventories — part of investment. With an unplanned decrease in inventories, firms are anxious to restore inventories to their desired levels. To achieve this objective, firms increase their production. As they do so, real GDP begins to rise.

So far, we've worked out two effects of a fiscal policy action that increases aggregate expenditure. The first of these effects is an increase in *equilibrium* expenditure and real GDP. We illustrated this effect in Fig. 30.5(a). The second effect, which we have just described, is an unplanned decrease in inventories that initiates a process of rising real GDP.

To keep track of what happens next, it is important to recall the distinction between actual real GDP and equilibrium real GDP. Actual real GDP is determined by actual expenditure — planned and unplanned expenditure. Equilibrium real GDP is determined by planned expenditure — by the *AE* curve. As the economy continues to adjust to a fiscal policy expansion, actual real GDP continues to increase. But what happens to equilibrium real GDP? As we are about to discover, it declines because of influences feeding back from the money market.

The increase in actual real GDP increases the demand for real money. As a consequence, the demand curve for real money shifts to the right and the interest rate rises. A higher interest rate decreases planned investment and makes the *AE* curve start to shift downward. As the *AE* curve shifts downward, equilibrium expenditure and equilibrium real GDP decrease. Let's see how the interest rate changes induced by an increasing real GDP bring about the new equilibrium.

Induced Changes in the Interest Rate and Investment As actual real GDP increases towards its new equilibrium level, the demand for real money also increases. The demand curve for real money starts to shift to the right from MD_0 in Fig. 30.5(b). With the demand for money increasing and the supply of money constant, the interest rate begins to rise. The rising interest rate lowers investment. There is a movement along the investment demand curve, as shown in Fig. 30.5(c), and planned investment falls to $37.5 billion.

Convergence to New Equilibrium With lower investment, autonomous expenditure and aggregate expenditure begin to fall. These changes are shown in Fig. 30.5(a). As the aggregate expenditure curve shifts down, equilibrium real GDP decreases. The new equilibrium occurs where the rising actual real GDP becomes equal to the falling equilibrium real GDP.

In Fig. 30.5(a) this equilibrium is $325 billion where aggregate expenditure curve AE_2 intersects the 45° line. Equilibrium real GDP has increased by $25 billion. At this higher level of real GDP, the demand for money has increased to MD_1 raising the interest rate to 6 per cent in Fig. 30.5(b). At this interest rate, investment is $37.5 billion in Fig. 30.5(c).

The net increase in autonomous expenditure is $12.5 billion, the initial fiscal policy package increase of $25 billion minus the decrease in investment of $12.5 billion. The increase in equilibrium real GDP of $25 billion is twice the net increase in autonomous expenditure (that is, two times $12.5 billion equals $25 billion).

The Aggregate Demand Curve Shifts Because equilibrium expenditure has increased at the original price level, the aggregate demand curve has shifted to the right, as shown in Fig. 30.5(d).

R E V I E W

An increase in government purchases of goods and services or a decrease in taxes affects aggregate demand by increasing autonomous expenditure. This action sets up the following sequence of events:

- Aggregate expenditure increases.
- Equilibrium expenditure and equilibrium real GDP increase.
- Unplanned decreases in inventories occur.
- Actual real GDP begins to increase.
- Increasing actual real GDP increases the demand for money and shifts the demand curve for real money to the right.

- The shifting demand curve for real money increases the interest rate.
- The rising interest rate decreases planned investment, which partly offsets the initial increase in autonomous expenditure arising from the fiscal policy action.
- Decreasing planned investment decreases equilibrium expenditure and equilibrium real GDP.
- Rising actual real GDP and falling equilibrium real GDP converge.
- In the new equilibrium, the real GDP and interest rate that make the quantity of real money demanded equal the quantity supplied also make aggregate expenditure equal to real GDP.
- The increase in equilibrium expenditure, at the original price level, means that the aggregate demand curve has shifted to the right. ■

Crowding Out and Crowding In

We have just discovered that an increase in government purchases of goods and services generates a decrease in investment. This phenomenon is called 'crowding out'. **Crowding out** is the tendency for an increase in government purchases of goods and services to increase interest rates, thereby reducing investment. The increase in government purchases *crowds out* investment.

Crowding out may be partial or complete. Partial crowding out occurs when the decrease in investment is less than the increase in government purchases. This is the normal case. Increased government purchases of goods and services increase real GDP, which increases the demand for real money, and so interest rates rise. Higher interest rates decrease investment. But the effect on investment is smaller than the initial change in government purchases.

Complete crowding out occurs if the decrease in investment equals the initial increase in government purchases. For complete crowding out to occur, a small change in the demand for real money must lead to a large change in the interest rate, and the change in the interest rate must lead to a large change in investment.

Another influence of government purchases on investment that we've not considered so far works in the opposite direction to the crowding out effect and is called 'crowding in'. **Crowding in** is the tendency for an increase in government purchases of goods and services to *increase* investment. This effect works in two ways. First, increased government purchases in a recession may create expectations of a more speedy recovery and bring an increase in expected profits. With higher expected profits, the investment demand curve shifts to the right and investment increases despite higher interest rates. A second source of crowding in is increased government purchases of public capital. Such expenditure may increase the profitability of private capital and lead to an increase in investment. For example, suppose the government increased its expenditure and built a new highway that cut the cost of transporting a farmer's produce to a market that was previously too costly to serve. The farmer may now purchase a new fleet of refrigerated trucks to take advantage of the newly available profit opportunity.

The Exchange Rate and International Crowding Out

We've seen that an increase in government purchases or a decrease in taxes leads to higher interest rates. But a change in interest rates affects the exchange rate. Higher interest rates make the dollar rise in value against other currencies. With interest rates higher in the Australia than in the rest of the world, funds flow into Australia and people around the world demand more Australian dollars. As the dollar rises in value, foreigners find Australian-made goods and services more expensive and Australians find imports less expensive. Exports fall and imports rise — net exports fall. The tendency for an increase in government purchases to decrease net exports is called **international crowding out** — foreign spending on domestic goods and services is crowded out by domestic government spending. The decrease in net exports offsets, to some degree, the initial increase in aggregate expenditure brought about by an expansionary fiscal policy.

R E V I E W

Crowding out, the tendency for an increase in government purchases of goods and services to increase interest rates thereby reducing investment, may be partial or complete. The normal case is partial crowding out — the decrease in investment is less than the increase in government purchases.

Crowding in, the tendency for an increase in government purchases of goods and services to increase investment, may occur in a recession if fiscal stimulation brings expectations of economic recovery and higher profits or if the government purchases public capital that complements private capital and so hastens economic recovery.

International crowding out, the tendency for an increase in government purchases or a decrease in taxes to decrease net exports, occurs because fiscal expansion increases interest rates and makes the dollar rise in value against other currencies. A higher dollar increases imports and decreases exports. ■

The Relative Effectiveness of Monetary and Fiscal Policy

We've now seen that equilibrium aggregate expenditure and real GDP are influenced by both monetary and fiscal policy. But which policy is the more potent? Which has larger 'bang per buck'? This question was once at the centre of a controversy among macroeconomists and, later in this section, we will look at the controversy and see how it was settled. Let's begin by seeing what determines the relative effectiveness of monetary and fiscal policy.

The Effectiveness of Monetary Policy

The effectiveness of monetary policy depends on two key factors:

- The sensitivity of the demand for money to the interest rate
- The sensitivity of investment demand to the interest rate

We're going to discover how these two factors influence the effectiveness of monetary policy by studying Fig. 30.6.

Monetary Policy Effectiveness and the Demand for Money The effectiveness of monetary policy is measured by the magnitude of the increase in equilibrium real GDP resulting from a given increase in the money supply. Other things being equal, this effect is bigger, the less sensitive is the demand for money to the interest rate. Fig. 30.6(a) shows why.

The figure shows two demand curves for real money, MD_A and MD_B. Along the demand curve MD_A the quantity of real money demanded is less sensitive to a change in the interest rate than along the demand curve MD_B.

If the demand curve for real money is MD_A, an increase in the money supply that shifts the real money supply curve from MS_0 to MS_1 decreases the interest rate from 5 per cent to 3 per cent. Planned investment increases from \$50 billion to \$100 billion. Contrast this outcome with what happens if the demand curve for real money is MD_B. In this case, the same increase in the money supply lowers the interest rate from 5 per cent to only 4 per cent and investment increases to only \$75 billion.

The larger the increase in investment, the larger is the resulting increase in equilibrium real GDP. Thus with the demand curve for real money MD_A monetary policy is more effective than with the demand curve for real money MD_B.

We have previously discussed the sensitivity of demand with respect to price changes in terms of elasticities. In this context, the lower the elasticity of demand for money with respect to changes in the interest rate, the more effective is monetary policy.

Monetary Policy Effectiveness and Investment Demand Other things being equal, the effect of a change in the money supply on equilibrium real GDP is bigger, the more sensitive is investment demand to the interest rate — the more elastic is investment demand with respect to changes in the interest rate. Figure 30.6(b) shows why.

The figure shows two investment demand curves, ID_A and ID_B. Along the demand curve ID_A investment is more sensitive to a change in the interest rate than along the demand curve ID_B.

With the demand curve for real money MD_A, an increase in the money supply that shifts the real money supply curve from MS_0 to MS_1 decreases the interest rate from 5 per cent to 3 per cent. If the investment demand curve is ID_A, planned investment increases from \$50 billion to \$100 billion. Contrast this outcome with what happens if the investment demand curve is ID_B. The same decrease in the interest rate increases planned investment from \$50 billion to only \$75 billion.

The larger the increase in investment, the larger is the resulting increase in equilibrium real GDP. Thus with the investment demand curve ID_A monetary policy is more effective than with the investment demand curve ID_B.

Figure 30.6 Monetary Policy Effectiveness

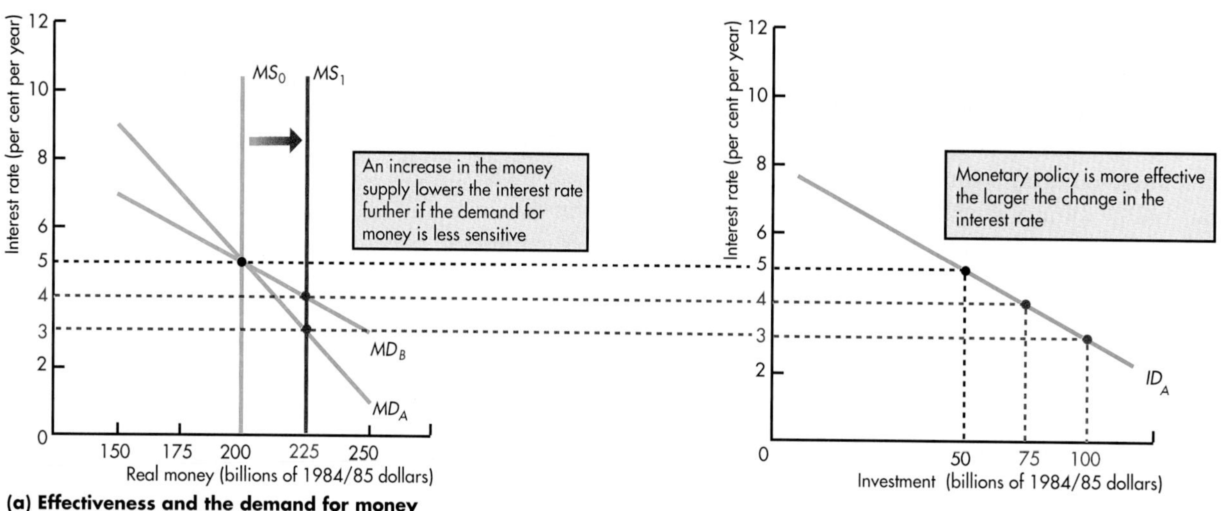

(a) Effectiveness and the demand for money

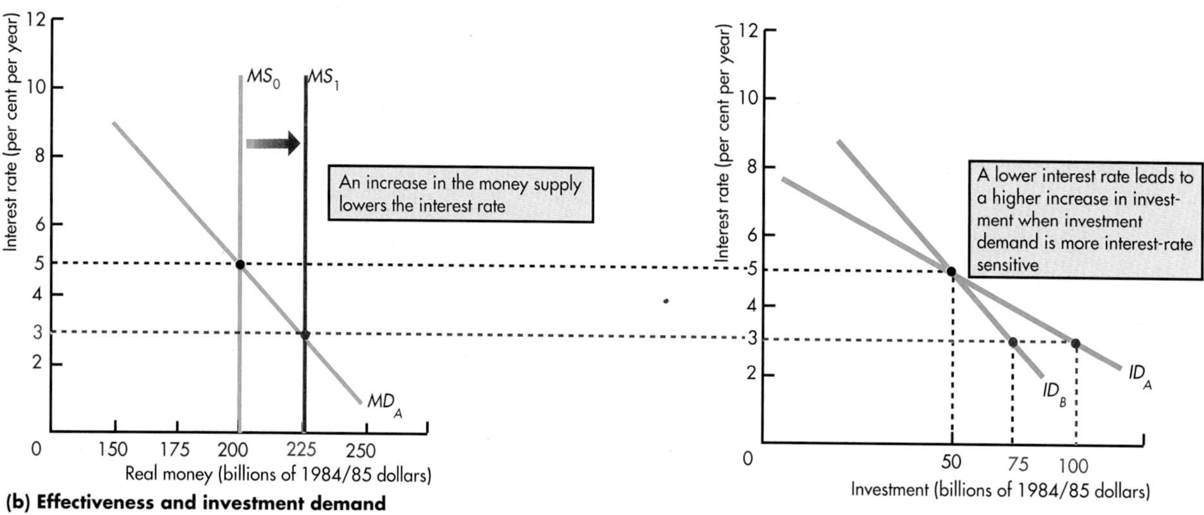

(b) Effectiveness and investment demand

In part (a), along the demand curve for real money MD_A the quantity of real money demanded is less sensitive to a change in the interest rate than along the demand curve MD_B. With the demand curve MD_A, an increase in the money supply that shifts the real money supply curve from MS_0 to MS_1 lowers the interest rate from 5 per cent to 3 per cent and increases planned investment from $50 billion to $100 billion. With demand curve MD_B, the same increase in the money supply lowers the interest rate to only 4 per cent and increases planned investment to only $75 billion. The larger the increase in investment, the larger is the resulting increase in equilibrium real GDP. So with demand curve MD_A monetary policy is more effective than with MD_B.

In part (b), along the investment demand curve ID_A planned investment is more sensitive to a change in the interest rate than along the investment demand curve ID_B. With the demand curve for real money MD_A, a shift in the real money supply curve from MS_0 to MS_1 lowers the interest rate from 5 per cent to 3 per cent. With investment demand curve ID_A investment increases from $50 billion to $100 billion, but with investment demand curve ID_B investment increases to only $75 billion. The larger the increase in investment, the larger is the resulting increase in equilibrium real GDP. So monetary policy is more effective with investment demand curve ID_A than with ID_B.

The Effectiveness of Fiscal Policy

The effectiveness of fiscal policy depends on the same two factors as the effectiveness of monetary policy:

- The sensitivity of investment demand to the interest rate
- The sensitivity of the demand for money to the interest rate

But other things being equal, the less effective is monetary policy, the more effective is fiscal policy. Let's see why by studying Fig. 30.7.

Fiscal Policy Effectiveness and Investment Demand The effectiveness of fiscal policy is measured by the magnitude of the increase in equilibrium real GDP resulting from a given increase in government purchases of goods and services (or decrease in taxes). Other things being equal, this effect is bigger the less sensitive is investment demand to the interest rate — the less interest-rate elastic is the demand for investment. Figure 30.7(a) shows why.

The figure shows two investment demand curves, ID_A and ID_B. Along the demand curve ID_A planned investment is more sensitive to a change in the interest rate than along the demand curve ID_B.

An increase in government purchases increases real GDP and increases the demand for money. The demand curve for real money shifts from MD_0 to MD_1. This increase in the demand for money increases the interest rate from 5 per cent to 6 per cent. If the investment demand curve is ID_A, investment decreases from $50 billion to $25 billion. Contrast this outcome with what happens if the investment demand curve is ID_B. The same increase in the interest rate decreases investment from $50 billion to $37.5 billion.

The decrease in investment decreases autonomous expenditure, offsetting to some degree the increase in government purchases — crowding out occurs. Therefore the larger the decrease in planned investment, the smaller is the increase in equilibrium real GDP resulting from a given increase in government purchases. Thus with the investment demand curve ID_A fiscal policy is less effective than with the investment demand curve ID_B.

Fiscal Policy Effectiveness and the Demand for Money Other things being equal, the bigger the effect of fiscal policy on equilibrium real GDP, the more sensitive the demand for money to the interest rate — the more interest-rate elastic is the demand for money. Figure 30.7(b) shows why.

The figure shows two alternative initial (blue) demand curves for real money, MD_{A0} and MD_{B0}. Along the demand curve MD_{A0} the quantity of real money demanded is less sensitive to a change in the interest rate than along the demand curve MD_{B0}.

An increase in government purchases increases real GDP and increases the demand for money, shifting the demand curve for real money to the right. If the initial curve is MD_{A0} the new curve is MD_{A1}; if the initial curve is MD_{B0} the new curve is MD_{B1}. Notice that the size of the shift to the right is the same in each case. In the case of MD_A, the increase in the demand for money increases the interest rate from 5 per cent to 6 per cent. With investment demand curve ID_A, planned investment decreases from $50 billion to $25 billion. In the case of MD_B the increase in the demand for money increases the interest rate from 5 per cent to 5.5 per cent. With investment demand curve ID_A, investment decreases from $50 billion to $37.5 billion.

A decrease in investment decreases autonomous expenditure, offsetting to some degree the increase in government purchases. Therefore the smaller the decrease in investment, the larger is the increase in equilibrium real GDP resulting from a given increase in government purchases. Thus with the demand for real money curve MD_A fiscal policy is less effective than with the demand for real money curve MD_B.

A Comparison of Monetary and Fiscal Policy Effectiveness We have seen that, other things being constant, conditions that tend to make fiscal policy effective also tend to make monetary policy ineffective. Table 30.1 summarizes this discussion.

Interest Rate Sensitivity of Demand for Money and Investment Demand What determines the degree of sensitivity of the demand for money and investment demand to interest rates? The answer is the degree of substitutability between money and other financial assets and the degree of substitutability between capital and labour.

Because money performs a unique function that other financial assets do not perform — it facilitates the exchange of goods and services — money is an imperfect substitute for other financial assets. Therefore we hold money even though it has an op-

Figure 30.7 Fiscal Policy Effectiveness

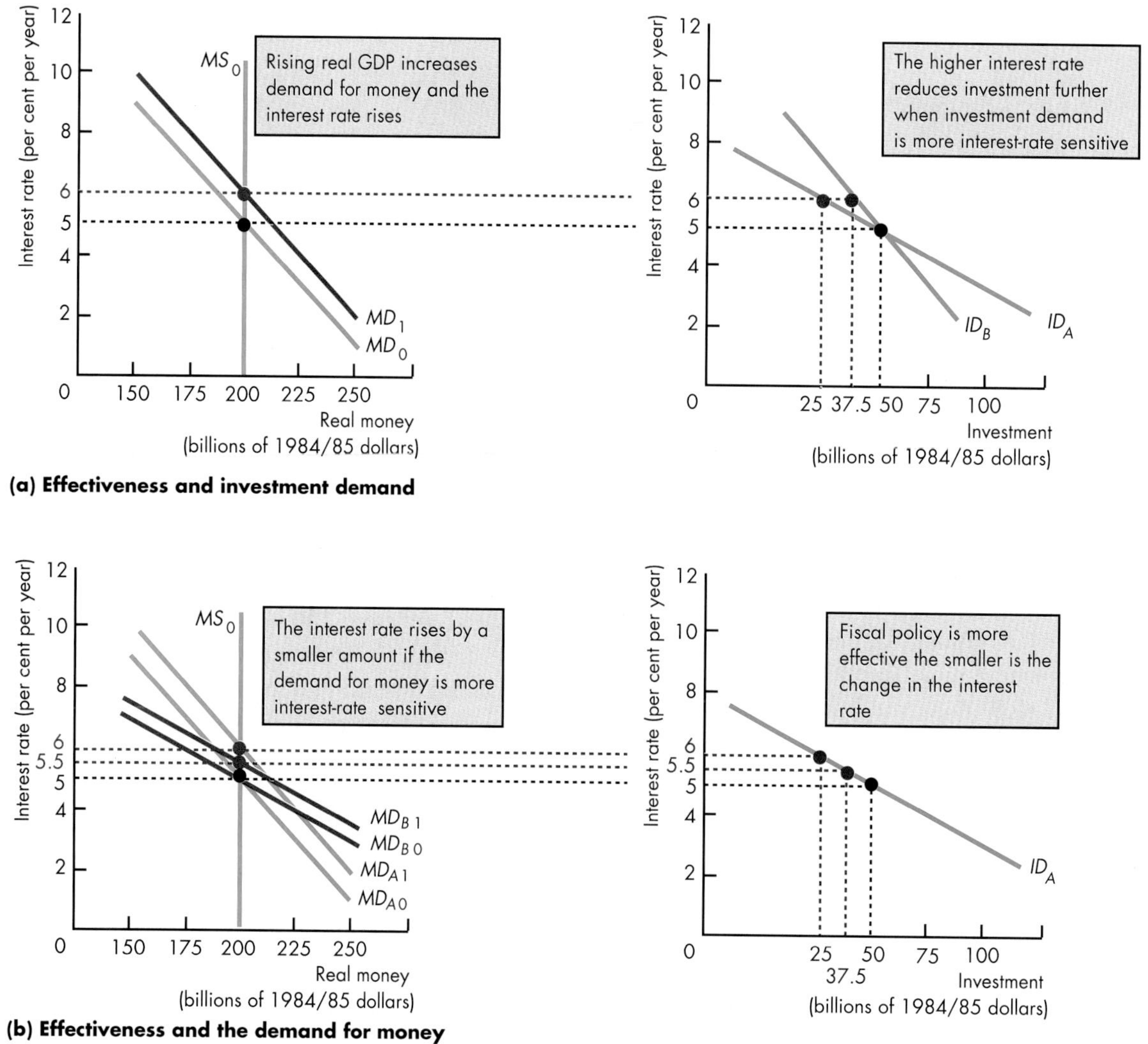

(a) Effectiveness and investment demand

(b) Effectiveness and the demand for money

In part (a), along the investment demand curve ID_A the level of planned investment is more sensitive to a change in the interest rate than along the demand curve ID_B. An increase in government purchases increases real GDP and shifts the demand curve for real money from MD_0 to MD_1, raising the interest rate from 5 per cent to 6 per cent. With investment demand curve ID_A investment decreases from $50 billion to $25 billion, but with demand curve ID_B investment decreases to only $37.5 billion. The larger the decrease in investment, the smaller is the increase in equilibrium real GDP resulting from a given increase in government purchases. So fiscal policy is less effective with investment demand curve ID_A than with ID_B.

In part (b), along the demand curve for real money MD_A the quantity of real money demanded is less sensitive to a change in the interest rate than along the demand curve MD_B. An increase in government purchases increases real GDP and the demand curve for real money shifts to the right — MD_{A0} shifts to MD_{A1} and MD_{B0} shifts to MD_{B1}. The size of the shift to the right is the same in each case. In case *A* the interest rate rises from 5 per cent to 6 per cent and, with investment demand curve ID_A, investment decreases from $50 billion to $25 billion. In case *B*, the interest rate rises to 5.5 per cent, and investment decreases to only $37.5 billion. The smaller the decrease in investment, the larger is the increase in equilibrium real GDP resulting from a given increase in government purchases. So fiscal policy is less effective with the demand curve for real money MD_A than with MD_B.

Table 30.1 Conditions for Policy Effectiveness

		Interest rate sensitivity of the demand for money: High	Interest rate sensitivity of the demand for money: Low
Interest rate sensitivity of investment demand	**High**	—	Monetary policy effective Fiscal policy ineffective
	Low	Monetary policy ineffective Fiscal policy effective	—

portunity cost. But the amount that we hold decreases as its opportunity cost — the interest rate — increases. The degree to which a change in the interest rate brings a change in the quantity of money held depends on how easily other financial assets can be substituted for money.

It has been claimed that financial market deregulation, which we discussed in Chapter 28, has reduced the effectiveness of monetary policy. This could have occurred because many accounts providing the services of money now pay interest, reducing the opportunity cost of money. Thus there is less substitution out of 'money' when interest rates rise. In other words, the demand curve for money is now less responsive to interest rate changes. Offsetting this development, of course, is the fact that interest rates are freer to adjust and so are now more variable — they rise and fall by larger amounts in deregulated markets. The net impact of financial market deregulation on the effectiveness of monetary policy is therefore uncertain.

Investment is the purchase of capital — of productive buildings, plant and equipment. The substitute for capital is labour. But it is an imperfect substitute. The amount of capital used, and the amount of investment undertaken, increase as the interest rate decreases. The degree to which a change in the interest rate brings a change in investment depends on how easily labour can be substituted for capital.

REVIEW

The effectiveness of monetary and fiscal policy depends on the sensitivity of investment demand and the demand for money to variations in the interest rate. These sensitivities are usually described in terms of elasticities. The conditions that make monetary policy effective — low sensitivity of money demand and high sensitivity of investment demand to changes in the interest rate — tend to make fiscal policy ineffective. And the conditions that make fiscal policy effective — high sensitivity of money demand and low sensitivity of investment demand — tend to make monetary policy ineffective. ■

Our discussion of the effectiveness of monetary policy and fiscal policy concerned the long-run effects of policy changes. But the choice between using monetary policy or fiscal policy to achieve a certain goal also depends on how quickly those long-term goals can be achieved. Let's now discuss the lags that arise between the implementation of a policy and the realization of its desired effects. These lags can be different for monetary policy and fiscal policy.

The Lags of Monetary and Fiscal Policy

Monetary and fiscal policy actions do not have an instantaneous effect on aggregate demand. Instead they operate with a time lag. That is, their effects are spread out over time. There are four important time lags:

- A policy formation lag
- An autonomous expenditure lag
- An induced expenditure lag
- A price adjustment lag

The policy formation lag describes the time it takes for policymakers to decide that a macroeconomic problem exists, to decide on appropriate action, and then to implement it. Since the lag is mainly the result of information gathering and administrative processes it is sometimes called an 'inside' lag. The remaining three lags comprise the total time it takes for the implemented policy to work its way through the economy to achieve the intended results. Since these lags are usually outside the control of policymakers they are called 'outside' lags. Let's now examine each in more detail.

Policy Formation Lag A policy formation lag is the result of the time it takes for policymakers to identify a problem, agree upon a solution and then to actually implement the chosen policy. With both fiscal and monetary policy, we can identify two components of the policy formation lag, which we will call the 'recognition' and 'action' lags. The former is the time it takes for the Reserve Bank or the government to assess a developing problem with sufficient confidence to take action on it. Having decided a problem requires some attention, which policy instrument — monetary or fiscal — should be used? In arriving at a decision, the current and recent performance of the economy has to be carefully assessed and a consensus established on its most likely future course. Often there are confusing and contradictory signals about the current state and future direction the economy is taking. Agreement must be reached, not only on current economic performance, but also on the economic goals and the best actions to take for achieving those goals.

Most importantly, because the effects of the policy actions operate with long outside lags (which we will discuss below), the Reserve Bank and the government must *forecast* the state of the economy at the time when all the effects of its current actions will have been realized. That is, the policymaker has to behave in some ways like an electric power company. The power company knows that if it is to meet the demand for electric power in 1997, it must set some plans in place here and now to build additional generating capacity that will come on stream in that year. If the time lag from the policymaker's action to a change in equilibrium real GDP takes two years, the policy actions in 1990 must be geared to the best available forecasts of the state of the economy in 1992. The policymaker, like the electric power company, must take actions today that will put in place the correct level of aggregate expenditure to maintain stable prices not today but two years from today.

Generally speaking, the monetary policy formation lag is much shorter than that for fiscal policy because of monetary policy's shorter action lag. The Reserve Bank can, and does, operate daily in the official money short-term market and can implement changes in monetary policy almost immediately.

Fiscal policy has formation lags that are longer than those for monetary policy. To implement changes in government expenditure on goods and services, or in taxes, the entire legislative process must be completed. This process, which involves Cabinet and parliament, as well as many committees, interest groups and lobby groups, creates a long action lag, which operates on a time frame that makes fine adjustments to fiscal policy for macroeconomic stabilization purposes virtually impossible.

The remaining three outside lags all arise because it takes time for any given policy to work its way through the economy.

Autonomous Expenditure Lag Both fiscal and monetary policy influence aggregate expenditure initially through their effect on autonomous expenditure. When autonomous expenditure rises or falls, the aggregate expenditure curve shifts and equilibrium real GDP changes. But fiscal and monetary policy affect autonomous expenditure in different ways. Let's examine the differences.

Some fiscal policy actions have an immediate effect on autonomous expenditure and so on aggregate expenditure. For example, a change in government purchases of goods and services has an immediate impact on the markets in which the government is buying the additional goods and services. An increase in government spending directly adds to the level of autonomous spending. Thus, at least for changes in government purchases of goods and services, the fiscal policy autonomous expenditure lag is short.

Monetary policy also has an impact on autonomous expenditure, but through a rather more indirect channel. Monetary policy's immediate or direct impact is in the money market. It is only as interest rates change, which usually happens very rapidly, that autonomous expenditure begins to change. But the effects of interest rates on planned investment can take some time to operate. The length of time between a change in interest rates and the change in autonomous spending can also be variable. Longer still are the effects of changing exchange rates, as a result of changing interest rates, on net exports. Thus changes in monetary policy only indirectly affect the level of autonomous spending and so the monetary policy autonomous expenditure lag can be both long and uncertain.

Induced Expenditure Lag A given change in autonomous expenditure induces a change in actual real GDP, which then induces a change in consumption expenditure and in equilibrium expenditure. This induced change is the multiplier effect that we studied in Chapter 26. But the multiplier effect takes time to operate, so there is a second outside lag. We described the elements of this time lag in Chapter 26. Let's briefly recall them here. The chain of events begins with a change in firms' inventories. Only when firms adjust output to restore their inventories to their desired levels does real GDP change. And not until real GDP has changed is there a change in induced expenditure. A change in induced expenditure changes real GDP yet further. Eventually, the multiplier process comes to an end when aggregate planned expenditure, once again, is equal to real GDP. The induced expenditure lag is the same for both monetary and fiscal policy changes, which work through changing autonomous expenditure.

Fiscal policy involving a tax cut does not have a direct effect on autonomous expenditure but does have an immediate effect on disposable income. However, its effect on consumption expenditure is also drawn out over time in the same way as the multiplier process slows down the impacts of a change in autonomous expenditure.

Price Adjustment Lag A third outside lag that occurs is the lag between a change in equilibrium expenditure and a change in prices. An increase in equilibrium expenditure shifts the aggregate demand curve to the right. With a new aggregate demand curve, the price level begins to increase. But the increase in prices is slow at first and only begins to speed up when the higher price level induces higher prices of factors of production, which, in turn, start to shift the short-run aggregate supply curve upward.

REVIEW

There is a lag — a passage of time — from the moment a problem is recognized, a corrective policy decided upon, the policy implemented and the effects felt on equilibrium real GDP. This lag can be quite long and is often variable, which complicates the task of predicting the effects of any given policy. The entire lag for either fiscal and monetary policy can be broken down into a policy formation lag, an autonomous expenditure lag, an induced expenditure lag and a price adjustment lag.

There are differences in the way the lags operate with fiscal or monetary policy. Generally speaking, fiscal policy has an immediate effect on aggregate expenditure — a short autonomous expenditure lag — followed by a long drawn out effect as interest rates change and other components of aggregate expenditure adjust in response to the changing interest rates. In the case of monetary policy, there is no immediate effect on aggregate demand — a long autonomous expenditure lag. The effect gradually builds up as more and more firms and households respond to the changing interest rates and other money and financial market conditions. However, monetary policy can have a much shorter policy formation lag than fiscal policy. ■

The analysis of the effects of monetary and fiscal policy on aggregate expenditure that we have presented in this chapter was for several years, in the 1950s and 1960s, extremely controversial. It was at the heart of the Keynesian–monetarist controversy. (The Keynesian–monetarist controversy of today is different from that of the 1950s and 1960s; we'll discuss the current controversy — about how labour markets work — in Chapter 31.) The Keynesian–monetarist controversy was an interesting and important episode in the development of modern macroeconomics. Let's take a look at the essentials of the dispute and see how it was resolved.

The Keynesian–Monetarist Controversy

The Keynesian–monetarist controversy is an ongoing dispute in macroeconomics between two broad groups of economists. **Keynesians** are macroeconomists whose views about the functioning of the economy represent an extension of the theories of John Maynard Keynes, published in Keynes's *General Theory.* Keynesians regard the economy as being inherently unstable and as requiring active government intervention to achieve stability. They assign a low degree of importance to monetary policy and a high degree of importance to fiscal policy. Monetarists are macroeconomists who assign a high degree of importance to variations in the quantity of money as the main determinant of fluctuations in aggregate demand and regard the economy as inherently stable. But, because of the lags in monetary policy and the uncertainty surrounding the timing of its effects, some monetarists argue that a stable rate of growth of the money supply, with little active intervention, will reduce the variability in aggregate demand and so stabilize the economy. The founder of modern monetarism was Milton Friedman. (Keynes and Friedman are discussed in Our Advancing Knowledge, pp. 184–185.)

The nature of the Keynesian–monetarist debate has changed over the years. In the 1950s and 1960s, the debate focused almost exclusively on the relative effectiveness of fiscal policy and monetary policy in changing aggregate demand. Although it is a simplification, we will be able to see more clearly the essence of the controversy if we distinguish three views:

- Extreme Keynesianism
- Extreme monetarism
- The intermediate position

Extreme Keynesianism The extreme Keynesian hypothesis is that a change in the money supply has very little or no effect on the level of aggregate demand, and a change in government purchases of goods and services or in taxes has a large and predictable effect on aggregate demand.

There are two circumstances in which a change in the money supply has no effect on aggregate demand. They are

- A vertical investment demand curve
- A horizontal demand curve for real money

If the investment demand curve is vertical, planned investment is completely insensitive to interest rates. In that situation, even if monetary policy changes interest rates, those changes do not affect aggregate expenditure and monetary policy is impotent.

A horizontal demand curve for real money means that people are willing to hold any amount of money at a given interest rate — a situation called a **liquidity trap.** With a liquidity trap, a change in the quantity of money affects only the amount of money held. It does not affect interest rates. With an unchanged interest rate, investment is unchanged and monetary policy is impotent.

Extreme Monetarism The extreme monetarist hypothesis is that a change in government purchases of goods and services or in taxes has very little or no effect on aggregate demand and that a change in the money supply has a large and predictable effect upon aggregate demand. There are two circumstances which support the predictions of an extreme monetarist:

- A horizontal investment demand curve
- A vertical demand curve for real money

If an increase in government purchases of goods and services induces an increase in interest rates that is sufficiently large to reduce investment by the same amount as the initial increase in government purchases, then fiscal policy has no effect on aggregate demand. This is the outcome of complete crowding out that we described earlier in this chapter. For this result to occur, either the demand curve for real money must be vertical — a fixed amount of money is held regardless of the interest rate — or the investment demand curve must be horizontal — any amount of investment will be undertaken at a given interest rate.

The Intermediate Position The intermediate position is that both monetary and fiscal policy affect aggregate demand. Crowding out is not complete, so that fiscal policy does have an effect. There is no liquidity trap and investment does respond to interest rates, so monetary policy affects aggregate demand. This position is the one that now appears to be correct. Let's see how economists came to this conclusion.

Sorting Out the Competing Claims The dispute between monetarists, Keynesians and those taking an intermediate position had a number of components. The most important was a disagreement about the magnitudes of two economic parameters:

- The sensitivity of investment demand to interest rates
- The sensitivity of the demand for real money to interest rates

If investment demand is highly sensitive to interest rates and the demand for real money is hardly sensitive at all, then monetary policy is powerful and fiscal policy relatively ineffective. The world then looks similar to the claims of extreme monetarists. If the demand for real money is highly sensitive to interest rate changes and investment demand is very insensitive, then fiscal policy is powerful and monetary policy is relatively ineffective. The world then looks similar to the claims of the extreme Keynesians.

Using statistical methods to study the demand for real money and investment demand, and using data from a wide variety of historical and national experiences, economists were able to settle this dispute. Neither extreme position turned out to be supported by the evidence, and the intermediate position was the one that won.

An intermediate position does not always win in scientific matters. Indeed, scientific progress is at its most exciting when logically possible situations are shown, empirically, not to occur. But in this particular dispute that outcome did not arise. The demand curve for real money does slope downward. So does the demand curve for investment. Neither of these demand curves is vertical or horizontal, ruling out the extreme Keynesian and monetarist hypotheses.

This particular controversy in macroeconomics is now behind us, but other controversies are still around. One concerns the relative magnitudes of the multiplier effects of monetary and fiscal policy. Another concerns the time lags of those effects. But the major outstanding controversy that divides Keynesians and monetarists concerns how the labour market works. We'll meet that controversy in the next chapter.

REVIEW

The early controversy between Keynesian and monetarist economists was the result of disagreement over whether fiscal policy or monetary policy was most effective. This debate depended on different views about the sensitivity of money demand and investment demand to changes in interest rates. In the extreme case, if the demand for money is completely insensitive to changes in the interest rate or investment demand is extremely sensitive, monetary policy is effective and fiscal policy is ineffective. In the opposite extreme case, if the demand for money is extremely sensitive to changes in the interest rate and investment demand is completely insensitive, fiscal policy is effective and monetary policy is ineffective. These extremes do not occur in reality. ■

Influencing the Composition of Aggregate Demand

If aggregate expenditure is to be increased, there is a choice of methods for increasing it. Either the money supply can be increased or fiscal policy can be expansionary (an increase in government purchases or a tax cut). If there is an increase in the money supply, as we have seen above, the increased aggregate expenditure comes along with lower interest rates. Lower interest rates, in turn, result in a higher level of investment. However, if aggregate expenditure is stimulated by fiscal policy, the increased aggregate expenditure comes along with higher interest rates. If crowding in does not occur, higher interest rates mean lower investment. Thus the method by which aggregate expenditure is increased has an important effect on its composition.

With an increase in aggregate expenditure resulting from an increase in the money supply, both investment and consumption expenditure increase while government purchases of goods and services are unchanged. If aggregate expenditure is increased by an increase in government purchases of goods and services, consumption expenditure also increases but investment decreases. If the increase in aggregate expenditure is brought about by a tax cut, consumption expenditure increases and investment decreases. In this case, government purchases remain constant.

Assigning Monetary and Fiscal Policy Goals

The different effects on the composition of aggregate demand resulting from different policies for changing aggregate demand have meant that the government has, at different times, relied more heavily on one policy tool rather than the other. Sometimes the emphasis on particular policies has been a source of tension between the various branches of government responsible for fiscal and monetary policies, or between the government and private business or employee representative groups.

For example, in response to the rising unemployment and low growth in the early 1980s, the government adopted an expansionary fiscal policy, coupled with a wages and prices policy. This particular policy mix, which did not make active use of monetary policy, resulted from the National Economic Summit Conference held shortly after the election of the Hawke Labor government in 1983.

While the policy was apparently successful in stimulating growth and reducing unemployment, it was also associated with a rising imbalance on the trade account — imports were rising faster than exports. To counter this, the government reversed the direction of fiscal policy to the extent that the $8 billion deficit in 1983/84 turned into an $8 billion surplus in 1989/90. But this meant that the government, through the Reserve Bank, had to rely on monetary policy as the tool for demand management purposes. Monetary policy became the so-called 'swing instrument'. That is, monetary policy was actively used in an attempt to manage the level of equilibrium aggregate expenditure.

Tight monetary policy in 1988/89 and 1989/90 was so effective in reducing aggregate demand that by late 1990 the economy had gone into recession. This has prompted criticisms suggesting that monetary policy is a 'blunt instrument', particularly with respect to its effects on investment, which have implications for longer run growth. While always administering the government's policies, the Governor of the Reserve Bank has suggested, on occasion, that monetary policy might be better directed at the longer term goal of inflation, rather than for short-term demand management purposes.

In Chapter 33 we discuss the policies of the 1980s in considerably more detail.

Real GDP and the Price Level

We've now studied the effects of monetary and fiscal policy on equilibrium expenditure and real GDP at a given price level. But the effects that we've worked out occur at each and every price level. Thus the monetary and fiscal policy effects that we've studied tell us about changes in aggregate demand and shifts in the aggregate demand curve.

But when aggregate demand changes, both real GDP and the price level change. To determine the amounts by which each change, we need to look at both aggregate demand and aggregate supply. Let's now do this, starting with the short-run effects of monetary and fiscal policy.

The Short-Run Effects on Real GDP and the Price Level

When aggregate demand changes and the aggregate demand curve shifts, there is a movement along the short-run aggregate supply curve and both real GDP and the price level change. These changes are illustrated for an increase in aggregate demand in Fig. 30.8. Initially, the aggregate demand curve is AD_0 and the short-run aggregate supply curve is *SAS*. Real GDP is $300 billion and the GDP deflator is 130.

Now suppose that fiscal and monetary policy changes increase aggregate demand, shifting the aggregate demand curve to AD_1. At the initial price level (GDP deflator equal to 130) real GDP would increase to $325 billion. This increase is one we studied earlier in this chapter. But real GDP does not actually increase to this level. The reason is that the price level increases, bringing a decrease in the quantity of real GDP demanded. The higher level of aggregate demand puts upward pressure on the prices of all goods and services, and the GDP deflator rises to 140. At the higher price level, the real money supply decreases.

Figure 30.8 Policy-Induced Changes in Real GDP and the Price Level

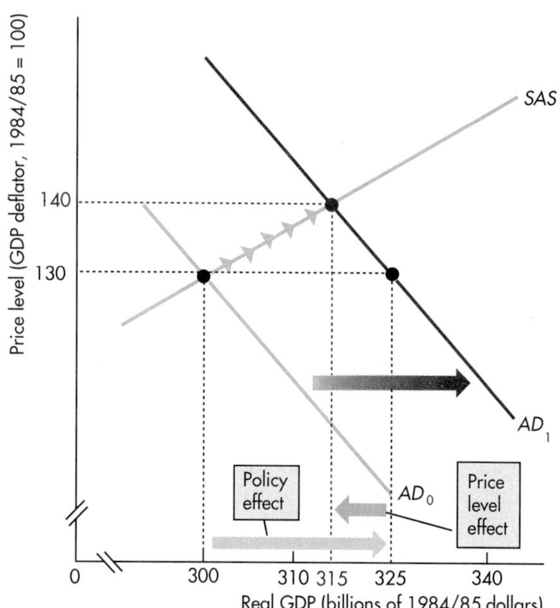

Initially aggregate demand is AD_0 and short-run aggregate supply curve is *SAS*. Real GDP is $300 billion and the GDP deflator is 130. Monetary and fiscal policy changes shift the aggregate demand curve to AD_1. At the initial price level (GDP deflator equal to 130) real GDP rises to $325 billion. But the price level increases, bringing a decrease in the real money supply. The decrease in the real money supply increases the interest rate, decreases investment, and decreases equilibrium expenditure and real GDP. The increase in real GDP from $300 billion to $325 billion is the result of the initial policy-induced increase in aggregate demand at a given price level; and the decrease in real GDP from $325 billion to $315 billion is the result of the decrease in the real money supply induced by the higher price level.

A decrease in the real money supply resulting from a rise in the price level has exactly the same effects on real GDP (and the interest rate) as a decrease in the real money supply resulting from a decrease in the nominal money supply brought about by the Reserve Bank's monetary policy. We've already seen what these effects are. A decrease in the real money supply increases the interest rate, decreases investment, and decreases equilibrium expenditure and real GDP.

The increase in real GDP from \$300 billion to \$325 billion is the result of the initial policy-induced increase in aggregate demand at a given price level; and the decrease in real GDP from \$325 billion to \$315 billion is the result of the decrease in the real money supply induced by the higher price level.

The exercise that we've just conducted for an increase in aggregate demand can be reversed to see what happens when there is policy-induced decrease in aggregate demand. Real GDP decreases and the price level falls.

The effects that we've just worked out are short-run effects. Let's now look at the long-run effects of monetary and fiscal policy.

The Long-Run Effects on Real GDP and the Price Level

The long-run effects of monetary and fiscal policy depend on the state of the economy when the policy action is taken. Again, we'll concentrate on the case of an increase in aggregate demand. If, initially, unemployment is above its natural rate and real GDP is below its long-run level, fiscal and monetary policy may be used to restore full employment. Figure 30.8 can be used again to show this case. Suppose that long-run aggregate supply is \$315 billion. The increase in aggregate demand moves the economy from below full employment to full employment and that is the end of the story. The short-run and the long-run adjustments are the same. The expansionary government fiscal policy in 1983/84 and 1984/85 was an example of such a policy action. Policy was used to move the economy from a serious recession into a period of expansion.

In contrast, suppose that a policy-induced increase in aggregate demand occurs when the economy is already fully employed with real GDP at its long-run level. Such a situation may have occurred in 1987/88 when monetary policy was loosened as the economy was approaching full employment. In this case, what are the long-run effects?

The answers are seen in Fig. 30.9. The long-run aggregate supply curve is *LAS*. Initially, the aggregate demand curve is AD_0 and the short-run aggregate supply curve is SAS_0. Real GDP is \$300 billion and the GDP deflator is 130.

Suppose that changes in fiscal and monetary policy increase aggregate demand and shift the aggregate demand curve to AD_1. At the initial price level (GDP deflator equal to 130) real GDP would increase to \$325 billion — the increase we studied in Fig. 30.8. But, as we've just seen, real GDP does not actually increase to this level. The higher price level decreases the real money supply and raises the interest rate. As a result investment, equilibrium expenditure and real GDP decrease. The new short-run equilibrium is where real GDP is \$315 billion and the GDP deflator is 140.

Figure 30.9 The Long-Run Effects of Policy-Induced Changes in Real GDP and the Price Level

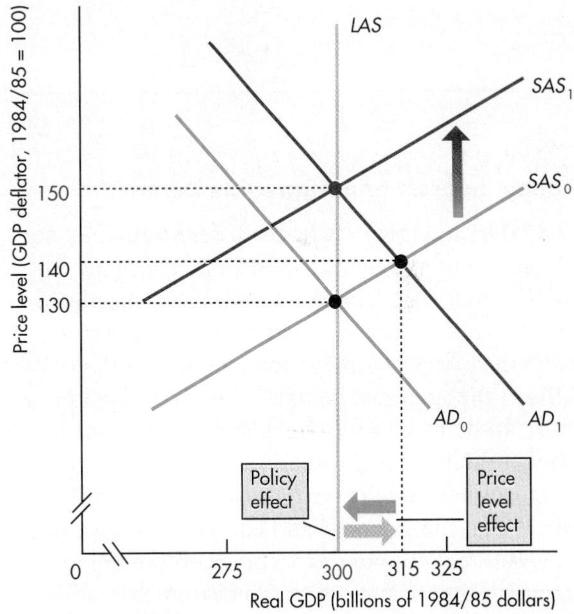

The long-run aggregate supply curve is *LAS*. Initially the aggregate demand curve is AD_0 and the short-run aggregate supply curve is SAS_0. Real GDP is \$300 billion and the GDP deflator is 130. Monetary and fiscal policy changes shift the aggregate demand curve to AD_1. The new short-run equilibrium is where real GDP is \$315 billion and the GDP deflator is 140. Because real GDP is above its long-run level, wages increase and the short-run aggregate supply curve begins to shift upward to SAS_1. The new long-run equilibrium is where the GDP deflator is 150 and real GDP is back at its original level.

But real GDP is now above its long-run level and unemployment is below its natural rate. A shortage of labour puts upward pressure on wages. And as wages increase, the short-run aggregate supply curve begins to shift upward. It shifts upward until it has reached SAS_1. At this stage, the GDP deflator has increased to 150 and real GDP is back at its original level. Thus in the long run an expansionary fiscal and monetary policy at full employment brings inflation but no additional real GDP.

REVIEW

A policy-induced change in aggregate demand changes both real GDP and the price level. The amount by which each changes depends on aggregate supply. In the short run, with an expansionary policy, both real GDP and the price level increase, but the increase in real GDP is smaller than would occur at a fixed price level. In the long run, the effects of monetary and fiscal policy depend on the state of the economy when the policy action is taken. Starting from a position below long-run real GDP, fiscal and monetary policy may restore full employment, increasing real GDP and the price level. But starting from full employment, an expansionary fiscal and monetary policy brings inflation and no additional real GDP. ■

■ We have now studied the detailed effects of monetary and fiscal policy on real GDP, interest rates and the price level. We've seen what determines the relative effectiveness of monetary and fiscal policy and how the mix of these policies can influence the composition of aggregate expenditure. But we've also seen that the ultimate effects of these policies on real GDP and the price level depend not only on the behaviour of aggregate demand but also on aggregate supply. Our next task is to turn to the aggregate supply side of the economy and to study the determination of long-run and short-run aggregate supply, employment and unemployment.

SUMMARY

Money, Interest and Aggregate Demand

Real GDP and the price level are determined by the interaction of aggregate demand and aggregate supply (Chapter 24). Monetary and fiscal policy influence aggregate demand. To look at their effects we freeze the price level and study the magnitudes of the shifts of the aggregate demand curve at a given price level. To do this we use the aggregate expenditure model (of Chapters 25 and 26). In this model the aggregate expenditure curve tells us aggregate expenditure at a given price level and equilibrium aggregate expenditure corresponds to a point on the aggregate demand curve. Thus when equilibrium expenditure changes, the aggregate demand curve shifts.

Equilibrium expenditure depends on autonomous expenditure and one of the components of autonomous expenditure, planned investment, varies with the interest rate. The higher the interest rate, other things held constant, the lower is investment, and hence the lower is autonomous expenditure and equilibrium expenditure. Therefore equilibrium expenditure and real GDP depend on the interest rate.

The interest rate is determined by equilibrium in the money market. The demand for real money depends on both real GDP and the interest rate. The higher the real GDP, other things held constant, the greater is the demand for real money and the higher is the interest rate. Therefore the interest rate depends on real GDP.

Both real GDP and the interest rate are determined simultaneously as shown in Fig. 30.1. Equilibrium real GDP and the interest rate are such that they give money market equilibrium and make aggregate planned expenditure equal to real GDP. (pp. 329–332)

Monetary Policy and Aggregate Demand

The main transmission channel of monetary policy is the interest rate. A decrease in the money supply increases the interest rate. The higher interest rate decreases planned investment, and lower investment reduces aggregate planned expenditure. A decrease in aggregate expenditure causes equilibrium real GDP to fall. Actual real GDP begins to fall. A fall in actual real GDP decreases the demand for real money. The demand curve for real money shifts to the left and interest rates fall. Falling interest rates lead to an increase in planned investment and aggregate expenditure starts to rise. Equilibrium real GDP rises. The falling actual real GDP and rising equilibrium real GDP converge at a new equilibrium. Such an equilibrium is a situation in which real GDP and the interest rate take on values that make the quantity of real money demanded equal the quantity supplied and aggregate expenditure equal real GDP.

Other transmission channels for monetary policy are the real balance effect, the wealth effect and the exchange rate effect. A change in the quantity of real money has a direct effect on aggregate expenditure. A change in wealth also has a direct effect on aggregate expenditure. A change in the exchange rate changes Australian demand for foreign-made goods and services and foreign demand for Australian-made goods and services. (pp. 332–337)

Fiscal Policy and Aggregate Demand

A change in government purchases of goods and services or taxes has a direct effect on aggregate demand through its effect on aggregate expenditure. But fiscal policy changes real GDP and also changes interest rates. Therefore fiscal policy has an indirect effect on investment. An increase in government purchases of goods and services or a tax cut that increases aggregate expenditure increases equilibrium real GDP and makes actual real GDP begin to rise. Rising actual real GDP increases the demand for real money and increases interest rates. Higher interest rates lower investment — the crowding out effect. In an extreme situation crowding out could be complete. That is, the decrease in investment could be sufficient to offset the initial increase in aggregate planned expenditure resulting from the fiscal policy action. In practice, complete crowding out does not occur.

An opposing effect is 'crowding in', an increase in investment resulting from an increase in government purchases of goods and services. Such an effect may occur in a recession if fiscal stimulation brings expectations of economic recovery and higher profits or if the government purchases public capital that strengthens the economy.

Fiscal policy also influences aggregate demand through the exchange rate. An increase in government purchases or a cut in taxes tends to increase interest rates and make the value of the dollar rise against other currencies. When the dollar strengthens, Australians buy more imports and foreigners buy fewer Australian-made goods, so net exports decline. (pp. 337–341)

The Relative Effectiveness of Monetary and Fiscal Policy

The relative effectiveness of monetary and fiscal policy on aggregate demand depend on two factors: the sensitivity of the demand for money to the interest rate and the sensitivity of investment demand to the interest rate. The less sensitive the demand for real money and the more sensitive investment demand to the interest rate, the larger is the effect of a change in the money supply on aggregate demand. The more sensitive the demand for money and the less sensitive investment demand to the interest rate, the larger is the effect of a fiscal policy change on aggregate demand.

The original Keynesian–monetarist controversy concerns the relative effectiveness of monetary and fiscal actions in influencing aggregate demand. The extreme Keynesian position is that only fiscal policy affects aggregate demand and monetary policy is impotent. The extreme monetarist position is the converse — that only money policy affects aggregate demand and that fiscal policy is impotent. This controversy was the central one in macroeconomics in the 1950s and 1960s. As a result of statistical investigations, we now know that neither of these extreme positions is correct and that both monetary and fiscal actions influence aggregate demand. Controversy remains about the relative effectiveness of the two types of policy and the precise timing of their effects.

The mix of monetary and fiscal policy influences the composition of aggregate demand. If aggregate demand increases as a result of an increase in the money supply, interest rates fall and investment increases. If aggregate demand increases as a result of an increase in government purchases of goods and services, interest rates rise and investment falls. These different effects of monetary and fiscal policy on aggregate demand create some political tensions. (pp. 341–350)

Real GDP and the Price Level

When aggregate demand changes, both real GDP and the price level change by amounts determined by both aggregate demand and aggregate supply. When a monetary or fiscal policy-induced increase in aggregate demand occurs, the aggregate demand curve shifts to the right. The magnitude of the shift of the aggregate demand curve is equal to the effect of the policy change on aggregate demand at a given price level. In the short run, real GDP and the price level increase. The rise in the price level decreases the real money supply. The effects on real GDP (and the interest rate) of a decrease in the real money supply are the same regardless of whether the nominal money supply decreases (Reserve Bank's monetary policy) or the price level rises.

The long-run effects of monetary and fiscal policy depend on the state of the economy when the policy action is taken. Starting out with unemployment above its natural rate and real GDP below its long-run level, fiscal and monetary policy may restore full employment. But starting out from full employment, with real GDP at its long-run level, a policy-induced increase in aggregate demand increases the price level and leaves real GDP unchanged. (pp. 350–352)

KEY TERMS

Action lag, p. 346
Autonomous expenditure lag, p. 346
Crowding in, p. 340
Crowding out, p. 340
Induced lag, p. 347
Inside lag, p. 346
International crowding out, p. 340
Keynesian, p. 347
Liquidity trap, p. 348
Monetarist, p. 348
Outside lag, p. 346
Policy formation lag, p. 346
Price adjustment lag, p. 347
Wealth effect, p. 336

PROBLEMS

1 In the economy described in Fig. 30.1, suppose there is an increase in the money supply of $25 billion.
   a) Work out the immediate change in the interest rate.
   b) What is the immediate change in investment?
   c) What is the immediate effect on aggregate planned expenditure?
   d) What is the ~~immediate~~ effect on equilibrium real GDP?
   e) What happens to inventories?
   f) What is the economy's new equilibrium?

2 In the economy described in Fig. 30.1, suppose that the government introduces a fiscal policy that decreases its purchases of goods and services by $25 billion.
   a) Work out the initial change in equilibrium expenditure and real GDP.
   b) What happens to inventories?
   c) Explain how real GDP and the interest rate change.
   d) Explain how investment changes.
   e) What is the economy's new equilibrium?
   f) Explain how the economy converges to a new equilibrium.

3 There are two economies that are identical in every way except the following. In economy A, a change in the interest rate of 1 percentage point (for example, from 5 per cent to 6 per cent) results in a $100 billion change in the quantity of real money demanded. In economy B, the same change in the interest rate leads to a $50 billion change in the quantity of real money demanded.
   a) In which economy does a change in the quantity of real money have a larger effect on equilibrium real GDP?
   b) In which economy does an increase in government expenditure on goods and services have a larger effect on real GDP?
   c) In which economy is the crowding out effect weaker?

4 The government wants to increase aggregate demand, stimulate exports and increase investment. Explain whether it should seek to achieve this objective by increasing government purchases of goods and services, by cutting taxes or by increasing the money supply. Explain the mechanisms at work under the alternative policies that lead to your policy recommendation. What are the time lags in the effectiveness of the alternative policies?

Appendix to Chapter 30

The *IS–LM* Model of Aggregate Demand

This appendix presents the *IS–LM* model of aggregate demand. This model provides an explicit account of the derivation of the aggregate demand curve and of the effects of monetary and fiscal policy on aggregate demand. The material is not inherently difficult but it is of a higher level than the presentation in the chapter and is optional. Nevertheless, if you have the time and interest to study the appendix, you will emerge with a deeper and clearer understanding of aggregate demand and how it is influenced by monetary and fiscal policy.

Chapters 25, 26 and 28 contain the ingredients of the *IS–LM* model. First, we'll refresh our memory about equilibrium expenditure and real GDP flows. Second, we'll look at money market equilibrium. Then we'll bring these two things together.

Equilibrium Expenditure and Real GDP

Aggregate expenditure depends on real GDP because consumption, the biggest component of aggregate expenditure, increases as real GDP increases. The equilibrium flows of aggregate planned expenditure and real GDP occur when aggregate planned expenditure equals real GDP. But aggregate planned expenditure also depends on the interest rate. The higher the interest rate, the lower is planned investment. Thus the higher the interest rate, the lower is aggregate planned expenditure.

These ideas, which were discussed in greater detail in Chapters 25 and 26, are summarized in Fig. A30.1. Let's work through this figure carefully, starting with its table.

Begin by looking at the two columns headed 'Interest rate' and 'Autonomous expenditure'. Recall that investment is part of autonomous expenditure and that investment decreases as the interest rate rises. The table shows us how autonomous expenditure varies as the interest rate varies. For example, when the interest rate is 6 per cent, autonomous expenditure is $125 billion. When the interest rate falls to 5 per cent, autonomous expenditure rises to $150 billion.

Next, look at the last two rows of the table labelled 'Induced expenditure' and 'Real GDP'. Recall that induced expenditure is expenditure that depends on real GDP. It is that part of consumption expenditure that depends on real GDP minus imports. The numbers here tell us how induced expenditure varies as real GDP varies. For example, if real GDP is $250 billion, induced expenditure is $125 billion. If real GDP increases to $300 billion, induced expenditure rises to $150 billion.

Finally, look at the block of table labelled 'Aggregate planned expenditure'. Each number in this block tells us the level of aggregate planned expenditure at a specific combination of the interest rate and the level of real GDP. For example, row *b* tells us that when the interest rate is 5 per cent and when real GDP is $250 billion, aggregate planned expendi-

Figure A30.1 Aggregate Planned Expenditure, Flow Equilibrium and the *IS* Curve

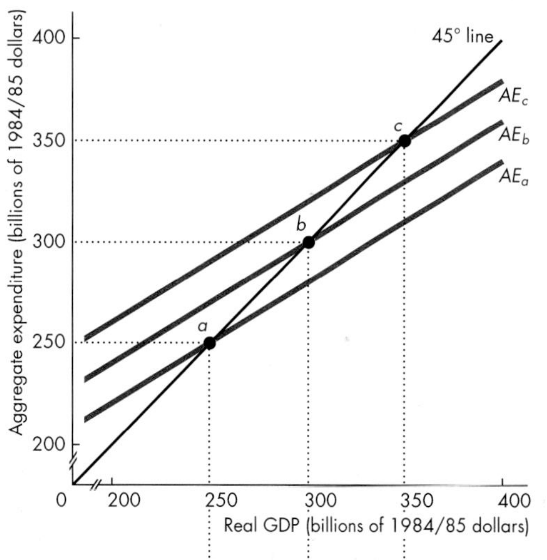

(a) Aggregate expenditure and real GDP

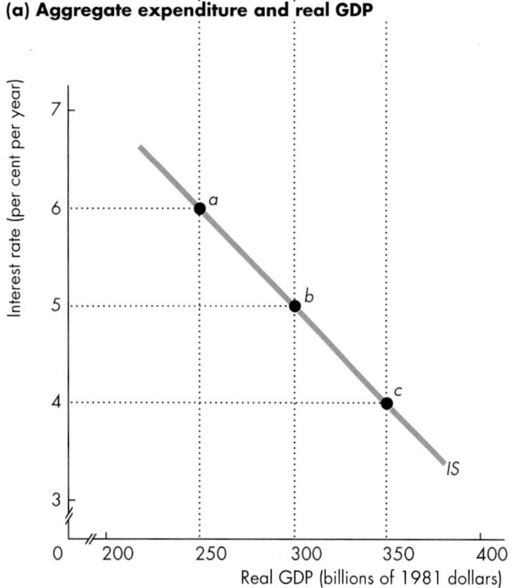

(b) The *IS* curve

The table shows the aggregate planned expenditure — the sum of autonomous expenditure and induced expenditure — that occurs at different combinations of the interest rate and real GDP. For example, if the interest rate is 6 per cent and real GDP is \$350 billion, aggregate planned expenditure is \$300 billion (top right number). Flow equilibrium — equality of aggregate planned expenditure and real GDP — is shown by the green squares. Each row *a*, *b* and *c* represents an aggregate expenditure schedule, plotted as the aggregate expenditure curves AE_a, AE_b and AE_c, respectively in part (a). Equilibrium expenditure positions are shown in part (a), where these *AE* curves intersect the 45° line and are marked *a*, *b* and *c*. Part (b) shows these same equilibrium positions but highlights the combinations of the interest rate and real GDP at which they occur. The line connecting those points is the IS curve.

	Interest rate (per cent per year)	Autonomous expenditure (billions of 1984/85 dollars)	Aggregate planned expenditure (billions of 1984/85 dollars)		
a	6	125	250	275	300
b	5	150	275	300	325
c	4	175	300	325	350
	Induced expenditure		125	150	175
	Real GDP (billions of 1984/85 dollars)		250	300	350

ture is \$275 billion — the sum of autonomous expenditure of \$150 billion and induced expenditure of \$125 billion. The other eight numbers in the top right section of the table are arrived at in the same way. Check that you can calculate them as the sum of autonomous expenditure and induced expenditure at the appropriate interest rate and real GDP.

The green squares in the table indicate positions of equilibrium expenditure. For example, look again at row *b*. It tells us that when the interest rate is 5 per cent, equilibrium expenditure is \$300 billion. At that interest rate, autonomous expenditure is \$150 billion. At real GDP of \$300 billion, induced expenditure is \$150 billion. Therefore aggregate planned expenditure is \$300 billion, which equals real GDP. This is an expenditure equilibrium. When aggregate planned expenditure exceeds real GDP, real GDP increases. At an interest rate of 5 per cent, if real GDP is \$250 billion, aggregate planned expenditure is \$275 billion — real GDP increases. When aggregate planned expenditure is below real GDP, real GDP falls. At an interest rate of 5 per cent, if real GDP is \$350 billion, aggregate planned expenditure is \$325 billion — real GDP falls. At an interest rate of 5 per cent, aggregate planned expenditure is equal to real GDP only when real GDP is \$300 billion. The other two green squares tell us equilibrium expenditure at interest rates of 6 per cent and 4 per cent.

The *IS* Curve

The *IS* curve shows combinations of real GDP and the interest rate at which aggregate planned expenditure equals real GDP. The name *IS* curve was suggested by the curve's inventor, the great English economist John Hicks. The letter *I* stands for Investment and *S* stands for Saving. When Hicks invented the *IS* curve, he used a model economy in which there was no government and no foreign sector, so that flow equilibrium occurs when investment equals saving. The label *IS* tells us that along that curve planned investment is equal to saving in such an economy. In an economy with a government and a foreign sector, the points on the *IS* curve are points at which planned injections into the circular flow of expenditure and income equal the planned leakages from the circular flow.

Figure A30.1 derives the IS curve. Figure A30.1(a) looks familiar, it is similar to Fig. 26.4 (p. 217). The 45° line shows all the points at which aggregate planned expenditure equals real GDP. Curves AE_a, AE_b, and AE_c are aggregate planned expenditure curves. Curve AE_a represents aggregate planned expenditure when the interest rate is 6 per cent (row *a* of the table). Curve AE_b shows aggregate planned expenditure when the interest rate is 5 per cent (row *b*) and AE_c shows aggregate planned expenditure when the interest rate is 4 per cent (row *c*).

There is just one expenditure equilibrium on each of these three aggregate planned expenditure curves. On curve AE_a, the expenditure equilibrium is at point *a*, where real GDP is $250 billion. The expenditure equilibrium on curve AE_b occurs at point *b*, where real GDP is $300 billion. The expenditure equilibrium on AE_c occurs at point *c*, where real GDP is $350 billion.

Figure A30.1(b) shows each expenditure equilibrium again but highlights the relationship between the interest rate and real GDP at the expenditure equilibrium. Its horizontal axis, like Fig. A30.1(a), measures real GDP. Its vertical axis measures the interest rate. Point *a* in Fig. A30.1(b) illustrates the expenditure equilibrium at point *a* in Fig. A30.1(a) of the figure (or in row *a* of the table). It tells us that if the interest rate is 6 per cent, the expenditure equilibrium occurs at a real GDP of $250 billion. Points *b* and *c* in Fig. A30.1(b) illustrate the expenditure equilibrium at points *b* and *c* of Fig. A30.1(a). The continuous line through these points is the *IS* curve.

It is often helpful to think of the relationships between two variables as one of 'cause' and 'effect'. For example, the investment demand curve tells us the level of investment (effect) at a particular interest rate (cause). The *IS* curve is *not* a 'cause and effect' relationship. Rather, it is a relationship that can be read in two ways. The *IS* curve that we have just derived tells us that if the interest rate is 6 per cent, then aggregate planned expenditure equals real GDP only if real GDP is $250 billion. But we can turn things around. If real GDP is $250 billion, the interest rate at which aggregate planned expenditure equals real GDP is 6 per cent. That is

The IS *curve shows combinations of the interest rate and real GDP at which there is an expenditure equilibrium.*

To determine the interest rate and real GDP, we need an additional relationship between those two variables. That second relationship between interest rates and real GDP comes from equilibrium in the money market.

Money Market Equilibrium

The quantity of money demanded depends on the price level, real GDP and the interest rate. The quantity of money demanded is proportional to the price level. If the price level doubles, so does the quantity of money demanded. Real money is the ratio of the quantity of money to the price level. The quantity of real money demanded increases as real GDP increases and decreases as the interest rate increases.

The supply of money is determined by the actions of the Reserve Bank, the banks and other financial intermediaries. Given those actions, and given the price level, there is a given quantity of real money in existence. Money market equilibrium occurs when the quantity of real money supplied is equal to the quantity demanded. Equilibrium in the money market is a stock equilibrium. Figure A30.2 contains a numerical example that enables us to study money market equilibrium.

Suppose that the quantity of money supplied is $200 billion. Also, suppose that the GDP deflator is 100 so that the quantity of real money supplied is also $200 billion. The real money supply is shown in the last row of the table. Money market equilibrium occurs when the quantity of real money demanded equals the quantity supplied — $200 billion. The quantity of real money demanded depends on real GDP and the interest rate. The table tells us about the demand for real money. Each row tells us how much real money is demanded at a given interest rate as real GDP varies, and each column tells us how much is demanded at a given real GDP as the interest rate varies. For example, at an interest rate of 6 per cent and with real GDP at $250 billion, the quantity of real money demanded is $150 billion. Alternatively, at an interest rate of 5 per cent and real GDP at $300 billion, the quantity of real money demanded is $200 billion. The rest of the numbers in the table are read in a similar way.

Money market equilibrium occurs when the quantity of real money demanded equals the quantity supplied — $200 billion. The green squares in the table highlight the combinations of interest rate and real GDP at which money market equilibrium occurs. If real GDP is $250 billion, the quantity of real money demanded is $200 billion when the interest rate is 4 per cent. Thus at real GDP of $250 billion and an interest rate of 4 per cent, the money market is in equilibrium. The other two green squares tell us the interest rate at which the quantity of real money demanded is $200 billion when real GDP is $300 billion and $350 billion respectively. That is, they illustrate the interest rates at which the money market is in equilibrium.

Figure A30.2 The Money Market, Stock Equilibrium and the *LM* Curve

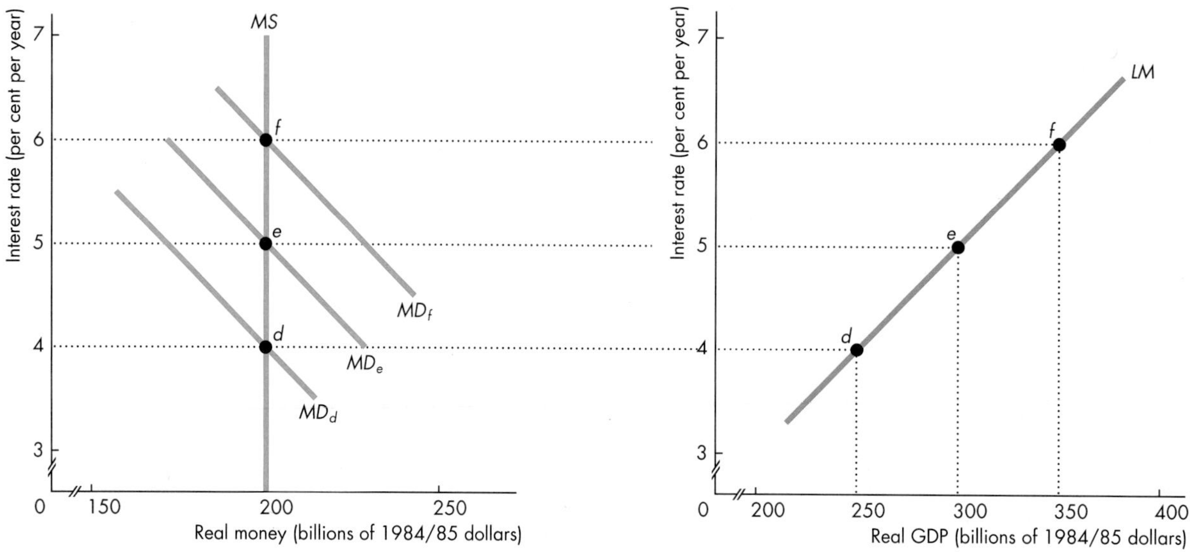

(a) Money market equilibrium

(b) The *LM* curve

The table shows the quantity of real money demanded at different combinations of the interest rate and real GDP. For example, if the interest rate is 6 per cent and real GDP is $250 billion, the quantity of real money demanded is $150 billion (top left number). Stock equilibrium — equality between the quantity of real money demanded and supplied — is shown by the green squares. Each column *d*, *e* and *f* represents a demand schedule for real money, plotted as the demand curves for real money MD_d, MD_e, and MD_f respectively in part (a). Money market equilibrium positions are shown in part (a), where these *MD* curves intersect the supply curve of real money *MS*, and are marked *d*, *e* and *f*. Part (b) shows these same equilibrium positions but highlights the combinations of the interest rate and real GDP at which they occur. The line connecting these points is the *LM* curve.

Interest rate (per cent per year)	Quantity of real money demanded (billions of 1984/85 dollars)		
6	150	175	200
5	175	200	225
4	200	225	250
Real GDP	250	300	350
Real money supply (billions of 1984/85 dollars)	200	200	200
	d	*e*	*f*

The *LM* Curve

The *LM* curve shows the combinations of real GDP and the interest rate at which the quantity of real money demanded equals the quantity of real money supplied. The name *LM* curve, like the name *IS* curve, was invented by John Hicks. The quantity of money demanded used to be called liquidity preference. The label *LM*, when first used, meant that liquidity preference (*L*) is equal to the quantity of money supplied (*M*).

Figure A30.2 derives the *LM* curve. Figure A30.2(a) shows the demand and supply curves for real mon ey. The quantity supplied is fixed at $200 billion so the supply curve *MS* is vertical. Each of the columns of the table labelled *d*, *e* and *f* is a demand schedule for real money — a schedule that tells us how the quantity of real money demanded rises as the interest rate falls. There is a different schedule for each level of real GDP. In Fig. A30.2(a), these three demand schedules for real money are graphed as demand curves for real money. That is, as MD_d, MD_e and MD_f. For example, when real GDP is $250 billion, the demand curve for real money is MD_d. Money market equilibrium occurs at the intersection of the supply curve and the demand curves for real money at points *d*, *e* and *f* in Fig. A30.2(a).

Figure A30.2(b) shows combinations of the interest rate and real GDP for which the money market is in equilibrium given different money demand curves. Points *d*, *e* and *f* in Fig. A30.2(b) illustrate the money market equilibrium represented by the green squares in the table and by those similarly labelled points in Fig. A30.2(a). The continuous line through these points is the *LM* curve. The *LM* curve shows the interest rate and real GDP at which money market equilibrium occurs when the real money supply is $200 billion.

Like the *IS* curve, the *LM* curve does not have a 'cause and effect' interpretation. The *LM* curve illustrated in Fig. A30.2(b) tells us that if the quantity of real money supplied is $200 billion and real GDP is $250 billion, then for money market equilibrium the interest rate is 4 per cent. It also tells us that if the quantity of real money supplied is $200 billion and the interest rate is 4 per cent, then for money market equilibrium real GDP is $250 billion. That is

> *The* LM *curve shows combinations of the interest rate and real GDP at which there is money market equilibrium.*

The Equilibrium Interest Rate and Real GDP

We now have two relationships between the interest rate and real GDP. The first — the *IS* curve — tells us the relationship between those two variables when aggregate planned expenditure equals real GDP. The second — the *LM* curve — tells us the relationship between real GDP and the interest rate when the quantity of real money demanded equals the quantity supplied. Neither of these two relationships, on its own, determines the interest rate or real GDP. Yet together they determine both real GDP and the interest rate (at a given price level). Let's see how.

Figure A30.3 brings together the *IS* curve and the *LM* curve to determine equilibrium real GDP and the interest rate. This equilibrium is the point of intersection of the *IS* curve and *LM* curve. Point *b* on the *IS* curve is a point of expenditure equilibrium. The interest rate and real GDP are such that aggregate planned expenditure equals real GDP. Point *c* on the *LM* curve is a point of money market equilibrium. The interest rate and real GDP are such that the quantity of real money demanded equals the quantity of real money supplied. At this intersection point, there is both flow equilibrium in the goods market and stock equilibrium in the money market. The equilibrium interest rate is 5 per cent and real GDP is $300 billion.

At all other points, there is either no expenditure equilibrium, or the money market is not in equilibrium, or both. At a point such as *a*, the economy is on its *IS* curve but off its *LM* curve. With real GDP at $250 billion and the interest rate at 6 per cent, the interest rate is too high or real GDP is too low for money market equilibrium. Interest rates adjust quickly and would fall to 4 per cent to bring about money market equilibrium, putting the economy at point *d*, a point on the *LM* curve. But point *d* is off the *IS* curve. At point *d*, with the interest rate at 4 per cent and real GDP at $250 billion, aggregate planned expenditure exceeds real GDP. By checking back to the table in Fig. A30.1, we can see that aggregate planned expenditure is $300 billion, which exceeds real GDP of $250 billion. With aggregate planned expenditure larger than real GDP, real GDP will increase. But as real GDP increases, so does the demand for real money and so does the interest rate. Real GDP and the interest rate would rise, and continue to do so, until the point of intersection of the *IS* and *LM* curves is reached.

The account that we have just given of what would happen if the economy was at a point like *a* or *d* tells us that the economy cannot be at such points. The forces that operate in such situations would be so strong that they would always push the economy to the intersection of the *IS* and *LM* curves.

The Aggregate Demand Curve

The aggregate demand curve traces the relationship between the quantity of real GDP demanded and the price level (the GDP deflator), holding everything else constant. Let's see how we can derive the aggregate demand curve from the *IS–LM* model. To derive the aggregate demand curve, we vary the price level and work out how equilibrium real GDP varies as we do so.

The role of the price level in the *IS–LM* model is in determining the quantity of real money supplied. The Reserve Bank determines the money supply as a certain number of

Figure A30.3 *IS–LM* Equilibrium

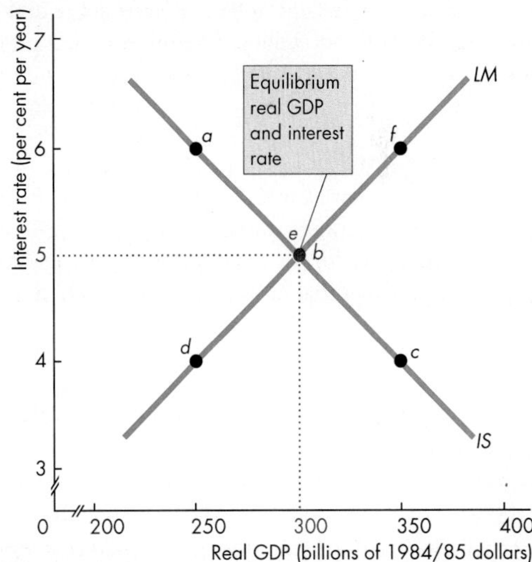

All points on the *IS* curve are points where aggregate planned expenditure equals real GDP. All points on the *LM* curve are points at which the quantity of real money demanded equals the quantity of real money supplied. The intersection of the *IS* curve and the *LM* curve determines the equilibrium interest rate and real GDP — 5 per cent and $300 billion. At this interest rate and real GDP, there is flow equilibrium in the goods market and stock equilibrium in the money market.

current dollars. The higher the price level, the lower is the real value of those dollars. Because the price level affects the quantity of real money supplied, it also affects the *LM* curve.[2] Let's see how.

The Effects of a Change in Price Level on the *LM* Curve

Let's begin by asking what happens if the price level, instead of being 100, is 114 — 14 per cent higher than before. The money supply is $200 billion. With a GDP deflator of 100, the real money supply is also $200 billion. But if the GDP deflator is 14 per cent higher, the real money supply is 14 per cent lower — $175 billion. (The real money supply is $200 billion divided by 1.14, which equals $175 billion.) We can see in the table in Fig. A30.2 that the quantity of real money demanded is $175 billion if real GDP is $300 billion and the interest rate is 6 per cent. Thus, a GDP deflator of 114, an interest rate of 6 per cent and real GDP of $300 billion determine a point on the *LM* curve. You can see this as point *g* in Fig. A30.4(a).

Next, suppose that the GDP deflator is lower than the original case — 89 instead of 100. Now the real money supply becomes $225 billion (the real money supply is $200 billion divided by 0.89, which equals $225 billion). Again for money market equilibrium we can see in the table of Fig. A30.2 what happens to the interest rate at a real GDP of $300 billion. With a GDP deflator of 89, the interest rate falls to 4 per cent in order to increase the quantity of real money demanded to $225 billion — equal to the real money supply. Thus, a GDP deflator of 89, an interest rate of 4 per cent and real GDP of $300 billion determine a point on the *LM* curve — point *h* in Fig. A30.4(a).

The *LM* Curve Shift

The example that we have worked through tells us that there is a different *LM* curve for each price level. Figure A30.4(a) illustrates the *LM* curves for the three different price levels we have considered. The initial *LM* curve has the GDP deflator equal to 100. This curve has been relabelled as LM_0 in Fig. A30.4(a). When the GDP deflator is 114 and real GDP is $300 billion, the interest rate that achieves equilibrium in the money market is 6 per cent. This equilibrium is shown as point *g* on curve LM_1 in Fig. A30.4(a). The entire *LM* curve shifts up to LM_1 in order to pass through point *g*. When the GDP deflator is 89 and real GDP is $300 billion, the interest rate that achieves equilibrium in the money market is 4 per cent. This equilibrium is shown as point h on the curve LM_2 in Fig. A30.4(a). Again, the entire *LM* curve shifts downward to LM_2 in order to pass through point *h*.

[2] In a more general version of the *IS–LM* model, the price level also affects the *IS* curve. Its effects come through the real balance effect on expenditure and the international substitution effect. In this appendix, we'll ignore those effects. In the real world, those effects reinforce the effects we are studying here.

Now that we have worked out the effects of a change in the price level on the position of the *LM* curve, we can derive the aggregate demand curve.

The Aggregate Demand Curve Derived

The aggregate demand curve shows how aggregate expenditure varies as the price level varies. We can derive the aggregate demand curve from the *IS–LM* model. Equilibrium in the *IS–LM* model determines real GDP for a given price level, such that the money market is in equilibrium and there is an expenditure equilibrium. Since there is an expenditure equilibrium, the equilibrium real GDP determined by the *IS–LM* model is also equal to aggregate expenditure. Therefore we can derive the aggregate demand curve by determining the equilibrium real GDP in the *IS–LM* model for a variety of different price levels.

Figure A30.4 shows the derivation. Figure A30.4(a) shows the *IS* curve and the three *LM* curves associated with the three different price levels (GDP deflators of 89, 100 and 114). When the GDP deflator is 100, the *LM* curve is LM_0. Equilibrium is at point *e*, where real GDP is $300 billion and the equilibrium interest rate is 5 per cent. If the GDP deflator is 114, the *LM* curve is LM_1 and equilibrium is at point *j*, where real GDP is $275 billion and the interest rate is 5.5 per cent. If the GDP deflator is 89, the *LM* curve is LM_2 and equilibrium is at point *k*, where real GDP is $325 billion and the interest rate is 4.5 per cent. At each price level there is a different equilibrium real GDP and interest rate.

Figure A30.4(b) traces the aggregate demand curve. The price level is measured on the vertical axis and real GDP on the horizontal axis. When the GDP deflator is 100, equilibrium real GDP is $300 billion (point *e*). When the GDP deflator is 114, equilibrium real GDP is $275 billion (point *j*). And when the GDP deflator is 89, real GDP demanded is $325 billion (point *k*). Each of these points corresponds to the same point in Fig. A30.4(a). The line joining these points in Fig. A30.4(b) is the aggregate demand curve.

Now that we have derived the aggregate demand curve and seen how it depends on flow equilibrium in the goods market and stock equilibrium in the money market, we can work out the effects on aggregate demand of changes in government expenditure on goods and services, taxes and the money supply. Let's begin with fiscal policy and work out its effects on aggregate demand.

Fiscal Policy and Aggregate Demand

A change in government purchases or in taxes shifts the *IS* curve and the aggregate demand curve. In Chapter 26 we worked out the magnitude of the change in aggregate planned expenditure resulting from a change in government purchases or in taxes when the interest rate is constant. In terms of the *IS–LM* model, these multiplier effects tell us how far the *IS* curve shifts. But the change in aggregate planned expenditure at a given interest rate is not the same thing as a change in aggregate demand. For, when aggregate planned expenditure

Figure A30.4 Deriving the Aggregate Demand Curve

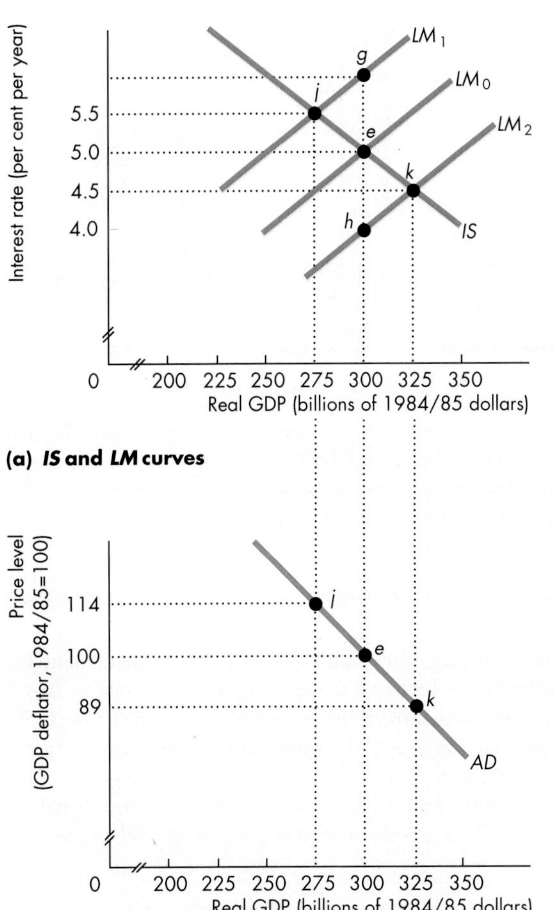

The position of the *LM* curve depends on the price level. In part (a), if the GDP deflator is 100, the *LM* curve is LM_0. If the GDP deflator increases to 114, the *LM* curve shifts to the left to LM_1. A lower real money supply requires a higher interest rate at each level of real GDP for money market equilibrium. For example, if real GDP is $300 billion, the interest rate has to increase from 5 per cent to 6 per cent (point *g*). If the price level falls, the real money supply increases and the *LM* curve shifts to the right to LM_2. If real GDP is $300 billion the interest rate falls to 4 per cent (point *h*) to maintain money market equilibrium. When the GDP deflator is 100, the *IS* and *LM* curves intersect at point *e* — at an interest rate of 5 per cent and real GDP of $300 billion. This equilibrium is shown again in part (b) at point *e* on aggregate demand curve *AD*. This point tells us that when the GDP deflator is 100, the quantity of real GDP demanded is $300 billion. If the GDP deflator is 114, the *LM* curve is LM_1. The equilibrium interest rate is 5.5 per cent and real GDP is $275 billion. A second point on the aggregate demand curve is found at *j*. If the GDP deflator is 89, the *LM* curve is LM_2, the interest rate is 4.5 per cent and real GDP is $325 billion. Hence another point on the aggregate demand curve is generated at point *k*. Joining points *j*, *e* and *k* gives the aggregate demand curve.

changes, the interest rate usually changes as well and that has further effects on expenditure plans.

Figure A30.5 illustrates three different effects of a change in fiscal policy. In all three parts of the figure, the same fiscal policy action takes place. There is either a rise in government purchases or a cut in autonomous taxes that shifts the *IS* curve from IS_0 to IS_1. In Fig. A30.5(a), the normal case, the *LM* curve is upward-sloping (LM_N). When the *IS* curve shifts, the interest rate increases and so does real GDP. But the increase in real GDP is smaller than the magnitude of the shift to the right of the *IS* curve. The reason is that the higher interest rate leads to a decrease in private investment, and this decrease in investment partially offsets the initial increased spending resulting from the fiscal policy action.

In Fig. A30.5(b), the *LM* curve is horizontal (LM_H). The *LM* curve is horizontal only if there is a 'liquidity trap' — a situation in which people are willing to hold any quantity of money at a given interest rate. When the *IS* curve shifts to the right, real GDP increases by the same amount as the shift to the right of the *IS* curve. Interest rates stay constant. In this case, the multiplier effect of Chapter 26 still operates.

In Fig. A30.5(c), the *LM* curve is vertical (LM_V). Although the *IS* curve shifts to the right by exactly the same amount as in Fig. A30.5(a) and (b), real GDP stays constant. Here, the interest rate increases. The higher interest rate leads to a decrease in private investment that exactly offsets the initial increase in expenditure resulting from the fiscal policy. There is complete crowding out. Complete crowding out occurs if the demand for real money is completely insensitive to interest rates. No matter what the interest rate, the quantity of real money demanded is a constant portion of real GDP.

Figure A30.5(b) corresponds to the extreme Keynesian prediction, Fig. A30.5(c) to the extreme monetarist prediction and Fig. A30.5(a) to the intermediate position.

Next, let's consider monetary policy.

Figure A30.5 Fiscal Policy and Aggregate Demand

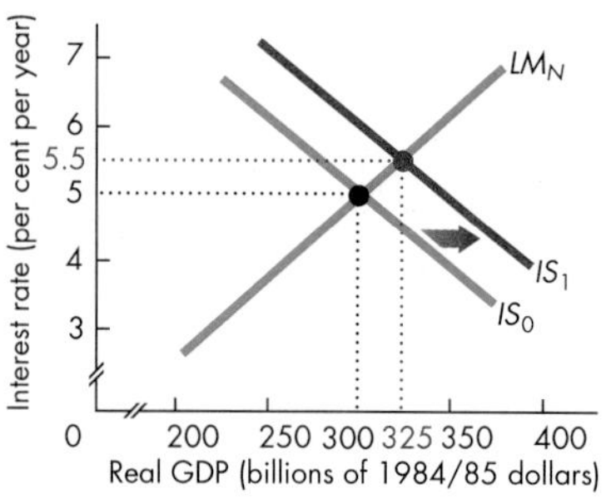

(a) Fiscal policy: normal case

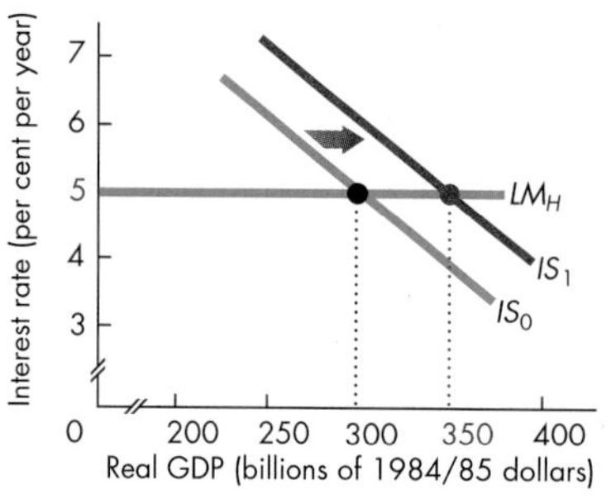

(b) Fiscal policy: maximum effect on GDP

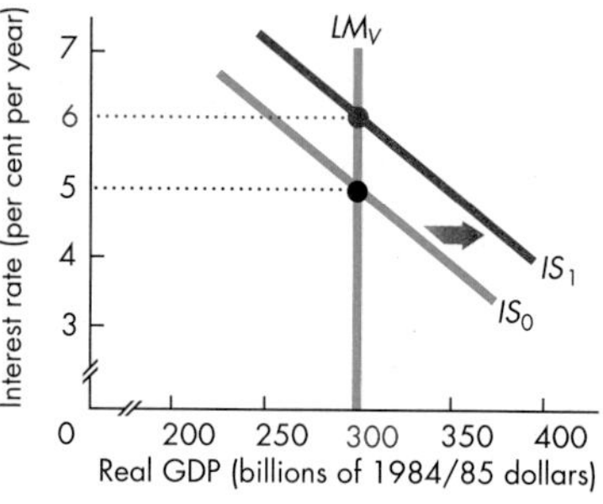

(c) Fiscal policy: no effect on GDP

An increase in government purchases or an autonomous tax cut shifts the *IS* curve to the right. The effects of fiscal policy on real GDP and the interest rate depend on the slope of the *LM* curve. In the normal case (part a), interest rates and real GDP rise. If there is a liquidity trap, the *LM* curve is horizontal — part *b* — and real GDP increases but interest rates stay constant. If the demand for money is insensitive to interest rates, the *LM* curve is vertical — part *c* — and interest rates rise but real GDP stays constant. In this case, there is complete 'crowding out'. The higher interest rate leads to a cut in investment that exactly offsets the initial fiscal policy action.

Monetary Policy and Aggregate Demand

We saw earlier in this appendix that when the *LM* curve shifts because of a change in the price level, equilibrium real GDP changes and there is a movement along the aggregate demand curve. But a change in the money supply also shifts the *LM* curve. If the *LM* curve shifts because there is a change in the nominal money supply, then the aggregate demand curve shifts. The magnitude of the change in aggregate demand — the shift in the aggregate demand curve — depends on two factors: the size of the shift of the *LM* curve and the slope of the *IS* curve. Figure A30.6 shows three possible cases. In each case, the *LM* curve shifts to the right by the same amount, from LM_0 to LM_1. In Fig. A30.6(a), the normal case, the *IS* curve is downward sloping (IS_N). When the

Figure A30.6 Monetary Policy and Aggregate Demand

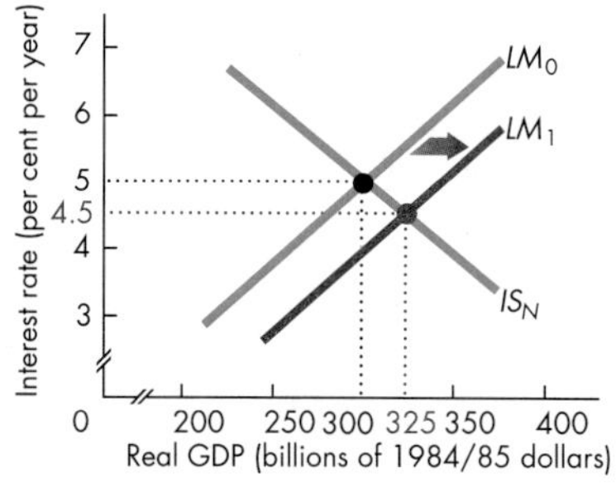

(a) Monetary policy: normal case

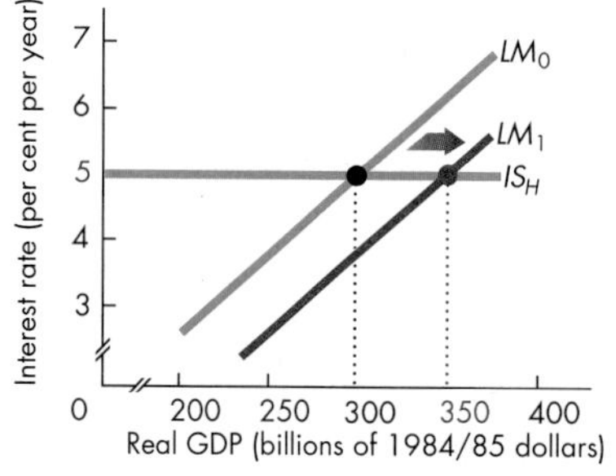

(b) Monetary policy: maximum effect on GDP

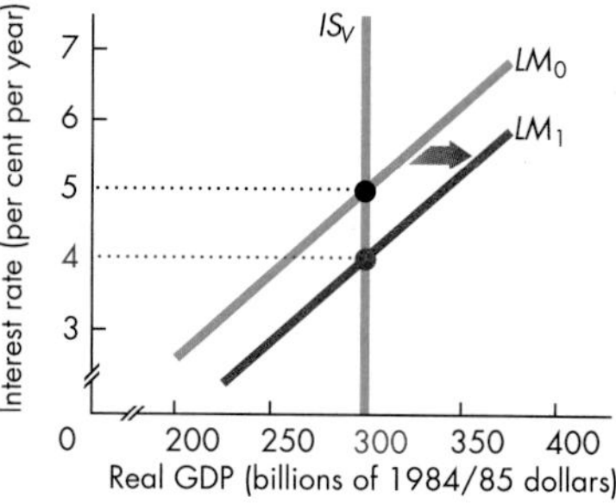

(c) Monetary policy: no effect on GDP

An increase in the money supply shifts the *LM* curve to the right. The effect of the monetary action on interest rates and real GDP depends on the slope of the *IS* curve. In the normal case, shown in part (a) interest rates fall and real GDP rises. The lower interest rates stimulate investment. In the special case, part (b), the *IS* curve is horizontal. The change in the money supply changes real GDP but leaves the interest rate constant. If investment demand is completely insensitive to interest rates, part (c), the *IS* curve is vertical and a change in the money supply lowers interest rates but leaves real GDP unchanged. In this case, the lower interest rate has no effect on investment, so there is no initial injection of additional expenditure.

money supply increases, the interest rate falls and real GDP rises. The rise in real GDP results from increased investment induced by the lower interest rate.

In Fig. A30.6(b), the *IS* curve is horizontal (IS_H). This situation arises if people retime their investment whenever the interest rate rises above or falls below 5 per cent. If the interest rate rises above 5 per cent, all investment stops; if the interest rate falls below 5 per cent, there is no limit to the amount of investment that people try to undertake. At 5 per cent, any amount of investment will be undertaken. In this case, a change in the money supply shifts the *LM* curve and increases real GDP but leaves the interest rate unchanged.

In Fig. A30.6(c), the IS curve is vertical (IS_V). This case arises if investment is completely insensitive to interest rates. People plan to undertake a given level of investment regardless of the interest cost involved. In this case, when the *LM* curve shifts, interest rates fall but the lower interest rate does not stimulate additional expenditure, so real GDP stays constant.

Figure A30.6(c) corresponds to the views of extreme Keynesians. A change in the money supply has no effect on real GDP. Figure A30.6(b) corresponds to the predictions of monetarists. A change in the money supply has a large and powerful effect on real GDP. Figure A30.6(a) is the intermediate position.

Chapter 31

Unemployment and Aggregate Supply

After studying this chapter, you will be able to:

- Explain why real GDP and employment fluctuate together.
- Explain how firms decide how much labour to employ.
- Explain how households decide how much labour to supply.
- Explain how wages, employment and unemployment are determined if wages are flexible.
- Explain how wages, employment and unemployment are determined if wages are 'sticky'.
- Derive the short-run and long-run aggregate supply curves.
- Explain the influences that shift the aggregate supply curves.

Jobs and Incomes

As our economy ebbs and flows through the business cycle, employment and unemployment and real GDP march in close step with each other. Sometimes the Australian economy is in a state of deep recession — real GDP has fallen and the unemployment rate is high. Such a situation prevailed in 1983 when, at one point during the year, more than 11 per cent of the workforce was without a job. In 1991, over 10 per cent of the workforce was unemployed. In both those periods of high unemployment, a large number of those unemployed were considered 'long-term unemployed'. That is, they had been unemployed for twelve months or longer. In contrast, at the end of 1989, the Australian economy had experienced six years of continuous recovery and unemployment was 6 per cent. Why does unemployment occur? Why, at times, are more than one in ten people of working age unsuccessfully looking for a job? What makes the unemployment rate rise and fall? Q More than 50,000 manufacturing jobs disappeared during 1990 as the recession and tariff cuts forced factories to close or lay off workers. But at one factory, an SPC cannery in Victoria, more than 650 workers negotiated pay cuts rather than lose their jobs. Why don't more firms and workers undertake such negotiations to avoid plant closures and unemployment? Q The opposite of unemployment is overtime working. Many firms routinely work overtime and when the economy is booming most firms are in that situation. But even while some firms are paying overtime to their workers, other people are still without jobs. Why? Why don't the unemployed get jobs and the employed work normal hours for normal wages? Why does full employment really mean some unemployment?

In this chapter we'll take a close look at the Australian labour market. We'll attempt to discover why the unemployment rate is sometimes unusually high and what brings high unemployment rates down. Our study of labour markets will take us to the heart of the current controversy in macroeconomics. The controversy is about how flexible the labour market is in bringing about changes in wages to equate the quantity of labour supplied with the quantity demanded. Some economists see the labour market as a highly flexible and sophisticated instrument that maintains equality between the quantities demanded and supplied on a continuous basis. In the view of these economists, unemployment arises mainly from frictions and from the fact that it takes time for labour to be re-allocated from one sector to another, or from one region of the country to another. That is, they explain fluctuations in unemployment as fluctuations in the natural rate of unemployment.

Another group of macroeconomists believe that wages do not adjust quickly enough to maintain equality between the quantity of labour supplied and the quantity demanded. In the view of these economists, wages are sometimes 'too high' and, as a consequence, the quantity of labour demanded is less than the quantity supplied and unemployment is above its natural rate.

Our study of the labour market will complete a further block in the macroeconomic jigsaw puzzle — the aggregate supply-side block. We'll return to the short-run and long-run aggregate supply curves that you met in Chapter 24 and see how those curves are related to the labour market. We'll discover that, along the long-run aggregate supply curve, the quantity of labour demanded equals the quantity supplied; and we'll see how the levels of employment and unemployment change as the economy slides along its short-run aggregate supply curve. But, to understand these connections, we must first study the relationship between employment and real GDP.

Figure 31.1 Short–Run Aggregate Production Function

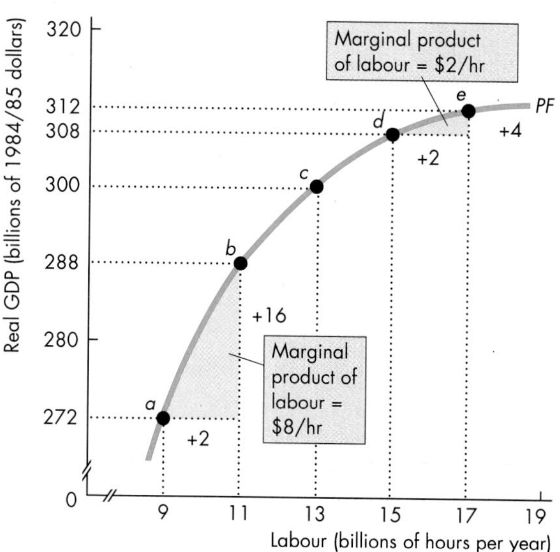

	Labour (billions of hours per year)	Real GDP (billions of 1984/85 dollars per year)
a	9	272
b	11	288
c	13	300
d	15	308
e	17	312

The short-run aggregate production function shows the level of real GDP at each quantity of labour input, holding constant the stock of capital equipment and state of technology. The table lists five points on a short-run aggregate production function. Each row tells us the amount of real GDP that can be produced by a given labour input. Points *a* to *e* in the graph correspond to the rows in the table. The curve passing through these points traces the economy's short-run aggregate production function. The marginal product of labour is highlighted in the diagram. As the labour input increases, real GDP also increases, but by successively smaller amounts. For example, a 2 billion hour increase in labour from 9 to 11 billion hours per year increases real GDP by $16 billion — a marginal product of $8 an hour. But a 2 billion hour increase in labour from 15 to 17 billion hours per year increases real GDP by only $4 billion — a marginal product of $2 an hour.

The Short-Run Aggregate Production Function

A **production function** shows how output varies as the usage of inputs is varied. A short-run production function shows how output varies when the quantity of labour employed varies, holding constant the quantity of capital and the state of technology. Although production functions exist for every kind of economic activity — building dams and highways or baking loaves of bread — the production function we will study in this chapter is the short-run aggregate production function. The **short-run aggregate production function** shows how real GDP varies as the quantity of labour employed is varied, holding the capital stock and state of technology constant.

The table in Fig. 31.1 records part of an economy's short-run aggregate production function (*PF*). In that table, we look at the aggregate quantity of labour, measured in billions of hours a year, over the range 9 billion hours to 17 billion hours. Through that range of employment, real GDP varies between $272 billion and $312 billion a year (measured in 1984/5 dollars).

The short-run aggregate production function is illustrated in the graph in Fig. 31.1. The labour input is measured on the horizontal axis and real GDP on the vertical axis. The short-run production function slopes upward, indicating that more labour input produces more real GDP.

The Marginal Product of Labour

The **marginal product of labour** is the additional real GDP produced by one additional hour of labour input, holding all other inputs and technology constant. We calculate the marginal product of labour as the change in real GDP divided by the change in the quantity of labour employed. Let's do such a calculation, using Fig. 31.1.

When the labour input increases by 2 billion hours from 9 to 11 billion hours per year, real GDP increases from \$272 billion to \$288 billion — an increase of \$16 billion. The marginal product of labour, over this range, is \$8 an hour (\$16 billion divided by 2 billion hours). Next, look at what happens at a higher level of labour input. When the labour input increases again by 2 billion hours per year, but from 15 million to 17 billion hours, real GDP increases but by much less than in the previous case — it increases by only \$4 billion. Now the marginal product of labour is only \$2 an hour (\$4 billion divided by 2 billion hours).

The marginal product of labour is measured by the slope of the production function. Figure 31.1 highlights this fact. The average slope of the production function between points *a* and *b* is \$8 per hour as we calculated above. Similarly, the average slope of the production function between points *d* and *e* is \$2 an hour.

Diminishing Marginal Product of Labour The most important fact about the marginal product of labour, apparent from the calculations that we've just performed and visible in the figure, is that it declines as the labour input increases. This phenomenon is called the diminishing marginal product of labour. The **diminishing marginal product of labour**, is the tendency for the marginal product of labour to decline as the labour input increases, holding everything else constant. Diminishing marginal product of labour is a feature of almost every production process. It arises because we are dealing with a *short-run* production function. As the quantity of labour employed is varied, all other inputs are held constant. Thus, although more labour can produce more output, the additional labour operates the same capital equipment — machines and tools — as a smaller labour force would. As more people are hired, the capital equipment is worked closer and closer to its physical limits and output cannot be increased in proportion to the increased labour input. This feature is present in almost all production processes and is also present in the relationship between aggregate employment and aggregate output — real GDP.

The fact that the marginal product of labour diminishes has an important influence on the demand for labour, as we shall see shortly. But first, let's look at some of the things that make the production function shift.

Economic Growth and Technological Change

Economic growth is the expansion of the economy's productive capacity. Every year, some of the economy's resources are devoted to developing new tech-

Figure 31.2 The Growth of Output

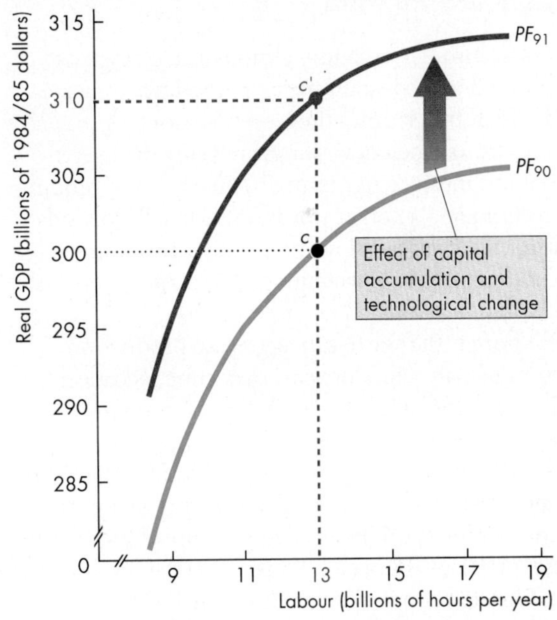

Output grows over time. The accumulation of capital and the adoption of more productive technologies make it possible to achieve a higher level of real GDP for any given labour input. For example, between 1990 and 1991 the production function shifts upward from PF_{90} to PF_{91}. A labour input of 13 billion hours a year produces \$300 billion of real GDP in 1990 (point c) and \$310 billion in 1991 (point c′).

nologies to achieve greater output from a given amount of labour input. Also, resources are devoted to building new capital equipment that incorporates the most productive technologies available. Because capital accumulates and technology advances, the short-run aggregate production function shifts upward over time. Figure 31.2 illustrates such a shift. The curve labelled PF_{90} is the same as the production function in Fig. 31.1. During 1990, capital accumulated and new technologies were incorporated into the new, and more productive, capital equipment. Some old and less productive capital wears out and is retired to the scrap heap. The net result is an increase in the productivity of the economy that results in an upward movement of the short-run aggregate production function to PF_{91}. When 13 billion hours a year of labour are employed, the economy can produce a real GDP of $300 billion in 1990 (point *c*). By 1991, that same quantity of labour can produce $310 billion (point *c′*). Each level of labour input produces more output in 1991 than in 1990.

Variable Growth Rates

Capital accumulation and technological change do not proceed at a constant pace. Sometimes they are rapid and at other times they are very slow. Also, there are times when new things are being discovered but not put into practice through innovation in production techniques. In other words, there may be periods of rapid invention but slow innovation. **Invention** is the discovery of a new technique. **Innovation** is the act of putting a new technique into operation.

Though the short-run aggregate production function usually shifts upward over time, occasionally it shifts downward — lowering the economy's production potential. Negative influences, or shocks, that make the aggregate production function shift downward are widespread droughts, major disruptions to international trade, widespread industrial unrest, major civil unrest or war. A serious disruption of international trade occurred in 1974 when the Organization of Petroleum Exporting Countries (OPEC) placed an embargo on oil exports, depriving the industrialized world of one of its most crucial natural resources. Firms could not obtain all the fuel they needed, and as a result, the labour force could not produce as much output as it normally would. As a consequence of that embargo, the short-run aggregate production function shifted downward in 1974.

Let's take a closer look at the short-run aggregate production function in Australia.

The Australian Short-Run Aggregate Production Function

We can examine the short-run aggregate production function in Australia by looking at the relationship between real GDP and aggregate employment.

Figure 31.3 measures real GDP on the vertical axis and the quantity of labour on the horizontal axis. The values of these two variables are plotted for each year between 1966/67 and 1990/91. For example, in 1966/67 non-farm labour hours were 8.6 bil-

Figure 31.3 The Australian Short-Run Aggregate Production Function, 1966/67–1990/91

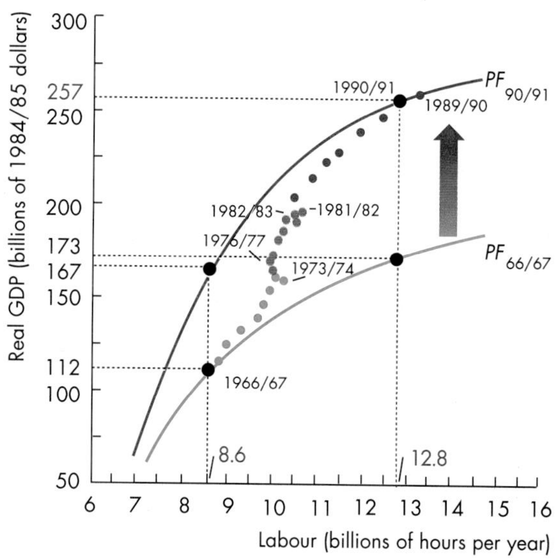

The points in the figure show real GDP and aggregate hours of labour employed in Australia for each year between 1966/67 and 1989/90. For example, in 1966/67 labour input was 8.6 billion hours and real GDP was $112 billion. In 1990/91 labour input was 12.8 billion hours and real GDP was $257 billion. The points do not lie on one short-run aggregate production function. Instead, the short-run aggregate production function shifts from year to year as capital accumulates and technologies change. The figure shows the short-run aggregate production functions for 1966/67 and 1990/91 — $PF_{66/67}$ and $PF_{90/91}$. The 1990/91 production function is 54 per cent higher than that for 1966/67. For example, the 8.6 billion hours of labour that produced $112 billion of real GDP in 1966/67 would have produced $167 billion of real GDP in 1990/91. Similarly, the 12.8 billion hours of labour that produced $257 billion of real GDP in 1990/91 would have produced only $173 billion of real GDP in 1966/67.

Source: Real GDP: see Fig. 22.4; Labour: based on calculations on NIF-105 Model Data, supplied by EconData's dX Data Service.

lion and real GDP was $112 billion; in 1990/91 labour hours were 12.8 billion and real GDP was $257 billion. These two points, together with the other points in the figure, do not all lie on the same short-run aggregate production function. Instead, they each lie on their own short-run aggregate production function. Each year the stock of capital equipment and the state of technology change, so that the economy's productive potential is usually higher than in the year before. The production function for 1966/67 is $PF_{66/67}$ and that for 1990/91is $PF_{90/91}$.

The 1990/91 short-run production function is 54 per cent higher than the 1966/67 aggregate production function. This fact means that, if employment in 1990/91 had been the same as it was in 1966/67, real GDP in 1990/91 would have been only $173 billion. Equivalently, if employment in 1966/67 had been the same as it was in 1990/91, real GDP in 1966/67 would have been $167 billion.

Note that the slope of the production function at 12.8 billion hours in 1990/91 is steeper than the slope of the production function at 8.6 billion hours in 1966/67. This indicates that the marginal product of labour has risen.

The difference between real GDP in 1990/91 and in 1966/67 is partly accounted for by an increase in capital stock and technological change that shifted the short-run aggregate production function upward, and partly by an increase in employment from 8.6 billion hours to 12.8 billion hours that produced a movement along the new short-run production function.

Figure 31.3 also indicates three periods, 1973/74 to 1977/78, 1980/81 to 1982/83 and 1989/90 to 1990/91, when the total quantity of labour employed, measured in total *hours* of labour, actually declined. The first period followed a negative external shock to oil prices. During the second period there was a high level of industrial unrest and a severe drought. The most recent decline was due to a monetary policy-induced recession. It is likely that the production function, itself, did not shift. In the period 1973/74 to 1977/78 the number of workers actually employed rose, but in the latter two periods, the number of workers employed fell. In all cases, the average hours worked by each person also fell significantly.

R E V I E W

A production function tells us how the output that can be produced varies as inputs are varied. A short-run production function tells us how the output that can be produced varies as the employment of labour varies, holding everything else constant. The short-run aggregate production function tells us how real GDP varies as total labour hours vary. The marginal product of labour — the increase in real GDP resulting from a one-hour increase of labour input — diminishes as the labour input increases.

The short-run production function usually shifts upward from year to year but, occasionally, it shifts downward. Capital accumulation and technological advances shift the short-run aggregate production function upward. Shocks such as droughts, disruptions of international trade, industrial unrest, or civil and political unrest shift the production function downward. The short-run aggregate production function in Australia shifted upward by 54 per cent between 1966/67 and 1990/91. ■

We've seen that the level of output in any given year depends on the position of the short-run aggregate production function and on the quantity of labour employed. But to determine the level of output we need to understand not only the influences on the short-run aggregate production function, but also those which affect the level of employment. To determine the level of employment, we need to study the demand for and supply of labour and how the market allocates labour to jobs. We'll begin by studying the demand for labour.

The Demand for Labour

The **quantity of labour demanded** is the number of labour hours hired by all the firms in an economy. The **demand for labour** is a schedule or curve that shows the quantity of labour demanded at each level of the real wage rate. The **real wage rate** is the wage per hour expressed in constant dollars — for example, the wage per hour expressed in 1984/85 dollars. The wage rate expressed in *current dollars* is called the **money wage rate.** The real wage rate is the money wage rate divided by the GDP deflator and multiplied by 100. A real wage rate expressed in 1984/85 dollars tells us what today's money wage rate would buy if prices today were the same as in 1984/85. For example, if today the money wage rate is $13.50 per hour and the GDP deflator is 141, the real wage rate is $9.57 ($13.50 divided by 141 and multiplied by 100 equals $9.57).

An example of a demand for labour schedule is shown in the table of Fig. 31.4. Row *d* tells us that at a real wage rate of $9 an hour, 15 billion hours of labour (per year) are demanded. The other rows of the table are read in a similar way. The demand for labour schedule is graphed as the demand for labour curve (*LD*). Each point on the curve corresponds to the row identified by the same letter in the table.

Figure 31.4 Demand for Labour

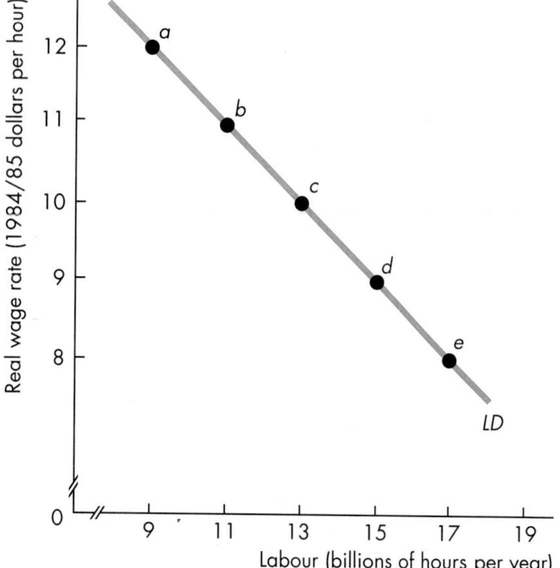

	Real wage rate (1984/85 dollars per hour)	Quantity of labour demanded (billions of hours per year)
a	12	9
b	11	11
c	10	13
d	9	15
e	8	17

The quantity of labour demanded increases as the real wage rate decreases, as illustrated by the labour demand schedule in the table and the demand for labour curve (*LD*). Each row in the table tells us the quantity of labour demanded at a given real wage rate and corresponds to a point on the labour demand curve. For example, when the real wage rate is $9 an hour, the quantity of labour demanded is 15 billion hours a year (point *d*). The demand for labour curve slopes downward because it pays firms to hire labour so long as its marginal product is greater than or equal to the real wage. The lower the real wage rate, the larger is the number of workers whose marginal product exceeds that real wage.

Why is the quantity of labour demanded influenced by the *real* wage rate? Why isn't it the *money* wage rate that affects the quantity of labour demanded? Also, why does the quantity of labour demanded increase as the real wage rate decreases? That is, why does the demand for labour curve slope downward? We're now going to answer these questions.

Diminishing Marginal Product and the Demand for Labour

Firms are in business to maximize profits. Each worker that a firm hires adds to its costs and increases its output. Up to a point, the extra output produced by the worker is worth more to the firm than the extra wages the firm has to pay. But each additional hour of labour hired produces less output than the previous hour — the marginal product of labour diminishes. As the amount of labour employed varies and the capital equipment employed is constant, more workers have to work the same machines and the plant operates closer and closer to its physical limits. Output increases, but it does not increase in proportion to the increase in labour input. As the firm hires more workers, it eventually reaches the point where the revenue from selling the extra output produced by an additional hour of labour equals the hourly wage rate. But, if the firm hires even one more hour of labour, the extra cost incurred will exceed the revenue brought in from selling the extra output. The firm will not employ that additional hour of labour. It stops at the point at which the revenue brought in by the last hour of labour input equals the wage rate.

To see why the real wage, rather than the money wage, affects the quantity of labour demanded, let's consider an example.

The Demand for Labour in a Brewery Suppose a brewery employs 400 hours of labour. The additional output produced by the last hour hired is 11 bottles of beer. That is, the marginal product of labour is 11 bottles of beer an hour. Beer sells for $1 a bottle, so the revenue brought in from selling these 11 bottles is $11. Suppose the money wage rate is also $11 an hour. This last hour of labour hired brings in as much revenue as the wages paid out, so it just pays the firm to hire that hour of labour. The firm is paying a real wage rate that is exactly the same as the marginal product of labour — 11 bottles of beer. That is, the real wage rate is equal to the money wage rate of $11 an hour divided by the price of beer, $1 a bottle.

To see why the real wage affects the quantity of labour demanded, let's work out what happens if the money wage rate increases to $22 an hour while the price of beer remains constant at $1 a bottle. The real wage rate has now increased to an equivalent of 22 bottles of beer — equal to the money wage of $22 an hour divided by $1 a bottle, the price of a bottle of beer. The last hour of labour hired now costs $22 but brings in only $11 of extra revenue. It does not pay the firm to hire this hour of labour. The firm cuts back the scale of its labour input until its marginal product brings in $22 of revenue. That occurs when the marginal product of labour is 22 bottles an hour — that is, 22 bottles at $1 a bottle sell for $22. The marginal product is again equal to the real wage rate. But to make the marginal product of labour equal to the real wage rate, the firm has to decrease the quantity of labour employed. Thus when the real wage rate increases, the quantity demanded decreases.

In this example, the real wage increased because the money wage increased with a constant output price. But the same outcome occurs if the money wage remains constant and the output price decreases. For example, if the wage rate remains at $11 an hour while the price of beer falls to 50 cents a bottle, the real wage is 22 bottles of beer and the brewery hires the amount of labour that makes the marginal product of labour equal to 22 bottles an hour.

To see why the money wage rate does *not* affect the quantity of labour demanded, suppose that the money wage rate and all prices double. The money wage rate increases to $22 an hour and the price of beer increases to $2 a bottle. In real terms, the brewery is in the same situation as before. It pays $22 for the last hour of labour employed and sells the output produced by that labour for $22. The money wage rate has doubled from $11 to $22 an hour but nothing *real* has changed. The real wage rate is still 11 bottles of beer. As far as the firm is concerned, 400 hours is still the right quantity of labour to hire. The money wage rate has changed but the real wage rate and the quantity of labour demanded have remained constant.

The Demand for Labour in the Economy The demand for labour in the economy as a whole is determined in the same way as in the brewery that we've just studied. Thus the quantity of labour demanded depends on the real wage rate, not the money wage rate, and the higher the real wage rate, the smaller is the quantity of labour demanded.

We now know why the quantity of labour demanded depends on the real wage and why the demand for labour curve slopes downward, but what makes it shift?

Shifts in the Demand for Labour Curve

When the marginal product of each hour of labour changes, the demand for labour curve shifts. The accumulation of capital and the development of new technologies are constantly increasing the marginal product of each hour of labour. We've already seen one effect of such changes. They shift the short-run aggregate production function upward, as shown in Fig. 31.2. At the same time, they make the short-run aggregate production function steeper. Anything that makes the short-run production function steeper increases the marginal product of each hour of labour — increases the extra output obtained from one additional hour of labour. At a given real wage rate, firms will increase the amount of labour they hire until the revenue brought in from selling the extra output produced by the last hour of labour input equals the hourly wage. Thus, as the short-run aggregate production function shifts upward, the demand for labour curve also shifts to the right.

In general, the demand for labour curve shifts to the right over time. But there are fluctuations in the pace at which the demand for labour curve shifts and these match the fluctuations in the short-run aggregate production function. Fluctuations in the production function produce changes in the demand for labour, which in turn produce fluctuations in employment, real GDP and the real wage rate.

Let's look at the demand for labour in Australia and see how it has changed over the period since 1966/67.

The Australian Demand for Labour

Figure 31.5 shows the real wage rate and the quantity of labour employed in each year between 1966/67 and 1990/91. For example, in 1990/91 the real wage was $10.18 an hour (in 1984/85 dollars) and 12.8 billion hours of labour were employed. The figure also shows two labour demand curves, one for 1966/67 ($LD_{66/67}$) and the other for 1990/91 ($LD_{90/91}$). Between 1966/67 and 1990/91, the production function shifted upward and the marginal product of labour increased.

Figure 31.5 The Australian Demand for Labour, 1966/67 to 1990/91

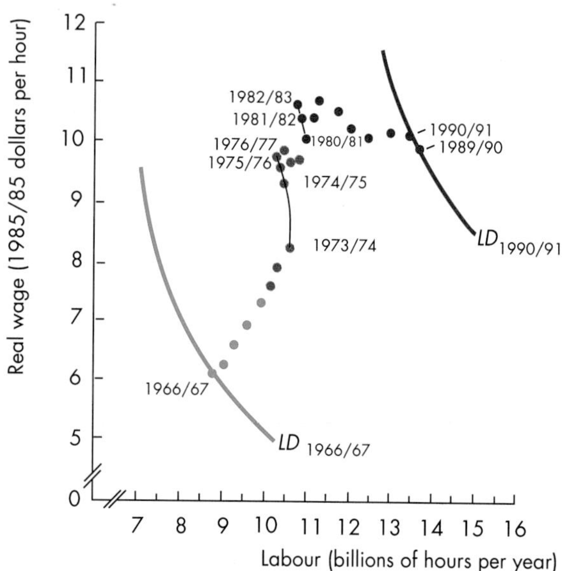

The figure shows the quantity of labour employed and real wages in Australia from 1966/67 to 1990/91. For example, in 1966/67 the real wage was $6.09 an hour and 8.6 billion hours of labour were employed. In 1990/91 the real wage was $10.18 an hour and 12.8 billion hours of labour were employed. These two points (and the points for the years between them) do not lie on a single demand for labour curve. The demand for labour curve has shifted as a result of shifts in the short-run aggregate production function. The figure shows the demand curves for 1966/67 and 1990/91 — $LD_{66/67}$ and $LD_{90/91}$. Over time, the demand for labour curve has shifted to the right.

Source: See Fig. 31.3

Again note the labour market outcomes for the periods from 1973/74 to 1977/78 and from 1980/81 to 1982/83. Each period was one in which labour markets allowed very large pay increases to workers — so-called 'wages breakouts'. The comparative size of the real wage increase in each instance is indicated by how far above the previous point the next one is. It seems that the real wage increase assigned to workers in the respective periods was so high that, even if the demand curve for labour shifted out as a result of technological progress and capital accumulation, the quantity of labour demanded fell. That is, there was a movement back along the demand curves in the periods from 1973/74 to 1977/78, from 1980/81 to 1982/83 and in 1990/91.

R E V I E W

The quantity of labour demanded by firms depends on the real wage rate. For an individual firm, the real wage rate is the money wage rate paid to the worker divided by the price for which the firm's output sells. For the economy as a whole, the real wage rate is the money wage rate divided by the price level. The lower the real wage rate, the greater is the quantity of labour demanded. The demand for labour curve slopes downward.

The demand for labour curve shifts because of shifts in the short-run aggregate production function. An increase in the capital stock or advances in technology embodied in the capital stock shift the short-run aggregate production function upward and increase the marginal product of labour. The demand for labour curve shifts to the right, but at an uneven pace. On some occasions, real wages increase faster than the demand curve shifts to the right. In such periods, the quantity of labour demanded falls. ■

Let's now turn to the other side of the labour market and see how the supply of labour is determined.

The Supply of Labour

The **quantity of labour supplied** is the number of hours of labour services that households supply to firms. The **supply of labour** is a schedule or curve that shows how the quantity of labour supplied varies as the real wage varies.

A supply of labour schedule appears in the table in Fig. 31.6. Row *a* tells us that, at a real wage rate of $8 an hour, 9 billion hours of labour (a year) are supplied. The other rows of the table are read in a similar way. The supply of labour schedule is graphed as the supply of labour curve (*LS*). Each point on the *LS* curve represents the row identified by the same letter in the table. As the real wage increases, the quantity of labour supplied increases. The supply of labour curve slopes upward.

But why does the quantity of labour supplied increase when the real wage increases? There are two reasons:

- Hours per worker increase
- The labour force participation rate increases.

Figure 31.6 The Supply of Labour

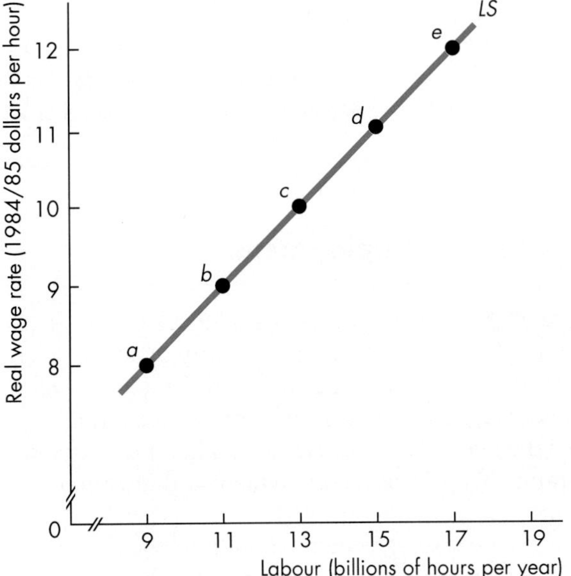

	Real wage rate (1984/85 dollars per hour)	Quantity of labour supplied (billions of hours per year)
a	8	9
b	9	11
c	10	13
d	11	15
e	12	17

The quantity of labour supplied increases as the real wage rate increases, as illustrated by the labour supply schedule in the table and the supply of labour curve (*LS*). Each row of the table tells us the quantity of labour supplied at a given real wage rate and corresponds to a point on the labour supply curve. For example, when the real wage rate is $9 an hour, the quantity of labour supplied is 11 billion hours a year (point *b*). The supply of labour curve slopes upward because households work longer hours, on the average, at higher wages and more households participate in the labour force. These responses are reinforced by intertemporal substitution — the retiming of work to take advantage of temporarily high wages.

The Determination of Hours per Worker

In choosing how many hours to work, a household has to decide how to allocate its time between work and other activities. If a household chooses not to work for an hour, it does not get paid for that hour. The real hourly wage rate that the household gives up is the opportunity cost of an hour of not working. What the household really gives up by not working is all the goods and services that it could buy with the hourly money wage. So the opportunity cost of an hour of time spent not working is the real hourly wage rate.

What happens to people's willingness to work if the real wage rate increases? Such a change has two opposing effects:

- A substitution effect
- An income effect

Substitution Effect The substitution effect of a change in the real wage rate works in exactly the same way that a change in the price of tapes affects the quantity of tapes demanded. Just as tapes have a price, so does time. As we've just noted, the real hourly wage rate is the opportunity cost of an hour spent not working. A higher real wage rate increases the opportunity cost of time and makes time itself a more valuable commodity. This higher opportunity cost of not working encourages people to reduce their non-work time and increase the time spent working. Thus, as the real wage rate increases, more hours of work are supplied.

Income Effect A higher real wage rate also increases people's incomes. As you know, the higher a person's income, the greater is the demand for all the different types of goods and services. One such 'good' is leisure — the time to do pleasurable things that don't generate an income. Thus a higher real wage rate also makes people want to enjoy longer leisure hours and supply fewer hours of work.

However, unless real GDP is growing as resource availability grows, there cannot be an aggregate income effect. At any point in time, total income is determined by the quantity of resources — labour and capital — actually employed. To increase the real wage for all workers, that is, increase the share of labour income in total income, non-labour income must fall. For example, following a general increase in real wages, the profits of firms fall and dividend income falls. But since workers, as a group, own the firms that generate dividend income, what they gain in increased wages they lose in reduced non-labour income.

Thus, in the aggregate, only a substitution effect exists and an increase in the real wage increases the market supply of labour. In consequence, the market labour supply curve slopes upward.

The Participation Rate

The **labour force participation rate** is the proportion of the working age population that is either employed or unemployed (but seeking employment). For a variety of reasons, people differ in their willingness to work. Some people have better productive opportunities at home and so need a bigger inducement to give up those activities and work for someone else. Other individuals place a very high value on leisure, and they require a high real wage to induce them to do any work at all. These considerations suggest that each person has a reservation wage. A **reservation wage** is the lowest wage at which a person will supply any labour. Below that wage, a person will not work or seek work in the labour force.

Those people who have a reservation wage below or equal to the actual real wage will be in the labour force, and those with a reservation wage above the real wage will not be in the labour force. The higher the real wage rate, the larger is the number of people whose reservation wage falls below the real wage. Hence, the higher the real wage rate, the higher is the labour force participation rate.

Reinforcing and strengthening the increase in hours worked per household and the labour force participation rate is an intertemporal substitution effect on the quantity of labour supplied.

Intertemporal Substitution

Households have to decide not only whether to work but *when* to work. This decision is based not just on the current real wage but on the current real wage relative to expected future real wages.

Suppose that the wage rate is higher today than it is expected to be later on. Suppose, for example, that a firm is offering lots of overtime now but the opportunity to work extra hours for premium pay is not expected to last. How does this fact affect a person's labour supply decision? It encourages more work today and less in the future. Workers might decide to work overtime now, and even postpone their annual holidays for a while. Thus the higher the real wage relative to what is expected in the future (other things being constant), the larger is the supply of labour.

Temporarily high real wages are similar to a high rate of return. If wages are temporarily high, people can obtain a higher rate of return on their work effort by enjoying a smaller amount of leisure and supplying more labour in such a period. By investing in some work now and taking the return in more leisure time later, they can obtain a higher overall level of consumption of goods and services and of leisure.

We've now seen why, as the real wage rate increases, the quantity of labour supplied increases — why the supply of labour curve slopes upward. Let's next bring the two sides of the labour market together and study the determination of wages and employment.

Wages and Employment

We have discovered that as the real wage rate increases the quantity of labour demanded declines and the quantity of labour supplied increases. We now want to study how the two sides of the labour market interact to determine the real wage, employment and unemployment.

There is disagreement about how the labour market works, and this disagreement is the main source of current controversy in macroeconomics. There are two leading theories about the labour market:

- Flexible wage theory
- Sticky wage theory

The flexible wage theory is an approach built on the assumption that labour is traded in markets that operate much like the markets for ordinary goods and services, with the real wage continuously and freely adjusting to keep the quantity demanded equal to the quantity supplied. The sticky wage theory is an approach based on the assumption that the dominant form of trading in the labour market is a wage contract that specifies a fixed money wage for a fixed period of time — hence the term sticky wages. If money wages are sticky, real wages do not continuously adjust to keep the quantity of labour demanded equal to the quantity supplied. Let's look at these two theories, beginning with the simpler — the flexible wage theory.

The Flexible Wage Theory

Most people's wages — money wages — are determined by wage contracts that usually run for one year but sometimes for two or three years. Doesn't this fact mean that wages are not flexible? Economists who regard the flexible wage theory as the appropriate one argue that there are many ways in which money wages, even those that are fixed by wage contracts, can and do adjust upward or downward and that they do so quickly enough to maintain labour market equilibrium. The mix of overtime and normal time work (overtime being paid at a higher wage rate) and bonus payments are the two principal means by which wage flexibility is achieved.

The flexible wage theory of the labour market assumes that these sources of wage adjustment are sufficient to achieve a continuous balance between the quantities of labour supplied and demanded. The economy remains at full employment.

Figure 31.7 illustrates the theory. The demand for labour curve is *LD* and the supply of labour curve is *LS*. This market determines an equilibrium real wage rate of $10 an hour and a quantity of labour employed of 13 billion hours. If the real wage rate is below its equilibrium level of $10 an hour, the quantity of labour demanded exceeds the quantity supplied. In such a situation, nominal wages will rise, since firms are willing to offer higher wages in order to overcome their labour shortages. At given prices, the real wage rate will continue to rise until it reaches $10 an hour, at which point there will be no shortage of labour.

If the real wage rate is higher than its equilibrium level of $10 an hour, the quantity of labour supplied exceeds the quantity demanded. In this situation, households are not able to get all the work that they want and firms will find it easy to hire labour. Firms will have an incentive to cut the wage and households will accept the lower wage to get a job. Alternatively, firms will raise prices to cover the higher costs of hiring labour. Either way, the real wage rate will fall until it reaches $10 an hour, at which point every household will be satisfied with the quantity of labour that it is supplying.

Figure 31.7 Equilibrium with Flexible Wages

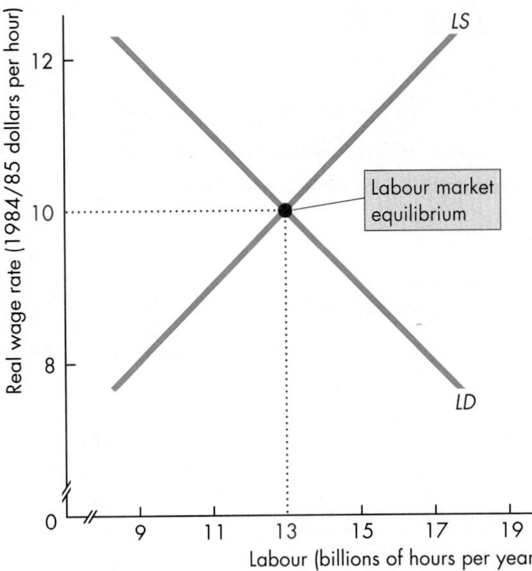

Equilibrium occurs when the real wage makes the quantity of labour demanded equal to the quantity supplied. This equilibrium occurs at a real wage of $10 an hour. At that real wage rate, 13 billion hours of labour are employed. At real wage rates below $10 an hour, the quantity of labour demanded exceeds the quantity supplied and the real wage rate rises. At real wage rates above $10 an hour, the quantity of labour supplied exceeds the quantity of labour demanded and the real wage rate falls.

Changes in Wages and Employment The flexible wage theory makes predictions about wages and employment that are identical to the predictions of the demand and supply model that we studied in Chapter 4. An increase in the demand for labour shifts the demand for labour curve to the right and increases both the real wage rate and the quantity of labour employed. An increase in the supply of labour shifts the supply of labour curve to the right, lowering the real wage rate and increasing employment.

The demand for labour increases over time because capital accumulation and technological change increase the marginal product of labour. The supply of labour increases over time because the population of working age is steadily increasing. Rightward shifts of the demand for labour curve are generally larger than shifts of the supply of labour curve so, over time, both the quantity of labour employed and the real wage rate increase. But real wages do not increase steadily each and every year and there are even examples of prolonged periods, such as from the mid-1980s to the late 1980s, when real wages declined. In some years, the nominal wage can actually fall while prices are rising, as occurred in 1990/91; this was the first time that average nominal wages had fallen since the 1960s.

Aggregate Supply with Flexible Wages In Chapter 24, we met the concept of aggregate supply and the long-run and short-run aggregate supply curves. What does the flexible wage theory of the labour market tell us about aggregate supply?

Recall the definitions of the short-run aggregate supply curve and the long-run aggregate supply curve. The short-run aggregate supply curve tells us how the quantity of real GDP supplied varies as the price level varies, holding input prices constant. The long-run aggregate supply curve tells us how the quantity of real GDP varies as the price level varies, when all input prices adjust by the same percentage as the price level.

According to the flexible wage theory of the labour market, the money wage rate adjusts to determine a real wage that brings equality between the quantity of labour demanded and the quantity supplied. If the prices of all other inputs also behave in the same way as the money wage rate, then all input prices change to preserve equilibrium in the various input markets. The aggregate supply curve generated by the flexible wage model of the labour market is the same as the long-run aggregate supply curve. It is vertical. Let's see why.

Figure 31.8 illustrates the derivation of the long-run aggregate supply curve. Figure 31.8(a) shows the aggregate labour market. The demand and supply curves shown are exactly the same as those in Fig. 31.7. And the equilibrium, with a real wage of $10 an hour

Figure 31.8 Aggregate Supply with Flexible Wages

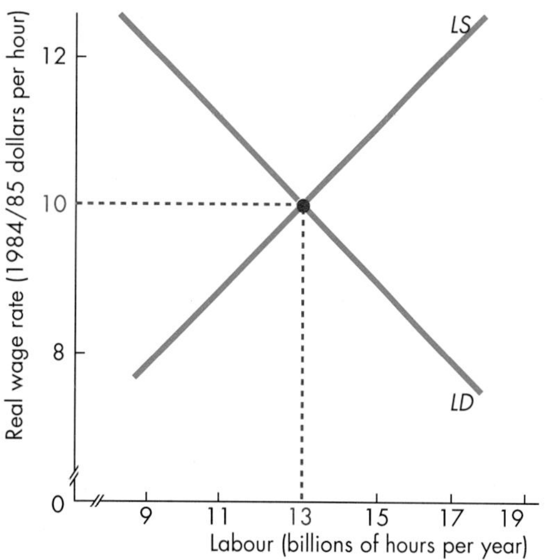

(a) Labour market

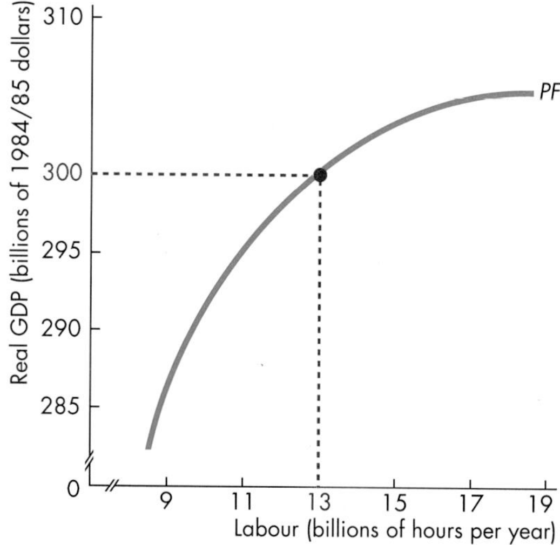

(b) Short-run aggregate production function

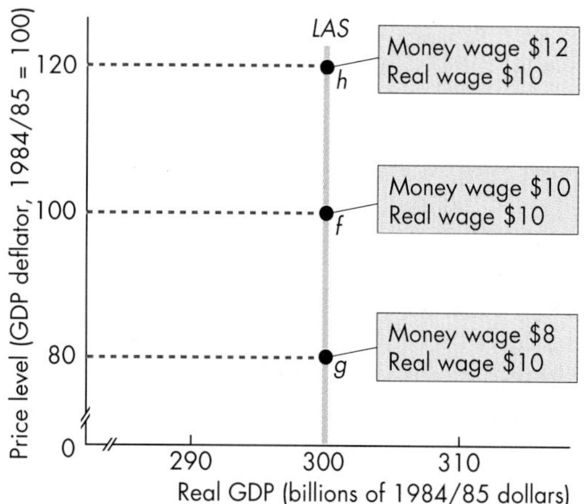

(c) Long-run aggregate supply curve

Labour market equilibrium determines the real wage and employment. The demand for labour curve (*LD*) intersects the supply of labour curve (*LS*) at a real wage of $10 an hour and 13 billion hours of employment — part (a). The short-run aggregate production function (*PF*) and employment of 13 billion hours determine real GDP at $300 billion — part b. Real GDP supplied is $300 billion regardless of the price level. The long-run aggregate supply curve is the vertical line (*LAS*), in part (c). If the GDP deflator is 100, the economy is at point *f*. If the GDP deflator is 120, money wages rise to keep real wages constant at $10 an hour, employment remains at 13 billion hours and real GDP is $300 billion. The economy is at point *h*. If the GDP deflator is 80, money wages fall to keep real wages constant at $10 an hour, employment remains at 13 billion hours and real GDP is $300 billion. The economy is at point *g*.

and employment of 13 billion hours, is exactly the same equilibrium that was determined in that figure.

Figure 31.8(b) shows the short-run aggregate production function. This production function is exactly the same as the one shown in Fig. 31.1. We know from the labour market — Fig. 31.8(a) — that 13 billion hours of labour are employed. Figure 31.8(b) tells us that when 13 billion hours of labour are employed, real GDP is $300 billion.

Figure 31.8(c) shows the long-run aggregate supply curve. That curve tells us that real GDP is $300 billion regardless of the price level. To see why, look at what happens to real GDP when the price level changes.

Start with a price level, measured by the GDP deflator, of 100. In this case, the economy is at point *f* in Fig. 31.8(c). That is, the GDP deflator is 100 and real GDP is $300 billion. We've determined, in Fig. 31.8(a), that the real wage rate is $10. With the GDP deflator of 100, the money wage (the wage in current dollars) is also $10.

What happens to real GDP if the price level falls from 100 to 80 (a 20 per cent fall)? If the money wage rate remains at $10, the real wage rate rises and the quantity of labour supplied exceeds the quantity demanded. In such a situation, the money wage rate will fall. It falls to $8 an hour. With a money wage of $8 and a GDP deflator of 80, the real wage rate is still $10 ($8 divided by 80 and multiplied by 100 equals $10). With the lower money wage but a constant real wage rate, employment remains at 13 billion hours and real GDP is constant at $300 billion. The economy is at point g in Fig. 31.8(c).

What happens to real GDP if the GDP deflator rises from 100 to 120 (a 20 per cent higher price level)? If the money wage rate stays at $10 an hour, the real wage rate falls and the quantity of labour demanded exceeds the quantity supplied. In such a situation, the money wage rate rises. It will keep rising until it reaches $12 an hour. At that money wage rate, the real wage is $10 ($12 divided by 120 and multiplied by 100 equals $10) and the quantity of labour demanded equals the quantity supplied. Employment remains at 13 billion hours, real GDP remains at $300 billion, which means that the economy is at point *h* in Fig. 31.8(c).

Points *f*, *g* and *h* in Fig. 31.8(c) all lie on the long-run aggregate supply curve. We have considered only three price levels. We could have considered any price level and we would have reached the same conclusion: a change in the price level generates a proportionate change in the money wage rate and leaves the real wage rate unchanged. Employment and real GDP are also unchanged. The long-run aggregate supply curve is vertical.

Fluctuations in Real GDP In the flexible wage theory of the labour market, fluctuations in real GDP arise from shifts in the long-run aggregate supply curve. Technological change and capital accumulation shift the short-run aggregate production function upward and also shift the demand for labour curve to the right. Population growth shifts the supply of labour curve to the right. These changes in economic conditions change equilibrium employment and real GDP and also shift the long-run aggregate supply curve. Most of the time these changes result in the long-run aggregate supply curve moving to the right — thus increasing real GDP. But the pace at which the long-run aggregate supply curve shifts to the right varies, leading to fluctuations in the growth rate of real GDP. Occasionally the short-run aggregate production function shifts downward. When it does so, the demand for labour curve shifts to the left, employment falls and the long-run aggregate supply curve shifts to the left — so that GDP falls.

R E V I E W

The flexible wage theory of the labour market maintains that the real wage rate adjusts sufficiently freely to maintain continuous equality between the quantity of labour demanded and the quantity of labour supplied. In such an economy there is only one aggregate supply curve — the vertical long-run aggregate supply curve. Fluctuations in employment, money wages and real GDP occur because of fluctuations in the supply of labour, and because of shifts in the short-run aggregate production function that bring fluctuations in the demand for labour. The most important source of fluctuations is the uneven pace of technological change and other occasional negative influences on the short-run aggregate production function.

With flexible wage theory, the real wage always adjusts to equate supply and demand in the labour market, and only 'voluntary' unemployment emerges. That is, the only people who are unemployed choose to be so. (We will discuss why they might do this later.) But many economists find it difficult to accept the view that measured unemployment, particularly at double digit levels, is all voluntary.

In addition, there are perceived problems with the flexible wage theory as an explanation of business cycles — the systematic fluctuations in GDP, which we discussed in Chapter 22. First, it is unlikely that the shifts in the long-run aggregate supply curve are systematic enough to explain business cycles. Second, and perhaps more important, there are several periods in the Australian experience that are difficult to explain with a flexible wage theory. These periods are 1973/74 to 1977/78 and 1980/81 to 1982/83, when employment was falling while the real wage was rising quite fast. If the reduced demand for labour was caused by a downward shift in the short-run production function, possibly because of the oil price rises that occurred in 1973 and 1979, then employment would certainly fall. But in order for the real wage to *rise*, the supply curve for labour must be shifting backward faster than the demand curve for labour. An explanation must be given for such behaviour. ■

We will discuss unemployment shortly. First, let's examine how the labour market works and employment varies when money wages are sticky.

The Sticky Wage Theory

Most economists, while recognizing the scope for flexibility in wages from bonuses and special overtime wage rates, believe that these sources of flexibility are insufficient to keep the quantity of labour supplied equal to the quantity of labour demanded. Basic money or nominal wage rates, they point out, rarely adjust more frequently than once a year, so that money wage rates are fairly rigid. And in Australia, money wages tend to be set, or at least ratified, in a complex industrial court system. Real wage rates change more frequently than do money wage rates because of changes in the price level, but it is argued, not with sufficient flexibility to achieve continuous full employment.

The starting point for the sticky wage theory of the labour market is a theory of the determination of the money wage rate — the wage that is 'sticky'. Generally speaking, firms like to pay as low a wage as possible. Workers like as high a wage as possible. But workers want to get hired and firms want to be able to find labour. Firms recognize that if they offer too low a wage there will be a labour shortage. Workers recognize that if they try to achieve too high a wage there will be a shortage of jobs — excessive unemployment. Workers also realize that if wages are set to clear the market, as flexible wage theory suggests, then not only will the money wage vary with fluctuations in the demand for or supply of labour, but so will equilibrium employment. Thus the income of workers — the wage times the level of employment— might vary quite considerably. In response to this potential volatility of income, we might expect that firms and workers could come to some agreement whereby the income of workers is stabilized. Let's see how.

Implicit Contracts An **implicit contract** is an informal arrangement between firms and workers whereby firms provide workers with insurance against fluctuating wages by agreeing to pay them a constant nominal wage. To the extent that other prices in the economy adjust slowly and are predictable then the real wage is also stable. But since firms are offering insurance, which is costly to maintain, they must somehow be collecting an insurance premium. There are two ways they do this:

- They pay workers less than the marginal product of labour, on average.
- They exercise full control over the number of workers employed.

This means that not only will the nominal wage be sticky, but employment will vary up and down along the demand for labour curve.

An alternative explanation for sticky wages results in workers being paid more than the marginal product. This approach is based on efficiency wages.

Efficiency Wages The **efficiency wage** approach is based on the idea that if a firm pays its workers more than the average wage paid by other firms and, at the same time, it threatens to fire workers who are exerting very little effort, then the average productivity of all workers employed by that firm rises. The firm will thus continue to increase the wage paid to workers until any further increase does not attract sufficient extra effort to cover the cost of the wage rise. Even though raising the wage increases the total wage costs of the firm, it reduces wage costs per unit of output because workers are producing more.

Having established an efficiency wage, the firm is reluctant to adjust the wage in response to changes in demand. Doing so would reduce the effort of all workers and so reduce the firm's profit. Thus firms will vary employment levels in response to demand shocks but not wages. Like the implicit contract theory, efficiency wage theory predicts that wages of workers will be stable but the level of employment will vary. It also predicts that firms will enter into long-term relationships with workers because workers with a short-term horizon will not have any incentive to increase effort. The threat of being fired is less punitive when workers expect to be on the job for a short time in any event.

Money Wage Determination Supposing that money wages are established in either an implicit contract or an efficiency wage framework, at what level are they set? To answer this, suppose that the labour demand and supply curves are the same as those used in Fig. 31.7. The real wage that achieves balance between the quantity demanded and quantity supplied is $10, as shown in Fig. 31.9. The money wage corresponding to this real wage depends on the price level. But when firms and workers agree to a money wage rate for a future contract, they do not know what the price level is going to be. All they can do is base the contract on their best forecast of future prices. Let's suppose that firms and their workers all have the same expectations about the future. In our example, we suppose that they expect the GDP deflator for the coming year to be 100. That being the case, firms and workers will be ready to agree to a money wage rate of $10 per hour.

Real Wage Determination The real wage rate that actually emerges depends on the actual price level. If the GDP deflator turns out to be 100, as expected, then the real wage rate is $10, as expected. In this case, employment is 13 billion hours — the quantity determined at the intersection of the labour demand (*LD*) and labour supply (*LS*) curves. But many other outcomes are possible. Let's consider two of them, one in which the price level turns out to be higher than expected and one in which it turns out to be lower than expected.

First, suppose that the GDP deflator turns out to be 83.3. In this case, the real wage is $12. That is, a money wage of $10 and a GDP deflator of 83.3 enables people to buy the same goods that a money wage of $12 buys when the GDP deflator is 100. Next, suppose that the GDP deflator turns out to be 125 instead of 100. In this case, the real wage is $8. A money wage of $10 with a GDP deflator of 125 buys the same quantity of goods that a real wage of $8 buys when the GDP deflator is 100. The three points *a, c* and *e* in Fig. 31.9 illustrate the relationship between the price level, the money wage and the real wage. If the money wage is constant at $10, the higher the price level the lower is the real wage. If the real wage is different from $10, how is the level of employment determined?

Figure 31.9 A Labour Market with Sticky Money Wages

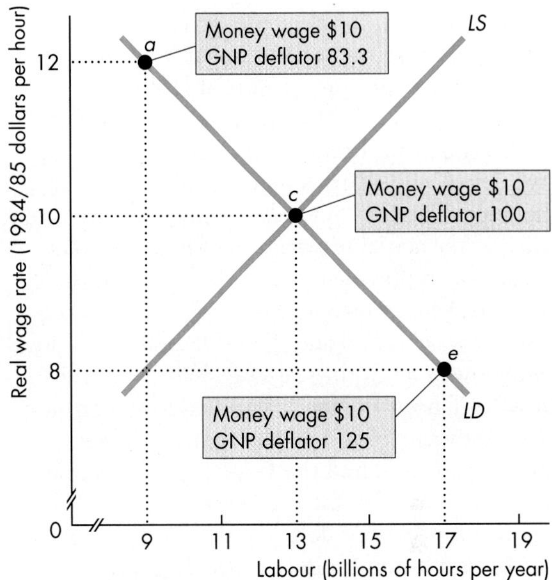

The labour demand curve is *LD* and the labour supply curve is *LS*. The money wage is set to achieve an expected balance between the quantity of labour demanded and the quantity supplied. If the GDP deflator is expected to be 100, the money wage rate is set at $10 an hour. The labour market is expected to be at point *c*. The quantity of labour employed is determined by the demand for labour. If the GDP deflator actually turns out to be 100, then the real wage is equal to $10 and the economy does operate at point *c*, employing 13 billion hours of labour. If the GDP deflator turns out to be 83.3, then the real wage is $12 an hour and the quantity of labour demanded falls to 9 billion hours. The economy operates at point *a*. If the GDP deflator is 125, then the real wage is $8 an hour and employment increases to 17 billion hours. The economy operates at point *e*.

Employment with Sticky Wages The sticky wage theory implies that the quantity of labour actually demanded determines employment. Provided firms agree to pay the agreed wage, households contract to supply whatever labour firms demand. The agreed wage is usually determined before events are actually realized and so must be based on firms' and households' expectations of the future state of the labour market and other variables. One way this is achieved is to base the contracted wage on the wage that would emerge if wages actually were flexible, given the demand for and supply of labour. Thus the labour supply curve *LS* is used to calculate the money wage rate that corresponds to the real wage households expect, for example, given that they expect the price level to be 100, but it does not represent a constraint on the amount of labour that firms can employ. At the money wage of $10, contracts are such that households are obliged to supply whatever labour firms demand for the duration of the wage contract. Since the quantity of labour demanded at the actual real wage determines employment, actual employment is determined from the demand for labour curve in Fig. 31.9. Thus, when the money wage is $10 and the GDP deflator is unexpectedly low at 83.3, the real wage is $12 and the quantity of labour demanded and employment are 9 billion hours (point *a* in the figure). When the money wage is $10 and the GDP deflator is unexpectedly high at 125, the real wage is $8 and both the quantity of labour demanded and employment are 17 billion hours (point *e* in the figure).

Aggregate Supply with Sticky Wages When money wages are sticky, the short-run aggregate supply curve slopes upward. Figure 31.10 illustrates why this is so. Let's start by looking at Fig. 31.10 (a) which describes the labour market. The three equilibrium levels of real wages and employment, which we discovered in Fig. 31.9, are shown again here. The money wage rate is fixed at $10 an hour. If the price level is 100, the real wage rate is also $10 an hour and 13 billion hours of labour are employed — point *c*. If the price level is 83.3, the real wage rate is $12 an hour and employment is only 9 billion hours — point *a*. If the price level is 125, the real wage rate is $8 an hour and employment is 17 billion hours — point *e*.

Figure 31.10(b) shows the short-run aggregate production function. We know from the labour market, shown in Fig. 31.10(a) that at different price levels, different quantities of labour are employed. Figure 31.10(b) tells us how these employment levels translate into real GDP. For example, when the employment level is 9 billion hours, real GDP is $272 billion — point *a*. When the employment level is 13 billion hours, real GDP is $300 billion — point *c*, and when employment is 17 billion hours, real GDP is $312 billion — point *e*.

Figure 31.10(c) shows the aggregate supply curves. The long-run aggregate supply curve, *LAS*, is the one we've already derived in Fig. 31.8(c). The short-run aggregate supply curve, *SAS*, is derived from the labour market and production function we've just examined. To see why, first focus on point *a* in all three parts of the figure. At point *a*, the price level is 83.3. From the labour market as shown in Fig. 31.10(a) we know that in this situation the real wage is $12 an hour and 9 billion hours of labour are employed. At this employment level we know from the production function as shown in Fig. 31.10(b) that real GDP is $272 billion. That's what point *a* in Fig. 31.10(c) is telling us — when the price level is 83.3, real GDP supplied is $272 billion. The other two points, *c* and *e*, are interpreted in the same way. At point *e*, the price level is 125 so the real wage rate is $8 an hour and 17 billion hours of labour are employed (Fig. 31.10(a)). This employment level produces a real GDP of $312 billion. Points *a*, *c* and *e* are all points on the short-run aggregate supply curve. Note that this curve, unlike the one in Chapter 24, is *curved.* As the price level rises, real GDP increases but, because of the diminishing marginal product of labour, the increments in real GDP become successively smaller. The straight line *SAS* curve we have been using is an approximation to this curve.

The short-run aggregate supply curve intersects the long-run aggregate supply curve at the expected price level — where the GDP deflator is 100. At a price level higher than that expected, the quantity of real GDP supplied exceeds its long-run level and at a price level lower than that expected, the quantity of real GDP supplied falls short of its long-run level.

Fluctuations in Real GDP All the factors that lead to fluctuations in long-run aggregate supply in the flexible wage theory apply to the long-run aggregate supply curve of the sticky wage theory. But, in addition, employment and real GDP can fluctuate because of movements along the short-run aggregate supply curve. These movements occur because of changes in real wages. Real wages change in the sticky wage theory when the price level moves but the contractually determined money wage rate stays constant.

R E V I E W

The sticky wage theory emphasizes the importance of labour market contracts that fix the money wage

Figure 31.10 Aggregate Supply with Sticky Wages

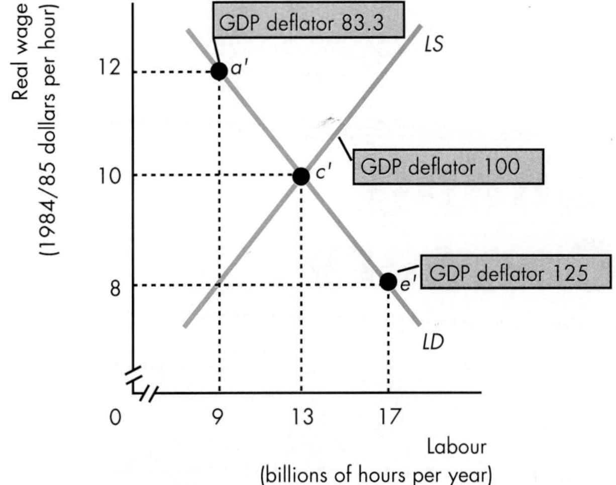

(a) Labour market

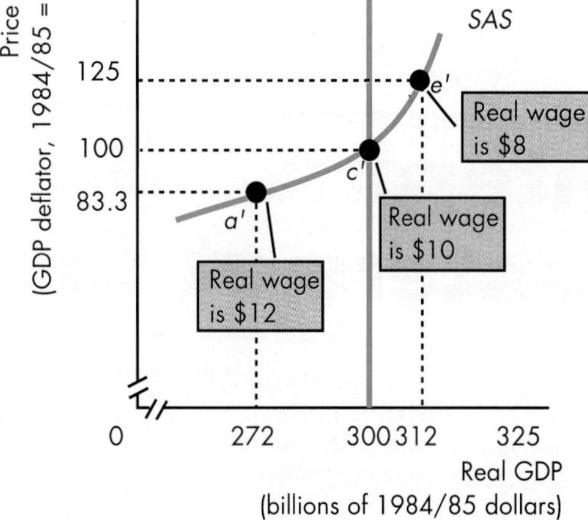

(c) Aggregate supply curves

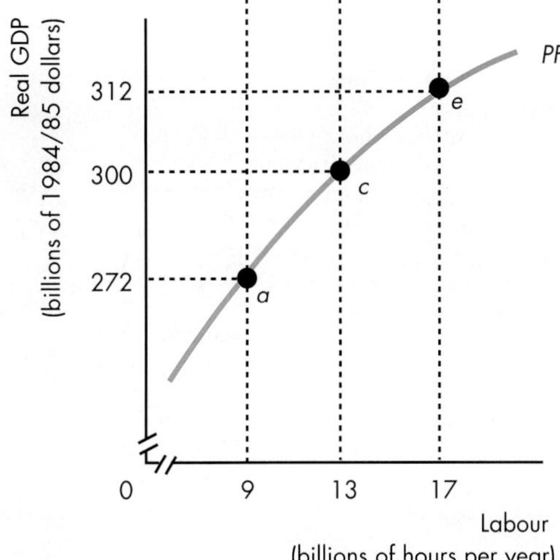

(b) Short-run aggregate production function

The money wage is fixed at $10 an hour. In part (a), the demand for labour curve (*LD*) intersects the supply of labour curve (*LS*) at a real wage rate of $10 an hour and 13 billion hours of employment. If the GDP deflator is 100, the economy operates at this point — *c*. In part (b), the short-run aggregate production function (*PF*) determines real GDP at $300 billion. This is long-run aggregate supply (*LAS*), in part (c). If the GDP deflator is 83.3, real wages are $12 an hour and the economy is at point *a* — employment is 9 billion hours, as in part (a) and real GDP is $272 billion, as in part (b). The economy is at point *a* on its short-run aggregate supply curve (*SAS*) in part (c). If the GDP deflator is 125, real wages are $8 an hour and the economy is at point *e* — employment is 17 billion hours — part (a) and real GDP is $312 billion — part (b). The economy is at point *e* on its short-run aggregate supply curve in part (c).

rate, making it insensitive in the short run to price level changes. The money wage is set on the basis of expectations about the price level over the course of the wage contract. If the price level turns out to be the same as expected, the real wage is the same as it would be if wages were flexible. If the price level turns out to be lower than expected, the real wage is higher than in the flexible wage case. If the price level is higher than expected, the real wage is lower than in the flexible wage case.

The level of employment is determined by the demand for labour. When the real wage is higher than expected, employment falls; when the real wage is lower than expected, employment increases. These movements in the level of employment result in changes in the level of real GDP and are represented as movements along the short-run aggregate supply curve. A higher than expected price level lowers the real wage, increases employment and increases real GDP; a lower than expected price level increases the real wage, lowers employment and lowers real GDP. ■

So far, although we have been examining models of the labour market, we have used those models

Achieving Wage Flexibility

Enterprise Bargaining Masters at the Cannery

One thing the debate over the SPC dispute has shown is the buzz-phrase 'enterprise bargaining' is one of the most misused and misunderstood terms in the industrial relations arena.

As a slogan, 'enterprise bargaining' was coined by the Business Council of Australia in its 1989 report *A Better Way of Working*.

But as a feature of industrial relations, enterprise bargains have been commonplace in Australia for decades, involving both over-award deals in good economic times and cost-cutting measures in bad.

Recent agreements in the vehicle industry to cope with falling demand brought forward annual leave and rostered days off.

SPC has had enterprise bargaining for years; the new agreement cuts labour costs by a similar amount to the original agreement without touching any award conditions — because it makes savings by reducing over-award deals, work practices and plain rorts from previous bargains.

The main SPC union, the Food Preservers' Union, are past masters of enterprise bargaining and SPC's previous management took a short-term approach to industrial relations, resolving disputes with expedient deals outside the award system.

Consider the following current SPC practices, none of which is an award condition and all of which are the result of past enterprise bargaining.

- The shiny allowance: paid to fork-lift drivers to compensate for glare from fruit cans.
- The three-prong allowance: an over-award allowance paid to driver of fork lifts with three prongs.
- Leading hands: under their awards, several workers qualify for a leading-hand allowance of about $15 a week for supervisory duties during the picking season but under an enterprise deal they are paid the allowance all year.
- Straight over-award payments: these range from about $55 a week for production workers to $130 a week for maintenance workers.
- The '1978 adjustment': the rationale for this over-award payment cannot be recalled clearly by most managers or union officials.
- Meal allowances: some trades workers at SPC are entitled to crib time and a meal allowance under their award if they are rostered for a shift with less than 24 hours' notice but under a work practice they have been paid the allowance regardless of whether they have less than 24 hours' notice.
- Working hours: although the main award covering SPC, the Food Preservers' Interim Award, prescribes 40 hours as the ordinary weekly working hours, production workers work a 38-hour week in the form of a 19-day month.
- Sick leave: most seasonal employees who work during the 10-week picking season have five days' sick leave entitlement but under an over-award arrangement they have been paid out at the end of the season for untaken sick leave.

Financial Review
Friday, 4 January 1991
By Mark Davis

The Essence of the Story

- SPC is a fruit cannery located at Shepparton, Victoria. The company employs about 700 permanent and seasonal workers. The workers at the plant are represented by various unions, the main one being the Food Preservers' Union.
- Late in 1990, a new board of directors of the company discovered that it was facing a $10 million loss in 1990. Faced with the prospect of either cutting costs or shutting down the plant, the management of the company entered into negotiations with its employees through their unions.
- Management initially proposed a package including:
  - A reduced number of rostered days off
  - Reduced weekend penalty pay rates
  - Reduced pro-rata sick leave entitlements for seasonal workers
  - Reduced crib and meal allowances
- All these cuts would have meant a loss in award conditions.
- However, the unions rejected the possibility of the erosion of award conditions.
- Nonetheless, a deal that enabled SPC to cut nearly $2 million in labour costs over 1991 was possible because of the proliferation in over-award arrangements which had occurred in the plant and some of which are listed in the story.
- The deal struck between management and unions provided for the following cost-cutting measures over the 12 months of 1991:
  - Reductions in over-award payments under a formula that take account of different shift and overtime work patterns
  - Overtime and shift penalty amounts to be calculated on award pay rates and not over-award rates
  - Staggered non-award rest breaks to minimize the disruption to production (rather than scrapping them altogether)
  - Non-union staff employees not covered by awards to give up annual leave loadings
  - Suspension of rostered days off
- The company also agreed to implement a profit-sharing arrangement where workers would be paid an annual bonus amounting to 10 per cent of after-tax profit, or 50 per cent of productivity gained over the previous year, whichever is higher.

Background and Analysis

- It is often claimed that the existence of the award structure of wage determination in Australia imparts an inflexibility to wages that renders the flexible wage description of the labour market irrelevant. And certainly unions are very reluctant to see an erosion of award conditions.
- But the proliferation of over-award payments and conditions, which indicate upward flexibility of wages, also provides a buffer through which labour costs can be significantly reduced without affecting the underlying award conditions.
- Thus, 'wages', appropriately measured, may in fact be much more flexible than is suggested by the institutional arrangements in which base payments are determined.
- The flexibility of over-award payments, both upward and downward, also means that many companies have been engaging in 'enterprise bargaining' for quite some time.

Conclusion

- In May 1991, the management of SPC announced that, because of the reductions in costs achieved over 1991 (which appeared to be larger than initially estimated) and because of productivity increases generated by restructuring, the company, which lost $25.6 million in 1990, would return a profit in 1991. The company would therefore return all the conditions lost in the cost-cutting agreement and would pay out accrued 'lost' earnings to workers, in the first pay period in December.

to determine the level of employment and wages but have ignored unemployment. How is unemployment determined?

Unemployment

We discovered in Chapter 22 that unemployment is an ever-present feature of economic life and that the unemployment rate sometimes rises to a level that poses a massive problem for millions of families. Yet the labour market models that we have just been studying seem to ignore this important phenomenon. They determine the real wage rate and aggregate hours of labour employed but don't say anything about *who* supplies the hours. Unemployment arises when some people in the labour force are working zero hours but are seeking work. Why does unemployment exist? Why does its rate vary?

There are four main reasons why unemployment arises:

- It may pay firms to vary the number of workers employed rather than the number of hours per worker, when they wish to vary employment.
- Firms have imperfect information about people looking for work.
- Households have incomplete information about available jobs.
- Wage contracts prevent the wage adjustments that would be needed to keep the quantity of labour demanded equal to the quantity supplied.

The flexible wage theory places emphasis on the first three of these sources of unemployment. The sticky wage theory acknowledges the importance of these factors but regards the fourth factor as the most significant cause of unemployment and of variations in its rate. First, we'll examine the sources of unemployment that are present regardless of whether wages are flexible or sticky. Then we'll see how wage stickiness generates yet more unemployment.

Indivisible Labour

If it were profitable to do so, firms would vary the amount of labour they employ by varying the hours worked by each person on their payrolls. For example, suppose that a firm employs 400 hours of labour each week and has 10 workers, each working 40 hours. If the firm decides to cut back its production and reduce employment to 360 hours, it might either lay off one worker or cut the hours of each of its 10 workers to 36 hours a week. In most production processes, the profitable reaction for the firm is to lay off one worker and keep the remaining workers' hours constant. There is an optimum or efficient number of hours for each worker. Work hours in excess of the optimum level result in decreased output per hour as workers become tired. Employing a larger number of workers for a smaller number of hours each also lowers output per hour, since workers take time to get started up and there are disruptions to the production process caused by workers leaving and arriving. It is for these reasons that labour is an economically indivisible factor of production. That is, taking account of the output produced per hour, it pays firms to hire labour in indivisible lumps. As a consequence, when the demand for labour changes, the number of people employed changes rather than the number of hours per worker.

Being fired or laid off would not be important if an equally good job could be found right away. But finding a job takes time and effort — it has an opportunity cost. Firms are not fully informed about all the potential workers available to them and households are not fully informed about all the potential jobs available to them. As a consequence, both firms and workers have to search for a profitable match. Let's examine this source of unemployment.

Job Search and Unemployment

Because households are incompletely informed about available jobs, they find it efficient to devote resources to searching for the best available job. Time spent searching for a job is part of unemployment. Let's take a closer look at this source of unemployment by examining the labour market decisions that people make and the flows that arise from those decisions. Figure 31.11 provides a schematic summary of this discussion.

Labour Market Decisions and Flows The population is divided into two broad groups: those in the labour force (L) and those not in the labour force. Those not in the labour force fall into three groups: full-time students, homemakers and children, and retirees. The labour force consists of two broad groups: the employed (E) and the unemployed (U).

Decisions made by the demanders of labour and the suppliers of labour result in nine types of flows that change the number of people employed and unemployed. These flows are shown by the ar-

Figure 31.11 Labour Market Flows

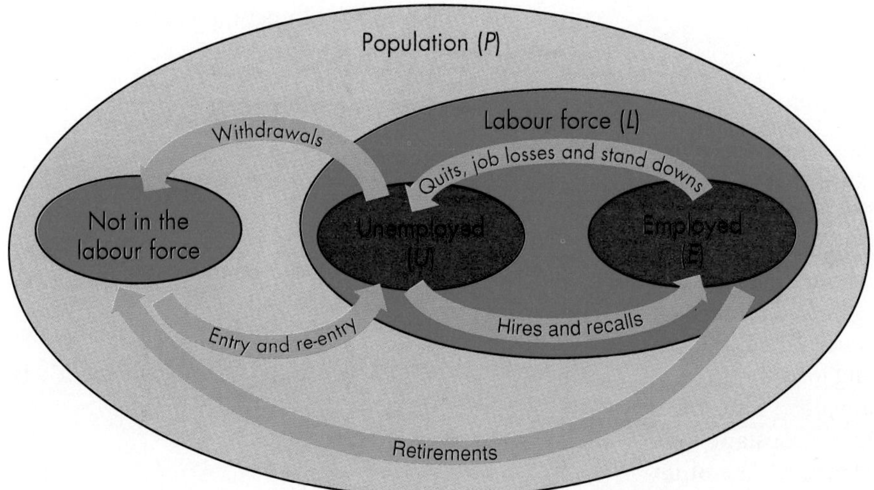

The population is divided into two groups: those in the labour force and those not in the labour force. The labour force, in turn, is divided into those employed and those unemployed. The figure shows the flows between the labour force and the rest of the population and between the employed and the unemployed. New entrants from full-time schooling flow into the unemployment pool. As these new entrants are hired, they flow out of the unemployment pool. Flows from employed to unemployed occur as a result of people resigning, being fired or stood down. Flows occur in the opposite direction as a result of hires and recalls. Workers sometimes withdraw temporarily from the labour force to become homemakers or to go back to full-time study. Others retire permanently. Those who have temporarily withdrawn from the labour force re-enter and search for a job. They flow in through the unemployment pool. The quantity of unemployment depends on the scale of the flows and on the length of time that people remain in the unemployed category. The greater the entry flow and the greater the rate of resignations, sackings and stand downs, the higher is the average rate of unemployment.

Source: Australian Bureau of Statistics, *The Labour Force, Australia*, December 1990, ABS Catalogue No. 6203.0.

rows in the figure. Let's look at each of these decisions and see how the flow that results from it affects the amount of unemployment and employment.

There are two ways in which a person not in the labour force can become unemployed. Full-time students can decide to leave school, enter the labour force and search for a job; or homemakers can decide to change their activities by entering or re-entering the labour force and seeking a job. Usually, when such people enter the labour force, they start off as unemployed.

There are three ways in which employed workers may become unemployed. An employer may stand down (lay off) workers temporarily; an employer may fire workers; or workers may decide to quit their current job to find a better one. Each of these decisions results in a fall in employment and a rise in unemployment.

There are three ways in which people can leave the pool of unemployment. They may decide to withdraw from the labour force temporarily (to bring up children, become homemakers, go back to full-time study or simply become discouraged and stop searching for employment). They may be recalled from temporary layoff. They may be hired in a new job.

Finally, people can leave the labour force and unemployment by retirement.

At any one moment, there is a stock of employment and unemployment and, over any given period, there are flows between the labour force and the rest of the population and between employment and unemployment. In December 1990, for example, there were 8.6 million people in the labour force — 64.6 per cent of the population aged 15 years and over. Of these, 704,600 (8.1 per cent of the labour force) were unemployed and 7.9 million (91.9 per cent of the labour force) were employed. Of the 704,600 unemployed, 23 per cent were looking for their first full-time job and 18.7 per cent were looking for part-time work. Nearly 18 per cent had quit their previous jobs. The largest flow into the pool of unemployed were job losers — unemployed people who left their last job involuntarily because they were laid off, fired, retrenched, injured or in temporary jobs. A further 2.3 per cent were stood down.

Unemployment with Flexible Wages

Natural Rate of Unemployment According to the flexible wage model of the labour market, all the unemployment that exists arises from the sources we've just reviewed. In the labour market there is a balance between the quantity of labour demanded and the quantity of labour supplied. And for a given labour force, there is a balance between the number of workers who are losing or leaving jobs and the number of workers who are finding jobs. Thus the total number of unemployed people is constant and the unemployment rate equals the **natural rate of unemployment**. By elaborating on this idea of balance we gain some insight into how large the natural rate of unemployment is and what causes it to change. Let's see how.

Since everyone in the labour force (L) is either employed (E) or unemployed (U) then:

$$L = E + U$$

But, as we have already observed, the labour market is a dynamic changing environment. There is a steady flow of people into the pool of employed and, at the same time, there is a steady flow into the pool of unemployed. Suppose, for the moment, that the size of the labour force is constant. Suppose also that the number of people who find new jobs is a constant fraction η of the total pool of unemployed people. For example, it might be the case that over every period 15 per cent of unemployed people find a job. Thus, the new addition to the employed workforce is given by

$$\text{Change in employed} = \Delta E = \eta U$$

where Δ stands for 'change in'. In addition, suppose that the number of people who lose or leave jobs equals a constant fraction s of the pool of employed workers. For example, 1 per cent of employed people might lose or leave jobs every period. Thus, the total number of newly unemployed is given by

$$\text{Change in unemployed} = \Delta U = sE$$

Under the assumptions of the flexible wage model, the economy is at the natural rate of unemployment when the number of newly unemployed just equals the number of people finding jobs so that both the total number of unemployed and employed is unchanged. That is

$$\Delta E = \Delta U$$

But this means that

$$\eta U = sE$$

From the definition of the labour force

$$E = L - U$$

Therefore, the natural rate of unemployment u^*, is[1]

$$u^* = \frac{s}{s+\eta} \times 100$$

For example, if 1 per cent of all employed workers leave or lose a job in any period ($s = 0.01$) and 15 per cent of all unemployed workers find a job ($\eta = 0.15$), then the natural rate of unemployment is

$$u^* = \frac{0.01}{0.01 + 0.15} \times 100 = 6.25 \text{ per cent}$$

Figure 31.12 illustrates such a situation. The labour force — everyone who has a job and all those who are looking for one — is larger than the supply of labour.[2] The supply curve of labour tells us only about the quantity of labour available with no further job search. Others in the workforce are still looking for information about jobs and are thus not ready to accept just any job. Equilibrium occurs at the real wage rate that makes the quantity of labour supplied — not the labour force — equal to the

[1] The calculation is as follows: substitute $E = L - U$ into $\eta U = sE$. That is

$$\eta U = sE = s(L - U)$$

Solve for U^*, the natural level of unemployment

$$U^* = \frac{s}{s+\eta} L$$

The unemployment rate is defined as $100 \times (U/L)$, which after substitution yields the equation in the text.

[2] It would normally be the case that the size of the labour force also depended positively on the real wage. For simplicity we have assumed that the labour force is given at any point in time and does not respond to changes in the real wage. Thus we have drawn the labour force curve vertical.

quantity of labour demanded. Unemployment arises from the fact that information about jobs and workers is costly and it takes time for people without work to find an acceptable job, and for employers to find acceptable workers. There are constant flows of people into and out of the pools of employed and unemployed workers.

According to the flexible wage theory, fluctuations in unemployment are caused by fluctuations in labour market flows that arise on both the supply side and demand side of the labour market and thus cause fluctuations in the natural rate of unemployment.

Supply Side Events The supply side of the labour market is influenced by the size and age distribution of the population. A large increase in the proportion of the population of working age brings an increase in the rate of entry into the labour force and a corresponding increase in unemployment as the new entrants take time to find the best available jobs. The increase in the labour force shifts the labour-force curve to the right. This factor has been important in the Australian labour market in recent years. A bulge in the birth rate occurred in the early 1950s following World War II. This bulge resulted in a bulge in new labour market entrants in the 1970s, increasing the natural rate of unemployment. As the birth rate declined, the bulge passed and the number of new labour market entrants in the 1980s declined, lowering the natural unemployment rate.

For a given population and age structure, rising real wages might also induce some people currently in household activities into the workforce. In this case the participation rate rises. The **participation rate** is the percentage of the working age population in the labour force. That is

$$\text{Participation rate} = \frac{L}{P} \times 100$$

The participation rate has risen steadily in Australia since World War II as women continue to enter the workforce. Since most new entrants enter the pool of unemployed first, a rise in the participation rate increases the natural rate of unemployment.

The supply of labour curve can also shift as workers' expectations of the wage they might get change. For example, suppose that the economy is expanding rapidly. If wages are beginning to rise, currently unemployed workers who are searching for a job might be induced to search a little longer because the chances of finding the 'right' job have risen. Thus the rate of new job finding, η, falls and

Figure 31.12 Unemployment with Flexible Wages

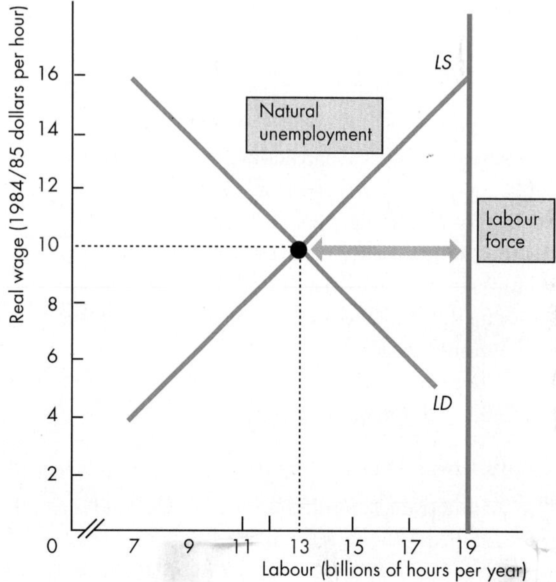

The labour force is 19 billion hours a year. Some members of the labour force are immediately available for work at a given real wage rate and this amount determines the supply of labour (*LS*). Other members of the labour force are searching for the best available job. Equilibrium occurs at the real wage rate that makes the quantity of labour supplied equal to the quantity demanded. The labour force minus the quantity of labour employed is unemployment. The economy is at full employment and unemployment is at its 'natural' rate.

the natural rate of unemployment rises. In addition, workers who have a job might be induced to quit and look for a better job — s rises — and the natural rate of unemployment rises further. Offsetting or sometimes reinforcing these supply side influences on the natural rate of unemployment are demand side disturbances. Let's examine some now.

Demand Side Events Cycles in unemployment arise from the fact that the scale of hiring, firing and job quitting ebbs and flows with the fluctuations in real GDP — with the business cycle. These labour market flows and the resulting unemployment are strongly influenced by the pace and direction of technological change. When some firms and sectors of the economy are expanding quickly and others are contracting quickly, labour turnover increases. This means large flows between employment and unemployment, and the pool of those temporarily unem-

Unemployment: Waste or 'Natural'?

Ever since the Great Depression and the subsequent publication of Keynes's *General Theory* (see Our Advancing Knowledge, pp. 620–621), most macroeconomists have believed that fluctuations in unemployment have been caused by fluctuations in aggregate demand and are an avoidable waste of resources. Sticky money wages that do not adjust to changes in aggregate demand are seen as the source of fluctuations in real GDP and unemployment.

Okun's Law

The quantitative relationship between output and unemployment is called 'Okun's Law', named after Arthur Okun.

Arthur Okun (1929–1979) did his graduate work in economics at Columbia University and taught for several years at Yale. But most of Okun's professional career was spent in Washington, DC. He became a member of Kennedy's Council of Economic Advisors in 1964. He became chairman of the Council in 1968 and so became President Lyndon B. Johnson's senior economic advisor. After he left the CEA, he spent the rest of his life as a research economist at the Brookings Institution. Okun was a compassionate and articulate exponent of Keynesian macroeconomics.

Arthur Okun

The relationship that intrigued Arthur Okun was the following: deviations of real GDP from trend, the 'output gap', very closely tracks the difference between the natural rate and the actual unemployment rate. This observation has led economists to conclude that fluctuations in aggregate demand produce fluctuations in output which lead to fluctuations in unemployment. This cause-and-effect relationship is Okun's Law.

This consensus has been challenged in recent years by real business cycle theorists and by those economists focusing on sectoral shifts as sources of cyclical unemployment.

Real Business Cycle Theory

Real business cycle theory is a revival of a very old branch of macroeconomics developed by Edward Prescott of the University of Minnesota, Finn Kydland of Carnegie-Mellon University, and John Long and Charles Plosser of the University of Rochester. Real business cycle theory explains aggregate fluctuations as the consequence of fluctuations in the pace of technological change. According to real business cycle theory, fluctuations in employment and real GDP are the best possible response to real changes affecting the economy.

The concept of indivisible labour, discussed in this chapter (p. 820) has been incorporated into real business cycle theories by Richard Rogerson of the University of Rochester. Gary Hansen of the University of California at Los Angeles has shown that an artificial economy incorporating these ideas, which can be modelled on a computer, produces fluctuations in output, employment and unemployment similar to those that we observe in the United States economy.

Sectoral Shifts

The possible importance of sectoral shifts as a cause of unemployment has been suggested by David Lilien of the University of Southern California. Lilien calculated the scale of sectoral shifts by measuring the amount of labour turnover across 21 major sectors of the US economy. He discovered that this measure of labour turnover was strongly correlated with the actual unemployment rate and was able to explain most of the rise in unemployment in the 1970s.

Lilien's results and interpretation have been challenged by Katharine Abraham (of the Brookings Institution and the Massachusetts Institute of Technology) and Lawrence Katz (of the University of California, Berkeley) who show that sectoral shifts are correlated with aggregate demand. They argue that Arthur Okun's original conclusion — that unemployment is caused primarily by aggregate demand fluctuations — is broadly correct.

The Keynesian Resurgence

In recent years, there has been a burst of research activity aimed at providing a theoretical foundation for the Keynesian idea that unemployment is wasteful. Carl Shapiro of Princeton University and Joseph Stiglitz of Stanford University have suggested the efficiency wage hypothesis (p. 814 in this chapter). Recall that the central idea of this hypothesis is that firms can get greater effort from their workers by paying them a higher wage. But a higher wage results in unemployment — an excess of the quantity of labour supplied over the quantity demanded. Indeed, it is the fear of unemployment that generates the greater effort from workers who are paid an efficiency wage.

Assar Lindbeck, of the University of Stockholm, and Dennis Snower, of the University of London, have developed what they call the 'insider–outsider' theory of employment and unemployment. Their idea is that people who have jobs don't care about people who are unemployed and negotiate wages with their employers that preserve their own employment level but do not enable 'outsiders' to get in.

Peter Diamond of the Massachusetts Institute of Technology has suggested that job search, of the type discussed in this chapter (p. 820), can create 'multiple equilibrium' levels of unemployment. If a large number of firms are looking for a large number of workers, the chances of each side finding a good match are high and unemployment is low. If a small number of firms are looking for a small number of workers, the chances of matches being made are much lower and unemployment is high. Diamond's ideas have been developed by Olivier Blanchard and Lawrence Summers of Harvard to explain the difference between European unemployment (persistently high) and US unemployment (falling throughout the 1980s). Their idea is given the name 'hysteresis'. Loosely, hysteresis applied to unemployment means that the unemployment rate depends on its previous level. A large shock to the economy can create a high unemployment rate that then persists until another large shock knocks the economy back to a low unemployment rate.

The debate among economists about the causes of unemployment is not just of academic interest. It is crucial for the design and conduct of macroeconomic stabilization policy. If real wages are flexible enough to ensure that all unemployment is 'natural unemployment', and fluctuations in actual unemployment are fluctuations in natural unemployment, then aggregate demand policy has no role to play. There is only one aggregate supply curve — the vertical long-run aggregate supply curve. Fluctuations in real GDP, employment and unemployment are all associated with shifts in this vertical aggregate supply curve. Monetary and fiscal policy can be used to influence aggregate demand and shift the aggregate demand curve. But these shifts will not affect real GDP, employment and unemployment. They will affect only the price level (and inflation rate).

On the other hand, if wages are not sufficiently flexible, and if some unemployment results from sticky wages, the short-run aggregate supply curve slopes upward and a role may exist for managing the level of aggregate demand to achieve full employment. A fall in aggregate demand can produce a fall in real GDP and an increase in unemployment. This fall in aggregate demand can, in principle at least, be offset by an appropriate increase in the money supply, an increase in government purchases of goods and services or a tax cut.

Economists remain a long way from agreement about the causes of unemployment and the reasons for its sometimes high and constantly fluctuating rate.

ployed increases at such a time. In addition, if the impacts of the business cycle are unevenly distributed over the economy, so that job creation is concentrated in a different part of the country than where job destruction is occurring, then the pool of unemployed temporarily increases further.

According to the sticky wage model of the labour market, there is an additional source of unemployment that has to be added to the natural rate of unemployment that occurs in a flexible wage labour market. Let's see what it is.

Unemployment with Sticky Wages

With sticky money wages, unemployment does not necessarily equal its natural rate. If the real wage rate is above its full-employment level, the quantity of labour employed is less than the quantity supplied and unemployment is above its natural rate. Such a situation is shown in Fig. 31.13. The money wage rate is \$10 an hour. If the GDP deflator is 100 there is full employment — unemployment is at its natural rate — point *c*. If the GDP deflator is 83.3, the real wage rate is \$12 an hour and the quantity of labour demanded is 9 billion hours — point *a*. Unemployment is above its 'natural' rate. If the GDP deflator is 125, the real wage rate is \$8 an hour and the quantity of labour demanded is 17 billion hours — point *e*. Unemployment is below its 'natural' rate.

Fluctuations in aggregate demand bring fluctuations in the price level. These fluctuations move the economy (upward and downward) along its demand for labour curve. At the same time, unemployment fluctuates around its natural rate. According to the sticky wage theory, fluctuations in unemployment arise primarily from the mechanism just described. Changes in the real wage rate arising from a sticky money wage rate and a changing price level result in movements along the labour demand curve and movements along the short-run aggregate supply curve. The rate of job creation and destruction also fluctuates but those fluctuations are the result of aggregate demand fluctuations.

Those economists who emphasize the role of sticky wages in generating fluctuations in unemployment usually regard the natural rate of unemployment as constant — or changing slowly. Fluctuations in the actual unemployment rate are fluctuations around the natural rate. Notice that this interpretation of fluctuations in unemployment contrasts with that of the flexible wage theory. A flexible wage model predicts that *all* changes in unemployment are fluctuations in the natural rate of unemployment.

Figure 31.13 Unemployment with Sticky Money Wages

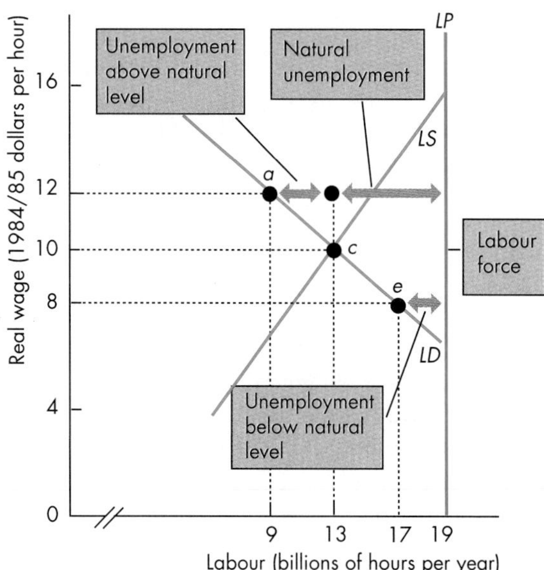

The money wage rate is set at \$10 an hour in anticipation that the GDP deflator will be 100. If the deflator turns out to be 83.3, the real wage rate is \$12 an hour. At this higher real wage rate, the quantity of labour demanded falls short of the quantity of labour supplied and unemployment is above its natural rate. If the deflator turns out to be 125, the real wage rate is \$8 an hour. At this lower real wage rate, the quantity of labour demanded exceeds the quantity of labour supplied and unemployment is below its natural rate. Fluctuations in the price level, with sticky money wages, cause fluctuations in the level of unemployment.

If most of the fluctuations in unemployment *do* arise from sticky wages, aggregate demand management can moderate those fluctuations in unemployment. By keeping aggregate demand steady so that the price level stays close to its expected level, the economy can be kept close to full employment.

The controversy about unemployment, and some recent attempts to improve our understanding of the phenomenon, are dealt with in Our Advancing Knowledge on pp. 388–389. The alignment of macroeconomists in this controversy is similar to that in the older Keynesian–monetarist controversy that we discussed in the previous chapter. Monetarists tend to take the view that wages are flexible and that unemployment is frictional or 'natural'. Keynesians take the view that wages are sticky and that some unemployment arises from insufficient wage flexibility. Unlike the old Keynesian–monetarist aggregate demand controversy, this controversy is still not settled. We have not yet found the 'acid test' that enables economists on both sides of the debate to set out a research agenda that can, in principle, settle their differences.

■ We have now studied the labour market and the determination of long-run and short-run aggregate supply, employment, wages and unemployment. Our next task is to bring together the aggregate demand and aggregate supply sides of the economy again and see how they interact to determine inflation and business cycles. We are going to pursue these tasks in the next two chapters.

SUMMARY

The Short-Run Aggregate Production Function

The short-run aggregate production function tells us how real GDP varies as the aggregate quantity of labour employed changes, with a given stock of capital equipment and a given state of technology. As the labour input increases, real GDP increases but by diminishing marginal amounts. The short-run aggregate production function shifts as a result of capital accumulation and technological change. These factors cause the short-run aggregate production function to shift upward over time. Occasionally the production function shifts downward because of negative influences such as restrictions on international trade. The Australian short-run aggregate production function shifted upward by 54 per cent between 1966/67 and 1990/91. (pp. 366–369)

The Demand for Labour

Firms choose how much labour to demand. The lower the real wage rate, the larger is the quantity of labour hours demanded. In choosing how much labour to hire, firms aim to maximize their profits. They achieve this objective by ensuring that the revenue brought in by an additional hour of labour equals the hourly wage rate. The more hours of labour that are employed, the lower the revenue brought in by the last hour of labour. Firms can be induced to increase the quantity of labour hours demanded, either by a decrease in the price of labour — the wage rate — or by an increase in the revenue brought in — by an increase in the price of output. Both a decrease in wages and an increase in prices result in a lower real wage. Thus the lower the real wage, the higher is the quantity of labour demanded.

The relationship between the real wage and the quantity of labour demanded is summarized in the demand for labour curve, which slopes downward. The demand for labour curve shifts as a result of shifts in the short-run aggregate production function. (pp. 369–372)

The Supply of Labour

Households choose how much labour to supply. They also choose the timing of their labour supply. A higher real wage rate encourages the substitution of work for leisure and a higher participation rate. A high current wage relative to expected future wages encourages more work in the present and less in the future — the intertemporal substitution effect. Taking all these forces together, the higher the real wage rate, the greater is the quantity of labour supplied. (pp. 372–374)

Wages and Employment

There are two theories of labour market equilibrium, one based on the assumption that wages are flexible and the other based on the assumption that they are sticky. Under the flexible wage theory, the real wage rate adjusts to ensure that the quantity of labour supplied equals the quantity demanded.

With flexible wages, the aggregate supply curve is vertical — the long-run aggregate supply curve. The quantity of real GDP supplied is independent of the price level. The long-run aggregate supply curve shifts as a result of shifts in the supply of labour curve and shifts in the short-run aggregate production function that lead to shifts in the demand for labour curve.

With sticky money wages, real wages do not adjust to balance the quantity of labour supplied and the quantity demanded. Money wages are set to make the expected quantity of labour demanded equal to the expected quantity supplied. The real wage depends on the money wage contracted and the price level. The level of employment is determined by the demand for labour, with households agreeing to supply the quantity demanded. Fluctuations in the price level relative to what was expected generate

Measuring Unemployment

Participation Rate Blurs the Jobless Figures

How much will unemployment rise as new job opportunities dry up? This, of course, will depend on how many people are thrown out of work.

But it will also hinge on the 'labour force participation rate' because of the way that the Australian Bureau of Statistics categorises the labour market.

When it conducts its monthly survey of households, the ABS counts people as employed if they work for payment for at least one hour a week.

People are unemployed if they do not have a job and if they are 'actively' looking for paid work.

The jobless rate is a percentage of employment plus unemployment — the labour force.

The participation rate comes in here by measuring the labour force as a proportion of the population aged 15 years or more.

Hence, 63.6 per cent of the working age population were either 'employed' or 'unemployed' last month.

The remaining 36 per cent, mainly those on unpaid home duties, students and the retired, are classified as not in the labour force.

The importance of this for unemployment can be neatly shown in the accompanying updated versions of graphs devised by Professor Bob Gregory of the Australian National University.

Unemployment rises (or falls) if employment growth is lower (or higher) than the growth in the labour force, such as when the jobless rate jumped from 6 per cent to 10 per cent in 1982–83.

When job growth slows or turns negative, those people previously in work do not all become unemployed.

Some of them drop out of the labour force and become 'discouraged workers' or the 'hidden unemployed'. This acts to push the participation rate down and dampen the rise in official unemployment.

Conversely, when the economy creates lots of new jobs, they are not all filled from the pool of unemployed.

Many of the new jobs are taken by people previously outside the labour force who effectively bypass unemployment, thus lifting the participation rate.

This 'cyclical.' behaviour is most pronounced for females, because they tend to be the 'secondary' part-time bread-winner for families and do most of the unpaid housework.

The graphs also reflect the longer-term participation rate trends, as shown by the much stronger growth in the female labour force over the 1980s.

In Australia, as in most advanced economies, trend female participation is rising due to changing social attitudes, the impact of contraception on reducing the size of families, more available child care and labour-saving household appliances (such as dishwashing machines, clothes driers and microwave ovens).

In the mid-to-late 1980s, two other factors were important.

One the supply side, real wage cuts and increased housing costs encouraged more married women to enter the job hunt, particularly for part-time employment.

On the demand side, most of the new jobs created were in the female dominated and labour intensive services sector, such as tourism, retailing and data processing.

Thus, the participation rate for females has jumped from 44 per cent to above 52 per cent since the early 1980s — explaining why very strong job growth in the 1980s made only modest inroads into measured unemployment.

However, for males the participation rate has fallen over the 1980s from 79 to 75 per cent.

Many of the older men retrenched in the 1982–83 recession have become 'discouraged' from looking for work; retirement (although this may be levelling off); and, until the late 1980s, relatively few extra jobs were created in manufacturing.

As the job market weakens, a cyclical easing in the participation rate will tend to dampen the rise in measured unemployment.

But, if high interest rates produce a deep manufacturing and construction recession in 1990, official unemployment could still rise relatively sharply from 6 per cent towards 8 per cent. The retrenched male workers would tend to keep the participation rate up by staying in the labour force.

However, if the economy is going into mainly a 'retail recession', the outcome is more uncertain.

If married women workers go out of the labour force and back to the kitchen as female jobs dry up, the participation rate will fall more and official unemployment might not even reach 7 per cent.

This happened in the 1970s when the job market weakened.

But, if the squeeze on family incomes and the taste for the working life keep retrenched married women in the job hunt, then the participation rate will not fall and unemployment could rise above 7 per cent.

***Financial Review*, Friday, 8 June 1990**
By Michael Stutchbury

The Essence of the Story

- The participation rate is the total number of employed people plus unemployed people (the labour force) expressed as a percentage of the working age population.
- The unemployment rate is the total number of unemployed people expressed as a percentage of the labour force.
- Thus the unemployment rate can change because either the total number of unemployed people changes, given the size of the labour force, or because the size of the labour force itself changes, that is, the participation rate changes.
- The participation rate is subject to two types of influences:
  - Secular or long-term trend influences
  - Cyclical or short-term influences
- There have been a number of long-term influences that have changed the participation rate for males and females:
  - Changing social attitudes, improved contraception methods, cheaper child care, and cheaper household labour-saving devices have made it easier for women to enter the labour force (a substitution effect).
  - Declining real wages and increasing costs of housing have further induced women to enter the labour force (an income effect).
  - The increased availability of jobs in the services sector, where employment is female dominated, has increased the probability that a woman entering the labour force will find a job.
  - On the other hand, the number of jobs in the manufacturing sector, where employment is predominantly male, has declined.
- These changing influences have caused a long-run increase in the female participation rate from 44 per cent in the early 1980s to over 52 per cent in 1990. But the male participation rate has declined over the same period from 79 per cent to 75 per cent.

Background and Analysis

- The most important cyclical influence on the participation rate is the variation of the real wage over the business cycle. The effects are depicted in part (a) of the figure. *LF* is the labour force curve. The labour force varies with the real wage because when the real wage increases more people will find it worthwhile to look for a job. Conversely, when the real wage declines, some people will find that their time is more valuable in non-market activity and will leave the labour force.
- The initial demand for labour is LD_0 and the supply of labour is LS_0. In the initial equilibrium the size of the labour force is F_0 and L_0 are actually employed at a real wage w_0. The unemployment rate is:

$$u_0 = \frac{F_0 - L_0}{F_0} \times 100$$

- If the demand for labour decreases, that is, LD_0 shifts to the left to LD_1, the real wage falls to w_1. Some people decide that their time is better spent in non-market activity and leave the labour force. F_0 falls to F_1. The unemployment rate rises to:

$$u_1 = \frac{F_1 - L_1}{F_1} \times 100$$

- We should not treat those people who have left the labour force as 'discouraged workers' simply because they found their time more valuable in other activities. However, there is an important discouraged worker effect, which arises for different reasons. Part (b) of the figure depicts what happens.
- When the unemployment rate rises, some workers who are looking for a job come to believe that they will never find one because there are now so many people looking for work. They leave the labour force, discouraged by the activity of searching for a job, even though they might not have any productive activities to undertake outside the market. Thus the labour force curve shifts to the left, from LF_0 to LF_1. This also shifts the labour supply curve to the left from LS_0 to LS_1. As a result of the quantity $F_0 - F_1$'. discouraged workers leaving the labour force, the reported unemployment rate is lower than it would otherwise have been, the labour force is smaller and the real wage is higher.

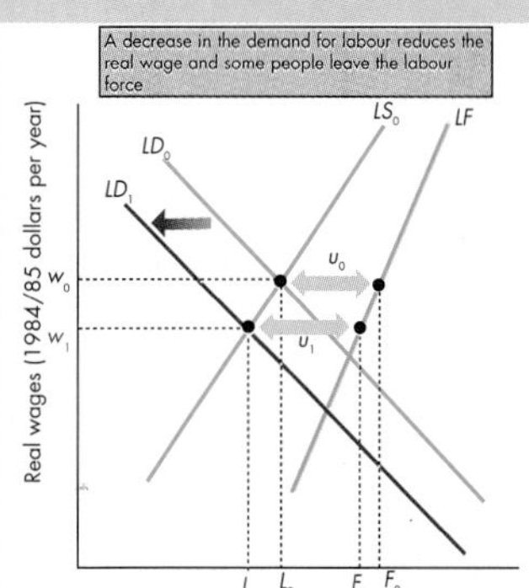

(a) Procyclical participation rate

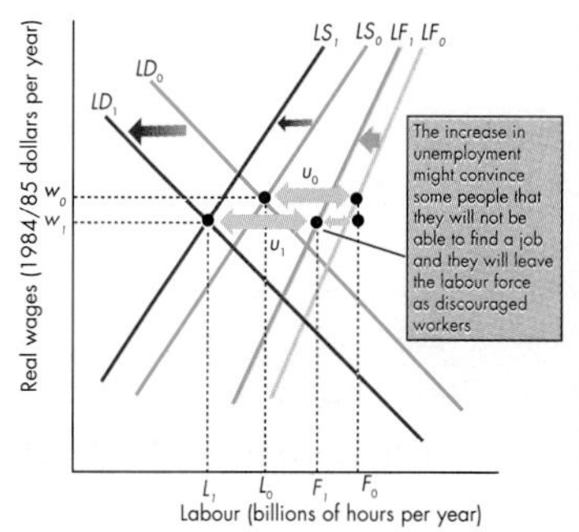

(b) The discouraged-worker effect

fluctuations in the quantity of labour demanded and in employment and real GDP. The higher the price level relative to what was expected, the lower is the real wage. The lower the real wage, the greater is the quantity of labour demanded and the greater is employment and real GDP.

With sticky money wages, the short-run aggregate supply curve slopes upward. The higher the price level, the higher is the quantity of real GDP supplied. (pp. 374–384)

Unemployment

The labour market is in a constant state of change or labour turnover. Labour turnover creates unemployment. New entrants to the labour force and workers re-entering after a period of homemaking must take time to find a job. Some people quit an existing job to seek a better one. Some are laid off and others are fired and forced to find another job. The pace of labour turnover is not constant. When technological change is expanding one sector and leading to a contraction of another sector, labour turnover increases. Finding new jobs and moving takes time, and the process of adjustment may create overtime and unfilled vacancies in the expanding sector but unemployment in the contracting sector. Workers' expectations of the type of job they might get and at what wage also affect the rate of labour turnover.

Even if wages are flexible, unemployment arising from labour market turnover cannot be avoided. The rate of unemployment arising from this source is the natural unemployment rate. In labour markets with flexible wages, all the fluctuations in unemployment are fluctuations in the natural rate arising from changes in the rate of labour turnover.

If wages are sticky, unemployment arises for all the same reasons as in the case of flexible wages and for one additional reason. With sticky wages the real wage may not move quickly enough to keep the quantity of labour demanded equal to the quantity supplied. In such a case, if the real wage rate is 'too high', the level of employment is below full employment and unemployment rises above its natural rate. If real wages are 'too low', the quantity of labour demanded and employed rises and unemployment falls below its natural rate. (pp. 384–391)

KEY TERMS

Demand for labour, p. 369
Diminishing marginal product of labour, p. 367
Efficiency wage, p. 378
Implicit contract, p. 378
Innovation, p. 368
Invention, p. 368
Labour force participation rate, p. 374
Marginal product of labour, p. 367
Money wage rate, p. 369
Natural rate of unemployment, p. 386
Production function, p. 366
Quantity of labour demanded, p. 369
Quantity of labour supplied, p. 372
Real wage rate, p. 369
Reservation wage, p. 374
Short-run aggregate production function, p. 366
Short-run production function, p. 366
Supply of labour, p. 372

PROBLEMS

1 Use the following information about an economy to answer problems a) to f). The economy's short-run production function is:

Labour hours	Real GDP
1	20
2	38
3	54
4	68
5	80
6	90
7	98
8	104

Its demand and supply schedules for labour are:

Real wage rate	Labour hours demanded	Labour hours supplied
6	8	2
8	7	3
10	6	4

12	5	5
14	4	6
16	3	7
18	2	8
20	1	9

a) If real wages are flexible, how much labour is employed and what is the real wage rate?
b) If the GDP deflator is 120, what is the money wage rate?
c) If real wages are flexible, what is the aggregate supply curve in this economy?
d) If money wages are sticky and if the GDP deflator is expected to be 100, what is the money wage rate in this economy?
e) Find three points on the short-run aggregate supply curve of this economy when money wages are at the level determined by your answer to part d).
f) Calculate the real wage rate at each of the three points that you have used in your answer to part e).

2 There are two economies, each with constant unemployment rates but with a great deal of labour market turnover. In economy A, there is a rapid pace of technological change. Twenty per cent of the workforce is either fired or quits every year and 20 per cent is hired every year. In economy B, only 5 per cent is fired or quits and 5 per cent is hired. Which economy has the higher unemployment rate? Why?

3 There are two economies, Flexiland and Fixland. These economies are identical in every way except that, in Flexiland, real wages are flexible and maintain equality between the quantities of labour demanded and supplied. In Fixland, wages are sticky in such a way that, on the average, the quantity of labour demanded equals the quantity supplied.
a) Explain which economy has the higher average unemployment rate.
b) Explain which economy has the largest fluctuations in unemployment.

Chapter 32

Expectations and Inflation

After studying this chapter, you will be able to:

- Explain why inflation is a problem.
- Explain how increasing aggregate demand generates a price–wage inflation spiral.
- Explain how decreasing aggregate supply generates a cost–price inflation spiral.
- Explain why it pays to make accurate forecasts of inflation.
- Explain how inflation expectations are formed.
- Explain how inflation expectations affect *actual* inflation.
- Explain the relationship between inflation and interest rates.
- Explain the relationship between inflation and unemployment.

Wanted: A Crystal Ball

In 1980/81 there was strong growth in Australia. Both firms and unions agreed that a mining boom was imminent. The high level of confidence prompted firms to undertake investment on a large scale. Unions were able to negotiate large pay increases on the anticipation of continued strong growth and consequent price increases. But the unexpected happened. The rest of the world went into recession in 1981/82 as a result of tight monetary policies in the United States and Europe. The mining boom did not eventuate, prices did not rise as expected and real wages stayed very high. In effect, the less-than-expected inflation landed firms with a 10 per cent real wage increase. A recession followed. Suppose that by a supreme effort of self-discipline you have saved $100 for a rainy day. On 1 January 1990, you put your $100 in a 15-year Commonwealth government bond, with an annual yield of 13 per cent. If you re-invest the interest income each year, you will have $625 to spend on 1 January 2005. Is that a good deal? Should you run out and buy bonds? That depends on what $625 buys in the year 2005. With no inflation, your $100 will have grown into enough to buy a good VCR or a modest stereo system. If inflation averages 13 per cent, however, $625 in the year 2005 will buy the same amount of goods as $100 did in 1990. If inflation averages 20 per cent, a restaurant meal that today costs $40 will cost nearly $620 in 2005. No matter how much you like the meal, it will not be a good deal, over 15 years, to shrink $100 into today's equivalent of $40. You have a terrific opportunity to buy a unit for $100,000 financed by a twenty year loan at a fixed interest rate of 10 per cent a year. If you take the opportunity, you are committed to making monthly payments for the next twenty years of $965. You know that you can only just squeeze this amount out of your current budget. But you believe that inflation will average around 6 per cent a year raising your income by at least that amount each year. If you're right the loan will be easy to repay, at least after a year or two of inflation. If you're wrong you'll just not be able to keep up with repayments and do all the other things you want to do with your income. These are examples of situations in which inflation has a big effect on our lives. To make good decisions we need good forecasts of inflation, and not just for the next year but for many years into the future. To forecast inflation we need to know what causes it. Why does the pace of inflation rise and all? Why do the best made plans go awry when it comes to inflation? How do people form expectations about inflation? Do those expectations influence the economy? How do inflation expectations affect interest rates?

This book will not tell you whether Commonwealth government bonds are a good deal today or whether or not to take out that twenty year fixed interest rate loan today. To do that, we would need a crystal ball. But this chapter will help you to understand the forces that generate inflation. It will also help you to understand how inflation expectations are formed and how the performance of the economy — real GDP, the GDP deflator and interest rates — depends on the extent to which inflation is correctly anticipated.

The forces that determine inflation (and real GDP growth) are studied using the aggregate demand–aggregate supply model. In that model, inflation — a rising price level — can result from increasing aggregate demand, decreasing aggregate supply or a combination of the two. Before embarking on a study of the causes of inflation let's remind ourselves of what inflation is and why it is a problem.

Inflation

We're now going to use our macroeconomic model of aggregate demand and aggregate supply to study the causes of inflation. First, recall that the inflation rate is the percentage rise in the price level. That is

$$\text{Inflation rate} = \frac{\text{Current year's price level} - \text{Last year's price level}}{\text{Last year's price level}} \times 100$$

Let's write this equation in symbols. We'll call this year's price level P_1 and last year's price level P_0, so that

$$\text{Inflation rate} = \frac{P_1 - P_0}{P_0}$$

This equation shows that there is a connection between the inflation rate and the price level. For a given price level last year, the higher the inflation rate, the higher is the price level this year.

The inflation rate is a measure of the rate at which money is losing value and this fact is the source of the inflation problem. But the nature of the problem depends on whether inflation is anticipated or unanticipated.

Anticipated Inflation

If money loses value at a rapid but anticipated rate, it does not function well as a medium of exchange. In such a situation resources are wasted. As a result, people may search for alternative means of payment (for example, foreign currency) or resort to barter. Instead of concentrating on the activities at which they have a comparative advantage and exchanging the results of their efforts, people may find it more profitable to search for ways to avoid holding and using too much money — to avoid the loss in the value of money induced by inflation.

Anticipated inflation only becomes a serious problem at very high inflation rates. But there are many examples of costly anticipated inflations around the world. Israel had such an inflation in the 1980s. And Bolivia has such an inflation in the 1990s. The closest Australia has come to such a situation was in the mid-1970s when the inflation rate averaged more than 15 per cent a year.

Unanticipated Inflation

Unanticipated inflation is a problem even at low inflation rates. It redistributes wealth between borrowers and lenders and income between employers and employees. An unanticipated increase in the inflation rate transfers real buying power from lenders to borrowers and an unanticipated decrease in inflation transfers resources in the opposite direction. An unanticipated increase in inflation also decreases real wages and increases real GDP and employment, while an unanticipated decrease in inflation increases real wages and decreases real GDP and employment. Unanticipated fluctuations in the inflation rate produce fluctuations in the economy — fluctuations in real GDP, employment and unemployment.

Much of this chapter explains why unanticipated inflation has these effects. It also explains how unanticipated inflation arises by studying the formation of inflation expectations. Let's begin by looking at the unanticipated inflation that results from an increase in aggregate demand.

Demand Inflation

Inflation resulting from an increase in aggregate demand is called **demand-pull inflation.** Such inflation may arise from any source that increases aggregate demand. Let's look at some of them.

Sources of Increasing Aggregate Demand

Any of the factors reviewed in Chapter 24 can lead to an increase in aggregate demand, but the most important of these for generating ongoing increases in aggregate demand are:

- Increases in the money supply
- Increases in government purchases of goods and services

When aggregate demand increases, the aggregate demand curve shifts to the right. Let's trace the effects of such an increase.

Inflation Effect of an Increase in Aggregate Demand

Suppose that last year the GDP deflator was 130 and real GDP was $300 billion. Suppose also that the economy's capacity output last year was $300 billion, so that the economy was at full employment. Figure 32.1(a) illustrates the economy last year. The aggregate demand curve last year was AD_0, the aggregate supply curve was SAS_0 and the long-run aggregate supply curve was *LAS*.

In the current year, aggregate demand increases to AD_1. Such a situation arises if the Reserve Bank loosens monetary policy, or the government increases its purchases of goods and services or cuts taxes. The economy moves to the point where the aggregate demand curve AD_1 intersects the short-run aggregate supply curve SAS_0. The GDP deflator increases to 135 and real GDP increases to $325 billion. The economy experiences 3.85 per cent inflation (a GDP deflator of 135 compared with 130 in the previous year) and a rapid expansion of real GDP.

Wage Response

The economy cannot produce at an above full-employment level of real GDP for long. With unemployment below its natural rate, there is a shortage of labour. Wages begin to increase, and the short-run aggregate supply curve starts to shift to the left. Prices rise further and real GDP begins to fall. With no further change in

Figure 32.1 Demand-Pull Inflation

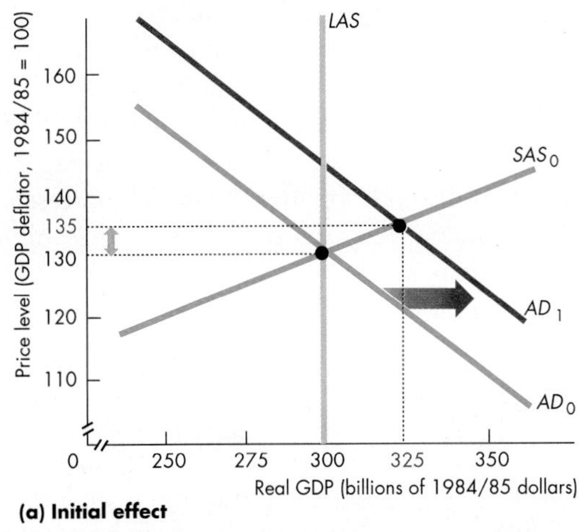

(a) Initial effect

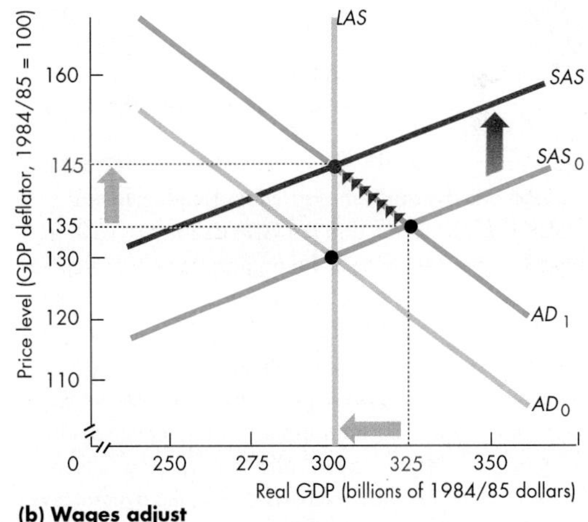

(b) Wages adjust

In part (a), the aggregate demand curve is AD_0, the short-run aggregate supply curve is SAS_0 and the long-run aggregate supply curve is *LAS*. The GDP deflator is 130 and real GDP is $300 billion, its long-run level. Aggregate demand increases to AD_1 (because the Reserve Bank increased the money supply or the government increased its purchases of goods and services). The new equilibrium occurs where AD_1 intersects SAS_0. The economy experiences inflation (the GDP deflator rises to 135) and real GDP increases to $325 billion.

In part (b), starting from above full employment, wages begin to rise and the short-run aggregate supply curve shifts to the left to SAS_1. The price level rises further and real GDP returns to its long-run level.

aggregate demand — the aggregate demand curve remains at AD_1 — this process comes to an end when the short-run aggregate demand curve has moved to SAS_1 in Fig. 32.1(b). By this time, the GDP deflator has increased to 145 and real GDP has returned to its long-run level, from which it started.

A Price–Wage Inflation Spiral

The inflation process we've just studied eventually comes to an end when, for a given increase in aggregate demand, wages have adjusted enough to restore the real wage rate to its full-employment level. But suppose that the initial increase in aggregate demand

Figure 32.2 A Price–Wage Inflation Spiral

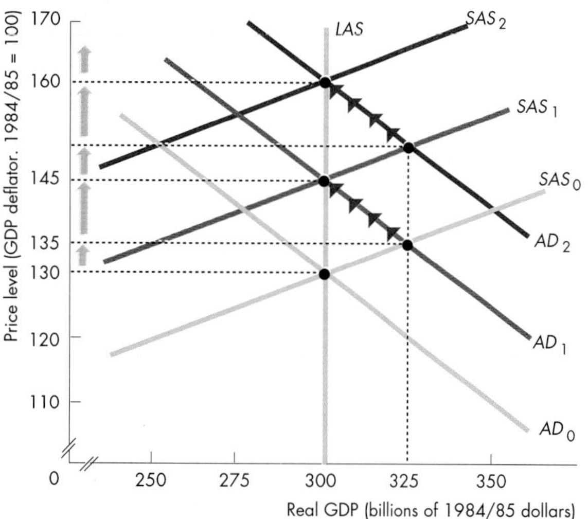

The aggregate demand curve is AD_0, the short-run aggregate supply curve is SAS_0 and the long-run aggregate supply curve is *LAS*. Real GDP is $300 billion and the GDP deflator is 130. Aggregate demand increases, shifting the aggregate demand curve to AD_1. Real GDP increases to $325 billion and the GDP deflator rises to 135. With real GDP above its long-run level, wages begin to rise, shifting the short-run aggregate supply curve to SAS_1. The GDP deflator increases to 145 and real GDP returns to its full-employment level. As aggregate demand continues to increase, the aggregate demand curve shifts to AD_2. The GDP deflator increases further, real GDP exceeds its full-employment level and wages continue to rise. As the short-run aggregate supply curve shifts to SAS_2, the GDP deflator increases to 160. As aggregate demand continues to increase, the price level rises, generating a chronic demand-pull inflation. Real GDP fluctuates between $300 billion and $325 billion. But if aggregate demand increases *at the same time* as wages increase, real GDP remains at $325 billion as the demand-pull inflation occurs.

resulted from a large government budget deficit, financed by the Reserve Bank, creating more and more money. If such a policy remains in place, aggregate demand will continue to increase year after year. The aggregate demand curve will keep shifting to the right, putting continual upward pressure on the price level. The economy will experience *chronic* demand-pull inflation.

Figure 32.2 illustrates a perpetual demand-pull inflation. The starting point is the same as that shown in Fig. 32.1. The aggregate demand curve is AD_0, the short-run aggregate supply curve is SAS_0 and the long-run aggregate supply curve is *LAS*. Real GDP is $300 billion and the GDP deflator is 130. Aggregate demand increases, shifting the aggregate demand curve to AD_1. Real GDP increases to $325 billion and the GDP deflator rises to 135. With real GDP above its long-run level, there is a shortage of labour and the wage rate rises, shifting the short-run aggregate supply curve to SAS_1. The GDP deflator increases to 145 and real GDP returns to its full-employment level.

But aggregate demand continues to increase, shifting the aggregate demand curve to AD_2. The GDP deflator increases further, real GDP exceeds its full employment level and wages continue to rise. As the *SAS* curve shifts to SAS_2, the GDP deflator increases further to 160. As aggregate demand continues to increase, the price level rises continuously, generating a chronic demand-pull inflation. Real GDP fluctuates between $300 billion and $325 billion.

In the price–wage inflation spiral that we've just described, aggregate demand increases and wages increase in response in a continuing cycle — first aggregate demand increases, then wages, then aggregate demand, and so on. If, after the initial increase in aggregate demand that took real GDP to $325 billion, aggregate demand continues to increase *at the same time* as wages increase, real GDP remains above its long-run level at $325 billion as the demand-pull inflation proceeds.

On the other hand, if aggregate demand continues to increase at the same time as wages increase, *after* real GDP has returned to its long-run level of $300 billion, then demand-pull inflation would proceed with no gain in output.

Inflation in Beenleigh You may better understand the inflation process we've just described by considering what is going on in an individual part of the economy, such as a Beenleigh brewery. Initially when aggregate demand increases, the demand for beer increases and the price of beer rises. Faced with a higher price for its output, the brewery works overtime and increases production. Conditions are good for workers in Beenleigh and the brewery finds it hard to hang on to its best people. To do so it has to offer higher wages. As wages increase, so do the costs of the brewery.

What happens next depends on what happens to aggregate demand. If aggregate demand remains constant — as in Fig. 32.1(b) — the firm's costs are increasing but the price of beer is not increasing as quickly as its costs. Production is scaled back. Eventually, wages and costs increase by the same amount as the price of beer. In real terms, the brewery is in the same situation as it was initially, before the increase in aggregate demand. It produces the same amount of beer and employs the same amount of labour.

But if aggregate demand continues to increase, so does the demand for beer and the price of beer rises at the same rate as wages. The brewery continues to operate above full employment and there is a persistent shortage of labour. Prices and wages chase each other upward in an unending price–wage spiral.

R E V I E W

Demand-pull inflation results from any initial factor, such as an increase in the money supply, an increase in government purchases of goods and services, a decrease in taxes, an increase in profit expectations, an increase in foreign income or a decrease in the value of the dollar, that increases aggregate demand. Initially, the increase in aggregate demand increases the price level and real GDP. With real GDP above full employment, wages rise, decreasing short-run aggregate supply. If aggregate demand remains constant at its new level, the price level rises further and real GDP returns to its long-run level. If aggregate demand continues to increase, wages chase prices in an unending price–wage inflation spiral. ■

Anticipating Increases in Aggregate Demand

At some point in the inflation process, people will recognize the inflationary environment in which they are living and *anticipate* the inflation. When that happens there is an important change in the behaviour of both the price level and real GDP. We'll look at this case later in the chapter, but before doing so, let's look at how shocks to aggregate supply create inflation.

Supply Inflation and Stagflation

Inflation can result from a decrease in aggregate supply. Let's look at the main reasons why aggregate supply might decrease.

Sources of Decreasing Aggregate Supply

There are two main reasons why aggregate supply might decrease. They are:

- An increase in wage rates
- An increase in the prices of key raw materials

These disturbances increase costs and induce firms to reduce supply. Inflation caused by rising costs is called **cost-push inflation**. Other things remaining the same, the higher the cost of production, the smaller is the amount produced at a given price level. Rising wages, with a constant price level, lead firms to decrease the quantity of labour employed and to cut back on production. But increases in the

Figure 32.3 Cost-Push Inflation

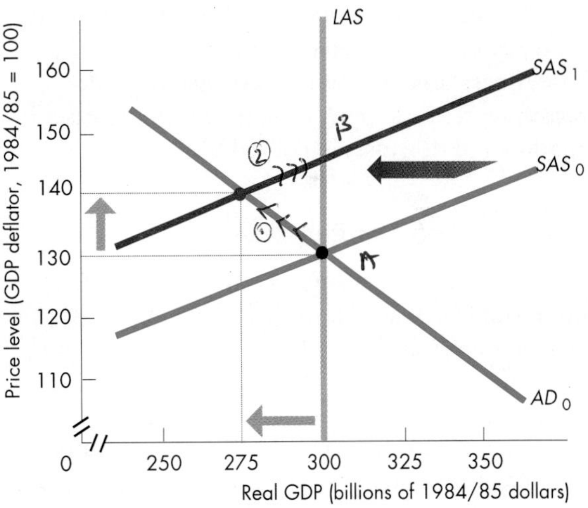

Initially the aggregate demand curve is AD_0, the short-run aggregate supply curve is SAS_0 and the long-run aggregate supply curve is *LAS*. A decrease in aggregate supply (resulting from an across-the-board increase in wages) shifts the short-run aggregate supply curve to SAS_1. The economy moves to the point where the new short-run aggregate supply curve SAS_1 intersects the aggregate demand curve AD_0. The GDP deflator increases to 140 and real GDP decreases to $275 billion. The economy experiences inflation and a contraction of real GDP — *stagflation*.

prices of other key inputs such as oil or other energy sources have a similar effect. When aggregate supply decreases, the short-run aggregate supply curve shifts to the left. Let's see what that does to the price level.

Inflation Effect of a Decrease in Aggregate Supply

Suppose that last year the GDP deflator was 130 and real GDP was $300 billion. Long-run real GDP was also $300 billion. This situation is shown in Fig. 32.3. The aggregate demand curve is AD_0, the short-run aggregate supply curve is SAS_0 and the long-run aggregate supply curve is *LAS.*

In the current year, aggregate supply decreases, shifting the short-run aggregate supply curve to SAS_1. Such a situation might arise if there is a sharp across-the-board increase in wages. The economy moves to the point where the new short-run aggregate supply curve SAS_1 intersects the aggregate demand curve AD_0. The GDP deflator increases to 140 and real GDP decreases to $275 billion. The economy experiences 7.7 per cent inflation (a GDP deflator of 140 compared with 130 in the previous year) and a contraction of real GDP. This combination of rising prices and falling output is known as **stagflation.**

The situation that developed in Australia in 1974/75 and again in 1981/82 was similar to what we've just described (refer back to Fig. 31.5). At those times, large increases in average wages decreased aggregate supply, bringing sharp increases in inflation and decreases in real GDP.

Figure 32.4 Aggregate Demand Response to Cost Push

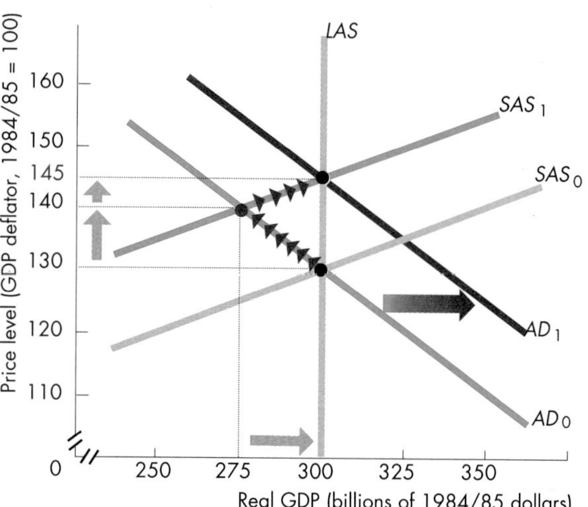

Initially the aggregate demand curve is AD_0, the short-run aggregate supply curve is SAS_0 and the long-run aggregate supply curve is *LAS*. A decrease in aggregate supply shifts the short-run aggregate supply curve to SAS_1. The GDP deflator rises from 130 to 140 and real GDP decreases from $300 billion to $275 billion. The economy experiences stagflation. The economy may be stuck at an unemployment equilibrium. If the Reserve Bank or government responds by increasing aggregate demand to restore full employment, the aggregate demand curve shifts to the right to AD_1. The economy returns to full employment, but at the expense of higher inflation. The price level rises to 145.

Aggregate Demand Response

When the economy is stuck at an unemployment equilibrium such as that shown in Fig. 32.3, there is often an outcry and a call for government action to restore full employment. Such action includes an increase in government purchases of goods and services, a tax cut or an increase in the money supply. Any one of these actions, or a combination of them, increases aggregate demand and shifts the aggregate demand curve to the right. Figure 32.4 shows an increase in aggregate demand that shifts the aggregate demand curve to AD_1 and restores full employment, but at the expense of a still higher price level. The price level rises to 145.

A Cost–Price Inflation Spiral

Compare the situation illustrated in Fig. 32.4, where the price level is 145, with the economy's initial situation in Fig. 32.3, where the price level is 130. In each case, real GDP is $300 billion, there is full employment and the *real wage* is the same. The only difference is that price level and nominal wages are higher. The price level has increased 11.5 per cent and the economy has experienced inflation. Throughout this inflationary process, real wages were higher than initially. It was this higher cost of labour that triggered the inflation and the monetary response that increased aggregate demand and pulled inflation even higher. But the subsequent inflation also wiped out the real wage gains that started the process off.

Suppose now that workers, seeing the real wage fall, decide to increase it yet again. Figure 32.5 continues the story. The short-run aggregate supply curve now shifts to SAS_2 and another bout of stagflation ensues. The price level rises again — to 155 — and real GDP falls — to $275 billion. Unemployment rises above its natural rate. If the Reserve Bank

Figure 32.5 A Cost–Price Inflation Spiral

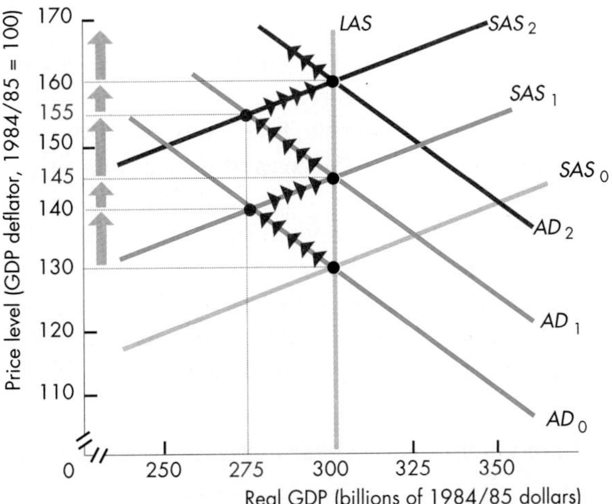

When a cost increase (such as an increase in the world oil price) decreases short-run aggregate supply from SAS_0 to SAS_1, the GDP deflator rises to 140 and real GDP decreases to $275 billion. The Reserve Bank and government respond with an increase in aggregate demand from AD_0 to AD_1. The GDP deflator rises again to 145 and real GDP returns to $300 billion. The cost-push force is applied again shifting the short-run aggregate supply curve to SAS_2. Stagflation is repeated and the GDP deflator now rises to 160. The Reserve Bank and government respond again and a cost–price inflation spiral ensues. Inflation has again become chronic.

responds again with a further increase in the money supply, aggregate demand increases and the aggregate demand curve shifts to AD_2. The price level rises even higher — to 160 — and full employment is restored. If the Reserve Bank does not respond, the economy remains below full employment until the initial price increase that triggered the stagflation is reversed.

You can see that the Reserve Bank is in a dilemma. If it increases the money supply to restore full employment, it invites another wage increase that will result in a further increase in the money supply. Inflation will continue at a rate decided by the unions, which are negotiating on behalf of workers. The economy again experiences chronic inflation. But if the Bank keeps a tight rein on money supply growth, the economy operates with a high level of unemployment. The Reserve Bank has often faced such a dilemma in Australia because the wage-setting process operates in an institutional environment, where wage increases are decided on outside the flexible wage labour market described in the previous chapter.

Cost-Push Inflation in Beenleigh What is going on in the Beenleigh brewery when the economy is experiencing cost-push inflation? When the average wage of other workers increases, so do the wage demands of the Beenleigh workers. Thus the costs of the brewery rise. The higher costs increase the price of beer, decreasing demand for Beenleigh beer, which ultimately leads to a decrease in the quantity produced. The brewery lays off some workers. This situation will persist until either the Reserve Bank increases aggregate demand — some of which falls on beer — or the real wage falls. If the Reserve Bank increases aggregate demand, the demand for beer increases and so does its price. The higher price of beer brings higher profits, because real wage costs are lowered, and the brewery increases its production. The brewery rehires the laid-off workers. If the Reserve Bank resists the pressure to increase aggregate demand, eventually the real wage falls and beer production gradually increases. This adjustment might take a much longer time than would occur when demand is increased.

R E V I E W

Cost-push inflation results from any initial factor, such as an increase in the money wage rate, an increase in the world price of a key raw material or a disruption of world trade, that decreases aggregate supply. The initial effect of a decrease in aggregate supply is an increase in the price level and a decrease in real GDP — stagflation. If monetary or fiscal policy increases aggregate demand to restore full employment, the price level rises further. If aggregate demand remains constant, the economy stays below full employment until the initial price rise is reversed. If the response to stagflation is always an increase in aggregate demand, a freewheeling cost-push inflation takes place at a rate determined by the speed with which costs are pushed upward. ■

Inflation Expectations

As we saw in the chapter opener, failing to anticipate the inflation rate is costly. Let's now take a closer look at inflation expectations. What exactly are the costs of unanticipated inflation? And how does the anticipation of inflation affect the actual course of inflation?

The Cost of Wrong Forecasts

Our inability to know the future, combined with our need to make forecasts about it, inevitably imposes costs on us. The more wrong we are in assessing the future price level, the more expensive our mistake will be. To see why errors in forecasting inflation are expensive, let's review what we have learned about the process of unanticipated inflation. And let's do this by returning to the brewery in Beenleigh.

Wages When we looked at the effects of demand inflation we saw that, initially, the price of beer and of other goods increases but the money wage doesn't change. The real wage rate falls and the brewery increases production. Workers begin to quit the brewery to find jobs that pay a higher real wage rate, one closer to that prevailing before the burst of inflation. This outcome imposes costs on both the firm and the workers. The firm operates its plant at a high output rate and incurs overtime costs, high labour turnover rates, and higher plant maintenance and parts replacement costs. The workers wind up feeling cheated. They've worked overtime to produce the extra output and, when they come to spend their wages, they discover that prices have increased so that their wages buy a smaller quantity of goods and services than anticipated.

Contrast this outcome with what might have happened if the burst of inflation had been correctly anticipated. In this case, the money wage rate at the brewery increases at the same rate as prices — the price of beer and the price level generally. The real wage rate, employment and output remain constant. Anticipated inflation is virtually costless.

Interest Rates Just as firms and workers incur costs from wrong forecasts of the price level, so do borrowers and lenders. Interest rates are determined on the basis of some expectation of the future value of money, which, in turn, depends on the future course of the price level. If inflation turns out to be unexpectedly high, borrowers gain and lenders lose. But what borrowers gain is less than what lenders lose. Both groups will regret the scale of borrowing and lending that took place. Borrowers wish they had borrowed more and lenders wish they had lent less.

If inflation turns out to be lower than expected, lenders gain and borrowers lose. Again, both groups regret the scale of borrowing and lending. In this case, lenders wish they had lent more and borrowers wish they had borrowed less. Again, the gains of the lenders are not sufficient to match the losses of the borrowers.

Costs occur regardless of whether price expectations turn out to be wrong on the up side or the down side. Wrong expectations impose costs on firms and households and the larger the forecasting error, the larger are those costs. The costs of wrong forecasts, like any other costs, are something to be minimized. These costs arise from scarcity in the same way that all other costs arise from scarcity. In this case, what is scarce is information. Nevertheless, although the costs of wrong forecasts cannot be entirely avoided, they can at least be made as small as possible.

Minimizing the Losses from Wrong Expectations

Lacking complete information, people cannot be right all the time. But they can use all the information available to them to make their forecasting errors as small as possible. That is, they can make a rational expectation. A **rational expectation** is a forecast based on all the available information. A rational expectation has two features. First, the range of the forecast error is as small as possible. No information that might narrow the range of uncertainty has been wasted. Given what is known, the range of uncertainty cannot be made smaller. Second, a rational expectation is correct *on the average.* This does not mean that a rational expectation is an accurate forecast each and every time a forecast is made. Rather, it means that people will not consistently make a forecast that turns out to be always too high or too low. Making forecasts that consistently err on one side or the other would finally be recognized and an adjustment made, which gets you closer to the right forecast. That is, simply by looking at past forecast errors, people could avoid being wrong in one direction. Since the costs of wrong forecasts occur regardless of whether expectations are too high or too low, the best that can be done is to make a forecast that has an equal chance of being too high or too low.

How do people actually form expectations? And, in particular, how do they form a rational expectation?

How People Form Expectations in the Real World

Different people devote different amounts of time and effort to forming expectations. Some people specialize in forecasting and even make a living by selling their forecasts. For example, investment advisers forecast the future prices of shares and bonds. Banks, large share and commodity brokers, government agencies and private forecasting firms make macroeconomic forecasts about inflation.

Specialist forecasters stand to lose a great deal by making wrong forecasts. They have a strong incentive, therefore, to make their forecasts as accurate as possible — minimizing the range of error and at least making them correct on the average. Furthermore, organizations that stand to lose by having wrong forecasts invest a good deal of effort in checking the forecasts of the professionals. For example, all the large banks, some of the major unions, government departments and most large private-sector producers of goods and services devote a lot of effort not only to making their own forecasts but also to checking their forecasts and comparing them with the forecasts of others.

In contrast to the specialists, most individuals devote little time and effort to making forecasts. Instead, they get their forecasts either by buying them from specialists or by mimicking people who appear to have been successful.

How Economists Predict People's Forecasts

Economics is a discipline concerned with predicting the choices people make. Since an important determinant of people's choices is their expectations of such phenomena as inflation, then to predict people's choices we also have to predict their expectations. How do economists set about that task?

They assume that people are as rational in their use of information and in forming expectations as they are in all their other economic actions. This idea leads economists to the rational expectations hypothesis. The **rational expectations hypothesis** is the proposition that the forecasts which people make are the same as the forecasts which would be made by an economist using the relevant economic theory together with all the information available at the time the forecast is made. For example, to predict people's expectations of the price of orange juice, economists use the economic model of demand and supply, together with all the available information about the positions of the demand and supply curves for orange juice. To make a prediction about people's expectations of the price level and inflation, economists use the economic model of aggregate demand and aggregate supply.

Let's see how we can use the model of aggregate demand and aggregate supply to work out the rational expectation of the price level.

The Rational Expectation of the Price Level

To form a rational expectation of the price level, we use the aggregate demand and aggregate supply model to forecast the state of the economy in much the same way that meteorologists use a model of the atmosphere to forecast the weather. But there is an important difference between the meteorologist's model of the atmosphere and the economist's model of aggregate demand and aggregate supply. Tomorrow's weather will not be affected by our forecast of it. We may forecast a sunny day or a torrential downpour, but the outcome is independent of that forecast. But the consensus forecast of the price level might affect the actual price level. We must take this fact into account when working out a rational expectation of the price level.

We'll now calculate a rational expectation of the price level using Fig. 32.6 to guide our analysis. The aggregate demand and aggregate supply model predicts that the price level is at the point of intersection of the aggregate demand and short-run aggregate supply curves. To forecast the price level, therefore, we have to forecast the positions of these curves.

Let's begin with aggregate demand. Suppose that we have forecasted all the things that influence aggregate demand. We then have a forecast of the position of the aggregate demand curve. This forecast is given by the expected aggregate demand curve (*EAD*).

Our next task is to forecast the position of the short-run aggregate supply curve, but here we have a problem. We know that the position of the short-run aggregate supply curve is determined by two things:

- Long-run aggregate supply
- The money wage rate

The short-run aggregate supply curve intersects the long-run aggregate supply curve at the full-employment price level. So we need a forecast of long-run aggregate supply. To make such a forecast we must forecast all the factors that determine long-run aggregate supply. Suppose that we have made the best forecast we can of long-run real GDP and that we expect long-run aggregate supply to be $300 billion. The *expected* long-run aggregate supply curve is *ELAS* in Fig. 32.6.

Figure 32.6 A Rational Expectation of the Price Level

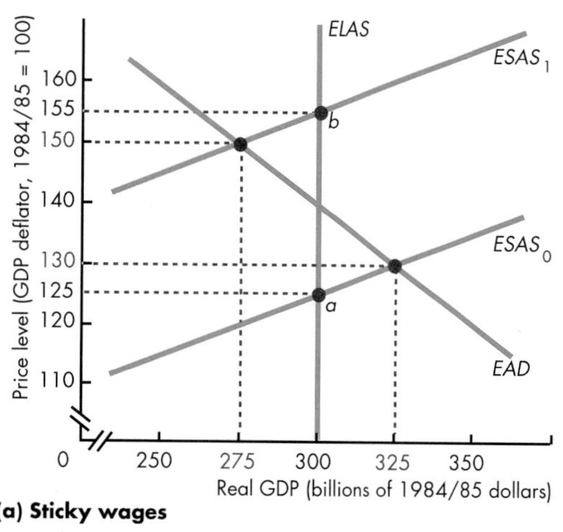

(a) Sticky wages

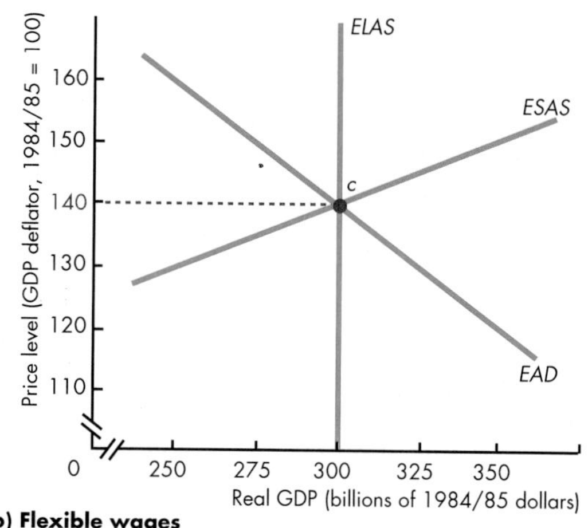

(b) Flexible wages

The rational expectation of the price level is the best available forecast. That forecast is constructed by forecasting the expected aggregate demand curve (*EAD*) and the expected short-run aggregate supply curve (*ESAS*). The rational expectation of the price level occurs at the point of intersection of curves *EAD* and *ESAS*.

But forecasts of the long-run aggregate supply curve *ELAS* and the money wage rate are needed to forecast the position of *ESAS*. In part (a), wages are sticky and do not respond to price level expectations so the position of the expected short-run aggregate supply curve depends on *ELAS* and the fixed money wage. With a low money wage rate, the expected short-run aggregate supply curve is $ESAS_0$, the full-employment price level is 125 (point *a*) and the rational expectation of the price level is 130. With a high wage, the expected short-run aggregate supply curve is $ESAS_1$, the full-employment price level is 155 (point *b*) and the rational expectation of the price level is 150.

In part (b), wages are flexible and respond to the expected price level. The rational expectation of the price level is at the point of intersection of *EAD* and *ELAS* — point *c*. The money wage rate is determined by this price level and the expected short-run aggregate supply curve *ESAS* passes through point *c*.

The final ingredient we need is a forecast of the money wage rate. Armed with this information, we have a forecast of the point on *ELAS* at which the short-run aggregate supply intersects. The forecast of the money wage rate depends on the degree of wage flexibility, and we need to look at two cases:

- Sticky money wages
- Flexible money wages

Rational Expectation with Sticky Money Wages

With sticky money wages, it is easy to forecast the position of the short-run aggregate supply curve. Its position is determined by the known and fixed money wage rate. Given that fixed wage rate, and given the expected long-run aggregate supply curve *ELAS*, there is an expected short-run aggregate supply curve. Figure 32.6(a) illustrates such a curve as $ESAS_0$. The point at which this curve intersects *ELAS*, point *a*, is at the price level at which full employment would occur.

The rational expectation of the price level is the point of intersection of *EAD* and $ESAS_0$, a price level of 130. The rational expectation of inflation is calculated as the percentage change from the previous period's actual price level to the expected value of the current period's price level. There is also a rational expectation of real GDP, $325 billion. Given the money wage rate and the expected short-run aggregate supply curve $ESAS_0$, the rational expectation is that the economy will be in a state of above full employment.

Figure 32.6(a) also shows another case — one in which the expected short-run aggregate supply curve is $ESAS_1$. Here, the money wage rate is higher. It is such that, for full employment, the GDP deflator would have to be 155, at point *b* in the figure. In this case, the rational expectation of the price level is 150 and the economy is expected to be in an unemployment equilibrium with a real GDP of $275 billion.

Rational Expectation with Flexible Wages

When wage flexibility is taken into account, it is harder to forecast the position of the short-run aggregate supply curve because wages have to be forecast. Furthermore, wages depend on the expected price level, the variable we are trying to forecast. There seems to be a big problem. To forecast the price level, we need a forecast of wages. And to forecast wages, we need a forecast of the price level.

The problem is solved by finding a forecast of the price level that makes the forecast of both the expected aggregate demand and expected short-run aggregate supply curves intersect at that same forecasted price level. There is only one such price level. It is that at which the expected aggregate demand curve intersects the expected long-run aggregate supply curve. This case is shown in Fig. 32.6(b). If money wages adjust in response to changes in the expected price level, they move to a level that makes the expected short-run aggregate supply curve *ESAS* in Fig. 32.6(b). We forecast the position of the short-run aggregate supply curve at the same time as forecasting the price level and the two forecasts are consistent with each other. Our forecast of the price level is a GDP deflator of 140 and *ESAS* is our forecast of the short-run aggregate supply curve.

Theory and Reality

The analysis that we have just conducted shows how economists work out a rational expectation. But do other people form expectations of the price level by using that same analysis? We can imagine that graduates of economics might, but it seems unrealistic to attribute such calculations to most people. Does this fact make the whole idea of rational expectations invalid?

The answer is no! In performing our calculations, we have been building an economic model. That model does not seek to describe the actual thought processes of people. Its goal is to make predictions about *behaviour*, not mental processes. The *rational expectations hypothesis* states that the forecasts which people make, regardless of how they make them, are on average the same as the forecasts that an economist makes using the relevant economic theory.

Now that we know what macroeconomic rational expectations are and how rational expectations of the price level and output are calculated, let's go on to see how actual real GDP and the actual price level are determined and compare them with their rational expectations.

R E V I E W

Wrong inflation forecasts impose costs on firms and workers, and borrowers and lenders. If inflation is higher than expected, real wages and real interest rates are lower than expected. Firms and borrowers gain and workers and lenders lose. If inflation is lower than expected, redistribution goes in the opposite direction. But there is not just a redistribution. Decisions made and actions taken to produce, to work, to borrow and to lend are different than they would have been had people acted with correct information about inflation. To minimize forecasting errors, people use all available information and form a *rational expectation.* Real world specialist forecasters use data and statistical models to generate expectations. Others either buy forecasts from specialists or copy people who seem to be successful.

Economists predict people's expectations using the rational expectations hypothesis — the hypothesis that the forecasts that people make are the same as those made by an economist using the relevant economic theory, together with all available information. A rational expectation of inflation uses the aggregate demand and aggregate supply model to forecast the future price level. ■

Rational Expectations Equilibrium

So far in this chapter we have discovered how unanticipated inflation results from changes in aggregate demand and aggregate supply and we have seen how real GDP and unemployment are also influenced by these forces. We have also studied the determination of inflation expectations — the way people try to *anticipate* inflation. Our next task is to bring these two things together. That is, we want to see how the economy works when there are disturbances to aggregate demand or aggregate supply and *at the same time* people are doing the best they can to anticipate changes. Such a situation is called a rational expectations equilibrium. A **rational expectations equilibrium** is a macroeconomic equilibrium based on expectations that are the best available forecasts. The rational expectations equilibrium occurs at the intersection of the aggregate demand and short-run aggregate supply curves.

Let's look at such situations and see how they come about using Fig. 32.7. The figure has three parts. Figure 32.7(a) contains people's forecasts of the economy and Fig. 32.7(b) and (c) show two alternative outcomes that differ from the forecast. The forecast in Fig. 32.7(a) is exactly the same as that seen in Fig. 32.6. The forecasted or expected price level is 140. In Fig. 32.7(b), we work out what happens when aggregate demand turns out to be different from expected aggregate demand. The long-run aggregate supply curve (*LAS*) and the short-run aggregate supply curve (*SAS*) in Fig 32.7(b) are identical to the expected long-run aggregate supply curve (*ELAS*) and the expected short-run aggregate supply curve (*ESAS*) in Fig. 32.7(a). The point at which these curves intersect — point *c* — is the same in each part of the figure and occurs when the GDP deflator is 140 and real GDP is $300 billion.

Figure 32.7 (b) shows what happens when actual aggregate demand turns out to be lower than expected. Such an outcome might arise from an *unexpected* slow-down in the rate at which the Reserve Bank is creating money, an *unexpected* fall in foreign demand for Australian exports, an *unexpected* tax increase or an *unexpected* reduction in government purchases of goods and services. The actual aggregate demand curve is *AD*. Equilibrium is determined where the actual aggregate demand curve intersects the short-run aggregate supply curve. The GDP deflator is 135 and real GDP $275 billion. With actual aggregate demand below its expected level, the price level is below its expected level and real GDP is below its long-run level.

Figure 32.7(c) shows what happens when aggregate supply turns out to be less than expected but aggregate demand is the same as expected. The aggregate demand curve (*AD*) in Fig. 32.7(c) is identical to the expected aggregate demand curve in Fig. 32.7(a). But the short-run aggregate supply curve is further to the left in Fig. 32.7(c) than the expected short-run aggregate supply curve in Fig. 32.7(a). Such a situation could arise because of an *unexpected* increase in the price of materials. Again, the equilibrium occurs where the aggregate demand curve intersects the short-run aggregate supply curve. In this case, that equilibrium is at a GDP deflator of 145 and real GDP of $275 billion. The actual price level is higher than expected because short-run aggregate supply is lower than expected and the economy is again below its long-run level of output.

Sticky Versus Flexible Wages

Do the outcomes just described depend on whether wages are sticky or flexible? This is a difficult question to answer because even if wages are flexible, they cannot respond to what is not known and not expected. The issue then turns to how quickly wages respond once it becomes clear that expectations of either demand or supply were wrong. With sticky wages, the outcome is expected to last until new wages are agreed upon. In a complex institutional framework, such as operates in Australia, this adjustment may take some time. With flexible wages, there is a presumption that as soon as either excess supply or excess demand pressures

Figure 32.7 Rational Expectations Equilibrium

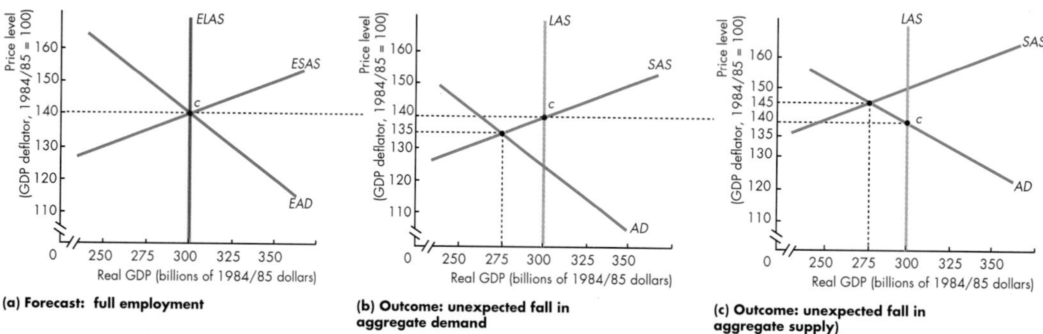

(a) Forecast: full employment

(b) Outcome: unexpected fall in aggregate demand

(c) Outcome: unexpected fall in aggregate supply)

The rational expectation of the price level is calculated in part (a). It occurs at the intersection of curves *EAD* and *ELAS* (point *c*). If long-run aggregate supply turns out to be as expected but aggregate demand is lower than expected, as in part (b), real GDP falls below capacity and the price level falls below its expected level. If aggregate demand turns out to be as expected but long-run aggregate supply is lower than expected, as in part (c), the price level rises above its expected level and real GDP falls.

emerge in the labour market, wages adjust to ensure that a full-employment equilibrium is quickly established.

Individuals in a Rational Expectations Equilibrium

The key characteristic of any economic equilibrium is that all the people in the economy, all of whom are trying to do the best they can for themselves, have reached a situation in which they cannot make a reallocation of their resources that they regard as superior to the one they have chosen.

Each household or firm sees itself as a small part of the overall economy. Those firms and households with sufficient market power to influence prices have exerted that influence to their maximum possible advantage. But most households and firms are not able to exert a significant effect on the prices that they face. Each household and firm does its best to forecast those prices relevant to its own actions.

Armed with its best forecasts, or rational expectations, each household works out how many chickens, microwaves and suits to buy, how much to spend on cars and plumbing, how much money to have in the bank and how many hours a week to work. These decisions are expressed, not as fixed quantities, but as demand and supply schedules.

On the other side of the markets, firms, also armed with their rational expectations, determine how much new capital equipment to install (investment), how much output to supply and how much labour to demand. Like households, firms don't express their decisions as fixed quantities. Instead they express them as demand schedules for factors of production and supply schedules of output.

In equilibrium, prices, wages and interest rates are determined in the markets for goods and services, labour and money at levels that ensure the mutual consistency of all the plans of individual households and firms trading in these markets. The quantities demanded and supplied in each market balance.

In a rational expectations equilibrium, each person is satisfied that there is no better action he or she could currently take. But such an equilibrium is not static. The economy constantly changes. You could imagine the economy at each point that we observe as a frozen frame in a video: in the frame, the supply and demand curves in the markets for all the different goods, services and factors of production all intersect, determining their prices and quantities at that moment. Economists try to understand what is happening by stopping the video to take a closer look at it.

We've now seen how unexpected changes in aggregate demand and aggregate supply affect both the price level and real GDP, even when people are doing their best to anticipate these changes. Let's now see how things work out when forecasts are correct — when people get lucky and correctly anticipate the future.

Anticipated Inflation

If people could correctly anticipate the future course of inflation, they would never agree to a wage contract in which the wage rate was fixed. Wages would change in line with prices. We'll study anticipated inflation, therefore, using the flexible wage model only.

Suppose that last year the GDP deflator was 130 and real GDP was \$300 billion. Suppose also that the economy was at full employment and its long-run real GDP last year was \$300 billion. Figure 32.8 illustrates the economy last year. The aggregate demand curve last year was AD_0, the aggregate supply curve was SAS_0 and the long-run aggregate supply curve was *LAS*. Since the economy was in equilibrium at long-run real GDP, the actual price level equalled the expected price level.

To simplify our analysis, let's suppose that at the end of last year long-run real GDP was not expected to change, so that this year's expected long-run aggregate supply is the same as last year's. Let's also suppose that aggregate demand was expected to increase, so that the expected aggregate demand curve for this year is EAD_1. We can now calculate the rational expectation of the price level for this year. It is a GDP deflator of 145, the price level at which the new expected aggregate demand curve intersects the expected long-run aggregate supply curve. Wages increase as a result of the expected increase in the price level and the short-run aggregate supply curve shifts to the left. In particular, given that the expected price level increased by 11.5 per cent, the short-run aggregate supply curve for next year (SAS_1) shifts upward by that same percentage amount (11.5 per cent) and passes through the long-run aggregate supply curve (*LAS*) at the expected price level.

If aggregate demand turns out to be the same as expected, the actual aggregate demand curve AD_1 is the same as EAD_1. The intersection point of AD_1 and SAS_1 determines the actual price level — where the GDP deflator is 145. Between last year and this year, the GDP deflator increased from 130 to 145 and the economy experienced an inflation rate of 11.5 per cent.

Inflationary Expectations

Recession has Cut Inflationary Expectations

Hopes that the inflation cycle has been broken have been supported by the latest broad survey of manufacturing industry, which reveals falling inflationary expectations and a widespread fall in output prices not seen since the 1960s.

The December quarter survey of industrial trends, by the Confederation of Australian Industry and Westpac, suggests that the present recession is going to be at least as long, and as damaging, as the recession of 1982–83.

The survey of 246 manufacturers found no evidence of an imminent economic turn-around. The survey drew a picture of the manufacturing sector which parallels the 1982–83 recession, except that output and new orders have fallen for longer than in the previous recession — suggesting that this recession could be more protracted.

Just over half of the manufacturers surveyed expected that costs would remain stable in the June quarter, and the proportion expecting costs to increase fell compared with the previous survey.

This indicates that inflationary expectations are falling, which is a crucial breakthrough in efforts to permanently lock in a low inflation rate.

For the first time since 1964, more manufacturers reported that their average selling price had declined rather than risen.

The result is probably an indication of the heavy discounting used to clear stocks in some sectors, particularly the car industry.

But manufacturers are forecasting that average selling prices will rise once discounted stock is sold.

Demand continues to be weak with new orders in the March quarter worse than expected.

Output did not improve and is not expected to pick up in the near term.

The survey found that more than half of the respondents expected a deterioration in business conditions over the next six months while 70 per cent of manufacturers reported they were running plant below capacity.

Capital investment plans were weak for the fifth consecutive quarter and more than 60 per cent of respondents said that numbers employed fell in the March quarter.

None of the groups expected an increase in output for the June quarter.

Financial Review
Friday, 8 March 1991
By Tim Dodd

The Essence of the Story

- In 1990/91, the Australian economy was experiencing a severe recession.
- An indicator of the depth of this recession was that output and new orders had fallen for a longer period than in the recession of 1982/83. Another indicator was that 70 per cent of manufacturers reported that they were operating their plant below capacity.
- One consequence of the recession, however, was that costs had remained stable, or in some cases had fallen, and manufacturers expected this to continue in the short run.
- As a result, for the first time since 1964, prices had fallen rather than risen.
- There was some concern, however, that once discounted stock had been sold and the economy began to pick up, prices would again rise.

Background and Analysis

- The thrust of the story is that the recession, though unfortunate, had yielded one positive outcome in breaking inflationary expectations. Indeed, policy discussions at the time of the article, and after, were focused on how to maintain low inflationary expectations.
- Prior to the recession, workers and managers of firms had expected prices to rise — inflationary expectations were high.

Part (a) of the figure depicts the situation. SAS_0 is the initial short-run aggregate supply curve. AD_0 is the initial aggregate demand curve. Equilibrium occurs at the intersection of SAS_0 and AD_0, at point *a*, which is at the full-employment level of output on the long-run aggregate supply curve, *LAS*.

- Anticipating higher prices, workers negotiate for higher nominal wages. The short-run aggregate supply curve shifts upward to SAS_1. Firms' costs rise and so their prices begin to rise.

- In the absence of any other policy changes, the rising prices would reduce the quantity of real GDP demanded and real output would fall. To avoid this outcome, with its associated rise in unemployment, policy is changed to accommodate the rise in costs. For example, by increasing the money supply, the Reserve Bank shifts the aggregate demand curve to the right, to AD_1. The new equilibrium occurs at point *b*. Thus prices rise, output is unchanged, and the anticipation of inflation was shown to have been correct. That is, the high inflationary expectations have been realized.

- Because workers' inflationary expectations were correct before, they still hold those expectations for the next period and again negotiate for nominal wage increases. The short-run aggregate supply curve shifts upwards from SAS_1 to SAS_2, as shown in part (b) of the figure.

- Suppose for other reasons, for example, because the trade balance deficit increases, monetary policy is unexpectedly tightened. Instead of shifting to the right, as would occur if the newly negotiated wage rises were to be accommodated, the aggregate demand curve shifts to the left, to AD_2 in part (b) of the figure.

- Equilibrium now occurs at point c — prices have not risen but real output has fallen well below the full employment level.

- To the extent that workers do not expect any price rises in the future, they will not negotiate for nominal wage increases and the short-run aggregate supply curve will remain fixed at SAS_2. At this point, inflationary expectations have been broken. But any attempt to change policy to shift the aggregate demand curve to the right might simply spark a renewed push for wage increases which would yield the outcome seen in part (a) of the figure, but at below-capacity output levels. Anticipating the effects of the expansionary demand-management policy would boost inflationary expectations back to their previous levels.

- Note from the story that firms expect some price rises as stocks are run down. They will gradually increase output to replenish stocks and the economy will move along SAS_2 from point *c* to point *d*. If this occurs, then with fixed nominal wages, the price rise will reduce the real wage and employment will rise as the economy returns to its full-employment output level. How these price rises are handled will be important for the economy. If they are automatically reflected in nominal wages, for example, by a return to full wage indexation, then the short-run aggregate supply curve will resume its upward drift, possibly thwarting the return to full-employment output levels.

Conclusion

- In the context of this story, it is easy to see why there was such a vigorous debate in late 1991 about whether or not the government should have stimulated the economy more by loosening monetary policy more than it had already done. What the government feared was that by deliberately shifting the aggregate demand curve to the right, inflationary expectations would be re-ignited. The government wanted to avoid this at *any* level of real output, but it might even have occurred before the economy had returned to full employment.

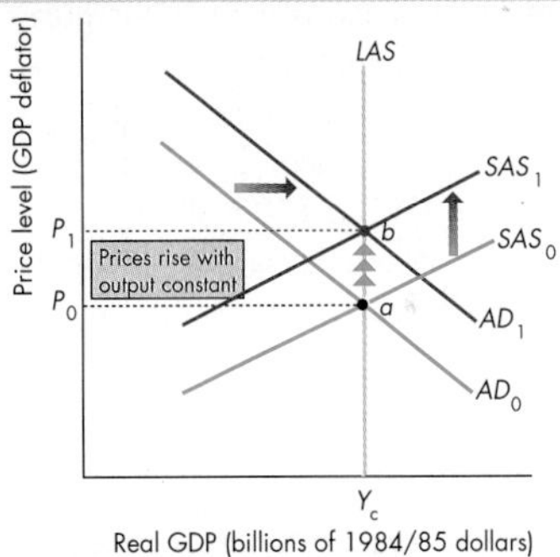

(a) Inflationary expectations high

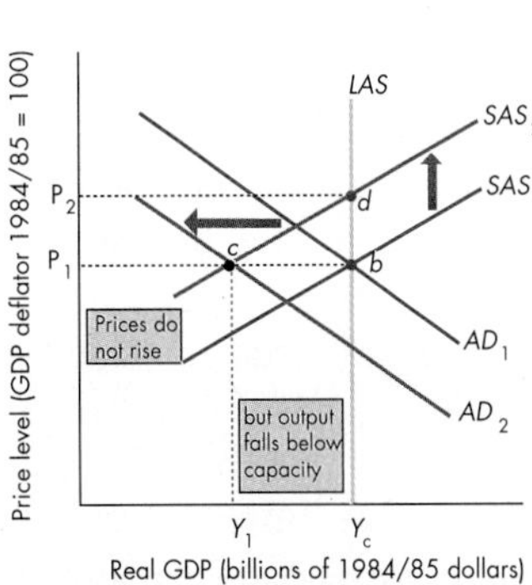

(b) Inflationary expectations broken

Figure 32.8 Anticipated Inflation

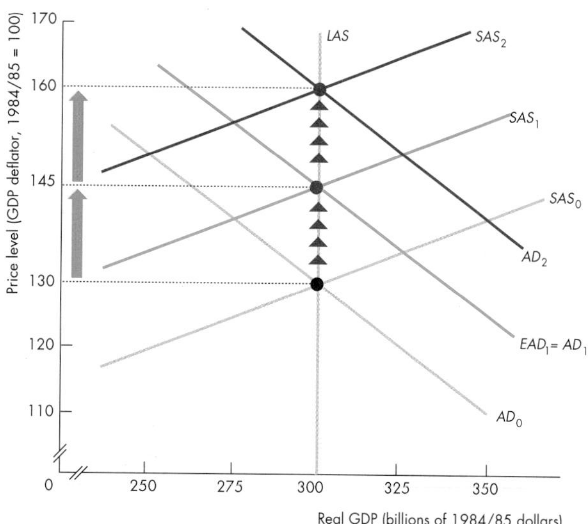

The actual and expected long-run aggregate supply curve (*LAS*) is at a real GDP of \$300 billion. Last year, aggregate demand was AD_0 and the short-run aggregate supply curve SAS_0. The actual price level was the same as that expected — a GDP deflator of 130. This year aggregate demand is expected to rise to EAD_1. The rational expectation of the GDP deflator changes from 130 to 145. As a result, the short-run aggregate supply curve shifts up to SAS_1. If aggregate demand actually increases as expected, AD_1 is the same as EAD_1, the actual aggregate demand curve AD_1 is the same as the expected aggregate demand curve. Equilibrium occurs at a real GDP of \$300 billion and an actual GDP deflator of 145. The inflation is correctly anticipated. In the next period the process continues with aggregate demand increasing as expected to AD_2 and wages rising to shift the short-run aggregate supply curve to SAS_2. Again, real GDP remains at \$300 billion and the GDP deflator rises, as anticipated, to 160.

In this example, inflation was anticipated. The price level was expected to rise from 130 to 145 — an expected inflation rate of 11.5 per cent. The price level did exactly what it was expected to do, so the actual inflation rate was 11.5 per cent as well.

What caused the inflation? The immediate answer is the anticipated and actual increase in aggregate demand. Because aggregate demand was expected to increase from AD_0 to EAD_1, the short-run aggregate supply curve shifted up from SAS_0 to SAS_1. Because aggregate demand actually did increase by the amount that was expected, the actual aggregate demand curve shifted from AD_0 to AD_1. The combination of the anticipated and actual shifts in the aggregate demand curve to the right produced an increase in the price level that was anticipated. In the next period, the process continues with aggregate demand increasing, as expected, to AD_2 and wages rising to shift the short-run aggregate supply curve to SAS_2. Real GDP remains at \$300 billion and the GDP deflator rises, as expected, to 160.

Only if aggregate demand growth is correctly foreseen will the economy follow the course described in Fig. 32.8. If the expected growth rate of aggregate demand is different from its actual growth rate, the expected aggregate demand curve will shift by a different amount from the actual aggregate demand curve. The inflation rate will depart from its expected level and, to some extent, there will be unanticipated inflation. It is this type of inflation that we studied in the first part of this chapter.

Inflationary Expectations and Policy Credibility

What would have happened if the aggregate demand curve had not shifted up to EAD_1 in Fig. 32.8 as expected? In this case we would have had the same outcome as we described in Fig. 32.4. The short-run aggregate supply curve would have shifted up because people expected prices to rise but the aggregate demand curve would have remained at AD_0. The price level would have risen but output and employment would have fallen. The Reserve Bank and the government would then be faced with the choice of boosting aggregate demand, in effect fulfilling the inflationary expectations, or of allowing the unemployment equilibrium to gradually work itself out.

Such a situation, as just described, could arise simply because inflation had been occurring in the past and people think that it is likely to continue in the future. If the past inflation had been the result of past expansionary monetary or fiscal policies, could the Reserve Bank or the government halt inflation, without causing unemployment, simply by telling people that it was no longer continuing with the expansionary policies?

The answer to this question is yes, if the policymakers have credibility with the public. For example, if the Reserve Bank was always believed, it could simply announce that money growth will fall next year and, consequently, the rate at which the aggregate demand curve shifts to the right will be reduced. Thus inflation will be reduced. Firms and workers would build the lower rate of inflation into their expectations and there would be no surprise when inflation actually was lower next year. Real GDP would be unaffected.

Why does this not happen in practice? Perhaps because the public has little confidence in the Reserve Bank's or the government's ability to actually carry out such a promise. If policymakers have little credibility with respect to future commitments on inflation, then a recession to 'break the stick of inflation' might be a likely outcome.[1]

REVIEW

A *rational expectations equilibrium* is a macroeconomic equilibrium based on expectations that are the best available forecasts. It describes how real GDP and the price level are determined when people are doing the best they can to anticipate the levels of aggregate demand and short-run aggregate supply.

In a rational expectations equilibrium, if aggregate demand is lower than expected, real GDP and the price level are lower than expected. If long-run aggregate supply is lower than expected, the price level is higher and real GDP lower than expected. These outcomes do not depend on whether wages are sticky or flexible. Even flexible wages cannot respond to the unknown and unexpected, and unemployment or above full employment can occur in a rational expectations equilibrium.

If people do correctly anticipate changes in aggregate demand and aggregate supply, the result is anticipated inflation. The price level changes at an anticipated rate, and real GDP and unemployment are unchanged. If expectations of inflation are systematically built into people's actions then the ability of policymakers to stop inflation by announcing a change in policy depends on their credibility with the public. ■

Interest Rates and Inflation

There have been massive fluctuations in interest rates in the Australian economy in recent years. In the early 1960s, corporations could raise long-term capital at interest rates of 5 per cent a year. By the end of the 1960s that interest rate had risen to 7 per cent a year. During the 1970s, the interest rates paid by firms for long-term loans fluctuated between 7 and 14 per cent. During the 1980s, interest rates hit the high teens. Why have interest rates fluctuated so much, and why were they so high in the late 1970s and early 1980s?

To answer these questions, it is necessary to distinguish between nominal interest rates and real interest rates. **Nominal interest rates** are those actually paid and received in the marketplace. **Real interest rates** are the rates that nominal interest rates translate into when the effects of inflation are taken into account. If the nominal interest rate is 15 per cent a year and prices are rising by 10 per cent a year, the real interest rate is only 5 per cent a year.[2] If you made a loan of $100 on 1 January 1990, it's true you'd have $115 to spend on 1 January 1991, but you'd need $110 to buy the same goods that $100 would have bought a year earlier. All you've really made is $5 — the difference between the $110 you need to buy $100 worth of goods and the $115 that you've got.

When we studied how interest rates are determined in Chapter 28, we analysed an economy in which the price level was constant. In such an economy, there is no difference between the nominal and real interest rate. There is just one interest rate and its level ensures that the quantity of money demanded equals the quantity of money supplied.

But we know that, in the real world, the price level is rarely constant and, most of the time, it is increasing. What are the effects on interest rates of a rising price level and of expectations of the price level continuing to rise? These are the questions that we are now going to answer.

Expectations of Inflation and Interest Rates

Let's begin our exploration of the relationship between inflation expectations and interest rates by imagining two economies that are identical in every way except for one: one of the economies has no inflation and the other economy has a 10 per cent inflation rate. In each case, the behaviour of the price level is correctly anticipated. That is, in the first economy there is no inflation and none is expected. In the second economy, there is 10 per cent inflation and a 10 per cent inflation rate is expected. In both economies, the real interest rate is 5 per cent. What is the difference in the nominal interest rates in these two economies?

In the zero-inflation economy the nominal interest rate is 5 per cent a year — the same as the real

[1] This is a 1991 quote from the then Federal Treasurer, Paul Keating.

[2] Recall from our discussion in Chapter 25 that the real interest rate is approximately equal to the nominal interest rate minus the rate of inflation.

interest rate. What is the nominal interest rate in the second economy? The answer is 15.5 per cent a year. Why?

First, let's look at things from the point of view of lenders. People who make loans recognize that the value of the money that they have lent is falling at a rate of 10 per cent a year. Each year the money buys 10 per cent less than it would have bought the year before. Lenders will want to protect themselves against such a loss in the value of money by asking for a higher interest rate on the loans that they make.

Let's now look at the situation from the point of view of borrowers. People who borrow recognize that in an economy that is inflating at 10 per cent a year, the money they use to repay what they have borrowed will be worth 10 per cent less each year than it was worth the year before. They will recognize that lenders need to be protected against the falling value of money and willingly agree to a higher interest rate.

But how much higher will the interest rate be that borrowers and lenders agree to? First, they will agree to add 10 percentage points because the value of the money borrowed and lent is expected to fall at a 10 per cent annual rate. Second, they will recognize that even the interest payment will buy less at the end of the year than at the beginning of the year. To allow for that factor, they will add 10 per cent of the interest rate. Since the interest rate is 5 per cent when there is zero inflation, 10 per cent of the interest rate is half a percentage point. So the total amount that they will agree to add to the real interest rate of 5 per cent is 10.5 percentage points. Thus the nominal interest rate is 15.5 per cent.

The nominal interest rate equals the real interest rate plus an allowance for the expected rate of inflation that is slightly higher than that expected inflation rate. The higher the expected inflation rate, the higher is the nominal interest rate. When inflation and interest rates are low, the nominal interest rate approximately equals the sum of the real interest rate and the expected inflation rate.

By considering the behaviour of borrowers and lenders, you can see that it makes sense for the nominal interest rate to rise above the real interest rate by an amount slightly larger than the expected inflation rate. We studied the determination of interest rates in Chapter 28, and discovered that it is the demand for real money and the supply of real money that determine interest rates. But which interest rate — the nominal interest rate or the real interest rate — is it that equates the quantity of real money demanded with the quantity supplied? (In Chapter 28, these two interest rates were the same because we assumed there was no inflation.)

To answer this question, we need to determine the opportunity cost of holding money, for it is that opportunity cost that adjusts to make the quantity of money demanded equal to the quantity supplied. There are two components to the cost of holding money: one is the fall in the value of money resulting from inflation; the other is the real interest rate that could have been earned by reducing money holding and making loans or investing in real capital — plant and equipment. Thus

$$\text{Opportunity cost of holding money} = \text{Expected inflation rate} + \text{Real interest rate}$$

But we know the nominal interest rate is also approximately equal to the expected inflation rate plus the real interest rate. We've discovered, therefore, that the opportunity cost of holding money is the nominal interest rate. It is the nominal interest rate that adjusts in the money market to ensure that the quantity of money demanded equals the quantity available. The higher the expected inflation rate, the higher is the opportunity cost of holding money and the lower is the quantity of money people plan to hold.

Inflation and Interest Rates in Australia

What is the actual relationship between inflation and interest rates in Australia? That relationship is illustrated in Fig. 32.9. The interest rate measured on the vertical axis is that paid by the Commonwealth government on long-term bonds — the 10-year Treasury bond rate. Each point on the graph represents a year in recent Australian history between 1970 and 1990. The data groups together in distinct categories. The first group includes the points indicating interest rates and inflation rates in the early 1970s and the late 1970s. This group is clustered along the line labelled 'real interest rate of 0.7 per cent', which is the average real interest rate over those years. There is a clear positive relationship between inflation and nominal interest rates. As anticipated, inflation rose in these years, and interest rates rose to maintain the real interest rate at 0.7 per cent. At the time, the highly regulated financial market and the method of selling government bonds (see Chapter 35) prevented the real interest rate from rising further.

In the mid-1970s, there was a burst of high inflation. Clearly, the high inflation was not incorporated into interest rates, as the real interest rate became significantly negative. You can see that the

Figure 32.9 Inflation and the Interest Rate

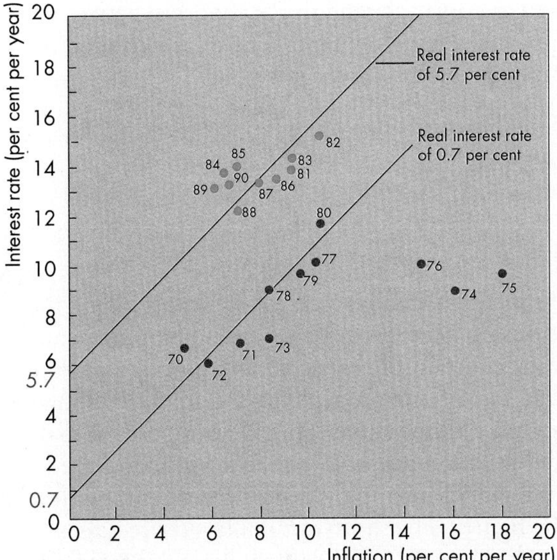

Other things being equal, the higher the expected inflation rate, the higher is the interest rate. A graph showing the relationship between the interest rate on government bonds and the actual inflation rate reveals that the influence of inflation is a strong one. But another strong influence can be seen at work in Australia. That is the effects of regulated financial markets, which placed a ceiling on interest rates prior to 1980. When the ceilings were removed, the average level of the real interest rate rose.

Source: Inflation: see Fig 22.2; Interest rate: 10 Year Treasury Bond Rate, Series FIRCMTBLO, RBA Bulletin Database, supplied by EconData's dX Data Service.

points for 1974, 1975 and 1976 lie well to the right of the 0.7 per cent real interest rate, where the inflation rate is greater than the nominal interest rate. That is, savings held in the form of government bonds lost value in terms of purchasing power over the period. Nominal interest rates did not rise to incorporate the higher levels of inflation because government regulations did not permit it.

As we observed in Chapter 27, the first major moves to deregulate the finance markets occurred in 1980 with the removal of deposit rate ceilings and the introduction of tendering for government bonds. In the deregulated market, from 1981 onwards, a positive relationship between inflation and interest rates is again apparent. The points representing inflation and interest rates for the 1980s are all clustered along the line labelled 'real interest rate of 5.7 per cent', which is the average real interest rate for the period. Thus it would seem that financial market deregulation led to savers being compensated by an average of an extra 5 percentage points during the 1980s compared with the 1970s.

We discussed the process of financial deregulation in Chapter 28. Now you can see one of the important forces behind it. Because of relatively high inflation in the 1970s, savers were not being compensated for deferring consumption and lending money. The solution was to allow interest rates to be flexible enough to allow market expectations about inflation to be fully incorporated. This required deregulation of interest rates, and financial markets generally.

Money Supply and Interest Rates Again

We have seen that high nominal interest rates and high expected inflation rates go together. We have also seen that high expected inflation can be the product of a high anticipated money supply growth rate. Thus a high anticipated growth rate of the money supply can bring not only a high anticipated inflation rate but also high interest rates.

In Chapter 28, when we studied the effects of the Reserve Bank's actions on interest rates, we concluded that an increase in the quantity of money *lowers* interest rates. How can both of these conclusions be correct? How can an increase in the anticipated growth rate of the money supply increase interest rates while an increase in the quantity of money lowers them?

The answer lies in the time scale of the adjustments of interest rates to a change in the money supply. If the Reserve Bank takes an unexpected action that increases the quantity of money, the immediate effect of that action is to lower interest rates. Lower interest rates are needed to bring the quantity of money demanded into equality with the quantity supplied. But if the Reserve Bank continues to increase the money supply, and keeps on increasing it year after year at a faster pace than real GDP is growing, people will come to expect that increase in the money supply and the inflation that goes with it. In these circumstances, they will not be willing to make loans unless they obtain a return on them that sufficiently compensates them for the loss in the value of money due to inflation.

Thus it is an *unanticipated* increase in the money supply that brings a *fall* in interest rates. An *anticipated* and ongoing increase in the money supply *increases* interest rates. The decrease in interest rates following an increase in the money supply is an immediate but temporary response. The increase in interest rates associated with an increase in the growth rate of the money supply is a long-run response.

R E V I E W

The nominal interest rate is the rate actually paid and received in the marketplace. The real interest rate is the rate *really* paid and received when the effects of inflation are taken into account. The real interest rate is approximately equal to the nominal interest rate minus the inflation rate. The nominal interest rate is approximately equal to the expected real interest rate plus the expected inflation rate. It is also the rate that makes the quantity of money demanded equal to the money supplied. ■

Inflation over the Business Cycle: The Phillips Curve

We've seen that a speed-up in aggregate demand growth that is not fully anticipated increases both inflation and real GDP growth. It also decreases unemployment. Similarly, a slow-down in the growth rate of aggregate demand that is not fully anticipated slows down both inflation and real GDP growth and increases unemployment. We've also seen that a fully anticipated change in the growth rate of aggregate demand changes the inflation rate and has no effect on real GDP or on unemployment. Finally, we've seen that a decrease in aggregate supply increases inflation and decreases real GDP growth. In this case, unemployment increases.

The aggregate demand–aggregate supply model that we have used to obtain these results gives predictions about the level of real GDP and the price level. Given these predictions, we can work out how unemployment and inflation have changed. But inflation and unemployment are not placed at the centre of the stage in the aggregate demand–aggregate supply model. An alternative way of studying inflation focuses directly on the joint movements in inflation and unemployment. Let's look at this alternative approach.

The Phillips-Curve Approach

A macroeconomic model that focuses directly on inflation and unemployment is based on a relationship known as the Phillips curve. The Phillips curve is so named because it was popularized by New Zealand economist A. W. Phillips when working at the London School of Economics in the 1950s. A **Phillips curve** is a curve showing the relationship between inflation and unemployment. There are two time frames for Phillips curves:

- The short run
- The long run

The Phillips Curve in the Short Run

The **short-run Phillips curve** is a curve showing the relationship between inflation and unemployment, holding constant the expected inflation rate and the natural rate of unemployment. Figure 32.10 shows a short-run Phillips curve (*SRPC*). Suppose the expected inflation rate is 10 per cent a year and the natural rate of unemployment is 6 per cent, point *a* in the figure. The short-run Phillips curve passes through this point. If the unemployment rate falls below its natural rate, inflation rises above its expected rate. This joint movement in the inflation rate and the unemployment rate is illustrated as a movement up the short-run Phillips curve from point *a* to point *b* in Fig. 32.10. Similarly, if unemployment rises above the natural rate, inflation falls below its expected rate. In this case, there is movement down the short-run Phillips curve from point *a* to point *c*.

This negative relationship between inflation and unemployment along the short-run Phillips curve is explained by the aggregate demand–aggregate supply model. Suppose that, initially, inflation is anticipated to be 10 per cent a year and unemployment is at its natural rate. This situation is illustrated by the aggregate demand–aggregate supply model in Fig. 32.1 and by the Phillips curve approach as point *a* in Fig. 32.10. Suppose that now an unanticipated increase in the growth of aggregate demand occurs. In Fig. 32.1 the aggregate demand curve shifts to the right more quickly than expected. Real GDP increases, the unemployment rate decreases and the price level starts to increase at a faster rate than expected. There has been a movement from point *a* to point *b* in Fig. 32.10. If the unanticipated increase in aggregate demand is temporary, aggregate demand growth slows to its previous level. When it does so, the process is reversed and the economy moves back to point *a* in Fig. 32.10.

A similar story can be told to illustrate the effects of an unanticipated decrease in the growth of aggregate demand. In this case, an unanticipated

Figure 32.10 The Short-Run Phillips Curve

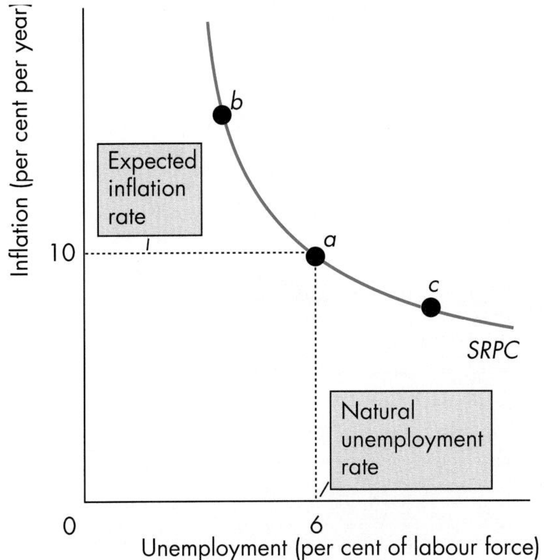

The short-run Phillips curve *SRPC* shows the relationship between inflation and unemployment at a given expected inflation rate and given natural unemployment. With an expected inflation rate of 10 per cent a year and a natural unemployment rate of 6 per cent, the short-run Phillips curve passes through point *a*. An unanticipated increase in aggregate demand lowers unemployment and increases inflation — a movement up the short-run Phillips curve to point *b*. An unanticipated decrease in aggregate demand increases unemployment and lowers inflation — a movement down the short-run Phillips curve to point *c*.

slow-down in the growth of aggregate demand reduces inflation, slows real GDP growth and increases unemployment. There is a movement down the short-run Phillips curve from point *a* to point *c*.

The Phillips Curve in the Long Run

The **long-run Phillips curve** is a curve showing the relationship between inflation and unemployment, when the actual inflation rate equals the expected inflation rate. The long-run **Phillips curve** is vertical at the natural rate of unemployment — the **natural rate hypothesis.** The natural rate hypothesis was proposed independently in the mid-1960s by Edmund Phelps (now at Columbia University but then a young professor at the University of Pennsylvania) and by Milton Friedman. It is sometimes given the alternative name, the **Phelps–Friedman hypothesis.** A long-run Phillips curve is shown in Fig. 32.11 as the vertical line *LRPC.*

If the expected inflation rate is 10 per cent a year, the short-run Phillips curve is $SRPC_0$. If the expected inflation rate falls to 8 per cent a year, the short-run Phillips curve shifts downward to $SRPC_1$. At points *a* and *d*, inflation is equal to its expected rate and unemployment is equal to its natural rate. The distance by which the short-run Phillips curve shifts downward when the expected inflation rate falls is equal to the change in the expected inflation rate. Points *a* and *d* lie on the long-run Phillips curve *LRPC.* This curve tells us that any inflation rate is possible at the natural unemployment rate so long as that inflation is expected.

To see why the short-run Phillips curve shifts when the expected inflation rate changes let's do an

Figure 32.11 The Short-Run and Long-Run Phillips Curves

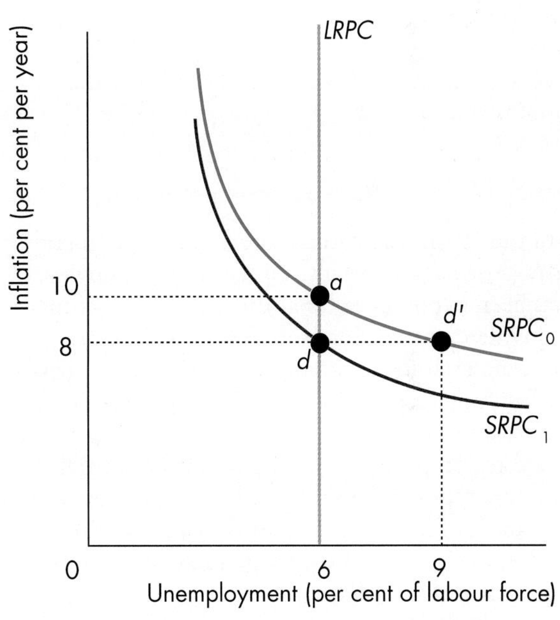

The long-run Phillips curve is *LRPC*, a vertical line at the natural unemployment rate. A decrease in inflation expectations lowers the short-run Phillips curve shifting it down by the amount of the fall in the expected inflation rate. Here, when expected inflation falls from 10 per cent a year to 8 per cent a year, the short-run Phillips curve shifts from $SRPC_0$ to $SRPC_1$. The new short-run Phillips curve intersects the long-run Phillips curve at the new expected inflation rate at point *d*. If the fall in inflation was, at first, unanticipated, nominal wages would continue to rise at 10 per cent a year, real wages would rise and the economy would move from point *a* to point *d'*.

experiment. The economy is at full employment and there is a fully anticipated inflation of 10 per cent a year. Now suppose that the Reserve Bank and the government begin a permanent attack on inflation by slowing money supply growth and cutting the deficit. Aggregate demand growth slows down and the inflation rate falls to 8 per cent a year. At first, this drop in inflation is unanticipated, so wages continue to rise at their original rate, shifting the short-run aggregate supply curve to the left at the same pace as before. Real GDP falls and unemployment increases. In Fig. 32.11, the economy moves from point *a* to point *d′* on short-run Phillips curve $SRPC_0$.

If the actual inflation rate remains steady at 8 per cent a year, eventually this rate will come to be expected. As this happens, wage growth slows down and the short-run aggregate supply curve moves to the left less quickly. Eventually it shifts to the left at the same pace at which the aggregate demand curve is shifting to the right. When this occurs, the actual inflation rate equals the expected rate and full employment is restored. Unemployment is back at its natural rate. In Fig. 32.11, the short-run Phillips curve has shifted from $SRPC_0$ to $SRPC_1$ and the economy is at point *d*.

Variable Natural Rate of Unemployment

Until the 1970s, the natural rate of unemployment was regarded as a constant. In recent years, however, it has been hypothesized that the natural rate of unemployment varies. Some of these variations arise from changes in the amount of labour market turnover resulting from technological change, which leads to job switching from firm to firm, sector to sector and region to region. A change in the natural rate of unemployment shifts both the short-run and the long-run Phillips curves. Such shifts are illustrated in Fig. 32.12. If the natural rate of unemployment increases from 6 per cent to 9 per cent, the long-run Phillips curve shifts from $LRPC_0$ to $LRPC_1$, and if expected inflation is constant at 8 per cent a year, the short-run Phillips curve shifts from $SRPC_1$ to $SRPC_2$. Because the expected inflation rate is constant, the short- run Phillips curve $SRPC_1$ intersects the long-run curve $LRPC_0$ (point *d*) at the same inflation rate as the short-run Phillips curve $SRPC_2$ intersects the long-run curve $LRPC_1$ (point *e*).

Figure 32.12 A Change in the Natural Rate of Unemployment

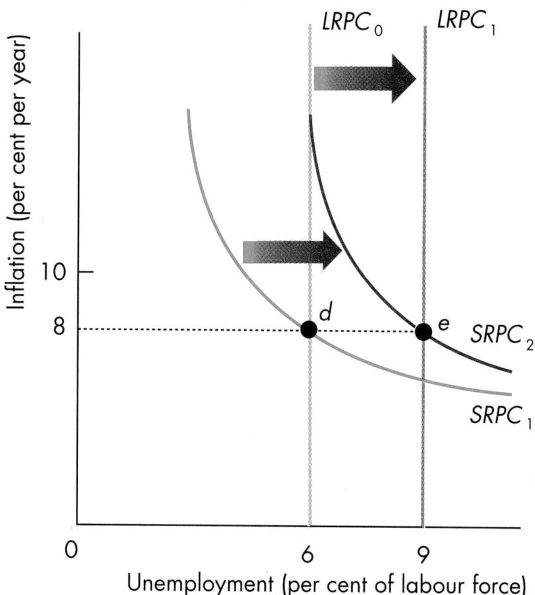

A change in the natural rate of unemployment shifts both the short-run and long-run Phillips curves. Here the natural rate of unemployment increases from 6 per cent to 9 per cent and the two Phillips curves shift right to $SRPC_2$ and $LRPC_1$. The point at which the new long-run Phillips curve intersects the new short-run Phillips curve — point *e* — is the expected inflation rate.

The Phillips Curve in Australia

Figure 32.13 shows the relationship between inflation and unemployment in Australia. Begin by looking at Fig. 32.13(a), a scatter diagram of inflation and unemployment since 1967/68. Each dot in the figure represents a combination of inflation and unemployment for a particular year. As you can see, starting in 1967/68 until 1973/74, unemployment was roughly constant as inflation was rising rapidly. From 1973/74 to 1974/75 inflation continued to rise rapidly as unemployment began to rise. Unemployment consistently rose between 1974/75 and 1983/84, falling steadily thereafter. However, the behaviour of inflation over this period is quite different. Between 1974/75 and 1978/79 inflation fell from very high levels to around 10 per cent per year — still high by international standards. The inflation rate hovered around 10 per cent a year until 1983/84 when it fell to around 7 per cent a year, and stayed there during the rest of the 1980s.

Just how to interpret these data using a Phillips curve analysis is a difficult task, and no single explanation will satisfy everybody. However, there are some important institutional changes that occurred at

Figure 32.13 Phillips Curves in Australia

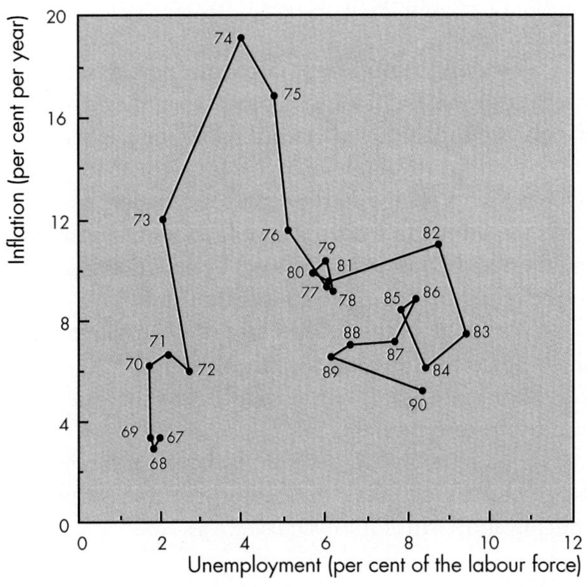

(a) The time series sequence

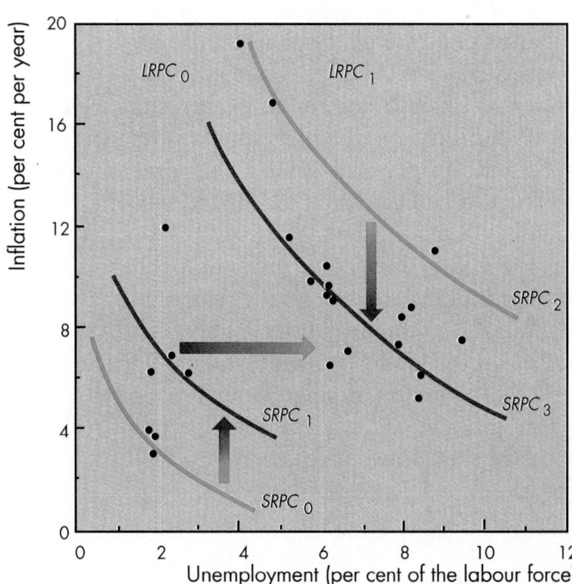

(b) An interpretation

In part (a), each dot represents the combination of inflation and unemployment for a particular year in Australia. There is no clear relationship between the two variables. Part (b) interprets the data in terms of shifting long-run and short-run Phillips curves. The long-run Phillips curve in the late 1960s and early 1970s is shown by *LRPC*0, at a natural rate of unemployment of 2 per cent. The short-run Phillips curve shifts upwards as anticipated inflation increases. Sometime between the early 1970s and the mid-1970s, the natural rate of unemployment rose to 6 per cent, shifting the long-run Phillips curve to *LRPC*1. Wage indexation, first introduced in 1975, abandoned in 1978 and introduced again in 1983, has fixed expectations of inflation in each of the associated periods and is thus associated with a different short-run Phillips curve.

Source: See Figs. 22.2 and 22.7.

some of the break points noted above, and these help to pin down an interpretation. But note that, like many explanations in economics, this particular interpretation of the data is not the only possible one.

Figure 32.12(b) explains the data as the result of shifts in both the short-run and the long-run Phillips curve. That is, in terms of both changing inflation expectations and a changing natural rate of unemployment.

We begin with a long-run Phillips curve — natural rate of unemployment — of 2 per cent. This is indicated by the initial long-run Phillips curve *LRPC*0. The initial short-run Phillips curve is shown by *SRPC*0, with equilibrium inflation around 4 per cent a year. Inflation expectations are also 4 per cent a year. For various reasons, inflation rose between 1967/68 and 1970/71 but workers were aware of the changes and expectations adjusted rapidly. The short-run Phillips curve shifted upward to *SRPC*1.

Between 1972/73 and 1974/75 inflation rose rapidly. Part of the increase was the result of the oil price increases engineered by OPEC and part was the result of competitive wage claims by unions generating a rapid cost-push inflation. To break the wage–price spiral the government introduced wage indexation in April 1975. Nominal wages were set with reference to the previous period's inflation rate. Inflation expectations were thus contained by fixing them to a previously determined figure.

Over this period, the natural rate of unemployment rose from 2 per cent to 6 per cent. Why the natural rate of employment rose is not fully understood but it may be closely related to the surge in the labour force resulting from the new entry of the baby-boom generation. In any event, the long-run Phillips curve shifted to $LRPC_1$. With expectations of relatively high inflation continuing, the short-run Phillips curve settled down at $SRPC_2$. Wage indexation was abandoned in 1978/79 and inflation then stabilized around 10 per cent a year, which appears to have been fully anticipated. In 1981/82, the government experimented with decentralized wage bargaining. Wages, inflation and unemployment all rose rapidly.

In 1983, the government introduced a new form a wage indexation through the Accord process. Throughout this period, real wages fell, which brought down the level of unemployment. The Accord process apparently brought about a marginal reduction in inflation, and in inflation expectations, shown by the shift down of the short-run Phillips curve to $SRPC_3$.

R E V I E W

The short-run Phillips curve shows the relationship between inflation and unemployment at a given expected inflation rate and natural rate of unemployment. An unanticipated burst of aggregate demand growth increases inflation and decreases unemployment — a movement up the short-run Phillips curve. An unanticipated slow-down in aggregate demand growth reduces inflation and increases unemployment — a movement down the short-run Phillips curve.

The long-run Phillips curve, the relationship between inflation and unemployment when the actual inflation rate equals the expected inflation rate, is vertical at the natural rate of unemployment — the natural rate hypothesis. A change in the expected inflation rate shifts the short-run Phillips curve (up for an increase in inflation and down for a decrease) by an amount equal to the change in the expected inflation rate.

A change in the natural rate of unemployment shifts both the short-run and the long-run Phillips curves (to the right for an increase in the natural rate and to the left for a decrease).

The relationship between inflation and unemployment in Australia can be interpreted in terms of shifting short-run Phillips curves. ■

■ We have now completed our study of inflation and the relationship between the inflation rate and the interest rate. Our next task, which we'll pursue in Chapter 33, is to see how the same aggregate demand and aggregate supply model that we have used to study inflation also helps us to explore and interpret fluctuations in real GDP and explain recessions and depressions.

S U M M A R Y

Inflation

Inflation is a problem because it results in a fall in the value of money. The nature of the problem depends on whether the inflation is *anticipated* or *unanticipated*. Anticipated inflation reduces the effectiveness of money as a medium of exchange. Unanticipated inflation is a problem because it redistributes wealth between borrowers and lenders and redistributes income between employers and employees. Unanticipated fluctuations in the inflation rate produce fluctuations in real GDP, employment and unemployment. (p. 398)

Demand Inflation

Demand-pull inflation arises from increasing aggregate demand. Its origin can be any of the factors that shift the aggregate demand curve, the most important of which are an increasing money supply and increasing government purchases of goods and services. When the aggregate demand curve shifts to the right, other things remaining the same, both real GDP and the GDP deflator increase and unemployment falls. With a shortage of labour, wages begin to increase and the short-run aggregate supply curve shifts to the left, raising the GDP deflator still more and decreasing real GDP.

If aggregate demand continues to increase, the aggregate demand curve keeps shifting to the right and the price level keeps on rising. Wages respond, aggregate demand increases again and a price–wage inflation spiral unwinds. (pp. 399–401)

Supply Inflation and Stagflation

Cost-push inflation can result from any factor that decreases aggregate supply but the most important of these are increasing wage rates and increasing prices of key raw materials. These sources of a decreasing aggregate supply bring increasing costs that shift the short-run aggregate supply curve to the left. Firms decrease the quantity of labour employed and cut back production. Real GDP declines and the price level rises. If no action is taken to increase aggregate demand, the economy remains below full employment until the initial price increase that triggered the stagflation is reversed.

Reserve Bank or government action to restore full employment (an increase in the money supply or in government purchases of goods and services or a tax cut) increases aggregate demand and shifts the aggregate demand curve to the right, resulting in a still higher price level and higher real GDP. If the original source of cost-push is still present, costs rise again and the short-run aggregate supply curve shifts to the left again. If the Reserve Bank or the government responds again with a further increase in aggregate demand, the price level rises even higher. Inflation proceeds at a rate determined by the cost-push forces. (pp. 401–403)

Inflation Expectations

Different people devote different amounts of attention to forming expectations — some specialize in the activity and others simply follow someone else's forecast. The rational expectation of the price level can be found by using the theory of aggregate demand and aggregate supply to forecast the state of the economy. People do not use the theory of aggregate demand and aggregate supply explicitly to make their forecasts of the price level. They use a variety of methods. The rational expectations hypothesis states that, regardless of how people actually go about calculating their expectations, the expectations that they form are on the average, the same as the forecast that an economist would make using the relevant economic theory. (pp. 403–407)

Rational Expectations Equilibrium

A rational expectations equilibrium is a macroeconomic equilibrium based on expectations that are the best available forecasts. The rational expectations equilibrium occurs at the intersection of the aggregate demand and short-run aggregate supply curves. A rational expectations equilibrium may be a full employment equilibrium but other possibilities can occur. Aggregate demand and aggregate supply may be higher or lower than expected. The combination of these possibilities means that output may be higher or lower than capacity and the price level higher or lower than expected. Regardless of which of these states the economy is experiencing, in a rational expectations equilibrium no one would have acted differently, given the state of affairs in which they made their choices.

When changes in aggregate demand and aggregate supply are correctly anticipated, their only effects are on the price level — inflation is anticipated. (pp. 407–413)

Interest Rates and Inflation

Expectations of inflation affect nominal interest rates. The higher the expected rate of inflation, the higher is the nominal interest rate. Borrowers will willingly pay more and lenders will successfully demand more, as the anticipated rate of inflation rises. Borrowing and lending and asset-holding plans are made consistent with each other by adjustments in the real rate of interest — the difference between the nominal rate of interest and the expected rate of inflation. (pp. 413–416)

Inflation over the Business Cycle: the Phillips Curve

Phillips curves describe the relationships between inflation and unemployment. The short-run Phillips curve shows the relationship between inflation and unemployment, holding constant the expected inflation rate and the natural rate of unemployment. The long-run Phillips curve shows the relationship between inflation and unemployment, when the actual inflation rate equals the expected inflation rate. The short-run Phillips curve slopes downward — the lower the unemployment rate, the higher is the inflation rate, other things remaining the same. The long-run Phillips curve is vertical at the natural rate of unemployment — the natural rate hypothesis.

Changes in aggregate demand, with a constant expected inflation rate and natural unemployment rate, bring movements along the short-run Phillips curve. Changes in inflation expectations bring shifts in the short-run Phillips curve. Changes in the natural unemployment rate bring shifts in both the short-run and long-run Phillips curves.

There is no clear relationship between inflation and unemployment in Australia, but the joint movements in those variables can be interpreted in terms of shifting short-run and long-run Phillips curves. (pp. 416–420)

KEY TERMS

Cost-push inflation, p. 401
Demand-pull inflation, p. 399
Long-run Phillips curve, p. 417
Natural rate hypothesis, p. 417
Nominal interest rate, p. 413
Phelps–Friedman hypothesis, p. 417
Phillips curve, p. 416
Rational expectation, p. 404
Rational expectation equilibrium, p. 407
Rational expectations hypothesis, p. 405
Real interest rate, p. 413
Short-run Phillips curve, p. 416
Stagflation, p. 402

PROBLEMS

1 An economy has the following expected aggregate demand and short-run aggregate supply curves:

Price level (GDP deflator)	GDP demanded (billions of 1984/85 dollars)	GDP supplied (billions of 1984/85 dollars)
80	5	1
100	4	3
120	3	5
140	2	7

The long-run aggregate supply is $4 billion.
a) What is the expected price level?
b) What is the expected real GDP?
c) Are money wages expected to be fixed?

2 In the economy of problem 1, the expected price level increases to 120.
a) What is the new *SAS* curve if wages are fixed?
b) What is the new *SAS* curve if wages are flexible?
c) In parts (a) and (b), is real GDP expected to be above or below full employment?

3 In 1992, the expected aggregate demand for 1993 is as follows:

Price level (GDP deflator)	Expected real GDP demanded (billions of 1984/85 dollars)
120	4.0
121	3.9
122	3.8
123	3.7
124	3.6

In 1992, the long-run real GDP is $3.8 billion and the real GDP expected for 1993 is $3.9 billion. Calculate the 1992 rational expectation of the price level for 1993 if money wages are
a) Fixed
b) Flexible.

4 The economy in problem 3 has the following short-run aggregate supply schedule:

Price Level (GDP deflator)	Real GDP supplied (billions of 1984/85 dollars)
120	3.2
121	3.5
122	3.8
123	4.1
124	4.4

a) Under what conditions is this short-run aggregate supply schedule consistent with your answer to problem 3?
b) Calculate the actual and expected inflation rate if the aggregate demand curve is expected to shift upward by 10 per cent and if it actually does shift upward by that amount.

Chapter 33

Expansions and Contractions

After studying this chapter, you will be able to:

- Describe the causes of the expansions and contractions of the Australian economy in the 1980s.
- Describe the course of money and interest rates as the economy expands and contracts.
- Describe the labour market in recession.
- Compare and contrast the flexible and sticky wage theories of the labour market in recession.
- Describe the economy in the contraction phase of the Great Depression between 1929 and 1933.
- Compare the economy of the 1930s with that of today and assess the likelihood of another Great Depression.

What Goes Up Must Come Down

The first half of the 1920s were prosperous years for Australians and for the citizens of all the major industrial countries. After the horrors of World War I, the economic machine was back at work, producing such technological marvels as cars and aeroplanes, telephones and vacuum cleaners. Houses and apartments were being built at a frantic pace. Australian GDP grew at an average annual rate of 6.5 per cent. But while the rest of the world continued to enjoy prosperity, the Australian economy stagnated in the second half of the 1920s, with real GDP actually falling 2.5 per cent over the years 1925/26 to 1928/29. Compounding Australia's troubles was the unprecedented stock market crash in October 1929. Overnight, the values of stocks and shares trading on Wall Street, and in London, Paris and Berlin, fell by up to 30 per cent. In the four succeeding years there followed the worst contraction in recorded history. By 1933, world output had fallen to only two-thirds of its 1929 level. In Australia, real GDP fell by 10 per cent; unemployment increased to 20 per cent of the labour force; and prices were down 29 per cent. The cost of the Great Depression, in terms of human suffering, will never be fully known. The cost went far beyond the hardship faced by those having no jobs. Families were unclothed, hungry and homeless; social tensions and crime increased. As a result of the conditions, political attitudes that were to dominate the next 40 years of Australian history were formed. What caused the Great Depression? In October 1987, stock markets in Australia and throughout the world again crashed. The crash was so steep and so widespread that it has been dubbed a stock market 'meltdown' — conjuring up images of the nuclear catastrophes at Three Mile Island and Chernobyl. This severe and widespread stock market crash caused some commentators to draw parallels between 1987 and 1929 — the eve of the greatest economic depression in history. Were there similar forces at work in Australia and the world economy then that might have caused another Great Depression in the 1990s? Why didn't world economies react in the same way in 1987 as they did in 1929? During the 1980s Australia experienced three complete business cycles, that is, three full sequences of expansion and contraction. Were all the cycles triggered by the same cause or were there a variety of causes?

In this chapter, we're going to use the macroeconomic tools that we have studied in the previous chapters to interpret the dramatic events that we have just discussed. We're going to unravel some of the mysteries of business cycle behaviour in Australia, of recession and depression, and assess the likelihood of a serious depression such as that of 1930s ocurring again. We're going to begin by examining the 1980s.

Australia's Economic Performance in the 1980s

The decade leading up to the 1980s was mixed in terms of Australia's economic performance. The 1970s started well for Australia, with strong growth in the 1960s continuing until 1973/74. The only warning sign of possible future difficulties was the rate of inflation rising from 3 per cent to 7 per cent a year between 1970 and 1973. Between 1974 and 1979, economic performance deteriorated. Inflation averaged nearly 10

Figure 33.1 Australian Macroeconomic Performance in the 1980s

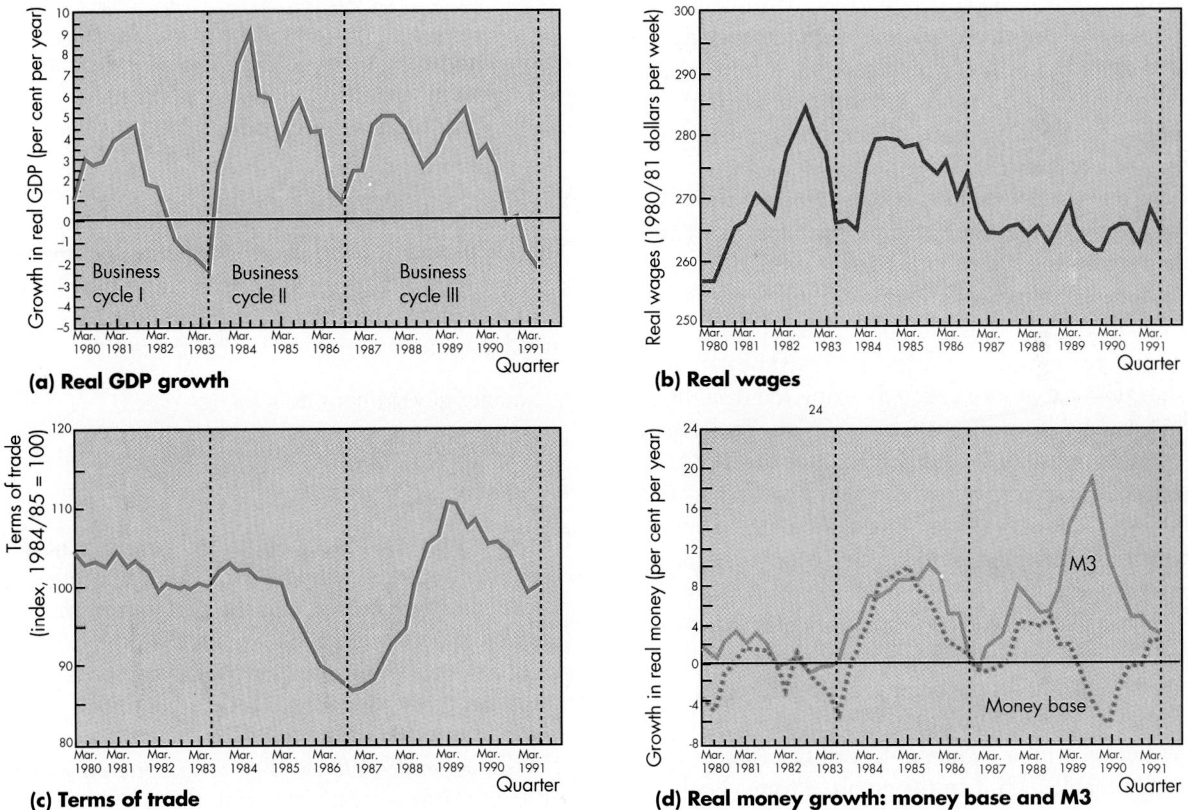

Part (a) shows the behaviour of real GDP from the March quarter 1980 to the March quarter 1991. Three complete business cycles are evident. The first two business cycles lasted just over three years and the third lasted nearly five years. The first and third business cycles ended with GDP contracting, that is, in recession. The second business cycle ended with a slow-down in economic growth, not a fall in the level of real GDP.

Part (b) shows the behaviour of real wages, measured in 1980/81 dollars, over the 1980s. A very sharp increase occurred during the first business cycle, with a gradual decline in real wages since then.

Part (c) shows the behaviour of the terms of trade. The major changes in the terms of trade were a sharp decline in the second half of the second business cycle and then an equally sharp rise in the first half of the third business cycle.

Finally, part (d) shows the behaviour of the real money supply, both the money base and M3, measured in 1984/85 dollars. The sharpest changes in both the money base and M3 occurred in the third business cycle.

Source: Real GDP growth: See Fig. 22.5; Real wages: Average Weekly Earnings Deflated by CPI, Series VNEQ.AC_WAR$ and VNEQ.V181_PCPI, from NIF-IOS Model Data; Terms of trade: see Fig. 29.8; Real money: Series DMAMB and DMAM3U, Reserve Bank Bulletin Database, supplied by EconData's dX Data Service.

per cent a year over the ten years to 1979, compared with the OECD average of 8 per cent. Real GDP grew at an average rate of 2.4 per cent a year compared to 3.3 per cent for OECD countries as a whole. Unemployment had risen from around 1 per cent of the labour force in 1970 to nearly 6 per cent by the end of 1979. But, as we will see below, there was a mood of optimism in the country as it entered the 1980s.

Over the 1980s, Australia experienced three complete business cycles. That is, measuring the fluctuations in real GDP from trough to trough, there were three periods of expansion, peak, contraction and trough — the characteristics of cycles as we described them in Chapter 22. Figure 33.1 shows the behaviour of real GDP and three other important variables contributing to the expansions and contractions of the economy.

While there were many short-term variations in the economy, in Fig. 33.1(a) three business cycles are evident, spanning the periods March 1980 to June 1983, June 1983 to September 1986 and September 1986 to June 1991. The first two cycles lasted just over three years, and the third cycle lasted nearly five years. GDP actually contracted during the troughs of the first and third business cycles — the economy experienced *recession* — but this was not the case at the end of the second business cycle. That is, although the economy slowed down and entered a trough in the second business cycle, it did not experience a recession.

Figure 33.1 also shows three variables that contributed to the economic fluctuations of the 1980s. Figure 33.1(b) shows the behaviour of real wages measured in 1980/81 dollars. A sharp rise in real wages between June 1980 and December 1982 is the most noticeable feature of the graph. From March 1983 onwards, that increase in real wages has been gradually eroded, although the rate of real wage erosion has varied considerably.

The terms of trade were introduced in Chapter 24, as a measure of the ratio of the prices received for Australian exports relative to the prices paid for imports into Australia. Figure 33.1(c) shows a very large drop in the terms of trade beginning in March 1985 and continuing until March 1987. Over the next two years, the terms of trade grew even faster than they had fallen in the previous two years. And then they declined rapidly again.

Finally, Fig. 33.1(d) shows the behaviour of the real money supply. The percentage changes in both the money base and M3, measured in 1984/85 dollars, are graphed. In the first two business cycles, the real money supply appears to rise and fall with changes in real GDP. Recall that the 1980s was a decade of financial deregulation (described in Chapters 27 and 28) and the effects of some of the changes were not always anticipated. The effects of deregulation might account for the most noticeable feature of the graph — the behaviour of the money base and M3 during the third business cycle. While the rate of growth of the real money base fell sharply during 1988, real M3 grew very strongly. Then the rate of growth of M3 collapsed while the money base growth rate increased.

The behaviour of these variables probably paints a confused picture. Let's look at each business cycle episode separately, focusing on the major changes that occurred each time.

The 1980–1983 Business Cycle

The 1970s had not ended well for Australia. Inflation was high, GDP growth was low and unemployment was rising. The Fraser government had adopted a 'fight inflation first' strategy that comprised:

- Smaller government deficits
- Targets for monetary growth rates
- Calls for real wage cuts

Unfortunately the reductions in the government deficits were not always achieved, the monetary targets were frequently exceeded, and the calls for real wage cuts were generally ignored. Nonetheless, the 1980s began optimistically because there was a widespread expectation that there was going to be another mining boom, as had occurred in the early 1970s.

The year 1980/81 was one of strong growth because of a large increase in autonomous business investment. (We considered the effects of a change in autonomous spending in Chapter 26.) Over the year, investment in plant and equipment rose by 17 per cent and investment in non-dwelling construction rose by 27 per cent, even though interest rates also rose during the year. Most of the increase in investment was in base metals manufacturing and mining developments. The effects of this increase in autonomous investment are shown in Fig. 33.2. For 1979/80 the aggregate demand curve (AD_{79})and the short-run aggregate supply curve (SAS_{79}) are shown. The economy began the decade below capacity, with real GDP of $187 billion in 1984/85 dollars and the GDP deflator at 66. Thus the intersection of AD_{79} and SAS_{79} occurs to the left of the long-run aggregate supply curve (not shown in the figure).

Figure 33.2 The 1980–83 Business Cycle

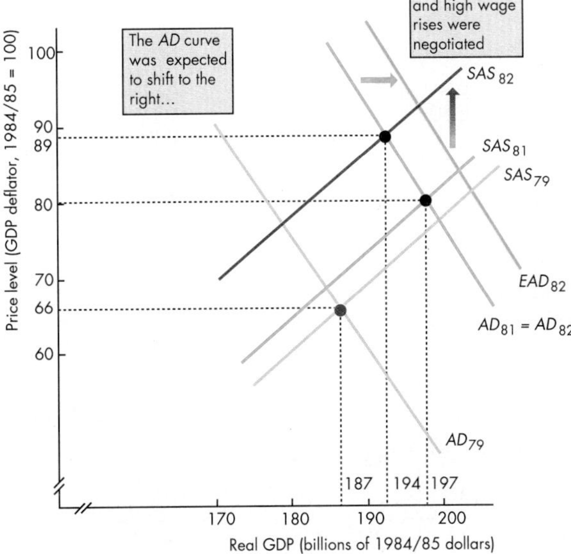

The economy began at the intersection of the SAS_{79} and AD_{79}. Real GDP was $187 billion in 1984/85 dollars. Strong investment in the mineral resources sector, as firms expected higher future profits due to an anticipated mining boom, shifted the aggregate demand curve to the right. By 1981/82 it had shifted up to AD_{81}. Real GDP grew strongly to $197 billion. Prices also rose, with the GDP deflator rising to 80, a 21 per cent increase since 1979/80. Anticipating higher prices and continued strong demand, and expecting to benefit from the strong economy, unions negotiated large real wage increases. These negotiations were based on an expected aggregate demand curve EAD_{82}. As the wage increases were granted, the costs of firms rose, shifting the short-run aggregate supply curve up to SAS_{82}. The mining boom did not eventuate, and demand remained stagnant at AD_{81}. Consequently, real GDP fell to $194 billion even though prices continued to rise. This combination of falling output and rising prices is known as stagflation.

Throughout 1980/81 and 1981/82, autonomous business investment increased as firms expected higher future profits as a result of the anticipated mining boom. The aggregate demand curve shifted to the right, so that by 1981/82 it was at AD_{81}. Real GDP had grown strongly to $197 billion and the GDP deflator had also risen strongly by 21 per cent from 66 to 80. That is, inflation averaged 10 per cent a year for 1980/81 and 1981/82.

Anticipating continued strong economic growth, in December 1981 the metals trade unions negotiated large wage increases that became the standard of reference for other union wage negotiations. This was possible because in 1981 the government experimented with decentralized wage bargaining, abandoning the earlier practice of centralized wage setting through the Industrial Relations Commission. Within twelve months, 90 per cent of all employees covered by Federal and State awards had received proportionate pay increases. This increased the costs of firms, shifting the short-run supply curve to SAS_{82}.

The wages negotiated by the unions were based on an expected aggregate demand curve EAD_{82}. However, unfortunately for Australia, the rest of the world entered a recession caused by very tight monetary policy in the United States. Thus the anticipated mining boom did not eventuate. In fact, the terms of trade declined in 1982/83, as shown in Fig. 33.1(c), because the prices of minerals and metals exported by Australia fell. At the same time, Australia experienced an unexpectedly severe drought. The combination of a decline in the terms of trade and a decrease in agricultural exports because of the drought meant that aggregate demand did not expand as expected. But the higher wages had already been granted and could not be rescinded. Thus real GDP fell to $194 billion, while prices continued to rise. The country had entered into a recession. Unemployment rose by almost 50 per cent in 1982/83.

We met the combination of falling output and rising prices in Chapter 32 where we termed it *stagflation.*

The National Economic Summit In March 1983, the Hawke Labor government was elected. Within six weeks it had called for a National Economic Summit Conference, attended by representatives from the Federal and State governments, employer groups and unions. The Summit represented an attempt to identify a commonly accepted approach to the simultaneous reduction of both unemployment and inflation. In other words, the Labor government attempted to find an economic strategy based on consensus. Ultimately, the Summit resulted in a remarkable degree of consensus among the divergent groups. It was agreed, and announced in a Summit communiqué, that the government should adopt a policy mix comprising:

- A return to centralized wage fixing
- A boost to business profits, generated by real wage restraint
- Fiscal expansion, reversing the trend of the late 1970s.

The 1983–1986 Business Cycle

The second complete business cycle in the 1980s lasted from June 1983 to September 1986. The cycle began from a deep recession and ended, not with another recession, but rather with a slow-down in economic growth. Of prime concern in March 1983 was the combined problem of high inflation and high unemployment — stagflation. The approach resulting from the National Economic Summit was adopted by the Hawke government.

The arrangements relating to wages were formalized in the Wages Accord, which restricted wage increases and emphasized the role of productivity improvements as a basis for wage rises in excess of the national average. By restricting nominal wage growth, the Accord significantly slowed the upward movement of the short-run aggregate supply curve. This is seen in Fig. 33.3 by the small year-to-year upward shifts in the *SAS* curves. At the same time, the government expanded its purchases of goods and services. Government spending rose from 26 per cent of GDP in 1981/82 to 30 per cent of GDP in 1983/84 and 1984/85. In 1984/85, the Federal government deficit rose to over $8 billion dollars or 4.1 per cent of GDP. The increase in government expenditure is reflected in the shift to the right of the aggregate demand curve to AD_{83} and then to AD_{84}.

Referring back to Fig. 33.1(b), the effects of nominal wage restraint coupled with strong growth and rising prices are evident from the sustained fall in real wages over the 1983/84 to 1985/86 period.

Figure 33.3 The Expansion of 1983–1985

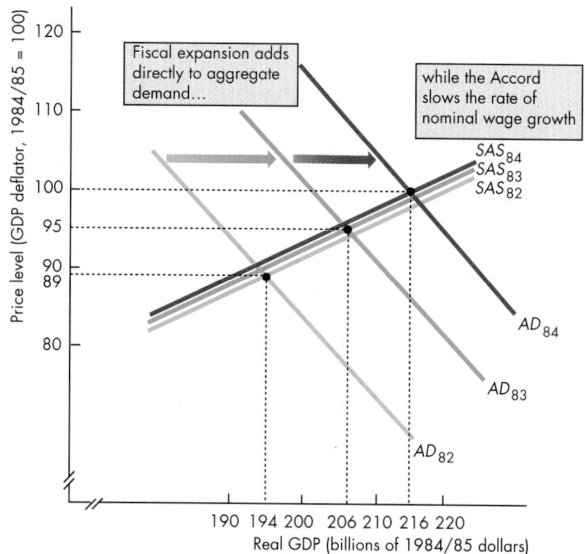

The Wages Accord restricted the growth in nominal wages, significantly slowing the upward movement of the short-run aggregate supply curve. Between 1982 and 1984, the SAS curve exhibited small upward shifts relative to the shifts of the aggregate demand curve. The shifts in the aggregate demand curve were the result of the fiscal expansion undertaken by the government which directly added to aggregate demand, shifting the aggregate demand curve out to AD_{83} and then to AD_{84}. With the price level rising faster than nominal wages, real wages fell.

The 1985/86 Contraction The cycle ended with a sharp slow-down in economic growth because of a collapse in the terms of trade in 1985/86. The prices received for Australian mineral and commodity exports fell dramatically because of the world-wide collapse of oil prices in 1985. World demand for Australia's products, many of which are energy substitutes for oil, declined. The decline in net exports caused a shift to the left in the aggregate demand curve. At the same time, Australia's balance of payments deteriorated causing widespread concern within the government and elsewhere. While the economy slowed down considerably, it did not experience negative growth because the decline in real wages and associated increase in business profitability meant that private investment continued at a high level, offsetting, in part, the deteriorating export performance.

A Banana Republic? The deterioration in export demand meant that net exports declined. At the same time there was a sharp devaluation of the Australian dollar so that the deficit on the trade account, and associated accumulation of foreign debt (see Chapter 37), continued to cause grave concern within the government. When the May 1986 current account figures were released, indicating a continued poor performance, despite the currency depreciations, the Federal Treasurer Paul Keating was prompted to suggest that, if Australia did not change policy, it risked becoming a Latin American style 'banana republic' characterized by high inflation and a weak currency.

In response to this predicament, government policy changed dramatically. The new direction primarily involved a reversal of the expansionist fiscal policies, recommended in the Summit communiqué, supported by a further decline in real wages sufficient to restore international competitiveness.

The 1986–1990 Business Cycle

Just as the downturn that ended the second business cycle was caused by an unexpected drop in the terms of trade, the new upswing into the third business cycle was stimulated by an unexpected resurgence in the terms of trade. In fact, where the terms of trade declined by 13.5 per cent between March 1985 and March 1987, they rose by 27 per cent between March 1987 and March 1989. At the same time, real wages continued to fall following the Treasurer's 'banana republic' remark, lowering the costs of producing output. And, on the basis of looser monetary policy, interest rates fell sharply in 1987/88. Lower interest rates further stimulated aggregate demand.

These developments are shown in Fig. 33.4 where the aggregate demand curve (AD_{86}) and short-run aggregate supply curve (SAS_{86})for 1986/87 are shown. Real GDP was $231 billion in 1984/85 dollars and the GDP deflator was 115. The resurgence in the terms of trade is shown by a shift to the right in the aggregate demand curve to AD_{87}. The Accord was still managing to restrain nominal wage growth so the upward shifts in the short-run aggregate supply curves from year to year were modest. Short-run equilibrium real GDP increased to $224 billion and the GDP deflator index rose to 124.

The stock market crash in October 1987 prompted fears of a recession along the lines of the 1930s depression. To avoid such an outcome, monetary policy was loosened in 1987/88, interest rates continued to fall and aggregate demand received another exogenous boost. All the while, the terms of trade were still rising strongly. By 1988/89, the aggregate demand curve had shifted to AD_{88}, equilibrium GDP had risen to $251 billion and the GDP deflator had risen to 136.

By this stage, the government had cut back sharply on government spending, turning the previously large government deficit into a surplus. (This turn of events is discussed in more detail in Chapter 35.) We might have expected this turn-about to shift the aggregate demand curve back to the left, reducing GDP. In fact, any such effects were more than offset by a resurgence in private investment, as business profitability continued to rise due to declining real wages and interest rates.

The strong growth up to mid-1989 led to a large influx of imports, which contributed to renewed anxieties about the balance of payments and external debt. But since the government had already set a path for fiscal policy, which was to maintain a surplus, its only option for restraining demand was to tighten monetary policy. As is evident from Fig. 33.1(d), this began in mid-1988 but it was some time before the effects began to be felt. The problem was that the removal of SRD requirements on banks (see the discussion of financial deregulation in Chapter 28) provided a separate large boost to M3 as banks brought much of their off-balance sheet banking back on to their books. That is, they replaced their bill market borrowing with direct borrowing from depositors. Thus, while the money base was contracting, M3 was expanding and the extent of the monetary tightening was not recognized. However, the underlying tightening of the money base was reflected in rising interest rates.

Figure 33.4 The Expansion of 1987–1989

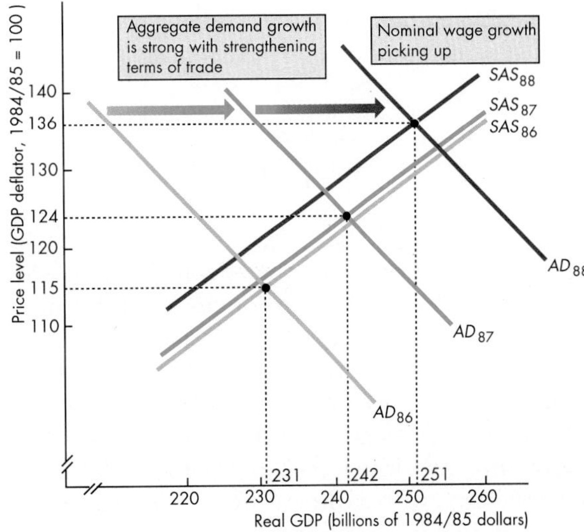

Equilibrium real GDP in 1986/87 is at the intersection of the aggregate demand curve, AD_{86}, and the short-run aggregate supply curve, SAS_{86}. The GDP deflator is 115. The sharp increase in the terms of trade, which rose by 27 per cent between March 1987 and March 1989, is shown by a relatively large shift to the right of the aggregate demand curve — to AD_{87}. The restraining effects of the Accord are seen by the relatively small upward shift in the short-run aggregate supply surve to SAS_{87}.

Throughout 1988/89, the terms of trade continued to strengthen. Additionally, in response to the stock market crash of October 1987, the Reserve Bank loosened monetary policy in late 1987 and the first half of 1988. The aggregate demand curve continued to shift to AD_{88}. By 1988/89, real GDP had risen to $251 billion and the GDP deflator had risen to 136.

Coincidentally, monetary policy was being tightened at the same time as the terms of trade ceased their upward rise and began to turn down. These two developments very quickly reduced aggregate demand, and real GDP growth fell precipitously in the second half of 1989. By late 1990, the economy had entered into what turned out to be a severe recession.

REVIEW

There have been three business cycles in Australia over the 1980s and each had its origin in a different set of circumstances. The first was caused by expectations of a mining boom that provided the stimulus for very large real wage increases in 1981/82. When the boom did not eventuate and a drought occurred, the economy went into recession. The second business cycle began with a commitment to consensus and cooperation between employers and unions, resulting in real wage cuts and profit increases, coupled with a large increase in government expenditure. Very strong growth followed but was halted by a sudden collapse in the terms of trade. A reversal in the terms of trade, coupled with falling real wages and interest rates, initiated the upswing in 1987/88. Looser monetary policy provided an additional boost to the upswing.

Of the three contractions that followed the expansions of the 1980s, only the last can be said to have been policy induced. It resulted directly from tight monetary policy. However, in fairness to the Reserve Bank, the financial deregulation of the 1980s may have obscured the monetary picture sufficiently that it was difficult to see the full effects of current policies as they were applied. ■

These problems aside, however, what is the normal reaction of money and interest rates over a business cycle? Let's answer these questions by considering the behaviour of money, interest rates and expenditure in more detail.

Money, Interest Rates and Expenditure over the Business Cycle

A feature common to all three business cycles over the 1980s was that interest rates rose well into the business cycle as the economy grew strongly. As the rate of GDP growth then fell, and even as the economy moved into recession, interest rates continued to rise. By the time GDP had

Figure 33.5 Interest Rates over the Business Cycle

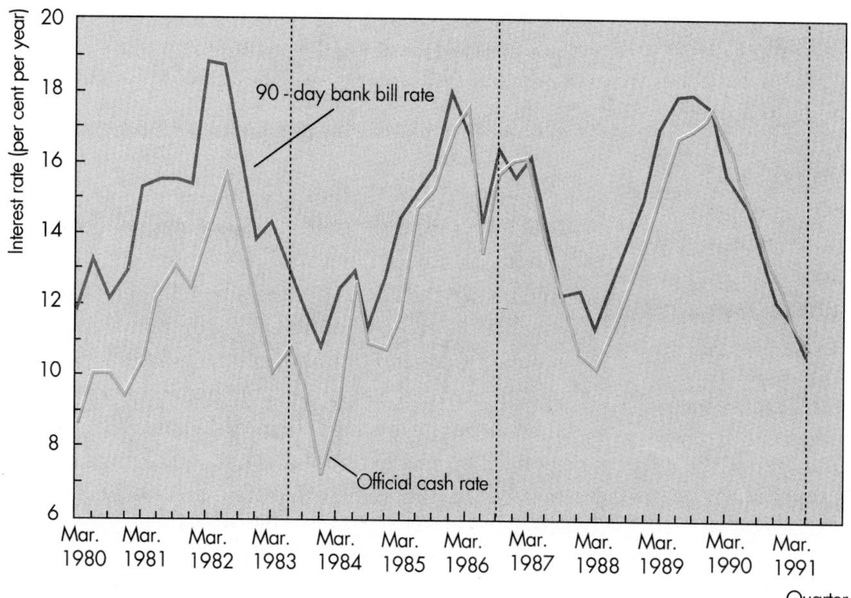

The figure shows the official cash rate — the interest rate influenced directly by the Reserve Bank — and the 90-day bank bill rate. Both move very closely together. In the second and third business cycles, interest rates continued to fall as the economy began to expand. But as the expansion continued, interest rates rose in all instances. They stopped rising only after GDP growth had peaked.

Source: Cash rate: Series FIRMMADWA; Bank bill rate: Series FIRMMBAB90, Reserve Bank Bulletin Database, supplied by EconData's dX Data Service.

reached its trough, interest rates were falling, and they continued to fall after the new expansion had begun. Figure 33.5 shows the changes in interest rates over the 1980s. The official cash rate — the interest rate directly affected by Reserve Bank policy — and the 90-day bank bill rate are shown. Both interest rates move very closely together.

Referring back to Fig. 33.1(d), we see that there appears to be a tendency for the real money supply to rise during expansions and then to fall during contractions. How is this behaviour related to the behaviour of interest rates? To find out, let's study the money market over the first business cycle of the 1980s. Figure 33.6 contains the relevant analysis.

Figure 33.6(a) shows the money market over the expansion phase of the 1980–83 business cycle. The real money supply expanded as output grew between March 1980 and March 1982, rising from $72 billion (M3 in 1984/85 dollars) in 1980 to $73 billion in 1981 and to $74 billion in 1982. This is shown by a shift to the right in the supply of money curve from MS_{80} to MS_{81} to MS_{82}. But the rise in real GDP over the same period increased the demand for money faster than the supply of real money. Thus interest rates rose, reaching 13.8 per cent in March 1982.

Figure 33.6(b) shows what happened on the down side of the cycle. With the overseas recession and drought at home, aggregate demand failed to rise, and the increase in costs caused by high wages and high interest rates actually reduced real GDP. The real demand for money fell from MD_{82} to MD_{83}.

Although the nominal quantity of money continued to rise, albeit more slowly than before, prices rose faster and the real money supply fell — from

Figure 33.6 The Official Cash Rate and Real Money over a Cycle

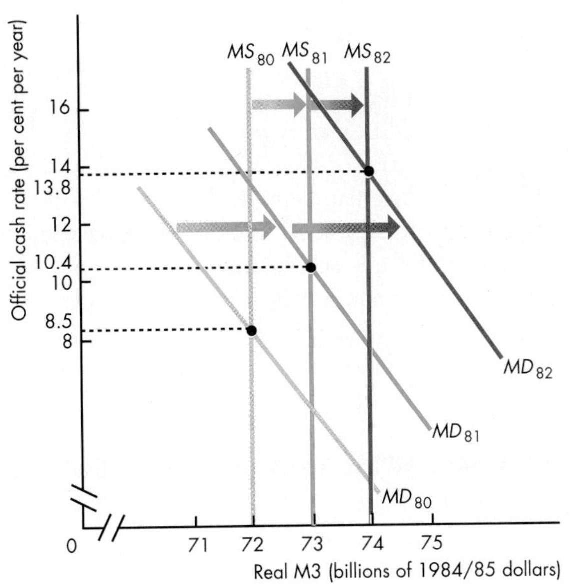

(a) The expansion

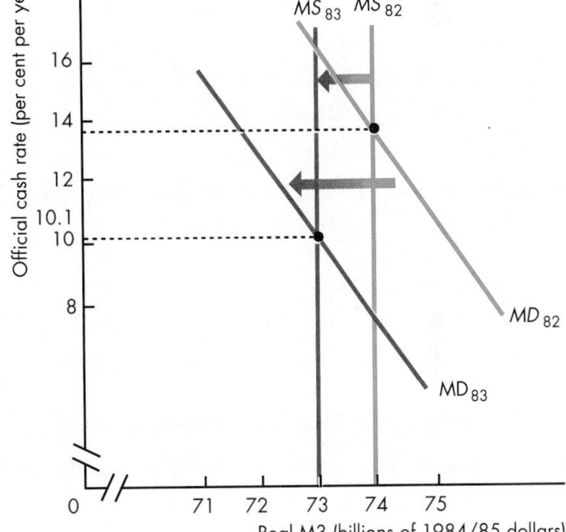

(b) The contraction

During the course of the 1980–83 business cycle, the real money supply and real output moved in the same direction. As output grew, the real money supply expanded, and vice versa. Part (a) shows the expansion phase of the cycle. In 1980, the real money supply (M3 in 1984/85 dollars) was $72 billion, shown by MS_{80}. The demand for money was MD_{80}. Between 1980 and 1982, the real money supply expanded slowly. But the growth in aggregate demand increased the demand for money faster, shifting the demand for money curve from MD_{80} to MD_{81} to MD_{82}. By 1982, interest rates had risen to nearly 14 per cent.

Part (b) of the figure shows the events in the money market during the contraction phase of the business cycle. The combination of a recession overseas, drought at home, high wage costs and high interest rates reduced aggregate demand and led to a decline in real GDP. Thus the demand for money fell from MD_{82} to MD_{83}. Even though the nominal supply was still rising, albeit slower than before, prices were rising faster and the real money supply fell — the money supply curve shifted to the left from MS_{82} to MS_{83}. Because the real money supply fell as the economy went into recession, interest rates did not fall by as much as they otherwise would have.

MS_{82} to MS_{83}. Because the demand for money fell faster than the supply of real money, interest rates fell.

The pattern in the next two cycles was slightly different. In both cases, the real money supply rose in the early stages of the expansion and interest rates fell. The fall in interest rates boosted the initial forces that had started the economy on its upswing — the new consensus-based approach to policy leading to greater business profitability, increased government spending in 1983/84 and the strong terms of trade in 1987/88. But as the expansion got stronger, increasing real GDP led to increased demand for money and interest rates rose.

While the collapse of the terms of trade in 1985/86 brought an end to the expansion in the second business cycle of the 1980s, declining rates of growth in nominal money aggregates, coupled with rising prices, meant that the real money supply contracted at the same time as the real demand for money fell. Consequently, interest rates stayed high in 1986 even though growth had slowed considerably.

On the other hand, the third business cycle of the 1980s, which received a large early boost as the real money supply expanded, was abruptly brought to an end by a deliberate use of tight monetary policy. The real money base contracted severely from mid-1988, as the Reserve Bank halted injections of new cash into the system, but prices continued to rise. As we noted earlier, real M3 continued to rise as banks re-arranged some of their financing arrangements, but it too fell precipitously in late 1989 and throughout 1990. By early 1990, as the effects of the tight monetary policy were becoming apparent, policy was loosened by allowing the money base to grow more rapidly, but by then demand was falling very fast and interest rates were tumbling.

Booms and Busts We have seen that there have been a number of reasons why the economy has exhibited cyclical behaviour. Additionally, it would seem that the characteristic behaviour in Australian money markets is for interest rates to fall early in an expansion, providing an additional boost to growth, and then to rise as the expansion strengthens. At this point, either the high interest rates reinforce some event that dampens the expansion and moves the economy into a contraction, or monetary policy is independently tightened in an attempt to halt the rise in aggregate demand. The pro-cyclical behaviour of the real money supply suggests that there is a strong possibility that monetary policy actually amplifies the cyclical fluctuations in real GDP, first by loosening and boosting the expansion phase, and then by declining as the economy contracts and deepening the contraction phase. Perhaps this is one reason why the Australian economy has, at times, been called a 'boom–bust' economy.

Why would monetary policy be managed so that it added to the volatility of real GDP? The answer is that, rather than being an intentional policy, it may be the unintentional result of other policies. In particular, if the Reserve Bank is targeting the interest rate, the exchange rate or some other variable, then unexpected changes in the economy might cause it to expand or contract the money supply when it might not otherwise have chosen to do so.

Table 33.1 Expenditure in the 1982/83 Contraction

	Y	**=**	**C**	**+**	**I**	**+**	**G**	**+**	**EX**	**–**	**IM**	**+**	**SD**
			(billions of 1984/85 dollars)										
1981/82	195	=	119	+	38	+	50	+	28	–	36	+	–4
1982/83	193	=	120	+	28	+	51	+	28	–	33	+	–1
Change	–2	=	+1		–10		+1		+0		–3		+3
Percentage change	–1.0		+0.8		–26.3		+2		0		–8.3		

Source: Australian Bureau of Statistics, *National Income and Expenditure Accounts* (Canberra, ABS, 1989).

We will discuss this problem in depth in Chapter 34, where we analyse stabilization policies.

As we have noted, the behaviour of interest rates is a very important determinant of aggregate expenditure. Let's look more closely at how aggregate expenditure changed in the 1982/83 recession.

Changes in Expenditure

When the economy is in a recession, real GDP falls and real aggregate expenditure also falls. (Recall that, in equilibrium, real GDP and real aggregate expenditure are equal to each other.) But the main component of aggregate expenditure that falls is investment — see Table 33.1. Investment falls for two reasons. First, an increase in real interest rates (that is, in interest rates relative to expected inflation) increases the opportunity cost of buying new capital equipment. Second, expectations of recession lead to a downward revision of profit expectations, and that too lowers investment. For these two reasons, investment falls. During the 1982/83 recession, investment (in 1984/85 dollars) fell from $38 billion by 1981/82 to $28 billion in 1982/83, a decline of over 26 per cent. In that downturn, both private consumption expenditure and government expenditure rose.

A decrease in investment has two effects. First, it decreases aggregate expenditure and aggregate demand. Second, it results in the capital stock growing less quickly and a slow-down in the pace at which new technologies are introduced. This aspect of the investment slow-down feeds back to slow down the growth of aggregate supply. But in the short-run, it is the effect of decreased investment on aggregate demand that dominates.

As you can see from Table 33.1, between 1981/82 and 1982/83 the only other component of aggregate demand to fall was imports, which fell by 8 per cent. During that particular downturn, exports did not change. There is a connection between the decrease in imports and the decrease in investment. Much of Australia's investment consists of specialized equipment made in other countries. When investment declines, the demand for Boeing aeroplanes and Caterpillar earthmovers from the United States, for high-tech instruments from West Germany and for electronic components from Japan declines.

The fact that our exports did not decline does not mean that the Australian recession was not strongly influenced by events in the rest of the world. Recall that the expansion in 1980/81 and 1981/82 was caused by the expectation of a mining boom. The fact that our exports did not *increase* was sufficient to generate a climate of pessimism, as it signalled that the anticipated mining boom was not going to occur.

We've now reviewed the events of the 1982/83 recession in terms of the aggregate demand–aggregate supply model, events occurring in the money market and the components of aggregate expenditure. Next, we're going to examine the labour market.

One of the main reasons why people fear contractions, and especially recessions, is that they are associated with a high unemployment rate. What happens in the labour market during expansions and contractions? Why does unemployment increase during contractions? Let's now examine these questions.

Business Cycles and the Australian Labour Market

Figure 33.7 provides a description of the main events. The large rise in real wages, which in this graph are measured on the right axis in 1980/81 dollars per week, began in mid-1980 and continued through 1982. Unemployment, shown on the left axis, began to rise early in 1982 and continued to grow throughout 1983. Apart from a sudden fall and rise in 1983, real wages gradually fell until 1990, as did unemployment. By early 1990, real wages had fallen to almost their 1980 level. Although these longer run trends dominate the data, there appears to be a small increase in real wages, with an associated increase in unemployment, at the end of the second and third business cycles of the 1980s.

Throughout most of this period, the labour force grew steadily at an average annual rate of 2 per cent. However, as we will see below, there were periods when the labour force fell.

In Chapter 31, we discussed the controversy among economists about how the labour market works and about its ability to act as a coordinating mechanism to bring about an equality between the quantities of labour demanded and supplied. Let's see how we can interpret the events occurring in the Australian labour market over the 1980–83 business cycle, using the sticky wage theory and the flexible wage theory, and see why economists do not agree on how the labour market functions. Figure 33.8 depicts the analysis.

The Expansion in 1981/82

The years 1980/81 and 1981/82 were a period of strong growth in real GDP because planned investment growth was strong. Confidence was high as

Figure 33.7 Unemployment and Real Wages over the 1980s

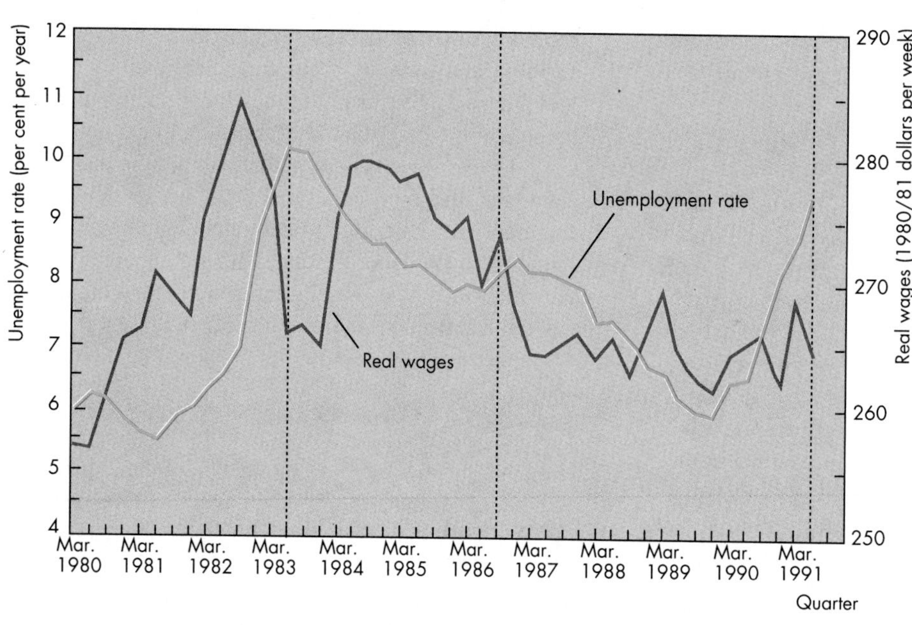

The behaviour of real wages, in 1980/81 dollars a week, is dominated by the sharp rise in 1980/81 and 1981/82. Thereafter, real wages (shown on the right axis) gradually fell until the real wage in early 1990 was almost back at its 1980 level. Unemployment (shown on the left axis) follows a similar pattern, though with a lag. Unemployment was steady in 1980/81 and 1981/82, even as real wages were rising. Then unemployment rose sharply, falling only gradually as real wages fell.

Source: See Figs. 22.7 and 31.1.

firms were anticipating higher future profits from an imminent mining boom. In 1981/82, the government also abandoned centralized wage setting through the Industrial Relations Commission and experimented with decentralized wage setting. Expectations of higher real wages, as a result of real GDP growth, naturally ensued and individual unions negotiated for higher nominal and real wages. The negotiations were not always smooth and 1981/82 saw an unusually high level of industrial disputation. In part, it reflected the process of competitive wage claims pushed by different unions as they struggled to maintain wage parity in an environment where average wages were rapidly rising. Firms ultimately conceded to higher wages because they expected to get higher prices for their output.

Figure 33.8(a) shows the situation. The demand curve for labour in March 1981 is shown as LD_{81}. The supply of labour curve is LS_{81} and the total labour force is shown by LF_{81}. Equilibrium was at point *a* where employment was 11.3 billions hours and the real wage, in 1984/85 dollars, was $266 per week. The total labour force was 11.8 billion hours. The unemployment rate was around 5 per cent, which we will assume is roughly the natural rate of unemployment. Thus the economy was at a full-employment equilibrium.

As a result of the high rate of investment, the short-run production function rose and shifted the labour demand curve to the right to LD_{82}. At the same time, the labour force, mainly through immigration, increased from 11.8 billion hours to 12 billion hours. The increase in the labour force was reflected in a shift to the right of the labour supply curve to LS_{82}. Employment rose to 11.4 billion hours and the real wage rose to $276 a week, shown by point *b*. Under our assumptions, the economy is still at the natural rate of unemployment.

The Contraction in 1982/83

As noted, the mining boom did not eventuate because the United States and other major countries went into recession. Demand for Australian-made products not only did not rise, as was expected, but actually fell. The result was a significant fall in planned investment. Aggregate demand fell and prices did not rise as expected. At the same time, Australia was experiencing an unexpected but severe drought. Coupled with a very high level of industrial unrest, the short-run production function temporarily shifted down. Thus the demand for labour curve shifted back to the left. Our explanation of the impact on the

Figure 33.8 Alternative Explanations of the Labour Market over the Business Cycle

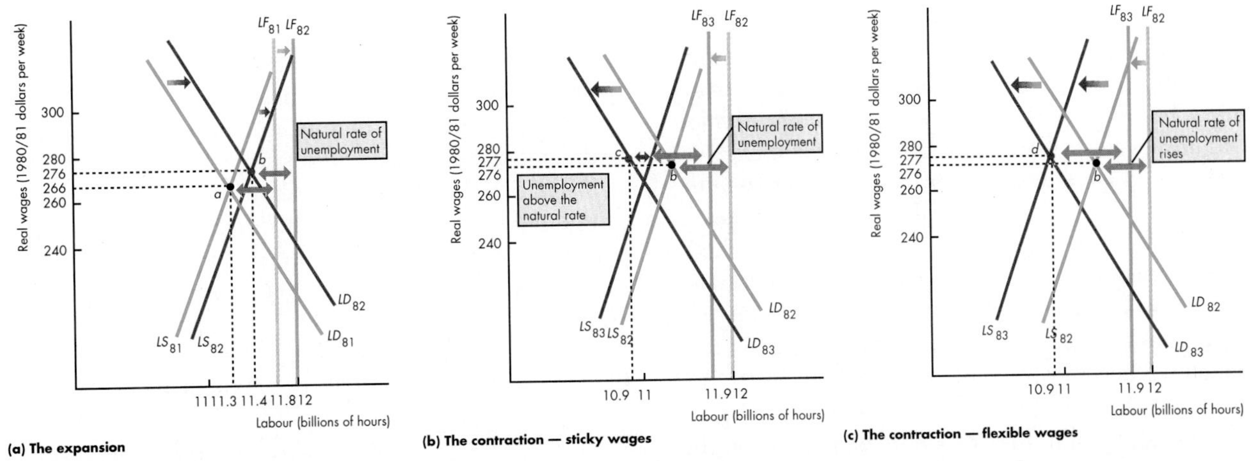

(a) The expansion

(b) The contraction — sticky wages

(c) The contraction — flexible wages

Part (a) shows the job market as planned investment was growing rapidly. The short-run production function was rising and the demand for labour increasing. The labour force and the supply of labour increased marginally. Starting from equilibrium at point *a*, the labour demand curve shifted to the right from LD_{81} to LD_{82}. The labour supply curve also shifted to the right from LD_{81} to LD_{82}. Employment and real wages rose, and the economy remained at a full-employment equilibrium at point *b*.

Part (b) shows how the labour market reacted to decline in the demand for labour with sticky wages. The labour demand curve shifted back to the left to LD_{83} but real wages did not fall. Unemployment rose and some workers became discouraged and left the workforce. The labour supply curve shifted to the left to LS_{83}. Equilibrium occurred at point *c*, with a substantial increase in unemployment.

Part (c) interprets the same events using a flexible wage approach. With expectations of higher real wages, unemployed workers increased their *reservation wages* and searched for longer than before. Some employed workers were induced to quit jobs they were in and join the search for higher wages. As a result the supply of labour curve shifted to the left to LS_{83}. Unexpectedly, and at the same time, the demand for labour fell. Many job searchers were caught unawares and expectations were slow to adjust. The new equilibrium occurred at point *d*.

labour market depends on whether wages are sticky or flexible. Let's discuss the alternative scenarios.

The Sticky-Wage Theory Figure 33.8(b) considers adjustments in the labour market under the assumption of sticky wages. The labour supply and demand curves, as they were in 1982, are reproduced from Fig. 33.8(a). As the short-run production function shifted down, the demand for labour fell and the labour demand curve shifted back to the left to LD_{83}. Because nominal wages were sticky, the real wage did not fall to eliminate the unemployment that subsequently developed. In fact, real wages rose marginally to $277 a week. However, the rise in unemployment did have an effect on the supply of labour because, with more people competing for a smaller number of jobs, the chances of any of the unemployed finding a job were diminished. Thus some left the labour force — the discouraged worker effect — and the labour force actually fell from 12 billion hours (LF_{82}) to 11.9 billion hours (LF_{83}). This decline was reflected in a shift to the left in the supply of labour curve to LS_{83}.

The new equilibrium in the labour market occurred at point *c* on the demand for labour curve, LD_{83}. Unemployment rose to near 10 per cent, which was about double the natural rate. But measured unemployment understated the true level of unemployment because of the discouraged worker effect.

This account of the labour market, emphasizing the effects of sticky wages, is probably the one that most Australian economists regard as correct. But it is also possible to explain the facts of the 1980–83 business cycle based on a flexible wage theory. Let's see how.

A Flexible-Wage Interpretation Figure 33.8(c) offers an explanation of the behaviour of the labour market during the 1980–83 business cycle using a flexible wage theory. In this case we use the job search explanation of the natural rate of unemployment first introduced in Chapter 31. Recall that, in that model, unemployment arose because it takes time for people without work to find an acceptable job. Information is costly, particularly information regarding other job opportunities. So workers, who might be unsure of their prospects of finding a new job and unsure about the wage they might be offered, might be tempted to search for longer than usual in the hope of attracting a good job offer. As more workers search for longer, measured unemployment rises. Let's apply this approach to the job market in 1981/82.

Recall that 1980–82 was a period of rising expectations regarding future income and a period in which workers, through individual unions, were given the opportunity to negotiate their own wage outcomes. With industrial action, which was on the rise, apparently successful in securing real wage increases (as shown in Fig. 33.7), expectations of further wage increases were widespread. This behaviour shifted the supply of labour curve to the left to LS_{83} for the following reason: anticipating further wage rises, unemployed workers lifted their reservation wages so that, in order to be willing to supply the same amount of labour as before, they had to be offered a higher wage. In addition, some worker already in jobs may have been induced to quit and to search for a higher paying job.

However, unexpectedly, and for reasons already discussed, the demand for labour curve shifted back to the left as the supply curve shifted. With many workers caught unawares, expectations were slow to adjust so a new equilibrium wage and level of employment was established at point *d*. In effect, the natural rate of unemployment rose because workers had expectations that turned out to be unrealistic in the new circumstances.

Which Theory? Each of the approaches to explaining the facts is based on fundamentally different assumptions about how the labour market works, and choosing between them is very difficult. Nonetheless, most economists in Australia appear to have accepted the sticky wage explanation of the labour market for a variety of reasons.

First, the labour market in Australia is highly institutionalized, which naturally imparts rigidity to wages. Apart from being highly unionized, the labour market is dominated by bodies such as the Industrial Relations Commission (IRC) through which most wage outcomes are ratified, if not originated. Indeed, it was because of these various institutions that the Hawke Labor government was able to press for an Accord based on a consensus approach, which recognized the need to reduce real wages and improve business profitability.

Second, if unemployment developed because of unrealistic expectations formed during a period of rapid wage growth, then, as it became obvious that the boom had passed, expectations should have adjusted rapidly, shifting the labour supply curve to the right and quickly reducing unemployment. In fact, unemployment did fall, but only slowly, over the rest of the decade as real wages were eroded. And this decline in real wages and reduction in unemployment coincided with the initiation of the Wages Accord.

Third, it is difficult to reconcile a decrease in the labour force, as was observed in 1983, with a period when expectations were of significant wage increases. If anything, such expectations should have increased the labour force as more people were attracted into the labour force by higher real wages. That is, we might have expected to see an increase in the participation rate and a shift to the right of the labour-force curve, LF_{83}.

The Wages Accord

In mid-1983, the government entered into an agreement with trade unions to restrain nominal wage growth. This agreement, known as the Wages Accord, effectively imposed real wage decreases on workers because the price level was allowed to rise faster than wages.

The most commonly accepted explanation of the Accord follows from Fig. 33.8(b), which describes the labour market with sticky wages. With the economy in recession and the labour market stuck at an equilibrium — point *c* in Fig. 33.8(b) — unemployment would have remained high because the individual unions, which had bargained for high nominal wage increases, had no incentive to reduce wages to eliminate unemployment. Any one union initiating such a change would merely have lost ground relative to other unions. Thus it was reasoned that a consensus to bring down real wages could only be achieved if *all* unions agreed to a consistent plan of action. Hence the Accord was formulated so that all unions acted in the same manner. It was negotiated with the government on behalf of the individual unions by the main national union body, the Australian Council of Trade Unions (ACTU). The effects of the Accord can be seen in Fig. 33.7, which shows a gradual decline in real wages accompanied by a gradual decline in unemployment from mid-1983. On these grounds, the Accord has been judged a success.

However, this conclusion is not universally accepted, and some economists have criticized the Accord as being unnecessary and only adding to existing rigidities in the labour market. These economists argue that the Accord merely institutionalized wages at a level they would have reached in any case under the weight of unemployment. That is, adopting the flexible wage theory approach, as wage expectations became more realistic, wages would have fallen to eliminate the large pool of unemployment. The Accord simply slowed this process down.

These questions are far from being resolved, although the weight of opinion lies with the sticky wage approach. The big question, however, is not really whether or not wages are flexible in Australia, as most people agree that they are not, but rather, whether the institutions in the labour market could be re-organized so that wages become more flexible in a way that benefits employers and employees alike. A major part of the debate focuses on the desirability of small enterprise-based unions as opposed to large industry-based unions.

R E V I E W

The 1980s opened with large increases in real wages, growing employment and constant unemployment. Then the demand for labour collapsed, employment fell, unemployment rose, but real wages did not fall. Two competing theories have been offered to explain the facts.

The first, sticky-wage theory, explains the rise in unemployment as the result of high real wages caused by high nominal wage increases granted to workers, the result of aggressive union action. With this approach, the Wages Accord was a necessary policy initiative required to coordinate the actions of workers so that real wages could be gradually reduced.

The second explanation, flexible-wage theory, is based on workers holding unrealistic wage expectations when the demand for labour fell unexpectedly. As a result, the natural rate of unemployment temporarily rose. In this scenario, the institution of the Accord merely acted to remove wage flexibility and so prolong the adjustment that would otherwise have occurred without intervention.

Most economists accept the sticky-wage theory as the more appropriate explanation of the Australian labour market. ■

Another Great Depression?

Following the slow-down associated with the terms-of-trade collapse in 1985/86, the Australian economy moved into a period of strong growth. Then, in October 1987, there occurred the biggest stock market crash to hit the Australian economy (and, indeed, the world economy) since that of 1929 — the crash that had heralded the Great Depression. On Wall Street the magnitude of the 1987 crash was almost identical to the 1929 crash — the Dow Jones index fell 34 per cent. This similarity was so striking that some commentators concluded that the closing years of the 1980s and the early 1990s would resemble the Great Depression of the early 1930s. A book that fed such fears, and that otherwise would have passed almost unnoticed, temporarily became a bestseller.[1]

But the world economy continued as if nothing had happened, and in Australia the years 1987/88 and 1988/89 were years of very strong growth. Why did the Australian economy shrug off the events of October 1987, whereas the world economy moved into the Great Depression following the events of October 1929? What was the Great Depression like? Just how bad did things get in the early 1930s? What would the Australian economy look like in the 1990s if those events were to be repeated? Once we've charted the broad waters of the Great Depression, we'll examine why it happened and consider the question of whether it could happen again.

What the Great Depression Was Like

At the beginning of 1929, the United States and other economies were apparently operating at near full capacity. It was only as events unfolded during that year, prior to the Wall Street crash, that it became clear that probably all was not as well as people had hoped. The Australian economy, on the other hand, was already in a weak position by early 1929. The four years up to 1928/29 had seen real GDP fall by nearly 2 per cent, and unemployment had risen to nearly 7 per cent of the workforce. In essence, the Australian economy began sliding into recession before the Great Depression had begun elsewhere. The events following the world-wide stock market crash, in which most shares lost, on average, nearly one-third of their values within two weeks, led to four years of monstrous depression —

[1] Ravi Batra, *The Great Depression of 1990* (New York: Simon and Schuster), 1987.

depression so severe that it came to be called the Great Depression.

The dimensions of the Great Depression in Australia can be seen from Fig. 33.9. Figure 33.9(a) shows the situation beginning in 1924/25, which was the last year of a period of rapid growth. The economy was on its short-run aggregate supply curve SAS_{24} and aggregate demand curve AD_{24}. Real GDP was $31.6 billion dollars (in 1984/85 dollars) and the GDP deflator was 5.5 (1984/85 = 100). (Real GDP, at the end of the 1980s, was some eight times its 1924/25 level and the GDP deflator is about 23 times its level of that year.)

Between 1924/25 and 1928/29, the terms of trade in Australia fell by more than 20 per cent. At the time, Australia exported mainly wool, and the decline reflected a world-wide decline in demand for Australian wool. Thus the aggregate demand curve shifted back to AD_{28}. Throughout the period 1924/25 to 1928/29, nominal wages rose at the same rate as the price level, maintaining a constant real wage, so that the short-run aggregate supply curve moved up to SAS_{28}. As a consequence of the decline in demand and the rise in costs, real GDP fell and prices rose. In other words, Australia experienced stagflation.

With the economy already in poor shape, the economic collapse in the rest of the world had a disastrous impact on the Australian economy. The most immediate impact was felt through the terms of trade, which fell by another 40 per cent in the two years between 1928/29 and 1930/31. This decline in

Figure 33.9 The Great Depression

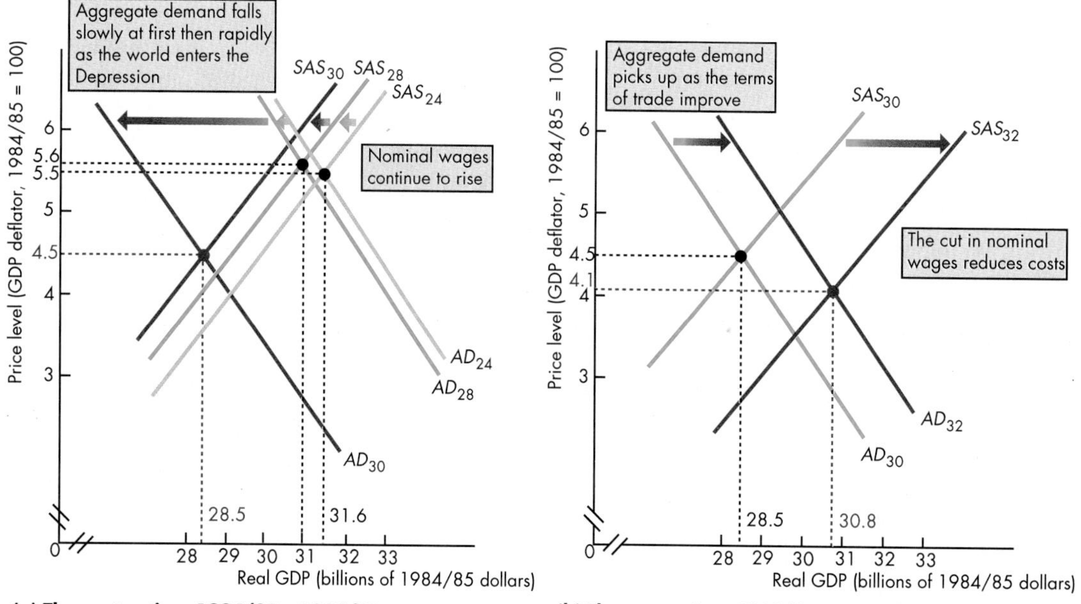

(a) The contraction: 1924/25 - 1930/31

(b) The expansion: 1930/31 - 1932/33

In 1924/25, real GDP was $31.6 billion (in 1984/85 dollars) and the GDP deflator was 5.5 (1984/85 = 100) — at the intersection of SAS_{24} and AD_{24} shown in part (a). Falling terms of trade over the next four years as world demand for Australian wool declined resulted in a shift back in the aggregate demand curve to AD_{28}. Rising nominal wages shifted the short-run aggregate supply curve up to SAS_{28}. Real GDP fell by 2 per cent and prices rose — there was stagflation.

The economic collapse in the rest of the world in 1929/30 had a big impact on Australia. Our terms of trade fell by another 40 per cent. Domestic private investment fell, as confidence collapsed, and the aggregate demand curve shifted back to AD_{30}. The short-run aggregate supply curve shifted to SAS_{30}. By 1930/31, real GDP had fallen to $28.5 billion, an 8 per cent decline, and prices had fallen by 20 per cent.

Part (b) shows that, between 1930/31 and 1932/33, the economy began to pick up very slowly. The terms of trade rose marginally, investment stopped falling and real GDP rose to $30.8 billion as aggregate demand increased — the aggregate demand curve shifted to the right from AD_{30} to AD_{32}. Falling nominal wages shifted the short-run aggregate supply curve to the right from SAS_{30} to SAS_{32}. However, unemployment had risen to nearly 20 per cent of the workforce.

export income shifted the aggregate demand curve back to the left. As a result of deteriorating conditions, business confidence plummeted and domestic private investment likewise plummeted, falling by nearly 60 per cent. For these and other reasons, by 1930/31 the aggregate demand curve had shifted back to AD_{30}. Nominal wages continued to rise. The short-run aggregate supply shifted back to SAS_{30}. By 1930/31 real GDP had fallen another 8 per cent to $28.5 billion (in 1984/85 dollars) and prices had fallen by nearly 20 per cent. Unemployment had risen to more than 16 per cent.

Figure 33.9(b) shows that, between 1930/31 and 1932/33, there was a slight improvement. The terms of trade stopped falling and even rose a little. Business confidence slowly picked up and domestic investment rose. The aggregate demand curve began to slowly edge to the right again to AD_{32}. Nominal wages fell, shifting the short-run aggregate supply curve downward to SAS_{32}, although real wages remained constant. By 1932/33, the economy was growing very slowly again.

Although the Great Depression brought enormous hardship, the distribution of that hardship was very uneven. Twenty per cent of the workforce had no jobs at all. At that time there were virtually no organized social welfare and unemployment programmes in place. So, for many families, it was a very difficult time if members of the household were unemployed. But, for the 80 per cent of the labour force who had jobs, it was a very different story. It's true that wages fell. But, at the same time, the price level fell by even more. Hence real wages for those who had jobs increased, even through the contraction years of the Great Depression.

You can begin to appreciate the magnitude of the Great Depression if you compare it with the 1982/83 recession that we studied earlier in this chapter. From June 1982 to June 1983 real GDP fell by 5 per cent. In comparison, from 1928/29 to 1930/31, real GDP fell by almost 10 per cent. In September 1983, unemployment stood at over 10 per cent, whereas in 1931/32 it was nearly 20 per cent. Thus, even though the 1982/83 recession was severe, conditions were much worse during the Great Depression. Of course the biggest difference concerns the *duration* of the poor conditions. Real GDP grew very strongly in 1983/84 following the recession. But, by 1934/35, real GDP had only recovered enough to reach the level previously attained in 1926/27!

Let's consider the causes of the particularly long duration of the Great Depression, first by looking at events in the rest of the world, then by looking at domestic money, fiscal and wages policies.

The Great Depression in the Rest of the World

The late 1920s were years of economic boom in North America and parts of Europe. New houses and apartments were built on an unprecedented scale, new firms were created and the capital stocks of most nations expanded. But these were also years of increasing uncertainty. The main source of increased uncertainty was the world economy, which was going through tumultuous times. The patterns of world trade were changing as the United Kingdom, the traditional economic powerhouse of the world, began its long period of relative economic decline, and new economic powers such as Germany and Japan were emerging. International currency fluctuations and the introduction of restrictive trade policies by many countries (see Chapter 36) further increased the uncertainty faced by firms.

This environment of uncertainty led to a slowdown in consumer spending in the United States, especially on new homes and household appliances. By the northern hemisphere autumn of 1929, the uncertainty had reached a critical level and contributed to the stock market crash. The stock market crash, in turn, heightened people's fears about economic prospects in the foreseeable future. Fear fed fear. Investment collapsed and the building industry almost disappeared. An industry that had been operating flat out just two years earlier was now building virtually no new houses and apartments. It was this drop in investment, and a drop in consumer spending on durables, that led to the initial decrease in aggregate demand. This decrease in consumer demand spilled over into large decreases in imports, which of course were, in part, Australia's exports.

The Deepening Depression At this stage, what was to become the Great Depression in the rest of the world, was no worse than many previous recessions had been. What distinguishes the Great Depression from other previous recessions (and subsequent ones) are the events that followed, between 1930 and 1933. But, even to this day, economists have not come to an agreement on how to interpret those events. One view, argued by Peter Temin,[2] is that spending continued to fall in the United States for a wide variety of reasons — in-

[2] Peter Temin, *Did Monetary Forces Cause the Great Depression?* (New York: W.W. Norton, 1976).

The Task of Managing Policy

Lessons from the Cycle

Looking back over the second half of the 1980s, a number of observations can be made.

As the economy accelerated out of the 1986 slow-down, its likely path was clouded by the stock market crash of October 1987, that saw the largest market disruption since the crash of 1929. Understandably concerned to ensure the stability of the world financial system and minimize the possible real effects on activity, monetary authorities stood ready to support the financial system. This led Central Banks world-wide to err on the side of easier credit conditions. As events turned out, the confidence effects of the crash and its impact on activity proved to be much less significant than expected by governments and financial markets world-wide.

In Australia's case, monetary policy was eased substantially in 1987 as part of a policy reweighting which involved significant fiscal tightening. After the stockmarket crash, Australia was one of the first countries to tighten policy with an increase of around 1 percentage point in official short-term interest rates during April–May 1988. With the benefit of hindsight, however, the initial and subsequent tightening in 1988 may have been unduly cautious as subsequent data indicated that the terms of trade were moving substantially in our favour and demand was picking up. Earlier adjustment may have lessened the extent of subsequent policy tightening. In addition, the announcement effects (and immediate impact on expectations) were not as pronounced as they might have been.

Overlaying all this, the policy trade-off between monetary and fiscal policy in the upswing proved less favourable than was expected. Fiscal policy was not moderating demand pressures as effectively as expected. The impact of the asset price boom on demand was at the same time not fully appreciated.

Over the cycle, the interpretation and operation of monetary policy were complicated by the effects of financial deregulation and innovation as well as asset price swings. The upswing in the terms of trade, the asset price cycle and the upswing in non-dwelling construction worked to offset the effects of tighter monetary policy during late 1988 and 1989.

In deregulated financial markets, private sector expectations play a much more important role in determining the speed of the transmission of monetary policy changes to the real economy. In particular, judgements about the likely future course of interest rates — and the economy more generally — affect the response of business decisions to changes in current interest rates. One factor which bears on these judgements is the perceived willingness of governments to sustain policy changes to their desired end. As a result:

- the degree of 'policy credibility' can be important in determining both the size of required policy adjustments and the speed of the flow-through effects;
- announcement effects, where the changes in interest rates and their relation to the policy stance are immediately and clearly articulated, can be important — especially as borrowers and lenders are coming to terms with the 'new environment'; and
- continued adherence to defined policy objectives can help build credibility minimising confused signals and inappropriate policy adjustments.

Given the difficulties of assessing and interpreting the impact of monetary policy in such an environment, it is necessary to guard against the danger of over-reacting to current and short-term developments in judging the setting of policy. While, for the reasons mentioned above, the length and distribution of the impact of changes in monetary policy are difficult to predict, an average lag of the order of a year seems to be involved. If such lags are not allowed for, monetary policy can have unintended, and possibly pro-cyclical, effects.

That said, Australian and international experience shows that setting policy successfully in such a prospective framework is a very significant challenge, not least because of the limited availability of genuinely forward-looking statistical and other information that provides a reliable guide to future trends. The recent cycle has been a reminder of those difficulties.

Not all of the key lessons of the past cycle relate to what may be perceived as policy shortcomings. One of the key policy lessons of the 1980s was the powerful positive effects on investment, employment and growth potential associated with real wage restraint and improved levels of profitability.

Overall, the past five years have provided a clear reminder of the difficulties that macroeconomic policy faces when economic events are unusually difficult to predict, where economic trends are not easily discernible and where policy responses operate with substantial and uncertain lags. Those circumstances will always confront, in varying degree, an internationally open economy like Australia's. This points to the advantages of relating policy more to the medium-term and assigning policy instruments to their area of greatest effectiveness. Such a framework entails:

- monetary policy clearly enunciated and focused on reducing inflation and inflationary expectations but remaining very much alive to the implications of settings for domestic demand;
- fiscal policy targeted towards contributing to an appropriate balance between domestic demand and production, particularly through its contribution to raising national savings; and
- wages policy aimed at restraining aggregate wage pressures to maximize employment growth and contribute to progress on inflation, while increasing labour market flexibility.

It is important to appreciate that a policy focus on such medium-term objectives does

***The Budget Statements, 1991–92*: Extract from Statement 2**
By the Treasury Department

not rule out the desirability or likelihood of policy changes in response to changing economic circumstances. Quite clearly, the need for such policy adjustments will remain. However, such changes need to be cognisant of the difficulties of fine tuning given the lags and uncertainties involved in economic systems.

A necessary corollary of the medium-term objectives for macroeconomic policy is the need for flexible goods and labour markets to enable the smooth and timely adjustments to external influences and other factors. This need is heightened in Australia's case by our susceptibility, as a commodity exporter, to movements in the commodity prices. Greater flexibility in goods and labour markets can significantly ease the adjustment costs associated with economic cycles, as well as increase medium-term growth potential via more efficient utilisation of both labour and capital. Lack of flexibility, on the other hand, by inhibiting the relocation of resources within the domestic economy, can magnify dislocation costs and result in a lower long-term growth path.

The Essence of the Story

As the economy emerged from the 1985/86 slow-down (caused by the collapse in the terms of trade) a number of changes and disruptions occurred, which made assessing the impact of policy very difficult. These included:

- The stock market crash in October 1987
- A 'policy reweighting', which saw active use of fiscal policy de-emphasized and greater emphasis placed on monetary policy as the tool for short-term demand management purposes
- Financial market deregulation

■ Expectations of policy, particularly monetary policy, proved to be critical. The issue of 'policy credibility' emerged in several guises:

- How did credibility, or lack thereof, affect the size of required policy changes?
- Could policy announcements, by themselves, be effective?
- Would adherence to well-defined, unchanging policy objectives improve the policymakers' credibility?

■ The lack of information on the current and future state of the economy significantly increased the difficulty of formulating appropriate policies.

■ For all these reasons, policy settings may not have been correct in the late 1980s; in particular, monetary policy was too loose in 1987 and 1988 and then too tight for too long in 1989 and 1990. There was even a danger of policy becoming 'pro-cyclical' (see pp. 432–433).

■ Given the difficulties inherent in fine-tuning policy for short-run demand management purposes, the Treasury's preferred approach consists of placing less reliance on a short-run demand management approach in favour of a more stable 'medium-term' approach consisting of:

- Focusing monetary policy at reducing inflation
- Focusing fiscal policy at raising national savings
- Focusing wages and incomes policy at increasing employment, and labour market flexibility

■ The third goal is appropriately thought of as a 'supply side' target.

Background and Analysis

■ The Treasury is advocating assigning policy to achieve medium-term goals and is suggesting that changing policy settings to achieve short-run goals, while legitimate in some circumstances, is a very difficult task and is often subject to very costly error.

■ We address these same issues, of how policy should be determined and assigned, in terms of 'fixed rules' and 'feedback rules' in the next chapter.

Table 33.2 Expenditure in the Contraction Phase of the Great Depression

	Y	=	C	+	I	+	G	+	EX	–	IM
			(billions of 1966/67 dollars)								
1928/29	6.2	=	4.7	+	0.6	+	1.2	+	1.0	–	1.3
1930/31	5.7	=	4.0	+	0.2	+	0.9	+	1.1	–	0.6
Change	–0.5	=	–0.7		–0.4		–0.3		+0.1		– 7
Percentage changes	–8		–14		–60		–23		+10		– 52

Source: R. Maddock and I.W. McLean (eds), *The Australian Economy in the Long Run* (Cambridge: Cambridge University Press, 1987).

cluding a continuation of increasing pessimism and uncertainty. According to Temin's view, the continued contraction resulted from a decrease in investment demand and a fall in autonomous expenditure. Milton Friedman and Anna J. Schwartz have argued that the continuation of the contraction was almost exclusively the result of the subsequent worsening of financial and monetary conditions.[3] According to Friedman and Schwartz, it was a severe cut in the money supply, caused by households' withdrawing deposits from banks and reversing the money creation process (which we discussed in Chapter 28) that lowered aggregate demand, prolonging the contraction and deepening the depression.

Although there is disagreement about the causes of the contraction phase of the Great Depression, the disagreement is not about the elements at work but about the degree of importance attached to each. Everyone agrees that increased pessimism and uncertainty lowered investment demand, and everyone agrees that there was a massive contraction of the real money supply. Temin and his supporters assign primary importance to the fall in autonomous expenditure and secondary importance to the fall in the money supply, while Friedman, Schwartz and their supporters rank the monetary influences well in front of any other factors.

From Australia's point of view, the events in the rest of the world had a direct influence: first, through their impact on export incomes; second, through effects on confidence; and third, through effects on domestic interest rates and monetary policy.

Government Policy and the Depression in Australia

The Components of Expenditure Let's look at the contraction of aggregate demand in Australia a bit more closely. The key facts about the composition of aggregate expenditure are shown in Table 33.2. As you can see, just as in the case of the 1982/83 recession, the major decline in spending came from investment. In the Great Depression, the decline in investment was a near-total collapse — a 60 per cent decline. It is this decline in investment expenditure that Peter Temin emphasizes in his interpretation of world-wide events. In Australia's case, fiscal policy was also contractionary, with government spending declining by 23 per cent between 1928/29 and 1930/31. While exports rose by 10 per cent between 1928/29 and 1930/31, they had fallen by 10 per cent between 1928/29 and 1929/30 and had fallen continuously in the period before that, between 1926/27 and 1928/29.

It is apparent from Table 33.2 that fiscal policy was contractionary during the Great Depression. So was monetary policy. Let's look at the policy responses of the Australian government.

Fiscal Policy The role of the government in the early 1930s was very different from its role in the 1980s. The average tax rate was only 12 per cent, social welfare payments totalled only 3 per cent of

[3] Milton Friedman and Anna J. Schwartz, *A Monetary History of the United States 1867–1960* (Princeton: Princeton University Press, 1963).

GDP and there were no unemployment benefits. By 1928/29, the government was running large deficits as a result of spending on public works during the 1920s. These projects were funded by borrowings from London, and the interest payments on this debt absorbed nearly 60 per cent of total taxation receipts. With the contraction in world trade as a result of the depression in the United States and Europe, the government lost a major source of revenue — tariffs — and the resultant increase in the budget deficit in 1930/31 and 1931/32 was viewed as a crisis. In May–June 1931, the Commonwealth and State governments met and agreed to the Premiers' Plan, which was based on a 20 per cent cut in government spending, just when the Depression was at its deepest. On top of this, taxes were increased so that they rose from 12 per cent of GDP in 1928/29 to 17 per cent of GDP in 1932/33. This increase in taxation receipts occurred despite the collapse of the income tax base as GDP contracted, because the government imposed an assortment of new taxes — Federal sales tax, primage duties, special taxes on property incomes and unemployment relief taxes.

The combination of reduced government spending and higher taxes had a contractionary impact on the economy, perhaps prolonging what might otherwise have been a typical and short-lived recession. On the other hand, the government's attention to the deficit probably increased lender confidence in the way the government was handling the situation, which enabled the government to continue borrowing in what was otherwise a very fragile international capital market.

Monetary Policy In the 1920s and 1930s, Australia did not have a well developed central bank, although the Commonwealth Bank performed some of the functions of a central bank — primarily in note issue and as the government's banker. To a large extent, monetary policy was operated by a small group of private banks. These banks held reserves, known as 'London Funds', in banks in London. These reserves were, effectively, the country's foreign exchange holdings.

With the continued collapse of export prices in 1929/30, the current account deficit increased and reached around 10 per cent of GDP in 1930/31. (By comparison, the current account deficit in 1991 was 4 per cent of GDP.) Contributing to this deficit was the large component of interest on the government's debt, which rose to 25 per cent of export income in 1930/31. These developments placed a severe drain on the London Funds, which the domestic banks quickly sought to rebuild. They did this by raising interest rates on deposits to attract new funds, by reducing the availability of loans, and by selling less foreign exchange. The reduction in loans reduced domestic consumption and investment, and the reduction in sales of foreign exchange reduced the country's ability to finance imports. In other words, monetary policy tightened considerably.

The magnitude of the tightening can be gauged by the behaviour of real interest rates, which rose because nominal interest rates were increased and also because domestic prices were falling. Averaging 4 per cent a year in 1929, *real* interest rates rose to more than 23 per cent by the end of 1930 and stayed at more than 15 per cent throughout 1931. (Real interest rates averaged 7 per cent over 1990/91.)

Only after the exchange rate was devalued, during 1931, did the monetary pressures ease as the induced improvement in net exports replenished stocks of foreign exchange.

Wages Policy In the 1920s and 1930s, Australia already had a highly institutionalized labour market. A variety of Commonwealth and State courts and tribunals had power over wages because of their ability to set award rates of pay. The most important of these was the Commonwealth Conciliation and Arbitration Court (now the IRC).

Although the courts only had power over nominal wages, they were concerned mainly about maintaining real wages. This was achieved by a system of full wage indexation for past price changes. Thus when the recession began to take hold and prices fell, nominal wages fell too but real wages stayed constant, and in some cases even rose slightly. In an attempt to reduce *real wages*, on 1 February 1931, the Commonwealth Court reduced the basic wage and all other awards covered by its hearing by 10 per cent. The intent was to engineer a 10 per cent reduction in the real wage, with indexation continuing thereafter. However, this, and other attempts, to cut the real wage failed. Not even unemployment of 20 per cent or more of the labour force managed to bring down real wages.

A Combination of Policies The depression started in Australia well before it began in the rest of the world, because of the steadily declining demand for Australian wool from 1925/26 onward. This was reflected in the deteriorating terms of trade and reduced export incomes. When the Depression hit other countries, these negative shocks were amplified in Australia. However, it seems that a combination of tight monetary policy, tight fiscal policy and real wage rigidity were the main factors explaining the remarkable longevity of the Great Depression and its accompanying high rates of unemployment.

The Stock Market Crash

What role did the stock market crash of 1929 play in producing the Great Depression? It certainly created an atmosphere of fear and panic in Australia and other countries, and probably also contributed to the overall air of uncertainty that dampened investment spending. It also reduced the wealth of shareholders, encouraging them to cut back on their consumption spending (the real balance effect). But the direct effect of the stock market crash on consumption, although a contributory factor to the Great Depression, was not the major source of the drop in aggregate demand. It was the collapse in investment, arising from increased uncertainty, that brought about the 1930 decline in aggregate demand.

The stock market crash was a predictor of severe recession. It reflected the expectations of shareholders concerning future profit prospects. As those expectations became pessimistic, the prices of shares were bid lower and lower. That is, the behaviour of the stock market was a consequence of expectations about future profitability, and those expectations were lowered as a result of increased uncertainty.

The stock market crash of 1987, being so large in magnitude, prompted the same concerns as arose in 1929. Economists feared that a large negative real balance effect would significantly reduce consumption demand. This fear, once conveyed to business people, might itself have been sufficient to reduce business confidence and cause a reduction in investment. The feared decline in both consumption and investment would have reduced aggregate expenditure, and real GDP would have declined. Fortunately, a repeat of the Great Depression did not occur. The economies of Australia, the United States and others continued to grow as if nothing had happened. Why were these economies so robust after the 1987 crash? Let's see why.

Can it Happen Again?

Since, even today, we have an incomplete understanding of the causes of the Great Depression, we are not able to predict such an event or to be sure that it cannot occur again. But there are some important differences between the economy of the 1990s and that of the 1930s that make a severe depression much less likely today than it was 60 years ago. The most important features of the economy that make severe depression less likely today are:

- Taxes and government spending
- A reactive central bank
- Consensus-based wages policy
- Multi-income families

Let's examine these in turn.

Taxes and Government Spending The government sector was a much less important part of the economy in 1928/29 than it is today. On the eve of that earlier recession, government purchases of goods and services were 17 per cent of GDP. In contrast, today they are more than 24 per cent. Government transfer payments were only around 3 per cent of GDP in 1929. These payments have grown to nearly 10 per cent of GDP today.

A larger level of government purchases of goods and services means that, when recession hits, a large component of aggregate demand does not decline. Government transfer payments, however, are the most important economic stabilizer. When the economy goes into recession and depression, more people qualify for unemployment benefits and social security. As a consequence, although disposable income decreases, the extent of the decrease is moderated by the existence of such programmes. Consumption expenditure, in turn, does not decline by as much as it would in the absence of such government programmes. But this limited decline in consumption spending further limits the overall decrease in aggregate expenditure, thereby limiting the magnitude of an economic downturn.

A Reactive Central Bank The Reserve Bank is now very aware of the role of monetary policy in influencing the course of the economy. Rather than contracting monetary policy, as occurred in the Great Depression, the Reserve Bank would quickly move to expand the money supply and reduce interest rates if a second Depression was foreshadowed.

Of course, this readiness can lead to false steps, as the expansion of the money supply after the 1987 stock market crash showed. Recall that, in this instance, the economy continued to grow strongly and the Reserve Bank's actions boosted that growth.

Consensus-Based Wages Policy The events following the 1982/83 recession indicate that a consensus-based strategy, which involves unions in the discussion and planning process, can succeed in reducing real wages. This is exactly what has happened over the last several years. Such an outcome appeared impossible in the 1930s.

Multi-Income Families At the time of the Great Depression, families with more than one wage earner were much less common than they are today. The labour force participation rate in 1929 was around 55 per cent, while today it is 67 per cent. Thus even if the unemployment rate increased to 20 per cent today, 54 per cent of the adult population would actually have jobs. During the Great Depression, only 44 per cent of the adult population had work. Multi-income families have greater security than single-income families. The chance of both (or all) income earners in a family losing their jobs simultaneously is much lower than the chance of a single earner losing work. With greater family income security, family consumption is likely to be less sensitive to fluctuations in family income that are seen as temporary. Thus when aggregate income falls, it does not induce a cut in consumption. For example, during the 1982 recession, as real GDP fell by 3 per cent, personal consumption expenditure fell by only 2 per cent.

For the four reasons we have just reviewed, it appears that the economy has better shock-absorbing characteristics today than it had in the 1920s and 1930s. Even if there is a collapse of confidence leading to a fall in investment, the recession mechanism that is now in place will not translate that initial shock into the large and prolonged fall in real GDP and the rise in unemployment that occurred 60 years ago.

Because the economy is now more immune to severe recession than it was 60 years ago, even a stock market crash of the magnitude that occurred in 1987 had barely noticeable effects on spending. A crash of a similar magnitude in 1929 resulted in the near collapse of investment (especially in housing) and consumer durable purchases. In the period following the 1987 stock market crash, investment and spending on durable goods hardly changed. Of course, over that period, the terms of trade were rising strongly, real wages were falling and business confidence was very high.

None of this is to say that there might not be a deep recession or even a great depression in the 1990s. Such an event might occur if there was again a confluence of the negative shocks that occurred in the late 1920s and early 1930s. For example, a big fear in Australia in 1991 was that a collapse in the terms of trade, on top of the monetary policy induced recession, could send the economy into prolonged recession. But it would take a very severe shock to trigger such a prolonged recession.

■ We have now completed our study of the working of the macroeconomy. We've studied the macroeconomic model of aggregate demand and aggregate supply and we've learned a great deal about the workings of the markets for goods and services, labour, and money and financial assets. We have applied our knowledge to explaining and understanding the problems of unemployment, inflation and business cycle fluctuations.

In the next part of the book we will study two aspects of macroeconomic policy — the policies that governments can take to stabilize the economy and the policy toward the government's budget deficit.

S U M M A R Y

Australia's Economic Performance in the 1980s

There have been three business cycle fluctuations in Australia over the 1980s. The first was caused by expectations of a coming boom leading to real wage increases for workers. When the boom did not eventuate and the country suffered a severe drought at the same time, the economy went into recession. A consensus-based wages policy, aimed at cutting real wage increases, coupled with expansionary fiscal policy lifted the economy back into expansion.

A collapse in the terms of trade precipitated the second contraction in economic growth. In this instance, growth remained positive but slowed sharply, and the economy did not go into recession.

A subsequent rapid improvement in the terms of trade, coupled with an expansionary monetary policy, stimulated the third upturn. It was a very tight monetary policy, conducted in a rapidly changing monetary environment, that led to the most recent recession. (pp. 425–430)

Money, Interest Rates and Expenditure over the Business Cycle

Interest rates tend to rise during an expansion phase of a business cycle and they continue to rise after the economy has turned down. Interest rates fall only after the economy has considerably weakened, and often continue to fall as a new expansion begins. It may be that policies adopted by the Reserve Bank have led to the money supply rising during expansions and falling during contractions. Such behaviour may make business cycle behaviour more volatile.

Because of the effects of interest rates and the impact of the business cycle on confidence, investment is the component of expenditure that changes most during a cycle. (pp. 430–433)

Business Cycles and the Australian Labour Market

There is controversy about the behaviour of the labour market during a recession. According to the sticky-wage interpretation of events, real wages do not adjust to bring equality between the quantities of labour demanded and supplied. When the economy goes into recession, the quantity of labour supplied exceeds the quantity demanded and unemployment exceeds its natural rate. According to the flexible-wage interpretation of events, real wages do adjust to maintain continuous equality between the quantities of labour demanded and supplied. Unrealistic expectations might reduce the supply of labour, as employed workers quit to find new higher paying jobs and unemployed workers extend their search activity.

The weight of opinion in Australia is in favour of sticky-wage theories as a reasonable explanation of the labour market. In this light, the Wages Accord is seen as a necessary circuit breaker in a system which stimulated competitive wages claims. (pp. 433–437)

Another Great Depression?

The Great Depression that began in 1929 lasted longer and was more severe than any recession before it or since. The Great Depression started in Australia when the economy had already experienced several years of weak growth, as the world demand for Australian exports declined. The Great Depression began in the United States with increased uncertainty and pessimism that brought a fall in investment (especially in housing) and purchases of consumer durables. Increased uncertainty and pessimism also brought on the stock market crash, which added to the pessimistic outlook and led to further spending cuts. There then followed a near total collapse of the US financial system. Banks failed and the money supply fell, resulting in a continued fall in aggregate demand. Expectations of falling prices led to falling wages, but the fall in aggregate demand continued to exceed expectations and real GDP continued to decline.

The Great Depression in the rest of the world had a direct influence on the Australian economy through its effects on export earnings, confidence, and monetary and fiscal policy. (pp. 437–445)

PROBLEMS

1 Analyse the changes in the interest rate during the 1983–86 business cycle by drawing a diagram of the money market showing shifts in the demand and supply curves for real money. What policy changes could have prevented interest rates from rising? What would the effects of such actions have been on real GDP and the price level?

2 During the 1982/83 recession, real wages and employment decreased. How can these events be explained by the sticky-wage theory? How can they be explained by the flexible-wage theory?

3 Compare and contrast the events that took place between 1929 and 1933 with those of the period from 1980 to 1982.

4 List all of the features of the Australian economy in 1990 and 1991 that you can think of that are consistent with a pessimistic outlook for the 1990s.

5 List all of the features of the Australian economy in 1990 and 1991 that you can think of that are consistent with an optimistic outlook for the 1990s.

6 How do you think the Australian economy is going to evolve over the next year or two? Explain your predictions, drawing on the pessimistic and optimistic factors that you have listed in the previous two questions and on your knowledge of macroeconomic theory.

Part 12

Macroeconomic Policy

Talking with John Nevile

John Nevile is Professor of Economics at the University of New South Wales, a position he has held since 1965. After taking a first degree from the University of Western Australia, he completed his PhD at the University of California, Berkeley. He has returned several times to Berkeley as an academic visitor. In addition, he has been a visiting academic at Harvard University, the University of Southampton and the University of British Columbia. He has also been a consultant for the International Monetary Fund. Professor Nevile has published over fifty books and articles covering a wide range of topics. In 1962 he developed and published the first econometric model of the Australian economy. He has served on a number of government advisory bodies.

How would you describe your underlying approach to economics?

Economics is concerned with real-life problems, not with technique for its own sake, or theory whose main claim is its elegance. In particular, economics is about two things, efficiency and equity or fairness. Adam Smith understood this. His great book on efficient production, *The Wealth of Nations,* was built on the foundations of another book, *The Theory of Moral Sentiments.* Many modern economists, who are followers of Adam Smith, put all the emphasis on efficiency and leave equity questions to others, such as politicians or social policy specialists. I believe economists should not opt out of the equity debate. They have insights that others do not have. For example, in the environment debate, politicians and social policy specialists are unlikely, by themselves, to realize that, unless we take steps to change the situation, the cost of the greening of Australia is likely to be borne disproportionately by the less well off in our society, not by rich business people.

At the same time, economists should be constantly reminding non-economists that efficiency is also important. It is no good having the fairest distribution of income in the world, if the average level of income in a country is the lowest in the world.

It appears that much of your work has particular policy applications in mind. Is this a conscious choice following from your basic beliefs?

It is certainly a conscious choice to work in areas of economics that are immediately relevant to policy questions. This is partly because I see economics as a study concerned with improving the lot of people, but it is also because I find this part of economics more interesting, more congenial to me personally. If it is any good, the most abstract theory must be relevant to real problems. I'm not saying that I have the interests of others more at heart than do many theorists. It's more that I do the sort of economics that I enjoy doing.

Yet you have been critical of the current dominance of economic rationalists in the policy debate. Is this because you do not like the direction of the debate or because you think that the so-called rationalists themselves begin from a particular philosophical stance, one which they do not admit to?

I believe that policy prescriptions by economists flow from a mixture of theoretical ideas and empirical judgements. In this complex and uncertain world, empirical judgements are heavily influenced by our underlying beliefs. The so-called economic rationalists do not seem to realize, and certainly do not acknowledge, that their empirical judgement that market failure is rare, is heavily influenced by their underlying distrust of large or active government, which they fear will reduce individual freedom.

Do you think it is possible to conduct a 'value-free' analysis in economics?

There may be a few areas in which it is possible to conduct a value-free analysis in economics, but work on most of the interesting questions very much reflects people's values. The interesting questions involve empirical judgements, which cannot be settled objectively in some vast social laboratory and, hence, necessitate the economist making personal judgements, which are inevitably influenced by her or his own values. The question I already alluded to, how common is market failure in a capitalist economy, is a good example. Economists who place a high value on personal liberty are suspicious of government intervention and regulation, which they see as decreasing personal liberty. It is not surprising that such economists, generally, make the professional judgement that market failure is rare. Given the values they hold, the costs of unnecessary government intervention are high, so it is responsible to be cautious when claiming that market failure exists.

Other economists are more concerned about the cost of not intervening when it is beneficial to do so. If there is market failure, the people who suffer are the economically weak, who may receive very low levels of real income as a result of market failure. This is particularly the case when market failure leads to high levels of involuntary unemployment. Economists who put a high value on income security for all are far more likely to make the professional judgement that market failure is an important problem in an unregulated capitalist economy.

Under these circumstances, what advice would you offer would-be policy analysts?

Be aware of the values that you hold, and the potential they have to affect the conclusions that you reach.

You have made major contributions in the area of fiscal policy. What has been the major thrust of this work?

I think that the major thrust is twofold. First, that fiscal policy is important for the whole economy and does affect what happens to variables like unemployment and inflation. Second, that the figure everyone talks about — the Federal budget deficit — is a very bad indicator of the effect of fiscal policy on the economy. We need fairly sophisticated measures of fiscal policy if we are to have any hope of predicting the effects of fiscal policy on the economy. If we don't use these measures, we will end up with nonsense statements of this sort — 'In the year 1991–92, we must cut government expenditure to restore discipline to fiscal policy' — in circumstances in which the change from surplus to deficit is because the recession has both reduced tax revenues and increased social security payments.

'Infrastructure' appears to be a new buzzword. But you have been commenting on the structure of government spending for some time. Do we pay enough attention to how the government spends our money?

If we mean the public at large, no we certainly do not. Most members of the public have very little idea of how much the government spends on this and how much on that; despite the fact that, as you say, it is our money.

'Economics is concerned with real-life problems, not technique for its own sake'

Do you see some, or all, government spending as a complementary capital input into the private production process?

Some government spending is a complementary capital input into the private production process. Roads, ports and airports are good examples of this sort of spending. Some government spending is capital input into the public production process, for example, hospitals. Some is current expenditure on public production, for example, spending on administration or police salaries. Some is very necessary support for the disadvantaged in our community, through the social security system, and some is just waste, like the traditional vote-winning expenditure on some dams in rural Australia.

You have also been a supporter of the Wages Accord. Do you see a major role for the unions in participating in policy determination?

I think that all groups in society should be able to participate in policy determination, in the sense that they should have the chance to put their views and have them carefully and sympathetically listened to. The unions are only in a special position in that they have the possibility of being a major force in making our economy function better, or a major force in making it work less well. Under the Accord, the government has given a great deal of sympathetic consideration to union views, and the response of the unions has greatly improved the working of the Australian economy.

'Some government spending is a complementary capital input into the private production process'

What have been the benefits of the Accord?

The Accord has restrained wage claims without the necessity for continual very tight macroeconomic policy. This has had two benefits. First, inflation has been lower. In round figures, the highest rate of inflation, over a whole year, while Hawke has been Prime Minister, is the same as the lowest rate of inflation we experienced when Fraser was Prime Minister, despite Fraser's avowed policy of 'fighting inflation first'. Second, the Accord has restrained wage claims so much that real wages have actually fallen over the period of the Accord, stimulating employment.

Would labour market deregulation, whatever that may mean, make the conduct of economic policy easier and more predictable?

If labour market deregulation means relying completely on enterprise bargaining with no centralized supervision this would not make the conduct of economic policy easier or more predictable, particularly in the transition period, which could be expected to last a decade. Unions and employers would reach wage bargains at the enterprise level which reflected the relative power of each side and which paid no attention to ramifications outside the firm or for the common good.

Returning to your philosophical position as an economist, were these values arrived at as a professional? Or were they developed in your youth?

Both. They were certainly developed and made sharper as a result of my professional training and experience, but they grew out of and reflect values that I grew up with. I was born in the worst part of the Great Depression of the 1930s. My parents were not only personally affected by the Depression, but were very concerned by what they saw happening about them. My father, in particular, was somewhat left-wing with Fabian tendencies and, when I was old enough to be interested in such things, my home was filled with books on economics and politics by writers with the sort of views my father shared. So I grew up believing that economics was important as a means of improving the welfare of people and with a concern for the least well off in society.

'The Accord has restrained wage claims so much that real wages have actually fallen . . . stimulating employment'

Why did you become an economist?

Partly no doubt because of the background I have just described and subtle influences from my parents, but also because I liked the subject and discovered that I was good at it.

Chapter 34

Stabilizing the Economy

After studying this chapter, you will be able to:

- Describe the goals of macroeconomic stabilization policy.
- Describe the key players whose actions influence economic stability.
- Explain how the state of the economy affects the popularity of the government.
- Explain how the government and the Reserve Bank can influence the economy.
- Distinguish between fixed rules and feedback rules for stabilization policy.
- Explain the debate among economists over fixed rules and feedback rules.
- Review the stabilization successes and failures of the recent past and the challenges of the present and future.

Who's in Charge

People panic when things go very wrong and turn to their political leaders for reassurance and action. Thus it was, in the depths of the Great Depression, that our grandparents turned to the Scullin government to deliver them from that economic holocaust and establish an economic order that would banish such horrors forever. Fifty years later, when Robert Hawke arrived in Canberra, part of his political agenda was to unleash the forces of competition, enabling free people in free markets to find their own economic progress and prosperity. But when the Australian economy fell into recession in 1990/91, the cry went out again, 'Who's in charge'? Who *is* in charge of the Australian economy? When economic growth falters, what can and what does government do about it? What does the government do about other macroeconomic ills such as high inflation and high unemployment? Is it possible that the government's own actions inadvertently contribute to these problems? In December 1972, with inflation rising but unemployment steady, the Liberal government led by W. McMahon was rejected by the electorate, ending 23 years of continuous Liberal–Country Party rule. The Whitlam Labor government came to power amid high hopes of social and economic change in Australia. Just three years later, with both unemployment and inflation high, the electorate soundly rejected the Whitlam government, installing a Liberal–Country Party coalition government under Malcolm Fraser. And then in 1983, with inflation again high and unemployment even higher than it was in 1975, the Hawke Labor government was elected to lead the country, ending eight years of coalition rule. How important was the economy in determining these election outcomes? And what aspects of the economy do voters care about? Do they mainly fear unemployment, worrying little about inflation? Or is inflation the source of nightmares and unemployment less important? Although we all want security — security of employment, security of lifetime savings that will not be wiped out by inflation — how much security can the government actually provide?

In this chapter, we're going to study the problems of stabilizing the Australian economy — of avoiding inflation, high unemployment, and wildly fluctuating levels and growth rates of economic activity. At the end of the chapter you will have a clearer and deeper understanding of the macroeconomic policy problems facing Australia today and of the political debate concerning those problems.

The Stabilization Problem

The stabilization problem is to deliver a macroeconomic performance of strong economic growth that is as smooth and predictable as possible. Solving this problem involves specifying targets to be achieved and then devising policies that result in getting as close as possible to those targets.

Macroeconomic Policy Targets

The targets of stabilization policy are the specific values of macroeconomic variables that policymakers seek to achieve. There are five main macroeconomic policy targets:

- Unemployment at its natural rate
- Steady and sustainable growth in real GDP
- Low and predictable inflation
- Stable exchange rates between the dollar and foreign currencies
- Appropriately balanced international trade

We defined the first three targets of macroeconomic policy in Chapter 22. There we discovered that keeping unemployment close to its natural rate and keeping real GDP growth steady avoids the costs of excessive unemployment and of excessive bottlenecks in the economy. When unemployment is above its natural rate, output is lost, there is a slowdown in the accumulation of human capital and, if unemployment is high and prolonged, serious psychological and social problems arise for the unemployed workers and their families. When unemployment falls below its natural rate, labour and other resources do not move to their most productive uses as quickly as they otherwise would. We also discovered in Chapter 22 that low and predictable inflation increases the usefulness of money as a measuring rod for conducting transactions, especially those that are spread out over time, such as borrowing and lending or working for an agreed wage.

The fourth target of macroeconomic policy — stable exchange rates between the dollar and other foreign currencies — is not just a goal of Australian stabilization policy, but is also a goal of world stabilization policy because it provides a stable environment for world trade. To understand some Australian stabilization policy actions that have occurred in recent years, we cannot ignore the importance of this international goal.

The fifth target of macroeconomic policy is also an international target. It is the attainment of a satisfactory trade balance with the rest of the world. In some circumstances a trade surplus is optimal, while in other circumstances a trade deficit is optimal. Like the exchange rate targets, we cannot ignore this target of macroeconomic policy if we want to understand the contemporary stabilization policy problem. But we'll return to this aspect of policy in Chapter 37.

The five targets of macroeconomic stabilization policy are not independent of each other. As we have already seen, in Chapter 22, unemployment and real GDP fluctuate together. Similarly, inflation and the foreign exchange value of the dollar move together, although, as we saw in Chapter 29, movements in these two variables are not as precisely linked as those of real GDP and unemployment. Nevertheless, other things being equal, if the inflation rate goes up by 1 per cent, the dollar loses 1 per cent of its value against the currencies of other countries. Finally, the balance of trade deficit fluctuates with the state of the economy, although its movements depend on a large number of other factors, including the state of the world economy.

The links between the five macroeconomic policy targets make it useful, for many purposes, to divide the targets into two groups:

- Real targets
- Nominal targets

The **real targets** of macroeconomic policy are unemployment at its natural rate, steady and sustainable growth in real GDP and balanced international trade. The **nominal targets** of macroeconomic policy are low and predictable inflation and stable foreign exchange rates.

Macroeconomic Performance Indexes

There are various ways in which macroeconomic performance can be summarized. The ones that we'll consider are indexes that combine, in some way, the real targets and the nominal targets of macroeconomic policy. All the indexes can be stated in terms of a combination of unemployment (real target) and inflation (nominal target). The different indexes place different weights on these two variables. Let's begin by considering one of the best known indexes, although one that has absolutely no scientific basis — the so-called misery index.

Misery Index The **misery index** (MI) is an index of macroeconomic performance equal to the sum of the inflation rate and the unemployment rate. That is

$$\text{MI} = \text{Inflation rate} + \text{Unemployment rate}$$

An increase in the misery index is 'bad', and a decrease in the misery index is 'good'. The weights attached to inflation and unemployment in the misery index are equal. That is, an increase in the inflation rate of 1 percentage point is just as bad as an increase in the unemployment rate of 1 percentage point. The misery index was devised as a political slogan by the Democratic Party in the United States in 1975, during the closing years of a Republican administration. It was subsequently used by the Republicans themselves against Jimmy Carter, a Democratic President, and versions of it surface in Australian discussions from time to time.

The misery index is supposed to provide a measure of the extent to which the real and nominal macroeconomic policy targets have been missed. The higher the inflation rate, the less is the success in achieving low and predictable inflation and a stable dollar. The higher the unemployment rate, the less is the success in keeping unemployment close to its natural rate and in keeping real GDP growth steady.

A second index of macroeconomic performance, and one that does have some scientific basis, is based on voter behaviour.

Wages Policy and the Accord

Voter Behaviour The effects of economic performance on voter behaviour have been studied most thoroughly by Ray Fair of Yale University, using data on US presidential elections. By studying the outcome of all the presidential elections between 1916 and 1984, Fair discovered the following:

- For each 1 percentage point increase in the real GDP growth rate, the incumbent political party gets a 1 percentage point increase in voter share.
- For each 3 percentage point increase in the inflation rate, the incumbent political party gets a 1 percentage point decrease in voter share.

Thus voters in the United States apparently place more weight on GDP growth than they do on inflation. That is, if GDP growth fell by 1 percentage point, in order to maintain its share of voters, the incumbent government would need to reduce inflation by 3 percentage points.

There are no studies of the relationship between Australian voting behaviour and the state of the Australian economy that lead to such clear-cut conclusions as those discovered by Fair concerning US voters. Nevertheless it is clear that the state of the economy affects the popularity of the government. We can use such links between the state of the economy and voter behaviour to construct a voter unpopularity index (UPI). If we use the numbers discovered by Fair by way of example, our voter unpopularity index is as follows:

$$\text{UPI} = \underset{\text{rate}}{\text{Inflation}} - \left(3 \times \underset{\text{growth rate}}{\text{Real GDP}}\right)$$

Politicians seek to make the UPI as low as possible — that is, they seek to avoid unpopularity. The idea behind this index is similar to that of the misery index. It combines the real and nominal aspects of macroeconomic performance into a single index that tells us whether performance is better or worse, as indicated by its effects on voter behaviour. The higher the inflation rate and the lower the real GDP growth rate, the more unpopular is the government.

In order to compare the unpopularity index with the misery index, we need a relationship between unemployment and real GDP growth. We saw such a relationship — Okun's Law — in Our Advancing Knowledge, pp. 388–389. Okun's Law states that, for each 2 percentage points that real GDP falls relative to trend, the unemployment rate increases by 1 percentage point, other things being equal. Using Okun's Law together with Fair's voter popularity findings, an unpopularity index becomes

$$\text{UPI} = \underset{\text{rate}}{\text{Inflation}} + \left(6 \times \underset{\text{rate}}{\text{Unemployment}}\right)$$

What this equation tells is that, on the average, voters care six times as much about unemployment of a given percentage as they do about inflation of that same percentage, other things being equal. This means that if the unemployment rate increases by 1 percentage point, to maintain its popularity the government would have to find a way of lowering the inflation rate by 6 percentage points. Thus unemployment matters a great deal for electoral popularity. If inflation increases by 1 percentage point, the government would have to find a way of lowering the unemployment rate by one-sixth of one percentage point in order to maintain its popularity.

A third index of macroeconomic performance is based on nominal GDP.

Nominal GDP Target James Tobin of Yale University, John Taylor of Stanford University and James

Meade of Cambridge University have all suggested that a useful operating goal for macroeconomic policy is to keep the growth rate of nominal GDP steady. Many Australian economists accept this as a useful and achievable goal. Nominal GDP is the current dollar value of the final goods and services produced. Thus nominal GDP increases when real GDP increases and when prices increase. The following simple equation tells us the connection between nominal GDP, real GDP and inflation:

$$\text{Nominal GDP growth rate} = \text{Real GDP growth rate} + \text{Inflation rate}$$

If the inflation rate increases by 1 percentage point, nominal GDP growth remains steady only if the real GDP growth rate falls by 1 percentage point. Loosely speaking, if policymakers choose stabilizing the growth rate of nominal GDP as a goal, they place equal weight on inflation and real GDP growth. The nominal GDP target, then, is a bit like Fair's voter unpopularity, except that the weight placed on real GDP growth is not three times that placed on inflation but equal to that placed on inflation. This defines the stabilization policy index (SPI). Using Okun's Law gives:

$$\text{SPI} = \text{Inflation rate} + \left(2 \times \text{Unemployment rate}\right)$$

A comparison of SPI and MI shows that a nominal GDP target places twice as much importance on unemployment as does the misery index.

Performance Indexes since 1960 The macroeconomic performance of Australia since 1960, as measured by the three performance indexes that we have just reviewed, is set out in Fig. 34.1. (All the indexes have been scaled to have the same average values.) As you can see, all three indexes tell the same broad story. Macroeconomic performance generally improved between 1960/61 and 1964/65. It then started to deteriorate, and continued to do so all the way through to 1974/75. Then, from 1975/76 to 1977/78, a brief period of improvement was followed by a further severe deterioration through to 1983/84. Since 1983/84, the macroeconomic performance of Australia has improved according to all three indexes. But it deteriorated again with the 1990/91 recession.

It is interesting to note that, on the last three occasions when the government has changed hands, the unpopularity index was peaking. This might indicate that the Australian electorate places a heavier emphasis on unemployment than inflation as an indicator of economic misery. Thus we might expect Australian governments to be more concerned about unemployment, and policies that reduce it, rather than concentrating on inflation.

Figure 34.1 Indexes of Macroeconomic Performance

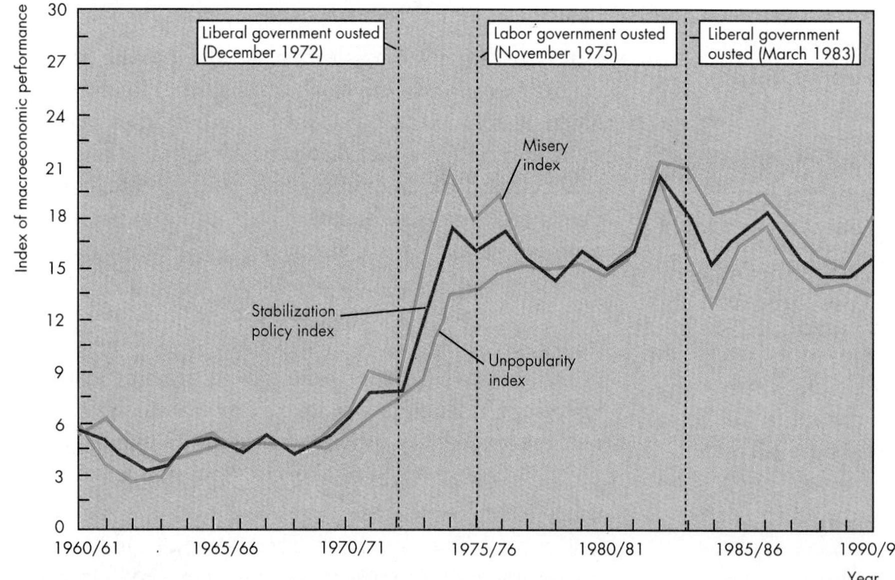

The voter popularity of a government depends in part on macroeconomic performance. The more strongly the economy grows and the lower the inflation rate, the more popular is a government. Three indexes of performance are graphed here. The misery index, which was invented for political purposes, is simply the sum of inflation and unemployment. An unpopularity index, which is based on election results, measures voter unpopularity. A stabilization policy index measures the closeness with which nominal GDP targets are achieved.

Source: Authors' calculations.

Of course, indexes such as these have limitations. They tell us nothing about the distribution of economic misery or prosperity. They also do not take into account variations in the natural rate of unemployment. There are times when unemployment is high because an unusually large amount of re-allocation of labour and other resources is taking place. At such times, the high unemployment rate reflects the fact that a larger number of people are voluntarily relocating to their highest value jobs. Such indexes also do not take into account the extent to which inflation is anticipated or unanticipated. As we've seen, this distinction makes a crucial difference to the costs of inflation and the people on whom those costs fall.

Nevertheless, although the indexes that we've reviewed are crude, they all point in a similar direction. And the state of the economy, as summarized in such indexes, has an important effect on the actions of policymakers.

But who are the policymakers?

The Key Players

Two key players formulate and execute macroeconomic stabilization policy in Australia:

- The Commonwealth government of Australia
- The Reserve Bank of Australia

In addition there are two other main groups of people that have some influence over the conduct of policy. These are:

- The Australian Council of Trade Unions (ACTU)
- Various employer organizations.

The influence of the representatives of employers and workers vary over time and also with the political party in government. Their influence can be direct, as when they are specifically invited to participate in policy discussion or through other means of formal consultation, or it can be indirect, achieved through more informal lobbying activities.

The Government of Australia

The Commonwealth government is the main player in implementing the nation's fiscal policy. To a lesser extent, State and Local governments have some influence. Fiscal policy has two elements:

- Spending plans
- Tax laws

At the national level, these elements determine the Commonwealth government's budget deficit or surplus. The Commonwealth government's fiscal policy is brought together and announced in the Commonwealth Budget. The **Commonwealth Budget** is a statement of the government's financial plan, itemizing programmes and their costs, tax revenues and the proposed deficit or surplus. The expenditure side of the Budget is a list of programmes, together with the amount that the government plans to spend on each programme and a forecast of the total amount of government expenditure. Some expenditure items in the Commonwealth Budget are directly controlled by government departments. Others arise from decisions to fund particular programmes, the total cost of which depends on actions that the government can forecast but not directly control. For example, farm subsidies depend on farm costs and prices. Some transfer payments depend on the state of the economy.

State and local governments also have taxing and spending powers, and thus contribute to the nation's fiscal policy. Together, the Commonwealth, State and local governments comprise what is called the **general government** sector. The Commonwealth government raises more than three-quarters of all general government revenue but spends only about one-half. A useful measure of the net fiscal position of the general government sector is the public sector borrowing requirement. The **public sector borrowing requirement (PSBR)** is a measure of total outlays less total revenues and indicates how much the government sector, as a whole, will be borrowing from capital markets.

The various governments make decisions about revenue by enacting tax laws. As in the case of some important items of government expenditure, they cannot control with precision the amount of tax revenue that they will receive. The amount of tax paid is determined by the actions of the millions of people and firms who make their own choices about how much to work, spend and save, and also on the overall state of the economy.

We will discuss budget deficits and surpluses, and associated borrowings in detail in Chapter 35.

There are competing views about how fiscal policy should be run. Some economists would like to see the general government balance its budget. That is, manage a zero PSBR. If the general government was starting with a deficit, one way of balancing the budget would be to increase government revenue. But there are two competing views about how this objective might be achieved. One, associated with the 'supply side' view, is that lower tax rates will increase revenue by stimulating economic activity, increasing the incomes on which taxes are paid by enough to ensure that lower tax rates, combined with higher incomes, bring in higher revenue. The other view is that revenue can only be increased by increasing tax rates or introducing new taxes. But whether a government should operate, on average, with a budget deficit, balance or surplus is itself an unsettled question.

The Reserve Bank of Australia

The Reserve Bank is the nation's central bank. The main features of the Reserve Bank are described in Chapter 28. The Bank influences the economy by trading in markets in which it is one of the major participants. The two most important groups of such markets are those for government debt and those for foreign currency. Its decisions to buy and sell in these markets influence interest rates, the value of the dollar in terms of foreign currencies and the amount of money in the economy. These variables that the Reserve Bank can directly influence, in turn, affect the conditions in which the millions of firms and households in the economy undertake their own economic actions. But the Reserve Bank itself operates under severe constraints — constraints imposed by the spending and taxing decisions made by the Commonwealth and State governments.

The Australian Council of Trade Unions

The ACTU is the major central trade union body in Australia. It was formed in 1927 after failed attempts to create a single large radical union in Australia. Today the ACTU represents over 150 affiliated unions with a total membership of 2.6 million workers — about 80 per cent of all union members and over 40 per cent of the workforce. Other important members of the ACTU are the various Trades and Labour Councils in each state. The principal decisionmaking body of the ACTU is the biennial congress. Any decisions made at this congress bind future actions of the ACTU. Policy decided upon at the biennial congress is then implemented by the Federal Executive of the ACTU.

The role of the ACTU is to

- Help affiliated unions resolve disputes.
- Present submissions to the National Wage Case or other hearings on behalf of affiliated unions.
- Present submissions to the Federal government on economic, legal and industrial issues that affect members of affiliated unions.
- Provide other services and advice to affiliated unions regarding various workplace-related and social issues, for example, on occupational health and issues relevant to safety, and migrant or women workers.

More recently, the ACTU has been directly involved with the government in the implementation of wages policy via the Accord. Later in this chapter, we discuss some of the issues associated with wages policy in Australia.

Employer Organizations

Employer representation is much more fragmented than is employee representation through the ACTU, and so is less likely to be as effective. There are three main organizations representing employers. These are:

- The Confederation of Australian Industry (CAI)
- The Business Council of Australia (BCA)
- The Australian Chamber of Manufacturers (ACM).

In addition, there are smaller organizations representing particular industry groups.

We've now reviewed the effects of macroeconomic performance on political popularity and have also described the key players in the policymaking game. Let's now turn our attention to the methods used for stabilizing the economy.

The Policy Instruments

Having identified the stabilization problem and the people who attempt to deal with it, we need to specify the means at their disposal — the policy instruments. The policy instruments are often referred to as the arms of economic policy, a phrase designed to emphasize that policymakers view all of the instruments of policy as parts of a coordinated whole, working towards a common end.

There are four policy instruments at the disposal of policymakers:

- Fiscal policy
- Monetary policy
- Wages and incomes policy
- Trade and industry policy.

The first two arms of policy — fiscal and monetary policy — are traditional tools actively used by most governments around the world. The latter two arms of policy are less traditional and more controversial in their application. Wages and incomes policy has been used for many years in Australia and has recently become a major part of the Hawke, then Keating, governments' approach. Trade and industry policy has also been around for a long time in the Australian policy debate. Most recently it has re-emerged under various guises, such as supply-side policies and micro-economic reform.

Evidence of this four-way approach to macroeconomic policy can be found in the Commonwealth government's assessment of policy settings for the 1991/92 year, which accompanied the 1991/92 Budget. In a section of *Budget Statement 2*, dealing with the policy framework, the government outlines its plans for the coming year for monetary policy, fiscal policy and wages policy.[1] A separate section of *Statement 2* deals with the contribution of micro-economic reform.

Until recently, it had been customary to refer to a fifth arm of policy — external policy or exchange rate policy. However, as we discussed in Chapter 29, when the Reserve Bank fixes the exchange rate, it loses control of the money supply. Thus exchange rate policy is really a particular version of monetary policy and it gets little independent attention in today's floating exchange rate environment.

We have discussed the operation of fiscal and monetary policy in some detail already. Let's review those discussions and elabourate on the other policies. A detailed discussion of the recent history of fiscal policy is deferred to Chapter 35.

Fiscal Policy

As we have just discussed, fiscal policy is a choice of spending plans and tax laws, which together form the government's budget. And as we saw in Chapter 26 and Chapter 30, changes in fiscal policy, whether changes to taxation receipts or changes to the level of government purchases of goods and services, have a multiplier effect on the level of equilibrium expenditure and hence shift the aggregate demand curve. In this context, fiscal policy is widely thought of as a demand management tool.

The approach adopted by governments to the use of fiscal policy has changed a great deal. Fiscal policy is now seen more as a policy instrument intended to influence medium-term savings and consumption habits, rather than as a tool for fine-tuning aggregate demand for the purposes of short-term macroeconomic stabilization. The latter approach to fiscal policy was characteristic of the 1970s. We will defer further discussion of changes in fiscal policy to Chapter 35.

Monetary Policy

Monetary policy, like fiscal policy, is a demand management tool. As we saw in Chapter 28 and Chapter 30, changes in the money supply affect interest rates, which then cause the level of autonomous spending to change, changing the equilibrium level of expenditure. At given prices, this means that the aggregate demand curve shifts.

As with fiscal policy, the approach to monetary policy has undergone changes over the years. For a long time, monetary policy was seen as an instrument more appropriate to the task of controlling the long-run rate of inflation. But, as the government gradually pinned fiscal policy to medium-term and longer term goals, monetary policy was increasingly diverted to short-term demand management goals. For example, the recession of 1990/91 was induced by tight monetary policies applied during 1988/89. We will discuss this episode in some detail below.

Wages and Incomes Policies

Australian labour markets have operated with some form of a wages and incomes policy since the very early 1900s. From 1907, when the first basic wage was introduced, to 1953, wages and incomes policies were seen as a tool for administering social justice, rather than as a tool for managing the macroeconomy. For example, the first basic wage, granted in 1907, was based on the concept of the perceived needs of a husband, wife and three children. This concept continued to evolve into the 1980s with the concept of a social wage — the overall consumption package of wage earners including after-tax wage and social wel-

[1] Department of the Treasury, *Budget Statement 2* (Canberra: AGPS, 1991), pp. 2.43–2.46.

fare provisions. From 1953 on, however, the wage system increasingly became concerned with the 'economy's capacity to pay' or the impact of wage increases on inflation. Indeed, by the late 1980s, wages and incomes policies were viewed primarily as ways to limit wage increases to alleviate inflationary pressures.

At times, during the mid-1980s in particular, wages policies have been directed at external goals. For example, high real wages were seen as a cause of the balance of payments collapse in the mid-1980s and thus wage restraint was apparently necessary in order to restore international competitiveness and so improve the level of net exports.

The primary vehicle for Australian wages and incomes policies has been some form of wage indexation. The basic wage was indexed from 1907 to 1953, adjusted every quarter by the Commonwealth Arbitration Court (which subsequently became the Commonwealth Arbitration Commission and then the Industrial Relations Commission) in line with rises in the cost of living. From 1953 to 1965, basic award wages were still set by the Arbitration Commission but not with reference to the rate of inflation. In the period 1965–1972, award wages were set by the Commission on the basis of inflation plus productivity increases. The change in the attitude of the Commission over this period was seen by some to be an attempt to regain control over the wage-setting system as more wages were being adjusted outside the Commission through higher over-award payments.

In 1973 and 1974, wages exploded to such an extent that, even though prices were rising rapidly, nominal wage growth far outstripped inflation and real wages grew very rapidly. In late 1974, unemployment rose rapidly and the Arbitration Commission exerted more control over the wage system by re-introducing indexation in early 1975. The return to indexation was not without controversy and arguments both for and against were heard.

Pro-Indexation First, indexation was seen as the only way of controlling competitive wage increases as prices rose and various income groups succeeded in getting wage increases of their own. It was suggested that strong unions were in a position to demand, and get, wage increases that would then flow-on to other unions. Flow-ons, whereby one union was granted rises already given to another union, were based on the Australian notion of *comparative wage justice*, which meant maintaining wage parities. Indexation would break this cycle by giving everyone the same pay raise at the same time.

Second, indexation was seen as a means of reducing inflation by cutting non-wage components of prices such as indirect taxes. Cutting these would bring reductions in prices, which would then feed through to reductions in wages, thus winding down the wage–price spiral.

Anti-Indexation There were a number of arguments offered against indexation. First, if indexation was imposed when prices were rising rapidly, it would simply institutionalize the prevailing rate of inflation. Put another way, indexation fixed real wages and, if they were initially set at a level that generated unemployment, then indexation removed the flexibility, which would ultimately have reduced the real wage and eliminated the unemployment.

Second, indexation would make the economy susceptible to external shocks as they occurred through the exchange rate. Any change in foreign prices, which was passed on to domestic prices, either directly or indirectly through changes in the exchange rate, would, under indexation, be passed on to wages.

Some of the objections to indexation were overcome in the period 1975 to 1981 because the Commission rarely granted increases to fully offset rises in prices. Thus indexation was partial. The system of partial indexation was not well received and finally collapsed in 1981. The government then adopted a policy of non-intervention in the labour market, encouraging decentralized collective bargaining. As we discussed in Chapter 33, this led to another wages explosion in 1981 and 1982, inevitably leading to a reintroduction of some form of indexation in 1983. This occurred under the banner of the Prices and Incomes Accord, which the newly elected Hawke government negotiated with the unions.

The principles behind the Accord were somewhat different from those behind previous forms of indexation. In particular, the desire to reach a consensus between employers and employees was important and this was achieved by adopting a policy-formation strategy that encompassed all the key players in the economy. We will examine the Accord and its effects later in this chapter.

Trade and Industry Policy

A trade and industry policy covers a multitude of initiatives not specifically falling under any of the three policies we have just discussed — fiscal, monetary or wages and incomes policies. The earliest trade and industry policies in Australia began in Victoria in the 1850s with successful arguments in favour of tariff protection as a means to reduce unemployment. A well-known report published in 1929, named the Brigden Report after its primary author, advocated tariff protection as a means for securing higher real wages for workers. This propensity to protect Australian industry from foreign competition continued up to the early 1970s.

Protection from external competition was also coupled with restrictions on domestic or internal competition. The two airline or duopoly model for interstate air services; government-owned or government-backed monopolies in postal services and telecommunications, electricity provision and other utilities; restrictions on banking and finance practices, wharf facilities and many agricultural industries are just some examples of how government regulations have affected decisionmaking in industry.

Debate about Australia's current and future industry policy has continued on a number of fronts and the term microeconomic reform has been coined to indicate the breadth and scope of some of the proposals. These include scaling back tariffs to somewhere near zero by the year 2000; abolishing quotas on foreign imports; financial deregulation; introducing competition into many government-controlled and/or government-monopolized industries; introducing user-pays principles into other areas where the government provides services to the public; and reform of the labour market. There are many other industry-specific reforms proposed. Some of these initiatives have already been implemented, such as deregulation of financial markets and of the domestic aviation industry.

Microeconomic reform is not generally viewed as a policy instrument for achieving short-term macroeconomic stabilization goals. Rather, it achieves two other goals. First, it is a way of getting more output from the same amount of inputs. As we discussed in Chapter 24, the reforms, if successfully implemented on a broad enough scale, will shift the long-run aggregate supply curve to the right, increasing output and employment and reducing prices. Second, the reforms will render the Australian economy more flexible, adaptable and more able to absorb and withstand disturbances from the international economic environment. In this respect, the reforms will make the other arms of policy more effective in achieving their goals.

As is the case with the exercise of the other arms of policy, there is debate over how Australia's trade and industry policy should proceed. On one side of the argument are those who recommend the complete removal of all impediments to international and domestic competition, forcing the private sector to adapt and allowing the market to choose who will survive and who will not. Such a view has been labelled a *laissez faire* approach to industry policy and is rejected by some on the grounds that other countries do not follow this approach but, rather, actively encourage the development of certain industries. On this basis, a corporatist approach is recommended with an industry policy comprising much of the microeconomic reform discussed above but coupled with planned industry assistance to targeted sectors. The choice of which sectors to target is seen as the consensual outcome of a process of wide-ranging discussion and negotiations.

REVIEW

The stabilization problem is to deliver strong economic growth that is as smooth and predictable as possible. To achieve this goal, targets of stabilization policy are specified. These include unemployment at its natural rate, steady and sustainable growth in real GDP, low and predictable inflation, a stable exchange rate and balanced international trade.

The key players who formulate and execute macroeconomic policy are the Commonwealth government and the Reserve Bank of Australia. In addition the ACTU, as a representative of workers, and various representative groups for employers participate in the debate.

The tools of macroeconomic policy stabilization are monetary and fiscal policies, wages and incomes policies, and trade and industry policy. Monetary and fiscal policies are demand management tools, while wages and incomes policies and industry policies are more supply-side management tools. There is considerable debate about how to exercise policy with each of the four instruments. ■

We have now identified the stabilization policy problem, the people whose job it is to solve the problem and the means at their disposal. But we also know that there is not a consensus about how to go about using the policy instruments to achieve the policy goals. Much of the disagreement ultimately comes down to the following question: should the government adopt an activist or a non-activist approach to policy? Let's now discuss some of these issues.

Alternative Approaches to Stabilization Policy

There are obviously many different monetary, fiscal, wages and even industry policies that can be pursued. To understand the policies that are adopted, it is convenient to classify all possible policies into two broad categories:

- Fixed rules
- Feedback rules

Fixed Rules and Feedback Rules

A **feedback rule** specifies how policy actions respond to changes in the state of the economy. An everyday example of a feedback rule is that governing your actions in choosing what to wear and whether or not to carry an umbrella. You base those actions on a forecast of the day's temperature and rainfall. (With a fixed rule, you either always or never carry an umbrella.) A stabilization-policy feedback rule is one that changes policy instruments, such as the money supply, interest rates or taxes, in response to the state of the economy. For example, the Reserve Bank pursues a feedback rule if an increase in unemployment causes it to engage in an open market operation aimed at increasing the money supply growth rate and lowering interest rates. The Reserve Bank also pursues a feedback rule if an increase in the inflation rate triggers an open market operation aimed at cutting the money supply growth rate and raising interest rates. Feedback rules are characteristic of *activist* stabilization policies.

A **fixed rule** specifies an action to be pursued independently of the state of the economy. There are many examples of fixed rules in everyday life. Perhaps the best known one is that which keeps the traffic flowing by having us all drive on the left. The best known fixed rule for stabilization policy is one that has long been advocated by Milton Friedman (see Our Advancing Knowledge, pp. 184–185). He proposes setting the quantity of money growth at a constant rate, year in and year out, regardless of the state of the economy. Friedman proposes this rule because he believes that, with a low enough rate of growth of the money supply, it is possible to hold the *average* inflation rate at zero. Fixed rules are characteristic of *non-activist* stabilization policies.

The key distinction between a fixed rule and a feedback rule is that, with a fixed rule, policy instruments are set without regard to whether the economy is depressed, booming, or moving into recession or recovery, while, with a feedback rule, policy instrument settings are changed in direct response to the state of the economy.

Expectations and Policy Rules We saw in Chapter 32 that inflation expectations play an important role in determining the actual inflation rate and the level of real GDP. Expectations of inflation, in turn, depend, in part, on expectations about changes in aggregate demand. These expectations, in turn, depend on expectations about stabilization policy. But expectations about stabilization policy obviously depend on the stabilization policy rules that are being pursued. If the Reserve Bank pursues a fixed rule, such as Friedman's constant money supply growth rate rule, the Bank's actions will be expected to keep aggregate demand growing at its average rate. (Other factors might be expected to speed up or slow down the growth rate of aggregate demand, but the Reserve Bank's own actions will not be expected to have such an effect.) Alternatively, if the Bank always lowers interest rates and speeds up the growth of aggregate demand when unemployment rises to some trigger point, and always increases interest rates and slows the growth of aggregate demand when inflation rises to some trigger point, then forecasts about the future growth of aggregate demand will incorporate the effects of the forecasted change in the Bank's monetary actions.

Let's study the effects of a fixed rule and a feedback rule for the conduct of stabilization policy by examining how the price level and real GDP (and employment and unemployment, since both move with real GDP) behave under two alternative rules.

The Two Rules in Action

We'll study a model economy that starts out at full employment and has no inflation. Figure 34.2 illustrates this situation. The economy is on aggregate demand curve AD_0 and short-run aggregate supply curve *SAS*. These curves intersect at a point on the long-run aggregate supply curve, *LAS*. The GDP deflator is 100 and real GDP is $300 billion. Now let's see what happens if there is a change in aggregate demand. Suppose that there is an unexpected and temporary fall in aggregate demand.

Perhaps there is a wave of pessimism about the future that results in a fall in investment demand, or perhaps there is a recession in the rest of the world that leads to a fall in exports. Regardless of the origin of the fall in aggregate demand, the aggregate demand curve shifts to the left, to AD_1 in the figure. Because the fall in aggregate demand is unantici-

Figure 34.2 A Fall in Aggregate Demand

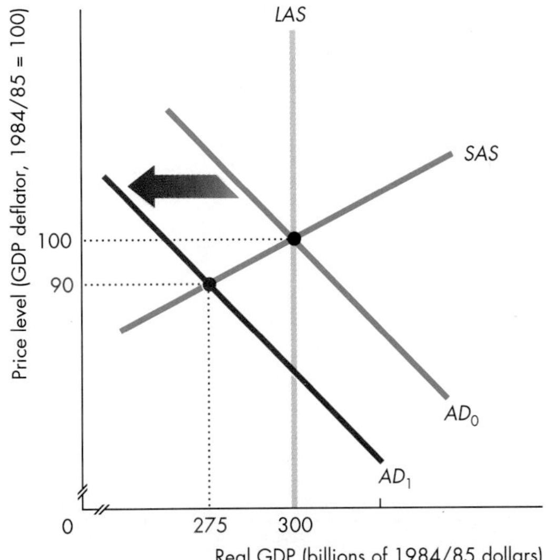

The economy starts out at full employment on aggregate demand curve AD_0 and short-run aggregate supply curve *SAS*, with the two curves intersecting on the long-run aggregate supply curve *LAS*. Real GDP is $300 billion and the GDP deflator is 100. A fall in aggregate demand (due to pessimism about future profits, for example) unexpectedly shifts the aggregate demand curve to AD_1. Real GDP falls to $275 billion, and the GDP deflator falls to 90. The economy is in a depressed state.

pated, expected aggregate demand remains at AD_0, so the expected GDP deflator remains at 100. The short-run aggregate supply curve stays at *SAS*. Aggregate demand curve AD_1 intersects the short-run aggregate supply curve *SAS* at a GDP deflator of 90 and a real GDP of $275 billion. The economy is in a depressed state. Real GDP is below its long-run level and unemployment above its natural rate.

The fall in aggregate demand from AD_0 to AD_1 is not permanent. But, at the same time, it is not purely temporary — aggregate demand only gradually increases to its original level of AD_0. That is, as confidence in the future improves, firms' investment picks up, or as economic recovery proceeds in the rest of the world, exports gradually rise. Thus the aggregate demand curve gradually returns to AD_0, but it may take a good deal of time to do so.

If neither investment nor exports increase, it may be necessary for nominal wages to fall, which would shift the SAS curve down. At lower real wages, firms would be willing to employ more labour and increase output. However, this adjustment process could take even longer than the gradual re-adjustment of the demand curve. To keep our analysis simple, we will assume that demand recovers before costs are reduced.

We are going to work out how the economy responds under two alternative monetary policies during the period in which aggregate demand gradually increases to its original level: a fixed-rule policy with the money supply constant, and a feedback-rule policy that stimulates aggregate demand by increasing the money supply. Figure 34.3 illustrates the analysis.

First, we'll consider what happens with a fixed rule.

Fixed Rule When aggregate demand falls to AD_1, the money supply growth rate is held constant. (In this example, the growth rate of the money supply is zero so the money supply remains constant.) No special measures are taken to bring the economy back to full employment. But recall that we are assuming that aggregate demand gradually increases because of other factors and eventually returns to AD_0. As it does so, real GDP and the GDP deflator gradually increase. The GDP deflator gradually returns to 100 and real GDP to its long-run level of $300 billion, as shown in Fig. 34.3(a). Throughout this process, the economy experiences more rapid growth than usual but beginning from a state of excess capacity. Unemployment remains high until the aggregate demand curve has returned to AD_0.

Let's contrast this adjustment with what occurs under a feedback-rule monetary policy.

Feedback Rule Under the feedback rule that we are analysing, the money supply increases whenever there is a fall in aggregate demand and decreases whenever there is a rise in aggregate demand. When aggregate demand falls to AD_1, the Reserve Bank increases the money supply to shift the aggregate demand curve back to AD_0, as shown in Fig. 34.3(b). As the other forces that increase aggregate demand respond, the Reserve Bank gradually cuts back on the money supply, holding the aggregate demand curve steady at AD_0. Real GDP jumps back to its full-employment level and the GDP deflator jumps back to 100.

Under a fixed-rule policy, the economy goes into a recession and stays there for as long as it takes the aggregate demand curve to return to its original position. Under a feedback-rule policy, the economy is pulled out of its recession quickly by the policy action. The price level and real GDP fall and rise by exactly the same amounts in the two cases, but real

Figure 34.3 Two Monetary Policies

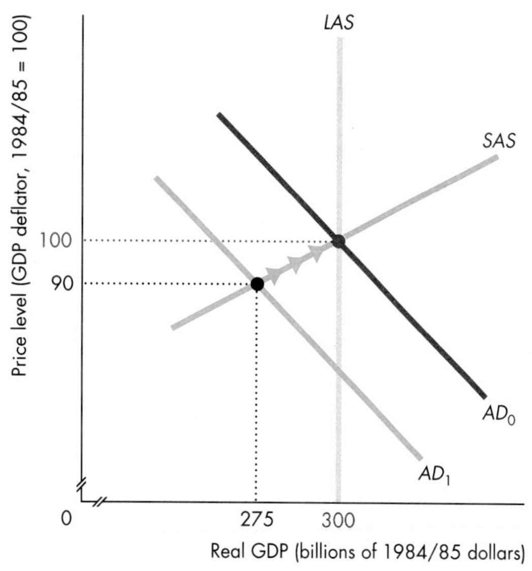

(a) Fixed rule

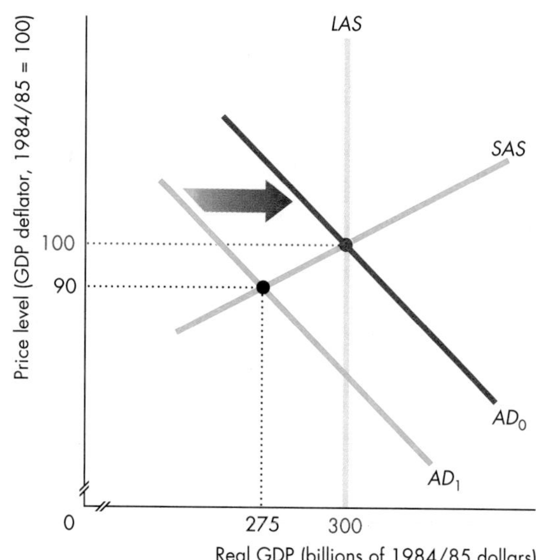

(b) Feedback rule

The economy is in a depressed state with a GDP deflator of 90 and real GDP of $275 billion. The short-run aggregate supply curve is *SAS*. A fixed-rule monetary policy — part (a) — leaves the aggregate demand curve initially at AD_1, so the GDP deflator remains at 90 and real GDP at $275 billion. As other influences on aggregate demand gradually increase, the aggregate demand curve shifts back to AD_0. As it does, real GDP rises back to $300 billion and the GDP deflator increases to 100. A feedback-rule monetary policy — part (b) — increases the money supply, shifting the aggregate demand curve instantly from AD_1 to AD_0. Real GDP returns to $300 billion and the GDP deflator returns to 100. The money supply is then gradually decreased as the other influences on aggregate demand increase its level. As a result, the aggregate demand curve is kept steady at AD_0 and real GDP stays at $300 billion.

GDP stays below its long-run level for longer with a fixed rule than it does with a feedback rule.

Advantages of Feedback Rules

The example just considered highlights the advantage of pursuing a feedback policy rule, in this case a monetary policy feedback rule, as opposed to following a fixed rule. With a feedback rule, the economy can be more quickly brought back to a full-employment equilibrium, thus avoiding the costs and pain associated with the forgone output and high unemployment that would necessarily arise while waiting for the economy to self-correct. And there are many economists who doubt that the economy self-corrects in any case. As we discussed in Chapter 31 and Chapter 33, whether or not we believe the economy is inherently stable — self-correcting — depends, in large part, on how we view the way the labour market operates. If wages are sticky, not flexible, then an unemployment equilibrium might persist for a long time. If wages are flexible, then the economy probably self-corrects very quickly and unemployment is quickly eliminated.

However, it is reasonable to ask why the Reserve Bank can't use a feedback rule to keep the economy close to full employment with a stable price level all the time? Of course, unforecasted changes — such as the fall in aggregate demand in our example — will knock the economy from time to time. But, by responding with an active change in the quantity of money, can't the Reserve Bank minimize the damage from such a shock? In other words, why is there any controversy about feedback rules versus fixed rules at all? The answer is that there are problems with trying to implement feedback rules — problems that some economists believe are insurmountable. Let's look at some of the issues.

Implementing Feedback Rules — the Problems

Despite the appearance of the superiority of a feedback rule, many economists remain convinced that a fixed rule works best. These economists assert that

- Feedback rules require greater knowledge of the economy than we have.
- Feedback rules introduce unpredictability.
- Feedback rules generate bigger fluctuations in aggregate demand.
- Aggregate supply shocks, not aggregate demand shocks, cause most economic fluctuations.

We'll look briefly at each of these assertions.

Knowledge of the Economy Although the aggregate demand–aggregate supply model of the economy provides us with a useful tool for both understanding and predicting aggregate fluctuations, it is not a precise tool. We can predict the general direction in which the economy will move, following a change in one of the factors that influence aggregate demand or aggregate supply. But we cannot predict, with any certainty, either the magnitude of the change or its precise timing. As we discussed in Chapter 30, the multiplier effects of monetary and fiscal policy actions take place over a prolonged period of time, with uncertain lags, and are influenced by far more factors than can be kept track of.

Also, we have a limited knowledge of the precise way in which the labour market works. The degree of wage flexibility, the economy's capacity level of real GDP and the natural rate of unemployment are all magnitudes that can only be estimated and about which there is uncertainty and disagreement.

To make matters worse, we rarely know where the economy is at any point in time. The relevant data is often collected only quarterly and they are subsequently revised, so that it is at least three months, and sometimes six or nine months, before we know where we were when a policy was adopted.[2]

Lacking a precise model of the economy that makes exact predictions about the quantitative effects of policy actions and of other exogenous influences, we are not able to design feedback rules that can be guaranteed to smooth out fluctuations. We may easily end up designing rules that make fluctuations more severe.

The second problem with feedback rules, that they can introduce unpredictability, emerges largely because of our limited knowledge of the economy. Let's see how.

[2] Someone once described controlling the economy as being like driving a car using only the rear-vision mirror: you do not know where you are, or where you are going, but you have generally got a good idea of where you have been.

Unpredictability of Feedback Rules As we just saw, the operation of feedback rules requires that policymakers have detailed knowledge of the economy — a knowledge that many economists believe we do not currently possess. However our knowledge of how economies operate is changing all the time. That knowledge changes either because more knowledge is actually acquired or simply because current knowledge is interpreted differently as fashions change. But as the knowledge base changes and grows, the types of feedback rule employed by policymakers also change and this introduces uncertainty and unpredictability into the operation of policy. Let's see how.

Many economic decisions require people to look ahead. For example, to make decisions about long-term contracts for employment (wage contracts) and for borrowing and lending, people have to anticipate the future course of prices — the future inflation rate. To make a forecast of inflation, it is necessary to forecast future demand. But as we have ascertained, important determinants of aggregate demand are monetary and fiscal policies. Thus it is important that people making decisions in markets can reliably predict the future course of policy.

Operating with feedback rules does not, by itself, add to the uncertainty surrounding policymaking, except insofar as the feedback rules are not well specified or if they unexpectedly change. Unfortunately, it appears to be the case that the feedback rules used to implement policy in Australia are rarely well specified, and, as a result, they appear to change frequently as attention shifts from one perceived problem to another. It seems that at different times the Reserve Bank and the government have emphasized different variables as targets of feedback policies, including interest rates, money growth rates, the rate of inflation, the rate of growth of real GDP and unemployment. Additionally, the exchange rate and the balance of payments or the level of external debt have figured prominently. Some of this uncertainty arises because the Reserve Bank and the government can disagree over which variables are the most important variables to target.

The effects of this uncertainty and unpredictability are evident when economic commentators and analysts seem to overreact to the slightest bit of economic news, no matter how trivial. That piece of news might be unimportant in itself, but it may also hold clues as to the course of future policy.

Economists disagree on whether the fluctuations induced by the policymakers' unpredictability are big enough to offset the potential stabilizing influ-

Guessing Future Policy Directions

Nobody Dances to the BOP Anymore

The BOP dropped again yesterday for yet another month but did anyone really care?

It says a lot about how Australia has grown up, how we have become used to being a deficit country and how financial markets believe economic policy is formulated.

The monthly balance of payments figures appear to have gone to that graveyard of economic fashion. Remember that thing called M3?

Just a few years back the monthly figures were the biggest event for the financial community. The Australian dollar sometimes swung by more than 1c or more, interest rates sometimes moved by a whole percentage point and banks cut or increased their loan rates 'on the back of the BOP'.

Just a few years back the *Herald* ran a series of articles about how the precious figures were being leaked. Every second month rumours abounded of how someone had the jump on the 11.30 am release.

In one instance the Australian Federal Police were called in to investigate the 'leaking of commercially sensitive information' to operators in the Sydney Futures Exchange. There were reports of 'uncharacteristic trading'.

In 1988, when the monthly deficits became bigger each month, the *Herald* ran a piece which tried to capture the mood in the dealing room.

It began: 'It was 11.23 am, and suddenly no-one wanted to deal. Seven minutes before the release of the official October trade figures, the phones in the Bankers Trust dealing room on the 40th floor of Australia Square were eerily quiet. Dealers paced up and down like expectant fathers.

But the mood yesterday was very different.

'You used to be shivering in your boots at 11.29', one domestic market dealer said yesterday.

'Today, I was having a coffee and chat when the figure came out. There was a sell-off for about 30 seconds. Everyone used it to get long and that was it'.

And, according to one foreign exchange dealer, the last 12 monthly figures brought only minor moves in the dollar.

It seems that financial markets are focusing more on unemployment and the quarterly consumer price index than anything else. Unemployment figures are a key indicator because they could break the government's resolve to continue to run a reasonably tough monetary policy.

The CPI is now king because a much lower inflation trend is expected over the next six months. While some of this is already factored in, the Government could be expected to cut rates further once lower inflation is confirmed.

The trend also reflects more reliance on quarterly figures such as the national accounts and the consumer price index.

No longer are the markets dazzled by a saw tooth BOP.

The Sydney Morning Herald
Tuesday, 7 May 1991
By Paul Cleary

The Essence of the Story

- The balance of payments figures for April 1991 were apparently not very good (the current account deficit got bigger) but, unlike past experiences, the bad news had little impact on financial markets.
- The balance of payments figures appear to have gone out of fashion with traders in money markets, in the same way that the monetary growth figures did some years ago.
- Now markets appear to be more concerned with the quarterly release of unemployment and inflation figures.
- The value of the news releases, concerning whatever figure the markets happen to be concentrating on at the time, is evidenced by the significant impact they can have on the exchange rate and interest rates, and by the quantity of resources devoted to keeping them secret until the appropriate time or in tracking down leaks.

Background and Analysis

- Why would the release of isolated economic statistics generate so much interest and activity? And why do certain figures go in and out of fashion?

- The release of monthly money growth or balance of payments statistics, or of quarterly inflation or unemployment statistics, do not contain much information for markets. What the releases apparently do is to signal the future course of monetary policy.

- For example, suppose the markets are considering the possibility of a change in monetary policy. There have been many instances of such speculation in recent times, for example, in late 1991. At that time, the economy was in recession or perhaps emerging from recession; nobody was quite sure. If it became clear that the economy was not recovering, markets expected the Reserve Bank to loosen monetary policy. If the economy was in fact recovering, and either rising inflation or reduced unemployment appeared to verify this, then the markets expected the Reserve Bank to maintain its current monetary policy.

- How could traders benefit from this information? Suppose that the new figures showed a rise in unemployment, at a time when unemployment was expected to remain steady or fall. Market expectations of an easing of monetary policy were then strengthened. Recall from our discussion in Chapter 28 that the Reserve Bank loosens monetary policy by entering the market and undertaking an open market purchase of Commonwealth government securities (CGS). This action drives up bond prices, and interest rates on government securities decline. But if you were holding government securities when the Reserve Bank undertook its open market operation then you would have benefited from capital gain — the rise in the price of government securites required to reduce their yield (recall our discussion of the relationship between bond prices and interest rates in Chapter 28).

- Thus to make money you need to be ahead of the market — to anticipate what it will do. If nobody has inside information, and all traders attempt to benefit from the release of the same news item, only those few traders who make the first deals will benefit as all traders, acting together, will force bond prices up or down as they attempt to take a position in the market in anticipation of future Reserve Bank action.

- You can see the value of 'inside information'. Knowing what the news releases will reveal and knowing how the markets will react permits you to take a position well in advance and thus benefit from the market action.

- But why would markets place more value on different information at different times? Because traders in those markets believe that the Reserve Bank itself bases its monetary policy actions on different indicators. When the Bank was targeting money growth rates, the release of news that the most recent month's growth rate of money was above the targeted average growth rate for the year indicated to the financial markets that the Bank would have to reduce monetary growth rates — tighten monetary policy — at some time in the near future in order to achieve its yearly target. Then monetary targeting was abandoned and the balance of payments became an indicator of how rapidly aggregate expenditure was growing relative to the aggregate output. As long as the balance of payments was not improving, monetary policy was expected to remain tight. As the economy went into recession, tight monetary policy in response to excess demand no longer became the focus. Instead, when and by how much monetary policy would be loosened became important. Hence the change in unemployment levels became a focus. But at the same time, the Reserve Bank did not want to stimulate a resurgence in inflationary expectations so the CPI also needed watching.

- By adopting an approach to policy whereby policy stances are determined by short-run economic conditions, markets become accustomed to trying to predict the next change in policy. If done correctly, and early enough, large profits can be made from taking the right position in the bond market. In such an environment, apparently innocuous economic statistics take on an importance far beyond their intrinsic value.

ence of the predictable changes they make. No agreed measurements have been made to settle this dispute.

Variability of Aggregate Demand with Feedback Rules Some economists argue that aggregate demand will not only be more unpredictable but will also fluctuate more with a feedback rule. The main thrust of the argument is that stabilization policies affect aggregate demand with a time lag that is long and impossible to predict. As a consequence, any policy action taken today will be inappropriate for the state of the economy at that uncertain future date when the policy's effects will be felt.

For example, when the Reserve Bank puts on the monetary brake, the first effect is that interest rates increase. Some time later, higher interest rates produce a slow-down in investment and the purchases of consumer durable goods. Later still, the fall in expenditure reduces income, which, in turn, induces lower consumption expenditure. The sectors in which the spending cuts occur vary, and so does the impact on employment. It can take anywhere from nine months to two years for an initial action by the Bank to cause a change in employment, real GDP and the inflation rate. Thus, to smooth the fluctuations in aggregate demand, the Bank needs to take actions today, based on a forecast of what will be happening over a period stretching more than a year into the future. It is no use taking actions a year from today to influence the situation that then prevails. It's too late. Any actions taken then will have their effect two further years into the future.

This problem may be accentuated if the Reserve Bank uses an inappropriate variable to judge the stance of monetary policy. Whether or not a particular variable is appropriate often depends on where the disturbances to the economy are coming from, and, as we discussed above, we do not always get this information in a timely fashion. For example, let's consider the outcome of using interest rates as a guide to monetary policy when the economy is subject to demand shocks.

Suppose, for example, the Reserve Bank was targeting interest rates. How does it achieve this? Consider the example in Fig. 34.4. The real money supply is MS_0 and the demand for money is MD_0. Equilibrium in the money market occurs at an interest rate of 10 per cent and a real quantity of money of $100 billion. Suppose that the Reserve Bank is targeting the interest rate at 10 per cent: if the interest rate edges up, the Bank would respond by increasing the real supply of money; if the interest rate fell, the Bank would contract the real money supply.

Now suppose that, unbeknown to the Reserve Bank, equilibrium expenditure and real GDP have grown and the demand for money increases. That is, the demand curve shifts upward to MD_1, but the Reserve Bank is not immediately aware of this development. It simply observes a rise in interest rates and, interpreting this as a signal of unexpectedly tight money, the Bank increases the supply of real money, shifting the supply curve to MS_1. Why, you ask, should the Reserve Bank interpret a rise in interest rates as a result of tighter money? Recall from Chapter 28 that the money multiplier depends on both the actions of households and banks. If either sector decides to increase its holding of cash, the money

Figure 34.4 Targeting the Interest Rate

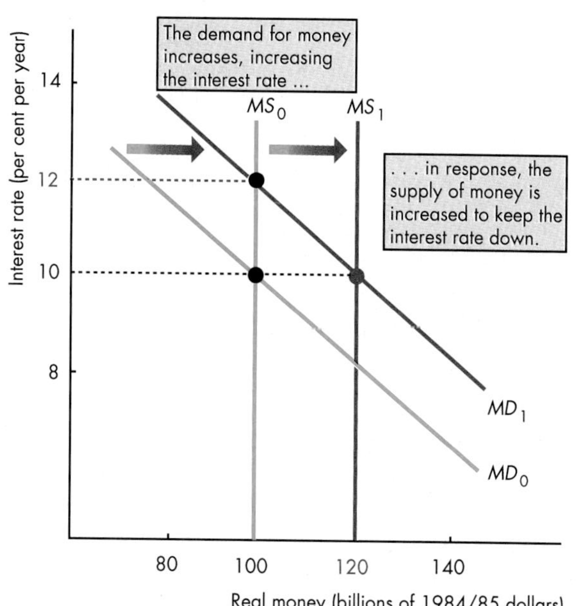

Suppose the Reserve Bank is targeting the interest rate at 10 per cent. If the demand for money curve is MD_0, the Reserve Bank will set the money supply at MS_0. The money market clears at an interest rate of 10 per cent and a quantity of real money of $100 billion. If the interest rate rose, then the Bank would increase the quantity of real money supplied, and would do the opposite if the interest rate fell.

Suppose that, unbeknown to the Reserve Bank, the demand for money increased, shifting out to MD_1. Other things being equal, the interest rate would rise to 12 per cent. Seeing this, the Bank would interpret the rise as due to an unexpected tightening of monetary policy and would expand the quantity of real money to MS_1. Interest rates would fall back to 10 per cent.

multiplier falls and the money supply contracts. The Bank at this stage has no reliable evidence as to why the demand for money has risen and the rise in interest rates could just as well been caused by a falling money multiplier.

After increasing the supply of money, the interest rate falls back to 10 per cent. Now, if the increase in the demand for money was the result of an unanticipated disturbance that was expanding aggregate demand — for example, a strong rise in the terms of trade, as occurred in 1987/88 — then the looser monetary policy further boosts aggregate demand by holding down interest rates. In this example, monetary policy contributes to a more rapid expansion than would otherwise have occurred. This behaviour could explain the money supply reactions we observed in Fig. 33.1 in Chapter 33.

Why would the Reserve Bank target interest rates, or any other such variable, and not the money itself? One reason is that central banks world-wide have lost confidence in the information contained in monetary aggregates, particularly since financial deregulation. As we saw, some of the deregulatory moves themselves contributed to large variations in monetary aggregates, even though there was no policy change. Unfortunately, however, because interest rates are determined by both the demand for and supply of money, they might not be good indicators of policy. Unobserved disturbances to the demand for money, such as unexpected growth in real GDP, might induce the wrong monetary policy response and the Bank's own actions can become a major source of fluctuations.

We earlier noted that another reason why economists do not agree on monetary policy is that they do not agree about the sources of aggregate fluctuations. Those advocating feedback rules believe most fluctuations in real GDP come from changes in aggregate demand. Those advocating fixed rules believe that aggregate supply fluctuations are the dominant ones. Let's now see how aggregate supply fluctuations affect the economy under a fixed rule for monetary policy and under a feedback rule for monetary policy, and see why those economists who believe that aggregate supply fluctuations are the dominant ones also favour a fixed rather than a feedback rule.

Stabilization Policy and Aggregate Supply

There are a number of reasons why aggregate supply fluctuations can cause problems for a stabilization feedback rule. We dealt with one important reason in Chapter 32 when we discussed *cost-push inflation.* Recall that when wages or the prices of other inputs rose, the short-run aggregate supply curve shifted to the left, and short-run equilibrium occurred with higher prices and reduced real output. An unemployment equilibrium emerged. The difficulty for feedback policy rules arises when the high level of unemployment invokes an expansionary fiscal or monetary response from the government or Reserve Bank. The policy might succeed in stimulating demand to the extent that a full-employment equilibrium is re-established. But if nothing else changes, the conditions that caused the short-run aggregate supply curve to shift to the left are likely to be unchanged and the process repeats itself. (See Fig. 32.5.)

A second, related problem for feedback stabilization policy rules arises with permanent changes in supply. Let's see how by considering the effects of a slow-down in capacity growth.

Some economists believe that fluctuations in real GDP (and in employment and unemployment) are caused, not by fluctuations in aggregate demand, but by fluctuations in the growth rate of long-run aggregate supply. These economists have developed a new theory of aggregate fluctuations called real business cycle theory. **Real business cycle theory** is a theory of aggregate fluctuations based on flexible wages and random shocks to the economy's aggregate production function. The word 'real' draws attention to the idea that it is real things — random shocks to the economy's real production possibilities — rather than nominal things — the money supply and its rate of growth — that are, according to the theory, the most important sources of aggregate fluctuations.

According to real business cycle theory, there is no useful distinction to be made between the long-run aggregate supply curve and the short-run aggregate supply curve. Because wages are flexible, the labour market is always in equilibrium at the natural rate of unemployment. The vertical long-run aggregate supply curve is also the short-run aggregate supply curve. Fluctuations occur because of shifts in the long-run aggregate supply curve. Normally, the long-run aggregate supply curve shifts to the right — the economy expands. But the pace at which the long-run aggregate supply curve shifts to the right varies. Also, on occasion, the long-run aggregate supply curve shifts to the left, bringing a decrease in aggregate supply and a fall in real GDP.

As we demonstrated in Chapter 32, in these circumstances, economic policy that influences the aggregate demand curve has no effect on real GDP. But it does affect the price level. However, if a feedback policy is used to increase aggregate demand every time real GDP falls, and if the real business cycle theory is correct, the feedback monetary policy will make price level fluctuations more severe than they otherwise would be. To see why, consider Fig. 34.5.

Imagine that the economy starts out on aggregate demand curve AD_0 and long-run aggregate supply curve LAS_0 at a GDP deflator of 100 and with real GDP equal to $300 billion. Now suppose that long-run aggregate supply falls to LAS_1. (An actual fall in long-run aggregate supply could occur as a result of a severe drought, as occurred in 1981/82, other natural catastrophes or perhaps as the result of a disruption of international trade such as the OPEC embargo of the 1970s.) With a *fixed rule* for the money supply, the fall in the long-run aggregate supply has no effect on the Reserve Bank and no effect on aggregate demand. The aggregate demand curve remains AD_0. Real GDP falls to $275 billion and the GDP deflator increases to 120.

Figure 34.5 Monetary Policy and Aggregate Supply: A Capacity Decrease

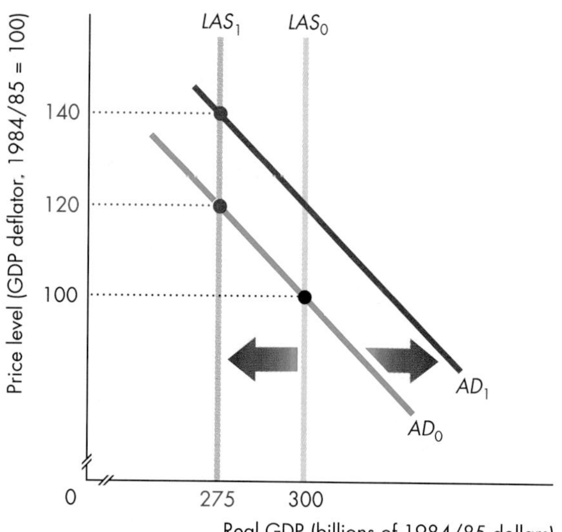

A fall in capacity output shifts the long-run aggregate supply curve from LAS_0 to LAS_1. Real GDP falls to $275 billion and the GDP deflator rises to 120. With a fixed money supply rule, aggregate demand stays at AD_0, and that is the end of the matter. With a feedback rule, the Reserve Bank increases the money supply, intending to increase real GDP. Aggregate demand moves to AD_1, but the long-run result is an increase in the price level — the GDP deflator rises to 140 — with no change in real GDP.

Now suppose that the Reserve Bank uses a feedback rule. In particular, suppose that when real GDP falls, the Bank increases the money supply to increase aggregate demand. In this example, the Bank increases the money supply and shifts the aggregate demand curve to AD_1. The Bank's goal is to bring real GDP back to $300 billion. But the long-run aggregate supply curve has shifted, and so capacity output has fallen to $275 billion. The increase in aggregate demand cannot bring forth an increase in output if the economy does not have the capacity to produce that output. So, real GDP stays at $275 billion but the price level rises still further — the GDP deflator goes up to 140.

You can see that, in this case, the attempt to stabilize real GDP using a feedback rule for monetary policy has no effect on real GDP but generates a substantial price level increase.

We've now seen some of the shortcomings of using a feedback rule for monetary policy. Some economists believe that these shortcomings are serious and urge policymakers to implement fixed rules.

Advantages of Fixed Rules

Since the case for adopting feedback rules is that it is too costly to sit back and do nothing whenever a problem emerges, the case for fixed rules must be that the costs of pursuing feedback rules are so high as to make them greater than the costs of doing nothing. That is, pursuing feedback rules not only does not improve matters, it must actually make matters worse. These additional costs, as we have just seen, are the increased unpredictability and increased variability of real GDP and unemployment.

To support the case for non-activism — fixed rules — you must also believe that the economy is inherently stable — self-correcting — so that problems that emerge from unforeseen disturbances quickly work through markets and do not bring about an extended period of high unemployment or low GDP growth.

Economists tend to disagree on both these issues. Those who believe that the economy is not self-correcting usually advocate a flexible approach to policy with the adoption of feedback rules. Conversely, those economists who believe that the economy is self-correcting usually believe that it is too difficult to implement workable feedback rules and so advocate fixed rules.

As you probably have guessed by now, the division of economists between those who advocate activist policies implemented by feedback rules and those who advocate non-activist policies implemented by fixed rules closely parallels the division of economists along Keynesian and monetarist lines. Keynesian economists are usually more activist and, as evidence of their success, point to the fact that fluctuations in real GDP have declined significantly since World War II when feedback rules first came into use. (Refer back to Fig. 22.5 to verify this assertion). Monetarist economists explain the reduction in the variability of real GDPs world-wide as the result of increasing world trade, which tends to disperse localized disturbances, and the rapid growth in the service sector of most Western economies. In support of their position, they point to instances where feedback policies apparently worsened matters because the policymakers made mistakes. A prominent example coming to light in Australia is the period from 1987 to 1991, which we discuss below.

Stabilizing the Australian Economy

So far in this chapter we've studied the theory of stabilization policy. It is now time to turn to an examination of stabilization policy in practice. We'll begin this examination by studying the Reserve Bank's monetary targeting policies of the 1970s and early 1980s.

The Reserve Bank's Monetary Targeting

From 1976/77 through to 1984/85, the government, through the Reserve Bank, pursued a policy of announcing ahead of time its target range for the growth rate of the M3 definition of the money supply. By pinning down the future behaviour of the money supply with the announced projections, the government was following a fixed rule for monetary policy. These projections of future growth were announced in August, at Budget time, by the Treasurer. The projection referred to the rate of growth of M3 over the twelve months to the following June.

When the Bank embarked upon this policy, the rate of growth of M3 was running at more than 20 per cent a year, and it had been highly volatile up to that point. Inflation was well into double digits with little sign of relief. The Bank's plan was to squeeze the inflation out of the economy by gradually slowing down the growth rate of the money supply. In the first year, M3 growth was supposed to decline to the 10–12 per cent a year range.

The Reserve Bank's target range for the growth rate of M3 and the actual outcome are illustrated in Fig. 34.6. As you can see, in the first year of monetary targeting, the Bank planned that the money supply should grow at between 10 and 12 per cent a year, and in fact achieved 11 per cent. By 1977/78, the rate of growth of M3 had been brought down to 8 per cent a year. Thereafter, the rate of growth of M3 consistently exceeded the target range.

The actual growth rate of M3, shown in the figure, indicates that the Reserve Bank comfortably met its targets in 1977 and 1978 but failed to get the growth rate of M3 inside the target range again. By the end of 1984, growth in M3 was well above the predicted range. The government took the view that the recent deregulation of financial markets — abolition of controls on interest rates, introduction of new banks and foreign banks, and floating the exchange rate — were all measures that might have been expected to cause M3 to grow. So, when the actual M3 growth rate looked like being double the targeted rate, the government abandoned any further attempts to target the money supply.

Using a Checklist

By abandoning any attempt to adhere to pre-set targets, the Reserve Bank effectively chose to drop monetary management by fixed rules in favour of adopting feedback rules. The question it then faced was: what variables should be considered when deciding on current monetary policy?

It seems that this was a difficult question to answer because, as many commentators have noted, the objectives of the Reserve Bank appeared to have changed many times over the rest of the decade.[3] In 1984, monetary policy was targeted at real GDP and therefore concerned with maintaining economic activity (with the Accord assigned to control inflation). In 1985/86, the external imbalance caused by the collapse of the terms of trade came to the forefront. In 1987, concern centred around the effects of the October stock market crash. By 1988/89, worries about inflation and a renewed concern for the external account surfaced. And by 1990/91 the looming recession was again the focus of monetary policy. The Reserve Bank justified these 'moving targets' by

[3] The Reserve Bank is constantly reviewing its own behaviour, both through internally sponsored research and by sponsoring externally produced research. A very good assessment of monetary policy over the 1980s is contained in 'Money and Finance', a paper written by Ross Milbourne and presented at a Reserve Bank sponsored conference in 1990. The collection of papers, including Milbourne's, were published in Stephen Grenville (ed.), *The Australian Macro-Economy in the 1980s* (Sydney: Reserve Bank, 1990).

The Quantity Theory and Monetarism

David Hume

The quantity theory of money has had a long and chequered history. Its first statement — that a change in the quantity of money brings about a proportional change in the price level — was made by the French philosopher Jean Bodin in the early seventeenth century. Its first clear statement in the English language was by David Hume. Hume was an extraordinary philosopher and economist who lived in Edinburgh, Scotland, from 1711 to 1776. He died in the year that Adam Smith's *Wealth of Nations* was published. Hume was a close friend of Adam Smith and had enormous influence on him.

A milestone in the development of the quantity theory of money was the contribution of Henry Thornton, a British monetary economist and legislator who lived in London from 1760 to 1815. While a member of the British parliament, Thornton wrote his impressive *An Enquiry into the Nature and Effects of the Paper Credit of Great Britain.* In this book, he developed the notion of the quantity of money and its velocity of circulation, the two key elements in the modern statement of the quantity theory of money.

The first major American contribution to the development of the quantity theory was that by Irving Fisher (see Our Advancing Knowledge pp. 184–185). Born in Saugerties, New York, in 1867, Fisher spent his entire professional career at Yale University. His book, *The Purchasing Power of Money,* published in 1911, provided extensive evidence on the long-run proportionality between the quantity of money and the general level of prices.

The quantity theory of money was never popular with everyone. It was particularly unpopular with John Maynard Keynes (see Our Advancing Knowledge, pp. 184–185). Keynes argued that there was only the loosest connection between the quantity of money and the price level. He described the lack of a connection with the ancient proverb, 'there's many a slip twixt cup and lip'. Keynes's views on the lack of a connection between money and the price level were so forcefully expressed that he was able to attract a very large following and his views became dominant in the 1950s and early 1960s.

Throughout the postwar years, the University of Chicago's Milton Friedman (see Our Advancing

Knowledge, pp. 184–185) had been working on his version of the quantity theory of money. In a monumental work with Anna J. Schwartz, *A Monetary History of the United States 1867–1960*, published in 1963, the role and importance of money in explaining fluctuations in the US economy was presented and argued. In 1956, Friedman had also published what was to become a landmark paper, 'The Quantity Theory of Money: A Restatement'.[1] In that paper, Friedman argued that the quantity theory of money, in its modern form, is a theory about the demand for money. There is, argued Friedman, a stable demand curve for real money, which depends on the interest rate (the opportunity cost of holding money) and real income. Variations in the nominal money supply can produce short-run variations in real GDP and interest rates but, in the long run, all their effects are felt only on the price level.

Stemming from his views about the importance of money in influencing aggregate expenditure, Friedman formulated what has become a famous rule — the '*k* per cent rule'. Friedman advocated that the money supply should grow steadily year after year at a rate (*k*) equal to the average growth rate of real GDP. On the average, inflation will be zero. The economy will fluctuate but the fluctuations will be as small as they can possibly be made and smaller than those arising from active attempts to stabilize aggregate demand. Friedman's views were given the name 'monetarism' by Karl Brunner, another proponent of Friedman's version of monetary theory and another advocate of steady money supply growth rules.

Brunner arrived in the United States in the 1950s from Switzerland and spent his teaching and research career at the University of California, Los Angeles (UCLA), Ohio State University and the University of Rochester. Brunner and his lifelong collaborator Alan H. Meltzer (of Carnegie-Mellon University) founded the 'Shadow Open Market Committee'. This committee meets to make recommendations about monetary policy and open market operations that parallel those of the Federal Open Market Committee, the group that makes the real decisions.

Today, monetarism has some following among economists working in central banks and advising governments, not only here in Australia but around the world. One of the leading younger monetarists, Michael Darby of UCLA, was a member of the administration's team of economists at the White House during Reagan's presidency.

But the quantity theory of money has always had its dissenters. Modern critics of the quantity theory of money include Thomas Sargent of Stanford's Hoover Institution, Bruce Smith of the University of Western Ontario and Neil Wallace of the University of Minnesota. These scholars argue that the quantity of money is not the most important variable determining the general price level except in special circumstances. Only because there are legal tender laws and legal restrictions on bank reserve holdings does the quantity of money take on a special significance. More generally, they argue, it is the total value of outstanding government debt that is the important nominal magnitude for determining the general price level. Tests of their views remain controversial and more reasearch will have to be undertaken before it can be said that the foundations of the quantity theory of money have been destroyed.

---

[1] M. Friedman, 'The Quantity Theory of Money: A Restatement', in M. Friedman (ed.), *Studies in the Quantity Theory of Money* (Chicago: University of Chicago Press, 1956)

Figure 34.6 Monetary Targeting

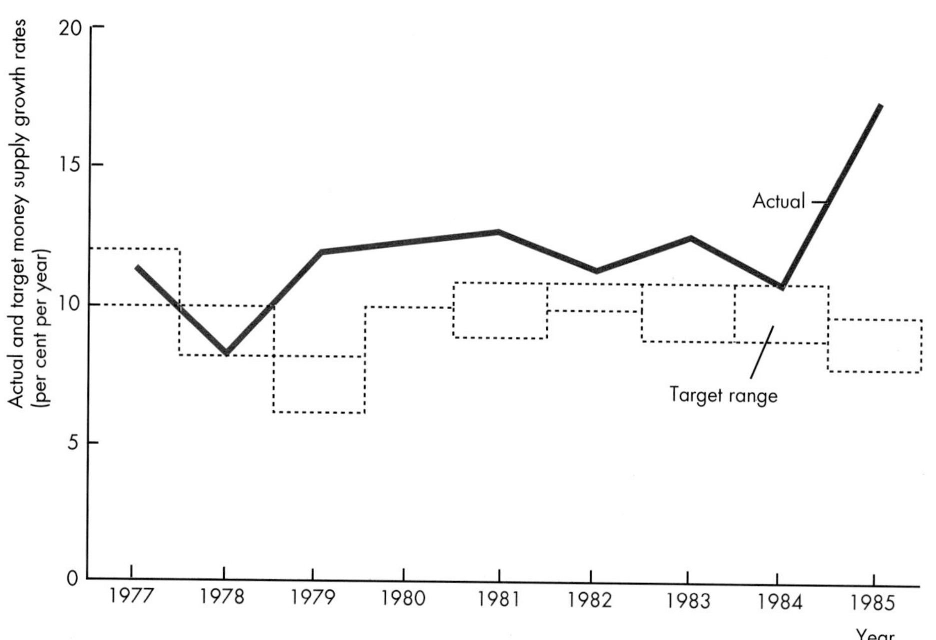

From 1976/77 to 1984/85, the Treasurer announced projected growth rates, or targets, for M3. This target range is shown in the figure. Except for the first two years of targeting, the actual growth rate of M3 remained outside the target range. In 1985, when the actual growth rate of M3 was running well ahead of the projection, the government abandoned money growth targeting. Since the abandonment of targeting, in 1985, M3 growth has been highly volatile.

Source: V. Argy, T. Brennan and G. Stevens, 'Monetary Targeting: The International Experience', *Economic Record*, 1989, 66, pp. 37–72.

stressing that it looked at a whole range of variables before deciding on a monetary policy choice. At one point, this approach became known as the *checklist approach*, whereby the Reserve Bank ran down a checklist of indicators of the economic health of the country. At any particular time, some variables on the checklist might be further from their targeted values than other variables and so they would warrant particular attention.

Destabilizing Monetary Policy, 1987/88 to 1990/91?

As we discussed in Chapter 33, the real money supply rises during expansions and falls during contractions of real GDP. And, if the Reserve Bank is using interest rates and the exchange rate as indicators of monetary policy, it is easy to see why. In 1987/88, the economy started out in a very sluggish state because of the prior collapse in the terms of trade. The terms of trade then began to rise rapidly. Aggregate demand also rose, along with interest rates, as equilibrium GDP increased.

Then, in October 1987, the stock market crash caused fears of a contraction in aggregate demand because of the real balance effect. To prevent this, the Reserve Bank loosened monetary policy in anticipation of another slow-down. But, the terms of trade were still growing strongly and real wages were falling so that business confidence was high. Thus autonomous expenditure rose and real GDP grew very strongly. In the words of various government and Reserve Bank economists, everyone underestimated the strength of the recovery.

As the strong growth caused a large increase in imports in 1988/89 and 1989/90, the monetary policy focus changed and was now directed at reducing consumption expenditure so as to bring down the demand for imports. Monetary policy was tightened. This was accomplished by open market sales of Commonwealth government securities, which slowed the rate of growth of the money base. (Refer back to Chapter 28 to refresh your memory on open market operations.) As the growth rate of the money base slowed, the growth rate of M3 accelerated because of the impact of the removal of SRD requirements. The Reserve Bank was getting conflicting signals about the stance on monetary policy. On the one hand, interest rates rose to record levels but, on the other hand, the growth rates of broader monetary aggregates were also very high. While the authorities pondered over monetary policy, investment demand collapsed in 1990/91. As we saw in Chapter 24 and Chapter 33, investment is the component of aggregate demand most sensitive to high interest rates. Consumption also slowed down but, because the high interest rates induced an appreciation of the exchange rate, import demand remained strong. Thus the tight monetary policy continued to be directed at the level of net exports, even though both aggregate demand and equilibrium GDP were falling.

Early in 1990, it became apparent just how tight monetary policy really was as the adjustments by banks to the removal of SRDs had finished and the rate of growth of M3 fell very quickly. Monetary policy was loosened throughout 1990 and 1991 in an attempt to halt the rapid slide of the economy. But we know that there are long and variable lags in the transmission of monetary policy and, by 1991, the economy was in the deepest recession encountered since the Great Depression. It appears that the conduct of monetary policy greatly contributed to this outcome.

Of course, these conclusions are easy to arrive at with the benefit of hindsight. But this is precisely the point argued by those economists advocating simple fixed-rule policies. It appears from Reading Between the Lines (pp. 440–441) that key advisers in the Treasury might be coming to the same conclusion.

Wages Policy and the Accord

Unlike many other countries, Australia has always had some form of wages and incomes policy as an important tool for stabilizing the economy. This is possible in Australia because of the centralized bargaining system that has operated here since early this century. Generally speaking, wages policies have been seen as the most direct way the government has of controlling inflation and they have usually been implemented through some form of complete or partial wage indexation.

The centrepiece of wages policies during the 1980s was the Prices and Incomes Accord. This was an agreement reached between the government and the ACTU regarding the determination of future wages. The Accord was different in its approach, compared with previously adopted wages policies, because it reflected a change in the philosophy underlying a wages policy. An important ingredient in the new approach is thought to be the notion of an 'encompassing group'. This term was popularized by American economist Mancur Olson to express the view that interest groups act in a more socially responsible way when they represent the interests of a broader range of people, that is, when they encompass a wider range of views.[4] It has been argued that, by 1983, the ACTU had become more encompassing, representing about 80 per cent of all unionists and about 40 per cent of the workforce. Similarly, by forming a few peak bodies, employer groups had also become more encompassing. Thus, when the Hawke government adopted its consensus-based approach to economic management in 1983, it found willing partners in both employee and employer representatives. As a first step, it was able to secure voluntary wage restraint in exchange for establishing the Prices Surveillance Authority.

In light of our earlier discussion, an interesting question is whether or not wages policy in Australia operated as a fixed rule or a feedback rule? Let's answer this question by reviewing the evolution of the Accord process.

Accord Mark I The first version of the Accord operated from mid-1983 to September 1985. It reintroduced full wage indexation, with nominal wages being tied to the consumer price index but without allowing for catch-up for the real wage erosion that had occurred during the wages freeze imposed by the Fraser government in the second half of 1982. The wages freeze was imposed after the failure of the Fraser government's experiment with decentralized bargaining in 1981/82, which had allowed a real wage explosion.

The goal of the Accord was to seek agreement on how to break the spiral in wages caused by the extensive flow-on practices in the Australian labour market, which contributed to competitive wage claims. Thus the Accord can be seen as wages policy by a fixed rule, with discretionary wage rises eliminated.

Accord Mark II The economic recovery in 1983–85 and subsequent collapse in the terms of trade caused a widening trade deficit. Since this was interpreted as the result of a loss in competitiveness, it was agreed that real wages had to fall. This meant abandoning full indexation of wages. Thus, in September 1985, the Treasurer and the ACTU negotiated a package comprising less than full wage indexation in return for tax cuts and increases in superannuation to be paid for by employers.

[4] M. Olson, *The Rise and Decline of Nations: Economic Growth, Stagflation and Social Rigidities* (New Haven: Yale University Press, 1982).

Accords Mark III to Mark VI Following the Treasurer's 'Banana Republic' comments of May 1986, the wage rises and tax cuts promised under Accord Mark II were postponed. Accord Mark III saw the total elimination of wage indexation and the introduction of a 'two-tier' system of small across-the-board pay increases coupled with productivity-based increases, which were to be the result of restructuring and efficiency improvements.

The various Accords since then have all comprised various packages of pay increases, tax cuts and superannuation payments negotiated between the Treasurer and the ACTU. In 1991, Accord Mark VI was current and it contained elements of all of those.

Fixed or Feedback Rule? The Accord started out as a fixed-rule policy, which removed the discretionary power of individual unions to pursue their own pay increases. In this respect it halted the inflationary spiral of competitive wage increases, which were subsequently accommodated by the Reserve Bank. But the rule changed six times in six years. Can it still be considered as fixed? In reality, all fixed rules are ultimately flexible, that is, feedback rules, unless measures are taken to restrict the ability of policymakers to change the rules in the future. Thus the question of how to conduct policy does not really hinge on 'fixed versus feedback' rules, but, rather, it is a question of how often and by how much should policymakers react to changing economic circumstances.

■ We have now looked at the implementation of policy in Australia. In the next chapter, we will examine in some detail the changing face of fiscal policy in Australia.

SUMMARY

The Stabilization Problem

The targets of macroeconomic policy fall into two categories: real and nominal. The real targets are to keep unemployment at its natural rate, achieve steady and sustained growth in real GDP and maintain balanced international trade. The nominal targets are to achieve low and predictable inflation and stable exchange rates between the dollar and foreign currencies. Indexes of macroeconomic performance combine the real and nominal targets into a single measure. Three such measures are the misery index, an unpopularity index based on voter behaviour, and a stabilization policy index based on a nominal GDP growth target. All three indexes paint a similar picture of Australian's macroeconomic performance: steady performance through 1969/70 and rapid deterioration after that. All indexes peaked in 1974/75, improving rapidly until 1977/78. They deteriorated again until 1983/84 and have shown improvement since. The government of Australia typically changes hands as the unpopularity index peaks. (pp. 452–455)

The Key Players

The key players in the formulation and execution of macroeconomic policy are the Commonwealth government, the Reserve Bank, the Australian Council of Trade Unions and various employer representative groups. The Commonwealth government, along with the State and Local governments, makes the nation's fiscal policy while the Reserve Bank makes the nation's monetary policy. The government of Australia, in consultation with the ACTU, makes wages policy. (pp. 455–456)

The Policy Instruments

There are four policy instruments at the disposal of policymakers. These are fiscal policy, monetary policy, wages and incomes policy, and trade and industry policy. Fiscal and monetary policies are demand management tools, while wages and incomes policies and industry policies are tools for influencing aggregate supply. (pp. 456–459)

Alternative Approaches to Stabilization Policy

There are two broad types of stabilization policy: fixed rules and feedback rules. Since expectations about aggregate demand affect wages and other costs, and therefore affect short-run aggregate supply, expectations about policy, as well as actual policy actions, influence the course of the economy.

Fixed-rule policy permits the aggregate demand curve to fluctuate as a result of all the independent forces that influence demand. As a result, there are fluctuations in real GDP and the price level. Feedback-rule policy adjusts the money supply to offset the effects of other influences on aggregate demand. An ideal feedback rule would keep the economy at full employment with stable prices.

Some economists argue that feedback rules require greater knowledge of the economy than we have, introduce unpredictability, generate bigger fluctuations in aggregate demand and are ineffective in the face of aggregate supply shocks. But operating with fixed rules may entail long periods of high unemployment and low real GDP growth, if the economy is not inherently or rapidly self-correcting.

Economists disagree about the choice between fixed rules and feedback rules, usually along the same lines that Keynesians and monetarists disagree. (pp. 460–469)

Stabilizing the Australian Economy

During the period 1976/77 to 1984/85, the Reserve Bank pursued a policy of announcing its money supply growth target and gradually slowing down that target growth rate with a view to squeezing out inflation, without causing serious unemployment or recession. At first the policy worked, when the growth rates of all the monetary aggregates were in line with each other. By the late 1970s, however, the policy failed and the Bank rarely achieved its money growth target thereafter. Accepting the proposition that financial market deregulation had made some of the monetary aggregates unstable, the Reserve Bank abandoned money growth targeting in 1985. Money growth rates subsequently increased in volatility, and may even have contributed to business cycle ups and downs.

Wages polices, through the various versions of the Accord, have been directed at eliminating inflation. The Accord began as a fixed rule but ended up as a feedback policy because of the continual adjustments to the policy as the economic environment evolved. (pp. 469–474)

KEY TERMS

Checklist, p. 469
Commonwealth budget, p. 455
Comparative wage justice, p. 458
Feedback rule, p. 460
Fixed rule, p. 460
Flow-ons, p. 458
General government sector, p. 455
Laissez faire, p. 459
Misery index, p. 453
Nominal targets, p. 452
Public sector borrowing requirement (PSBR), p. 455
Real business cycle theory, p. 467
Real targets, p. 452
Social wage, p. 457
Stabilization policy index, p. 454
Targeting interest rates, p. 466
Unpopularity index, p. 453
Wages and incomes policy, p. 457

PROBLEMS

1 The economy is experiencing 10 per cent inflation and 7 per cent unemployment. Set out policies for the Reserve Bank and the government of Australia to pursue that will lower both inflation and unemployment. Explain how and why your proposed policies will work. How might the ACTU contribute to the recovery?

2 The economy is booming and inflation is beginning to rise, but it is widely agreed that a massive recession is just around the corner. Weigh the advantages and disadvantages of the Bank pursuing a fixed rule and a feedback rule monetary policy.

3 You have been hired by the prime minister to draw up a plan that will maximize the chance of his being re-elected.

a) What are the macroeconomic stabilization policy elements in that plan?
b) What do you have to make the economy do in an election year?
c) How important is it to keep inflation in check?
d) How important is it to prevent unemployment from rising?
e) What policy actions would help the prime minister achieve his objectives?

In dealing with this problem, be careful to take into account the effects of your proposed policy on expectations and the effects of those expectations on actual economic performance.

Chapter 35

Federal Deficits and Surpluses

After studying this chapter, you will be able to:

- Explain why, between the early 1950s and 1986/87, the government of Australia spent more each year than it raised in taxes, and why the position has since changed.
- Distinguish between the Federal deficit and Federal debt.
- Distinguish between the *nominal* deficit or surplus and the *real* deficit or surplus.
- Distinguish between the *nominal* deficit and the *structural* deficit, and why deficits appear to be bigger than they really are.
- Describe the different means available for financing a deficit and what a government does with a surplus.
- Explain the links between deficits or surpluses and monetary policy.
- Explain why a deficit can cause inflation.
- Explain why a deficit can be a burden on future generations.

Spendthrifts or Skinflints in Canberra

In every year from 1949/50 up to, and including, 1986/87, the Commonwealth government spent more than it raised in taxes. In 1975/76, when spending exceeded tax receipts by $3.5 billion, the gap was nearly 5 per cent of GDP. On occasion, the gap between spending and receipts had grown to nearly $8 billion. The excess of spending over tax receipts is called the Federal deficit. From 1987/88 to 1990/91, the Commonwealth government spent less than it received, for example, saving more than $8 billion dollars in 1989/90. But, by 1991/92, the government was again spending more than it received. The excess of receipts over expenditure is called the Federal surplus. Why have we had Federal deficits? How did they become surpluses? And why did the surpluses disappear? Large deficits mean that the Commonwealth government is rapidly building up debt. Just how large were the deficits really? How large did the stock of accumulated debt get? Does the fact that the government has a surplus mean that is is paying off its debt? How can we gauge the scale of deficits and surpluses when there is so much inflation going on? How big were the deficits when we adjust for changes in the value of money? Some countries, such as Bolivia, Chile, Brazil and Israel, have had large government deficits and runaway inflations. In an earlier era, following World War I, Germany suffered an enormous budget deficit as a result of being required to make payments to France, and other former enemies, in compensation for damage inflicted during the war. That deficit produced a hyperinflation — defined as an inflation of more than 50 per cent a month — where German prices rose by as much as 30,000 per cent a month. The fact that deficits have, at other times and places, produced extraordinary inflations raises the question for us today: did the government's deficits cause inflation? Does a surplus mean an end to inflation? Do deficits somehow make it harder, or even impossible, and surpluses make it easier, for the Reserve Bank to control the money supply and keep inflation in check? When we incur a personal debt, that debt has to be repaid. Thus, when we incur a debt, we incur a self-imposed burden to repay the debt with interest. This fact leads to worries that when the nation incurs a debt as a result of a government deficit, a burden is being placed, not just on ourselves at a later date, but on our children and grandchildren. Do deficits create a burden on future generations?

In this chapter, we're going to study what became the hottest economic topic of the 1980s. We're going to examine the origins of the Federal deficits and surpluses, gauge their true scale, and explain why deficits are feared and why they constitute a problem. We'll also discuss some of the measures that have been taken to eliminate deficits. By the time you've read this chapter, you'll be able to explain what fiscal policy is all about.

The Sources of the Deficit or Surplus

What exactly is the surplus or deficit? The government of Australia's budget surplus or **deficit** is the difference between the revenue the government collects and its outlays in a given time period. Normally the period of time over which we measure the government's surplus or deficit is a year. According to the Budget Papers '**outlays** are a measure of the cost of providing non-marketable goods and services (commonly referred to as [expenditure on] public goods and services) that are distributed using collective public choice rather than through the operation of the market'. That is, outlays are a measure of the resources used by the government in providing services to the public for which it does not directly charge. It includes the government's total expenditure on purchases of goods and services, transfers and interest on the government's debt. **Revenue** consists of tax receipts, net of refunds, and non-tax receipts such as interest and dividends but excludes receipts from user charges, assets sales and repayments of advances and loans. The latter two are offset against outlays.

If revenue exceeds outlays, the Federal government has a surplus. If outlays exceed revenue, the government has a deficit. Thus we can define the government's deficit or surplus as follows:

Surplus = Revenue – Outlays,
if revenue > outlays

Deficit = Outlays – Revenue,
if revenue < outlays

If the surplus or deficit is zero, in other words if taxes and expenditures are equal, the government's budget is balanced. A **balanced budget** is a government budget that is neither in surplus nor in deficit.

Government debt is the total amount of borrowing that the government has undertaken and the total amount that it owes to households, firms and foreigners. Government debt is a *stock*. It is the accumulation of all the past deficits, minus all the past surpluses. The government deficit or surplus is a *flow*. It is the flow that adds to or subtracts from the stock of outstanding debt. Thus if the government has a deficit, its debt is increasing. If the government has a surplus, its debt is decreasing. If the government has a balanced budget, its debt is constant.

The Federal Budget since 1953/54

The Federal government's deficit, measured as a percentage of GDP, is shown in Fig. 35.1. The deficit or surplus is shown as a percentage of GDP, rather than in billions of dollars, so that we can see its importance in relation to the scale of the economy. After all, because of economic growth and inflation, GDP in 1990/91 was almost forty times what it was in 1953/54.

As Fig. 35.1 illustrates, for most of the period 1953/54 to 1990/91 the government operated at a deficit. That deficit reached 4.7 per cent of GDP in 1975/76, following several years of expansionary fiscal policy under the Whitlam Labor government. The budget was almost balanced in 1980/81 and 1981/82, as a result of the government's 'fight inflation first' policy. But, facing electoral defeat, the Fraser government significantly boosted spending in 1982/83. This trend was continued, following the change of government in 1983 and the subsequent National Economic Summit (recall our discussion in Chapter 33). The deficit expanded rapidly to 4.1 per cent of GDP in 1983/84, declining thereafter. In 1987/88, a small surplus was achieved. The surplus continued to grow and by 1989/90 reached 2.2 per cent of GDP, just over $8 billion. It was predicted that the surplus would be 2 per cent of GDP in 1990/91, but the unexpected severity of the recession greatly reduced the amount of the surplus to just 0.5 per cent of GDP. In the 1990/91 Budget Papers, the Treasury Department forecast a deficit of 1.2 per cent of GDP in 1991/92. We will discuss why a downturn in economic activity reduces the size of a surplus or increases a deficit a little later in this chapter.

The effect of the deficit on the government's debt is shown in Fig. 35.2. As you can see, after being relatively high following the Korean War in the early 1950s, the Federal debt, as a percentage of GDP, has since declined. It fell steadily to about 25 per cent in the mid-1980s and then declined to less than 15 per cent in 1989/90. The dollar value of the debt peaked in 1986/87 and has fallen since as the government has run surpluses.

The government has occasionally borrowed with foreign currency denominated debt. Borrowings have been in US dollars, deutschmarks, Swiss

Figure 35.1 Revenue, Expenditure and the Deficit (–) or Surplus (+)

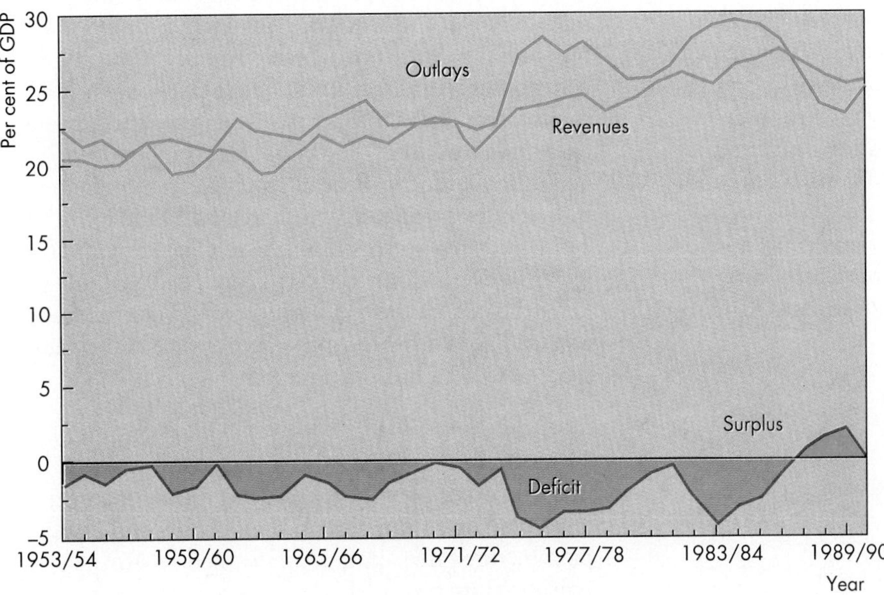

The figure records the Federal government's revenue, expenditure and deficit or surplus, from 1953/54 to 1990/91. Deficits have characterized the government finances for most of the period. Between 1987/88 and1990/91, the Federal government operated with a surplus. A deficit was forecast for 1991/92 due in large part to the recession.

Source: Budget Statements, Budget Paper No. 1 (Canberra: AGPS, 1991), p. 5.15.

francs and UK pounds sterling. However, the foreign component of the government debt has always been small, usually less than one-fifth of the total. In 1990/91, the balance of foreign currency denominated government debt was about 10 per cent of the total stock of outstanding government debt.

Why does the Federal government sometimes have a deficit, sometimes a surplus? Where do defi-

Figure 35.2 The Federal Government Debt

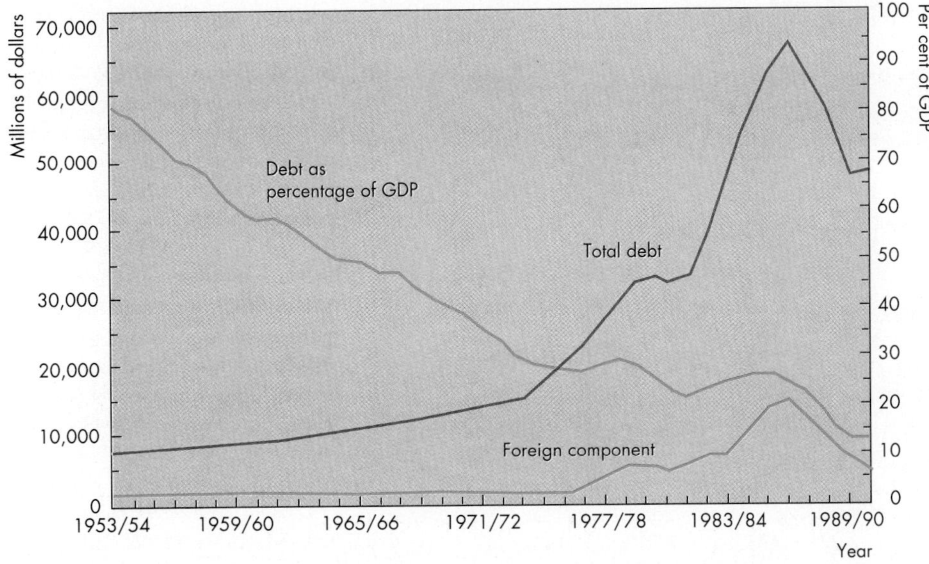

The Federal government debt, as a proportion of GDP (right-hand scale), has declined since 1953/54. The rate of decline was steady until the mid-1980s and then accelerated, as the government turned deficits into surpluses. The foreign component of the debt has typically been less than one-fifth of the total amount outstanding. Currently it stands at a little under 10 per cent.

Sources: 1953/54 to 1984/85: W.E. Norton and C.P. Aylmer, *Australian Economic Statistics 1949–50 to 1986/87* (Reserve Bank of Australia, 1988); 1985/86 to 1991/92: see Fig. 35.1.

cits come from? Some answers can be obtained by glancing back to Fig. 35.1. In that figure, you can see that, when the deficit grew large in 1974/75 and 1975/76, it was because expenditure grew much faster than before. The surpluses achieved in the late 1980s were the result of sharp reductions in expenditure (outlays), coupled with steady growth in taxes (revenues). Total revenues have steadily increased as a percentage of GDP, although there was a reduction during the late 1980s.

Why haven't government revenue and expenditure stayed in line? Let's answer this question by looking at the Federal government's revenues and outlays in a bit more detail.

Federal Government Revenue

There are three broad categories of Federal government revenue:

- Indirect taxes
- Direct or income taxes
- Other income

These elements of Federal government revenue are illustrated in Fig. 35.3. Let's look at each of them.

Indirect Taxes Indirect taxes are taxes on the goods and services that we buy. These are taxes assessed on producers, relating to the production and sales of goods and services. An example of an indirect tax is the sales tax, which currently is the largest contributor to indirect taxes. These taxes also include the customs duties that we pay when we import goods from other countries, and excise taxes on petroleum and other products. Federal government receipts from indirect taxes declined as a share of GDP until 1971/72, then increased reaching 8 per cent of GDP by 1986/87. Indirect taxes have since declined slightly. Over the period, the composition of indirect taxes has also changed with sales taxes contributing a much larger share of total indirect tax receipts.

Direct Taxes Direct taxes are income taxes paid by individuals on their labour and capital incomes, taxes paid by companies on their profits and taxes paid by foreigners on incomes earned in Australia (withholding taxes). These taxes have fluctuated much more than the other components of Federal government revenue, but the overall trend since the late 1950s has been upward. Between 1949/50 and 1986/87 the average tax rate on personal income rose from 7.6 per cent to 23.9 per cent. There has been a slight decline in tax revenue from individual income as a share of GDP since 1986/87, although taxes on

Figure 35.3 Federal Government Revenue

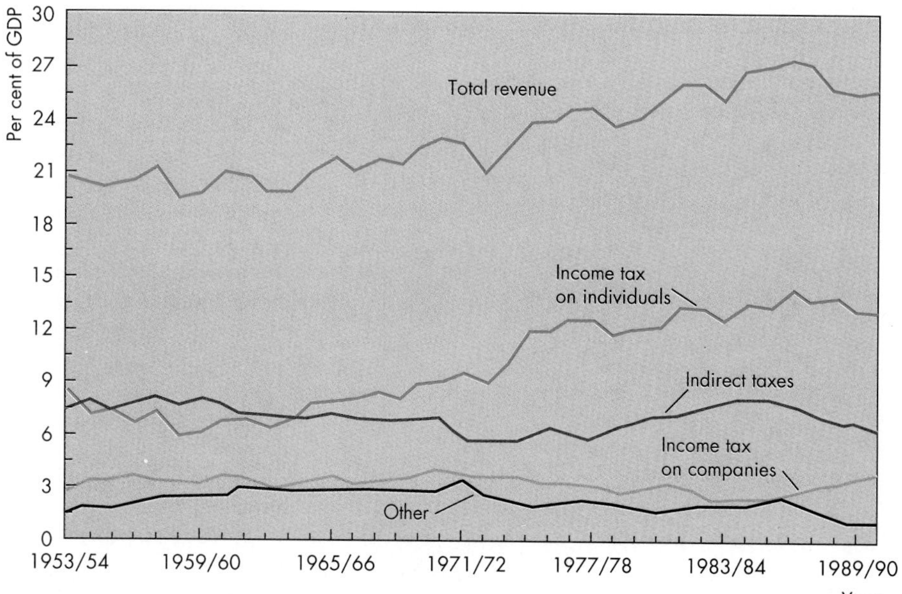

Four categories of Federal government revenue are shown: two components of income taxes — on individuals and companies — indirect taxes and other income, which includes interest income from loans to the State and local governments. Indirect taxes fluctuate slightly, increasing steadily from 1972/73 to 1986/87. Since 1987/88, indirect taxes have declined as a share of GDP. The largest item of government revenue, and the one that fluctuates most, is direct taxes, and the biggest component of direct taxes is taxes on individuals — mainly PAYE tax. Since 1959/60, income tax on individuals has increased from 6 per cent to nearly 15 per cent of GDP.

Source: See Fig. 35.1.

individuals still constitute 80 per cent of all direct tax collections. Even though the company tax rate has been reduced, taxes paid by firms have increased in recent years, at least up until 1989/90, because of strong growth and high profits. It appears that tax collections are down significantly in 1990/91 as a result of the recession, because both personal and company incomes are down.

Other Income Other income is mainly interest income received by the Federal government from loans to the State, territory and local governments. Also included here is income from public trading enterprises. This source of government income is not large and has steadily declined. It is expected to decline further as the States assume responsibility for the refinancing of their own debt under arrangements agreed at the 1990 Premiers' Conference, Loan Council meeting.[1]

Total Revenue When all three of the components of the Federal government revenue are added together, we find that their total has grown from around 20 per cent of GDP in the early 1950s to over 25 per cent of GDP in the late 1980s. Revenue peaked at nearly 28 per cent of GDP in 1986/87. Recent trends have been for revenue to decline slowly as a percentage of GDP.

Next, let's consider outlays.

Outlays

We will examine government outlays by dividing its expenditure into five categories:

- Expenditure on goods and services
- Personal benefits payments
- Grants to State, territory and local governments
- Other subsidies and transfers
- Interest payments and other

Figure 35.4 shows the behaviour of four of these items of expenditure over the years between 1953/54 and 1990/91. Let's examine each in turn.

Expenditure on Goods and Services Commonwealth government expenditure on goods and services includes both current expenditures — salaries and other expenses incurred in the day-to-day operation of the government — and capital expenditures — purchases of new fixed assets and purchases less sales of second-hand fixed assets plus stocks. It includes the cost of the Federal government administration, all the main Federal departments, including such items as national defence, roads and transport, and environmental protection. Generally speaking, defence spending accounts for about half of total expenditure on goods and services. The total resources devoted to these activities, as a share of GDP, has declined slowly since 1967/68.

Personal Benefits Payments In 1989/90, personal benefits payments became the largest component of Commonwealth government outlays. As a share of GDP, they have increased in spurts since 1953/54. There was a large boost in the years 1973/74 and 1974/75 and then again in 1982/83 and 1983/84. These payments include outlays on medical, unemployment, and invalid benefits and the age pension. Also included are payments to students, family allowances and widows' pensions. Of these, payments for medical benefits are expected to continue to grow very strongly.

Grants to States and Other Subsidies Grants to State, territory and Local governments are usually the largest item of expenditure for the Commonwealth government. Including advances, or loans, often at subsidized interest rates, total Commonwealth government transfers to State and local governments have averaged around 30 per cent of total outlays over the last 15 years. Also included in this item are subsidies, payments to producers and transfers overseas. Transfers overseas include payments made to and on behalf of Papua New Guinea, and other grants made under bilateral aid projects.

Interest Payments and Other This is the smallest component and comprises mainly interest payments on outstanding Commonwealth government debt. These payments grew quickly during the 1980s up to 1986/87. Since then they have declined, both in absolute terms and as a fraction of GDP, as government surpluses have reduced the stock of outstanding government debt, even though interest rates have been rising.

Total Outlays Total government outlays, expressed as a percentage of GDP, have risen over the past 30 or so years. This upward trend was steady through to 1972/73. In 1973/74, there was a rapid

[1] The Loan Council consists of the prime minister, who usually nominates the treasurer in his stead, and the State premiers, or their representatives, who meet to coordinate government borrowing.

Figure 35.4 Commonwealth Government Outlays

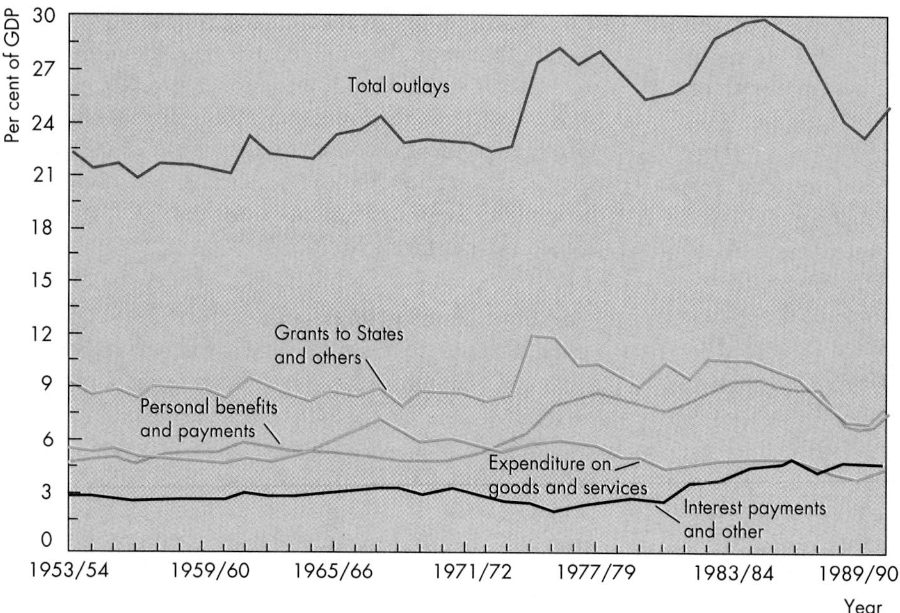

Four categories of Federal government outlays are shown: expenditure on goods and services, personal benefits payments, grants to State and local governments, and interest payments. Expenditure on goods and services (the operation of the Federal government including national defence) has not fluctuated much and, since 1967/68, has been a slowly declining percentage of GDP. Personal benefits payments have increased the most, following strong and permanent increases in the early 1970s to the mid-1970s and then again in the early 1980s. Grants to the States have fluctuated a lot but, following large increases in 1973/74 and 1975/76, they are now back to levels prevailing in the 1960s. Debt interest payments increased as the level of government debt rose over the 1980s but have declined recently as the government has accumulated surpluses.

Source: See Fig. 35.1.

increase in personal payments benefits and transfers to the States. Some of this was eroded in the early 1980s, but another rapid increase occurred in 1982/83 and 1983/84. Between 1986/87 and 1989/90, there has been a rapid decline in government outlays. This decline was arrested, and ultimately reversed, by the recession of 1990/91.

The Evolving Budget

The story of the budget can now be told in simple and straightforward terms. Revenue collections have grown steadily throughout most of the period from 1953/54 on. Up until 1972/73, outlays grew at about the same pace, although the budget was usually in deficit of 1 to 2 per cent of GDP. In 1973/74, government spending increased rapidly and the deficit approached 5 per cent of GDP. Spending was subsequently curtailed and the budget neared balance in 1980/81 and 1981/82. But again, in 1982/83 and 1983/84, spending increased much faster than receipts and the budget deficit rose to near 5 per cent of GDP. Between 1986/87 and 1989/90, however, Commonwealth government outlays have fallen as a share of GDP as spending and transfers were cut. In 1987/88, the Federal government achieved a surplus for the first time in 35 years. This surplus was short-lived as the effects of the recession caused large increases in government transfers and spending.

Why have government outlays fluctuated so much that the budget has at times been in large deficit but now is in large surplus? What events triggered these changes? The event that provoked the first rapid increase in government outlays was the election of the Whitlam Labor government in late 1973. The government was elected on a mandate of change and the economy fully expected the transformation. However, a new government was elected in 1975 and re-elected in 1978 on a platform of smaller government. Hence the reversal in the late 1970s. But, facing defeat at the polls, the Fraser government undertook, to no avail, a last-ditch spending increase. As we discussed in Chapter 33, the Hawke Labor government was elected in 1983. Once again, consensus was reached for continued large increases in government spending as one way of boosting economic activity. Only when it became evident that the fiscal stimulus was spilling over into an increase in imports did the fiscal stance change. We will discuss the relationship between the government deficit and the trade deficit in Chapter 37.

The Budget and the Business Cycle

There is an important relationship between the size of the deficit or surplus and the stage of the business cycle through which the economy is passing. We defined the business cycle, in Chapter 22, as the ebbs and flows of economic activity measured by the percentage deviation of real GDP from trend. We also saw that fluctuations in GDP from trend match very closely fluctuations in unemployment from the natural rate.

To see the connection between the budget surplus or deficit and the business cycle, look at Fig. 35.5. This figure shows the Federal government deficit (as a percentage of GDP) and the unemployment rate for the 38 years between 1953/54 and 1990/91. Note that unemployment is graphed on the right-hand axis, which has been inverted. As you can see, there is a close relationship between these two variables. When the unemployment rate increases, so does the deficit; when the unemployment rate decreases, so does the deficit. A change in the unemployment rate by an amount equal to 1 per cent of the labour force changes the deficit by an amount equal to somewhat more than 1 per cent of GDP.

Why does the deficit become larger when the unemployment rate increases and the economy goes into recession? Why does the deficit recede as unemployment falls and the economy recovers? Part of the answer lies on the spending side and part on the taxation side of the government's account.

The scale of government spending and taxes depends on the state of the economy. The government passes tax laws defining tax *rates*, not *dollars* to be paid in taxes. As a consequence, the taxes that the government collects depend on the level of income: if the economy is in a recovery phase of the business cycle, tax collections rise; if the economy is in a recession phase of the business cycle, tax collections fall.

Spending programmes behave similarly. Many government programmes are related to the state of well-being of individual citizens and firms. For example, when the economy is in a recession, unemploy-

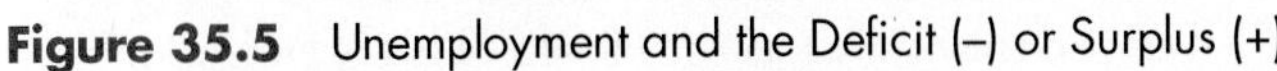

Figure 35.5 Unemployment and the Deficit (–) or Surplus (+)

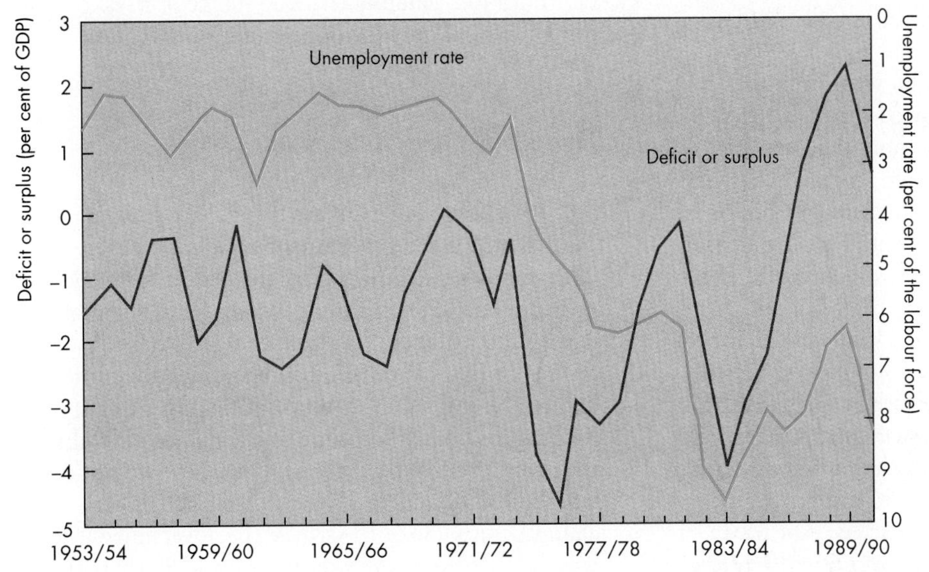

Recession leads to higher unemployment and recovery to lower unemployment. There is a close connection between the business cycle and the deficit. In recovery, lower unemployment reduces government transfer payments and so lowers total outlays. Additionally, the tax base grows, increasing total revenues. Overall the deficit falls or the surplus increases during an expansion. Just the reverse happens during a contraction.

Sources: The Deficit: see Fig. 35.1.

ment is high, economic hardship from poverty increases and a larger number of firms and farms experience hard times. Transfer payments increase as the government responds to the increased economic hardship. When the economy experiences boom conditions, expenditure on programmes to compensate for economic hardship declines.

Because of both these factors, the deficit rises when the economy is in a depressed state and falls when the economy is in a state of boom.

The Surplus in Expansion and Recession

In 1987/88 there was unexpectedly strong growth. As we discussed in Chapter 33, the terms of trade grew unexpectedly and strongly in conjunction with a loose monetary policy and buoyant business confidence. Thus economic activity grew more strongly than was anticipated. This meant that the tax base, both individual and corporate, grew strongly. As a result, the Commonwealth government had expected to collect $78.8 billion in revenues but in fact collected $80.8 billion, $2 billion extra. At the same time, demands on the government for transfers declined and total outlays, which were expected to be $78.9 billion, were only $78.7 billion. Thus the budget, estimated to be $177 million in deficit, actually ended up more than $2 billion in surplus.

As the strong growth continued into 1988/89, outlays ended up marginally higher than expected but revenues were considerably higher, so again the surplus was nearly $0.5 billion dollars more than anticipated.

Recall, however, that tight monetary policy was imposed throughout 1988/89 and into 1989/90. Coupled with this, there was a downturn in the terms of trade, and growth slowed through 1989/90. Outlays grew by $237 million more than expected. More importantly, the slow-down in growth slowed tax collections and revenues were nearly $1 billion less than first estimated. In the end, the surplus in 1989/90 was just over $8 billion, still a record, but the government had predicted over $9 billion.

The year 1990/91 developed into the major recession. As a result, the tax base shrank and tax collections were over $4 billion less than predicted. On top of this, with much larger payments in the form of unemployment benefits than were originally anticipated, outlays were over $2 billion more than predicted. The budget surplus, predicted to be $8.1 billion was actually $1.9 billion, over $6 billion less than expected. This downward trend was expected to accelerate, with the government predicting, in August 1991, that the budget deficit in 1991/92 would be nearly $5 billion.

R E V I E W

The Federal government has gone through several periods of large deficits caused by steady growth in revenues being overwhelmed by large increases in the rate of growth of spending. The components of total outlays that grow fastest, under an expansionary fiscal policy, are personal benefits payments and grants to State and local governments. Such increases occurred in 1973/74 and 1974/75, and again in 1982/83 and 1983/84. Between 1986/87 and 1989/90, the government reined in spending, and the budget went from large deficit to large surplus. However, the surplus evaporated under the influence of the 1990/91 recession.

The deficit or surplus is related to the business cycle. Other things being equal, the stronger the economy, the lower is the deficit. In the economic boom of 1987/88 and 1988/89, the strong growth contributed to the first surplus achieved by a government in over 30 years. The subsequent recession saw the surplus almost disappear, although further large surpluses had been predicted. ■

We've now seen where the deficit and surplus come from and how they relate to the business cycle. But are they as big as they look? This is an important question, gauging the true stance of fiscal policy, to which we'll now turn our attention.

The Real Deficit or Surplus

Inflation distorts many things, not least of which is the government's budget balance. To remove the inflationary distortion from the measured deficit or surplus, we need a concept of the real budget balance. The **real budget balance** is the change in the real value of outstanding government debt. The real value of outstanding government debt is equal to the market value of the debt divided by the price level. We are going to see how we can calculate the real deficit and how such a calculation changes our view of the size of the government's deficit. But before we do that, let's consider real deficits in more personal terms by examining the real deficit of a family.

The Real Deficit of a Family In 1960, a young couple (perhaps your parents) ran a deficit to buy a new house. The deficit took the form of a mortgage. The amount borrowed to cover the deficit — the difference between the cost of the house and what the family had available to put down as a deposit — was $20,000. Today, the children of that couple are buying their first house. To do so, they too are incurring a deficit. But they're borrowing $140,000 to buy their first house. Is the $140,000 deficit (mortgage) of the 1990 house buyer really seven times as big as the deficit (mortgage) of the 1960 house buyer? In dollar terms, the 1990 borrowing is indeed seven times as big as the 1960 borrowing. But in terms of what money will buy, these two debts are almost equivalent to each other. Inflation in the years between 1960/61 and 1989/90 has raised the prices of most things to about seven times what they were in 1960/61. Thus a mortgage of $140,000 in 1989/90 is really the same as a mortgage of $20,000 in 1960/61.

When a family buys a new home and finances it on a mortgage, it has a deficit in the year in which it buys the home. But in all the following years, until the loan has been paid off, the family has a surplus. That is, each year the family pays to the lender a sum of money, part of which covers the interest on the outstanding debt, but part of which *reduces* the outstanding debt. The reduction in the outstanding debt is the household's surplus. Inflation has another important effect here. Because inflation brings higher prices, it also brings a lower real value of outstanding debts. Thus the real value of the mortgage declines by the amount paid off each year plus the amount wiped out by inflation. Other things being equal, the higher the inflation rate, the faster the mortgage is really paid off, and the larger is the household's real surplus.

The Government's Real Deficit or Surplus

This line of reasoning applies with equal force to the government. Because of inflation, the government's deficit (if it is a deficit) is not really as big as it appears. To see how we can measure the deficit and correct for the distortion of inflation, we'll work through a concrete numerical example. First, look at Case A in Table 35.1 — a situation in which there is no inflation. Government expenditure, excluding debt interest, is $17 billion and taxes are $20 billion. Thus if the government didn't have interest to pay, it would have a surplus of $3 billion. But the government has outstanding debt of $50 billion and interest rates are running at 4 per cent a year. Thus the government must pay $2 billion of debt interest (4 per cent on $50 billion). When we add the $2 billion of debt interest to the government's other spending, we see that the government's total expenditure is $19 billion, so the government has a $1 billion surplus. The government's debt falls to $49 billion — the $50 billion outstanding at the beginning of the year is reduced by the surplus that the government has run. Ignore the last two rows of Table 35.1 for the moment.

Next, let's look at this same economy with exactly the same spending, taxes and debt but in a situation in which the inflation rate is 10 per cent a year — Case B in Table 35.1. With 10 per cent inflation,

Table 35.1 How Inflation Distorts the Deficit

	Case A	**Case B**
Government expenditure (excluding debt interest)	$17 billion	$17 billion
Taxes	$20 billion	$20 billion
Government debt	$50 billion	$50 billion
Market interest rate	4 % a year	14 % a year
Inflation rate	0 % a year	10 % a year
Real interest rate	4 % a year	4 % a year
Debt interest paid	$2 billion	$7 billion
Surplus (+) or deficit (–)	+ $1 billion	–$4 billion
Government debt at end of year	$49 billion	$54 billion
Real government debt at end of year	$49 billion	$49 billion
Real surplus (+) or deficit (–)	+ $1 billion	+ $1 billion

Inflation distorts the measured deficit by distorting the debt interest payments made by the government. In this example, the real interest rate is 4 per cent a year and government debt is $50 billion, so debt interest in real terms is $2 billion. With no inflation, Case A, the actual debt interest paid is also $2 billion. At 10 per cent inflation, Case B, interest rates rise to 14 per cent a year (in order to preserve a real interest rate of 4 per cent), and debt interest increases to $7 billion. The deficit increases by $5 billion from a surplus of $1 billion to a deficit of $4 billion. This deficit is apparent, not real. With 10 per cent inflation, the real value of the government's debt falls by $5 billion, offsetting the deficit of $4 billion, and resulting in a $1 billion real surplus.

the market interest rate will not be 4 per cent a year, but 14 per cent. The reason why the interest rate is higher by 10 percentage points is that the real value of outstanding debt declines by 10 per cent a year. Lenders — the households, firms and foreigners who are buying government debt — know that the money that they will receive in repayment of the loans they are making to the government will be worth less than the money that they are lending out. The government also recognizes that the money that it will use to repay its debt will have a lower value than the money that it borrows. Thus the government and the people from whom it borrows readily agree to a higher interest rate that compensates for these foreseen changes in the value of money. So, with a 14 per cent interest rate, the government has to pay $7 billion in debt interest — 14 per cent of $50 billion. When the $7 billion of debt interest is added to the government's other spending, total expenditure is $24 billion, $4 billion more than taxes. Therefore the government has a deficit of $4 billion. At the end of one year, the government's debt will have increased from $50 billion to $54 billion.

The difference between the two situations that we've just described is a 10 per cent inflation rate. Nothing else is different. What the government is actually spending and receiving is the same and the real interest rate is the same in the two cases. But, at the end of one year, government debt has increased to $54 billion in Case B and has fallen to $49 billion in Case A. However, the real debt is the same in the two cases. You can see that, by keeping in mind that although government debt increases to $54 billion in Case B, the prices of all things have increased by 10 per cent. If we deflate the government debt in Case B to express the debt in constant dollars instead of current dollars, we see that real government debt has actually fallen in Case B to $49 billion. ($54 billion divided by 1.1 — 1 plus the proportionate inflation rate — equals $49 billion.) Thus, even in Case B, the real situation is that there is a surplus of $1 billion. Inflation makes it appear that there is a $4 billion deficit when really there is a $1 billion surplus.

The numbers in Table 35.1 are, of course, hypothetical. They deal with two imaginary situations. But the calculations that we've just done provide us with a method of adjusting the Federal government deficit to eliminate the effects of inflation and reveal the real deficit. How important is it to adjust the Australian deficit for inflation in order to obtain an inflation-free view of the deficit or surplus?

Figure 35.6 Real and Nominal Deficits or Surpluses

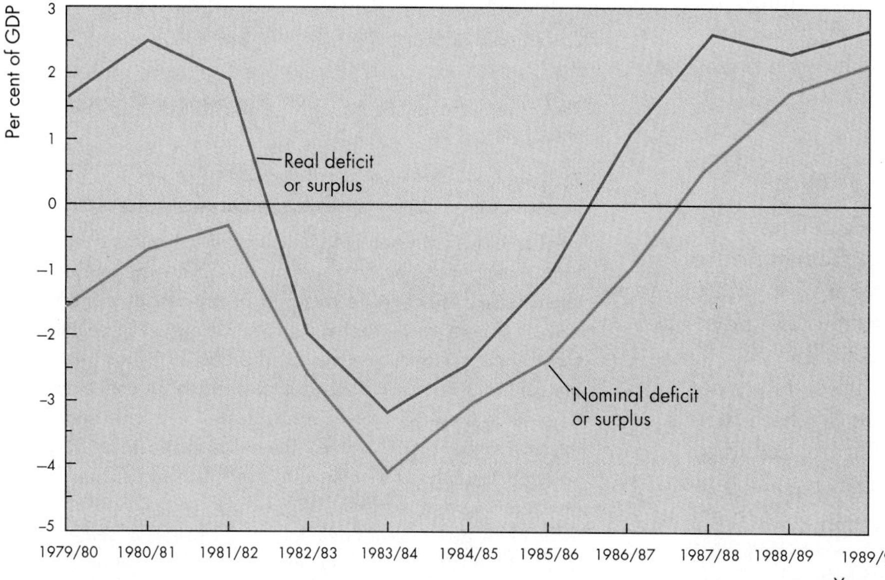

The real deficit removes the effects of inflation on interest rates from the outstanding value of government debt and also the effects of exchange rate changes on debt and payments denominated in foreign currencies. The real deficit and the nominal deficit follow a similar path, but the real deficit is lower than the nominal deficit, or the real surplus is higher than the nominal surplus.

Source: T. Makin, 'The Real Federal Budget Imbalance', *Economic Record* (66), September 1990, pp. 249–253.

Real and Nominal Federal Deficits and Surpluses in Australia

Figure 35.6 provides an answer to the above question. The data is provided from work done by Tony Makin at the University of Queensland. The nominal and real deficits or surpluses of the Federal government are plotted alongside each other. In calculating the real deficit, Makin accounted not only for the fact that inflation erodes the real value of government debt, but also for the effects of exchange rate depreciations on the value of government debt held in foreign currencies. Referring back to Fig. 35.2 we see that up to 15 per cent of total government debt has been denominated in foreign currencies — US dollars, UK pounds, Swiss francs, German deutschmarks and Japanese yen. When the Australian dollar depreciates, the value of this foreign debt, and interest payments on it, increase in terms of the domestic currency. When the domestic currency strengthens, the debt commitment, and payments thereon, decline.

As you can see from Fig. 35.6, the real deficit or surplus closely follows changes in the nominal deficit or surplus, but is consistently more positive. In fact, using the real measure, the Federal government actually ran surpluses in the late 1970s and early 1980s, as a result of consciously tight fiscal policies. The achievement of surpluses in the late 1980s actually occurred one year earlier when we consider the real surplus.

Thus, correcting for nominal distortions shows that the government has had a consistently tighter fiscal policy than the nominal figures would indicate.

Let's now go on to examine some other aspects of deficits and surpluses.

Financing a Deficit

To finance a deficit, the government sells bonds. But the effects of bond sales depends on who buys the bonds. If they are bought by the Reserve Bank, they bring an increase in the money supply. If they are bought by anyone other than the Reserve Bank, they do not bring a change in the money supply. When the Bank buys government bonds it pays for them by creating new money (see Chapter 28). We call such financing of the deficit 'money financing' or 'monetizing' the debt. **Money financing** or **monetizing the debt** is the financing of the government deficit by the sale of bonds directly to the Reserve Bank, which results in the creation of additional money. All other financing of the government's deficit is called debt financing. **Debt financing** is the financing of the government deficit by selling bonds to anyone (households, firms or foreigners) other than the Reserve Bank.

Let's look at the consequences of these two ways of financing a deficit, starting with debt financing.

Debt Financing First, suppose that the government borrows money by selling bonds to households and firms. In order to sell a bond, the government must offer the potential buyer a sufficiently attractive deal. In other words, the government must offer a rate of return high enough to convince people to lend their money.

Let's suppose that the going interest rate is 10 per cent a year. In order to sell a bond worth $100 and cover its deficit of $100, the government must promise not only to pay back the $100 at the end of the year but also to pay the interest of $10 accumulated on that debt. Thus, to finance a deficit of $100 today, the government must pay $110 a year from today. In one years time, in order simply to stand still, the government would have to borrow $110 to cover the cost of repaying, with interest, the bond that it sold a year earlier. Two years from today the government will have to pay $121 — the $110 borrowed plus 10 per cent interest ($11) on that $110. The process continues, with the total amount of debt and total interest payments growing year after year.

Money Financing Next, consider what happens if, instead of selling bonds to households and firms, the government sells bonds to the Reserve Bank. There are two important differences in this case compared with the case of debt financing. First, the government winds up paying no interest on these bonds; second, additional money is created.

The government ends up paying no interest on the bonds bought by the Reserve Bank because the Bank, although an independent agency, pays its residual profits to the government. Thus, other things being equal, if the Bank receives an extra million dollars from the government in interest payments on government bonds held by the Bank, the Bank's profits increase by that same million dollars and flow back to the government. Second, when the Bank buys bonds from the government, it uses newly created money to do so. This newly created money flows into the banking system in the form of an increase in the monetary base and enables the banks to create more money by making additional loans (see Chapter 27 and Chapter 28).

As we saw in Chapter 24 and Chapter 32, an increase in the money supply causes an increase in aggregate demand. Higher aggregate demand eventually brings a higher price level. Persistent money financing leads to continuous increases in aggregate demand and to inflation.

Debt Financing and Money Financing in Australia

The government's financing arrangements, like many other aspects of financial market behaviour, have undergone changes during the 1980s as part of the deregulatory process. The significant changes occurred between 1979 and 1982. We will look at debt and money financing prior to and following these dates.

Prior to 1979 As we discussed above, money financing is accomplished by the government borrowing directly from the Reserve Bank, which prints new cash to pay for the new government liabilities. Debt financing is accomplished by the government borrowing directly from the public. Prior to 1979, the government used two different types of security to tap these different sources of funds.

Treasury Bills were the security the government sold directly to the Reserve Bank to avoid its accounts going into debit. Effectively, by buying these bills, the Reserve Bank provided the government with an overdraft facility. Treasury Bills were short-term bills, of less than 91 days' maturity, which were seldom traded publicly before 1966, and then only with trading and savings banks, and they were not publicly traded thereafter. There was never a secondary market in Treasury Bills.

The government sold a variety of securities to the markets whenever it used debt financing. These included Special Bonds and Australian Savings Bonds, Treasury Notes and Treasury Bonds. The latter two securities are the most important for the purposes of funding government outlays. *Treasury Notes*, like Treasury Bills, are short-term securities. They are discount bonds, that is, they sell at less than their face value and pay no coupon. Until December 1979 Treasury Notes were available 'on tap', that is, an investor could buy as many as he or she wanted at a price (and hence yield) determined by the Loan Council. Since December 1979, Treasury Notes have been sold under a tender system — the Reserve Bank, acting as the agent of the Commonwealth government, calls for bids from the public and then sells them to the highest bidder(s). Treasury Notes can be redeemed before maturity by selling them to the Reserve Bank at a discount from the market price, or by selling them directly in the market. Thus they are very liquid assets.

Treasury Bonds are a collection of securities of longer maturity than Treasury Notes. Treasury Bonds are the most important source of government funds. Until 1979, they were issued in periodic loan raisings. From April 1980 to July 1982, new securities were issued under a tap system, as were Treasury Notes prior to December 1979.

While the quantity of outstanding Treasury Bonds is considerably larger than the stock of Treasury Notes, the latter, being of shorter maturity and hence more liquid, are traded in much larger volume in secondary markets. Treasury Notes are the basic money market instrument and are actively traded between banks, authorized dealers and other non-bank financial intermediaries.

To indicate the relative importance of money financing compared to debt financing, Fig. 35.7 shows, as a percentage of the deficit or total amount to be financed, the quantity of Treasury Bills (money financing) and other securities (debt financing) sold between 1959/60 and 1979/80.

Figure 35.7 illustrates the extent to which debt financing and money financing had been used to cover the Federal government deficit in Australia over the 20 years prior to the introduction of the tender system. As you can see, money financing has been used in a very limited way. In some years, such as 1960/61 and 1962/63, government securities were sold to the market to raise funds used to redeem Treasury Bills from the Reserve Bank. Note that in many years, particularly between 1970/71 and 1973/74, the total amount raised from the market exceeded the amount of the deficit, the funding requirement. In those years, the government was raising additional cash to add to its own cash balances held at the Reserve Bank.

A problem with the tap system of debt financing used at the time was that, with prices of government debt set by the Loan Council, interest rates paid by the government could get seriously out of line with market rates. The discrepancy became more apparent when other interest rates were deregulated but rates on government debt were not. This introduced unnecessary uncertainty into government financing activity because, when yields on government debt fell too far below market rates, the government had difficulty in raising the necessary finance. For this reason, the sale of Treasury Notes by tender was intro-

Figure 35.7 Debt and Money Financing Prior to the Tender System

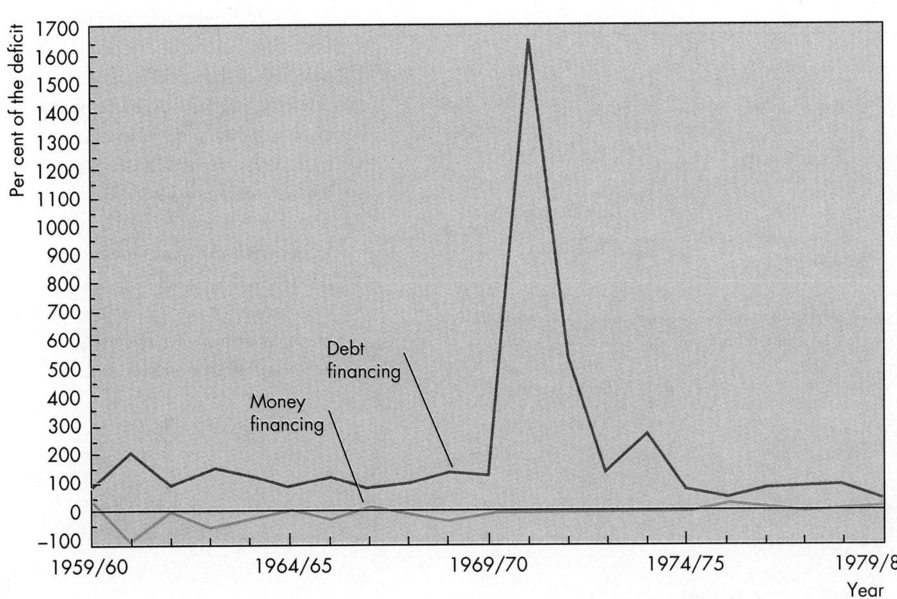

Sales of Treasury Bills direct to the Reserve Bank and other securities, mainly Treasury Notes and Bonds, to the public, as a percentage of the deficit, are shown. It is apparent that money financing has been used sparingly. On occasions, such as 1960/61 and 1962/63, debt has been sold to the public to raise funds to redeem Treasury Bills from the Reserve Bank. On occasions, where the total funds raised exceed 100 per cent of the deficit, the government was adding to its cash balances. The years 1970/71 to 1973/74 were years during which the government's cash balances grew enormously.

Source: See Fig. 35.2.

duced in December 1979 and the sale of Treasury Bonds by tender was introduced in July 1982.

Additionally, the government abandoned the practice of selling Treasury Bills directly to the Reserve Bank and redeemed $2.5 billion in outstanding Bills between 1980 and 1982.

We will discuss reasons for forgoing the opportunity of money financing below.

Debt Financing after 1982 By abandoning the practice of selling bonds directly to the Reserve Bank, the government left itself with only debt financing by tender as an option for fundraising after 1982. Figure 35.8 shows how sales of government debt were allocated between domestic and foreign markets. As you can see, overseas borrowing was never very important compared with sales of debt in the domestic market.

When the Commonwealth government turned its finances from deficit into surplus in 1987/88, it now had funds to dispose of. This was done by retiring outstanding government debt. In 1989/90, for example, with an $8 billion surplus, the government repaid:

- $2.8 billion of Treasury Bonds
- $1.9 billion of Australian Savings Bonds
- $1.3 billion of Treasury Notes
- $2.7 billion of overseas debt

Since the total repayments exceed the value of the surplus, the government also used nearly $500 million of its cash balances. Retiring overseas debt, that is, debt denominated in foreign currencies, is viewed as an important goal. As Fig. 35.8 shows, in 1988/89 the government actually repaid more overseas debt than domestic debt.

The conduct of fiscal policy in Australia has undergone two important transformations since the late 1970s. The first major decision was to abandon money financing of the deficit in the late 1970s and early 1980s. The second was to convert the deficit into a surplus, a decision taken in 1986 with the goal achieved in 1987/88. Let's review the arguments behind each of these decisions.

Money Versus Debt Financing

What are the pros and cons of financing a deficit by issuing debt or creating money? In comparing these two methods of covering the deficit, it is clear that debt financing leaves the government with a continuing obligation to pay interest — an obligation that gets bigger each year if the government keeps running deficits. When the government uses money financing, it pays its bills and that is the end of the matter. (The government pays interest to the Reserve Bank, but the Bank pays its profits to the gov-

Figure 35.8 Debt Financing Under the Tender System

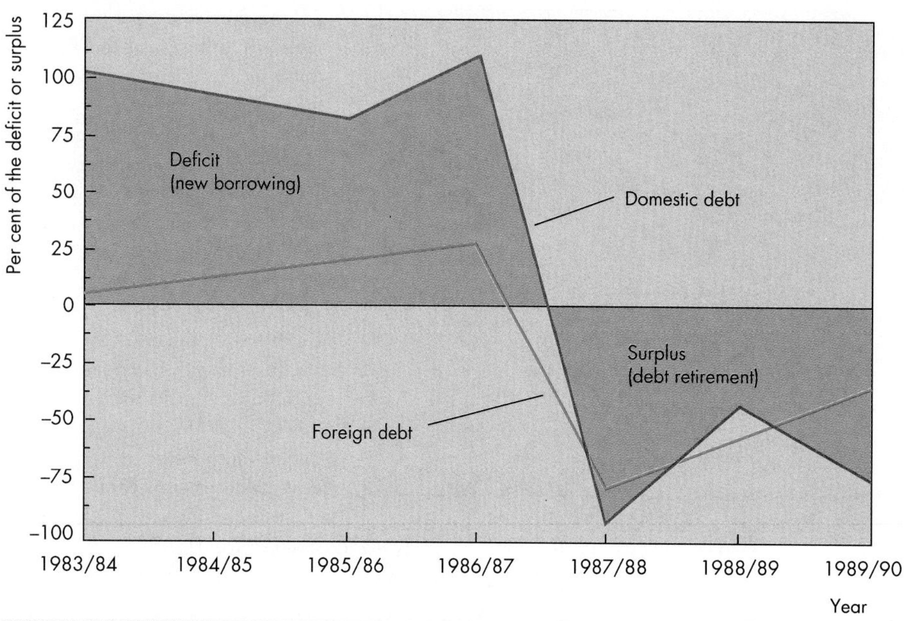

After 1982, all government deficit financing was debt financing. The majority of that debt was sold in the domestic market. Sales of overseas debt, denominated in foreign currencies, never exceeded 25 per cent of the deficit. After 1986/87 the turnabout of the government's finances from deficit to surplus meant that the government was retiring debt rather than issuing it. In 1988/89 the government actually retired more foreign debt than domestic debt.

Source: See Fig. 35.2.

ernment, so the government has no continuing interest obligation.) Thus there is a clear advantage, from the government's point of view, in covering its deficit by money financing rather than by debt financing. Unfortunately, this solution causes inflationary problems for everybody else.

But the alternative, debt financing, is not problem-free. Financing the deficit through bond sales to households, firms and foreigners increases the scale of debt and associated interest payments. The larger the debt and interest payments, the bigger the deficit problem becomes, and the greater is the temptation to end the process of debt financing and begin to finance the deficit by selling bonds to the Reserve Bank — money financing. This ever-present temptation is what leads many to fear that deficits are inflationary, even when they are not immediately money financed.

It has even been suggested, recently, that debt financing is more inflationary than money financing. Let's examine this proposition more closely.

Unpleasant Arithmetic

To compare the effects of financing a government deficit with debt issue as against money creation, suppose that the government has a deficit of a given size, which it plans to maintain indefinitely. Initially, the government covers its deficit by creating money and, consequently, the economy experiences inflation. The inflation rate depends on the size of the deficit. The larger the deficit, the larger is the sum of money that will have to be created and the faster will aggregate demand increase. The faster aggregate demand increases, other things being equal, the higher will be the inflation rate.

Suppose the economy is experiencing steady inflation as a result of a money-financed deficit and the government tries to slow the inflation by slowing down the growth rate of the money supply and covering its deficit by selling bonds to the public. It makes no changes in its spending and taxing policies, so that the deficit, excluding debt interest, remains constant. But the deficit, including debt interest, begins to grow. Furthermore, everyone understands this fact. The people to whom the government wants to sell bonds fully realize that, with a continuing deficit financed by bond sales, the deficit will have to increase to cover the additional interest payments arising from the growing national debt. They will also reason that, at some point, the amount of government debt outstanding will have grown so large that the interest burden on it will be larger than the government is willing to pay. At that point, they continue to reason, the government will do what it can do here and now —

cover its deficit by money financing. But the key difference is that to cover the deficit here and now by money financing only requires that the deficit, excluding debt interest, be money financed. The longer the government attempts to cover its deficit by debt financing, the larger is the deficit (the original deficit plus the additional interest burden) that will ultimately have to be paid for by creating money.

Thus, people continue to reason, at some future time the government will resort to creating money and there will be rapid inflation. At that time, the government bonds that are being bought today will lose value so rapidly as to make them almost worthless. Hence, if government bonds are going to be bought today, the interest rate on them must be sufficient to compensate for the foreseen future loss in their value resulting from the inflation that will eventually arise. And, in anticipation of a fall in the value of money, people will reduce the amount of money that they plan to hold here and now. This reduction in the demand for money will lead to an increase in the demand for goods and so to rising prices.

This argument was first advanced by Thomas Sargent (of the Hoover Institution at Stanford University) and Neil Wallace (of the University of Minnesota). They called their calculations 'unpleasant monetarist arithmetic'. It is unpleasant arithmetic because deferring the date at which a deficit is financed by money creation worsens the inflation that will ensue. It is unpleasant *monetarist* arithmetic because it constitutes a direct attack on the central proposition of monetarism — inflation is caused by the growth rate of the money supply. If the money supply growth rate is contained, inflation will not erupt. The unpleasant monetarist arithmetic calculations point out that the deficit must be sufficiently small to provide confidence in the ability and willingness of the government, and the Reserve Bank, to continue to keep money supply growth in line with the growth in the economy's capacity to produce goods and services. A deficit that is too large to reinforce that expectation will be inflationary.

But, for the deficit to be the problem that Sargent and Wallace say it is, it must be a truly persistent phenomenon. A deficit that is large and that lasts even for a decade does not inevitably have to produce inflation. If expectations are widely held that the deficit is going to be brought under control at some reasonably near future date then the unpleasant arithmetic is not relevant.

We have now reviewed the relationship between deficits and inflation. Deficits are not inevitably inflationary. But the larger the deficit and the longer it persists, the greater the pressure and the greater the temptation to cover the deficit by creating money, thereby generating inflation. This was one of the considerations of the government when it decided to eliminate the deficit and generate a surplus. But it was by no means the most important consideration. Let's review what the other considerations were.

Arguments Against a Deficit

There are three reasons for choosing not to run persistent deficits:

- They are inflationary.
- They impose a burden on future generations.
- They contribute to the trade deficit.

We have just discussed the interaction between deficits and inflation. In Chapter 37 we will discuss the relationship between the government deficit and the trade deficit. Let's now discuss the proposition that running deficits today places a burden on future generations.

A Burden on Future Generations?

It is a common and popular cry that 'we owe it to our children to control the deficit'. Is this popular view correct? How would the deficit burden future generations? We've already examined one way in which the deficit might leave a burden on future generations — the burden of inflation. But when people talk about the deficit as a burden on future generations, they usually mean something other than inflation.

For example, somebody has to pay the interest on the huge national debt that the deficit creates. The government will pay the interest with money it takes from the people as taxes. Taxes will have to be raised. Won't those taxes burden future generations?

Wait, though: don't the people who pay the taxes also receive the interest? If so, how can the deficit be a burden to future generations? It might be a burden to some members of the future generation, but it must be a benefit to others, so that, in the aggregate, it is neither a net cost nor net benefit.

Although, in the aggregate, the interest paid equals the taxes collected, there may be important redistributional effects. For example, one feature of our past deficits is that some government debt was sold to American, European and Japanese investors.

So part of the future burden of the current deficit is that future Australian taxpayers will have to provide the resources with which to pay interest to foreign holders of Australian government debt.

There's another way in which today's deficit can make people poorer tomorrow: by slowing today's pace of investment and reducing the stock of productive capital equipment available for future generations. This phenomenon is called crowding out.

Crowding Out *Crowding out* is the tendency for an increase in government purchases of goods and services to bring a decrease in investment (see Chapter 30, p. 340). If crowding out does occur, and if government purchases of goods and services are financed by government debt, the result is that the economy has a larger stock of government debt and a smaller stock of real capital. Unproductive government debt replaces productive real capital.

Whether or not crowding out actually occurs is a controversial issue. Let's see why it might be important. In order for crowding out to occur, a deficit has to result in lower private investment, so that future generations have a smaller capital stock than they otherwise would have had. This drop in investment will lower their income and, in a sense, be a burden to them. (They will still be richer than we were, but not as rich as they would have been if they had a larger stock of productive machines.) Let's examine how the deficit might be a burden to future generations as a result of lowering investment today.

As we saw in Chapter 25, the scale of investment depends on its opportunity cost, that is, the real interest rate. Other things being equal, the higher the real interest rate, the less firms will want to invest in new plant and equipment. For a government deficit to crowd out investment, it must be the case that a deficit causes interest rates to rise. Some people believe that a deficit does increase interest rates because the government's own borrowing represents an increase in the demand for loans with no corresponding increase in the supply of loans. Figure 35.9 shows what happens in this case. Figure 35.9(a) shows the demand and supply curves for loans. Initially, the demand for loans is D_0 and the supply of loans is S_0. The real interest rate is 3 per cent, and the quantity of loans outstanding is $100 billion. Figure 35.9(b) shows investment. At a real interest rate of 3 per cent, investment is $50 billion.

Figure 35.9 The Deficit, Borrowing and Crowding Out

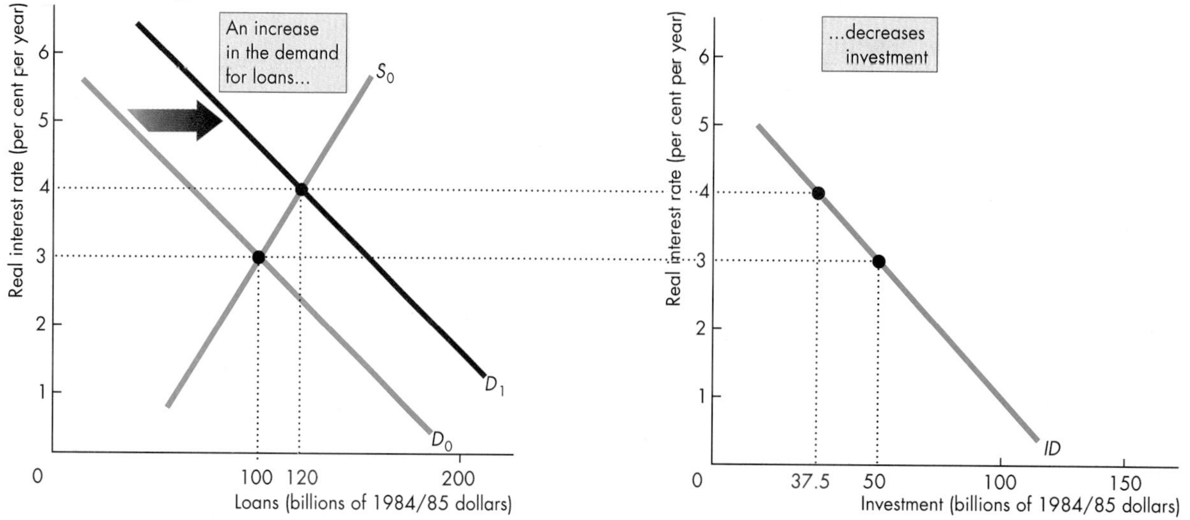

(a) The market for loans

(b) Investment

Part (a) shows the market for loans. The demand for loans is D_0 and the supply is S_0. The quantity of loans outstanding is $100 billion and the real interest rate is 3 per cent. Part (b) shows the determination of investment. At an interest rate of 3 per cent, investment is $50 billion. The government runs a deficit and finances the deficit by borrowing. The government's increase in demand for loans shifts the demand curve to D_1. The interest rate rises to 4 per cent and the equilibrium quantity of loans increases to $120 billion. The higher interest rate leads to a decrease in investment in part (b). The government deficit crowds out capital accumulation.

Now, suppose that the government runs a deficit. To finance its deficit, the government borrows. There is an increase in the demand for loans. The demand curve for loans shifts from D_0 to D_1. There is no change in the supply of loans, so the real interest rate increases to 4 per cent and the quantity of loans increases to $120 billion. Note that the increase in loans that occurs in equilibrium is smaller than the increase in the demand for loans. That is, the demand curve shifts to the right by a larger amount than the increase in loans that actually occurs. The higher interest rate brings a decrease in investment and a lower capital stock. Thus the increased stock of government debt crowds out some productive capital.

Does a deficit make real interest rates rise as shown in Fig. 35.9? Many economists believe so, and they have some pretty strong evidence to point to. Real interest rates in Australia in the 1980s, in precisely the years in which we had a large real deficit, have been higher than at any time since the Great Depression. Furthermore, there is a general tendency for real interest rates and the real deficit to fluctuate in sympathy with each other.

It is this relationship that leads some economists to predict that a higher real deficit means higher real interest rates, lower investment and a smaller scale of capital accumulation. Because of its effects on real interest rates, the real deficit and the accumulation of paper debt crowd out the accumulation of productive physical capital. As a consequence, future output will be lower than it otherwise would have been and so the deficit burdens future generations.

Crowding In Offsetting the effects of crowding out are the influences which lead to crowding in. These influences, first discussed in Chapter 30, can occur for two reasons. First, government spending on capital works can complement private investment, raising the marginal product of private capital and so inducing further private investment. Second, increased government spending might have important expectational effects, creating the expectation of a future increase in aggregate spending, which will induce firms to invest more today.

Recognizing the effects of crowding in, some evidence is accumulating overseas to suggest that the composition of government spending is important. It has been suggested that government spending on social infrastructure works complements private investment and so leads to crowding in, while government spending on current consumption leads to crowding out.

Figure 35.10 Ricardian Equivalence

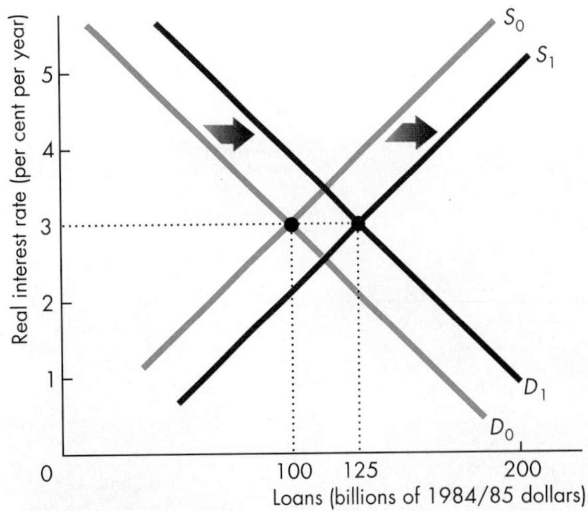

Initially, the demand for loans is D_0 and the supply of loans is S_0. The equilibrium quantity of loans is $100 billion and the real interest rate is 3 per cent. An increase in the government deficit, financed by borrowing, increases the demand for loans and shifts the demand curve to D_1. Households, recognizing that the increased government deficit will bring increased future taxes to pay the additional interest charges, cut their consumption and increase their saving. The supply curve of loans also shifts to the right to S_1. The equilibrium quantity of loans increases to $125 billion, but the real interest rate stays constant at 3 per cent. There is no crowding out of investment.

Ricardian Equivalence Some economists do not believe that deficits crowd out capital accumulation. On the contrary, they argue, debt financing and paying for government spending with taxes are equivalent. The level of purchases of goods and services matters, but not the way in which it is financed.

The first economist to advance this idea (known as Ricardian equivalence) was the great English economist David Ricardo (see Our Advancing Knowledge, pp. 494–495). Recently, Ricardo's idea has been given a forceful restatement by Robert Barro of Harvard. Barro argues as follows: if the government increases its purchases of goods and services but does not increase taxes, people are smart enough to recognize that higher taxes must be paid later in order to cover the higher spending and interest payments on the debt that is being issued today.

David Ricardo and the Deficit

David Ricardo

The economic landscape of England at the end of the eighteenth century was an exciting and rapidly changing one. Britain had left the Gold Standard in 1797 and, by 1799, the price of gold was rising rapidly; equivalently, the value of paper money was falling rapidly. That same year, a 27-year old, stockbroker, on a weekend visit to Bath, happened upon a copy of *The Wealth of Nations* (see Our Advancing Knowledge, pp. 20–21), a book of which he was to become 'a great admirer'. The young man in question was David Ricardo (1772–1832), the greatest economist of his time.

Born in London in 1772 into a devout Jewish family, Ricardo began his career at the age of 14, working for his father, a wealthy stockbroker. At 21, Ricardo displeased his father in the extreme by marrying a Quaker and was banished from the family business and disinherited. Continuing to work on his own as a stockbroker, Ricardo demonstrated real brilliance, amassing a fortune of £775,000 — equivalent to $2.4 billion (yes, billion) in today's money.

Ricardo made important contributions to a host of economic problems and issues, ranging from the value of money to the theories of value, exchange and international trade, and laid the foundations of modern public finance theory. His most significant work was *On the Principles of Political Economy,* published in 1817. Although he was a practical man, this book, and many of Ricardo's other writings, dealt with abstract and difficult matters of theory — matters that remain controversial even today among historians of economic thought.

But much of Ricardo's work, even though it is theoretical, has practical consequences. His contribution that has the most relevance for us in this chapter is that on public debt and on what has come to be called Ricardian equivalence. The idea of Ricardian equivalence was set out in a brief paper entitled 'Funding System' that was first published in the relatively obscure *Supplement to the Fourth, Fifth, and Sixth Editions of the Encyclopaedia Britannica.*

Ricardo's interest in public debt and government deficits was sparked by the enormous deficit incurred by Great Britain during the Napoleonic Wars, which ended in 1815. At its peak, in 1815, the British government's budget deficit was £35 million, almost one half of its annual revenue from taxes. Thus it was while discussing the appropriate way in which to finance a war that Ricardo offered his thoughts on debt and taxes. Although his words are open to several interpretations, Ricardo is usually held to have asserted that, if people take full account of the future tax burden that will have to be imposed in order to pay the interest on public debt, then financing government purchases with current taxes is equivalent to financing it with debt and paying interest on that debt in perpetuity. But Ricardo also expressed his belief that people do not in fact make such rational calculations when making decisions on whether to consume or save.[1] As consequence, tax financing of government purchases leads to lower private consumption and lower interest rates than does debt financing.

Interest in Ricardo's work was revived in the mid-1970s by Robert Barro (then at the University of Chicago, and now at Harvard University). Using a model economy in which each generation takes account of the effects of its own actions on the consumption possibilities of the succeeding generations, Barro showed some of the conditions under which Ricardo's equivalence theorem holds.[2] But, as Barro pointed out, almost every other model in use at that time assumed that debt and taxes were *not* equivalent.

The issue of Ricardian equivalence took on an extremely practical note when, in the early 1980s, in the face of an already large deficit, US President Ronald Reagan proposed cutting taxes. Some economists claimed that Ricardian equivalence was a valid description of the US economy, and that a tax cut that increased the deficit would have no adverse effects. Interest rates would *not* increase, and private saving would rise to finance the increased amount of government debt outstanding. Others (the majority) claimed that Ricardian equivalence was an abstract idea of little or no practical relevance, and that a tax cut would stimulate aggregate demand, resulting in a deficit that would create a debt, which would be a burden on future generations. In the majority, and among Barro's most vocal critics, were Martin Feldstein, Chairman of President Reagan's Council of Economic Advisers, and Nobel Laureate James Buchanan.

A whole series of studies of the issue, undertaken during the 1980s, has failed to come to a decisive conclusion, although one of the most recent of these studies, by Paul Evans of Ohio State University,[3] suggests that US consumers are indeed Ricardian — that Ricardian equivalence is a 'reasonable approximation'. But the issue has not been settled.

[1] Gerald P.O'Driscoll, Jr, 'The Ricardian Nonequivalence Theorem', *Journal of Political Economy*, vol. 85, 1977, pp. 207–10.

[2] Robert J.Barro, 'Are Government Bonds Net Worth?' *Journal of Political Economy*, vol. 82, no. 6, 1974, pp. 1095–1117.

[3] Paul Evans, 'Are Consumers Ricardian? Evidence for the United States', *Journal of Political Economy*, vol. 96, no. 5, 1988, pp. 983–1004.

Recognizing their future tax burden, people will cut their consumption now, increasing their saving, so as to ensure that when the higher taxes are finally levied by the government, sufficient wealth has been accumulated to meet those tax liabilities, without a further cut in consumption. The scale of increased saving matches the scale of increased government spending.

Figure 35.10 illustrates this case. Initially, the demand for loans is D_0 and the supply of loans S_0. The real interest rate is 3 per cent and the quantity of loans outstanding is $100 billion. The government runs a deficit and finances that deficit by borrowing. The demand curve for loans shifts to the right to D_1. At the same time, using the reasoning of Ricardo and Barro, there is a cut in consumption and an increase in the supply of loans. The supply curve shifts to the right to S_1. The quantity of loans increases from $100 to $125 billion and the real interest rate stays constant at 3 per cent. With no change in the real interest rate, there is no crowding out of investment.

Some economists argue that Ricardian equivalence breaks down because people take into account only future tax liabilities that will be borne by themselves, and not those borne by their children and their grandchildren. Proponents of the Ricardian equivalence proposition argue that it makes no difference whether future tax liabilities are going to be borne by those currently alive or by their descendants. If the taxes are going to be borne by children and grandchildren, the current generation takes account of those future taxes and adjusts its own consumption, so that it can make bequests on a large enough scale to enable those taxes to be paid.

Laying out the assumptions necessary for Ricardian equivalence leaves most economists convinced that the proposition cannot be empirically relevant. Yet there is a perhaps surprising amount of evidence to support it. In order to interpret the evidence, it is important to be clear that Ricardian equivalence does *not* imply that real interest rates are unaffected by the level of government purchases of goods and services. A high level of government purchases, other things being equal, brings a higher real interest rate. The Ricardian equivalence proposition implies that real interest rates are not affected by the way in which a given level of government purchases is financed. Regardless of whether it is financed by taxes or by borrowing, real interest rates will be the same.

Whether the deficit does affect real interest rates remains unclear. If people do take into account future tax burdens (and not just their own but their children's and grandchildren's future tax burdens), then saving will respond to offset the deficit and the deficit itself will have little or no effect on real interest rates and capital accumulation. If people ignore the implications of the deficit for their own and their descendants' future consumption possibilities, the deficit will indeed increase real interest rates. The jury remains out on this question.

■ We have now almost completed our study of macroeconomics and of the challenges and problems of stabilizing the economy. In this study, our main focus has been the economy of Australia. We have taken into account the linkages between Australia and the rest of the world, but international economic relations have not been our main concern. In the remaining chapters, we are going to shift our focus and study some vital international issues. First, in Chapter 36, we examine the international exchange of goods and services. Second, in Chapter 37, we study the financing of international trade and the determination of our balance of payments, including the effects of government deficits on the balance of payments. Third, we turn our attention to the problems of the poor developing countries of the Third World. Fourth, and finally, we examine economic systems different from our own, such as those of in the Soviet Union and China and look at the momentous events taking place in Eastern Europe.

SUMMARY

The Sources of the Deficit or Surplus

Until 1987/88, the Federal government spent more than it collected in taxes. That is, the Federal government operated at a deficit, which was usually around 1–2 per cent of GDP. In 1973/74 and 1974/75, there was a sharp increase in outlays, mainly in the form of increased personal benefits payments and increases in grants to the States. As revenue collections continued on their steady upward path, the deficit narrowed until 1982/83 and 1983/84, when spending again increased rapidly. Fiscal policy direction was reversed in 1985/86 and, by 1987/88, the government achieved its first surplus in more than 35 years.

The deficit or surplus fluctuates in sympathy with the business cycle. When the economy is in a recovery, taxes increase and transfer payments decrease as a percentage of GDP. The deficit declines or the surplus increases. When the economy goes into recession, taxes decrease and transfer payments increase as a percentage of GDP, and so the deficit increases or the surplus declines. Thus, when the economy entered a recession in 1990/91, the government's surplus vanished and was replaced by a substantial deficit. (pp. 478–484)

The Real Deficit or Surplus

Inflation distorts the deficit by overstating the real interest burden carried by the government. Adjusting the deficit for this fact, and measuring the real deficit, reveals that the apparent deficit in the early 1980s was actually a surplus. (pp. 484–487)

Financing a Deficit

To finance a deficit the government sells bonds. If the bonds are bought by the Reserve Bank then the debt is being monetized. If anyone other than the Reserve Bank buys the bonds then the deficit is debt financed. Continued debt financing leads to an escalating level of debt. Money financing leads to an increase in the money supply and a consequent increase in aggregate demand.

Prior to 1979, the government undertook a substantial amount of money financing. Between 1979 and 1982, the system changed so that all government debt is sold by tender on the market.

The argument against monetizing the debt is that it is ultimately inflationary because of the continued increases in the money supply. But similar arguments have been made against debt financing because there is a belief that, ultimately, the government will resort to monetizing the debt as its level escalates. (pp.487–491)

Arguments Against a Deficit

There are three reasons for choosing against running persistent deficits: deficits are inflationary, they impose a burden on future generations and they contribute to the trade deficit.

Whether the deficit is a burden on future generations is a controversial issue. Some economists believe that the deficit causes real interest rates to rise, thereby lowering investment and the amount of capital that we accumulate. As a consequence, future output will be lower than it otherwise would have been and future generations will be 'burdened' with the effects of the deficit.

Other economists argue that government expenditure affects interest rates but the way in which that expenditure is financed does not. They suggest that, if government spending is financed by borrowing, people will recognize that future taxes must increase to cover both the spending and the interest payments on the accumulated debt. And, in anticipation of those higher future taxes, saving will increase and consumption will decrease in the present. Thus the burden of increased government expenditure — not the burden of the deficit — is spread across all generations. (pp. 491–496)

KEY TERMS

Balanced budget, p. 478
Budget surplus or deficit, p. 478
Debt financing, p. 487
Direct taxes, p. 480
Expenditure, p. 481
Government debt, p. 478
Indirect taxes, p. 480
Monetizing the debt, p. 487
Money financing, p. 487
Outlays, p. 478
Real budget balance, p. 484
Revenue, p. 478
Ricardian equivalence, p. 493
Tender system, p. 488

PROBLEMS

1 You are given the following information about an economy. When unemployment is at its natural rate, which is 5.5 per cent, government spending and taxes are each 20 per cent of GDP. There is no inflation. For each 1 percentage point increase in the unemployment rate, government spending increases by 1 percentage point of GDP and taxes fall by 1 percentage point of GDP. Suppose that the economy experiences a cycle in which the unemployment rate takes the following values.

Year	Unemployment rate
1	5
2	6
3	7
4	6
5	5
6	4
7	5

a) Calculate the actual deficit (as a percentage of GDP) for each year.

b) Is the actual deficit related to the business cycle?

2 Government expenditure, excluding debt interest, in an economy is $8.5 billion. Taxes are $10 billion. The government has an outstanding debt of $25 billion. Interest rates are 24 per cent a year and there is a 20 per cent inflation rate. Calculate the following:

a) The debt interest that the government pays.

b) The government's budget surplus or deficit.

c) The value of the government debt outstanding at the end of the year.

d) The government's real deficit.

e) The real value of its debt outstanding at the end of the year.

Part 13

The World Economy

Talking with Max Corden

Professor Max Corden is one of Australia's best known economists. He is now Professor of International Economics in the School of Advanced International Studies at the Johns Hopkins University in Washington, DC. Before that he was an adviser to the International Monetary Fund and Professor of Economics in the Research School of Pacific Studies at the Australian National University. Earlier, for nine years, he was Reader in International Economics at Oxford University. Christopher Findlay talked to Professor Corden about his work on issues in international economics and macroeconomic policy.

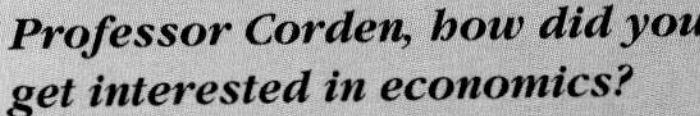

Professor Corden, how did you get interested in economics?

I was always interested in political and social issues. I saw economics as a way of helping to understand those issues. I had studied economics at Melbourne High School and I did a Commerce degree at the University of Melbourne. At that time, I also wanted a career in business. I worked for a newspaper for a while but after a couple of years I had a strong desire to travel to England. I won a scholarship to the London School of Economics and that revived my interest in the academic study of economics.

Australia has a long history of protecting industry by tariffs. Yet by the end of the 1990s the bulk of protection of this type will have disappeared. What were some of the factors that contributed to this shift in policy?

Recent events are part of a process of a long-run decline in the level of tariffs in Australia. A number of factors contributed. One was a world-wide trend to liberalization which Australia has been slow to imitate. Another was a shift in thinking in Australia about protection. The previous thinking was that protection was a good thing, so much so that being called a 'free trader' was a term of abuse. People like Alan Wood (writing then for the Australian Financial Review), Bert Kelly (a Liberal member of Parliament), Richard Boyer at the old Tariff Board and I argued for tariff reductions in those debates. After that debate, opinion shifted. The general belief developed that lower tariffs or even free trade were desirable, but the time was not ripe. A big step forward came with the Whitlam government and the establishment of the Industries Assistance Commission. This was the 1970s and early 1980s. But private interest groups were still strong. Finally the Hawke/Keating government finished off the job at the start of the 1990s.

There's been a debate in Australia about a range of new forms of industry assistance, like export subsidies. Are there any new arguments for industry assistance in these forms?

No, there are no new arguments. The same criticisms apply to them as apply to tariffs. But you have to remember that none of my work says that non-intervention is the best policy. It says that free trade is best but that there are also circumstances where it might pay to intervene with domestic taxes or subsidies to correct some sort of failure in the market. The problem is to make sure that proposals for intervention, whatever the form, are in the national interest, and that they are not the result of private interest pressures.

The question has often been asked, 'where do the jobs come

from?' when protection is cut. How do you tackle that question?

Economists should not claim to predict where the jobs will come from. We are trying to design a system to give signals to which numerous decentralized decisionmakers will respond. As relative prices change due to cuts in protection, new opportunities are created in other parts of the economy. We can make guesses about where the jobs will be but we have to wait to see the result. I often draw people's attention to the tremendous growth of the workforce in the 1970s when more women entered the workforce in Australia. The same question was asked: where will the jobs come from? It was difficult to predict, but all those people did find jobs. The same process has found jobs for the large numbers of immigrants to Australia.

Your name is associated with the idea of the 'conservative social welfare function'. What is that and why is it important?

This idea is helpful for explaining the actual trade policies of many countries. In its simplest form it says that the goal of policy is often to avoid any significant reductions in real income of any significant section of the community. It comes close to saying that the existing income distribution is best, so that's why it can be called a conservative function, that is, a conservative scheme for weighting the importance of the interests of different groups in the society. This notion helps explain first why tariffs are used to protect industries under pressure to decline. It also helps explain the reluctance to take off tariffs again once they are imposed. And it helps to explain why economies which are growing rapidly have less trouble reducing protection.

You have worked in a number of different areas during your academic career. How have you chosen the topics for your research?

I have always been interested in issues that were relevant to policy. I got interested in protection in the 1960s because it was relevant. The rest of the world was moving and we were not. In the 1970s, I got interested in macro policy because of all the disturbances in the world economy. In Australia, in the second half of the 1970s, the central problem was to understand unemployment. There were interesting intellectual challanges in all these topics too.

Commenting on Australian macroeconomic experience, you once said that 'Keynesianism is a guide only for short-run policy, and not for medium or long-run policy'. Can you explain?

In the short run, the Phillips curve is not vertical. The level of unemployment can be reduced by fiscal or monetary expansion. The basic Keynesian message does apply over a two-year period, say. But in the long run you can't decrease unemployment by printing more money, for example. The level of employment depends on real wages and on productivity. Persistent monetary expansion will only lead to inflation. The move to this position was the big intellectual shift of the mid-1970s in the macroeconomic policy debate.

Shocks from the rest of the world like changes in the terms of trade are difficult to manage for a small open economy like Australia. Is that the biggest macro policy management problem we face?

Some fluctuations in the performance of the economy are unavoidable. We can't actually intervene to completely sterilize the effects of shocks from the world economy. But the issue for Australia is not the existence of fluctuations. It is the level of unemployment. Why is there such high unemployment? It varies in the range from 6 to 10 per cent of the workforce. We should be able to get a range of 2 to 5 per cent. We know now there is a link between real wages and unemployment. For that reason, I would say that the biggest source of problems in managing the Australian economy is the inadequately flexible labour market.

You argued that a reason for the shift in protection policy was a greater public awareness of its costs. Is public awareness of the costs of various outcomes (for example, high inflation) also important in the management of the macro economy?

A widespread understanding of economic principles is vital for policy change. That's why the universities in Australia play a role in teaching economics and contributing to that understanding.

You said once that wage restraint under the Accord was impressive and that union leaders had 'learnt from the model'. Can you explain?

The Accord reflected a process of learning, especially from the experience of the wages booms in 1974/75 and 1980/81, that real wages are connected to the level of unemployment. In that sense, the leadership 'learnt from the model'. But the Accord is not a long-run solution to the labour market problem. It does not deal with what I call the 'structural rigidities', those factors which contribute to high levels of unemployment.

What would be your comment to someone starting out their study of economics?

Economics is a fantastically interesting subject. It illuminates so much of the real world. For example, a central problem is mass poverty in developing countries, and economics offers some simple ideas for reducing, even eliminating, it. To make the world a better place, it is vital to understand economics.

Chapter 36

Trading with the World

After studying this chapter, you will be able to:

- Describe the trends and patterns in international trade.
- Explain comparative advantage.
- Explain why all countries gain from international trade.
- Explain how prices adjust to bring about balanced trade.
- Explain how economies of scale and diversity of taste contribute to gains from international trade.
- Explain why trade restrictions lower the volume of imports and exports, and reduce our consumption possibilities.
- Explain why we have trade restrictions even though they lower our consumption possibilities.

Australia and the World Economy — A New Era?

Since ancient times, people have striven to expand their trading as far as technology allowed. The maritime nations of southern Europe, the Middle East and North Africa had flourishing trades in the Mediterranean 5000 years ago. Roman coins have been found in the ruins of ancient Indian cities. Marco Polo opened up the silk route between Europe and China in the thirteenth century. Merchants of Venice imported goods from the entire known world in the fifteenth century. We're not sure when Australia became part of the world economy. Adventurers like Dutchman Abel Tasman and Englishman William Dampier located the continent in the seventeenth century, although trade did not develop until European settlement in the last decade of the eighteenth century. Today, container ships laden with cars and machines, bulk ships carrying coal and iron ore, and Boeing 747s stuffed with fresh fruit from the Riverland, live Tasmanian lobsters and cheeses from Victorian dairies carry billions of dollars' worth of goods. Not only merchandise but also services are traded internationally. We export education services to students from Asia. Australians import tourist services when they holiday in Hong Kong or Bali. Why do people go to such great lengths to trade with those in other nations? What does the pattern of international trade look like today? And what have been the recent trends in international trade? International trade obviously brings enormous benefits. It enables us to buy a wide range of manufactured goods such as cars, VCRs, TVs, PCs and textiles that are available at lower prices from other countries. It also enables our producers — workers and the firms that employ them — in export industries to earn more by expanding the markets for their products. But international trade also has its costs. An increase in the penetration of imports into Australian markets for textiles, clothing and motor vehicles will reduce employment in those industries. Do the benefits of international trade make up for the cost of jobs displaced by foreign competition? Could we, as some industry commentators often claim, improve our economy by restricting imports? The rich countries of the European Community, Japan, the United States and the rapidly industrializing economies of Asia import vast quantities of raw materials from resource-rich developed countries such as Australia, as well as from other developing economies. To pay for these raw material imports, they sell manufactured goods to the countries supplying their resources. Do resource suppliers become poorer when they sell their bauxite, coal and iron ore and buy Boeing jets, PCs or textiles in return? The wages earned by the workers in the textile and electronics factories of Southeast Asia and China are incredibly low compared with wages in Australia. Obviously, these countries can make manufactured goods much more cheaply than we can. How can we possibly compete with countries that pay their workers a fraction of Australian wages? Are there any industries where we have an advantage?

Australia has a long history of protecting local industry against foreign competition by taxing imports. An import tax is called a tariff. We had one of the highest average tariff rates among the rich countries in the world. But from the mid-1970s, tariffs and other forms of protection have been cut and, on current plans, by the end of the 1990s, manufacturing sector protection will have virtually disappeared. What are the effects of trade restrictions? What explains the dramatic change in Australia's policy towards international trade in manufactures? Are we at the start of a new era in Australian trade policy?

In this chapter, we're going to learn about international trade. We'll begin by looking at some facts about international trade, examining the patterns of imports and exports and trends in the main items that Australia buys from and sells to other countries. Then we will discover how *all* nations can gain by specializing in producing the goods and services at which they have an advantage compared with other countries and by exchanging some of their output with each other. We'll discover that all countries can compete in something, no matter how high their wages. We will also explain why, despite the fact that international trade is beneficial, countries restrict trade. We'll discover who suffers and who benefits when international trade is restricted.

Patterns and Trends in International Trade

The goods and services we buy from people in other countries are called **imports**. The goods and services that we sell to people in other countries are called **exports.** What are the important things that we import and export? As we'll see, Australia is unusual for a high income country. Most of the rich countries of the world export *and* import a lot a manufactured goods. We don't. We export a lot of raw materials and agricultural products and we import a lot of manufactures. Let's look at the pattern of Australian trade in more detail.

Australia's International Trade

Table 36.1 classifies Australian trade into four categories: agriculture, mining, manufacturing and services. The table has three sections: exports, imports and the **balance of trade**, which is the value of exports minus the value of imports. If the balance is positive then the value of exports exceeds the value of imports, and Australia is a **net exporter**. If the balance is negative, the value of imports exceeds the value of exports, and Australia is a **net importer**.

Within each section of the table is shown data for two years, 1984/85 and 1989/90. Against each number in the first two sections of the table has been added the percentage of that item in either total exports or imports. These are the numbers in brackets.

The data in Table 36.1 highlight a number of points:

- Australia is a large net exporter of the output of the agricultural and mining sectors.
- The importance of the agricultural and mining sectors in exports fell from 46 per cent to 35 per cent.
- The importance of manufactures in exports rose by over 7 percentage points and the importance of services rose by over 5 points, which highlights the relatively rapid growth of exports of manufactures and services over this period.
- Australian imports are dominated by manufactures; they account for about 70 per cent of the total, while services account for over 20 per cent.
- The overall trade balance is negative, that is, Australia is a net importer of all goods and services.

Figure 36.1 shows the composition of Australia's exports over a longer period. Apart from the changes in the last five years of the 1980s, which we

Table 36.1 Australian Exports and Imports, 1984/85 and 1989/90 (thousands of dollars)

Industrial Sector	Exports 1984/85		Exports 1989/90		Imports 1984/85		Imports 1989/90		Balance of trade 1984/85	Balance of trade 1989/90
Agriculture [a]	6,245	(18.3)[b]	7,305	(12.5)	427	(1.2)	598	(0.9)	5,818	6,707
Mining[c]	9,326	(27.4)	11,835	(20.3)	1,127	(3.1)	1,436	(2.2)	8,199	10,399
Manufacturing	13,578	(39.8)	27,537	(47.2)	26,448	(71.6)	48,325	(72.6)	-12,870	-20,788
Services	4,938	(14.5)	11,719	(20.1)	8,924	(24.2)	16,197	(24.3)	-3,986	-4,478
Total	34,087	(100.0)	58,396	(100.0)	36,926	(100.0)	66,556	(100.0)	-2,839	-8,160

a Includes forestry, fishing and hunting.
b The numbers in parentheses are percentages.
c Includes oil and gas.

Source: ABS, *Exports, Australia. Annual Summary Tables*, 1989/90, No. 5424.0; ABS, *Imports, Australia. Annual Summary Tables*, 1989/90, No. 5426.0; ABS, *Balance of Payments Australia*, 1989/90, No. 5303.0.

have just examined, the figure highlights the longer trends of the declining importance of agricultural exports and the rising importance of minerals between the 1960s and the 1980s.

Australia's trade pattern is dramatically different from other rich countries. In those other economies, manufactures usually account for about the same share of exports and imports. Their share is usually in the range of 70 to 80 per cent (that is, excluding services). In Australia those kinds of goods also account for 90 per cent of merchandise imports, but they make up only about 60 per cent of our mer-

Figure 36.1 The Changing Composition of Australian Exports since 1960[a]

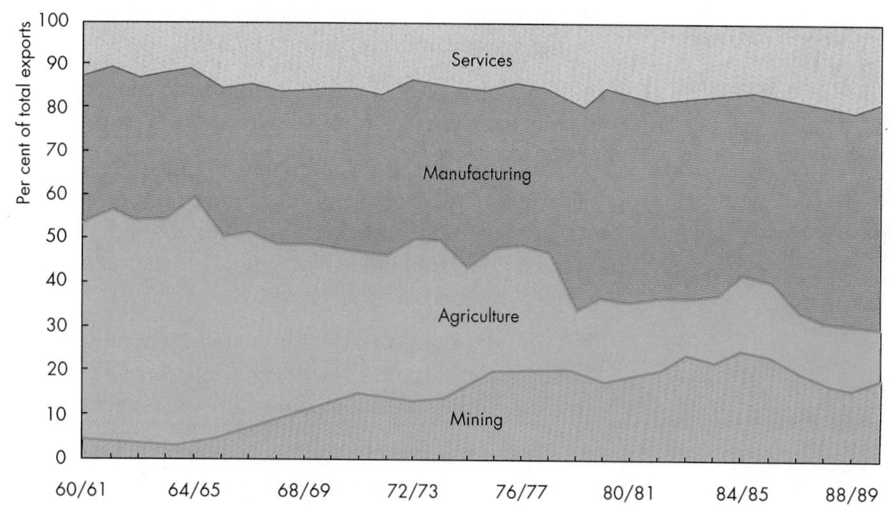

Three changes are evident in the composition of Australian exports over the last three decades. First, the share of agricultural exports has fallen. Second, the share of minerals in exports rose between the 1960s and the 1980s. Third, more recently, the shares of both services and manufactures in exports have increased.

[a] There is a break in the data between 1977/78 and 1978/79 due to a change in the system of classifying goods into the four categories. In particular, some processed agricultural products are reclassified as manufactures rather than as agriculture.

Source: ABS, *Exports, Australia. Annual Summary Tables*, 1980/90, No. 5424.0.

chandise exports. Agriculture and mining account for a much smaller share of world trade than they do of Australian exports. They make up about a quarter of total world merchandise exports, but about 40 per cent of our merchandise exports. This suggests we are relatively highly specialized in the production and export of those kinds of goods. We'll discuss later some reasons for this apparently unusual pattern of specialization in Australian trade.

Table 36.2 lists some of the major exports of Australia. The items are listed according to the value of net exports in 1989/90. The biggest net export item in that year was coal. Wool was still ranked third, despite the drop in wool prices in 1989 and 1990. The biggest net import item was electrical equipment, which includes things like office machines, stereo gear and so on. Other big import items were cars and industrial machines. There are many items which the data says we both import and export! These are shown in the middle of the table. Examples are petroleum products and iron and steel. We even export some of the big import items like electrical equipment and cars.

Trade in Services Roughly 20 per cent of our exports and imports are services. The components of our services trades are shown in Table 36.3. 'Shipment' refers to the carriage of freight to and from Australia. When we export goods from Australia, the ship carrying those goods might be an Asian-owned vessel. When we pay the Asian company for those shipment services, that counts as an import of the service. When a foreign firm pays an Australian airline for carrying fresh produce, then that is an export of shipment services. Australia is a net importer of shipment services.

'Travel' refers to tourist spending. When Australians travel to Singapore, we are importing services. When Japanese tourists visit Australia, we are exporting tourism services to Japan. The travel item includes only spending at the destination, for example, the hotel bills and other services bought by Japanese in Australia. 'Other transportation' refers to the

Table 36.2 Major Items in Australian Merchandise Exports and Imports, 1989/90 (billions of dollars)

	Exports	Share (per cent)	Imports	Share (per cent)	Balance
Coal	5.82	12.5	0.02	0.04	5.80
Aluminium/alumina	5.03	10.8	0.15	0.3	4.88
Wool	4.05	8.7	0.15	0.3	3.90
Meat	2.67	5.7	0.01	0.02	2.66
Wheat	2.56	5.5	0.00	0.0	2.56
Gold	2.84	6.1	0.28	0.6	2.56
Iron ore	2.21	4.7	0.06	0.1	2.15
Iron and steel	0.75	1.6	1.04	2.0	–0.29
Petroleum oils and products	2.01	4.3	2.51	5.0	–0.50
Scientific instruments	0.25	0.5	1.14	2.3	–0.89
Paper products	0.16	0.3	1.30	2.6	–1.14
Textile yarn and products	0.18	0.4	1.95	3.9	–1.77
Other transport equipment	0.60	1.3	2.80	5.6	–2.20
Road vehicles	0.55	1.2	5.06	10.0	–4.51
Industrial machinery	0.80	1.7	5.73	11.4	–4.93
Electrical equipment	1.17	2.5	8.08	16.1	–6.91
Other items	15.03	32.2	20.07	39.9	–5.04
Total	46.68	100.0	50.35	100.0	–3.67

Source: See Table 36.1.

Table 36.3 Australian Trade in Services: 1984/85 and 1989/90 (thousands of dollars)

	Exports		Imports		Balance	
	1984/85	**1989/90**	**1984/85**	**1989/90**	**1984/85**	**1989/90**
Shipment	395	535	2,539	3,269	–2,144	–2,734
Other transportation	2,096	3,446	2,097	3,420	–1	26
Travel	1,359	4,337	2,618	5,086	–1,259	–749
Other services	1,088	3,401	1,670	4,422	–582	–1,021
Total	4,938	11,719	8,924	16,197	–3,986	–4,478

Source: ABS, *Balance of Payments Australia*, 1985, 1990, No. 5303.0.

travel to and from the destination. For example, when Australians travel on Qantas there is no international transaction, export or import. But when Japanese tourists fly with Qantas, Australia is exporting these services to Japan. At the same time, some Australians will fly with Japan Airlines or with ANA. In that case, we are importing transportation services from Japan. This item is roughly in balance.

'Other services' includes mainly business services traded with the rest of the world, for example, engineering services, education, health and accountancy. Australia is also a net importer of these services. However, the growth in exports of this item, along with the export or services to foreign tourists visiting Australia, has contributed to the rise in the services share of exports.

Geographic Patterns Table 36.4 lists Australia's major trading partners at the start of the 1990s. Countries are listed according to their im-

Table 36.4 Geographical Patterns of Australian Exports and Imports in 1989/90

	Exports	**Share (per cent)**	**Imports**	**Share (per cent)**	**Balance**
Japan	12.81	(31.2)	9.87	(19.2)	2.94
Western Europe	6.85	(16.7)	11.32	(22.0)	–4.47
United States	5.35	(13.0)	12.37	(24.1)	–7.03
ASEAN	4.98	(12.1)	2.97	(5.8)	2.01
Korea	2.68	(6.5)	1.25	(2.4)	1.42
New Zealand	2.60	(6.3)	2.17	(4.2)	0.43
Taiwan	1.83	(4.5)	1.95	(3.8)	–0.12
Hong Kong	1.32	(3.2)	0.85	(1.6)	0.48
Eastern Europe	1.25	(3.0)	0.55	(1.1)	0.70
China	1.19	(2.9)	1.24	(2.4)	–0.05
Rest of the World	0.22	(0.5)	6.79	(13.2)	–6.57
Total	41.08	(100.0)	51.33	(100.0)	–10.25

Source: ABS, *Exports, Australia, Annual Summary Tables*, 1989/90, No. 5424.0; ABS, *Imports, Australia, Annual Summary Tables*, 1989/90, No. 5426.0.

Figure 36.2 The Changing Direction of Australian Exports since 1950

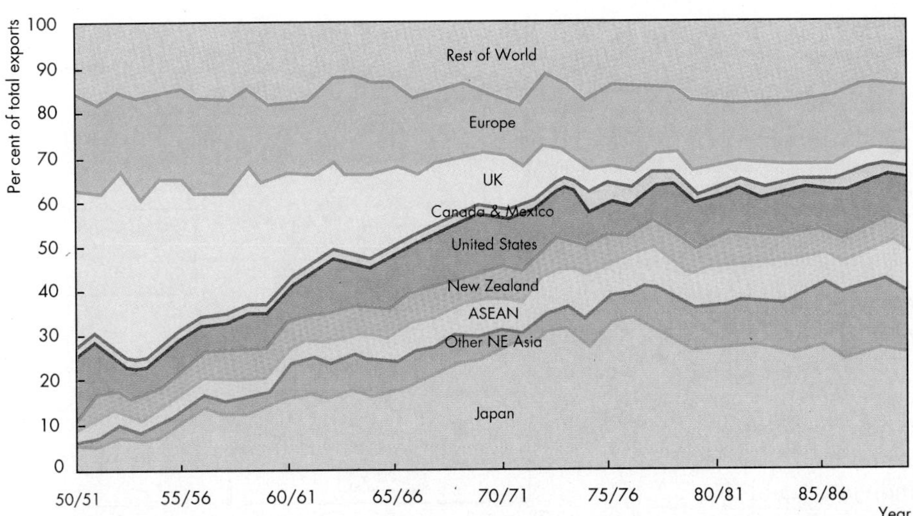

Australia has transformed itself over the four decades since the 1950s into an exporter to Asia. The Asian share of our exports is now up to 60 per cent, some 6 times more than in the 1950s. Japan is the major market, taking just over 30 per cent of exports. More recently, other Asian economies have become more important. Britain now accounts for less than 10 per cent, compared with more than 30 per cent in 1950.

Source: See Table 36.4.

portance in our exports. Japan is our biggest export market, followed by Western Europe, members of the Association of Southeast Asian Nations (ASEAN) (which includes Singapore, Malaysia, Thailand, the Philippines and Indonesia) and the United States. If we add together all the major Asian markets, then they account for about 60 per cent of our exports. The major sources of imports at the start of the 1990s were the United States, Japan and Europe.

Figure 36.2 shows the share of exports by country since 1950/51. There has been a massive re-orientation of Australian exports in the four decades since World War II. At the start of the 1950s, Europe accounted for more than half our exports, but their share has fallen to about 20 per cent. The bulk of this decline in the importance of exports to Europe has been the dramatic decline in the importance of the United Kingdom. The Asian share has risen from less than 10 per cent to 60 per cent, initially be-

Figure 36.3 The Balance of Trade as a Percentage of GDP, 1950/51–1990/91

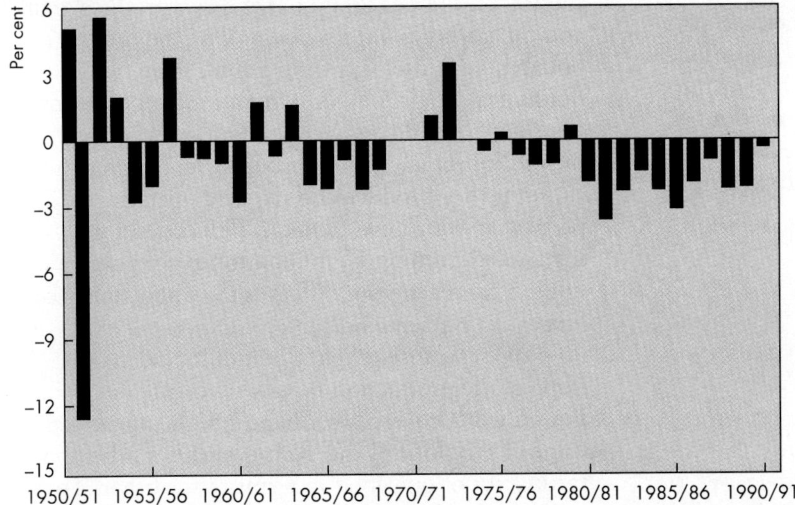

The balance of trade fluctuated around zero since the 1950s, but since 1980 imports have grown faster than exports and a persistent deficit has emerged.

Source: See Table 36.3.

cause of a rapid growth in the share of Japan in exports, then, since the mid-1970s, a higher share for the rest of Northeast Asia, and, from the mid-1980s, a rising share for the ASEAN countries.

The Balance of Trade

The overall balance of trade in goods and services is shown in Figure 36.3. The balance fluctuated around zero up to the mid-1970s, but since 1980/81 there has been a persistent deficit.

The Balance of Trade and International Borrowing When people buy more than they sell, they have to finance the difference by borrowing. When they sell more than they buy, they can use the surplus to make loans to others. This simple principle, which governs the income and expenditure and borrowing and lending of individuals and firms, is also a feature of our balance of trade: if we import more than we export, we have to finance the difference by borrowing from foreigners. When we export more than we import, we make loans to foreigners to enable them to buy goods in excess of the value of the goods they have sold to us.

This chapter does *not* cover the factors that determine the balance of trade and the scale of international borrowing and lending that finance that balance. It is concerned with understanding the volume, pattern and directions of international trade rather than its balance. So that we can keep our focus on these topics, we'll build a model in which there is no international borrowing and lending — just international trade in goods and services. We'll find that we are able to understand what determines the volume, pattern and direction of international trade and also establish its benefits and the costs of trade restrictions within this framework. This model can be extended to include international borrowing and lending, but such an extension does not change the conclusions we'll reach here about the factors that determine the volume, pattern and directions of international trade.

Let's now begin to study those factors.

Opportunity Cost and Comparative Advantage

Let's apply the lessons that we learned in Chapter 3 about the gains from trade between Kylie and Jason, to the trade between nations. We'll begin by recalling how we can use the production possibility frontier to measure opportunity cost.

Figure 36.4 Opportunity Cost in Pioneerland

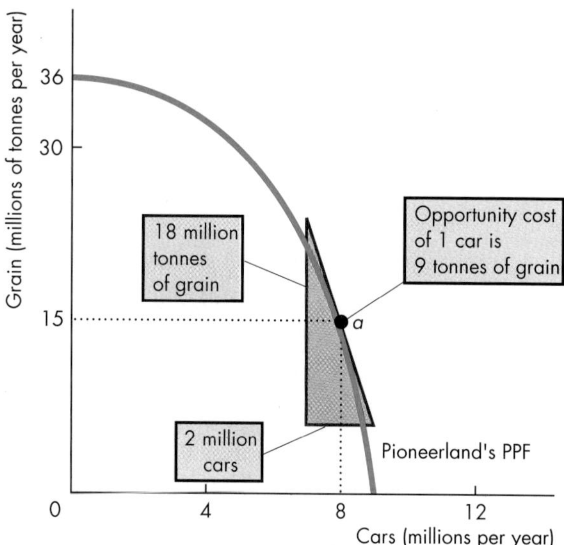

Pioneerland produces and consumes 15 million tonnes of grain and 8 million cars a year. That is, it produces and consumes at point *a* on its production possibility frontier. Opportunity cost is measured as the numerical value of the slope of the production possibility frontier. At point *a*, 2 million cars cost 18 million tonnes of grain. Equivalently, one car costs 9 tonnes of grain or 9 tonnes cost one car.

Opportunity Cost in Pioneerland

Pioneerland (a fictitious country) can produce grain and cars at any point inside or along the production possibility frontier shown in Figure 36.4. (We're holding constant the output of all the other goods that Pioneerland produces.) The Pioneers (the people of Pioneerland) are consuming all the grain and cars that they produce and they are operating at point *a* in the figure. That is, Pioneerland is producing and consuming 15 million tonnes of grain and 8 million cars each year. What is the opportunity cost of a car in Pioneerland?

We can answer that question by calculating the slope of the production possibility frontier at point *a*. For, as we discovered in Chapter 3, the numerical value of the slope of the frontier measures the opportunity cost of one good in terms of the other. To measure the slope of the frontier at point *a*, place a straight line tangential to the frontier at point *a* and

Figure 36.5 Opportunity Cost in Magic Empire

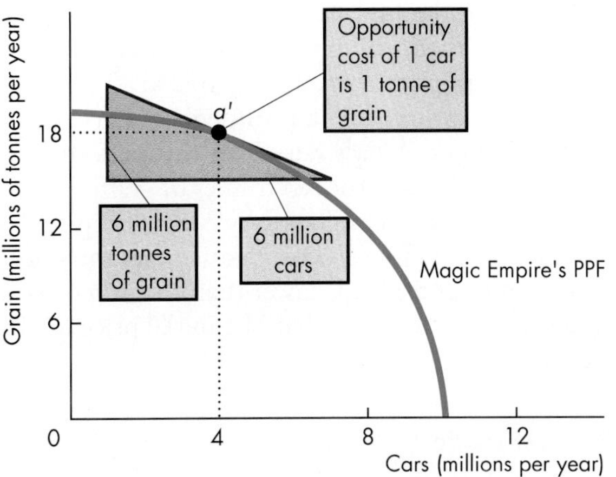

Magic Empire produces and consumes 18 million tonnes of grain and 4 million cars a year. That is, it produces and consumes at point *a*′ on its production possibility frontier. Opportunity cost is measured as the slope of the production possibility frontier. At point *a*′, 6 million cars cost 6 million tonnes of grain. Equivalently, one car costs 1 tonne of grain or 1 tonne costs one car.

calculate the slope of that straight line. Recall that the formula for the slope of a line is the change in y divided by the change in x as we move along the line. Here, y is millions of tonnes of grain and x is millions of cars. So the slope (opportunity cost) is the change in the number of tonnes of grain divided by the change in the number of cars. As you can see from the red triangle in the figure, at point *a*, if the number of cars produced increases by 2 million, grain production decreases by −18 million tonnes. Therefore the slope is 18 million divided by 2 million, which equals −9. To get one more car, the people of Pioneerland must give up 9 tonnes of grain. Thus the opportunity cost of one car is 9 tonnes of grain. Equivalently, 9 tonnes of grain cost one car.

Opportunity Cost in Magic Empire

Now consider the production possibility frontier in Magic Empire (another fictitious country and the only other country in our model world). Figure 36.5 illustrates its production possibility frontier. Like the Pioneers, the Magicians (the people in Magic Empire) consume all the grain and cars that they produce. Magic Empire consumes 18 billion tonnes of grain a year and 4 million cars, at point *a*′.

We can do the same kind of calculation of opportunity cost for Magic Empire as we have just done for Pioneerland. At point *a*′, one car costs 1 tonne of grain, or, equivalently, 1 tonne of grain costs one car.

Comparative Advantage

Cars are cheaper in Magic Empire than in Pioneerland. One car costs 9 tonnes of grain in Pioneerland but only 1 tonne of grain in Magic Empire. But grain is cheaper in Pioneerland than in Magic Empire: 9 tonnes of grain cost only one car in Pioneerland while that same amount of grain cost nine cars in Magic Empire.

Magic Empire has a comparative advantage in car production. Pioneerland has a comparative advantage in grain production. A country has a **comparative advantage** in producing a good if it can produce that good at a lower opportunity cost than any other country. Let's see how opportunity cost differences and comparative advantage generate gains from international trade.

The Gains from Trade

If Magic Empire bought grain for what it costs Pioneerland to produce it, then Magic Empire could buy 9 tonnes of grain for one car. That is much lower than the cost of growing grain in Magic Empire, for there it costs nine cars to produce 9 tonnes of grain. If the Magicians buy at the low Pioneerland price, they will reap some gains.

If the Pioneers buy cars for what it costs Magic Empire to produce them, they will be able to obtain a car for 1 tonne of grain. Since it costs 9 tonnes of grain to produce a car in Pioneerland, the Pioneers would gain from such an activity.

In this situation, it makes sense for Magicians to buy their grain from Pioneers and for Pioneers to buy their cars from Magicians. Let's see how such profitable international trade comes about.

Reaping the Gains from Trade

We've seen that the Pioneers would like to buy their cars from the Magicians and that the Magicians would like to buy their grain from the Pioneers. Let's see how the two groups do business with each other, concentrating attention on the international market for cars.

Figure 36.6 illustrates such a market. The quantity of cars traded internationally is measured on

Figure 36.6 International Trade in Cars

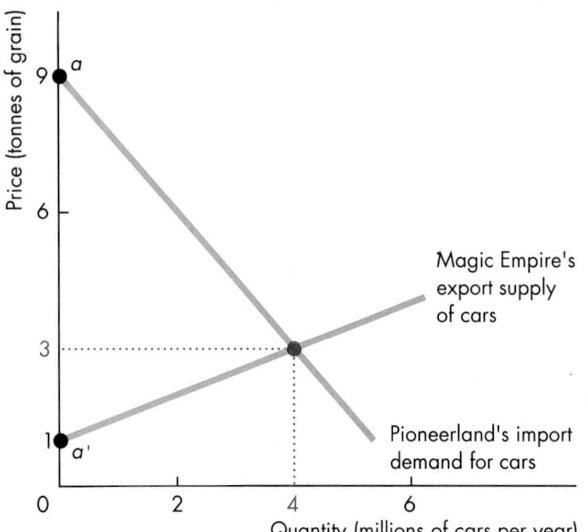

As the price of a car decreases, the quantity of imports demanded by Pioneerland increases — Pioneerland's import demand curve for cars is downward sloping. As the price of a car increases, the quantity of cars supplied by Magic Empire for export increases — Magic Empire's export supply curve of cars is upward sloping. Without international trade, the price of a car is 9 tonnes of grain in Pioneerland (point *a*) and 1 tonne of grain in Magic Empire (point *a'*). With free international trade, the price of a car is determined where the export supply curve intersects the import demand curve — a price of 3 tonnes of grain. At that price, 4 million cars a year are imported by Pioneerland and exported by Magic Empire. The volume of grain exported by Pioneerland and imported by Magic Empire is 12 million tonnes a year, the quantity required to pay for the cars imported.

the horizontal axis. On the vertical axis we measure the price of a car but it is expressed as its opportunity cost — the number of tonnes of grain that a car costs. If no international trade takes place, that price in Pioneerland is 9 tonnes of grain, indicated by point *a* in the figure. Again, if no trade takes place, that price is 1 tonne of grain in Magic Empire, indicated by point *a'* in the figure. The points *a* and *a'* in Fig. 36.6 correspond to the points identified by those same letters in Figs 36.4 and 36.5. The lower the price of a car (in terms of tonnes of grain), the greater is the quantity of cars that the Pioneers import from the Magicians. This fact is illustrated in the downward-sloping curve that shows Pioneerland's import demand for cars.[1]

The Magicians respond in the opposite direction. The higher the price of cars (in terms of tonnes of grain), the greater is the quantity of cars that Magicians export to Pioneers. This fact is reflected in Magic Empire's export supply of cars — the upward-sloping line in the figure.[2]

The international market in cars determines the equilibrium price and quantity traded. This equilibrium occurs where the import demand curve intersects the export supply curve. In this case, the equilibrium price of a car is 3 tonnes of grain. Four million cars a year are exported by Magic Empire and imported by Pioneerland. Notice that the price at which cars are traded is lower than the initial price in Pioneerland but higher than the initial price in Magic Empire.

Balanced Trade

Notice that the number of cars exported by Magic Empire — 4 million a year — is exactly equal to the number of cars imported by Pioneerland. How does Pioneerland pay for its cars? By exporting grain. How much grain does Pioneerland export? You can find the answer by noticing that for one car Pioneerland has to pay 3 tonnes of grain. Hence, for 4 million cars they have to pay 12 million tonnes of grain. Thus Pioneerland's exports of grain are 12 million tonnes a year, given our assumption of balanced trade. Magic Empire imports this same quantity of grain.

Magic Empire is exchanging 4 million cars for 12 million tonnes of grain each year and Pioneerland is doing the opposite, exchanging 12 million tonnes of grain for 4 million cars. Trade is balanced between these two countries. The value received from exports equals the value paid out for imports.

Changes in Production and Consumption

We've seen that international trade makes it possible for Pioneers to buy cars at a lower price than they can produce them for themselves. It also enables Magicians to sell their cars for a higher price, which is equivalent to saying that Magicians can buy grain for a lower price. Thus everybody seems to gain. Magicians buy grain at a lower price and Pioneers buy cars at a lower price. How is it possible for every-

[1] The slope of Pioneerland's import demand curve for cars depends on that country's production possibility curve and on the tastes of the citizens of Pioneerland.

[2] The slope of Magic Empire's export supply curve depends on that country's production possibilities curve and on the tastes of the citizens of Magic Empire.

Figure 36.7 Expanding Consumption Possibilities

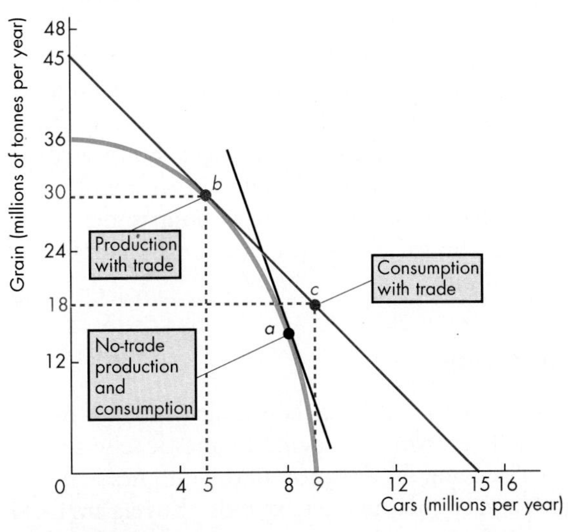

(a) Pioneerland

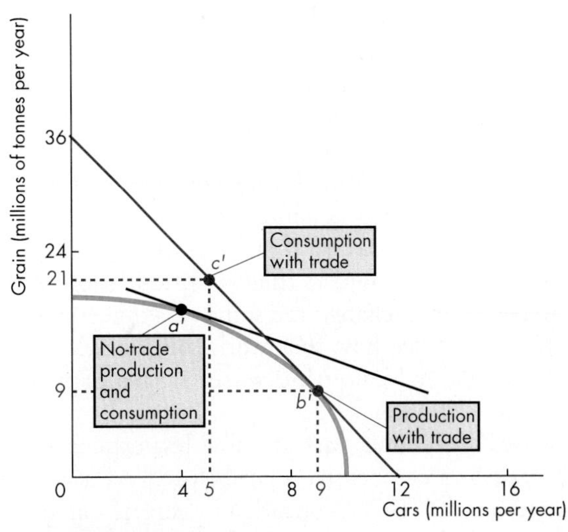

(b) Magic Empire

With no international trade, the Pioneers produce and consume at point *a* and the opportunity cost of a car is 9 tonnes of grain (the numerical value of the slope of the black line in part (a)). Also, with no international trade, the Magicians produce and consume at point *a′* and the opportunity cost of 1 tonne of grain is one car (the numerical value of the slope of the black line in part (b)).

Goods can be exchanged internationally at a price of 3 tonnes of grain for one car along the red line. In part (a), Pioneerland decreases its production of cars and increases its production of grain, moving from *a* to *b*. It exports grain and imports cars, and it consumes at point *c*. The Pioneers have more of both cars and grain than they would if they produced all their own consumption goods — at point *a*. In part (b), Magic Empire increases car production and decreases grain production, moving from *a′* to *b′*. Magic Empire exports cars and imports grain, and it consumes at point *c′*. The Magicians have more of both cars and grain than they would if they produced all their own consumption goods — at point *a′*.

one to gain? What are the changes in production and consumption that accompany these gains?

An economy that does not trade with other economies has identical production and consumption possibilities. Without trade, the economy can only consume what it produces. But with international trade an economy can consume different quantities of goods from those that it produces. The production possibility frontier describes the limit of what a country can produce but it does not describe the limits to what it can consume. Figure 36.7 will help you to see the distinction between production possibilities and consumption possibilities when a country trades with other countries.

First of all, notice that the figure has two parts, part (a) for Pioneerland and part (b) for Magic Empire. The production possibility frontiers that you saw in Figs 36.4 and 36.5 are reproduced here. The numerical values of the slopes of the two black lines in the figure represent the opportunity costs in the two countries when there is no international trade. Pioneerland produces and consumes at point *a* and Magic Empire produces and consumes at *a′*. Cars cost 9 tonnes of grain in Pioneerland and 1 tonne of grain in Magic Empire.

With international trade, Magic Empire can sell cars to Pioneerland for 3 tonnes of grain each. Pioneerland can buy cars from Magic Empire for that same price. Thus both countries can exchange cars for grain or grain for cars at a price of 3 tonnes of grain per car. These trading possibilities are illustrated by the red lines with identical slope in both parts of Fig. 36.6.

With international trade, the producers of cars in Magic Empire can now get a higher price for their output. As a result, they increase the quantity of car production. At the same time, grain producers in Magic Empire are now getting a lower price for their grain and so they reduce production. Producers in Magic Empire adjust their output until the opportunity cost in Magic

Empire equals the opportunity cost in the world market. Opportunity cost in the world market is identical for both countries and is determined as the numerical value of the slope of the red lines in Fig. 36.6 — one car costs 3 tonnes of grain. For Magic Empire, the opportunity cost of producing a car equals the world opportunity cost at point *b′* in Fig. 36.6(b).

But the Magicians do not consume at point *b′*. That is, they do not increase their consumption of cars and decrease their consumption of grain. They sell some of their car production to Pioneerland in exchange for some of Pioneerland's grain. But to see how that works out, we first need to look at Pioneerland to see what's happening there.

In Pioneerland, cars are now less expensive and grain more expensive than before. As a consequence, producers in Pioneerland decrease car production and increase grain production. They do so until the opportunity cost of a car in terms of grain equals the cost on the world market. They move to point *b*, in part (a). But the Pioneers do not consume at point *b*. They exchange some of their additional grain production for the now cheaper cars from Magic Empire.

The figure shows us the quantities consumed in the two countries. We saw in Fig. 36.6 that Magic Empire exports 4 million cars a year and Pioneerland imports those cars. We also saw that Pioneerland exports 12 million tonnes of grain a year and Magic Empire imports that grain. Thus Pioneerland's consumption of grain is 12 million tonnes a year less than it produces and its consumption of cars is 4 million a year more than it produces. Pioneerland consumes at point *c* in Fig. 36.7(a).

Similarly, we know that Magic Empire consumes 12 million tonnes of grain more than it produces and 4 million cars fewer than it produces. Thus Magic Empire consumes at *c′* in Fig. 36.7(b).

Calculating the Gains from Trade

You can now literally 'see' the gains from trade in Fig. 36.7. Without trade, Pioneers produce and consume at *a* (part (a)) — a point on Pioneerland's production possibility frontier. With international trade, Pioneers consume at point *c* (in part (a)) — a point *outside* the production possibility frontier. At point *c*, Pioneers are consuming 3 million tonnes of grain a year and 1 million cars a year more than before. These increases in consumption of cars and grain, beyond the limits of the production possibility frontier, are the gains from international trade.

But Magicians also gain. Without trade, they consume at point *a′* (part (b)) — a point on Magic Empire's production possibility frontier. With international trade, they consume at point *c′* — a point outside the production possibility frontier. With international trade, Magic Empire consumes 3 million tonnes of grain a year and 1 million cars a year more than without trade. These are the gains from international trade for Magic Empire.

Gains for All

When Pioneers and Magicians trade with each other, potentially everyone can gain. Domestic sellers add the net demand of foreigners to their domestic demand, and so their market expands. Buyers are faced with domestic supply plus net foreign supply, and so have a larger total supply available to them. As you know, prices increase when there is an increase in demand and they decrease when there is an increase in supply. Thus the increased demand (from foreigners) for exports increases their price and the increased supply (from foreigners) of imports decreases their price. Gains in one country do not bring losses in another. Everyone, in this example, gains from international trade. So, in answer to our earlier question of whether countries supplying resources become poorer when they sell their raw materials to buy manufactured goods, the answer is 'no'. They gain because they are trading according to their comparative advantage.

Absolute Advantage

Suppose that in Magic Empire, fewer workers are needed to produce any given output of either grain or cars than in Pioneerland. In this situation, Magic Empire has an **absolute advantage** over Pioneerland. A country has an absolute advantage if its output per unit of inputs of all goods is higher than that of another country. With an absolute advantage, isn't it the case that Magic Empire can outsell Pioneerland in all markets? Why, if Magic Kingdom can produce all goods using fewer factors of production than Pioneerland, does it pay Magic Empire to buy *anything* from Pioneerland?

The answer is that the cost of production in terms of the factors of production employed is irrelevant for determining the gains from trade. It does not matter how much labour, land and capital are required to produce 1 tonne of grain or a car. What matters is how many cars must be given up to produce more grain or how much grain must be given up to produce more cars. That is, what matters is the opportunity cost of one good in terms of the other good. Magic Empire may have an absolute advantage in the production of all things, but it cannot have a comparative advantage in the production of all goods. The statement that the opportunity cost of cars in Magic Empire is lower than in Pioneerland is identical to the statement that the opportunity cost of grain is higher in Magic Empire than in Pioneerland. Thus *whenever opportunity costs diverge, everyone has a comparative advantage in something.* All countries can gain from international trade.

R E V I E W

When countries have divergent opportunity costs, they can gain from international trade. Each country can buy goods and services from another country at a lower opportunity cost than it can produce them for itself. Gains arise when each country increases its production of those goods and services in which it has a comparative advantage (of goods and services that it can produce at an opportunity cost that is lower than that of other countries) and exchanges some of its production for that of other countries. All countries gain from international trade. Everyone has a comparative advantage at something. ■

Gains from Trade in Reality

The gains from trade that we have studied between Pioneerland and Magic Empire in grain and cars are taking place in a model economy — in an economy that we have imagined. But these same events occur every minute of every day in real world economies. Indeed, the model is a close caricature of Australian trade, if we swap Australia for Pioneerland. Australia also exports resource-based goods like grain and buys manufactured goods like cars from the rest of the world. The model leads to the hypothesis that the basis for Australia's trade pattern is the difference in opportunity costs of producing 'grain' or 'cars' between Australia and the rest of the world. In other words, our production possibility frontier is a different shape. Why?

Australia's frontier is a different shape because we have a very different set of endowments of the factors of production — in particular, more natural resources compared with labour. For example, consider the differences in population density in Australia compared with our trading partners in Asia. In Australia there are on average two people for every square kilometre. In Indonesia there are over 90, in the Philippines about 200, in Korea over 400, in Taiwan about 550 and over 300 in Japan. As a consequence these economies will have very different-looking production possibilities from ours. These differences, combined with their proximity, and their rapid growth has meant two things for Australia. First, it has swung our trade towards Asia, away from Europe. Second, it has encouraged our specialization in resource-intensive exports. Thus the model helps explain some of the significant features of Australia's trade that we identified earlier.

Therefore much of the international trade that we see in the real world takes precisely the form of the trade that we have studied in our model of the world economy. But as we saw earlier in this chapter, a lot of world trade involves the international exchange of manufactured goods. Those sorts of goods account for 70 to 80 per cent of world merchandise trade and, what is more, the rich countries trade these goods intensively with each other. They get about 85 per cent of their manufactured goods from other rich countries. That is, despite their apparently similar resource endowments and therefore despite what we would expect would be a similar-looking set of production possibilities, two-way trade in the same product groups is the dominant form of trade. Even within Australia's manufactured goods sectors, there is a lot of two-way trade. The phenomenon occurs not only in the manufactured goods trades but also in services trades. As we saw earlier, Australia is both a large exporter and importer in many of the traded service categories. Why do countries exchange the same types of goods or services with each other? Can our model of international trade explain such exchange?

A Puzzle

At first thought it seems puzzling that countries would exchange similar manufactured commodities. Let's look at an example of one manufactured good where this sort of trade in the world market is important, namely, cars. They are produced using technologies that are widely available. Skilled workers to operate car plants and the finance to build them would be available in high-income countries. If all the big car-consuming high-income countries have car plants of the same technology with enough skilled workers to operate them, why don't they produce all the cars that their consumers want to buy? Why doesn't the international car trade disappear?

Diversity of Tastes The first part of the answer to the puzzle is that people have a tremendous diversity of tastes. Some people prefer sports cars like old MGs, some prefer a big limousine, some prefer a station wagon, and some a hatchback. In addition to the size and type of car, there are many other dimensions in which cars vary. Some have low fuel consumption, some have high performance, some are spacious and comfortable, some have a large boot, some have four-wheel drive, some have front-wheel drive, some have a manual transmission, some have automatic transmission, some are durable, and so on. People's preferences vary across all these dimensions.

The tremendous diversity in tastes for cars means that people would be dissatisfied if they were forced to consume from a limited range of standardized cars. People value variety and are willing to pay for it in the marketplace.

But the puzzle is not solved. Even if people value variety why can't car plants in each consuming country pump out the mix of cars that will sell in the marketplace?

Economies of Scale The second part of the answer to the puzzle is economies of scale. *Economies of scale* are the tendency, present in many manufacturing processes, for the average cost of production to be lower the larger the scale of production. In such situations, larger and larger production runs lead to ever lower average production costs. Many manufactured goods, including cars, experience economies of scale. For example, if a car producer makes only a few hundred (or perhaps a few thousand) cars of a particular type and design, it has to use production techniques that are much more labour-intensive and much less automated that those actually employed to make hundreds and thousands of cars of a particular model. With low production runs and labour-intensive production techniques, costs are high. With very large production runs and automated assembly lines, production costs are much lower. But to obtain lower costs, the automated assembly lines have to produce a large number of cars.

It is the combination of diversity of tastes and economies of scale that produces such a large amount of international trade in similar commodities. Diversity of tastes and the willingness to pay for variety do not guarantee that variety will be available. It could simply be too expensive to provide a highly diversified range of different types of cars, for example.

Relying on their domestic market alone, car producers may not be able to reap economies of scale. Although the current variety of cars could be made available, it would be at a very high price, and perhaps at a price that no one would be willing to pay. But with international trade, each manufacturer of cars has the whole world market to serve. Each producer specializes in a limited range of products and then sells its output to the entire world market. This arrangement enables large production runs on the most popular cars and feasible production runs even on the most customized cars demanded only by a handful of people.

The situation in the market for cars is also present in many other industries, especially those producing specialized machinery and specialized machine tools. International exchange of similar but slightly differentiated manufactured goods is a highly profitable activity.

This type of trade can be understood in terms of the model of international trade that we studied earlier. Although we might think of cars as a single commodity, we have to think of each type of car as a different good. Different countries then have a comparative advantage in some of these 'goods', in this case because of economies of scale associated with specialization in producing just a few types. Scale economies are the source of the differences in opportunity costs between countries.

Can we also answer the question of which types of cars will be exported and which type imported by a particular country? In the previous model we saw that the Magic Empire exports grain and imports cars. The origins of its comparative advantage in grain lay in the shape of its production possibility frontier. Now in the car trade we have identified the source of differences in opportunity cost and therefore the origins of international trade. But what determines the directions of trade?

Suppose there are just two types of cars, big four-wheel drive ones and small front-wheel drive ones. Suppose that a bigger share of consumers in Pioneerland prefer big four-wheel drives and more consumers in Magic Empire like small cars, even if the prices of those cars were just the same. Will this pattern of domestic preferences affect the pattern of trade? If there were no costs of shipping cars between the two countries, it would not matter where cars of a particular type were made. The pattern of trade will reflect the accidents of history. But there are costs of transport. In that case, a car maker is more likely to specialize in production of cars preferred in the home market. The reason is that the car producer will then be able to undercut imports with a lower delivered cost of a car. In this example, Pioneerland will export big four-wheel drives and Magic Empire will export small front-wheel drives. The patterns of trade in these sorts of goods are therefore influenced by the diversity of tastes between countries.

This section has highlighted the influence of a number of factors on differences in opportunity costs between countries. A wide range of conditions in the exporting economy are important for its international competitiveness and pattern of trade. The Reading Between the Lines (pp. 516–517) provides an illustration of the range of factors that can be important.

Where Will the Jobs Come From?

You can see that comparative advantage and international trade bring gains regardless of the goods being traded. It's true that if we increase our imports of cars and produce fewer cars ourselves, jobs in our car-producing sector disappear. Or if we import more textiles and clothing from low-wage countries, then jobs in those sectors also disappear. The question is often asked, if we open up even more to international trade, will there be new jobs to take the place of the jobs lost? The answer is that jobs in other sectors, sectors in which we do have a comparative advantage and from which we export to the rest of the world, will expand. *After the adjustment is completed*, those whose jobs have been lost will find employment in the expanding sectors, and usually at higher wages than they had before. As a result of the gains from trade, those workers will also be able to buy imported goods at prices lower than those available before trade.

The adjustment process is not immediate. For example, an increase in car imports and the corresponding relative decline in domestic car production will not immediately bring greater wealth to the displaced car workers. It takes time to find a better job. It takes time for the export sectors to recognize the new opportunities and to increase their capacity. Thus the gains from specialization and trade are available in the long run. In the short run, adjustment costs are borne by groups associated with sectors where we do not have a comparative advantage.

The short-run costs of making the transition have been a barrier to capturing the long-run benefits of trade. Partly because of the costs of adjustment to changing patterns of international trade, and for other reasons, governments intervene in international trade, restricting its volume. Let's examine what happens when governments restrict international trade. We'll contrast restricted trade with free trade. We'll see that free trade brings the greatest possible benefits. We'll also see why, in spite of the benefits of free trade, governments restrict trade.

Trade Restrictions

Governments restrict international trade in order to protect domestic industries from foreign competition. The restriction of international trade is called **protection.** There are two methods of protection that are employed by governments:

- Tariffs
- Non-tariff barriers

A **tariff** is a tax that is imposed by the importing country when a good crosses an international boundary. A **non-tariff barrier** is any action other than a tariff that restricts international trade. Examples of non-tariff barriers are quantitative restrictions on the volume of imports.

The History of Protection

Protection became an issue in Australia in the days of the gold rushes of the 1850s. The gold discoveries caused the population of Australia to double from 0.5 million in 1852 to 1 million in 1858. The deposits were depleted in the 1860s and people began to worry about the employment of the much bigger workforce. Even then they were asking 'where will the jobs come from?'. Protection was proposed as one solution. The idea was to promote local manufacturing by protecting it from competition from imports. At that time, each State — or colony, as they were then — had power over its own tariffs, including tariffs on imports from the other States. There was a fierce debate over this issue, which carried on until Federation in 1901. At that time, barriers to trade between the colonies were removed and a common set of external tariffs was adopted. Despite the earlier debates, a consensus during the first decade of Federation emerged in favour of protection.

From Federation until the end of World War II, tariffs rose steadily. The average tariff in 1909 was just over 20 per cent. By 1940, the average general tariff on imports was about 60 per cent (al-

Sources of Comparative Advantage

Rugby Starts the Ball Rolling in NZ

While David Ricardo's theory of comparative advantage explained why England should stick to producing cloth and Portugal to making wine, the latest trade model tells us why the New Zealand All Blacks are the world's best at rugby.

The ideas of current trade and competition guru, Harvard's Michael Porter, have been embraced in a book by Graham Crocombe, co-authored by Michael Enright and by Porter, called *Upgrading New Zealand's Competitive Advantage*.

According to Porter, companies gain and sustain competitive advantage in global markets through the dynamic process of improvement, innovation and upgrading. In Porter's 'complete system', there are four broad determinants of the competitive advantage of a nation's companies:

- Factor conditions, or the inputs necessary to compete in an industry, such as natural resources, labour, capital and infrastructure.
- Demand conditions, where a sophisticated and critical local market forces companies to lift their performance and also anticipate foreign demand.
- Relate and supporting industries, or so-called clusters of world class related industries providing technology, ideas, individuals and potential competitors.
- Company strategy, structure and rivalry, which encompasses the conditions in a nation governing how companies are created, organized and managed (deriving from culture, religion, education and social norms) and the nature of domestic rivalry.

As well, there are two other variables. Chance events (such as pure invention, technological breakthrough, wars) and government (at all levels) can influence the four other determinants, which are mutually dependent and re-inforcing.

National advantage comes when this dynamic system is unique. The task for NZ business is to find those industries where it can build and sustain broad-based competitive advantage.

All so esoteric, isn't it? But to get the message across to the punters, Crocombe uses the example of NZ rugby to show the complete system at work and how a small country can achieve competitive advantage.

'Why, for over a century, have the All Blacks been the team to beat in international competition?', he asks.

First, the basic factors.

NZ has a mild winter and rugby can be played throughout the year. It has thousands of rugby fields. And NZ men are larger than average, which helps in contact sports.

But these factors (while necessary) are not sufficient for sustained international dominance and advanced factors are far more important.

For instance, Crocombe says the level of rugby knowledge in NZ is 'unparalleled' and it is a leader in specialist sports medicine and training. As well, it is innovative on the field (e.g. the 'rolling maul'). In terms of inputs, then, NZ is favourably positioned for success.

Although a small country, NZ has favourable demand conditions when it comes to rugby. Rugby is the national sport (indeed, 'a passion'), which leads to a very knowledgeable spectator base which can be a 'harsh judge of performance and warm rewarder of excellence'.

From this pre-eminence, a number of related and supporting industries have developed. Media coverage is unparalleled and relatively large markets for rugby videos, books and specialist magazines have developed. International matches and coaching clinics attract tourists. Rugby supplier, Canterbury International, is a major exporter. The rival code, Rugby League, provides a source of new ideas.

Naturally, the passion for rugby helps it attract and motivate the country's most talented sportsmen. An All Black is a national hero. There are clear incentives for teams and individuals to excel.

The intensity of the rivalry in New Zealand rugby (at all levels, schools, clubs, provincial and international) is both fierce and unique.

Put all this together and the determinants work together as a system in NZ rugby. Crocombe argues that this system is most difficult for other nations to replicate and therefore provides the basis for sustained international success.

***Australian Financial Review*, Thursday, 23 May 1991**
By Tom Dusevic

The Essence of the Story

- New Zealand is internationally competitive in rugby (union).
- Analysts have identified the sources of New Zealand's rugby competitiveness in terms of a group of variables, all of which reinforce each other.
- The variables include factor endowments, demand conditions, corporate organization and the nature of domestic competition, characteristics of related industries, chance and government influence.
- The challenge for a business sector that wants to be internationally competitive is to seek out those parts of the economy in which similar systems operate.

Background and Analysis

- The argument in the article is that a relatively large endowment of those 'factors of production' used intensively in the production of some good or service is necessary for an economy to be internationally competitive in that activity. But it is not enough.
- In the case of rugby, the relevant factors include the weather conditions (which, in the case of this outdoor game, permit the time to play and practice), the size and strength of the potential players and the stock of capital which is specific to the sector (like playing fields). But these relatively rich endowments of factors used intensively in the building up of rugby teams are not enough for those teams to be winners.
- Also required is a set of domestic demand characteristics that encourage local firms to produce a product which is exportable, that is, which has characteristics in demand by foreign suppliers. In the rugby setting, this means a capacity to define and then identify players of high quality.

  In addition, the suppliers of complementary inputs need to be efficient.
- Competitiveness in one sector can be undone by lack of efficiency elsewhere. If inputs to the sector are of high cost compared with those of international competitors, then the sector itself will lose competitiveness. Examples in the rugby case are the skills in the sports medicine sector in New Zealand, and the effectiveness of the local media in generating and spreading ideas about the game.
- Domestic competition is also important. The competitive pressure makes exporters more efficient and more likely to be internationally competitive. Potential international competitiveness is therefore not frittered away by inefficient production processes. Therefore the All Blacks are more competitive because the national side is selected from a vigorous domestic competition.
- The article does not spell out the roles that can be played by governments. One example might be the efficient provision of infrastructure which would not otherwise be provided, for example, in the rugby case, publicly available playing fields or coaching time in the school system.
- In summary, particular factor endowments are necessary for international competitiveness in particular sectors. The existence of those endowments remains a reasonable predictor of the pattern of competitiveness and therefore specialization in production. But those endowments are not enough. Other conditions, especially features of domestic demand, the international competitiveness of suppliers of complementary products and the degree of competition in the domestic market, are also important. Governments can also have an influence.

though imports from Britain were subject to a preferential tariff by this time of about 30 per cent).

There was a switch in protection policy prompted by the fluctuations in the trade balance in the early 1950s, which are evident in Fig. 36.3. The rise in wool and other raw materials prices associated with the Korean War pushed exports up in 1950/51. Imports responded to the growth in income, and to the rise in domestic prices, but with a lag. They boomed in 1951/52 just as export revenues fell. The Menzies government feared a balance of payments crisis and imposed direct controls on imports. These quantitative controls were implemented by a system of licences. Licencing remained until 1960. When it was dropped, tariffs were raised to replace the protective effects of the licences.

The steady rise in tariffs since Federation, the use of licencing and its replacement by further tariff increases are illustrations of the highly protectionist stance in Australia over that long period. Australia became one of the most highly protected rich countries, especially after the 1920s.

The mid-1970s were a turning point in Australia's protection history. All tariffs were cut by 25 per cent in 1973 and further cuts in the later 1970s brought the total reduction to 40 per cent.

Despite the cuts in the general tariff level, some industries received offsetting support from non-tariff barriers. From 1974, quotas were applied to the imports of textiles, clothing, footwear and motor vehicles. The level of protection received by these industries increased by a large amount as a result of the imposition of quotas. Quotas on motor vehicle imports were removed in April 1988 and in a major policy statement in May 1988, a plan was announced to phase out quotas on imports of textiles, clothing and footwear (TCF) by July 1995.

May 1988 marked an acceleration of the change in Australian tariff policy. At that time, tariffs in excess of 15 per cent on imports other than the TCF or motor vehicles sector were to be reduced to 15 per cent and tariffs between 15 and 10 per cent were to be reduced to 10 per cent in a series of steps by 1992.

There was a further acceleration of change in March 1991. In a major Industry Statement, the government announced that tariff cuts were to be extended beyond 1992, with both 15 and 10 per cent tariffs to be cut to 5 per cent by 1996. In addition, the tariff on motor vehicle imports was to be cut from 40 per cent in 1989/90 to 15 per cent by the year 2000. The end of TCF quotas was brought forward to 1993 and tariffs were to fall from the range of 30 to 50 per cent in 1992 to a range of 10 to 25 per cent by the year 2000.

We can illustrate the impact of these policy shifts after we have looked at how tariffs and quotas work.

How Tariffs Work

To determine the effects of tariffs and the effects of eliminating tariffs, such as the process under way as a result of the May 1988 and March 1991 policy statements, we need to know how tariffs work. To analyse them, we're going to return to the example of trade between Pioneerland and Magic Empire. We're going to work with this model economy rather than the real economy for two reasons. First, we'll find it easier to understand the basic principles involved in the working of tariffs and their elimination. Second, we are less emotionally involved in the affairs of the Pioneers and Magicians than we are in our own affairs. Thus we shall be able to be more

Figure 36.8 The Effects of a Tariff

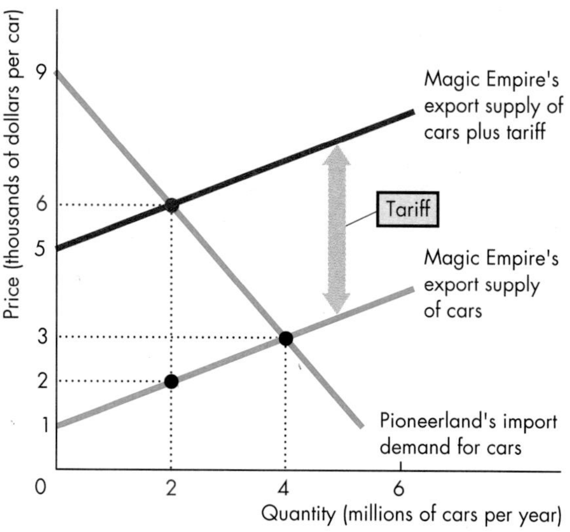

Pioneerland imposes a tariff on car imports from Magic Empire. The tariff increases the price that Pioneers have to pay for cars. It shifts the supply curve of cars in Pioneerland upward. The distance between the original supply curve and the new one is the amount of the tariff. The price of cars in Pioneerland increases and the quantity of cars imported decreases. The government of Pioneerland collects a tariff revenue of $4000 per car — a total of $8 billion on the 2 million cars imported. Pioneerland's exports of grain decrease since Magic Empire now has a lower income from its exports of cars.

clear-headed in focusing on the purely economic aspects of the tariff issue.

Let's return, then, to Pioneerland and Magic Empire. Suppose that these two countries are trading cars and grain in exactly the same way that we analysed before. Magic Empire exports cars and Pioneerland exports grain. The volume of car imports into Pioneerland is 4 million a year and cars are selling on the world market for 3 tonnes of grain. Let's suppose that grain costs $1000 dollars a tonne so, equivalently, cars are selling for $3000. Figure 36.8 illustrates this situation. The volume of trade in cars and their price are determined at the point of intersection of Magic Empire's export supply curve of cars and Pioneerland's import demand curve for cars.

Now suppose that the government of Pioneerland, perhaps under pressure from car producers, decides to impose a tariff on imported cars. In particular, suppose that a tariff of $4000 per car is imposed. (This is a huge tariff, but the car producers of Pioneerland are pretty fed up with competition from Magic Empire.) What happens?

The first part of the answer is obtained by studying the effects on the supply of cars in Pioneerland. Cars are no longer going to be available at the Magic Empire export supply price. The tariff of $4000 must be added to that price — the amount paid to the government of Pioneerland on each car imported. As a consequence, the supply curve in Pioneerland shifts in the manner shown in Fig. 36.8. The new supply curve becomes that labelled 'Magic Empire's export supply of cars plus tariff'. The vertical distance between Magic Empire's export supply curve and the new supply curve is the tariff imposed by the government of Pioneerland.

The next part of the answer is found by determining the new equilibrium. The new equilibrium occurs where the new supply curve intersects Pioneerland's import demand curve for cars. That equilibrium is at a price of $6000 a car and with 2 million cars a year being imported. Imports fall from 4 million to 2 million cars a year. At the higher price of $6000 a car, domestic car producers increase their production. Domestic grain production decreases to free up the resources for the expanded car industry.

The total expenditure on imported cars by the Pioneers is $6000 a car multiplied by the 2 million cars imported ($12 billion). But not all of that money goes to the Magicians. They receive $2000 a car or $4 billion for the 2 million cars. The difference — $4000 a car or a total of $8 billion for the 2 million cars — is collected by the government of Pioneerland as tariff revenue.

Obviously, the government of Pioneerland is happy with this situation. It is now collecting $8 billion that it didn't have before. But what about the Pioneers? How do they view the new situation? The demand curve tells us the maximum price that a buyer is willing to pay for one more unit of a good. As you can see from Pioneerland's import demand curve for cars, if one more car could be imported, someone would be willing to pay almost $6000 for it. Magic Empire's export supply curve of cars tells us the minimum price at which additional cars are available. As you can see, one additional car would be supplied by Magic Empire for a price only slightly more than $2000. Thus since someone is willing to pay almost $6000 for a car and someone is willing to supply one for little more than $2000, there is obviously a gain to be had from trading an extra car. In fact, there are gains to be had — willingness to pay exceeds the minimum supply price — all the way up to 4 million cars a year. Only when 4 million cars are being traded is the maximum price that a Pioneer is willing to pay equal to the minimum price that is acceptable to a Magician. Thus restricting international trade reduces the gains from international trade.

It is easy to see that the tariff has lowered Pioneerland's total import bill. With free trade, Pioneerland was paying $3000 a car and buying 4 million cars a year from Magic Empire. Thus the total import bill was $12 billion a year. With a tariff, Pioneerland's imports have been cut to 2 million cars a year and the price paid to Magic Empire has also been cut to only $2000 a car. Thus the import bill has been cut to $4 billion a year. Doesn't this fact mean that Pioneerland's balance of trade has changed? Is Pioneerland now importing less than it is exporting?

To answer that question, we need to work out what's happening in Magic Empire. We've just seen that the price that Magic Empire receives for cars has fallen from $3000 to $2000 a car. Thus the price of cars in Magic Empire has fallen. But the relative price of grain has increased. With free trade, the Magicians could buy 3 tonnes of grain for one car. Now they can buy only 2 tonnes for a car. With a higher price of grain, the quantity demanded by the Magicians decreases. As a result, Magic Empire's import of grain declines. But so does Pioneerland's export of grain. In fact, Pioneerland's grain industry suffers from two sources. First, there is a decrease in the quantity of grain sold to Magic Empire. Second, there is increased competition for inputs from the now expanded car industry. Thus the tariff leads to a contraction in the scale of the grain industry in Pioneerland. The tariff hurts the export sector.

It seems paradoxical at first that a country imposing a tariff on cars would hurt its own export industry, lowering its exports of grain. It may help to think of it this way: foreigners buy grain with the money they make from exporting cars. If they export fewer cars, they cannot afford to buy as much grain. In fact, in the absence of any international borrowing and lending, Magic Empire has to cut its imports of grain by exactly the same amount as the loss in revenue from its export of cars. Grain imports into Magic Empire will be cut back to a value of $4 billion, the amount that can be paid for by the new lower revenue from Magic Empire's car exports. Thus trade is still balanced in this post-tariff situation. Although the tariff has cut imports, it has also cut exports, and the cut in the value of exports is exactly equal to the cut in the value of imports. The tariff, therefore, has no effect on the balance of trade — it simply reduces the volume of trade.

The result that we have just derived is perhaps one of the most misunderstood aspects of international economics. On countless occasions, politicians and others have called for tariffs in order to remove a balance of trade deficit or have argued that lowering tariffs would produce a balance of trade deficit. They reach this conclusion by failing to work out all the implications of a tariff. Because a tariff raises the price of imports and cuts imports, the easy conclusion is that the tariff strengthens the balance of trade. But the tariff also changes the *volume* of exports as well. The equilibrium effects of a tariff are to reduce the volume of trade in both directions and by the same value on each side of the equation. The balance of trade itself is left unaffected.

Learning the Hard Way The analysis we have just worked through leads to the clear conclusion that tariffs cut both imports and exports and make the country worse off. Australians have not found that conclusion easy to accept. Time and again in our history we have imposed high tariff barriers on international trade so that Australia became one of the most protectionist high-income countries in the world. Whenever tariff barriers are increased, trade collapses. The most vivid historical example of this interaction of tariffs and trade occurred during the Great Depression years of the early 1930s when the world's largest trading nation, the United States, increased its tariffs, setting up a retaliatory round of tariff changes in many countries. The consequence of this period of very high tariffs was an almost complete disappearance of world trade.

Let's now turn our attention to the other range of protectionist weapons — non-tariff barriers.

Non-tariff Barriers

There are two important forms of non-tariff barriers:

- Quotas
- Voluntary export restraints

A **quota** is a quantitative restriction on the import of a particular good. It specifies the maximum amount of the good that may be imported in a given period of time. A **voluntary export restraint** is an agreement between two governments in which the government of the exporting country agrees to restrain the volume of its own exports. Voluntary export restraints are often called VERs.

Non-tariff barriers have become important features of international trading arrangements in the period since World War II and there is now general agreement that non-tariff barriers are a more severe impediment to international trade than tariffs.

It is difficult to quantify the effects of non-tariff barriers in a way that makes them easy to compare with tariffs, but some studies have attempted to do just that. Such studies try to assess the tariff rate that would restrict trade by the same amount as the non-tariff barriers do. With such calculations, non-tariff barriers and tariffs can be added together to assess the total amount of protection. As we saw earlier, quotas have been important instruments of protection in the motor vehicle industry and at the start of the 1990s were still important in the textile, clothing and footwear industries in Australia. In the textile and clothing industries in the rest of the world, an international agreement called the Multifibre Arrangement establishes quotas on a wide range of textile products. The trade in agricultural products is also subject to extensive quotas. Voluntary export restraints are particularly important in regulating the international trade in cars between Japan and North America.

How Quotas and VERs Work

To understand how non-tariff barriers affect international trade, let's return to the example of trade between Pioneerland and Magic Empire. Suppose that

Figure 36.9 The Effects of a Quota

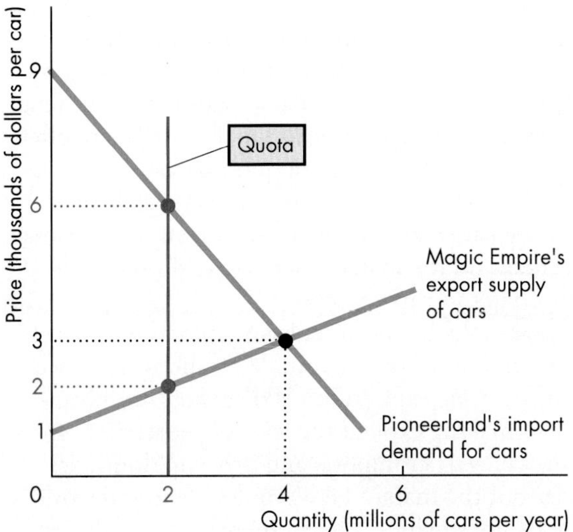

Pioneerland imposes a quota of 2 million cars a year on car imports from Magic Empire. That quantity appears as the vertical line marked 'Quota'. Since the quantity of cars supplied by Magic Empire is restricted to 2 million, the price at which those cars will be traded increases to $6000. Importing cars is profitable since Magic Empire is willing to supply cars at $2000 each. There is competition for import quotas since they are so profitable.

Pioneerland imposes a quota on car imports. Specifically, suppose that the quota restricts imports to not more than 2 million cars a year. What are the effects of this action?

The answer is found in Fig. 36.9. The quota is shown by the vertical red line at 2 million cars a year. Since it is illegal to import more than that number of cars, car importers buy only that quantity from Magic Empire producers. They pay $2000 a car to the Magic Empire producer. But what do they sell their cars for? The answer is $6000 each. Since the import supply of cars is restricted to 2 million cars a year, people with cars for sale will be able to get $6000 each for them. The quantity of cars imported equals the quantity determined by the quota.

Importing cars is now obviously a profitable business. An importer gets $6000 for an item that costs only $2000. Therefore the right to import is extremely valuable and the existence of that rent creates very strong incentives to compete for the right to import. This sort of competition is an example of 'rent seeking'. It will take different forms depending on the method used to allocate the rights to import. In Australia at the start of the 1990s the only remaining quotas are those on textiles, clothing and footwear. Those quotas used to be allocated between importing firms according to the level of imports in previous periods. But starting in 1982, increasing proportions of the quota were allocated by auction. Importers had to bid for the right. For example, in Fig. 36.9, importers would bid up to $4000 for the right to import a car.

The value of imports — the amount paid to Magic Empire — declines to $4 billion, exactly the same as in the case of the tariff. Thus with lower incomes from car exports and with a higher price of grain, Magicians cut back on their imports of grain in exactly the same way they did under a tariff.

The key difference between a quota and a tariff lies in who gets the profit represented by the difference between the import supply price and the domestic selling price. In the case of a tariff, that difference goes to the government. In the case of a quota, that difference goes to the person who has the right to import under the quota regulations. If, however, the quotas are auctioned, then the government also gets the difference between the import supply price and the domestic selling price. The quota is just like a tariff except that the government regulates in the first instance the volume of imports rather than the tax rate on imports.

A voluntary export restraint is like a quota except that the quotas are allocated to each exporting country, not to importers. The effects of VERs are similar to those of quotas but differ from them in that the gap between the domestic price and the export price is captured not by domestic importers but by the foreign exporter. The government of the exporting country has to establish procedures for allocating the restricted volume of exports among its producers. The incentives to seek rents leads to competition within that export quota allocation system.

R E V I E W

When a country opens itself up to international trade and trades freely at world market prices, it expands its consumption possibilities. When trade is restricted, some of the gains from trade are lost. A country may be better off with restricted trade than with no trade but not as well off as it could be if it engaged in free trade. A tariff reduces the volume of imports, but it also reduces the volume of exports. Under both free trade and restricted trade (and without international borrowing and lending), the value of imports equals the value of exports. With restricted trade, both the total value of exports and the total value of imports are lower than under free trade, but trade is still balanced. ■

Why Quotas and VERs Might Be Preferred to Tariffs

At first sight, it seems puzzling that countries would ever want to use quotas and even more puzzling that they would want to use voluntary export restraints. We have seen that the same domestic price and the same quantity of imports can be achieved by using any of the three devices for restricting trade. However, a tariff provides the government with a source of revenue; a quota, which is allocated administratively and not auctioned, provides domestic importers with an economic profit; and a voluntary export restraint provides the foreigner with an economic profit. Why, then, would a country use a quota or a voluntary export restraint rather than a tariff?

There are two possible reasons. First, a government can use quotas to reward its political supporters. Under a quota, licences to import become tremendously lucrative. So the government bestows riches on the people to whom it gives licences to import. Second, quotas are more precise instruments for holding down the volume of imports. As demand fluctuates, the domestic price of the good fluctuates but not the quantity of imports. You can see this implication of a quota by going back to Fig. 36.9. Suppose that the demand for imports fluctuates. With a quota, these demand fluctuations simply produce fluctuations in the domestic price of the import but no change in the volume of imports. When imports are subject to a tariff, fluctuations in demand lead to no change in the domestic price but to large changes in the volume of imports. Thus if for some reason the government wants to control the quantity of imports and does not care about fluctuations in the domestic price as domestic demand fluctuates, it will use a quota.

Why would a government use voluntary export restraints rather than a tariff or quota? The government may want to avoid a tariff or quota war with another country. If one country imposes a tariff or a quota, that might encourage another country to impose a similar tariff or quota on the exports of the first country. Such a tariff and quota war would result in a much smaller volume of trade and a much worse outcome for both countries. A voluntary export restraint can be viewed as a way of achieving trade restrictions to protect domestic industries but with some kind of compensation to encourage the foreign country to accept that situation and not retaliate with its own restrictions. Finally, VERs are often the only form of trade restriction that can be legally entered into under the terms of the General Agreement on Tariffs and Trade (GATT), an international agreement on the management of world trade (described later in this chapter).

Australia has been replacing quotas with tariffs as instruments of protection. Why the switch back to tariffs? One explanation is that there are advantages in making explicit the level of protection. A quota will restrict imports and drive up domestic prices, but the margin between domestic and world prices is not obvious. When there's a tariff, the gap is obvious. Also there was a desire to transfer the quota rents to the community, via the government, instead of leaving them in the hands of importers. The interim step in achieving both objectives was to auction the right to import.

Dumping

Dumping is the selling of a good in a foreign market for a lower price than in the domestic market. Dumping could occur for a number of reasons. It could reflect the disposal of an occasional surplus. It could reflect the predatory intentions of a foreign supplier who wants to drive out local competitors then exploit monopoly power. It could reflect monopoly power of an exporter in its home market, where it can charge a high price, and its willingness to meet the competition in the export market by charging a lower price. A low price may be all the foreign markets will bear, given the availability of substitutes. Under GATT, dumping is illegal and anti-dumping duties may be imposed on foreign producers. The danger is that the anti-dumping provisions can be abused and become another instrument of protection. In Australia, if local producers can show that (a) imported goods are being sold below their 'normal value', which is usually the price of that good in the exporter's domestic market and (b) they have been injured by dumping, then an anti-dumping duty (tariff) can be imposed. Australia has taken more anti-dumping actions than most other countries. Examples in 1988 and 1989 included cement from Korea, coloured pencils from Brazil, evaporated milk from Canada and outboard motors from Belgium. There were five cases of the imposition of new anti-dumping duties in 1989/90 but there were still over 20 instances of duties from previous years still in force. Not only have there been a lot of anti-dumping cases in Australia, but also the anti-dumping duties which applied in these cases were also relatively high compared with the long-run targets for cutting tariff levels. Anti-dumping actions could lead to significant protection for Australia industry, contrary to the objective of industry policy.

Measurement of the Effects of Protection

Australian economists have made a large contribution to the analysis of the effects of protection and the measurement of those effects. In particular, W.M. Corden's pioneering work on the theory and measurement of protection, and its application to the measurement of the extent of protection in Australia, has had an important impact on the economic analysis of protection policy.

In our analysis of the effects of protection, we saw how the imposition of a tariff or quota leads to higher prices for the imported product in the protected market than in the world market. In Figs 36.8 and 36.9, this gap was $4000. The protective effect of a tariff or quota, or a combination of both, is summarized in a measure called the **nominal rate of protection**, which is the percentage by which the domestic price exceeds the border price. In Figs 36.8 and 36.9, the nominal rate of protection is 200 per cent (that is, 4000/2000, since the world price is $2000). This rate is a measure of the impact of protection on consumers of cars.

Firms, as we saw, gain from the protection applied to the goods they produce. The nominal rate tells us the percentage by which the producers' gross receipts from current output are increased by protection. But in a real economy, the production relationships are much more complicated than the ones we depicted in our model. There are many more products and some are not sold to consumers but are used as inputs into the production of other products. Therefore producers of cars gain from protection of their products. But if they use inputs that are also protected, then they will lose. What matters to producers is not just the effects of protection on their outputs but the net effect of protection on the difference between their gross receipts and the cost of their inputs, that is, their value added. That depends on the protection on their products relative to the protection on their inputs. This impact is measured by the **effective rate of protection**, a concept developed by Corden. It measures the percentage change in value added that results from protection.

Why is this concept important? Factors of production will flow between sectors of the economy according to their rewards. Protection policy that has a big effect on value added in a particular industry compared with others will attract resources. Therefore the allocation of resources is determined by the relative effective rates of protection. It is the differences in the effective rates of protection which are important. For example, the effective rate of protection for underwear in 1989/90 was about 250 per cent. For the mining industry, the effective rate was nearly minus 2 per cent. That means that in the mining industry, inflated costs of inputs due to protection caused the value added to shrink.

Effective rates are plotted in Fig. 36.10. These rates are calculated by the Industry Commission (IC) and reported each year in its annual report. The method used by the IC includes the effect on value added of a wide range of industry policies, not only tariffs and quotas but also subsidies and other policies which affect prices. As a result, the IC measures are called rates of 'assistance', a broader concept than the rate of protection. Figure 36.10 illustrates the trend in protection which we identified earlier. By the year 2000, the average effective rate is planned to be 5 per cent.

The trend since 1973 is a reversal of the pattern of high protection for the previous 70 years. Why was trade restricted for so long and why have those restrictions been relaxed in the last two decades in Australia?

Why is International Trade Restricted?

There are many reasons why international trade is restricted. We've just seen one reason — to offset the effects of dumping. Even in these cases, it does not obviously benefit a country to protect itself from cheap foreign imports. However, more generally, we've seen that international trade benefits a country by raising its consumption possibilities. Why do we restrict international trade when such restrictions lower our consumption possibilities?

The key reason is that consumption possibilities increase *on the average,* but not everyone shares in the gain and some people even lose. Free trade brings benefits to some and costs to others, with total benefits exceeding total costs. This uneven distribution of costs and benefits is the main reason why a more liberal international trade is hard to achieve. In

Figure 36.10 Effective Rates of Assistance to Manufacturing, 1968-2001[a]

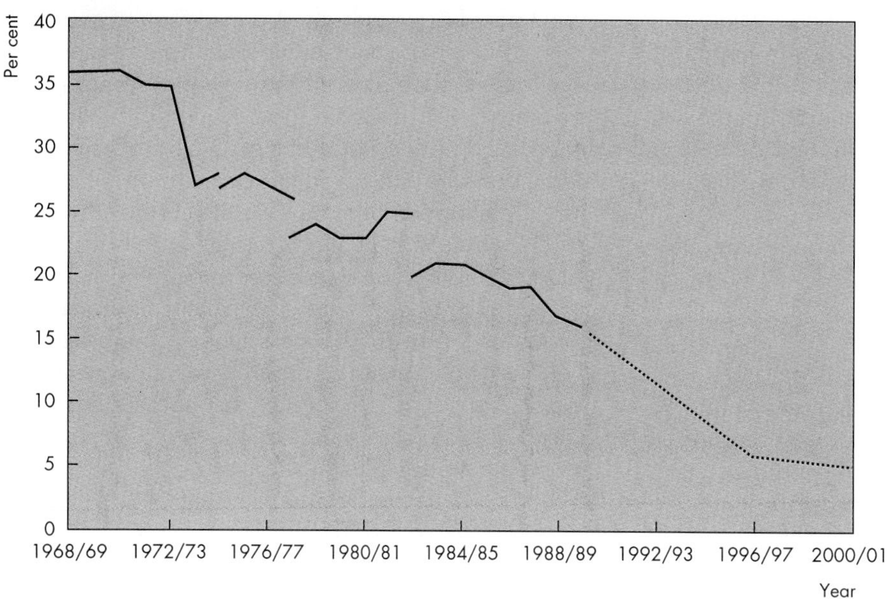

The effective rate of assistance to manufacturing has fallen since 1973. By the end of the century the average effective rate is planned to be 5 per cent. The trend since 1973 has been a decline, but the rate of decline accelerated at the end of the 1980s.

[a] The breaks in the series are due to changes in the weights used to form the averages.

Source: Industry Commission, *Annual Reports*, various issues.

this circumstance, the model of the supply of and demand for regulation can also be applied to the case of protection.

Returning now to Pioneerland and Magic Empire, we can see that the benefits from free trade accrue to all the producers of grain and to those producers of cars who would not have to bear the costs of adjusting to a smaller car industry. The costs of free trade are borne by those car producers and their employees who have to move and become grain producers. The number of people who gain will, in general, be enormous compared with the number who lose. Because the number who gain will be large, the gain per person will be rather small. The loss per person to those who bear the loss will be large. Since the loss that falls on those who bear it is large, it will pay those people to incur considerable expense in order to lobby against free trade. On the other hand, it will not pay those who gain to organize to achieve free trade. The gain for any one person is too small for that person to spend much time or money on a political organization to achieve free trade. The loss from free trade will be seen as being so great by those bearing that loss that they will find it profitable to join a political organization to prevent free trade. Each group is optimizing — weighing benefits against costs and choosing the best action for themselves. The anti-free trade group will, however, undertake a larger quantity of political lobbying than the pro-free trade group.

Compensating Losers

If, in total, the gains from free international trade exceed the losses, why don't those who gain compensate those who lose so that everyone is in favour of free trade? To some degree, such compensation does take place. It also takes place indirectly as a consequence of unemployment compensation arrangements. But, as a rule, only limited attempts are made to compensate those who lose from free international trade. The main reason why full compensation is not attempted is that the costs of identifying the losers would be enormous. Also, it would never be clear whether or not a person who has fallen on hard times is suffering because of free trade or for other reasons, and perhaps for reasons largely under the control of the individual. Furthermore, some people who look like losers at one time may, in fact, wind up gaining. The young textile industry worker who loses her job cutting cloth and becomes a computer assembly worker resents the loss of work and the need to move. But a year or two later, looking back on events, she can count herself fortunate. She's made a move that has increased her income permanently and given her greater job security.

It is partly because we do not, in general, compensate the losers from free international trade that protection has been such a popular feature of our national economic and political life.

The Political Outcome

The political outcome that emerges from this activity is one in which a modest amount of restriction on international trade occurs and is maintained. Politicians react to constituencies pressing for protection and find it necessary, in order to get re-elected, to support legislative programmes that protect those constituencies. The producers of protected goods are far more vocal and much more sensitive swing-voters than the consumers of those goods. The political outcome, therefore, leans in the direction of maintaining protection.

We have seen that even in the year 2000, there will still be some residual protection in Australian manufacturing, particularly in industries like textiles, clothing and footwear (TCF), as well as motor vehicles. Why have these industries been relatively highly protected and why is that protection lingering? In terms of our model of the political market, they have been effective in demanding assistance. There are a couple of reasons why this is so. The TCF industries employ relatively large numbers of workers who tend to be concentrated in a small number of regions in Australia, even located in marginal electorates. This leads to stronger support from Federal and State governments. Second, the TCF sector is labour-intensive. More people therefore face greater costs of adjustment in a rapid movement to free trade. As a result, the industries attract sympathy from the rest of the community. The rewards from a lobbying campaign are greater than for some other manufacturing industries.

Why is the overall level of protection falling in Australia? The hypothesis from our political model of the market for protection would be that the losing groups from protection increased their level of political activity. The losers include consumers, who are large in number and for whom the average cost is small. As a result, they are not likely to have become a potent political force. In the discussion of the effects of motor vehicle protection in Pioneerland on that economy's grain producers, we saw that other producers also lose from protection. In particular, we saw that in Australia, the big losers have been the miners. Producer groups like these are more likely to be politically effective than consumer groups. Why? Because they are smaller and because the average gain from action is likely to be greater. An important contributor to the incentive for these groups to act has been the increasing awareness in Australia of the costs of protection to consumers and, more importantly, of the costs of protection of some producers to others.

Industry Policy Debates in the 1990s

Now that protection cuts have been announced, what policy instruments will become the focus of attention of industry lobby groups seeking assistance? One possibility is that while less attention will be given to protection, more attention will be given to reducing input costs in order to raise value added. Tariff cuts will help on that side as well. In addition, industry lobby groups will give attention to the costs of other services they consume, such as transport and communications. These are sectors of the economy that are highly regulated and in which there are government-owned firms. In the 1990s, therefore issues about regulation, privatization and competition policy are likely to become relatively more important than issues of protection. Another topic of debate is the tax system. Questions asked are the extent to which lower rates would stimulate investment and whether particular industries should receive preferential treatment.

International Agreements

The temptation on governments to impose tariffs is a strong one. First, tariffs provide revenue to the government. Second, they enable the government to satisfy special interest groups in import-competing industries. But, as we've seen, free international trade brings enormous benefits. While on the one hand free trade brings benefits, on the other hand governments face the political temptation to restrict trade. There is also the possibility that other countries will retaliate in kind. These circumstances have led countries to enter into a multilateral agreement whose goal is the enhancement of free international trade: the **General Agreement on Tariffs and Trade**. GATT is an international agreement designed to limit government intervention to restrict international trade. It was negotiated immediately after World War II and was signed in October 1947. Its goal is to establish agreed rules that maintain and promote a liberal trading order and to provide an organization to settle disputes when countries allegedly break those agreed rules. The Secretariat of GATT itself is a small organization located in Geneva, Switzerland.

What is the rationale for an international agreement? We saw in our analysis of the effects of protection how car industry protection in Pioneerland hurts the export sector in that economy. The grain exporters have the incentive to lobby against protection. That incentive will be increased if the anti-protection lobby in Pioneerland can simultaneously cut protection applying in other countries against its exports of agricultural products. That is, the incentive to lobby will be greater if the cut in car industry protection in Pioneerland occurs as part of an agreement to cut all protection in other countries too. The agreement to move at the same time in more than one country therefore mobilizes the countervailing force of the export groups in the political market in each economy and makes a movement to free trade a more likely outcome.

Since the formation of GATT, several rounds of negotiations have taken place that have resulted in general tariff reductions. One of these, the Kennedy Round that began in the early 1960s, resulted in large tariff cuts. Further tariff cuts resulted from the Tokyo Round that took place between 1973 and 1979. The most recent GATT tariff round, the Uruguay Round, has been more ambitious in attempting to achieve less restricted trade in services and agricultural products. These were items which were previously regarded as too politically sensitive to make them worth including on the GATT agenda. Australia has taken a strong interest in the Uruguay Round. The desire to have some influence in those negotiations, in order to try to cut protection of agricultural markets in our trading partners, has also been a contributor to the cuts in protection for the manufacturing sector in Australia. It certainly helps Australia when making a strong argument against protection in GATT.

In addition to the multilateral agreements under GATT, some important bilateral and regional trade agreements lower trade barriers between the countries involved. One of these is the agreement on Closer Economic Relations (CER) between Australia and New Zealand. An important new bilateral agreement is the Canada–United States Free Trade Agreement which may be extended to include Mexico in a North America Free Trade Agreement (NAFTA). Another important arrangement of this type is Europe 1992. **Europe 1992** is the process of creating an integrated, single market economy among the member nations of the European Communities. After 1992, the European Communities will be the largest, single, integrated economy in the world, larger even than the United States, and even bigger if some of the other European economies join it.

■ You've now seen how free international trade enables everyone to gain from increased specialization and exchange. By producing goods in which we have a comparative advantage and exchanging some of our own production for that of others, we expand our consumption possibilities. Placing impediments on that exchange when it crosses national borders restricts the extent to which we can gain from specialization and exchange. By opening our country up to free international trade, the market for the things that we sell expands and the price rises. The market for the things that we buy also expands and the price falls. All countries gain from free international trade. As a consequence of price adjustments, and in the absence of international borrowing and lending, the value of imports adjusts to equal the value of exports.

In the next chapter, we're going to study the ways in which international trade is financed and also learn why international borrowing and lending that permits unbalanced international trade arises. We'll discover the forces that determine the Australian balance of payments.

S U M M A R Y

Patterns and Trends in International Trade

Australia is a net exporter of agricultural products and minerals. In recent years the exports of manufactures and services have grown more rapidly, but Australia is still a net importer of these items. The share of manufactures in imports is similar to that in other high-income economies, but their share in Australian exports is much less. The explanation lies in Australian comparative advantage relative to our trading partners, particularly those in Asia. Asia has dramatically displaced Europe, and the United Kingdom in particular, as a market for Australian exports during the last three decades. (pp. 503–508)

Opportunity Cost and Comparative Advantage

When opportunity costs differ between countries, the country with the lowest opportunity cost of producing a good is said to have a comparative advantage in that good. Comparative advantage is the source of the gains from international trade. A country may have an absolute advantage, but cannot have a comparative advantage, in the production of all goods. Every country has a comparative advantage in something. (pp. 508–509)

The Gains from Trade

Countries can gain from trade if their opportunity costs differ. Through trade, each country can obtain goods at a lower opportunity cost than it could if it produced all goods at home. Trading allows consumption to exceed production. By specializing in producing the good in which it has a comparative advantage and then trading some of that good for imports, a country can consume at points outside its production possibility frontier. Indeed, every country can do that.

In the absence of international borrowing and lending, trade is balanced as prices adjust to reflect the international supply and demand for goods. The world price is established at the level that balances the production and consumption plans of the trading parties. At the equilibrium price, trade is balanced and domestic consumption plans exactly match a combination of domestic production and international trade.

Comparative advantage explains the enormous volume and diversity of international trade that takes place in the world. But much trade takes the form of exchanging similar goods for each other — one type of car for another. Such trade arises because of economies of scale in the face of diversified tastes. By specializing in producing a few goods, having long production runs and then trading those goods internationally, consumers in all countries can enjoy greater diversity of products at lower prices. (pp. 509–515)

Trade Restrictions

A country can restrict international trade by imposing tariffs or non-tariff barriers, such as import quotas and voluntary export restraints. All trade restrictions raise the domestic price of imported goods, lower the volume of imports, and reduce the total value of imports. They also reduce the total value of exports by the same amount as the reduction in the value of imports.

All trade restrictions create a gap between the domestic price and the foreign supply price of an import. In the case of a tariff, that gap is the tariff revenue collected by the government. But the government raises no revenue from a quota. Instead, domestic importers who have a licence to import increase their profit. A voluntary export restraint by a trading partner has similar effects to a quota on imports, except that a higher price is received by the foreign exporter rather than the domestic importer.

The trend in Australia is towards low levels of protection by the year 2000, belatedly matching the levels in other rich countries. There is still some variation around this trend, in particular, some residual higher levels of protection for industries like textiles, clothing, footwear, motor vehicles and parts. The shift in policy dates from the first major tariff cuts in Australia's history in 1973. The explanation for the reform lies in the greater awareness among losing groups of the burdens placed on them by protection and their levels of political activity. Governments have restricted trade because restrictions help the producers of the protected commodity and the workers employed by those producers. Because their gain is large enough and the loss per consumer small enough, the political equilibrium can favour restricted trade. These factors explain the variation around the downward trend in protection. (pp. 515–526)

K E Y T E R M S

Absolute advantage, p. 512
Balance of trade, p. 503
Comparative advantage, p. 509
Dumping, p. 522
Effective rate of protection, p. 523
Europe 1992, p. 526
Exports, p. 503
General Agreement on Tariffs and Trade, p. 525
Imports, p. 503
Net exporter, p. 503
Net importer, p. 503
Nominal rate of protection, p. 523
Non-tariff barriers (NTBs), p. 515
Protection, p. 515
Quota, p. 520
Tariff, p. 515
Voluntary export restraint, p. 520

PROBLEMS

1 a) Using Fig. 36.4, calculate the opportunity cost of cars in Pioneerland at the point on the production possibility frontier at which 4 million cars are produced.
   b) Using Fig. 36.5, calculate the opportunity cost of a car in Magic Empire when it produces 8 million cars.
   c) With no trade, Pioneerland produces 4 million cars and Magic Empire produces 8 million cars. Which country has a comparative advantage in the production of cars?
   d) If there is no trade between Pioneerland and Magic Empire, how much grain is consumed and how many cars are bought in each country?

2 Suppose that the two countries in problem 1 trade freely.
   a) Which country exports grain?
   b) What adjustments will be made to the amount of each good produced by each country?
   c) What adjustment will be made to the amount of each good consumed by each country?
   d) What can you say about the price of a car under free trade?

3 Compare the total production of each good produced in problems 1 and 2.

4 Compare the situation in problems 1 and 2 with that analysed in this chapter. Why does Magic Empire export cars in the chapter but import them in problem 2?

5 The following figure depicts the international market for wheat.

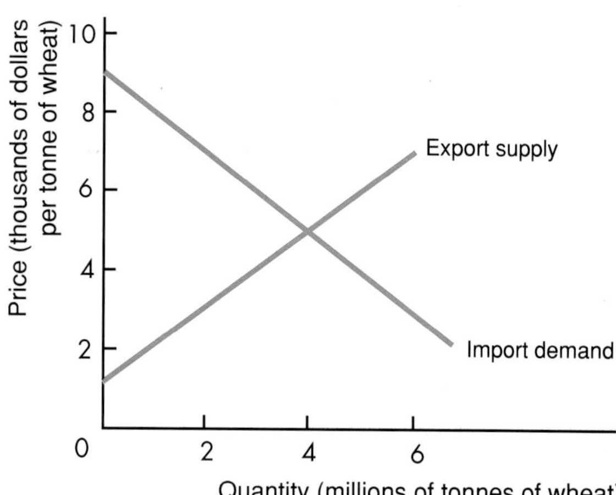

   a) What is the world price of wheat if there is free trade between these countries?
   b) If the country that imports wheat imposes a tariff of $2000 per tonne, what is the world price of wheat and what quantity of wheat gets traded internationally? What is the price of wheat in the importing country? Calculate the tariff revenue.

6 If the importing country in problem 5(a) imposes a quota of 3 million tonnes, what is the price of wheat in the importing country? What is the revenue from the quota and who gets this revenue?

7 If the exporting country in problem 5(a) imposes a voluntary export restraint (VER) of 3 million tonnes of wheat, what is the world price of wheat? What is the revenue of wheat growers in the exporting country? Which country gains from the VER?

8 Suppose that the exporting country in problem 5(a) subsidizes production by paying its farmers $1000 a tonne for wheat harvested.
   a) What is the price of wheat in the importing country?
   b) What action might wheat growers in the importing country take? Why?

Chapter 37

The Balance of Payments and the Dollar

After studying this chapter, you will be able to:

- Explain how international trade is financed.
- Describe a country's balance of payments accounts.
- Explain what determines the amount of international borrowing and lending.
- Explain why Australia is an international borrower.
- Explain the links between the exchange rate and the balance of payments.

For Sale: Australia

For most of us, economic life centres on the city and country in which we live. But for an increasing number of chief executive officers, marketing managers, accountants, lawyers and many other professionals, the economy is the world — there is a truly global economy. In this global economy, Australian assets are increasingly the target of foreign investors. More and more often, it seems, foreigners are buying Australian assets, sometimes to the dismay of local residents. In recent years, some very well known Australian brands have been bought by foreign firms. Speedo, the cossie manufacturer, has been bought by a British firm. And related companies that make Stubbies, King Gee, Pelaco and Formfit clothing have been sold to the American frozen cakes and dessert giant Sara Lee. Driza-Bone was sold to a British firm. Local beers, Castlemaine, Tooheys and Cascade, are owned by a New Zealand firm and Fosters beer is part-owned by a Japanese firm. Even Vegemite is now owned by a foreign company. US interests own very large tracts of Australian farming and grazing land, and while Japanese interests own considerably less land, it is concentrated in tourist locations. What is causing this foreign invasion of Australia? On the other side of the coin, Rupert Murdoch, whose News Corp Ltd grew from relatively small Australian roots, now runs a truly global media and publishing empire. Other Australian companies, Dunlop Pacific and BHP to name just two, are heavily involved in foreign operations. Why do some Australian firms undertake so much of their business in other countries? 'Dollar hurts exporters' read a headline in the *Sydney Morning Herald*, 10 April 1991. The story went on to say that the strong dollar had made 'exporters worse off than other producers, providing little incentive to invest in export industries'. Further, the dollar 'had significantly encouraged imports'. Why is a strong dollar a boon to importers but a problem for exporters? Does the strength of the dollar affect our balance of trade with the rest of the world? 'Dollar plunges on news of trade deficit' or 'Dollar surges on news of trade surplus'. Headlines such as these are commonplace and seem to be telling us that the strength of our dollar depends, in part, on the balance of our international trade. Does the balance of international trade affect the strength of the dollar? Or is it the other way around — that is, is it that the strength of the dollar affects our international trade balance?

In this chapter, we investigate the questions that have just been posed. We begin by reviewing the way in which international trade is financed and study the structure of the accounts in which our international activities are recorded — the balance of payment accounts. We study the forces that determine the balance of our international trade and the scale of our international borrowing and lending. We also study the links between the balance of trade and the exchange rate.

Financing International Trade

When David Jones imports Toshiba television sets from Japan, it does not pay for those TVs with Australian dollars — it uses Japanese yen. When Benetton imports designer sweaters from Italy, it pays for them using Italian lire, and when China buys wool from Australia, it pays for it using Australian dollars. Whenever we buy goods from another country, we use the currency of that country in order to make the transaction. It doesn't make any difference what the item being traded is — it can be a consumer good or a capital good, a building or even a firm.

We're going to study the markets in which transactions in money, in different types of currency, take place. But first we're going to look at the scale of international trading and borrowing and lending and at the way in which we keep our records of these transactions. Such records are called the balance of payments accounts.

Balance of Payments Accounts

A country's **balance of payments accounts** record all transactions between domestic residents and foreigners. Credit entries are used to record exports of goods and services, income receivable and financial transactions involving either a reduction in the country's holdings of foreign financial assets or an increase in its foreign liabilities, because each activity generates a flow of funds into the country. Debit entries are used to record imports of goods and services, income payable and financial transactions involving either an increase in foreign financial assets or a decrease in foreign liabilities, all activities with an associated outflow of funds. The accounts adopt standard **double-entry bookkeeping** procedures in which every transaction is represented by two entries of equal and opposite value. For example, a transaction involving the purchase of a foreign good will introduce into the accounts a record of the imported good (a debit entry) and a record of the means of payment, possibly by running down foreign assets (a credit entry). In keeping with this double-entry bookkeeping system, in Australia, there are two accounts. These are:

- Current account
- Capital account

Current Account The **current account** records:

- Balance on goods and services, or net exports
- Net income
- Net unrequited transfers

The *balance on goods and services* is related to what we called net exports in Chapter 25 and the balance of trade in Chapter 36. In fact it is both these things and more. Broadly speaking, it is the difference between the value of goods and services exported to foreigners and value of goods and services imported from foreigners. But the accounts break the balance on goods and services into two components: the *balance on merchandise trade* — these are exports and imports of visible goods such as cars, wheat, wool, computers and television sets — and *net services.* As we discussed in Chapter 36, net services are the balance of trade in invisible goods, such as airline trips, cargo freight, and banking and insurance services.

Net income is the difference between income earned by Australian residents from foreigners (recorded as credits) and income earned by foreigners from Australians (recorded as debits). It includes investment income, dividends and interest, for example, other property income, rent and royalties, and labour income.

Net unrequited transfers are recorded when resources (goods, services or financial assets) are provided without something of economic value being provided in return. For example, if Australia grants foreign aid to a country, in the form of a gift of real resources, the gift is treated as an export (a credit) and an offsetting entry (a debit) is recorded in unrequited transfers. In addition to foreign aid, migrant's transfers, gifts, donations, pensions and taxes are included.

Figure 37.1 shows the behaviour of the components of the current account since 1953/54 in part (a), and the overall current account balance in part (b). All individual items are expressed as percentages of GDP. The figure shows that the Australian current account has consistently been in deficit. However, only in recent years is this a result of imports of goods exceeding exports of goods. Up to the early

1980s, the merchandise trade account was usually in surplus. But the deficits on the net services, net income and net unrequited transfers accounts were sufficient to convert the current account into a consistent deficit. It is clear from the figure, however, that most of the variations in the current account were the result of variations in the merchandise trade balance.

Net income is the most consistently large negative component of the current account. Reflecting payments to foreigners from investment in Australia and loans made to Australians, it has grown rapidly over the 1980s as the interest payments on the outstanding external debt have grown.

Figure 37.1 Components of the Current Account

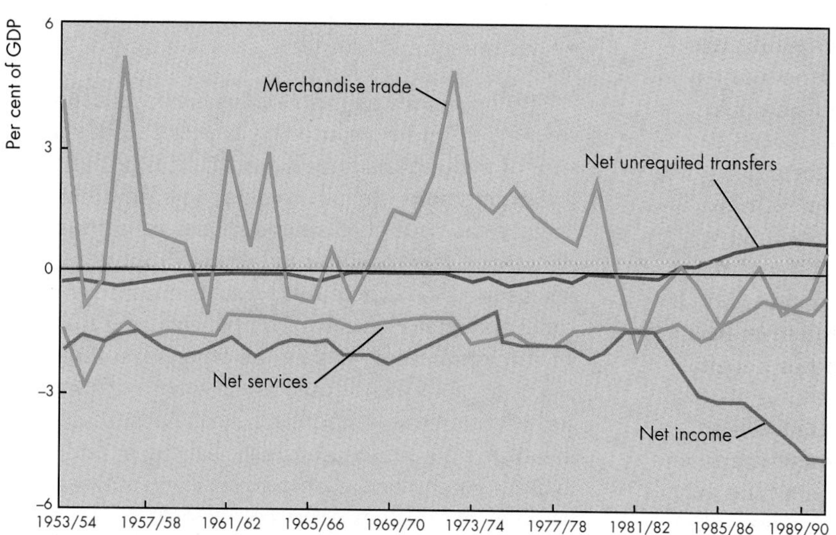

(a) The components of the current account

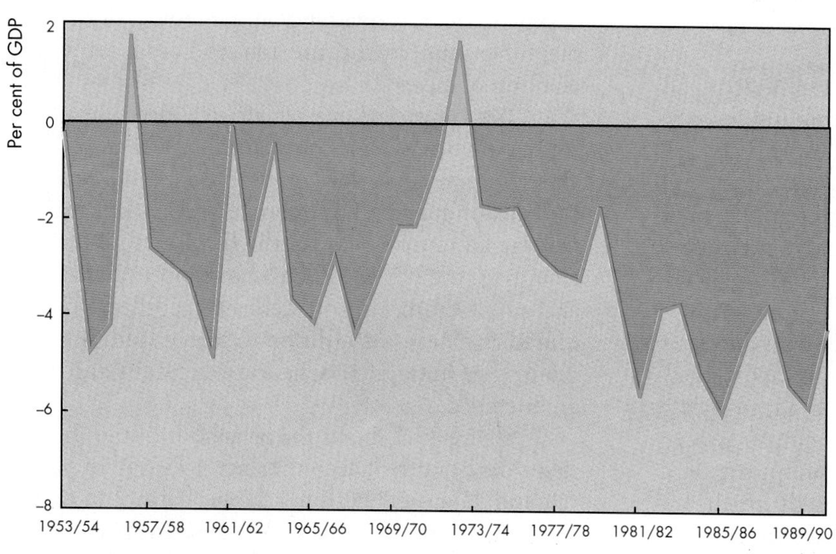

(b) The current account balance

For the entire period shown, variations in the current account are mainly caused by variations in the balance on merchandise trade (see part (a)). For most of the period up to the early 1980s, the merchandise trade account was in surplus. Since then the account has turned into deficit. A consistently large component of the current account has been net income. Reflecting income returned to foreigners derived from investments in Australia, it has grown rapidly over the 1980s as the interest bill on outstanding foreign debt has grown. Net services have also been consistently in deficit, although this has decreased in recent years. The transformation of unrequited transfers from a deficit to a surplus reflects the influence of the business immigration programme.

Overall, the Australian current account has consistently been in deficit (see part (b)). This deficit has shown a tendency to grow as a percentage of GDP over the 1980s.

Source: ABS, *Balance of Payments, Australia,* 1988/89, No. 5303.0; *Balance of Payments, Australia,* June Quarter, 1991, ABS No. 5302.

Unrequited transfers have recently turned from deficit to surplus, mainly due to the business immigration programme attracting income into the country.

Capital Account The **capital account** records all financial transactions — capital flows — involving Australian claims on and liabilities to foreigners. Because the balance of payments accounts adopt the convention of double-entry bookkeeping, the capital account records how the transactions occurring in the current account are financed. If the current account was in surplus, that is, Australia generated more current income from its external transactions than it paid out, then it would be acquiring claims on foreigners or accumulating foreign assets through a capital outflow, and the capital account would be in deficit. In effect, Australia would be lending to the rest of the world so that they can, on balance, buy our goods and services. Conversely, if the current account was in deficit, that is, Australia was on balance paying out more current income to foreigners than it was earning, then the capital account must be in surplus. Australia would be accumulating liabilities or claims by foreigners on Australian assets through a capital inflow. In this case, the rest of the world would be lending to Australia so that it could, on balance, purchase foreign goods. Thus the capital account records all international borrowing and lending transactions. The *capital account* balance records the difference between the amount that a country lends to and borrows from the rest of the world.

The capital account records the sector from which capital flows originate. These are:

- The balance on official transactions
- The balance on non-official or private transactions

The accounts also record the direction of the capital flows: inward for Australians borrowing from foreigners and outwards for Australians lending to foreigners. And the type of capital: direct investment (where equity is traded), portfolio investment (which is mainly loans) and other forms of investment.

The **balance on official transactions** is broken down into those transactions arising from the general government and those from the Reserve Bank. The general government sector covers all borrowing and lending by Commonwealth, State and Local governments, and their instrumentalities. Public business enterprises are excluded here, and are included in the non-official sector. We will discuss the Reserve Bank's role below.

The **non-official balance** includes the transactions of everyone else. An important distinction is between inward and outward flows of capital. Thus the accounts record foreign investment in Australia and Australian investment abroad.

Figure 37.2 shows the behaviour of the components of the capital account since 1953/54 (in part (a)), excluding the Reserve Bank transactions, and the overall balance (in part (b)). For most of the period, Australian investment abroad has been minimal, while foreign investment in Australia has been substantial. Its effect on the overall balance on the capital account is evident, with the consistent surplus generated on the capital account indicating a sustained increase in liabilities owed to foreigners. In recent years the flow of capital from Australia to foreign countries has increased markedly and this has slowed the rate of growth of the capital account surplus as a share of GDP.

Borrowing abroad by the government sector has contributed to the capital account surplus on only a few occasions — the late 1970s and mid-1980s, for example.

Australia's Balance of Payments Accounts

Table 37.1 shows the Australian balance of payments accounts in 1990/91. As you can see from the table, Australia had a current account deficit of $15.8 billion in 1990/91, down from a deficit of $22.3 billion in 1989/90. Even though we exported more than we imported, and had a surplus on unrequited transfers, we paid a lot more investment income to foreigners than we received from them.

How did we pay for our current account deficit? We paid by borrowing from abroad. The capital account tells us by how much. In 1990/91, we borrowed a total of $13.3 billion from the rest of the world. $18.1 billion was borrowed by private firms or individuals, but offsetting this was $1.8 billion lent by the various levels of government. In addition, a total of $1.5 billion was lent by private domestic citizens to foreigners, so the net amount of borrowing by private firms and individuals and the government was $14.8 billion.

The Reserve Bank purchased $1.5 billion in foreign assets. Most of these transactions were in foreign exchange, although the Bank can trade in gold, SDRs — a currency established by the International Monetary Fund (IMF) and used for transactions between governments — and other facilities held at the IMF. A negative number means that the Reserve Bank has been selling Australian dollars and buying

Figure 37.2 Components of the Capital Account

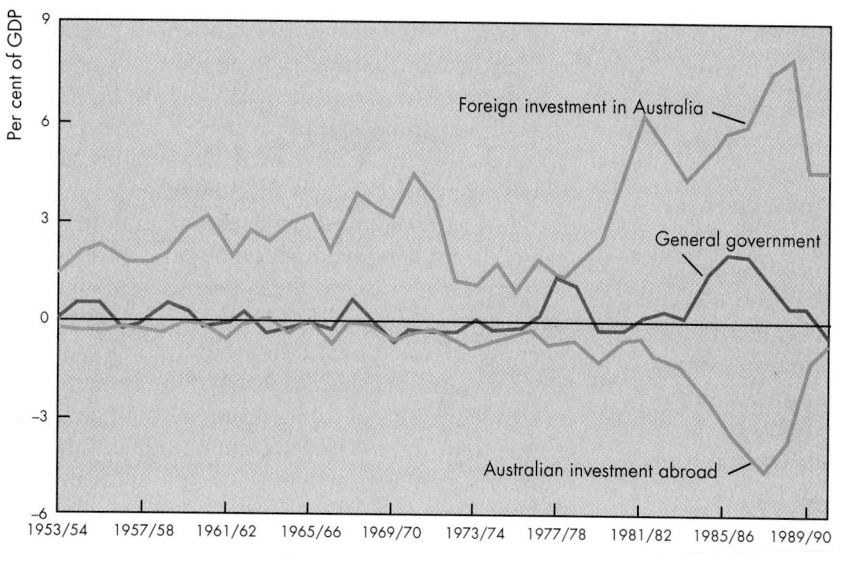

(a) The components of the capital account

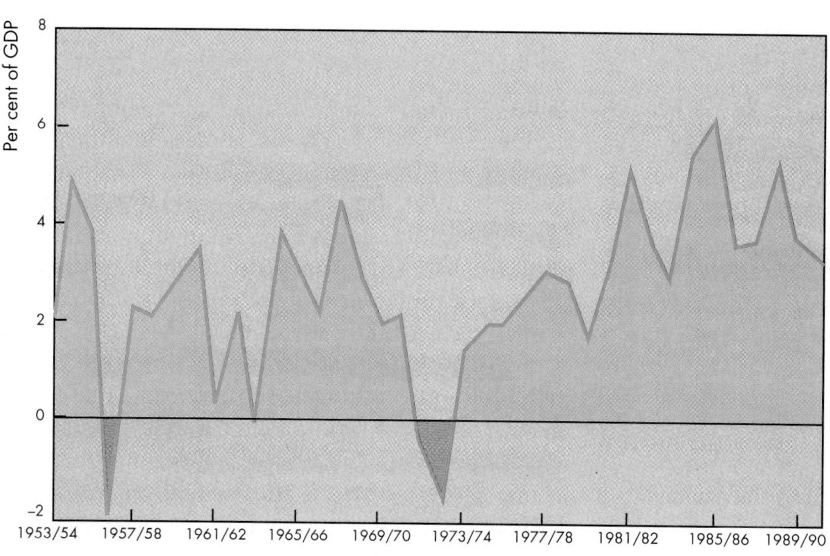

(b) The capital account balance

The influence of foreign investment coming into Australia is apparent (see part (a)). It has been large and positive, indicating an accumulation of Australian liabilities owed to foreigners. Since the early 1980s, a flow of investment from Australians to foreign countries has resulted in the capital account surplus stabilizing at about 3 per cent of GDP (see part (b)). The government sector has contributed to the foreign capital inflow on only a few occasions.

Source: See Fig. 37.1.

foreign currencies. This was a practice necessary when Australia operated under a fixed exchange rate. When the dollar was floated, the need for interventions in the foreign exchange market was removed. However, the Reserve Bank attempts to dampen some of the fluctuations that occur in exchange rates and so intervenes in the foreign exchange market regularly.

The final figure in the table is interesting, because its size varies a lot. It is the *balancing item.* Recall that the balance of payments accounts record all transactions as a double entry. For example, if some Australian goods are sold to a Japanese firm, which pays the exporter with a note drawn on their Japanese bank, the accounts record a credit for the exports but a debit,

Table 37.1 Australia's Balance of Payments Accounts in 1990/91 (billions of dollars)

Current account		
Imports of goods and services	–49.3	
Exports of goods and services	51.8	
Balance on merchandise trade		2.5
Net services		–3.5
Net income		–17.3
Net unrequited transfers		2.5
Current account balance		–15.8
Capital account		
General government	–1.8	
Reserve Bank	–1.5	
Total official		–3.3
Foreign investment in Australia	18.1	
Australian investment abroad	–1.5	
Total non-official		16.6
Capital account balance		13.3
Balancing item		2.5

Source: ABS, *Balance of Payments, Australia*, June Quarter 1991, 5302.0.

of equal value, for the accumulation of foreign assets received as payment. Since we are able to collect data on exports and imports and data on capital flows separately, we should be able to arrive separately at a measure of either the current account or the capital account. These numbers should be equal as every current account transaction is backed by an offsetting capital account transaction. In practice they are not because of errors in reporting transactions, or because of differences in timing. Payment may well be received some time after the exports have been delivered. The balancing item is included to ensure the accounts add up. In 1990/91 the balancing item was $2.5 billion. But in 1989/90 it was $7.7 billion, or more than one-third of the current account deficit.

The numbers in Table 37.1 give you a snapshot of the balance of payments accounts in 1990/91. In that year, Australia had a balance of trade deficit, a current account deficit and a large capital account surplus. It also had a deficit on the official transactions of the Reserve Bank. Was 1990/91 a typical year?

This question is answered in Fig. 37.3, which shows the history of Australia's balance of payments accounts going back to 1950/51. As you can see in part (a), the current account balance is almost a mirror image of the capital account balance. The balancing item has grown significantly in recent years. Part (b) shows the net transactions of the Reserve Bank. It is apparent that the Reserve Bank has been, and continues to be, actively involved in the foreign exchange market. Where the Bank's net transactions are negative, it is selling Australian dollars and buying foreign exchange as it increases the supply of Australian dollar-denominated assets and attempts to hold down the value of the dollar. Where the net transactions are positive, it is selling foreign exchange and buying Australian dollars as it attempts to hold up the dollar's value. The Reserve Bank operated to hold up the value of the Australian dollar in the periods 1973/74 to 1979/80 and 1984/85 to 1985/86. It acted to hold down the value of the dollar in the periods 1980/81 to 1983/84 and 1986/87 to 1990/91.

When the Reserve Bank is selling Australian dollars, its holding of foreign exchange reserves increases. When the Bank is buying Australian dollars, it is running down official reserves.

Let's try to deepen our understanding of the balance of payments accounts and the way in which they are linked together by considering the income and expenditure, borrowing and lending, and the bank account of an individual.

Individual Analogy An individual's current account records the income from supplying the services of factors of production and the expenditure on goods and services. Consider, for example, Heather. In 1989 she earned an income of $25,000. Heather has $10,000 worth of investments that earned her an income of $1000. Heather's current account shows an income of $26,000. Heather spent $18,000 buying goods and services for consumption. She also bought a new house, which cost her $60,000. So Heather's total expenditure was $78,000. The difference between her expenditure and income is $52,000 ($78,000 minus $26,000). This amount is Heather's current account deficit.

To pay for expenditure of $52,000 in excess of her income, Heather either has to use the money that she has in the bank or take out a loan. In fact

Figure 37.3 The Balance of Payments

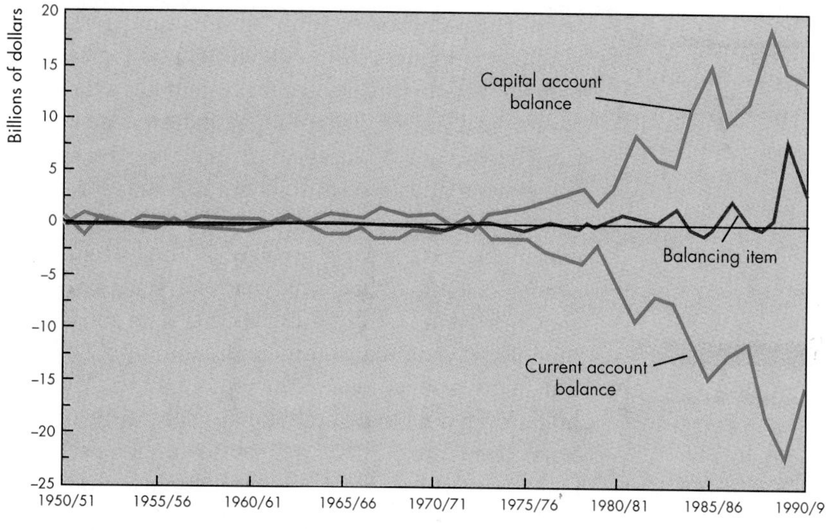

(a) Current and capital account balances

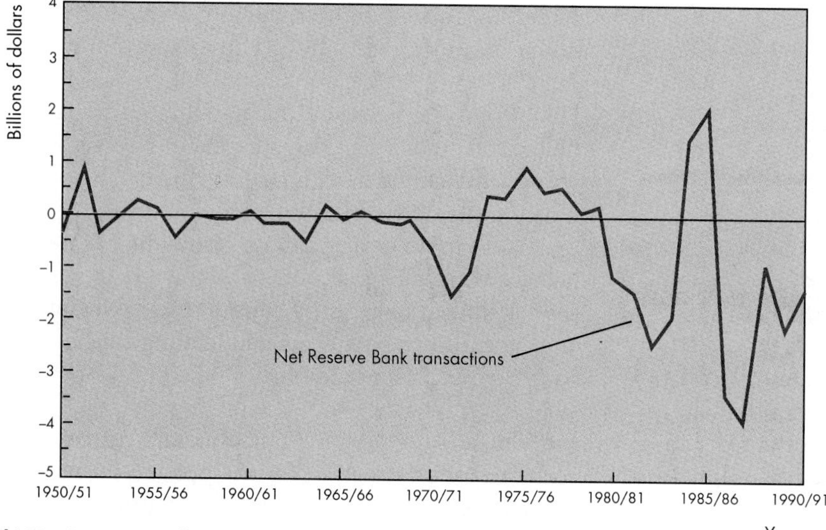

(b) Net Reserve Bank transactions

Part (a) shows the capital and current account balances, along with the balancing item. The current account balance is typically negative, but it has grown substantially negative over the 1980s. The capital account balance mirrors the current account balance, and is typically positive, indicating a net capital inflow.

Part (b) shows the net transactions of the Reserve Bank. When the net transactions are positive, as in 1973/74 to 1979/80 and 1984/85 to 1985/86, the Bank is selling foreign exchange and buying Australian dollars as it holds up the value of the currency. When the Bank's transactions are negative, as in the periods 1980/81 to 1983/84 and 1986/87 to 1990/91, the Reserve Bank is selling Australian dollars and buying foreign currency as it attempts to hold down the value of the dollar.

Source: See Fig. 37.1.

Heather took a mortgage of $50,000 to help buy her house. This was the only borrowing that Heather did, so her capital account surplus was $50,000.

With a current account deficit of $52,000 and a capital account surplus of $50,000, Heather is still $2000 short. She got that $2000 from her own bank account. Her cash holdings decreased by $2000.

Heather's supply of factors of production is analogous to a country's supply of exports. Her purchases of goods and services, including her purchase of a house, are analogous to a country's imports. Heather's mortgage — borrowing from someone else — is analogous to a country's foreign borrowing. Heather's purchase of the house is analogous to a country's foreign investment. The change in her own bank account is analogous to the change in the country's official reserves.

What determines a country's current account balance and its scale of international borrowing or lending?

International Borrowing and Lending

A country may be a

- *Net borrower* or a *Net lender*

and a

- *Debtor nation* or a *Creditor nation*

Borrower or Lender A country that is borrowing more from the rest of the world than it is lending to it is called a **net borrower**. Similarly, a **net lender** is a country that is lending more to the rest of the world than it is borrowing from it. A net borrower might be going deeper into debt or might simply be reducing its net assets held in the rest of the world. The total stock of foreign investment determines whether a country is a debtor or creditor.

Debtor or Creditor A **debtor nation** is a country that during its entire history has borrowed more from the rest of the world than it has lent to it. It has a stock of outstanding debt to the rest of the world that exceeds the stock of its own claims on the rest of the world. A **creditor nation** is a country that has invested more in the rest of the world than other countries have invested in it. Australia is a debtor nation. A debtor nation is one whose net receipts of interest on debt are negative: payments made by the country exceed its interest receipts.

Because Australia has been a borrower from foreigners, its level of net foreign liabilities has risen from around $26 billion dollars in 1980 to $167 billion dollars in June 1990, or 45 per cent of GDP. Of this large total, nearly $130 billion was in the form of loans from foreigners. Only $40 billion was in the form of equity holdings or **direct foreign investment**. This stock of foreign liabilities in Australia requires nearly 25 per cent of total export earnings to finance interest and dividend repayments.

Stocks and Flows At the heart of the distinction between a net borrower/net lender and a debtor/creditor nation is the distinction between flows and stocks. Borrowing and lending is a flow. It is an amount borrowed or lent per unit of time. Debts are stocks. They are amounts owed at a point in time. The flow of borrowing and lending changes the stock of debt. But the outstanding stock of debt depends mainly on past flows of borrowing and lending, not on the current period's flows. The current period's flows determine the change in the stock of debt outstanding.

Australia is not the only net borrower nation. It is in the company of lower income countries that are at an earlier stage of economic development, such as the Philippines and Thailand. And like Australia, these countries not only are net borrowers, they are also debtor nations. That is, their total stock of borrowing from the rest of the world exceeds their lending. The debt of these developing countries has grown from less than a third to more than half of their gross domestic products during the 1980s and has given rise to what has been called the 'third world debt crisis'.

The majority of countries, in fact, are net borrowers, including, in recent years, the United States. But a small number of countries are huge net lenders. Examples of net lenders are the oil-rich countries, such as Saudi Arabia and Venezuela, and developed economies, such as Japan and West Germany. On balance, since the world is a closed economy, the amount borrowed in the world must equal the amount lent.

Borrowing to Consume or Invest

Should Australia be concerned about being a net borrower? The answer to this question is usually thought to depend on what we do with the borrowed money. If we borrow to consume, then it is believed that we may have a problem. If we borrow to invest in additional capital equipment, provided that investment generates a high enough return, we do not have a problem — in fact, we reap benefits from our international borrowing.

It's easy to see why people believe that borrowing to consume may lead to problems while borrowing to invest does not by considering the case of an individual. Suppose you borrow $1000 to take a vacation to Bali in your final year of university. When you finish university and start working, you're going to have to repay that $1000 loan plus the interest on it. To make those repayments, your consumption will have to be reduced (when you quit university) to pay for your extra consumption splurge in your final year. Contrast this situation with one in which you borrow $1000 to invest in a profitable business venture. The investment pays you your $1000 plus another $200 back in a year from now. You have to repay your loan plus the interest on it. But the total amount that you owe is less than the return you've made on your investment.

In the first example, borrowing to consume, the day of reckoning came and you had to cut back on consumption later in order to repay your loan and the interest on it. In the second case, you put the loan to work and not only do you not have to cut back on future consumption, you can actually consume more in the future as a result of having taken a loan and used it to make a sound investment.

The analogy of the individual is often applied to the country. If Australia borrows heavily from the rest of the world to pay for vacations and other consumption activities — including government consumption — the country will run into difficulties in the future and be forced to cut back its level of consumption in order to eventually repay its loans and pay the interest on them. If, on the other hand, Australia borrows huge amounts of funds from the rest of the world to develop and profit from its vast human and physical resource base, then by generating more rapid economic growth than would otherwise have been possible, Australians become richer, are able to repay their international debts, together with the interest on those debts, and still wind up with more consumption than before.

Australia's International Borrowing

Is Australia borrowing from the rest of the world to finance consumption or investment? This is a very difficult question to answer. One approach is to look at the levels of saving and investment in Australia. If investment is greater than saving, then it might be the case that most overseas borrowing is used to finance investment. If this is true we might expect to see an increase in income in the future sufficient to repay the current borrowings. Otherwise, if savings are greater than investment, and our borrowings are used to finance consumption goods, then such an increase in future income might not be forthcoming. Future consumption would have to be reduced so that the currently incurred debt can be repaid. The figures for Australia are mixed. The private sector balance, savings minus investment, fluctuated between surplus and deficit for most of the 1960s. For much of the 1970s it was in surplus, sliding into deficit in the 1980s (see Fig. 37.5). But do these numbers really tell us about whether we are borrowing and importing for investment or not?

In fact it does not matter whether overseas borrowings are used for investment projects or simply to finance end consumption. A country could consume 100 per cent of its income and borrow overseas to import all its capital requirements. Or that same country could use all its domestic output for investment purposes and borrow to import all its consumption goods. In both cases, what is important is whether or not the investment undertaken is enough to provide the necessary growth in income to pay off the borrowings while sustaining the current consumption levels.

Figure 37.4 Net Investment Income Payable Abroad

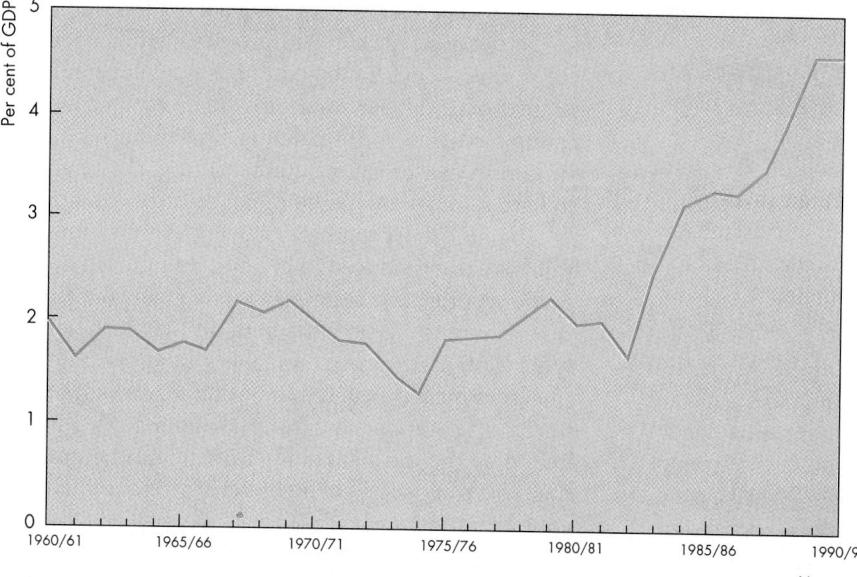

Income payable abroad, as a share of GDP, to service all foreign investment in Australia from 1960/61 to 1990/91 is shown. Up to 1983/84 the share was roughly constant. As foreign investment grew, domestic income grew as fast. However, since 1983/84 the share of domestic income payable abroad has doubled. This could indicate that less of the foreign investment has actually been used in productive investments in Australia and GDP growth has not kept pace with income payable abroad.

Source: See Fig. 37.1.

What are the facts for Australia? Figure 37.4 provides some information on this issue. It shows the income necessary to service all foreign investment in Australia, both equity and borrowings, as a percentage of GDP. If the ratio is roughly constant, as it was from 1960/61 to 1982/83, then even though foreign investment was increasing, domestic income was rising just as fast. Thus there was enough productive investment to provide the income growth necessary to repay the borrowing without having to cut consumption. But from 1982/83 on, the ratio has risen steeply. Since capital accumulation has remained roughly constant as a share of GDP over the entire period, and interest rates were just as high in the early 1980s as they were in the late 1980s, then we might conclude that since 1983/84 there has not been sufficient investment. Or, equivalently, there has been too much consumption. Income growth has not kept up with income payable abroad to service our holdings of foreign liabilities. It is this observation that has made the issue of Australia's foreign debt such a contentious one. This is discussed further in the Reading Between the Lines (pp. 540–542)

Let's now turn to an examination of the factors that determine the scale of our international borrowing and the size of our current account balance.

R E V I E W

When we buy goods from the rest of world, or invest in the rest of the world, we use foreign currency. When foreigners buy goods from us or invest in Australia, they use Australian currency. We record international transactions in the balance of payments accounts. The current account shows our exports and imports of goods and services and net transfers to the rest of the world. The capital account shows our net foreign borrowing or lending. The Australian current account has nearly always been in deficit — Australia is usually a net borrower. This borrowing over an extended period has meant that Australia has accumulated a large stock of foreign liabilities, mainly in the form of foreign debt. However, up to 1982/83 domestic investment was sufficient to produce the necessary income growth required to service the debt so that income paid overseas remained a constant fraction of GDP. Since 1982/83 this ratio has increased and this could be signalling an increase in consumption financed by borrowing abroad. ■

Current Account Balance

What determines the current account balance and the scale of a country's net foreign borrowing or lending? To answer that question, we need to begin by recalling and using some of the things that we learned about the national income accounts.

Sector Balances

Table 37.2 is going to refresh your memory and summarize the necessary calculations for you. Part (a) lists the national income variables that are needed, with their symbols. Their values in Australia in 1990/91 are also shown. Part (b) presents two key national income equations.

First, equation (1) reminds us that gross domestic product is the sum of consumption expenditure, investment (both private and public), government purchases of goods and services, and net exports (the difference between exports and imports). We have also included the statistical discrepancy as a separate item. Equation (2) reminds us that aggregate income is used in a number of ways. It can be consumed, saved, paid to the government in the form of taxes (net of transfer payments) or paid overseas as income payable on net foreign liabilities or unrequited transfers. Equation (1) tells us how our expenditure generates our income. Equation (2) tells us how we dispose of that income.

Part (c) of the table takes you into some new territory. It examines the sectoral balances: either the surpluses or deficits of the private, government and foreign sectors. To obtain these surpluses and deficits, first subtract equation (2) from equation (1) in Table 37.2. The result is equation (3). By re-arranging equation (3), we obtain a relationship for the current account — exports minus imports minus total net income paid overseas — that appears as equation (4) in the table.

Notice that the current account, in equation (4), is made up of three components. The first is taxes minus government spending on both goods and services and investment. The second is private saving minus private investment. These items are the surpluses or deficits of the government and private sectors. The statistical discrepancy balances the equation.

The **government sector surplus or deficit** is the difference between taxes (net of transfer payments) and government sector purchases of goods and services plus government sector investment. If taxes (net of transfer payments) exceed government sector purchases of goods and services and investment, the gov-

The Issue of the Foreign Debt

Hopes High on Stabilizing Foreign Debt

Increasing confidence is emerging within the Federal government that Australia's foreign debt may now be stabilizing years earlier than expected, and as a result not just of recession but of genuine change in the economy.

The Minister for Finance, Mr Willis, yesterday referred to one of the generally overlooked forecasts of last month's budget that foreign debt as a proportion of gross domestic product could stabilize this financial year —when he argued that Australia could emerge from recession with a structural improvement in its trade position.

The fact that more has not been made of this forecast — after years in which the buildup of foreign debt and the associated current account problem has dominated the thinking of economic policymakers — partly reflects the caution of the new Treasurer, Mr Kerin, in calling a premature end to the debt crisis.

The fact that the prospect of debt stabilization partially reflects the recession and the unwinding of the borrowing binge of the 1980s has also limited the extent to which the Government has crowed about it.

But Mr Willis, speaking to a Metal Trades Industry Association conference in Canberra, argued that the forecast fall in the current account deficit from 4 per cent of gross domestic product last financial year to 3.5 per cent this year 'could lead us this year to the point of stabilisation of our foreign debt as a percentage of GDP, something we previously thought to be years away'.

He said the constraints of the balance of payments had been a very limiting factor for the Australian economy.

'The fact that we have run up against the constraints of the balance of payments and current account, and increased foreign debt is a major reason why we went into recession,' he said.

Mr Willis argued that while the improvement in the current account from a point where it represented 6 per cent of GDP in 1989/90, 'has been helped by the impact of recession on imports, it is not only that, it is far from just that.

'Our export performance has been improved enormously and it flows from the fact that our competitiveness has been improved by about 18 per cent since 1982/83.

'It will be further improved by lower inflation rates than our trading partners this year.

'Our exports of manufacturing goods have in fact doubled in real terms since 1982/83.

'We have run away with a 112 per cent increase, an annual rate of 11.3 per cent and last year, they increased by 20 per cent.

'Our export base is therefore being rapidly broadened and the Third World pattern of exports which was left to us by the previous government, in which we had overwhelming reliance on primary products for our exports, is rapidly becoming a relic of the past'.

Foreign Debt to GDP Ratios

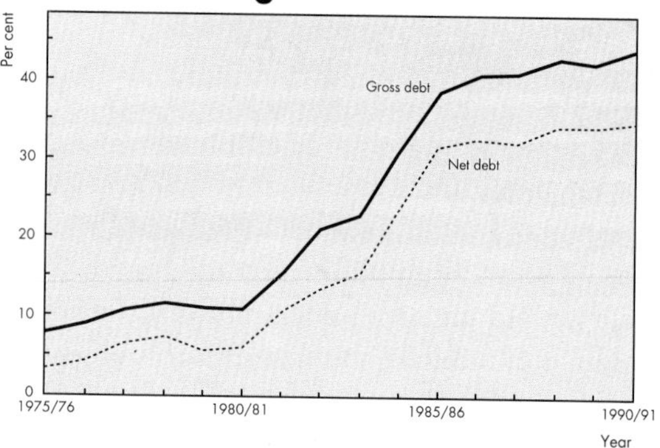

The assessment of the Treasurer in the Budget papers of the prospects for debt stabilization was modest, saying only that 'reflecting the improved current account performance, there is the prospect that the ratio of net external debt to GDP may begin to stabilise in 1991/92'.

But other advice flowing to the Cabinet is a little more confident. Other departments, such as Foreign Affairs and Trade, are pointing out to their ministers that the net debt to GDP ratio has actually remained about 34 per cent for the past three years.

The Department of Foreign Affairs and Trade attributes this relative stability to the decline in the current deficit and a switch in foreign investment from debt to equity.

The Australian,
5 September 1991
By Laura Tingle

The Essence of the Story

- The rising level of the foreign debt has been a major concern of the government, and others, for some time now, to the extent that it has been called the 'debt crisis'.
- The underlying cause of the rising debt levels has been the large current account deficits run by Australia and it was in response to these that monetary policy was tightened over the period 1988/89, ultimately sending the economy into recession.
- It was predicted at the time that even if the current account 'improved' it might take years for the level of foreign debt to stabilize.
- Now it appears that the level of the debt will stabilize much more quickly than first thought. This has occurred because of the unexpected severity of the recession and because of a fundamental change occurring in the export sector.

Background and Analysis

- A country runs a current account deficit if its total use of goods and services for all purposes, consumption and investment, private and public exceeds its total production. But this requires the country to borrow from the rest of the world to finance the excess of resource use over resources availability. Hence, consistent current account deficits mean that the country consistently builds up debt owed to the rest of the world.
- Australia has historically been a current account deficit country. This has been explained by the fact the Australia is a relatively young country with vast mineral and agricultural resources which are being developed. It would place considerable strain on domestic resources if all such development had to be financed from domestic funds. So many capital goods for investment purposes are imported, financed by foreign borrowing.
- But this issue became very contentious in the late 1980s. The cause of concern was the fact, as seen in the graph, that the level of net foreign debt as a percentage of GDP rose rapidly from around 10 per cent to nearly 35 per cent between 1980/81 and 1985/86. The debate has been vigorous, with the two sides being: i) the debt is a problem which policy should address, versus ii) the debt is not a problem unless someone can identify a source of market failure which has led to excessive levels of debt, and thus, it is counterproductive to address domestic policy towards the level of debt.
- The 'debt is a problem' camp have raised the following issues:
  - A high level of foreign debt makes the economy vulnerable to the effects of large devaluations, which increase the domestic value of the debt and its servicing, and so increase the possibility of large-scale bankruptcies.
  - If the foreign borrowing is used for investment in sectors of the economy which do not produce export goods, or is used for domestic consumption purposes, then the country may end up in a 'debt trap.' That is, because repayments on the debt are growing but exports are not, the country may end up having to borrow abroad just to meet debt repayments.
  - High levels of borrowing for unproductive purposes impose an 'externality' on other borrowers because the risk premium attributable to the country rises. All borrowers thus have to pay higher interest rates on their borrowing.
  - The high level of debt may induce a large depreciation in the future which will ultimately be inflationary.
- Against these arguments are the following considerations, many of which are associated with Professor John Pitchford from the Australian National University:
  - The debt is comprised mainly of private borrowings by domestic firms from foreign banks. These transactions are carried out under normal

business conditions and presumably are subject to the same scrutiny as would occur if the firms had borrowed from domestic banks. Some projects will fail and some will succeed, as is always the case, but there is nothing special about the fact that some of the borrowings are from foreigners.

- The economy is flexible and capable of adjusting even if the level of foreign debt is preceived to be excessive. If this occurs through higher interest rates, borrowing for marginal projects will be deterred and only those projects which are highly likely to yield strong future income growth will proceed. Such would be the case if all borrowing were sourced from domestic funds.
- Similarly with respect to the issue of vulnerability, both lenders and borrowers are aware of the additional risk attributable to the possibility of exchange rate variations. Any participants in a commercial deal who do not look at all the associated risks probably should not be in that business.
- In essence, the debate has revolved around whether or not those involved in the foreign transactions are capable of making sound business judgements on their own behalf, or whether they should in some way be regulated.

A Resolution?

- In 1988/89 policy-makers appeared to side with the 'debt is a problem' proponents because, as the reading suggests, the tight monetary policy of 1990 was largely in response to the large current account deficits. Hence the recession of 1990/91.
- But the graph appears to show that the level of the net debt had already stabilized from 1985/86 onwards at around 34 per cent of GDP. Since it has not grown over the ensuing five years, the foreign borrowings apparently have yielded sufficient growth in income to meet the debt-servicing requirements. And throughout this entire period the exchange rate steadily appreciated, in contrast to predictions of a large devaluation.
- And finally, the comments from Mr Willis concerning the changing manufactured goods export base support the view that many of the commercial decisions made in recent years which have been financed by foreign borrowings have been sound ones.
- If this view is correct, then the conclusion that it is counterproductive to target domestic monetary and fiscal policy at the current account, and associated debt levels, prevails.

Table 37.2 Determination of the Current Account Balance and Net Foreign Borrowing (billions of dollars)

	Symbols and equations	In 1990/91
(a) Variables		
Gross domestic product (GDP)	Y	379
Consumption expenditure	C	230
Private investment	I_p	72
Government investment	I_g	9
Government purchases of goods and services	G	67
Exports of goods and services	EX	65
Imports of goods and services	IM	66
Net income payable abroad	NI	17
Net unrequited transfers	TR	–2
Statistical discrepancy	SD	2
Saving	S	65
Taxes, net of transfer payments	T	69
(b) National income and expenditure		
Aggregate expenditure	(1) $Y = C + I_p + I_g + G + SD + EX - IM$	
Uses of income	(2) $Y = C + S + T + NI + TR$	
Difference between (1) and (2)	(3) $0 = I_p + I_g - S + G - T + EX - IM - NI - TR + SD$	
(c) Sectoral balances		
Current account	(4) $(EX - IM - NI - TR) = (T - G - I_g) + (S - I_p) - SD$	
	$-16 = -7 - 7 - 2$	
Government sector	$T - G - I_g = 69 - 67 - 9 = -7$	
Private sector	$S - I_p = 66 - 72 = -6$	

Note: The exports and imports data are collected on a different basis for the national accounts than for the balance of payments. Hence the numbers are different from those given in Table 37.1.

Source: ABS, *Australian National Accounts, National Income and Expenditure*, June Quarter 1991, No. 5206.0 and ABS Time Series Service, supplied through EconData's dX Data Service.

ernment sector has a surplus. If government sector purchases of goods and services plus investment exceed taxes, net of transfer payments, the government sector has a deficit. The government sector deficit examined here is different from the Federal government deficit or surplus examined in Chapter 35. The government sector, sometimes called general government, includes the Federal government, the State governments and local governments.

The **private sector surplus or deficit** is the difference between private saving and investment. If saving exceeds investment, the private sector has a surplus to lend to other sectors. If investment exceeds saving, the private sector has a deficit that has to be financed by borrowing from other sectors.

Bookkeeping and Behaviour

The calculations that we've just performed are really nothing more than bookkeeping. We've simply manipulated the national income and balance of payments accounts. We've discovered that the current account balance equals net exports plus net transfer payments from the rest of the world less net income paid abroad. We've also discovered that the current account is equal to the sum of the deficits of the government and private sectors. But what determines those other two deficits? Why, for example, isn't the private sector in a surplus equal to the government sector deficit so that the current account deficit is zero? Does an increase in the government sector deficit always bring an increase in the current account deficit?

Government Sector Balance and Current Account

You can see the answer to this question by looking at Fig. 37.5. That figure shows the general government budget balance, the private sector balance and the current account balance since 1971/72. Recall from Table 37.2 that the current account balance is the sum of the government sector balance and the private sector balance. Any observed deviation from this rule is accounted for by the statistical discrepancy. As you can see from the figure, there is no clear tendency for the current account deficit to get bigger or smaller as the government's budget deficit gets bigger or smaller. In some years, 1975/76 to 1979/80 for

Figure 37.5 The Three Balances

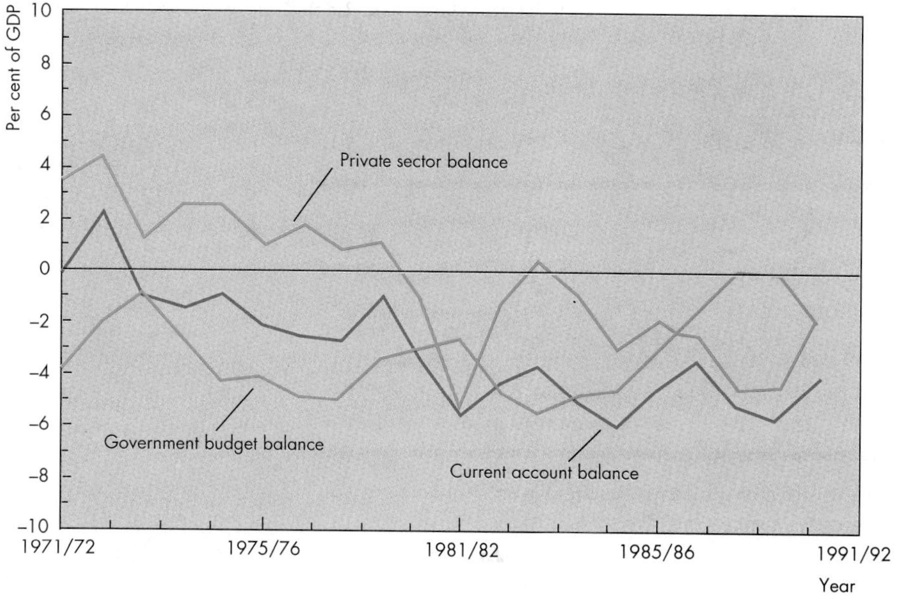

The current account balance is equal to the sum of the private sector balance (saving minus investment) plus the government sector balance (government spending minus taxes) plus the statistical discrepancy. The relationship between these three balances is illustrated here. The private sector balance and the current account have a closer relationship than does the government sector balance and the current account. There are a number of years when the government sector balance and the current account move in opposite directions.

Source: See Table 37.2.

example, the two accounts move in the same direction. In other years they do not.

On the other hand, there appears to be a much closer relationship between the private sector balance (savings minus investment) and the current account. In all but a few years these two accounts moved in the same direction.

Probably the strongest relationship appearing in Fig. 37.5 is that between the government sector balance and the private sector balance. Whenever the government sector balance is improving, taxes minus government spending are becoming less negative, the private sector balance is deteriorating and savings minus investment are declining. Thus these two balances appear to be negatively related.

What causes the relationship that we can see in Fig. 37.5 between the three balances? Let's begin to answer this question by looking at the effects of the government sector balance on the private sector balance.

Effects of Government Sector Balance on Private Sector Balance

It is not surprising that there are fluctuations in the private sector balance. As we've just seen, that variable is the gap between saving and investment. As we learned in Chapter 25, one of the main influences on the level of saving is disposable income. Anything that increases disposable income, other things being equal, increases saving and increases the private sector surplus. Savings also depend on the interest rate. Whenever the interest rate rises, current consumption is postponed as people save more for future consumption — the intertemporal substitution effect. In that same chapter, we learned that investment depends on the interest rate and on expectations of future profits. Again, other things being equal, anything that lowers interest rates or increases future profit expectations increases investment and decreases the private sector surplus.

But when the government changes its taxes or spending — changing its deficit — there are some effects on income and interest rates that, in turn, influence private sector saving and investment and the private sector surplus or deficit. An increase in government purchases of goods and services or a tax cut — either of which will increase the government deficit — tends to increase GDP and the interest rate. The higher GDP stimulates additional saving, but the higher interest rate dampens investment plans and further stimulates saving. Thus, to some degree, an increased government sector deficit induces an increased private sector surplus. This accounts for the observed relationship in Fig. 37.5. But the effect of the government deficit on the private sector surplus occurs only if the government's actions do indeed stimulate higher income and higher interest rates.

When the economy is operating close to capacity, as it is most of the time, the higher government deficit does not produce a higher level of real GDP. Also, internationally mobile capital lessens the effect of increased government spending on interest rates. Thus the two mechanisms by which an increase in the government sector deficit can increase the private sector surplus can, at times, be relatively weak.

Effects of Government Sector Balance on Current Account Balance

Since the current account balance equals the sum of the government sector balance and the private sector balance, any change in the government balance that does not influence the private sector balance must have its effect on the current account balance. But how does that effect come about? The easiest way of seeing the effect is to consider what happens when there is full employment. An increase in government purchases of goods and services or a tax cut leads to an increase in aggregate expenditure and an increase in aggregate demand. But with the economy at full employment there is no spare capacity to generate a comparable increase in output. Part of the increased demand for goods and services, therefore, spills over into the rest of the world and imports increase. Also, part of the domestic production going for export is diverted to satisfy domestic demand. Exports decrease. The rise in imports and the fall in exports increase the current account deficit. The excess of imports over exports leads to a net increase in borrowing from the rest of the world. But the economy does not operate precisely at full employment. Nor does foreign capital flow in at a fixed interest rate. Thus the link between government sector deficit and the current account deficit, **called the twin deficits hypothesis**, is not a precise one.

The Twin Deficits Hypothesis It was precisely this line of reasoning, except in reverse, which prompted the government to reverse fiscal policy in 1985/86. At that time the current account was worsening and the government was running large deficits as a result of policies adopted following the National Economic Summit Conference (see Chapter 33). The government reasoned that by cutting spending and generating a surplus on its own account, the current account would improve as exports rose and imports fell. However, this did not occur. From Fig. 37.5 we see that, in fact, as the government deficit turned into a surplus from 1986/87 on, the current account actually worsened to record very high deficits. Why were the government's predictions so wrong?

Well, as we noted above, the relationships between the various accounts are loose and depend in part on just where the economy is in the business cycle and on other events. As we observed in Chapter 33, from 1986/87 on there was strong growth in the economy as a result of the strong improvement in the terms of trade. For a couple of years, 1986/87 to 1987/88, this improved the current account. But coupled with loose monetary policy and lower interest rates, declining real wages and consequent increased business profitability which boosted business confidence and investment, GDP grew strongly. As both consumption and investment grew rapidly they spilled over into increased imports. Then in 1988 the Reserve Bank tightened monetary policy. As interest rates rose, the demand for Australian dollar-denominated assets rose and the exchange rate appreciated. Exports became more expensive to foreigners and imports became cheaper at home. The current account thus worsened. So, the twin deficits hypothesis did not fail. Rather, there were enough other disturbances and changes in the economy to overpower what might otherwise have been predicted to occur.

R E V I E W

The mechanism whereby the government balance deficit influences the private sector deficit and the current account deficit is as follows:

- An increase in government spending or a tax cut increases the government deficit.
- An increased government deficit increases GDP and raises interest rates.
- Higher GDP increases saving and higher interest rates cut investment and further increase savings, so the private sector surplus increases.
- The closer the economy is to full employment, the weaker is the influence of the government sector deficit on the private sector surplus.
- A higher government sector deficit, by increasing domestic aggregate demand, increases the demand for imports and diverts goods destined for export to domestic uses.
- Net exports fall and the current account deficit increases. ■

Net Exports and the Dollar

Exporters don't like a strong dollar and importers don't like a weak dollar. Why? Does the strength of the dollar affect the volume of our exports and imports? And does it affect the balance of trade — our net exports? Or does causation run the other way? That is, is the strength of the dollar itself determined by the balance of trade? In other words, does a balance of trade surplus lead to a strengthening of the dollar and a balance of trade deficit to a weakening of the dollar? These are the questions we are going to tackle in this section. We'll begin by looking at the connection between Australian-dollar prices and the foreign exchange rate.

Prices and the Exchange Rate

In order to understand the relationship between prices and the exchange rate, it is first necessary to refresh our memory about the important distinction between two concepts of price: relative price and absolute price. Relative price, recall, is the price of one good in terms of another. In Chapter 36, we studied a model economy in which there were just two goods, grain and cars. In that economy, the relative price is the number of tonnes of grain that are exchanged for a car. The absolute price of a good or service is the number of dollars for which it trades. The absolute price depends on the price level or, equivalently, on the value of money. The value of money is in turn determined by the amount of money supplied relative to the amount demanded.

Relative prices are determined by demand and supply and, in the case of goods and services that are traded internationally, by demand and supply in the world market, not the domestic market of any individual country. Money prices are determined partly by relative prices and partly by the value of money in an individual country. Each country has its own money prices that depend on the value of that country's money.

Let's consider an example in a model economy similar to the one we studied in Chapter 36. As in that earlier model, there are two goods: grain and cars. Suppose that one car exchanges for 1 tonne of grain on the world market. That is the relative price of cars and grain. The price of a car in terms of grain is 1 tonne or the price of 1 tonne of grain is 1 car.

The dollar price of cars and grain is going to depend on the value of money. If the value of money is such that $1000 buys 1 tonne of grain, then $1000 is the money price of grain. The money price of a car is $1000. That is, the ratio of the two money prices equals the relative price. If the value of money is such that 1 tonne of grain costs $4000, then a car costs $4000.

Money Prices in Two Countries

Money prices can differ from one country to another because of differences in the value of money. The example set out in Table 37.3 shows the connection between the prices in two countries and the exchange rate between the two currencies. In this example, we continue to use grain and cars and the two countries in question are Australia and the United States. Suppose that the world relative price of cars and grain is the same as in the previous section: one car costs 1 tonne of grain. Suppose that the value of money in the United States is such that 1 tonne of grain costs $4000. One car costs $4000. These are the world market prices expressed in US dollars. The world market prices expressed in Australian dollars depend on the exchange rate between the Australian dollar and the US dollar. Three examples are set out in the table. At an exchange rate of A$1.75 per US$1 (an exchange rate that is lower than we have ever experienced) the $4000 tonne of grain in the United States costs $7000 in Australia and the $4000 car in the United States costs $7000 in Australia. The other two examples give the prices in Australia, expressed in Australian dollars, at exchange rates of A$1.25 per US$1 and A$0.75 per US$1.

The key message from Table 37.3 is that prices in Australia, expressed in Australian dollars, depend on world market prices and on the value of the Australian dollar in terms of other currencies. The higher foreign exchange value of the Australian dollar against other currencies, the lower is the Australian-dollar price of a good.

Prices of Exports and Imports

You can now see why exporters like a weak dollar and importers like a strong dollar. If the Australian dollar is weak, the price received by an exporter, in Australian dollars, is high. If the Australian dollar is strong, the price received by an exporter is low. For example, suppose we export grain. With a strong dollar at A$0.75 per US$1, the grain exporter receives only $3000 a tonne. With a weak Australian dollar, at, say, A$1.75 per US$1, the exporter receives $7000 a tonne. The importer likes a strong dollar for the same reason. With a strong dollar — at A$0.75 per US$1 — a car costs only A$3000. But with a weak dollar, at A$1.75 per US$1, that same car costs $7000 Australian dollars.

Table 37.3 Australian and US Dollar Prices and the Exchange Rates

World market prices in US dollars:

Grain	$4000 a tonne
Cars	$4000 each

World market prices in Australian dollars:

	Australian dollar price	
Exchange rate	**Grain**	**Cars**
A$1.75 per US$1	$7000	$7000
A$1.25 per US$1	$5000	$5000
A$0.75 per US$1	$3000	$3000

The Dollar and the Balance of Trade

There is an important connection between the dollar and the balance of trade that arises from the relationship we've just studied between prices and the value of the dollar. Australian demand and supply for the goods that we export and import depend on their prices in Australia. Other things being equal, the higher the price of any good, the more of it will be produced and the less of it consumed. Equivalently, the higher the price of a good, the larger is the quantity supplied and the smaller is the quantity demanded.

Let's study the connection between prices, the exchange rate and the balance of trade by returning to a model economy. The model economy produces and consumes two goods: grain and cars. It exports grain and it imports cars, but it produces and consumes some of each of the goods. The markets for the two goods are illustrated in Fig. 37.6. Focus first on part (a) of the figure. In the market for grain (left part) the supply curve is *Sx* and the demand curve is *Dx*. In the market for cars (right part) the demand curve is *Dm* and the supply curve is *Sm*. The relative price of cars and grain, determined on the world market, is 1 tonne of grain per car, as before. Suppose that the price of these goods on the world economy is US$4000 a tonne for grain and US$4000 each for cars. Also, suppose that the exchange rate between the Australian dollar and the US dollar is A$1.75 per US$1 (the first example of Table 37.2). In this situation, the price of grain in Australian dollars is $7000, so that the quantity of grain demanded in Australia is 3000 tonnes and the quantity supplied is 8000 tonnes. Five thousand tonnes are exported and total exports are $35 million (5000 tonnes at $7000 a tonne). Also the price of a car in Australian dollars is $7000, so that the quantity of cars demanded is 5000 and the quantity of cars supplied is 4000. Australia imports 1000 cars and its imports are $7 million (1000 cars at $7000 a car equals $7 million). In this situation, Australia has a balance of trade surplus or positive net exports.

Next, look at part (b) of Fig. 37.6. This part illustrates what happens if the Australian dollar is more valuable than the US dollar — the case where A$0.75 equals US$1. In this case, the Australian-dollar price of grain is $3000 a tonne and that of a car is $3000. At $3000 a tonne, the quantity of grain supplied by Australian growers is 6000 tonnes a year and the quantity demanded is 5000 tonnes a year. One thousand tonnes are year are exported and total exports are $3 million. At a price of $3000 a car, the quantity of cars demanded in Australia is 7000 a year, and the quantity supplied is 2000 a year. Five thousand cars a year are imported at $3000 a car, so imports are $15 million. In this situation, Australia has a balance of trade deficit or negative net exports.

We've established that with a high value for the dollar, we import more than we export, and with a low value for the dollar, we export more than we import. In between these two situations is one in which exports and imports are equal in value. This case is illustrated in Fig. 37.6(c). Here, A$1.25 equals US$1, so that the prices in Australian dollars are $5000 a tonne for grain and $5000 for a car. At these prices, the quantity of grain supplied by Australians is 7000 tonnes and the quantity demanded is 4000 tonnes. Australia exports 3000 tonnes of grain at $5000 a tonne, so total exports are $15 million. At $5000 a car, the quantity of cars supplied in Australia is 3000 a year and the quantity of cars demanded is 6000 a year. Australia imports 3000 cars a year at $5000 a car, so the total imports are $15 million. In this situation, the balance of trade and net exports are each zero.

Equilibrium Exchange Rate

How is the exchange rate determined? What is the equilibrium exchange rate? This question is answered in Chapter 29, where we studied the forces that determine the exchange rate. The exchange rate is determined to make the quantity of Australian-dollar assets demanded equal to the quantity of Australian-dollar assets supplied. It is not determined by the balance of trade. Indeed, causation goes the other way around. The exchange rate is determined in asset markets — markets for Australian-dollar assets — and, given the exchange rate that is determined in those markets, the Australian-dollar prices of the goods it exports and imports are determined. And given those prices, its balance of trade is determined.

However, there are important feedbacks from the trade balance to the assets markets in which the exchange rate is determined. For example, suppose Australians decided that they liked foreign goods better than Australian goods, so that imports rose for no other reason than the change in attitudes. To purchase the increased imports Australia has to purchase increased foreign exchange. Net demand for Autralian dollar-denominated assets would fall and the exchange rate would depreciate. Thus, while the exchange rate is an important determinant of the trade balance, some causation works back the other way.

The exchange rate and trade balance determined in equilibrium have to be consistent with the analysis that we conducted above, where we discovered that the current account is equal to the sum of the private sector and government sector balances. This consistency is achieved because of some important interdependencies between the demand and supply curves in the markets for goods and services that are imported and exported and the market for Australian-dollar assets. Let's explore one such interdependency by working out what happens if business confidence increases to such an extent that there is an investment boom. Such an event occurred in the early 1980s and again in the years 1987/88 to 1988/89.

The Private Sector Balance, Net Exports and the Exchange Rate

Let's begin by supposing that business in Australia expects an export boom, as occurred in 1980/81 and 1981/82, or that real wages have fallen and overall profitability has increased, as occurred over the mid-1980s. Either or both of these events boost business confidence so much that there is a big increase in

Figure 37.6 Exports, Imports and the Dollar

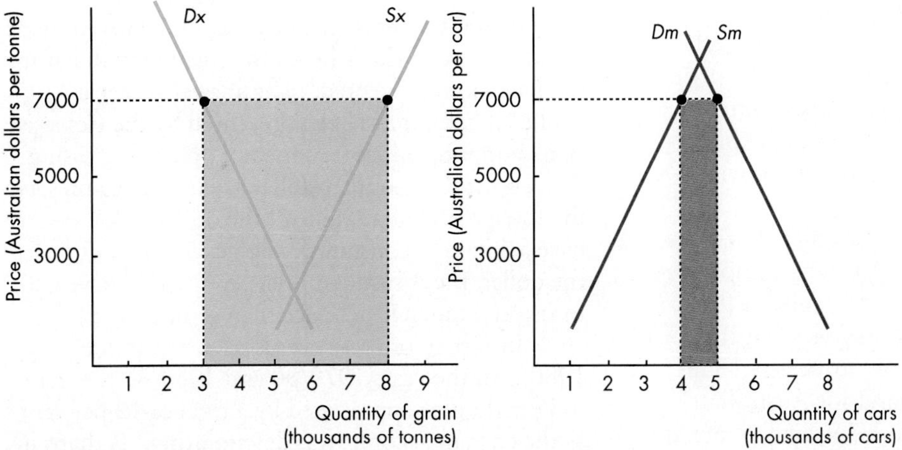

(a) Exports greater than imports

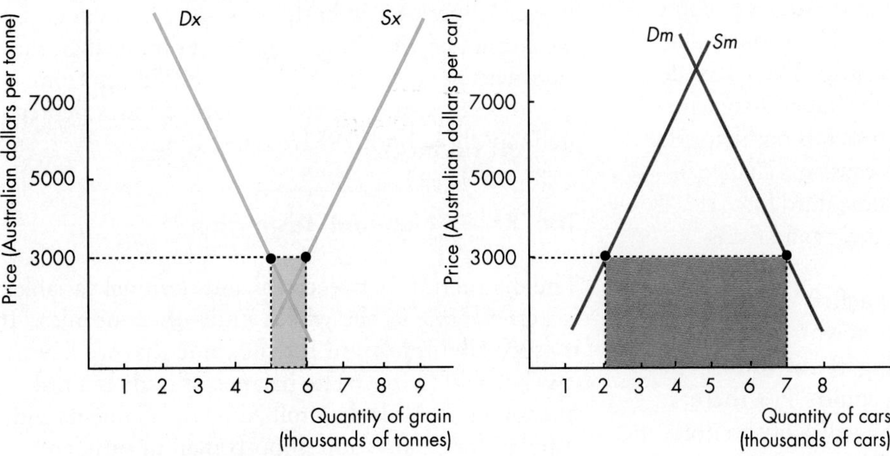

(b) Imports greater than exports

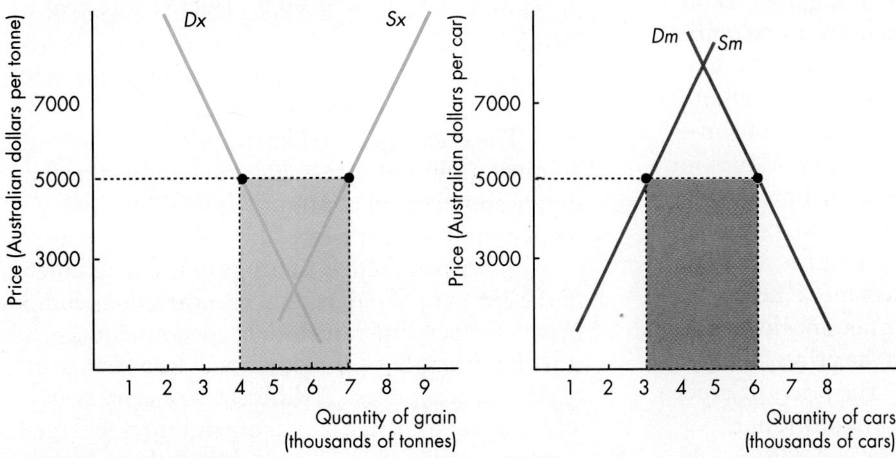

(c) Exports equal imports

The foreign exchange value of the dollar influences Australian-dollar prices. Other things being equal, the higher the Australian-dollar price of a good, the lower is the quantity demanded by Australians and the larger is the quantity supplied by Australians. The figure illustrates two goods, grain, which is exported, and cars, which are imported. When the exchange rate is A$1.75 per US$1, the price of grain is A$7000 a tonne and the price of a car is A$7000. The demand curve for grain is *Dx* and the supply curve is *Sx*. The demand curve for cars is *Dm* and the supply curve is *Sm*. At the exchange rate of A$1.75 per US$1 (part a), Australia has an excess of exports over imports (compare the shaded areas in the two parts of the figure). When the exchange rate is A$0.75 per US$1, the Australian-dollar prices are $3000 a tonne for grain and $3000 for a car. In this situation (part b), imports are greater than exports. When the exchange rate is A$1.25 per US$1, the Australian-dollar price of grain is $5000 a tonne and that of a car is $5000. The value of exports and the value of imports are equal (part c).

autonomous investment. As a result, expenditure increases and real GDP rises, as does the price level. If the private sector had begun in balance, as it was in 1979/80, then, because investment increases, it moves into deficit. To be sure, the increase in real GDP increases saving. And the increase in the price level reduces the real money supply causing interest rates to rise. The rise in real interest rates further stimulates savings, but not enough overall to wipe out the private sector deficit.

The rise in interest rates has another effect. Because interest rates have risen in Australia compared with foreign countries, they attract a capital inflow. Foreigners want to lend to Australians so that they can benefit from the high rates of return here. This leads to an increase in the demand for Australian dollar-denominated assets and the exchange rate appreciates. But we have just shown above that this will worsen the trade balance as imports become relatively cheaper to Australians and exports become relatively more expensive overseas. Net exports decline as the exchange rate appreciates. These two developments are a consequence of the initial change in the demand for investment by firms. It is not that a deteriorating balance of payments is causing a change in the value of the dollar. It is that some third force is causing both the balance of trade deficit and rising value of the dollar.

Could the balance of trade deficit be corrected by forcing the value of the dollar down? From the analysis that we conducted in Fig. 37.6, you might be tempted to conclude that it could. For there, we discovered that the lower the value of the dollar, the larger the value of net exports. But such a conclusion would be incorrect, for it would be holding constant too many other things that could not in fact be constant. It's important to recognize that along the demand and supply curves for exports and imports that appear in Fig. 37.6 all other influences on the quantities demanded and supplied (other than the price of the good in question) are held constant. To force the value of the dollar down, the Reserve Bank would have to increase the supply of Australian-dollar assets — it has to conduct open market operations that make more money available in Australia. In so doing, it not only lowers the value of the dollar, but increases the prices of all goods and services in Australia. The prices of exports and imports relative to the prices of other, non-traded goods and relative to wages and other production costs, do not change and so the balance of trade does not change.

Stabilizing the Exchange Rate

We've seen that forcing down the value of the Australian dollar could not have prevented the balance of trade deficit that emerged in the early 1980s. But could the rise in the value of the Australian dollar itself have been prevented? The answer is that it could. It could have been prevented by the Reserve Bank adopting a looser monetary policy, increasing the supply of Australian-dollar assets so as to preserve the foreign exchange value of the dollar. However, to have achieved a constant foreign exchange value of the dollar, the Australian price level would have had to rise at a much faster pace than it did.

In fact all of these events occurred in the early 1980s. In the years 1979/80 and 1980/81 the trade weighted index appreciated by a total of 12 per cent as the current account was deteriorating. Perhaps in response to this event, the money supply grew very rapidly in 1980/81 and 1981/82, with M3 growing at over 12 per cent in both years. As a consequence, the consumer price index registered double digit rates of growth in both 1981/82 and 1982/83, up from previous years, and the trade weighted index depreciated rapidly in both 1981/82 and 1982/83.

The 'Real'/'Nominal' Distinction

The distinction between real and nominal variables is a crucial one in the whole study of economics. It is especially important for the topic that we have just been studying. The balance of trade is a real phenomenon. It is determined by the demands and supplies for exports and imports that, in turn, are determined by the factors of production, technologies and preferences. The volume of trade is determined by the forces we discussed and described in Chapter 36. Its balance is determined by our intertemporal choices, by decisions both in the private and government sectors concerning consumption and saving.

The exchange rate, like the price level, is a nominal magnitude. Its value is determined by the supply and demand of nominal quantities — of money and financial assets.

Whenever there is a change in real magnitudes in the economy — an increase in autonomous components of expenditure, including government expenditure, for example — then there will be a change in relative or real prices. A different monetary policy with the same change in real expenditures will rarely produce a different real result but, rather, will affect only all nominal quantities, including the exchange rate.

■ You've now discovered what determines a country's current account balance and the foreign exchange value of its currency. An important influence on the current account balance is the level of autonomous expenditures, including government sector deficit.

In the final two chapters, we're going to look at some further global economic issues. First, in Chapter 38, we'll examine the problems faced by developing countries as they seek to grow. Then, in Chapter 39, we'll look at countries that operate with economic systems that are different from our own: the command economies of the Commonwealth of Independent States, Eastern Europe and the People's Republic of China, and the economy of Japan.

SUMMARY

Financing International Trade

International trade, borrowing and lending are financed using foreign currency. A country's international transactions are recorded in its balance of payments accounts. The current account records receipts and expenditures connected with the sale and purchase of goods and services, as well as net transfers to the rest of the world; the capital account records international borrowing and lending transactions, including those by the government and the Reserve Bank. The Reserve Bank's transactions typically lead to a change in international reserves. (pp. 531–536)

International Borrowing and Lending

A country that borrows more from the rest of the world than it lends to it is a net borrower; a country that lends more to the rest of the world than it borrows from it is a net lender. Borrowing and lending are flows. Borrowing increases debt and a debtor nation is one that has borrowed more than it has lent throughout its entire history. A creditor nation is one that has lent more than it has borrowed throughout its history. Historically, Australia has been a net borrower from the rest of the world and is a debtor nation. Australia has used its international borrowing to develop its economic resources and increase its level of income. Only since 1983/84 has the rate of growth of income fallen behind the rate of growth of Australia's obligations to the rest of the world. (pp. 537–539)

Current Account Balance

The current account balance is equal to the government balance plus the private sector balance, allowing for the statistical discrepancy. Fluctuations in the trade balance appear to arise mainly from fluctuations in the private sector balance. As the private sector deficit has grown in the 1980s, so the trade deficit has also grown. (pp. 539–546)

Net Exports and the Dollar

The higher the foreign exchange value of the dollar, the lower are the prices, in Australian dollars, received by exporters and paid by importers. Other things being equal, the higher the foreign exchange value of the dollar, the smaller the volume of exports and the larger the volume of imports. Although the foreign exchange value of the dollar affects imports and exports and the balance of trade, the value of the dollar itself is only indirectly influenced by the balance of payments. It is determined by the demand and supply of Australian-dollar assets in the world economy. But there are important links between the demand for and supply of Australian dollars and the balance of payments. For example, an increase in private sector spending increases real GDP and prices. Interest rates rise and the increase in the demand for Australian-dollar assets causes an increase in the value of the Australian dollar. The rise in real GDP and the higher exchange rate bring an increase in demand for foreign goods and an increase in the balance of trade deficit (or a decrease in the balance of trade surplus). (pp. 546–551)

KEY TERMS

Balance of payments accounts, p. 531
Balance on official transactions, p. 533
Capital account, p. 533
Creditor nation, p. 537

Current account, p. 531
Debtor nation, p. 537
Direct foreign investment, p. 537
Double-entry bookkeeping, p. 531
Government sector surplus or deficit, p. 539
Net borrower, p. 537
Net lender, p. 537
Non-official balance, p. 533
Private sector surplus or deficit, p. 544
Twin deficits hypothesis, p. 545

PROBLEMS

1 The citizens of Pioneerland, whose currency is the choo, conduct the following transactions in 1980:

	Billions of choos
Imports of goods and services	250
Exports of goods and services	397
Borrowing from the rest of the world	80
Lending to the rest of the world	20
Increase in official holdings of foreign currency	3

a) Set out the three balance of payments accounts for Pioneerland.
b) Does Pioneerland have a flexible exchange rate?

2 You are told the following about Ecoland, a country whose currency is the turky, and whose exchange rate is flexible:

	Billion turkies
GDP	50
Consumption expenditure	30
Government purchases of goods and services	12
Investment	11
Exports of goods and services	10
Government budget deficit	2

Calculate the following for Ecoland:
a) Imports of goods and services.
b) Current account balance.
c) Capital account balance.
d) Taxes (net of transfer payments).
e) Private sector deficit/surplus.

Part 14

Growth, Development and Comparative Systems

Talking with Helen Hughes

Professor Helen Hughes is Executive Director of the National Centre for Development Studies at the Australian National University. Before that she worked in the World Bank in Washington DC. Christopher Findlay spoke to Professor Hughes about current issues in the Australian economy, and about her experiences as a professional economist.

Suppose a Martian economist came to Australia to do an economic survey. What would be the Martian's expectations?

Based on the endowment of natural resources per head, the Martian would expect that Australia would be a very rich country, a highly educated country, a country whose population would be fluent in all the languages of the region and whose economy would be highly integrated into the East Asian economy.

Does Australia satisfy those expectations?

No it doesn't. In terms of per capita income Australia is sixteenth or seventeenth in the world. After World War II, Australia was third, after World War I it was second and in 1900 it was the leading country in per capita income terms. In relative terms the Australian standard of living has slipped. The Australian workforce is relatively poorly trained. Australian language skills are very weak and we have missed the opportunities created by the 1980s economic boom in Asia. Australia's international orientation, measured by the ratio of merchandise exports to GDP, should be much higher than the current level of about 15 per cent.

'In relative terms the Australian standard of living has slipped'

Apart from the resource-based industries, like mining or agriculture, what sectors of the economy would you expect to be internationally competitive?

Australia would find it difficult to compete in standardized products, which require mass production and marketing, even if Australian manufacturing was highly efficient. Our strength should be in niches where design skills can be exploited. Current examples of international competitiveness include some fashion clothing, precision instruments and medical innovations such as the bionic ear. There are some success stories, but fewer than our Martian would have expected.

What are some of the factors that explain the gap between expectations and performance?

One of the paradoxes of economics is that a resource-rich country tends to grow slowly. Australia is not the only example. Petroleum-rich countries have had notable growth difficulties. Instead of having to work hard to grow, Australians have been able to relax, enjoy a relatively high amount of leisure and still be reasonably well off. Natural resources reduce the urgency of adopting the good economic policies necessary to raise economic performance. Australia is, in fact, the 'unlucky country'. In a poor country everybody knows, for example, that two to three shifts have to be worked to utilize investment effectively, that trams have to run all night to service shift workers and that shops have to stay open at times when people come home from work. In Australia, shift work is largely confined to continuous processors such as petrochemicals and steel, and most capital is only used about 25 per cent of the time available.

'Australia is, in fact, the 'unlucky country''

What has been the contribution, if any, of Australian economic policies to this attitude?

A historical perspective is useful. In Australia, the rural sector did not need much labour. Innovations in technology such as fencing, after the gold rushes, led to the release of even more labour. How were the people no longer able to make a living on the diggings and unable to find jobs in agriculture to be employed? Australia chose to protect manufacturing industry. Expansion through import substitution rather than through specialization for export markets was seen as a way of absorbing all that labour. But as a result of protection from competition in the rest of the world, Australians were able to relax. Australian producers have looked inwards, not outwards. They became progressively less internationally competitive. Australia would have to change its trade policies and reduce indirect protection through regulation to become internationally competitive.

'Australian producers have looked inwards, not outwards'

Apart from trade policies, are there other institutional arrangements in the Australian economy in need of major reform?

The industrial relations system is a major barrier to efficiency. The focus is on the avoidance and settlement of disputes. 'Conciliation and arbitration' has had detrimental effects. It has led to inefficient work practices such as those which leave capital under-utilized. The margins between skilled and unskilled wages are too narrow. People with low skills are not encouraged to make the personal investment necessary to raise their skills. Skilled workers leave trades essential to competitiveness to become taxi drivers. Resources are used less productively than they should be used. Traditionally, in the 1900s, the industrial relations system had an important role to play in providing a floor to workers' income levels. Australia now has a sophisticated social welfare system to play that role. We now need a system of industrial relations that puts less weight on welfare and more on productivity. Industrial peace is an essential component of productivity.

'The industrial relations system is a major barrier to efficiency'

Turning now to your own background, how did you become interested in economics?

I switched from science to economics in high school as I became more interested in the way the society worked than in natural phenomena. I studied economics at Melbourne University. Being a woman in the Australia of the 1950s I needed a PhD and so, after I wrote a Masters thesis at Melbourne University on the steel industry, I went to the London School of Economics.

On your return, was it difficult to get a job as an economist?

When I came back to Australia with a PhD, I could not get an academic job. One of my referees, who had supervised my Masters thesis, took the view that my responsibilities to my two small children made it undesirable that I should work full-time. The public service at that time did not permit married women to work. Business was more liberal. I worked in market research for a couple of years. My first academic employer in Australia was an Englishman who was not as prejudiced as Australian men against women. It was not until I became one of the most senior economists at the World Bank that economists in Australia started to treat me as an equal.

'economists have to be more committed to equality than they now are'

What sort of impact has your work and your achievement of a senior position had on your personal life?

There's a positive and negative side. The positive side is that the experience has made me, and other professional women who had to fight for their rights, much tougher. The experience has made me, and others like me, more abrasive than I would have liked to be. I fortunately have still had a very rich and fulfilling family life, so the cost has not been too great.
Is there discrimination against women in taking up positions as professional economists, and if so what can be done about it?
Yes, there is discrimination. In Australian universities, the proportion of women in senior positions is much smaller than in more junior positions. Women account for about 10 per cent at best, and 4 or 5 per cent more commonly, of positions of reader or above. Female academics suffer substantial disadvantages in comparison to males. To solve the problem, economists have to be more committed to equality than they now are. Care has to be taken not to bias student selections against women. Most schoolgirls are not informed that maths is an essential prerequisite to taking economics. Women have to be encouraged to take postgraduate degrees. Some lecturers still tell sexist jokes to test women students. If they were not prejudiced against women they would instead tell students of successful women economists and demonstrate to them the intellectual and material rewards of the economics profession. Women have to be convinced that it is wise to invest in themselves. Tokenism is obviously no cure and has a backlash.

'In relative terms the Australian standard of living has slipped'

Would that be your advice to a woman starting out on a study in economics — invest in yourself?

Yes. There are enormous rewards in investing in higher study. The satisfaction of making a social contribution as an economist is enormous. Opportunities for women have opened up in the public service, in universities and in business. Economics consists of highly sophisticated, intellectually challenging tools and requires a thorough knowledge of society. I work very hard because the problems thrown up by economic analysis are constantly fresh and affect everyone's life. It is impossible to be bored.

If you are interested in reading more about Professor Hughes' views on the Australian economy, you can read her article entitled 'Too Little, Too Late: Australia's Future in the Pacific Economy' in the December 1988 issue of *Australian Economic Papers*.

Chapter 38

Growth and Development

After studying this chapter, you will be able to:

- Describe the international distribution of income.
- Explain the importance of economic growth.
- Explain how the accumulation of capital and technological progress bring higher per capita incomes.
- Describe the sources of high growth in our neighbours in East Asia and contrast their experience with that of Australia.
- Explain the possible effects of population control, foreign aid, free trade and demand stimulation on economic growth and development.
- Evaluate policies designed to stimulate economic growth and development.

Catching Up

'Never before in human history have economies grown as fast for so long as in Northeast Asia over the past four decades'.[1] In each decade, economic output more than doubled in Japan, Hong Kong, the Republic of Korea, Taiwan and the People's Republic of China. As a result, there has been a shift in the centre of gravity of production and trade towards this part of the world. More recent rapid growth in Southeast Asia as well has reinforced the importance of East Asia in the world. Why did these economies grow so fast for so long? Can we learn something from their experience? In the 1870s, living standards in Australia were the highest in the world. We were *number one.* Economic output per person in Australia was over 40 per cent higher than in the United Kingdom and over 80 per cent higher than in the United States. Now, we are ranked about number 18. Other economies caught up to us and then passed us. Why did this happen? As Australia lost its number one spot, the United States took over and became the lead country. By the end of the 1980s, Japan was challenging for the top spot. Real incomes in Japan were then about 70 per cent of those in the United States. The most dramatic examples of the convergence of incomes in some countries have occurred since the end of World War II. In Japan, per capita income at that time was a mere 17 per cent of that in the United States. Other countries have also caught up to the United States. In the late 1940s, France's per capita income was 47 per cent and Germany's 40 per cent of the US levels. Yet, today, per capita income — income per person — in these countries is also about 70 per cent of that of the United States. Why have these economies grown more quickly than the United States in the past few decades? While there has been a convergence in living standards among some economies, others have missed out. In 1984, for example, people all over Australia saw images of starving Ethiopian children on their television screens. In a surge of sympathy, they donated millions of dollars, most visibly through a rock concert benefit called Live Aid. The people of many other countries also responded generously. While the flow of aid didn't eliminate the hunger, it saved many thousands of lives. A success? Only, sadly, in the short run. Three years later, Ethiopia was as poor as ever, and it again suffered a devastating famine. The *average* person in Ethiopia has an income that is equivalent to about $2 a week. And Ethiopia, like all other countries, has an unequal distribution of income, so the poorest people in

---

[1] These were the opening words of an influential report by Australian National University economist Professor Ross Garnaut entitled *Australia and the Northeast Asian Ascendancy,* commissioned by the Hawke government and published in 1989.

that country have much less than $2 a week. These poorest of the world's people have no shelter, they wear rags for clothes and they spend most of their lives in hunger. Why are so many countries, like Ethiopia, chained to poverty? Why are there such differences in income between the poorest and richest countries? Does foreign aid help these countries? Why hasn't it alleviated their poverty?

The world's population has passed 5 billion inhabitants. These billions of people are unevenly distributed over the earth's surface. More than 4 billion live in the world's poor countries and only 1 billion in the rich industrial countries. It is estimated that by the year 2025, world population will exceed 8 billion, with close to 7 billion living in the poor countries and only 1.4 billion in the industrial countries. The governments of poor countries are constantly seeking new and more effective methods of containing their population growth rates, though with limited success. Why is the population growth rate so rapid in poor countries? What are the effects of rapid population growth on economic growth and development?

By the end of the 1980s, nearly US$50 billion worth of official aid a year was given by rich countries to developing countries. Australia is a generous donor, but Japan and the United States each provide about ten times more than Australia, and between them account for about 40 per cent of total aid payments. The recipients of this aid are the poor countries of Africa, Latin America and Asia. A lot of Australia's aid goes to Pacific Island nations. What are the effects of foreign aid on economic growth and development? Some poor countries try to encourage growth and development by protecting their domestic industries from international trade and foreign competition. Other countries adopt an outward-looking orientation, engaging in freer trade with the rest of the world. What kind of international trade policy gives a developing country the best chance of rapid and sustained economic growth?

In this chapter, we'll tackle some of the questions just posed. They are all aspects of one of those 'big' questions posed in Chapter 1: what causes differences in wealth among nations, making the people in some countries rich and in others poor? We don't fully understand the answer to this question. But there are some things that we do know. We'll review that knowledge in this chapter. We'll also review some of the ideas people have advanced about what can be done to speed up the growth of poor countries. Some strategies truly help poor countries, but others have mixed results and may even hurt their development.

The International Distribution of Income

When we studied the distribution of Australian income, we observed that there is a great deal of inequality. In 1988, the poorest 20 per cent earned 5 per cent of total income, while the richest 20 per cent earned 43 per cent. As we will see, the differences in income within a country, large though they are, look insignificant when compared with the differences among the nations. Let's see how income is distributed among the nations of the world.

The World Bank divides the economies of the world into three groups, low-income, middle-income and high-income economies.

The high-income economies have per capita GDP values of at least US$6000. That category includes Hong Kong, Singapore, New Zealand and Australia as well as even higher-income economies like the United States and Japan. This group accounts for nearly 75 per cent of world GDP but only about 16 per cent of world population.

The middle-income economies have incomes from US$600 to US$6000. This group includes the Philippines, PNG, Thailand, Malaysia and Korea. It accounts for 11 per cent of global GDP and 21 per cent of world population.

The low-income economies include those with incomes lower than US$600. Examples are India and China. The poorest countries in the world include Ethiopia, Bangladesh, Laos and Nepal. This group accounts for 5 per cent of world GDP and 57 per cent of global population.

There are other categories of economies. The poorest countries are sometimes called underdeveloped countries. An **underdeveloped country** is a country in which there is little industrialization, limited mechanization of the agricultural sector, very little capital equipment and low per capita income. In many underdeveloped countries, large numbers of people live on the edge of starvation. Such people devote their time to producing the meagre supplies of food and clothing required for themselves and their families. They have no surplus to trade with others or to invest in new tools and capital equipment. One of the most publicized of the poor countries is Ethiopia, where thousands of people spend their lives trekking across parched landscapes in search of meagre food supplies.

A **developing country** is one that is poor but is accumulating capital and developing an industrial and commercial base. The developing countries have a large and growing urban population and have steadily growing incomes. Examples are India, China, Egypt and Mexico.

Newly industrialized economies (often called NIEs) are countries in which there is a rapidly developing broad industrial base and per capita income is growing quickly. Their incomes are a much higher proportion of those of the high-income countries. Examples of such countries are South Korea and Taiwan. Thailand and Malaysia are rapidly making the transition into this group.

Industrial countries are countries that have a large amount of capital equipment and in which people undertake highly specialized activities, enabling them to earn high per capita incomes. These are the countries of Western Europe, Canada and the United States, Japan, and Australia and New Zealand, as well as Singapore and Hong Kong.

The World Lorenz Curve

A **Lorenz curve** plots the cumulative percentage of income against the cumulative percentage of population beginning with the shares of income accruing to the poorest economies. If income is equally distributed, the Lorenz curve is a 45° line running from the origin. The degree of inequality is indicated by the extent to which the Lorenz curve departs from the 45° line of equality. Figure 38.1 shows two Lorenz curves: one curve depicts the distribution of income among families in Australia, and the other depicts the distribution of average per capita income across countries.

As you can see, the distribution of income among countries appears to be more unequal than the distribution of income among families within Australia. Forty per cent of the world's people live in countries whose incomes account for less than 10 per cent of the world's total. The richest 20 per cent of the people live in countries whose incomes account for more than 70 per cent of the world's total income. Inequality in income is even more severe than that apparent in Fig. 38.1, for the world Lorenz curve tells us only how unequal average incomes are among countries. Inequality within countries is not revealed by the world Lorenz curve.

Although there are many poor people in the world, there are also many whose lives are undergoing dramatic change. They live in countries in which

Figure 38.1 Lorenz Curve for Australia and the World, 1988

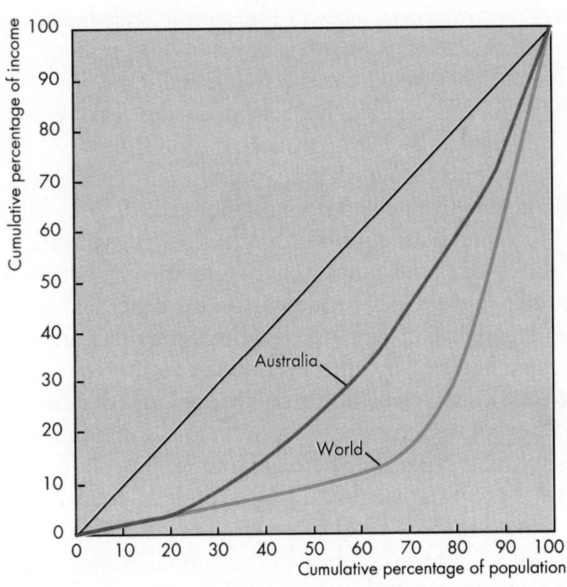

The cumulative percentage of income is plotted against the cumulative percentage of population. If income were distributed equally across countries, the Lorenz curve would be a straight diagonal line. The distribution of per capita income across countries is even more unequal than the distribution of income among families in Australia.

Source: Robert Summers and Alan Heston, 'The Penn World Table (Mark 5): An Expanded Set of International Comparisons, 1950–1980', *Quarterly Journal of Economics*, May 1991.

rapid economic growth is taking place. As a result of economic growth and development, millions of people now enjoy living standards undreamt of by their parents and inconceivable to their grandparents. Let's look at the connection between income level and the rate of economic growth.

Growth Rates and Income Levels

Poor countries can and do grow into rich countries. Poor countries become rich countries by achieving high growth rates of real per capita income over prolonged periods of time. Over the years, a small increase in the growth rate pays large dividends. A slowdown in the growth rate, maintained over a number of years, can result in a huge loss of real income.

The importance of economic growth and its effects on income levels are vividly illustrated by our own recent experience. In Australia in the early 1960s, aggregate income, measured by real GDP, was growing at nearly 6 per cent a year. Around 1973/74, GDP growth slowed down. The path actually followed by Australian GDP growth is shown in Fig. 38.2(a). The path that would have been followed if the pre-1973 growth trend had been maintained is also shown in that figure. By 1989, Australian real GDP was about a third below what it would have been if the 1960s growth rate had been maintained.

When poor countries have a slow growth rate and rich countries a fast growth rate, the gap between the rich and the poor widens. On the other hand, the experience in East Asia has been one of a narrowing gap between income levels in the region compared with the rich countries like the United States. This is because the rates of growth in the region have been higher than elsewhere. Figure 38.2(b) shows how the gap has narrowed for a sample of countries.

In Fig. 38.2(b), income levels are expressed as a proportion of the incomes in the United States. The data on income in this chart has been adjusted to allow for price differences between countries. They are real income measures. Since the mid-1960s, incomes in Australia and New Zealand have been about 60 per cent of those in the United States. Their relativities have not changed much at all. But look at Japan. By the late 1980s, its income has risen to Australian levels. Other East Asian economies are also catching up to us and to the United States. The example shown in the figure is Singapore. Taiwan and Korea are at an earlier stage of development.

For a low-income country to catch up to a rich country, it is necessary for its growth rate to exceed that of the rich country. Could a low-income country, such as China, achieve an income level equal to that in Australia? How long would it take? In 1985, per capita income in China in real terms was about 18 per cent of that in Australia. In the 1980s, Australia experienced an average per capita income growth rate of 2.0 per cent a year. If that growth rate is maintained and if per capita income in China also grows at 2.0 per cent a year, China will remain at 18 per cent of Australian income levels forever. The gap will remain constant. If per capita income in Australia were to grow at 2 per cent and if China could maintain a per capita income growth rate at twice that level — 4 per cent a year — China would catch up to Australia in per capita income levels in about 90 years. If China could do even twice as well as that — maintaining an 8 per cent a year growth rate in per capita incomes — the people of China would have income levels as high as those in Australia within your own lifetime — in about the year 2020. If China could pull off a miracle and make per capita income grow at 12 per cent a year, it would take just 18 years to catch up to Australia.

Growth rates as high as 10 per cent are not unknown. As we pointed out in the introduction, Japan grew in excess of 10 per cent a year, on the average, for almost 20 years following World War II. Recently China has, indeed, experienced per capita income growth of about 10 per cent a year, a rate which, if sustained, doubles per capita income every seven years. Even the poorest countries in the world would catch up to the industrial countries in a matter of 30 or 40 years if they could achieve and maintain growth rates of this level.

The key, then, to achieving high per capita income in a short time is to attain and maintain a high economic growth rate. The poor countries of today will join the rich countries of tomorrow only if they can find ways of attaining and maintaining rapid growth.

Clearly, the question of what determines a country's economic growth rate is a vital one. What does determine a country's economic growth rate? Let's turn to an examination of this crucial question.

Inputs, Technological Progress and Economic Growth

In the aggregate, income equals the value of output. Thus to increase average income, a country has to increase its output faster than its

Figure 38.2 Growth Rates and Income Levels

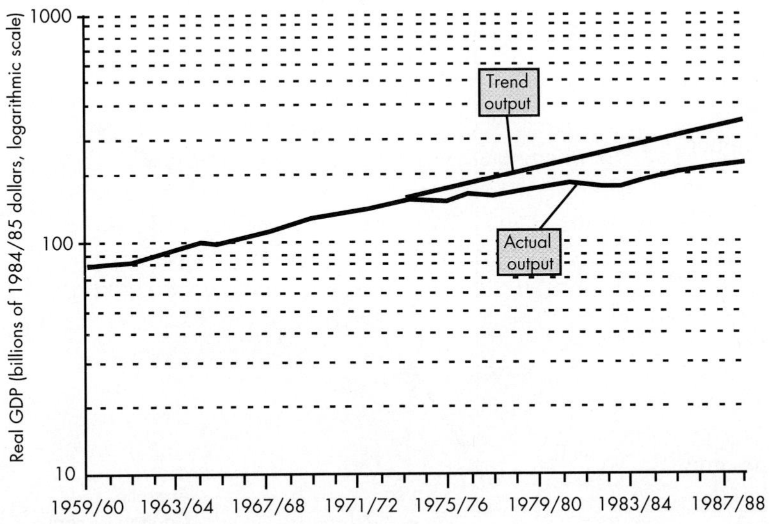

(a) Australian output loss from growth slowdown

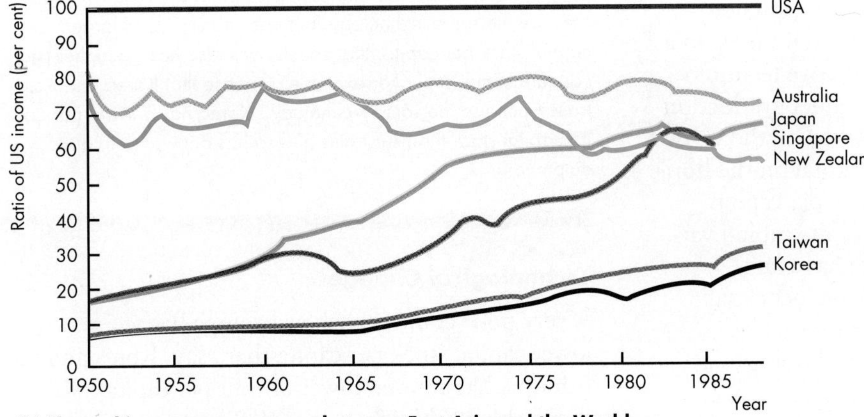

(b) The real income gap narrows between East Asia and the World

A fall in the growth rate of real income in Australia after 1973 has resulted in real GDP being about 33 per cent below what it would have been if the pre-1973 growth rate had been maintained. Small changes in the growth rate maintained over a long period lead to large changes in income levels. The figure also shows (part (b)) the real income levels in a sample of countries relative to income per head in the United States. Australian incomes have maintained their relative levels and NZ incomes have declined slightly. In Asia, income levels are catching up. Japan has already caught up with Australia. By the late 1980s, Singapore also had reached the real income levels of Australia and New Zealand.

Source: ABS, *Year Book Australia 1990*: Summers and Heston.

population. A country's output depends on its resources or inputs, and the techniques it employs for transforming inputs into outputs. This relationship between inputs and outputs is the *production function.* There are three inputs:

- Land
- Labour
- Capital

Land includes all the natural, non-produced inputs such as land itself, the minerals under it and all other non-produced resources. The physical quantity of these inputs is determined by nature, and countries have no choice but to put up with whatever natural resources they happen to have. But the economic significance of those endowments can change over time and thereby contribute to income growth. They might become better off as a result of discoveries of new deposits of natural resources. Furthermore, there are times at which those prices of unprocessed raw materials are rising quickly, and such times bring temporary income growth to resource-rich countries. We'll look at the relationship between resource endowments and growth, and the Australian experience, in a later part of this chapter.

Another source of increased output is a sustained increase in *labour* inputs. That is, a country can produce more output over the years simply because its population of workers grows. But for each successively larger generation of workers to have a higher *per capita* income than the previous generation, per capita output must increase. Population growth, on its own, does not usually lead to higher per capita output.

The input most responsible for rapid and sustained economic growth is capital. There are two broad types of capital: physical and human. *Physical capital* includes such things as highways and railways, dams and irrigation systems, tractors and ploughs, factories, trucks and cars, and buildings of all kinds. *Human capital* is the accumulated knowledge and skills of the working population. As individuals accumulate more capital, their incomes grow. As nations accumulate more capital per worker, labour productivity and output per capita grow.

To study the behaviour of per capita output, we use the per capita production function. The **per capita production function** shows how per capita output varies as the per capita stock of capital varies, in a given state of knowledge about alternative technologies. Figure 38.3 illustrates the per capita production function. Per capita output is measured on the vertical axis and the per capita stock of capital on the horizontal axis. The curve *PF* shows how per capita output varies as the amount of per capita capital varies. A rich country such as Australia has a large amount of per capita capital and a large per capita output. A newly industrialized country such as Korea which has access to the same technologies as Australia has a smaller capital stock and so a lower per capita output. Capital stock here is defined to include both human and physical capital.

Figure 38.3 The Per Capita Production Function

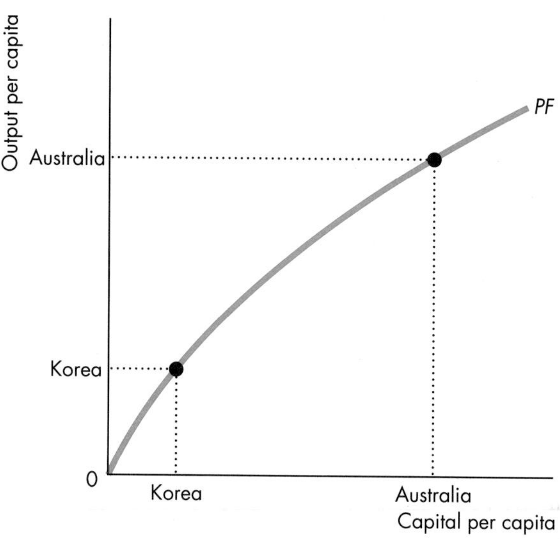

The per capita production function (*PF*) traces how per capita output varies as the stock of per capita capital varies. If two countries use the same technology, but one country has a larger capital stock per capita, that country will also have a higher per capita income level. For example, suppose that Korea and Australia each use the same technology. Korea has a lower per capita capital stock than Australia and so has a lower per capita output rate.

Capital Accumulation

By accumulating capital, a country can grow and move along its per capita production function. The greater the amount of capital (per capita), the greater is output (per capita). But the fundamental *law of diminishing returns* applies to the per capita production function. That is, as capital per capita increases, output per capita also increases but by decreasing increments. The diminishing returns to capital can, in fact, be offset because the per capita production function is constantly shifting upward as a result of improvements in technology. Let's see how technological change affects output and economic growth.

Technological Change

A very poor country such as Ethiopa has an even lower capital stock per capita than, say, Korea and so Ethiopia has an even lower output per capita. We didn't show Ethiopia in Fig. 38.3 because at such low levels of capital stock, it's also likely that Ethiopa won't even have access to the same technologies as either Korea or Australia.

Typically, rich countries use more productive technologies than do poor countries. That is, even if they have the same per capita capital, the rich country produces more output than the poor country. For example, a farmer in a rich country might use a 10-horsepower tractor, whereas a farmer in a poor country might literally use ten horses. Each has the same amount of 'horsepower', but the output achieved using the tractor is considerably more than that produced by using ten horses. The combination of better technology and more per capita capital accentuates still further the difference between the rich and poor countries.

Figure 38.4 illustrates the importance of the difference that technological advance makes in the catching-up process. Imagine that the year is 1950. The United States and Japan have access to different technologies shown by the dated per capita production functions. With a larger per capita stock of capital and access to more productive technology, the United States produces a larger per capita output than Japan. But by 2010 Japan has caught up, for two reasons. One is the accumulation of capital, but that is not the only reason. If technology had stayed the same in Japan, output per capita in Japan in 2010 would only reach the level of the United States in 1950. The difference is due to technological change. Japan has caught up to the technological frontier of the United States.

The faster the pace of technological advance, the faster the production function shifts upward. For example, in Fig. 38.4, the rate of technological change was faster in Japan than in the United States. The faster the pace of capital accumulation, the more quickly a country moves along its production function. Both of these forces lead to increased per capita output. A poor country becomes a rich country, partly by moving along its production function and partly by adopting better technology, thereby shifting its production function upward.

Figure 38.4 Technological Change

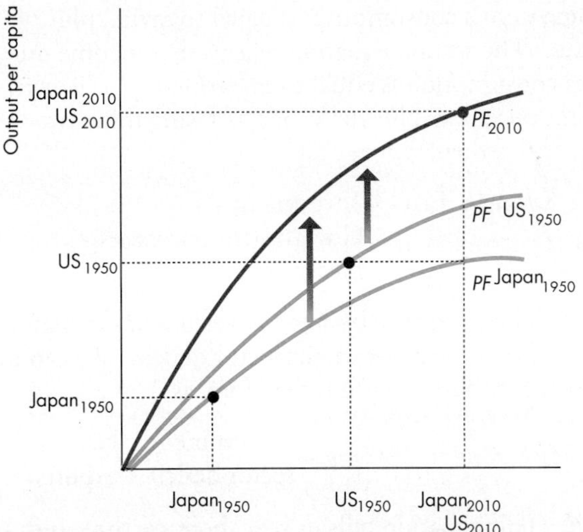

In 1950 the United States and Japan have different capital per capita levels of capital per person as well as facing different production functions. By 2010, the Japanese capital stock per person is the same as that of the United States but that alone was not enough to equalize incomes. Japan also caught up to US technology by 2010.

Technology transfer is at the heart of the catching-up process. As we suggested in the discussion of Fig. 38.4, the adoption of new technology promotes convergence. The transfer of ideas could even be reciprocal, but it is the low-income economies who have more to gain from the leaders rather than the reverse. The transfer of technologies is not costless and we'll look in the next section at some characteristics of economies which lower the barriers to the exchange of ideas.

REVIEW

There is enormous inequality in the world. The poorest people in the poorest countries live on the edge of starvation. The poorest fifth of the world's people consume less than one-twentieth of total output and the richest fifth consume about three-quarters of the total output. Nations can become rich by establishing and maintaining high rates of economic growth over prolonged periods. Economic growth results from the accumulation of capital relative to the workforce and the adoption of increasingly efficient technologies. The more rapidly capital is accumulated relative to workforce growth and the more rapid is the pace of technological change, the higher the rate of economic growth. Small changes in economic growth rates, maintained over a long period, make large differences to income levels. ■

Contributors to Economic Growth

The prescription for economic growth seems straightforward: poor countries can become wealthy by accumulating capital and adopting the most productive technologies. Is this all there is to it? Are there other conditions that have to be met?

One strategy for tackling this question is to look at the experience of a group, sometimes called a 'club', of high-growth economies and try to identify the contributors to their good performance. If we can do that, we might also be able to tackle another major issue in economics. That is, if the cure for abject poverty is so simple, why haven't more poor countries joined the 'high-income club'? Why are there so many poor people in the world today?

We do not know the answers to all these questions. If we did, we would be able to solve the problem of economic underdevelopment and there wouldn't be any poor countries. But we do understand some of the reasons for strong growth.

Which economies shall we study? From an Australian perspective the obvious candidates are the economies of East Asia, that is, not only the economies of Northeast Asia which we mentioned at the opening of this chapter but also Singapore, Malaysia, Indonesia, Thailand and the Philippines, all economies in Southeast Asia and members of ASEAN, most of which have also been growing rapidly.[2]

Capital Accumulation

The importance of the connection between capital accumulation and output growth is illustrated in Fig. 38.5(a). Capital accumulation is measured by the percentage of output represented by investment. (Recall that investment is the purchase of new capital equipment.) The figure shows the relationship between GDP growth and the investment rate in a sample of countries over the 1980s. The experience in East Asia is compared with the performance of three high-income countries around the Pacific, that is, Australia, New Zealand and the United States, and with the performance of the OECD countries, the Latin American countries and the South Asian economies.

The data is summarized by the trend line which indicates that every 5 to 6 percentage points in the investment rate add another percentage point to the GDP growth rate. There is, however, wide variation in this ratio. Some countries achieve much higher GDP growth rates than others with the same investment rates, that is, the productivity of investment varies a lot between economies. Some of the reasons were identified in our discussion of Fig. 38.4. Figure 38.5(b) shows what has been happening to investment over time in two extreme cases, Singapore and Ethiopia, compared with Australia. Fast-growing Singapore invests more than 30 per cent of its income. Slow-growing Ethiopia invests less than 5 per cent. The investment rate in Australia has fluctuated around 25 per cent.

Figure 38.5 only captures part of the investment story. As we explained above, it's not only the accumulation of physical capital that matters. The accumulation of human capital is also important. Recent research suggests that the stock of human capital provides an important explanation of the differences in income levels between economies. The problem is that the stock of human capital and the rate at which it is growing are very difficult to measure. It should include all the training of the population that is potentially part of the workforce, not only secondary school, college and university education but also on-the-job training. Imagine trying to measure all that!

High Saving Rate

As we have seen, capital accumulation is itself one of the main engines of economic growth. How is that capital accumulated? Let's start with some identities to see if we can say where the capital comes from.

As we saw in Chapter 23, there are just three things that people can do with their income: consume it, save it or pay it in taxes. That is

$$\text{Income} = \text{Consumption} + \text{Saving} + \text{Taxes}$$

We also saw in Chapter 23 that, in aggregate, the value of output equals income. An economy's output consists of consumption goods, capital goods, goods and services bought by the government and net exports (exports minus imports). Expenditure on capital goods is investment, and expenditure on goods and services bought by the government is called government purchases of goods and services. Thus

$$\begin{aligned}\text{Income} = {} & \text{Consumption} + \text{Investment} + \\ & \text{Government purchases} + \text{Net exports}\end{aligned}$$

The first of the above equations tells us that income minus consumption is equal to saving plus taxes. The second equation tells us that income minus consumption is equal to investment plus government purchases plus net exports. Using these two equations then, we see that

$$\begin{aligned}\text{Saving} + \text{Taxes} = {} & \text{Investment} + \\ & \text{Government purchases} + \\ & \text{Net exports}\end{aligned}$$

The difference between government purchases and taxes is the government sector deficit. We can rearrange the last equation, therefore, as

$$\text{Investment} = \text{Saving} - \frac{\text{Government}}{\text{sector deficit}} - \frac{\text{Net}}{\text{exports}}$$

This equation tells us that there are three influences on the pace at which a country can accumulate capital (can invest): private saving, the government sector deficit and net exports. If net exports are negative — imports exceed exports — they are financed by borrowing from the rest of the world (or by foreign investment). Other things being equal, the pace of capital accumulation is faster

[2] There are other economies within the East Asia region, for example Vietnam, Laos, Burma and Cambodia. But our focus is on the large and relatively open economies in the region.

Figure 38.5 Investment and Growth

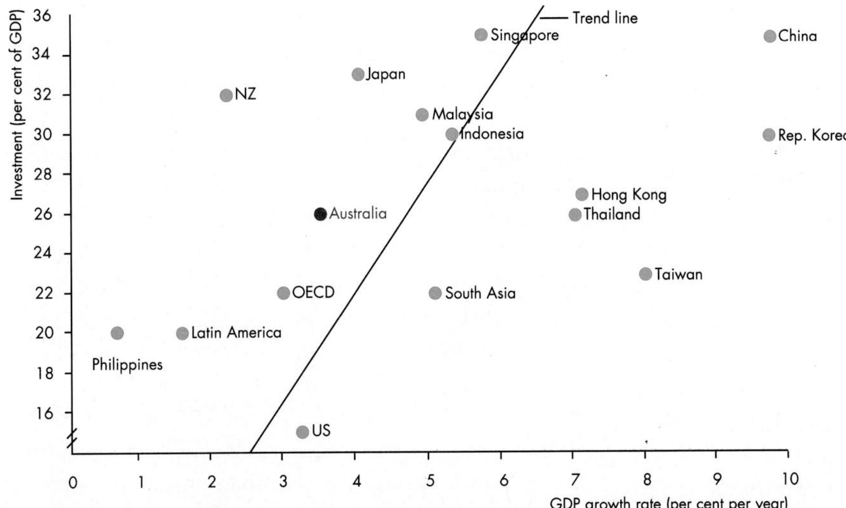

(a) Growth rate of GDP and the investment rate, 1980–89

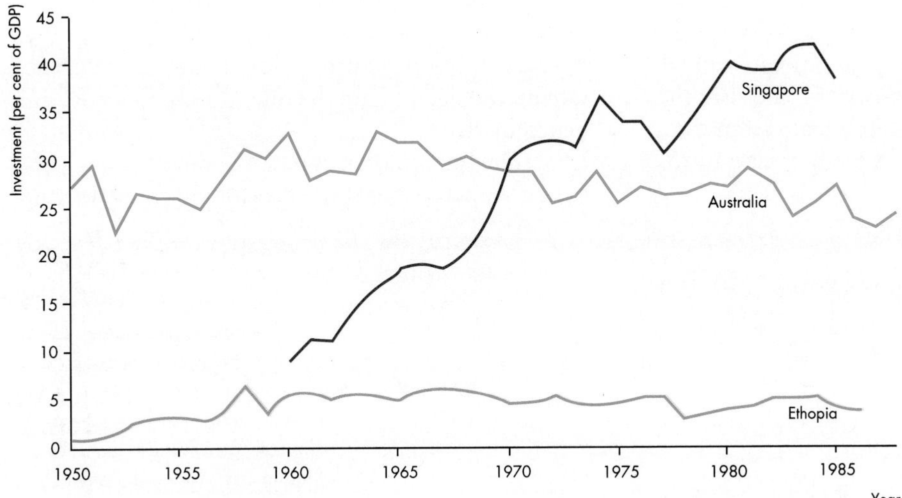

(b) Investment rates, 1950–1988

There is a positive relationship between the share of output going to investment (the investment rate) and real growth of GDP between 1980 and 1989. The trend line shows that every 5 to 6 percentage points extra on investment adds about one percentage point to the GDP growth rate. The fast-growing East Asian economies lie in the top right-hand corner of the diagram. Many also lie to the right of the trend line, indicating that their investment is highly productive (part (a)). Investment in Singapore has increased dramatically since 1960, while that in both Ethiopia and Australia has been almost constant (part (b)). High investment rates have led to higher growth rates.

Source: The World Bank, *World Development Report*, 1991: Summers and Heston.

- the larger the volume of private saving,
- the larger is government saving (that is, the smaller the government sector deficit or the larger the government sector surplus),
- the larger the borrowing (or investment) from the rest of the world.

The fraction of income that people save depends on the income level. Very poor people save nothing. As income rises, some part of income is saved. The higher the income level, the higher is the proportion of income saved. These patterns in the relationship between income and saving crucially affect the pace at which a country can grow.

Domestic saving is by far the most important component of the sources of financing investment. Figure 38.6 shows the savings rates in a sample of economies over the 1980s, relative to investment rates. In this figure, savings is defined to include both private saving and the government surplus (an increment to savings) or deficit (a subtraction). You can see a number of features in the figure. First, the savings rates for the East Asian economies are generally higher than those in other economies. Second, there is a strong correlation between the savings rate and the investment rate. Third, many East Asian economies now lie above the 45° line. (Note that the origin is missing from the figure.) This means they are running external surpluses.

International Debt

Poor countries often go into debt with the rest of the world. As we have just seen, a country incurs a debt when its net exports are negative. In that case, the current account deficit provides additional financial resources to domestic saving, which enable the country to accumulate capital at a faster pace than would otherwise be possible. A country that has a current account surplus is one that is accumulating capital at a slower pace than its domestic saving permits. Such a country uses part of its saving to accumulate capital — and thereby increases productivity — and uses the other part to pay interest on or repay loans from the rest of the world and to reduce its level of debt, or to expand net assets held abroad.

High savings rates and current account surpluses means that the East Asian economies are either paying off their debts, as in Korea, or have already done so and become net lenders to the rest of the world, like Japan and Taiwan.

The East Asian experience illustrates how a poor country that borrows heavily from the rest of the world and uses the borrowing to invest in productive capital will not become overburdened by debt provided the growth rate of income exceeds the interest rate on the debt. In such a situation, debt interest can be paid out of the higher income and there is still some additional income left over for additional domestic consumption or capital accumulation. The same principles apply to the use of foreign investment to finance capital accumulation. In East Asia, Singapore in the previous periods and Thailand and Indonesia more recently have made much use of foreign resources in the form of investment flows. We'll look at the role of foreign investment and trade in another section below.

Countries that borrow from the rest of the world and use the resources to invest in projects that have a low rate of return — lower than the interest rate on the debt — are the ones that become overburdened by debt.

The burden of international debt became particularly onerous for some developing countries dur-

Figure 38.6 Savings and Investment Rates, 1980–1989

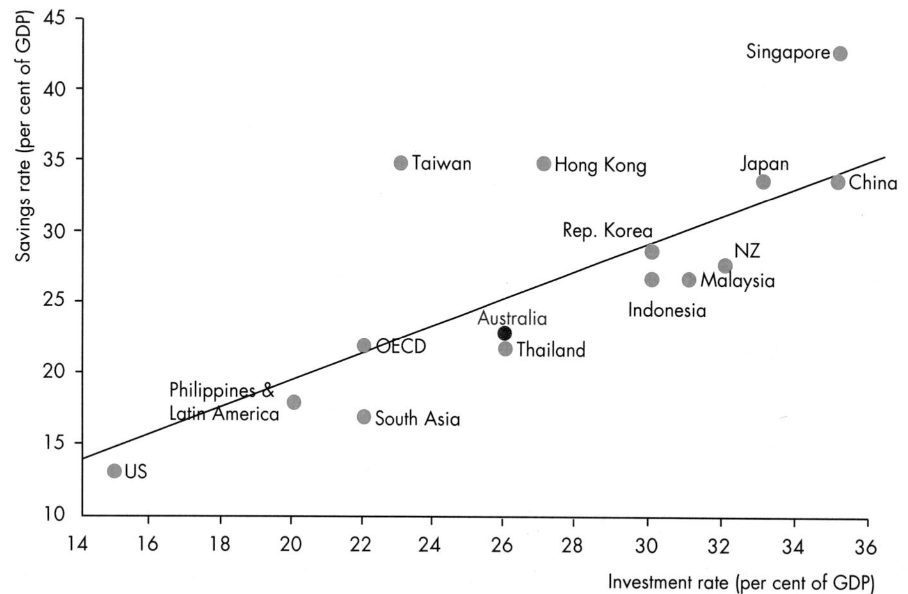

As we would expect, there is a strong correlation between total domestic savings (government and private) and the investment rate. The savings rates are generally high in East Asia and many East Asian economies now have savings rates which are higher than their investment rates. Those economies have external surpluses.

Source: The World Bank, *World Development Report*, 1991.

ing the 1980s. For example, the Latin American countries accumulated international debts of almost half a trillion dollars. Many of these debts were incurred during the 1970s when raw material prices were rising quickly. From 1973 to 1980, the prices of most raw materials increased, on the average, by close to 20 per cent a year — a rate much higher than the interest rates on the international debt being accumulated. In such a situation, countries producing raw materials, hungry for capital, borrowed on an enormous scale. In the early years of the 1980s, raw material prices collapsed. Huge international debts had been incurred, but the revenue with which to repay those debts was not coming in. To add a further burden, real interest rates increased sharply during the 1980s. Today, because of the combination of sagging raw material prices and higher interest rates, many poor countries have a crippling burden of international debt.

Instead of debt, another form of transfer of resources to low-income countries is foreign aid. How can it help the process of capital accumulation?

Foreign Aid

The idea that foreign aid helps economic development arises from a simple consideration. If a country is poor because it has too little capital, then by being given aid it can accumulate more capital and achieve a higher per capita output. Repeated applications of foreign aid year after year can enable a country to grow much more quickly than it could if it had to rely exclusively on its own domestic saving. On this line of reasoning, the greater the flow of foreign aid to a country, the faster it will grow.

Some economists suggest that foreign aid will not necessarily make a country grow faster, but the consensus is that foreign aid can help economic development if the resource flow is properly managed. The same rules apply to aid as to debt, that is, the projects in which aid is invested must be profitable ones. Aid is often profitably applied to investment projects that would not normally be undertaken by the private sector. The creation of human capital in the education systems of low-income countries is one example.

Aid is the principal form of transfer of funds to low-income countries. In 1989 aid accounted for nearly two-thirds of new flows of resources to low-income countries. The share of aid in resource flows to the poorest countries was even higher, at about 80 per cent. So the flow of aid can be important, but aid alone will not make a decisive difference to growth rates.

Population Growth

One of the impediments to economic development and rapid and sustained growth in per capita income is rapid population growth. In the past 20 years, world population has been growing at an average rate of 2 per cent a year. At a population growth rate this high, world population doubles every 37 years. That population stood at more than 5 billion at the end of 1988. But the pattern of population growth is uneven. Rich industrial countries have relatively low population growth rates, often less than 0.5 per cent a year, while the poor, underdeveloped countries have high population growth rates, in some cases exceeding 3 per cent a year.

Why is fast population growth an impediment to economic growth and development? Doesn't a larger population give a country more productive resources, permit more specialization, more division of labour and therefore yet greater output? These benefits do indeed stem from a large population. But when the population is growing rapidly and a country is poor, there are two negative effects on economic growth and development that outweigh the benefits of a larger population. They are:

- An increase in the proportion of dependants to workers.
- An increase in the amount of capital devoted to supporting the population rather than producing goods and services.

Some facts about the relationship between the number of dependants and population growth are shown in Fig. 38.7. The number of dependants is measured, on the vertical axis, as the percentage of the population under 15 years of age. As you can see, the higher the population growth rate, the larger is the percentage of the population under 15 years of age. In a country such as Australia, where the population growth rate is about 1.4 per cent a year, about one person in five (22 per cent) is under 15 years of age. In countries such as the Philippines or Malaysia, which have among the highest population growth rates in East Asia (of 2.5 per cent a year or higher), close to 40 per cent of the population is under 15 years of age.

Let's see why there is a connection between the population growth rate and the percentage of young people in the population. A country might have a steady population because it has a high birth rate and an equally high death rate. But the same steady population growth rate could occur with a low birth rate and a low death rate. Population growth rates increase when either the birth rate increases or the death rate decreases. Historically, it is a fall in the death rate with a relatively high and constant birth rate that has led to population explosions. The fall in the death rate mainly takes the form of a fall in the infant mortality rate, and it is this phenomenon that results in an enormous increase in the proportion of young people in the population.

In a country with a large number of young people, capital resources are directed toward providing schools, hospitals, roads and housing rather than irrigation schemes and industrial capital projects. Such a use of scarce capital resources is obviously not wasteful and does bring great benefits, but it does not add immediately to the economy's capacity to produce goods and services out of which yet additional capital accumulation can be provided.

The Underdevelopment Trap

The obstacles to economic development are so severe that some economists have suggested that there is a kind of poverty trap that applies to countries — the underdevelopment trap. The **underdevelopment trap** is a situation in which a country is locked into a low-income situation that reinforces itself. A low level of capital per worker (both physical and human capital) results in low output per worker. Low productivity, in turn, produces low per capita income. Low per capita income results in low saving. With low saving, there is a low rate of capital accumulation. Capital accumulation can barely keep up with population growth, so the stock of capital per worker remains low and the cycle repeats itself.

Population Control

Almost all developing countries use population control methods as part of their attempt to break out of the underdevelopment trap. Population control programmes have two key elements: the provision of low-cost birth control facilities and the provision of incentives encouraging people to have a small number of children. These methods meet with some, but limited, success. One of the most highly publicized programmes of population control is that employed in China. In that country, families are strongly discouraged from having more than one child. Despite this policy, the population of China continues to grow and forecasts, released in 1989, suggest that by the year 2000 the population will have grown above its target level by an amount equal to seven times the entire population of Australia.

Thus important though they are, population control methods, by themselves, are not likely to

Figure 38.7 Population Growth and Number of Dependants

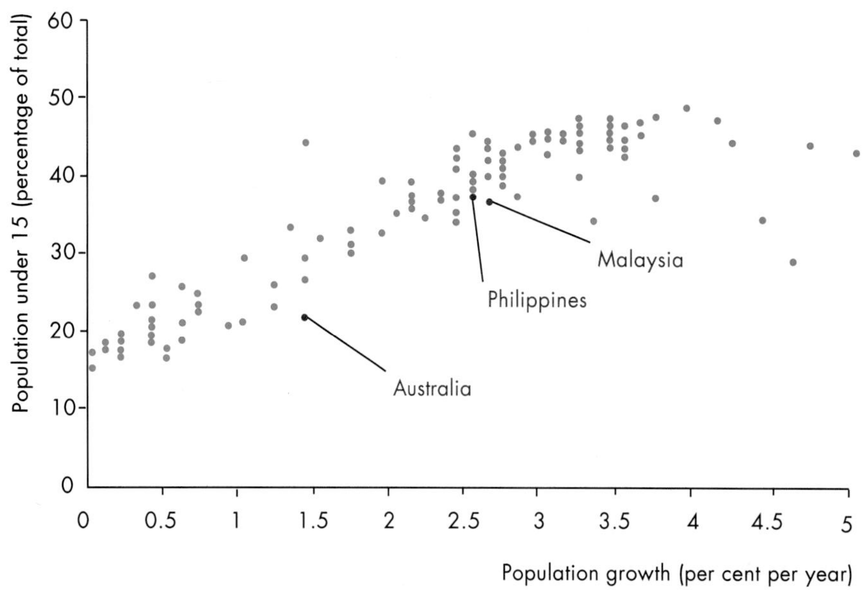

Each point represents a country. It shows the percentage of the population that is under 15 years of age (measured on the vertical axis) and the population growth rate (measured on the horizontal axis). The number of young people in the population is strongly influenced by the population growth rate. In countries such as Australia where the population growth is slower, about a fifth of the population is under 15 years of age, while in fast-growing countries such as Malaysia or the Philippines about 40 per cent of the population is under 15 years of age.

Source: The World Bank, *World Development Report*, 1991.

yield success in the fight against underdevelopment and poverty. A more common experience is that other initiatives to promote growth and raise incomes will simultaneously cut the rate of population growth.

A factor that has made a decisive difference to growth in many countries, especially in East Asia, is international trade policy. Let's now turn to an examination of the effects of international trade and investment on growth and development.

Trade and Development

Figure 38.8 illustrates the high positive correlation between merchandise export growth and GDP growth. It also highlights the point that the East Asian economies are generally clustered in the top right-hand corner of the chart. Also, over the period of the 1980s shown in the chart, the growth rate of exports for these economies usually exceeded that of GDP. That means the ratio of exports to GDP, a commonly used indicator of the degree of international orientation of an economy, must be increasing. Why is there a positive relationship between trade and growth?

The simple reason is that, as we saw in Chapter 36, specialization in domestic production and trade in the world market generates real income gains compared with a policy of self-sufficiency. As we saw in Chapter 36 also, access to the world market helps to exploit economies of scale. These are some of the static gains from trade. They generate real income, so they contribute to higher standards of living. But there are also some dynamic gains from trade.

For example, penetration of the market by imports is an important source of competition, especially in relatively small economies like Australia. Competition with other firms in a global market prods local firms to produce efficiently, to innovate and to adopt new technologies. These pressures help to ensure that the economy really does stick to the production function in Fig. 38.3. That function is after all a frontier. It is possible for an economy to drop below the frontier, a gap which represents opportunities lost. Trade also pushes economies to move to higher production functions, as we supposed happened in Japan (see Fig. 38.4).

A complementary contribution of trade is that it generates the funds with which to buy new technologies or obtain more capital. The foreign suppliers of capital or technology will want to be paid in their own currency. Strong export growth generates the foreign exchange that is required. An economy with strong export growth is far less likely to fall into the underdevelopment trap. If exports are growing rapidly it means that firms are specializing in production of goods in which this economy is internationally com-

Figure 38.8 GDP Growth and Export Growth, 1980–1989

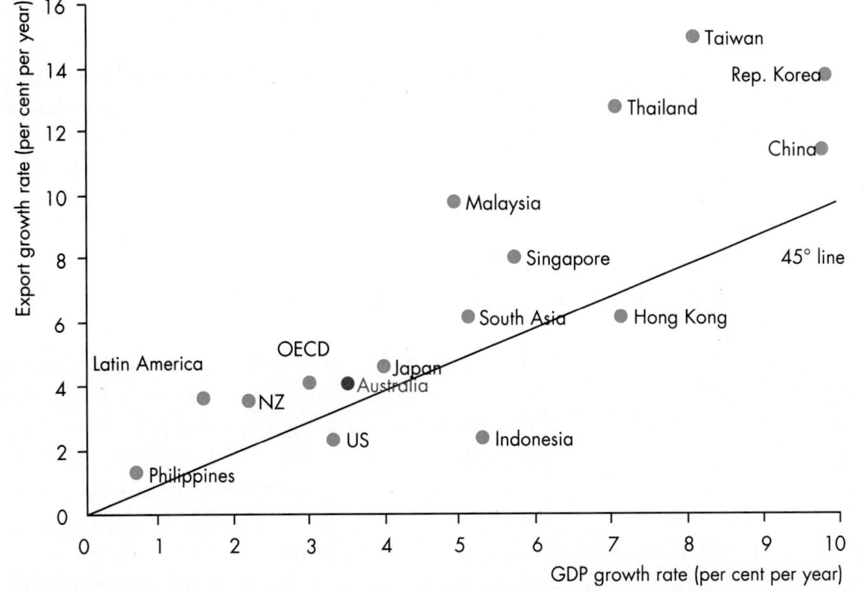

Annual average real growth in exports is positively correlated with real GDP growth over the 1980s. Furthermore the trend is for trade to grow faster than output, especially in the high-growth economies. The East Asian economies generally have higher export growth rates than the slow-growing economies.

Source: The World Bank, *World Development Report,* 1991.

petitive. Production decisions are not being distorted, by protection for example (see Chapter 36). As a result, any capital that is borrowed or supplied by foreign investors is more likely to be invested in profitable projects, so the repayments will not be a burden.

Foreign Investment

Foreign investment is the capital supplied by equity holders in a project. It is another source of capital inflow, alongside debt and aid. It is distinguished from debt because the suppliers of the capital are also equity holders, or owners, in the project which is financed. Compared with suppliers of debt, the foreign investors will only get a return if the project is profitable. As a result, they also bear some of the risks. This is an advantage of equity over debt. On the other hand, foreign investors do have some control over the project and in some economies that degree of foreign control is seen as a disadvantage. But in either case, the supplier of the capital will expect repayment and reward. Switching from equity to debt finance will not avoid that.

Foreign investment has some other side benefits. In many cases, foreign technology will only be supplied in a package with capital and management. That is, foreign owners of a new technology may only supply if they can also be part-owners of the project in which it is used. This gives them greater control over the use of their new technology. Debt finance will not have this side benefit.

Structural Change

The East Asian experience highlights another role for foreign investment. As economies grow and accumulate capital, the sorts of industries in which they are competitive change. According to the theory we developed in Chapter 36, this is because the relative opportunity costs change as capital accumulates and labour becomes relatively scarce. The East Asian experience has also been that new suppliers keep emerging to take over old markets, as, for example, Korea and Taiwan took over some of Japan's markets in textiles and clothing; now China and some ASEAN countries are doing the same to them. Foreign investment facilitates this process. Countries losing competitiveness can invest in new locations where the industry is competitive. Both sides gain. The old competitor finds a new base from which to continue to supply its markets. The host economy to the foreign investment is helped into a new export industry. It will also be able to export back to the market in the home economy of the foreign investor. Penetration of the home economy market is made easier by the presence of a partner from that economy.

The sequencing of development in East Asia accelerated this process of structural change. Economies in the region are at widely different stages of development. Some are net exporters of capital, that is, domestic savings exceed investment; others net importers. This means there are suppliers of capital within the region for those economies still trying to maintain high investment rates. The flows of capital also have the sorts of trade-promoting effects that we just discussed.

Trade and foreign investment have therefore been important components of the success of rapidly growing East Asian economies. They are critical to the process of the diffusion of technology from high-income economies to the laggards. They provide an instrument for managing and financing the transfer of technologies and they promote a competitive environment in which entrepreneurs have stronger incentives to transfer and to adopt those technologies.

Another important influence on growth is the capacity to maintain good macroeconomic management of the economy, not always an easy task even in periods of rapid growth. We'll now look at a number of aspects of macroeconomic policy and their contribution to growth.

Aggregate Demand Stimulation and Growth

It is often suggested that growth and development can be stimulated by expanding aggregate demand. The suggestion takes two forms. Sometimes it is suggested that if the rich countries stimulate their own aggregate demand, their economies will grow more quickly and, as a consequence, commodity prices will remain high. High commodity prices help poor countries and so stimulate their income growth and economic development. It is also often suggested that poor countries can make themselves grow faster by stimulating their own level of aggregate demand.

Can stimulating aggregate demand in the rich countries help the poor countries? Can aggregate demand stimulation in poor countries help them grow? The answer is to both these questions is almost certainly no, but let's see why. As we discovered when we studied the theory of aggregate demand and aggregate supply in Chapter 24, changes in aggregate income can occur as a result of either a change in aggregate demand or a change in aggregate supply. But aggregate demand changes affect output and income in the short run only. That is, when wages and other input prices are fixed, a change in aggregate demand changes both output and the price level. But in the long run, a change in aggregate demand leads to a change in the prices of goods and services and of factors of production. Once input prices have adjusted in response to a change in aggregate demand, income returns to its capacity level. Changes in per capita capacity income can be brought about only by changes in per capita productivity — which, in turn, is brought about by changes in the stock of per capita capital and in the state of technology.

This macroeconomic model of aggregate demand and aggregate supply applies to all countries, rich and poor alike. If rich countries stimulate aggregate demand by persistently allowing it to grow at a pace faster than capacity growth, they will generate inflation. If they allow it to grow at a pace similar to the growth of capacity, prices will be stable. In recent history, we have seen rich countries generating rapid inflation and moderate inflation. The 1970s was a decade of rapid inflation. During that decade, commodity prices also increased quickly, enabling many developing countries to increase the pace of capital accumulation and income growth. The 1980s was a decade of moderate inflation. It is this decade that brought falling raw material prices and the burden of large international debt for many developing countries.

Don't the facts of the 1970s and 1980s support the conclusion that rapid aggregate demand growth and inflation in the rich countries help the poor countries? They do not. Rather, they provide an example of what can happen, over a limited time period, when there is a previously unexpected increase or decrease in the growth rate of aggregate demand. In the 1970s, there was an unexpectedly rapid increase in aggregate demand. As a consequence, many countries experienced increasing inflation and increasing output growth. In the 1980s, there was an unexpectedly severe contraction of aggregate demand in the rich countries, resulting in falling inflation and a slowdown in output growth (and in some countries, including Australia, a fall in output). Unexpected fluctuations in the inflation rate can produce fluctuations in output growth — precisely what happened in the 1970s and 1980s. But sustained aggregate demand growth and sustained steady inflation are not capable of producing sustained growth in output.

Developing countries can make aggregate demand grow at a rapid or a moderate rate. The more rapidly aggregate demand grows, relative to the growth of capacity, the higher is the inflation rate. Some developing countries inflate quickly and others slowly. We might expect there to be a relationship, namely that lower inflation rates would promote long-run growth. In Chapter 22, we looked at some of the problems that can be caused by inflation. In this chapter, we have stressed that high-growing economies have high investment rates and high savings rates. Both will be reduced by the problems of

Figure 38.9 GDP Growth and Inflation, 1980–1989

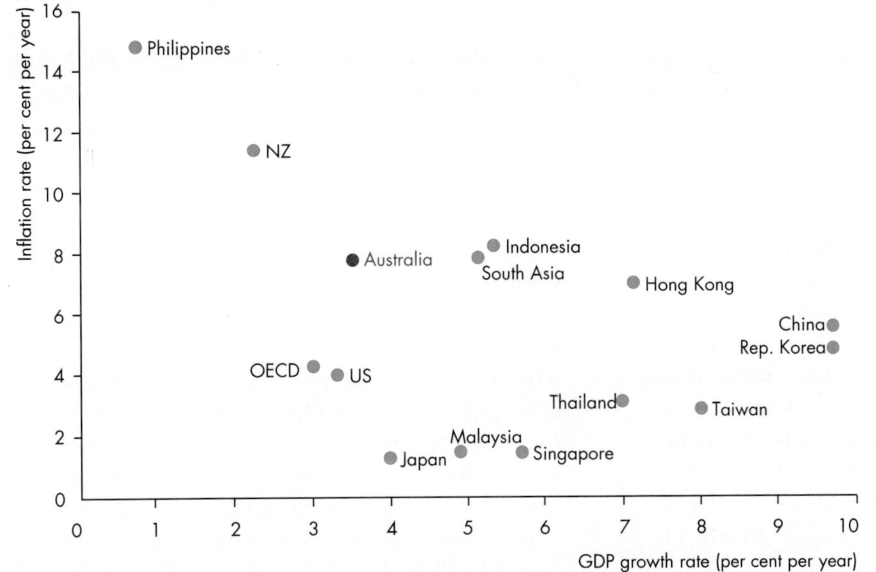

Each point in the figure represents a country or a region. It shows the GDP growth rate plotted against the annual inflation rate. There appears to be an inverse relation in the 1980s between the inflation rate and the pace of economic growth. The outliers, whose experience reinforces this result, are the Philippines (shown in the figure) and the Latin American countries (not shown).

Source: The World Bank, *World Development Report*, 1991

unanticipated inflation. Even anticipated inflation, in the absence of indexing systems, will inhibit savings and investment. We would expect that over a long time, high growth rates of GDP would not be consistent with sustained high inflation rates.

Figure 38.9 shows these two variables over the 1980s for the sample of countries and regions we have used in this chapter (with one exclusion). There appears to be a negative relationship. The East Asian experience is that, with the exception of Indonesia, high growth has been sustained with low inflation rates. It is the high-income and slow-growing economies that have higher inflation rates. An outlier in this figure is the Philippines. The other outlier not shown is the group of Latin American countries. Over the 1980s, the average annual rate of inflation in those economies was 117 per cent a year, while average annual GDP growth was 1.5 per cent. This data suggests that the management of aggregate demand so that inflation rates are kept low is an important contributor to the capacity of an economy to sustain high growth of GDP over a longer period.

An East Asian Model

Is there an East Asian model of development? It is certainly the case that there are low-income countries which are not in East Asia but which still have grown quickly. There are also some East Asian economies which have not grown quickly. So being in the East Asian region is neither necessary nor sufficient for high growth. But there are some common experiences in the region which highlight the important contributors to growth. We've seen that to grow quickly, a country must accumulate capital at a rapid pace. To do so it must achieve a high saving rate and use foreign funds, either debt or equity, in high-return activities. The most rapidly growing developing countries have a high pace of capital accumulation and obtain a high return on their capital by pursuing an open trade policy, thereby ensuring that they produce those goods and services in which they have a comparative advantage. An open economic policy also promotes the transfer of technology and the management of structural changes associated with growth. They achieve low population growth rates, which means that the accumulation of more capital for each worker is not held back. They also have clever macroeconomic policies which keep inflation rates under control, while they sustain high rates of output growth. These are the common elements of the East Asian experience.

Settler Economies: Resources and Growth

The Australian experience is of course very different from that in East Asia. The East Asian economies are densely settled. They are labour-abundant economies, while other economies, like Australia, are not. In comparison Australia has a large endowment of land, as we defined it earlier in this chapter, that is, not only the land itself but all the minerals underneath. Is there a difference in the path of development for a country like Australia which is resource-abundant, not labour-abundant?

Some countries well endowed with resources have attained very high income at the early stages of their development. University of Adelaide economic historian Ian McLean has coined the phrase 'settler economies'. **Settler economies** are economies which have abundant resources and small populations whose relatively high incomes at early stages of development attract a large inflow of other factors of production, such as immigrant labour. The high levels of prosperity of these economies are not always sustained. Australia is an example. As we noted earlier, income per head in Australia was higher than anywhere else in the world in 1870. Since then our position has dropped away, so that as shown in Fig. 38.2 Australian incomes are now only about 60 per cent of those in the United States.

The obvious source of high income in Australia at the end of last century was the existence of resources which could be converted into exportable items. Typically resource-rich economies had to rely on export markets because their own populations were small relative to the abundance of their resources. The small size of the domestic market has some other implications which help explain the slowdown in growth in settler economies. Because their populations were generally small, these sorts of economies, as their name suggests, usually relied on immigrant labour. The high levels of immigration made it more likely that there would be a smaller proportion of the population which was not working. As a result, and as long as the rate of immigration was not so high as to swamp the benefits of the resource endowment, the population would be relatively more productive and so the measured income per head would be higher in such an economy. But as the immigration flow slowed, the population would assume a more normal composition and as happened in Australia, we would expect to see the growth of income per head slow down.

Do the 'settler economies' necessarily make a transition to highly industrialized economies? That is, they can be high income, but do they eventually have to decrease the relative size of their resource sector in order to sustain their income levels? As long as they keep finding sufficient quantities and qualities of highly valued natural resources, the settlers could continue to earn high incomes. But otherwise we would expect to see the gradual transformation of the structure of the economy. Wealth accumulated during the resource boom period of development would be re-invested in other sectors of the economy to sustain further growth.

In this regard, Australia was lucky in the 1960s and 1970s. Discoveries of new deposits and higher prices added to incomes. If new resources keep being discovered then the resource-abundant country which adds to its labour force by migration can sustain high incomes and growth. Even agricultural land could be made more productive by the application of the results of research and development. This process was also important in New Zealand.

Australia has tried other ways of augmenting the demand for labour and therefore wages and incomes. The idea in the first decade of this century, after the experience of a recession in the 1890s, was to promote the manufacturing sector through protection. The hope was that a bigger manufacturing sector which used a lot of labour would, under protection, grow and create the demand for labour to support high wages without unemployment, even while maintaining a relatively large migration programme. The expectation that wages could be kept high was the basis of the development of the Australian industrial relations system. But as we saw in Chapter 36, protection also has its costs, and the argument in this chapter is that an inward or protection industry policy does not usually lead to high growth.

The transition to industrialization in Australia has been held up by the resource wealth that emerged in the 1960s and 1970s, partly a result of the growth in East Asia that we have just examined. Other settler economies in which the resource endowment relative to population was lower have managed the transition to industrialization and also to sustained growth. The United States is the outstanding example. It, too, was once relatively resource-rich but eventually became a net importer of raw materials. The reasons for this transformation and the industrial success of the United States are still the focus of research by economists.

There is one key difference between the United States and Australia that might help to explain our different experiences. This difference is that the states of the United States together comprised a large and highly integrated economy with a big population. Each US state could be thought of as a separate settler economy, but one which followed free trade not protectionist policies. If so, this is another example of our earlier observations about the role of trade as a stimulus to growth. What would Australia have been like if instead of adopting a protectionist position, we had looked outward in the 1920s? Whatever our previous strategy, can we now make the most of the opportunities created by sustained growth in East Asia and integrate ourselves into that regional economy?

S U M M A R Y

The International Distribution of Income

There is enormous inequality in the international distribution of income. The poorest countries have average per capita income levels of 4 to 9 per cent of that in the United States. Half of the world's population earns only 15 per cent of world income and the richest 20 per cent of the world's population earns 55 per cent of income. (pp. 558–560)

Growth Rates and Income Levels

Poor countries become rich by achieving and maintaining high rates of per capita income growth for prolonged periods. Rich countries grow at about 1.5 per cent per year. Poor countries that have a slower growth rate than that fall further behind. Poor countries that achieve a growth rate higher than 1.5 per cent per year close the gap on the rich countries. High and sustained growth makes a dramatic difference in a short time span. The experience in East Asia has been rapid growth, so much so that Japan by the end of the 1980s had caught up to income levels in industrial countries, and other economies in the region were rapidly approaching those levels. (p. 560)

Inputs, Technological Progress and Economic Growth

Per capita income growth results from the growth in per capita capital and in technological change. The greater the fraction of income invested in new capital equipment and the faster the pace of technological change, the higher is the rate of economic growth. (pp. 560–563)

Contributors to Growth

Important contributors to growth in successful economies appear to include (i) a high domestic savings rate, (ii) the use of foreign resources, either through debt or equity, but invested in profitable projects, (iii) a low population growth rate, (iv) an internationally orientated trade policy, and (v) careful macroeconomic management that keeps down inflation rates. (pp. 563–572)

Settler Economies

These are sources of success in all economies. Settler economies, which are well endowed with resources relative to population, tend to follow a different development path. Australia is an example of this sort of economy and so was the United States. Australia's relatively high resource wealth has slowed down the shift to industrialization. But an inward-looking trade policy in Australia may also have been a constraint. (pp. 572–573)

KEY TERMS

Developing country, p. 559
Foreign investment, p. 570
Industrial country, p. 559
Newly industrialized economy, p. 559
Per capita production function, p. 562
Settler economy, p. 572
Underdeveloped country, p. 559
Underdevelopment trap, p. 568

PROBLEMS

1 Per capita income in Indonesia in real terms is now about 12 per cent of that in Australia. If incomes in Indonesia are growing at about 7 per cent a year and at about 2 per cent a year in Australia, how many years will it take for Indonesian incomes to catch up to Australian incomes?

2 Siliconia is a poor country with no natural resources except sand. Per capita income is $500 a year and this entire income is consumed. Per capita income is constant — there is no economic growth. The government sector has a balanced budget and there are no exports or imports. Then, one day, the price of silicon increases and Siliconia is able to export sand at a huge profit. Exports soar from zero to $400 (per capita). Per capita income increases to $1000 a year and per capita consumption increases to $600 a year. There are still no imports and Siliconia has a current account surplus of $400 per capita.

a) What happens to investment and the growth rate in Siliconia?
b) If Siliconia imports capital goods equal in value to its exports, what will be its investment?
c) What will be its current account balance?
d) If the government sector of Siliconia runs a budget deficit of $100 (per capita), what will be its investment?

3 Discuss some of the factors which might contribute to the variation in GDP growth rates for given investment rates, illustrated in Fig. 38.5. Consider, for example, why most high-income countries tend to be to the left of the trend line? Could this effect contribute to the convergence in income levels observed in Fig. 38.2(b)?

Chapter 39

Comparing Economic Systems

After studying this chapter, you will be able to:

- Explain why the economic problem of scarcity is common to all economic and political systems.
- Describe the various political systems that have been proposed to deal with the economic problem.
- Explain the difference between capitalism, socialism and market socialism.
- Describe the varieties of capitalism in Australia, the United States, Japan and Western Europe
- Describe the main features of the economy of the former Soviet Union.
- Explain the economic restructuring — or Perestroika — being undertaken in the former Soviet Union and identify the sources of problems in the first round of reforms.
- Describe the economic reforms being undertaken in China and discuss the issues that emerged at the end of the 1980s.

Perestroika

From Moscow and Beijing to Washington, London, Canberra and Tokyo, dramatic changes are taking place in the way governments manage their nations' economies. In Moscow, it is called *perestroika* — restructuring. At the June 1987 meeting of the Central Committee of the Communist Party, Mikhail Gorbachev presented his model for the 'radical restructuring of economic management' in the former Soviet Union. With an almost religious intensity, he preached his message in meetings with ordinary Russians and proclaimed the virtues of 'working an extra bit harder'. Then in the July 1991 meeting of the Central Committee, Gorbachev argued that the time had come for the party to embrace private ownership of property and a free-market economy. This call for faster economic reform stimulated the processes for political reform and, following a failed coup, in October 1991 the Soviet Union was dismantled and replaced by the Commonwealth of Independent States (CIS). In Beijing, widespread reforms are being encouraged and implemented. These reforms began in the agriculture sector in 1978. In 1984 the decision was made in China to extend the reforms to urban industry as well. The extent of the market as a device for allocating resources has increased, although in some sectors bureaucratic allocation systems persist. China has experimented with a so-called two-track system, with markets operating alongside a planning system for some goods. Changes in government economic management are less dramatic in Washington, London, Canberra and Tokyo than those in the Soviet Union and China. But change, nevertheless, is in the air. In Australia, that change has taken the form of a steady process of deregulation, a process begun during the Fraser government years when there were the first enquiries into deregulation of the banking system and then accelerated after the election of the Hawke government in 1983. A similar process of deregulation began even earlier in the United States. In Great Britain and many other Western European countries, deregulation has been accompanied by the selling off of state-operated businesses such as railways, telecommunications and public utilities to private enterprise. In Japan, change is taking place that results in a greater liberalization of the Japanese economy and of its international trading and financial relations. What are the main differences in the economic systems of the old Soviet Union and China, and of Australia, the United States, Western Europe and Japan? What exactly are capitalism and socialism? Why are the socialist countries undergoing such massive changes in their methods of economic management? Why are countries in Western Europe and Japan privatizing large parts of their economies? How do the alternative economic systems of capitalism and socialism work? Can a single country successfully combine the two different economic systems?

In this chapter, we're going to describe some of the key differences in the economic systems of the world's major countries. We will learn how capitalist and socialist economies operate. We'll examine some of the diversity among the capitalist economies: Australia, the United States, Japan and Western Europe. We'll study the economic system of the former Soviet Union and see why *perestroika* is taking place. We'll examine the reforms in China and describe its economic goals. In the cases of China and the Soviet Union we will also see that the reforms have led to some serious economic problems. These problems occurred almost immediately in the Soviet case but much later in the Chinese case. We'll look at the origins of those problems and identify some common challenges that face reforming socialist economies.

The Fundamental Economic Problem

The first thing we learn when we begin to study economics is that the source of all economic problems is the universal fact of *scarcity*. In embarking on a study of comparative economic systems, it will be worthwhile to review and reinforce our understanding of the implications of scarcity.

Scarcity

Scarcity arises because we all want to consume more goods and services than the available resources make possible. The *production possibility frontier* describes the limits to what we can produce; it separates the attainable from the unattainable (see Chapter 3). Our consumption possibilities are maximized if we arrange our economic affairs in such a way that we produce at a point on our production possibility frontier. The first aspect of solving the economic problem, therefore, involves getting on to the frontier.

Getting on to the Production Possibility Frontier

If we operate at a point on the production possibility frontier rather than at some point inside it, we produce more of all goods. We cannot take it for granted, however, that we will automatically operate on the frontier. We might waste resources. For example, resources are wasted if we produce more of some perishable commodity at a given moment than can be quickly consumed. Some of the commodity rots and may as well not have been produced. Therefore the resources used to produce that commodity are wasted.

Another more subtle, yet more important, form of waste arises if productive resources are combined in a way that makes the cost of production higher than it needs to be. For example, electricity can be generated by using coal, oil or nuclear power as the energy source. If the cost of producing a megawatt of electricity is lowest using nuclear power, but instead coal and oil are used, then productive resources are wasted. Don't forget, however, that in economics the word 'cost' includes all costs. In the case of power production, the costs include environmental costs such as pollution, the hazard of nuclear accident and contamination, and many other costs not borne by the producer of electricity.

Different economic systems use different methods to get the economy to a point on its production possibility frontier. We will look at those methods in the next section. Once the economy is on its production possibility frontier, no more of any one good can be produced without producing less of some other good. It is this fact that gives rise to the concept of *opportunity cost.* The opportunity cost of producing one more unit of any particular good is the amount of some other good or goods forgone. Because it is only possible to produce more of one good by producing less of another good, a second aspect of solving the economic problem involves getting to the right point on the frontier.

Producing the Right Quantities of Goods and Services

Determining how much of each of the various goods and services to produce requires that people's preferences of the alternatives be taken into account. For example, if people place a high value on clean air and a low value on quick and convenient transportation, we would produce fewer cars and highways and have more stringent methods of controlling exhaust emission. If people value vacations on the moon highly and place little or no value at all on any of the other things that we currently produce and consume, then we would use an enormous amount of our resources to build lunar transportation systems and holiday resorts! If we all become addicted to fruit and ice cream and refuse to eat meat, Hungry Jacks and McDonald's fast-food outlets would either go out of business or radically change their range of products. The ice cream makers like Streets would be booming.

The way in which individual preferences influence the quantities of goods and services produced varies from one economic system to another. As we'll see shortly, our own economic system takes individual consumers' preferences as the dominant force determining what is produced. But there are other systems in which individual preferences play a limited role and the government's planning agency plays the dominant role.

Getting on to the production possibility frontier and choosing the right point on it are two aspects of solving the economic problem. There is a third aspect: determining the distribution of economic well-being.

The Distribution of Economic Well-Being

An economy could be at a point on the production possibility frontier and further, that point could be one that exactly reflects consumers' preferences concerning the values of the various goods. At that point, production of more of any one good and less of any other good would make somebody worse off. There are, however, many such points possible, each of which is associated with a different distribution of economic well-being. One such point is where everyone is equally well off. Another is where 90 per cent of the population is almost starving and the other 10 per cent are living in enormous luxury. Economic systems, in effect, make decisions about who gets what. Some economic systems favour, in principle at least, considerable equality in the distribution of economic well-being. Other systems favour equality of opportunity but pay little attention to the distribution that results from equal opportunities.

R E V I E W

The best we can do in the face of scarcity is to get ourselves on to the production possibility frontier. The point on the frontier that we go to depends on whose preferences determine which goods and services the economy produces and on how the economic system distributes well-being. No economic system can abolish the economic problem. Each system, at best, can only help people cope with scarcity. ■

Let's see how different economic systems cope with the fundamental economic problem.

Alternative Economic Systems

Economic systems vary in two dimensions:

- Who owns capital and land
- Who allocates resources

Figure 39.1 summarizes the possibilities. Capital and land may be owned entirely by individuals, entirely by the state or by a mixture of the two. Resources may be allocated entirely by markets, entirely by government economic planners or by a mixture of the two. The two highlighted corners of the figure represent two idealized extreme cases: capitalism and socialism.

Capitalism is an economic system based on private ownership of capital and land and on market allocation of resources. **Socialism** is an economic system based on state ownership of capital and land and on a centrally planned allocation of resources. **Central planning** is a method of allocating resources by command. It involves plans being made by a central planning authority and then communicated to the various production and distribution organizations in the country. The plans are monitored by a large team of bureaucrats. Hardly any country has ever used an economic system that precisely corresponds to one of these extreme types, but the United States and Japan come close to being capitalist economies, while the former Soviet Union was closest to being a socialist economy. The difficult problem facing the new Commonwealth of Independent States is just how to move from socialism to capitalism. China was a socialist economy but it too is moving towards a combination of planning and market forces to allocate resources.

A number of countries including China combine private and state ownership and market allocation and planning in unusual ways. **Market socialism** (also called **decentralized planning**) is an economic system that combines socialism's state ownership of capital and land with capitalism's market allocation of resources. Yugoslavia, Hungary and

Figure 39.1 Alternative Economic Systems

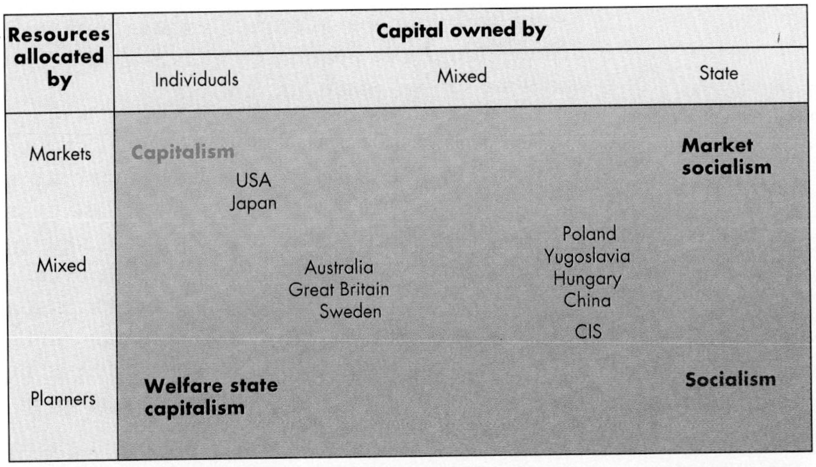

Resources allocated by	Capital owned by		
	Individuals	Mixed	State
Markets	Capitalism USA Japan		**Market socialism**
Mixed		Australia Great Britain Sweden	Poland Yugoslavia Hungary China CIS
Planners	**Welfare state capitalism**		**Socialism**

Under capitalism, individuals own capital — farms and factories, plant and equipment — and resources are allocated by markets. Under socialism, the state owns capital, and resources are allocated by a planning and command system. Market socialism combines state ownership of capital with a market allocation of resources. Welfare state capitalism combines private capital ownership with a high degree of state intervention in the allocation of resources.

Poland are other examples of market socialist economies. In such economies, the planners communicate a set of prices to the various production and distribution organizations and then leave those organizations free to produce whatever quantities they choose at those prices. For some goods, they will go even further and let the prices be determined by market forces as well.

Another combination is welfare state capitalism. **Welfare state capitalism** combines capitalism's private ownership of capital and land with a heavy degree of state intervention in the allocation of resources. Australia, the United Kingdom and other Western European countries provide examples of such economies.

Because of the extraordinary changes that are taking place, especially those in Eastern Europe, the position occupied by each country in Fig. 39.1 is itself undergoing change. The new CIS and other Eastern European countries are moving away from central planning toward market socialism and, to a lesser degree, away from market socialism and toward capitalism. The capitalist countries themselves are moving in the direction of even greater reliance on the unregulated market as the means of allocating resources.

Since all the economic systems in Fig. 39.1 are made up of a combination of capitalism and socialism, let's examine these two extreme types a bit more closely.

Capitalism

Let's describe a country that has a pure (hypothetical) form of capitalism. Such a country is one in which a concern for individual liberty is paramount. Its foundation is the establishment and enforcement of individual property rights. Each individual owns what he or she has produced or legitimately acquired. Resources are legitimately acquired as a result of buying them from a willing seller or receiving them as a gift. These are the only ways in which resources can be transferred between individuals. Any other method of transferring resources is illegal. Preventing illegal transfers is the only proper role of the state. No other economic action by any individual or group of individuals may be blocked by the force of the state. All individuals are free to form coalitions or groups to buy and sell whatever goods and services they choose and in whatever quantities they choose.

Governments may be viewed as coalitions among individuals that provide certain types of goods and services. Furthermore, if a government can offer better terms than any other coalition so that people choose to trade with it rather than with some other group, then a government may legitimately undertake economic actions. A government may not, however, coerce individuals in any way other than to prevent them from attempting to violate other people's property rights.

In capitalist economies, the allocation of resources is determined by individual choices expressed through markets. *What* is produced is determined by consumers' preferences; *how* goods are produced is determined by profit-maximizing firms; *for whom* goods are produced is determined by individual decisions on the supply of factors of production and by the market-determined prices at which those factors of production trade.

Socialism

Socialism is an economic system based on the political philosophy that the private ownership of capital and land enables the rich (owners of capital and land) to exploit the poor (workers who have no capital and land). To avoid such exploitation, capital and land are owned by the state. Individuals are permitted to own only their *human capital* and capital equipment used for consumption purposes such as consumer durable goods. All other capital is owned by the state. Thus the state owns all factories and farms and the plant and equipment to operate them. All labour works for the state and all consumption goods and services are produced by and bought from the state.

Under socialism, some people are wealthier (and have higher incomes) than others, but gross inequalities of wealth arising from the ownership of massive industrial and commercial complexes are not permitted. The principles governing the distribution of income are 'from each according to his ability, to each according to his contribution'. That is, the state pays each individual a wage that reflects the state's own opinion of the value of the output of the individual.

A variant of socialism is communism. **Communism** is an economic system based on the state ownership of capital and land, on central planning and on distributing income in accordance with the rule 'from each according to his ability, to each according to his need'. The word communism has been commonly used to describe the old Soviet-style socialism. In ordinary speech, the words communism and socialism are virtually interchangeable. It is worthwhile keeping the two words distinct, however, when thinking about economic systems.

In socialist (and communist) economies, resources are allocated not by markets but by central planners, and it is their preferences and priorities that determine *what, how* and *for whom* the various goods and services are produced.

The Pros and Cons of Capitalism

Advantages of Capitalism The major advantages of capitalism arise because each individual's judgement about his or her own well-being is paramount in determining what economic actions take place. Each individual decides how much work to do and for whom to work, how to spend time away from work, and how to dispose of the income made from selling his or her resources. Individual incentives are strong. Adam Smith wrote:

> As every individual ... endeavours as much as he can both to employ his capital in the support of domestic industry and so to direct that industry that its produce be of the greatest value; every individual necessarily labours to render the annual revenue of society as great as he can ... He intends only his own gain, and he is in this, as in many other cases, led by an invisible hand to promote an end which was no part of his intention. [1]

Adam Smith went on to reject any detailed state intervention in economic life:

> The statesman, who should attempt to direct private people in what manner they ought to employ their capitals, would not only load himself with a most unnecessary attention, but assume an authority which could safely be trusted, not only to no single person, but to no counsel or senate whatever, and which would nowhere be so dangerous as in the hands of a man who had the folly and presumption enough to fancy himself fit to exercise it. [2]

Disadvantages of Capitalism A major disadvantage of capitalism is seen, even by those who support this economic system, as arising from the fact that the historical distribution of endowments is arbitrary and indeed is often the result of illegitimate transfers. For example, the European colonizers of Australia and North America took land from the native people of those continents. Because there have in the past been illegitimate transfers — violations of private property rights — the current distribution of wealth has no legitimacy. If there were no large inequality in the distribution of wealth, its historical origins would not be a matter of much concern. But the fact that wealth is distributed very unequally leads most people to the conclusion that there is a role for state intervention to redistribute income and wealth.

[1] Adam Smith, *The Wealth of Nations* (New York: Random House, 1937), p.423.

[2] *Ibid.*

A further disadvantage of capitalism arises from the belief that some people do not, in fact, know what is good for them and will, if left to their own devices, make the wrong choices. We all agree that children should not be permitted to exercise complete freedom of choice. Most people would also extend some restrictions to the mentally ill, the senile and to those who are addicted (or even potentially addicted) to dangerous drugs. Some advocates of socialism go further, arguing that socialist planners are able to make better choices than people would make for themselves.

We have reviewed some arguments against capitalism that might be used to persuade people that such a system is not desirable. But there is a more fundamental problem with capitalism: it has an internal contradiction.

The Contradiction Private property rights can be enforced only if the state has a monopoly on coercion. If the state were simply competing with others to enforce property rights, then every time a disagreement arose between two parties each would hire its own enforcers to settle the dispute. Battles would ensue. Only when a single supplier of coercive power has emerged victorious can private property rights be successfully enforced without indulging in a process of open physical violence and conflict. The state is the monopolist in the provision of coercion for enforcing property rights. But once the state has achieved that monopoly position, there is no way of preventing it from expanding its range of coercive activities further. There is no check on those individuals who hold offices of state and who exercise the state's powers. Furthermore, there is no way of preventing private individuals and coalitions of private individuals from attempting to persuade the state to use its powers in a broader manner.

Whether it is because of the persuasiveness of the arguments against capitalism or because of the fundamental internal contradiction in the system, capitalism is a hypothetical rather than an actual economic system. No country ever has or ever will experience that pure form of economic organization. It is a philosophical ideal or reference point against which to compare actual systems. If we could have such a system and if we could remedy the historical violations of property rights, then some people would agree that we would have done the best we could to solve the economic problem. But such a solution is simply not available to us. It is for this reason that most capitalist economies include some element of state ownership and control of economic activity.

Varieties of Capitalism

There is no unique model of capitalism. Most of this book illustrates and elaborates the principles of economics, using examples drawn from our own capitalist economy, Australia. But not all capitalist economies look like Australia. In this section, we take a quick look at some of the key differences among the capitalist economies and some of the trends that are emerging in those countries.

Japan

Japan's economic performance since World War II is known as the 'Japanese economic miracle'. Emerging from war with per capita incomes less than 20 per cent of those in the United States, Japan has transformed itself into an economic giant challenging for the top spot. The most spectacular growth period occurred in the 25 years from 1945 to 1970, when per capita income increased eightfold. Today, the Japanese have a dominant position in world markets for cars and computers, audio and video equipment and a whole range of 'high-tech' commodities. The camera-laden Japanese tourist is now a common a sight in Asia, Australia and Europe. What has led to this transformation of Japan into one of the world's richest and most powerful economies? Is there something different about Japanese capitalism that distinguishes it from Western capitalism?

The fast-growing East Asian economies all have characteristics such as a high savings and investment rate, an outward-orientated trade policy and good macroeconomic management. Japan shares these characteristics.

Not only has there been a high rate of capital accumulation in Japan, there has also been a high rate of accumulation of human capital, especially in the applied sciences. Going along with a high rate of capital accumulation, both physical and human, has been a high rate of technological advance with a capacity to adopt the best technologies available, wherever in the world they might have been developed. These characteristics are the heart of the 'catching-up' process of growth, whereby poor countries which can sustain rapid economic growth eventually catch up to developed countries.

The economic system in Japan is similar to that in Australia. People are free to pursue their ideas, to own firms, to hire labour and other inputs, and to sell their outputs in relatively free markets. That is, Japan employs capitalist methods of resource allocation. But many scholars argue that alongside these capitalist features, the Japanese economic system has some extra dimensions.

Markets and Firms Either firms or markets can be used to coordinate production. In economies like Australia or the United States, transactions tend to be organized in one or the other of these forms. The features of a market transaction are the pursuit of individual private interest by the participants in the transaction as they respond to price signals. Both parties are free to enter the transaction or not and there is no compulsion to repeat the transaction at another time, as, for example, when you go to the vegetable market to buy potatoes. On the other hand, within the firm, decisions on resource allocation are made by the management with the objective of pursuing common interests, and the relationships tend to be fixed and continuing. The best example is the employment relationship.

In Japan, however, there is evidence from research by economists of greater use of an 'intermediate' form of organization. The features of this type of organization are for example a commitment to a long-term relationship but also the ever present threat of exit. Therefore it lies somewhere between the market mechanism and organization within the firm. Commonly cited examples are the long-term links between the car makers and their component suppliers. The long-term relationship adds to the likelihood of profits from investment in new technologies, for example, which involve fixed and sunk costs. In the absence of the long-term relationship, the parts maker might not make the investment, fearing that the life of the contract would not be long enough to pay back the investment with interest. But while a long-term relationship might be necessary for this investment to occur, it is not enough. Indeed, the parts makers might think they can exploit such a relationship instead and shirk on cost-cutting investments. The threat of the ending of the relationship, if certain conditions are not met, is important because it provides the incentive to actually undertake those sorts of investments and to cut costs. The instances of these kinds of intermediate forms of organization studied so far in Japan suggest that it has been possible to find the right balance between commitment and threat. Japanese industries have as a result built up a network of long-term business relationships with independent companies. This **networking** has the benefits explained of encouraging cost-cutting innovation. Networking is the key distinction of Japanese-style capitalism.

These sorts of relationships are not unique to Japan — they exist in the manufacturing sector in Australia too — but they appear to be more common in Japan. They occur in financial transactions in Japan as well as those related to the transfer of goods. The reasons for their prevalence and their benefits and costs are the topics of continuing research.

Government Another special feature of the Japanese economy is the role played by government. The Japanese government is the smallest in the capitalist world. The total scale of government is less than one-fifth of the economy. That is, government spending accounted for slightly less than one-fifth of GDP. This contrasts with a government sector (of all levels) that accounts for about 40 per cent of GDP in Australia. The relatively small scale of government in Japan means that taxes are low and therefore not a major discouragement to work, to saving and to accumulating capital.

There is a variety of ways in which the Japanese government intervenes in the economy, but the vehicle of government intervention that has attracted most attention is the **Ministry of International Trade and Industry** (MITI), a government agency responsible for stimulating Japanese industrial development and international trade. There is a debate about the role of MITI in Japanese economic development. One school of thought sees Japan as a capitalist system but one which is guided by the state. This perspective is encapsulated in the phrase 'Japan Inc', that is, a triumvirate of politicians in the ruling Liberal Democratic Party, central government bureaucrats and the leaders of big business. Among the bureaucrats, those in MITI play a central role in this model. They identify the winning industries of the future and help the adjustment processes of industries in decline. Their strategies are embodied in Japanese **industry policy**, that is, using government policy instruments to provide some industries with advantages relative to others.

The 'Japan Inc' model is not universally accepted. Another view is that Japanese industry policy is neither central to performance of the economy nor effective. Scholars who support this view argue that factors behind the catch-up process we listed above are much more important contributors to growth in Japan. Industry policy is not central. They also argue that the process of policymaking in Japan is much more complicated than suggested by the 'Japan Inc' model. MITI does not have sole control over industry policy. These are other groups with strong interests and MITI must compete for influence against those other interest groups, both within the bureaucracy and in the private sector. That is, they argue that the model of the political process implicit in the 'Japan Inc' perspective is too simple. A more complex model is needed such as that we used to explain the persistence of protection (see Chapter 36) or the existence of regulation. Finally they point to the evidence that the results of MITI's intervention in the marketplace have been mixed. Some industries have been targeted successfully but others have not.

The aluminium industry provides an important example to Australia of MITI's errors and accommodation to private sector pressures for adjustment. In the 1960s, MITI made a decision to promote the aluminium industry. This industry is highly energy-intensive and it seemed an odd choice for such a resource-poor economy. In the mid-1970s, MITI's hopes were dashed when the price of oil increased dramatically, and the smelting of bauxite to create aluminium became inefficient in Japan. Within two years, Japan's bauxite-smelting industry had been closed down, and Japan was importing all its aluminium from Australia. But it was the private sector which fixed the adjustment timetable. The results of research by Australian economists indicates that MITI was following not leading the retreat.

One feature of Japanese industry policy deserves emphasis. Industries which are losing competitiveness have generally not been protected by restrictions on imports through tariffs or quotas. This is because Japan has become such an important part of world trade that the rest of the world closely monitors policy changes in Japan. Trade barriers which reduce the access of other countries to the Japanese market attract trenchant criticism. An example is the beef and rice sectors in Japan, which have been highly protected. After strong criticism from Australia and the United States, the level of protection even in those industries has begun to fall. The forms of support for declining industries include instead:

- the provision of direct subsidies, for example for research and development, or to provide incentives to scrap excess capacity;
- the provision of low-interest loans, to finance adoption of new technologies, to facilitate offshore relocation or to carry existing stocks of output of the industry;
- sanctioning the closure of plants and encouraging the mergers of firms, even with the effect of creating a greater degree of concentration in the industry.

The evidence is that even when government subsidies are paid, they are much less than the losses borne by the enterprises involved. Furthermore, when an industry is declining, MITI usually releases an 'adjustment plan'. But as we suggested in the case of aluminium, that plan may be simply endorsing what has already happened in the private sector rather than leading the way. In summary, the adjustment in declining industries seems to be driven by the private sector, not by government.

The issue of the centrality and efficacy of Japanese industry policy is the subject of continuing empirical work by economists and other social scientists.

Welfare State Capitalism

Capitalism in Western Europe and Australia has characteristics different from that in the United States or Japan. It is welfare state capitalism. Australia as well as the countries of Western Europe, many of which now belong to the European Community, are basically capitalist market economies in the sense that most productive resources are owned by private individuals and most resources are allocated by individuals trading freely in markets for both goods and services and factors of production. But the scale of government and the degree and direction of government intervention are larger in these countries than in the United States and much larger than in Japan.

In Australia and the European countries, government expenditure and taxes range between 40 and 50 per cent of GDP, Australia being at the bottom end of that scale. These high tax rates create disincentives that result in less work effort and lower saving rates than in countries with lower taxes. Many Western European countries also have a large, nationalized industry sector. A **nationalized industry** is an industry owned and operated by a publicly owned authority that is directly responsible to the government. Railways, airlines, gas, electricity, telephones, radio and television broadcasting, banking and finance, coal, steel and even cars are among the list of industries that are either wholly or partly publicly owned in some European countries. In Australia, the tradition has been for the government to nationalize some industries, for example, the public utilities, but also to own enterprises that compete with private sector firms in other industries. Not included in these measures of the extent of government intervention are the effects of regulation or protection which affect relative prices and therefore the allocation of resources.

What were the origins of such a high degree of government intervention in Australia? This is a major issue in Australian economics and one which attracts research effort by Australian economists. One clue to the answer might lie in the trend of the relative size of government compared with GDP. The ratio of government outlays to GDP was about 13 per cent at the turn of the century compared to about 40 per cent now. That is, as Australians became richer, their spending on government services increased faster than their incomes. This trend reflects the emergence of welfare state capitalism in Australia. As Australians became richer, they were prepared to devote more resources to equity and security objectives. Some equity objectives were pursued via government spending programmes. Policies of protection and regulation to offset the uncertainties of less regulated markets were also adopted. The role of government ownership was to avoid problems of private firms exploiting market power and to equalize prices and quality of various services across the whole population.

These forms of intervention of welfare state capitalism, that is expenditure programmes, market regulation and government ownership, create costs and reduce the level of GDP and GDP growth. That reduction in growth is the price paid for the pursuit of the other objectives. As we noted in earlier chapters, there is a now a trend towards deregulation and reductions in protection in Australia. This process is not unique to Australia either. Increasingly in recent years, European governments have also been selling state-owned enterprises. The process of selling state-owned enterprises is called **privatization**. There has also been a retreat, in some countries, from very high tax rates. From these events in Australia and elsewhere we infer that there has been a shift in national preferences concerning the trade-off between equity objectives and the generation of wealth. We would expect to see a fall in the government share of GDP in those economies as a result. In terms of Fig. 39.1, the welfare capitalism economies are moving towards the left-hand corner of the box.

Far more dramatic has been the change in the management of the economies of Eastern Europe. These economies are also shifting out of the socialism corner of the box in Fig. 39.1. There is a belief that the socialist methods such as those once employed by the Soviet Union and China cannot deliver sustained economic growth. Let's take a closer look at socialism, first in the Soviet Union and then in China.

The Former Soviet Union/New CIS

The Soviet Union, or the Union of Soviet Socialist Republics, was founded in 1917 following the Bolshevik revolution led by Vladimir Ilyich Lenin. The Union survived until October 1991 when it was dismantled and replaced by a voluntarily joined Commonwealth of Independent States (CIS). The CIS is a vast, resource-rich and diverse nation. Its land area is three times that of Australia; its population is approaching 300 million; it has vast reserves of coal, oil, iron ore, natural gas, timber and almost every other mineral resource; it is a nation of enormous ethnic diversity, with Russians making up only 50 per cent of the population and the remaining population including many European, Asian and Arabic ethnic groups; it has a Pacific frontage as well as a European one.

History

A compact economic history of the Soviet Union appears in Table 39.1. Although the nation was founded in 1917, its modern economic management system was not put in place until the 1930s. The architect of this system was Joseph Stalin. The financial, manufacturing and transportation sectors of the economy had been taken into state ownership and control by Lenin. Stalin added the farms to this list. He abolished the market and introduced a command planning mechanism, initiating a series of five-year plans that placed their major emphasis on setting and attaining goals for the production of capital goods. The production of consumer goods was given a secondary place and personal economic conditions were harsh. With emphasis on the production of capital goods, the Soviet economy grew quickly.

By the 1950s, after Stalin's death, steady economic growth continued but the emphasis in economic planning gradually shifted away from capital goods toward the production of consumer goods. In the 1960s, the growth rate began to sag and by the 1970s and early 1980s, the Soviet economy was running into serious problems. Productivity was actually declining, especially in agriculture but also in some industries. Growth slowed to a lower rate than was being achieved in Western capitalist countries, and the Soviet Union began to fall further behind its superpower rival, the United States. It was in this situation that Mikhail Gorbachev came to power with plans to restructure the Soviet economy, based

Table 39.1 A Compact Summary of Key Periods in the Economic History of the Soviet Union

Period	Main economic events/characteristics
1917–1921 (Lenin)	• Bolshevik Revolution • Nationalization of banking, industry and transportation • Forced requisitioning of agricultural output
1921–1924 (Lenin)	• New Economic Policy (NEP) • Market allocation of most resources
1928–1953 (Stalin)	• Abolition of market • Introduction of command planning and five-year plans • Collectivization of farms • Emphasis on capital goods and economic growth • Harsh conditions
1953–1970 (Khrushchev to Brezhnev)	• Steady growth • Increased emphasis on consumer goods
1970–1985 (Brezhnev to Chernenko)	• Deteriorating productivity in agriculture and industry • Slowdown in growth
1985–87 (Gorbachev)	• The *Perestroika* campaigns
1987–88	• Reforms of the economic system
1990–91	• Economic crisis • Formation of Commonwealth of Independent States

on the idea of increased individual accountability and rewards based on performance.

Gorbachev's reforms involved a number of steps. The first of these was *Perestroika* (or 'restructuring') which was really a series of campaigns. The themes of these campaigns were to:

- Raise the rate of investment so as to retool and modernize industry
- Give greater emphasis to quality in production
- Unleash human initiative and make the bureaucracy more accountable

But these campaigns did not have much real effect on the economy, and the growth rate of the USSR continued to fall. Average annual real growth of output was only 2 per cent in 1986 and 1987, less than the average of the first five years of the 1980s (see Fig. 39.2). More substantial reforms began in 1987. From this time, a greater degree of autonomy was given to enterprises to determine output and set wages. There was also some dismantling of the traditional planning system. Let's see what the main elements of that system were. Then in a later section we'll explain why the process of reform seems to have coincided with even worse economic performance in the USSR, in particular, negative growth in 1990 (see Fig. 39.2), culminating with political upheaval and a firmer resolve to adopt market-based systems.

Planning and Command System

The State Committee for Economic Planning, whose acronym in Russian is **GOSPLAN**, was responsible for drawing up and implementing the state's economic plans. Every five years, this committee drew up a five-year plan, a broad outline of the general targets and directions set for a period of five years. Each year, GOSPLAN drew up an annual plan. The **annual plan** was a month-by-month set of targets for output, prices, inputs, investment, and money and credit flows. The plans were approved by the former Communist Party and then communicated to the individual enterprises — farms and factories — that produced the goods and services. Enterprises were overseen both by the ministries responsible for the various industries and by local party organizations.

The state enterprise was the basic production unit in the Soviet economy. An enterprise was run by a state-appointed director who was in charge of all the enterprise's operations but was required to follow the instructions imposed by the economic plans. State enterprises operated in both the industrial and agricultural sectors of the economy.

The annual plan was organized around five basic balances:

1 Consumer goods
2 Labour
3 Credit
4 Capital goods
5 Materials

1. Consumer Goods Balance Consumer goods balance is the achievement of a balance between the

Figure 39.2 Real Output Growth in the former USSR

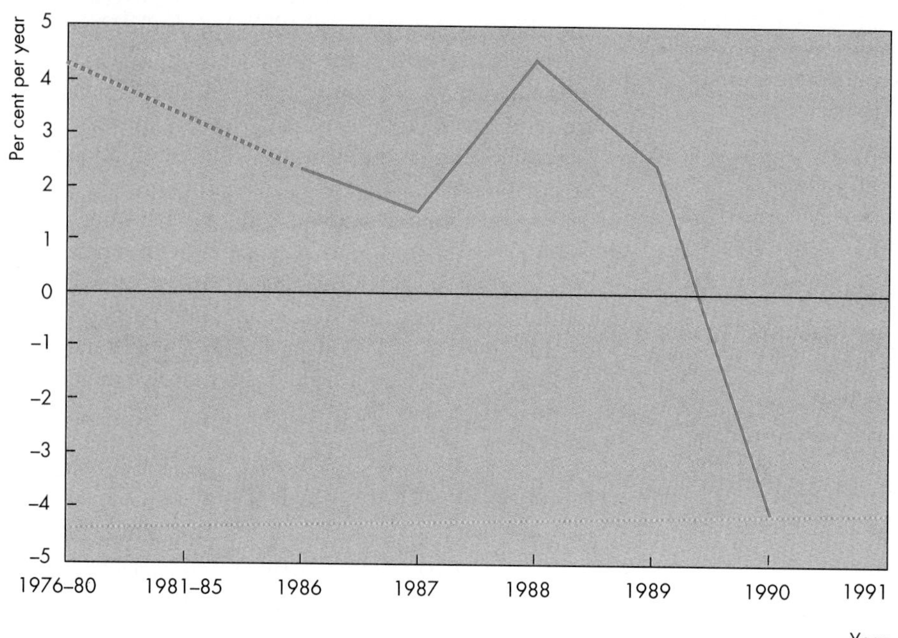

Real output growth in the former USSR was at least 3 per cent a year between 1976 and 1985, although the average was falling. The reform period since 1985 is characterized by even lower growth rates on average, and negative growth in 1990.

Source: IMF and others, *The Economy of the USSR: Summary and Recommendations*, World Bank, Washington DC, 1990.

quantities supplied and demanded for each individual category of consumer goods and services. The planners had three ways of achieving consumer goods balance: changing output, changing incomes and changing prices. Figure 39.3 illustrates these three possibilities. The demand for some good (say, shoes) is D_0; the quantity of shoes that the planners intend to produce is Q_0; the supply curve is S_0; and the cost of producing shoes is C. If the price of shoes is set by the planners at C there will be an excess of the quantity demanded over the quantity supplied — equal to Q_1 minus Q_0. The planners will not have achieved consumer goods balance in the market for shoes. They can achieve a balance by increasing production to Q_1, in which case the supply curve will shift to the right to S_1 (part (a)). They can also achieve a balance by imposing higher income taxes, thereby reducing after-tax income and lowering the demand for shoes (part (b)). They will have to increase taxes by enough to shift the demand curve to the left from D_0 to D_1. At a price of C, the quantity of shoes demanded equals the quantity supplied (Q_0).

In practice, although these two methods of achieving consumer goods balance were available to the Soviet planners, they were not the main methods used. The easiest way of achieving consumer goods balance, and the one most frequently used, was to adjust the price. Soviet planners adjusted prices by imposing turnover taxes. The **turnover tax** in the former Soviet Union was a tax on a consumer good designed to make its market price high enough to achieve a balance between the quantity demanded and the quantity supplied. In this example (Fig. 39.3(c)), a turnover tax sufficient to increase the price to P ensures consumer goods balance in the market for shoes. We'll indicate again below how price rises were used in 1991 in an attempt to achieve a balance in consumer goods markets.

2. Labour Balance Labour balance was the achievement of a balance between the quantities supplied and demanded for each individual category of labour services. It was achieved, in the short run, by adjusting wage rates. Large differentials in wages were necessary to achieve labour balance. In the long run, labour balance was also influenced by the planners' ability to direct resources allocated to education and training, favouring the acquisition of skills in short supply.

3. Credit Balance Credit balance was the achievement of a balance between the quantities of

Figure 39.3 Consumer Goods Balance in the Planning System

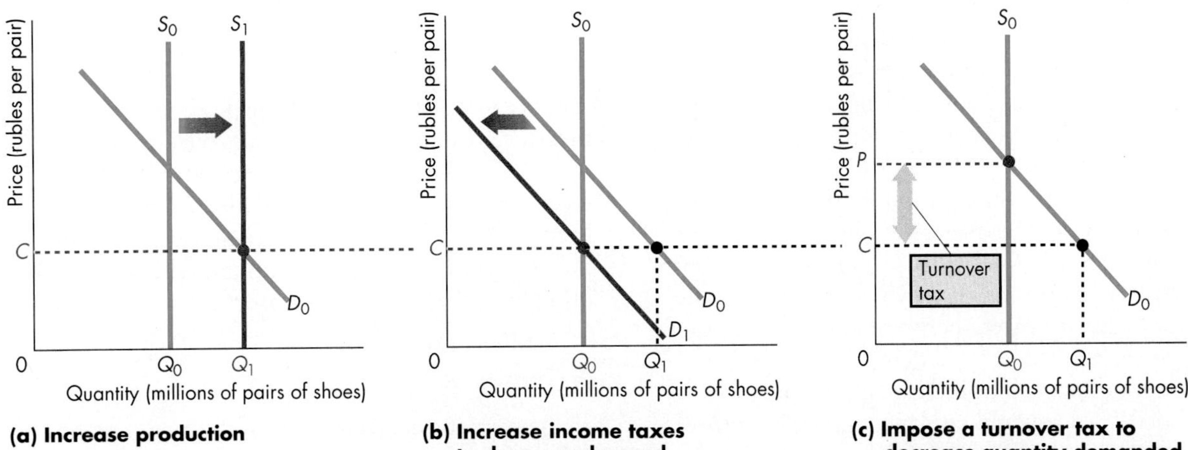

(a) Increase production

(b) Increase income taxes to decrease demand

(c) Impose a turnover tax to decrease quantity demanded

The cost of producing a consumer good (say, shoes) is *C*. The demand for shoes is D_0, and the quantity produced is Q_0. Three ways of achieving consumer goods balance are available. In part (a), the decision to increase output results in a shift in the supply curve to S_1. When the price is *C* and the quantity of shoes produced and consumed is Q_1, consumption goods balance is achieved. In part (b), income taxes are increased, reducing after-tax income. The demand for shoes decreases and the demand curve shifts to the left to D_1. The price is *C* and the quantity of shoes produced and consumed is Q_0. In part (c), the planners impose a turnover tax on shoes. A tax equal to the difference between *P* and *C* is imposed, raising the price of shoes to *P*. The quantity demanded decreases to Q_0 and consumer goods balance is achieved. Soviet planners used the turnover tax more frequently than the other two methods for achieving consumer goods balance.

credit supplied and demanded. The banking system in the Soviet Union was owned and controlled by the state. Credit balance was achieved by the state banking system making available the credit that the planners decided was required.

4. Capital Goods Balance Capital goods balance was the achievement of a balance between the quantities supplied and demanded of each type of capital good. The central planners decided how to allocate the scarce capital goods available and, through their control of credit, influenced the demand for capital goods by individual production enterprises.

5. Materials Balance Materials balance was the achievement of a balance between the quantities demanded and supplied for each and every raw material and intermediate good used in the production of final consumer goods and capital goods. This balancing exercise was the most complex aspect of Soviet planning. There were literally billions of raw materials and intermediate goods and the detailed plans for the material balances filled 70 volumes, or 12,000 pages, each year.

An example of a simplified materials balance schedule is set out in Table 39.2. There are just three materials. (The actual Soviet plans used to consider more than 30,000 separate materials at the central planning level, and a further 50,000 at the regional and local levels.) There are three sources of any material used in the production process: production, inventories and imports. There are three broad categories of uses of any raw material or produced input: an intermediate input into the production of other goods, final domestic use either for consumption or investment purposes, and exports. For each material, a detailed plan showing the balance between the quantity supplied and the quantity demanded was drawn up. For example, the first row of the table shows that 490 tonnes of coal are produced and 10 tonnes are taken from inventory. The quantity supplied is 500 tonnes of coal. The quantity demanded is made up of 50 tonnes as inputs in the coal industry itself, 300 tonnes to produce electric power, 50 tonnes to extract chemicals that are converted into nylon, 75 tonnes for domestic heating and the 25 tonnes exported. The total quantity demanded is 500 tonnes. The second row of the table shows the plan for electric power and the third row that for nylon.

Table 39.2 shows a balance between the quantity demanded and the quantity supplied of each material. Suppose that there is an excess of the quantity demanded over the quantity supplied of electric power. What could the Soviet planners do in such a situation? They could plan to produce more electric power or plan to produce less coal and less nylon, thereby reducing the amount of electric power demanded, or reduce the quantity of electric power for final domestic use. The Soviet planners usually chose the last of these options. If they were to increase the output of electric power, there would then be an increase in the quantity of coal demanded in the electric power industry. The increase in the quantity demanded of coal would result in a shortage in the coal sector that would require further adjustments in that sector. To balance the quantity supplied and quantity demanded of electric power by reducing the amount going to some other industry would result in that industry failing to achieve its targets. So instead, the shortage was passed on to the domestic sector.

The Market Sector

Although the economy of the former Soviet Union was a planned one, a substantial amount of economic activity took place outside the planning and command economy, and the market sector expanded under Gorbachev's reforms. The most important component of the market sector was in agriculture. It is estimated that there are 35 million private plots worked by rural households. These private plots constituted less than 3 per cent of the agricultural land of the old Soviet Union but produce close to 25 per cent of total agricultural output and one-third of all the meat and milk produced. Some estimates suggest that the productivity on private plots was 40 times that of state enterprise farms and collective farms.

There were other economic activities undertaken by Soviet citizens outside the planning systems. Many of these were legal but some were not. Often they involved the illegal buying and selling of goods brought in illegally from abroad.

Performance

These were the characteristics of the Soviet economy before the reforms of the late 1980s. As Fig. 39.2 shows, the Soviet growth rate had been low and falling over the previous decade. What were the sources of this poor performance?

Shortage In his book *Economics of Shortage* Janos Kornai argues that enterprises in planning systems are subject to a 'soft budget constraint'. This means that they are encouraged by the planning system to expand output at any cost. They are not concerned with the costs of inputs. They hoard materials, use them inefficiently and ignore the scope for saving materials through innovation. These features lead to shortages, and shortages breed more shortages, as enterprises hoard more and more. High ratios of in-

Table 39.2 Materials Balance

	Quantity supplied			Quantity demanded				
				Intermediate goods			Final goods	
Material	**Production**	**Inventories**	**Imports**	**Coal**	**Electric power**	**Nylon**	**Domestic**	**Foreign**
Coal (tonnes)	490	10	0	50	300	50	75	25
Electric power (kilowatt-hours)	10,000	0	0	2,000	1,000	1,500	5,500	0
Nylon (metres)	20,000	200	2,000	0	0	0	22,200	0

Materials can be supplied from production, inventories or imports. They are demanded as an input in the production of intermediate goods, for final domestic consumption or for export. Plans were drawn up to ensure that the quantity supplied equals the quantity demanded. To achieve materials balance, Soviet planners can increase production, decrease inventories, increase imports, decrease the quantity demanded as an intermediate good, decrease final demand or decrease exports. Reductions in final domestic demand were the main method employed for achieving materials balance.

puts to outputs and of inventories to outputs retard growth.

Lack of Specialization The problems of obtaining supplies encourages enterprises to be self-sufficient. They try to make everything they need. This means they try to produce goods or services in which they do not have a competitive advantage. They might also produce at small scale, less than the level at which average costs are minimized. As a consequence, the advantages of specialization are lost.

Risk Aversion Managers in Soviet-style enterprises tend to be risk-averse. They do not have incentives to innovate to raise production capacity. Their incentives are instead to achieve an output as close as possible to that anticipated by the planning system in the current period. They are not rewarded for raising the profits of their enterprise over a longer period. Innovation is very risky in this setting. The outcome is uncertain and, in the short run, the delays that might be induced by innovating inhibit the attainment of current output targets.

Distorted Information Flows In capitalist economies, information is collected in markets and conveyed by prices. In centrally planned economies, information is conveyed in reports. Since the evaluation of a person's performance is based on these reports, there are strong incentives to distort them and to misrepresent the facts. This meant that planning decisions were being based on what University of South Queensland economist Craig Littler calls 'a fantastic pyramid of deception'.

In these circumstances, the attainment of the production possibility frontier was highly unlikely. All these factors led to poor economic performance. The gap between the Soviet Union and the rest of the world became increasingly obvious. The response by the Soviet leadership was to seek reform.

The Reforms of 1987 and 1991

At the June 1987 meeting of the Central Committee of the Communist Party, Mikhail Gorbachev announced substantial reform, the key element of which was a greater degree of autonomy to enterprises, and a dismantling of some parts of the command system. The next major event in the economic reform process was the announcement in February 1991 of massive increases in consumer goods prices. This was followed in August 1991 by a conservative coup which tried but failed to unseat Gorbachev. The coup was followed by another major reform to the relations between the various republics which made up the USSR and which we will look at in a moment. The other main economic problems in 1991 were the very high rates of inflation and the slowdown in growth. What had gone wrong with the reform programme?

Problems in Soviet Reform

The main issue is the sequencing of the reforms. The first step was to give enterprises more autonomy, including that of setting wages. But while the reforms gave enterprises more autonomy they did not actually impose an equal amount of responsibility on enterprise management. The enterprises responded by offering workers higher wages. They made these offers because they wanted to be sure that they had enough labour to meet the output targets they had been given from the planning system. Unfortunately, the wage increases exceeded the growth in labour productivity. In capitalist enterprises, such offers would contribute to much lower profits, even losses. Despite this problem, the Soviet enterprises were able to pay higher wages because the state had cut back the tax rate on enterprises' profits. Even more importantly, the state had made available all the credit they wanted to cover their losses. On the surface the first stage of reform was an increase in enterprise autonomy. But actually it amounted to a massive increase in the money supply.

In a capitalist economy, the effect of an increase in the money supply would be a rise in the general level of prices. In the Soviet Union this did not happen, at least straightaway, because the state retained control over prices. Consumer goods prices were kept low. So the workers had higher money incomes and prices were low. The result was still excess demand, but instead of rising prices, the excess demand was reflected in other developments which have had severely disruptive effects on the Soviet economy. It's those disruptive effects which caused the growth rate to drop. Let's look at some of those effects.

Queuing When the price system is not working, and there is excess demand, then the supply available is allocated by other means. One is by queueing. Another is by the exploitation of influence and nepotism. These allocation mechanisms are less efficient than the use of money, and they lead to a great deal of anger and resentment among consumers.

Barter Another outcome is a greater use of barter. The first round of reforms were hoped to decentralize decisionmaking in the Soviet Union. But because money cannot be used as a means of exchange, enterprises started to barter with each other rather than buy and sell at going prices. Enterprises located in regions that cannot offer attractive bartering terms can be denied access to goods and services. For example, there were fears of food shortages in Russian cities in their winter of 1990/91. The problem was not the availability of food, but that the purchasers could only offer rubles in exchange, which the food-supplying regions did not want.

Hoarding When money loses its value as a means of exchange, people will also tend to hoard. This too is inefficient. There are huge costs involved in stockpiling, for example, households buying up a year's supply of tea or salt, for their own consumption or to barter.

The Black Market Trading might still occur with money as the medium of exchange, but in black markets. Those markets, which are strictly illegal, might produce prices close to market clearing levels but those markets have higher transactions costs than would occur in free markets, if only because of the efforts taken by participants to avoid detection, or by the state to apprehend the arbitragers.

Barriers to Trade As we noted, the former Soviet Union was made up of 15 republics. There are significant ethnic differences between them which were suppressed prior to Gorbachev's leadership when the republics were under the control of the national government in Moscow. The reforms have released the tensions between the republics and Moscow and, by the end of 1990, all 15 declared that they wanted to be independent or sovereign states. This movement towards political autonomy coincided with the economic problems outlined so far. One effect was attempts by the various Republican governments to pursue more independent policies. Free trade within the Soviet Union broke down as local governments put up barriers to try to control the terms of the barter trade.

Strikes by Workers Workers were faced with the frustrations of having large money incomes but being unable to spend that income to buy goods and services. Instead they must hoard, queue and deal in black markets. The costs of these forms of trade, the uncertainties involved and the frustrations contributed to high levels of workers' strikes, which in turn disrupted the production process. Strikes in critical raw material industries, such as coal production, had wide-ranging effects on production in other industries.

Options for Reform

All the above events have contributed to the slowdown in the Soviet Union. What could be done to solve the problems? One important institutional development occurred following the reinstatement of Gorbachev after the August coup. In October 1991, most of the republics agreed to endorse a new treaty for an 'economic union' and soon after the Commonwealth of Independent States was constituted. One of the objectives of this treaty will be to develop market relations between the republics and to remove barriers to trade between them. But what about the inflation problem? We can lay out the options using Fig. 39.3. The first is to increase output. This would require an increase in productivity that shifted supply curves to the right (see Fig. 39.3(a)). But productivity gains may not be possible without further rises in wages. That would mean another injection of money into the system, so the original problem will re-appear.

The second option is to cut back the money supply. The main sources of money supply growth have been the funding of enterprise losses and the provision of subsidies to consumers. Consumer prices are low, as we saw already, and in many cases less than cost. The difference is made up by subsidies from the central government. So a cut in the money supply would require further reforms on consumer goods pricing and enterprise responsibility for their own losses. Sometimes this latter reform is called giving the enterprises a **hard budget constraint,** as opposed to the 'soft budget constraint' under which they now operate. **Soft budget constraint** means that enterprise losses are not the responsibility of the enterprise and its managers, but instead they are borne by the government's budget.

The third option is to raise prices, that is, to pursue the old policy of a turnover tax. This was in fact the option chosen in February 1991. Food prices rose by an average of 240 per cent and consumer goods by 175 per cent. This has the double benefit of reducing the real value of the outstanding stock of money and also cutting back the size of the government subsidies, and therefore the growth of the money supply.

But there are some offsets. Consumers resist higher prices leading to lower real incomes. Attempts to raise prices can, for example, lead to even greater problems of industrial unrest. As a result, the central government, at the same time as raising prices, proposed to pay compensation to consumers to some degree. If compensation were paid, the problem of inflation would persist.

A failure to tackle the issue of enterprise losses will also lead to problems. First, there is no incentive to become more productive. Second, the accumulating losses lead to further money supply growth. If inflation cannot be controlled, then people will not be willing to hold money, so it will not be possible to reinstate money as a medium of exchange. A market mechanism will not work efficiently unless that happens.

And finally, there is the issue of defining and allocating property rights as enterprises previously owned by the state are handed back to private ownership. Apart from the administrative difficulties this process imposes, there is the issue of who would want many of the assets of some firms. On some estimates, up to 40 per cent of the capital stock in the CIS is so old as to have no market value. If this is the case, no one would accept the stock as a gift. As we noted above, those inefficient enterprises are still operating supported by subsidies from the state.

In summary, we have seen that reform is not as simple as giving enterprises more autonomy. A little bit of reform can lead to worse outcomes in the short run than no reform at all. Successful reform requires:

- Moving to a 'hard budget constraint', that is, enterprise responsibility as well as autonomy
- Reform of the pricing system
- Control of the money supply to avoid inflation and thereby to support the use of money as a medium of exchange
- Proper definition and allocation of property rights

A failure to move on all these fronts creates not only severe economic problems, even leading to falls in output, but also to severe political disruption. The CIS is particularly vulnerable to these political problems because of the diversity of its population.

These are some of the issues which the CIS is tackling in its reform process. Let's see what happened in the process of reform of the Chinese economy.

China

China is the world's largest nation, with a population of more than a billion people. Chinese civilization is ancient and has a splendid history, but the modern nation — the People's Republic of China — dates only from 1949. A compact summary of key periods in the economic history of the People's Republic is presented in Table 39.3.

Modern China began when a revolutionary Communist movement, led by Mao Zedong, captured control of China, forcing the country's previous leader, Chiang Kai-shek (Jiang Jie-shi), on to the island of Formosa — now Taiwan. Like the former Soviet Union, China is a socialist country. But unlike the former Soviet Union, China is not so industrialised. Agriculture in the Chinese economy is still a relatively important source of output and employment.

During the early years of the People's Republic, the country followed the Soviet model of economic planning and command. Urban manufacturing industry was taken over and operated by the state, and the farms were collectivized. Also, following the Stalin model of the 1930s, primary emphasis was placed on the production of capital equipment.

Figure 39.4 shows the growth since the early 1950s of income per capita in China. Over the quarter-century from 1952 to 1977, income per cap-

Table 39.3 A Compact Summary of Key Periods in the Economic History of the People's Republic of China

Period	Main economic events/characteristics
1949	• People's Republic of China established under Mao Zedong
1949–1952	• Economy centralized under a new communist government
	• Emphasis on heavy industry and 'socialist transformation'.
1952–1957	• First five-year plan
1958–1960	• The Great Leap Forward: an economic reform plan based on labour-intensive production methods
	• Massive economic failure
1966	• Cultural revolution
1976	• Death of Mao Zedong
1978	• Reforms of Deng Xiaoping: liberalization of agriculture and introduction of individual incentives
	• Growth rates accelerate
1985	• Inflation rates accelerate
1989	• Democracy movement; government crackdown
	• Slowdown in economic growth

ita grew at an annual average real rate of about 4 per cent a year. This is a reasonable growth rate, but it reflects the very high rate of accumulation of capital in China over this period. The high rate of capital accumulation was a product of the planning system, and did not reflect the voluntary savings decisions of households. This strategy limited growth in the supply of goods available for consumption. While the average growth rate over the period was reasonable, China's economic history since 1949 is punctuated by periods of great turbulence. The first of these was the Great Leap Forward.

In 1958, Mao Zedong set the Chinese economy on a sharply divergent path from that which the Soviet Union had followed. Mao called his new path the Great Leap Forward. The **Great Leap Forward** was an economic plan based on small-scale, labour-intensive industrialization. The Great Leap Forward paid little or no attention to linking individual pay to individual effort. Instead, a revolutionary commitment to the success of collective plans was relied on. The Great Leap Forward was an economic failure. Income per person fell, as illustrated in Fig. 39.4, and the diversion of labour out of agriculture led to a slump in output. There was a famine at this time in which millions of people, maybe as many as 30 million, perished.

The next shock came in the late 1960s during the period of the Cultural Revolution, just as incomes had caught up to their levels before the Great Leap Forward. Mao unleashed a political campaign which had both immediate and longer-run effects. The immediate effect was to disrupt the management of enterprises and other institutions in the economy. Income per head fell in the first year of the Cultural Revolution. An effect of the political campaign was to denounce productive managers, engineers, scientists and scholars, and banish them to the life of the peasant. Schools and universities were closed and the accumulation of human capital was severely disrupted. The growth rate of income per capita over the decade up to the mid-1970s was less than 3 per cent a year.

The slowdown in growth contributed to a re-evaluation of economic policy. The Chinese, for reasons of national security, were concerned about slipping too far behind other large economies, such as the United States or the former Soviet Union. Years of isolation had also denied China access to foreign technology, without which they could not easily catch up. The desire to catch up led to a reorientation of policy under the leadership of Deng Xiaoping.

The 1978 Reforms

By 1978, two years after the death of Mao Zedong, the new Chinese leader, Deng Xiaoping, proclaimed major economic reforms. Collectivized agriculture was abolished. Agricultural land was distributed among households on long-term leases. In exchange for a lease, a household agreed to pay a fixed tax and contracted to sell part of its output to the state. But the household made its own decisions on cropping patterns, the quantity and types of fertilizers and other inputs to use. Private farm markets were liberalized and farmers received a higher price for their produce. Also, the state increased the price it paid to farmers, especially for cotton and other non-grain crops.

The results of the reforms of Deng Xiaoping have been astounding. Annual growth rates of grain output doubled, rising to 5 per cent in the period to 1985. Annual growth rates of output of cotton and oil- bearing crops increased to 17 per cent and 14 per cent respectively, compared with less than 1 per cent prior to 1978. By 1984, a country that six years earlier had been the world's largest importer of agricultural products became a food exporter, at least for a short time! Overall, the growth rate of per capita income doubled (see Fig. 39.4).

The reforms not only produced massive expansion in the agricultural sector. Increased rural incomes brought an expanding rural industrial sector which operated completely outside the planning system. By the late 1980s, it accounted for about half the value of output in Chinese rural areas, that is, it had become as important as agriculture. It also accounted for about a quarter of national output value. The ownership of these enterprises is not well defined. But they can be thought of as being jointly owned by all the people in their surrounding communities, rather like a cooperative, although the 'shares' cannot be bought and sold.

The growth in rural industry was made possible by the emergence of a market economy operating alongside the planning system. In agriculture, households have obligations to the plan, but excess output could be sold on the free market, always at much higher prices. Urban manufacturing continued to operate mainly under the plan, receiving raw materials from the planning system and providing output back to that system. But it too could sell excess output on free markets. As we mentioned, manufacturers in rural China both bought and sold inputs and outputs on free markets. Consumers too could buy products from the state distribution system, and from the free markets.

Figure 39.4 Economic Growth in China

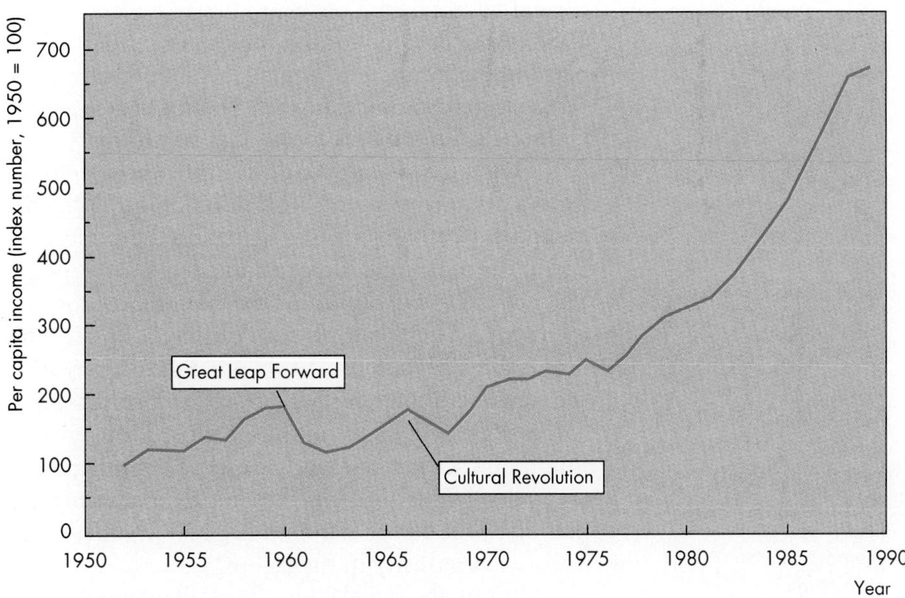

Income per head grew at about 4 per cent in real terms between 1952 and 1977. After the reforms of 1978, however, that growth rate more than doubled. Income growth has been more stable since 1978. In previous periods there were severe shocks to growth such as the Great Leap Forward and the Cultural Revolution.

Let's see how this system worked. Figure 39.5 shows the market for shoes. Enterprises selling shoes have an obligation to supply shoes to the state distribution system. The state has contracted to buy a quantity of Q_0 and price P_0 from all producers in the market who are tied to the planning system. Once this obligation is fulfilled, firms can sell on the free market.

The quantity Q_0 is distributed through the planning system. Those goods can be sold at a price above or below P_0, the level being at the discretion of the planners. The demand curve in the free market is shown as D in section (b) of the figure. This is the demand curve after the quantity Q_0 has been distributed. The supply curve S is the supply curve of those firms in the industry willing to deal in the free market, once the obligation to supply Q_0 to the state system has been met. In practice many of the firms operating in the free market may be more efficient than those tied to the planning system. The market clearing price is P_1. The quantity Q_0Q_1 is transacted at the market clearing price.

This system is called **two-tier pricing.** It has the political attraction to the planners of being able to supply at least some goods in the state system at prices the planners determine. It has the economic advantage of not affecting incentives at the margin. But once the market exists, the planners have a major problem trying to keep the planning system going. There are very strong incentives to switch goods out of the planning system (where they yield P_0 to producers) into the market (where they yield P_1). This sort of 'corruption' was a major issue in China by the end of the 1980s.

By the end of the 1980s, nearly all agricultural products were distributed under this two-tier system. One exception was cotton; another was grain, where volumes transacted at free-market prices were relatively small. As we'll see, this led to some problems in China. The same two-tier system applied to lots of industrial products except for a few raw materials regarded as critical inputs, like cotton, but also energy.

China has gone even further that the Soviet Union in other areas as well. It has a more open international trading system and is encouraging foreign investment and joint ventures. This was part of the so-called 'open door' policy, which dates from the early 1970s. Its original motivation was to increase China's access to foreign technology and capital. In addition, China is experimenting with formal capital markets and now has a stock market.

There is another way in which the Chinese economy employs a variety of systems of resource allocation. Motivated partly by political considerations, China is proclaiming the virtues of what it calls the 'one country, two systems' approach to economic management. The political source of this

Figure 39.5 Two-Tier Pricing

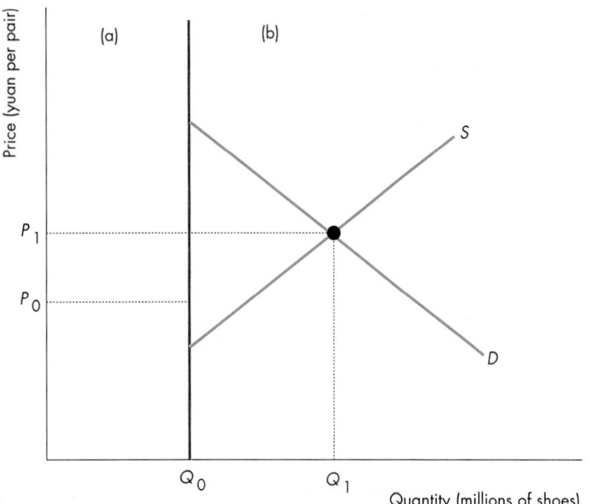

Two prices apply in this market. One is the price at which the state planning system acquires products from producers. The other is the price which rules in the free market. The latter is much higher, which creates strong incentives to try to undermine the planning system. At the margin, however, marginal cost and marginal evaluations of extra output are equalized.

movement is the existence of two capitalist enclaves in which China has a close interest: Taiwan and Hong Kong. China claims sovereignty over Taiwan. As such, it wants to create an atmosphere in which it becomes possible for China to be 'reunified' at some future date. Hong Kong, a British crown colony, is currently leased by Britain from China and that lease terminates in 1997. When the lease expires, Hong Kong will become part of China. Anxious not to damage the economic prosperity of Hong Kong, China is proposing to continue operating Hong Kong as a capitalist economy. With Hong Kong and Taiwan as part of the People's Republic of China, the stage will be set for the creation of other capitalist 'islands' in such dynamic cities as Shanghai.

Issues in the Chinese Reforms

Average annual income growth doubled in real terms in the decade after the reform compared with the period since 1952. But in the late 1980s, a number of problems emerged. Inflation rates started in rise. Before 1985 the annual inflation rate was generally less than 3 per cent (1980 being an exception at 6 per cent). But after 1985, inflation rates accelerated, reaching a peak of about 25 per cent at the end of 1988. This was followed by a dramatic slowdown in growth in China. In 1989, income per head increased by less than 2 per cent in real terms over 1988. Associated political turbulence in China culminated in the massacre in Beijing in June of that year. What factors contributed to these political and economic upheavals? Let's go back to the original reforms.

The success of the reforms in the early 1980s reflects a number of factors. The Chinese government raised the purchase prices of agricultural products and at the same time increased the degree of responsibility of farm households for the management of their land. They changed both the level of prices and farm autonomy and responsibility. Productivity in the rural sector increased as a result, so that real incomes increased. Since output increased, the initial round of price increases did not set off an inflationary cycle. Higher real incomes in the rural sector also permitted the accumulation of capital, which was reinvested in industry in the countryside.

But by the mid-1980s, the sequencing of reforms started to get out of kilter. The outcome was like that in the former Soviet Union, that is, a more rapid increase in the money supply and a higher rate of inflation. There were two main factors which led to a faster growth rate of money supply.

First, in the agriculture sector, the degree of autonomy at the farm level was still increasing, with farmers being given even more autonomy than before over which crops to plant. In contrast, the reform of the marketing system for grain in particular had slowed down. Grain prices were still controlled by the government. Meanwhile, higher incomes and the growth of industry had increased the demand for other agricultural products, like tobacco, cotton and sugar, which were substitute uses for agricultural land. In some cases, their prices were more flexible and rose relative to the price of grain. As a result, the profitability of growing other crops increased, farmers switched into other crops and grain output started to fall. Falling grain output set off alarm bells in the minds of the Chinese leadership, since grain shortages at the going planning system prices in urban areas would have led to political unrest. The government responded by pushing up the prices it paid the farmers for grain, but at the same time it tried to hold down consumer prices. By 1989, prices paid for grain from the state distribution system by urban consumers were less than half the prices paid to farmers. The difference was made up by subsidies from the state budget. As competition from other crops increased, these subsidies grew. The growth in these subsidies increased the money supply.

Second, despite the growth in rural industry, urban industry was still an important part of the economy. Unlike rural industry, urban industry continued to operate under a 'soft budget constraint'. As the general level of prices rose, its wage bill increased, but much faster than productivity growth, so that losses increased. These losses were bankrolled by the state budget, which led to further increases in the money supply.

Wages were rising, but not fast enough to keep up with the general level of prices. By 1989, real incomes in urban China started to fall. This led to more vocal urban protests. Complaints about these economic problems coincided with those about the slow pace of political reform, as well as those about the corruption associated with the two-tier pricing system. These forces culminated in the popular demonstrations in Beijing in 1989 in which a wide variety of people, workers as well as students and intellectuals, participated. The government, shocked by such a widespread threat to its authority, reacted with a great deal of force.

On the economic front, the government had already initiated a policy of slowing down the growth of the money supply. It did this by imposing much tighter controls on lending through the banking system. The credit squeeze was so tough that the growth rate of the economy slumped in 1989.

In summary, compared with the former Soviet Union, China found the first stages of reform much easier. The reason was that the first stages focused on the agricultural sector, where simultaneous movement on pricing and management autonomy, as well as responsibility, were possible. Eventually, problems of sequencing the reforms led to political and economic problems in China. But the importance of the agricultural sector in China and the growth of rural industry, which operates outside the plan, under a 'hard budget constraint', brightens the immediate prospects for further reform and therefore a return to high growth in China. The major problems in the 1990s are the reform of the pricing of agricultural products to urban residents and the tightening of budget constraints on urban enterprise.

REVIEW

What can we say about the process of reform of centrally planned economies? Some general observations are possible. First, the sequencing of reform will vary with the resource endowments and the stage of development of the reforming. China, for example, has followed a different path from the Soviet Union. Second, economic reforms tend to be cyclical. As the Soviet and Chinese experiences demonstrate, some reform steps can lead to further problems and a slowdown in reform. Third, the adoption of a reform programme, and the experience of some initial successes, create a powerful set of expectations in the community. Those expectations can be a force to crash through later problems and barriers to further reform, like those experienced by both China and the former Soviet Union. ■

SUMMARY

The Fundamental Economic Problem

No economic system can abolish the fundamental economic problem of scarcity. Each system attempts to get the economy on to its production possibility frontier, choose a point on the frontier, and distribute the gains from economic activity. (pp. 577–578)

Alternative Economic Systems

Economic systems vary in two dimensions: who owns capital and land and who allocates resources. Under capitalism, capital and land are privately owned and resources are allocated by markets. Under socialism, capital and land are owned by the state and resources are allocated by a command planning system.

Capitalism is based on the political philosophy that individual liberty is paramount. Individual preferences guide the production of goods and services. Socialism is an economic system based on the political philosophy that the private ownership of capital and land enables the wealthy to exploit the poor. The goods and services produced under socialism reflect the preferences not of individual consumers but of central planners.

Welfare state capitalism combines private ownership of capital and land with a large degree of state intervention. Market socialism combines state ownership of capital with market-determined prices.

All countries employ economic systems that contain some elements of capitalism and socialism. The United States and Japan come closest to being capitalist economies and the former Soviet Union is an example of a socialist economy. Australia and the countries of Western Europe employ welfare state capitalism. China has also moved in the direction of market socialism. (pp. 578–581)

Varieties of Capitalism

Japan is the capitalist economy whose performance has been most spectacular. Its performance has been based on a strong reliance on the free market and capitalist methods of production, a small scale of government and low taxes, and pro-business government intervention. Japanese capitalism also has some distinctive features, especially the extent of networking.

Capitalism in Australia and Western Europe has larger elements of government intervention than capitalism in Japan or the United States. Government expenditure and taxes are higher and many industries are publicly owned or nationalized. In recent years, there has been a shift to privatization, deregulation and lower taxes in these economies. (pp. 581–584)

The Former Soviet Union/New CIS

The CIS is a vast, resource-rich Commonwealth that used a socialist economic system with a central planning and command mechanism. Soviet planning was managed by GOSPLAN, based on a series of detailed plans for consumer goods, labour, credit, capital goods and materials. Since 1987, the former Soviet Union embarked upon a process of economic restructuring called *Perestroika.* This restructuring involved a move away from central planning and command toward decentralized incentives and market prices. The first round of reforms in the Soviet Union led to slower not faster growth. The reason is that problems in sequencing the reforms led to rapid growth in the money supply, a failure of money as the medium of exchange and a breakdown in the resource allocation system. Consequently, political reform followed with the break-up of the Soviet Union and the formation of the Commonwealth of Independent States. Each of the new constituent countries of the CIS has voted to move faster towards a market-based economy. (pp. 584–591)

China

Since the foundation of the People's Republic of China, economic management has been through turbulent changes. At first, China used the Soviet system of central planning. It then introduced the Great Leap Forward, which in turn degenerated into the Cultural Revolution. China at first grew quickly, with heavy reliance on state planning and capital accumulation, but growth slowed and, at times, per capita income actually fell. In 1978, China revolutionized its economic management, placing greater emphasis on private incentives and markets. As a consequence, productivity grew at a rapid rate and per capita income increased. The growth rate slumped at the end of the 1980s, following a period of high inflation in China. The accelerating level of prices also reflects problems of sequencing reform, in particular, the retention of soft budget constraints for urban industry and regulated distribution systems for some agricultural products in urban China. (pp. 591–595)

KEY TERMS

Annual plan, p. 585
Capitalism, p. 578
Central planning, p. 578
Communism, p. 580
Decentralized planning, p. 578
Five-year plan, p. 585
GOSPLAN, p. 585
Great Leap Forward, p. 592
Hard budget constraint, p. 590
Industry policy, p. 582
Market socialism, p. 578
Ministry of International Trade and Industry (MITI), p. 582
Nationalized industry, p. 583
Networking, p. 582
Privatization, p. 584
Socialism, p. 578
Soft budget constraint, p. 590
Two-tier pricing, p. 593
Turnover tax, p. 586
Welfare state capitalism, p. 579

GLOSSARY

Above full-employment equilibrium A situation in which macroeconomic equilibrium occurs at a level of real GDP above long-run aggregate supply.

Absolute advantage A person has an absolute advantage in the production of a product if he or she is more productive than another person in the production of that product. A country has an absolute advantage in the production of a product if its output per unit of inputs for that product is higher than that of another country.

Aggregate consumption function The relationship between real consumption expenditure and real GDP.

Aggregate demand The entire relationship between the aggregate quantity of goods and services demanded — real GDP demanded — and the price level — the GDP deflator — holding everything else constant.

Aggregate demand curve A curve showing the quantity of real GDP demanded at each price level, holding everything else constant.

Aggregate demand schedule A list showing the quantity of real GDP demanded at each price level, holding everything else constant.

Aggregate expenditure The expenditure that economic agents undertake in given circumstances.

Aggregate expenditure curve A graph of the aggregate expenditure schedule.

Aggregate expenditure schedule A list of the level of aggregate planned expenditure at each level of real GDP.

Aggregate quantity of goods and services demanded The total quantity of final goods and services demanded — it covers products demanded by consumers' expenditure, government purchases, investment and net exports.

Aggregate quantity of goods and services supplied The sum of the quantities of all the final goods and services produced by all the firms (and government departments) in the economy.

Annual plan A plan of the former Soviet government specifying month by month targets for output, prices, inputs, investment and money and credit flows.

Anticipated inflation An inflation rate that has been, on average, correctly forecast.

Arbitrage The activity of buying at a low price and selling at a high price in order to make a profit on the margin between the two prices.

Asset Anything of value that a household, firm, or government owns.

Assumptions The foundation on which a model is built.

Authorized money market dealers A select group of nine dealers with a special relationship with the Reserve Bank.

Automatic stabilizer A mechanism that decreases the size of fluctuations in aggregate expenditure that result from fluctuations in components of aggregate expenditure.

Autonomous expenditure The sum of those components of aggregate planned expenditure that are not influenced by real GDP.

Autonomous expenditure multiplier or **the multiplier** The amount by which a change in autonomous expenditure must be multiplied to calculate the resulting change in equilibrium expenditure and real GDP.

Autonomous tax multiplier The amount by which a change in autonomous taxes must be multiplied to determine the change that it generates in equilibrium expenditure and real GDP.

Autonomous taxes Taxes whose yields do not vary directly with real GDP.

Average propensity to consume The ratio of consumers' expenditure to disposable income.

Average propensity to save The ratio of saving to disposable income.

Axes The scale lines on a graph.

Balanced budget A government budget that is in neither surplus nor deficit.

Balanced budget multiplier The amount by which equal changes in government purchases and taxes must be multiplied to determine the change that they generate in equilibrium expenditure and real GDP.

Balance of payments accounts A record of a country's international transactions.

Balance of trade The value of exports minus the value of imports.

Balance on official transactions Transactions arising from the general government and those from the Reserve Bank.

Balance sheet A list of assets and liabilities.

Bank A bank is a firm, regulated under the Banking Act 1959 to receive deposits and make loans.

Barter The direct exchange of goods for goods.

Base period The period against which the current period is compared in any index.

Broad money M3 plus borrowings from private sector non-bank financial institutions less the latter's holdings of currency and bank deposits.

Budget surplus or budget deficit The difference between government sector revenue and expenditure in a given period of time. If revenue exceeds expenditure, the government sector has a budget surplus. If expenditure exceeds revenue, the sector has a budget deficit.

Business cycle The periodic but irregular up and down movement in economic activity measured by fluctuations in real GDP and other macroeconomic variables.

Capital accumulation The growth of capital resources.

Capital goods Goods that can be used many times before they eventually wear out. Examples of capital goods are plant, buildings, vehicles and machinery.

Capital stock The stock of plant, buildings, vehicles and machinery.

Capitalism An economic system based on the private ownership of capital and land used in production and on the market allocation of resources.

Central bank A public authority charged with regulating and controlling a country's monetary and financial institutions and markets.

Central planning A method of allocating resources by command.

Ceteris paribus Other things being equal, or other things remaining constant.

Change in demand A shift of the entire demand curve for a product that occurs when some influence on buyers' plans, other than the price of the product, changes.

Change in supply A shift in the entire supply curve for a product that occurs when some influence on producers' plans, other than the price of the product, changes.

Change in the quantity demanded A movement along a demand curve for a product that results from a change in the price of the product.

Change in the quantity supplied A movement along the supply curve for a product that results from a change in the price of the product.

Cheque account A loan by a depositor to a bank, the ownership of which can be transferred.

Clearing house The institutions in each state that work out the net position of each bank at the end of the day.

Closed economy An economy that has no links with any other economy.

Command mechanism A method of determining *what, how* and *for whom* goods and services are produced, based on the authority of a ruler or ruling body.

Commodity money A physical commodity valued in its own right and also used as a medium of exchange.

Commonwealth budget A statement of the government's financial plan.

Communism An economic system based on state ownership of capital and land, on central planning, and on distributing income in accordance with the following rule: from each according to his or her ability, to each according to his or her need.

Comparative advantage A person has a comparative advantage in producing a product if he or she can produce that product at a lower opportunity cost than anyone else. A country has a comparative advantage in producing a product if it can produce that product at a lower opportunity cost than any other country.

Competition A contest for command over scarce resources.

Complement A product that is used in conjunction with another product.

Consumer price index Measures the average level

of prices of the goods and services typically consumed by a metropolitan Australian household.

Consumption The process of using up goods and services.

Consumption expenditure The total expenditure by households on consumption goods and services.

Consumption function The relationship between consumers' expenditure and disposable income.

Consumption goods Goods that can be used just once. Examples are pickled onions and toothpaste.

Consumption smoothing The levelling out of consumption patterns by varying savings.

Contraction A business cycle phase in which there is a slowdown in the pace of economic activity.

Convertible paper money A paper claim to a commodity (such as gold) that can be converted into the commodity at a guaranteed price. The paper claim circulates as a medium of exchange.

Cooperation People working with others to achieve a common end.

Coordinates Lines on a graph running perpendicularly from a point to the axes.

Coordination mechanism A mechanism that makes the choices of one individual compatible with the choices of others.

Cost-push inflation Inflation that has its origin in cost increases.

Countercyclical A variable exhibiting a negative correlation with GDP.

Creditor nation A country that during its entire history has invested more in the rest of the world than other countries have invested in it.

Crowding in The tendency for an increase in government purchases of goods and services to increase investment.

Crowding out The tendency for an increase in government purchases of goods and services to increase interest rates, thereby reducing — or crowding out — investment expenditure.

Currency The bills and coins in use today.

Currency appreciation The increase in the value of one currency in terms of another currency.

Currency depreciation The fall in the value of one currency in terms of another currency.

Currency drain The tendency of some loans to leave the banking system.

Current account A record of receipts from the sale of goods and services to foreigners, the payments for goods and services bought from foreigners, and property income (such as interest and profits) and current transfers (such as gifts) received from and paid to foreigners.

Current account balance The net value of all the items on the current account.

Current deposit Deposits in banks that are at call.

Curve Any relationship between two variables plotted on a graph, even a linear relationship.

Cyclical unemployment Unemployment arising from a slowdown in the pace of economic expansion.

Debt financing The financing of the government sector deficit by selling bonds to anyone (households, firms, or foreigners) other than the Reserve Bank.

Debtor nation A country that during its entire history has borrowed more from the rest of the world than it has lent to it. It has a stock of outstanding debt to the rest of the world that exceeds the stock of its own claims on the rest of the world.

Decentralized planning or **market socialism** An economic system that combines socialism's state ownership of capital and land with capitalism's market allocation of resources.

Decisionmaker Any person or organized group of persons that make economic choices.

Deficit The government balance if total expenditure exceeds total revenues.

Deflation A downward movement in the average level of prices.

Demand The entire relationship between the quantity demanded of a product and its price.

Demand curve A graph showing the relationship between the quantity demanded of a product and its price, holding everything else constant.

Demand for labour A schedule or curve showing the quantity of labour demanded at each level of the real wage rate, holding everything else constant.

Demand for real money The relationship between the quantity of real money demanded and the interest rate, holding constant all other influences on the amount of money that people wish to hold.

Demand schedule A list of the quantities of a product demanded at different prices, holding everything else constant.

Demand-pull inflation The inflation resulting from an increase in aggregate demand.

Depreciation The fall in the value of capital or the value of a durable input resulting from its use and from the passage of time.

Depression A deep business cycle trough.

Desired reserve ratio The ratio of reserves to deposits that banks regard as necessary in order to be able to conduct their business.

Developing country A country that is poor but is accumulating capital and developing an industrial and commercial base.

Diminishing marginal product of labour The tendency for the marginal product of labour to decline as the labour input increases, holding everything else constant.

Direct taxes Income taxes paid by individuals on their labour and capital incomes.

Discouraged workers People who do not have jobs and would like to work, but have stopped seeking work.

Disintermediation The movement of funds between different types of deposits as interest rates change.

Disposable income Original income plus transfer payments minus taxes.

Dissaving Negative saving; a situation in which consumers' expenditure exceeds disposable income.

Domestic factor incomes The sum of wages, salaries and supplements and the net operating surplus of private trading enterprises, public trading enterprises, general government and financial enterprises.

Double coincidence of wants A situation that occurs when person A wants to buy what person B is selling, and person B wants to buy what person A is selling.

Double counting Counting the expenditure on both the final product and the intermediate goods and services used in its production.

Double entry book-keeping A procedure whereby every transaction is represented by two entries of equal and opposite value.

Dumping The sale of a good in a foreign market for a lower price than in the domestic market or for a lower price than its cost of production.

Economic activity What people do to cope with scarcity.

Economic growth The persistent expansion of a country's production possibilities.

Economic model An artificial or imaginary economy, or part of an economy.

Economic theory A generalization that enables us to understand and predict economic choices.

Economic welfare A comprehensive measure of the general state of well being and standard of living.

Economics The study of how people use their limited resources to try to satisfy unlimited wants.

Economizing Making the best use of scarce resources.

Economy A mechanism that allocates scarce resources among competing uses.

Effective rates of protection Measures the percentage change in value added that results from protection.

Efficiency wage An approach to wage determination based on the idea that if a firm pays its workers more than the average wage paid by other firms and, at the same time, it threatens to fire workers who are exerting very little effort, then average productivity of all the workers employed by the firm rises.

Employment The number of adult workers (aged 15 and older) who have jobs.

Endowment The resources that people have.

Equation of exchange An equation that states that the quantity of money multiplied by the velocity of circulation of money equals the price level multiplied by real GDP.

Equilibrium A situation in which everyone has economized — that is, all individuals have made the best possible choices in the light of their own preferences and given their endowments and the available technologies — and in which those choices have been coordinated and made compatible with the choices of everyone else. Equilibrium is the solution or outcome of an economic model.

Equilibrium expenditure The level of aggregate planned expenditure that equals real GDP.

Equilibrium price The price at which the quantity demanded equals the quantity supplied. At this price, opposing forces exactly balance each other.

Europe 1992 The process of creating an integrated, single market economy among the member nations of the European Community.

European monetary system A nearly fixed exchange rate system involving most of the members of the European Community.

Excess reserves The difference between a bank's actual reserves and its desired reserves.

Exchange settlements accounts Accounts held by each bank at the Reserve Bank.

Expansion A business cycle phase in which there is a speedup in the pace of economic activity.

Expected inflation rate The rate at which people, on average, believe that the price level will rise.

Expenditure approach A measure of GDP obtained by adding together consumers' expenditure, investment, government purchases of goods and services and net exports.

Exports Goods and services sold by people in one country to people in other countries.

Factor cost The cost of all the factors of production used to produce a good or service.

Factor market A market in which factors of production are bought and sold.

Factors of production The economy's productive resources — land, labour and capital.

Feedback rule A rule that states which policy instruments will be used and how each instrument will respond to the state of the economy.

Fiat money An intrinsically worthless or almost worthless commodity that serves the functions of money.

Final goods and services Goods and services that are not used as inputs in the production of other goods and services but are bought by their final users.

Financial innovation The development of new financial products and methods of borrowing and lending.

Financial intermediary A firm that takes deposits from households and firms and makes loans to other households, firms and governments.

Firm An institution that buys or hires factors of production and organizes them to produce and sell goods and services.

Fiscal policy The government's attempt to vary its purchases of goods and services and its taxes to smooth the fluctuations in aggregate expenditure.

Five-year plan A plan of the former Soviet government specifying in broad outline the general economic targets and directions for a period of five years.

Fixed exchange rate An exchange rate which is pegged by the country's central bank.

Fixed rule A rule in place and maintained regardless of the state of the economy.

Flexible exchange rate An exchange rate which is determined by market forces in the absence of central bank intervention.

Flow equilibrium A situation in which the quantity of goods or services supplied per unit of time equals the quantity demanded per unit of time.

Flow theory of the exchange rate The proposition that the exchange rate adjusts to make the flow supply of dollars equal to the flow demand for dollars.

Foreign exchange controls Controls on the flow of money into and out of a country.

Foreign exchange market The market in which the currencies of different countries are exchanged for one another.

Foreign exchange rate The rate at which one country's money exchanges for another's.

Foreign investment The capital supplied by equity holders in a project.

Forward contract A contract entered into at an agreed price to buy or sell a certain quantity of any commodity (including currency) at a specified future date.

Forward exchange rate The exchange rate in a forward contract.

Frictional unemployment Unemployment arising from new entrants into the labour market and from job turnover caused by technological change.

Full employment A situation in which all unemployment is frictional.

Full-employment equilibrium A macroeconomic equilibrium at a point on the long-run aggregate supply curve.

GDP deflator A price index that measures the average level of the prices of all the goods and services that make up GDP. It is calculated as nominal GDP divided by real GDP, multiplied by 100.

General Agreement on Tariffs and Trade An agreement that limits government taxes and other restrictions on international trade.

General goverment sector The Commonwealth, State and local government.

General skills Those skills that have the effect of raising the productivity of the workers in any enterprise.

Goods and services All the valuable things that people produce. Goods are tangible and services are intangible.

Goods market The market in which goods and services are traded.

GOSPLAN The Soviet planning committee that was responsible for drawing up and implementing the state's economic plans.

Government An organization that provides goods and services and redistributes income and wealth.

Government purchases multiplier The amount by which a change in government purchases of goods and services must be multiplied to determine the change in equilibrium expenditure and real GDP that it generates.

Government sector surplus or deficit The difference between taxes (net of subsidies, transfer payments and debt interest) and government sector purchases of goods and services. If taxes exceed purchases, the government sector has a surplus. If purchases exceed taxes, the government sector has a deficit.

Great Leap Forward An economic plan for post revolutionary China based on small-scale, labour intensive production motivated by revolutionary zeal.

Gresham's Law The tendency for bad money to drive out good money. Bad money is debased money; good money is that which has not been debased.

Gross domestic product The value of output produced in a country in a period of time.

Gross domestic product at factor cost The sum of wages, salaries and supplements and gross operating surplus.

Gross investment The value of new capital equipment purchased in a given time period. It is the amount spent on replacing depreciated capital and on making net additions to the capital stock.

Household Any group of people living together as a decisionmaking unit.

Human capital The accumulated skill and knowledge of human beings. It is the value of education and acquired skills.

Hyperinflation High inflation rates.

Implications The outcome of a model that follows logically from its assumptions.

Imports Goods and services bought by people in one country from people in other countries.

Income approach Measures GDP by adding together all incomes paid by firms and government departments to households for the services of production they use.

Indexing A technique that links payments made under a contract to the price level.

Index of a real exchange rate Measures changes in the exchange rate after allowing for changes in prices.

Indirect tax A tax on the production or sale of a good or service. Indirect taxes are included in the price paid for the good or service by its final purchaser.

Induced expenditure The sum of those components of aggregate planned expenditure that vary as real GDP varies.

Induced taxes Taxes that vary directly with real GDP.

Industrial country A country that has a large amount of capital equipment and in which people undertake highly specialized activities, enabling them to earn high per capita incomes.

Industry policy Government policy instruments to provide some industries with advantages relative to others.

Inferior good A product, the demand for which decreases when consumer incomes increase.

Inflation An upward movement in the average level of prices.

Inflationary gap The difference between long run real GDP and actual GDP when actual is above its long run level.

Inflation rate The percentage change in the price level.

Injections Expenditures that add to the circular flow of expenditure and income — investment, government purchases of goods and services and exports.

Innovation The act of putting a new technique into operation.

Intellectual property The intangible product of creative effort, protected by copyrights and patents. This type of property includes books, music, computer programs and inventions of all kinds.

Interest rate parity A situation in which interest rates are equal across all countries once differences in risk are taken into account.

Intermediate goods and services Goods and services that are used as inputs into the production of another good or service.

International crowding out The tendency for an increase in government purchases to decrease net exports.

International Monetary Fund An international organization that monitors members' balance of payments and exchange rate activities.

International substitution The substitution of domestic products for foreign products or of foreign products for domestic products.

Intertemporal substitution The substitution of products now for products later or of products later for products now.

Invention The discovery of a new technique.

Inventories The stocks of raw materials, semi-finished products and unsold final goods held by firms.

Investment The purchase of new plant, buildings, vehicles and machinery, and additions to inventories in a given time period.

Investment demand The relationship between the level of investment and the real interest rate.

Investment demand curve A curve showing the relationship between the real interest rate and the level of planned investment, holding everything else constant.

Investment demand schedule The list of quantities of planned investment at each real interest rate, holding everything else constant.

Keynesian A macroeconomist whose beliefs about the functioning of the economy represent an extension of the theories of John Maynard Keynes. A Keynesian regards the economy as being inherently unstable, and as requiring active government intervention to achieve stability. A Keynesian assigns a low degree of importance to monetary policy and a high degree of importance to fiscal policy.

Labour The brain-power and muscle-power of human beings.

Labour force The total number of employed and unemployed workers.

Labour force participation rate The proportion of the working age population that is either employed or unemployed (but seeking employment).

Land Natural resources of all kinds.

Law of one price A law stating that any given commodity will be available at a single price.

Leakages Income that is not spent on domestically produced goods and services — savings, taxes (net of transfer payments including debt interest) and imports.

LGS convention A system under which each bank held a certain ratio of liquid assets and government securities to their deposits.

Liability A debt — something that a household, firm or government owes.

Linear relationship The relationship between two variables depicted by a straight line on a graph.

Liquidity The degree to which an asset can be instantly converted into cash at a known price.

Liquidity trap A situation in which the demand curve for real money is horizontal at a given interest rate and people are willing to hold any amount of money at that interest rate.

Loan A commitment of a fixed amount of money for an agreed period of time.

Long-run aggregate supply The relationship between the aggregate quantity of final goods and services (real GDP) supplied and the price level (the GDP deflator) when there is full employment — that is when unemployment is at its natural rate.

Long-run aggregate supply curve A curve showing the relationship between the quantity of real GDP supplied and the price level when wage rates change along with the price level to achieve full employment.

Long-run Phillips curve Shows the relationship between inflation and unemployment when the actual inflation rate equals the expected inflation rate.

Lorenz curve A curve that shows the cumulative percentage of income or wealth against the cumulative percentage of population.

M0 (base money) Holdings of notes and coins by the private sector + deposits of banks with the Reserve Bank + Reserve Bank liabilities to the private non-bank sector.

M1 Notes and coins held by the private non-bank sector + current deposits with banks.

M3 M1 + all other bank deposits of the private non bank sector.

Macroeconomic equilibrium A situation in which the quantity of real GDP demanded equals the quantity of real GDP supplied.

Macroeconomics The branch of economics that studies the economy as a whole. It is concerned with aggregates and averages of behaviour rather than with detailed individual choices.

Macro short run The period over which the prices of goods and services change in response to changes in demand and supply, but wages and possibly other input prices do not change.

Macro long run The period sufficiently long enough for all prices and wages to have adjusted to any disturbance so that the quantities demanded and supplied are equalled in all markets.

Managed exchange rate An exchange rate, the value of which is influenced by the central bank's intervention in the foreign exchange market.

Marginal product of labour The change in total product (output) resulting from a one-unit increase in the quantity of labour employed, holding the quantity of all other inputs constant.

Marginal propensity to consume The fraction of the last dollar of disposable income that is spent on consumer goods and services.

Marginal propensity to consume out of real GDP The change in consumption expenditure divided by the change in real GDP.

Marginal propensity to import The fraction of the last dollar of real GDP spent on imports.

Marginal propensity to save The fraction of the last dollar of disposable income that is saved.

Marginal propensity to spend on domestic goods and services or marginal propensity to spend The fraction of the last dollar of real GDP spent on domestic goods and services.

Marginal tax rate The fraction of the last dollar of income paid to the government in taxes (net of any extra transfer payments received from the government).

Market Any arrangement that facilitates buying and selling (trading) of a good, service, factor of production or future commitment.

Market mechanism A method of determining *what, how* and *for whom* goods and services are produced, based on individual choices coordinated through markets.

Market price The price that people actually pay for a good or service. Such prices include indirect taxes but are net of subsidies.

Market socialism or decentralized planning An economic system that combines socialism's state ownership of capital and land with capitalism's market allocation of resources.

Medium of exchange Anything that is generally acceptable in exchange for goods and services.

Microeconomic reform The attempt to increase output from given inputs of labour, capital and materials by making markets work more efficiently.

Microeconomics The branch of economics that studies the decisions of individual households and firms, and the way in which individual markets work. Microeconomics also studies the way in which taxes and government regulation affect people's economic choices.

Ministry of International Trade and Industry A Japanese government agency responsible for stimulating Japanese industrial development and international trade.

Misery index An index of macroeconomic performance equal to the sum of the inflation rate and the unemployment rate.

Mixed economy An economy that relies partly on the market mechanism and partly on a command mechanism to coordinate economic activity.

Monetarist A macroeconomist who assigns a high degree of importance to variations in the quantity of money as the main determinant of aggregate demand and who regards the economy as inherently stable.

Monetary base The level of bank reserves plus the amount of cash held by the public.

Monetary exchange A system in which some commodity or token serves as the medium of exchange.

Monetary policy The attempt to control inflation and the foreign exchange value of the domestic currency and to moderate the business cycle by changing the quantity of money in circulation and adjusting interest rates.

Monetary theory of the exchange rate The proposition that the exchange rate adjusts to make the stock of a currency demanded equal to the stock supplied.

Money A medium of exchange.

Money financing The financing of the government sector deficit by the sale of bonds to the Reserve Bank which results in the creation of additional money.

Money multiplier The amount by which a change in the monetary base must be multiplied to determine the resulting change in the quantity of money.

Money wage rate The wage rate expressed in current dollars.

Multiplier The change in equilibrium real GDP divided by the change in autonomous expenditure which caused GDP to change.

Nationalized industry An industry owned and operated by a publicly owned authority directly responsible to a government.

Natural rate hypothesis The hypothesis that the long run Phillips curve is vertical at the natural rate of unemployment.

Natural rate of unemployment The unemployment rate when the economy is at full employment and the only unemployment is frictional.

Negative relationship A relationship between two variables that move in opposite directions.

Net borrower A country that is borrowing more from the rest of the world than it is lending to it.

Net domestic product Indirect taxes less subsidies added to domestic factor incomes.

Net exports function The relationship between a country's net exports and its real GDP, holding constant real GDP in the rest of the world, prices and the exchange rate.

Net exporter A country whose value of exports exceeds its value of imports.

Net exports The expenditure by foreigners on Australia produced goods and services minus the expenditure by residents on foreign-produced goods and services.

Net importer A country whose value of imports exceeds its value of exports.

Net investment Net additions to the capital stock — gross investment minus depreciation.

Net lender A country that is lending more to the rest of the world than it is borrowing from it.

Networking Japanese industries' networks of long term business relationships between companies.

Newly industrialized country A country where there is a rapidly developing broad industrial base and where per capita income is growing quickly.

Nominal GDP The output of final goods and services valued at current prices.

Nominal interest rate The interest rate actually paid and received in the marketplace.

Nominal quantity of money The quantity of money measured in current dollars.

Nominal targets Macroeconomic policy targets of low and predictable inflation and stable foreign exchange rates.

Non-callable deposits One per cent of total deposits held on deposit at the Reserve Bank.

Non-convertible note A banknote that is not convertible into any commodity and that obtains its value by government fiat.

Non-official balance The transactions of those not included in the official balance.

Non-tariff barrier Any action other than a tariff that restricts international trade.

Non-traded good A good that cannot be traded over long distances.

Normal good A product the demand for which increases when income increases.

Normative statement A statement about what *ought* to be. An expression of an opinion that cannot be verified by observation.

Official cash rate The interest rate determined in the official money market.

Official money market Transactions between the Reserve Bank and the authorized dealers.

Open economy An economy that has economic links with other economies.

Open market operation The purchase or sale of commonwealth government securities by the Reserve Bank.

Opportunity cost The best forgone alternative.

Optimizing Balancing benefits against costs to do the best within the limits of what is possible.

Origin The zero point that is common to both axes on a graph.

Outlays Total government expenditure.

Paradox of thrift The fact that an increase in saving leads to an increase in the income of an individual but may lead to a decrease in aggregate expenditure and real GDP. The paradox arises because an increase in saving occurs with no increase in investment.

Participation rate The percentage of the working population in the labour force.

Payments system The process by which banks settle transactions amongst themselves.

Peak The upper turning point of a business cycle — the point at which the economy is turning from expansion to contraction.

Per capita production function A curve showing how per capita output varies as the per capita stock of capital varies, with a given technology.

Perpetuity A bond that promises to pay a certain fixed amount of money each year for ever.

Phelps–Friedman hypothesis *see* **Natural rate hypothesis**

Phillips curve Shows the relationship between inflation and unemployment.

Portfolio balance theory of the exchange rate The proposition that the exchange rate adjusts to make the stock of financial assets denominated in units of that currency demanded equal to the stock supplied.

Positive relationship A relationship between two variables that move in the same direction.

Positive statement A statement about what *is*. Something that can be verified by careful observation.

Preferences A ranking of likes and dislikes and the intensity of those likes and dislikes.

Price index A measure of the average level of prices in one period as a percentage of their level in an earlier period.

Price level The average level of prices as measured by a price index.

Price stability A situation in which the average level of prices is moving neither up nor down.

Prime assets Liquid assets held by banks that are instantly convertible.

Prime assets ratio A ratio equal to a fixed percentage of a bank's assets, under which the bank must maintain its prime assets.

Private debt money A loan that a borrower promises to repay in cash on demand.

Private enterprise An economic system that permits individuals to decide on their own economic activities.

Private sector surplus or deficit The difference between saving and investment. If saving exceeds investment, the private sector has a surplus. If investment exceeds saving, the private sector has a deficit.

Privatization The process of selling a public corporation to private shareholders.

Production The conversion of natural, human and capital resources into goods and services.

Production approach A way of measuring GDP by summing the value added of each firm in the economy.

Production function A relationship showing how output varies as the employment of inputs is varied.

Production possibility frontier The boundary between attainable and unattainable levels of production.

Productivity The output per unit of input. For example, labour productivity can be measured as output per hour of labour.

Property Anything of value.

Property rights Social arrangements that govern the ownership, use and disposal of property.

Protection The restriction of international trade.

Public sector borrowing requirement Refers to the government sector borrowing requirement plus the borrowing requirement of the nationalized industries.

Purchasing power parity A situation that occurs when money has equal value across countries.

Quantity demanded The amount of a good or service that consumers plan to buy in a given period of time.

Quantity of labour demanded The number of labour hours hired by all the firms in an economy.

Quantity of labour supplied The number of hours of labour services that households supply to firms.

Quantity of money The quantity of cash, bank deposits and building society deposits held by households and firms.

Quantity supplied The amount of a good or service that producers plan to sell in a given period of time.

Quantity theory of money The proposition that an increase in the quantity of money leads to an equal percentage increase in the price level.

Quantity traded The quantity actually bought and sold.

Quota A restriction on the quantity of a product that a firm is permitted to sell or that a country is permitted to import.

Rational choice The best possible course of action from the point of view of the individual making the choice.

Rational expectation The best forecast that can be made on the basis of all the available and relevant information. A rational expectation is one in which the expected forecast error is zero and the range of error is as small as possible.

Rational expectations equilibrium A macroeconomic equilibrium based on expectations that are the best available forecasts.

Rational expectations hypothesis The hypothesis that the forecasts people make, regardless of how they make them, are on average the same as the forecasts that an economist would make using the relevant economic theory.

Real balance effect The influence of a change in the quantity of real money on the quantity of real GDP demanded.

Real budget balance The change in the real value of outstanding government debt.

Real business cycle theory A theory of aggregate fluctuations based on the existence of flexible wages and random shocks to the economy's aggregate production function.

Real exchange rate The ratio of the price index in one country to the index in another.

Real GDP The output of final goods and services valued at prices prevailing in the base period.

Real interest rate The interest rate minus the expected inflation rate.

Real money The quantity of goods and services that a given amount of money will buy.

Real money balance effect The influence of a change in the quantity of real money on the quantity of real GDP demanded.

Real targets Macroeconomic policy targets of unemployment at its natural rate, steady growth in real GDP, and balanced international trade.

Real wage rate The wage rate expressed in constant dollars.

Recession A contraction in the level of economic activity in which real GDP declines in two successive quarters.

Recessionary gap The difference between long-run real GDP and actual GDP, when actual GDP is below its long run level.

Relative price The ratio of the price of one good to the price of another. It is expressed as the number of units of one product that one unit of another product will buy.

Replacement investment The purchase of replacements for worn out or depreciated capital.

Required reserves The minimum reserves that a bank is required to hold.

Reservation wage The lowest wage rate at which a person or household will supply any labour to the market. Below that wage, a person will not work.

Reserve Bank of Australia Australia's central bank.

Reserve ratio The fraction of a bank's total deposits that are held in reserves.

Reserves Cash holdings in a bank's vault plus the bank's deposits with the Reserve Bank.

Revenue Money collected by the government in taxes.

Saving function The relationship between saving and disposable income.

Scarcity The universal state in which wants exceed the amount that available resources can produce.

Scatter diagram A diagram which plots the value of one economic variable that is associated with the value of another.

Self-sufficiency A state that occurs when each individual consumes only what he or she produces.

Settler economy Economies which have abundant resources and small populations whose relatively high incomes at early stages of development attract a large inflow of other factors of production, such as immigrant labour.

Short-run aggregate production function The relationship showing how real GDP varies as the quantity of labour employed varies, holding the capital stock and the state of technology constant.

Short-run aggregate supply The relationship between the aggregate quantity of final goods and services (real GDP) supplied and the price level (the GDP deflator), holding everything else constant.

Short-run aggregate supply curve A curve showing the relationship between the quantity of real GDP supplied and the price level, holding everything else constant.

Short-run aggregate supply schedule A list showing the quantity of real GDP supplied at each price level, holding everything else constant.

Short-run Phillips curve Shows the relationship between inflation and unemployment holding the expected inflation rate and the natural rate of unemployment constant.

Short-run production function The relationship showing how the maximum output attainable varies as the quantity of the variable input varies, holding the quantity of the fixed input and the state of technology constant.

Simple money multiplier The amount by which an increase in bank reserves must be multiplied to calculate the effect of the increase in reserves on total bank deposits, when there are no losses of cash from the banking system.

Slope The change in the value of the variable measured on the *y*-axis divided by the change in the value of the variable measured on the *x*-axis.

Socialism An economic system based on state ownership of capital and land and on a centrally planned allocation of resources.

Specialization The production of only one product or a few products.

Stagflation A situation in which real GDP stops growing or even declines while inflation accelerates.

Standard of deferred payment An agreed measure in which contracts for future receipts and payments are written.

Stock equilibrium A situation in which the entire available stock of an asset is willingly held.

Store of value Any commodity that can be held and sold at a later time.

Structural unemployment The unemployment that results when industry concentrated in a particular region declines.

Subsidy A payment made by the government to producers of goods and services.

Substitute A product that may be used in place of another product.

Supply The entire relationship between the quantity supplied of a product and its price.

Supply curve A graph showing the relationship between the quantity supplied and the price of a product, holding everything else constant.

Supply of labour A schedule or curve showing how the quantity of labour supplied varies as the real wage varies.

Supply schedule A list of quantities supplied at different prices, holding everything else constant.

Surplus The government balance if the total revenues exceed total expenditures.

Targetting interest rates Monetary policy designed to fix nominal interest rates.

Tariff A tax on an import by the government of the importing country.

Tastes An individual's attitudes or preferences towards goods and services.

Tax on expenditure A tax on the production or the sale of a good or service.

Technological progress The development of new and better ways of producing goods and services.

Technology The method for converting resources into goods and services.

Terms of trade The ratio of the Australian price of Australian goods exported to the Australian price of foreign goods imported.

Time-series consumption function The relationship between real consumers' expenditure and real disposable income over time.

Time-series graph A graph showing the value of a variable on the *y*-axis plotted against time on the *x*-axis.

Trade-weighted index Shows the value of the dollar against a basket of other currencies.

Transfer payment A payment made by the government to households.

Transfer payments multiplier The amount by which a change in transfer payments must be multiplied to determine the change that it generates in equilibrium expenditure and real GDP.

Trend A general tendency for a variable to rise or fall.

Trend real GDP A measure of the general upward

tendency or drift of real GDP that ignores its fluctuations.

Trough The lower turning point of a business cycle — the point at which the economy turns from contraction to expansion.

Turnover tax An old Soviet tax on a consumer good designed to make its market price high enough to achieve a balance between the quantity demanded and the quantity supplied.

Two-part tariff A pricing arrangement that results in consumers facing a bill with two parts.

Unanticipated inflation Inflation that catches people by surprise.

Underdeveloped country A country in which there is little industrialization, limited mechanization of the agricultural sector, very little capital equipment, and low per capita income.

Underdevelopment trap A situation in which a country is locked into a low per capita income situation that reinforces itself.

Underground economy Legal economic transactions hidden to avoid income tax obligations.

Unemployment The number of adult workers who are not employed and who are seeking jobs.

Unemployment equilibrium A situation in which macroeconomic equilibrium occurs at a level of real GDP below long-run aggregate supply.

Unemployment rate Unemployment expressed as a percentage of the labour force.

Unit of account An agreed measure for stating the prices of goods and services.

Value added The value of a firm's output minus the value of the inputs bought from other firms.

Value of money The amount of goods and services that can be bought with a given amount of money.

Velocity of circulation The average number of times a dollar is used annually to buy the goods and services that make up GDP.

Voluntary export restraint A self-imposed restriction by an exporting country on the volume of its exports of a particular good. Voluntary export restraints are often called VERs.

Wants The unlimited desires or wishes that people have for goods and services.

Wealth effect The effect of a change in real wealth on aggregate planned expenditure.

Welfare state capitalism An economic system combining capitalism's private ownership of capital and land with a heavy degree of state intervention in the allocation of resources.

***x*-axis** The horizontal scale on a graph.

***x*-coordinate** A line running from a point on a graph horizontally to the *y*-axis. It is called the *x*-coordinate because its length is the same as the value marked off on the *x*-axis.

***y*-axis** The vertical scale on a graph.

***y*-coordinate** A line running from a point on a graph vertically to the *x*-axis. It is called the *y*-coordinate because its length is the same as the value marked off on the *y*-axis.

INDEX

Key concepts and pages where they are defined appear in boldface

A

Above full-employment equilibrium, 156–7
Abraham, Katharine, 389
Absolute advantage, 55–6, 512–13
Accord *see* Wages Accord
ACM *see* Australian Chamber of Manufacturers
Action lag, 346
Actual reserves, 255
Aggregate consumption function, 182–6
Aggregate demand, 140–4, 146–7, 165, 226–7, 232, 329–32, 352
  anticipating increases in, 401
  changes in, 144
  effect of change in, 157
  fall in, 461
  fiscal policy and, 337–41, 353, 360–1
  full employment and, 230–1
  increasing, 399
  inflation effect, 399
  influencing composition of, 349
  IS–LM model, 355–63
  monetary policy and, 332, 352–3, 362–3
  quantity of money and, 256
  response to inflation, 402
  unemployment and, 229–30
Aggregate demand curve, 140
  autonomous expenditure and, 227–8
  derived, 360
  shifts in, 146–7, 334, 339
  slope, 141
Aggregate demand schedule, 140
Aggregate demand shocks, 157, 160
Aggregate demand stimulation and growth, 570–2
Aggregate economic activity, 131–6
Aggregate expenditure, 115–16, 118, 125, **194**, 207, 226–7, 232
  components of, 174–5, 200
  fluctuations in components, 175
  price level and, 226–7
  real GDP and, 194–8, 201
  relative volatility of components, 174–5
  relative importance of components, 174
Aggregate expenditure curve, 195–6, 210
  slope, 197
Aggregate expenditure schedule, 195–6
Aggregate fluctuations, 157, 160
Aggregate income, 115–16, 118, 125
Aggregate planned expenditure, 356
Aggregate production, 125
Aggregate quantity of goods and services demanded, 140
Aggregate quantity of goods and services supplied, 147
Aggregate supply, 147–54, 165, 329
  changes in, 154
  decreasing, 401–2
  effect of change in, 160–1
  flexible wages and, 375–7
  inflation effect, 402
  monetary policy and, 468
  quantity of money and, 256
  stabilization policy and, 467–8
  sticky wages and, 380–1
Aggregate supply curve, 150
Aggregate supply schedule, 150
Aid, foreign *see* Foreign aid, 567
Alternative economic systems, 578–81, 595–6
Annual plan, 585
Anticipated inflation, 96, 398, 409, 412
  problem of, 97–8
APC *see* Average propensity to consume
APS *see* Average propensity to save
Arbitrage, 314–16, 318, 322
Arrival of goods, 130–1
Asset prices, interest rates and, 287–8
Assets, 248, 250
Assumptions, 18
Australia
  'banana republic', 428–9
  business cycle 1980–1983, 426–8
  business cycle 1983–1986, 428
  business cycle 1986–1990, 429–30
  contraction, 428, 431–2, 434–5
  economic performance, 425–46, 454–5
  expansion, 428–9, 433–4
  Federal budget *see* Federal budget
  macroeconomic performance, 425–6
  real GDP growth, 425–6
  real money growth, 425–6
  real wages, 425–6
  stabilizing economy, 469–74
  stagflation, 438
  terms of trade, 425–6, 438
Australian Chamber of Manufacturers, 456
Australian Council of Trade Unions, 436, 455–6
Australian economy
  1989/90, 160–2
  aggregate demand, 161–2
  aggregate supply, 161–2
  trends and cycles in, 160–6
Australian Notes Act 1910, 244
Authorized money market dealers, 249, **274**
Automatic stabilizer, 218–19
  government deficit and, 219, 222
Autonomous consumption, 207
Autonomous expenditure, 195, **196**, 197
  aggregate demand curve and, 227–8
  change in, 210–11, 228
  increase in, 210–11
Autonomous expenditure lag, 346
Autonomous expenditure multiplier, 212, 231
Autonomous taxes, 217
Autonomous tax multiplier, 217–18, 232
Average propensity to consume, 178
  Australian, 181
Average propensity to save, 178–9
Averages, 180
Axes, 28

B

Backing, 243
  fractional *see* Fractional backing
Balanced budget, 478
Balanced budget multiplier, 218, 232
Balanced trade, 510
Balance on goods and services, 531
Balance on merchandise trade, 531
Balance on official transactions, 533

Balance of payments, 536
  individual analogy, 535–6
Balance of payments accounts, 531
  Australian, 533–6
Balance sheet, 248
  of all banks, 249–50
Balance of trade, 503
  international borrowing and, 508
  dollar and, 547–8
  percentage of GDP, 507–8
Balancing item, 534
Bank bills of exchange, 246
Bank lending, quantitative limits, 268–9
Banking Act 1945, 265
Banking Act 1959, 248, 264
Banks, 248–51
  Australian, 255–6
  failure, 255
  limited entry to other markets, 269
  money creation and, 253–5
  panic, 255
  USA, 255–6
Barriers to trade, 590
Barro, Robert, 493, 495
Barter, 60, 240, 590
Base money *see* M0
Base period, 94, 126, 128
BCA *see* Business Council of Australia
Below full-employment equilibrium, 155–6
Best alternative forgone, 9, 48
Best deal available, 76
Black market, 590
Blanchard, Olivier, 389
Bodin, Jean, 470
Bookkeeping, 544
Boom, 432–3
Boom–bust economy, 432–3
Borrowers, 96–7
  minimizing cost of monitoring, 252
Borrowing
  for consumption, 537–8
  international, 316–18, 537–9, 551
  for investment, 537–8
Branch banking, 255–6
Brigden Report, 459
Broad money, 244–6, 260
Brumberg, Richard, 185
Brunner, Karl, 471
Buchanan, James, 495
Budget deficit, 478–9
  arguments against, 491–7
  Australian, 486–7
  crowding in and, 493
  crowding out and, 492
  financing, 487–91, 497
  future and, 492
  inflation and, 485
  sources of, 478–84, 496–7
  unemployment and, 483
Budget surplus, 478–9
  Australian, 486–7
  expansion and, 484
  recession and, 484
  sources of, 478–84, 496–7
  unemployment and, 483
Business Council of Australia, 456
Business cycle, 101–2, 109–10
  in Australia, 425–33
  Australian labour market and, 433–7, 446
  economic welfare and, 135
  expenditure and, 430–3, 446
  Federal budget and, 483–4
  inflation and, 107–8, 416–21
  interest rates and, 430–3, 446
  money and, 430–3, 446
  phases of, 102
  stock market and, 106–7
  unemployment and, 106
Bust, 432–3

C

CAI *see* Confederation of Australian Industry
Capital, 14, 561–2
  existing, 189
  human, 562
  investment and, 189
  ownership of, 578–81
  physical, 562
Capital account, 533
  balance, 533–4
  components of, 534
Capital accumulation, 51–2, 562, 564
Capital adequacy, 267
Capital goods, 46
Capitalism, 57, 578, 579–80
  advantages, 580
  disadvantages, 580–1
  in Japan, 581–3
  state monopoly on coercion, 581
  varieties of, 581–4, 596
  welfare state *see* Welfare state capitalism
Capital stock, 120, 123, 153
Cars, international trade in, 510, 514
Cash management trusts, 249
Central bank, 264–5
  independent, 266
  reactive, 444
  subservient, 266
Central planning, 578
CER *see* Closer Economic Relations
Certificates of deposit, 246
***Ceteris paribus*, 40**
Change in demand, 69
Change in quantity demanded, 69
Change in quantity supplied, 73
Change, rates of, 32
Change in supply, 73
Checklist, 469, 472
Cheque account, 244, 246–7
Cheques, 244, 246–7
China, 591–6
  compared with Commonwealth of Independent States, 595
  Cultural Revolution, 592
  economic growth, 593
  economic history, 591–2
  economic reform, 592–5
  Great Leap Forward, 592
  inflation, 594
  money supply, 595
  wages, 595
Choice, 8
Circular flow, 114–20, 135–6
CIS *see* Commonwealth of Independent States
Clark, Colin, 184
Classical macroeconomics *see* macroeconomics, classical
Clearing House, 273
Clipping, 242
Closed economy, 16
Closer Economic Relations, 526
Coffee, 84
Command mechanism, 14
Commodity money, 242–3
  advantages, 242
  disadvantages, 242–3
Commonwealth Bank, 244
Commonwealth Bank Act
  1911, 264
  1945, 265
Commonwealth budget, 455
Commonwealth government of Australia, 455
Commonwealth of Independent States, 584–91, 596
  barriers to trade, 590
  barter, 590
  black market, 590
  capital goods balance, 587

compared with China, 595
consumer goods balance, 585–7
credit balance, 586–7
distorted information flows, 589
economic performance, 588–9
economic reform, 589–91
growth, 586
hoarding, 590
history, 584–5
labour balance, 586
lack of specialization, 589
main economic events, 585
market sector, 588
materials balance, 587–8
queuing, 589
risk aversion, 589
shortages, 588–9
Communism, 580
Comparative advantage, 54–5, 509
opportunity cost and, 508–9, 526–7
Comparative wage justice, 458
Competition, 9
Complement, 68
Components of money, 246
Confederation of Australian Industry, 456
Consumer Price Index, 126–8, 130–1
Consumer prices, 123
Consumption, 5, **46**, 120, 184–5
changes in, 510–12
function of disposable income, 183
function of real GDP, 183
Keynesian theory of, 184
wealth and, 185
Consumption expenditure, 114, 174–86, 196, 200–1
Australian, 181
real, 182
Consumption function, 177–8
aggregate *see* Aggregate consumption function
Australian, 180–2
saving function and, 178
shifts in, 181–2
Consumption goods, 46
Consumption possibilities, expanding, 511–12
Consumption smoothing, 226
Contraction, 102
Contracts, implicit *see* Implicit contracts
Convertible paper money, 243
fractionally-backed, 243
Cooperation, 9
Coordinates, 28
Coordination mechanisms, 13, 14–15
Coordination, of market, 15
Corden, W. M., 523
Cost of living, 130–1
Cost–price inflation spiral, 402–3
Cost-push inflation, 401–2, 467
Countercyclical, 225
Cournot, Antoine-Augustin, 78–9
CPI *see* Consumer price index
Credit, 245
Credit cards, 247–8
Credit cooperatives, 249
Creditor nation, 537
Crime, increase in, 105
Crowding in, 340, 493
Crowding out, 340, 492–3
Currency, 244
Currency, 246
Currency appreciation, 298
Currency depreciation, 298
Currency drain, 255
Current account, 531
Australian, 532
components of, 531–2
Current account balance, 108, 539–46, 551
Current deposits, 250
Curve, 35, 38
Cycles, 162–3
Cyclical unemployment, 104

D

Darby, Michael, 471
Debasement, 242
Debit card accounts, 246
Debit cards, 248
Debt
international, 566–7
overseas, 489
Debt financing, 487
in Australia, 488–9
compared with money financing, 489–90
inflation and, 490
tender system, 490
Debtor nation, 537
Decentralized planning, 578
Decisionmakers, 13
Deferred payment, standard of *see* Standard of deferred payment
Deficit, 108
Deflation, 94
Demand, 66–9, 84–5
change in, 67, 69–70, 76–7, 85
effect of change in, 77
law of, 66, 78–9
Demand curve, 66–7
movement along, 68
for real money, shifts in, 285–6
shift in, 68–70
and willingness to pay, 75–6
Demand for labour, 369, 391
Australian, 371–2
in brewery, 370–1
diminishing marginal product and, 370
in economy, 371
Demand for labour curve, shift in, 371
Demand for money, 293
in Australia, 286
Demand for real money, 284–6
Demand inflation, 399–401, 420
Demand-pull inflation, 399
chronic, 400
Demand schedule, 66–7
change in, 70
Deng Xiaoping, 592
Deposits, 245–6, 255
current, 246
interest-bearing current, 246
non-interest-bearing, 246
Depreciation, 122–3, 191
Depression, 102; *see also* Great Depression
Deregulation
financial markets, 270
monetary policy effectiveness and, 345
Desired reserve ratio, 253
Desired reserves, 255
Developing country, 559
Development
East Asian model, 572
trade and, 569–70
Diamond, Peter, 389
Diminishing marginal product, 370
Diminishing marginal product of labour, 367
Direct foreign investment, 537
Direct quote, 297
Direct taxes, 480–1
Disappearance of goods, 130–1
Discouraged workers, 103
Disintermediation, 278
Disposable income, 118, 144, 176, 179
Australian, 181
real, 182
taxes and, 217
Dissaving, 177

Diversity of tastes, 514
Dollar
  balance of trade and, 547–8
  exports and, 549
  imports and, 549
  net exports and, 546–51
Dollar cost, 8
Dollar-denominated assets
  market for, 305–6
  shift in supply curve, 304–5
Dollar prices, exchange rates and, 547
Domestic factor incomes, 122
Double coincidence of wants, 60, 240
Double counting, 124
Double-entry bookkeeping, 531
Dumping, 522–3
Dupuit, Arsène-Jules-Émile Juvenal, 78–9

E

Earnings, 5
Economic activity, 7–8
Economic equality, 134
Economic growth, 51, 52–3
  contributors to, 563–72, 574
Economic models, 18–22
  assumptions, 18–19
  implications, 19, 22
  macroeconomic, 22
  microeconomic, 22
  theory and reality, 22–3
Economics, 8
Economic science, 17, 24
  beginnings of, 20–1
Economic systems, alternative *see* Alternative economic systems
Economic theory, 18, 23
Economic welfare, 131, 131–6
  business cycle and, 135
  comparisons, 135
  real GDP and, 134–5
Economic well-being, distribution of, 578
Economies
  capitalist, 579–80
  socialist, 580
Economies of scale, 514–15
Economizing, 8
Economy, 12, 24
  stabilizing, 452–75
Effective rate of protection, 523
Efficiency wage, 378–9
Employer organizations, 456
Employers, 97
Employment, 102
  changes in, 375
  full *see* Full employment
  sticky wages and, 379–80
  wages and, 374–84, 391, 394
Endowment, 19
Environmental damage, 134
Equation of exchange, 257
Equilibrium, 19, 75
  changes in, 210
  convergence to, 198, 334–5
  money market, 357–9
Equilibrium expenditure, 198–201, 218, 227–8, 331
  constant interest rate, 332–3, 337–8
  interest rates and, 330
  real GDP and, 199–200, 355–7
Equilibrium GDP, price level and, 228–31
Equilibrium interest rate, real GDP and, 330
Equilibrium price, 75
Europe 1992, 526
European Monetary System, 319
Evans, Paul, 495
Excess reserves, 253
Exchange, 56–61
  medium of *see* Medium of exchange
Exchange rate
  in Australia, 268
  Australian dollar, 145, 299
  and demand for $A-denominated assets, 302–3
  determination, 300–14, 322
  dollar prices and, 547
  equilibrium, 548
  fixed *see* Fixed exchange rate
  flexible *see* flexible exchange rate
  fluctuations, managing, 310–11
  foreign *see* Foreign exchange rate
  forward *see* Forward exchange rate
  international crowding out and, 340
  managed *see* Managed exchange rate
  prices and, 546–7
  real *see* Real exchange rate
  recent history, 298–300
  and Reserve Bank of Australia, 267–8
  stabilizing, 550
  stable, 452
  and supply of $A-denominated assets, 303–4
Exchange rate effect, 336–7
Exchange rate regime
  foreign exchange reserves and, 307
  terms of trade and, 310–11
Exchange settlement accounts, 273
Expansion, 102, 163
Expectations, 146, 185
  formed by people, 404–5
  optimistic, 189, 206
  pessimistic, 189, 206
  policy rules and, 460
  wrong, 404
Expected future income, 176
Expected inflation rate, 96
Expenditure, 114–15, **481**
  Australian, 433
  business cycle and, 430–3, 446
  changes in, 433
  equal to real GDP, 198
  equality with income, 115–16, 118
  equilibrium *see* Equilibrium expenditure
Expenditure approach, 120, 125
Expenditure round, 215
Export growth, GDP growth and, 569
Exports, 192–3, 196, 210, **503**
  Australian, 504
  composition of, 504
  dollar and, 549
  geographical pattern, 507
  merchandise, 505
  net *see* Net exports
  prices of, 547
  quotas and, 521
  real, 194
  tariffs and, 518–20
External cost, 8

F

Factor cost, 123
Factor markets, 15
Factors of production, 14
  prices of, 72
Fair, Ray, 453
Families, multi-income, 445
Federal budget, 478–80, 482–4
  business cycle and, 483–4
  history, 482–3
  unemployment and, 483
Feedback rules, 460–3, 474
  advantages of, 462
  knowledge of economy and, 463
  problems, 462–3

unpredictability of, 463, 466
variability of aggregate demand with, 466
Feldstein, Martin, 495
Fiat money, 244
in Australia, 244
inflation and, 244
Final goods, 124
Final goods and services, 98
Finance companies, 249
Financial Corporations Act 1974, 264
Financial enterprises, 122
Financial innovation, 248, 252–3, 285
Financial intermediaries, 248–56, 260
economic functions of, 251–2
Firms, 14, 114–15, 117, 119
Fiscal policy, 216, 455, 457
adjustment process, 337–9
aggregate demand and, 337–41, 353, 360–1
assigning goals, 349–50
convergence to equilibrium, 338–9
effect on GDP, 362
initial effect, 337
interest rate and, 339
investment and, 339
real GDP and, 339
with unemployment, 229–30
Fiscal policy effectiveness, 343–5, 353
compared with monetary policy, 343, 345
demand for money and, 343
investment and, 343
Fiscal policy multipliers, 216–23, 231–2
Fisher, Irving, 184, 470
Five-year plan, 585
Fixed exchange rate, 268, 298, 303, 306, 319
interdependence with, 318–19
Fixed rules, 460–2, 468, 474
advantages of, 468–9
Flexible exchange rate, 268, 298, 303, 306, 321
independence with, 320–1
Flexible wages
aggregate supply and, 375–7
rational expectation and, 407
Flexible wage theory, 374–8, 435–6
labour market equilibrium, 375
Flow, 478, 537
Flow equilibrium, 288, 356
Flow-ons, 458
Flow theory of the exchange rate, 301–2
Forecasts, 346
interest rates and, 404
predicted by economists, 405
wages and, 404
wrong, 404
Foreign aid, 567
Foreign borrowing, 117
Foreign currency assets, 250
Foreign currency liabilities, 250
Foreign exchange, 297–323, 322
controls, 269
Foreign exchange market, 297
Foreign exchange rate, 96, 145, 193, **297**
Foreign exchange regimes, 298
Foreign investment, 570
in Australia, 534
Foreign sector, 116
Forward contract, 316
Forward exchange rate, 316
Fractional backing, 243–4
in Australia, 243–4
Free banking, 244
Frictional unemployment, 104
Friedman, Milton, 185, 442, 460, 470–1
Full employment, 104–5, 256
aggregate demand and, 230–1
macroeconomic equilibrium and, 155–7
Full-employment equilibrium, 156
Fundamental economic problem, 577–8, 595
Funds, minimizing cost of, 251–2

G

Gains from trade, 55, 61, 509–13, 527
Australia, 513
calculating, 512
real world, 513
GATT *see* General Agreement on Tariffs and Trade
GDP *see* Gross domestic product
GDP deflator, 126, 127–9, 132, 140
GDP growth
export growth and, 569
inflation and, 571
General Agreement on Tariffs and Trade, 522, **525**
General financiers, 249
General government sector, 455
Gold, 243
Goods
prices of and demand, 67
prices of and supply, 71–2
producing right quantity of, 577–8
Goods and services, 46
Goods markets, 15
Gorbachev, Mikhail, 584–5, 589
GOSPLAN, 585
Government, 6, **14**
Government accounts, 108, 110
Government borrowing, 117
Government budget balance, 544
Government budget, changes in, 305
Government debt, 478–9
Government deficit, 219, 222
Australian, 313
Government expenditure, 120, 481–2; *see also* Outlays
Government policy, 144
Government purchases, 116, 174–5, 210, 216
crowding in and, 340
crowding out and, 340
increasing, 399
Government purchases multiplier, 216, 217–18, 232
Government revenue, 222, 480–2
other, 481
total, 481
Government sector, 116
Government sector balance, 544–5
effect on current account balance, 545
effect on private sector balance, 545
Government sector deficit, 564
Government sector surplus or deficit, 539, 543–4
Government spending, 444
Government surplus, Australian, 313
Graphing data, 28
Graphs, 40
in economic models, 35–40, 41
misleading, 29–30
more than two variables, 40–2
single variable, 28
time-series *see* Time-series graphs
two variables, 28–9
Great Depression, 437–46
in Australia, 437–9
Australian government policy, 442–4
autonomous expenditure and, 442
components of expenditure, 442
contraction phase, 442

fiscal policy, 442–4
government spending in, 443
monetary policy, 443–4
money supply and, 442
multi-income families, 445
outside Australia, 439, 442
possibility of recurrence, 444–5
tariffs and, 520
unemployment and, 439
wages policy, 443–4
Great Leap Forward, 592
Greenbacks, 244
Gresham, Sir Thomas, 242
Gresham's law, 242
Gross domestic product, 98–101, 109
Australian, 99, 100, 120
declining, 102
expenditure approach, 120–1
factor incomes approach, 124
income approach, 121–3
nominal *see* Nominal GDP
real *see* Real GDP
production approach, 126
trend real *see* Trend real GDP
Gross domestic product at factor cost, 122
Gross investment, 122, 186
Growth, 100, 162–3
aggregate demand stimulation and, 570–2
investment and, 565
resources and, 572–3
technological change and, 367–8
Growth rates, 560
income levels and, 561, 573
variable, 368

H

Hall, Robert, 185
Hansen, Gary, 388
Hard budget constraint, 590
Hicks, John, 357–8
High-income economies, 558
Hoarding, 590
Hours per worker, determination of, 373
Household production, 134
Households, 13, 114–15, 117–19
Houses, 84
Human capital, 46, 105
loss of, 105
Human dignity, 105
Hume, David, 470

Hyperinflation, 98
hysteresis, 389

I

IC *see* Industry Commission
IMF *see* International Monetary fund
Implications, 19
Implicit contract, 378
Imports, 193, 196, **503**
Australian, 504
autonomous, 207
dollar and, 549
merchandise, 505
prices if, 547
quotas and, 521
real, 194
tariffs and, 518–20
Incentives, 153–4
Income, 114, 114–25, 68
categories of, 121
determination, algebra of, 207
equality with expenditure, 115–16, 118
foreign, 145–6
international distribution, 558–60, 573
loss of, 105
per capita, 562
Income approach, 121, 125
Income and expenditure accounts, 118–19
Australian, 120–5, 136
Income levels, 560
growth rates and, 561, 573
Indexing, 98
Indirect quote, 297
Indirect taxes, 123, 480, **480**
Indivisible labour *see* Labour, indivisible
Induced changes in real GDP *see* Real GDP, induced changes in
Induced expenditure, 195, **196**, 197
Induced lag, 347
Induced taxes, 217, 219
absence of, 219
Industrial country, 559
Industrial Relations Commission, 436
Industry Commission, 523
Industry policy, 582
Inferior goods, 68
Inflation, 6, **94,** 109, 126–31, 136, 162–3, 241, 398–407, 420
anticipated *see* Anticipated inflation
Australian, 95–6
Australian interest rates and, 414–15
Beenleigh brewery and, 400–1, 403
budget deficit and, 485
business cycle and, 107–8, 416–21
debt financing and, 490
demand *see* Demand inflation
expected, 187–9, 205–6
GDP growth and, 571
high, 398
interest rates and, 413–16, 421
Korean War and, 95
low and predictable, 452
money financing and, 490
Phillips-curve approach, 416–18
problem of, 96
relative price changes and, 128–30
spirals, 400–3
supply *see* Supply inflation
unanticipated *see* Unanticipated inflation
value of money and, 96
wage response, 399–400
wrong forecasts, 404
in 20th century, 94–5
Inflationary gap, 155–6
Inflation expectations, 403–7, 421
and interest rates, 413–14
and policy credibility, 412–13
Inflation rate, 95, 398
change in, 319–20
price level and, 95
Injections, 119
Innovation, 368
financial *see* Financial innovation
Inputs, 560–2, 574
Inside lag, 346
Intellectual property, 57
Interdependence, 318–19
Interest, 329–32, 352
Interest rate parity, 316–18
Interest rates, 142, 144, 176, 187, 320
asset prices and, 287–8
business cycle and, 430–3, 446
changes induced by fiscal policy, 339
changes induced by monetary policy, 334
changing, 290–1
controls, 269
determination of, 286–94
equilibrium, 359
high, 187–8
inflation and, 413–16, 421
inflation forecasts and, 404
investment and, 187, 331

low, 187–8
money supply and, 415–16
opportunity cost and, 283–4
real *see* Real interest rate
sensitivity of demand for investment, 343, 345
sensitivity of demand for money, 343, 345
short-run aggregate supply and, 152
Intermediate goods, 124
Intermediate goods and services, 99
International accounts, 108–10
International agreements, 525–6
International borrowing, Australian, 538–9
International crowding out, 340
International Monetary Fund, 298, 533
International specialization, 193
International substitution, 143
International substitution effect, 226
International trade, 6, 503–27
Australian, 503–8
balanced, 452
compensating losers, 524–5
diversity of tastes and, 514
financing, 551
financing, 531–51
gains from, 509–13, 527
geographic patterns, 506–8
jobs and, 515
patterns, 503–8, 526
political outcome, 525
reasons for restrictions, 523–4
services, 505–6
trends, 503–8, 526
Intertemporal substitution, 142
of labour, 374
Intertemporal substitution effect, 226
Invention, 368
Inventories, 120
Inventory changes, unplanned, 198–9
Investment, 114, 120, 123, 186–92, 201, 204–6
change in, 332
changes induced by fiscal policy, 339
determination of, 186–9
expected inflation and, 187–9
gross Australian, 191
growth and, 565
interest rate and, 187, 331
net *see* Net investment
real, 190
replacement *see* Replacement investment
saving and, 566
savings accounts, 246
unplanned, 333
Investment abroad, Australian, 534
Investment demand, 189–90, 206
Australian, 191–2
Investment demand curve, 189–90
Australian, 192
Investment demand schedule, 189–90
IS curve, 356–7, 361
IS–LM equilibrium, 359
IS–LM model, 355–63

J

Japan, 581–3
firms, 582
government, 582
industry policy, 582
markets, 582
Jenkin, Fleeming, 79
Job search, 384–6
Jobs, international trade and, 515

K

Katz, Lawrence, 389
Keating, Paul, 428
Keynes, John Maynard, 159, 184–5, 470
Keynesian, 347
Keynesianism, 389, 469
compared with monetarism, 348–9
extreme, 348
Keynesian macroeconomics *see* Macroeconomics, Keynesian
Keynesian–Monetarist controversy, 347–9
intermediate position, 348
Kuznets, Simon, 184
Kydland, Finn, 388

L

Labour, 14, 561–2
demand for *see* Demand for labour
indivisible, 384
intertemporal substitution, 374
marginal product of *see* Marginal product of labour
supply of *see* Supply of labour
Labour force, 102, 153
withdrawal from, 385
Labour force participation rate, 374, 387
Labour market
Australian, 433–7
decisions, 384–6
equilibrium, flexible wages, 375
flexible wage theory, 435–6
flows, 384–6
sticky wage theory, 379, 435–7
Lags, 146, 466
fiscal policy and, 345–7
monetary policy and, 345–7
see also individual lags
***Laissez faire*, 459**
Land, 14, 561
ownership of, 578–81
Lardner, Dionysius, 79
Law of demand *see* Demand, law of
Law of one price, 314
Law of supply *see* Supply, law of
Leakages, 119
Leisure time, 134, 373
Lenders, 96–7
Lending, international, 316–18, 537–9, 551
LGS convention, 267, 270
Liability, 249–50
Life-cycle hypothesis, 184–5
Lilien, David, 388–9
Linbeck, Assar, 389
Linear relationship, 35
Liquidity, 245–6, 267
of cash, 245
of cheques, 245
creating, 252
deposits, 245–6
Liquidity trap, 348
LM curve, 358–9, 361
effect of change in price level, 360
shift in, 360
Loan, 251
Long, John, 388
Long-run aggregate supply, 151–2
change in, 153–4
Long-run aggregate supply curve, 151
shift in, 154
vertical, 151
Long-run Phillips curve, 417–19
Lorenz curve, 559
Australia, 559

world, 559
Low-income economies, 559

M

M0, 244–6, 260
M1, 244–6, 260
multiplier, 279–80
M2, 246
M3, 244–6, 260, 469
Australia, 425–6, 431
multiplier, 279–80
Macroeconomic equilibrium, 154, 154–60, 165–6
in Australia, 156–7
full employment and, 155–7
types of, 156
Macroeconomic long-run, 147
Macroeconomic performance, 163–5
Macroeconomic performance indexes, 452–3
since 1960, 454–5
Macroeconomic policy targets, 452
Macroeconomics, 22
classical, 158–9
evolution of, 158–9
Keynesian, 159
modern, 159
Macroeconomic short-run, 147
Macroeconomic time frames, 147
Managed exchange rate, 268, 298, 303, 306
Mao Zedong, 592
Marginal–average relations, 180
Marginal cost, 8–9
Marginal product of labour, 367
Marginal propensities, slopes, 180
Marginal propensity to consume, 179, 197
Australian, 181
calculating, 178
Marginal propensity to consume out of real GDP, 186
Marginal propensity to save, 179
calculating, 178
Marginal propensity to spend, 197
increase in, 223
Marginal propensity to import, 197
Marginal tax rate, 219
change in, 222–3
Market, 15
Market coordination *see* Coordination, of market
Market mechanism, 15
Market price, 123
Market socialism, 578
Markets, world, 318
Marshall, Alfred, 79
Maximum points, 37
Meade, James, 453–4
Measurement, 17–18
Medium of exchange, 60, 240
Meltzer, Alan H., 471
MI *see* Misery index
Microeconomic reform, 163, 164, 165, 459
and prices, 164
problems, 164–5
and real output, 164
Microeconomics, 22
Middle-income economies, 558
Minimum liquid assets ratios, 269
Minimum points, 37
Minimum supply price, 71, 76
Ministry of International Trade and Industry, 582–3
Misery index, 453–4
MITI *see* Ministry of International Trade and Industry
Mixed economy, 15
Model economy, 46, 114–18; *see also* Economic models
Modigliani, Franco, 185
Monetarism, 469, 470–1, 491
compared with Keynesianism, 348–9
extreme, 348
Monetary base, 272
Monetary exchange, 60–1
Monetary independence, 318–23
Monetary policy, 264, 267, 457
adjustment process, 332–4
aggregate demand and, 332–7, 352–3, 362–3
aggregate supply and, 468
assigning goals, 349–50
Australian, 291–2, 311–18, 321
changes in, 304–5
destabilizing, 472–3
easing, 291
effect on GDP, 362
exchange rate and, 307, 310–13
expansionary, 307
feedback rules, 460–3
fixed rules, 460–2
goals, 304
relative effectiveness, 341–50, 353
tightening, 291
tools after deregulation, 270–1
tools prior to deregulation, 268–70
transmission channels, 336–7
and variations in terms of trade, 311–13
Monetary policy
effectiveness, 341–2
compared with fiscal policy, 343, 345
demand for money and, 341
deregulation and, 345
investment and, 341
Monetary targeting, 469, 472
Monetary theory of the exchange rate, 302
Monetizing the debt, 487
Money, 50, 60, 144–5, **240**, 240–61, 329–32, 352
in AD–AS model, 257
in Australia, 244–8
broad *see* Broad money
business cycle and, 430–3, 446
cheques and, 246–7
convertible paper *see* Convertible paper money
creation by banks, 253–5
credit cards and, 247–8
defined, 240
demand for, 281–6
fiat *see* Fiat money
forms of, 242–4
functions of, 240, 260
influences on holding, 282–4
measures of, 244–6
motives for holding, 281–2
price level and, 256–61
private debt *see* Private debt money
quantity theory of *see* Quantity theory of money
relative sizes of measures, 247
Money base, Australia, 425–6
Money financing, 487–8
compared with debt financing, 489–90
inflation and, 490
Money market, 330–2
open market operations and, 274–5
unofficial *see* Unofficial money market
Money market corporations, 249
Money market equilibrium, 288–90, 357–9
Money multiplier, 275, 279–80
Australian, 278–80
calculating, 280
Money prices in two countries, 547
Money supply
change in, 332
decrease in, 290
equilibrium real GDP and, 333
increase in, 290
increasing, 399

initial effect of change in, 332
interest rates and, 415–16
Money value, 128
Money wage determination, 379
Money wage rate, 369
MPC *see* Marginal propensity to consume
MPS *see* Marginal propensity to save
Multiplier, 212, 212–16. 227–33; *see also* individual multipliers
Australian, 224–6, 232
calculating, 212–13
marginal propensity to spend and, 212–14
process, 215, 276
real GDP and, 225
recession and, 225–6
recovery and, 225–6
size of, 214–16

N

NAFTA *see* North America Free Trade Association
National Economic Summit Conference, 427, 545
National Security (Banking) Regulations 1939–41, 265
Nationalized industry, 583
Natural rate hypothesis, 417
Natural rate of unemployment, 104, 434, **386–7**, 417–19, 452
variable, 418
Negative relationship, 35–6
Negative saving *see* dissaving
Neo-classical synthesis, 159
Net borrower, 537
Net domestic product, 123
Net exporter, 503
Net exports, 102, **118**, 174–5, 192–4, 196, 201, 564
dollar and, 546–51
exchange rate and, 548–50
Net exports function, 193–4
Net foreign borrowing, 543
Net importer, 503
Net income, 531
Net investment, 122, 186
Net investment income payable abroad, Australian, 538
Net lender, 537
Net operating surplus, 122
Net present value, 204–6
calculating, 204–5
Net Reserve Bank transactions, 536
Net services, 531
Net unrequited transfers, 531
Networking, 582
Newly industrialized economy, 559
Nominal deficit, 486–7
Nominal GDP, 99, 127–9
growth rate, 454
target, 453–4
Nominal interest rate, 205, **413**
Nominal quantity of money, 282
Nominal rate of protection, 523
Nominal surplus, 486–7
Nominal targets, 452
Non-callable deposits, 270–1
Non-convertible note, 272
Non-official balance, 533
Non-tariff barriers, 515, 520–1
international trade and, 521
Non-traded good, 315
Normal goods, 68
Normative statements, 17
North America Free Trade Association, 526
NTB *see* Non-tariff barriers

O

Observation, 17–18
Official cash rate, 274, 431
Official money market, 274
Okun, Arthur, 105, 388–9
Okun's Law, 105, 388–9, 453–4
OMO *see* Open market operations
Open economy, 16
Open market operations, 271–3
model of, 273
money market and, 274
multiplier effect, 275–8
Opportunity cost, 8, 47–51, 61, 98, 187, 508–9, 577
comparative advantage and, 508–9, 526–7
increasing, 49–50
interest rates and, 283–4
measuring, 48–9
on production possibility frontier, 49
Origin, 35
omitting, 30–2
Other things being equal *see Ceteris paribus*
Outlays, 478, 479, 481–2
expenditure on goods and services, 481
grants and subsidies, 481
interest payments, 481
other, 481
personal benefits payments, 481
total, 481–2
Output, growth of, 367
loss of, 105
Outside lag, 346

P

PAR *see* Prime assets ratio
Paradox of thrift, 212
Participation rate *see* Labour force participation rate
Passbook accounts, 246
Pastoral finance companies, 249
Patience, degree of, 176
Payments system, 273–4
Peak, 102
Per capita production function, 562
Perestroika, 585
Permanent building societies, 249
Permanent income hypothesis, 185
Perpetuity, 287
Phelps–Friedman hypothesis, 417
Phillips, A. W., 416
Phillips curve, 416, 416–21
in Australia, 418–20
Planned investment, 174–5, 196, 210
change in level of, 305
Plosser, Charles, 388
Policy credibility and inflation expectations, 412–13
Policy, fiscal *see* Fiscal policy
Policy formation lag, 346
Policy instruments, 456–9, 474
Policymakers, 455–6, 474
Policy rules, expectations and, 460
Policy targets, macroeconomic *see* Macroeconomic policy targets
Population, 68
age distribution, 387, 567–8
control of, 568–9
growth, 567–8
growth, dependants and, 567–8
Portfolio balance theory of the exchange rate, 302
Positive relationship, 35–6
Positive statements, 17
Poverty, 6–7
Precautionary motive, 281
Preferences, 19
Prescott, Edward, 388
Present value, 204, 206
Price, 67, 71–2
current, 142

exchange rate and, 546–7
foreign, 145
predicting changes in, 76–84, 86
as regulator, 74
relative, 193
Price adjustment lag, 347
Price comparisons, 241
Price determination, 74–6, 78–9, 86
Price index, 94, 126–7
Price level, 94–5, 126–31, 136, 227–33
aggregate expenditure and, 226–7
decreasing, 142–3
determination of, 154–5
effect on *LM* curve, 360
equilibrium GDP and, 228–31
increasing, 142–3
inflation rate and, 95
long-run effects, 351–2
money and, 256–61
policy-induced changes, 350–1
rational expectation of, 405–6
real GDP and, 350–4
short-run effects, 350–1
Prices and Incomes Accord, 458
Price stability, 94
Price–wage inflation spiral, 400–1
Prime assets, 251
Prime assets ratio, 251, 267, 270
Principle of effective demand, 159
Private debt money, 244
Private enterprise, 57
Private sector balance, 544–5
net exports and, 548–50
Private sector surplus or deficit, 544
Private trading enterprises, 122
Privatization, 584
Producer prices, 123
Production, 5, **46**
changes in, 510–12
physical limit, 151–2
Production approach, 123, 125
Production function, 366
technological change and, 563
Production possibilities, 47
changing, 51–6, 61
real world, 50–1
Production possibility frontier, 46–8, 61
cost of shifting, 51
getting on to, 577
shape, 50
Productivity, 55–6
Profit
expected, 189, 228
investment and, 189
Property, 56
Property rights, 56–7
consequences of absence, 57
in private enterprise capitalism, 57
limited by regulation, 57
limited by taxes, 57
Protection, 515
in Australia, 518
history of, 515, 518
industry policy and, 525
measuring effects of, 523
Prudential supervision, 266–7
PSBR *see* Public sector borrowing requirement
Public sector borrowing requirement, 455
Public trading enterprises, 122
Purchasing power parity, 315–16

Q

Quality improvements, 132
Quantity demanded, 66
change in, 69–70
Quantity of labour, 366, 369
employed in Australia, 372
real wage rate and, 372–3
Quantity of labour demanded, 369–70
Quantity of labour supplied, 372
Quantity of money, 141
Quantity of money demanded
interest rates and, 282–3
price level and, 282
Quantity of real money demanded, real GDP and, 282
Quantity supplied, 69, 71
change in, 73–4
Quantity theory, 470–1
Quantity theory of money, 257, 257–9
historical evidence, 259
international evidence, 259
Quantity traded, 66
predicting, 76–84
Quotas, 520–1
compared with tariffs, 522
effects of, 521
exports and, 521
imports and, 521

R

Rational choice, 19
Rational expectation, 404
flexible wages and, 407
sticky money wages and, 406
Rational expectations equilibrium, 407, 407–13, 421
flexible wages and, 408–9
individuals and, 409
sticky wages and, 408–9
Rational expectations hypothesis, 405, 407
Raw material prices, increasing, 401
Raw materials, availability of, 153
Reagan, Ronald, 495
Real balance effect, 226, 336
Real budget balance, 484
Real business cycle theory, 388, **467**
Real deficit, 484–7, 497
of family, 485
of government, 485–6
Real exchange rate, 315
Real GDP, 99, 99–101, 127–9, 131–5, 136, 196, 215, 227–33
aggregate expenditure and, 194–8, 201
Australian, 193
changes in quantity demanded, 143
changes induced by monetary policy, 333–4
changes induced by fiscal policy, 339
determination of, 154–5
economic welfare and, 134–5
equilibrium and, 198–9
equilibrium expenditure and, 355–7
equilibrium interest rate and, 359
fluctuations in, 156, 377, 380
importance of, 100–1
interest rates and, 330
long-run effects, 351–2
multiplier and, 225
physical limit, 151
policy-induced changes, 350–1
price level and, 350–4
short-run effects, 350–1
sustainable growth, 452
in 20th century, 101
underground, 131, 134
Real income, changes in, 285
Real interest rates, 187, 190, 205–6, **413**
Real money, 141
demand for *see* Demand for real money
Real money balances effect, 141, 143

Real/Nominal distinction, 550
Real surplus, 484–7, 497
 of government, 485–6
Real targets, 452
Real wage determination, 379
Real wage rate, 374
Real wages, Australian, 434
Real world money multipliers, 255
Recession, 102, 484
 Australia, 426
 multiplier and, 225–6
Recessionary gap, 156
Recovery, multiplier and, 225–6
Relative price, 129
Relative price changes, 128–30
Replacement investment, 186
Reserve Bank Act 1959, 264
Reserve Bank of Australia, 251, 256, **264**, 264–81, 293, 444, 455–6, 536
 actions, 291
 Administrative division, 266
 assets, 271
 balance sheet, 271–3
 Board, 265
 constitutional position, 266
 Deputy Governor, 265
 Economic Policy/Research division, 266
 exchange rate and, 267–8
 Financial Institutions division, 265–6
 Financial Markets division, 266
 functions, 266–7
 Governor, 265
 interest rates and, 290–1
 international constraints, 267–8
 liabilities, 271
 monetary targeting, 469
 origins, 264–5
 predicting actions, 291–3
 senior staff, 265–6
 structure, 265–6
Reserve ratio, 253
Reserve requirements, 270–1
Reserves, 251, 253–4
 excess *see* Excess reserves
Resources
 growth and, 572–3
 wasted, 577
Retirement, 385
Revenue, 478–9
Ricardian equivalence, 493, 493–6
Ricardo, David, 493–5
Risk
 concentration of, 267
 pooling, 252
Rogerson, Richard, 388

S

Sargent, Thomas, 471, 491
Saving, 118, 174–86, 200–1
 investment and, 566
 private, 564–5
Saving function, 177–8
 consumption function and, 178
Saving rate, high, 564–6
Say, Jean-Baptiste, 158–9
Say's Law, 158–9
Scaling, logarithmic, 34
Scarcity, 7, 24, 577
Scatter diagram, 32–5
Schwartz, Anna J., 442, 471
Sector balances, 539, 543–4
Self sufficiency, 54
Services, producing right quantity of, 577–8
Settler economy, 572–4
Shapiro, Carl, 389
Share prices, 106–7
Short-run aggregate production function, 366–9, 391
 Australian, 368–9
Short-run aggregate supply, 147, 150
 changes in, 152–4
 interest rates and, 152
 wages and, 152
Short-run aggregate supply curve, 147
 depression range, 150–1
 intermediate range, 151
 shift in, 152–4
Short-run aggregate supply schedule, 147
Short-run Phillips curve, 416, 416–19
Short-run production function, 366
Simple money multiplier, 255
Slope, 38–42
 across arc, 39–40
 defined, 38
 negative, 39
 at a point, 38–9
 positive, 39
Smith, Adam, 20–1, 470
Smith, Bruce, 471
Snower, Dennis, 389
Socialism, 578, 584–95
Social wage, 457–8
Soft budget constraint, 590
Soviet Union *see* Commonwealth of Independent States
Specialization, 54
Speculative motive, 282
Spending decisions, 329–30
SPI *see* Stabilization policy index
SRD ratio, 270
SRD *see* Statutory reserve requirements
Stabilization policy
 activist, 460
 aggregate supply and, 467–8
 alternative approaches, 474–5
 alternative approaches, 460–9
 non-activist, 460
Stabilization policy index, 454
Stabilization problem, 452–5, 474
Stage in life, 176, 185
Stagflation, 107, 402, 420–1
Standard of deferred payment, 241
Standard of living, 135
Statement savings account, 246
Statistical discrepancy, 121
Statutory reserve requirements, 269; *see also* SRD ratio
Sterilization, 310
Sticky money wages, 390
 rational expectation and, 406
Sticky wages
 aggregate supply and, 380
 employment and, 379–80
 unemployment and, 390–1
Sticky wage theory, 378–81, 435–6
Stiglitz, Joseph, 389
Stock, 478, 537
Stock equilibrium, 288, 358
Stock market
 business cycle and, 106–7
 market crashes, 437, 444
Store of value, 241–2
Straight line, 38–9
Structural change, 570
Structural unemployment, 104
Subsidy, 123
Substitutes, 67, 141
Substitution effects, 130
Summers, Lawrence, 389
Suppliers, number of, 72
Supply, 69–70, **71**, 72–4, 85–6
 change in, 71, 73–4, 77, 80, 85
 effect of change in, 80
 law of, 71, 78–9
Supply curve, 71–2
 and minimum supply price, 76
 movement along, 72–3
 shift in, 72–3

Supply and demand, change in both, 80–1, 84
Supply inflation, 401–3, 420–1
Supply of labour, 372, 391
  income effect, 373
  substitution effect, 373
Supply schedule, 71–2
  change in, 73
Surplus, 108

T

Targeting interest rates, 466
Tariffs, 515, 518–20
  compared with quotas, 522
  compared with voluntary export restraints, 522
  effects of, 518
  exports and, 518–20
  Great Depression and, 520
  imports and, 518–20
Tastes, 68
Tax, indirect *see* Indirect tax
Tax multiplier, 217–18
Tax rate, marginal *see* marginal tax rate
Taxes, 183, 186, 444
  autonomous *see* Autonomous taxes
  disposable income and, 217
  induced *see* Induced taxes
Taylor, John, 453
Technological progress, 5, **51**, 51–2, 562–3, 574
  growth and, 367–8
  production function and, 563
Technology, 19, 72, 153
Technology transfer, 563
Temin, Peter, 439, 442
Tender system, 488
Terms of trade, 145
  Australian, 311–13
  changes in, 310–11
  fluctuations in, 311–13
Thornton, Henry, 470
Thrift, 211–12
  paradox of *see* Paradox of thrift
Time cost, 8
Time lags *see* lags
Time-series, comparing, 32
Time-series consumption function, 182
Time-series graphs, 28–32
  misleading, 29–30
  relationships in, 33
Tobin, James, 453
Trade, development and, 569–70
Trade and industry policy, 458–9
Trade restrictions, 515–27
Trade routes, aboriginal, 60
Trade-weighted index, 299–301
Transactions motive, 281
Transfer payments, 116, 183, 186, 219
  absence of, 219
Transfer payments multiplier, 216–17, 232
Transmission channels, 336–7
  exchange rate effect, 336–7
  real balance effect, 336
  wealth effect, 336
Treasury bills, 488–9
Treasury bonds, 488–9
Treasury notes, 488
Trend, 29
Trend real GDP, 100
Trough, 102
Turnover tax, 586
Twin deficits hypothesis, 545–6
Two-tier pricing, 593–4

U

Unanticipated inflation, 96, 398
Underdeveloped country, 559
Underdevelopment trap, 568
Underground economy, 131, 134
Underground real GDP *see* Real GDP, underground
Unemployment, 5–6, **102**, 102–6, 110, 384–94, 388–9, 394
  aggregate demand and, 229–30
  Australian, 102–4, 427, 434
  budget deficit and, 483
  budget surplus and, 483
  business cycle and, 106
  calculating, 386–7
  costs of, 105
  cyclical *see* Cyclical unemployment
  defined, 102
  demand side events, 387, 390
  equilibrium, 256
  Federal budget and, 483
  flexible wages and, 386–90
  frictional *see* Frictional unemployment
  and inflation time series, 419
  job search and, 384–6
  measuring *see* Measuring unemployment
  natural rate of *see* Natural rate of unemployment
  reasons for, 384
  sticky wages and, 390–1
  structural *see* Structural unemployment
  supply side events, 387
  types of, 103–4
  voluntary, 377
  wage indexation and, 458
  ways of becoming, 385
Unemployment rate, 102, 386
Unit of account, 240–1
  absence of, 241
Unit banking, 255–6
Unofficial money market, 274
Unpopularity index, 453
UPI *see* Voter unpopularity index
USSR *see* Commonwealth of Independent States

V

Value added, 123, 123–5
Value of money, 96
Value of output, 116
Value, store of *see* Store of value
Variable growth rates *see* Growth rates, variable, 368
Variables
  independent, 37–8
  relationships between, 35–7
Velocity of circulation, 257, 282–3
  high, costs of, 283
  high, benefits of, 283
  M1, 287
  M3, 287
VER *see* Voluntary export restraints, 520–1
Voluntary export restraints, 520
  compared with tariffs, 522
Voter behaviour, 453
Voter unpopularity index, 453–4

W

Wage bargaining
  centralized, 427
  decentralized, 427
Wage expectations, unrealistic, 103
Wage indexation, 419–20, 458
Wage rates, 160
  increasing, 401
  money *see* Money wage rate
  real *see* Real wage rate
  short-run aggregate supply and, 152
Wages, 5, 121–2

changes in, 375
efficiency, *see* efficiency wages
employment and, 374–84, 391, 394
inflation forecasts and, 404
response to inflation, 399–400
Wages Accord, 161, 428–9, 436–7, 473–4
Mark I, 473
Mark II, 473
Mark III to Mark VI, 474
Wages and incomes policy, 457–8
Wages policy, 473–4
consensus-based, 445
Wage theory
flexible *see* Flexible wage theory
sticky *see* Sticky wage theory
Wallace, Neil, 471, 491
Wants, 66
Waste, 577
Wealth, 6–7, 144–5, 176
Wealth effect, 336
Wealth of Nations, 20–1
Welfare state capitalism, 579, 583–4
Willingness to pay, 67, 75–6
Workers, 97
discouraged, 103
part-time, 103

***x*-axis, 28**
***x*-coordinate, 28**

***y*-axis, 28**
***y*-coordinate, 28**

The publisher wishes to thank the following for permission to reproduce material in this book.

Photo Credits

Adam Smith (p.20), Jean-Baptiste Say (p.158), David Hume (p.470), David Ricardo (p.494): Mary Evans Picture Library. Antoine-Augustin Cournot (p.78): Historical Picture Service. Irving Fisher (p.184): Irving Fisher Papers, Manuscripts and Archives Department, Yale University Library. Arthur Okun (p.386): John Neubauer.

Interviews

Michael Parkin (p.viii): Jeremy Jones Photography. Douglas McTaggart (p.vii), Chris Findlay (p.vii), Heinz Arndt (pp.1–3), Sir Leslie Melville (pp.235–7), John Nevile (pp.447–9), Max Corden (pp.499–500), Helen Hughes (pp.553–5): Mishka Golski. James Tobin (pp.89–91), Robert E. Lucas Jr. (pp.169–71): Marshall Henrichs. Geoff Harcourt (pp.325–6): Dona Haycroft.

Text Credits

Parrot cartoon (p.7): © *1985 The New Yorker Magazine Inc.* Hydro-scheme: forests lose but ozone wins (pp.10–11); Soviet trading via barter (pp.58–9); Breakfast cereal producers cash in on health concerns (pp.82–3); National accounting for sustainable GDP, (pp.132–3); Deepening business gloom casts doubt on '91 revival (pp.148–9); Export sector economy's prop (pp.220–1); Participation rate blurs the jobless figures (pp.382–3); Enterprise bargaining masters at the cannery (pp.392–3); Recession has cut inflationary expectations (pp.410–11); Rugby starts the ball rolling (pp.516–7): © *Financial Review.* Nobody dances to the BOP anymore (pp.464–5), © *The Sydney Morning Herald.* Budget statements 1991–92, extract from statement 2 pp.2.31–2.33; *Treasury Dept, Commonwealth of Australia,* copyright reproduced by permission. Hopes high on stabilizing Foreign debt (pp.540–2), © *The Australian.* Aboriginal trade routes (p.60), © R.M. and C.H. Berndt, *The World of the First Australians,* Ure Smith, Sydney (1977).